D0765566

FACTS ABOUT
THE AMERICAN WARS

Edited by
John S. Bowman

THE H.W. WILSON COMPANY
NEW YORK AND DUBLIN

A New England Publishing Associates Book
1998

NEW ENGLAND
PUBLISHING
ASSOCIATES

Copyright © 1998 by New England Publishing Associates, Inc. and John S. Bowman

Copy-Editing: Barbara Jean DiMauro
Design and Page Composition: Ron Formica
Photo Researcher: Victoria Harlow
Editorial Administration: Ron Formica
Proofreading: Margaret Heinrich Hand
Indexing: Julianne Means

Library of Congress Cataloging–in–Publication Data
    Facts about the American wars / edited by John S. Bowman
    p. cm.
    Includes bibliographical references (p. 726) and index
    ISBN 0-8242-0929-X
    1. United States—History, Military—Miscellanea.
    I. Bowman, John Stewart, 1931 –
    E181.F28 1997
    904.7—dc21   97-40298
                                              CIP

CONTENTS

War	Page	War	Page

ILLUSTRATIONS CREDITS

The illustrations on pages 220 and 241 are provided courtesy of the Cartographic & Architectural Branch, National Archives.

The illustrations on pages 669, 684, and 711 are provided courtesy of the Defense Visual Information Center.

The illustrations on pages 78, 79, and 299 are provided courtesy of the Geography & Map Division, Library of Congress.

The illustrations on pages 132, 183, 301, 312, 335 are provided courtesy of John S. Bowman.

The illustrations on pages 14 and 337 are provided courtesy of the Prints & Photographs Division, Library of Congress.

The illustrations on pages 47, 70, 75, 84, 90, 136, 148, 153, 194, 197, 231, 232, 234, 240, 252, 261, 266, 309, 321, 333, 357, 363, 391, 401, 403, 443, 453, 462, 466, 473, 480, 483, 581, and 587 are provided courtesy of the Still Picture Branch, National Archives.

The illustration on page 9 is provided courtesy of the University of Massachusetts at Amherst.

The illustrations on pages 449, 478, 479, and 693 are provided courtesy of the U.S. Army.

The illustrations on pages 616, 622, 631, and 633 are provided courtesy of the U.S. Department of Defense.

The illustrations on pages 7, 41, 44, 143, 400, 469, 585, 625, 678, 682, and 709 are provided courtesy of the USMA Library.

PREFACE

To use *Facts About the American Wars* as an effective reference tool, you will find it helpful to understand the premises, issues, and decisions behind the contents of each of the sections found within the chapters.

WARS

Deciding what constitutes a "war" and what does not is far from clear-cut. Granted, there are many cases in U.S. history where war was formally declared by Congress and formally ended by a peace agreement or treaty. However, far more of the numerous fatal conflicts in American history fall into a gray area between a skirmish or "police action" and a full-scale war. To cite the most obvious, deadly hostilities between European settlers and Native Americans occurred with great frequency for a period of some 275 years, from the early 17th century to the 1890s; while some of these hostilities were organized and intense enough to be called wars by anyone's standards others hardly rose above the level of a local, if deadly, feud over land rights. Another case in point is the many U.S. interventions in the Caribbean region particularly, but in other parts of the world as well. Some were literally police actions or debt-collection missions; others were large enough in scale to warrant classification as a war, whatever the political authorities of the time chose to call it.

I could find no single test that clearly divided wars from lower-level conflicts. The length of time the hostilities lasted was not a good test, as some conflicts lasted for only a few days. The number of casualties could not be the deciding factor either: Some conflicts that are universally described as wars included only a few killed or wounded.

In the end, we had to make judgment calls, excluding simple "police" or "punitive" actions by U.S. military units even if they took some hostile fire and bore some casualties. Sponsorship by the United Nations has not per se ruled out inclusion — the Korean and Persian Gulf wars are found in this book — but we decided that most UN-sponsored international relief or peacekeeping operations, such as those in Somalia and Bosnia, could not be accurately described as "American wars." (This is not to denigrate the seriousness of these operations or the tragedy of the casualties.)

Perhaps the most reliable test for deciding what should and should not be included in this book is one that measures the opposition. As a general principle, if the enemy of the U.S. forces was a relatively well organized and an officially sponsored military force engaged in fighting U.S. military units, we believe the conflict qualifies as a "war."

DATES OF WAR

Although some wars have a universally agreed-upon beginning and/or ending, many do not. Wars do not always or even usually begin with a formal declaration or a major confrontation; often, a series of events culminates in what is generally recognized as a state of war. Historians can sometimes agree on a single event that marked the commencement of a true war and sometimes not. The dates given in this book are those that make the best sense and have the support of most historians.

Likewise, not all wars end with a single event: The fighting simply tapers off or a temporary cease-fire signed between commanders on the battlefield turns out to be the end, even if formal negotiations by diplomats to resolve the conflict by a peace treaty drag on for years after the fighting stops. Again, we have picked the dates that are supported by most historians.

In the case of the major world wars, even though the United States did not enter as a belligerent at the outset, the United States was so directly affected that we use the dates generally accepted by historians as marking the beginning of the war, rather than the date the United States entered the war.

ALTERNATE NAMES

Many wars have true alternate names, while others may simply be known by a more popular or a more specialized name. While the United States gave its own name to a certain conflict, the other belligerents involved may have used a different name for the same conflict. We have tried to provide all common alternates that show up in printed works.

SIGNIFICANCE

Each war tends to hold some special place in the history of the United States and in the lives and minds of Americans. This is what this section attempts to characterize. The historical significance was not always perceived by contemporaries of the war in question— they were either too close to events to see it or some time needed to pass for the repercussions of the war to become apparent. Whether contemporaries were aware of it or only later history has revealed it, the broader impact of each war is described here.

BACKGROUND

Wars are usually the culmination of events with deep historical roots or explanations. This section provides the deeper and broader historical context for the war in question. In some instances, this means going back many decades, even centuries; in other instances it may only require a summary of a brief period leading up to the war.

CAUSES OF THE WAR

This section provides the more immediate, specific causes of the war, what historians call the "proximate" causes: the incidents that quite directly led to the hostilities. Sometimes this is a dramatic, single incident, but more often it is a mounting series of incidents. Inevitably, too, opposing sides often disagree on these causes, each blaming the other; we have tried to be objective in presenting these causes.

PREPARATIONS FOR WAR

This section sets forth the steps, if any, that the warring parties took, sometimes in the long term but more usually in the short term, as they prepared for the onset of war: building up their armed forces, gearing up the machinery of war, making last-minute diplomatic efforts, and such.

DECLARATION OF WAR

Some of America's wars involved formal declarations by the president and Congress, but most did not. Before there was an independent United States, the colonists tended to slip into hostilities, often because of events in Europe. In the case of several wars of more recent years, the president found some other means of committing armed forces. The same holds true for the countries involved in a war against the United States: In many cases, these countries did not make a formal declaration of war. Whatever the approach, this section explains it.

COMBATANTS

This section lists the various nations or peoples that joined in the war and sets forth what is known about each side's armed forces—the numbers of personnel, the numbers and types of armaments, and such. Precise figures are not always available, but we provide what is reported by respected historians. In particular, many wars involved militia or improvised civilian units or guerrilla forces, and often their numbers never were accurately known.

GEOGRAPHIC AND STRATEGIC CONSIDERATIONS

As the various sides go into a war, they face certain geographic conditions that will play a role in the conduct of the war and its outcome: the actual terrain or climate of the battlefields, the physical challenges of ambitious campaigns, the distances between homelands and the sites of war. In addition, each side has certain strategic goals and has certain plans to attain those goals, often conditioned by the geographic features. Beyond such geographic factors, opposing sides consider many elements while planning how to gain their ends: the availability of natural resources, personnel, manufacturing capacity, the enemy's access to resources, etc. When relevant, such considerations are discussed in this section.

BATTLES AND CAMPAIGNS

The chronologies found under this heading are the heart of this work. Every effort has been made to list all the major events and assign specific dates to them. Pinning all events down to particular days is not always easy; there are considerable discrepancies in major sources, and no amount of effort can resolve them. Moreover, some important developments did not begin or end on a specific day. Some events simply cannot be pinned down to anything closer than a month.

Major operations and campaigns are usually described in full under the opening day's date, but if important incidents during the campaign warrant it they are covered in separate entries.

Every effort has been made to list the event under the day in the time zone where the event took place (not on the day it became known in the United States). In a few instances involving events overseas we have provided the time or date in the United States for clarification or to avoid confusing the reader. Unless otherwise noted, the date and time given refer to the Eastern Time Zone. Likewise, on rare occasions, we have provided the date within the time zone in the United States that the event took place: that is, if an event occurred in California and it was on a different day there than in Washington, we have tried to clarify the date for readers.

Wherever relevant—and this pertains to major wars—the chronologies are subdivided into the major "theaters"; these have usually been agreed upon by historians writing on these wars. We have tried to provide a reasonable number of such accepted subdivisions without offering so many that they would end up confusing the user. Thus, in World War I, it made the most sense to combine all events in the former colonial holdings of Germany, even though they stretched from Africa to China. Similarly, in the Vietnam War, the events in Laos and Cambodia, with occasional spillover into Thailand, are treated under one heading.

In general we treat the naval actions under a separate heading. In the case of World War II, with so many actions in so many spheres, the air war is also treated under its own heading. Special subheadings are used in a few other wars where doing so helps readers to see the connections between related events.

HOME FRONT

In all instances, this refers to governmental actions and civilian actions only in the United States that are directly related to the war. (Other nations' "home fronts" are treated under INTERNATIONAL DEVELOPMENTS.) In occasional instances, however, we also list events of major importance even though they may not have had a direct bearing on the war (e.g., the first man walking on the moon that occurred during the Vietnam War).

INTERNATIONAL DEVELOPMENTS

Most of America's wars involved other nations directly or indirectly. In the late-20th century, the UN and other international institutions became involved with wars. This section lists only those events abroad or on an international level that bear most directly on America's role in the war. Thus, during World War II there were thousands of decisions and episodes in nations throughout the world that had some bearing on the war, but we have included only those that had the most direct relationship with U.S. participation in the war.

NEGOTIATIONS AND PEACE TREATY

Not all wars ended with negotiations—some (especially those involving Native Americans) just tapered off and stopped—but most wars did involve some negotiations, however brief, between the warring parties. Cease-fires and armistices are technically different from peace treaties, although in the case of earlier American wars they were sometimes nearly indistinguishable. In the case of major wars, there was usually some formal meeting to work out what was intended to be a long-lasting peace. Often these peace treaties were negotiated years after the end of hostilities. This section sets forth the relevant details about both the negotiations and the treaties, if any, that resulted.

RESULTS OF THE WAR: CASUALTIES, COSTS, CONSEQUENCES

Casualties: Precise figures for casualties are surprisingly difficult to nail down. There are tremendous differences among even the most reputable sources; indeed, even "official" figures differ from book to book. We have tried to provide the most reasonable figures and estimates based on examining the varying sources. In the case of earlier wars, there was never any official tally kept or reported of the dead and wounded, and there is certainly no reliable way to determine such numbers long after the events. Even for the most recent wars, officials and historians rarely agree upon casualty figures, particularly when it involves civilian deaths. Even with military personnel, there is often confusion about exactly who may have been present and who may have been "lost" in combat. This problem is even more serious in dealing with America's enemies in these wars.

The word "casualties" as used in standard military histories usually refers to not only the dead and wounded but also the missing in action. The figures given in the immediate aftermath of a battle almost always have to be adjusted, as some reported dead show up in hospitals, some reported missing turn up dead, and so on. To further complicate matters, in major wars there are large numbers of personnel who die from disease, accidents, and other causes (including suicide); some reported as wounded may die of their wounds a decade or more later. We have tried our best to limit our casualty counts to the dead and wounded in combat, but make the necessary adjustments and comments where relevant. To cite some examples, we recognize the important role of disease in several wars; we recognize the many who died in prison camps during several wars; and we discuss the issue of those missing in action in the Vietnam War.

There is also the special issue of those in the military killed by "friendly fire." Although not generally openly discussed by Americans until the Vietnam War, deaths or wounds accidentally caused by one's own or allied forces have been a part of warfare from earliest times. The U.S. military, in fact, estimates the historical rate of American casualties due to friendly fire at about 15-20 percent. (In the Persian Gulf War, the rate was 24 percent.) If such deaths or wounds were directly related to a combat situation, they are included in the official casualty figures.

It is widely accepted that the major shift to civilian targets, with the resultant dramatic increase in civilian casualties, commenced in World War I and then reached its climax in World War II. (The concept of "total war" often traced to the American Civil War refers less to civilian casualties than to the utilization of all a nation's resources—drafting soldiers, shifting to a war economy, employing railroads and telegraph, requisitioning food and animals, etc.) In fact, civilians have almost always been affected by the violence of warfare: The Thirty Years War in Europe (1618-1648) is notorious for the toll it took on civilians, while in several of the early American frontier wars, there were far more civilian than military casualties. But in terms of absolute numbers, there is no denying that high civilian casualties are largely a modern phenomenon; it occurred again in the Vietnam War and in the Panama invasion but was far less significant in the Persian Gulf War. Aerial bombing (euphemistically referred to as "strategic bombing"), missiles, rockets, heavy artillery, napalm, and land mines are said to be the "causes" of civilian casualties, but of course the decision to employ these weapons against or around civilians is taken by human beings.

We have not attempted to quantify one category of civilian casualties: rapes. Unfortunately this has been a part of warfare from the beginning of time; if there is any question as to whether it persists, one has only to read the press reports from Bosnia or eastern Africa in the 1990s. The victims of rape should be counted among the civilian wounded, but there is rarely any solid evidence upon which to base such figures. (One notable exception might be the so-called comfort women of the Japanese military during World War II: the many thousands of females from lands captured by the Japanese, such as Korea and the Philippines, who were held in houses and raped by Japanese servicemen.)

Costs: This has proven to be one of the most difficult elements to come up with precise figures for. Only recently have historians tried to determine the cost of wars. Many wars have not had "price tags" calculated by professionals. Different sources often give wildly conflicting figures depending upon what is included in their calculations. We base our figures on the best available figures or estimates. Note, too, that we have generally converted them into the values of 1990 dollars. An attempt has been made to limit the costs to the most direct material costs (military personnel wages, armaments, destroyed property, physical infrastructure, and such), but we have also tried to indicate that, at least with major wars, there are indirect long-range costs (medical expenses, refugee resettlements, veterans' benefits, etc.) that can be even higher than the direct costs.

Consequences: Under this heading, we start with the most immediate results of the war on those directly involved: changes in territory, changes in government, the fate of important leaders, etc. Then we move on to the next level of results—the war's effects on the economy and society of those involved. Finally, where relevant, we deal with the less tangible but no less important consequences—usually in a longer time frame.

MILITARY INNOVATIONS, TACTICS, EQUIPMENT

Many, but by no means all, wars saw the introduction of new armaments—breech-loading rifles, for instance, or machine guns or tanks—which then often allowed for new tactics. These and all other such innovations are listed in this section. Sometimes inventions came about independent of any military need but were quickly adopted by the military: the railroad and the telegraph, to name just two. Sometimes a major scientific breakthrough lay behind a technology that was adapted for warfare: radar, for example, or the atomic bomb. In another sphere, many new medical techniques were developed during wars.

Meanwhile, whether because of these new armaments and technologies or simply because of the applications of new concepts, there were often changes in strategies. An example of this was the introduction of the airplane, and then in turn the aircraft carrier. This led to great naval battles fought entirely by airplanes.

Then, too, there were some innovations that came about primarily because certain military leaders made a conceptual breakthrough: The American colonists' adoption of Indian guerrilla tactics was one such instance; the German use of fast-moving armored columns in what was called *Blitzkrieg* was another.

LEGENDS AND TRIVIA

Most wars generated at least a few unusual individuals or events that have entered popular or folk history. Often misconceptions persist about some of these popular tales. The most important ones are discussed here, with special attention given to separating the facts from the myths.

NOTABLE PHRASES

Almost every war has produced some well-known and oft-quoted phrases. Many of these are misquoted or misattributed, or at least the facts and dates are not well known. The most familiar of these quotations are explained under this heading.

SONGS

Music has long been associated with wars. Many of the songs discussed in this section were directly written in response to the war being discussed. In some instances, the music involved may not have been directly influenced by the war, but still became intertwined with the images from a war. The Vietnam War is such an example, where 1960s rock and roll music became a virtual soundtrack to the war. This section discusses some of the better and lesser-known facts about the music associated with individual wars.

HISTORICAL PERSPECTIVES AND CONTROVERSIES

Every war has generated at least one or two issues that have continued to engage historians or be debated by the wider public. The major ones are set forth here in the spirit of clarifying the various positions, not of settling these questions.

CIVILIAN AND MILITARY BIOGRAPHIES

Under this heading we provide brief sketches of the principals of each war. These do not attempt to lay out all the facts about the lives of these people, but focus on those facts relevant to the person's role in the war. In a few instances, an individual may appear under two wars, with the focus on the role during each one.

FURTHER READING

The listings found under this heading are not intended to be exhaustive or scholarly but rather to provide a selection of books that would interest the general reader who wants to round out or fill in his or her understanding of various aspects of the war.

John S. Bowman
December 1997

INTRODUCTION

If questioned, most Americans would probably say they think their country should be recognized as one of the least warlike in recorded history. That may or may not be, since such things are impossible to objectively measure, but as a people, Americans have certainly had their share of wars—and these wars have dramatically affected U.S. history. In the years between 1600 and 1775, the people of the land that came to be known as the United States of America fought in eight major colonial wars; since their revolution, Americans have fought at least ten major wars. These figures exclude the numerous smaller wars throughout the centuries and the 150 or so "interventions" abroad by U.S. military units in the years since 1800.

Not counting the 17th-century colonial wars on the one end (as being both continual and often poorly defined) and the Cold War on the other end (also constant and not conventional), if all the months between January 1700 and December 1997 in which Americans were engaged in at least one war (as detailed in this volume) were added together, they would occupy some 30 percent of that total time span.

Wars, then, have to be recognized as critically important in factors shaping U.S. history. And it is fair to say that wars have been important in the lives of many if not most Americans. Whether female or male, child or adult, civilian or service personnel, pacifist or militant, progovernment or rebel, victor or loser, native or immigrant, most Americans in the course of their history have in some way been touched by warfare. Yet most Americans remain at best uncertain, at worst ill informed, about the role that wars have played in their history.

Why is this so? Probably for the simple reason that no people like to think of themselves as prone to fight wars. That is another way of saying that people are idealistic (although cynics might say hypocritical). Americans are taught to believe that war is bad and, therefore, would like to deny that their nation has engaged in such conduct—even if it did so for 30 percent of three centuries. But that at once raises the question:

Are all wars, in fact, bad? Or, to turn the question around: Is there such a thing as a just war? For that matter, is a justifiable war always the same as a just war?

A TYPOLOGY OF WARS

This book does not pretend to provide definitive answers to such questions, which, after all, have eluded historians and psychologists, sociologists, biologists, anthropologists, and philosophers for centuries. Inevitably, though, a book full of so many facts does raise questions beyond its foundation of details. One question that might arise from any survey of all U.S. wars is whether they can be typed in the neutral way of political scientists. That is, can the wars be pried loose from the specifics of their historical contexts—the ideologies, quarrels, prominent individuals, national or ethnic differences—and be seen as belonging to certain fundamental categories? It would appear that they can be and that something might be learned from such an exercise.

To start at the beginning would require an objective observer to take an overview of the many conflicts engaged in by the early settlers in the New World—roughly speaking, those during the 1500s and 1600s. In the end, the causes of those many wars seem reducible to two types. As outsiders, or newcomers, the colonists fought Native Americans for the simple goal of moving in on their territory and resources. And as Europeans competing to establish settlements in North America, the colonists fought each other in order to impose their own communities, religions, and economies on the newfound land.

Although this may seem somewhat simplistic, it does appear that those were the two causes of most of the wars in North America not only through the 1600s but even until the American Revolution. That said, there need to be a few adjustments, or close-ups of the typing of those many wars. For example, colonists sometimes enlisted Native Americans to fight alongside them against other colonists, and many of those Native American tribes had been fighting with each other over hunting grounds for centuries before the colonists arrived on the scene. For another example, it would probably be assumed that the basic conflict was between Roman Catholic nations and Protestant nations, but that was not entirely the case: Protestant English fought Protestant Dutch; Catholic French fought Catholic Spanish.

But there was one conflict during the 1600s that was not fought for either of those two goals—Native American territory or imperialist competition. That was Bacon's Rebellion: Minor though it was, it prefigured the American Revolution in that it was a revolt against the British colonial establishment by other Englishmen unhappy with the policies of their government. So, in fact, Bacon's Rebellion and the American Revolution might be seen as two versions of a third type: conflict over self-government.

In the wake of the American Revolution, two new types of wars emerged. Type four was seen in the so-called quasi-war with the French: The United States as a nation-state went to war to protect its rights, freedoms, and commerce. The War of 1812 could also be seen as another such type-four war. And the fifth type of war emerged with the Barbary Wars: The United States as an international policeman, set forth to take care of a foreign troublemaker that the rest of the world seemed unable or unwilling to deal with.

The Indian wars of the 1800s belong to type one: No matter how much they were disguised by various causes, they came down to a fight over territory and resources. The Mexican War, however, introduced a sixth type of war: a war to take territory from another sovereign nation. (Native Americans, of course, might argue that all of the Indian wars were essentially that type.) It seems fair to say that the Mexican War was the only such purely acquisitive war in U.S. history, although some might argue that the Spanish-American War belongs to this type.

The Civil War then becomes type seven—just what its name signifies: a war between two sets of Americans over a domestic political difference. Again, that was the only one of its type for Americans.

The Spanish-American War could be said to be a combination of the Quasi-War, the Barbary Wars, and the Mexican War: The United States set out to respond to an attack on its property (accepting the explosion of the USS *Maine*) and to punish the oppressive Spanish, but it ended up taking territory (Puerto Rico, Guam, the Philippines). Some might argue that there are other similarly ambiguous wars in U.S. history.

We think it makes sense to place the Spanish-American War in a new, eighth type: a Monroe Doctrine war. Namely, that special category of wars (and many interventions) in which the United States simply asserted that it was taking military action to stop what it regarded as a threat to the peace and security of the Western Hemisphere: This type includes the later wars in the Dominican Republic, Grenada, and Panama.

World War I could be said to come closest to type five (the Barbary Wars): the United States as international policeman yet, as with the Barbary Wars, there was also an element of self-interest—the losses to German submarines were quite similar to the losses to the Barbary pirates. World War II was another expression of this type. However, in that instance, the attack on Pearl Harbor turned the United States into a full participant in an all-out war for total victory. Even if the United States perceived itself as a policeman punishing "outlaw" nations in World War II, the metaphor admittedly seems forced, given the massive scale of American mobilization and the global scope of the conflict.

Some might argue that the Korean War was still another version of the type-five war: the United States as international policeman taking on Communism instead of Fascism (or Barbary pirates). The Vietnam War was yet another variant of the type five war. As was the Persian Gulf War, that time substituting Saddam Hussein's Iraq for Communism.

As has been admitted, those types of wars were not always absolutely distinct or "pure." The Barbary Wars against international terrorists of their day were not totally altruistic: They were also fought to protect American lives and commercial traffic. Likewise, Americans fought the War of 1812 not just to protect "freedom of the seas" but also to dispel actual invaders: Indeed, it was the only war that the United States fought to get rid of foreign invaders on its sovereign territory. And there is no denying that there were ambiguities in almost all the wars or that some historians might adopt a different system of typology—one, for instance, stressing ideology or less overt goals.

But by and large, it seems to us that all the American wars can fit this typology rather well. What this says about U.S. history is left to each of us to determine, but it does seem to suggest that behind all the elaborate details, wars remain stubbornly similar. In any case, it should make everyone think twice about U.S. history. For instance, Americans today are engaged in a debate over whether their country should become the world's policeman, as though this would be an entirely new role: In fact, it is a role that the United States has long played. A variant of that role is the many occasions that the United States has gone to war to enforce its self-proclaimed Monroe Doctrine. Above all, the recognition that the United States has fought wars to take territory should help dispel the myth of American "exceptionalism"—that is, the notion that the United States has been quite different from other countries in history.

THE AMERICAN ELEMENT

If U.S. wars turn out to be reducible to basic types, which in turn are probably universal types shared by other nations, the question then arises: Have Americans brought anything distinctive to war? Start with the colonial wars of the early and mid-1600s, with the small enclaves of largely English-colonial towns sprinkled in Virginia, Maryland, Connecticut, and Massachusetts. Pilgrim and Puritan in the North, Royalist and Anglican or Catholic in the South, Quaker in Pennsylvania, and amalgamated Dutch-English in New York, the inhabitants of those colonies were sometimes pious, sometimes acquisitive, and almost always fiercely individualistic, great believers in self-sufficiency. Back in Europe, those colonists had relied on the protection provided by powerful monarchs—mainly in the form of small, professional armies and navies. Once ashore in the New World, however, those colonists (Quakers excepted) quickly accepted that every man should have his own musket and that every settlement should be protected by a fort or stockade. For the most part, the enemy were the Native Americans and at times their European allies. With the basic belief in the requirement for self-protection came a corollary belief that manhood was contingent upon the ability to fight and die in defense of one's family, town, and way of life. It is questionable whether that introduced the first

"American angle" to warfare: In a way, the formation of local militias was a regression rather than an advance, a return to the days before nation-states organized professional armed forces. Yet, the encouragement and use of local militias comprised of volunteers motivated by the defense of their homes and owning their own weapons was a radical departure from military theory and practice in the 1600s. An armed populace with military training would have been perceived as a dangerous threat by every European government of the day.

The series of French and Indian wars (1689–1763) gave a new shape to the colonists' belief in the necessity and virtue of combat. Their attitudes toward military service were fully developed by 1763, which coincidentally saw the end of the French and Indian War and the start of Pontiac's War, one of the most serious Native American assaults upon American settlements. By 1763, most Americans (again, with the important exception of the Pennsylvania Quakers) believed it was imperative that any man over the age of 16 be able to load, shoot, and reload his musket. A corollary of that was that virtually every household had at least one weapon propped in a corner. To be sure, most Americans probably would have had a firearm for hunting, but on the American frontier, there was long the possibility of having to use that firearm against a fellow human. Needless to say, the need for firearms grew stronger the farther an individual moved westward; townsfolk had more built-in protections from surprise attacks than did people along the frontier.

There was another distinctive American aspect to wars of that era. In fighting against the (often) French-Catholic or Indian foe, citizens from the 13 colonies began to work together more frequently. In fact, Benjamin Franklin's famous expression "Join or die" was coined in 1754, the year the last and most important of the French and Indian Wars began. What is essential to realize is that as British colonists fought against the French, Spanish, and Native Americans to win control of the eastern seaboard, they became American rather than English-American. Although one can argue that many peoples originally came together to defend themselves and then stayed together to form nations, it had been a long time since a new nation emerged from that kind of mutual assistance.

By the time of their revolution, then, the people who came to be known as Americans had, if not invented, at least revived two dimensions of war that would characterize conflicts in the modern world: the citizen soldier and a society built around shared fighting. The era of the American Revolution then combined those two dimensions in what was a distinctly American ideal: the triumph of the citizen militia. Historians still debate whether it was the Continental Army (organized professionals) or the state/town militias (part-time soldiers) who won the Revolutionary War. But there is no doubt that the appearance of the self-reliant militia (most familiar as the Minutemen and exemplified by the statue at Concord Bridge) signaled a new departure in the military history of the modern European-American world.

The American militiaman was soon imitated by the citizen army of the French Revolution, with the idea that free citizens, bearing their own arms, were the best defenders of a nation. That notion gained prominence in the half century that followed the American and French revolutions. The United States's northern neighbor, incidentally, followed suit: The Canadian militia gained prominence during the War of 1812, when Canadian citizens were called out to defend their territory against U.S. invaders.

Up to the end of the War of 1812, Americans had been able to tell themselves that they were bringing another new dimension to modern warfare: They believed they were fighting for high ideals—at the very least, for self-defense and at best, for democratic freedoms. They did not see themselves fighting—as were their cousins in Europe—for territorial gain, dynastic power, ego, obscure quarrels. Americans believed that they were fighting for some sort of higher purpose: to establish a city on a hill, to bring Christianity to the heathen, to keep Roman papism out of the New World, to throw off the tyranny of a foreign government and allow free men to determine their own society. (Although it must be said that in the Southwest, the first Americans were fighting to establish Roman Catholicism and Spanish power among the heathen.) Today, we regard that as largely self-deception tinged with self-righteousness; Americans were also fighting for territory and resources and power, exactly like their European cousins. But at the time, Ameri-

cans seemed to be adding a new aspect to warfare—a crusade—a notion that Europeans had long before abandoned.

With the War of 1812, Americans took a new turn with their wars: They went on the offensive against foreign states.* Starting with the attempted invasions of Canada during the War of 1812 and then accelerating into the U.S. invasion of Mexico in the mid-1840s, Americans were openly turning to war to advance national aims and territorial expansion. By then, too, increasing numbers of Americans were accepting that the wars with Native Americans were quite frankly also territorial wars. But even as they adopted that new frankness about war aims, Americans were adding a new ideal to replace the old one of Christian values. It was called *Manifest Destiny*, an ideal that was invoked throughout the 19th century to claim that some larger force (with Divine Providence or historical determination implied or stated) wanted the United States to spread the Stars and Stripes across North America from the Atlantic to the Pacific.

Manifest Destiny may be seen as simply an extension of the concept that motivated the first settlers—to create a city on a hill—but it did give Americans the sense that they were fighting for a high ideal, just as the Monroe Doctrine (and its several corollaries) gave Americans the sense that they were fighting for an ideal, that the United States was a disinterested participant, a force for good in the world. President Woodrow Wilson invoked that spirit in World War I with his goal: "The world must be made safe for democracy." Americans also felt good about entering World War II because it was a "just war." And, finally, Americans felt good about fighting in places such as Korea to stop the spread of Communism. Perhaps the final American contribution to modern warfare might be said to be an element of naive idealism: war as a noble cause.

AIMS OF THIS BOOK

These are only a few of the speculations that this book may inspire in the minds of its users and readers. But although the compilers are happy if the book prompts such profound questions, that is not its primary aim. This book has the more practical but no less challenging goal

---

* Native Americans have argued that Americans had been attacking foreign states from the day they set foot in the New World. Some historians, such as John Keegan, have disputed the comparison, stating that nomadic societies are not territorial states in any meaningful sense of the term.

of laying out all the important facts about all the American wars.

Just as important, the facts are set forth in clearly defined categories so that anyone can proceed quickly and easily to a subhead to get a clear answer to any of the basic questions that might arise: Was a war known by other names? What were the immediate incidents that led to the war? Was there a formal declaration of war—and when? How many troops were involved—on both sides? Exactly when and where were specific battles fought? What weapons were employed? How much did a war cost in terms of dollars? How true are the legends inspired by the war? Just who were some of the individuals whose names we associate with the war?

Those and countless other questions can be answered by referring to this book. The facts set forth in this book are drawn from so many different and often obscure (or at least specialized) sources that we can in all modesty claim that there is no other single volume that contains all these facts. Indeed, although there may be single or multivolume histories of individual wars that have most of the facts about that particular war spread throughout hundreds of pages and hundreds of thousands of words, such specialized volumes often make it difficult to pin down many of the specifics that are laid out so clearly here.

Historians interested in broader themes and issues often have little interest in pinning down, for instance, the exact location of a battle or the number of casualties.

At the same time, we would be less than honest if we did not admit that it has not always been easy to come up with simple answers and straightforward facts. It is the nature of history that some facts are simply not known and probably never can be known. This is particularly true of casualties and dollar costs: Official sources have often been unable to agree on such details, and historians have often shown little interest in such details. Even the smaller wars have unknowns when it comes to exact numbers killed or wounded, not to mention those missing in action. In recognition of such problems, we discuss these issues in the preface—and we try throughout the book to indicate unknowns or estimates or disagreements.

In the end, then, these facts and any speculations they may inspire are designed to help people arrive at some better understanding of the role of wars in U.S. history.

John S. Bowman
Samuel Willard Crompton
December 1997

FRANCO-SPANISH WAR IN FLORIDA

DATES OF WAR

September 4–October 12, 1565

ALTERNATE NAMES

Huguenot-Catholic War

SIGNIFICANCE

Although often overlooked in discussions of American wars, the conflict between the French and the Spanish in Florida was the forerunner of a long series of wars in North America, and its outcome had a major impact on later developments. In prefiguring those later wars, the Franco-Spanish War in Florida signaled that the age-old European conflicts would be carried over to the Americas. Moreover, the Spaniards' devastating defeat of the French in that war encouraged the French to refocus their colonization efforts far to the north, in what are now the Canadian provinces of Nova Scotia and Quebec.

BACKGROUND

The background of the Franco-Spanish War in Florida lay in religious and economic developments in Europe. During the 16th century, France was one of several European countries that experienced a religious crisis: the challenge of the Protestant Reformation. John Calvin, a Frenchman who had settled in Geneva, Switzerland, was a leader of that movement, and his views on the Christian church and on society had a far reaching influence. Calvin's followers in France became known as *Huguenots*. Like many of the early Protestants of Europe, in addition to seeking changes in the teachings of the Roman Catholic Church, the Huguenots demanded a more active role in the French government and economy. Seeking relief from the persecutions they suffered in France, many Huguenots were eager to establish a colony in the New World.

French Huguenot colonists, led by Jean Ribaut and René Goulaine de Laudonnière, made two efforts to establish a colony in what became the southeastern United States. The first, Charlesfort, was founded on present-day Parris Island, South Carolina, in 1562. Ribaut went back to France for supplies and more colonists, but when he did not return when promised, the colonists in Charlesfort abandoned the site and returned to France. Then in 1564, Laudonnière led a second expedition and established a colony of about 300 people at Fort Caroline on the south bank of the St. Johns River, 10 miles east of present-day Jacksonville, Florida. Ribaut was planning to send supplies and reinforcements to the new colony when early in spring 1565 he learned that Spain was sending a fleet against Fort Caroline.

CAUSES OF THE WAR

At the root of the Franco-Spanish War in Florida were religious rivalries between French Huguenots and Spanish Roman Catholics, which were exacerbated by the conflicting colonial ambitions of France and Spain. Detesting what it considered the heresy of Protestantism, Spain was determined to keep 100 percent of its population 100 percent Catholic. Beyond that, Spain wanted to prevent other European countries from establishing colonies in the New World, which in the early 1500s was largely a Spanish domain. Although Spain had shown little interest in colonizing the Atlantic coast of Florida since Juan Ponce de León first visited it in 1513, Spain was uneasy about the French gaining a foothold in that territory. When reports came back that the French at Fort Caroline had captured a Spanish ship anchored in the St. Johns River and had then sailed to the West Indies to raid Spanish ships, Spain decided to eliminate the French presence in Florida.

PREPARATIONS FOR WAR

King Philip II of Spain appointed Pedro Menéndez de Avilés captain general of Florida and ordered him to ready a fleet to sail to the

New World. Learning of this, Jean Ribaut speeded up his preparations and sailed from France in May 1565.

DECLARATION OF WAR

There was no official declaration of war by either party, but King Philip II officially sanctioned the Spanish expedition led by Menéndez.

COMBATANTS

French Huguenots: A small minority (10 percent) of the population of France, the Huguenots tended to belong to the prosperous upper middle classes. They were ambitious and hardworking, and they wanted to create a lasting colony in the New World; many of them had brought their wives and children to the New World. By 1565, there were some 285 Huguenots (including women and children) in the colony at Fort Caroline. The men were expected to take up arms in an emergency, but few of them were experienced soldiers. They were reinforced by another 500 men who arrived with Ribaut in August 1565.

Spanish Catholics: The 800 Spaniards who arrived in Florida with Menéndez included some 300 professional soldiers and sailors in the pay of King Philip II; the other men were colonists prepared to take up arms. But most of the men, in addition to their loyalty to the crown, shared a deep hatred for Protestant sects, which increased the fervor with which they fought.

GEOGRAPHIC AND STRATEGIC CONSIDERATIONS

Neither party knew much about the land over which it fought; only the coastal region had been viewed by a few explorers and sailors. To the Huguenots, the stretch of the Atlantic coast they settled seemed a fertile, almost tropical paradise. Yet to the Spanish, who already had settlements along that coast, it was a land of mixed blessings—rich in vegetation and wildlife but full of disease, allegedly rich in gold that seemed free for the taking but already inhabited. The French Huguenots were interested in the accessible harbors and rivers; in the warm climate and plentiful water; and, above all, in the "free" and seem-

ingly boundless land. (Like the Spaniards, they showed no consideration for the natives already living there.) Although the French were already in place in their colony, the major consideration in the hostilities to follow was which fleet (that of Ribaut or that of Menéndez) would arrive first off the coast of Florida.

BATTLES AND CAMPAIGNS

May 1565: Jean Ribaut sailed from France with seven ships and some 500 colonists in order to reinforce and resupply the colony that had been established in 1564.

June 29, 1565: Pedro Menéndez de Avilés sailed from Cadiz, Spain, with ten ships and some 1,500 Spaniards, including some 800 fairly experienced soldiers and sailors; his goals were to wipe out the French colony in Florida and to establish a Spanish colony in its place. His fleet was heavily damaged by a storm, and he had to go first to Puerto Rico. He set out again from Puerto Rico on August 15 with only five ships and some 800 men, who were charged with eliminating the French to prepare the way for other Spanish colonists.

August 28, 1565: Jean Ribaut's fleet arrived at Fort Caroline on the St. Johns River.

September 4, 1565: The Spanish fleet approached the coast of Florida and encountered the French fleet, which had disembarked its passengers. The French sailed back to the St. Johns River for safety.

September 8, 1565: Menéndez and his men landed on the shore of the Matanzas River and built a fort they named San Augustin. That fort became present-day St. Augustine, Florida, the oldest city in the United States.

September 10, 1565: Intending to attack the new Spanish settlement to the south, Jean Ribaut embarked with 600 men aboard his largest ships and sailed from Fort Caroline.

September 11–12, 1565: As the two fleets prepared for battle, a major storm came up, and the French ships were blown far off course to the south, some as far as present-day Cape Canaveral. All the ships were wrecked along the coast between the Matanzas Inlet and present-day Cape Canaveral.

September 17, 1565: Menéndez led 500 of his men out of San Augustin and marched by land toward French Fort Caroline.

September 20, 1565: Menéndez attacked Fort Caroline, which was thinly defended in the absence of Ribaut's fleet. The Spanish took the fort; about 135 French were killed in the battle or executed, about 40 escaped (among them Laudonnière), and some 40 women and children were taken prisoner (and later sent to France).

September 23, 1565: Having renamed the French fortress Fort San Mateo, Menéndez left the St. Johns River and marched back to San Augustin.

September 29, 1565: Meeting a group of about 265 Frenchmen who had been shipwrecked in the storm on September 11–12, Menéndez and his men persuaded them to surrender and then killed them near the Matanzas River ("river of slaughters") south of San Augustin.

October 12, 1565: Jean Ribaut and about 350 of his men were stranded on an Atlantic beach near the Matanzas River and were discovered by Menéndez's troops. A series of negotiations followed, but those soon broke down. About 200 Frenchmen fled into the wilderness but Ribaut and some 150 others surrendered, hoping for mercy. The Spaniards killed all except about 15 who demonstrated they were Roman Catholics (see Notable Phrases, below). That abruptly ended the hostilities as well as the French presence in Florida.

NEGOTIATIONS AND PEACE TREATY

There were no negotiations and no peace treaty. Since the Franco-Spanish War in Florida was seen as an affair between the crown of Spain and a group of religious dissidents, the government of France had little interest in aiding the French Huguenots.

RESULTS OF THE WAR (Casualties, Costs, Consequences)

The Spanish suffered relatively few casualties in the brief Franco-Spanish War in Florida, but the French lost some 600 people. No historian has even tried to estimate the financial cost, but France again was the loser. In the short term, the Spanish also paid a price. Dominique de Gourgues, a French soldier-adventurer, was so incensed by news of the massacre of the Huguenot colony at Fort Caroline that, in 1568, he fitted

out three ships and sailed to Florida. With the aid of some natives, he captured Fort San Mateo (the former Fort Caroline) and killed all the Spanish troops (see Notable Phrases, below). Nonetheless, the brief war established Spain as the foremost military and colonial power in what is now the southeastern United States for 200 years. France, which had hoped to establish a colonial foothold in that region, was expelled and afterward concentrated its colonization efforts in present-day Canada.

MILITARY INNOVATIONS, TACTICS, EQUIPMENT

There were no innovations in the brief Franco-Spanish War in Florida. Most of the soldiers carried the standard weapon of the day, the harquebus—a heavy, rather crude early form of the rifle. Other weapons included pistols, swords, and pikes (iron-pointed staffs). None of those weapons was at all effective at long range. The professional soldiers wore metal helmets and breastplates; some carried shields. The Spanish already had shown their ability to organize military expeditions and send them across the Atlantic Ocean to capture native peoples who did not have firearms. That minor operation in Florida, however, was the first time that one European power organized what was essentially an amphibious invasion to fight another European force in the New World.

NOTABLE PHRASES

I do this not to Frenchmen but to Lutherans.

There is a story often repeated (but with absolutely no evidence) that Pedro Menéndez de Avilés erected a sign with those words near the graves of the Frenchmen killed near the Matanzas River. (Lutherans was the name commonly applied to all Protestants in those days.) Menéndez's point was that the Huguenots had died not because they were French but because they were Protestants—that is, virtual heathens. Perhaps inevitably, it also has been claimed (again with no evidence) that after de Gourgues destroyed Fort San Mateo in revenge (see Results of the War, above), he erected a sign: *Hanged not as Spaniards but as traitors, robbers, and murderers.*

HISTORICAL PERSPECTIVES AND CONTROVERSIES

Francis Parkman, the 19th-century American historian, made the first and most detailed study of the Franco-Spanish War in Florida (see Further Reading, below). Although various details have since been discovered, no historians have disputed Parkman's thesis that the religious and political animosities of 16th-century Europeans were simply carried over to the New World in the Franco-Spanish War in Florida. Modern historians, however, are apt to take a more skeptical view of the religious motives of the participants in that war. Accounts by the Spanish and French long stressed the religious dedication and even idealism of the participants, but more recent accounts by historians are inclined to emphasize the participants' desire for political power and commercial profit.

CIVILIAN AND MILITARY BIOGRAPHIES

Laudonnière, René Goulaine de (flourished 1562–1582)—sailor, colonizer: Laudonnière was born to a noble family in Poitou, France. He was a convert to the Huguenot faith. Serving as a lieutenant to Jean Ribaut, he sailed to North America in 1562 to establish the first colony at Charlesfort, then returned to France with Ribaut. In April 1564, Laudonnière sailed from France to command the new colony he established at Fort Caroline in Florida. The colony was torn apart by dissension, and the colonists were about to abandon it when, in August 1565, Ribaut arrived with ships, supplies, and reinforcements. In the fighting with the Spanish that ensued, Laudonnière escaped from Fort Caroline, made his way to one of the French ships, and reached France in 1566. He retired to his estate. His account of the French colonies came out in 1587 in an English translation by Richard Hakluyt, the English publisher of voyages of discovery.

Menéndez de Avilés, Pedro (1519–1574)— sea captain, colonizer: Menéndez was born in Avilés, Spain. He became such a successful sea captain that by the age of 35 he was the captain general of Spain's West Indies fleet. On the invitation of King Philip II, he set out to drive out the French colonists in Florida. He not only wiped out the colony but also established the fort that would become St. Augustine, Florida. For the next few years he sailed around the Caribbean, the Gulf coast, and up the Atlantic coast to Chesapeake Bay, helping to establish Spanish settlements. After the Spanish Jesuit colony on the shores of Chesapeake Bay was wiped out by local Indians in 1571, Menéndez returned to the Chesapeake Bay area and hanged eight of the alleged murderers.

Ribaut, Jean (1520–1565)—sailor, colonizer: Ribaut was born in Dieppe, France. He was a Protestant. Ribaut led the first colonizing effort on Parris Island. After he returned to France in 1562, he found the Protestants and Catholics essentially at war and so fled to England. There, he published an English translation of his report on the colony and conditions in the New World. Accused of seeking to steal some ships that were intended to bring an English colony to Florida, Ribaut was briefly imprisoned in the Tower of London. In 1565 he sailed with his French expedition to reinforce Fort Caroline, but that led to disaster and his death.

FURTHER READING

Lowery, Woodbury. *The Spanish Settlements within the Present Limits of the United States: Florida, 1562–1574.* New York: G. P. Putnam's Sons, 1905.

Parkman, Francis. *Pioneers of France in the New World.* Boston: Little, Brown Co., 1897.

Tebeau, Charlton W. *A History of Florida.* Coral Gables, Fla.: University of Miami Press, 1971.

THE COLONIAL WARS

DATES OF WARS

1609–1689

ALTERNATE NAMES

Canadian-Indian conflicts (1609–1689). Anglo-French conflicts (1613–1632). Virginian-Indian Wars (1622 and 1644). Pequot War (1636–1637). Dutch-Indian Wars (1642–1645). Dutch-Swedish Wars (1648–1655). Anglo-Dutch Wars (1652–1674). King Philip's War (1675–1676). Bacon's Rebellion (1676).

SIGNIFICANCE

Soon after they landed on the eastern shores of North America, the English, French, Swedish, and Dutch settlers began to make war on one another and on the Native Americans. That series of conflicts (known collectively as the Colonial Wars) was extremely important in the early history of North America. Two primary results emerged: First, the European victories over the Native Americans ensured the survival of European settlements in North America. Second, the victories of the French and English colonists over the Dutch and Swedish settlers ensured that France and England would be the two European countries foremost in colonization of eastern North America. In a broader sense, those early conflicts also set a pattern that characterized the history of the formation of the United States of America—namely, a sense that the original English-American colonies had a manifest destiny to conquer and control North America. Even Bacon's Rebellion (see p. 16), which might at first seem an exception to that pattern, was part of the process of imposing English authority: Nathaniel Bacon and Sir William Berkeley, governor of Virginia, did not disagree over the need to remove the Indians—only in how to do so.

BACKGROUND

The background for the Colonial Wars lay in the conflict between the European settlers in eastern North America and the Native American tribes and in the rivalries among the different groups of European settlers. In general, the issue was control of land and resources, but some of those rivalries were carried over from and influenced by events in Europe—events often far removed from concerns of the colonists. (Bacon's Rebellion was something of an exception in that it grew out of local, even personal issues.) Quite aside from that, the English, French, Dutch, and Swedish settlers never seemed to consider the possibility that there was more than enough land to go around; they perceived the territory in the New World in terms of monopolies. That approach was completely foreign to the Native Americans, who for the most part did not think in terms of ownership of land; they believed humankind should enjoy the fruits of the land, but not possess that land individually or collectively. Specifically, when they made treaties with the settlers regarding land the Indians believed they were simply agreeing to share the land—not deed it over to exclusive use of the Europeans. Out of the different beliefs that informed the Europeans and Native Americans, and out of the European power rivalries that had existed in Europe for hundreds of years, grew the Colonial Wars.

CAUSES OF THE WARS

The causes of the 17th-century hostilities known as the Colonial Wars may be divided into two groups. One group comprises conflicts that were essentially extensions of hostilities among the European states to their New World colonies. Those include the Anglo-French conflicts of 1613–1632, the Dutch-Swedish Wars of 1648–1655, and the Anglo-Dutch Wars of 1652–1674. Those conflicts were rooted in European power politics. The other group comprises those conflicts that were truly home-grown. They involved hostilities between the colonists and neighboring Indians. Those include the Canadian-Indian conflicts of 1609–1689, the Virginian-Indian Wars of 1622 and 1644; the Pequot

War of 1636–1637, the Dutch-Indian Wars of 1642–1645, and King Philip's War of 1675–1676. The one exception—Bacon's Rebellion (1676)—was a transitional conflict in two senses: a transition between the two types of wars and a transition to the type of hostility that eventually culminated in the American Revolution. The immediate causes of each of those wars are explained below under the heading for the war.

PREPARATIONS FOR WARS

In general, it may be said that the Colonial Wars occurred accidentally and incrementally rather than through decisive planning. Examples would include the French-Iroquois wars that grew out of the actions of Samuel de Champlain in 1609. He had never intended that assisting the Algonquin Indians in one fight would turn the Iroquois into long-standing enemies.

However, there were at least three occasions when European-Indian wars were deliberate. The Indian attacks on the Virginia colony in 1622 and 1644 were planned and led by the Indian chief Opechancanough. In 1675, the war that became known as King Philip's War was led by Metacomet (known to the English-Americans as King Philip), until the conduct and strategy of the war became larger than he could manage. For their part, the Europeans in North America also seemed to wander into their wars and only afterward pursue them with some organized planning. Thus, colonial settlements erected fences and outposts and assigned guards as part of a routine defensive policy, but not until hostilities broke out were true militias organized. Even when those hostilities were part of wars being fought in Europe by the motherlands, the colonies were for the most part left to fend for themselves.

DECLARATIONS OF WAR

In most cases, there were no formal declarations—at least as the Colonial Wars developed in the New World: Episode followed episode, incident followed incident, and people found themselves engaged in war. Exceptions to that are discussed in the particular Colonial Wars.

COMBATANTS

The combatants for the most part were French,

British (that is, Scottish, Welsh, even Irish, as well as English), Dutch, and Swedish settlers, and the Native Americans they encountered, ranging from the Abenaki Indians in Canada to the Powhatan Indians in Virginia. The European settlers sometimes organized the equivalent of militias but often fought as little more than isolated individuals. In some cases, troops from Europe were involved, such as in 1664, when English soldiers captured New York from the Dutch; in 1666, when French soldiers attacked the Iroquois villages; and in 1676, when English troops arrived in Virginia to help put down Bacon's Rebellion.

GEOGRAPHIC AND STRATEGIC CONSIDERATIONS

The geographic circumstances of the Colonial Wars were formed by the Atlantic coastline of North America to the east and the foothills of the Appalachian Mountains to the west; the other geographic factors were the major rivers that flowed into the Atlantic—such as the St. Lawrence, Connecticut, Hudson, and Delaware.

If the English settlers had any advantage over other Europeans it was primarily due to their numbers and their sense that they were determined, even destined, to colonize the New World.

Strategically, the Europeans fought to preserve their settlement enclaves along or near the coast, and the Native Americans usually fought with the intent of pushing the Europeans back to, if not into, the ocean. The Europeans also fought one another—sometimes with great ferocity—to determine which of them would hold the choicest parcels of land and control the most lucrative trade routes. What separates the Colonial Wars from many other wars in American history is a survival dimension to the fighting: The losers truly lost territory for all time. Had the Native Americans under Metacomet (King Philip) prevailed, for instance, the New England settlers might indeed have found themselves confined to the Atlantic coastline.

Canadian-Indian Conflicts: 1609–1689

As the French moved out from their settlements in Acadia and Quebec, they increasingly came into contact, and then conflict, with the Iroquois nations who inhabited the area of

This map of 1702 from Cotton Mather's Magnalia Christi Americana *shows the colonies of New England and New York at that time. Note that most settlements were concentrated along the coasts and rivers.*

present-day upstate New York. The conflicts were based upon trade rivalries (primarily for the beaver trade) and Indian enmities (the French became allied with the Abenaki and other Algonquin Indians, who were enemies of the Iroquois).

BATTLES AND CAMPAIGNS

July 9, 1609: Samuel de Champlain, who founded Quebec in 1608, led a group of Abenaki warriors to victory in a fight with the Iroquois at the junction of Lake George and Lake Champlain in present-day New York State. (That junction later became the site of Fort Ticonderoga.) Champlain won the day through his use of a French harquebus, a matchlock gun (neither the Algonquins nor the Iroquois had any firearms), but he earned the lasting enmity of the Iroquois.

1642–1661: Numerous attacks by the Iroquois Indians against the small French settlements along the St. Lawrence River nearly wiped out the colony of New France. Using a hit-and-run strategy, the Iroquois caused many casualties (in 1660–1661, 58 French settlers were killed and 59 were captured, out of a total population

of no more than 3,000 persons in the colony) and great suffering to the settlers of New France.

July 23, 1665–October 5, 1666: The Marquis de Tracy, a French army veteran, had arrived in French Canada in 1664 to direct a campaign against the Iroquois, who constantly interfered with French attempts to hunt and trade for furs in the territory south of Canada. He set out south from Quebec City in July 1665 and built a series of six forts all the way down to Lake Champlain. In January 1666, he sent out a force to intimidate the Iroquois and their allies, the Mohawks; the French did not inflict many casualties but the Iroquois sent delegates to negotiate peace in May and July; Tracy, hearing of atrocities (including the murder of a nephew) committed by Mohawks, imprisoned the delegates. That September Tracy led a punitive expedition against the Mohawks down into what would become New York State. They burnt the Indian villages, destroyed crops, and seized goods of any use, then claimed all the territory for France before returning to Quebec in October. Tracy then hanged one of the Iroquois and sent the others back to bring word of the French victory.

NEGOTIATIONS AND PEACE TREATY

The French and the Iroquois signed a treaty in 1667, ending years of warfare. But it was only a temporary peace, marked by numerous incidents. Eventually, in August 1684, the Iroquois entered into an official alliance with England, represented by Thomas Dongan, the governor of the English colony of New York. Dongan openly encouraged the Iroquois to move in on the French-Algonquin fur trade. Then, on August 5, 1689, some 1,500 Iroquois warriors made a ferocious attack on the French settlement of LaChine near Montreal—the largest and most devastating attack ever made by Indians on the French. The French suffered at least 200 persons killed, wounded, and taken prisoner; 56 of the 77 homes in the settlement were destroyed. The attack greatly weakened French morale, which only partly was bolstered by the appearance of the Count de Frontenac as the new governor. That and similar episodes led Frontenac to decide that he and his Algonquin allies should take the offensive against the English and their Iroquois allies—thus leading to the first of the French and Indian Wars (1689–1763).

Anglo-French Conflicts: 1613–1632

CAUSES OF THE WARS

Long before establishing their settlements in North America, England and France had a history of competition and hostility. To their early contacts in North America, English and French settlers brought the baggage of territorial disputes, commercial competition, colonial rivalry, dynastic claims, and religious animosity. It is impossible to single out any one of those factors as decisive in instigating the hostilities in North America. For example, religious differences certainly played a role: England had embraced Protestantism since the reign of King Henry VIII, but France had remained firmly Catholic, and each nation's faithful tended to demonize the other's. But it would be hard to separate that religious element from nationalistic and commercial motives when examining the early conflicts between the French and the English colonies in North America. And although they may appear as merely sporadic and somewhat "antiquarian" when set against major wars of American his-

tory, the English-French conflicts are among those wars that shaped the American colonies.

BATTLES AND CAMPAIGNS

July 1613: Sir Samuel Argall, the lieutenant governor of the Virginia colony, led a sea raid by Virginian colonists against the small French settlement of Port Royal in French Acadia (present-day Nova Scotia). After burning Port Royal, Argall and his party arrived off Mount Desert Island in present-day Maine, where on July 13 they attacked and captured the settlement of French Jesuits called St. Saveur. Argall eradicated the settlement and sailed back to Jamestown with 15 French prisoners.

November 1613: On his way home, Argall stopped at Manhattan Island and forced the tiny Dutch settlement to fly the English flag and acknowledge the authority of King James I.

1627–1629: Relations between England and France had been deteriorating for some years over several issues, particularly because of England's distrust of France's alliance with Hapsburg Spain and because of Cardinal Richelieu's treatment of the French Protestants, the Huguenots. England's new young king, Charles I, was greatly under the influence of George Villiers, the 1st Duke of Buckingham, and by early 1627 Buckingham was plotting an uprising in France that would rely on aristocrats unhappy with Richelieu as well as Huguenots. On June 27, 1627, Buckingham set sail with a British fleet, arriving at the island of Ré off La Rochelle, the Huguenots' main port, on July 10. Buckingham's plan was to starve the French garrison into submission with a siege. That failed in October when a large French force arrived and drove the British away. The French troops then laid siege themselves against the Huguenots in La Rochelle. Charles felt he should avenge this defeat and called on his Parliament for financial support for a new expedition under Buckingham; he was assassinated on August 14, 1628, so the fleet that sailed in September was led by the Earl of Lindsey. However, La Rochelle capitulated to the government forces on October 18, so England entered into peace negotiations with France. (It was the events of this war and its major participants, Buckingham and Richelieu, that Alexandre Dumas memorialized in *The Three Musketeers.*)

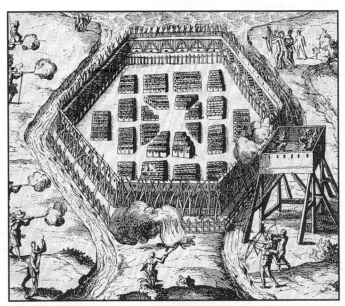

An engraving based on a sketch by Samuel Champlain shows the French and their Indian allies attacking an Iroquois village on Lake Onondaga in central New York in October 1615. Champlain was wounded in the attack.

July 21, 1629: As part of the Anglo-French war in Europe, the Kirke brothers (four English merchants and privateers) captured Quebec from the French defender, Samuel de Champlain. For the next three years, Quebec was a private colony of the Kirke family. That same year Sir Alexander Stewart, under a royal grant from King James I of England, built a new fort at Port Royal to secure Acadia, and renamed Acadia Nova Scotia for the English.

NEGOTIATIONS AND PEACE TREATIES

1632: The Treaty of Saint Germain-en-Laye was signed between France and England. Under its terms, Quebec and Acadia (Nova Scotia) were returned to France. Although there would be sporadic fighting between English and French merchants in the Bay of Fundy and Acadia for many years, there was no official resumption of warfare until 1689, when the French and Indian Wars began.

Virginian-Indian Wars: 1622 and 1644

CAUSES OF THE WARS

As the English settled in the Chesapeake Bay region of Virginia, they encountered a mixture of friendship and hostility from the Indians of that area. Loosely allied in the Powhatan confederacy, the Indians seemed willing to negotiate with the English on equal terms, but they resisted any attempt to be turned into vassals of the English king. Almost from the beginning, therefore, there were inevitable clashes and incidents as the English began to intrude on Indians' territory and resources.

December 10, 1607: The English had established their first permanent colony in Virginia—Jamestown—in May 1607. Capt. John Smith, the effective leader of the colony, went on an expedition in search of food supplies for the winter and was captured by the Indians. He later claimed he had been rescued from imminent execution by Pocahontas, the daughter of the Indian chief Powhatan. (Although one of the most frequently repeated tales of colonial history, there is no evidence to support it.) That was the start of a tenuous alliance of good will between the Virginia settlers and the Indians, lasting until 1622.

October 5, 1609: Capt. John Smith was injured in a gunpowder explosion. He returned to England, leaving the Virginia colony under less capable leadership. Many of the colonists died of malnutrition during the subsequent winter. For the next few years, the Jamestown settlement was in danger of collapse because of failures of leadership and difficulties in producing enough food to feed the colonists.

April 1613: The Jamestown colonists seized Pocahontas and held her hostage to force the release of English held by the local Indians. During captivity, she was converted to Christianity and given the name Rebecca. In 1614 she married the English colonist John Rolfe, who had introduced tobacco growing to the colony in 1612. Pocahontas accompanied Rolfe back to England and died there in 1617.

March 1618: Powhatan died in Virginia. He was succeeded as leader of the Powhatan confederacy by Chief Opechancanough.

BATTLES AND CAMPAIGNS

March 22, 1622: On Good Friday, Opechancanough's band of Indians began a headlong surprise attack on the English settlers in Virginia. Of a total population of some 1,200 colonists, 347 were killed at 31 different sites on the opening day of the war. Among the dead was John Rolfe, who had returned to Virginia after the death of Pocahontas. The English immediately retaliated with a series of raids on the Indians.

August 1, 1622: The Virginia Company of London sent a letter to the English colonists of Virginia urging them to wage war against the Indians. The company also sent 16 ships with 800 new settlers to make up for the early losses.

January 20, 1623: The English settlers in Virginia had gained the upper hand in the Indian war and were able to report to London that "in all places we have slain diverse [Indians], burned their towns, destroyed their wares and corn." The Indian losses in the war soon exceeded those of the English. Relations between the two settled down to a wary cooperation, marred only by occasional minor incidents.

March 18, 1644: Opechancanough's Indians rose against the English settlers in Virginia for a second time. The new attacks endangered the life of the Virginia colony, but Gov. William Berkeley led the colonists to victory during the two years of conflict that followed and emerged a hero. By 1646, the defeated Indians were forced to cede all the lands between the James and York Rivers in Virginia. Opechancanough was cap-

tured and taken to Jamestown, where he was killed prior to trial by an irate soldier (1646). The Indians of Virginia were gradually subdued and pushed off their lands, but there were no additional, concerted wars.

The Pequot War: 1636–1637

CAUSES OF THE WAR

As the Puritans of Massachusetts Bay spread further into Massachusetts, Connecticut and Rhode Island, they ran into conflicts with Indians who were willing and able to resist the encroachments of the white man on their territory. The Pequots of southern Connecticut and Rhode Island had established themselves as the dominant tribe among the Indians of that area. After 1635, the Pequots encountered a new rival—the English settlers. And unlike the Wampanoag, led by Massasoit, the Pequot were unwilling to cede territory and resources to the English.

BATTLES AND CAMPAIGNS

July 20, 1636: New England trader John Oldham was abducted and killed by Pequot Indians who lived in the area of present-day southern Connecticut and Rhode Island. (Oldham was said to have cheated Indians in trade deals). Oldham's death caused the English to carry out a series of punitive expeditions against the Pequots.

August 24, 1636: Massachusetts Bay governor John Endecott organized a military force against the Pequots. At that time, the only English settlement in southern Connecticut was a fort at present-day Old Saybrook; the commander there, Lion Gardiner, chastised Endecott, saying, "You come here to raise these wasps around my ears, and then you will take wing and fly away."

May 26, 1637: English captains John Mason and John Underhill led a colonial attack on the major Pequot stronghold near present-day Mystic, Connecticut. Using firearms and setting fire to wigwams, the Puritans killed 500 Pequot men, women, and children.

June 5, 1637: Capt. John Mason led a New England force against a sizable Pequot camp, this one near Stonington, Connecticut. Once again, the English won the day and destroyed the village in the aftermath of the battle.

July 28, 1637: A combined force of colonists from Massachusetts Bay, Plymouth, and Connecticut attacked and massacred a Pequot settlement near present-day Fairfield, Connecticut, putting an end to the Pequot War. The tribe was near extinction, and the English settlers of New England enjoyed peaceful relations with the Indians for nearly 40 years.

Dutch-Indian Wars: 1642–1645

CAUSES OF THE WARS

The Dutch who settled New Amsterdam (present-day New York City) in 1626 and subsequently extended their settlements up the Hudson River to Fort Orange (present-day Albany), into Pennsylvania and Delaware, and into present-day Hartford, Connecticut, were primarily intent on making profits from trade. Inevitably, though, their assertive and expansive ways brought them into conflict with the Indians.

BATTLES AND CAMPAIGNS

January 21, 1642: Willem Kieft, the director general of New Netherland, called a meeting of representatives of the leading 12 families in New Netherland. Kieft urged "the Twelve" to sanction warfare against the Indians of the lower Hudson River valley. For their part, those Indians felt menaced by Dutch encroachment on their lands and by the rise of the Iroquois tribes to their north in the Mohawk River valley.

March 1642: Following an unsuccessful Dutch campaign, Jonas Bronck, a Dutch settler, negotiated a truce with the Indians that lasted for one year.

February 1643: Wilhelm Kieft launched an attack against Hudson River valley Indians at Pavonia. Some 80 Indians were murdered. Following this brutality (and the breaking of the one-year truce), the Indian tribes rose in fury and soon confined the Dutch entirely to Manhattan Island and Fort Orange.

September 29, 1643: Connecticut colonist (and veteran of the Pequot War) Capt. John Underhill led a force of English militiamen to the aid of the Dutch, who were beleaguered by attacks from the Indians of the lower Hudson River valley.

December 25–26, 1643: Indians living along the Hudson River fled from attacks from Mohawk Indians and sought safety in Dutch settlements, but the Dutch massacred them. Other Indians retaliated by raiding Dutch settlements.

NEGOTIATIONS AND PEACE TREATY

August 9, 1645: Peace was formally made between the Dutch of New Netherland and the Indians of the Hudson River valley. Facilitated by Mohawk Indians (of the Iroquois Nation), the peace ended three years of hostilities. On July 28, 1646, Willem Kieft was removed from his position as director general of the New Netherland colony, largely because of his ill-considered Indian policy that had led to the wars.

Dutch-Swedish Wars: 1648–1655

CAUSES OF THE WARS

New Sweden was founded in 1638 when Peter Minuit, a Dutchman in the service of Sweden, led a small group of Swedish (and some Dutch) colonists to settle on land along the Delaware River purchased from the Indians. The first colony was established at Fort Christina (present-day Wilmington, Delaware). The Swedes who came to the New World were few in number, but they were determined to create a lasting settlement based on farming and fur trading. However, they ran into the expansionist ambitions of Dutch New Netherland to their north. As early as November 1640, Dutch colonists had settled along the Delaware River close to Fort Christina. But the situation radically changed when on May 11, 1647, Peter Stuyvesant arrived in New Amsterdam and assumed the position of director general of the colony of New Netherland.

BATTLES AND CAMPAIGNS

April 27, 1648: Peter Stuyvesant ordered the construction of Dutch Fort Beversrede at present-day Philadelphia, Pennsylvania. Meanwhile, Johan Bjornsson Printz, governor of the colony of New Sweden, was building a series of Swedish forts, concluding with Fort New Krisholm near the mouth of the Schuylkill River. There was increasing competition between the Dutch and Swedes for control of the Delaware River area.

May 1648: Swedish troops from Fort

Krisholm attacked, captured, and burned Dutch Fort Beversrede.

November 1648: After Dutch troops rebuilt Fort Beversrede, Swedish troops again burned it down. The Dutch hung on to the land and, in 1651, built Fort Casimir on the Delaware River near present-day New Castle, Delaware.

July 19, 1651: Dutch colonists from New Amsterdam occupied their newly constructed Fort Casimir. The Dutch hoped to be able to control the trade routes to the Swedish colony of New Sweden.

November 5, 1651: Johan Classen Rising, governor of New Sweden, defeated a Dutch force and captured Fort Casimir. Total casualties were one Swedish soldier killed.

September 26, 1655: Peter Stuyvesant, director general of New Netherland, recaptured Fort Casimir from the Swedes, virtually ending Swedish influence on the continent of North America. Stuyvesant, however, did not enjoy his victory for long; he was beleaguered by encroachments by English settlers from Connecticut.

Anglo-Dutch Wars: 1652–1674

CAUSES OF THE WARS

Essentially, Anglo-Dutch Wars stemmed from conflicts in Europe, in the East Indies, and on the world's oceans. In particular, the wars arose out of England's attempt to claim sovereignty over all the seas and thus the right to interfere with the expanding Dutch colonial and commercial empire. That rivalry was particularly direct and bitter in North America. The border between Dutch New Netherland and the English colonies of Connecticut and Massachusetts was vague. Because of their larger populations, the English colonies sometimes encroached on New Netherland (the encroachments generally took place under the auspices of private settlers), but it took the passage of the Navigation Act by the British Parliament on October 16, 1651, to bring things to a head: The act stated that no goods could be imported from the English colonies into England on non-English ships—effectively, that meant Dutch ships. Not only the Dutch colonists but also the English colonists objected to this infringement on their right to ship their goods as they saw fit. The precipitating event of the war, however, occurred in Europe.

BATTLES AND CAMPAIGNS: FIRST ANGLO-DUTCH WAR (1652–1654)

May 1652: Dutch and English ships fought a battle off the coast of England; the Dutch, under Adm. Maarten Tromp, were defeated. At issue was the right of the Dutch to engage freely in sea trade in the North Sea.

July 8, 1652: England declared war on Holland.

June 2, 1653: Relations between the English colonies that formed the New England Confederation (in 1643) and the Dutch colony known as New Netherland had deteriorated, aggravated by the outbreak of the war between their mother countries. The New England Confederation voted to make war against New Netherland, but the Massachusetts Bay Colony refused to go along with this action.

July 5, 1653: Troops of English colonists from Connecticut took over the Dutch Fort Good Hope at present-day Hartford, Connecticut. This was the only military action that took place in North America during the First Anglo-Dutch War.

April 1654: The English and Dutch signed the Treaty of Westminster in April 1654. The basic issues were left undecided, so the peace treaty amounted to little more than an armistice.

June 20, 1654: New England colonists were about to attack the Dutch settlement at New Amsterdam when they received word that the English and Dutch had signed a peace treaty ending their war in Europe. For the next decade, relations between the Dutch and English colonies in the Northeast remained in a state of guarded tension.

BATTLES AND CAMPAIGNS: SECOND ANGLO-DUTCH WAR (1665–1667)

March 12, 1664: King Charles II of England made a grant of land to his younger brother, James, the Duke of York. The grant gave authority to James over all the land between the Connecticut and Delaware Rivers in North America, ignoring the claims of the English colony in Connecticut and the now-defunct Swedish claim to the Delaware area.

August 29, 1664: Four English ships arrived off New Amsterdam, the Dutch colony on Manhattan Island. The fleet was commanded by Col. Richard Nicolls, who had been commissioned by the Duke of York to capture the Dutch colony of New Netherland.

September 7, 1664: Peter Stuyvesant, the director general of New Netherland, surrendered New Amsterdam and Manhattan Island to the English naval forces under Col. Richard Nicolls that had blockaded the colony for little more than a week. Stuyvesant was eager to fight, but the Dutch populace of Manhattan Island was unwilling. The area was soon renamed New York in honor of the Duke of York.

September 20, 1664: English colonel George Cartwright accepted the Dutch surrender of Fort Orange (present-day Albany, New York). Following this takeover, the English made efforts to befriend the Iroquois Indians of upper New York.

February 23, 1665: Col. Richard Nicolls, the Duke of York's deputy in America, ordered the annexation of all property that belonged to the Dutch West Indies Company in what had been New Netherland.

March 4, 1665: England declared war on the Netherlands, formally starting the Second Anglo-Dutch War.

June 1667: A Dutch fleet penetrated the Thames estuary and destroyed the English fleet docked at Chatham.

July 31, 1667: The English and Dutch signed the Peace of Breda, formally ending the Second Anglo-Dutch War. Although the Dutch gained something by having their rights as neutral traders recognized, the treaty gave England sovereignty over New Netherland.

BATTLES AND CAMPAIGNS: THIRD ANGLO-DUTCH WAR (1673–1674)

The seeds of this particular phase of the Anglo-Dutch Wars were planted in 1670, when King Louis XIV of France, wanting to challenge the expansive Dutch, signed the Treaty of Dover with King Charles II of England in secret. The French occupied much of the Dutch republic in 1672, but the Dutch navy continued to defeat the English at sea. The war took on international dimensions, mainly on the high seas, but there were some repercussions for North America.

August 7–12, 1673: A Dutch naval force of 23 ships carrying 1,600 men bombarded the English garrison at New York until the English surrendered. The Dutch did not formally hand back the city to the English until November 10, 1674.

August 15–17, 1673: Dutch military units moved up the Hudson River and took over many of the English (formerly Dutch) settlements all the way up to Fort Orange. Many English settlements on eastern Long Island and in New Jersey also submitted to Dutch rule.

February 19, 1674: The English and Dutch signed the Second Treaty of Westminster, ending the Third Anglo-Dutch War. The largely victorious English formally regained possession of the entire New York area, but they were forced to drop their claims of sovereignty over the seas and to grant the Dutch certain fishing rights.

King Philip's War: 1675–1676

CAUSES OF THE WAR

Following the arrival of the Pilgrims (1620) and the Puritans (1630) in Massachusetts, the English colonists lived for a number of years in peace with their Indian neighbors, led by the Wampanoag sachem Massasoit. The Pequot War, fought in southern Connecticut, did not disturb the peace in the Massachusetts colonies, but when Massasoit died in 1662 he was succeeded by his son Metacomet (known to the colonists as King Philip), who had no liking for the English. King Philip began almost immediately to plot against the colonists, but it took years of deteriorating relations between the English colonists and the Massachusetts Indians before full-scale war broke out.

BATTLES AND CAMPAIGNS

April 10, 1671: Following a series of minor hostilities between Wampanoag Indians and Massachusetts colonists, the leaders of Plymouth Colony forced Wampanoag sachem King Philip to turn over some of his arms to the colonists.

September 29, 1671: Realizing that the colonists had greater military strength than he had, King Philip signed a new accord with the commissioners of Plymouth Colony, agreeing to accept and follow the advice of the commissioners in matters of war and the sale of Indian lands.

1671-1675: Tensions continued to build between the Wampanoag Indians and the Plymouth Colony.

June 8, 1675: Plymouth colonists tried and

This engraving of a conflict in King Philip's War, which appeared in 1810, depicts the colonists in clothing not of their time and carrying long rifles which they did not have in the 17th century. But it is correct in showing the advantage that guns gave the colonists over the Native Americans with their bows and arrows.

executed three Wampanoag Indians who had been implicated in the murder of John Sassamon, an Indian who had converted to Christianity. The trial brought a new level of accusations against King Philip; the notion that he had developed a conspiracy to overthrow the English colonists grew rapidly after the trial.

June 20–25, 1675: King Philip led the Wampanoag Indians in a series of sporadic attacks against Swansea in Plymouth Colony, the town that was closest to Wampanoag territory on the Mount Hope peninsula in Rhode Island. The conflict that became known as King Philip's War began.

June 28, 1675: Colonial soldiers from Boston and Plymouth united in a force that swept through the Mount Hope area. The colonists found that King Philip and his people had fled from the peninsula by canoes to present-day Pocasset, Massachusetts.

July 1675: King Philip and his Wampanoag warriors slipped through forested areas of the colonial lines and made their way to central Massachusetts, where they met and formed an alliance with the Nipmuck Indians. That made the conduct of the war even more serious for the English: Confronted at first by only one tribe, they now found that the war had erupted on a new front and that the number of Indians under King Philip's command had increased.

August–November 1675: At least 150 English colonists in the north country of Maine were killed or captured in attacks by the Abenaki Indians of that area.

August 2–5, 1675: King Philip's Wampanoag and Nipmuck warriors carried out a siege of Brookfield, Massachusetts. Following the relief of the town on August 5 by colonial forces, King Philip withdrew to the north.

August 19, 1675: King Philip led his warriors in an attack on Lancaster, Massachusetts.

September 1, 1675: Taking the fight farther to the west, King Philip and his warriors attacked the settlements of Deerfield and Hadley in the Connecticut River valley. The Indians were turned back at Hadley under circumstances that appeared nearly miraculous. (See "The Angel of Hadley" under Legends and Trivia, p. 20.)

September 2, 1675: The Wampanoag and Nipmuck Indians attacked the settlement known as Squakeag (present-day Northfield, Massachusetts). Although that attack was fended off, the colonists eventually evacuated the settlement on September 6.

September 12, 1675: Indian forces attacked Falmouth (present-day Portland), Maine. That attack demonstrated that the war, which had begun as a local affair in Rhode Island and Massachusetts, had spread to many parts of colonial New England.

September 18, 1675: Indian forces won a major victory at "Bloody Brook," 2 miles south of Deerfield, Massachusetts. Colonial troops, who had been recruited from the town of Essex, Massachusetts, lost 64 of their best fighting men in an ambush; the bodies were thrown into the brook. Following this disaster, Deerfield was abandoned.

October 5, 1675: King Philip's warriors attacked colonists at Springfield, Massachusetts, but were repulsed.

October 30, 1675: The "praying Indians" (as the Massachusetts colonists called the Indians who converted to Christianity) of Natick and Waban, Massachusetts, were taken away under guard to Deer Island in Boston Harbor, where they remained for the rest of the war. An eminent 20th-century historian later proclaimed that the "treatment of the converted 'praying' Indians was no worse than that of the United States to Japanese-Americans in World War II."

December 19, 1675 ("The Great Swamp Fight"): Josiah Winslow led colonial troops in an attack on the Narragansett Indian stronghold near present-day South Kingston, Rhode Island. Caught by surprise, the Indians fled into a nearby swamp. Although many of the Indian warriors managed to escape, more than 300 women and children were killed in what became known as the "Great Swamp Fight."

Winter 1675–1676: King Philip's warriors wintered at present-day Schagticoke, New York, 20 miles north of present-day Albany on the Hudson River. That placed King Philip's warriors on the edge of the territory of the Mohawk Indians, the most warlike of the Five Nations of Iroquois.

January–June, 1676: King Philip's warriors were attacked several times by Mohawk warriors from the New York area. Those attacks weakened King Philip's ability to conduct his campaigns against the English settlements in Massachusetts.

February 10, 1676: Following weeks of hunger from low food supplies, King Philip and his warriors attacked Lancaster, Massachusetts, where they took a number of captives, chief among them Mary Rowlandson (see Legends and Trivia, p. 20).

February 21, 1676: King Philip's warriors gained a victory in their attack on Medfield, Massachusetts, killing 20 settlers.

March 26, 1676: Indian forces led by King Philip attacked a settlement, 5 miles north of Plymouth. Although the invaders were driven off, they killed 42 settlers. King Philip's warriors returned to Plymouth six weeks later, and burned 16 houses.

May 18, 1676 ("The Great Falls Fight"): English captain William Turner led 180 colonists in an attack on an encampment of King Philip's warriors at a section of the Connecticut River that has since become known as Turner's Falls, Massachusetts. The English achieved complete surprise and killed many of the Indians in their wigwams; others were killed while trying to escape in their canoes. The Indian losses were heavy, 200 killed and wounded, but the English also suffered casualties. On their return to Hatfield, the English were ambushed several times by Indians seeking revenge. The day's battle has remained controversial among many historians. Some have characterized the fight as a massacre; others have declared that the English action was commonplace in the warfare of the 17th century.

June 12, 1676: English captain John Talcott led a combined force of Connecticut River valley colonists and Mohegan Indians in a battle against King Philip's warriors near Hadley, Massachusetts. Following that battle and a subsequent defeat at Marlboro, Massachusetts, the Indians began to surrender in large numbers.

June 19, 1676: The government of the Massachusetts Bay Colony issued a special declaration of mercy. Although the declaration made no promises as to what would happen to Indian leaders, rank-and-file Indian warriors were encouraged to surrender with a promise of clemency.

June 27, 1676: A spectacular mass surrender of Indians (180 Nipmucks) occurred in Boston.

July 3, 1676: Capt. John Talcott led his men to victory over the Narragansett Indians near present-day Warwick, Rhode Island. The colonists killed or captured 67 Indians.

July 20, 1676: Capt. Benjamin Church led a colonial force against Wampanoag warriors near present-day Bridgewater, Massachusetts. Church's men prevailed in the fighting; 173 Indians were killed or captured.

July 31, 1676: The wife and nine-year-old son of King Philip were captured by colonial troops under the command of Capt. Benjamin

Church. A considerable debate ensued as to whether the family members should be put to death or sold into slavery in the West Indies. Although historians have generally accepted the view that King Philip's wife and son were sold into slavery, some evidence came to light in the 1990s that a Puritan minister may have hidden the woman and child, and that they went to live in northern New England, where many Indians today claim to be their descendants.

August 12, 1676: King Philip was surprised, shot, and killed by an Indian named Alderman, who was fighting with the colonial troops. The action took place in a swamp near present-day Bristol, Rhode Island, where the war had begun 14 months earlier. King Philip's body was decapitated and quartered; the head was stuck on a pole and displayed outside Plymouth, as a warning to the Indian tribes of New England (see Notable Phrases, p. 20 for Church's response to the death of King Philip).

NEGOTIATIONS AND PEACE TREATY

There was no formal treaty between the colonists and the Wampanoag and Nipmucks. But on April 12, 1678, Sir Edward Andros, acting on behalf of the Duke of York, signed the Peace of Casco in Pemaquid, Maine. This ended the fighting between colonists and Indians in Maine, fighting that had dragged on intermittently after the death of King Philip and was essentially a continuation of King Philip's War. The end of the war in the north country gave relatively advantageous terms to the Abenaki Indian tribes of that area, but it effectively ended the power of the New England tribes.

Bacon's Rebellion: 1676

CAUSES OF THE WAR

In 1675, the colony of Virginia was governed by Sir William Berkeley, the hero of the 1644 Indian war against Opechancanough. In 1675, however, Berkeley was accused of failing to pursue the Susquehannock Indians who were attacking and killing settlers on the western and northern frontiers of Virginia. Berkeley was charged with having a personal interest in the fur trade with the Indians. Among the leaders of the frontier settlers was 28-year-old Nathaniel

Bacon, a planter who had connections at court in England. Fed up with Berkeley's lack of action, Bacon decided to move on his own.

BATTLES AND CAMPAIGNS

May 10, 1676: Nathaniel Bacon led an unauthorized campaign against the Occaneechee Indians, alleged to be harassing settlers along the Roanoke River. Returning from his attack on the Indian villages, Bacon wrote "wee have left all nations of Indians where wee have bin ingaged in a civill warre against themselves."

May 26, 1676: Gov. William Berkeley declared Bacon a traitor, since he had engaged and fought the Indians without a proper commission to do so. When Bacon arrived in Jamestown to assume his elected position in the Virginia House of Burgesses, he was arrested.

June 5, 1676: Governor Berkeley pardoned and released Bacon after he agreed to submit to the governor's authority.

June 23, 1676: Berkeley and Bacon came into conflict again. Bacon assembled some 600 men and led them into Jamestown, where he asked the governor sign a commission for a war against the Indians. Berkeley was forced to submit, given the size of Bacon's army. Berkeley also was forced to agree to publicly retract the charge that Bacon had performed traitorous acts.

June 25, 1676: The Virginia assembly (composed of the Governor's Council and the House of Burgesses) ended its session, having passed the seven resolutions that became known as the "June laws," reforms that in general provided for greater protection for the planters from the wishes and desires of the royal governor. Bacon then set out to take on the Indians again.

July 29, 1676: Bacon led his militia back to the Virginia frontier and fought against the Susquehannock Indians. Governor Berkeley declared Bacon a rebel, calling him "Oliver Bacon," in reference to the fact that Bacon had forced laws on the Virginia assembly in a manner that resembled Oliver Cromwell's intimidation of the English Parliament during the 1650s. As Bacon grew in the size of his forces and in the territory he controlled, Governor Berkeley fled to the eastern shore of Virginia in an effort to rally those loyal to him.

August 3–11, 1676: Bacon and his followers held a convention at Middle Plantation in Virginia. Bacon drew up an oath of allegiance, which stated that the signers agreed to prosecute the war against the Indians with all means at their disposal; pledged to resist any efforts by Governor Berkeley to reassert his authority in the colony; and pledged to resist troops that might be sent from England until a letter from Bacon stating his case to King Charles II arrived in London. Sixty-nine prominent members of the colony signed that document, which has been viewed by many historians as proof that Bacon's Rebellion was in some ways a precursor to the events of the American Revolution 100 years later.

September 2, 1676: In an early morning surprise attack, loyalist colonel Philip Ludwell captured the ship *Rebecca*, which previously had been supporting Bacon's cause in Chesapeake Bay. That loss of naval power was grievous to Bacon's cause, since the loyalists gained control of the waters in and around Jamestown.

September 7, 1676: Encouraged by his success on the naval front, Governor Berkeley reoccupied Jamestown.

September 14, 1676: The rebel forces, led by Bacon, started a siege of Jamestown.

September 16, 1676: The loyalist defenders of Jamestown attempted a sortie, trying to break the siege of the town. Some 700 loyalists made a headlong charge against the rebel earthworks (earthen embankments used for fortification); the loyalists were repulsed quickly, with few losses to either side.

September 17, 1676: Bacon employed a screen to prevent Governor Berkeley from using cannon fire. Placing several wives of loyalists on top of the rebel earthworks, Bacon dared the governor to fire into "these ladyes white Aprons."

September 18, 1676: Having effectively screened the construction of his earthworks, Bacon started cannon fire against Jamestown.

September 19, 1676: Seeing the impossibility of defending the town, Governor Berkeley and his loyalist followers fled the town and escaped by ship to safety.

September 20–21, 1676: Nathaniel Bacon, "Governor by Consent of the People," entered Jamestown in triumph. Knowing that the loyalist control of Chesapeake Bay would soon render his position untenable, Bacon reluctantly ordered his men to set the town on fire at nightfall. By the morning of September 21, the rebels had

set fire to the governor's five houses, the church, and state houses, and had destroyed property that totaled approximately 45,000 English pounds.

Late September 1676: Bacon called together his followers at Green Spring, Berkeley's plantation, and tried to get them to take an oath to fight the king's forces. Many refused. Bacon became more autocratic and destructive in his operations.

October 20, 1676: Bacon's rebel forces had gained full control of the valleys between the James and York Rivers in Virginia. The loyalist troops of Governor Berkeley were ineffectual on the eastern shore of Virginia (present-day Maryland), but Berkeley had the support of the owners and captains of ships and conducted a naval battle that successfully isolated Bacon's forces.

October 26, 1676: Bacon died, probably from influenza. His followers buried him in a swampy area, seeking to prevent Berkeley from exhuming the body for retribution.

November–December 1676: The rebellion continued, but it lacked the force and unity that had been provided by Bacon. On November 21, Capt. Thomas Grantham arrived with his ship, *Concord*, and began to negotiate a truce among the two warring factions. He persuaded Berkeley to offer a pardon to all who surrendered immediately, but he was able to persuade only a few of Bacon's followers to do so. Berkeley went on and tried and executed the more prominent leaders he captured.

January 9, 1677: William Drummond, one of Bacon's leading coconspirators, was caught by loyalist forces. He received a half-hour trial on January 15 and was hanged the same day.

January 29, 1677: The first English ship carrying trained soldiers as reinforcements for Governor Berkeley arrived in Chesapeake Bay. (Within the next two weeks, a total of 1,100 English soldiers arrived in Virginia—one of the first appearances of redcoats in the colonies.) On the ship also were two royal commissioners, Adm. John Berry and Col. Francis Moryson, assigned to investigate the rebellion: Word had reached England that Berkeley bore some responsibility for the civil war in Virginia.

February 11, 1677: English colonel Herbert Jeffreys arrived in Virginia and took command of the 1,100 men assembled there. In his discussions with Governor Berkeley (whom he had been sent to replace), Colonel Jeffreys learned that Berkeley had executed two dozen rebel leaders.

Although Jeffreys disapproved of the way Berkeley had handled affairs, he himself sat on courts that tried and executed eight rebel leaders.

May 5, 1677: Sir William Berkeley departed the colony for England, leaving Colonel Jeffreys in control of the government of Virginia.

HOME FRONTS

There were two home fronts during the 17th-century Colonial Wars: the European homelands of the various colonists, and the communities of colonists who were engaged in the hostilities in North America. Those home fronts experienced the wars in quite different ways. In Europe—in England, in France, in the Netherlands, in Sweden—only a relatively few people at the center of things were directly affected by events in the New World. The courts, political figures, and military men were involved in the major developments to the extent that they were responsible for organizing armed forces and paying them. Yet even those decision makers were far more concerned about the European aspects of several of the wars: During the 1600s, those four nations were constantly engaged in conflict, both internal and among themselves and other nations. In the larger cities and seaports of those countries, those engaged in trade and shipping with the American colonies were aware of events. Certain manufacturers—of gunpowder and armaments, of ships and ship supplies—saw their orders rise or fall. But the mass of people in Europe were barely affected by the hostilities in North America. From king to commoner, word of events in the Americas was slow to reach Europe. Newspapers, which appeared in Europe early in the 1600s, did not circulate widely, certainly not among the largely illiterate masses.

The home front in the American colonies was affected quite differently: Although a few of the battles were fought in locales removed from civilian populations, in most cases there was virtually no distinction between the battlefields and the home front in the colonies. Settlements were relatively few and far between, so warfare centered on these. Whether it was the various militia (or occasionally imported troops) attacking other nationals' settlements or colonists fighting Indians, the home front was the battlefield. Forts were settlements and vice versa; the settlers were the combatants and vice versa. A battle

was fought, and, depending on the victor, the settlers picked up their lives as before or found their settlement ravaged and/or controlled by foreign rulers. Thus, throughout the century, most colonists lived with the possibility of war at their doorstep: They did not need newspapers to tell them they were living in a war zone.

NEGOTIATIONS AND PEACE TREATIES

In general, there were few peace treaties during the Colonial Wars—the exceptions have been noted—and most of them were treaties signed in Europe by the mother countries. There were some treaties between Indians and Europeans, but they generally followed the pattern of King Philip's humiliating agreement (September 29, 1671) to follow the lead of the Plymouth Colony. One of the few treaties with Indians that proved effective (though only for a few years) was the Peace of Casco (April 12, 1678), which effectively ended King Philip's War.

RESULTS OF THE WARS (Casualties, Costs, Consequences)

The Canadian-Indian conflicts were much more serious, for both French Canada and the Iroquois. New France was nearly wiped out during the 1650s; only a thin line of white settlers managed to hang on to the three key towns of Quebec, Three Rivers, and Montreal. In the fighting that took place between 1609 and 1689, the French suffered approximately 300 persons killed, wounded, and captured, of a total population between 2,000 and 3,000. The Iroquois suffered similar losses and were hard pressed to make up for the warriors they lost in the fighting.

The early Anglo-French conflicts produced relatively light casualties. Few Englishmen or Frenchmen died in the desultory raids that went on from 1613 to 1632; the major lasting result of the conflicts was that the French were confirmed in their status as the colonial power that held Quebec and the St. Lawrence River.

The Virginian-Indian Wars were comparable to the Canadian-Indian Conflicts in terms of the losses suffered. The Virginia colonists suffered approximately 500 persons killed, wounded, and missing in 1622, and perhaps 600 such losses in 1644. However, the Virginians inflicted at least twice as many casualties on the Indians and broke the power of the Virginia tribes in the process. The monetary losses to the English cannot be effectively calculated, beyond stating that two years' tobacco crops were seriously affected by the fighting.

The Pequot War produced little suffering for the colonists of New England. At a loss of no more than 100 men killed, wounded, and missing, the colonists inflicted losses of up to 1,000 on the Pequot Indians and completely reduced the independent status of that tribe.

The Dutch-Indian Wars were extremely costly for both sides. The Dutch in New Netherland suffered at least 500 persons killed, wounded, missing, and captured, and the Indian tribes suffered losses that were approximately equal to those of the Dutch. The trade of New Netherland suffered greatly between 1642 and 1645. The colony was close to complete collapse when Peter Stuyvesant took control in 1647.

The Dutch-Swedish Wars produced very few casualties. Probably no more than a total of 20 persons were killed, wounded, and missing on both sides during the sporadic fighting that went on from 1648 to 1655. The economic cost was greater; New Sweden, of course, lost its very existence, and New Netherland was again weakened through warfare.

The Anglo-Dutch Wars were primarily European affairs; the action in North America was a sideshow to the conflict over maritime and trade rights that went on in the North Sea and the English Channel. In America, the Dutch lost their New Netherland colony, which never had been prosperous (at least as far as the Dutch West India Company was concerned). On a broader scale, however, the third Anglo-Dutch War was quite important; England replaced the Netherlands as the primary carrier of merchant goods, and the France of Louis XIV became the most dangerous European nation as far as the English were concerned. This led, in 12 years time, to the start of the French and Indian wars.

The losses to the English colonists during King Philip's War were extreme. The English suffered at least 1,000 killed, wounded, and missing. (It has been claimed that in proportion to the population, the casualties were greater than those in any war in U.S. history.) Twelve towns and 1,200 houses in New England were destroyed in the course of the war; the monetary cost was assessed at 100,000 English pounds. For the Indians, the losses were even more severe; as many as 3,000 Indians were killed or wounded during the war, and the Indians of southern New England remained demoralized and poverty stricken for the rest of the colonial period. The best estimates of the damage caused by the war indicate that New England Indians did not return to their prewar standard of living until 1775.

In Bacon's Rebellion, the English colonists' losses were caused by their fellow Englishmen: In effect, it was America's first civil war. Approximately 500 Virginians lost their lives during the rebellion. The economic costs were considerable, but the social ones were even greater: Recent historians have concluded that Bacon's Rebellion put an end to the practice of bringing indentured servants to Virginia and increased the number of Africans who were brought to America, which transformed the economy of the upper South to one of plantation slavery.

MILITARY INNOVATIONS, TACTICS, EQUIPMENT

European Americans: During the Colonial Wars, the European-Americans (English, French, Dutch, and Swedes)—both colonists and the occasional regular troops from Europe—generally used the equipment they had brought from Europe. That equipment ranged from Samuel de Champlain's harquebus, a matchlock gun used in 1609, to the cutlass, sword, and musket that had become common by the time of King Philip's War. In no way can the European Americans be said to have been pioneers in their armaments; they employed the best weaponry they could import, but they seldom improved upon that weaponry. In terms of tactics, the European settlers gained steadily during the period of the Colonial Wars. Although the Indians generally outperformed the Europeans in the woods, the Europeans proved quite expert at sieges and at cornering their foes (exemplified in the Pequot War and King Philip's War). The European-American style of fighting developed from the Thirty Years' War in Europe (1618–1648)—a series of wars that emphasized ruthless prosecution of warfare, heedless of distinctions between military and civilian targets.

Native Americans: Prior to the arrival of the Europeans, the most effective weapons of the

Indians had been bows-and-arrows, and toma-hawks. During the Colonial Wars, the Indians continued to use those weapons; by around 1650, the Indians had also acquired many fire-arms, but they always remained at a crucial dis-advantage when it came to such armaments. In terms of tactics, the Indians were masters of "bush warfare"; their greatest advantage lay in their mobility, with which they consistently out-performed the European Americans. However, the single greatest weakness of the Native Ameri-cans lay in the fact that their sachems, or chiefs, did not have the type of absolute authority that a European American commander had in times of war. Even "King Philip" never had the power of a European American commander; as a sachem, he had to gain and continue to hold the accep-tance of his councillors and his warriors in a way that no European American governor or military leader had to.

LEGENDS AND TRIVIA

On September 1, 1675, Hadley, a settlement in west-central Massachusetts, repulsed an attack by King Philip's warriors. Some time after the attack, a legend sprang up that in the thick of the fighting—when the English defenders were dis-couraged—a white-bearded man whom no one knew emerged with a sword and rallied the colo-nists, leading them to a successful defense. The idea spread that the helpful stranger was none other than William Goffe, one of the infamous 59 regicides, the men who had condemned King Charles I to death in 1649. There is no doubt that Goffe and his fellow regicide Edward Whalley did spend time in Hadley, but the notion that Goffe appeared as the **"Angel of Hadley"** has yet to be proved or disproved. Although mod-ern scholarship has generally found the notion fatuous, it should be emphasized that both Goffe and Whalley had been military men under Cromwell and that either of them could conceiv-ably have rallied a populace in a time of crisis.

Mary White Rowlandson was captured by King Philip's warriors at Lancaster, Massachu-setts, on February 10, 1676. She spent 82 days in Indian captivity before she was ransomed on May 2, 1676. She saw King Philip several times; he asked her to smoke tobacco with him, but she declined. Her writing emphasized the hand of Divine Providence, but she also recognized some of the positive qualities of her Indian captors. Her book, *The Sovereignty and Goodness of God* was published in 1682, and went into 40 editions. It was one of the most widely read tracts in the New England colonies prior to the Revolution.

NOTABLE PHRASES

Great, doleful, naked, dirty beast.

Those were the words of Capt. Benjamin Church when he found the body of King Philip on August 12, 1676. Their significance lies in the fact that that feeling became the central attitude of many New Englanders to the Indian.

How miserable that man is, that Governs a People when Six parts of Seaven at least are Poore Endebted Discontented and Armed.

Gov. William Berkeley's letter to Thomas Ludwell (dated July 1, 1676) indicated the frus-tration that Berkeley and other royal governors faced when trying to apply English models of government to colonies that were inhabited by poor and desperate men. It was, of course, largely from the ranks of such men that Nathaniel Bacon was able to draw his support.

That old fool has hanged more men then I have for the death of my father.

Those are supposedly the words of King Charles II in reference to Sir William Berkeley, governor of the royal colony of Virginia; they have never been substantiated. If the king did pronounce those words, they were meant to con-demn Governor Berkeley for his widespread use of the gallows in the wake of Bacon's Rebellion; it is estimated that Berkeley summarily tried and executed 26 men before the royal commissioners interceded.

SONGS

The American colonists of the 17th century had little time or inclination for composing songs. If they sang anything beyond psalms and hymns, it was the traditional folksongs of their native lands—"Chevy Chase," "Barbara Allen," and others still sung today. Printed music was ex-tremely rare in America before the Revolution.

Instead, words were printed on sheets (or in volumes) with only the name of the traditional melody. The first book known to have been printed in the colonies, *The Whole Booke of Psalmes of 1640* (better known as *The Bay Psalm Book*), contained only the words of the biblical psalms (translated into English) with directions on how to sing them.

HISTORICAL PERSPECTIVES AND CONTROVERSIES

The Colonial Wars have stirred considerable controversy among American historians for three centuries. The key questions that have been debated are as follows:

Why did the white men (European Americans) generally prevail in the conflicts, considering that the Native Americans long outnumbered them?

Historians used to be content to view the Colonial Wars through the lenses of the great Puritan writers Cotton Mather and William Hubbard. Those two historians of that period consistently referred to the hand of Divine Providence; they believed that God intended the Puritans to gain and hold New England and that he paved the way for the victories over the Native Americans. In part because few serious historians examined those wars, that view simply survived as part of a broader sense that it was America's manifest destiny to defeat the Indians. Although not all historians put it in those words, that view was seldom challenged until the mid-20th-century, when historians Douglas Edward Leach and Alden T. Vaughan took a more scientific and materialistic approach; they emphasized, for instance, the strength of European-American technology. A still later generation of American historians (among them Francis Jennings and Stephen Saunders Webb) described the Colonial Wars (particularly King Philip's War) in a much broader context; Jennings and Webb emphasized the influence of the Iroquois Nations, and both sought to de-emphasize the Boston-Plymouth-Hartford triangle as the heart of European America during King Philip's War. The colonists' victories over the Native Americans are today seen as far more complex and more problematic.

Why did the English and French emerge as the two colonial peoples to beat in North America and the Dutch simply fade after their initial efforts?

Between 1620 and 1640 the United Provinces of the Netherlands possessed by far the largest merchant marine in the world—some 10,000 ships—and given their maritime strength and commercial success, it seems the Dutch should have thrived in North America. Historians such as Henri and Barbara Van der Zee have reiterated the old line that the Dutch colonies failed to last because of low immigration and short-sighted colonial policies. The argument runs that the Dutch (and Swedish) colonies were founded on the desire for mercantile profits and that even the leaders of those colonies (men such as Stuyvesant, Kieft, and Minuit) were not fully committed to the success of their territorial domains. However, some historians point out that the successful English colonies also suffered from short-sighted management and that the French colony suffered as much from low rates of immigration as did any of its rivals. Perhaps it simply was that the Dutch decided to direct their energies elsewhere.

What lasting effects did the Colonial Wars have on the American character? Were they, for example, a formative time for the development of an American style of warfare?

Although many historians have sought to address those questions, none have done so with the thoroughness and conviction of Richard Slotkin. Writing in the 1970s, Slotkin portrayed the Colonial Wars as fundamentally important in the development of the American frontier mythology, the American form of hero worship, and the American approach to violence. Making links between the heroes of the Colonial Wars (John Mason, Benjamin Church, and others) and the European-American approach to the wilderness and frontier fighting, Slotkin set forth a powerful thesis that the American character, American mythology, and the American approach to warfare were all determined to a considerable extent by the Colonial Wars. In a more extreme variation on that, historian Stephen Katz has discussed the similarities and differences between the genocide practiced by the Puritans in the Pequot War and King Philip's War and the genocide practiced by Hitler's Third Reich in the 20th century.

What was the true nature of Bacon's Rebellion? Did it really come from and go to something fundamental in the American experience or was it only an isolated episode involving some individuals operating out of self-serving and egotistical motives?

Bacon's Rebellion has continued to fascinate historians on several levels. Thomas J. Wertenbaker started the debate in 1914; he was followed by Wilcomb E. Washburn in 1957 and Virginia Carson in 1976. Historians such as Wertenbaker portray Bacon's Rebellion as a precursor to the bid for independence in 1776; others see Bacon as a hotheaded, power-hungry young upstart; still others believe that Bacon played only a supporting role and that the rebellion was actually a conflict between races (white, Indian, black) and classes. In recent years, the most influential commentators have been Edmund S. Morgan and Stephen Saunders Webb; each has emphasized that Bacon's Rebellion was far larger and had greater consequences than previously had been seen.

CIVILIAN AND MILITARY BIOGRAPHIES

FRENCH

Champlain, Samuel de (1567–1635)—soldier, explorer: Samuel de Champlain was born in France. He came to North America in 1601 and spent most of his life there, exploring and colonizing. He had to surrender to the English privateer Kirke brothers in 1629, but he returned to Quebec in 1633. He died there in 1635, secure in his status as the "Father of New France."

DUTCH

Kieft, Willem (1597–1647)—director general: Willem Kieft was born in the Netherlands. He served as governor of New Netherland from 1638–1645. His arrogant temperament and hasty approach to decisions contributed to the Dutch-Indian Wars (1642–1645), which were disastrous for the colony. He died in a shipwreck off the coast of Wales.

Stuyvesant, Peter (1592–1672)—director general: Peter Stuyvesant was born in the Netherlands. He was governor of New Netherland from 1646 to 1664. He defeated the Swedes in Delaware. He was eager to fight against the English invasion of New Netherland in 1664, but the people were not willing to fight. He retired and lived the life of a gentleman farmer.

ENGLISH

Bacon, Nathaniel (1647–1676)—rebel: Nathaniel Bacon was born of a good family in England. He settled in Virginia around 1670. He soon became the leader of the disaffected settlers on the frontier and opposed Gov. William Berkeley. The uprising he led, generally known as Bacon's Rebellion, remains controversial in American historiography, as does Bacon's character and behavior.

Berkeley, Sir William (1608–1677)—governor: William Berkeley was born in England. He was knighted in 1639 and settled in Virginia in 1642. He was a hero to the colony during the Indian war of 1644, but his later policies caused much discontent. In the aftermath of Bacon's Rebellion, he showed no mercy to the rebels and was called back to England in some disgrace.

Church, Benjamin (1639–1718)—soldier: Benjamin Church was born in Plymouth Colony. He was the first true American frontier hero. Generally hailed for his pursuit of King Philip in 1676, Church became a symbol of the American belief that European Americans could indeed "beat the Indians at their own game," fighting in the woods.

Smith, John (?1580–1631)—soldier, colonist: John Smith was born in England. He had an adventurous career, which included fighting against the Turks. He settled in Jamestown in 1607 and immediately emerged as the leader of the embattled colony. Smith's favorite saying was "He that does not work, neither shall he eat." Smith was effective in helping the Jamestown colony to survive its early years. He went to England in 1609 but later returned to map and chart the coast of New England.

NATIVE AMERICAN

Metacomet, or "King Philip" (?1642–1676)—sachem: Metacomet was chief of the Wampanoag Indians. He led the Indian revolt that became known as King Philip's War. It is not clear to historians whether he was the true architect of events or whether he responded to situations as they arose. He was hunted down and killed in 1676.

Opechancanough (1556–1646)—sachem: Opechancanough was a Powhatan Indian. He was the younger brother of Powhatan. He succeeded to the leadership of his people upon the death of his brother in March 1618, and he reaffirmed the peaceful intentions of his people toward the English settlers. But he was a consummate conspirator and organizer; he masterminded the surprise attacks of 1622 and 1644 on the Virginia colony. Captured in 1646, he was brought to Jamestown and was killed by an irate soldier while awaiting trial.

FURTHER READING

Axtell, James. *The Invasions Within: The Contest of Cultures in Colonial North America.* New York: Oxford University Press, 1985.

Bourne, Russell. *The Red King's Rebellion.* New York: Oxford University Press, 1990.

Carson, Jane D. *Bacon's Rebellion.* Jamestown, Va.: Jamestown Foundation, 1976.

Jennings, Francis. *The Invasion of America: Indians, Colonialism, and the Cant of Conquest.* New York: W. W. Norton & Co., 1976.

Josephy, Alvin M. *The Patriot Chiefs.* New York: Viking Press, 1961.

Leach, Douglas Edward. *Flintlock and Tomahawk: New England in King Philip's War.* New York: Macmillan Publishing Co., 1958.

Mather, Cotton. *Magnalia Christi Americana.* London: T. Parkhurst, 1702.

Melvoin, Richard I. *New England Outpost: War and Society in Colonial Deerfield.* New York: W. W. Norton & Co., 1989.

Morgan, Edmund S. *American Slavery, American Freedom: The Ordeal of Colonial Virginia.* New York: Norton, 1975.

Morgan, Ted. *Wilderness at Dawn: The Settling of the North American Continent.* New York: Simon & Schuster, 1993.

Slotkin, Richard. *Regeneration Through Violence.* Middletown, Conn: Wesleyan University Press, 1973.

Van der Zee, Henri and Barbara Van der Zee. *A Sweet and Alien Land: The Story of Dutch New York.* New York: Viking Press, 1978.

Vaughn, Alden T. *New England Frontier: Puritans and Indians, 1620–1675.* Boston: Little, Brown Co., 1965.

Washburn, Wilcomb E. *The Governor and the Rebel.* Chapel Hill: University of North Carolina Press, 1957.

Webb, Stephen Saunders. *1676: The End of American Independence.* New York: Alfred A. Knopf, 1984.

Wertenbaker, Thomas J. *Torchbearer of the Revolution: The Story of Bacon's Rebellion and Its Leader.* Princeton, N. J.: Princeton University Press, 1940.

THE PUEBLO REVOLT OF 1680

DATES OF WAR

August 10, 1680–December 1696

ALTERNATE NAMES

Popé's Revolt

SIGNIFICANCE

The revolt of the Pueblo Indians in what is now New Mexico was one of the few successes enjoyed by Indians in repelling Europeans. Although eventually Spanish rule in what is now New Mexico was restored, the Spanish never again viewed their control of the area with complacency and even allowed the Pueblo Indians a certain amount of religious freedom. At the same time, that local and limited war established that, in the end, Indians would be powerless against the arms and organized forces of the Europeans.

BACKGROUND

The background of the Pueblo Revolt lay in Spanish colonialism and its impact on native peoples. In 1598, Juan de Oñate started the first Spanish settlement in the province of what later became New Mexico; he named the settlement San Juan de los Caballeros. The Indians of the area lived in stone or adobe communal dwellings called pueblos (Spanish for "villages"), and so the Spanish and other Europeans took to calling the natives Pueblo Indians. By 1680, the population of the colony (mostly Spanish Mexicans) had risen to about 3,000 persons, and the population of the Pueblo Indians had fallen from an estimated 60,000 people (in 1600) to about 17,000. The reasons for the decline of the native peoples were several: diseases brought by Europeans, droughts and famine, and an onerous system of forced labor imposed by the Spanish.

The natives also had to endure forced religious conversion. The Spanish colony was dominated by Roman Catholic priests, who felt their duty was to convert the Indians to Christianity.

Not content to set up their missions and churches, the priests did everything possible to keep the Indians from worshiping in their own way. There had been several incidents over the decades in which the Indians had tried to rise up against the Spanish, but none had amounted to anything before the Pueblo Revolt of 1680.

CAUSES OF THE WAR

In 1675, Gov. Juan Francisco Trevino feared that the Pueblo Indians were planning an uprising, so he briefly imprisoned 47 natives, many of them medicine men who functioned as priests and leaders of their people. Four were hanged; the rest were whipped, then released. One of the medicine men released was Popé, who lived in the San Juan de los Caballeros pueblo. After his release, Popé moved to the Taos Pueblo, where he began to plan a coordinated Indian uprising against the Spanish, scheduled to begin on August 12, 1680.

PREPARATIONS FOR WAR

Popé sent runners, each carrying a piece of knotted rope, to each of the many Pueblo villages; each piece of rope was part of a secret code. When the last knot in the last rope was untied, the revolt would begin. Spanish governor Antonio de Otermin learned of the plot on August 9, when two Pueblo Indians were arrested and confessed to the plot. Otermin sent messengers to various Mexican authorities in the area and told them to prepare to defend their people. But word of that reached Popé and his fellow plotters before the day was out, and they decided to strike at once. As a result, the colonists had almost no chance to make preparations.

DECLARATION OF WAR

Since the Pueblo Revolt was intended as a surprise assault, the Pueblo Indians naturally made no formal declaration. The Spanish authorities simply responded with force.

COMBATANTS

Pueblo Indians: An estimated 5,000 Pueblo men eventually participated in the uprising. They greatly outnumbered the Spanish, but they were not warriors and had no tradition of organized warfare. Although some of them did have guns and ammunition, they were poorly armed compared to the Spanish.

Spanish-Mexicans: Among the settlers, there were probably as many as 1,500 able-bodied men, some of whom were professional soldiers. But the settlers were scattered throughout a large area when the revolt broke out; most of them were caught by surprise and were primarily concerned with saving their families.

GEOGRAPHIC AND STRATEGIC CONSIDERATIONS

The journey from Mexico City to the San Juan de los Caballeros pueblo and the other Mexican settlements in the Santa Fe area was a 1,500-mile, six-month one. Moreover, the Indians were completely familiar with every square inch of the land and knew all its resources and limitations. If the Pueblos could catch the colonists off guard, they could fight them without fear that any reinforcements coming from the south would arrive in time to make a difference.

BATTLES AND CAMPAIGNS

August 10, 1680: When the Indians realized that the Spanish governor had learned of their plan, the Pueblo Revolt began precipitously. Indians in villages throughout present-day upper New Mexico rose, killing priests and settlers. The first blood (that of Franciscan Friar Juan Pio and a soldier) was shed in the Indian village of Tesque.

August 15, 1680: Pueblo forces surrounded Santa Fe, the capital and center of activity in the province. Following an offer to pardon the rebels (which was met with derision), Governor Otermin led his fewer than 100 soldiers outside the palace and fought against the Indians. The battle lasted for hours before the Spanish withdrew into the palace after inflicting many casualties with their superior firepower.

August 18, 1680: The besieging force of Pueblos cut off the water supply to the governor's palace in Santa Fe.

August 20, 1680: Following 36 hours without water, Otermin led his soldiers in a desperate attack on the Indians. The Spanish killed 300 Indians and captured an additional 47, all of whom were executed after summary trials.

August 21, 1680: Having decided that it was hopeless to hold Santa Fe, Otermin led about 1,000 soldiers and civilians out of the town. They expected to have to fight their way through the Indians, but, instead, the Indians simply observed the Spanish as they set off for the south. During the next four weeks, that group of soldiers and colonists slowly and arduously made its way, generally following the Rio Grande. Along the way they were joined by about 1,400 other colonists fleeing the Indians.

September 19, 1680: The Spanish refugees led by Governor Otermin reached La Salienta just north of El Paso del Norte (present-day El Paso, Texas). On arrival, Otermin counted some 2,520 refugees, including several hundred Pueblo Indians who had stayed loyal to the Spanish. He also reported that 21 priests and 380 settlers had been killed during the revolt (some historians believe that the total was much higher).

1681–1691: The Spanish remained at El Paso del Norte, creating a permanent settlement there. They made occasional forays into San Juan de los Caballeros, but found that the Pueblo Indians were able to repel any serious attacks.

Between 1681 and 1691, the Pueblo Indians destroyed almost every trace of Mexican-Spanish rule and of Roman Catholicism—archives, vestments, religious articles, and all missionary structures and churches. Popé was said to have demanded that any Indians who had been baptized be washed clean. He also wiped out all traces of the written and spoken Spanish language. During that same period, however, Popé instituted a harsh regime, and in 1685, he was deposed by Luis Tupatu of the Picuris pueblo. Then, in 1688, Tupatu was deposed by the Indians of his pueblo, and Popé returned to prominence, again imposing his harsh regime. Meanwhile, the Pueblo Indians found themselves attacked by the more aggressive Apache Indians. When Popé died around 1690, the spirit of resistance went out of the Pueblo Indians.

February 22, 1691: Diego de Vargas Zapata Lujan, from one of the most prominent families in Spain, took office in El Paso del Norte as the new governor of the territory.

Fall 1692: Vargas undertook a thorough reconnaissance of the territory and determined that altough the Pueblos were still hostile to Spanish rule, they would not resist with the type of unity they had displayed in 1680.

October 4, 1693: Vargas left El Paso del Norte with 100 soldiers, 70 families, and 18 priests, heading north for the province that had been lost in the revolt 13 years earlier.

December 30, 1693: Following two weeks of negotiations just outside Santa Fe, the Spanish stormed the town and captured it, losing only one man in the battle; the Indians suffered nine killed.

Fall 1694: By the fall of 1694, the Spanish under Vargas had established a tenuous hold over the province.

June 4, 1696: Five missionaries and 21 Spanish settlers were killed in an uprising by the Pueblo Indians. Although that uprising was serious, it lacked the coordination of the revolt of 1680.

December 1696: The last Pueblo resistance was put down.

NEGOTIATIONS AND PEACE TREATY

Once the Spanish suppressed the last resistance by the Pueblo Indians, they saw no need to engage in any negotiations.

RESULTS OF THE WAR (Casualties, Costs, Consequences)

The Spanish suffered at least 400 people killed during the Pueblo Revolt. The Spanish also lost most of the structures they had built in San Juan de los Caballeros during their first century there. The Pueblo Indians probably had fewer of their people killed, but when the war was over, they had lost their land and their independence. The Spanish soon moved back in, rebuilt their homes and missions, and restored their colonial administration. They did, however, relax their efforts to subject the Indians to forced labor; and although the Catholic missionaries tried to convert the Indians, the civil authorities allowed the Indians to pursue their own religion. Compared to many parts of North America, relations between the European colonists and the natives were fairly harmonious during the ensuing centuries.

MILITARY INNOVATIONS, TACTICS, EQUIPMENT

There were no innovations employed in the Pueblo Revolt. Many of the Indians as well as the colonists had European firearms, but both sides soon ran short of ammunition. And although some of the colonists had horses, those provided virtually no advantage because the Pueblo Indians didn't approach in large formations. The Indians fought a guerrilla warfare—relying on surprise, ambush, and sabotage (such as cutting off the water supply to the government palace in Santa Fe).

LEGENDS AND TRIVIA

Popé claimed he had communicated with three fiends, or devilish spirits believed in by the Pueblo Indians. Popé declared that he was inspired by visits from those deities and that he had been appointed by the spirits to free his people from Spanish rule.

NOTABLE PHRASES

They were saying that now God and Santa Maria were dead, they were the ones whom the Spaniards worshiped, and that their own god who they obeyed had never died.

Francisco Gomez, a Mexican-Spanish army officer, reported that the Pueblo Indians who revolted on August 10, 1680, said those words to him when he inquired as to the motivation for their uprising.

HISTORICAL PERSPECTIVES AND CONTROVERSIES

Although the Pueblo Revolt has attracted some historians over the years, it remains little known to most Americans in comparison to uprisings led by such Indians as King Philip (see Colonial Wars, p. 13) and Pontiac (see Pontiac's War, pp. 57-62). The absence of knowledge about the Pueblo Revolt from popular culture may have little to do with any resentment about the Indians having achieved at least temporary success. Rather, that absence may reflect the bias that has long existed in telling America's history from the point of view that stresses the English settlements along the Atlantic coast. In recent years, however, the Pueblo Revolt has begun to attract more attention, along with the increased recognition given to the role of Hispanics in settling North America. Some historians, among them Andrew L. Knaut, have begun to study the Pueblo Indians' numerous attempts to revolt prior to 1680. Even though those rebellions were also unsuccessful, they cast a new light on relations between the natives and the European colonists.

CIVILIAN AND MILITARY BIOGRAPHIES

Popé (?–?1690)—Indian leader: Little is known about Popé other than that he was a medicine man who was offended by the Spanish disdain for the religious practices of the Pueblos. He preached against the Spanish to the Pueblo people and believed that the Pueblo gods disapproved of the Spanish. He masterfully organized the Pueblo Revolt (and is said to have killed his own son-in-law, who he thought betrayed news

of the planned revolt). But he failed as a leader of his people, becoming autocratic and arbitrary.

FURTHER READING

Hackett, Charles W. *The Revolt of the Pueblo Indians of New Mexico and Otermin's Attempted Reconquest, 1680–1682.* Albuquerque, N. Mex.: University of New Mexico Press, 1942.

Knaut, Andrew L. *The Pueblo Revolt of 1680: Conquest and Resistance in Seventeenth-Century New Mexico.* Norman, Okla.: University of Oklahoma Press, 1995.

Spicer, Edward. *Cycles of Conquest: The Impact of Spain, Mexico, and the United States on the Indians of the Southwest, 1533–1960.* Tucson, Ariz.: University of Arizona Press, 1962.

TUSCARORA WAR

DATES OF WAR

September 22, 1711–April 1713

ALTERNATE NAMES

None.

SIGNIFICANCE

The Tuscarora War eliminated the Tuscarora Indians in eastern North Carolina not only as a fighting force but also as a presence, thereby opening that colony to further settlement by Europeans. Beyond that, other tribes in what would become the southeastern United States were intimidated by what happened to the Tuscarora.

BACKGROUND

During the first half-century of European settlement in North Carolina (1650–1700), the Tuscarora were quite friendly to the European settlers. The English had been the first to arrive, settling near the border with Virginia; gradually the Europeans began to move southward down the coast to the land between the Pamlico and Neuse Rivers. Some French Huguenots also moved into that area. A noticeable change in relations between the Indians and the Europeans began around 1700, as white encroachment on the Indians' hunting lands increased. And some of the colonists engaged in deceitful trading practices with the Indians. White slave traders (from South Carolina in particular) preyed upon the Tuscarora villages, kidnapping Indians and selling them into slavery either in other colonies or in the Caribbean.

CAUSES OF THE WAR

By the early 1700s, the Tuscarora Indians were becoming increasingly unhappy with the growing presence of European settlers in their region. Then, in 1710, a Swiss colonizer, Baron Christopher de Graffenried, brought approxi-

mately 400 German and 1,200 Swiss Protestants to the coast of North Carolina. The immigrants settled on the confluence of the Neuse and Trent Rivers and founded New Bern. Graffenried claimed he paid for the land three times (once to the colony's proprietors, once to the colony's governor, and once to an Indian chief), but the establishment of such a large colony clearly represented a new level of pressure on the Tuscarora. The fact that the New Bern settlement was going through difficult times during its first year, experiencing food shortages and a typhoid fever epidemic, probably did little to encourage the Indians to take up arms against the settlers. Likewise, the Tuscarora probably were not particularly influenced by the dissension that had escalated during 1710–1711 to almost a civil war among various factions in the colony.

PREPARATIONS FOR WAR

On September 10, 1711, Graffenried was on a scouting expedition with John Lawson, an Englishman who was also instrumental in establishing the colony at New Bern, when they were detained by 60 Tuscarora warriors. They were brought to the council fire at the main Tuscarora village, Catechna (sometimes spelled Cotechny), near Snow Hill in present-day Greene County, North Carolina. Lawson entered into an argument with Chief Hancock and was tortured and killed.

Whether because of that act or because the Tuscarora were already prepared to strike, 12 days later hundreds of Tuscarora warriors attacked the white settlements in northeastern North Carolina. Although the initial attacks killed many of the Swiss and German colonists, Graffenried, who was being held prisoner, agreed to keep the settlers at New Bern neutral in the ensuing hostilities.

COMBATANTS

Europeans: There were about 5,000 European colonists (including women and children) in northeast North Carolina, most of them English. Hundreds of the English, however, were Quakers, whose pacifism compelled them to refuse to participate in the hostilities. Graffenried had promised his Tuscarora captors that the German and Swiss colonists in and around New Bern would not take an active part in the war; in fact, as the war dragged on, many of them did take up arms, and by January 1712, Graffenried broke his truce with the Indians and committed both men and cannon to the war. In the end, though, it was the volunteer troops from South Carolina (including hundreds of allied Indians) who defeated the Tuscarora.

Tuscarora Indians: The Tuscarora population of an estimated 4,000, including a fighting force of 1,200 warriors, lived in 15 different Indian settlements. On some occasions, they were aided by other Indians living in the region, but it was the Tuscarora who organized and prepared to take the offensive.

GEOGRAPHIC AND STRATEGIC CONSIDERATIONS

Given their intimate knowledge of the land and their mobility, the Tuscarora seemed to have the advantage, since they could strike at the whites and then retire inland. In reality, the longer the war lasted, the more the Indians were at a disadvantage, since the North Carolinians were supported by forces from the adjacent colony of South Carolina.

BATTLES AND CAMPAIGNS

September 22, 1711: Hundreds of Tuscarora warriors (as well as Indians from other tribes) struck the white settlements near the Neuse, Trent, and Pamlico Rivers in northeastern North Carolina. The Indian attacks lasted three days, at the end of which the whites counted 130 persons killed and between 20 and 30 taken prisoner. Several settlements, including New Bern and Bath Town, were severely damaged.

October 1711: As the attacks continued intermittently, the settlers saw their crops destroyed, their property plundered, their homes burned. In desperate straits, the North Carolina settlers appealed for help from other colonies. Virginia refused to send troops into North Carolina, but it did offer a bounty for every hostile

Tuscarora captured. The New York colonists persuaded the Seneca Indians (relatives of the Tuscarora) not to intervene in the war. South Carolina agreed to send a force, and at the end of the year Col. John Barnwell with 50 white soldiers and about 350 allied Indians (mainly Yamasee) marched some 300 miles north to help the North Carolinians.

January 1712: Barnwell arrived at New Bern, North Carolina, where he assembled a strike force totaling about 650 colonists (including 50 German colonists) and Indian allies.

January 30, 1712: Barnwell's mixed settler-Indian force stormed the Tuscaroras' Fort Narhantes (present-day Fort Barnwell). The whites suffered 7 killed and 32 wounded, and their Indian allies suffered 6 killed and 28 wounded; they inflicted 62 deaths on the Tuscarora and took 30 prisoners as well as the fort itself.

February 9, 1712: Barnwell's force arrived at Bath Town, North Carolina, and paused to gather supplies and reinforcements.

February 27, 1712: Having recruited another 200 North Carolinians, Barnwell left Bath Town and headed for Catechna, the main settlement of the Tuscarora Indians.

March–April 1712: Barnwell and his men made two attacks on Catechna; both attacks were repulsed by the Tuscarora.

April 17, 1712: Barnwell and the Tuscarora Indians at Catechna agreed to a cease-fire, providing that the Tuscarora free all the captives they held and deliver their chief, Hancock, to the English. Hancock escaped to Virginia, where he was taken prisoner by Upper Tuscarora chief Tom Blunt (sometimes spelled Blount), who had remained friendly with the European settlers.

May 1712: Barnwell returned to South Carolina by ship. In his absence, some of his men invited a large number of Tuscarora to meet with them at Core Town, North Carolina. The Indians, who had come in peace, were attacked by the whites; between 40 and 50 Indians were killed, and nearly 200 women and children were seized to be sold as slaves.

Summer and fall 1712: The Tuscarora War flared anew, largely because of the actions of Barnwell's men. Although the fighting strength of the Tuscarora was much reduced, they carried out raids against isolated settlements. A yellow fever epidemic made the North Carolinians even more desperate. The governor of North Carolina appealed once again to the colony of South Carolina.

March 1713: Col. James Moore of South Carolina arrived in North Carolina with a force of 33 white soldiers and about 900 Indian allies.

March 20–23, 1713: Moore carried out a siege of the Tuscarora Fort Nohoroco near the Indian settlement of Catechna. Moore and his men stormed the fort on March 23 and won a complete victory after what has been described as one of the most desperate and deadly hand-to-hand actions ever recorded in warfare between Indians and whites. The white troops under Moore (who had been reinforced by North Carolina recruits) suffered 22 killed and 36 wounded; their Indian allies suffered 35 killed and 58 wounded. The Tuscarora losses were much greater; at least 200 died within the burning fort; 166 were captured, tortured, and killed outside the fort; and 392 were taken prisoner and were later sold into slavery. Moore and his men took 192 scalps.

NEGOTIATIONS AND PEACE TREATY

There were no formal negotiations immediately after the Tuscarora were defeated at Fort Nohoroco, but it was such a complete catastrophe for the Tuscarora that their will to fight quickly evaporated.

April 1713: Chief Tom Blunt of the Upper Tuscarora (who had not joined in the war) signed a preliminary treaty with the settlers that provided a reservation for his people on the lower Roanoke River in North Carolina.

February 11, 1715: Representatives of the European settlers in North Carolina and the Tuscarora Indians signed a treaty. The Indians agreed to live on a reservation near Lake Mattamuskeet in present-day Hyde County, North Carolina, but many of them migrated north.

RESULTS OF THE WAR (Casualties, Costs, Consequences)

The colonists and their Indian allies counted some 500 dead and several score missing. Many houses and barns were burned and cattle and crops destroyed. The war also disrupted trade and led the North Carolina government to run up great debts, which undermined the local currency. New Bern was seriously damaged but was soon rebuilt and served as the capital of the colony of North Carolina until 1776. In the long run, the colony emerged stronger. Once the Tuscarora had been cleared out of North Carolina, colonists began to move in and settle on the Tuscarora land.

The Tuscarora lost between 500 and 600 killed, and another 600 were taken prisoner. Although the Tuscarora were granted a reservation in North Carolina, most of them fled northward during the ensuing years to join their relatives, the Seneca Indians in northern New York. In 1722, the Tuscarora were accepted into the Iroquois confederacy as the Sixth Nation.

MILITARY INNOVATIONS, TACTICS, EQUIPMENT

There were no innovations in the Tuscarora War. The settlers and militia carried the basic muskets and pistols of the period. The Indians had some guns but relied mostly on bows-and-arrows and tomahawks.

HISTORICAL PERSPECTIVES AND CONTROVERSIES

There never has been much disagreement among historians about the facts of the Tuscarora War. The work of Douglas Letell Rights remains an important source for understanding the basic chronology of the war. Little new documentary evidence has turned up; what has changed are attitudes about the evidence. In the early contemporary accounts by participants and observers, the Indians were portrayed as absolute savages with no right on their side. In more recent times, historians have attempted to consider both sides of the conflict, noting, for instance, that it was an Englishman who boasted of the Europeans taking 192 scalps after the battle at Fort Nohoroco (see Battles and Campaigns, March 20-23, 1713, above).

CIVILIAN AND MILITARY BIOGRAPHIES

Barnwell, John (c. 1671–1724)—colonial official: John Barnwell was born in Ireland. He imigrated to South Carolina in 1701. He led a

South Carolina force of whites and Indians in the Tuscarora War, and in 1712, he negotiated a cease-fire with the Tuscarora. After the war, he returned to South Carolina, where he often was referred to as "Tuscarora Jack" for his victories in the war.

Hancock (?–1713)—Tuscarora chief: Nothing is known of Hancock's early years. He began the Tuscarora War by killing John Lawson and sending his warriors to the September 1711, massacre of white settlers. It is believed that he was betrayed in 1712 by Upper Tuscarora Indians who turned him over to the whites, who promptly executed him.

FURTHER READING

Lefler, Hugh T., and William S. Powell. *Colonial North Carolina: A History*. New York: Charles Scribner's Sons, 1973.

Rights, Douglas Letell. *The American Indian in North Carolina*. Durham, N. C.: Duke University Press, 1947.

THE FRENCH AND INDIAN WARS

DATES OF WARS

May 29, 1689—February 10, 1763

ALTERNATE NAMES

What are commonly summed up as the French and Indian Wars in American history were actually four separate wars: King William's War (1689–1697), Queen Anne's War (1702–1713), King George's War (1744–1748), and the French and Indian War (1754–1763). In Europe, those conflicts were known respectively as the War of the League of Augsburg (1689–1697), the War of the Spanish Succession (1702–1713), the War of the Austrian Succession (1744–1748), and the Seven Years' War (1756–1763). In addition to these four wars, there was the War of Jenkins's Ear (1739–1744), which is so inextricably involved with the same principals and issues that it is included here.

SIGNIFICANCE

What Americans know as the French and Indian Wars were extensions of European conflicts. But the French and Indian Wars played an important role in the formation of a distinctive North American culture and character. In the process of fighting against French and Spanish foes in North America, English soldiers and the American colonists grew to understand one another better and, simultaneously, to recognize the differences that were emerging between two distinct peoples— the English and the Americans.

When the wars began in 1689, England had ten colonies on the continent of North America, and France had New France and Acadia (eastern coastal Canada). Spain held present-day Florida. When the wars ended in 1763, England emerged as the clear winner, with her colonies stretching from Hudson Bay to the southern tip of Florida. France retained only two tiny islands off the coast of Newfoundland, and Spain had yielded Florida to England. What would become the United States was embarked on a course that was set by English-based culture and the English language.

BACKGROUND

Traditional animosities, trade and imperial rivalries, dynastic succession, and religious differences contributed to the French and Indian Wars. There had been a long-standing animosity between the French and English people. Starting as early as the Hundred Years' War (1337–1453), this animosity poisoned relations between the two most influential European powers. In North America, both countries had planted colonies early in the 17th century, and small conflicts had developed between French Canada and New England (see Colonial Wars, pp. 5–23). England, France, and Spain were increasingly competing for trade and territory on a broader world stage, and those rivalries were only intensified by developments in New France, New England, and New Spain during the 17th century. Central to the jockeying for power among those great powers was the question of who would inherit the thrones of various countries. Intermarriage among royal families could lead to one country's "inheriting" another, and that could not be tolerated by those left out. Then, too, there was the issue of religious differences: England had become a mainly Protestant nation, and France and Spain had remained Roman Catholic, and there were constant occasions for those nations to clash while promoting their faiths. New England and the other English colonies were founded on Protestant principles, and New France and New Spain were created in the wake of the Catholic Counter-Reformation of the 16th century. It should also be noted, as described below, fighting in North America began only after hostilities commenced in Europe; the exception was the French and Indian War that began in North America in 1754 but did not commence in Europe until 1756.

CAUSES OF THE WARS

The causes of each of the conflicts known collectively as the French and Indian Wars were specific, although all stemmed from the rivalry between the major colonial powers—England,

France, and Spain—for dominance along the eastern seaboard of North America and their attempts to enlist Native American allies in their struggles. Colonial rivalries in other parts of the world as well as jousting among the major powers in Europe were contributing factors. The immediate causes of each specific conflict are recounted below under the heading for each war.

PREPARATIONS FOR WAR

As was the case with several of the 17th-century Colonial Wars, the French and Indian Wars in the Americas were largely extensions of European power politics. The wars not only had different names in Europe—and in some instances different time spans—but also were fought in quite different ways in Europe: Many more nations were involved, and those nations organized full-scale preparations, centralized their commands and strategies, and committed large professional armies and navies to great battles. With a few exceptions, the wars did not take on nearly that dimension in the Americas, but there was an escalation toward that kind of organized warfare. For the most part, the French and Indian Wars were fought by the colonial militias—part-time soldiers, called out only when there was some specific threat or operation; cannons and most other weapons had to be imported, and there was not even the capacity to make gunpowder in North America until early in the 1800s.

King William's War began with attacks by Indians on English settlements, then broadened when the Comte de Frontenac sent out war parties of French settlers to accompany the Indians. The English colonists responded only with their militias, although in one instance—the disastrous expedition led by William Phips in 1690—they organized an ambitious force. Queen Anne's War, again, was fought mostly by colonists and Indians, until in 1711 the Walker Expedition to Quebec involved 5,000 professional soldiers brought over from England. That, too, also ended in disaster. Then followed the long peace of 1713–1740, but during that period the French and English were busy building or enlarging their network of forts in their American colonies: The French began the fort at Louisbourg, Nova Scotia, in 1720 and built Fort Niagara in 1726, Fort St. Frederic (later Crown Point) on Lake Champlain in 1731, and Fort Vincennes (later Fort Stanwix) in 1733. During King George's War, the French under Duc d'Anville sent a large fleet to America in 1747, but it met the same disastrous fate as had the Phips and Walker expeditions.

The final war in the series represented a new development in warfare in North America. For the first time, the major European powers committed large professional military forces to operations in North America, with all that involved in the way of planning and supplies. Gen. Edward Braddock had some 700 regular English troops when in 1755 he walked into an ambush in western Pennsylvania; in 1757, Montcalm had 8,000 men, about one-quarter French regulars, when he captured Fort William Henry, defended by some 2,300 British regulars and militia; in 1758, 8,000 English troops were sent to take Fort Louisbourg; in 1758 the English attacked Fort Carillon with 16,000 men, about half of them regulars; and in 1759, 9,000 English regulars were under Wolfe's command at the battle to take Quebec. (The English defeated 4,000 French regulars as well as 12,000 French-Canadian militia.) It was during that time that the French and English built several of the major forts that would later play a role in the American Revolution—in particular, the French built Fort Carillon (which became Fort Ticonderoga) and Fort Duquesne (replaced by English Fort Pitt), and the English built Fort William Henry on Lake George.

The pattern was clear: War in the New World gradually took on a grand scale, and that scale dictated that preparation for war be systematic and thorough.

DECLARATIONS OF WAR

In the New World itself, there were no formal declarations of war by any of the participants; they simply took up arms based on local situations or because they had news of events in Europe. In their European phases, however, all those wars did involve formal declarations, which are listed below under the heading for each war.

COMBATANTS

In the course of the French and Indian Wars, there were five groups of combatants: English regular troops, French troops (colonial and regulars), Spanish troops, Native American warriors (mostly Iroquois and Algonquin), and the colonial forces of of the 13 English colonies.

English: Soldiers transported from England and soldiers enlisted from the English colonies were the most numerous in North America. From 1689 until 1763, the English colonists outnumbered their French and Spanish rivals. The English regular troops were on their way toward acquiring a fearsome reputation, and the victories of the English army under the Duke of Marlborough during the War of the Spanish Succession would add greatly to England's international reputation for fighting prowess.

French: The French army of Louis XIV was the largest in the European world, ranging from 200,000 in peacetime to 400,000 in wartime. However, very few of those French troops fought in North America. The brunt of the American fighting was borne by the "Troops of the Marine," a small corps of veterans; French-Canadian habitants ("tillers of the soil"); and coureurs du bois, ("runners of the forests"), referring to the French-Canadians who lived and hunted in the American forests in ways learned from the Indians.

Spanish: The Spanish regular troops were few in number. Spain still held an enormous empire during the French and Indian Wars, but the bulk of the Spanish forces fought in the Caribbean and the Gulf of Mexico, and few were allotted to fight for Spanish Florida.

Native American (Iroquois and Algonquin): The Iroquois tribes (five nations until the 1720s, six nations after the 1720s) lived in present-day New York State. Their influence was extensive. Despite the small size of their forces (some 3,000 warriors at their peak strength), the Iroquois held the balance of power between New France, New England, and New York. The Iroquois warriors dominated the Mohawk River Valley, Lake George, Lake Champlain, and the routes of the fur trade through those areas. The English colonists of New York and New England formed an uneasy alliance with the Iroquois during that period. The Iroquois' Algonquin rivals lived in northern New England, Acadia, and near French settlements along the St. Lawrence River. Algonquin tribes, such as the Abenakis and Micmacs, had become closely allied to New France and soon found that their long-standing hostility toward the Iroquois paralleled the French rivalry with the English.

Colonial Troops: Starting in 1690, troops recruited from the English colonies played an important role in the wars. Although they were looked down on by their English counterparts and were denied the sweetness of the ultimate victories in Canada (English regular troops claimed those honors), the colonial fighters of the 13 colonies gained important battle training during the wars and, some historians have argued, became more "American" in the process of fighting.

GEOGRAPHIC AND STRATEGIC CONSIDERATIONS

A map of colonial America in 1690 shows New France stretching from the mouth of the St. Lawrence River to beyond the Great Lakes. (By 1720, it extended intermittently down the Mississippi basin to present-day New Orleans and the Gulf of Mexico.) New Spain loomed ominously northward from Mexico well up into the entire western flank of North America. (Spain also controlled the Gulf of Mexico and held claim to Florida and much of present-day Georgia.) The map shows the English colonies (ten in number in 1690; three others were added by 1732) holding a continuous but narrow area along the eastern seaboard, ranging from South Carolina to present-day Maine (then part of Massachusetts).

Each side held some important geographic advantages. The French had an advantage in holding the St. Lawrence River and the mouth of the Mississippi River; those riverine settlements had access to the coast and to the interior. Given the French skill with canoes and their generally good relations with the Indians, French fur traders, colonizers, and soldiers generally held an important advantage in mobility.

The Spanish colonies benefited from having enemies on only one side—the English to their north. The Spanish, therefore, had virtually unrestricted access to the outside world from the sea. Generally speaking, the French and Spanish did not fight each other, although they did vie for control of the lower Mississippi valley and the waters offshore.

The English colonies held the advantage of interior lines. As the colonies were laid out in a connected manner, they could communicate and provide assistance to each other quite easily. Fortunately for the French and Spanish, the English colonists often chose to obstruct one another, rather than cooperate with one another. The English colonies, however, all had more or less unrestricted access to the Atlantic coast and thus easy contacts with England and its powerful navy.

The Iroquois Indians possessed the advantage of being in the middle of New France, New England, and New York. No strategic planner could afford to ignore the Iroquois, and although the Iroquois generally supported the English colonists, they maintained a certain detachment and signed a temporary treaty with the French in 1702.

The Algonquin Indians (principally the Abenaki Indians of northern New England) had the advantage of being close to the French settlements along the St. Lawrence River, where they obtained guns, ammunition, clothes, and food from their French allies.

Strategically, all the combatants in North America were to a large extent dependent on events in Europe. Although the combatants tried with great effort to defeat their foes, they ultimately were at the mercy of European policy makers and diplomats. The prime example of this was the requirement under the Treaty of Aix-la-Chapelle (1748) that Louisbourg be returned to the French, even though the New England volunteers had conquered it.

King William's War: 1689–1697

CAUSES OF THE WAR

In November 1688, William of Orange, the political leader of the Netherlands, and his wife, Mary of England, replaced Mary's father, King James II of England, in the Glorious Revolution. King James II fled to France, where he was welcomed by King Louis XIV. Louis XIV, or the "Sun King," as he was known, vowed to fight to restore the Catholic James to his throne in England. Two factors thus brought about the War of the League of Augsburg (known in America as King William's War): the change of political leadership in England, and King Louis XIV's desire for territorial gain. Louis XIV's land grabs had already brought him into conflict with the Netherlands, the Holy Roman Empire, various small German states, and Spain. Together, those groups formed the League of Augsburg in 1686 (named after the city in southwestern Germany). After the French attacked the German state known as the Palatinate in 1688, England joined those countries in 1689, and the League of Augsburg became known as the Grand Alliance. King Louis XIV now found himself at war with the English.

DECLARATION OF WAR

England declared war on France on May 29, 1689.

BATTLES AND CAMPAIGNS

August 5, 1689: Some 1,500 Iroquois warriors made a ferocious attack on the French settlement of La Chine, near Montreal—the largest and most devastating attack ever made by Indians on the French. The French suffered at least 200 killed, wounded, and taken prisoner, and 56 of a total 77 homes in the settlement were destroyed. Although totally independent of events in Europe, that attack and other similar attacks soon led to an extension in North America of France's war with England in Europe.

October 16, 1689: The Comte de Frontenac arrived at Quebec City and assumed his post as the new governor of New France. A seasoned soldier, the comte had been instructed by King Louis XIV to design a strategy that would capture the English colony of New York. Realizing that the king's plan was too ambitious for his slender resources (New France had a population of only 12,000 French colonists), Frontenac decided instead to send out three war parties of French and Indians to harass the English frontier.

February 9, 1690: French and Indian fighters descended on the settlement of Schenectady, New York, in the early morning hours. The French and Indians laid waste to the town, burned most of the houses, then retreated northward, having struck the opening blow of King William's War in the New World (indeed, of the entire series of French and Indian Wars). This attack was soon followed by attacks on Salmon Falls, New Hampshire, and Falmouth, Maine (then a part of Massachusetts).

May 1, 1690: Delegates from the colonies of Connecticut, Massachusetts, Plymouth, and New York met at Albany, New York, for a military conference. They decided to make a two-pronged attack on French Canada. One military force (made up of militia and Iroquois Indians) marched northward along Lake Champlain and seized Montreal, and a second left Boston by ship and made a surprise descent on Quebec.

May 11, 1690: Massachusetts soldiers under the leadership of Sir William Phips captured Port Royal, a French fort near present-day Annapolis Royal, Nova Scotia. Phips and his men violated the terms of the surrender as they plundered the Catholic chapel and took much loot from Port Royal home to Boston.

May 20, 1690: A force of French and Indians destroyed the English settlement at Casco, Maine.

August 9, 1690: Emboldened by its success against Port Royal, the colony of Massachusetts launched a naval force that sailed against Quebec. Sir William Phips led 2,200 men onto 32 ships at Nantasket Roads, outside Boston Harbor. The Puritan armada set sail before nightfall.

August 1690: Fitz-John Winthrop of the Connecticut colony led about 1,000 militiamen to Wood Creek, at the head of Lake Champlain, with the intention of joining a large force of Iroquois warriors. Winthrop was disappointed by the small number of Indians there; fewer than 100 Iroquois warriors came to the rendezvous spot. Suffering from an outbreak of smallpox and seeing that the Indians lacked canoes for a movement over Lake Champlain, the militia disbanded and returned home.

August–October 1690: Frontenac, expecting an attack on Montreal, spent two months in that city preparing for an attack he suspected would come by way of Lake Champlain. Around October 1, 1690, he learned from his Abenaki allies that an English fleet had reached the St. Lawrence and was headed toward Quebec. Frontenac departed immediately and reached Quebec on October 4.

October 6, 1690: Sir William Phips led his fleet of 32 ships into the basin of the St. Lawrence River at Quebec. Having succeeded against Port Royal by issuing a summons, Phips tried again. He sent ashore Capt. Thomas Savage, who was brought to the Chateau St. Louis in the Upper Town of the city. Savage delivered Phips's message, which demanded surrender of the town within one hour's time. In response to the demand, Frontenac gave a ringing reply, "Tell your general that I have no answer to give other than through the barrels of my muskets and the mouths of my cannon." (See Notable Phrases, p. 51).

October 7–12, 1690: Phips carried out a half-hearted siege of Quebec. He landed 1,300 men, who found their way blocked by the St. Charles River and the French defending army (3,000 men in all). Phips himself launched a cannonade against the Lower Town of Quebec. The French gunners, firing from the Upper Town, caused damage to Phips's ships, while Phips's cannon shots caused little damage to the city. Phips broke off the siege

and headed home to Boston. On the return trip, his men suffered from hunger, cold, and smallpox.

November 19, 1690: Phips and the majority of his fleet made their way into Boston Harbor. The Massachusetts colony had lost 500 men, four ships, and 50,000 English pounds on this endeavor.

October 22, 1692: A 14-year-old French Canadian girl, Madeleine Jarret de Vercheres, led her brothers and a handful of other settlers in a successful defense of Vercheres, 20 miles below Montreal on the St. Lawrence River. Fending off an attack by the fierce Iroquois warriors, Madeleine Jarret de Vercheres became a hero to the French Canadian population (see Legends and Trivia, p. 51).

1692–1694: Phips, now the governor of the Massachusetts Bay Colony, had Fort William Henry constructed at Pemaquid Point in present-day Maine. Intended to intimidate the local Abenaki and Micmac Indians, the fort instead prompted the French in Canada to try to capture the stronghold.

August 15, 1694: Colonial representatives from Connecticut, Massachusetts, New Jersey, and New York signed a peace treaty with the Iroquois Indians in Albany. This was clearly an effort to keep the Iroquois from joining the French.

August 15, 1696: A French-Indian force, led by Pierre LeMoyne d'Iberville, captured Fort William Henry. The 100 English defenders were attacked by Indians after the surrender, and only the removal of the English to a nearby island saved their lives.

March 15, 1697: French-Indian forces conducted a raid against the English settlement of Haverhill, Massachusetts. Having made a successful raid, the Indians withdrew with a number of captives, among them Hannah Dustin and her two children. Some 30 miles away from Haverhill, Dustin awoke her fellow captives and set upon their sleeping captors. The audacious Puritan woman and her compatriots killed and scalped at least ten Indians and brought the scalps home to Haverhill and collected a bounty (See Legends and Trivia, pp. 50–51).

NEGOTIATIONS AND PEACE TREATY

The Treaty of Ryswick (Holland), signed on September 30, 1697, ended the War of the League of Augsburg and thus King William's War—not because of anything that had happened in North

America but because the European powers had temporarily resolved their differences. Although the news would not reach North America for several months, the war had ended—at least as far as North America was affected. Under the terms of status quo ante bellum ("the state existing before the war"), all territorial gains made during the war, including the English conquest of Port Royal and the French capture of Pemaquid, were negated.

Queen Anne's War: 1702–1713

CAUSES OF THE WAR

Few observers expected the Treaty of Ryswick to produce anything more than a temporary truce, both in Europe and in North America. As events turned out, it was the death of King Charles II of Spain (October 1, 1700) without an heir that precipitated the next round of hostilities. Louis XIV decided that his grandson, Philip of Anjou, should inherit the Spanish throne and unite the countries of France and Spain under one ruler. The other European powers did not want France to become so powerful, and with King William of England taking the lead, the war, known in Europe as the War of the Spanish Succession and in America as Queen Anne's War, commenced in 1702.

DECLARATION OF WAR

England declared war on France on May 4, 1702. This was soon followed by a series of declarations that allied France and Spain against the so-called Grand Alliance of England, the Netherlands, Prussia, Austria, and most of the other states of the Holy Roman Empire.

BATTLES AND CAMPAIGNS

September 10, 1702: The Carolina Assembly (Carolina was not separated into North and South until 1712) voted to send an expedition to take Spanish St. Augustine in Florida. A mixed force of 500 colonists and Indians burned and pillaged the town in December, but the key fortress resisted the attacks.

August 10, 1703: Initiating the war in northern New England, a group of Abenaki Indians began a series of attacks on several English settlements in Maine.

February 28–29, 1704: French Canadians and Abenaki Indians attacked and destroyed the frontier settlement of Deerfield, Massachusetts. The French-Indian forces came from Canada on snowshoes in the dead of winter. The French-Indian force killed at least 50 settlers and captured another 100. The sufferings, endurance, and eventual return of some of these captives would be enshrined in Deerfield pastor John Williams's book *The Redeemed Captive.*

July 1–28, 1704: Col. Benjamin Church, a leading veteran of King Philip's War, led a force of New England colonists in a successful attack on a number of French settlements in Acadia (present-day Nova Scotia). That not only wiped out a source of supplies for the Abenaki Indians but also gave the English control of the prosperous fishing industry based in Acadia.

1704: Gov. James Moore of the English colony of Carolina led a force of colonists and friendly Indians in attacking and leveling 13 of the 14 Spanish missions in the Appalachian Indian territory of present-day South Carolina and Georgia. Spain had long claimed the Carolina territory and had constructed those missions during the 17th century. By eradicating them, Moore and his fellow Englishmen broke the bonds of Spanish influence with the Indians and served notice that English Americans were determined to fight for what they regarded as their proper southern border with Spanish Florida.

August 24, 1706: French and Spanish troops from St. Augustine, Florida, and Havana, Cuba, combined forces and attacked Charles Town, Carolina. The Carolina settlers were able to fend off the attack.

March 6, 1707: Queen Anne of England endorsed the Act of Union between England, Wales, and Scotland. From that date on, the English people, country, and empire were more accurately described as the British people, country, and empire.

September 21, 1707: Abenaki Indians attacked the English settlement at Winter Harbor, Maine.

August 29, 1708: A French Canadian and Indian force descended on the frontier settlement of Haverhill, Massachusetts, and killed virtually all the inhabitants of that town.

December 21, 1708: A force of French and Algonquin captured the English settlement at St. John's, Newfoundland. That gave the French control over the North Atlantic coastline.

October 16, 1710: A combined English and colonial military force besieged the French stronghold of Port Royal, Acadia. The attack was successful, and the English conquerors renamed the settlement Annapolis in honor of Queen Anne.

June 1711: With the support of the English government in London, British Col. Francis Nicholson called a meeting of New England governors at New London, Connecticut, to develop a strategy for conquering French Canada.

July 30, 1711: A British fleet of 9 warships and 60 transports departed from Nantasket Roads on the edge of Boston Harbor. Led by Adm. Sir Hovenden Walker, the fleet carried 5,000 English veteran troops and nearly 2,500 New England militiamen. The destination of this force was Quebec City. Expectations of success were high; the English troops on this expedition were veterans of victorious campaigns in the European theater.

August 22, 1711 (The Walker Expedition): Seven English transport ships and one storeship ran aground at the mouth of the St. Lawrence River near Egg Island. Some 740 English troops and 150 sailors drowned. Following the disaster, Admiral Walker gave up hope of success and on September 16 led the fleet back to Boston, then to England, without ever having struck a blow against French Canada.

September 22, 1711: More or less independent of the war between the English and the French, the Tuscarora Indian War began with a massacre of English settlers on the Chowan and Roanoke rivers in Carolina (see Tuscarora War, pp. 29–32). A subsequent attack on the German colonists at New Bern, Carolina, led to the abandonment of that settlement.

January 30, 1712: The colonial militia of Carolina, assisted by Indian allies, attacked the Tuscarora on the Neuse River. Sixty-two of the Tuscarora were killed in the fighting.

May 9, 1712: Carolina was officially separated into North Carolina and South Carolina.

March 23, 1713: South Carolina militia captured the Tuscarora stronghold of Fort Nohoroco. That capture virtually ended the war for the Tuscarora Indians, who soon moved north and joined the Five Nations of the Iroquois (which became the Six Nations of the Iroquois).

NEGOTIATIONS AND PEACE TREATY

The Treaty of Utrecht (Holland), signed by England and France on April 11, 1713, effectively ended Queen Anne's War in North America. (The fighting ended in Europe, but the rulers of Spain and Austria continued to feud, and hostilities broke out again between those two countries in 1717.) The terms were advantageous to the English and Dutch, but painful for the French. England gained control of Acadia (Nova Scotia), Newfoundland, and Hudson Bay territory. France kept control of Cape Breton Island and islands in the St. Lawrence, and Spain yielded Gibraltar to England. However, Philip of Anjou was recognized as King of Spain, with the condition that the Bourbon family of France and Spain would never allow one individual to rule the two kingdoms simultaneously.

The Abenaki Indians of northern New England signed their own peace treaty with Massachusetts Governor Joseph Dudley in Portsmouth, New Hampshire on July 13, 1713.

The 'Long Peace': 1713–1740

Although France, Spain, England, and the Netherlands were at peace between 1713 and 1740, there were a number of minor conflicts in North America during that time.

April 15, 1715: Thousands of Yamasee, Creek, Choctaw, and Catawba Indians attacked exposed settlements in South Carolina. The frontier families raced to Charles Town for protection.

January 1716: Aided by Cherokee Indians, the South Carolina settlers defeated the Yamasee Indians northwest of Port Royal, South Carolina.

Summer 1718: French settlers founded the town of New Orleans, near the mouth of the Mississippi River. That small beginning to what would become the French colony of Louisiana threatened the growth of a stronger French hold in North America and the encirclement of the English colonies.

1720: French engineers began the construction of the fortress at Louisbourg on the eastern side of Cape Breton Island off the northern tip of Nova Scotia.

1726: Lawrence Armstrong, the English governor of Nova Scotia (formerly known as Acadia) demanded an oath of allegiance to England from the Acadian settlers. The Acadian habitants made a counter demand, insisting on neutrality in any future fighting between England and France. The matter was left unsettled.

March 9, 1728: South Carolina militiamen intruded into Spanish Florida and attacked the Yamasee Indian settlement of Nombre de Dios, directly under the guns of the Spanish fortress at St. Augustine.

1730: Gov. Richard Phillips of Nova Scotia sent to England a statement that he had gained for England the complete allegiance of the Acadian population. Some historians believe that Phillips made a verbal promise to the Acadians that they would never be called for military service.

1731: As part of their policy of expansion, the French built Fort St. Frederic at present-day Crown Point, New York, on the western side of Lake Champlain.

February 12, 1733: British Col. James Oglethorpe landed in present-day Savannah, Georgia, and began to lay out that town and the colony of Georgia. Georgia, the last of the 13 colonies to be settled, was intended as a haven for debtors and as a buffer zone between South Carolina and Spanish Florida.

March 1738: The governor of Spanish Florida, Don Manuel de Montiano, proclaimed that all slave runaways from the English colonies would be freed, armed to fight, and resettled in Fort Moosa, 3 miles north of St. Augustine.

The War of Jenkins's Ear: 1739–1744

CAUSES OF THE WAR

Although nearly 30 years of peace among England, France, and Spain ensued after the Treaty of Utrecht (1713), there were numerous incidents and issues that created tension among those superpowers of the day. There was disagreement over the boundaries of the French and English territories in Canada. The Spanish and English disputed the boundary of Florida, and the Spanish accused the English of logging in Honduras. The English accused the Spanish of interfering in the slave trade in the Americas. The immediate cause of the War of Jenkins's Ear was that Spaniards boarded a English trading ship in the West Indies in 1733. The captain was Robert Jenkins, and he would later claim that he was tortured by the Spanish before they cut off his ear. Not until 1738 did he appear before Parliament to show that his ear had been severed. There was a storm of outrage, but Prime Minister Robert Walpole tried to negotiate a settlement with Spain; eventually,

though, Walpole was unable to persuade either the Spanish or his outraged countrymen to compromise, and he called for a declaration of war. Most historians have concluded that the true motive for England's embarking on this war was the desire of English merchants to seize portions of, or at least have free access to, the Spanish Empire in the Americas.

DECLARATION OF WAR

England declared war on Spain on October 19, 1739.

BATTLES AND CAMPAIGNS

January 1740: Gov. James Oglethorpe of the English colony of Georgia invaded Spanish Florida. With his western flank covered by friendly Indians, he captured Fort San Francisco de Pupo and Fort Picolata, both on the San Juan River.

June 13–July 10 1740: Governor Oglethorpe's Georgian troops and their Indian allies (totaling 2,000 men) laid siege to Spanish St. Augustine. Successful in ravaging the countryside around the fort, Oglethorpe found he was unable to capture the fort itself.

March 3, 1741: A combined English-American fleet arrived off Cartagena, a Spanish settlement on the northwestern coast of Colombia. Led by Adm. Edward Vernon, the fleet carried nearly 3,500 English Americans who had been recruited in the colonies.

April 17, 1741: Following an abortive attempt to capture Cartagena, Admiral Vernon reembarked his troops and sailed for North America. Due to scurvy and yellow fever, only 600 of the 3,500 troops returned to the colonies. George Washington's half-brother, Lawrence Washington, did return, and he named the family plantation Mount Vernon in honor of the British admiral.

May 1742: Some 3,000 Spanish troops from Cuba arrived in Florida. Those forces were intended to attack the English colony of Georgia in reprisal for the English attacks on Florida in January 1740.

May–June 1742: Aware of the danger of a Spanish attack, Gov. James Oglethorpe strengthened the defenses of Fort Frederica on St. Simons Island, south of Savannah, Georgia.

July 7–12, 1742 (Battle of Bloody Marsh): Spanish and Cuban troops, under the command of Florida governor Manuel de Montiano, landed on St. Simons Island and made an initial attack on English defenses there. In command of only 600 troops, Governor Oglethorpe conducted a brilliant defense that included two wilderness ambushes. By July 12, de Montiano gave up the attack and returned to Florida. The Battle of Bloody Marsh on St. Simons Island was crucial in defending the southern border of the 13 colonies. Some historians have likened its importance to that of the Battle of the Plains of Abraham at Quebec in 1759 (see September 13, 1759, p. 46).

King George's War: 1744–1748

CAUSES OF THE WAR

In 1744, France joined forces with Spain against England and Austria in what was the already ongoing War of the Austrian Succession. That came about when the Austrian ruler Charles VI died in 1740 and various European rulers objected to his having left his lands to his daughter, Maria Theresa. The kings of Prussia, Spain, and other European lands attacked Austria. When France also joined in the attacks, England and Holland saw that the balance of power was threatened and came to Austria's defense. In what was in some respects a continuation of the War of Jenkins's Ear—in that Spain and England simply continued their hostilities—the battlefronts extended to all of North America, as New France, Louisiana, and what was left of French Acadia, fought against the English-American settlers.

DECLARATION OF WAR

Having signed a pact with Spain, the French monarchy of King Louis XV declared war on England on March 15, 1744.

BATTLES AND CAMPAIGNS

May 14, 1744: Having learned on May 3 of the declaration of war, the French governor of Louisbourg at the fort on Cape Breton Island, Nova Scotia, sent 600 men south by ship to attack the English settlement at Canso, located on a peninsula of Nova Scotia opposite the southern tip of Cape Breton.

May 1744: The French troops captured Canso. The English garrison surrendered on the condition that the men be returned to Boston. Prior to their repatriation, the English were held for a time as prisoners at Louisbourg, where they assessed the fortress.

January 26, 1745: Massachusetts governor William Shirley proposed to the Massachusetts Council that troops be raised and vessels found to carry an army northward to capture Louisbourg and Cape Breton.

February 1745: Massachusetts merchant William Pepperrell was named commander of the expedition against Louisbourg. Before setting out on his mission, Pepperrell consulted with the English evangelist George Whitefield, who responded, "Nil Desperandum Christo Duce" ("Never despair while Christ is the Leader") (see Notable Phrases, p. 51).

March 24, 1745: The colonial land forces embarked from Boston and sailed for Canso, Nova Scotia.

March–May 1745: The colonial land forces trained and drilled at Canso without being detected by the French at Louisbourg.

April 30–June 16, 1745: The colonial troops, backed up by an English squadron of ships led by Adm. Peter Warren, besieged the fortress of Louisbourg. Built between 1720 and 1730, in the tradition of the great French military engineer Vauban, the fortress had two fatal flaws: It was vulnerable to attack from the sea, and it was situated in a low-lying area.

June 17, 1745: Louisbourg surrendered to the joint English-American forces under Pepperrell and Warren. In that, the single greatest exploit of American arms to date, the Americans had overcome a fortress that had been believed to be impregnable. When the news reached London, the guns of the Tower of London were fired in celebration and Pepperrell was made a baronet (the first native-born American to receive that honor). Massachusetts was even reimbursed for the expenses of the expedition. During the siege, the Americans suffered 130 killed and 300 wounded; the official French estimate was 50 killed and 80 wounded.

1745–1747: Massachusetts militiamen held Louisbourg. In contrast to their relatively low casualties during the siege, the New Englanders lost nearly 1,200 men to smallpox during this holding period.

November 28–29, 1745: A French and Indian force marched overland from Fort St. Frederic on Lake Champlain to the English village of

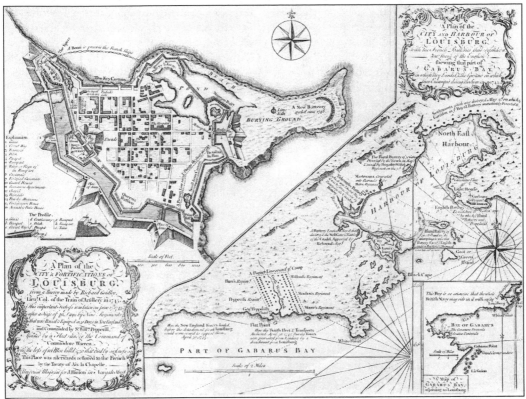

This map and plan from 1745 shows the city and fort of Louisbourg on the island of Cape Breton, Nova Scotia, right after they were taken from the French by an expedition of British colonists from New England. The Treaty of Aix-la-Chapelle (1748) that concluded King George's War (War of the Austrian Succession in Europe) returned Louisbourg to the French.

Saratoga, New York. The French and Indians surprised the town and killed some 30 inhabitants.

June–October 1746: A large French fleet (65 ships, including transports and supporting ships) departed from Brest, France, carrying 3,000 troops. Commanded by the Duc d'Anville, the force was sent to recapture Louisbourg, to conquer Nova Scotia, and to strike against the English colonies along the North American coast. Along the way, the sailors were struck by smallpox, fever, and dysentery, and hundreds of them died before they arrived off the coast of New England in September. As they approached the coast of Nova Scotia, a terrible storm disabled several ships and one ran aground. The Duc d'Anville then died and was succeeded by his lieutenant admiral, who committed suicide. By October the fleet had turned around and was making its way back to France. Although no men were lost in combat, the French lost an estimated 2,000 to disease.

August 20, 1746: French and Indian forces besieged and captured English Fort Massachusetts in East Hoosack (present-day Adams), Massachusetts, near the borders of Massachusetts, New York, and Vermont. The surrender and subsequent destruction of the fort was a serious loss to Massachusetts, and many colonists feared that additional raids would follow in the aftermath of the siege.

NEGOTIATIONS AND PEACE TREATY

The Treaty of Aix-la-Chapelle, signed on October 18, 1748, ended the War of the Austrian Succession and thus also King George's War. The diplomats followed the basic principle of status quo ante bellum ("the state existing before the war")—Louisbourg was returned to France; Madras in India, which the French had conquered, was returned to England. New England colonists were outraged when they learned the terms of the treaty as New England militiamen had captured Louisbourg and had held it in spite of serious losses due to disease. The treaty negated that costly conquest to serve the broader interest of the mother country. Some historians have conjectured that the outrage in New England (shown in church sermons and in the newspapers) was one of the first significant steps that English Americans took in their long road toward independence from England. In recognition of that thesis, references hereafter will be made to the American colonists, instead of English-Americans or English colonists.

The French and Indian War: 1754-1763

CAUSES OF THE WAR

In the interval between King George's War and the French and Indian War (sometimes referred to as "the short peace") the American, French, and Spanish colonists continued to jockey for positions in North America. The prime zones of contention were Lake Champlain in upstate New York and the Ohio River valley. A series of episodes in those areas gradually pulled the English and French in North America into a war without any formal declaration.

1749: Alarmed by English intrusions into the Ohio River valley area, the government of New France sent Col. Celeron de Bienville south from Lake Erie to claim land and territory for France. During his expedition, Bienville buried lead plates at key spots along rivers, documenting the French claim to the land now occupied by Ohio, Indiana, and Illinois. That was the first stage of an ambitious French plan to build a string of forts to connect Lake Erie with the Ohio River valley.

April 1753: The governor of French Canada, the Marquis de Menneville, ordered the construction of a fort to be called Presqu'Isle at present-day Erie, Pennsylvania.

October 31, 1753: Concerned over the news that the French were building forts in the Ohio area, Virginia governor Robert Dinwiddie sent 21-year old George Washington, a major in the Virginia militia, to ascertain what the French intentions were.

December 1753: Washington reached the French headquarters near Erie, Pennsylvania, and was told to inform the English that the French intended to defend their claims to the Ohio River valley.

January 16, 1754: George Washington re-turned to Williamsburg, Virginia, and reported the French message. He also provided detailed maps of the region he had traveled through and urged Dinwiddie to build a fort at the junction of the Allegheny and Monongahela rivers (present-day Pittsburgh) where the Ohio River begins.

February–March 1754: Under the orders of Governor Dinwiddie, Capt. William Trent and a small force erected a tiny fort where the Allegheny and Monongahela Rivers joined to form the Ohio River.

BATTLES AND CAMPAIGNS

April 17, 1754: French forces captured the fort built by the Americans in February at the forks of the Ohio River and evicted the 41 defenders. The French proceeded to erect their own, more ambitious Fort Duquesne on the same site.

May 28, 1754: By then a lieutenant colonel, George Washington was assigned to lead a force of 150 Virginia militia to man a new fort at the head of the Ohio River. Enroute, in southwestern Pennsylvania (11 miles east of present-day Uniontown), he ran into a group of French troops under Lt. Joseph Coulon de Jumonville. In a short but sharp engagement, the French suffered 10 killed (including Jumonville), 1 wounded, and 21 prisoners; the Americans lost only 1 man. The 22-year-old Washington had struck the first blow of what would become known as the French and Indian War in North America.

July 3, 1754: Aware that the French held Fort Duquesne, Washington built Fort Necessity about 60 miles south of the French fort, at the Great Meadows in the southwestern corner of Pennsylvania (near present-day Uniontown). After the French launched an overpowering attack, Washington was forced to surrender. The French, however, allowed Washington and his men to evacuate Fort Necessity and retreat to Virginia.

February 20, 1755: English general Edward Braddock arrived in Virginia. Having come from England to take the position of commander in chief in North America, Braddock brought with him two English regiments. Braddock soon conferred with Washington and Benjamin Franklin; both urged him to consider the possibility that the French and the Indians would fight in a manner different from the European style of open-field warfare.

April 14, 1755: General Braddock began to assemble the troops he would lead in an attempt to capture Fort Duquesne. Braddock's force consisted of 1,400 British soldiers and 450 American troops under the command of Washington.

June 19, 1755: Two thousand New England militiamen and English troops captured French Fort Beauséjour in Nova Scotia. This conquest ended the French resistance in the Nova Scotia region.

July 9, 1755 (Braddock's Defeat): General Braddock marched straight into a trap laid by the French and Indians at a ravine 8 miles away from Fort Duquesne. Hiding behind trees and bushes, the French and Indians completely defeated the English troops, who, standing exposed and in bright red uniforms, were an easy target for the enemy. By the end of the day, the English had suffered 977 soldiers killed, wounded, and missing. (Braddock was wounded and later died.) Washington led the remnants of the English-American army back to Fort Cumberland in present-day Maryland. That battle, the single greatest disaster for the English and Americans during the war, had a profound effect on English and American troops.

September 5, 1755: Col. Charles Lawrence, the English governor of Nova Scotia, ordered all Acadians (French settlers) who refused to swear allegiance to King George II and England expelled from the colony. Between September and November 1755, some 6,000 Acadians were forcibly expelled from their homes. Some escaped to other parts of Canada; but most were shipped to the 13 English colonies, where they were received with disapproval. Some found their way to Louisiana and founded the Cajun culture of that area; others returned after many years to Nova Scotia and endured poverty in order to be reunited with their homeland (see Legends and Trivia, p. 51).

September 8, 1755: English-American trader and representative to the Mohawk Indians William Johnson led a force of 3,500 American colonists to victory over a French force of 1,400 men at the Battle of Lake George. Johnson had intended to attack Fort St. Frederic on Lake Champlain, but he was attacked by the French and Indians, led by Baron Dieskau of the French army. Defending their fortifications, the Americans stopped their opponents. The French suffered at least 200 men killed, wounded, and missing; the Americans suffered only half as many losses. Baron Dieskau was wounded and captured by the Americans. Johnson did not press on to Lake Champlain, and the battle ended in a draw along the Lake Champlain–Hudson River corridor. In reward for

his stance against the French, Johnson was made a baronet of England in 1756.

Fall 1755: Following the defeat of Baron Dieskau's forces, the French built a second fort to guard Lake Champlain. Fort Carillon, better known by its English name Fort Ticonderoga, was constructed on the western side of the lake. The fort soon became the keystone of French defenses on the Lake Champlain–Hudson River corridor.

December 1755: George Washington persuaded colonial assemblies to begin construction of a series of forts from the Potomac River in Virginia to Fort Prince George in South Carolina.

May 11, 1756: Louis Joseph, the Marquis de Montcalm, arrived at Quebec and took command of the French troops stationed there. Montcalm replaced Baron Dieskau.

May 15, 1756: While the English were fighting the French and their Indian allies in North America, the nations of Europe were once again choosing sides, this time over the right to own Silesia (now part of Poland and Czechoslovakia). When England became allied with Prussia in its quarrel with Austria over Silesia, Austria retaliated by making a treaty with France.

England declared war on France on May 15, 1756, making official a conflict that had been raging for two years in North America. That began what is known as the Seven Years' War in Europe (1756—1763). Warfare spread to India (where the English and French had competing trading outposts) and the Pacific (where the English took the Philippines from the Spanish in 1762).

August 14, 1756: The Marquis de Montcalm successfully led French troops against English Fort Oswego on the southern side of Lake Ontario. Following the English surrender, Montcalm and his men destroyed the fort, which had served as a seat and symbol of English power in the area (especially to the Iroquois who lived close by).

August 31, 1756: English general Daniel Webb withdrew his troops from the Mohawk River valley to the safety of Fort Edward on the Hudson River. Coming in the wake of the loss of Fort Oswego, that withdrawal further lowered English prestige among the Iroquois Indians.

June 29, 1757: In London, William Pitt became secretary of state for England (and effectively prime minister) and was given supreme control over the conduct of the war, both in Europe and in North America.

June 30, 1757: A British fleet and army reached

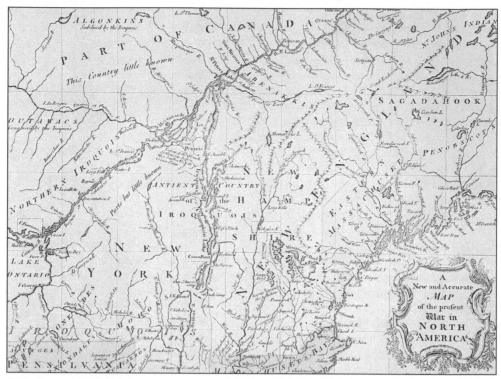

This map of 1757 shows the northeastern corner of North America as the French and Indian War (known in Europe as the Seven Years War) was raging. It does not include Nova Scotia or western Pennsylvania where important battles took place.

Halifax, Nova Scotia. Commanded by the Scottish Earl of Loudon, the force was intended to attack and capture Fort Louisbourg (which had been returned to French control by the Treaty of Aix-la-Chapelle in 1748).

August 3–7, 1757: Montcalm besieged Fort William Henry at the base of Lake George in northern New York. Montcalm's 8,000-man army used classic European-style siege tactics to envelop the fort, defended by 2,300 troops under Col. George Munro.

August 9, 1757: Having surrendered on honorable terms, the English garrison marched out of Fort William Henry and headed toward Fort Edward, 14 miles to the south. The capitulation agreement permitted the English to leave the scene. (Montcalm could not have provided food for so many prisoners.) As they exited the fort and began their march, the disarmed English and American troops were set upon by many of Montcalm's Indian allies, who were infuriated by the lack of enemy scalps they had taken in the campaign. A horrendous scene ensued in which Indian warriors attacked and scalped largely helpless En-

glish and colonial troops while French officers pleaded with their Indian allies to stop the killings. When the French finally managed to restore order, they found that at least 200 of the English and Americans had been killed and another 200 had been taken into captivity. This, one of the most grisly episodes in the entire war, was later memorialized in James Fenimore Cooper's *The Last of the Mohicans*. The massacre was a sorry event for Montcalm, as his greatest victory to date was spoiled by the actions of his allies.

September 1, 1757: The Earl of Loudon brought his English troops to New York City. Frustrated in his attempt to attack Louisbourg by the presence of a large French fleet, Loudon arrived in New York to find it in a state of near panic. Many settlers were convinced that Montcalm, victorious at Fort William Henry, would proceed south. Actually, Montcalm and his French and Indian forces already had begun to march back to Canada.

December 30, 1757: The new English prime minister, William Pitt, sent a series of directives to North America. Pitt replaced Lord Loudon as commander in chief with Gen. James Abercromby. Pitt also asked the governors of the northern colonies to gather a force of 20,000 men to be joined by English troops. Together the English-American troops were to make an all-out assault on Canada.

June 8, 1758: An English fleet of more than 100 vessels, commanded by Adm. Edward Boscawen, landed 8,000 troops under Gen. Jeffery Amherst and Gen. James Wolfe near the French fortress of Louisbourg on Cape Breton Island. The successful English landing almost guaranteed the English a victory, since their fleet controlled the waters off Louisbourg.

June 19, 1758: The English army began a siege of Louisbourg. In the next five weeks they expended 18,700 roundshot and 1,493 barrels of powder in a constant cannonade against the French fortress.

July 4, 1758: An army of 16,000 men (including English regulars and American militiamen) set out from the ruins of Fort William Henry in up-colony New York. Transported by canoes and boats, the English-American troops made their way up Lake George and were soon in a position to threaten the French fortress of Fort Carillon (known to the English as Ticonderoga).

July 6, 1758: English general George Augustus Howe was killed in a skirmish as he reconnoitered the area near Fort Carillon. Howe's death caused a general depression in the English-American army. An unusually adaptable English officer, Howe had taken to heart the lessons of Braddock's defeat and had worked well with American soldiers.

July 8, 1758: Gen. James Abercromby ordered an all-out attack by the English-American army on the French lines set up outside Fort Carillon. Sixteen thousand English and American troops attacked barricades set up by Montcalm and his 4,000 troops. Conducted on a hot day, the English-American attack turned into a complete disaster as wave after wave of English and American troops threw themselves furiously but unsuccesfully against the French lines. When the firing ended around 7 P.M., the English and Americans had 464 killed, 1,117 wounded, and 29 missing. The French suffered approximately 400 men killed or wounded.

July 9, 1758: General Abercromby ordered a retreat down Lake George, even though his mauled army still greatly outnumbered the French defenders. The French were amazed to witness this re-

treat. Soon afterward, Montcalm erected a cross to commemorate the victory won by his small army (see Notable Phrases, p. 52).

July 26, 1758: Louisbourg surrendered to the English army led by General Amherst. The French garrison suffered 411 killed; 5,637 men surrendered. The English suffered 195 killed and 329 wounded. The soldiers and sailors of the French garrison were sent to England as prisoners.

August 27, 1758: English forces led by Col. John Bradstreet captured French Fort Frontenac at the site of present-day Kingston, Ontario.

September 18, 1758: Gen. Jefferey Amherst replaced Abercromby as the English commander in chief in North America.

November 25, 1758: French troops used gunpowder demolition to damage Fort Duquesne shortly before the arrival of English and American troops under the command of Gen. John Forbes. Forbes avoided repeating the earlier mistakes of General Braddock: He cooperated with the American troops led by George Washington and marched slowly and with care through western Pennsylvania to avoid any possible ambushes. The loss of Fort Duquesne, combined with the loss of Louisbourg and Frontenac, made the French position in North America much more tenuous, and the aggressive strategy of the English, conceived by Prime Minister William Pitt, seemed to be on the verge of success. (Fort Duquesne was renamed Fort Pitt.)

June 27, 1759: Gen. James Wolfe and 9,000 troops, transported by a huge English fleet (49 warships and 119 transport and supply vessels), arrived at Quebec City. The English captains and pilots had accomplished an extraordinary feat in bringing the large ships of the fleet up the St. Lawrence River without the loss of a single man or ship. Wolfe found that the Marquis de Montcalm and the Marquis de Vaudreuil, governor of Canada, had gathered 16,000 troops (12,000 militia and 4,000 French regulars) to defend Quebec. The French troops were drawn up in a 20-mile radius on the northern side of the St. Lawrence River, making an attack difficult.

July 25, 1759: A combined force of American Colonials and Iroquois warriors, led by Gen. John Prideaux and Col. Sir William Johnson, captured Fort Niagara from the French.

July 27, 1759: French troops led by General Bourlamaque evacuated Fort Carillon (after destroying as much of it as they could) as the

English-American army led by Gen. Jefferey Amherst approached. A cautious and methodical general, General Amherst had showed no inclination to be drawn into a frontal assault such as General Abercromby had mistakenly made the year before.

At Quebec, the French defenders sent a small fleet of fire ships against the English fleet. English sailors managed to tow the fire ships aside, rendering the attack harmless. "Damn Jack, dids't thee ever take hell in tow before," became a cliché among the sailors of Adm. Charles Saunders's fleet.

July 31, 1759: The French forces led by General Bourlamaque evacuated Fort St. Frederic (after destroying much of it) and moved northward on Lake Champlain. Finally establishing a defensive line at Isle-aux-Noix at the northern head of Lake Champlain, Bourlamaque was able to report to Montcalm that he believed Amherst would not move farther north during that year. For his part, Amherst soon built English forts at the renamed Fort Ticonderoga (Fort Carillon) and Fort Crown Point (Fort St. Frederic).

English troops under General Wolfe went ashore at Beauport, 5 miles north of Quebec. The famed English Grenadiers made a charge uphill against the French defenders. The weather worked against the invaders; a sudden and heavy downpour soaked their gunpowder and made their footing treacherous. The French defenders poured volley after volley into the English ranks. By the time Wolfe called off the attack, the English had suffered 444 men killed, wounded, or missing; French casualties were minimal. Although far from conclusive, this defeat made General Wolfe's mission to capture Quebec more difficult.

August 1759: As he pondered his next move against Quebec, General Wolfe sent raiding parties into the interior to burn many French-Canadian farms. In addition, English cannons, set up at Pointe Lévis, on the south side of the St. Lawrence River, pounded the upper and lower towns of Quebec with cannon fire. Wolfe was trying to force the Marquis de Montcalm to bring his army out and fight, but Montcalm held his ground, confident that the coming winter would force the English to depart.

September 1–2, 1759: English troops on the northern side of Montmorency Falls were withdrawn to augment the English force stationed at Pointe Lévis, directly across from Quebec. Governor Vaudreuil was exultant, believing this action

was preliminary to a general British withdrawal, but Montcalm knew it was unlikely that Wolfe would leave without making a last attempt to capture Quebec.

September 11, 1759: General Wolfe landed his army 2 miles south of Quebec, an area that seemed impossible to penetrate because of the high cliffs. From deserters, Wolfe knew that the French were tiring from the long siege and the cannon fire, set up in August, that had left the lower Town in ruins.

September 12–13, 1759: General Wolfe led his men in an ascent from Anse de Foulon, 2 miles south of the city. Ascending the cliffs, the advance English guard overpowered a small French detachment at the top of the cliffs and cleared the way for the main body of troops to ascend the cliffs. By dawn, 4,500 English troops and a few field pieces of artillery were at the top of the cliffs. Wolfe soon chose his battle spot, an uneven patch of ground named for a farmer named Abraham.

September 13, 1759 (Battle of the Plains of Abraham): Seeing that the English had outsmarted him and had placed themselves on the heights to the rear of the city, Montcalm decided on an attack. Leading a force of equal size (about 4,500 men), Montcalm advanced toward the English lines. The French-Canadian militiamen advanced rapidly, throwing themselves to the ground after firing, but the French regulars advanced slowly while firing. Prepared by Wolfe for this moment, the English held their fire until the French were only 40 yards away—then the cry of "Fire" rang out. The British poured two devastating volleys into the French troops, then advanced. The French troops, both militia and regulars, ran, and the retreat turned into a rout. (Casualties on both sides were about equal—640 killed or wounded.) Wolfe, who was wounded twice, upon learning that the French were in retreat, ordered that they be cut off (this was not achieved). Soon after, Wolfe died from his wounds. Montcalm also was wounded. He made it to the city on horseback, but died a few hours later (see Notable Phrases, p. 52).

September 18, 1759: Following a flight from the city of Quebec by Governor Vaudreuil and the bulk of the French army, the Chevalier de Ramezay, left in charge of the city, surrendered Quebec to the English army under the command of Gen. James Murray.

October 11–12, 1759: A French squadron of

In the famous painting by Benjamin West, Gen. James Wolfe is portrayed dying at the moment of British victory at Quebec.

three small naval vessels was sunk by its crew on Lake Champlain, following a confrontation with a larger English squadron. That opened the way for an English advance up Lake Champlain the following spring.

April 23, 1760: The ice in the St. Lawrence River at Quebec broke up, heralding the start of spring. Of the 5,600 English troops still stationed at Quebec, 2,300 were on the sick list.

April 27, 1760: The Chevalier de Lévis, the French commander in Canada since the death of Montcalm, began a siege of Quebec. Lévis had brought the remnants of the French army northward from Montreal with the intent of capturing Quebec before the first supply ships from England could arrive.

April 28, 1760 (Battle of Sainte-Foy, sometimes called the Second Battle of the Plains of Abraham): Gen. James Murray led 3,000 of his troops out of Quebec and fought against 4,000–5,000 French troops at Sainte-Foy, only a mile away from the battleground of the Plains of Abraham. Murray almost duplicated the error of Montcalm in September 1759. By leaving the safety of the city walls, he exposed his men to a battle in the spring mud on the field at Sainte-Foy. When the day was over, both the English and French had suffered about the same number of casualties— some 1,000 killed, wounded, taken prisoner, or missing—but the battle thrust the English back into

the city walls and briefly revived hopes of the habitants of New France that they might be rescued from English rule.

April 29-May 15, 1760: The Chevalier de Lévis undertook a siege of Quebec. Lacking heavy siege artillery, Lévis was at the mercy of whatever ship first appeared off Quebec. On May 9, 1760, the English HMS *Lowestoft* appeared, dimming the French chances considerably. Lévis continued the siege until May 15, when the arrival of other English ships signaled the end of chances for a successful siege.

Summer 1760: A three-pronged English invasion force moved slowly toward Montreal, the last French-held city in Canada. Gen. Jeffery Amherst brought an army up the St. Lawrence River from Lake Ontario, Gen. James Murray led English forces southward from Quebec, and Col. William Haviland led English troops north from Fort Ticonderoga and Fort Crown Point.

September 6, 1760: The English forces of Amherst, Murray, and Haviland rendezvoused near Montreal.

September 8, 1760: The Marquis de Vaudreuil, governor general of French Canada, officially surrendered Montreal and all the remaining pockets of French resistance in Canada to the forces led by General Amherst. When Amherst refused to grant the customary honors of war to the defeated French garrison, the Chevalier de Levis ordered the regimental colors burned, rather than surrender the colors into the hands of the English.

November 29, 1760: English forces led by Maj. Robert Rogers accepted the surrender of the French outpost at Detroit.

1760–1761: Sporadic fighting continued in Europe and the Caribbean, even as peace negotiations began between France and England.

January 24, 1762: King George III declared war on Spain, anticipating that Spain would aid the defeated France.

Summer 1762: The English army and navy won important victories against Spain, capturing Havana in Cuba and Manila in the Philippines.

NEGOTIATIONS AND PEACE TREATY

During the early years of the war, none of the parties were inclined to seek peace. The Prussian and French victories of 1756 and 1757 affirmed their position; and although the English victories of 1758–1759 made the Bourbon dynasties of France and Spain eager to seek peace, they wanted peace on terms the English would not accept. The issue of a negotiated peace had as much to do with internal politics in England as it did with anything occurring on the battlefields. Certainly the hostilities in North America had little influence on William Pitt, England's secretary of state and the most powerful man in the government, who wanted to completely limit the power of France and Spain to oppose England in the future. But Pitt was strongly opposed by many others in the government, and when King George II died in October 1760, his grandson, George III, began to throw his weight behind Pitt's opponents.

Although the North American colonists, both French and English, occasionally signed treaties with Indians during this period, the French and Indian Wars in North America ended only with the signing of peace treaties in Europe. Those treaties are explained above under the heading for each war.

April 19, 1761: Etienne, the Duc de Choiseul, first minister to Louis XV of France, suggested that England and France send a representative to each other's capital to commence negotiations for peace. Pitt accepted and sent Hans Stanley, a relatively obscure member of Parliament, to Paris to serve as his representative.

May 31, 1761: Stanley arrived in France to begin negotiations. On the same date, Monsieur F. de Bussy arrived in England as the representative of the Duc de Choiseul.

June 24–26, 1761: Pitt met with the British cabinet to consider the terms offered by France. The French had given in on many issues, but they insisted on the return to them of Cape Breton Island at the mouth of the St. Lawrence River. Determined to break the French strength at sea and knowing that the French maritime strength depended in part on the fishing stations on Cape Breton, Pitt pushed his cabinet members to reject the proposals.

July 29, 1761: Hans Stanley delivered an ultimatum to Choiseul: Cape Breton must be given to England, but France would be allowed limited rights to fish in the waters off Canada's Atlantic coast.

August 1761: Pitt continued discussions of the peace terms with the cabinet throughout August. He finally yielded to the suggestion to concede France an island off Newfoundland to use as a fishing station. Stanley conveyed this concession to Choiseul in Paris, but Choiseul countered by requesting instead an island in the Gulf of St. Lawrence, more convenient for fishermen.

September 18, 1761: Opposition to Pitt was intensifying because of his insistence that England declare war against Spain to once and for all destroy Spain's threat to England's empire. Pitt formally proposed war against Spain, but cabinet members refused to go along with him and persuaded George III to support them.

September 30, 1761: With all efforts to break the stalemate in negotiations apparently having failed, Hans Stanley returned to England.

October 6, 1761: His policies and person under attack from all sides, William Pitt resigned as secretary of state of England. Within a month he was replaced by the Earl of Bute.

January–October 1762: On January 4, Bute and his government declared war against Spain, just as Pitt had proposed. In the months that followed, Bute and his closest advisers began to negotiate with France in secret through the Sardinian ambassador in London. Because Bute and his supporters were willing to concede more to the French than Pitt had been, England and France eventually came to terms.

November 3, 1762: Preliminary articles of had

peace between France and England were signed at Fontainebleau, France. Meanwhile, King Louis XV of France signed a secret treaty with Spain, ceding Louisiana (France's territory west of the Mississippi) and Isle d'Orleans (including the city of New Orleans) to Spain, ostensibly to reward Spain for its aid during the Seven Years' War. But it was really intended to keep England from gaining control of this vast territory.

February 10, 1763: The Treaty of Paris was signed by England, France, and Spain, concluding their roles in both the European and colonial phases of the war. The terms were severe for Spain and France. France yielded Canada to England (including Cape Breton) but was allowed to keep the islands of St. Pierre and Miquelon off the Atlantic coast and to maintain fishing rights in the Gulf of St. Lawrence and off the coast of Newfoundland. France yielded to England all territory east of the Mississippi, except the city of New Orleans (already promised to Spain). Spain yielded Florida to England, in return for retaining power in Cuba; Spain recovered Manila in the Philippines. France retained most of its islands in the Caribbean. Generally, England gained territory everywhere—North America, off the coast of Africa, in the Caribbean. Even in India, England's claims to territory were strengthened, and the French claims were greatly reduced.

February 15, 1763: Prussia and Austria signed a peace treaty at Hubertusburg, Austria, ending the Seven Years' War, essentially by restoring the disputed and conquered lands to their status before the war.

HOME FRONT

The European civilians experienced the French and Indian Wars in quite a different way from North American civilians. There were numerous battles all across Europe (and in India), but, with the exception of several sieges, they did not impact directly on the lives of civilians. Nevertheless, masses of Europeans paid dearly in lives, property, and taxes for the wars conducted by their rulers.

In North America, the French and Indian Wars had an immediate impact on many civilians. Several of the major battles were fought around forts or fortified settlements—Louisbourg (a constant target), Fort Carillon, Quebec City, Fort William Henry—but there were inevitably civilian casualties. Several major communities were devastated—Port Royal in Nova Scotia, Deerfield and Haverhill in Massachusetts, New Bern in North Carolina, St. Augustine in Florida—and dozens of lesser known settlements across New England, upper New York, South Carolina, and Georgia. Indian raids were apt to be on civilian settlements, but the Indians were by no means the only ones to disrupt the home front. One of the most notorious episodes involved the expulsion in 1755 of some 6,000 French Acadians not only from their settlements but also from Nova Scotia.

The casualties during the French and Indian Wars often numbered in the thousands, compared with the hundreds during the 17th century, and a large proportion of these casualties were militia—basically, civilians who were temporarily at war. In proportion to the total populations, their deaths had a terrific impact on their civilian communities. Certainly during the years of actual hostilities, colonists were well aware of war raging around them. If nothing else, the colonists had to pay for the wars in one currency or another. Ironically, it was the English, who emerged victorious at the end of the French and Indian Wars, who imposed new taxes and brought their colonists to a revolution.

RESULTS OF THE WARS (Casualties, Costs, Consequences)

During King William's War, the English and Americans suffered approximately 1,000 men killed, wounded, or missing. The French suffered about 400, and the Iroquois lost as many as 500 men. There are no definitive records for the monetary losses. However, the cost of the war can be suggested by the cost of the expedition against Quebec in 1690—50,000 English pounds.

Queen Anne's War proved to be more costly for all the combatants. Although there is no figure for the total English and colonial losses, one can point to the fact that 750 English troops and 150 English sailors were lost in just the Walker expedition of 1711. Monetary costs were high for both sides; the English government in London was better able to afford the high costs of the war, since the Bank of London (created in 1694) allowed the English to borrow money more effectively than the French could. In the colonies, the costs were enormous—the average Boston taxpayer paid 42 percent more in taxes in 1713 than he had in 1700, before the war began.

The War of Jenkins's Ear was very costly to the American colonials and to the Spanish. Somewhere between 2,000 and 3,000 Americans died (mostly from disease) during Admiral Vernon's expedition against Cartagena. The Spanish lost hundreds of men in the Battle of Bloody Marsh on St. Simon's Island, and great damage was done to the town of St. Augustine.

During King George's War, the casualties and losses for both sides increased. The New Englanders captured Louisbourg with light losses, but then 1,200 of them died from disease. The French fleet of the Duc d'Anville lost 2,300 men, mostly from disease. In addition, the border raids that were carried out by both sides caused hundreds of casualties.

The French and Indian War was better documented than the other conflicts. The English national debt more than doubled (to a total of 167 million English pounds) during the war, and thousands of English soldiers and sailors lost their lives in the conflict (on one day alone, July 8, 1758, the English suffered 1,600 casualties at Fort Carillon). The French and French Canadians suffered thousands of deaths from battle and disease, and the French-Canadian farmers of the St. Lawrence River valley lost many of their farms because of the "scorched earth" policy of General Wolfe in 1759.

The main outcome, though, was that when the series of wars known to Americans as the French and Indian Wars ended, England emerged as the supreme maritime and imperial power in the world.

MILITARY INNOVATIONS, TACTICS, EQUIPMENT

English: During Queen Anne's War, the English army developed the use of the flintlock musket, which was devastatingly accurate at short range. The English also pioneered the use of the bayonet, which increased the battle deaths of that war. In addition, the leadership and successes of John Churchill, later the Duke of Marlborough, replaced the static, fortress type of warfare practiced in King William's War with a more fluid, mobile type of fighting.

French: The French in the late 17th century were leaders in fortress design. The Marquis de Vaubaun led the way in developing forts in Europe that served as models for the fortress at Louisbourg. In North America, the French proved much more adaptable than the English to wilderness warfare, as was shown in their ambush of Braddock in 1755.

Spanish: No particular innovation emerged from the Spanish during the wars. However, a remarkable revitalization of the Spanish navy and imperial strategy took place during the reign of King Philip V. Some historians have attributed this resurgence to the influence of King Philip's second wife, Elizabeth de Farnese.

Native Americans: From the start of the wars to their finish, the Native Americans were outgunned by their European-American foes. One exception to this was the Six Nations of the Iroquois, who, until about 1715, were as well armed as their European foes. The Iroquois fell behind in equipment after 1715.

Americans: The Americans sought to keep up with all the new changes coming from Europe. They adapted readily to the flintlock musket but not to the use of the bayonet. The Americans slow to adapt to wilderness warfare, and even George Washington, who had once warned Braddock of the dangers involved in the European style of fighting, greatly admired the discipline of the English troops.

LEGENDS AND TRIVIA

Hannah Dustin (1657–1729) emerged as the quintessential Puritan female hero during the wars. On March 15, 1697, she, her one-week-old child, and the child's nurse, Mary Neff, were taken into captivity by Abenaki Indians, who attacked the town of Haverhill, Massachusetts. As the Indians took the prisoners northward, Dustin's baby was killed and she learned that she and her fellow captives would soon be required to run the gauntlet, a grueling and humiliating punishment. While camped at the confluence of the Contoocook and Merrimack Rivers, near present-day Concord, New Hampshire, Dustin awoke Mary Neff and an English boy (15-year-old Samuel Lennerdson). The English captives attacked and killed their ten sleeping captors. (It is believed that Dustin killed nine and the boy killed one). Scalping their Indian foes, they left the scene and made it safely home to Haverhill. They also went to Boston, where Dustin was awarded 25 pounds for the scalps. (Mary Neff and the boy were awarded 12.5 pounds each.)

Marie Madeleine Jarret de Vercheres (1678–1747) became the quintessential female hero on the French-Canadian side. Marie Madeleine was the daughter of a career officer in the French army. She and the fellow occupants of the fortified settlement of Vercheres (20 miles below Montreal on the St. Lawrence River) were surprised by an attack of Iroquois warriors on October 22, 1692. Marie Madeleine outran her foes and reached the fort, where she donned a soldier's hat, fired a cannon, and rallied her brother and a handful of other men to defend the fort. The Iroquois withdrew after two days. Marie Madeleine married in 1706 and remained a lasting hero to the French-Canadian population.

Evangeline is a fictional character created by the American poet Henry Wadsworth Longfellow. Inspired and saddened by the story of the Acadians who were ejected from their homeland in 1755, Longfellow wrote his poem *Evangeline: A Tale of Acadie* between November 1846 and March 1847. Although he had never seen Acadia or Louisiana, Longfellow brought the story to life in moving and poetic words. He described the Acadians prior to their expulsion as "Alike were they free from / Fear, that reigns with the tyrant, and envy, the vice of republics." His poem has remained an important part of American literature and has emerged as part of the ethos of the Acadian people. Statues have been erected to honor Evangeline in Grand Pré, Nova Scotia, and St. Martinville, Louisiana.

NOTABLE PHRASES

Tell your general that I have no answer to give other than through the barrels of my muskets and the mouths of my cannon.

Those were the words of the Comte de Frontenac at the battle of Quebec in 1690 (see October 6, 1690, p. 36) when asked to surrender. The quote was later repeated by generations of Canadian students. A more extended quotation concluded with: "He must learn that this is not the way to summon a man such as myself. Let him do his best, and I will do mine."

Nil Desperandum Christo Duce. ("Never despair while Christ is the leader.")

That was the slogan adopted by the Massa-chusetts expedition against Louisbourg in 1745 (see February 1745, p. 40). The words were provided by Rev. George Whitefield, who was at the time staying at the home of William Pepperrell in Kittery, Maine (then a part of Massachusetts). A fuller quotation included the ominous prediction of Whitefield that if he, Pepperrell, accepted leadership of the expedition, all the eyes of the widows and orphans would be upon him.

Fortified towns are hard nuts to crack, and your teeth are not accustomed to it.

In a letter to his brother in Boston, Benjamin Franklin expressed his doubts as to whether the New England forces could indeed capture Louisbourg. Written in 1745, those words displayed a more cautious part of Franklin that has seldom emerged in studies of this famous American. A fuller quotation is: "Fortified towns are hard nuts to crack, and your teeth are not accustomed to it. Taking strong places is a particular trade, which you have taken up without serving an apprenticeship to it. Armies and veterans need skillful engineers to direct them in their attack. Have you any? But some seem to think forts are as easy taken as snuff."

I heard the bullets whistle, and, believe me, there is something charming in the sound.

Virginia colonel George Washington wrote those words to his younger brother John Augustine Washington, on May 31, 1754, three days after George Washington had fought the first armed engagement of his life—the attack on French under Jumonville on May 28 (see p. 42). A fuller quotation is: "I fortunately escaped without any wound, for the right wing, where I stood, was exposed to and received all the enemy's fire, and it was the part where the man was wounded. I heard the bullets whistle, and, believe me, there is something charming in the sound."

I am sure I can save this country and no body else can.

Those were the words of William Pitt as he took the reins of leadership in England in 1757. Although the tone of the words indicates Pitt's arrogance, he was proved right in the four years that followed.

Quid dux? quid miles? quid strate ingentia ligna?
En signum! en victor! Deus hic, Deus ipse triumphat.

The Marquis de Montcalm had those words carved onto a cross he erected near the site of the French victory at Ticonderoga in 1758 (see July 9, 1758, p. 45). The loose translation given by historian Francis Parkman is:
Soldiers and rampart's strength are nought,
Behold the conquering Cross! Tis God the triumph wrought.

"The paths of glory lead but to the grave." Gentlemen, I would rather have written those words than have conquered Quebec.

Those words were attributed to Gen. James Wolfe. Wolfe is said to have spoken those words on September 12, 1759, as he and his men prepared for the final gamble of their campaign—the ascent of the heights at Anse de Foulon (see p. 46). Wolfe was quoting from poet Thomas Gray's "Elegy in a Country Courtyard."

Who run?
They sir, the French, they give way everywhere.
Now God be praised, since I have conquered, I will die in peace.

Supposedly, that was the conversation General Wolfe had as he lay dying on the battlefield of the Plains of Abraham on September 13, 1759. The scene at Wolfe's death was made immortal by a famous painting by Benjamin West a number of years later (see p. 47).

Oh My God, the Marquis is wounded!
It's nothing my friends, please don't concern yourselves.

Those two phrases were alleged to have been spoken when the Marquis de Montcalm rode into Quebec, when the Battle of the Plains of Abraham was over. The woman who spoke first was correct, as Montcalm was gravely wounded, and in spite of his response, he died within 24 hours.

Time enough to treat all of that, sir, when the Tower of London has been taken, sword in hand.

Those were the words of Prime Minister William Pitt, responding to the peace terms proposed by France and Spain in 1761.

SONGS

During the French and Indian Wars, most of the American colonists remained heavily influenced by the culture of their mother country. Inevitably, many of the songs that were popular in England became popular in the colonies—often as not introduced by the English troops who came over to fight in the Colonial Wars. Three of the most imperial of English songs appeared during that period. One such was "Rule, Britannia," composed in 1740 by Dr. Thomas Arne with words by James Thomson and David Mallet. The melody originally served as the conclusion of Arne's masque Alfred. "God Save the King" was also first sung in the colonies in the 1740s. The origin of both music and words remains in dispute, but one claimant to being its composer was Englishman Henry Carey; he is said to have sung it in 1740 in London at a dinner honoring Adm. Edward Vernon for his capture of Porto Bello, Panama, from the Spanish in 1739 in the War of Jenkins's Ear. (Later the colonists wrote their own words, "God save the 13 colonies.")

"The British Grenadiers," first published in 1750, was well known to colonists. (Its music was later used by Joseph Warren for his own patriotic song "Free America": "Oppose, oppose, oppose, oppose for North America!") Warren was killed at Bunker Hill, but his words continued to be sung.

Yet another song that was popular during the prerevolutionary era was "Heart(s) of Oak," written in 1759, with words by the great actor David Garrick, and music by William Boyce. In 1768, John Dickson (well-known author of *Letters from a Farmer in Pennsylvannia*) wrote new words and changed the title to "The Liberty Song." The song became known as America's first patriotic song, becoming the anthem of the more radical colonists.

One song specifically associated with the French and Indian Wars was a drinking song, "How Stands the Glass Around?" It became known as "Wolfe's Song," after Gen. James Wolfe, who sang it to his officers the night before attacking Quebec City. The song has remained a popular military drinking song to this day.

HISTORICAL PERSPECTIVES AND CONTROVERSIES

Scholarly debate about the French and Indian Wars has been long-lasting. Following are the main questions that have been addressed by historians from Francis Parkman to Francis Jennings:

Why did England and its American colonies win the final war? Was there something intrinsically stronger about the English colonies and the English form of government?

Historians of the 19th century, such as George Bancroft and Francis Parkman, tended to believe that England and its colonies prevailed because of a stronger moral and religious fiber. Anyone who has even browsed through Francis Parkman's works has been left with no doubt as to which side he believed should have prevailed; Parkman and many of his contemporaries believed that Anglo-Saxon government, the Protestant church, and the American militia were all superior to their French and Spanish Catholic rivals. Parkman occasionally showed some admiration for the French settlers, particularly for the *coureurs du bois* ("runners of the forest," that is, woodsmen), but on the whole, he held the belief that the French Canadians, conquered in 1760, had fared much better under English rule than they would have if they had stayed under the rule of France.

Many 20th-century historians followed this line as well. Samuel Eliot Morison followed Parkman in the belief that Canada was better off under English rule. Only since 1967, the year of the World's Fair in Montreal, and the subsequent resurgence of French-Canadian pride, has that basic thesis been questioned. Francis Jennings has sought to remove the romantic coloring from the Seven Years' War; his work has shown the war to have been a desperate and brutal conflict between three imperial systems: France, England, and the Iroquois tribes.

In any case, few historians today would presume to advance arguments about the superior moral or cultural fiber of one nation over another. Essentially, however, most historians have agreed on the salient and concrete reasons that England and its colonies won: greater population and the supremacy of the English navy. At the time of the last war (1754–1763), French Canada and French Louisiana had a total population of only 80,000; the English colonies had 1.5 million inhabitants. Meanwhile, the gradual emergence of the English navy as predominant in the Atlantic Ocean doomed New France, since the French colony could not receive supplies and reinforcements at the same rate as its English rivals did.

What military lessons were learned by the English Americans in the course of their victories?

That question has remained contentious. Douglas Edward Leach's work emphasized the importance of the French and Indian Wars, showing how the colonists learned to fight in the backwoods style and in the more traditional European style. (None other than George Washington was the best witness to that.) Francis Parkman and Samuel Eliot Morison went so far as to thank the French, Indians, and Spanish for providing stiff resistance; those historians seemed to believe that even the moral fiber of the Americans was enhanced by the wars.

Did the Fench and Spanish presence in North America leave behind a lasting legacy?

That question has provoked much discussion. Until perhaps the 1960s, the Anglo legacy was the only one emphasized in most books and classrooms. Under the influence of the so-called multiculturalism movement, the contributions of other peoples and traditions to North America are being recognized. Thus, historian Roger Kennedy recently has asserted that the evidence of France is "all around us," although we have a hard time seeing it because of the writings of traditional historians, who have emphasized military and political achievements to the exclusion of all other forms—artistic, architectural, cultural, etc. Kennedy's viewpoint seems likely to inspire further discussion of this topic, and recent works on Spain and the Spanish borderlands show that Spain had a long-lasting influence in Florida and the American southwest.

What was the Indian role in what has been called the French and Indian Wars?

Traditional historians responded to that question with claims such as, had the French not aligned themselves with the Algonquin Indians in their hostility to the Iroquois, the French might well have become the masters of eastern North America. That would seem to give the Indians a central role in the wars, and undoubtedly the Indians did play a prominent role in many engagements. A more recent response to that question comes from the work of Francis Jennings, who has openly declared that his multivolume studies of early America are intended to replace those of Francis Parkman. Jennings emphasizes the complexity of Indian life and declares that it is usually a mistake for European Americans to treat all the Indians of the 18th century together in a lump: Their motivations differed to the same extent that those of a Frenchman, Englishman, or American of that time period differed.

CIVILIAN AND MILITARY BIOGRAPHIES

ENGLISH

Amherst, Jefferey (1717–1797)—general: Jefferey Amherst was born in England. He was sent to America as commander in chief in 1758, replacing Gen. James Abercromby. Amherst led the successful siege of Louisbourg in 1758 and moved to capture Fort Carillon (Fort Ticonderoga) and Fort Crown Point in July 1759. He accepted the final French surrender at Montreal in September 1760 and emerged from the wars as a hero in England, though he was not always liked by the Americans. Following the wars, he enjoyed a distinguished reputation in England.

Howe, George Augustus (1722–1758)—general: George Howe was born in England. He was the older brother of William Howe and Richard Howe, who served on the English side in the American Revolution. An inspiring leader, he befriended the Americans under his command. When he was killed in a skirmish outside of Fort Carillon (Fort Ticonderoga) on July 6, 1758, the heart went out of the English-American army that had come to besiege the fort. The Massachusetts Bay Colony later spent 500 English pounds to erect a monument in his honor in Westminster Abbey.

Oglethorpe, James (1696–1785)—general, governor: James Oglethorpe was born in England. He founded the Georgia colony in 1733. The colony served both as a haven for debtors and as a buffer against Spanish Florida. He was a hu-

manitarian and a vigorous military leader. He led two expeditions against St. Augustine, and he deflected a dangerous Spanish expedition against his colony in July 1742.

Pitt, William (1708–1778)—prime minister: William Pitt was born in England. He was an influential Whig leader helped by King George II. He became prime minister in 1757, when England was at its lowest point in the Seven Years' War. He followed an American and imperial strategy, choosing to fight against France on the seas and in North America. Although supremely successful in that, he was removed from the post of prime minister by King George III. Pitt later became the Earl of Chatham.

Walker, Sir Hovenden (1656–1728)—admiral: Walker was born in England. He was named to command the joint English-American attack on Quebec in 1711. After seven of his ships went aground in the mouth of the St. Lawrence River, he returned to England. His flagship blew up in the harbor of Portsmouth, England, soon after his arrival there. Ever plagued by controversy, Walker moved to the Bahamas.

Wolfe, James (1727–1759)—general: James Wolfe was born in England. He learned his battle skills in the aftermath of Culloden and the Scottish rebellion of 1745. Known as a fierce and dedicated military leader, Wolfe directed the campaign that won Quebec in 1759. Perhaps less heroic than his reputation has made him out to be, James Wolfe has remained a hero to British imperialists.

AMERICAN

Johnson, William (1714–1774)—merchant, diplomat to the Indians: William Johnson was born in Ireland. He arrived in New York in 1741 and, while working as a fur trader, became the white person most trusted by the Mohawk Indians of the Six Nations of the Iroquois. He led American troops at the Battle of Lake George in 1755; he and his men defeated the French attackers and captured his opponent, Baron von Dieskau. Johnson received a baronetcy for that accomplishment. He went on to capture Fort Niagara in 1759. He was the superintendent of Indian Affairs (1756–1764) and remained the single most powerful individual on the New York frontier until his death.

Pepperrell, William (1696–1759)—merchant, general: William Pepperrell was born in Maine (then a part of Massachusetts). He was a successful merchant. In 1745 he was offered and accepted, leadership of the expedition against Louisbourg. During the siege, he was a model of courtesy and modesty, especially in his relations with Sir Peter Warren, who commanded the English squadron offshore. Pepperrell was made a baronet in recognition of the victory.

Phips, William (1650–1695)—shipowner, general, governor: William Phips was born in Maine (then a part of Massachusetts). He earned wealth, fame, and a knighthood for raising a sunken Spanish treasure ship in the Caribbean. He led a successful attack against Port Royal in May 1690 but failed to take Quebec in October 1690. He later served as the first royal governor of Massachusetts (1692–1694).

Rogers, Robert (1731–1795)—trader, explorer, soldier: Robert Rogers was born in Massachusetts. He became a frontier ranger, then a major of scouts for the British army in North America. He fought several sensational battles against the French and Indians in the Fort Ticonderoga area. On October 6, 1759, he led a daring raid against the Abenaki settlement of St. Francois, just over the Canadian border. During the American Revolution, he remained loyal to King George III.

FRENCH

Comte de Frontenac, Louis Baude (1622–1698)—governor of New France: Comte de Frontenac was born in France. He saw action in the Thirty Years' War before he served twice as governor of Canada (1672–1682, 1689–1698). A warrior in the old feudal style, he made mistakes (evidenced in his dealings with the Iroquois), but he enjoyed the supreme pleasure of repulsing the attack of the New England expedition under Sir William Phips in 1690.

King Louis XV (1710–1774)—king, great-grandson of King Louis XIV: Louis XV came to the throne at the age of five. Called "Louis the well beloved" in his early years, he became increasingly unpopular as the old regime in France began to break down under the stress of court finances and wars. Louis XV showed little interest in French Canada; upon receipt of the news that Canada had been lost to the English, his mistress, the Marquise de Pompadour, was alleged to have said, "Now the king can sleep."

Marquis de Montcalm, Louis Joseph (1712–1759)—general: The Marquis de Montcalm was born in France. He arrived in Canada in 1756 to serve as commander in chief. He won important victories at Oswego and Fort William Henry, but his reputation as an officer was damaged by the massacre at Fort William Henry in 1757. He repulsed the English attack on Fort Carillon in 1758, and he waged a skillful campaign against Gen. James Wolfe through the summer of 1759. Defeated (and mortally wounded) in the battle of the Plains of Abraham, Montcalm has remained a symbol to French-Canadian nationalists and an icon for romantic historians.

Vaudreuil, Pierre Rigaud de (1698–1778)—governor of New France: Pierre Rigaud de Vaudreuil was born in Canada. He was governor of Louisiana (1742–1753) and Canada (1755–1760). Jealous of the Marquis de Montcalm, he vied with Montcalm for leadership of the military forces. Following his surrender to Gen. James Amherst at Montreal on September 9, 1760, Vaudreuil was sent to France.

SPANISH

Philip of Anjou, later Philip V of Spain (1683–1746)—monarch: Philip of Anjou was born in France. He accended to the throne of Spain in 1702 in an action that soon set off the War of the Spanish Succession. Far from being a puppet of his grandfather, King Louis XIV, Philip V generally followed his own policies. In Philip's later years, Spain experienced a resurgence of its military and imperial strength.

Montiano, Manuel de (1685–1762)—governor of Spanish Florida: Manuel de Montiano was born in Bilbao, Spain. He served the Spanish crown for 27 years before becoming governor of Florida in 1737. He successfully defended the Castillo de San Marcos (the fort of St. Augustine) against expeditions sent by Georgia's English governor James Oglethorpe. Montiano launched an unsuccessful invasion of Georgia in 1742 and was defeated at the Battle of Bloody Marsh at St. Simon's Island. He left Florida in 1748 to become governor of Panama (1748–1758). After this, Montiano retired to Madrid.

FURTHER READING

Abbey, Kathryn. *Florida, Land of Change*. Chapel Hill: University of North Carolina Press, 1941.

Anderson, Fred. *A People's Army: Massachusetts Soldiers and Society in the Seven Years' War*. Chapel Hill, N.C.: Institute for Early American Studies, 1984.

Bird, Harrison. *Battle for a Continent: The French and Indian War 1754–1763*. New York: Oxford University Press, 1965.

Brasseaux, Carl A. *Acadian to Cajun, Transformation of a People, 1803–1877*. Jackson, Miss.: University Press of Mississippi, 1992.

Eccles, W. J. *France in America*. New York: Harper & Row, 1972.

Ferling, John. *Struggle for a Continent: The Wars of Early America*. Arlington Heights, Ill.: Harlan Davidson, 1993.

Fregault, Guy. *Canada: The War of the Conquest*. New York: Oxford University Press, 1969.

Gipson, Lawrence H. *The British Empire before the American Revolution* (8 volumes). New York: Alfred A. Knopf, 1960.

Harkness, Albert Jr. "Americanism and Jenkins's Ear," *Mississippi Valley Historical Review* XXXVII (1950): 61–90.

Kennedy, Roger. *Orders from France: The Americans and the French in a Revolutionary World*. Philadelphia: University of Pennsylvania Press, 1991.

Jennings, Francis. *Empire of Fortune: Crowns, Colonies & Tribes in the Seven Years' War in America*. New York: W.W. Norton Co., 1988.

Leach, Douglas Edward. *Arms for Empire*. New York: Macmillan Publishing Co., 1973.

Morison, Samuel Eliot. *The Oxford History of the American People*. New York: Oxford University Press, 1965.

O'Meara, Walter. *Guns at the Forks*. Englewood Cliffs, N. J.: Prentice Hall, 1965.

Parkman, Francis. *Count Frontenac and New France under Louis XIV*. Boston: Little, Brown Co. 1877.

——————. *Montcalm and Wolfe*. Boston: Little, Brown Co. 1884.

Peckham, Howard. *The Colonial Wars 1689–1762*. Chicago: University of Chicago Press, 1964.

Stacey, C. P. *Quebec, 1759: The Siege and the Battle*. Toronto: Macmillan Publishing Co., 1959.

Weddle, Robert S. *The French Thorn: Rival Explorers in the Spanish Sea, 1682–1762*. College Station: Texas A&M University Press, 1991.

Wright, J. Leitch. *Anglo-Spanish Rivalry in North America*. Athens: University of Georgia

PONTIAC'S WAR

DATES OF WAR

May 9, 1763–July 23, 1766

ALTERNATE NAMES

The Conspiracy of Pontiac. Pontiac's Rebellion.

SIGNIFICANCE

In one sense, Pontiac's War was an epilogue to the recently ended French and Indian War. In another, this brief war contributed to an increase in British-American tensions preceeding the American Revolution. Pontiac's War convinced British officials in London that a definite Indian frontier policy needed to be established; even as the conflict was under way, the Royal Proclamation of 1763 banned westward settlements beyond the Appalachian Mountains. But in the colonies, most settlers saw the war as evidence that they needed to push the boundaries of their settlements farther west. Those contradictory views would contribute to the conditions that culminated in the American Revolution. Pontiac's War also sent a message that few people at the time were able or willing to accept: that Indians were not going to step aside and let white people take over their land without a fight.

BACKGROUND

In the immediate aftermath of the French and Indian War (1754–1763), (see pp.42-50) France yielded its settlements and trading posts in present-day Ohio, Illinois, and Indiana to the British. Indian tribes in that region, such as the Ottawa and Shawnee, were accustomed to the light hand of the French authorities and civilians in their territories. The Indians disliked the introduction of British trade policies, which among other changes reduced the annual gifts of the French. The Indians also soon noticed the insatiable land hunger of the English settlers. For their part, many white colonists, who felt cooped up east of the Appalachian Mountains, saw the end of French control in those territories as the perfect opportunity for westward expansion.

CAUSES OF THE WAR

Sometime around 1762–1763, a Delaware Indian holy man, Neolin, known as "the Prophet," was preaching a stirring message to the tribes in the Ohio River valley. Calling on the Indians to turn away from white people's ways and seek a spiritual renewal, the Prophet caught the attention of Chief Pontiac of the Ottawa tribe. Pontiac altered the Prophet's message slightly, claiming that only the British and their colonial followers (English settlers) needed to be driven from Indian lands; the French, who had been in the area for nearly 100 years, could remain. Pontiac also overlooked the Prophet's requirement that the Indians reject all the customs of Europeans, including the use of guns.

Pontiac brought his version of the Prophet's ideas to a council of many tribes that was held at Ecorse on the Detroit River, 8 miles south of Detroit, in late April 1763. Little is known of the debates, which were lengthy, but the conclusion, reached on April 27, was that the tribes would arise at an appointed time and attack the British forts along the northwestern frontier.

PREPARATIONS FOR WAR

The British did not have much warning of the Indian uprising, but they had long been cautious in their dealings with the Indians. However, Gen. Jefferey Amherst, who was governor general of British North America, was supremely confident that his trained men could withstand any attack made by the Indians. He resisted suggestions that he be generous in offering gifts to the Indian chiefs to placate their anger over the growth of white settlements.

When a large force of Indians showed up at Fort Detroit on May 7, 1763, the British were on their guard, but they allowed Pontiac and about 300 warriors to enter the fort as a sign of good faith. In fact, the Indians were carrying guns underneath their clothes and were prepared to attack and seize the fort. But Maj. Henry Gladwin, the British commander, had anticipated that possibility; he had his 120-man garrison standing ready with their weapons. On that occasion, both sides observed the formalities of hospitality, and the Indians withdrew. But it soon became apparent that the Indians were prepared for an uprising. Within a few weeks large parties of different Indians attacked 11 British forts across a wide area.

DECLARATION OF WAR

Neither side made a formal declaration of war. The Indians conducted surprise attacks, and the British simply responded.

COMBATANTS

British and British-Americans: In 1763, Britain had approximately 15 forts across its northwestern frontier, ranging from Fort Bedford (in west-central Pennsylvania) to Fort Michilimackinac (on the straits dividing Lakes Huron and Michigan). Those forts were garrisoned by fewer than 1,000 soldiers, but the British were able to count on the assistance of thousands of English settlers who were establishing homes in the areas newly opened to settlement in the wake of the French and Indian War. There were also thousands of British troops in the colonies along the Atlantic seaboard who could be called on in an emergency.

Indians: The many tribes that Pontiac summoned to the war council, or at least the tribes he was in touch with, were able to summon between 2,000 and 3,000 warriors for combat. Although hardy and brave, those men were not truly the "soldiers" of Pontiac in the way that British soldiers were responsible to their leaders: Indian tribes were not acccustomed to coordinating their operations, and individual warriors had been known to depart from war at anytime.

GEOGRAPHIC AND STRATEGIC CONSIDERATIONS

The territory where Pontiac's War was fought—essentially a band below the Great Lakes—was vast and varied, but much of it was thickly wooded. That was of great advantage to the Indians, for they could move swiftly and unseen out of and back into the forest. The British troops were either bound to their forts or fought conventional battles on open fields as they had been taught, and the remote British forts were dependent on supplies getting through, whether by way of the Great Lakes or through the long trails from the Atlantic colonies. The two most important factors thus were those of surprise and speed. If Pontiac's tribes could surprise the British in their forts and capture them during the summer of 1763, the British would have no advance stations from which to strike the Indians.

BATTLES AND CAMPAIGNS

May 9, 1763: Pontiac and the Indians again approached Fort Detroit; but they were informed that only 50 of them would be admitted at any one time. Rebuffed, Pontiac and his warriors went to nearby Isle au Couchon (present-day Belle Isle), killed 24 steers, three soldier-herdsmen, and two settler families there. That was the first blood shed in Pontiac's War.

May 11, 1763: Pontiac's warriors came to within 60 yards of Fort Detroit before they were pushed back by musket fire. Pontiac then began a siege of the fort.

May 16, 1763: Seven Indians entered British Fort Sandusky on the south shore of Lake Erie peacefully. They then turned on the British and massacred the 20-man garrison.

May 28, 1763: British lieutenant Abraham Cuyler and 96 soldiers in ten boats were set upon by a large number of Indians at Point Pelee at the west end of Lake Erie. The attack caught the British off guard; Cuyler and about 20 men escaped in two boats; the other men were killed and their boats taken.

June 1, 1763: British Fort Ouiatenon (at present-day Lafayette, Indiana) was captured by an Indian force.

June 3, 1763: British Fort Michilimackinac, the northernmost post, was attacked and taken by Ojibwa and Sauk Indians, who killed 17 members of the garrison and took 15 others prisoner. The Indians had gained their entrance by a trick. Playing a game of baggataway (a form of lacrosse) outside the walls of the fort, one Indian knocked the ball inside the fort; his fellows pursued it as if the game were in earnest, but once inside the walls, they turned on the British with a vengeance.

June 4, 1763: British Fort Ligonier (in western Pennsylvania) was attacked by Indians. The garrison beat off the attack successfully, the only small-sized fort to do so during the entire war.

June 15, 1763: British Fort Pitt (present-day Pittsburgh) was threatened by Indians for the first time in the war.

June 18, 1763: Indians set Fort LeBoeuf (in present-day Waterford, Pennsylvania) on fire, using flaming arrows. The Indians proceeded to capture the fort, which was burned beyond further use.

June 20, 1763: Indians attacked the Presqu'-Isle Fort (at present-day Erie, Pennsylvania). Following a short siege, Ens. John Christie and his men agreed to depart from the fort. Most of the soldiers were massacred soon after they left the fort.

July 18, 1763: British colonel Henry Bouquet marched from Carlisle in eastern Pennsylvania with 480 soldiers, intending to relieve Fort Pitt. Not only was Bouquet's force smaller than he wished, but a number of his men were recovering from malarial fever they had contracted while serving in the Caribbean, prior to their reassignment to North America.

July 24, 1763: A Delaware Indian chief approached Fort Pitt and warned Capt. Simeon Ecuyer that other forts had fallen. Having heard the chief's suggestion that he yield the fort before he, too, was attacked, Ecuyer thanked the Delaware and assured him that the 338-man garrison would hold out against any attack. According to one story, Ecuyer then sent a present to the Delaware of two blankets and a handkerchief that had been issued to men in the fort suffering from smallpox. It is not known whether the Delaware then suffered an outbreak of the disease (see Legends and Trivia, p. 61).

July 28, 1763: Fort Pitt was attacked by Indians; following the failure of the direct assault, it was placed under siege.

August 5–6, 1763 (Battle of Bushy Run): On August 5, Colonel Bouquet, leading 400 Royal American and Scottish Highland troops, reached Bushy Run 20 miles east of Fort Pitt. The British advance guard was attacked by Delaware, Mingo, Shawnee, and Huron Indians, who were hoping for a surprise attack such as the one that had succeeded against Gen. Edward Braddock in 1755

(see French and Indian War, Battles and Campaigns, July 9, 1755, p. 43). Bouquet ordered a general charge; his men surged forward and cleared the Indians from the bushes. The Indians fell back, but because dusk was approaching, Bouquet did not pursue them, choosing instead to set up camp on Edge Hill. The British force suffered 60 men killed or wounded.

On the morning of August 6, the Indians completely encircled the British camp and attacked in waves against different parts of the British perimeter. Bouquet used a ruse to defeat those attacks. Pretending to retreat farther into their perimeter, the British drew the Indians into an attack on the western slope of Edge Hill, where two light infantry companies waited in reserve. A charge by the fresh troops dismayed the Indians, who fell back in confusion. The British then pursued the retreating Indians for two miles. The British suffered an additional 40 men killed or wounded; the Indian losses for the two days are unknown but are thought to have exceeded those of the whites.

August 10, 1763: Bouquet's troops entered Fort Pitt, bringing to an end the Indian siege.

August 15, 1763: The British schooner *Huron* arrived at Fort Detroit, bringing supplies and reinforcements from Fort Niagara.

October 1763: British major Henry Gladwin was ready to abandon Fort Detroit, which had been holding out against the Indian siege since May 11.

October 12, 1763: Faced with the disappearance of many warriors (who had gone home or to their hunting grounds for the autumn), some of the remaining Indians besieging Fort Detroit requested a truce with Gladwin, who refused.

October 31, 1763: Learning that the French would not provide troops and supplies for his cause, Pontiac declared an end to the siege of Fort Detroit and withdrew with his remaining warriors to the west. Other Indians maintained the siege until British colonel John Bradstreet arrived in August 1764. From that point on, the war essentially wound down through a series of negotiations. Pontiac allegedly tried to rouse an uprising among Indians living in French-held territory along the Mississippi River and tried to gain French support for continuing the war. He failed in both those aims and eventually went to Fort Detroit and made peace (see August 28, 1765, p. 60).

NEGOTIATIONS AND PEACE TREATY

August 1764: Col. John Bradstreet left Fort Niagara with 1,200 men in boats. Under orders from Gen. Thomas Gage (who had replaced Gen. Jefferey Amherst as commander in North America) to attack the Shawnee and Delaware villages south of Lake Erie, Bradstreet proceeded to the ruins of Presqu'Isle.

August 12–26, 1764: On August 12, Bradstreet met with representatives from the Shawnee and Delaware tribes at Presqu'Isle and drew up a treaty with them, even though Sir William Johnson, the British superintendent of Indian affairs, was the only man empowered to negotiate peace terms. Bradstreet went on to Fort Detroit, and relieved the siege on August 26.

August–September 17, 1764: British captain Charles Morris was sent to conclude a peace treaty with the Indians based in the Illinois territory. Along the way, he came upon an Indian encampment, where he met with Pontiac. After several more weeks of fruitless dealings with the Indians, Morris returned to Fort Detroit.

September 5–7, 1764: Bradstreet held a conference with chiefs from the Ottawa, Huron, Chippewa, and Potawatomi tribes in the fields outside Fort Detroit. He concluded what he regarded as a peace treaty to end the war, but it was not observed by the Indian tribes.

October–November 1764: Col. Henry Bouquet left Fort Pitt with 1,500 men, having been ordered by General Gage to conduct a punitive strike against the Indian villages in present-day Ohio. Bouquet went as far as the Muskingum River, where he engaged in a parley with several Indian chiefs and persuaded them to give up their captives, many of them women and children. After several more encounters with Indians, Bouquet returned to Fort Pitt, bringing with him more than 200 former captives and 100 Indian hostages he had taken as a guarantee that other British captives would be delivered to Fort Pitt.

August 28, 1765: Pontiac entered Fort Detroit in peace and smoked a pipe of peace with Indian agent George Croghan. Pontiac gave a speech in which he urged his "new father," the King of England, to be as gracious to him and his people as the King of France had been in the past (see Notable Phrases, p. 61). In a conference with Sir William Johnson, Pontiac promised to bring a formal conclusion to the war the following spring.

July 23, 1766: Johnson met with Pontiac and other Indian chiefs at Fort Ontario at Oswego on the southeastern side of Lake Ontario. Johnson and Pontiac concluded a formal treaty, thus ending Pontiac's War.

RESULTS OF THE WAR (Casualties, Costs, Consequences)

The British soldiers and colonial militia suffered heavy casualties in Pontiac's War: Estimates ran as high as 2,000. The financial costs have never been estimated, but they certainly added to the considerable debt Britain was runnning up to control its empire in North America. Indian casualties are unknown but overall were probably relatively light, as the Indians attacked by surprise or simply maintained sieges and did not engage in many battles.

The most surprising consequence of Pontiac's War was the Royal Proclamation of October 7, 1763, made by King George III on the advice of the parliamentary cabinet. It limited habitation by whites to east of a line along the north-south crest of the Appalachian Mountains, unless the Indians allowed settlers into that territory by treaties. It also required that all trade with Indians pass through licensed government agents. It seemed to promise a new era in good relations between settlers and Indians, but, in fact, the proclamation had almost no effect. Settlers moved into the off-bounds territory anyway, and the frequent treaties were merely window dressing for the taking of the Indians' land.

Ironically, the British emerged from Pontiac's War with somewhat better relations with the Indians, as they began to modify their strict dealings with the Indians and adopt some of the French policies. As a result, many Indians fought alongside the British in the American Revolution because they felt that if the British won, they would be more respectful of the Indians' rights than the colonists.

MILITARY INNOVATIONS, TACTICS, EQUIPMENT

Military operations employed nothing particularly new or innovative in Pontiac's War; the British forces were either defending forts or mounting small operations against the Indians, and both sides used conventional tactics. The British always had the advantage in weapons, but their cannons were never of much use against Indian tactics. Some of the Indians had muskets or pistols, but the Indians were no match for the British in numbers of firearms or availability of gunpowder.

LEGENDS AND TRIVIA

One of the most persistent stories to survive from the otherwise obscure Pontiac's War is the claim that Gen. Jefferey Amherst proposed distributing smallpox-infected blankets to the Indians. The fact is that sometime in early July 1763 Amherst wrote to Col. Henry Bouquet at Fort Pitt and asked: "Could it not be contrived to send the Small Pox [sic] among those disaffected tribes of Indians? We must on this occasion use every stratagem in our power to reduce them." Bouquet responded: "I will try to inoculate the [Indians] with some blankets that may fall in their hands, and take care not to get the disease myself. As it is a pity to expose good men against them, I wish we could make use of the Spanish method, to hunt them with English dogs, supported by rangers and some light horses, who would, I think, effectually extirpate or remove that vermin." Amherst responded: "You will do well to try to inoculate the Indians by means of blankets, as well as to try every other method that can serve to extirpate this execrable race." There is no evidence that Amherst or Bouquet ever executed that plan. However, Capt. Simeon Ecuyer, a Swiss-born soldier serving under the British, may have done something like that (see July 24, 1763, p. 59). Even if Ecuyer did infect the Indians with smallpox, it is unlikely that he was aware of Amherst's proposal to Bouquet. More likely, such a scheme was generally discussed among the British military at that time.

NOTABLE PHRASES

We have all smoked out of this pipe of peace.

In August 1765, Pontiac made a concluding speech at the peace ceremony held at Fort Detroit. As reported by George Croghan in his published journal, Pontiac said: "We have all smoked out of this pipe of peace. It is your children's pipe and as the war is all over and the Great Spirit

and Giver of Light. . . has brought us all together this day for our mutual good, I declare to all Nations that I have settled my peace with you before I came here and now deliver my pipe to be sent to Sir William Johnson, that he may know that I have made peace and taken the King of England for my Father."

HISTORICAL PERSPECTIVES AND CONTROVERSIES

The first, and still most prominent, historian to address the question of Pontiac's role in the conflict was the 19th-century American Francis Parkman, who divulged his point of view in the very title of his work: *The Conspiracy of Pontiac*. But Parkman was a historian of the old school, who wrote epic narratives that featured heroes and villains, great deeds and drama. Although Parkman did draw on all the contemporary sources—journals, letters, official reports—he undoubtedly elevated Pontiac's role and embellished Pontiac's life. Howard H. Peckham, writing a century later, drew a somewhat different conclusion: that Pontiac was indeed in charge of events in and around the Fort Detroit area, but that the war itself was quite beyond his control. Had Pontiac possessed such an influence, Peckham suggested, the attacks on the different small forts would have occurred simultaneously rather than in sequential order.

To this day, the question of Pontiac's role has remained unanswered in a definitive manner. To begin with, Indians did not recognize military leaders in the same manner that the whites did, and Pontiac was at most the first among a number of prominent chieftains. If, however, he did come up with the idea for the war and direct his fellow chiefs to assault the western forts in a coordinated manner, then he was one of the most powerful chieftains of Indian history, since the war stretched over a 600-mile front and involved Indians from at least a dozen different tribes. Some modern historians remain skeptical of that version of Pontiac's War and some of Parkman's embellishments but accept that Pontiac was the dominant figure in that war.

CIVILIAN AND MILITARY BIOGRAPHIES

Bouquet, Henry (1719–1765)—soldier: Henry

Bouquet was born in the Swiss canton of Berne. He became a mercenary and entered the British service in 1755. He led the relief column that lifted the siege of Fort Pitt (August 1763), was promoted to brigadier general (April 1765), and was sent to command British forces in Florida, where he died of malarial fever.

Gladwin, Henry (?–1791) —soldier: Henry Gladwin was born in England. He was sent to America with Gen. Edward Braddock in 1755. As commander of Fort Detroit during Pontiac's War, he bore one of the primary responsibilities for preventing the Indian war from turning into a rout of all British forces in the west. Gladwin's successful defense of Fort Detroit left Pontiac with no option other than to retire from the siege.

Pontiac (1720?–1769)—Indian chief: Nothing of Pontiac's early life is known for certain, but he may have been born somewhere in present-day Ohio. He became a prominent Ottawa chief. He fought alongside the French during the French and Indian War. He does not come into clear focus for historians until the siege of Fort Detroit, where he did not always agree with other Indians on how to deal with the British. After he concluded his own peace with the British in July 1766, he gave up trying to oust the British, despite rumors that he was intending to organize another uprising. Some accounts claim that he was murdered by a Peoria Indian in April 1769 in Cahokia (present-day St. Louis), but not all historians accept that.

FURTHER READING

Parkman, Francis. *The Conspiracy of Pontiac and the Indian War after the Conquest of Canada*. Boston: Little, Brown & Co., 1848.

Peckham, Howard H. *Pontiac and the Indian Uprising*. Princeton, N. J.: Princeton University Press, 1947.

LORD DUNMORE'S WAR

DATES OF WAR

April–October 1774

ALTERNATE NAMES

Dunmore's Expedition

SIGNIFICANCE

Lord Dunmore's War, a relatively minor episode, not much more than an expedition or a campaign, delivered a major message: The American frontier was not going to be easily regulated. The Royal Proclamation of 1763, the Treaty of Fort Stanwix of 1768, and an order from the British prime minister, Lord North, in 1774 expressly forbade the colonists to move into certain territories beyond the Appalachian Mountains. However, whether a noble British governor or a humble homesteader, a greedy land speculator or a pious Protestant, settlers were not to be stopped by laws, treaties, or proclamations from moving westward onto Indian lands.

BACKGROUND

As soon as the French and Indian War ended in 1763, there was great pressure from pioneer settlers and land speculators to move westward onto the lands that had long been considered the preserve of the French. The Royal Proclamation of 1763 forbade white settlement beyond the Appalachian Mountains, but that was ignored. Three separate groups claimed the fertile land of the upper Ohio River basin: the colony of Pennsylvania, the colony of Virginia, and the numerous Indian tribes who had used that area as their primary hunting grounds for generations. Virginia and Pennsylvania had long contested ownership of what eventually became western Pennsylvania. In 1773, the royal governor of Virginia, Lord Dunmore, decided to reclaim Fort Pitt (at present-day Pittsburgh) and use it as a base from which to assert control over western Pennsylvania. By early 1774, the decaying fort

was rebuilt and renamed Fort Dunmore; John Connolly was appointed by Dunmore to serve as colonel of the militia there.

CAUSES OF THE WAR

During the spring of 1774, there were several hostile encounters between Indians and white men who met in the disputed lands; several of them ended in Indian deaths. By April 21, Colonel Connolly was circulating a letter declaring that a war between the whites and the Indians seemed inevitable. Then, on April 30, white hunters attacked and murdered a group of Indians at Yellow Creek, Ohio, some 50 miles from Fort Dunmore. Eight Indians were killed, including a brother and a sister of Mingo chief Tachnecdorus, known to the whites as Chief Logan. He became the undying enemy of the white settlers. That incident caused an immediate uproar among the Indian tribes. By the time word of it reached Virginia, settlers and Indians throughout the region were preparing for war.

PREPARATIONS FOR WAR

There were no long-range preparations for the brief Lord Dunmore's War. However, Dunmore knew he was defying British policy and violating Indian treaties by giving land grants in the disputed territory to settlers. And by rebuilding Fort Pitt and assigning John Connolly to organize a militia, Dunmore was, in effect, preparing for war. As soon as Dunmore received authority from the Virginia House of Burgesses, he called out the militias throughout Virginia and organized an ambitious supply operation.

So far as can be known, the Indians did not make any long-term preparations. But in 1771, several tribes in the region had formed a loose confederation in anticipation of a conflict, so in that sense, they were prepared to fight together.

DECLARATION OF WAR

On May 13, 1774, the Virginia House of Burgesses in Williamsburg, Virginia, authorized Lord Dunmore to take all steps he deemed necessary "to repel the hostile and perfidious attempts of these savage and barbarous enemies." On June 10, Dunmore formally called for an organized attack on the Indians. The Indians did not make any formal declaration of war but simply responded to the attacks.

COMBATANTS

British-Americans: Dunmore did not use British regular army troops; instead, he called out the militia, the equivalent of today's National Guard, which by that time was well organized throughout the British colonies. Within three months, some 2,700 citizen-soldiers had come from several counties (mostly in Virginia and present-day West Virginia) to form a quite professional fighting force. Many of the men were veterans of the French and Indian War.

Indians: When the war began, the English settlers faced the possibility of fighting against the Delaware, Wyandot, Shawnee, and possibly even Iroquois tribes. The adroit diplomacy of missionaries in New York colony (who pacified the Iroquois) and Dunmore (who reached agreement with the Delaware and Wyandot) left the Shawnee tribe the only tribe solidly committed to the war effort. No accurate estimate can be reached as to how many Shawnee warriors existed at the time; the most the tribe was able to assemble for the largest battle was between 500 and 600 warriors.

GEOGRAPHIC AND STRATEGIC CONSIDERATIONS

The territory in dispute extended far beyond the boundaries of the present-day states of Virginia and Pennsylvania; it included the land that became the states of West Virginia, Kentucky, and Ohio. When the war began, the Indians appeared to be in a geographically favorable position. The Allegheny Mountains separated them from the major towns of Virginia and Pennsylvania, and the lightly equipped warriors were far better suited to making journeys across the mountains than were their white adversaries. However, the Virginia militia forces surprised the Indians by marching over the mountains of present-day West Virginia, and Dunmore used the fast-flowing Ohio River to bring another force into the Shawnee country by boat.

BATTLES AND CAMPAIGNS

June 10, 1774: As a result of the April 30 massacre at Yellow Creek, Ohio, in which white hunters savagely murdered several Indians, the Indians in the Ohio River basin seemed to pose a threat. Hearing that many settler families were fleeing from the mountain areas and congregating in the lowlands of Virginia, Governor Dunmore called out the militia of western Virginia. He ordered Andrew Lewis to assemble a force and prepare to march against the villages of the Shawnee Indians in a region of present-day Ohio.

July 1774: By July 1774, some 1,500 families had fled east to the more populated areas of Virginia and Pennsylvania.

July 10, 1774: Dunmore left Williamsburg, the capital of Virginia, and headed for the northwest region of Virginia, where he temporarily established his headquarters near Winchester.

July 24, 1774: Dunmore ordered Lewis, reputed to be the most experienced soldier in the southwestern counties of Virginia, to organize "a respectable body of men" from his region and to join him along the Ohio River to mount a joint attack on the Indians. Assuming the rank of general, Lewis immediately called on volunteers to assemble at what he called Camp Union, the site of present-day Lewisburg, West Virginia. In the ensuing weeks, hundreds of men, mostly from Virginia counties, gathered at Camp Union and were organized into well-disciplined units.

July 26–August 12, 1774: Col. Angus McDonald, commander of the northern Virginia militia, led 400 men from Fort Fincastle near present-day Wheeling, West Virginia, toward the Shawnee settlements in present-day Ohio. When McDonald and his men came near the Shawnee village of Wakatomica on the Muskingum River, the Shawnees managed to withdraw all their people while pretending to be negotiating a surrender. McDonald's men destroyed the settlement and its crops, then returned to Virginia. Following the loss of Wakatomica, the Indians along the frontier engaged in a series of attacks that took the lives of many settlers.

September 1774: Early in September, Dunmore arrived at Fort Dunmore (former Fort Pitt at present-day Pittsburgh) with about 1,000 men. There, he held a council with a number of Indian chiefs. Through adroit diplomacy, he gained the neutrality of at least some of the Delaware and Wyandot Indians, thereby making the war mainly a contest between his forces and the Shawnee warriors.

September 6–22, 1774: On September 6, the first 600 militiamen in Camp Union set out overland for the Kanawha River in the north-central corner of present-day West Virginia; they were followed during the next few days by another 900. By September 22, they had all met near the site of present-day Charleston, West Virginia. From there, they set out on foot and by boat down the Kanawha, the first stage on the way to their planned rendezvous with Dunmore's force.

Late September 1774: Dunmore led 700 troops on rafts and in boats from Fort Dunmore down the Ohio River; another 500 followed on land with wagons and supplies. By September 30, they had arrived at present-day Wheeling, West Virginia. They continued on, and by mid-October they all had gathered (joined by another 100 volunteers) and built a stockade at the site of present-day Hockingport, Ohio. Dunmore intended to mount a joint attack with General Lewis's force at a locale northwest of the newly built fort, about 35 miles south of present-day Columbus, Ohio.

October 6, 1774: The main body of Virginia militia troops under Lewis reached a triangular point of land at the confluence of the Kanawha and Ohio Rivers. There, Lewis stopped his march, waiting for news from Dunmore. Because the men found the area tranquil after their grueling journey, they called their encampment Camp Point Pleasant.

October 9–10, 1774: Approximately 500 Shawnee warriors led by Chief Keightughqua—known to the English as Cornstalk—crossed the Ohio River on rafts during the night. They arrived at a point one mile away from Camp Point Pleasant. Lewis's men were completely unaware of their approach. Early on the morning of October 10, two soldiers went out to hunt deer; they chanced upon the advancing Indians; one soldier was killed, the other ran back and aroused the camp.

October 10, 1774 (Battle of Camp Point Pleasant): Informed of the approaching Indians, Lewis immediately assigned his 800 militia troops to take their positions. A group of 150 men sent out to reconnoiter was thrown back by the Indians, with heavy losses (including the death of Lewis's brother, Charles). The battle was then joined by the main forces. Marked by a number of tactical errors on the part of the militia, the battle was in danger of being lost. Lewis found that his orders were often not followed, but some units did manage to execute a flanking movement that confused the Shawnees, who thought that reinforcements from Dunmore's army had arrived from the north. Cornstalk roamed all over the battlefield, exhorting his men and praising their courage; but by late morning, when he saw he could not overpower the militia forces, he withdrew his men. As the Indians retreated, however, they continued to take advantage of the terrain and the cover provided by the forest and slowed the militia's advance considerably throughout the day. The Virginians suffered 81 killed and some 140 wounded; the Indian losses are not certain (as they carried away most of their dead and wounded) but are assumed to have been comparable.

October 17, 1774: Coming within 15 miles of the Shawnee village on the Scioto River, Dunmore and his men were met by Matthew Elliott, a white trader, who led a delegation sent by Cornstalk and other chiefs to discuss peace terms with the governor. Dunmore quickly set up an encampment that he named Camp Charlotte (after his wife) and began negotiations that led to a tentative agreement.

October 17–23, 1774: Recovered from the battle, Lewis moved his force out from Camp Point Pleasant and headed for his rendezvous with Dunmore to carry out their joint attack against the Shawnee villages in present-day Ohio. He met Dunmore near Camp Charlotte on October 23 and, informed that the treaty had been concluded, set off for Virginia with his troops on October 25.

NEGOTIATIONS AND PEACE TREATY

October 19–20, 1774: At the end of two meetings at Camp Charlotte, the Indians agreed "to never again wage war against the frontier of Virginia," to cease hunting on (or even visiting, except for trading) the south side of the Ohio River, and to stop harassing travelers on the Ohio River. Dunmore and his staff agreed that no white people would hunt north of the Ohio River. In addition, the Indians agreed to give up the prisoners and black slaves they had taken in their raids and to return the horses and valuables they had seized during the war. It was understood that the settlement was temporary and that a full peace treaty would be negotiated at a general conference in the spring of 1775 between the tribal leaders and Dunmore at Pittsburgh. By then, however, Dunmore was trying to keep Virginia from entering the patriot camp in the Revolutionary War, so the conference was postponed for several weeks.

October 1775: Commissioners from Virginia and Pennsylvania negotiated the Treaty of Pittsburgh with chiefs of all the major tribes in the disputed region. The treaty confirmed the Ohio River as the boundary between Indian country to the north and the areas to the south that were to be open to white settlement. The Shawnee, Delaware, Mingo, Seneca, Wyandot, Potawatomi, and Ottawa tribes also agreed to remain neutral in the Revolutionary War then under way.

RESULTS OF THE WAR (Casualties, Costs, Consequences)

In the hostilities between April and October, the settlers counted at least 150 dead and at least that many wounded; the Indian casualties are not known but were probably at least that many. Hundreds of English and other European settlers were temporarily dislocated, but eventually they moved back and repossesssed the land.

Dunmore, elated with his victory, believed his personal popularity in the aftermath of the war would suffice to enable him to keep Virginia in the Loyalist camp as the patriots began to press their cause. The reverse occurred: Dunmore's arrogance pushed Virginia onto the patriot side, and he was recalled to England in July 1776. For the settlers along the Virginia and Pennsylvania frontiers, the war had the fortunate effect of keeping peace with the local Indians for at least the first crucial years (1775–1777) of the American Revolution. When the Revolution did break out on the frontier, the patriots were ready to cope with the dangers from the Indians. In fact, the famous campaigns of George Rogers Clark (see American Revolution, pp. 86-87, 89) were to some extent anticipated by Dunmore's War. Meanwhile, many of the men who fought under Dunmore ended up drawing on their experience

to fight against the British. Above all, Dunmore's brief war paved the way for white American settlers to cross the Appalachian Mountains and enter the fertile lands in the Ohio River valley.

NOTABLE PHRASES

I appeal to any white man to say if ever he entered Logan's cabin hungry and he gave him no meat; if ever he came cold and naked and he clothed him not....There runs not a drop of my blood in any living creature. This called on me for revenge. I have sought it. I have killed many. I have fully glutted my vengeance. For my country I rejoice at the beams of peace. But do not harbor a thought that mine is the joy of fear. Logan never felt fear. He will not turn on his heel to save his life. Who is there to mourn for Logan? Not one.

That is the heart of a speech allegedly delivered by the Mingo chief Logan (see Civilian and Military Biographies, p. 67) to Lord Dunmore at the time of the signing of the treaty ending Lord Dunmore's War. Many members of Logan's immediate family had been killed in the episode that triggered the war, and he wanted to explain why he would not participate in signing the treaty. Thomas Jefferson reproduced that speech in his *Notes on the State of Virginia* (1785) and said of it: "I may challenge the whole orations of Demosthenes and Cicero and of any more eminent orator, if Europe has furnished any more eminent, to produce a single passage superior to the speech of Logan, a Mingo chief, to Lord Dunmore, when governor of [Virginia]." Jefferson was challenged by some as to the authenticity of that speech, but in a letter, he claimed that Lord Dunmore had brought back a written record of the speech. Jefferson said he (Jefferson) recorded it in his notebook in 1774 after hearing the speech from someone who vouched for its authenticity. Jefferson also stated that the speech had been widely published in 1774 and that many schoolboys were thereafter required to learn it. Not until Jefferson was challenged in a newspaper in 1797 did he track down the fact that the speech had been delivered not to Dunmore but to Dunmore's emissary to Logan, Gen. John Gibson, who had in turn translated the speech. It was the translated version that Jefferson repeated.

HISTORICAL PERSPECTIVES AND CONTROVERSIES

Over the years, various people have raised the question of the war's name. One historian, Dale Van Every, argued in the early 1960s that it was one of the most ineptly named wars of American history: "It was a war provoked by frontiersmen, waged by frontiersmen, and won by frontiersmen for the sole benefit of frontiersmen." More recent studies, which have focused on all that Dunmore and his associates stood to gain from the war, disagree. Those more critical assessments suggest that the war was prompted more by the land hunger of Dunmore and his associates in land speculation, and by the traditional rivalry between Virginia and Pennsylvania, than by frontiersmen as that term is commonly understood. Dunmore's land grants to settlers were illegal under British policy. And it was Dunmore who assigned John Connolly to Fort Pitt, thus triggering the chain of events that aggravated the situation. It may not deserve to be called a war, but whatever it was, Dunmore was its chief architect.

CIVILIAN AND MILITARY BIOGRAPHIES

Cornstalk (1720?–1777)—Shawnee chief: Cornstalk was known to the Shawnee as Chief Keightughqua. He fought against English settlers in the French and Indian War, then fought in Pontiac's War. For a time after the end of the latter war, he was held hostage to guarantee the good behavior of the Shawnee. In 1774, he and his brother, Silver Heels, were true to the terms of their parole; rather than participate in the Indian attacks on settlers that resulted in Lord Dunmore's War, they escorted white traders to the safety of white forts. When, by mistake, a militiaman grievously wounded Silver Heels, Cornstalk tried to keep the peace, but when he saw the relentless pressure toward war, he resigned himself to his traditional role as war leader for his people. He led the Shawnee at the Battle of Camp Point Pleasant, where they came close to victory (see October 10, 1774, p. 65). After the war, he tried to befriend the American settlers, but some of them took him and his son hostage; Cornstalk and his son were killed after other In-

dians ambushed one of the colonists.

Logan (c. 1725-1780)—Mingo leader: Logan was born Tachnecdorus in Pennsylvania. He was named James Logan after a colonial trader and statesman admired by his Mingo father, Chief Shikellamy. Logan became a leader of the Mingo tribe that lived near the Ohio and Scioto Rivers. He was for long a good friend of the white settlers. After most of his immediate family were killed in the massacre at Yellow Creek on April 30, 1774 (see Causes of the War, p. 63), Logan joined in the war (and by some accounts collected 30 scalps). He refused to attend the treaty signing and fought alongside the British during the American Revolution. He was murdered on returning from Detroit. His later fame rested on the speech he was said to have delivered (see Notable Phrases, p. 66).

Murray, John, Earl of Dunmore (1732–1809)—colonial governor: Lord Dunmore was born in Scotland. He became royal governor of Virginia in 1771. Ambitious for his colony and for himself (he was involved in land speculation in the western areas where the war was fought), he led one of the two forces that won the war in 1774. He became so unpopular for his attempts to stem the revolutionary tide in Virginia that at one point (June 1775) he had to take refuge on a British ship offshore. After the battles of Lexington and Concord, he began to make war against the Virginian patriots, but in July 1776, he was recalled to England. From 1787 to 1796 he served as governor of the Bahamas.

FURTHER READING

Lewis, Virgil A. *History of the Battle of Point Pleasant.* Charleston, W. Va.: Tribune Printing Co., 1909.

Thwaites, Reuben Gold. *Documentary History of Dunmore's War, 1774.* Madison, Wis.: Wisconsin Historical Society, 1905.

Van Every, Dale. *Forth to the Wilderness: The First American Frontier, 1754–1774.* New York: William Morrow & Co., 1961.

THE AMERICAN REVOLUTION

DATES OF WAR

April 19, 1775–September 3, 1783

ALTERNATE NAMES

American Revolutionary War. The War of American Independence. United States War of Independence.

SIGNIFICANCE

The American Revolution involved a political-social confrontation and an armed conflict with England. Focusing on the armed hostilities makes it difficult to separate those two aspects when it comes to the Revolution's immediate and long-term impact on history. In addition to showing the effectiveness of an amateur military effort—the colonists often used what would become known as guerrilla tactics—the American Revolution sparked a new era, one in which men and women in many lands began to pursue the goals of "Life, Liberty, and the Pursuit of Happiness." The French Revolution was only the most dramatic instance of this new era in history. The American colonists' ability to fight and win their independence from the world's strongest maritime and imperial power gave hope to emerging revolutionary movements in South America and Europe. Within the 50 years following the American Revolution, Simón Bolivar and others effectively deposed the Spanish as the ruling power in South America in a revolution similar in spirit and in form to the American Revolution. Throughout the world, people who have revolted against foreign and domestic tyranny in the modern age have appealed to the American Revolution as a paradigm—both for its political strategies and its military tactics.

BACKGROUND

The origins of the American Revolution cannot be traced to one point in time or even to a few issues, but if a starting point could be identified, it would be 1763. At that time, England's national debt, the imposition of new taxes on the colonists, the concept of legislative representation, and the presence of foreign troops in the colonies were the most important and specific issues that led to the American Revolution.

With the end of the Seven Years' War (see pp. 42-50) in 1763, England had defeated France and Spain and had gained a large empire. At that time, England was the most powerful nation in the world, and many Americans were proud to proclaim themselves subjects of the British Empire. Yet during the Seven Years' War, the British national debt more than doubled, to reach the figure of 167 million English pounds (about $10 billion in 1990 dollars).

To alleviate the massive debt created by the Seven Years' War, several British prime ministers sought to impose new taxes on the American colonies. To the British leaders, it seemed logical that the Americans should pay new taxes: They were the ones who had benefited the most from the Seven Years' War, which resulted in the removal of France from Canada. And for the first time in many decades, England had a king, George III, who was prepared to take an active role in matters such as those. Believing passionately in the right of king and Parliament to legislate for the American colonies, King George III pushed the Sugar Act (April 1764), then the Stamp Act (March 22, 1765) through Parliament. The Sugar Act (officially the Revenue Act of 1764) increased some taxes already in effect, such as the taxes on imported sugar and on goods shipped first to England, then on to the colonies. The Sugar Act also added more taxes on wine and coffee and on cloth imported from other countries. The Stamp Act required the colonists to purchase special stamped paper for use in printing newspapers, pamphlets, and almanacs and to have a stamp embossed on documents such as ships' papers and insurance policies.

Although greatly resented, the Sugar Act taxes were hidden in the costs of exports and imports. But the Stamp Act imposed a direct tax on the colonists. Massachusetts politician Samuel Adams and the fiery Virginian orator Patrick Henry were foremost in protesting the Stamp Act. Adams organized the Boston Sons of Liberty in the summer of 1765, and similar groups soon sprang up in several major American cities. Those groups consisted of young men organized for the purpose of resisting the hated stamp tax. Stamp revenue officials were sometimes assaulted, and their homes were occasionally burned by zealous Boston Sons of Liberty. In Virginia, Patrick Henry gave an impassioned speech on the matter of the rights of British subjects. Although it is not certain whether Henry actually shouted "If this be treason, make the most of it," he was, at the very least, questioning the British system of the lack of colonial representation in Parliament.

American colonists resisted many of the new taxes, claiming they had no representation in Parliament and, therefore, were not obligated to pay taxes. British political theorists responded by drawing a distinction between virtual representation and actual representation. Under the British theory of virtual representation, every member elected to Parliament represented the interests of all the subjects of England and the empire, not just the narrow political interests of his own political district. American political theory, which had been developing since the mid-1600s, asserted that subjects could be taxed only when they had representatives in Parliament directly guarding their interests.

Patrick Henry and others were still far from calling for American independence from England; they were, instead, reasserting the glory of being an Englishman. An Englishman, Henry declared, had the right not to be taxed without his consent. The Virginia House of Burgesses approved Henry's views in the Virginia Resolves (May 30, 1765). James Otis, Henry, and Adams appeared to strike a common chord with many American colonists. The Stamp Act Congress met in New York City (October 7–25, 1765) and called taxation without representation as an affront to American rights as British subjects. In addition, a general boycott of British goods followed from the Stamp Act Congress. That boycott touched the pocketbooks of many British merchants, some of whom sat in Parliament.

Following the boycott, Parliament repealed the Stamp Act (March 18, 1765) but on the same day passed the Declaratory Act, which asserted that Parliament had the right to make laws and levy taxes on the colonies "in all cases whatsoever." Many Americans went wild with joy when they heard the news of the repeal. They were quick to overlook the implications of the Declaratory Act and commissioned statues of King George III and Prime Minister William Pitt.

Soon after the Declaratory Act was passed, however, a new British prime minister—Charles Townshend—proposed a series of new duties and levies on the colonies, which Parliament passed in 1767. Those new obligations placed additional duties on paint, lead, glass, and tea. Although the total sum of those taxes still left most American taxpayers paying less than their British cousins, the cry of "no taxation without representation" (see Notable Phrases, p. 105) went up in even greater force than during the Stamp Act period. Many Americans resumed both their boycott of British goods, particularly tea, and their attacks on the revenue officers who enforced the Townshend Acts. In response, England sent troops to the colonies.

British troops, known as "redcoats" and "lobsterbacks," first arrived in Boston in October 1768. Soon there were British soldiers in New York City and Charles Town, South Carolina. In their effort to prevent mob violence, the British soldiers often came into conflict with the local citizenry. Bostonians resented the presence of troops, many of whom were billeted (or staying) in American homes. Although British troops were soon sent to all the major American coastal cities, the focus of discontent was strongest in two areas: New York City and Boston.

The battle of Golden Hill took place in New York City on January 19, 1770. British soldiers chopped down an American liberty pole, one of many that had been set in place during the resistance to the Stamp and Sugar Acts. Following this action, a number of New York citizens fought 30–40 British soldiers. The citizens were armed with clubs and swords; the soldiers had bayonets. In the scuffle and skirmish, several Americans were wounded, but no one on either side was killed. That incident, usually overshadowed by the Boston Massacre, was, in fact, the first true armed conflict between American colonists and British troops in the years prior to the actual start of the Revolution.

The Boston Massacre took place on the cold, snowy night of March 5, 1770. British soldiers

A lithograph based on Paul Revere's famous engraving of the Boston Massacre of 1770 features Crispus Attucks at the center. It distorts the true nature of the British guards' actions.

standing guard at the Customs House (across from the still-standing State House) were pelted with snowballs and iceballs thrown by American patriots. No one is certain whether British captain Thomas Preston ordered "Hold your fire!" or "Fire!" But the result was that his men emptied their muskets into the crowd that had been taunting them. When the smoke cleared, five Americans lay dead, including Crispus Attucks, the first black man to lose his life in the patriots' conflict with the British. The shooting might have given way to a general conflagration, but royal governor Thomas Hutchinson, Samuel Adams, and John Hancock prevailed on the crowd to disperse for the night.

The next day, it was agreed that the British soldiers involved in the shooting would stand trial. In a show of support for the British/American system of justice, patriots John Adams and Josiah Quincy stepped forward to serve as defense counsels for the soldiers. At the end of the trial, on December 4, 1770, two British soldiers were found guilty of manslaughter and had their thumbs branded as punishment. The episode in front of the Customs House might never have gained such prominence had it not been for the

provocative engraving made by Paul Revere; it depicted the British soldiers lined up like an organized army and firing into the crowd of colonists. Copies of the engraving were distributed throughout the colonies and helped enforce the negative reputation of British rule.

For the next two years (1770–1772), a relative calm prevailed in British-American relations. A new British prime minister, Lord Frederick North, repealed the Townshend Acts (April 12, 1770), with the exception of the 3-penny tax on tea, even before the news of the Boston Massacre reached England. The mother country and her colonies appeared to recognize the seriousness of Golden Hill and the Boston Massacre and made efforts to back away from their hard-line positions, and the threat of revolution seemed to recede.

CAUSES OF THE WAR

The Gaspee Affair: On June 9, 1772, a British revenue ship, the *Gaspee*, ran aground off the coast of Rhode Island while pursuing an American ship engaged in smuggling. That night, Americans boarded the *Gaspee* and burned the ship after removing its crew. When British officials attempted to prosecute the American colonists, they found no Americans willing to testify. That enraged many British officials and led to a renewed tension in British-American relations.

Committees of Correspondence: On November 2, 1772, in response to the tension created by the Gaspee affair, Boston patriots activated a group, first proposed by Massachusetts legislators in 1764, know as the committee of correspondence. The committee's intent was to spread news of patriot activities; similar committees were soon formed in other colonies. The Virginia House of Burgesses formed a committee on March 12, 1773, and by February 1774 committees were established in every colony except North Carolina and Pennsylvania. Samuel Adams and Patrick Henry were among the important and articulate patriots whose speeches and writings were carried throughout the colonies by dispatch riders such as Paul Revere and William Dawes.

The Boston Tea Party (December 16, 1773): In response to the impending bankruptcy of the British East India Company, Lord North permitted that company to bypass the British middlemen and sell tea cheaply to American customers. Lord North thought the Americans would easily overlook the 3-penny tax that he had imposed on the tea. North believed that the Americans thought the price of tea was more important than principles such as no taxation without representation. North was not alone in that belief; many prominent Englishmen believed the American colonists were fond of their wallets. American patriots responded with great anger to the news and to the appearance of the ships carrying tea. In November 1773, in Philadelphia, a crowd of 8,000 people forced the captain of a tea ship to turn back to England; in Annapolis, Maryland, a brig carrying tea was burned to the waterline; in Charles Town, South Carolina, tea was allowed to be brought ashore but left to languish in a warehouse for three years. All those incidents served as examples of the solidarity that many Americans had come to feel about the subject of taxes and tea. It was, however, in Boston that events came to a most dramatic conclusion. Boston patriots asked royal governor Thomas Hutchinson to send three tea ships back to England. Hutchinson refused, but he urged the captains of the three tea ships not to unload their products, given the temper of the Boston crowd. A stalemate developed, which lasted several

days. The deadlock was broken on the night of December 16, 1773. Hundreds of Boston patriots (most of them members of the Sons of Liberty) dressed themselves as Mohawk Indians and boarded the three ships. In what came to be know as the Boston Tea Party, the patriots dumped 167 chests containing 90,000 pounds of tea, into Boston Harbor.

The Coercive Acts (also known as the Intolerable Acts): Outraged by the Boston Tea Party, British parliamentary leaders (Whigs and Tories alike) passed a series of acts to punish Boston for its actions. The Boston Port Act (March 31, 1774) closed Boston to all merchant shipping. The Massachusetts Government Act (May 20, 1774) put Massachusetts under the military rule of a new royal governor, Gen. Thomas Gage, and prevented the towns of Massachusetts from holding their annual town meetings. The Administration of Justice Act (May 20, 1774) required that British officials be tried in England, not in America, for any crimes they might commit. The Quartering Act (June 2, 1774) reinforced what had long been British policy: that American colonists were required to house and feed British troops when called upon to do so.

The First Continental Congress (September 5-October 26, 1774): In response to the Coercive Acts and to the general level of tension in British-American relations since the Gaspee affair, 56 delegates from 12 of the 13 American colonies met in Philadelphia. (Fearful of being involved in a risky enterprise, Georgia did not send a delegation.) Although the delegates adopted the Suffolk Resolves, which condemned the Intolerable Acts, and created the Continental Association, which made its own intolerable demands on Britain, the thrust of the congress was to improve British-American relations; there was almost no advocacy of a true political separation from England. The congress adjourned but resolved to reconvene on May 10, 1775, if relations did not improve.

PREPARATIONS FOR WAR

British-American relations deteriorated rapidly during the winter of 1774–1775. Virtually every community in eastern Massachusetts began to reorganize its militia, or volunteer units, by getting rid of members who were supporters of the British position. There had long been such militia under the British, but they existed to fight the French and Indians. The new units were organized specifically to be available at a moment's notice to resist unwanted moves by the British; they were called minutemen. Dependent on British arms and ammunition, in December 1774, Massachusetts militiamen attacked a British arsenal in Portsmouth, New Hampshire, and seized arms and ammunition.

Meanwhile, Gen. Thomas Gage, the British royal governor of Massachusetts, was asking his superiors in England to send more troops to the colonies. The more the redcoats settled in, the more the colonists resented the British presence. In the spring of 1775, Gage received instructions from England to seize all stores of weapons and gunpowder accessible to the American patriots in storehouses throughout New England. He decided to seize first the gunpowder supplies at Concord, Massachusetts, about 20 miles from Boston. In addition to seizing the gunpowder there, Gage intended to capture Samuel Adams and John Hancock, whom Gage correctly regarded as two of the principal promoters of anti-British activities. Adams and Hancock were known to be hiding at Lexington, the town adjacent to Concord. During the night of April 18–19, some 700 British troops in Boston were ferried across the Charles River to Cambridge, preparatory to marching to Concord.

The Boston patriots had been on their guard for some time. By April there were signs that the British army was planning to march on Concord. The leaders of the patriot movement in Boston decided on a simple signal should the British set off for Concord at night: The Code "one if by land, two if by sea" meant that one lantern would be hung in the belfry of the Old North Church in Boston if the British were marching out of the city by the peninsula (or neck) and that two lanterns would be hung in the belfry if the British were using boats to cross the Charles River to Cambridge. Waiting for the signal across the river would be the patriots of Charlestown. Two riders—Paul Revere, a silversmith and patriot, and Samuel Dawes, a tanner also experienced at riding for the patriot cause—would set off to ride to Lexington and Concord. Their assignment would be a double one: to rouse the minutemen along their routes to oppose the approaching British and to warn Samuel Adams and John Hancock.

Even before the lanterns were hung in the belfry late that night of April 18, 1775, Dawes and Revere set off for Lexington and Concord, taking different routes. Dawes went first and Revere followed. As Revere rode by the homes and shops along his route, he roused the minutemen; hundreds of them armed themselves quickly and departed for Lexington and Concord. Revere arrived in Lexington shortly before Dawes and was able to warn Samuel Adams and John Hancock in time for them to escape.

Then Revere and Dawes set off for Concord. By chance, they were joined by Samuel Prescott, a young doctor and patriot riding home after visiting with his lady friend. The three were approached by a small troop of British cavalry. Dawes escaped the British but was thrown from his horse and had to walk back to Lexington. Revere was captured and roughly questioned by the British but after about an hour was let free. Only Prescott escaped to ride on to Concord and warn the minutemen there. Meanwhile, other dispatch riders set out from Boston to rouse even more minutemen throughout eastern Massachusetts. Only a few hundred arrived in Concord in time to join the local minutemen in confronting the British that morning, but many hundreds were in position to attack the British as they retreated back to Boston the next day.

DECLARATION OF WAR

There was no formal declaration of war on either side. However, as early as February 9, 1775, England's Parliament declared the colony of Massachusetts to be in a state of rebellion, and on August 23, 1775, King George III declared all the American colonies to be in "open and avowed rebellion." For the colonists, the Declaration of Independence (July 4, 1776) served as the most appropriate substitute for a formal declaration of war. The reason for the ambiguity was that the British did not consider a colonial rebellion to be a true war, and many Americans did not become fully convinced of the need for independence until 1776.

COMBATANTS

There were six groups of combatants in the Revolutionary War:

American: The colonial army during the

Revolution was made up of militia and Continentals. Militia units were organized and paid for by either individual communities or the colony as a whole; in most cases, all able-bodied men were required to participate in their local militia. Most militia units retained their separate identities throughout the conflict—their own officers and organization. Some fought only within their own colony, but others were sent where needed. The Continentals were the troops authorized and paid for by the Continental Congress. At the outset of the war, the Continental Army was simply formed by designating the New England militias as such. As the war dragged on, the Continental Congress put out numerous calls for each colony to provide its quota, but it lacked the authority to enforce that call. In any case, many men enlisted for only six to nine months because they were farmers or craftsmen who could not leave their work and families for much longer. At its peak, the Continental Army numbered about 20,000 men. By the end of the war it was hard to distinguish between the militia and regulars: All had been essentially conscripted, or drafted, by one system or another. It is estimated that a total of 200,000 colonists served at least some time in the army during the Revolution but that at any given moment there were at most some 30,000 colonials, both militia and Continentals, under arms. Since those were spread throughout vast areas, there were seldom even as many as 10,000 available for a single campaign or battle.

At sea, the patriots could count on three forces: colonial navies, the Continental Navy, and private mercenaries. Most of the colonies maintained small navies, but they had only small ships, and few played any decisive roles in the war other than protecting merchant ships coming into and going out of their harbors. The Continental Navy was officially organized on October 1775; at its peak it had 10,000 men and 50 warships. The mercenaries were men, known as privateers, who served on private ships, often simply merchant ships with a few guns. The mercenaries were rewarded by being allowed to keep most of what they seized in battles with the British—the ships and their goods. Some 2,000 privateers participated in the colonists' cause.

It was also during the Revolution (November 1775) that America first authorized a group of men to fight aboard ships; those men were known as the Continental Marines. At the peak of the war, that force numbered only some 3,100 men.

British: The British army was considered among the best in the world. Its men, although often drafted from the bottom of British society, were fearsome fighters, particularly skilled in the use of the bayonet. At the peak of the Revolutionary War, there were 42,000 British troops available in North America. King George III also hired some 30,000 mercenaries from German states. Because more than half those soldiers came from the region of Hesse, all the Germans became known as Hessians. The British also had the support of some 50,000 Americans who remained loyal to King George. They were known as Loyalists (or Tories, a reference to those conservative British most supportive of the crown).

French: More motivated by hatred of England than by devotion to the American cause, France entered the American Revolution formally in February 1778. At the peak of the war, there were some 8,000 French troops fighting alongside the colonists, but altogether some 12,500 served in America. The French navy sent 63 warships on different occasions, and some 32,600 officers and men served on these ships. The French army was well-disciplined and high-spirited, but French troops did not play a crucial role until 1781, when they supported Washington in his threat to the British in New York City during the summer. Those French troops then moved south to join the French navy, and both played a decisive role in the victory at Yorktown that October.

Spanish: Spain entered the American Revolution in 1779, not as an ally of the Americans but as an ally of France and as a co-belligerent against the British. In now all-but-forgotten battles, the Spanish fought in the Gulf of Mexico, in Florida, and in the Illinois region.

Foreign adventurers: Thousands of Europeans came to the American colonies and offered their services. Some simply sought action, but many were inspired by the ideals of the Revolution as articulated by Benjamin Franklin, Thomas Jefferson, and Thomas Paine. The best known of those adventurers include the French Marquis de Lafayette, Polish Count Casimir Pulaski, Prussian Baron von Steuben, and German Johann ("Baron de") Kalb. There were countless anonymous individuals who brought experience and enthusiasm to the fighting.

Indians: The Native Americans of the eastern seaboard were split in their allegiances. Many stayed neutral, but the Mohawk and Seneca Indians of the Six Iroquois Nations joined with the British, and many of the Shawnee Indians of the Ohio region preyed upon American frontier settlements. Some Indians from the Abenaki, Oneida, Stockbridge, Potawatomi, and Tuscarora tribes fought with the colonists.

GEOGRAPHIC AND STRATEGIC CONSIDERATIONS

Both sides experienced some advantages and disadvantages in terms of geography. The Americans were defending their own land, which they knew well, but the rivers and bays on the Atlantic coast, including the Connecticut, Hudson, and Delaware Rivers, and Chesapeake Bay, made the Americans vulnerable to attacks from British ships. Once British troops headed inland, however, the colonists gained a distinct advantage from their knowledge of the terrain and their skill at fighting in the woods and on uneven ground.

The British and their allies had the great geographical advantage of the Atlantic Ocean and the seacoast of North America. British ships, usually uncontested at sea, were able to transport British, Hessian, and Loyalist troops up and down the seacoast of North America far more quickly than the Americans could march troops by land. The greatest geographical obstacle faced by the British was the great distance (3,000 miles) between England and North America. British commanders had to requisition their supplies far in advance, and ocean storms often disrupted British troop and supply movements.

Strategically, both sides had pluses and minuses. The Americans had the advantage of being able to fight on the defensive, and as long as they could hold on to the bulk of their territory, they would be perceived as the winners. The American commanders, George Washington foremost among them, believed it was necessary to hold on to the key coastal cities, and, therefore, the Americans could not fight a strictly backcountry war.

For their part, the British had the advantage of being able to choose where and when to launch their attacks. They could shift their focus, as they did in 1778, from northern to southern areas. The disadvantage the British labored under was a lack of time. The longer the Ameri-

can colonies remained unconquered, the more the world perceived them to be the victors. And the longer the struggle lasted, the more France and Spain were tempted to assist the American rebels as a way to avenge their own losses to the British during the Seven Years' War.

When the American Revolution began in 1775, there was no way of knowing that it would become a world wide war, involving France, Spain, and the Netherlands. (The Dutch did not fight in America, but their ships attacked British ships in European waters.) Therefore, at the outset, most neutral observers expected a war fought only between battle-hardened British and Hessian troops and undisciplined, inexperienced American militia forces. There was, therefore, a general worldwide consensus that the Americans would be overwhelmed by the size and professionalism of their foes.

BATTLES AND CAMPAIGNS: 1775

There were three areas of activity in 1775: northern theater (Canada, New England, New York, New Jersey, and Pennsylvania), southern theater (from Virginia to Georgia), and naval theater (primarily along the Atlantic coastline).

NORTHERN THEATER

April 19, 1775 (battles of Lexington and Concord): Following the midnight ride of Paul Revere, the advance guard of the British army marched onto the town green of Lexington, Massachusetts. Led by Capt. John Parker of Lexington, only 70-odd minutemen met them on the green that morning. British major John Pitcairn rode forward and shouted, "Disperse, ye rebels, disperse!" After a minute's hesitation, the Americans began to drift off the green, carrying their muskets with them. That affair might have come to a bloodless conclusion, but someone fired a shot. Soon, the green was covered with smoke from British and American muskets. No one knows who fired that first shot, but when the firing ended and the smoke cleared, eight Americans lay dead or dying on the green, ten others were wounded; only one British soldier was hurt. The British cheered and continued their march. The American Revolution had begun.

The overall British commander on the march, Lt. Col. Francis Smith, led his men to Concord,

This 1832 print of the Battle of Lexington on April 19, 1775, although somewhat exaggerated, rightfully shows colonial marksman picking off the massed British troops.

where they spent the morning destroying the military supplies the Americans had collected. Meanwhile, 400–500 American minutemen gathered on Punktasset Hill, overlooking the Concord River's North Bridge. Seeing smoke coming from the town and afraid that the British were about to set all Concord ablaze, the minutemen advanced down the hill to the bridge, where they met a small guard of British troops. Volleys of fire were exchanged, and the British withdrew with nearly 20 casualties.

Lieutenant Colonel Smith soon reorganized his men and began his march back to Boston. His mission had succeeded up to a point, and he wanted to be sure to reach Boston by nightfall. What Smith did not anticipate—and what many British officers would underestimate time and again during the war—was the skill, in particular the markmanship, of the Americans as fighters. As the British marched back to Charlestown, they were constantly fired upon by Americans hiding behind trees, rocks, and stone walls. By the time the British reached the protection of their naval fleet in Charlestown, they had suffered 273 casualties. American casualties ran only to 95.

April 20, 1775: Immediately after the British troops withdrew to Boston after the hostilities at Lexington and Concord, they began to strengthen their defensive positions around Boston. At the same time, thousands of New England militiamen and volunteers gathered in a ring around Boston; their leader was Gen. Artemas Ward. The Americans were unable to cut off the British from the sea, but they maintained such an effective siege by land that the British finally evacuated Boston on March 17, 1776.

May 10, 1775: Ethan Allen and the Green Mountain Boys, acting in concert with Benedict Arnold of Connecticut, seized the British Fort Ticonderoga, situated at the junction of Lake George and Lake Champlain in northeastern New York. Thundering, "Open in the name of the Continental Congress and the Great Jehovah," Ethan Allen took possession of the fort. That provided a significant morale boost for many Americans.

May 22, 1775: Three British major generals, Sir William Howe, Sir Henry Clinton, and John Burgoyne, arrived by ship in Boston to relieve General Gage as commanding officer in that city.

June 17, 1775 (Battle of Bunker Hill): During the night of June 16–17, American troops dug entrenchments on Breed's Hill on the Charlestown peninsula overlooking Boston.

When morning came and the British leaders saw the entrenchments, they resolved to attack at once, before the Americans could place artillery on the hill. Gen. William Howe landed 2,200 British troops on the peninsula in the early afternoon and personally led his men up Breed's Hill against the 1,200 American defenders. American general William Prescott told his men "Don't one of you fire until you see the whites of their eyes!" (see Notable Phrases, p. 106). Following Prescott's orders, the Americans fired with devastating effect when the British were only 40 yards away. Shattered by the musket fire, the British retreated down the slope. Howe re-formed his lines and led his men up the hill again, with much the same result. On their third attempt, the British succeeded in gaining the hill, largely because the Americans had run out of gunpowder and were forced to slip away. The British gained control of Breed's Hill, neighboring Bunker Hill, and the Charlestown peninsula at the cost of 1,054 men killed, wounded, or missing. The Americans suffered some 400 casualties. General Howe learned to be very cautious when it came to attacking entrenched American troops.

July 3, 1775: Arriving in Cambridge, Massachusetts from Virginia, George Washington officially took command of the Continental Army.

August 25, 1775: American brigadier general Richard Montgomery led American troops northward on Lake Champlain as part of a two-pronged attempt to capture Canada. The battle for the "14th colony" had begun.

September 25, 1775: Benedict Arnold (a colonel in the Continental Army) led American troops north from Fort Western (present-day Augusta, Maine), as the second wing of the American assault on Canada.

November 2, 1775: General Montgomery accepted the surrender of British Fort St. Johns on the Richelieu River in Canada, following a 55-day siege. The siege had cost the Americans precious time, and the Canadian winter was rapidly approaching.

November 9, 1775: Benedict Arnold led 675 of his original force of 1,200 men to Pointe Lévis, directly across the St. Lawrence River from Quebec City. To reach this point, Arnold had led his men through 350 miles of desolate wilderness in a march that historians would liken to that of Hannibal's march over the Alps. Arnold's men were exhausted and hungry, but he pushed them forward, and within three days, he had ferried his small army across the river and was in position to threaten Quebec City. Lacking siege weapons, he withdrew 30 miles to the south and waited for news of General Montgomery's men.

November 13, 1775: The citizens of Montreal surrendered their city to General Montgomery's American army. That significant American victory was marred by two factors. First, Col. Ethan Allen was captured by the British just prior to the city's surrender, and second, British governor general Sir Guy Carleton escaped from Montreal and traveled the St. Lawrence River to Quebec City to lead the defense of that place. Well liked by the French-Canadian population and by his own men, Carleton proved a formidable foe.

December 2, 1775: General Montgomery and Colonel Arnold joined forces near Quebec City. Each man had achieved near miracles in his respective section of the campaign, and they prepared to work together in an effort to take the grand prize—Quebec City.

December 5, 1775: Patriot colonel Henry Knox arrived at Fort Ticonderoga in New York and announced General Washington's plan to move almost all the working cannons and mortars back to Boston. Within two weeks, Knox set off with 60 cannons and mortars on 42 sledges drawn by 80 yoke of oxen. During almost five weeks of terrible winter conditions, Knox's troops dragged the cannons across New York and western Massachusetts.

December 31, 1775: In the early morning hours, Montgomery and Arnold launched an all-out, desperate attack on Quebec City. The attack was desperate because many of the American militiamen were ready to go home the next day when their enlistments were up. The fighting was intense. Montgomery was killed in the early stages of the battle, and his death took the heart out of many of his men. Arnold and Virginia leader Daniel Morgan forced their way into the city and fought hand-to-hand combat against the British defenders. Eventually, the Americans were overwhelmed by the resistance they met and withdrew, leaving Morgan a prisoner in the hands of the British. (He was released in a prisoner exchange in 1776.) Arnold was wounded in his left leg but managed to exit the city. With the death of Montgomery, Arnold became the officer in command of what was left of the American army. The Americans suffered 60 killed and 426 captured; the British, 5 dead and 13 wounded.

SOUTHERN THEATER

November 7, 1775: Lord Dunmore, the royal governor of Virginia, issued a proclamation urging black slaves to run away from their masters and join his British forces. Promising freedom to all escaped slaves who could reach his lines, Dunmore was ready to promote a race war in the American South in order to further the British cause there. In response to Lord Dunmore's action, George Washington announced that free blacks would be allowed into the ranks of the Continental Army as of January 1776.

December 11, 1775: Lord Dunmore, leading British and Loyalist troops (few blacks had yet reached his lines) was defeated at Great Bridge near Norfolk, Virginia, by a force of 900 North Carolina and Virginia patriots.

NAVAL THEATER

June 11–12, 1775: Word of the hostilities at Lexington and Concord in April had reached even the most distant points in Maine (then part of Massachusetts). On June 11, a British armed schooner, the *Margaretta*, put into the harbor of Machias, Maine, accompanying two transport sloops owned by a Loyalist merchant. Angry townsmen, including some sailors, led by Jeremiah O'Brien and Benjamin Foster, captured the two sloops; in attempting to escape, the *Margaretta* ran aground. The next day, the *Margaretta* was afloat, but O'Brien and Foster pursued it in one of the sloops. Firing on the *Margaretta* (and killing one British sailor), O'Brien and Foster captured it. That engagement became known as "the naval Lexington." O'Brien was later made a captain in the Massachusetts navy and participated in several actions against the British.

October 18, 1775: A British squadron sailed into the harbor of Falmouth (present-day Portland, Maine) and burned 139 houses. Actions such as that helped convince unsure Americans that freedom from British rule was a necessity.

HOME FRONT

June 15, 1775: The Continental Congress

named 43-year-old George Washington, a Virginia planter and a veteran of the French and Indian War, supreme commander of the new Continental Army. Washington declined to accept direct payment for his services, asking only for reimbursement of his expenses.

June 27, 1775: The Continental Congress voted to attempt to capture British-held Canada. American leaders reasoned that an American-held Canada would be an important bargaining chip to bring to the eventual peace negotiations.

October 13, 1775: The Continental Congress voted to outfit two ten-gun ships for the defense of the coastline. Some historians have used October 13, 1775 to mark the founding of the United States Navy.

November 10, 1775: The Continental Congress approved a resolution establishing two new battalions to be called the Continental Marines. Those were "sea soldiers," or men trained for combat and stationed aboard ships for engagements at sea and for quick excursions ashore. Commanded by Samuel Nicholas, those battalions are regarded as the first units of the United States Marine Corps.

December 11–13, 1775: The Continental Congress heard the report of the naval committee that had been formed on October 13, 1775. After debating the issues presented by the committee, the congress voted to build a squadron of 13 frigates (one for each of the rebelling colonies) at an estimated cost of $66,666 each. The new fleet was to include five 32-gun ships, five 28-gun ships, and three 24-gun ships.

December 21, 1775: The Continental Congress officially established the Continental Navy to harass British ships and to establish American control of the coastline.

December 22, 1775: Esek Hopkins, a Connecticut sailor, was named by the Continental Congress to command the Continental Navy.

BATTLES AND CAMPAIGNS: 1776

There were three areas of activity in 1776: northern theater, southern theater, and the naval theater.

NORTHERN THEATER

January 24, 1776: Col. Henry Knox arrived at Cambridge, Massachusetts, with 43 cannons

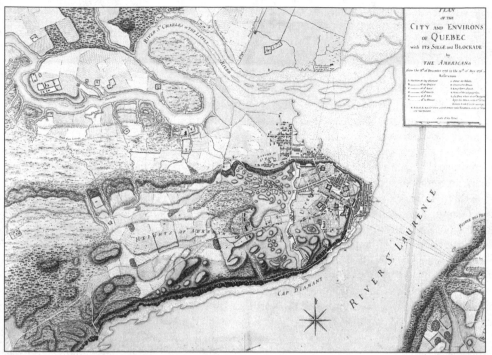

This plan shows Quebec City as it was when Benedict Arnold and Richard Montgomery led their American forces in the siege and blockade of the city between December 1775 and May 1776. (The plains of Abraham, where Montcalm and Wolfe fought in 1759 is to the left of the city.) The American colonists' expedition ended in total disaster.

and 16 mortars from Fort Ticonderoga. Placed around the city of Boston, the weapons intensified the difficult situation faced by the British troops and Loyalists under siege (see December 5, 1775, p. 76).

March 4–5, 1776: Led by Gen. John Thomas, American troops occupied Dorchester Heights overlooking Boston from the south. On the morning of March 5, General Howe resolved to capture the heights. Before a repeat of the battle of Bunker Hill could get under way, a storm set in, preventing the British attack on the heights.

March 17, 1776 (British evacuation of Boston): General Howe evacuated Boston, taking with him 9,000 British troops and at least 1,000 Loyalists, many of whom would never see their homes in Boston again. Americans cheered the bloodless liberation of the city, made possible by Colonel Knox's transportation of artillery from Fort Ticonderoga.

April 13, 1776: General Washington led the main body of his Continental forces south to New York City, correctly anticipating that General Howe would aim his next attack at that city.

May 6, 1776: Three British ships arrived in the harbor of Quebec City, bringing supplies and reinforcements to the garrison there. Still under the command of Benedict Arnold, the small American army, which had rested during the winter in the hope of capturing Quebec City in the spring, quickly retreated southward. By the end of June, the British had retaken Montreal and the last of the American soldiers had left Canada, thus ending the campaign for the "14th colony."

July 2, 1776: Gen. William Howe disembarked at Staten Island, New York, with thousands of British and Hessian troops. (This was the first appearance of Hessians in the war.) On July 12, 1776, Howe was joined by his brother, Adm. Richard "Black Dick" Howe, who commanded the British naval forces. Between them, the Howes gathered an army of more than 30,000 men and an enormous fleet which gave them a preponderance of strength over the American defenders of New York City (Manhattan Island). Washington had perhaps 20,000 men, but many of them were militia troops, engaged for only a three-month period.

August 27, 1776 (Battle of Long Island): General Howe led his British and Hessian troops

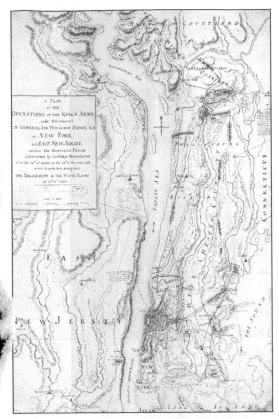

This map shows the section of the Hudson River and the major sites of operations by Gen. William Howe against the American forces between October 12 and November 26, 1776. White Plains, the site of a major battle on October 28, is the dark locale near the top right. New York City is shown at the tip of the peninsula, center bottom.

to a stunning victory over the American forces stationed at the western end of Long Island (present-day Brooklyn). Outflanking the Americans, Howe gained territory and caused between 1,000 and 2,000 casualties to the Americans at a cost of only 400 casualties to his own men. However, Howe did not follow up his attack the next day, and the American army was evacuated by boat to New York City.

September 15, 1776: British troops landed at several locations in New York City and soon won control of the city. Washington and his Continental troops escaped to the northern tip of Long Island.

September 22, 1776: A Connecticut schoolmaster and captain in the Continental Army, Nathan Hale was executed by the British. Caught behind the British lines on Long Island in civilian clothes, Hale was judged to be a spy. According to tradition (there is no historical record), before being hanged, Hale uttered the words that made him an American legend: "I only regret that I have but one life to lose for my country" (see Notable Phrases, p. 106).

October 11, 1776: Following the American withdrawal from Canada in May, Benedict Arnold built a makeshift American fleet on Lake Champlain. British general Guy Carleton had spent the summer of 1776 constructing a British squadron of ships, and the two opposing fleets came into action at Valcour Bay on Lake Champlain. Despite inspired leadership and heroic fighting, the Americans were defeated. Arnold burned his remaining ships and marched his men south. In delaying Carleton and his large army, Arnold had rendered an extremely important service to the American cause. He had prevented a British invasion from Canada.

October 28, 1776 (Battle of White Plains, New York): Northeast of New York City, Washington stopped to fight the British army. The Americans were outflanked and had to withdraw, although American casualties (150–350) were estimated to be fewer than those of the British.

November 16, 1776: Hessian soldiers stormed and captured Fort Washington on the northern tip of Long Island. Three thousand Americans were taken prisoner, and ammunition and supplies were lost to the Hessians.

November 20, 1776: American troops abandoned Fort Lee on the western bank of the Hudson River just minutes before British and Hessian troops arrived to storm the fort. The loss of Fort Washington and Fort Lee meant that the American position on the Hudson River was untenable; Washington led the remnants (4,000 men) of the Continental Army into New Jersey to escape further British attacks.

December 7, 1776: Washington led his tired, hungry, and footsore men across the Delaware River, just in time to escape the pursuit of British and Hessian troops under the command of Gen. Charles Cornwallis. Cornwallis went into winter quarters in New York City, confident that he could return in the spring and finish off what was left of the American resistance. Cornwallis left some 4,000 Hessian troops on the east bank of the Delaware River to keep an eye on the Americans.

December 25–26, 1776 (Battle of Trenton):

In the greatest gamble of his military career, Washington led his men back across the Delaware River. Catching the Hessian soldiers at Trenton completely by surprise (they were sleeping off the effects of having celebrated Christmas), Washington managed to inflict 100 casualties upon them and to capture 916 men after half an hour's fighting. The boost from this victory to American morale was invaluable.

December 31, 1776: In the wake of the victory at Trenton, many American militiamen serving with Washington agreed to reenlist for another six months.

SOUTHERN THEATER

February 27, 1776: A force of North Carolina patriots resoundingly defeated a detachment of Scottish-American Loyalists at Moore's Creek near Wilmington, North Carolina. The patriots took 900 prisoners and eliminated the possibility of a major Loyalist uprising in the South. (For more on the Scottish-American loyalties, see Flora MacDonald in Legends and Trivia, p. 105.)

June 28, 1776: British admiral Sir Peter Parker led an all-day bombardment of Fort Moultrie on Sullivan's Island in the harbor of Charles Town, South Carolina. The fort, made from palmetto logs, resisted the British cannonballs, which sank harmlessly into the spongy wood. By the end of the afternoon, the British had suffered 205 casualties and lost one ship. Parker withdrew his fleet, ending the British attack on Charles Town.

NAVAL THEATER

February 17, 1776: Esek Hopkins, commodore of the new Continental Navy, led the first fleet of eight armed ships out to sea. The first lieutenant on Hopkins's flagship, the *Alfred*, was John Paul Jones, a young Scot. Aboard also were 200 of the first marines. Hopkins had been ordered to confront the British fleet in Chesapeake Bay, but considering it too strong, he headed for the Bahamas.

March 19, 1776: The Continental Congress authorized American privateers to prey upon British commerce. The American ships operated under letters of marque—a license granted a private individual to outfit a ship with armaments to pursue enemy merchant ships.

May 9–16, 1776: Hopkins and his fleet captured Nassau in the Bahamas. The American marines briefly occupied Nassau before the fleet returned to Boston with a sizable amount of captured artillery, powder, and other stores.

May–October 1776: John Paul Jones had been given his first command, the *Providence*, in May and was promoted to captain in August. In August, he set sail from Nova Scotia to Bermuda and by October had captured eight British ships and sunk eight others.

HOME FRONT

January 4, 1776: Thomas Paine published his pamphlet *Common Sense* in Philadelphia. Calling for independence from England, Paine (who was born in England and had immigrated to America in 1774) declared that the freedom of America was a historic opportunity that had to be embraced. In the following six months, 300,000 copies of the pamphlet were sold.

July 4, 1776 (Declaration of Independence): The Second Continental Congress (in session May 10, 1775–December 12, 1776) officially endorsed the Declaration of Independence. Drafted by Virginian Thomas Jefferson, with revisions from several other delegates, the document drew upon various sources, including British political philosopher John Locke. One major difference was that Locke had championed the right of people to seek "life, liberty, and the preservation of property," and Jefferson wrote "Life, Liberty, and the Pursuit of Happiness."

INTERNATIONAL DEVELOPMENTS

March 1, 1776: The Comte de Vergennes, the foreign minister of France, wrote a secret dispatch to his Spanish counterpart suggesting that Spain join with France in secretly sending arms and ammunition to the American rebels.

December 21, 1776: Benjamin Franklin arrived in Paris and initiated a diplomatic mission to the court of King Louis XVI. Franklin's mission was to persuade the French to send soldiers and ships to aid the American patriots in their war against the British.

BATTLES AND CAMPAIGNS: 1777

The three areas of activity in 1777 were: northern theater, frontier theater, and naval theater.

NORTHERN THEATER

January 2, 1777 (Battle of Princeton): Upon learning of Washington's victory at Trenton, British general Cornwallis rushed south to New Jersey, seeking to defeat the newly revived American army. Moving rapidly, Cornwallis's troops soon pinned the American troops, with the Assinpunk Creek at their backs, near Trenton. Cornwallis paused for the night, and Washington left campfires burning to conceal his move to the north during the night. At dawn on January 3, Washington surprised the rear guard of Cornwallis's army at Princeton, New Jersey. The battle was even at the start, but Washington's leadership inspired his men, and the Americans prevailed and captured 323 British soldiers.

January 6, 1777: Evading any further contact with the British army, Washington led his tired but twice-victorious men into winter quarters at Morristown, New Jersey.

May 11, 1777: British general John Burgoyne arrived at Montreal. Burgoyne soon assembled an army of 8,000 British, Hessian, and Indian troops. Prior to his arrival in Canada, Burgoyne had drawn up a master plan for the defeat of the American colonies. Believing that New England was the heart and soul of the rebellion, Burgoyne called for three British armies to converge on Albany, New York, hold the line at the Hudson River, and thereby isolate the New England colonies from the middle and southern colonies. Approved by the British War Office in London, the plan called for Burgoyne to move with 8,000 men south from Montreal to Albany and for British colonel Barry St. Leger to leave Montreal, go to Lake Ontario, then approach Albany via the Mohawk River valley. General Howe was to bring the main body of British troops north from New York City to Albany. Burgoyne's plan was sound in concept. But would all the leaders follow the plan, and, if so, would the weather, geography, and circumstances permit the plan to proceed?

July 5–7, 1777: Burgoyne began the action in the northern area by laying siege to Fort Ticonderoga, which was defended by 2,500 Americans under Gen. Arthur St. Clair. Fort Ticonderoga was a strong position, but it was vulnerable because of the proximity of Mount Defiance, which loomed just south of the promontory on which the fort was located. Burgoyne's engineers accomplished an amazing feat in their method of hauling cannons to the summit of Mount Defiance. On July 4, patriot General St. Clair became aware of the cannons on top of the hill and ordered an immediate retreat from Fort Ticonderoga. The Americans escaped across a bridge of boats on Lake Champlain to the eastern side. Burgoyne entered the fort in triumph, and many of his men pursued the Americans into Vermont (then called the Hampshire Grants). In the ensuing battle at Hubbardton, Vermont, the retreating Americans fought the British army well, and only the arrival of reinforcements from Burgoyne prevented a minidisaster for the column of British and Hessian troops. The bulk of the American troops escaped southward and were able to regroup under the command of Gen. Philip Schuyler near Albany. Burgoyne's victory was celebrated in London. King George III is reported to have exulted, "I have beaten them! I have beat all the Americans!" when he heard the news of Fort Ticonderoga's fall.

July 1777: After the victory at Fort Ticonderoga, Burgoyne and his army marched south. Burdened by a supply train that included fine wines and other luxuries, Burgoyne and his men were slowed by thick underbrush and trees that had been felled by the American defenders led by General Schuyler. The march from Lake Champlain to Fort Edward on the Hudson River, which under ideal circumstances should have been completed in five days, took the British a total of 20 days. Meanwhile, large numbers of American militiamen from New York and western New England were gathering under the leadership of General Schuyler, then under the leadership of his replacement, Gen. Horatio Gates.

July 23, 1777: General Howe left New York City with 20,000 British troops aboard 267 British transport ships headed for Chesapeake Bay. It is unclear whether Howe willfully chose to disregard the plan of coordination with Burgoyne or if Howe had been given enough latitude by London to engage in his own campaign. In either case, Howe made his decision. Consistent with his earlier policy of holding Boston (1775–1776) and capturing New York City (1776), he sought to capture and hold Philadelphia, the seat of the Continental Congress, and, he believed, the heart and soul of the rebellion.

July 26, 1777: British colonel Barry St. Leger departed from Oswego on the southern side of Lake Ontario and headed for the Mohawk River valley and his rendezvous with Burgoyne at Albany. St. Leger had approximately 2,000 British troops, Loyalists, and Indians under his command. Joseph Brant, the Mohawk chief, was the leader of the Indians.

July 27, 1777: American Loyalist Jane McCrae was murdered and scalped by Indians serving with Burgoyne's army in upstate New York. The death of the young American woman, who had come to Burgoyne's camp to meet with her fiancé, a British or Loyalist officer, inflamed American patriots. They asked that if this could happen to an American Loyalist, what horrors could patriot Americans expect from the British and their Indian allies.

August 3, 1777: British colonel St. Leger and his forces arrived at American Fort Stanwix, near present-day Utica, New York. St. Leger demanded that the Americans surrender. Upon receipt of their refusal, he placed the fort under siege.

August 6, 1777 (Battle of Oriskany): Learning of the siege of Fort Stanwix, the population of the Mohawk River valley rallied to create a relief force. Led by Col. Nicholas Herkimer, 800 militiamen set out from Fort Dayton (near present-day Herkimen, New York), intending to raise the siege. About 6 miles from the fort, the American relief column marched straight into a British and Indian ambush in a ravine near Oriskany, New York. The fighting raged throughout the afternoon, and no mercy was asked for or given by either side. When the British and Indians finally withdrew, they left possession of the field to the Americans, who suffered the greater losses (200 killed, 50 wounded, 200 captured). The American relief column turned back to Fort Dayton. The battle, which some historians have called the bloodiest of the entire war, allowed the siege of Fort Stanwix to continue, but the morale of the Indians allied with St. Leger dropped considerably after the battle. Like many British commanders, St. Leger had assured the Indians that the Americans were a farming people unaccustomed to the sacrifices of warfare and that their fighting spirit was poor.

August 16, 1777 (Battle of Bennington): Worried about the lack of news from General Howe, Burgoyne sent a 1,000-man detachment of Hessian troops into Bennington, Vermont, to find supplies (livestock in particular) and to gather information about the enemy. The Hessians marched headlong into a force of some 2,600 militiamen led by Col. John Stark of New Hampshire. The Americans made a furious attack on the Hessians, using a complicated double-envelopment strategy. Stark's battle cry, "There they are! We'll beat them before night or Molly Stark will be a widow!" epitomized the American fighting spirit that had developed in the aftermath of the loss of Fort Ticonderoga and the death of Jane McCrae. Most impressive was the fact that the Hessian force was simply overrun by the American attack. A column of 600 reinforcements, sent by Burgoyne, threatened to turn the tide, but by nightfall, the British and Hessians had suffered 200 killed and 700 captured or missing; American casualties numbered only about 80. To make matters worse, Burgoyne's numbers were dwind-ling, but the Americans could replenish any losses they suffered through additional militia enlistments by the local inhabitants.

August 22, 1777: Colonel St. Leger lifted the siege of Fort Stanwix and began a disorderly retreat to Lake Ontario. St. Leger's decision was caused by two factors: First, he was aware that Benedict Arnold was approaching with a relief column from Fort Dayton (what St. Leger did not know was that Arnold had only 800 men), and second, St. Leger's Indian allies were terrified by rumors that Arnold was coming with men as "numerous as the leaves on the trees" and that smallpox was about to spread throughout the British camp. Abandoned by the Indians, who were his eyes and ears in the wilderness campaign, St. Leger began his retreat, thus removing the second wing of Burgoyne's three-pronged attack on New York (see May 11, 1777, p. 81).

August 23, 1777: Benedict Arnold led his relief column into Fort Stanwix. Arnold had commissioned Yon Host Schuyler, who was part Indian, to spread the news among the Indians and his ruse succeeded. Arnold was free to return to the Hudson River area and participate in what was expected to be a decisive battle against Burgoyne's men.

September 11, 1777 (Battle of Brandywine): Washington led the Continental Army in a defense of the Brandywine River in Pennsylvania against the oncoming British army under General Howe. The British troops, who had sailed up Chesapeake Bay during the month of August, were now marching on Philadelphia. In a battle that was strikingly reminiscent of the battle of

Long Island (1776), Howe made feints against the American center while sending men around the American left flank. Howe's battle tactics succeeded again, and the Americans were forced to withdraw, with approximately 1,200 men killed, wounded, or missing. (The young Marquis de Lafayette was among the wounded.) The British suffered 500 casualties.

September 19, 1777 (First Battle of Saratoga): General Burgoyne sent out an advance column of 1,500 men to probe the American lines near Freeman's Farm on the west bank of the Hudson River. The commander of the American forces, Gen. Horatio Gates, sent Col. Daniel Morgan with his highly skilled Virginia marksmen to stop the British. Burgoyne's men fought in an open field, surrounded by hundreds of American sharpshooters firing from the cover of the woods. By the end of the afternoon, Burgoyne had pulled his men back; they had suffered nearly 600 men killed, wounded, or missing. More important, the British had lost the initiative on the Hudson River.

September 21–22, 1777: Five British regiments made a bayonet attack on American troops under Col. Anthony Wayne at Paoli Tavern near Philadelphia. The Americans suffered 150 men killed or wounded; the British losses were negligible. Although the event was soon called the Paoli massacre by the Americans, the British use of the bayonet attack fell within the generally accepted rules of warfare at the time. Colonel Wayne escaped with his life and was deeply humiliated by the action. His revenge would come at the battle of Stony Point, New York, in 1779 (see July 15–16, 1779, pp. 87–88).

September 26, 1777: British troops entered Philadelphia, the original seat of the Continental Congress. That city was the focus of General Howe's campaign. However, Howe soon found that the American cause depended on the support of the citizenry rather than on the possession of a key city.

October 3, 1777: Having learned of the perilous position of Burgoyne's men on the Hudson River, British general Henry Clinton left New York City with 3,000 men, seeking to capture American territory and to create a diversion that would relieve the pressure on Burgoyne.

October 4, 1777 (Battle of Germantown): Washington threw his Continental Army units— some 11,000 troops—into a surprise attack on Howe's British army, which was situated at Germantown, Pennsylvania. The American attack fared well in its opening stage; the British fell back in confusion. The way was open for a full-scale battle, with the Americans holding the edge. However, an early morning fog confused Washington's units, some of which fired on other American troops by mistake. In addition, the British stubbornly defended a stone house on the American route, and the delay caused by the defense there threw off Washington's timetable. The Americans withdrew, having suffered 152 killed and 521 wounded; the British losses amounted to 537. Although technically a defeat, the battle served as a balm to American spirits; the Continentals had come close to winning a major battle.

October 7, 1777 (Second Battle of Saratoga, or Battle of Freeman's Farm): General Burgoyne again sent out an advance force to probe the American lines. The Americans again took their stand at Freeman's Farm. Burgoyne's men met with withering musket fire from American sharpshooters and were forced to retreat. After repulsing the British movement, the Americans went on the offensive. Led by Benedict Arnold on horseback, the Americans charged and captured the key Hessian defensive fortifications. Arnold was wounded in his left leg, the same leg that had been injured in the attack on Quebec City in 1775 (see pp. 76-77). American casualties for the day were 150; the British suffered 600 casualties, as well as the loss of their key position.

October 8, 1777: Burgoyne and his men retreated north to the village of Saratoga. Finding any retreat farther north blocked by thousands of American militiamen, Burgoyne camped, hoping that General Clinton's diversion to the south might yet improve his situation.

October 8, 1777: General Clinton captured American forts Clinton and Montgomery on the lower Hudson River.

October 17, 1777 (Convention of Saratoga): Burgoyne surrendered 5,700 officers and men to Gen. Horatio Gates at Saratoga. Realizing that Clinton's movement could not rescue him and that retreat to Canada was impossible, Burgoyne negotiated the convention, which allowed him and his men to be paroled to England on their honor not to serve against the Americans again during the war. The surrender removed any threat

A copy of the painting by John Trumbull depicts British general John Burgoyne (center left) surrendering to Gen. Horatio Gates (October 17, 1777) after the battle of Saratoga.

of British invasion of New York State during 1777 and gave a tremendous boost to American spirits throughout the country. It also made General Gates a national hero. Gen. Benedict Arnold, however, was convinced that his heroic activities at Saratoga and his lifting of the siege at Fort Stanwix had been overlooked in favor of Gates's accomplishments.

October 22, 1777: Americans successfully defended Fort Mercer, situated at present-day Red Bank, New Jersey, against an attack made by Hessian forces. The Hessian troops suffered 400 men killed and wounded; American losses came to fewer than 50 men.

November 20, 1777: The American garrison of Fort Mercer evacuated and withdrew to join with the bulk of the Continental Army under George Washington.

December 4, 1777: General Howe took his British, Hessian, and Loyalist troops into winter quarters in Philadelphia. Howe's fondness for parties and balls during his stay in Philadelphia soon gave rise to the belief that "Philadelphia had captured General Howe."

December 19, 1777: Washington led his Continental troops into winter quarters at Valley Forge, 20 miles from Philadelphia. One of the reasons there was difficulty in acquiring food and supplies was that the local merchants were reluctant to accept the Continental dollar, the newly issued paper money that was not backed by gold or silver.

FRONTIER THEATER

June 1, 1777: American brigadier general Edward Hand arrived at Pittsburgh, Pennsylvania, and began to organize a defense of the western frontier. Hand's presence was intended to show the frontier people that the Continental Congress had not forgotten them and the dangers under which they lived.

June–July, 1777: British colonel Henry Hamilton sent out British-Indian war parties from Fort Detroit. Although Hamilton instructed his war parties to make distinctions between soldiers and civilians, the taking of many scalps along the frontier that summer led to Americans calling Hamilton the "hair buyer."

October 1, 1777: Col. George Rogers Clark left Harrodsburg, Kentucky, for Williamsburg, Virginia, to propose to lead a small force of militiamen to capture British posts in the Illinois country (present-day Ohio, Indiana, and Illinois) and thereby prevent further attacks on the American frontier.

December 4, 1777: Col. George Rogers Clark, officially commissioned to carry out his plan, set off for the Illinois Territory. He and his forces traveled much of the way on riverboats.

NAVAL THEATER

American privateers continued to prey upon British commerce, taking far more ships than they lost to British cruisers. Although King George III and his ministers considered that merely a nuisance, some members of the British Parliament, merchants themselves or related to merchant families, felt the economic loss from the American raids on British commercial ships.

May 28–June 27, 1777: Capt. Lambert Wickes led four American ships on a daring and unprecedented raid into the Irish Sea, between England and Ireland. That cruise into the home waters of the enemy netted the Americans a prize of at least 14 ships before the American ships were forced to retire to the French port of St. Malo for safety.

June 1777: John Paul Jones was given command of the newly built *Ranger*, with 18 guns, and set sail for the waters off Britain, where he attacked British ships.

HOME FRONT

December 20, 1776–March 4, 1777: The session of the Continental Congress met in Baltimore, Maryland.

March 5, 1777–September 18, 1777: The Continental Congress returned to Philadelphia.

September 18, 1777: Mindful of the approach of General Howe's army, the Continental Congress left Philadelphia.

September 27, 1777: Seeking to find a secure place to locate, the Continental Congress met for one day only in Lancaster, Pennsylvania.

September 30, 1777: The Continental Congress met in York, Pennsylvania, where it remained until June 27, 1778.

INTERNATIONAL DEVELOPMENTS

June 27, 1777: The 20-year-old Marquis de Lafayette arrived in Philadelphia and offered his services to the Continental Congress. The congress originally was skeptical of the young man, but changed its view and bestowed the commission of major general on him, attaching him to the Continental Army, where he soon became chief aide-de-camp to General Washington.

December 17, 1777: During 1777, Benjamin Franklin continued his diplomatic mission to the court of King Louis XVI. When news of the American victory at Saratoga reached France, that country officially recognized the independence of the United States.

BATTLES AND CAMPAIGNS: 1778

There were four areas of activity in 1778: northern theater, southern theater, frontier theater, and naval theater.

NORTHERN THEATER

May 8, 1778: British general Henry Clinton arrived in Philadelphia, bringing the news that he had been named to replace General Howe as commander in chief of all British forces in North America. (Howe had asked to be replaced.)

June 18, 1778: Conscious that the new French-American alliance (see International Developments, p. 87) had made the British position more vulnerable, General Clinton departed from Philadelphia, leading the British-Hessian army by land toward New York City.

June 19, 1778: Washington led his men out of their winter quarters at Valley Forge. The Americans who had stayed with Washington during the winter of 1777–1778 had become a hardened, cohesive group, brought together by the sufferings they had endured during the winter and by the drilling and training they had undergone under Prussian captain Frederick von Steuben.

June 28, 1778 (Battle of Monmouth): Washington's troops caught up with Clinton's retreating force in Freehold, Monmouth County, New Jersey. It was a scorching 100-degree day, and the American attack fared poorly early in the battle, but there seemed to be no reason for Gen. Charles Lee to order the Americans to retreat. (This ill-fated decision led to his court-martial and dismissal from the army.) Sensing American weakness, British generals Clinton and Cornwallis turned about and attacked the American lines. There was the potential for a total rout, but the arrival of Washington at a key moment both inspired and shamed Lee's retreating men. Mounted on a white horse, Washington rallied Lee's shaken men, who then put up a stubborn resistance to the British. By midafternoon, the Americans had gained the upper hand, and only the arrival of evening and the exhaustion caused by the heat saved Clinton from a serious defeat.

Clinton, his army, and his baggage train safely retreated to New York City. This battle, the last large-scale battle of the revolution to be fought in the Northeast, displayed the courage and magnetism of General Washington. Commenting on how Washington had saved the day with his presence, the young Marquis de Lafayette exclaimed, "I thought that I had never seen so superb a man!"

July 10, 1778: A French fleet led by the Comte d'Estaing arrived in New York Harbor. D'Estaing's warships held an advantage in size over the fleet of British admiral Richard Howe, but the French ships were unable to cross the sandbar at the entrance of the harbor. Chagrined by his failure, d'Estaing left the area and sailed to Newport, Rhode Island, hoping to win a victory there (see Naval Theater, p. 87). For Washington, the New York Harbor episode was a dismal setback.

SOUTHERN THEATER

December 29, 1778: British general Augustine Prevost captured Savannah, Georgia. That was the first successful British initiative in the American South, and it signaled a new priority and direction for the British. General Clinton intended to hold the line in New York City but sent men to campaign in the South, where, he believed, there were large numbers of American Loyalists ready to flock to the aid of King George III's armies.

FRONTIER THEATER

May 30, 1778: Some 300 Iroquois Indian warriors, allied with the British, raided and burned Cobbleskill, New York. This raid was the start of a campaign of terror by Loyalists and Indians against American frontier settlements in New York and Pennsylvania.

June 30, 1778: George Rogers Clark, with his force of some 200 volunteers, sailed down the Ohio River to Fort Massac, close to where the Tennessee River joined the Ohio River. After a short rest, they set out overland to the settlement at Fort Kaskaskia (in present-day Illinois) some 120 miles to the northwest.

July 3, 1778 (Wyoming Valley Massacre): Loyalist colonel John Butler led 400 Loyalists and 600 Indians into the Wyoming valley in north-central Pennsylvania. American colonel Zebulon

Butler (no relation) commanded some 350 American militia at Forty Fort (near present-day Wilkes-Barre), where the valley's settlers had taken refuge. After half an hour's fighting, the Americans began a disorderly retreat that soon turned into a rout. Several hundred settlers and militia were killed, and many who escaped soon died of starvation. The Loyalists and their Indian allies proceeded to destroy most of the settlements in the valley.

July 4, 1778: On the second anniversary of the Declaration of Independence, Col. George Rogers Clark captured the British garrison at Fort Kaskaskia, at the junction of the Mississippi and Kaskaskia Rivers in the Illinois country. He and his band of frontiersmen swept down on the fort unexpectedly during the night.

July 20, 1778: George Rogers Clark captured the British post of Vincennes, on the Wabash River (in present-day Indiana). The combination of the captures of Fort Kaskaskia and Fort Vincennes left the British and Indians with no post south of Fort Detroit from which to launch their attacks on the American frontier settlements in Kentucky.

October 7, 1778: British colonel Henry Hamilton left Fort Detroit with a British-Indian force, intent upon reversing the losses that the British had suffered at the hands of Clark in the Illinois country.

November 11, 1778 (Cherry Valley Raid): In the autumn of 1778, the American militia in the Mohawk River valley of New York destroyed villages of Indians friendly to the British. In retaliation, Mohawk chief Joseph Brant and Loyalist captain Walter Butler (son of John Butler, who had led the Wyoming Valley raid) led a combined force of some 800 Indians and Loyalists against the settlement of Cherry Valley (about 50 miles west of Albany, New York). In the surprise attack, some 45 men, women, and children were killed and another 70 were wounded or captured. The attackers withdrew the next day, when some 200 patriot troops arrived.

December 17, 1778: British colonel Hamilton occupied Fort Vincennes, on the Wabash River, in a bloodless takeover. Rather than continue his campaign through the winter, Hamilton decided to wait until spring to finish off George Rogers Clark, who, camped at Fort Kaskaskia, was effectively cut off from supplies and reinforcements.

NAVAL THEATER

April 10–May 8, 1778: American captain John Paul Jones took the recently built 18-gun *Ranger* on a cruise off the eastern coast of England and Scotland. Jones took two merchant ships as prizes and then, on April 23, landed at Whitehaven, England, where he disabled the guns of the coastal defenses and burned a ship in the harbor. On April 24, he fought and captured the 20-gun HMS *Drake*, which he took to Brest, France. American privateer raids had taken 733 British ships since 1776, but the effect of Jones's presence in the coastal waters was extremely discomforting to the British, who were used to commanding all the waters around their home island.

July 9, 1778: A British naval force raided and burned Fairfield, Connecticut.

July 29, 1778: The French war fleet of the Comte d'Estaing arrived off British-held Newport, Rhode Island.

August 8, 1778: American troops led by Gen. John Sullivan arrived in the Newport area to begin a siege of that city. Working in conjunction with Admiral d'Estaing, Sullivan hoped to win a substantial victory, which had been denied Sullivan and many other commanders prior to this because of the British command of the sea.

August 9–11, 1778: Admiral d'Estaing sailed out of Narragansett Bay in order to meet the oncoming British fleet of Adm. Richard Howe. For two days, the fleets maneuvered and countermaneuvered, each seeking to gain and hold the weather gauge (to have the wind at their back and, therefore, to dictate the course of action). A major storm set in and scattered the ships of both fleets. The fighting that took place after the storm was haphazard. Following the storm and the limited fighting, both fleets sailed away to repair their sails and masts: the British to New York City and the French to Boston. To his anger and disgust, General Sullivan was forced to abandon the siege of Newport.

HOME FRONT

July 2, 1778: The Continental Congress met in Philadelphia in the wake of the British departure from that city (see June 18, 1778, p. 85). The Congress remained in Philadelphia for the rest of the war.

July 9, 1778: Delegates to the Continental Congress from Massachusetts, Rhode Island, Connecticut, New York, Pennsylvania, Virginia, and South Carolina signed the Articles of Confederation in Philadelphia. The other states announced they needed time to study the articles. The document linked the 13 states into a loosely knit confederation.

INTERNATIONAL DEVELOPMENTS

February 6, 1778: France signed a commercial and a military alliance with the United States. The two countries agreed to grant favorable trade status to each other, and, more important, the French pledged to fight until the Americans won their independence from England. For their part, the Americans promised not to seek a separate peace with England. The alliance, largely the handiwork of two men (Benjamin Franklin and the French foreign minister, the Comte de Vergennes), signaled a new departure in international affairs for the United States. However, the alliance had the potential to reopen old wounds; Americans and Frenchmen had fought against each other in the French and Indian Wars and reinstating cooperation between the two peoples would not be easy.

BATTLES AND CAMPAIGNS: 1779

There were four areas of activity in 1779: northern theater, southern theater, frontier theater, and naval theater.

NORTHERN THEATER

June 1, 1779: Ending a long period of British inactivity in the northern theater, Gen. Henry Clinton led 6,000 troops up the Hudson River valley from New York City. The troops were soon able to occupy the unfinished American forts at Stony Point and Verplancks Point on the Hudson River but failed to reach their ultimate destination of West Point, the strategic American fort that commanded the Hudson River.

July 5–11, 1779: Loyalist troops led by New York governor Thomas Tryon raided a number of towns in coastal Connecticut, burning Fairfield and Norwalk.

July 15–16, 1779 (Battle of Stony Point): Realizing the advantage gained by the British in holding Stony Point on the west bank of the Hudson River, Washington resolved to retake that position. Looking for a commander, he settled on Brig. Gen. Anthony Wayne, who had remained a favorite despite his defeat at Paoli Tavern in 1777 (see September 21–22, 1777, p. 83). Wayne led 300 light infantry troops in a silent, bayonet-only attack on the British position. The British surrendered after a 30-minute fight. The Americans suffered 15 men killed and 80 wounded; the British suffered 63 killed and more than 500 men taken prisoner. The successful operation raised American morale, and Anthony Wayne soon became known as "Mad Anthony" Wayne. The American defeat at Paoli Tavern was avenged. More important, the Continental troops serving on the Hudson River were gradually showing that they could equal and even surpass their British foes in almost every aspect of fighting.

July 25, 1779: The entire Massachusetts navy, which had been organized in September 1775 (and was distinct from the Continental Navy)—3 ships, 3 brigantines, 13 privateers, and 20 transports strong—arrived in Penobscot Bay. The Massachusetts navy intended to subdue a British base near present-day Castine, Maine (then part of Massachusetts). The ambitious enterprise was commanded by Massachusetts commodore Dudley Saltonstall. Paul Revere was in command of the American artillery.

August 12, 1779: A squadron of British ships sailed into Penobscot Bay, threatening the Massachusetts fleet anchored there. Acting in haste and fear, the Massachusetts sailors cut their cables and took their ships as far up the Penobscot River as they could. When they found they could go no farther, the crews scuttled and burned their ships, then started the long walk home to Massachusetts. Not a single ship of the Massachusetts navy escaped destruction, whether at the hands of its own men or of the British. The debacle was extremely costly to Massachusetts, and Commodore Saltonstall was dismissed from the service. Commander of artillery Paul Revere was court-martialed and acquitted.

August 19, 1779: American general Henry Lee captured Paulus Hook (present-day Jersey City), the last remaining British stronghold in New Jersey. The Americans suffered two men killed and three wounded, and the British suffered 50 casualties and 150 men taken prisoner.

October 11, 1779: British general Clinton evacuated the naval base at Newport, Rhode Island, and brought the garrison from there to New York City. Clinton was seeking to consolidate his forces in anticipation of a campaign in the American South.

October 17, 1779: Washington led the Continental Army into winter quarters at Morristown, New Jersey. During the winter of 1779–1780 (which was colder than the winter of 1777–1778 at Valley Forge), Washington's men suffered from poor supplies and low morale. The contrast between the comfortable British quarters in New York City and the desolate countryside around their winter camp had a strong negative effect on the American soldiers.

December 26, 1779: General Clinton embarked 8,700 troops on board transport ships in New York Harbor. Ten warships and 90 transport ships carried the army out to sea, where it endured heavy storms before reaching its destination—the coastal waters off South Carolina.

SOUTHERN THEATER

April 29, 1779: British general Prevost led 2,400 British troops and a body of Indian warriors across the Savannah River against American general William Moultrie, who retreated to Charles Town, South Carolina. Virtually all Georgia had fallen into British hands, and a British royal governor was installed in Georgia.

May 10, 1779: In one of the first military actions to be fought in Virginia since 1775, British naval forces captured and burned Portsmouth and Norfolk, Virginia.

May 11, 1779: A British attack on Charles Town, South Carolina, was repulsed by Brig. Gen. Casimir Pulaski, a Polish count who had become one of the most devoted foreign adventurers in the service of the American army.

June 19, 1779: American troops unsuccessfully attacked the rear guard of British troops under General Prevost at Stono Ferry, South Carolina. Prevost's men made their return to Savannah, Georgia, without being molested further.

September 8, 1779: French admiral d'Estaing dropped anchor at Tybee Bar, where the Savannah River enters the Atlantic Ocean. D'Estaing intended to cooperate with American general Benjamin Lincoln in an attempt to recapture Savannah, Georgia, which had fallen to the British in December 1778.

September 16, 1779: D'Estaing made a formal summons to British general Augustine Prevost to surrender Savannah to the French-American forces. Prevost skillfully played for time and continued to build his defense.

September 23, 1779: The formal siege of Savannah began.

October 9, 1779: French-American troops made a frontal assault on the British fortifications around Savannah. Worried by the approach of the hurricane season, which threatened the safety of his ships, d'Estaing persuaded General Lincoln to risk all in the attack. The French-American forces were repulsed with frightful casualties: 650 French and 150 Americans were killed, wounded, or missing; d'Estaing was wounded twice (neither wound was serious); Count Pulaski was mortally wounded; and the French fleet soon sailed away from the scene. The French-American alliance had suffered another setback, and many Americans began to seriously doubt the value of an alliance that had so far produced only failures: New York City, Newport, and Savannah.

FRONTIER THEATER

February 5, 1779: American colonel George Rogers Clark left Fort Kaskaskia in the Illinois country with some 170 men. Having learned that British colonel Hamilton had retaken Vincennes 240 miles to the east, Clark risked a journey through the winter-flooded Illinois country to try to catch Hamilton by surprise.

February 21, 1779: Clark and his men were ferried across the Wabash River close to their goal of Vincennes.

February 23–25 1779: Clark and his men attacked and captured the town of Vincennes during the evening of the 23rd. The British troops were isolated in Fort Sackville, and Clark convinced the British that he was leading a much larger force than he had. As Colonel Hamilton dragged out negotiations during the day of the 24th, Clark and his men killed four unfriendly Indians in full view of the fort. Finally, on the morning of the 25th, Hamilton and his men were allowed to walk out of the fort in a formal surrender and were taken prisoner. Hamilton and 27 of his men were sent to Virginia. Fort Sackville was renamed Fort Patrick Henry. With that triumph, Clark asserted American power west of the Al-

legheny Mountains and made the Kentucky frontier if not entirely secure, at least safer than it had been before his arrival.

April 1–30, 1779: American colonel Evan Shelby destroyed a group of Chickamagua Indian settlements in present-day Tennessee in retaliation for raids by those Indians against American settlements in Kentucky.

July 22, 1779: American militiamen pursued Indians led by Mohawk chief Joseph Brant on the east bank of the Delaware River near present-day Port Jervis, New York. Drawn into an ambush, the militia lost 130 men out of a total force of 150 men.

August 29, 1779: At Newtown, near present-day Elmira, New York, American general John Sullivan led 4,000 American troops in a battle against 800 Loyalists and Indians, led by Maj. John Butler and Chief Joseph Brant. Sullivan, who had been sent by General Washington to punish the Six Nations of the Iroquois for their part in aiding the British cause, then moved on to complete a march through the land of the Iroquois. During the next two weeks, Sullivan destroyed some 40 Indian villages, 1,500 fruit trees, and some 160,000 bushels of corn. Sullivan's march had a devastating effect on the subsequent ability and will of the Iroquois to resist the Americans.

September 1779: Spanish governor of Louisiana Bernardo Galvez led Spanish forces in the capture of British forts at Manhac, Baton Rouge, and Natchez. An able and energetic leader, Galvez intended to restore Spain to the status of a great colonial power on the Gulf of Mexico.

NAVAL THEATER

January 10, 1779: The French presented a dilapidated vessel to American captain John Paul Jones in France. Jones refitted the ship, mounted 42 guns, and named it the *Bonhomme Richard*, in honor of Benjamin Franklin, then famous for his *Poor Richard's Almanac.*

August 14, 1779: Capt. John Paul Jones led the *Bonhomme Richard* and six smaller ships out from Brest, France. He cruised through British waters until October 3 and returned to America as one of the outstanding heroes of the war.

September 23, 1779: Aboard the *Bonhomme Richard*, John Paul Jones attacked a British merchant convoy off the east coast of England near

An engraving made long after the battle in September 1779 depicts the hand-to-hand fighting as American seamen from the **Bonhomme Richard** *take over the British ship* **Serapis.**

Flamborough Head. In the afternoon, Jones engaged the British frigate *Serapis* in a one-on-one battle. Knowing that the British artillery was superior to his own, Jones brought his ship very close to the British ship and put grappling irons aboard his foe, locking the two ships together. As the afternoon wore on, British gunners fired round after round into the leaky American ship, and American sharpshooters in the masts shot down any British sailor who remained on deck. Given the stalemated nature of the battle, the British commander, Capt. Richard Pearson, hailed Jones and called on him to surrender.

Jones retorted, "I have not yet begun to fight!"(see Notable Phrases, p. 106) As nightfall approached, Captain Pearson did an about-face and surrendered his ship to Jones. Jones transferred his command to the *Serapis*, and the *Bonhomme Richard* sank. Although the victory did not change the fact that England's large navy continued to rule the waves, the story of Jones's

retort and victory gave a tremendous boost to American morale.

HOME FRONT

February 15, 1779: The Continental Congress set forth goals for a possible peace settlement with England. The goals were independence, complete British evacuation of American territory, and freedom of navigation on the Mississippi River (something that would later be challenged by England and Spain).

INTERNATIONAL DEVELOPMENTS

April 12, 1779: France and Spain signed the Treaty of Aranjuez in Spain, which provided for Spain to enter the war against England on the side of France. France pledged not to sign a treaty of peace with England until Spain had managed to recover the stronghold of Gibraltar, where the Mediterranean entered the Atlantic Ocean. Spain, which had lost Gibraltar in 1704, wanted desperately to regain the spot for strategic considerations and for national honor.

June 21, 1779: Spain formally declared war on England. King Charles III of Spain and his ministers did not recognize the independence of the United States nor did they pledge to fight with the Americans, but the entry of Spain and the Spanish fleet into the war gave the British war planners another factor to consider, especially in their home waters of the North Atlantic and the English Channel.

BATTLES AND CAMPAIGNS: 1780

There were four areas of activity in 1780: northern theater, southern theater, frontier theater, and naval theater.

NORTHERN THEATER

June 23, 1780 (Battle of Springfield, New Jersey): American general Nathaniel Greene led 1,000 American troops to a defensive victory over 5,000 British and Hessian troops led by Hessian general von Knyphausen in Springfield, New Jersey. The special bravery demonstrated by a Rhode Island regiment in holding a key bridge in Springfield was reminiscent to many of the American heroics at the bridge in Concord, Massachusetts at the start of the Revolution in 1775 (see April 19, 1775, pp. 74-75).

July 11, 1780: Five thousand first-rate French soldiers disembarked at Newport, Rhode Island. Commanded by the Comte de Rochambeau, a longtime soldier, the troops were intended to serve as allies and auxiliaries of the American forces. In a rare display of allied cooperation, Rochambeau was ordered by the French government to defer to Washington in matters of overall command. Unfortunately for the French-American alliance, Rochambeau's men and their accompanying squadron of ships were soon blockaded at Newport by a larger British fleet.

August 5, 1780: Benedict Arnold assumed command of West Point, the key American fortress that guarded the lower Hudson River valley from further incursion by British ships and soldiers. Embittered by what he saw as a lack of gratitude on the part of the Continental Congress for his remarkable service in 1775–1777, Arnold—even as he took command—conducted secret negotiations with British general Clinton to "turn coat" and hand West Point to the British forces.

September 23, 1780: Aide-de-camp to General Clinton Maj. John André was captured by American troops while behind American lines and out of uniform. André was returning from a secret meeting with Benedict Arnold, and sewn into his clothes were Arnold's plans for handing over the West Point fortress to the British.

September 25, 1780: Hearing the news that Major André had been apprehended by American troops and suspecting the worst, Benedict Arnold ran from West Point and made his way by boat to the British ship *Vulture* on the Hudson River. Arnold soon reached New York City, where he was received with cool correctness by General Clinton and the British officer corps. Upon learning that Arnold had defected to the British, General Washington was heard to exclaim, "Arnold! Whom now can we trust?"

October 2, 1780: Maj. John André was hanged as a spy by the American army. His death caused great sadness in the British camp, and a memorial was later erected in his honor in Westminster Abbey in London.

SOUTHERN THEATER

February 1, 1780: After surviving a winter storm at sea, the British fleet carrying General Clinton's army arrived off Charles Town, South Carolina.

March 14, 1780: Spanish governor Bernardo Galvez captured the British fort and port at Mobile in present-day Alabama.

April 8, 1780: British naval forces initiated an attack on Charles Town by sailing past the American guns at Fort Moultrie on Sullivan's Island in the harbor of that city. The British suffered losses of 27 men, negligible compared with the casualties they had suffered while bombing the fort in June 1776 (see p. 80). Charles Town was effectively isolated by the British.

May 6, 1780: American fort Moultrie fell to British forces encircling Charles Town. Clinton's army tightened its grip on Charles Town, using textbook siege tactics: digging trenches; employing cannons, mortar, and howitzers; and slowly grinding down the American ability to resist.

May 19, 1780 (Surrender of Charles Town): American general Benjamin Lincoln surrendered Charles Town to General Clinton. Included in the surrender were 5,466 officers and men, 6,000 muskets, 391 cannon, and a considerable store of ammunition. The surrender was the greatest single loss sustained by the Americans during the war. Clinton and his fellow British officers were jubilant, and they believed that the Loyalists in the American South would soon join the British cause.

May 29, 1780: British colonel of dragoons Banastre Tarleton (called "Benny" and "Bloody Tarleton" by the Americans) made a surprise attack on American troops led by Col. Alexander Buford at Waxhaws Creek, South Carolina. Tarleton's cavalrymen won the battle swiftly but continued to kill Americans after the white flag of surrender had been raised. The large American losses (113 men killed, 203 taken prisoner) and the savagery of the British attack made Tarleton the most hated British officer in North America. New slogans soon emerged on the American side—"Remember the Waxhaws!" and "Tarleton's quarter!"

June 5, 1780: British general Clinton sailed from Charles Town for New York City, leaving command of all British and Loyalist troops in the South to Gen. Charles Cornwallis.

June 13, 1780: Having learned of the disastrous American surrender of Charles Town, the Continental Congress named Horatio Gates, the victor of the Saratoga Campaign of 1777, to lead the American army of the South. Gates left Philadelphia almost immediately and rode south to take command.

July 25, 1780: Gates took command of what was left of the American army of the South— only 2,000–3,000 militiamen—at Coxe's Mill, North Carolina.

August 16, 1780 (Battle of Camden): American general Gates collided with British general Cornwallis at Camden, South Carolina. Gates, who had the reputation of being a fine tactician, had led his men (many of them untested recruits) from North Carolina. Cornwallis had marched north, seeking to defeat Gates. The battle was perhaps the most unfortunate for the Americans during the entire war. Gates's men fought stubbornly on the right flank (commanded by the Bavarian born American general, Johann de Kalb), but the American left flank disappeared as Gates's untested militia fled from a British bayonet attack. Gates himself escaped from the battle on horseback, his reputation ruined. The true American hero of the day was de Kalb, who fought and led his men with great valor until he collapsed, dying from 11 different wounds. When the day ended, Gates's army of the American South was completely shattered. The Americans suffered almost 1,000 men killed or wounded (British losses were only 215), and the militia forces soon melted away into the South Carolina backcountry, leaving almost nothing that could properly be termed an army. When news of the battle reached Philadelphia and the other northern cities, pessimism grew on the American side. The combination of the defeats at Charles Town, Waxhaws, and Camden weighed heavily on patriot morale throughout the fall of 1780.

August 18, 1780: British colonel Banastre Tarleton followed up the victory at Camden with a win over American general Thomas Sumter on the Catawba River in South Carolina. Suffering losses of only 15 men killed or wounded, Tarleton inflicted casualties of 150 men killed or wounded and took 500 Americans prisoner. Even neutral observers of the overall conduct of the war were forced to conclude that further American resistance in the South was unlikely.

September 8, 1780: Having gathered and concentrated his forces in the aftermath of the victory at Camden, British general Cornwallis began a full-scale invasion of North Carolina.

October 7, 1780 (Battle of Kings Mountain): On a hilltop in York County, South Carolina, just south of the border between North Carolina and South Carolina, British major Patrick Ferguson fought a fierce and desperate battle against American frontiersmen, who had gathered in the backcountry to resist his advance. Ferguson led 1,000 Loyalists, the western wing of General Cornwallis's invasion force. Ferguson was noted for his technical brilliance (he had invented a breech-loading rifle, one that was loaded at the base of the barrel, not at the muzzle) and for his dislike of all patriot Americans. He had prompted the attack by announcing that he would march through the backcountry and pillage those areas that were disloyal to the crown.

The backcountry American patriots (1,000 men led by Col. William Campbell of Virginia) charged the hillside a number of times. What unnerved Ferguson's men was the unerring marksmanship of the backwoodsmen. Disdaining to surrender to a "band of banditti," Ferguson led a suicidal charge down the hill; his body was pierced by at least ten different shots. Following his death, Ferguson's men tried to surrender. Many of the Loyalists were killed in cold blood by patriots who cried, "Tarleton's quarter!" The patriots suffered 28 killed and 60 wounded; Ferguson's column, made up almost entirely of Loyalists, suffered 157 killed, 163 wounded, and 698 taken prisoner. Not only had the backwoodsmen wiped out Ferguson's force, they also had eliminated the western wing of Cornwallis's invasion of North Carolina.

October 1780: Learning of the defeat of Ferguson, Cornwallis ordered a stop to the invasion of North Carolina.

October 14, 1780: After having solicited the advice of General Washington, the Continental Congress named Gen. Nathaniel Greene the new leader of the American army in the South.

December 2, 1780: General Greene arrived at Charlotte, North Carolina, and assumed command of what was left of the American southern army: 2,300 men, many of them militia. Greene had two strengths that were not obvious—his sound strategic sense and the brilliant tactical ability of his second in command, Col. Daniel Morgan, who had served with distinction at Quebec in 1775 and at Saratoga in 1777.

December 1780: Disregarding all the conventional rules of warfare, General Greene made a conscious decision to divide his numerically inferior force. Even though General Cornwallis was only 70 miles away with 5,000 men, Greene divided his small army into two sections, sending Daniel Morgan with half the army north while he led the other half south toward Cheraw, South Carolina. That strategy, one of the truly outrageous gambles undertaken by any general during the war, produced the effect that Greene desired. Cornwallis soon divided his army in two, sending a column under Colonel Tarleton after Morgan while he pursued Greene.

FRONTIER THEATER

January 28, 1780: Fort Narborough (renamed Fort Nashville in 1782) was established on the Cumberland River in present-day Tennessee to secure that area from attacks from Indians coming from present-day Ohio.

August 6, 1780: George Rogers Clark led a force of Virginia and Kentucky militiamen in an assault on the chief Shawnee Indian town of Chillicothe (in present-day Ohio). The Americans captured the town suffering a loss of 20 men killed, 40 wounded. The Americans reported taking 73 scalps.

NAVAL THEATER

June 1, 1780: American captain James Nicolson led the frigate *Trumbull* in a grueling two-and-one-half-hour fight with the British privateer *Watt* 250 miles south of Bermuda. The Americans suffered 6 killed and 32 wounded, and the British suffered 90 killed or wounded in a battle that rivaled that between the *Bonhomme Richard* and the *Serapis* in intensity. The British ship managed to escape after a chase of several hours.

HOME FRONT

March 18, 1780: The Continental Congress passed the Forty to One Act, which provided for continental paper money to become redeemable at one-fortieth its face value.

INTERNATIONAL DEVELOPMENTS

December 20, 1780: The United Provinces of the Netherlands (commonly known as Holland) initiated hostilities against England. The Dutch made no formal alliance with the Americans but simply were fighting for what they perceived were the rights of neutrals at sea. Although their formal declaration of war added another country to the list of England's enemies, the Dutch had little effect on the struggle taking place in North America.

BATTLES AND CAMPAIGNS: 1781-1782

There were four areas of activity in 1781 and 1782: northern theater, southern theater, frontier theater, and naval theater.

NORTHERN THEATER

January 1–8, 1781: A crisis developed among the troops of the Pennsylvania line of the Continental Army quartered in Morristown, New Jersey. Claiming rightfully that they were underpaid and poorly fed, troops of the Pennsylvania line (whose commander was Gen. Anthony Wayne) mutinied. Mortified by the mutiny, General Wayne both negotiated with the men and threatened them. On the first day of the mutiny, one of Wayne's officers was killed and two others were wounded. Wayne controlled his formidable temper and, at certain points, acted as a champion for the rights of his men. Following several days of quasi negotiations and quasi threats by Wayne, the mutiny was quelled. A board of sergeants was appointed to investigate the matter. The entire affair was extremely serious for General Washington and the Continental Army, occurring at a time when all the news coming from the southern front was bad and when France and Spain were showing signs of wearying of the war.

January 20, 1781: Troops of the New Jersey line of the Continental Army mutinied in Pompton, New Jersey. The mutiny was suppressed on January 27 by 600 men sent by General Washington, and two of the mutineers were executed.

March 6, 1781: Washington went to Newport, Rhode Island, to meet with the Comte de Rochambeau, leader of the 5,000-man French force. Speaking through interpreters, Washington and Rochambeau reached agreement on two basic points: Washington would serve as the overall commander of the French-American troops (when the two forces were united), and the French-American troops would plan to attack and recapture New York City sometime during 1781.

April 1781: In a letter to the Continental Congress, Washington laid out the desperate situation of the Continental Army. Referring to low supplies, low morale, and an overall sense of futility, Washington concluded with the statement, "We are at the end of our tether."

May 21, 1781: Washington and Rochambeau met at Wethersfield, Connecticut. The second meeting between the generals concluded with an agreement to unite the French and American troops and to move directly to the area surrounding New York City.

May 22, 1781: Washington learned that the French naval leader in the Caribbean, Adm. François Paul de Grasse, intended to bring all or part of his fleet northward during the summer months. Believing that de Grasse would come into New York Harbor, Washington intensified his preparations for a French-American assault on New York City.

June 1781: Washington brought the Continental Army from New Windsor, New York, to Peekskill, New York, and began tentative operations against King's Bridge on the Hudson River.

July 1781–August 14, 1781: Washington and Rochambeau jointly conducted a lengthy reconnaissance of the British defenses around Manhattan Island. Both men became gloomy about the prospect for a successful assault, given the strength of the British defenses. However, Washington's sense of desperation (given the hard winter at Morristown and the mutinies of January 1781) impelled him to believe that the French-American forces (united under his command) must attack the city.

August 14, 1781: Washington and Rochambeau received a lengthy dispatch from French admiral de Grasse. De Grasse sprang the surprising news that he would bring his ships to Chesapeake Bay, not to the New York City area.

August 14–15, 1781: During the night, Washington came to a momentous, albeit painful, decision. Given that de Grasse's ships were headed toward Chesapeake Bay and that New York City would be impervious to an attack that lacked naval support, Washington made the crucial decision to march the entire French-American army south to try to box in General Cornwallis at Yorktown, with his back to the Chesapeake Bay. Having greatly desired to launch an attack on New York City, Washington abandoned his greatest wish, to attempt what was realistically impossible,

given the circumstances.

August 21, 1781: The bulk of the French-American army departed from King's Bridge on the Hudson River and marched south toward Philadelphia and Chesapeake Bay. Washington left a scant 2,500 troops under Gen. William Heath to guard the American position on the Hudson River. In the absence of Washington and the main part of the Continental Army, Heath and his men constructed dummy fortifications and made feints against New York City. So successful were they in those efforts that General Clinton, safe inside New York City with 13,000 troops, made no move to take the offense.

September 1, 1781: The French part of the French-American army made a grand march through Philadelphia.

SOUTHERN THEATER

January 5–6, 1781: Benedict Arnold, who had become a general in the British army, brought 1,200 British troops to capture Richmond, Virginia. Having arrived off the coast of Virginia on December 30, 1780, Arnold intended to bring discomfort and disaster to the patriot cause in Virginia (a state that had suffered relatively little during the six years of war).

January 17, 1781 (Battle of Cowpens): American colonel Daniel Morgan inflicted a tremendous defeat on the British forces of Col. Banastre Tarleton. Knowing that his 1,000-man force was being pursued by a force of equal size under Tarleton, Morgan stopped and chose his battleground—the high rolling ground in Cowpens, South Carolina. With the Broad River to his back, Morgan left no avenue of retreat. Morgan arranged his troops in three distinct lines. The first line was composed of militia troops who were to fire two rounds at the British and then withdraw to the rear; the second line was made up of more seasoned Continental troops who were to engage the enemy in hand-to-hand fighting, if necessary; the third and last line was composed of Morgan's hard-core veterans and a small cavalry troop led by Col. William Washington (a second cousin once removed of Gen. George Washington).

Tarleton and his men arrived on the scene early in the morning of January 17. He and his troops had marched for days in pursuit of Morgan, but Tarleton did not allow his men to pause for breakfast. Having overcome American detachments at

Waxhaws and Camden with overwhelming attacks, Tarleton decided to make the same play at Camden and gave the order to attack at once.

As Tarleton's men charged up the slight incline toward the Americans, the first line of Morgan's men delivered two volleys, then retired to the rear in good order. Believing that their retirement was the sign of a general retreat, Tarleton threw all his reserve units against the American line. Instead of breaking under the strain, the second line of Morgan's men delivered volleys of musket fire, then came to grips with the advancing British, resulting in a fierce hand-to-hand contest. As the conflict raged, Colonel Washington led his cavalrymen around the British wings and encircled the British in a classic double envelopment—a maneuver military commanders have praised as the highest form of battle tactics since the Carthaginian general Hannibal employed it against the Romans. To his shock and disbelief, Tarleton found that his battle line was falling apart and that Colonel Washington's cavalrymen were upon him. Tarleton and Washington came into striking range of each other. They exchanged pistol fire and sword thrusts before Tarleton escaped from the contest and from the battle itself. The British could not believe the results of the one-hour's fighting, considering the confidence with which they had approached the battle. In what was the most tactically brilliant performance by any general on either side during the entire war, Morgan had nearly annihilated the British column. The British suffered 110 killed, 229 wounded, and 550 taken prisoner. The Americans suffered 12 killed and 60 wounded. Moreover, Tarleton's defeat erased the western wing of General Cornwallis's advance into North Carolina.

January 24, 1781: In the aftermath of Tarleton's defeat, General Cornwallis resolved to risk everything in an attempt to catch up with the retreating American troops under General Greene. Cornwallis made the decision to order his men at Ramsour's Mill, North Carolina, to burn all the baggage they could not carry. When news of this reached General Greene a few days later, he exclaimed, "Then he is ours!"

January 25–February 14, 1781 (Race to the Dan River): In a series of classic military maneuvers, Greene and Cornwallis engaged in a headlong race to reach the Dan River in North Carolina. Swollen by winter rains, the Dan would prove a formidable obstacle to whichever army came second to the scene: both generals were aware that there would be a limited number of boats to ferry troops across. Having lightened the load of his men, Cornwallis pressed forward with great urgency, and his dispatches, when they were read in New York City and in England, revealed the crucial importance of the race.

February 13–14, 1781: The American army of the South, led by General Greene and Colonel Morgan (who had recombined after the battle of Cowpens), reached the Dan River and made its way across in the only boats available. Approximately one hour after the last Americans had crossed the river, British troops burst through the woods on the southern bank of the river. The lag of three to four hours had made all the difference. Greene and his men were safe on the northern bank of the river, and Cornwallis and his troops (bereft of their baggage) stood helplessly on the southern bank. The race to the Dan River was followed with great interest by strategic planners in New York City and in London, and when they learned that Greene had won the race, many British became pessimistic.

March 15, 1781 (Battle of Guilford Court House): Led by General Greene, the American army of the South came to grips again with the British under Cornwallis and Tarleton. Greene had rested and regrouped his men on the northern bank of the Dan River, then recrossed the river and sought a battle with the British. Ever eager for battle, Cornwallis pushed his footsore and hungry men into battle, and the result was a fight seldom matched for ferocity throughout the war. The British, 2,300 strong, attacked the 4,000-man American army. Fought in a fashion similar to the Battle of Cowpens (again, the British attacked up a long, gradual incline), Guilford Court House proved to be a death trap for many British soldiers. At one point in the battle, when it seemed as though the Americans might break his lines and win a complete victory, Cornwallis ordered his cannons in the rear to fire into the melee of fighting soldiers. Numerous British as well as Americans were killed by that artillery fire. That desperate act technically saved Cornwallis from defeat, and at the end of the day, he held possession of the field, but at the cost of 143 killed and 389 wounded. American casualties were 78 killed, 183 wounded. When news of Cornwallis's victory reached London, Charles James Fox, the leader of the Loyal Opposition to His Majesty's Government, declared that "one more such victory would prove the ruin of the British army."

March 18, 1781: In the wake of the costly battle at Guilford Court House, Cornwallis began a slow retreat to the North Carolina coast. Greene did not pursue the British. Knowing that Cornwallis would seek to invade Virginia, Greene marched south to confront Cornwallis's subordinate, Lord Francis Rawdon, who had become the British commander in South Carolina in Cornwallis's absence.

April 25, 1781: Cornwallis led his battered and weary troops from Wilmington, North Carolina, and headed toward Virginia. Believing that he would be best served by remaining close to the coast (and hence close to the support of the British navy), Cornwallis resolved to combine forces with Benedict Arnold and to conquer Virginia.

At the same time, General Greene's men fought the British troops under Lord Rawdon at Hobkirk's Hill, South Carolina. Greene left possession of the field to the British but caused 200 casualties to Lord Rawdon's force—casualties that the British could not afford. Soon after that battle, Lord Rawdon moved farther south in a thinly disguised retreat. Greene wrote a letter to the French ambassador to the United States explaining his general approach to warfare in the American South: "We fight, get beat, rise and fight again."

May 9, 1781: Gov. Bernardo Galvez of Louisiana led Spanish troops in the capture of the British fort and town at Pensacola, Florida. The British surrender of 1,113 officers and men gave Galvez and the Spanish virtual control of the western section of Florida.

June 4, 1781: British colonel Tarleton (having come north with General Cornwallis) made a surprise cavalry descent on Charlottesville, Virginia. Tarleton sought to catch Virginia governor Thomas Jefferson napping there but missed Jefferson by only a few minutes.

June 1781: An American force of around 5,000 men commanded by Generals Lafayette, Wayne, and von Steuben feinted and retreated in a series of maneuvers against General Cornwallis's 7,000-man army in Virginia. Lafayette's mission was to contain Cornwallis and keep the British close to the seacoast.

July 6, 1781: In the battle of Green Spring Farm, Virginia, Lafayette came to grips with the larger army of General Cornwallis. Only reckless bravery on the part of General Wayne's men prevented a disaster for the Americans. As it was, they suffered 28 killed and 99 wounded.

August 1, 1781: Concluding a series of raids against towns and plantations in Virginia, General Cornwallis settled in at the coastal settlement of Yorktown, Virginia. Cornwallis believed that as long as he had access to the sea (and the British navy) he had nothing to fear from the American forces. What Cornwallis's confidence disguised was that after more than a year of campaigning in the American South, he had lost two major detachments of troops (those of Ferguson and Tarleton) and that he had been "exiled" north into Virginia, while General Greene was taking apart the gains the British had made in South Carolina during 1780.

August 1781: During the month of August, Cornwallis's men dug in at Yorktown. Lafayette's small American army, which was shadowing Cornwallis's army, grew through both reinforcements and militia recruitments.

August 30, 1781: A French fleet, with 28 ships of the Comte de Grasse, was sighted in Chesapeake Bay by British and American observers.

September 8, 1781: General Greene met the British forces under Col. Alexander Stewart at Eutaw Springs, South Carolina. In what was a trying day for Greene, his troops won the early part of the battle easily and proceeded to loot the British encampment. In the afternoon, the Americans were stunned by a successful British counterattack. The affair killed, wounded, and otherwise eliminated 600 men in both the British and the American forces. Greene again yielded possession of the field, but the British soon left the area and moved to a defensive line 12 miles north of Charles Town, South Carolina.

September 14–24, 1781: With the assistance of transport ships provided by the Comte de Grasse, Washington and Rochambeau brought their men down Chesapeake Bay to just outside Yorktown, where they combined forces with the Marquis de Lafayette. The encirclement of Cornwallis was complete. For his part, Cornwallis was aware of the dangers posed by the French-American forces, but he retained some hope that British general Clinton would soon depart New York City with a strong fleet and army to rescue the British cause in Virginia.

September 28, 1781: The siege of the tobacco town of Yorktown, Virginia, inhabited by Cornwallis's 7,000 troops, began in earnest. Eleven thousand American troops and 7,000 French soldiers and sailors surrounded the town.

October 6, 1781: The French-American forces established the first parallel of their siege fortifications outside Yorktown.

October 14, 1781: American and French troops stormed and captured two key British redoubts (fortifications) in night attacks. The attacks were planned and implemented by American colonel Alexander Hamilton and French colonel Guillaume Deux-Ponts. The capture of the two redoubts allowed American engineers to begin construction of a massive second-siege line—this one only 250 yards from the British lines.

That same day, British general Henry Clinton appeared off Chesapeake Bay with a sizable British fleet carrying 7,000 men. Before he could set his troops ashore and in position, he learned of the surrender of Cornwallis on October 19 and sailed back to New York City.

October 16, 1781: General Cornwallis sent 350 of his men on a night sortie against one of the American strongholds. The British briefly took possession of the redoubt and were able to spike (disable by caulking the firing holes) some French and American cannon before being forced to withdraw. The French-American engineers quickly repaired ths redoubt and brought up replacement guns, which were soon firing as many rounds as before into the British lines, making the sortie a costly escapade that had no significant result.

October 17, 1781: A British drummer boy appeared on the ramparts of the British defensive works at Yorktown and began to beat the "long roll," an internationally recognized signal for a flag of truce (or parley).

October 19, 1781: General Cornwallis surrendered 7,087 officers and men, 144 cannons, 30 transport ships, 15 galleys, a frigate, and 900 seamen to the French-American forces at Yorktown. Cornwallis pleaded illness and did not attend the surrender ceremony but sent his second in command, Gen. Charles O'Hara, who carried Cornwallis's sword, to surrender. The British and Hessian troops marched solemnly in front of the French-American victors, and the British bands played the song "The World Turned Upside Down." General O'Hara marched to the French commander, General Rochambeau, and tried to present Cornwallis's sword. Rochambeau shook his head and pointed to General Washington. O'Hara went to the American commander, who

declined to accept the sword, saying, "Never from so good a hand." Instead, Washington pointed O'Hara to American general Benjamin Lincoln, who had been forced to surrender to Clinton and Cornwallis at Charles Town in 1780. Thus, the American commander who had suffered the greatest single humiliation of the war (see May 19, 1780, p. 91) was accorded the honor of receiving the sword of Cornwallis. During the siege, the British suffered 156 killed and 326 wounded; the French suffered 60 killed, 107 wounded; the Americans suffered 20 killed, 56 wounded. The battle ended the major military operations of the British in the war, and from that point on British troops essentially disengaged themselves from combat on the North American continent.

FRONTIER THEATER

January 1781: Spanish troops captured British Fort St. Joseph in the Illinois country. Holding the fort for only 24 hours, the Spanish later used this conquest as a rationale for Spanish control of the Fort St. Joseph and Illinois River areas.

April–June 1781: Indian and Loyalist forces led by Joseph Brant and Col. William Butler conducted raids and attacks throughout the length and breadth of the Mohawk River valley in upstate New York. Fort Stanwix was blockaded, and in May, that post, which had withstood the siege of Colonel St. Leger in 1777 and which had remained a sign of the American determination to defend the frontier, was abandoned.

March 6–7, 1782: American colonel David Williamson led frontier troops in the massacre of 90 Christian Delaware Indians in the Gnadenhutten villages on the Muskingum River in the Ohio Territory. The Americans had suspected, incorrectly, that the Indians were helping the British and other Indian tribes in attacks on American frontier settlements in the region.

July 4–5, 1782: Five hundred Wyandot, Mingo, and Delaware Indians defeated American colonel William Crawford near Upper Sandusky in present-day Ohio.

August 19, 1782: American frontier fighters from Kentucky met and fought a collaboration of Indian and Loyalist fighters on the middle fork of the Licking River near present-day Lexington, Kentucky. The fight, soon to be known as "Blue Licks," was disastrous for the Americans; in 20 minutes they suffered 77 men killed or wounded.

November 1782: Seeking to revenge the defeat at Blue Licks, American colonel George Rogers Clark led 1,050 mounted men from the Kentucky area into Shawnee Indian lands in present-day Ohio, destroying Shawnee villages. On November 10, Clark and his men burned Chillicothe. They then returned to the mouth of the Licking River, ending a campaign that made 1782 the "Year of Sorrow" for the American frontier settlers and the Indians. Clark's campaign is regarded by some historians as the final military operation of the Revolution.

NAVAL THEATER

April 2, 1781: American naval captain John Barry, commanding the *Alliance*, captured two British privateers, the *Mars* and the *Minerva*, while returning from France to the United States.

May 29, 1781: Capt. Barry Nego captured two British men-of-war, the *Atlanta* and *Trepassy.*

August 5, 1781: As he had promised in a letter to George Washington and Jean Baptiste Rochambeau (a letter they received on August 14), French admiral de Grasse left Haiti, with his entire fleet of 28 ships, carrying 3,000 French troops and headed for Chesapeake Bay.

August 30, 1781: Admiral de Grasse anchored in Chesapeake Bay, thereby blocking British general Cornwallis from supplies and reinforcements.

September 5–8, 1781 (Battle of the Capes): Near Cape Henry and Cape Charles on Chesapeake Bay, Admiral de Grasse learned of the approach of 19 British ships under Adm. Thomas Graves and Adm. Samuel Hood. Rather than wait to defend his position in the bay, de Grasse ordered his captains to slip their cables and make sail to fight the British in the open sea. His hasty move meant that hundreds of French sailors (ashore helping the land forces) were unable to participate in the ensuing Battle of the Capes (sometimes called the Battle of Cape Henry). De Grasse brought out 24 ships to battle the enemy. The French superiority in numbers was at first nullified by the British possession of a favorable wind. A cautious leader, Admiral Graves engaged the French in a line-to-line and ship-to-ship formation that almost guaranteed the battle would be a draw. The French advance, led by Comdr. Louis de Bouganville (who would later rival Captain Cook as an explorer), confronted the British advance led by Adm. Francis Samuel Drake. During the battle, the French suffered 209 men killed or wounded, and the British suffered 336 men killed or wounded. For the next four days, the two fleets drifted slowly south by southeast. Then, on September 9, Admiral de Grasse reversed direction and returned to Chesapeake Bay, where he found, to his delight, that a squadron of eight French ships under Admiral de Barras had slipped by the British to join him. When the British fleet returned and saw the 32 French ships drawn up in battle formation in the bay, British admiral Graves asked his second in command, Admiral Hood, for advice. Hood, who had privately disparaged his chief's cautious approach to the Battle of the Capes, sent back the following remark: "Sir Samuel Hood would be very glad to send an opinion, but he really knows not what to say in the truly lamentable state we have brought ourselves." The British effectively left the field to the French.

HOME FRONT

February 20, 1781: The Continental Congress appointed Robert Morris superintendent of finance of the United States.

March 1, 1781 (Articles of Confederation): Following the ratification of the Articles of Confederation by the delegates of Maryland, the Continental Congress declared the Articles of Confederation had become the law of the land. On March 2, the Congress gave itself a new title: The United States in Congress Assembled.

July 21, 1781: Rebellious black slaves in Williamsburg, Virginia, set fire to the capitol and several other buildings.

December 31, 1781: The United States in Congress Assembled officially chartered the Bank of North America, one of the first institutions created by Robert Morris, to finance the war.

December 13, 1782: British forces departed Charles Town, South Carolina, taking with them 4,000 Loyalists and a significant number of blacks.

INTERNATIONAL DEVELOPMENTS

November 25, 1781: Official news of Cornwallis's surrender reached London. British prime minister Lord North reacted to the news by exclaiming, "O God! It's all over!"

November 27, 1781: Parliament convened in London. King George III's "Speech from the throne" sought to convey the news of Yorktown gently, but members of the Loyal Opposition began loud calls for the resignation of Prime Minister North.

March 4, 1782: The British Parliament passed a resolution that characterized as an enemy to the country and the king anyone who attempted to continue the war in North America. The instigator of this resolution was Charles James Fox, a staunch opponent of King George III and his Tory supporters.

March 20, 1782: British prime minister Lord North resigned his position, which he had held since January 1770. He was replaced by a ministry led by the Marquis of Rockingham.

July 1, 1782: The Marquis of Rockingham died, after only a brief tenure as prime minister of England. He was replaced by the Earl of Shelburne.

September 13, 1782: A French-Spanish naval armada attacked the British fortress of Gibraltar. The armada was largely destroyed by British artillery firing from Gibraltar. The result was that British popular opinion turned toward a vigorous prosecution of the war, at least as far as France and Spain were concerned.

NEGOTIATIONS AND PEACE TREATY

There were efforts to bring about a peace settlement soon after the war began in 1775. Three notable efforts were the Olive Branch Petition, the Howe Brothers Peace Commission, and the Carlisle Peace Commission, all of which failed. After the entrance into the war of France (1778), Spain (1779), and Holland (1780), efforts to make peace became infinitely more complicated. France wanted to strip away parts of the British Empire; Spain was adamant in its insistence on regaining Gibraltar (the fortress it had lost to England in 1704); and Holland perceived itself as defending the rights of neutrals at sea. To make matters even more convoluted, Austria and Russia offered to conduct mediation, offers that were spurned by King George III, who insisted that the British war with America was a "family matter." During 1781, all the countries involved conducted diplomatic negotiations (some of them secret, some of them open) with one another; each country tried to gain some advantage in a situation that had evolved into a deadlock. What changed the scenario was Cornwallis's surrender at Yorktown. Lord North's ministry fell soon after that surrender, and England became more amenable to negotiations with the Americans. The new British ministry, led first by the Marquis of Rockingham, and then by the Earl of Shelburne, adroitly created suspicion and then separation between the French and American allies. The Americans and British signed preliminary articles of peace in November 1782 and final articles of peace in September 1783.

July 5, 1775: The Continental Congress adopted the Olive Branch Petition, written by Pennsylvania delegate John Dickinson. The petition reiterated the Americans' grievances against England, but declared their intention and desire to bring about a lasting settlement with England.

November 9, 1775: The Continental Congress learned that King George III had refused to meet with Richard Penn (a descendant of Quaker leader William Penn), who had carried the Olive Branch Petition to London. That was extremely disappointing to many members of Congress, who had, up to that point, believed that only Parliament was uncompromising and that King George III was well disposed toward a peace with America.

March 1776: In London, British admiral Richard Howe informed the British colonial secretary, Lord George Germain, that he would serve against the Americans only if he and his brother, Gen. William Howe, were granted status as peacemakers along with their roles as military and naval commanders.

May 6, 1776: British admiral Richard Howe and his brother, Gen. William Howe, received their final instructions from London. The two brothers were authorized to act as special commissioners to the American rebels and were empowered to grant pardons to Americans and to lift trade restrictions on sections of the colonies that asked for clemency.

July 14, 1776: The Howe brothers, anchored off the coast of North America, issued a joint declaration of their intention to establish peace. They sent a copy addressed to "George Washington, Esq., etc. etc." to the American ships around New York City. Washington refused to consider a peace commission that did not even recognize his status as the American commander in chief.

September 11, 1776: American peace commissioners, led by Benjamin Franklin, met with Adm. Richard Howe on Staten Island. The Americans soon ascertained that Howe was empowered only to offer pardons, and, therefore, they broke off the conference.

November 1776: The Howe brothers gave up

on their peace mission, having been rebuffed by Washington, the Continental Congress, and the American public at large.

March 16, 1778: The British House of Commons passed two bills that were initiated by Prime Minister Lord North. The bills aimed at a reconciliation between Great Britain and North America. Cognizant of the signing of the French-American alliance (see International Developments, p. 87), Lord North offered many concessions to the Americans that amounted to home rule.

April 16, 1778: The Carlisle Peace Commission (headed by Frederick Howard, the fifth Earl of Carlisle) departed from Portsmouth, England.

June 11, 1778: The dispatches of the Carlisle Peace Commission reached the Continental Congress. The Continental Congress made a reply on June 17, 1778, to the effect that any negotiations between the United States and England had to be preceded by the withdrawal of all British soldiers and ships from North America. In order to prevent the British from winning popular sympathy, the congress printed and circulated copies of the dispatches throughout the states; the terms were rebuffed by most Americans, and copies were publicly burned in some cities.

September 27, 1779: The Continental Congress named John Jay minister plenipotentiary to Spain and John Adams minister plenipotentiary to negotiate with the British.

June 11, 1781: The Continental Congress formed a commission to negotiate peace with England. John Adams was the first named to the commission; John Jay was named second on June 13. Benjamin Franklin, Henry Laurens, and Thomas Jefferson were named to the commission on June 14. (Of the above, all served except Jefferson, who was occupied in Virginia.)

June 15, 1781: The Continental Congress wrote instructions to its peace commission abroad. The commissioners were directed to seek American independence and sovereignty, with most other points left open to the discretion of the commission. However, the commissioners were firmly instructed to consult with French diplomats on all the major issues of the peace and to "ultimately govern yourselves by their advice and opinion."

November 25, 1781: News of Cornwallis's surrender reached London. British prime minister Lord North saw the futility of continuing the war in North America, but his opinion was not shared by his monarch, King George III.

March 20, 1782: Lord North resigned and was replaced by Lord Rockingham.

April 12, 1782: Richard Oswald, the unofficial representative of Lord Rockingham, arrived in Paris and began talks with Benjamin Franklin. Oswald, who had spent a number of years in North America, established a rapport with Franklin, and the two men discussed everything from fishing rights to Canada. Franklin believed that England should yield Canada to the United States.

April 1782: John Jay departed from Madrid for Paris to join Benjamin Franklin and John Adams. During his two years at the court of King Charles III of Spain, Jay had met mainly with frustration; the Spanish were determined to obtain Gibraltar and to keep control of the mouth of the Mississippi River. The first of their desires had the potential to hold up the peace process, and the second was against the wishes of the Americans.

June 23, 1782: Jay arrived in Paris and added his voice to that of the American peace commission. Although Henry Laurens did play a role, it was essentially Jay, Adams, and Franklin who negotiated the peace.

August 10, 1782: A tense meeting was held at Versailles between the Comte de Vergennes and the American peace commissioners. Vergennes pressed upon the Americans his view that they should make reasonable and moderate demands during the negotiations. Vergennes felt strongly that the Americans would need to reimburse the Loyalists for the losses they had suffered during the war. After the meeting, Adams and Jay became firmer in joint resolution to negotiate a treaty for the United States with England directly (without the advice and opinion of France). Franklin pointed out that that was counter to their instructions of June 15, 1781.

September 13, 1782: The French-Spanish armada attempted and failed to capture Gibraltar. Following the debacle, Spanish diplomats remained firm in their insistence that Gibraltar must be returned to Spain.

September 19, 1782: The Shelburne ministry in London gave Richard Oswald formal authorization to negotiate with the Americans.

October 5, 1782: John Jay gave Richard Oswald a draft for a treaty between the United States and England.

October 28, 1782: Henry Strachey arrived in Paris from London. He became the second key commissioner for the British negotiating team.

November 1, 1782: Adams and Jay won Franklin over to their position regarding French advice and opinion. Franklin agreed to negotiate directly with the British and to withhold information about the negotiations from the Comte de Vergennes.

November 5, 1782: A new set of articles was exchanged between the American and British negotiating teams. Among the key issues were (1) Loyalist compensation, (2) fishing rights, (3) boundaries, and (4) terms of evacuation by British troops from North America.

November 30, 1782: The American and British peace commissions signed preliminary articles of peace in Paris. The terms were extremely favorable to the Americans. The United States of America was deemed fully independent, and the boundaries of the new country were set forth in full and generous detail. American fishermen were granted access to the Grand Banks off Nova Scotia and Newfoundland as well as the right to cut and dry their fish on the shores of Nova Scotia. (New Englander John Adams wrote home that "our Tom Cod are safe in spite of the malice of enemies, the finesse of allies, and the mistakes of Congress.") The United States was to extend from present-day Maine to Georgia (Florida was still being contested by Britain and Spain). The northern border between the United States and British Canada was drawn at the 45th parallel of north longitude (at the Vermont and New Hampshire borders), cut through the center of Lake Ontario and Lake Erie, extended out to the Lake of the Woods (in present-day Minnesota). The western boundary of the United States was agreed to be the Mississippi River (an agreement that provoked future conflict between the United States and Spain). In return for all those concessions, the Americans agreed only that the Continental Congress would "earnestly recommend" to the state legislatures that the states grant compensation to Loyalists for their properties. The tenth and final article of the treaty provided for ratification by both countries.

December 5, 1782: In a speech from the throne to Parliament, King George III announced that he had negotiated a treaty with the Americans and that he was ready to declare them "free and independent states." Some observers claimed the king almost choked back the words as he uttered them.

December 1782: The French and Spanish negotiating teams continued to negotiate with British. The Comte de Vergennes, conscious that

his strength had been weakened by the action of the Americans, pressed upon Spain the necessity of coming to terms. The Spanish held out for further concessions, but the British were determined that Spain should not have Gibraltar. King Charles III and the Spanish court remained adamant in their demand for Gibraltar, but the key Spanish diplomat, the Conde de Aranda, disobeyed his instructions and continued to negotiate. When challenged by King Charles and others on his action, Aranda gave a memorable reply: *"¿Una roca, Excelentisimo, quanto turbada tres Imperios?"* ("How long, your Majesty, can one rock disturb the peace of three empires?")

January 20, 1783: Preliminary articles of peace between Britain, Spain, and France were signed. Spain gained Florida, Minorca, and minor trade privileges in Honduras. France gained some trading posts in Africa and the right to fish in areas of the Grand Banks off Newfoundland. England yielded a great deal, but its losses were smaller than they might have been considering that it had been engaged in a worldwide war and the magnitude of its defeat.

February 4, 1783: The British proclaimed a cessation of hostilities.

February 20, 1783: Lord Shelburne resigned as British prime minister and was replaced by Charles James Fox, a maverick politician.

April 11, 1783: The Continental Congress declared itself satisfied with the results of the preliminary articles of peace.

September 3, 1783 (Treaty of Paris): The final, or definitive, articles of peace between the United States and England were signed at the Hotel d'York on Rue Jacob in the Quartier Latin in Paris. The definitive articles reflected the preliminary articles of November 30, 1782, in almost all respects, but September 3, 1783, is generally regarded as the end of the American Revolution.

November 22, 1783: John Thaxter Jr., private secretary to John Adams, arrived in Philadelphia with copies of the definitive peace treaty.

November 25, 1783: British general Sir Guy Carleton withdrew from New York City. The British withdrawal, which had been underway since April 1783, included the removal of thousands of Loyalists and hundreds (perhaps thousands) of blacks who had served with the British during the war. Although the peace treaty required Carleton to yield the blacks to America, he declared that to do so would be to break the word of Lord Dunmore (and that of King George III), who had promised freedom to those who joined with the British.

January 14, 1784: The Continental Congress formally ratified the peace treaty with England.

May 12, 1784: Formal ratifications were exchanged between the British and the American diplomats in Paris.

RESULTS OF THE WAR (Casualties, Costs, Consequences)

American: There is no absolutely reliable figure for how many Americans served in the American Revolution. Some estimates run as high as 200,000 Americans who put on a uniform. That figure is perhaps exaggerated, but it indicates the great spirit of the Americans. The fact is that many fought without uniforms.

Casualties and losses were better documented than the total number of men who served. About 6,800 American patriots lost their lives in direct combat; somewhere around 10,000 died in British prisons (most notoriously in the British prison ships in New York Harbor); and another 10,000 died from wounds or disease in American camps and hospitals.

Financial costs were considerable, especially when one considers that the United States had yet to establish a sound system of credit when the war began. It is generally accepted that the cost of the war to the Americans was $104,042,000; that figure does not include the numerous loans and gifts made to the United States by France, Holland, and even (though reluctantly) Spain. The debts incurred by the Continental Congress and by the individual state legislatures (one thinks here of the cost to Massachusetts for the failed Penobscot expedition in 1779; see August 12, 1779, p. 88) remained an important and sometimes divisive issue in the new nation for years to come.

Commercial costs as well were high for the United States. Although American privateers won more than they lost, at least 800 merchant vessels were captured or destroyed during the war.

It was in terms of territory that the U.S. truly triumphed. When the war began, the 13 colonies extended only about 200 miles westward from the eastern seacoast. The legendary forays of Daniel Boone and others into Kentucky had just begun. When the war ended in 1783, the new United States claimed, based on the Treaty of Paris, territory from the eastern seacoast to the Mississippi River.

British: Only in recent years have historians come to realize the tremendous efforts and sacrifices made by England and the British people during the war. Even though their royal navy dominated, the British lost some 2,000 navy and civilian ships. Nearly a quarter of a million men are known to have served between 1775 and 1783 (110,000 in the army, 107,000 in the navy, and 40,000 in the "fencibles," or British militia). The British also hired the services of 30,000 German troops.

It is believed that some 50,000 British troops were killed, wounded, or missing during the war. This included British troops who fought against the French and Spanish in India and the Caribbean as well as those who fought in North America. Nonetheless, the figure was large enough to justify the recent description of the American Revolution as "Britain's Vietnam."

When the war began in 1775, the British national debt stood at 127 million English pounds; when the war ended in 1783, the national debt had reached 232 million English pounds.

Territorial losses were undeniably major, but not decisive for the future of England. The "First British Empire" had started with the colonization in North America in the early 1600s, and although England retained the vast territory of Canada, it undeniably suffered a major blow with the loss of the 13 colonies. Yet, the "Second British Empire," starting in 1783 and accelerating with the Napoleonic Wars with France, would become greater in size and go on to greater glory than the first.

Hessian: Some 30,000 German mercenaries fought for the British in North America during the Revolution. They were furnished by the German regions of Brunswick, Hesse-Cassel, Hesse-Hanau, Anspach-Bayreuth, Waldeck, and Anhalt-Zerbst. Of those 30,000, only 17,313 returned. Of the 12,600 or so who did not return, about 1,200 were killed or wounded in battle, 6,400 died of illnesses or accidents, and 5,000 deserted.

French: The French mobilized fewer soldiers than they had during the Seven Years' War, but, eventually, some 12,500 French troops saw some service in North America, 1,000 of whom lost their lives there. The French spent a great deal of time, energy, and money refitting the French navy. Although the French navy performed poorly in North American waters during 1778–1780, it redeemed itself fairly well against the British navy elsewhere. It certainly helped the Americans with its successes at Chesapeake Bay and at Yorktown in autumn 1781 (see pp. 96-98), but by 1782, the French navy was suffering heavily at the hands of the British navy. By 1783, the French had lost about 1,100 sailors killed and wounded in North American waters and many more fighting the British in Europe, India, and the Caribbean. (Sailors were more crucial than soldiers because they had skills that made them harder to replace.) When the war ended in 1783, France had expended at least 2 billion livres (about $4 billion in today's terms). The Comte de Vergennes had succeeded in the aims of his "grand alliance." France, Spain, Holland, and the United States had fought the British to at least a draw. But the results were catastrophic for the court of King Louis XVI. The French expenditures were too great to be absorbed by the feudal type of tax system that France lived under, and the French Revolution in 1789 swept away almost all the gains that Vergennes had made during the American Revolution.

Spanish: Spain made great efforts during the war, efforts that have been overlooked by many American historians. The Spanish pressure on British Florida and the diversion of British resources to hold on to Gibraltar contributed a good deal to the winning of American independence. That, of course, was not what the Spanish King Charles III and his court wanted; more farseeing than Vergennes, they accurately predicted that a successful revolution might have an adverse effect on their colonies in North America. During the war, Spain spent more than a billion reales (about $125 million U.S. in today's terms), a cost that the Spanish court was able to afford at that time. The greatest loss to Spain was the humiliation of Gibraltar's remaining in British hands.

Loyalist: The American Loyalists, or Tories, suffered greatly during and after the war. More than 100,000 Loyalists left America, some voluntarily, some under duress. Very few ever received any compensation for the properties they had forfeited in North America. Many Loyalists moved to Nova Scotia, and some were among the first settlers of present-day New Brunswick, Canada. Those who went to England were perhaps the least fortunate, and discouraged American Loyalists bearing petitions seeking compensation from King George III remained a regular sight in London for years to come.

Indian: The Native Americans may have been the most unfortunate of the combatants in the war. Most of the Indians fought for Britain, and the heavy losses of men, villages, and food supplies were devastating to the Six Iroquois Nations. The Shawnee and Wyandot Indians of the Ohio region came out of the war strong enough to hold on to their lands for a time, but the Cherokee and Iroquois tribes were mortally wounded when the war ended.

MILITARY INNOVATIONS, TACTICS, EQUIPMENT

All the combatants in the American Revolution used weaponry that was standard during the 18th century, including the "brown Bess" musket (so named because of its walnut stock), bayonets, fieldpieces, mortars, and howitzers. In the areas of military innovation and tactics, however, nearly all the combatants tried new and truly creative approaches to old problems on the battlefield. The failure of many of those new devices and approaches should not be taken as a condemnation. Indeed, many unsuccessful attempts at innovation made during the war led to successful implementation within 20 or 30 years' time.

American: The major American innovations were the Kentucky rifle (also known as the Pennsylvannia rifle), the first known use of the submarine, and floating explosives. The Kentucky—or Pennsylvania—rifle had a longer than usual barrel with its bore incised with spiral grooves. The rifle gave far greater accuracy and encouraged men to concentrate on their marksmanship. As the Western world was slowly turning from muskets to rifles, there were few sharpshooters as accurate as those from the American frontier. The rifle was employed with considerable success in specific battles including those fought by Daniel Morgan and his men at Saratoga (see September 19, 1777, p. 83).

In 1776, American inventor David Bushnell of Connecticut introduced the use of a submarine in warfare. On September 9, 1776, he piloted his experimental *Turtle* in New York Harbor, seeking to sink the flagship of the British fleet. Bushnell located the British ship but was unable to position his hand drill so that he could bore holes in the British ship. That and Bushnell's second innovation—the floating of explosive kegs on the Delaware River in 1777—were failures, but Bushnell's efforts provided the inspiration for later American development of submarines and floating mines.

It was in tactics that the Americans were extremely successful. From the first day's fighting on the road back to Boston from Concord (see April 19, 1775, pp. 74-75), the Americans showed an ability to use natural obstacles (such as trees, brush, etc.) to hide themselves while inflicting casualties on the British. American surprise attacks were often successful during the war; examples of surprise attacks are the capture of Fort Ticonderoga in 1775 and Washington's victories at Trenton and Princeton. However, the American skill at backwoods fighting and the use of surprise were insufficient to win the war. George Washington knew that, and he wanted, above all, to win a European style of victory on American soil. This wish was realized in the Yorktown campaign (see pp. 96-97).

British: The British employed few technical innovations during the war. Had they paid greater attention to Maj. Patrick Ferguson's invention of a breech-loading rifle (see Battle of King's Mountain, October 7, 1780, p. 92), the British might have gained a true advantage over the Americans. Instead the British largely stayed with their brown Bess, a smooth-bore, flintlock musket. In terms of tactics, time and again, the British showed themselves to be masterful in the European style of warfare—moving large units about in disciplined maneuvers, lining up troops in rows that fired successive volleys, charging with fixed bayonets. The proof of that lay in the British victories at Long Island, White Plains, Brandywine, and Germantown, where, again and again, the British outflanked and defeated the Americans. In the end, though, the British appear to have suffered from strategic shortsightedness. Cornwallis's venture into Virginia in 1781 stands forth as a good example, as does the failure of Burgoyne's three-pronged invasion of New York City in 1777.

French: The French employed almost no technical innovations during the war, although it has been claimed that the French ships were better built than those of their British adversaries. The French high commanders (Rochambeau and de Grasse) did exhibit an uncommon ability to foresee strategic results at Yorktown.

Spanish: In their attack upon Gibraltar in 1782, the Spanish used floating batteries of cannons, which were not very successful.

Indian: Something that has been overlooked in many histories is the skill and tenacity with which many of the Indian tribes fought. Armed by the British with muskets and powder, the Indians were formidable rivals of the Americans in the Ohio and Illinois regions. Tactically, the Indians used roughly the same type of hit-and-run strategy that they had employed in the French and Indian Wars.

LEGENDS AND TRIVIA

A number of legends sprang up during and after the American Revolution. Indeed, to the generation of Americans born between 1780 and 1800, the Revolution remained the primary event of their history. Many of the legends arising from the American Revolution had at least some basis in reality; several of them are presented here.

Molly Pitcher appears to have been a composite developed from several different American patriot women who served during the war. The name derives from the claim that those women carried water in pitchers to the troops in the front lines. The legend of Molly Pitcher has also come to represent women such as Mary Ludwig Hays McCauley, who took over from her husband at the battle of Monmouth, New Jersey, after he had collapsed from heat exhaustion, and continued to fire his cannon. Another example is Margaret Corbin, who was said to have stepped into her husband's position when he was mortally wounded at the battle of Harlem Heights in September 1776.

More documentation exists on the subject of **Deborah Sampson** (1760–1827). Deborah Sampson was born in Plympton, Massachusetts. In 1781, she disguised herself as a man and enlisted in the Continental Army under the name Robert Shurtleff (or in some versions, Robert Sampson). She served in several engagements and was wounded twice. One wound led a doctor to discover her true sex. After the war, she married a Massachusetts farmer and accepted speaking engagements throughout New England.

One of the most interesting legends associated with the Revolution concerns **Flora MacDonald**, who was born in Scotland in 1722. There, she helped the Stuart pretender to the British throne, Prince Charles Edward (Bonnie Prince Charlie), escape from the British after the battle of Culloden in 1746. Flora and her husband immigrated to North Carolina in 1774. When the war began in 1775, the MacDonalds kept their allegiance to King George III. Flora and her husband returned to Scotland by the end of the war.

Jane McCrae was killed and scalped by Indians serving with Burgoyne's army (see July 27, 1777, p. 82), McCrae came to stand as a vivid reminder of the atrocities of the British and their Indian allies. The irony is that McCrae was engaged either to a British or a Loyalist officer and that she never intended for her name to become a rallying cry for the patriot cause.

NOTABLE PHRASES

There were a great many notable phrases that came out of or were inspired by the American Revolution.

Now, one of the most essential branches of English liberty is the freedom of one's house. A man's house is his castle; and whilst he is quiet, he is as well guarded as a prince in his castle. This right, if it should be declared legal, would totally annihilate this privilege.

Massachusetts politician James Otis delivered a strong argument against the British writs of assistance in 1761. The writs of assistance allowed British customs officials to enter and search any home in their pursuit of smuggled goods. Although the expression "a man's house is his castle" had been around for centuries, it was Otis's use that revived it to inspire the American colonists.

Caesar had his Brutus; Charles the First his Cromwell; and George III [interrupted by shouts of "Treason! Treason"]—may profit by their example. If this be treason, make the most of it.

On May 29, 1765, Patrick Henry addressed the Virginia House of Burgesses. Referring to the Stamp Act and to the perceived injustice of British taxes being laid on America, Henry gave an impassioned speech in which he appeared to warn that King George III might follow in the tyrannical path of Julius Caesar, who had been assassinated, and King Charles I of England, who had been beheaded by his subjects in 1649.

No taxation without representation!

The precise origin of that, the most widespread of the phrases made famous during the Revolution, is uncertain. The English expression "taxation without representation is tyranny" had been coined by English patriot John Hamden in 1637. In North America, John Adams attributed the source of the American phrase to James Otis, but Adams's assertion never has been proved. (What we do know Otis said is, "No parts of His Majesty's dominions can be taxed without their consent.") In any case, the phrase became popular and pervasive among the American colonists.

What is it that gentlemen wish? What would they have? Is life so dear or peace so sweet as to be purchased at the price of chains and slavery? Forbid it, Almighty God. I know not what course others may take, but as for me, give me liberty or give me death!

On March 23, 1775, Patrick Henry spoke to the second Virginia Convention. Referring to the fact that Britain was sending more ships and troops to the colonies, Henry asserted that the colonists would do better to die in resistance than to tamely accept the oppressive rule of King George III.

Hang a lantern aloft in the belfrey arch
Of the Old North Church tower as a signal light,
One if by land, and two if by sea;
And I on the opposite shore will be,
Ready to ride and spread the alarm
Through every Middlesex village and farm
For the country folk to be up and to arm.

Those were the words of poet Henry Longfellow in his narrative poem "Paul Revere's Ride," written in 1863. Revere and his fellow patriots did use that signal, and Revere himself wrote of the signal in a letter to Dr. Jeremy Belknap on April 16, 1775.

What a glorious morning for America!

Samuel Adams is alleged to have exclaimed those words when he heard the sounds of gunfire coming from Lexington on April 19, 1775.

By the rude bridge that arched the flood,
Their flag to April's breeze unfurled,
Here once the embattled farmers stood,
And fired the shot heard round the world.

Those lines are from a poem composed by Ralph Waldo Emerson for the dedication of a monument at the site of the battle of Concord, held on July 4, 1837.

In the name of the great Jehovah, and the Continental Congress!

That was the response of Ethan Allen, leader of the Green Mountain Boys, when, on May 10, 1775, he was asked by the British commander of Fort Ticonderoga on whose authority he was making an attack on the fort.

Men, you are all marksmen—don't one of you fire until you see the whites of their eyes.

It has been alleged that Col. William Prescott so ordered the American defenders at Bunker Hill (actually Breed's Hill) on June 17, 1775. But the same or similar expression has also been attributed to other military leaders, from Israel Putnam (also at Breed's Hill) to King Frederick II of Prussia (Frederick the Great) during the Seven Years' War in Europe and to Prince Charles of Prussia at a battle in 1745.

Let us therefore animate and encourage each other, and show the whole world that a Freeman, contending for liberty on his own ground, is superior to any slavish mercenary on earth.

From his headquarters in New York, George Washington addressed those words to his troops in his General Orders of July 2, 1776.

There, I guess King George will be able to read that.

As president of the Continental Congress, John Hancock was the first of the 56 delegates to sign the Declaration of Independence. Well aware that he was a wealthy man and that the Declaration pledged the lives, liberty, and possessions of all who participated, Hancock is said to have pronounced those words as he signed with an especially bold flourish. To this day, Americans refer to a signature as "a John Hancock."

I only regret that I have but one life to lose for my country.

Those were said to have been the last words of Nathan Hale, the Connecticut schoolmaster who was caught behind the British lines on Long Is-

land and was hanged as a spy (September 22, 1776). If he did say them, he may well have been inspired by the English author Joseph Addison (1672–1719), who in his drama *Cato* (Act IV, Scene 4) had written, "What pity is it / That we can die but once to serve our country."

These are the times that try men's souls. The summer soldier and the sunshine patriot will, in this crisis, shrink from the service of their country; but he that stands it now, deserves the love and thanks of man and woman. Tyranny, like hell, is not easily conquered; yet we have this consolation with us, that the harder the conflict, the more glorious the triumph.

Thomas Paine wrote those words (published in *The American Crisis* on December 23, 1776) while Washington and the remnants of the Continental Army were encamped on the south bank of the Delaware River, prior to the surprise victories at Trenton and Princeton. The words affirmed Thomas Paine's place as the most consistently eloquent writer on behalf of the American cause.

I have not yet begun to fight!

Those words did not actually appear in writing until 1825, when an account of the battle between the *Bonhomme Richard* and the *Serapis* was written by Richard Dale. In his official account of the battle, John Paul Jones wrote that when called upon by the British commander to surrender, "I answered him in the most determined negative." A longer rendition of Jones's words is, "Ay, ay, we'll do that when we can fight no longer, but you shall see yours come down first; for you must know, that Yankees do not haul down their colors till they are fairly beaten."

Witness to the world that I die like a man.

Those were the last words of British major John André before he was hanged as a spy by the Americans on October 2, 1780.

SONGS

A number of songs have been identified as either having their origin in the American Revolution or as having gained prominence because of the war.

The most famous American song from the period was, of course, "Yankee Doodle," around which much controversy revolves. It is unclear whether the music originated in England or in some other European country. In any case, it was sung in the 13 colonies at least 15 years before the Revolution—probably introduced by British soldiers. (The British troops were said to have played "Yankee Doodle" as they marched on the minutemen in Lexington and Concord.) But although the tune was known as "Yankee Doodle," the words were often quite different from those known today. By the time of the Revolution, the American colonists had made the tune their own, and it was evidently during the late 1770s that the words we know today became the standard version (although other words continued to be sung to the melody). The exact origin of the name Yankee is equally unclear: The best estimate is that it is based on the Dutch nickname for Jan and that by the early 1700s it was being applied derisively by the British to New Englanders; by 1784 the British were applying the term to all Americans.

"Chester," which has been called the "*Marseillaise*" of the American Revolution," was written by William Billings, who took his already admired psalm known as "Chester" and wrote a new set of more belligerent lyrics ("Let tyrants shake their iron rod") for it when the Revolution broke out.

Other important American songs were "Revolutionary Tea," "The American Hero," "God Save Great Washington," "Paul Jones's Victory," "Stony Point," "The White Cockade," and "The Girl I Left Behind Me."

"The Battle of the Kegs," written by Francis Hopkinson (and set to the tune of "Yankee Doodle"), memorialized the effort of the Americans to combine explosives with floating kegs.

On the British side, there were two songs that stood for different aspects of the conflict. For sheer nationalistic bravura, nothing quite equaled the famous "British Grenadiers." But their favorite march tune "The World Turned Upside Down," (based on a traditional folk melody), indicated the state that many British soldiers (and leaders) found themselves in when the Americans played the tune as Cornwallis surrendered to the enemy at Yorktown.

The French military tunes were generally more amorous than martial. Favorites that were played by French bands during the war included *"Auprès de ma blonde"* ("Near my blond"), *"Un Canadien Errant"* ("The Wandering Canadian"), and *"La Belle Catherine"* ("The Beautiful Catherine").

HISTORICAL PERSPECTIVES AND CONTROVERSIES

The American Revolution has been debated and discussed by historians, amateurs, patriots, and Loyalists since the war ended in 1783. Some of the major issues debated have been the following:

What were the true causes of the war? How could the English Americans, who in 1763 had celebrated their status within the British Empire, have chosen to separate in 1775?

No one satisfactory answer has emerged to those questions. One of the most distinguished historians of the colonial period, Bernard Bailyn, found what he believed to be the origins within the pamphlets and documents of the early rebel groups such as the Boston Sons of Liberty. Through those writings Bailyn traced the roots to the English civil war (1642–1645) and the English "Glorious Revolution" (1688). That is, Bailyn placed the American Revolution in the continuum of the development of Anglo-Saxon liberties and constitutional development. A different view was more recently proposed by Theodore Draper, who described the period 1765–1775 as one in which the English-American colonists developed and pursued their own "will to power." Believing that the American desire for self-government was based on a more primal, less rarefied approach to power and self-government, Draper offered students of the American Revolution an alternative model for consideration. Other historians (both British and American) have emphasized the folly of King George III and Lord North; that view has been promoted by Barbara Tuchman and William Seymour.

How did 13 disparate colonies manage to combine forces and defeat the greatest maritime and imperial power of the day?

For a long time, perhaps even until around 1990, the majority of Americans believed that the

Americans had won the Revolution through the superiority of (1) their moral cause and (2) the fighting qualities of their troops, in particular the militia. The belief that those qualities sufficed to win the war was given credence by 19th-century historians such as George Bancroft. A new historiography began to emerge early in the 20th century, influenced perhaps by the new relationship between the United States and Great Britain, who were allies during World War I.

Writers such as Samuel Flagg Bemis and Jonathan Dull began to emphasize the crucial importance of England's simultaneous conflict with France, Spain, and Holland; the French-American alliance; and even the assistance given indirectly by the Spanish navy. Dull, for instance, points out that without Spanish pressure on Florida, Minorca, and Gibraltar, the English would have had far greater resources to throw against the Americans. One author who has combined some of the 19th-and 20th-century views is Page Smith, who has made the Revolution much more accessible to the lay reader. Smith has echoed the 19th-century historians in his admiration for the fighting spirit of the patriots, at the same time being careful not to ascribe miraculous deeds to them. And although acknowledging the enthusiasm with which many foreigners fought for the cause of liberty, Smith argues that American independence was inevitable, whether it was supported by the European powers or not. But the debate over this subject promises to continue.

Was the war truly revolutionary? That is, did it bring into being a society markedly different from the one that had existed before?

That is probably the most controversial question of all. Again, no single answer has emerged from the writings of scholars over nearly 200 years. James Franklin Jameson's important and controversial theory was that the Revolution could better be understood as a social movement (Tory versus patriot, landowner versus tenant farmer) rather than as a unified struggle for constitutional liberties. Jameson's ideas might be linked to those of Charles Beard, who emphasized the economic motives of the whole Revolutionary enterprise, or to Carl Becker, who framed the question, Was the Revolution over home rule or who was to rule at home? This economic viewpoint—claiming, for instance, that the Sons of Liberty were motivated

by a desire to acquire the properties of wealthy Loyalists—remained popular through the middle decades of the 20th century. Then, around 1970, the "new social history," with its closer examination of local developments, began to emphasize the radicalism of the Revolution. By the 1990s, another approach was coming to the fore in the work of historians such as Gordon Wood. Claiming that the Revolution transformed a monarchical society into a democratic one, Wood brought his readers closer to the general view that had been promoted by the nationalist historians of the 19th century.

CIVILIAN AND MILITARY BIOGRAPHIES

AMERICAN

Adams, John (1735–1826)—diplomat: John Adams was born in Massachusetts. He served in the Continental Congress. In 1779 he was named by congress to lead the American peace commissioners; in this role, he vied with Benjamin Franklin for leadership. Known as a stubborn, relentless negotiator, Adams was pleased with the treaty results. He went on to serve as vice president (1789–1797) and then president (1797–1801) of the United States.

Adams, Samuel (1722–1803)—agitator: Samuel Adams was born in Massachusetts (the cousin of John Adams). He played a crucial role in promoting the patriot movement, especially the Boston Sons of Liberty. He served in the Continental Congress and was governor of Massachusetts (1794–1797). He became more conservative in his later years.

Arnold, Benedict (1741–1801)—general, traitor: Benedict Arnold was born in Connecticut. He became one of the outstanding American officers in the field. Victories at Fort Ticonderoga, Saratoga, and Fort Stanwix did not earn him what he believed was his due. He defected to the British in 1780 and tried to betray West Point. He served as a brigadier general in the British army but never achieved battlefield glory again. In 1783, he went to England where he lived for the rest of his life.

Clark, George Rogers (1752–1818)—soldier: George Rogers Clark was born in Virginia. Clark grew up on the frontier. In his mid 20s, he led the epic campaign that resulted in the extremely important capture of British posts in the Northwest

Territory. His later military career was less glorious, but he remained the archetypal American frontier hero.

Franklin, Benjamin (1706–1790)—publisher, diplomat, inventor: Benjamin Franklin was born in Massachusetts. He made his fortune in Philadelphia. Although he personally seemed in no haste to break from England, he became the ultimate representative (popular and diplomatic) of the Revolution abroad, and he was lionized by French society. He also served as the leader of the American peace commission (1781–1783). At the time of his death, he was the second most revered American, next to George Washington.

Gates, Horatio (1728–1806)—general: Horatio Gates was born in England. He came to America in 1772, and threw in his lot with the patriot cause. He was the overall American commander at Saratoga, and he became involved in a plot, known as the Conway Cabal, to take over Washington's place as commander in chief. He led the American southern army in its disastrous defeat at Camden (1780), then retired to his farm in Virginia.

Greene, Nathaniel (1742–1786)—general: Nathaniel Greene was born in Rhode Island. He served with his state militia before becoming a brigadier general in the Continental Army. He lost Fort Washington to the British in 1776, but later redeemed his reputation with spectacular success in the American South. Although he almost never won a battle, he fought and wore down the forces of General Cornwallis and Lord Rawdon. Greene's skillful strategy contributed greatly to Cornwallis's move into Virginia, thereby making the Yorktown campaign a possibility.

Hancock, John (1737–1793)—merchant, politician: John Hancock was born in Massachusetts. He inherited great wealth in the merchant trade. He was one of the early leaders in the patriot movement in Massachusetts. As president of the Continental Congress in 1776, he was the first to sign the Declaration of Independence. He later served as the first governor of Massachusetts (1780–1785), and again served as governor of Massachusetts from 1787 to 1793.

Henry, Patrick (1736–1799)—orator, statesman: Patrick Henry was born in Virginia. He served in the Virginia House of Burgesses and was governor of Virginia (1776–1780). Of his many impassioned speeches, two are cited in Notable Phrases (see p. 105). After the American Revolution, he becam a firm opponent of the United States Constitution, claiming that it would bring about a new type of tyranny.

Jefferson, Thomas (1743–1826)—intellectual, statesman: Thomas Jefferson was born in Virginia. He served in the Continental Congress and was the main writer of the Declaration of Independence in 1776. He served as governor of Virginia from 1779–1781 and was a delegate to the Continental Congress of 1783 to 1784. Jefferson was president of the United States (1801-1809), during which he vastly increased the size of the United States with the purchase of the Louisiana Territory from France (1803).

Jones, John Paul (1747–1792)—sailor: John Paul Jones was born in Scotland. He immigrated to America in 1773 and became a devout patriot. He led a daring privateer cruise in the Irish Sea (1778), and in 1779, he won the celebrated victory over the HMS *Serapis*. Jones later served briefly in the Russian navy. He died in Paris, but his remains were brought to the United States in 1905.

Knox, Henry (1750–1806)—general: Henry Knox was born in Massachusetts. Knox became the chief of artillery for the Continental Army. He did great service to the American cause by bringing cannons from Ticonderoga to Boston (1775–1776). He later served as the first United States secretary of war (1789–1794).

Marion, Francis (1732–1795)—general: Francis Marion was born in South Carolina. A brilliant partisan and guerrilla leader, he harassed the British in South Carolina, fighting from the swampy lowland country, thus becoming known as "the Swamp Fox." He became a legend in his own time in the American South for his battle skill and ability to evade the enemy.

Morgan, Daniel (1736–1802)—general: Daniel Morgan was born in New Jersey. He was the most truly homespun of the Continental leaders. He served with distinction at Quebec and with brilliance at Saratoga and Cowpens, which was the most tactically brilliant battle of the war. Morgan was known as the "Old Wagoner." He became a wealthy landowner in his retirement.

Montgomery, Richard (1738–1775)—general: Richard Montgomery was born in Ireland. He served in the British army before he immigrated to America in 1772. A fine battlefield commander, he led the western wing of the American attack on Canada in 1775. Montgomery captured Montreal and was killed in the attack on Quebec.

Morris, Robert (1734–1806)—financier: Robert Morris was born in England. He immigrated to America in 1747 and prospered as a merchant. Known as the "financier of the Revolution," he ran the finances of the young country from 1781 to 1784 and later served as a United States senator (1789–1795). He invested in western land speculation, lost his fortune, and spent three years (1798–1801) in debtors' prison.

Otis, James (1725–1783)—statesman: James Otis was born in Massachusetts. He was foremost in resisting the Sugar Act. A great admirer of England and of Anglo-Saxon government and law, he wanted to ensure that Americans would receive their full rights as British subjects. His moderate stance cost him leadership of the patriot faction; Samuel Adams became his replacement in that role.

Paine, Thomas (1737–1809)—writer: Thomas Paine was born in England. He immmigrated to Philadelphia in 1774. Encouraged by Benjamin Franklin, he published *Common Sense*, which became almost the Bible of the patriot cause. He later played a part in the French Revolution and alienated many of his former supporters. He died, nearly forgotten, in New York State.

Sullivan, John (1740–1795)—general: John Sullivan was born in Maine. He became one of the foremost, and unluckiest, American generals. Sullivan was outflanked at Long Island and at Brandywine by General Howe. He also led the failed American attack on Newport, Rhode Island, in 1778. He redeemed his reputation with his march through the Iroquois country in 1779.

Washington, George (1732–1799)—general, president: George Washington was born in Virginia. He saw service in the French and Indian War. Named commander in chief of the American army in 1775, he persevered through a great many defeats at the hands of the British. Although fundamentally conservative, he won his key victories at Trenton, Princeton, and Yorktown through his willingness to take risks. Washington was greatly esteemed in America and Europe. He went on to become the first president of the United States (1789–1797).

Wayne, Anthony (1745–1796)—general: Anthony Wayne was born in Pennsylvania. He became one of the true firebrands on Washington's staff; his daring actions in battle gained him the sobriquet "Mad Anthony." After suffering the humiliation of defeat at Paoli's Tavern (1777), he went on to win the battle of Stony Point (1779).

After the war, he led the American army in a campaign against the Indians in the Ohio region.

BRITISH

Burgoyne, John (1722–1792)—general, playwright: John Burgoyne was born in England. He was sent to America in 1775. He devised a three-pronged strategy to defeat the colonists but failed in the implementation. Forced to surrender at Saratoga, he returned to England, where he continued to write plays; *The Heiress* was a signal triumph in 1786.

Carleton, Sir Guy (1724–1808)—governor, general: Sir Guy Carleton was born in Ireland. He became the British governor of Quebec in 1775. He defended that province against the Americans in 1775–1776. Carleton served as the last British commander in chief in North America (1782–1783).

Clinton, Sir Henry (1738–1795)—general: Sir Henry Clinton was born in England. He was sent to America in 1775 to serve as Howe's second in command. He was promoted to commander in chief in 1778. Aside from his capture of Charles Town, South Carolina, in 1780, the British cause did not prosper during his tenure.

Cornwallis, Charles (1738–1805)—general: Charles Cornwallis was born in England. He was sent to America in 1776 to serve as leader of the British vanguard under General Howe. Cornwallis was promoted to commander of British forces in the South. He was outmaneuvered by General Greene and forced to move into Virginia. He surrendered a large army at Yorktown in 1781 but was not censured. He went on to a distinguished career, serving in Ireland and India.

Gage, Thomas (1720–1787)—general: Thomas Gage was born in England. He served as British commander in chief in North America (1774–1775). A solid military man but a poor commander in chief, he was unable to fulfill the orders sent to him from London to forestall the patriot movement by seizing gunpowder and supplies.

King George III (1738–1820)—king: King George III was born in England. He ascended to the throne in 1760. Throughout the American Revolution, he remained obdurate, believing that he could triumph over the Americans. The loss of the war caused him great pain. He reigned until 1811 (when he was declared insane). Well intentioned but obstinate, King George III was indeed the "king who lost America."

Germain, Lord George (1716–1785)—secretary of state for the colonies: Lord George Germain was born in England. He served in the Seven Years' War in Europe and became the number one policy maker for the Revolutionary War in America (1775–1782). In this position, Germain had total control of the British army in America. As such, he frequently argued with the British generals fighting in the field.

Hamilton, Henry (c. 1734–1796)—soldier, governor: Born in Dublin, Ireland, he had served as an officer in the British army in Canada during the Seven Years' War. He resigned from the army in 1775, and that same year was appointed the civil governor of the British fort/outpost at Detroit. For the next few years he authorized raids by pro-British Indians against Americans living along the northeastern frontier; this gained him the label of "the hair buyer," because he allegedly paid the Indians for Americans' scalps, he seems to have done nothing different from others on both sides of the frontier wars. As word of the victories of George Rogers Clark and his Virginia militia in Illinois country reached him in 1778, Hamilton took it upon himself to lead an expedition to seize the fort/outpost at Vincennes in December 1778. But Clark's force attacked without warning and forced Hamilton to surrender with his entire garrison on February 25, 1779. Hamilton was held prisoner in Virginia for 18 months, many of them in irons, before he was allowed to return to England.

Howe, Richard (1726–1799)—admiral: Richard Howe was born in England. He was the older brother of William Howe, rising to the rank of admiral. Eager to be a peace commissioner to America, he nevertheless pursued the war with diligence and skill.

Howe, Sir William (1729–1814)—general: Sir William Howe was born in England. He became commander in chief in North America (1775–1778). A brilliant battle tactician but a poor strategist, he let several opportunities to defeat the Americans pass by. Recalled in 1778, he returned to England and continued his career in the British military.

North, Lord Frederick (1732–1792)—prime minister: Lord North was born in England. He was prime minister of Britain from 1770 to 1782. Although a strong believer in the right of king and Parliament to legislate for the colonies, North was never an enthusiastic leader during the American Revolution. He resigned as prime minister shortly after the British were defeated at Yorktown.

Tarleton, Banastre (1754–1833)—colonel of Dragoons: Banastre Tarleton was born in England. He was probably the most reckless (and some would say bloodthirsty) British officer in North America. He annihilated American troops during several battles in the South before he met his match in Gen. Daniel Morgan at Cowpens. No one could deny Tarleton's courage; he fought with total abandon, whether he was winning or losing, sick, well, or wounded.

FRENCH

de Grasse, François (1722–1788)—admiral: François de Grasse was born in France. He headed the French fleet in the Caribbean (1781–1782). Acting on his own initiative, he made the daring and crucial decision to bring his fleet to Chesapeake Bay and blockade Cornwallis there. He had the misfortune to lose the Battle of the Saintes in the Caribbean in April 1782; he was taken prisoner and sent to England.

Marquis de Lafayette, Marie Joseph Paul Yves Roch Gilbert du Motier (1757–1834)—general: Lafayette was a blue-blooded French aristocrat. He was drawn to America to fight for liberty. Greatly loved by George Washington, Lafayette became a major general in the Continental Army. After the war, he played important roles in two French revolutions—those of 1789 and 1830. He was known as the "hero of two worlds." Lafayette made a triumphal tour of the United States in 1825.

Rochambeau, Jean Baptiste (1725–1807)—general: Jean Baptiste Rochambeau was born in France. He was a veteran of many campaigns before he was sent to Newport, Rhode Island, in 1780. He collaborated with Washington in the successful Yorktown campaign. During the French Revolution, he narrowly escaped the guillotine. He was honored in his old age by Napoleon Bonaparte.

Vergennes, Charles Gravier (1717–1787)—French foreign minister: Charles Gravier Vergennes was born in France. He rose to the top of the French diplomatic corps and was the true architect of the Grand Alliance between France, Spain, and the United States. Never a true lover of the idea of American independence, he undertook to manage the war in order to harm England and redress the balance of power in Europe that had resulted since the end of the Seven Years' War.

SPANISH

de Galvez, Bernardo (1746–1786)—governor of Louisiana: Bernardo de Galvez was born in Spain. He served as governor of Louisiana from 1776 to 1783. He had served in the Spanish army before his appointment as governor of Spanish Louisiana. Galvez energetically prosecuted the Spanish war against England. He captured Baton Rouge, Natchez, and Pensacola, thereby ensuring that the Treaty of Paris (1783) would return Florida to Spain.

NATIVE AMERICAN

Brant, Joseph (1742–1807)—Mohawk chieftain: Joseph Brant was born in the Ohio area. He became a tribal leader at an early age. Brant sided with the British during the war. He spent a year in London (1775–1776), then returned to lead Indian and Tory forces in raids against patriots in the Mohawk River valley. Brant won many victories, but his cause was lost as supplies and assistance from the British dwindled. With the end of the Revolution, he resettled in Canada.

FURTHER READING

Alden, John Richard. *The American Revolution.* New York: Harper & Row Pubs. Inc., 1954.

Aptheker, Herbert. *The American Revolution, 1763–1783.* New York: International Pubs. Co., 1960.

Bailyn, Bernard. *The Ideological Origins of the American Revolution.* Cambridge, Mass.: Harvard University Press, 1967.

Bancroft, George. *History of the United States of America.* Boston: Little, Brown & Co., 1839, 1874.

Becker, Carl Lotus. *The Eve of the Revolution.* New Haven, Conn.: Yale University Press, 1918.

Bemis, Samuel Flagg. *The Diplomacy of the American Revolution.* New York: Appleton-Century-Crofts, 1935.

Billias, George. *George Washington's Generals.* New York: William Morrow & Co., 1964.

_____. *George Washington's Opponents.* New York: William Morrow & Co., 1969.

Brandt, Claire. *Man in the Mirror.* New York: Random House, 1994.

Draper, Theodore. *A Struggle for Power: The American Revolution.* New York: Random House, 1996.

Dull, Jonathan R. *A Diplomatic History of the American Revolution.* New Haven, Conn.: Yale University Press, 1985.

Fischer, David Hackett. *Paul Revere's Ride.* New York: Oxford University Press, 1994.

Flood, Charles Bracelen. *Rise, and Fight Again.* New York: Dodd Mead & Co., 1976.

Fowler, William M. Jr. *Rebels Under Sail: The American Navy During the Revolution.* New York: Charles Scribner's Sons, 1976.

Jameson, John Franklin. *The American Revolution Considered as a Social Movement.* Princeton, N.J.: Princeton University Press, 1926.

Miller, John. *Origins of the American Revolution.* Boston: Little, Brown, & Co., 1943.

Morison, Samuel Eliot, ed. *Sources and Documents Illustrating the American Revolution, 1764–1788.* New York: Oxford University Press, 1965.

_____. *The Peacemakers: The Great Powers and American Independence.* New York: Harper & Row, 1965.

Morris, Richard B. *The American Revolution Reconsidered.* New York: Harper & Row, 1967.

Neumann, George C. *The History of Weapons of the American Revolution.* New York: Harper & Row, 1967.

Peckham, Howard. *The Toll of Independence: Engagements and Battle Casualties of the American Revolution.* Chicago: University of Chicago Press, 1974.

(continued on p. 113)

Quarles, Benjamin. *The Negro in the American Revolution*. Chapel Hill, N.C.: University of North Carolina Press, 1961.

Seymour, William. *The Price of Folly: British Blunders in the War of American Independence*. London: Brassey's, 1995.

Smith, Page. *A New Age Now Begins: A People's History of the American Revolution*. New York: McGraw Hill, 1976.

Tuchman, Barbara. *March of Folly*. New York: Ballantine Books, 1985.

_____. *The First Salute*. New York: Alfred Knopf, 1988.

Van Every, Dale. *A Company of Heroes: The American Frontier, 1775–1783*. New York: William Morrow & Co., 1962.

Wood, Gordon. *The Radicalism of the American Revolution*. New York: Random House, 1993.

Wood, William J. *Battles of the Revolutionary War, 1775–1781*. Chapel Hill, N.C.: Algonquin Bks. of Chapel Hill, 1990.

NORTHWEST TERRITORY INDIAN WAR

DATES OF WAR

September 30, 1790–August 3, 1795

ALTERNATE NAMES

None.

SIGNIFICANCE

The United States had recently won its independence from Great Britain, the most powerful nation in the world. In fighting the colonists in the American Revolution, Britain had enlisted as many Native Americans as it could. Now the fledgling nation showed that it was ready to go on the attack against the Indians and their British patrons. The Northwest Territory Indian War also indicated that the new nation would not regard treaties made with the Indians as serious obligations.

Some historians treat the Northwest Territory Indian War as a series of separate campaigns, but the war is best understood as a war for control of the Northwest Territory.

BACKGROUND

With the Treaty of Paris (1783), which concluded the American Revolution, the United States gained what became known as the Northwest Territory. This territory included the land that eventually became the states of Ohio, Indiana, Illinois, Michigan, Wisconsin, and part of Minnesota. The British, however, held on to several of their forts at sites inside United States territory: four in New York (Pointe au Fer, Ogdensburg, Oswego, and Niagara) and two in Michigan (Detroit and Michilimackinac). Originally, the British government said it simply wanted to help the British fur traders conclude their business. (Such forts often served as trading posts as well as military stations.) Then Britain tried to persuade the Americans to agree to a buffer zone between Canada and the American territory; the British proposed that this zone would be occu-

pied solely by Indians. When the Americans refused, Britain changed its reason for keeping the forts, saying the forts would stay until Americans paid off their debts to British subjects.

There long had been fighting in the Northwest Territory between the Indians and the increasing numbers of white settlers, and the end of the American Revolution only intensified that fighting. In 1787, the Confederation Congress officially organized the Northwest Territory and appointed as its first governor Arthur St. Clair, a veteran officer who had fought in the Revolution and who was active in western Pennsylvania politics. St. Clair had personal as well as patriotic motives for trying to suppress the Indians; he was a shareholder in the Ohio Company, which intended to sell the land to settlers.

CAUSES OF THE WAR

The first American administration had just come into office in 1789 under President George Washington, who signed the first U.S. treaty with Indians (those of the Northwest Territory) on June 1, 1789. Although the terms of the treaty were respectful of Indians' rights, the administration soon came to believe that the Indians were becoming a threat. Many Americans, especially those living on the frontier, were convinced that the British were encouraging the tribes in their hostility toward the Americans. The British claimed that they were simply trading guns and gunpowder to the tribes as Europeans always had. In any case, a state of uneasiness prevailed on the northwestern frontier between 1783 and 1790. During that time, some 1,500 American settlers in the Northwest Territory were killed or driven off by Indian raids. As early as September 16, 1789, Washington asked Congress to pass an act enabling him as commander in chief to call on the militias of Virginia and Pennsylvania to supplement the federal troops needed to defend American lives and property in the Northwest Territory. By 1790, Washington and Congress came to feel that direct action had to be taken against the Indians.

PREPARATIONS FOR WAR

The initial preparation the U.S. government made was what any new nation might have been expected to make: the government established a national army.

Henry Knox, a hero of the Revolution, was appointed secretary of war on September 12, 1789. On September 29, 1789, the new Congress legalized the army it had inherited from the Articles of Confederation government. Congress provided for an authorized strength of 840 men in one infantry regiment, augmented by another 160 in four companies of artillery. Brig. Gen. Josiah Harmar, a veteran of the American Revolution, was named commander of the army.

In March 1790, Congress added four additional infantry companies to the regiment that existed, bringing the strength of the authorized force to 1,216 men.

Harmar, like St. Clair, was an investor in the Ohio Company, which planned to develop the Northwest Territory. In June 1790, the two men presented a plan for a punitive expedition by the federal Army to quell the hostile Indians to Knox, who in turn received the support of President Washington. Although Washington continued to try to negotiate peace with the Indians, he was under great pressure from settlers all across the frontier, who were threatening to mount their own militia war unless the new federal Army took some action.

DECLARATION OF WAR

There was no formal declaration of war by either side, but there was something close to one when Washington and Henry Knox authorized a punitive expedition against the Ohio Valley Indians (see Preparations for War, above). The Indians simply responded to U.S. forces as they came into Indian territory.

COMBATANTS

Americans: When the war began in 1790, the young United States had a standing Army that numbered only 1,216 men. Nonetheless, the Americans could draw upon a large (4 million) and growing population—although there were only about 4,200 white settlers in the Northwest Territory. In addition, the Americans had signifi-

cant advantages in artillery and weaponry, which the Indians could not hope to match.

Indians: Between 1790 and 1794, warriors from the Wyandot, Delaware, Shawnee, Miami, Ottawa, Chippewa, and Potawatomi tribes (and certain other, smaller tribes) fought against the Americans. At their peak strength, the Indians could muster several thousand warriors. Led by their most prominent chiefs—Little Turtle, Black Wolf, and Blue Jacket—the Indians made formidable foes when fighting in the woodlands north and west of the Ohio River. Many of them had muskets and pistols acquired from many years of trading with Europeans. One primary military weakness, however, lay in the manner of Indian leadership: Even a chief as renowned as Little Turtle could not command his warriors in the way an American captain or major could; Indian chiefs were forced to cajole and persuade their followers to follow their directives.

GEOGRAPHIC AND STRATEGIC CONSIDERATIONS

The area in which the three major battles were fought was a sparsely inhabited, largely wooded land in present-day Indiana and Ohio. It was not a particularly difficult terrain, but it was hundreds of miles overland from any of the major settlements that could provide troops and supplies for an organized military offensive. It was a considerable challenge for the Americans to penetrate that interior; just cutting trails for the supply wagons consumed a great deal of time and resources. By the end of June 1790, Knox had authorized a two-pronged expedition against the Indians of the Ohio River valley. One force was to come from the east, the other from the west; together they would drive out or at least suppress the Indians in that region, then establish a permanent fort on the upper Maumee River.

BATTLES AND CAMPAIGNS

September 30–October 10, 1790: As part of the two-pronged plan, the western force of 330 men, commanded by Maj. John F. Hamtramck, set out from Fort Knox (present-day Vincennes, Indiana) heading up the Wabash River. The force soon began to run short of food; a few of the militia officers refused to continue, so the entire force turned around and went back to Fort Knox.

October 1790: The eastern force was headed by Brig. Gen. Josiah Harmar. He set out to the northwest from Fort Washington (near present-day Cincinnati) on the Ohio River with 343 regular troops (one quarter of the entire regular U.S. Army) and 1,133 militiamen. General Harmar's goal was to reach the Maumee River and wipe out the several Indian villages near present-day Fort Wayne, Indiana.

October 13–19, 1790: Harmar's force reached several of the villages of the Miami Indians. The Indians had fled, but Harmar's men destroyed five of the villages and a cache of 20,000 pounds of corn.

October 19, 1790: One detachment of Harmar's troops was ambushed by Indians after it separated from the main body of the American Army. The American militiamen in the detachment broke and ran, leaving the regular troops to be hit hard by the attack.

October 21–23, 1790: On October 21, Harmar sent a detachment of 400 men to one of the main Indian villages to attack any Indians who might have returned to their town. Instead this force was ambushed in much the same manner as the detachment had been on October 19. On October 23, seeing that his forces were demoralized and that the first frosts were heralding an early winter, Harmar gathered his force and set off for Fort Washington.

November 3–6, 1790: Harmar arrived at Fort Washington on November 3. On November 6, he sent a report to Secretary of War Knox in which he listed the casualties of his expedition as 12 officers, 183 noncommissioned officers and privates killed, and 31 men wounded. Harmar claimed to have killed about 200 Indians (but many historians have concluded that Harmar exaggerated his estimates of Indian losses); he claimed that his campaign had been successful and blamed the heavy casualties he had sustained on the undisciplined militia.

March 4, 1791: Motivated by a desire to revenge Harmar's defeat, Congress voted to create a second infantry regiment, increasing the Army to some 2,200 men. President Washington replaced Harmar as commander of the U.S. Army with a new general, Arthur St. Clair, who was allowed to retain his post as governor of the Northwest Territory. St. Clair was instructed to raise a force of some 3,000 regulars and militia and build a fort in the Indian territory where

Harmar had been, then to "strike [the Indians] with great severity." The construction of such a fort was a clear violation of the U.S. government's treaty with the Indians.

May 1791: Annoyed by the claims that the militia had been responsible for the failure of Harmar's expedition, a militia colonel in Kentucky territory, Charles Scott, organized about 750 volunteers. They crossed the Ohio River and went into present-day Indiana, where they destroyed a number of Indian villages. Col. James Wilkinson led a second such expedition in August.

September 6, 1791: St. Clair had spent the summer trying to organize his Army, but by the time he set out on September 6, the Army was still only partially trained and was inadequately supplied with food, gear, and transport. The long train of some 2,700 men set out north from Ludlow's Station near Fort Washington on the Ohio River. St. Clair's force moved slowly, because it was accompanied by more than 300 camp followers and because St. Clair insisted that his troops build a wide road as they traveled, as well as a series of forts along their route.

September 15, 1791: St. Clair's force built Fort Hamilton on the Miami River only 23 miles north of Fort Washington.

October 12, 1791: St. Clair's force stopped again, to build Fort Jefferson some 50 miles farther north of Fort Hamilton.

October 24, 1791: St. Clair's force marched from Fort Jefferson, north toward the villages of the Miami Indians.

November 4, 1791 (St. Clair's Defeat): Camped along an eastern fork of the Wabash River on the border with present-day Indiana, St. Clair's Army had advanced only about 100 miles north of Fort Washington in two months. (St. Clair had become so ill that he was carried on a litter slung between two horses.) The Army had shrunk to about 1,450 men because of desertions and because St. Clair had left garrisons at the two forts he had built. Moreover, St. Clair had spread out his force and failed to post adequate guards. Just before dawn, some of the units were attacked by 1,500 Miami warriors led by Chief Little Turtle. The Indians had the advantage of surprise and concealment, and the American units were surrounded before they had a chance to organize. After desperately resisting for two hours, the Americans began a pell-mell retreat to Fort Jefferson some 25 miles to the south. St.

Clair tried to organize the retreat, but it was too late to maintain the cohesiveness of the force.

After he arrived back at Fort Washington, St. Clair examined his Army and determined his losses to be 637 men killed and 263 wounded— nearly two-thirds of the men who had been engaged in the battle. The Army also had lost six artillery pieces, 316 packhorses, 384 tents, 1,200 muskets and bayonets, and quartermaster's stores valued at $38,810 (about $500,000 in 1990 dollars). In terms of casualties alone, it was the single greatest defeat suffered by the U.S. Army in any of its conflicts with the Indians. (In proportion to the size of the force engaged, the casualty rate would not be surpassed until the loss of the Philippines to the Japanese in 1942.)

March 5, 1792: Congress authorized recruiting to bring the original two infantry regiments of the Army up to full strength and established the basis for three new infantry regiments to be enlisted for a period of three years. That brought the official strength of the Army up to 5,280 officers and enlisted men; it also had a new name: Legion of the United States (with four legions of 1,280 men each).

President Washington replaced St. Clair with Anthony Wayne, a hero of the American Revolution. Wayne was promoted to major general and commander of the American Army and was charged with organizing and leading the new Army into Indian country.

Summer 1792–fall 1793: Determined not to repeat the errors of the two previous expeditions, General Wayne set about to thoroughly train the American troops. He also made sure that each officer had a copy of the handbook for military practice prepared by Baron Friedrich Wilhelm von Steuben, a hero of the American Revolution. President George Washington tried to negotiate new terms with the Indians in the Northwest Territory, but neither side would yield on the basic differences over exclusive rights to the land.

September 11, 1793: General Wayne set out northward from Fort Washington with 3,000 men. Over 600 of the men were mounted riflemen from Kentucky.

December 25, 1793: Upon reaching the site of St. Clair's defeat in November 1791, Wayne's men had to bury the bones of many of the dead in order to clear a space to erect their tents. Wayne immediately ordered his men to begin building Fort Recovery (in present-day west-central Ohio on the border with present-day Indiana), in part to show his determination to recover the ground lost by the defeats of 1790 and 1791.

Winter 1793–spring 1794: Wayne sent emissaries to the Indians, seeking to bring them to negotiation. The Indians did not respond to his request. Wayne began to move his force northward at the rate of 10 to 12 miles a day.

Late spring 1794: Some 2,000 warriors gathered at Au Glaize (present-day Defiance, Ohio), the central village of the Miami tribe; they came from as far away as southern Canada and the villages of the Cherokee in northern Tennessee. Among the many chiefs present was Little Turtle, one of the leaders in the defeats of Harmar and St. Clair.

June 30–July 1, 1794: On June 30, Little Turtle's warriors attacked a train of packhorses moving north from Fort Recovery and killed or wounded some 40 Americans. Emboldened by their success, the Indians attacked Fort Recovery. Although Wayne and the main body of his troops were no longer there and although they were outnumbered ten to one, the American garrison turned back all the attacks on the fort during a two-day fight.

July 1794: Discouraged by the setback at Fort Recovery, Little Turtle began to counsel the tribes to seek peace; he eventually was replaced as the leader of the combined tribal force by Black Wolf, a Shawnee leader, and Blue Jacket, recognized as a leader by the Ottawa, Chippewa, and Potawatomi. Meanwhile, the British governor of Canada, Sir Guy Carleton, had ordered troops to build yet another fort in American territory, Fort Miami at the rapids of the Maumee River (southwest of present-day Toledo, Ohio). Carleton promised the Indians that the British would join them in their war against the Americans.

General Wayne marched about 60 miles north of Fort Recovery into Au Glaize, where he built the aptly named Fort Defiance. He was about 40 miles from Fort Miami, where some 1,600 Indian warriors had gathered.

August 1794: Wayne made numerous feints along the Maumee River toward Fort Miami. Wayne knew the Indians had a policy of fasting before an anticipated battle; each feint by Wayne prompted the Indians to fast, after which they lost their physical strength.

August 20, 1794 (Battle of Fallen Timbers): General Wayne led his 2,000-man Army along the west bank of the Maumee River, heading northeast toward British Fort Miami. Around 1,600 Indians commanded by Blue Jacket lay in wait for the Americans at a place near a fort called Fallen Timbers. A few years earlier, a tornado had knocked down hundreds of trees along the banks of the river, leaving what seemed to be a perfect site for an Indian ambush of the white soldiers.

Wayne was prepared for just such an ambush. Wayne's troops were also more than ready. The first assault the Indians made was allowed to pass through the main body of American troops; it was then destroyed by the rear guard of the American Army. Wayne then ordered a general advance, with bayonets fixed. As the Indians withdrew into the tangle of fallen trees, many of them tripped over the trees and fell. Wayne had sent the mounted Kentucky riflemen around the right flank of the Indian position; when the mounted troops attacked, the Indians panicked and retreated. Confusion and disorder spread throughout the Indian lines, and within an hour the battle was over. Many Indians fled to the walls of British Fort Miami, but the British commander, Maj. William Campbell, refused to open the gate to his supposed allies or to send out his troops to aid the Indians. After the Indians scattered into the wilderness, American militia units set about burning Indian villages and destroying Indian crops.

The Americans suffered 44 killed and 87 wounded in the battle; the Indians suffered about 50 killed and at least as many wounded. Although minor by measures such as duration, area fought over, and casualties, the Battle of Fallen Timbers had an enormous impact on Indian morale; not until after the confederacy forged by Tecumseh, a Shawnee chief, in 1807 would the Indians of the Northwest Territory fight in earnest against the Americans.

NEGOTIATIONS AND PEACE TREATY

Following his victory at Fallen Timbers, General Wayne returned to Fort Recovery and sent out messengers to the Indian tribes, summoning the chiefs to meet him in a conference scheduled for the following year.

August 3, 1795: Wayne met representatives of the major tribes at Fort Greenville, in west-central Ohio, close to the border with present-day Indiana. A total of 87 chiefs, representing the Wyandot, Delaware, Shawnee, Miami, Ottawa, Chippewa, Potawatomi, Kickapoo, Weea, Eel River, Piankeshaw, and Kaskaskia tribes, signed the ten-article Treaty of Fort Greenville with Wayne. The conditions of the treaty provided that all prisoners on either side be returned; that specific Indian lands, amounting to much of the land between the Ohio River and the southern boundary of the Great Lakes, be ceded to the United States; that the United States specifically relinquish claims to other Indian lands; and that the Indians receive goods valued at $20,000 and annual payments of $9,500 forever.

The treaty ended most of the warfare in the Northwest Territory until the uprising in 1811 led by Tenskwatawa, Tecumseh's brother.

RESULTS OF THE WAR (Casualties, Costs, Consequences)

Excluding the many civilian settlers who were killed in Indian raids during the Northwest Territory Indian War, U.S. military and militia forces counted some 1,000 dead and another 500 wounded. Historians believe the Indians suffered only about 200 dead and as many wounded. Although the United States won the war, it was one of the few wars against Indians in which the American forces suffered more casualties than did the Indians.

The American victory allowed for the expansion of white settlements into a large part of the Northwest Territory—and paved the way for the next phase of the westward expansion. The Indian presence in the Northwest Territory was greatly reduced after the Treaty of Fort Greenville. And the threat of a war between the United States and Great Britain, which had backed the tribes to a limited extent, was temporarily avoided—although tensions along the frontier helped bring on the War of 1812.

Not widely recognized as a result at the time was the dramatic increase in the size and strength of the newly established U.S. Army during the war. A country that had won its independence from Great Britain through the use of a largely volunteer militia found that its new status as an independent nation required the development of a regular army as well as militia forces. In 1802, an academy for training Army officers was established at West Point in New York.

MILITARY INNOVATIONS, TACTICS, EQUIPMENT

The major innovation of the Northwest Territory Indian War, already cited above, was the buildup and utilization of a regular U.S. Army. After the American Revolution ended in 1783, there had been a major national debate about whether the United States needed or even wanted to have a federal standing army. After the Northwest Territory Indian War, few opposed a regular U.S. Army.

Up to the time of the war, and for many years after, Americans, including the military, had to purchase most of their armaments abroad because of the lack of manufacturing facilities for such items. The American experience in the Northwest Territory demonstrated the need for domestic production of military equipment. In 1794, the U.S. government established the first federal armory, or arsenal, at Springfield, Massachusetts. That armory manufactured the first military musket produced in the United States. That same year, the government established its second armory at Harper's Ferry, Virginia.

Rifles—guns with the interior of the barrel rifled—had been used (and made) in some parts of North America since the early 1700s. Rifles with extra long barrels—known as Kentucky rifles because they were associated with the frontiersmen and pioneers of the Kentucky Territory—were used first during the American Revolution. Many of the militia and soldiers in the Northwest Territory Indian War preferred the Kentucky rifle over the old-fashioned and less accurate smoothbore guns.

SONGS

The events in the Northwest Territory did not give rise to any memorable songs: Disasters such as those under Harmar in 1790 and St. Clair in 1791 were not apt to inspire Americans to sing out. And the victory at Fallen Timbers, although now recognized as decisive, was in its day too minor and remote to result in any outpouring of music. The closest thing to a popular song was a poem that accompanied a woodcut engraving that circulated during the war; the engraving depicted British leaders paying money for American scalps brought to them by the Indians. The verse beneath the picture was:

Arise Columbia's Sons and forward press
Your Country's wrongs call loudly for redress.
The savage Indian with his scalping knife
Or tomahawk may seek to take your life.
By bravery aw'd they'll in a dreadful fright
Shrink back for refuge to the woods in flight.
Their British leaders then will quickly shake
And for those wrongs shall restitution make.

HISTORICAL PERSPECTIVES AND CONTROVERSIES

The ability of the Indians to inflict defeats on Brig. Gen. Josiah Harmar and Gen. Arthur St. Clair in 1790 and 1791 respectively has been the subject of debate since the two men returned from their disasters and tried to justify their conduct. Harmar tried to blame the undisciplined militia and the fact that he had been under pressure to move before he had had time to train his men. But it was Harmar himself who had urged that the campaign be carried out, and he had had many years' experience fighting alongside militia. St. Clair also defended himself on the grounds that he had been pressured to rush ahead with his expedition. That may have been true, but once he arrived at the site of the attack, he failed to take the basic precautions that almost certainly would have saved his men from massacre. Secretary of War Henry Knox, who was as responsible as anyone for promoting these two expeditions, offered the excuses that Harmar and St. Clair had set out too late in the campaign season and that each was poorly supplied. Those are the explanations echoed by many historians. None of those explanations, however, recognizes the extent to which the leadership of the Indians contributed to their victories. Chief Little Turtle, for example, was one of the most effective war chiefs ever to fight against the Americans east of the Mississippi River.

CIVILIAN AND MILITARY BIOGRAPHIES

Little Turtle (c. 1752–1812)—Miami chief: Little Turtle was known to the Miami as Chief Michikiniwa. He was born near present-day Fort Wayne, Indiana. Renowned for his skill as an orator as well as a warrior, he was one of the principal leaders in the Indian victories over Generals Harmar and St. Clair. In 1794, however, he became discouraged after the repulse of his men at Fort Recovery. He urged his people to seek peace, lost favor with many, and was not in command at the Battle of Fallen Timbers (where the Shawnee Blue Jacket led the warriors). He later visited Philadelphia, met George Washington, had his portrait painted by Gilbert Stuart, and became something of a hero to many Americans.

St. Clair, Arthur (1736–1818)—soldier, politician: Arthur St. Clair was born in Scotland. He was sent to America in 1758 to fight with the British in the French and Indian War. He settled in western Pennsylvania and served with distinction in the American Revolution (although he was removed from service in the field after surrendering Fort Ticonderoga in 1777). He was named governor of the Northwest Territory in 1787. After the disastrous defeat in 1791, he was absolved from blame by a congressional committee. He returned to govern the Northwest Territory, but he did so with such a heavy hand that President Thomas Jefferson removed him from office in 1802.

Wayne, Anthony (1745–1796)—soldier: Anthony Wayne was born in Pennsylvania. He was a surveyor and tanner before joining the Continental Army in 1776 as a colonel. He participated in numerous battles throughout the American Revolution; was with Washington at Valley Forge (1777–1778); and after helping defeat the British at Yorktown, fought against the Indians in Georgia (1782–1783). After Generals Harmar and St. Clair were defeated, President Washington appointed Wayne a major general in 1792 and assigned him to move against the Indians in the Northwest Territory. Wayne carefully organized the campaign that resulted in the victory at Fallen Timbers (see August 20, 1794, p. 118). He negotiated the Treaty of Fort Greenville in 1795. He died in Erie, Pennsylvania, the following year. For his careful reorganization of the Army and preparation for the Battle of Fallen Timbers, he has sometimes been referred to as the "father of the regular army."

FURTHER READING

Guthman, William H. *March to Massacre: A History of the First Seven Years of the United States Army*. New York: McGraw-Hill, 1970.

Millett, Allan R., and Peter Maslowski. *For the Common Defense: A Military History of the United States of America*. New York: Free Press, 1984.

Reuter, Frank T. *Trials and Triumphs: George Washington's Foreign Policy*. Fort Worth, Texas: Texas Christian University Press, 1983.

QUASI-WAR WITH FRANCE

DATES OF WAR

July 7, 1798–October 1, 1800

ALTERNATE NAMES

The Undeclared Naval War with France. The War with France.

SIGNIFICANCE

Fought against the first official ally of the United States, the Quasi-War with France provoked mixed feelings among many Americans, who felt a debt of gratitude to France for its considerable aid during the American Revolution. The war gave other Americans a surge of national pride and increased confidence in the skill of the U.S. naval forces. At the same time, the war so exacerbated the differences between the Federalists and the Republicans that the American political scene was at once and forever changed from George Washington's vision of a nonpartisan nation.

BACKGROUND

The French revolutionary wars, which raged in Europe from 1792 until 1802, pitted France against a coalition of powers, including Great Britain, Prussia, Russia, and the Austrian Empire, that were determined to restore the monarchy to France. (After around 1802, the wars continued as the Napoleonic Wars.) On April 22, 1793, President George Washington made an official proclamation of American neutrality in the fighting between revolutionary France and Great Britain. Many Frenchmen saw that as a betrayal of the commitments expressed in the 1778 treaties of commerce and alliance between France and the United States, which had been signed during the American Revolution; those treaties had seemed to promise lasting cooperation between the two nations. In the United States, many followers of Thomas Jefferson (who as vice president was becoming the unofficial head of

the opposition party, known as the Republican Party) favored the French cause. The followers of Alexander Hamilton (head of the emerging Federalist Party) believed either in neutrality or in siding with the British.

CAUSES OF THE WAR

In 1794, the United States signed the Jay Treaty with Great Britain; that settled several outstanding issues between the two nations (and guaranteed Britain's withdrawal from its forts along the northern frontier of the United States) and reaffirmed U.S. neutrality in Britain's ongoing conflict with France. There was an outburst of anger against the United States in France, and the Directory government of France (in power 1795–1799) authorized the seizure of American merchant vessels on the high seas. Between July 1796 and July 1797, the French seized 316 American ships. (During those years, the British also were seizing American ships; they not only took the cargoes, but also impressed, or kidnapped, American sailors, whom they considered to still be British subjects. In effect, by signing the Jay Treaty, the U.S. postponed the resolution of that problem until the War of 1812.) In response to France's conduct, the newly elected American president, John Adams, sent three commissioners to France to negotiate better relations between the two countries.

Elbridge Gerry, John Marshall, and Charles C. Pinckney all arrived in Paris by October 4, 1797. The French foreign minister, Charles Maurice de Talleyrand-Perigord, designated three agents to deal with the Americans. Between October 17 and October 28, the Americans met with these men, who were referred to in official reports only as X, Y, and Z (see Legends and Trivia, pp. 125-126). The French agents made insulting proposals, pressed the commissioners for a bribe if they wanted to speak directly with Talleyrand, and demanded a "loan" of $250,000 to France. Charles C. Pinckney retorted with, "Not a sixpence, sir" (see Notable Phrases, p. 126). Frustrated by the negotiations, the U.S. commissioners ended their negotiations on March 3, 1798; on April 1, they demanded their passports and left France.

PREPARATIONS FOR WAR

The American Navy had literally been put out of existence in 1785, after of the American Revolution. But in 1794, mainly because of the activities of the Barbary pirates (see Barbary Wars, pp. 128-138), the U.S. Congress authorized the construction of six new frigates. The U.S. Navy was formally founded on May 3, 1798, when the Navy Department was established; the first secretary of the navy, Benjamin Stoddert, went immediately to work to build up the Navy.

The U.S. Army also had been allowed to shrink, to about 3,300 men, after the end of the fighting in the Northwest Territory. But in July 1798, Congress authorized the creation of a special 4,000-man Provisional Army, to be headed by George Washington. He came out of retirement to oversee the new force but died in December 1799, before the Quasi War with France ended. Congress also authorized an enlargement of the volunteer militia forces to 10,000.

Along with the establishment of the new U.S. Navy, Congress reconstituted the United States Marine Corps, and on July 11, 1798, President Adams signed the bill that marked the official establishment of the Marine Corps, a division of the Navy, assigned to provide fighting forces in any naval engagements and to provide landing forces when necessary.

With those provisions made, the U.S. government was prepared to take action against French ships.

DECLARATION OF WAR

President Adams learned of the outrageous French demands on March 4, 1798. On April 3, he released to Congress the so-called XYZ Affair correspondence to show how badly the French were behaving. There was mounting protest, especially by Federalists, and on June 21 Adams sent a special message to Congress stating that he was going to break off diplomatic relations with France. On July 7, Congress passed a law setting aside all treaties with France. Two days later, Congress passed and Adams signed an "act further to protect the commerce of the United States," allowing American ships

(government or private) to seize armed French ships wherever they might find them. Adams could have asked for and received a formal declaration of war, but he held back and what began was, therefore, called the Undeclared Naval War with France, or the Quasi-War with France.

COMBATANTS

Americans: By the time President Adams signed the act allowing American ships to seize French ships, the U.S. Navy could count on only the six frigates authorized in 1794, three of which had been launched. The other three were rushed into construction. In 1799, Congress voted to construct six more ships of the line and some dozen other smaller vessels; by the end of the war, the Navy had acquired 15 frigates and had built, bought, or leased approximately 35 other vessels. The navy had some 6,700 officers and enlisted men in service, although that still left many of the ships undermanned or staffed by inexperienced personnel. Although the U.S. had a small Navy compared to France's, its frigates, at least, had been built by the finest naval architects and shipbuilders, and American timber proved to be among the best in the world for seaworthiness and resistance to gunfire. In addition, some 365 American merchant ships were commissioned as privateers; outfitted with guns, they roamed the oceans seeking French ships.

During the war, the Provisional Army built up to some 3,600 men, but it was never called on to do anything except remain in a defensive mode.

The Marine Corps quickly was built up to some 1,100 men. Marines served aboard all major ships and took an active role in many engagements, both at sea and on land.

French: The French navy was about ten times larger than the U.S. Navy in numbers of warships and personnel, but most French ships were involved elsewhere in fighting the British. In fact, most of the engagements between Americans and French at sea involved privateers and/or merchant ships of the two nations. The French navy, which had generally been ranked second to the British navy throughout the 18th century, declined during the years following the French Revolution, which began in 1789. The far superior British navy took a heavy toll on French warships during the Quasi-War with France, and France had to rely increasingly on privateers.

British: Although the British were occupied in their own war against the French, they were so pleased to have American ships attacking their enemy that the Royal Navy effectively helped to guard the U.S. coastline. Often, the Royal Navy provided escorts for American ships. Yet the British continued to stop American ships and impress sailors. The most scandalous case was in November 1798, when British ships boarded the USS *Baltimore*, a 20-gun American frigate, and took away five of the crew; the *Baltimore*'s captain, Isaac Phillips, was forced to resign from the Navy.

GEOGRAPHIC AND STRATEGIC CONSIDERATIONS

The Quasi-War with France was almost entirely fought at sea, for the most part in the Caribbean Sea; some engagements occurred off the Atlantic coast of the United States, and the U.S. Navy did send ships as far as the Mediterranean Sea and the Indian Ocean. When the war began, the French had the advantage of having many ships in the Caribbean. That initial edge was soon replaced, however, by the large number of American merchantmen who were outfitted in American ports and sent to the Caribbean as privateers. The French had access to far fewer friendly ports in the Western Hemisphere. The Americans were also aided by the willingness of the British to allow American ships to use their Caribbean ports for refuge, recovery, and reprovisioning.

As the war continued, the Americans enjoyed an even greater advantage, as the French lost battles at sea to the British in the Atlantic and Mediterranean. At the Battle of the Nile (August 1, 1798), the British delivered a devastating blow to the French navy, which increased the pressure within France to bring about a diplomatic end to its naval war with the United States.

BATTLES AND CAMPAIGNS

July 7, 1798: American captain Stephen Decatur Sr., commanding the sloop USS *Delaware*, engaged and captured the French schooner *Croyable* off Egg Island, New Jersey, and renamed it the USS *Retaliation*.

August 23, 1798: The USS *Delaware* and the USS *United States* captured the French schooner *Sans Pareil* near Martinique in the Caribbean.

September 5, 1798: The USS *Delaware* and the USS *United States* captured the French sloop *Jaloux* north of Puerto Rico.

November 20, 1798: Off the Caribbean island of Guadeloupe, the French ships *L'Insurgente* and *Volontaire* captured the USS *Retaliation*, formerly the French schooner *Croyable*. The American commander, Lt. William Bainbridge, and his 250-man crew remained prisoners of the French until February 1799.

February 3, 1799: The USS *United States* captured the French schooner *L'Amour de la Patrie* near Martinique.

February 4, 1799: The USS *United States* captured the French privateer *Tartuffe* near St. Lucia in the Caribbean.

February 9, 1799: American captain Thomas Truxtun led the 48-gun USS *Constellation* in a battle against the 44-gun *L'Insurgente* south of the island of Nevis in the Caribbean. The French ship surrendered after a short but sharp fight in which the Americans suffered one killed and two wounded; the French lost 58 men killed or wounded.

March 1, 1799: The USS *Montezuma* captured the French brig *Les Amis* south of Puerto Rico.

March 5, 1799: The USS *Delaware* captured the French schooner *Marsouin* near Havana, Cuba.

March 14, 1799: The USS *Constellation* captured the French schooner *Union* near Dominica in the Caribbean.

February 1–2, 1800: The USS *Constellation*, still under the command of Capt. Thomas Truxtun, met the 54-gun *La Vengeance* off Guadeloupe. A five-hour battle ensued, during which the French captain twice signaled he wished to surrender, but both times his signal was missed by the Americans. *La Vengeance* limped off into the darkness and escaped capture, but it was a spent vessel, and half the 320-man crew had been killed or wounded. The American losses were 25 killed and 14 wounded. Although his ship was severely damaged and he did not have a prize to bring home to port, Truxtun's victory (his second) was seen as one of the most important indications that the United States was winning the war, and Truxtun became a national hero.

May 11, 1800: The island of Santo Domingo in the Caribbean belonged to the Spanish and was supposed to be neutral, but it was well known that French forces took refuge there. The French were holding the British ship *Sandwich* in the harbor of Puerta Plata on Santo Domingo. Eighty U.S. marines on the USS *Constitution* off Puerta Plata commandeered an American vessel, the *Sally*, and hiding below decks, sailed into the harbor. They quickly overwhelmed the French and Spanish, stormed and captured the Spanish fort, spiked its guns, and sailed away with the *Sandwich*. It was the first combat landing on foreign soil by U.S. Marines.

June 1800–April 1801: Peace negotiations were under way in Paris, and eventually the treaty was signed. But ships at sea did not receive word of that peace treaty for many months, and attacks by French, American, and British ships continued in several parts of the world. In particular, the fighting between U.S. ships and French privateers in the Caribbean continued until official word of the end of the war reached all the ships in the Caribbean in April 1801.

NEGOTIATIONS AND PEACE TREATY

Almost from the start of the Quasi-War with France, French foreign minister Charles Talleyrand indicated a willingness to discuss peace negotiations. (In 1798, Dr. George Logan, a Quaker from Pennsylvania, traveled on his own to Paris to try to engage Talleyrand in peace negotiations.) The willingness of France to negotiate a peace treaty was accentuated by the overthrow of the Directory government of France (November 9, 1799) in a coup d'état led by Napoleon Bonaparte. Napoleon Bonaparte led the new government as the First Consul of France and was anxious to end hostilities with the U.S. The French government let the U.S. government know that it was willing to commence negotiations.

February 1799: President Adams appointed three peace commissioners: William Vans Murray, the American ambassador to the Netherlands; Chief Justice Oliver Ellsworth; and William R. Davie, former governor of North Carolina.

March 8, 1800: Napoleon Bonaparte formally received the three American peace commissioners in Paris.

April 2, 1800: Formal peace negotiations between France and the United States began.

September 30, 1800: The American commissioners reached an agreement with the French.

September 30–October 1, 1800: In Paris, on September 30, the Treaty of Mortefontaine (also known as the Convention of 1800) was agreed to and dated; it was not formally signed until the next day. The treaty (with its 27 articles) mutually abrogated the Franco-American treaties of amity and commerce of 1778 (see American Revolution, p. 87) but restored normal diplomatic relations. The United States agreed to negotiate payments for American merchant ships that had been seized by the French.

December 16, 1800: President John Adams submitted the treaty to the Senate.

January 23, 1801: The Senate rejected the treaty by a vote of 16 in favor and 14 against (less than the two-thirds required), with two senators not voting.

February 3, 1801: President Adams submitted the treaty again, and the Senate approved it (with reservations) by a vote of 22 in favor and 9 against, with one senator not voting.

July 31, 1801: Ratifications of the treaty were exchanged in Paris.

December 21, 1801: President Thomas Jefferson proclaimed the Convention of 1800 as the law of the land.

RESULTS OF THE WAR (Casualties, Costs, Consequences)

No official figures for the casualties in the war are available, in part because so many of the engagements occurred in remote areas of the sea and involved privateers rather than official Navy ships. Casualties simply were not recorded. But the U.S. Navy lost about 50 men killed in combat, with perhaps double that number wounded; the French suffered at least 250 combat casualties. In addition, many more men were lost at sea in accidents. In the fall of 1800, for example, three American ships vanished, presumably in a storm, and more than 400 men were lost.

Historians have never put a dollar value on the cost of the Quasi-War with France to the United States. American merchant shipowners alone filed claims for about $12 million (some $1.2 billion in 1990 dollars) for losses in French seizures. The U.S. government later paid that debt. Many American privateers and naval crews actually profited from the sale of the ships and cargoes seized. But the war certainly cost the U.S. government the equivalent of several billion in 1990 dollars, not including the cost of the expensive new frigates. During the war, the Republicans in Congress tried to resist the enlargement of the armed forces but failed. That meant, however, that the Federalists had to increase revenue, so they voted for taxes on land, houses, and even slaves. (That led to a virtual rebellion in some Pennsylvania counties, but President Adams suppressed the rebellion by sending in 500 Army troops.)

In the short term, the Quasi-War with France resulted in a U.S. national military establishment that many Americans had hoped their country could avoid. The U.S. Navy, for instance, had built dry docks and purchased timberlands to provide wood for constructing its ships. It ended up with a fleet of some 40 ships. The Navy was drastically cut back, as were the Army and the Marines, by the new Republican administration that took over under President Jefferson in 1801. But the Navy Department nonetheless existed, as did the U.S. Marine Corps. And in 1802, the U.S. Military Academy was founded at West Point in New York (where, since 1796, there had been a small, informal school to train engineers and artillerymen).

Just as the new United States had challenged the British in the Northwest Territory Indian War, it had taken on the powerful nation of France in the Quasi-War with France. Americans were signaling that they would not be bullied when it came to their claims for respect. But in the long term, the war won only half a loaf for Americans: They were rid of the French menace at sea but still faced British attacks and insolence. As Britain and France continued their war, the British also continued raiding American ships and impressing American seamen until the end of the War of 1812 (see War of 1812, pp. 139-165).

MILITARY INNOVATIONS, TACTICS, EQUIPMENT

The Quasi-War with France, although a minor war, actually saw several major developments in the American military. Not only were the U.S. Navy and the U.S Marine Corps made permanent services, but the United States began to commit itself to maintaining a permanent military by establishing such facilities as shipyards. The first arsenals for handheld weapons had been established in 1794, but when the Quasi-War with France commenced, the American military was dependent on foreign nations for heavy weapons, such as naval cannons. By the end of the war, American foundries were beginning to provide heavy weapons.

One major innovation was the production of extra-heavy-duty wooden frigates that were larger in dimension and stronger in their construction than comparable British and French ships. (It was one of those ships, the USS *Constitution*, that gained the name "Old Ironsides" during the War of 1812.) Among other features, the American ships had gangways on both sides, which added strength to the hulls and provided a second gun deck. And the U.S. Navy was quick to borrow from other navies whatever was most useful: During the Quasi-War with France, for the first time, U.S. warships used carronades, short, lighter cannons capable of smashing heavy balls into enemy vessels at close range.

LEGENDS AND TRIVIA

The infamous **XYZ Affair** began when the three American commissioners went to Paris in October 1797 to negotiate better relations with the French (see Causes of the War, p. 121). Instead of being allowed to deal directly with the French foreign minister, Charles Maurice de Talleyrand, they found themselves approached by several men who, it soon became apparent, were agents of Talleyrand. Because the negotiations were supposed to be secret, the American commissioners and President John Adams chose to refer to the three men in official reports as X, Y, and Z. (In fact, at the outset, there were four such men, and they were actually called W, X, Y, and Z; but W dropped out of the negotiations.) At least two of those men had spent some time in America (and were married to American women), where they had been acquainted with at least one of the American negotiators. X was Jean Conrad Hottinguer, a Swiss financier; Y was Pierre Bellamy, also Swiss, who had been educated as a clergyman but had gone into banking; and Z was Lucien Hauteval, a wealthy French sugar planter from the West Indies. What all three men had in common besides their wealth was a desire to exploit the troubles between the United States and France to make more money. When they made it clear that the negotiations would go nowhere unless the Americans paid a bribe, the offended Americans broke off discussions and returned to the United States. President Adams thereupon published all the documents in the case, exposing the scandalous behavior of the French and arousing a storm of anger against the French.

NOTABLE PHRASES

Millions for defense, but not one cent for tribute!

That became the rallying cry of Americans during 1798. It is believed that Robert Goodloe Harper delivered it as a toast to John Marshall (one of the three United States commissioners who had returned from Paris) on June 18, 1798. Many people mistakenly believed that was the response of Charles C. Pinckney in Paris to French representative Jean Conrad Hottinguer's statement, "You do not speak to the point, it is money; it is expected that you will offer money."

All three American representatives (Marshall, Pinckney, and Elbridge Gerry) replied, "We have given an answer to that demand."

Hottinguer responded, "No you have not. What is your answer?"

"Not a sixpence, sir" said Pinckney, outraged at the very idea of having to pay money in order to speak to the French foreign minister. (Some sources claim that Pinckney said, "Not a penny! Not a penny!")

SONGS

Although the Quasi-War with France itself did not inspire any memorable music, two songs became popular during that era. Perhaps the biggest hit of the day, and still well known, was "Hail, Columbia." The words were by Joseph Hopkinson, son of the famous musician-poet-lawyer Francis Hopkinson; the melody was that of a well-known tune of the day, "The President's March." Joseph Hopkinson's song was introduced on April 25, 1798, at a theater in Philadelphia; President Adams was said to have been present. It was adopted by Adams's Federal supporters and soon assumed the status of an unofficial national anthem. For decades, Army and Navy bands frequently played that song on formal occasions.

John Adams was not the type of person who inspired much fervor (except among his Republican enemies), but one of the most popular songs of the period, dated to 1798, was known as "Adams and Liberty." The words were by Robert Treat Paine, a signer of the Declaration of Independence and a justice on the Massachusetts supreme court; he set his words to an old British drinking song known as "To Anacreon in Heaven." That music (credited to an Englishman, John Stafford Smith) would be familiar today because the music was adopted some 16 years later for the "Star-Spangled Banner," written by Francis Scott Key.

HISTORICAL PERSPECTIVES AND CONTROVERSIES

Various historians have debated whether the Quasi-War with France was merely a minor incident in U.S. history or whether it had a profound impact on future events. It is hard to imagine, some argue, that much would have been different had the U.S. never gone to war with France over the issue of the seizing of American ships. Sooner or later that practice would almost certainly have come to an end. The British practice of impressment was a much larger and more vexing problem.

Yet, most historians agree that the war had a major impact on the development of the U.S. Navy and naval tradition: Almost all the naval leaders in the Barbary Wars and in the War of 1812 gained their experience in the naval war with France. Politically, the difference of opinion over whether the United States should build a national military establishment led to the emergence of the two parties, the promilitary Federalists and the antimilitary Democratic-Republicans. The debate was so intense that Adams and his Federalists passed several legislative acts that were among the more shameful abridgements of civil liberties in U.S. history—all the more so because the Federalists' primary motivation was to exploit anti-French sentiment to discredit Jefferson for their own political gain. The Alien Act (June 25, 1798) gave the president the power to deport, even during peacetime, any foreigner considered potentially dangerous or treasonous to the U.S. The Sedition Act (July 11, 1798) made it a crime to write, speak, or in other ways try to arouse discontent with the government. Those acts not only led to the downfall of Adams after one term but also served as a warning against the danger of any government intent on suppressing political dissent. Indirectly, then, the Quasi-War with France resulted in a sharp and permanent turn in American political life.

CIVILIAN AND MILITARY BIOGRAPHIES

Talleyrand-Perigord, Charles Maurice de (1754–1838)—diplomat: Talleyrand was born in Paris. He was educated for a career in the Catholic Church. When the French Revolution broke out in 1789, Talleyrand, a bishop, emerged as a moderate supporter of its aims and in 1790 was elected president of the National Assembly. When the revolution became more radical, his loyalty was suspect, and between 1794 and 1796, he lived in exile in America. He returned to France in 1796 and, as the most adroit and ruthless diplomat of the era, managed to serve the Directory, the Consulate, the French Empire under Napoleon, the restored government of King Louis XVIII after Napoleon's downfall, and the constitutional monarchy of Louis Philippe. Talleyrand's high-handed approach to the American commissioners in 1797 was one of his few clear blunders. He remained instrumental in French international affairs for another generation.

Truxtun, Thomas (1753–1822)—naval officer: Thomas Truxtun was born in New York. He briefly served in the Royal Navy before becoming a successful privateer commander during the American Revolution. In 1786, he took the first ship from Philadelphia to China. He entered the new U.S. Navy as a captain (1794) and supervised the construction of the USS *Constellation* in Baltimore. He helped establish a professional code of conduct for the U.S. Navy and published several training manuals. He captained the USS *Constellation* in the two most notable ship-to-ship actions of the Quasi-War with France.

FURTHER READING

De Conde, Alexander. *The Quasi-War: The Politics and Diplomacy of the Undeclared Naval War with France, 1797–1801*. New York: Charles Scribner's Sons, 1966.

Guttridge, Leonard F, and Jay D. Smith. *The Commodores: The U.S. Navy in the Age of Sail*. New York: Harper & Row, 1969.

Palmer, Michael A. *Stoddert's War: Naval Operations During the Quasi-War with France, 1798–1801*. Columbia, S. C.: University of South Carolina Press, 1987.

Stinchcombe, William C. *The XYZ Affair*. Westport, Conn.: Greenwood Press, 1980.

THE BARBARY WARS

DATES OF WARS

May 14, 1801–June 10, 1805; March 2, 1815–June 30, 1815.

ALTERNATE NAMES

The Wars with Tripoli and Algiers. Tripolitan and Algerian Wars. The North African Wars.

SIGNIFICANCE

Through standing up to the extortionist demands of the Barbary States—the sultanates that conducted piracy along the coast of North Africa—the United States gained respect among the nations of the world. Not even 15 years old, the U.S. had undertaken its first action as an international "policeman" by challenging distant rulers on behalf of the principle of freedom of the seas. During the Barbary Wars, the U.S. Navy developed and nurtured an elite corps of daredevil seamen and officers who went on to win many victories against the British during the War of 1812.

BACKGROUND

The background and setting of the Barbary Wars lay in European power politics, Mediterranean shipping traditions, and the international policies of the young United States. Starting in the 1500s, the Arab-Berber peoples of the North African coast had developed skills in piracy, hostage-taking, extortion, and double-dealing. The pirates were based primarily in Algiers, Tunis, and Tripoli. Throughout the 18th century, the pirates routinely received tribute from the major European nations—Britain, France, Denmark, Sweden, Spain—so that their merchant ships could sail peacefully in the Mediterranean. (Most European powers found it advantageous to pay tribute rather than confront the Barbary States.)

When the United States won its independence from England in 1783, it found that its ships were no longer protected under the British treaty with the pirates. By 1795, some 115 American seaman

were being held hostage by Algerian pirates. Therefore, on September 5, 1795, the United States negotiated a treaty under which the U.S. agreed to pay the pirates $1 million to ransom the prisoners and to pay Algeria a tribute of $642,500 as well as naval stores worth $21,600. That humiliating treaty was followed by similar treaties with Tripoli (November 4, 1796) and Tunis (August 28, 1797) and served as the basis for United States–Barbary relations until 1801, when the arrogance of the pasha of Tripoli brought the two countries into a state of war. (The pasha, Yusuf, had deposed his brother Hamet Karamanli in 1796.)

From 1797 to 1800, the United States was engaged in an undeclared naval war with France, so U.S. ships in foreign waters had to fend off French attacks and plots that further complicated their dealings with the Barbary pirates. Britain, not especially happy to see a growing American presence on the seas, stood by and let the United States take on the Barbary States alone.

CAUSES OF THE WARS

The causes of the two conflicts known as the Barbary Wars were fairly straightforward: the demands for payments of tribute and the mistreatment of American seamen by the Barbary Coast pirates. Both of those had been endured for many years before specific incidents, recounted below under the heading for each war, provoked the United States to take up arms.

PREPARATIONS FOR WAR

The United States did not enter into the Barbary Wars with much discussion, knowledge, or preparations for military operations. In both cases, American presidents somewhat precipitously decided to take action. The specific preparations made for the two wars are described below under the heading for each war.

DECLARATIONS OF WAR

There were no formal declarations of war by

any of the parties in the first of the Barbary Wars; the leaders simply authorized their armed forces to commence hostilities. In the second of the wars, however, the United States did make a formal declaration of war. The specifics are recounted below under the heading for each war.

COMBATANTS

There were essentially three combat forces in the Barbary Wars: the U.S. Navy, the Tripolitan and Algerian navies, and an army organized by William Eaton.

U.S. Navy: The U. S. Navy was small but efficient. As a result of legislation signed by George Washington in 1794, six large frigates (including the USS *Constitution*) had been constructed during the late 1790s. Built more solidly than even their British counterparts, the frigates carried as many as 50 guns (as opposed to the standard 44). There were about 45 other ships in the Navy by 1800, and more ships were added as the wars continued. Like any military service, the U.S. Navy had its share of sluggards, but its sailors and officers had won most of the battles, in which they fought in the undeclared naval war with France and morale was high.

It should be noted that in 1798 the U.S. formally established the United States Marine Corps and that most warships carried at least a small contingent of marines; they participated in boarding actions in sea fights. Marines played crucial roles in several actions during the Barbary Wars.

Tripolitan and Algerian Navies: Although they did not maintain navies in the modern sense of highly centralized, organized, and disciplined fleets, Tripoli and Algiers had a long tradition of fighting at sea. However, the Barbary fleets were made up largely of feluccas and xebecs—ships well designed for sailing and fighting on the Mediterranean but no match for large frigates. Their sailors and officers were cramped by a lack of up-to-date naval technology (for example, the short but powerful cannons known as carronades and copper sheathing on the bottoms of the vessels). The sailors and officers of the Barbary fleets paid little attention to the importance of gunnery practice. In addition, the Barbary tradition of warfare relied heavily on boarding enemy ships and fighting hand to hand—a style that was ill-suited to the era of long-range 24-pounder guns.

The Barbary States were named after the Berbers, the people (known in Arabic as Barbar) who had long inhabited the North African coast. During the seventh and eighth centuries, the Arabs had conquered and mixed with the Berbers and introduced the Islamic religion to the region. And from the 16th century, the Ottoman Turks tended to hold the real power over the Barbary States. Berber, Arab, Tripolitan, Turk, and others had become so intermixed that it was virtually impossible to assign individuals to one or another of those ethnic groups.

"General" Eaton's Army: William Eaton had been the U.S. consul in Tunis (1799–1803). During and after his tenure, he argued that only a strong American land force could break the power of the Barbary States and free the United States from paying tribute. When he was finally sent back to North Africa to organize such a force in 1804, he personally led a small corps of nine Americans (one U.S. Navy midshipman and eight U.S. Marines), a couple dozen soldiers of fortune and rogue adventurers of various nationalities, a troop of some 40 Greek mercenaries from Egypt, and hundreds of Arabs and Berbers in an epic march across Egypt into Tripoli (present-day Libya). In several engagements with the Tripolitan forces, that ragtag army administered such stinging defeats that many historians credit Eaton's actions with bringing the Tripolitan War to an end.

GEOGRAPHIC AND STRATEGIC CONSIDERATIONS

The Barbary States had the major advantage of fighting in their home waters, the Mediterranean: Their forces had ready access to supplies and safe havens; they knew the seas and the weather, and they were highly mobile. By contrast, the Americans had to send ships, men, and equipment more than 3,000 miles from American seaports. Just to take on sufficient water could involve long cruises and long stays in neutral ports around the Mediterranean. On the other hand, the Barbary States were vulnerable to bombardment from American ships, as when the U.S. Navy ventured into the harbor of Tripoli.

Another strategic factor was the attitude of other nations. At Gibraltar and elsewhere around the Mediterranean were the ships of many powerful nations; all had some interest in the outcome of the wars. When the first war began, most neutral observers expected the Tripolitans to win.

When the war went in the direction of the Americans, many neutrals were delighted to see damage done to the pirates, who had for so long made shipping difficult, dangerous, and expensive.

The War with Tripoli: 1801–1805

CAUSES OF THE WAR

From October 19–November 8, 1800, Mustapha II, the dey (or ruler) of Algiers, forced the USS *George Washington* to carry goods and slaves to Constantinople. The goods and slaves were the dey's tribute to the Turks, but that tribute reminded Americans of their humiliation of paying tribute to the Barbary Coast powers.

Irritated by delays in tribute and by the apparent reluctance of the Americans to indulge his whims, the pasha of Tripoli sent a group of men to cut down the American flagpole outside the American consulate in Tripoli. This took place on May 14, 1801.

PREPARATIONS FOR WAR

Thomas Jefferson, inaugurated president of the United States in March 1801, was widely regarded as opposed to building a permanent military and engaging in international adventures. But years before, when serving as the American ambassador to France, he had decided that the Barbary powers should not be paid tribute. Shortly after becoming president, and without seeking congressional approval, Jefferson sent a squadron of ships to the Mediterranean to observe the situation there. That was before he received word that the pasha of Tripoli had cut down the American flagpole.

DECLARATION OF WAR

Although there was never a formal declaration of war by the United States in response to the pasha of Tripoli's action in cutting down the American flagpole on May 14, 1801, on February 6, 1802, the U.S. Congress authorized President Thomas Jefferson to use naval force to protect American vessels against the Tripolitan pirates. This Act for the protection of the commerce and seamen of the United States, permitted the president and the Navy to use force at sea and so served as an informal declaration of war.

BATTLES AND CAMPAIGNS

June 2, 1801: Commodore Richard Dale sailed from Norfolk, Virginia, with a squadron of American ships (three frigates and one sloop of war) headed for the Mediterranean. Although President Jefferson claimed that the squadron's mission was to observe conditions, its real purpose was to show the flag—that is, to suggest to the Barbary pirates the potential power of the United States. Dale was also authorized to defend American ships from attack by any of the Barbary powers.

July 24, 1801: Having learned that the pasha of Tripoli had declared war on the United States, Commodore Dale established a loose blockade around the harbor of Tripoli.

August 1, 1801: The USS *Enterprise* (12 guns and 90 men) under the command of Lt. Andrew Sterrett fought the Tripolitan ship *Tripoli* (14 guns and 80 men). The three-hour battle concluded with the surrender of the *Tripoli*, which was in ruins. The Tripolitans suffered 20 dead and 30 wounded; the Americans lost not a single man. The lopsided nature of the battle was attributed to the Americans' skill at gunnery, something that the American crews had worked on since leaving the United States.

September 3, 1801: Commodore Dale abandoned the blockade of Tripoli and sailed for Gibraltar and then America.

Winter 1801–1802: United States ships in the Mediterranean were harassed occasionally by Barbary pirates, but there were no overt hostilities. The U.S. Navy maintained only a symbolic presence at Tripoli, not a full blockade.

February 6, 1802: The United States Congress authorized President Jefferson to use naval force to protect American vessels against the Tripolitan pirates. The Act for the Protection of the Commerce and Seamen of the United States Against the Tripolitan Cruisers permitted the president and the Navy to use force at sea but avoided an outright declaration of war against the pasha of Tripoli.

April 27, 1802: Capt. Richard Morris sailed from Hampton Roads, Virginia, in command of a squadron of six ships to protect American interests in the Mediterranean.

June 17, 1802: The Emperor of Morocco declared war on the United States over a minor matter that involved a single ship and trading rights.

By August, the issues were negotiated and peace was restored.

June 26, 1802: The U.S. merchant ship *Franklin* was captured by Tripolitan pirates and the captain and eight crew members were taken to Tripoli. It wasn't until September 22 that all the Americans were freed after payment of ransom.

Fall 1802–Spring 1803: The American situation in the Mediterranean deteriorated because of a series of personal feuds among American consuls and naval personnel. The Barbary leaders took advantage of that situation and demanded more tribute.

April 25, 1803: William Eaton, former American consul in Tunis, met with President Jefferson and Secretary of State James Madison. At that meeting, he urged Jefferson and Madison to pursue a much more aggressive campaign against the Barbary pirates. Sometime during the next year and a half, Eaton concocted a plan that involved an overland military expedition to depose the pasha of Tripoli. Eventually, Eaton received a special commission as U.S. Naval Agent on the Barbary Coast and returned there with a vague authorization to organize such an expedition.

May 13, 1803: The USS *John Adams* captured the emperor of Morocco's ship, the *Meshouda*, which previously had flown under the Tripolitan flag and which had been blockaded in Gibraltar for two years. That caused some concern among the Americans that Morocco might join in the war on the side of Tripoli.

May 23, 1803: Capt. Edward Preble was commissioned as commander of the American squadron in the Mediterranean; he replaced the largely ineffectual Capt. Richard Morris. (Capt. John Rodgers served as interim commander until Preble arrived in September.)

June 10, 1803: As the final action of his tenure as commodore in the Mediterranean, Captain Morris sent ashore a force of some 50 men, who managed to destroy most of the grain boats that lay outside the harbor of Tripoli. The Americans suffered 15 men dead or wounded; the Tripolitans lost twice as many.

October 5, 1803: Arriving on his flagship, the USS *Constitution*, Captain Preble met with the emperor of Morocco at Tangier Bay in Morocco. Preble asserted his authority as a United States naval officer and, with a show of naval might, persuaded the emperor to reaffirm the treaty of friendship between the United States and Morocco,

which was signed in 1786.

October 31, 1803: Commanded by Capt. William Bainbridge, the USS *Philadelphia* ran aground on an uncharted reef off the northeastern edge of the port of Tripoli. As the Americans worked frantically to rescue the ship, Tripolitan gunboats surrounded it. Bainbridge was forced to surrender the ship with its crew of 235 seamen, 41 marines, and 33 officers. The Tripolitans brought the captured ship and crew to Tripoli Harbor. The captives were placed in a stone warehouse that measured 50 feet by 20 feet. The *Philadelphia* was freed at high tide and towed into the harbor.

November 1803–February 1804: The Americans feared the Tripolitans would use the *Philadelphia* not only as their own fighting ship but also as a model to build frigates of their own. Preble realized that this could give the Barbary pirates a tremendous advantage.

December 13, 1803: The USS *Enterprise* and the USS *Constitution* captured the Tripolitan ketch *Mastico*, which the Americans renamed the *Intrepid*. Lt. Stephen Decatur was placed in command of the *Intrepid*.

February 16, 1804: Lt. Stephen Decatur performed what British admiral Horatio Nelson would call the most "daring act of the age." Disguising himself and others as Maltese sailors, Decatur led the ketch *Intrepid* into the harbor of Tripoli and, with a force that included U.S. Marines, boarded the captured USS *Philadelphia* and drove off its Tripolitan crew. After setting fire to the frigate, Decatur and his force escaped without the loss of a single man; the *Philadelphia* burned to the waterline before exploding.

April 29, 1804: While Capt. Edward Preble was occupied in trying to ransom the American captives from the *Philadelphia*, his ships captured a Tripolitan 16-gun brig.

August 3, 1804: After heavy bombardment from heavier U.S. Navy ships, six smaller American gunboats entered Tripoli Harbor and fought a desperate hand-to-hand battle against the crews of Tripolitan gunboats in what became known as the "battle of the gunboats." The Americans captured three gunboats and lost none of their own. The Tripolitans suffered 44 killed, 26 wounded, and 52 taken prisoner. American losses were a total of 14 men killed (including Lt. James Decatur, brother of Stephen) and wounded. Stephen Decatur emerged a hero once again. It was said that after being saved from death by a seaman

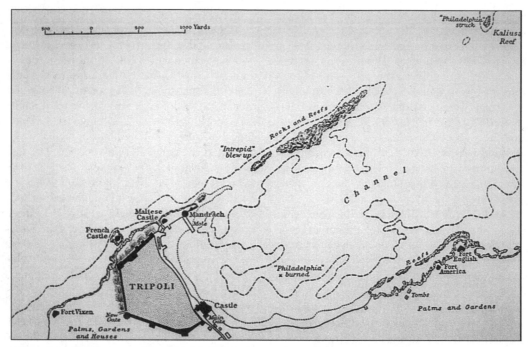

This plan of the city and fort of Tripoli on the Barbary Coast (now in Libya) shows the reef where the USS **Philadelphia** *went aground (October 31, 1803), the location in the harbor where it was burned by a daring American raid (February 16, 1804); and the location where the* **Intrepid** *exploded (September 3, 1804).*

named Daniel Frazier (see Legends and Trivia, p. 136), Stephen Decatur pursued a Tripolitan gunboat and, in hand-to-hand combat, killed the Tripolitan who had allegedly killed his brother James.

August 7, 1804: Captain Preble led his ship in a two-hour bombardment of the Fort of Tripoli. The Americans suffered 14 killed and 6 wounded; the Tripolitan losses are unknown.

September 3, 1804: American lieutenant Richard Somers and 12 of his men were lost in an attack against the harbor of Tripoli. The ketch *Intrepid* had been outfitted as an ammunition storehouse, or floating mine. The plan was for its volunteer crew to sail the ketch close to the Tripolitan ships, light fuses, and escape in rowboats. The ship exploded, however, before it could do much damage, and all the Americans were killed. Some historians have claimed that Somers deliberately set fire to the explosives and killed himself and his crew rather than be taken prisoner (he allegedly told others he would do so), but other historians believe that a Tripolitan shell hit the ship.

September 11, 1804: With the arrival of Capt. Samuel Barron at the head of a new squadron of ships, Capt. Edward Preble was replaced as commodore of the Mediterranean fleet and recalled to the United States. Barron was less aggressive than Preble and, leaving a few ships off Tripoli, he soon retired to Malta. The war against Tripoli once more slipped into a standoff.

November 26, 1804: William Eaton had returned to the Mediterranean with Captain Barron and arrived in Alexandria, Egypt. He was determined to find and ally himself with the deposed pasha of Tripoli, Hamet Karamanli, then proceed with his plan to attack Tripoli by land.

Mid-January 1805: Eaton met Hamet for the first time at Damanhur, Egypt. The two men agreed to combine their forces and make a land assault on Tripoli. Although Hamet was not a forceful leader—and even tried to abandon Eaton's expedition at several points along the way—Eaton needed him to justify the intervention by Americans in an assault on Tripoli.

March 8–April 25, 1805: Eaton and his collection of international adventurers—40 Greek mercenaries recruited in Alexandria, 300 mounted Arabs, 1 U.S. Navy midshipman, and 8 U.S. marines commanded by Lt. Presley N. O'Bannon—

set off from Alexandria. Eaton's first goal was Derna, a port city of Tripoli. Along the way, they were joined by more Arabs and Berbers (including their families), eventually building up to a total army of some 1,000. There were constant quarrels, desertions, and mutinies by the Arabs, and Eaton claimed he personally executed two Arabs to maintain discipline. The 600-mile trek took Eaton's force across the Egyptian and Tripolitan wastelands, usually within sight of the sea.

April 16, 1805: Eaton's force made a planned rendezvous with the USS *Argus* along the coast and received badly needed supplies.

April 25, 1805: Eaton's force reached the outskirts of Derna.

April 27, 1805: Having failed to persuade the governor of Derna to surrender (see Notable Phrases, p. 137), William Eaton and his men fought a sharp battle and gained control of Derna. They were well supported by the heavy guns of the USS *Argus* and the USS *Hornet*. Lt. Presley O'Bannon performed so heroically that Hamet Karamanli presented O'Bannon with his elaborate sword (which today serves as the pattern for the sword carried by U.S. Marine officers). Eaton reported only 14 "Christians" killed and wounded (including two U.S. Marines, who were killed).

May 13, 1805: William Eaton, Hamet Karamanli, and their forces were placed under siege in Derna by a force of 2,000–3,000 Tripolitans.

June 1–3, 1805: U.S. Navy ships off Tripoli commenced a heavy bombardment of Derna to force Pasha Yusuf to negotiate a peace. The pasha surrendered on June 3 and released the prisoners taken from the *Philadelphia*.

June 11, 1805: While Eaton and the Christian forces remained in Derna, the Arabs and Greeks under Hamet Karamanli (but with help of firepower from U.S. ships offshore) defeated their Tripolitan foes in a cavalry battle near Derna. That ended the War with Tripoli.

NEGOTIATIONS AND PEACE TREATY

There was little in the way of negotiation during the first two years of the War with Tripoli. It was not until late 1804, following the intensive American bombardment of Tripoli, that Pasha Yusuf began to put out feelers toward negotiations. The Spanish consul general in Tripoli, Don Joseph de Souza, served as the go-between for the pasha and the American diplomat in the Medi-

terranean, Col. Tobias Lear. Actual negotiations began in late May 1805, after Pasha Yusuf heard of the fall of Derna. Among other motives, Yusuf wanted to make sure that his brother, Hamet, would not be restored to the throne. Tobias Lear, Capt. Samuel Barron, and the other Americans involved were anxious to conclude a peace swiftly and were willing to set aside Hamet's claim—much to William Eaton's dismay.

June 4, 1805: Terms for a peace treaty were agreed to by the United States and Tripoli. The United States agreed to pay $60,000 for the release of the sailors taken from the USS *Philadelphia*. For its part, Tripoli agreed to grant most-favored-nation trade status to the United States, to not molest American merchant vessels, and to forgo demands for tribute payments. However, the purported goal of Eaton's campaign—to restore Hamet to the throne of Tripoli—was completely ignored.

June 10, 1805: The treaty was signed by Col. Tobias Lear and Pasha Yusuf.

September 1, 1805: The dey of Tunis, having been placed under blockade for 32 days by an American naval squadron commanded by Comdr. John Rodgers, agreed to stop harassing American ships and to send an ambassador to the United States to negotiate terms.

April 12, 1806: President Jefferson had submitted the treaty to the U.S. Senate on December 11, 1805, and after long and acrimonious debate, the U.S. Senate approved the treaty with the pasha of Tripoli. (The Senate voted to award Hamet a small sum of money in compensation for the failure to restore him to the throne of Tripoli. Hamet died an outcast in Egypt.)

The War with Algiers: 1815

CAUSES OF THE WAR

Even after treaties were signed between Tripoli and the United States and Tunis and the United States, the dey of Algiers continued to demand tribute (in the form of naval stores) from the United States. During the War of 1812 (1812–1815), while all American naval power was devoted to fighting against Great Britain, the dey of Algiers preyed upon American shipping in the Mediterranean. Insisting that he had not been paid proper tribute, he dismissed the American consul, Tobias Lear, in 1812, then seized an American merchant ship and enslaved its officers and crew. The United States was powerless to do much while engaged in a war with Great Britain, but immediately after the end of the war with Britain, President James Madison determined to put an end to the threat of hostility toward American merchant ships once and for all.

PREPARATIONS FOR WAR

During the War of 1812, it was recognized that the few heavily gunned U.S. frigates had performed respectfully, but the shortage of those and other large ships had left the U.S. Navy at an obvious disadvantage when confronting a major naval power. Six large ships, however, had been commissioned just as the war broke out, and one of those, the USS *Guerrière*, was ready for duty. The *Guerrière* was immediately assigned with the veteran USS *Constellation* to lead a squadron of nine ships to the Mediterranean. Outfitting this squadron was the extent of the preparations for this expedition.

DECLARATION OF WAR

February 23, 1815: President Madison sent a message to Congress recommending a declaration of war against the Barbary state of Algiers.

March 2, 1815: Congress officially declared war on Algiers.

BATTLES AND CAMPAIGNS

May 20, 1815: Capt. Stephen Decatur sailed from New York City in command of ten American ships headed for the Mediterranean to end the raids of the Algerian pirates.

June 15, 1815: Captain Decatur and his squadron arrived at Gibraltar after a remarkably fast crossing of the Atlantic Ocean.

June 17, 1815: The USS *Constellation* and the USS *Guerrière* fought against the 46-gun Algerian frigate *Mashuda*. The Americans captured the frigate, with losses of four killed and nine wounded. The Algerian losses were calculated at 30 killed, dozens wounded, 406 taken prisoner; among the dead was their famous admiral Hammida.

June 19, 1815: American sailors from Decatur's squadron boarded and captured the Algerian brig *Estedio*; 23 Algerians were killed and 80 were taken prisoner.

June 28, 1815: Captain Decatur's squadron arrived off the city of Algiers with both recently captured Algerian ships in tow. He threatened to bombard the city and attack every Algerian ship in sight unless the dey capitulated immediately and gave in to all American demands.

NEGOTIATIONS AND PEACE TREATY

June 29, 1815: Negotiations were opened between Cap. Stephen Decatur and the dey of Algiers through the office of the Swedish consul in Algiers.

June 30, 1815: A treaty of peace between Algiers and the United States was signed. The treaty required that the prisoners held by both sides be returned at once, forced the dey of Algiers to pay $10,000 in compensation for the American citizens and property that had been held by Algiers, and specifically disallowed any further form of tribute by Americans.

July 26, 1815: Decatur's squadron moved eastward along the coast and anchored off Tunis. Decatur demanded and received $46,000 in payment for two American ships that Tunisia had turned over to the British. The dey of Tunis also agreed to cease all interference with American shipping and to cease demands for tribute.

August 5, 1815: Decatur's squadron anchored off Tripoli, and Decatur received $25,000 in recompense for the Tripolitan role in the capture of two American ships. Yusuf Karmanli, still the pasha of Tripoli, again agreed to release all Americans without ransom, to cease raiding American shipping, and to stop demands for tribute.

November 12, 1815: Captain Decatur brought his squadron into New York Harbor, having conducted a remarkably swift and successful campaign in the Mediterranean.

December 26, 1815: The treaty with Algiers was ratified by the U.S. Senate.

HOME FRONT

During the years of the first Barbary War (1801–1805), the people of the United States were little aware of the events in the distant Mediterranean. Even the fastest passage to the Atlantic seaports required a month, and news then traveled slowly inland. Relatively small numbers of American sailors and marines were involved in the action, and few Americans except those involved in international commerce were directly affected by the suppression of the pirates—although nearly all Americans supported the notion of ridding their country of the odious tribute and humiliating hostage taking. That was what allowed the newly installed president, Thomas Jefferson, to obtain support for his actions in the Mediterranean, even as he drastically cut back the Navy and promised a less active role for the federal government. Most Americans' attention, however, was drawn not to Europe but to their own West: The Northwest Territory was being developed, and the Louisiana Purchase (1803) added a vast territory to the nation. In March 1804, Congress passed the Land Act which permitted anyone to buy a 160-acre tract at a low price and in installments over ten years. In May 1804, the Lewis and Clark expedition set out from St. Louis. The fledgling nation was heading away from its European nest.

The United States was just emerging from the War of 1812 with a mixture of relief and some exhilaration when President James Madison and Congress authorized the expedition to the Mediterranean, and the second of the Barbary Wars was practically over before most Americans knew about it. The U.S. fleet arrived off Algiers in mid-June; by August 5, Decatur had forced Algiers, Tunis, and Tripoli to agree to terms of a treaty; by November 12—just about the time the news of events in the Mediterranean was spreading through the United States—Decatur was bringing his victorious fleet into New York Harbor. During that brief period, Americans were preoccupied with a more immediate issue that also involved U.S. ships. On the Great Lakes, there were several incidents involving U.S. and Canadian ships (no shots were fired), and there were rumors that the British intended to build up their war fleet there. Just about the time Decatur's fleet was arriving home, Madison was instructing his ambassador to Britain to negotiate a compromise. The result was the Rush-Bagot Agreement (April 1817), limiting each country's naval forces on the Great Lakes.

NEGOTIATIONS AND PEACE TREATY

Both Barbary Wars ended with the United States negotiating formal treaties with the principal parties. The full details are recounted above under the heading for each war.

RESULTS OF THE WARS (Casualties, Costs, Consequences)

During the Barbary Wars the Americans suffered relatively few men killed or wounded. Although exact figures are not available, it is estimated that the total number of Americans killed was fewer than 100. The figure for the Barbary residents was much higher—at least 500 and perhaps as many as 1,000 persons were killed. Assuming that the United States would have had to maintain its Navy at about the same level with or without the Barbary Wars, the cost of the wars to the United States was relatively modest—some $500,000—especially considering that the U.S. had paid more than $2 million in tribute to the Barbary States. Although the United States action did not immediately end the predations of the Barbary pirates (the United States continued to pay tribute for another few decades), it announced to the world at large that the United States of America was prepared to go to great lengths to fight for what it valued.

MILITARY INNOVATIONS, TACTICS, EQUIPMENT

The United States gained several valuable military lessons during the otherwise minor Barbary Wars. To begin with, between 1794 and 1798, the U.S. built six frigates, five designed by the leading American shipbuilder, Joshua Humphreys of Philadelphia. Since he knew that American ships might often be outnumbered by powerful European navies, Humphreys built the frigates of extra strong cedar and oak to withstand heavy 24-pounder balls, allowed for extra cannons (sometimes 50 instead of the standard 44), and designed the sails so that the ships could escape when outgunned. The ships proved their worth in the Tripolitan War and were available for the War of 1812.

The United States also discovered the value of maintaining a small, mobile, and flexible marine corps. Whether in actions at sea (as with Decatur's burning of the *Philadelphia*) or on land (as with Eaton's attack on Derna), the U.S. Marine Corps proved its worth.

In the years after 1805, there were those who questioned whether the United States should maintain a large navy and a strong marinecorps; the actions of both in the Barbary Wars were often cited to support the need.

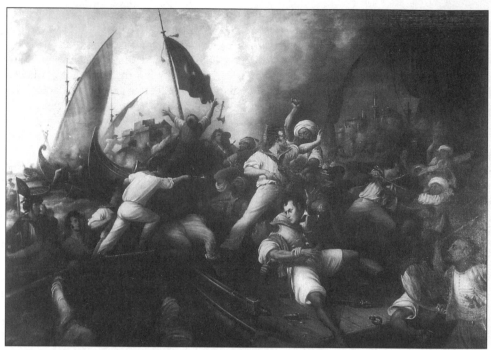

This painting depicts Lt. Stephen Decatur (struggling in foreground) and midshipman Thomas Macdonough (standing center) leading a boarding party on a Tripolitan ship during the attack on Tripoli, August 3, 1804.

LEGENDS AND TRIVIA

The **battle of the gunboats** (August 3, 1804) has long remained a symbol by which Americans recall the intrepid actions of the young U.S. Navy. In the 20th century, a U.S. destroyer was named the USS *Reuben James* in honor of an American sailor who was believed to have risked his life in order to save Lt. Stephen Decatur's life during the gunboat battle. However, extensive research has proved that the sailor who saved Decatur was Daniel Frazier, not Reuben James.

NOTABLE PHRASES

We mean to rest the safety of our commerce on the resources of our own strength and bravery in every sea.

President Thomas Jefferson wrote those words in a letter to Yusuf Karamanli, the pasha of Tripoli, on May 21, 1801. Noting that he was sending a squadron of observation to the Mediterranean, Jefferson also let Karamanli know that he, Jefferson, was determined to uphold the dignity of the American flag. Jefferson was generally thought of as a pacifist, but he was not against using military power against tyrants or thieves.

God, I thank thee that my children are Americans!

William Eaton wrote those words in his journal on February 1, 1805, in Egypt. Eaton had just been approached by an 11-year-old boy who had asked for help for his mother and four brothers and sisters. In his journal, Eaton reported that he had given all the money in his pocket to the boy.

My head or yours.

That was the succinct reply made by Governor Mustapha of Derna to William Eaton and Hamet Karamanli when they demanded the surrender of Derna on April 27, 1805. As it turned out, Governor Mustapha escaped from the city before it fell to the American-Berber force, and, therefore, neither leader actually lost his head.

Our country! In her intercourse with foreign nations may she always be in the right; but our country, right or wrong.

Those were the words of Capt. Stephen Decatur, offered as a toast in the city of Norfolk, Virginia, on April 4, 1816. A number of prior toasts had celebrated Decatur and the actions of the Navy in the Tripolitan and Algerian Wars. The statement has been used many times since.

SONGS

The official hymn of the United States Marine Corps refers to the "shores of Tripoli." The words reflect the achievements of Lt. Presley O'Bannon and the seven other marines who marched from Alexandria to Derna in March–April 1805. The song was accepted as the official song of the U.S. Marine Corps in 1929.

From the halls of Montezuma,
To the shores of Tripoli.
We fight our country's battles,
On the land as on the sea.
First to fight for right and freedom,
Then to keep our honor clean.
We are proud to claim the title of,
United States Marines.

It has been claimed that those original words (the fourth line was changed in 1942 to "In the air, on land and sea") were composed by an unknown marine after U.S. troops took Mexico City in 1847, but that has not been proved. The melody to which the words have been sung since at least 1918 is based on a song in the opera *Geneviève de Brabant* (1859, 1875), by Jacques Offenbach.

HISTORICAL PERSPECTIVES AND CONTROVERSIES

Although 19th century and early 20th century historians determined to assign blame would always be able to cast the Barbary Wars as just another chapter in Western imperialism, even the revisionist histories of the 1960s failed to find any rationale for the United States having to accept the piratical behavior of the Barbary States. There has been almost unanimous consensus among American historians that the wars were just, honorable, necessary, and beneficial to the United States. What also has been generally accepted is that the Tripolitan War served as a training ground for the U.S. Navy and Marine Corps. Few men have done as much to instill a winning tradition in

the American armed forces as did Edward Preble, Stephen Decatur, William Eaton, and Presley N. O'Bannon.

The only controversy that has emerged has been over the conduct of some of the officers of the U.S. Navy. There were two extremes. On the one hand, there were the overly cautious commodores, such as Richard Morris and Samuel Barron. Many historians feel that if those men had pursued the Barbary pirates and potentates more aggressively from the outset, the latter would have capitulated sooner. On the other hand, there were the reckless junior officers, such as Stephen Decatur. But if Decatur was foolish in his acceptance of a duel with a British official during the war, that activity has not served to dim the brilliance of his actions on the night of February 16, 1804 (see p. 131).

CIVILIAN AND MILITARY BIOGRAPHIES

AMERICAN

Bainbridge, William (1774–1833)—naval officer: William Bainbridge was born in New Jersey. He became a captain in the U.S. Navy in 1800. In 1800, he had the dubious distinction of being in command of the USS *George Washington* that was forced by the dey of Algiers to bring tribute to Constantinople. Then in 1803, he suffered a worse humiliation when his ship, the USS *Philadelphia,* ran aground off Tripoli. Taken prisoner with all his crew, he was held captive for two years. A court of inquiry was held, and he was cleared of any blame for the incident with the *Philadelphia.* In the War of 1812 he regained his reputation as captain of the USS *Constitution* in its victory over the British *Java.* When the war with Algiers began in 1815, Bainbridge was given command of the second squadron that sailed for the Mediterranean, but he arrived too late to play any significant role.

Decatur, Stephen (1779–1820)—naval officer: Stephen Decatur was born in Maryland. He joined the U.S. Navy in 1798. A lieutenant at the start of the Barbary Wars, he rose to captain through his brilliant performances in the burning of the USS *Philadelphia* and at the "battle of the gunboats." He went on to serve in the War of 1812 and to become a naval commissioner. He died in a duel with a fellow naval officer, James Barron.

Eaton, William (1764–1811)—consul, military leader: William Eaton was born in Connecticut. He served as U.S. consul in Tunis and negotiated a treaty between that country and the United States. In 1803, he returned to the United States and obtained permission to lead a risky expedition through Egypt and to strike at Tripoli from the land. He captured Derna in April 1805, but then endured the humiliation of seeing the United States negotiate with the usurper pasha of Tripoli. Eaton returned to the U.S. and was honored as a hero. He died a few years later.

O'Bannon, Presley Neville (1776–1850)—marine officer: Presley N. O'Bannon was born in Virginia. He led seven Marines who accompanied William Eaton on the epic campaign against Derna (1805). O'Bannon raised the Stars and Stripes over Derna, the first time the American flag had been raised over a foreign city. He retired from the Marines in 1807 and moved to Kentucky, where he served in both houses of the legislature.

Preble, Edward (1761–1807)—naval officer: Edward Preble was born in Falmouth, Massachusetts (then a part of Maine). He ran away to sea at 16 and was commissioned a lieutenant in 1798. He became commodore of the American squadron off Tripoli in 1803, and his actions contributed greatly to the U.S. victory in the War with Tripoli.

TRIPOLITAN

Karamanli, Yusuf (ruled 1796–1834)—pasha of Tripoli: In 1796, Yusuf Karamanli took over the position of pasha after murdering his oldest brother and deposing the next in line, his brother Hamet Karamanli. In 1801, Yusuf ordered the cutting down of the American flagpole, thus opening the War with Tripoli. He fought against the Americans with great gusto during the Tripolitan war but shrank from the prospect of a rematch during the Algerian war in 1815. He managed to keep his throne until 1834, when he abdicated in favor of

his children. He was the last of the Karamanli dynasty of Tripoli (1711–1834). Following his abdication, Tripoli was again ruled by the Ottoman Empire, which was based in Constantinople.

Karamanli, Hamet (?–1810)—exiled pasha of Tripoli: Hamet Karamanli ruled as pasha only one year (1795–1796) before being deposed and exiled by his younger brother, Yusuf. In 1805, while in Egypt, he was recruited by William Eaton to march against the city of Derna with the promise that the United States would restore him to power. Following the capture of that city and the end of the war, Hamet went into exile once again, with scant recognition of his services by the United States.

FURTHER READING

Allen, Gardner W. *Our Navy and the Barbary Corsairs.* Hamden, Conn.: Archon Books, 1965.

Edwards, Samuel. *Barbary General: The Life of William H. Eaton.* Englewood Cliffs, N. J.: Prentice Hall, 1968.

Guttridge, Leonard F., and Jay D. Smith. *The Commodores: The U.S. Navy in the Age of Sail.* New York: Harper & Row, 1969.

Martin, Tyrone G. *A Most Fortunate Ship: A Narrative History of Old Ironsides.* Chester, Conn.: Globe Pequot Press, 1980.

Tucker, Glenn. *Dawn Like Thunder: The Barbary Wars and the Birth of the U.S. Navy.* New York: Bobbs-Merrill Company, 1963.

Whipple, A. B. C. *To the Shores of Tripoli: The Birth of the U.S. Navy and Marines.* New York: William Morrow, 1991.

Wright, Louis B., and Julia H. MacLeod. *The First Americans in North Africa.* Princeton, N. J.: Princeton University Press, 1945.

THE WAR OF 1812

DATES OF WAR

June 18, 1812–February 17, 1815.

ALTERNATE NAMES

Mr. Madison's War. The War of Faulty Communication. The Second War of American Independence.

SIGNIFICANCE

The War of 1812 was one of the strangest and least conclusive wars in American history. Fought for a variety of reasons—including sailors rights and land hunger—the war came to involve the United States, Great Britain, British Canada, and a number of Native American tribes. The fighting ended in little more than a draw between the United States and Great Britain, yet the consequences for Canada and the Native Americans were very large. Although neither side could truly claim that it "won" the War of 1812, all combatants except Native Americans could point to some positive outcomes from the conflict. From the American point of view, the war was important in that it freed the United States from its junior status among the nations of the world and allowed it to expand westward with little concern over future invasion or encroachment.

BACKGROUND

The background and setting of the War of 1812 had its roots in the American Revolution, the Napoleonic Wars, maritime issues of neutrality and commerce, and conflicts between American settlers and Indian tribes in the Northwest Territory (present-day Indiana, Illinois, and Michigan).

Bad feelings between British subjects and American citizens remained from the American Revolution. In particular, the British refusal to evacuate forts along the Great Lakes reminded Americans of the fighting that had taken place between the two countries and of Britain's apparent contempt for the young American Republic.

For their part, the British probably would have forgotten about America if the Napoleonic wars had not come forth to create fresh dissension between the United States and Great Britain.

In 1793, Great Britain entered into what became a 20-year struggle against France. The Napoleonic Wars started when France was a revolutionary republic (1793–1799). They continued under the consulate regime, in which Napoleon Bonaparte was first consul (1799–1804), and culminated with the French empire under Emperor Napoleon (1804–1815). Wars between England and France dated back many centuries, but the intensity and scope of the Napoleonic Wars made the previous series of French and Indian Wars seem rather small. The British people perceived their conflicts with Napoleonic France to be a life-and-death struggle, and the British navy showed little respect for many neutral ships during the years 1793–1815.

Early on in the Napoleonic Wars, President George Washington declared the United States neutral (April 22, 1793). That wise move led to a period of grace for the United States, during which American merchant ships were permitted a larger share of the world's merchant cargo from port to port (1793–1806). However, as the Napoleonic Wars became more intense at the turn of the 19th century, the British Royal Navy entered into a program of impressment—taking sailors off neutral ships and impressing them into the service of the Royal Navy. The British, whose rationale was once an Englishman, always an Englishman, asserted that many deserters of the British navy were on American ships and that they could be taken off and returned to the British service at any time. Naturally, this policy and the practice of impressment led to outrage on the part of American shipowners and, eventually, on the part of the American public. The closest estimates indicate that between 1800 and 1812 approximately 2,500 American sailors were impressed into the British navy.

Finally, there was the matter of Native American–British relations in the Northwest Territory, which the United States had acquired under the Treaty of Paris, which ended the American Revolution. (The vast tract of land that comprised the Northwest Territory was eventually divided to form the states of Ohio, Indiana, Illinois, Michigan, Wisconsin, and part of Minnesota.) In an attempt to prevent further movement into the territory by American settlers, British forts on the Canadian shore of Lake Erie supplied guns and gunpowder to Indian tribes, such as the Shawnee, in present-day Ohio and Indiana. The British hoped to secure the southern border of Canada to prevent the United States from continuing to expand westward. The British found allies in men such as the Shawnee chief Tecumseh and his brother, "the Prophet," who sought to create a tribal confederacy to prevent further American expansion. In the eyes of American settlers in the Northwest Territory, the British policy of supplying weapons to the Native Americans was nothing short of encouraging murderous acts along the frontier.

CAUSES OF THE WAR

The immediate causes that led to the War of 1812 were:

The Orders in Council: Three specific British naval regulations issued from London (January 7, 1807; November 11, 1807; April 21, 1812) made it legal for British ships to search, fine, and seize neutral ships (mostly American) carrying cargo to Britain's enemies, principally Napoleonic France.

American responses: The United States Congress passed the Non Importation Act (April 18, 1806), the Embargo Act (December 22, 1807), the Non Intercourse Act (March 1, 1809), and Macon's Bill Number 2 (May 1, 1810), all intended to force Great Britain to allow the United States to pursue "free trade and sailors' rights" and to rescind the Orders in Council. The most important of the four acts was the Embargo Act, which made it illegal for any American ship to carry cargo from an American port to Great Britain. The act was, of course, designed to harm British commerce, but it hurt American shipping even more, especially in New England. A New Hampshire poet wrote

Our ships all in motion,
    Once whiten'd the ocean
They sailed and return'd with a cargo;
    Now doomed to decay
They are fallen a prey,
    To Jefferson, worms and embargo.

Naval clashes: Two clashes between American and British warships just off the U.S. East Coast inflamed American public opinion.

The Chesapeake-Leopold *Affair (June 22, 1807):* The frigate USS *Chesapeake*, sailing from Hampton Roads, Virginia, was accosted ten miles out to sea by the HMS *Leopold.* The British demanded to search the American ship for deserters; the American commander, Capt. James Barron, refused the insult to the American flag. Without warning, the British ship fired three broadsides into the American ship, killing three men and wounding 18 others. Captain Barron fired a token shot of resistance, then struck his flag and accepted the British boarding party, which took four men off the ship. The *Chesapeake* limped back into harbor, and American public opinion moved close to the point of war. Captain Barron was barred from naval service for five years. The British finally apologized for the affair five years later.

The Little Belt *Affair (May 16, 1811)*: The American frigate *President* sailed from Annapolis and encountered a British ship off Cape Henry. Thinking that they had found the British ship *Guerrière*, which had conducted numerous impressments, the Americans fired on the British vessel, causing 32 casualties. It turned out that the ship was actually the British sloop of war *Little Belt*, and with its 18 guns, it was no match for the American ship, which had 44 guns. The *Little Belt* affair further poisoned the air between the United States and Great Britain.

Conflicts with Native Americans: Indians along the northwest and southwest frontiers increasingly came into conflict with American settlers pushing westward. In many cases, the Indians had support from British agents and traders based in Canada.

In response to stories of a major Indian confederacy, under the leadership of Tecumseh, planning to strike at American pioneer settlements, Gen. William Henry Harrison led 1,000 American militiamen—most of them from Ohio—from Vincennes to the Indian stronghold of Prophetstown (September 26, 1811). In the absence of Tecumseh, who was in the South trying to recruit Creek warriors to his cause, Tecumseh's brother, known as "the Prophet," struck at Harrison on the banks of the Tippecanoe River on November 7, 1811. The fighting led to many casualties on both sides, but the American forces prevailed and proceeded to burn Prophetstown before returning home. The Indian confederacy had been dealt a severe, although not fatal, blow, and Harrison achieved national recognition for his leadership. (He would run for President in 1840 with the slogan "Tippecanoe and Tyler, Too.")

Congressional elections and 12th Congress of the United States: The 12th Congress, which convened on November 4, 1811, represented a new generation in American politics. The men of the 12th Congress were far too young to have participated in the American Revolution but were eager to uphold the dignity of the American flag. Among those young congressmen of 1811 were Henry Clay from Kentucky, elected Speaker of the House of Representatives; John C. Calhoun from South Carolina; Richard M. Johnson of Kentucky; and Felix Grundy from Tennessee. Those men soon became the leaders of the so-called War Hawks in the 12th Congress, calling for war with Great Britain in order to seize Canada and thereby free American pioneers from the threat of Indian raids supported by British weapons. In the debates that ensued in Congress between December 1811 and June 1812, the War Hawks contested with Federalists—mostly from New England—who claimed that war with the British would be a disaster.

PREPARATIONS FOR WAR

During the spring of 1812, in the aftermath of the *Little Belt* affair and the Battle of Tippecanoe, a call for war developed in the United States. President James Madison proposed, and Congress passed, a 60-day embargo on all shipping from U.S. ports (April 4, 1812). On April 10, 1812, Congress empowered the president to call up 100,000 militiamen from the states and territories to serve for six months. There was still some hope within the Madison administration that war could be avoided. Those hopes were pinned on the expected arrival of the USS *Hornet*, which was bringing diplomatic dispatches from Great Britain.

On May 19, 1812, the USS *Hornet* docked at New York City. Three days later, President Madison and his advisers had the British response, declaring a strict and stubborn adherence to the Orders in Council (see p. 140). That disappointment led Madison closer to war.

Unknown to Madison and to anyone in the United States, however, was the fact that the British prime minister, Spencer Perceval, had been assassinated on May 11, 1812 (the only assassination of a prime minister in British history). Following Perceval's death, the British Parliament began to reassess its maritime policy. On June 16, 1812, the British suspended the Orders in Council and on June 23, the orders were formally revoked. Had those actions occurred a few weeks earlier, war might have been avoided, but during the four to six weeks that it took for news to cross the Atlantic Ocean, the United States declared war.

DECLARATION OF WAR

President Madison sent a war message to Congress on June 1, 1812, citing impressment, the Orders in Council, economic blockades, and British influence over Indians in the Northwest Territory as reasons for war. Not a belligerent man, Madison was responding to pressure from the War Hawks in Congress and to the need for resolution of the conflicts over maritime affairs that had dragged on for several years.

The House of Representatives voted in favor of war on June 4, 1812, by a vote of 79-49. The Senate followed suit on June 17, 1812 by a vote of 19-13, making that the closest vote on any war ever cast by a U.S. Congress. Sectional differences were clearly visible in the voting; all 39 Federalist members of Congress (most from New England, where shipping and merchant interests were strong) voted against the war, and most congressmen from Pennsylvania and farther south (where frontier and agricultural interests predominated) voted in favor of war.

COMBATANTS

Americans: The American combatants were a mixture of regular Army soldiers, long-term militiamen (state-organized volunteers), short-term militia units, regular Navy sailors, and merchant sailors who converted their ships to privateers during the war.

As the war began, there were fewer than 7,000 men in the regular U.S. Army. Those troops had seen little or no action during their careers in the military, and they had yet to develop into a cohesive fighting force. The activities of certain regular Army officers, such as Winfield Scott, did much to change that during the war, but at the start, the American regular Army was small and untested.

Militia units, both long-term and short-term,

formed the core of American military forces. Victory in the American Revolution had created an almost mystical faith in the fighting abilities of the American militiaman. For the first year and a half of the war, the performance of the militia was disappointing both on the offense and on the defense. Gradually, some militia units worked their way up to a semiprofessional status, and by 1814, many of them performed well in battle.

The U.S. Navy was small, but its seven frigates were among the best designed and constructed in the world. Naval officers had earned their stripes in the undeclared naval war with France (1798–1800) (see pp. 121-127), in the Tripolitan War (1802–1805) (see pp. 130-133), and in actions such as those of the *Chesapeake* and *Little Belt* affairs. The American naval officers tended to be daring, sometimes to the point of foolhardiness. Despite its diminutive size (seven frigates, two sloops, three brigs, four schooners, and two bomb ketches), the U.S. Navy was confident of its abilities on a ship-to-ship basis.

The regular Navy was augmented by numerous privateers. Merchant ships could be turned into lightly armed privateer vessels that preyed upon British commerce. The advantages were obvious: The costs were small; the potential profits from seizing ships were large; and privateering involved individual enterprise rather than federal spending. One disadvantage was that privateer captains were loyal to their pocketbooks, and many of them backed away from engagements in which they might have inflicted more damage on the British but put themselves at greater risk. In general, the privateers performed a service similar to that of the American militiamen, and that involved many of the same limitations—lack of professionalism and reliability.

British: British regular army troops were considered to be among the best in the world. Under the leadership of the Duke of Wellington, they were in the process of defeating Napoleonic armies in Spain when the War of 1812 began. Few neutral observers believed that American soldiers— whether they were regular Army or militia—could stand up to Wellington's Invincibles. However, when the war began, Britain could spare only a small number of its men for American campaigns (a condition that changed after the abdication of Emperor Napoleon on May 14, 1814). In addition, the veterans of the Spanish campaigns found it difficult to adjust to the North American terrain.

Officers and sailors of the 600-ship British Royal Navy were considered to be far and away the best in the world. More than 20 years of sea fighting in the Napoleonic Wars had yielded victory after victory to the British navy. Conscious of their superiority over French, Spanish, Danish, and Dutch fleets, the British looked with utter contempt on the tiny American fleet.

Canadians: The Canadian soldiers were almost exclusively militiamen. When the war began, they had no tradition of service or of victory, such as the American militia had from their victory in the American Revolution. The Canadian militiamen were looked down on by the Americans and by their British regular army officers, but they proved to be stubborn and persistent in defense of their home soil.

Indians: The War of 1812 presented one last chance for the Indian tribes living east of the Mississippi River to combine against the Americans. Tecumseh and the Prophet failed to create a general Indian confederacy (due in part to General Harrison's victory at Tippecanoe, November 7, 1811), but the Shawnee Indians in the North and the Creek Indians in the South fought with great bravery and skill against the Americans during the war. The greatest weakness of the Indian warriors was that their culture worked against centralization and command, and even a powerful and respected chief such as Tecumseh had to use persuasion rather than command when organizing his men. Tecumseh also found that the British commanders with whom he was allied often offered little assistance to his cause. Only in the case of Gen. Isaac Brock did Tecumseh find a British leader worthy of the comment, "This is a man!"

GEOGRAPHIC AND STRATEGIC CONSIDERATIONS

When the war began in June 1812, most of the immediate advantages belonged to the Americans. The United States could strike at Canada before reinforcements could arrive from Britain, especially as the British were still involved in fighting a war against Napoleon.

The population of the United States (7.5 million) was far larger than that of British Canada (500,000), and the United States had a stronger military tradition deriving from the Colonial Wars and the Revolution. Given those factors, it seemed entirely likely that the riflemen of the American

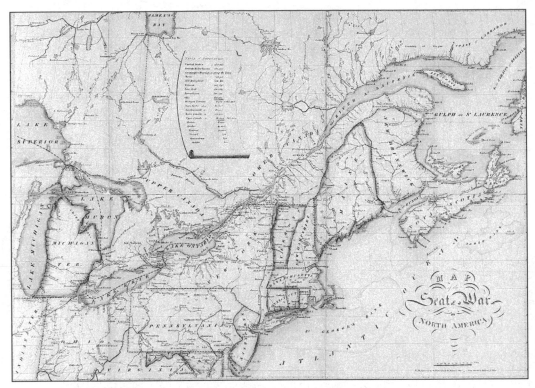

This 1815 map of the "seat" of the War of 1812 shows the extensive territory where the battles of the war were fought.

frontier (Kentucky and Tennessee especially) would be able to take Canada simply by marching northward. But what was the right route to take? Given the poor condition of the roads, transporting any large body of troops and supplying them at the front required a water route.

The most obvious was the Hudson River–Lake George–Lake Champlain–Montreal route, the very one that British general John Burgoyne had tried to use in 1777 (see American Revolution pp. 81-84). However, it was also the best-guarded route, and its very obviousness raised doubts.

There were at least two other possible invasion routes. The first was from Buffalo, New York, across the Niagara River into Ontario. The second was from Fort Detroit (site of present-day Detroit) across the Detroit River and into Ontario from the western point of entry. Either of those two routes seemed distinctly possible, as long as there was an American naval presence on Lake Erie. Lacking a naval force on Lake Erie, any full-scale invasion force would face the danger of having its supply lines cut by British vessels.

British and Canadian strategy was essentially

defensive when the war began. The British had only about 8,000 regular army troops in all of Canada, and it was, therefore, imperative to hold the main lines of defense until reinforcements could arrive from the mother country. The British were well aware of the three likely routes of invasion, and early on they deployed their small force of regular soldiers in areas in which they could be repositioned to meet whatever attack came. Key to the British defense strategy was maintaining a naval superiority on Lake Ontario, Lake Erie, and Lake Champlain.

In the southern states, Creek warriors went on the offensive against the Americans, and in the northern states, Tecumseh and his warriors aligned themselves with British general Brock to fight against the Americans at Fort Detroit. Although the Indians fought with great skill and stubbornness throughout the war, an element of defeatism crept into their ranks following the Battle of Tippecanoe on November 7, 1811, and the burning of Prophetstown.

In general, at the time of the declaration of war—June 1812, months before Britain could get its troops over to North America—the lay of the land, population factors, and the rapid mobilization of forces all seemed to be in the favor of the American cause.

BATTLES AND CAMPAIGNS: 1812

There were four areas of activity in 1812: western theater (Detroit, Lake Erie, Lake Michigan, and present-day Indiana and Illinois), Niagara theater (British and American military camps on either side of the Niagara River, stretching from Fort Niagara to Buffalo on the American side), Lake Champlain theater (traditional invasion route between Albany and Montreal), and the naval theater (which included battles on the Great Lakes). In all those theaters, the Americans had the initiative in 1812, and in they all took the offensive.

WESTERN THEATER

July 5, 1812: Brig. Gen. William Hull arrived at Fort Detroit with his army of 2,000 American militia troops, most of them recruited from the Ohio region. The 60-year old Hull was a veteran of the American Revolution. His orders were to cross into Canada and capture British fort Malden as a preliminary stroke to begin an invasion of present-day Ontario.

July 12, 1812: General Hull crossed the Detroit River into Canada.

July 16–August 7, 1812: On July 16, Hull's men came within 4 miles of Fort Malden, but Hull remained indecisive for weeks before finally ordering an attack on the fort on August 6. Hearing of the advance of British general Isaac Brock, Hull quickly canceled the attack and recrossed the Detroit River to take up a defensive position at Fort Detroit on August 7, 1812.

August 13, 1812: British general Isaac Brock arrived at Fort Malden and met with Shawnee chief Tecumseh, who had arrived with 600 Indian warriors. Men of like minds, Brock and Tecumseh decided to attack immediately, before Hull could receive reinforcements.

August 14, 1812: General Brock laid out cannons in preparation to bombard Fort Detroit, and British and Indian forces marched ceaselessly back and forth in front of the fort in an effort to intimidate General Hull.

August 15, 1812: Responding to Hull's orders to evacuate their fort, the American garrison of Fort Dearborn (present-day Chicago) marched out of the fort only to be set upon by approximately 500 Indian warriors. In the ensuing fight, 12 children, 12 civilian men, 1 captain, 2 officers, and 26 enlisted men were killed. The news spread further gloom throughout Americans along the northwest frontier.

August 16, 1812: General Hull surrendered Fort Detroit to British general Brock. Hull was overwhelmed by the British and Indian show of force and was preoccupied by the presence of his daughter and grandchildren within the fort. Of Hull's 2,000-man army, the militiamen were paroled by Brock (who did not want to have to feed such a large number); the regular army troops were prisoners of war in Canada. Following the surrender, Brock declared that Michigan was part of Great Britain. Hull was later court-martialed and sentenced to death, but his sentence was commuted by President Madison because of his service in the American Revolution. The loss of Fort Detroit was a great blow to American forces throughout the western area, and it allowed Tecumseh's Indian warriors to carry out a number of raids that would otherwise have been impossible.

August 22, 1812: William Henry Harrison was made a brigadier general with the responsibility to organize the American forces in the western area and to recapture Fort Detroit.

September 3, 1812: Indian forces in alliance with Tecumseh attacked an American settlement at Pigeon Roost in present-day Indiana, killing 20 American settlers.

September 4–September 16, 1812: Tecumseh led a siege of Fort Harrison in present-day Indiana. The fort's 70-man garrison, led by Capt. Zachary Taylor, managed to hold out against 600 warriors until Gen. William Henry Harrison arrived on September 12 to relieve the garrison. Taylor was promoted to major for his efforts. (He later served as a general in the Mexican War. He eventually became the ninth president of the United States in 1849.)

Third week of September 1812: In response to Indian attacks on American pioneer settlements, American troops attacked Ottawa, Potawatomi, and Miami Indian settlements in present-day Indiana, burning crops wherever they could.

Fall 1812: General Harrison recruited militia from Ohio and Indiana for the planned recapture of Fort Detroit. Thwarted, however, by autumn rains and a lack of supplies, Harrison had to stay in camp for the fall and plan for a spring offensive. As a face-saving gesture, he sent Gen. James Winchester north to scout the British lines. One of Winchester's detachments, led by Lt. Col. John Campbell, was surprised and attacked by Indians on December 8, 1812. The Americans suffered a loss of 10 dead and 48 wounded before they fought off the attack. That was the last action of 1812 in the western theater.

NIAGARA THEATER

October 1, 1812: Some 6,000 American troops, most of them militiamen, were assembled on the east bank of the Niagara River. The American commander was Gen. Stephen Van Rensselaer, who lacked military experience. His cousin, Col. Solomon Van Rensselaer, was his aide and military adviser. Across the river, Gen. Isaac Brock was in command, having hastened to Niagara after the fall of Fort Detroit. Brock had approximately 2,000 men under his command and was under strict orders to remain on the defensive.

October 8–9, 1812: American naval lieutenant Jesse Duncan Elliott led a night attack across the Niagara River. Elliott's men took two British brigs, the *Caledonia* and the *Detroit*, from under the guns of British fort Erie. The Americans set fire to the *Detroit* and brought the *Caledonia* to the American side.

October 13, 1812 (Battle of Queenstown Heights): Gen. Stephen Van Rensselaer sent 600 American troops across the Niagara River to capture the area known as Queenstown Heights. The initial crossing was a success, and the American boats returned to take reinforcements across the river. At that point, however, many American militiamen refused to cross because they were inexperienced volunteers who were frightened by the sight of the first wounded and by reports of Indians fighting beside the British. Although some reinforcements crossed, the position of the Americans at Queenstown Heights became precarious. British general Brock led a charge directly against the Americans on the Heights and was killed—an irreparable loss to the British cause. Later in the day, a second and third British attack succeeded, and the American lines crumbled, while their compatriots watched from the eastern side of the river. The American loss was very heavy: 90 killed, 100 wounded, and 958 men taken prisoner. The British losses were 14 killed, 84 wounded, and 15 missing, but the loss of General Brock weighed on the British morale and fighting spirit. Throughout the war, the British would not find another general as talented and as energetic. Soon after the battle, General Van Rensselaer retired from his command and was succeeded by Gen. Alexander Smyth.

November 28, 1812: American general Smyth led a halfhearted attack on the British lines across the Niagara River. The Americans were driven back, with a loss of 17 dead, 57 wounded, and 56 missing. The British losses were 15 killed, 47 wounded, and 32 missing. That was the last significant military action in the Niagara theater during 1812. No territory had changed hands on either side, and the Americans had learned that militiamen often refused to cross national or even state boundaries.

LAKE CHAMPLAIN THEATER

August 6–26, 1812: American general Henry Dearborn, who doubted the fighting spirit of his troops, arranged for a cease-fire with the British leaders in Montreal. The arrangement was terminated when President James Madison learned of it and ordered Dearborn to march north.

August–October 1812: General Dearborn collected an army of American militiamen at Greenbush near Albany, New York. The American troops were nearly all militiamen and were mostly from the state of New York. The New England states had refused to send militia, since they were opposed to the war on philosophical and commercial grounds.

November 16, 1812: Dearborn led his army of about 6,000 American troops from Plattsburg, New York, north to the Canadian border.

November 19, 1812: Dearborn was informed by the leaders of two-thirds of his militia units that their men were unwilling to cross the border into Canada. They would defend the United States but would not cross the international line. Dearborn was outraged but helpless in the face of the defiance of his men.

November 20, 1812: Lt. Zebulon Pike led 600 U.S. regular troops across the Canadian border in an attempt to save the honor of General Dearborn and the American cause. They were joined by some 400 American militiamen. Pike and his men captured a blockhouse from the British at La Cole Mill. Traveling separately, the American militia units also advanced on the blockhouse. In the fog and confusion, the American groups fired on each other, causing a total of 50 casualties before the mistake was known. Pike's men and the militia units recrossed the border, ending the campaign of 1812 in the Lake Champlain area.

NAVAL THEATER

August 19, 1812: The USS *Constitution* (44 guns) met the HMS *Guerrière* (38 guns) off the coast of Nova Scotia. The American commander, Capt. Isaac Hull (nephew of Gen. William Hull), outmaneuvered and outfought his British opponent, Capt. Richard Dacres. After two hours of fighting the British ship was completely dismasted. The British suffered 13 killed and 62 wounded; American losses were 7 killed, 7 wounded. The *Guerrière* surrendered and sank soon afterward. Hull returned to Boston on August 30, and the news spread that an American frigate had completely outclassed a frigate of the Royal Navy. The news was heralded in the United States, but in Great Britain it was received with a great deal of shock and disbelief.

October 18, 1812: The sloop of war USS *Wasp* (18 guns) met the British HMS *Frolic* (18 guns) 600 miles off the coast of Virginia. American captain Jacob Jones won a resounding victory in which 10 Americans were killed or wounded; the British suffered 90 casualties. Almost immediately after the battle, Captain Jones surrendered his battered vessel to a much larger British ship, but the event remained a victory to the American public.

October 25, 1812: Off the Madeira Islands, the USS *United States* (44 guns) met and defeated the HMS *Macedonian* (38 guns). American commander Stephen Decatur, a hero of the Tripolitan War (see Civilian and Military Biographies, p. 138), had trained his gunners and his sailors well, and they completely outshot and outmaneuvered their British opponents. The Americans suffered 6 men killed and 6 wounded; the British losses were 36 dead and 68 wounded. The *Macedonian* was brought into Newport, Rhode Island. It was the first British ship of war ever to be brought into an American port.

November 9, 1812: American vessels on Lake Ontario entered the British harbor at Kingston and fought a short battle there. Losses were low on both sides (one killed and four wounded for the Americans), but the American withdrawal was significant, and the United States did not enter the

harbor at Kingston again during the remainder of the war.

December 29, 1812: Off the coast of Brazil, the USS *Constitution,* commanded by Capt. William Bainbridge (Captain Hull had been made commander of the Charlestown Navy Yard), met the HMS *Java* (38 guns). After a four-hour battle, the *Java* surrendered, totally dismasted, and was later burned. The American ship won the nickname "Old Ironsides" because of the way in which her timbers resisted the British cannonballs. The Americans suffered 12 killed and 22 wounded; the British losses were 48 killed and 102 wounded.

BATTLES AND CAMPAIGNS: 1813

There were six theaters of action in 1813: western, Niagara, Lake Champlain, Great Lakes, naval, and southern.

WESTERN THEATER

January 22, 1813 (Battle of Raisin River): Gen. James Winchester led 1,300 American troops into Frenchtown on the Raisin River in present-day Michigan. Winchester and his men were attacked by 1,100 British and Indians under Gen. Henry Procter. The attack was a complete surprise, and the Americans suffered 300 dead, 27 wounded, and nearly all the rest of the army—including Winchester—taken prisoner. At least 30 American captives were massacred by Indians. The defeat struck a deep chord in the United States, and henceforth American troops often went into battle with the shout "Remember the Raisin," a warning that the enemy should expect no mercy.

April 28–May 8, 1813: British and Indian forces conducted an unsuccessful siege of Fort Meigs in present-day Ohio.

July 25–August 2, 1813: British and Indian forces besieged Fort Stephenson in present-day Ohio. Despite the fact that the British and Indians outnumbered the Americans five to one, the British and Indians withdrew without capturing the American fort.

September 27, 1813: Gen. William Henry Harrison's men reoccupied Fort Detroit, which had fallen to the British 13 months earlier. Harrison marched with his army in pursuit of British general Procter and the Shawnee chief Tecumseh, who had withdrawn by land and were marching on the north side of Lake Erie.

October 5, 1813 (Battle of Moraviantown, or Battle of the Thames River): General Harrison's men, mostly from Kentucky, began the battle with a cavalry charge. The British line broke almost immediately, but the Indians continued to resist for some time. The American victory was complete. Procter fled, and Tecumseh was presumed killed on the field (although his body was never recovered). The British suffered 12 dead, 22 wounded, and 600 men captured. The Americans suffered 12 men killed and 20 wounded. The Indian losses were unknown. The battle gave control of the western theater to the United States. Harrison did not follow up on his victory because most of his citizen-soldiers were eager to return home.

NIAGARA THEATER

May 27, 1813: American troops captured the British fort George at the northern end of the Niagara River. The loss of the fort and the number of British casualties (50 killed, 500 wounded) appeared to indicate that the Americans would triumph in the Niagara River valley.

June 5, 1813 (Battle of Stoney Creek, Ontario): A force of some 2,000 Americans had encamped along Lake Ontario near Hamilton. Through the Americans' laxity in mounting proper guards, a British force of 700 was able to approach the encampment. Caught by surprise just before dawn, the Americans engaged in hand-to-hand combat with the British. When the two American generals (William Winder and John Chandler) and four of their artillery were captured, the Americans retreated. When the British took over the encampment later that day, they seized valuable ammunition and stores. The Americans reported only 160 casualties; the British reported close to 210.

June 24, 1813 (Battle of Beaver Dams, or Battle of the Beechwoods, Ontario): After the Battle at Stoney Creek, the American force on the Canadian side of Lake Ontario still numbered almost 3,000. A detachment of some 700 set out to attack what they believed was a small British outpost near Fort George. However, a Canadian, Laura Secord, heard of the Americans' plan and walked some 20 miles through the American forces to warn the British (see Legends and Trivia, p. 159). As a result, a party of British and their Indian allies ambushed the Americans at Beaver Dams. After several hours of desperate

resistance, some 600 Americans surrendered to the British. Combined with their victory at Stoney Creek on June 5, the victory at Beaver Dams restored the morale and fighting spirit to the British in Canada. After the American defeat at Beaver Dams, Gen. Henry Dearborn was removed from command of the American forces in the Niagara theater, and the Americans pulled back to Fort George.

December 10, 1813: American forces evacuated and burned Fort George, which they had held since May 27. Before withdrawing across the Niagara River, they also burned Newark, Ontario.

December 18, 1813: British troops crossed the Niagara River and occupied Fort Niagara.

December 19–31, 1813: British troops captured Lewiston, Fort Schlosser, Black Rock, and Buffalo, all in upstate New York.

GREAT LAKES THEATER

During 1813, the British and Americans sought to build more ships in shipyards on Lake Erie and Lake Ontario. In the course of their building programs, both sides carried out raids against the other's shipyards and towns on the lakes.

February 22, 1813: British naval forces on Lake Ontario attacked Ogdensburg, New York.

March 27, 1813: Capt. Oliver Hazard Perry (U.S. Navy) reached Presque Isle and began to build an American fleet for Lake Erie.

April 27, 1813: American forces led by Gen. Zebulon Pike landed at York (present-day Toronto). The Americans won the battle, but soon lost many men in an explosion of a British powder magazine; Pike was among the 52 men who died. Another 180 men were wounded in the explosion. Enraged over this and suspecting that the explosion had been a British scheme, the American troops ravaged York for three days and, on April 29, burned the Government House. The Americans then withdrew from the area.

May 29, 1813: British forces attacked Sackett's Harbor, New York, on Lake Ontario. The British were repulsed and suffered casualties of 260 men; American losses totaled 160.

September 10, 1813 (Battle of Lake Erie): Capt. Oliver Hazard Perry, leading an American fleet of nine ships, fought and defeated a comparable British force, led by Capt. John Barclay. The battle was touch and go for hours. Perry's blue pennant proclaimed *Don't Give Up the Ship,* a

An 1840 lithograph depicts the September 10, 1813, battle on Lake Erie won by the American ships commanded by Oliver Hazard Perry.

rallying cry that had come from the loss of the USS *Chesapeake* on June 1, 1813 (see Naval Theater, below). When the day was over, Perry had won a complete victory at the cost of 21 Americans killed and 63 wounded; British losses were 44 killed and 103 wounded. Perry sent a dispatch to General Harrison, which became famous: "We have met the enemy, and they are ours" (see Notable Phrases, p. 159).

September 28, 1813 (Battle of York Bay): On Lake Ontario, following a running sea battle that left the British squadron bottled up in Burlington Bay, the U.S. squadron established a clear, although temporary, supremacy on the lake.

LAKE CHAMPLAIN THEATER

June 3, 1813: British forces captured two American brigs, giving the British naval superiority on Lake Champlain.

July 3, 1813: American general Wade Hampton reached Burlington, Vermont, and found that his militia forces were in a state of general chaos, preventing any quick attack on Canada.

July 30, 1813: Canadian militia along with British troops captured Plattsburg, New York. They burned public property, blockhouses, barracks, and military storehouses before they withdrew on August 3.

October 25–26, 1813: American forces led by Gen. Wade Hampton were repulsed by Canadian militia at Chateauguay, New York.

November 11, 1813: American forces led by Gen. Jacob Brown attacked and were repulsed by British troops at Chrysler's Farm, Ontario, thus ending any danger to Montreal in 1813.

NAVAL THEATER

February 24, 1813: The USS *Hornet* defeated the HMS *Peacock* near the coast of Brazil.

March 30, 1813: The British navy extended its blockade of the American coastline from Long Island to New Orleans.

June 1, 1813 (the "Infamous First of June"): The USS *Chesapeake*, commanded by Capt. James Lawrence, was defeated off the coast of Massachusetts by the HMS *Shannon*, commanded by Capt. Philip Broke, who had trained his gunners specifically for that meeting. Lawrence's dying words were, "Don't give up the ship" (see Notable Phrases, p. 159). On the same day, American captain Stephen Decatur led two U.S. ships out of New London, Connecticut, seeking to evade the British blockade and make his way to the open sea. Inexplicably, Decatur turned around just as he neared the eastern tip of Long Island and headed back to port. The result was that Decatur, one of the best American naval leaders,was blockaded throughout most of the remainder of the war.

August 14, 1813: The British HMS *Pelican* defeated and captured the 18-gun USS *Argus* off the coast of Wales.

September 4, 1813: The USS *Enterprise* met and defeated the HMS *Boxer* off the coast of Maine. The battle made it clear, once again, that American gunnery was pound for pound superior to that of the British.

SOUTHERN THEATER

Tensions between the Creek Indians and the American settlers had been building for some time. Tecumseh had encouraged the Creeks to strike against the Americans, who had indulged in "land grabs" in the South.

July 27, 1813 (Battle of Burnt Corn Creek): In the opening battle of the Creek War, Creek warriors overwhelmed American militia some 80 miles north of Pensacola, Florida.

August 30, 1812 (Massacre at Fort Mims): Fort Mims, a stockaded fort about 40 miles north of present-day Mobile, Alabama, was surrounded and captured by Creek warriors, who killed 400 of the 500 Americans there. The battle created a storm of anger in the American South, and soon American militia troops were converging on the Creek lands from several directions.

November 9, 1813 (Battle of Talladega): Leading a force of militiamen from Tennessee, Gen. Andrew Jackson defeated a large group of Creek warriors near Talladega in present-day Alabama. The battle left 17 Americans killed and 83 wounded; approximately 290 Indians were killed.

November 29, 1813: American general John Floyd captured the Indian village of Auttose (in present-day Alabama), killing at least 200 Indians. The American losses were 11 killed and 54 wounded.

As 1813 came to a close, the results were mixed for the United States. American forces had won important victories on the Great Lakes and had secured the western theater via the Battle of the Thames. The Niagara and Lake Champlain theaters were in deadlock, however, and British ships had made a comeback in ship-to-ship duels. In the southern war with the Creeks, the American militia had the advantage and were about to press for more victories.

BATTLES AND CAMPAIGNS: 1814–1815

In addition to important developments on the international stage, there were four theaters of action in 1814: Niagara, Lake Champlain, Chesapeake Bay, and Southern.

NIAGARA THEATER

July 3, 1814: American general Jacob Brown led his troops in an attack on British fort Erie, across the Niagara River from Black Rock. The British surrendered the fort in the afternoon, and American troops crossed the Niagara River in large numbers.

July 5, 1814 (Battle of Chippewa): American troops, led by General Brown and Brig. Gen. Winfield Scott, battled British forces led by Gen. Phineas Riall within earshot of Niagara Falls. In one of the hardest-fought battles of the entire war, Winfield Scott's men stood out as exceptionally well disciplined and able to maintain control under heavy fire. Watching the Americans defeat his soldiers, British general Riall exclaimed, "By God, those men are regulars!" He had been deceived into thinking that Scott's men were militia, since they wore gray uniforms. (The American success in the battle is commemorated by the gray uniforms worn by present-day cadets at West Point.) The British suffered 148 dead and 321 wounded; the American losses were 60 killed and 235 wounded.

July 25, 1814 (Battle of Lundy's Lane, or Battle of Niagara Falls): Gen. Jacob Brown led 2,600 American soldiers against 3,000 British troops at another site close to Niagara Falls. The five-hour-long battle produced frightening casualties for both sides. The British suffered 84 dead and 559 wounded, and the Americans suffered 171 dead and 572 wounded. Although the British maintained possession of the field, neither side could claim to have won the day. The overall effect of the battles of Chippewa and Niagara Falls was to blunt General Brown's offensive.

August 14–September 21, 1814 (Siege of Fort Erie): British troops made repeated attacks on American-held Fort Erie on the eastern side of the Niagara River. By the end of the unsuccessful siege, the British suffered a total of 2,300 casualties in the Niagara area during the months of July, August, and September.

November 5, 1814: American forces abandoned and blew up Fort Erie before recrossing the Niagara River to set up defensive positions on the American side. After two years of hard, bloody fighting in the Niagara theater, no significant territorial change had occurred.

LAKE CHAMPLAIN THEATER

August 31, 1814: British general Sir George Prevost led 11,000 British regulars—crack regiments from the Napoleonic Wars—across the Canadian border into New York State, seeking to capture Plattsburg, New York, then drive on to Albany. Prevost's supporting fleet on Lake Champlain—4 ships and 12 gunboats—was commanded by Capt. George Downie. Prevost was emboldened to make this assault by two factors: the size and strength of his army and the fact that New England farmers—who had opposed the war since its start—were willing to drive cattle north for sale to the British army.

September 3, 1814: American master commandant Thomas Macdonough led his fleet of four ships and ten gunboats into Plattsburg Bay. Macdonough, a veteran of the Tripolitan War, was keenly aware of the high stakes involved in a naval battle fought on Lake Champlain.

September 11, 1814 (Battles of Plattsburg and Lake Champlain): Captain Downie's British fleet attacked Macdonough's fleet at the same time that General Prevost's soldiers attacked across the Saranac River at Plattsburg. All the advantages were with the British on land, but at sea, the British ran into a young naval genius (Macdonough had studied the tactics of Lord Nelson and other sea fighters). The naval battle lasted two hours (8:30–10:30 A.M.). At the battle's end, the Americans had captured all four British warships and had inflicted casualties of 57 dead and 100 wounded. (Captain Downie was among the dead.) Hearing of this, General Prevost stopped the land attack, even though his men were very close to Plattsburg. An extremely cautious man, Prevost began a full-scale retreat to Canada, leaving behind valuable supplies and ammunition. The Lake Champlain theater—so long an area of frustration and humiliation for the Americans—had yielded the most dramatic American victory in the war. Macdonough's victory was, of course, reminiscent of Capt. Oliver Hazard Perry's victory on Lake Erie in 1813 (see September 10, 1813, pp.

147-148), but it also echoed of a much earlier naval battle, that of Valcour Island in 1776, in which Benedict Arnold had delayed a British invasion of New York by one year (see American Revolution, October 11, 1778, p. 99).

CHESAPEAKE BAY THEATER

July 12, 1814: Twelve British transport ships left France, carrying 3,000 veterans of the Spanish campaigns. Commanded by Gen. Robert Ross, those men were headed for the east coast of North America to harass and chastise "the savages," as the London *Times* referred to the Americans.

July 24, 1814: General Ross and his men arrived at Bermuda and began to plan an attack on the Chesapeake Bay area.

August 19, 1814: Following an aimless series of raids against hamlets along Chesapeake Bay, 4,000 British troops under General Ross landed near Benedict, Maryland. At that point, even the British commander was uncertain of what the British troops might accomplish, but the notion of taking the U.S. capital city was especially sweet in light of the fact that American troops had captured and burned York (Toronto) in April 1813.

August 22, 1814: American captain Joshua Barney, a veteran of the American Revolution, blew up his gunboat flotilla in the Patuxent River in order to avoid its capture by British ships.

August 24, 1814 (Battle of Bladensburg, Maryland): As General Ross's British troops approached the capital city of Washington, D.C., American defensive preparations went into full swing. Seven thousand American militiamen and the sailors of Captain Barney's defunct flotilla gathered to stop the British at Bladensburg, 7 miles from Washington. The battle was short. Although Ross's men were outnumbered, their discipline, determination, and equipment (especially the new Congreve rockets) overawed the American militiamen, who, in large part, fled the battlefield within half an hour (see Military Innovations, p. 158). General Ross had an open road to the American capital, at the cost of 64 men killed and 185 wounded; the American losses were 26 killed and 51 wounded.

August 24–25, 1814: As the British approached the capital, a number of dramatic scenes took place. The most memorable of those occurred minutes before the arrival of the British troops. First Lady Dolley Madison insisted on overseeing the arrangements to remove the now-famous Gilbert Stuart painting of George Washington from the White House (see Legends and Trivia, p. 159). The president and first lady escaped just before the invaders arrived; many congressmen and officials had left the city earlier in the day. Ross's men entered the capital city in the late afternoon, and British officers dined at the President's House, which was not then known as the White House. The British commander was wary of his victory, but his men were ecstatic. They burned large sections of the city that night, including the President's House, the Capitol, all the federal buildings, and several private homes. To a commander such as Ross, to be in the enemy's capital was the ultimate triumph, but Ross realized the slender margin of his success and withdrew from the city on August 26.

August 27, 1814: President Madison and most officials of the U.S. government returned to a blackened and charred Washington, D.C. Madison vowed to keep the city as the nation's capital. To appease the public need for a scapegoat for the disaster, he asked for and received the resignation of Secretary of War John W. Armstrong.

August 30, 1814: General Ross's British troops reembarked at Benedict, Maryland.

September 13–14, 1814 (Battle of Baltimore): Aware that Baltimore, Maryland, was the base for many American privateering ships, British general Robert Ross and Adm. George Cockburn planned and carried out a two-pronged assault on that city. Baltimore (population 40,000) had two weeks to prepare for the attack. General Ross was killed in a night maneuver on September 13, and with his death some of the vigor went out of his men. During the night of September 13–14, the British fleet carried out a ferocious bombardment of the American fort McHenry, located at the entrance to the harbor of Baltimore. Commanded by Maj. George Armistead and presided over by an enormous 42-by-30-foot American flag, the fort withstood at least 1,500 rounds of fire from the British ships. When dawn came, Francis Scott Key, an American lawyer on board a British ship who had just conducted an exchange of prisoners, saw the flag still flying and penned the words to the "Star Spangled Banner," which became the U.S. national anthem in 1931 (see Songs, p. 160). Key's words were dramatic and accurate; the British fleet withdrew and reembarked its soldiers without having captured the key port of Bal-

timore. During the bombardment, the fort's garrison suffered 4 men killed and 24 wounded. British losses also were light.

The Chesapeake Bay campaign of 1814 cost the two sides a roughly equal number of casualties (about 350 men dead on both sides) and a great amount of ill will between British and Americans. The burning of Washington, D.C., and the British attempt to arm slaves left a deep imprint on Americans in the Chesapeake Bay area.

SOUTHERN THEATER

January 22–January 26, 1814: In a continuation of the Creek war, American troops from Tennessee fought three battles over four days with Creek warriors near the Creek village of Emuckfau on the Tallapoosa River in upper Alabama. The American casualties were 17 killed and 132 wounded; the Creek losses were much higher.

March 27, 1814 (Battle of Horseshoe Bend on the Tallapoosa River): Creek Indians, ensconced within earthen fortifications near present-day Daviston, Alabama, were attacked by Gen. Andrew Jackson's militiamen from Kentucky and Tennessee. The battle was furious, but Jackson's tactics and the marksmanship of his men prevailed. Seven hundred Creek warriors were killed, compared with American casualties of 26 killed and 111 wounded. Following the battle, Creek chieftain Red Eagle walked into the American camp, found Jackson's tent, and surrendered. That capitulation put an end to Tecumseh's dream that Indians from the Great Lakes to the Gulf of Mexico would unite and fight the white man.

August 9, 1814 (Treaty of Fort Jackson): Gen. Andrew Jackson compelled Creek chieftains to sign a treaty that ceded 20 million acres of their land to the United States. Although a good many Creeks had remained neutral and some had even fought with the Americans against their brethren, the treaty made no distinction between friendly and unfriendly Creek Indians.

August 1814: British military planners in London determined that New Orleans should be seized. Troops were dispatched to a rendezvous point on Jamaica.

September 12–16, 1814: British naval forces were repulsed in their effort to capture the American port at present-day Mobile, Alabama. That preliminary maneuver in the overall British effort to take New Orleans cost the British 32 killed and

37 wounded; the American losses were 4 killed and 5 wounded.

September 1814: British agents approached Jean Laffite, the pirate leader of the buccaneers of Barataria, asking him to assist them in their move against New Orleans. Laffite weighed the possibilities, but rejected the British offer.

November 7, 1814: Gen. Andrew Jackson led American troops in the capture of Spanish-held Pensacola, Florida. Although the U.S. was certainly not at war with Spain, the British ships that had attacked present-day Mobile, Alabama, were at anchor in Pensacola harbor, and Jackson used this as the pretext for his capture of the town.

December 1814: General Jackson had assembled an army that can be described as either motley or hybrid in its composition. It included riflemen from Kentucky and Tennessee, Creoles and blacks from the bayou country, workers and street people from New Orleans, and pirates under the leadership of Jean Laffite, who had offered his services to Jackson under the condition he would receive a pardon from the U.S. government for his past offenses. Laffite's men brought much-needed ammunition and expertise with artillery.

December 2, 1814: Following the receipt of news that British forces were assembling in the Caribbean to plan an attack on New Orleans, Gen. Andrew Jackson arrived in New Orleans, having made a forced march from Pensacola, Florida. He found the city in a mild state of chaos and began to organize men, material, and supplies.

December 12, 1814: British army and navy forces arrived at Cat Island, 80 miles to the east of New Orleans. The British troops were led by Sir Edward Pakenham, a brother-in-law of the Duke of Wellington and a veteran of the Spanish campaigns. Pakenham's mission was to seize New Orleans and to hold the mercantile city hostage as a pawn for use in peace negotiations. Neither Pakenham nor Jackson was aware that the British and American diplomats in Ghent, Belgium, were inching close to a peace settlement.

December 14, 1814: British vessels overwhelmed and captured five American gunboats on Lake Borgne, about ten miles east of New Orleans. The U.S. commander, Lt. Thomas Catesby Jones, was wounded. The effect was that Jackson was kept in the dark about from where the British assault would originate.

December 16, 1814: Responding to difficulties in managing the civilian population of New Orleans (which had been under three flags in a dozen years), General Jackson proclaimed a state of martial law throughout the city.

December 23, 1814: The British advance guard—1,600 strong—crossed Lake Borgne, landed near Bayou Mazant, and made its way to the Villeré plantation, only 8 miles from New Orleans. To that point, the British secrecy had been perfect, but the news that the British forces were encamped soon spread to New Orleans and to General Jackson.

December 23–24, 1814: Learning of the British advance guard's placement so close to the city, General Jackson vowed, "By the Eternal! They shall not sleep on our soil" (see Notable Phrases, pp. 160-161). Rather than continue to build his defenses, Jackson went immediately on the offensive. Leading 2,100 troops, he made a night attack on the British position and caught the enemy largely by surprise. The fighting was sharp, and in the night fighting, the American sharpshooters held the advantage. When the Americans retired, leaving the British in possession of the field, the engagement had cost the British 46 killed, 167 wounded, and 64 missing; American losses were 24 killed, 115 wounded, and 74 missing.

December 24, 1814: On Christmas Eve, American and British diplomats signed the Treaty of Ghent, bringing the war to an end on paper (see Negotiations and Peace Treaty, p. 156).

December 25, 1814: The main body of British troops and its commanders, led by Sir Edward Pakenham, arrived at the Villeré plantation. By that time, General Jackson was well on his way to fortifying the Rodriquez Canal area, some 5 miles east of New Orleans.

January 1, 1815: British general Pakenham initiated a blistering artillery exchange between the British and American lines. The British suffered the greater casualties, which forced Pakenham to wait for reinforcements before launching his infantry attack. Despite the setback, the morale among British forces remained high. Pakenham's troops were confident that they would beat the Americans and enjoy the booty and splendor of New Orleans.

January 8, 1815 (Battle of New Orleans): At 8 A.M., in response to a rocket fired as a signal, the British army marched directly against Jackson's troops entrenched at the Rodriquez Canal. Marching in close ranks and carrying scaling ladders, the British were cut down again and again in the

This picture of the Battle of New Orleans, fought on January 8, 1815, is based on a sketch made by Andrew Jackson's engineer, who was present on the battle.

half-hour battle. Pakenham was killed early in the firing. The British casualties were horrific—192 killed, 1,265 wounded, and 484 missing—compared with the American losses of 13 killed, 13 wounded, and 19 missing. The carnage of the scene recalled the battle at Bunker Hill in 1775 and foreshadowed the grim fighting that would occur during battles such as Antietam during the American Civil War. The surviving British general, John Lambert, withdrew his men and departed the area on January 28, 1815. The Battle of New Orleans, the final land battle of the war, was an overwhelming triumph for Andrew Jackson, southern militia fighters, and the American belief in the fighting ability of its people.

HOME FRONT

Sectional differences figured prominently during the War of 1812. New England, dominated by merchants and tradesmen who could not import or export goods through the blockade, found the war a financial disaster and resisted participating to the greatest possible extent. That led to the Hartford Convention of 1814–1815, at which New England delegates considered altering the U.S. Constitution in order to prevent such a war from

happening again. Southern and western government leaders tended to favor the war, especially as they saw the bountiful land areas that could be taken from the Creek Indians and from the Spanish monarchy in Florida, Alabama, and Georgia. Areas such as Pennsylvania and Maryland were divided in their sympathies; Baltimore was one of the strongest prowar towns, but Philadelphia was much more ambivalent about the conflict.

June 18, 1812: President Madison made the official pronouncement that the United States was at war with Great Britain.

June 26, 1812: Massachusetts governor Caleb Strong declared a statewide public fast to protest the war, which he believed would harm the state's shipping interests. The Massachusetts House of Representatives issued the following statement: "Organize a *peace party* throughout your country, and let all party distinctions vanish."

July 2, 1812: Connecticut governor John Cotton refused to allow the militia of his state to serve in the U.S. Army. Massachusetts did the same on August 5, with the result that the U.S. Army in the Northeast fought at a considerable disadvantage throughout the war.

July 27, 1812: In Baltimore, Maryland, riots broke out. Prowar Republicans attacked the businesses and homes of antiwar Federalists. Nine Federalists were publicly beaten and stabbed with penknives as hot candle wax was dropped into their eyes. Due to the strength of the prowar movement in Baltimore, no one was punished for the actions, but the Federalists of Baltimore received national attention. And Alexander Hanson—one of the tortured Federalists—and his *Federal Republican* newspaper gained a wider readership.

December 3, 1812: James Madison was officially declared the winner of the 1812 presidential election. Madison defeated De Witt Clinton by an electoral vote of 128 to 89 (Clinton fared best in the North, and Madison did best in the southern and western states). In the congressional elections, the ruling Republican Party lost ground but maintained its majority status. Republican losses were particularly heavy in New York, Massachusetts, and New Hampshire. The proportion of seats that the Republicans held in the U.S. Senate fell from 82 percent to 78 percent; in the House, their majority fell from 75 percent to 63 percent. Among the new congressmen elected was Daniel Webster, a Federalist from New Hampshire. He made his congressional debut by assailing the Madison administration for bringing the U.S. into the war.

March 4, 1813: James Madison was inaugurated for his second term as president; Elbridge Gerry was inaugurated vice president.

May 24, 1813: The 13th U.S. Congress met for a special session (May 24–August 2, 1813). During that session, Congress heard many denunciations of the war policy. The most important issue, however, was the question of how to raise money to pay for the war. A $16 million loan was opened for subscriptions. Three wealthy merchants—David Parish, Stephen Girard, and John Jacob Astor—put up two-thirds of the sum. The U.S. treasury had to accept a 12 percent discount, meaning that only 88 dollars per hundred actually was received. That and other financial maneuvers prompted further criticism of the administration and the war.

December 17, 1813: President Madison signed an embargo into law. Even more prohibitive than the Embargo Act of 1807 (see Causes of the War, p. 140), the new embargo declared that all ships had to remain in port and prohibited the export of all goods and produce. The severity of the law resulted from Madison's fury over the illegal trade that flourished between New England merchants and British Canada and the piracy that

existed in the Gulf of Mexico, principally from the pirates of Barataria, led by Jean Laffite.

January 25, 1814: In response to petitions from the suffering citizens of Nantucket Island, Congress made special provisions regarding the Embargo Act of 1813. Nantucket was allowed to import food and fuel, and coasting vessels trapped away from home were permitted to return to port.

January 27, 1814: Congress passed legislation authorizing the U.S. Army to grow to the number of 62,773 men. At that time, the actual strength of the regular army stood at about 11,000 men.

April 14, 1814: Realizing the complete failure of the Embargo Act of 1813, Congress repealed the legislation with the encouragement of President Madison.

April 18, 1814: Congress adjourned. During the second session of the 13th Congress (December 1813–April 1814), Congress had increased the recruitment bounty for soldiers, appropriated money for a steam frigate, raised the bounty for prisoners of war, and authorized a new loan and new issue of treasury notes.

September 19, 1814: The 13th Congress met for its third and final session. Many congressmen were struck by the extent of the damage that the capital city had suffered during the British invasion (see August 24-25, 1814, pp. 150-151).

September 20, 1814: President Madison sent his State of the Union message to Congress. He appealed to the American patriotic spirit to make the sacrifices necessary to continue the war until an honorable peace could be negotiated.

October 17, 1814: In response to the war and to the damage done to commerce, the Massachusetts legislature called for a convention of the New England states to meet at Hartford to discuss their "public grievances and concerns" and to propose amendments to the U.S. Constitution.

December 1, 1814: President Madison submitted to Congress the new peace terms sent by the British. Based on the principle of *uti possidetis*, meaning that each side should maintain the territory it presently held, the terms would leave the eastern half of Maine in British hands, a matter that was wholly unacceptable to the congressmen from New England and their constituents.

December 15, 1814: The Hartford Convention convened in secret. Twenty-six Federalist antiwar delegates representing all the New England states met to discuss their grievances, the continuation of the war, and the pivotal issue of states' rights versus national sovereignty.

December 15, 1814–January 5, 1815: The delegates of the Hartford Convention met twice a day. George Cabot of Massachusetts was elected president of the convention. By January 5, 1815, the convention had adopted a series of resolutions that were intended to limit the power of the president and the Congress to bring the nation into war, to limit any and all embargoes to a two-month duration, and to limit the presidency to one term (or at least to ensure that the president could not be succeeded by a member of his home region). The convention disbanded on January 5, 1815 and sent three members to present its requests to the national government in Washington, D.C.

February 11, 1815: The delegates from the Hartford Convention learned of the Treaty of Ghent. Coming on the heels of the news of Jackson's victory at the Battle of New Orleans, the three delegates chose not to present their requests to the national government but rather to try to persuade Congress to reimburse the states for their militia costs.

February–March, 1815: Widespread rejoicing followed the news of the end of the war. Newspaper editorials claimed that the United States had triumphed and that the "second war of independence has been illustrated by more splendid achievements than the war of the revolution" (New York *National Advocate,* February 20, 1815).

July 3, 1815: American and British trade representatives signed a joint commercial agreement, ending discriminatory duties and permitting the United States to trade with the British East Indies. (No such agreement was reached regarding the British West Indies.)

NEGOTIATIONS AND PEACE TREATY

In a sense, negotiations began almost as soon as the war itself. During the summer of 1812, President Madison considered an armistice with Britain, and the news that the Orders in Council had been revoked caused some pause in the United States (see p. 140). However, the war had a momentum of its own, and it was not until August 1814 that American and British peace commissioners met in the Flemish town of Ghent. In the negotiations, the Americans held the advantage of seeking peace with honor, while the British delegates sought to win territory. In addition, the American commissioners were more independent and more assertive and were given greater latitude in negotiation than their British counterparts.

March 8, 1813: The Russian minister to the United States presented to Secretary of State James Monroe an offer from Czar Alexander I for formal mediation between the United States and Great Britain.

May 1813: President James Madison named James A. Bayard and Albert Gallatin as peace commissioners. Bayard and Gallatin arrived at St. Petersburg, Russia on July 21.

July 5, 1813: The British foreign secretary, Lord Castlereagh, declined the mediation offer of Czar Alexander I.

November 4, 1813: In response to Britain's need to concentrate on defeating Emperor Napoleon, Lord Castlereagh sent a letter to Secretary of State James Monroe proposing peace talks between the United States and Great Britain.

January 5, 1814: James Monroe sent a diplomatic note to Lord Castlereagh accepting direct negotiations.

January 18, 1814: The Senate confirmed President Madison's nomination of John Quincy Adams, James A. Bayard, Henry Clay, and Jonathan Russell as peace commissioners. Together with Albert Gallatin—who was confirmed on February 8, 1814—those men became the U.S. peace negotiators (hereafter referred to as U.S. peace commissioners).

April 11, 1814: Emperor Napoleon I formally abdicated his throne. Although Napoleon's personal ambition was by no means exhausted, France was worn out from the Russian campaign (1812–1813) and 20 years of fighting against the "old regime" monarchies of Europe. The abdication set off great rejoicing in Great Britain and created a dual response toward the Americans—some British people wanted relief from war taxes and constraints; others called for an offensive campaign to punish the United States.

June 27, 1814: President Madison wrote to the U.S. peace commissioners in the Flemish town of Ghent. Acknowledging the seriousness of the military situation and the fact that the fall of Napoleon had removed some causes of friction between the U.S. and Great Britain, Madison gave the commissioners leeway to sign a treaty that would not mention the issue of impressment.

August 8, 1814: The five U.S. peace commissioners met at Ghent with their British counterparts—Lord James Gamier, Henry Goulburn, and William Adams—for the first time. In that meeting, the British peace commissioners presented a long list of territorial demands (including land along the Great Lakes and creation of an Indian buffer state under British control). The U.S. peace commissioners promptly refused.

August 19, 1814: The British peace commissioners continued to push for territorial gains, based on the concept of *uti possidetis.* Knowing that adhering to that principle would mean the loss of parts of the Northwest Territory (and the northern half of Maine), the U.S. peace commissioners refused. Instead, they presented their demand for *status quo ante bellum*, meaning that all territory should return to the party that held it when the war began.

September 1814: September 1814 was the most optimistic month of the war for the British Ministry, led by Lord Liverpool. Having heard of the capture and burning of Washington, D.C., the British peace commissioners were obstinate in their calls for American territorial concessions. Diplomatic notes were exchanged between the two commissions, but no formal meetings were held.

October 21–24, 1814: The British peace commissioners presented a new, shorter list of demands to the Americans. The U.S. peace commissioners, conscious of the American victories at Baltimore and Lake Champlain, flatly refused.

November 1, 1814: The British Ministry sent orders to its fleet commanders in North American waters to cease the policy of burning American towns in revenge for the destruction of York (Toronto) in 1813.

November 9, 1814: The Duke of Wellington replied that he saw no way to win the American war without naval superiority on the Great Lakes (something that the British had been without since the victories of Perry and Macdonough on Lake Erie and Lake Champlain).

November 26, 1814: In a diplomatic note to the U.S. peace commissioners, the British Ministry abandoned for the first time its insistence on the principle of *uti possidetis.*

December 1, 1814: The British and American peace commissions met formally at Ghent, for the first face-to-face talks since August 19, 1814. The American commissioners were in an optimistic frame of mind, but the mood of the British diplomats ranged from discouragement to pessimism.

December 24, 1814: At 6 P.M. on Christmas Eve, the American and British peace commissioners signed and sealed the Treaty of Peace and Amity between His Britannic Majesty and the United States of America. Containing 11 articles, the document (1) officially ended the war, (2) abided by the principle of *status quo ante bellum* (each side would retain the territory that it had when the war began), (3) restored to the Native Americans to their lands as they owned them in 1811, and (4) set up four commissions to deal with specific questions such as the U.S.-Canada boundary and fishing rights on the Grand Banks. The treaty said nothing about impressment, neutral rights, or whether the British had the right to navigate the Mississippi River. In addition, the treaty would become operative only on the ratification of both countries, with the ratification documents to be exchanged in Washington, D.C.

December 26, 1814: In London, copies of the treaty were received. The British press responded with a mixture of disgust and relief at the prospect of peace after so many years of war.

December 27, 1814: The prince regent ratified the Treaty of Ghent.

January 2, 1815: Anthony Baker (British) and Henry Carroll (American) left Plymouth, England, on board the sloop of war HMS *Favourite* to bring the copies of the treaty to the United States.

February 11, 1815: The HMS *Favourite,* flying a flag of truce, came into New York Harbor, bringing copies of the Treaty of Ghent.

February 14, 1815: Copies of the Treaty of Ghent were delivered to Washington, D.C.

February 17, 1815: The U.S. Senate unanimously ratified the Treaty of Ghent. At 11 P.M., ratification documents were exchanged between the British and the American diplomats in Washington, D. C.

February 18, 1815: President Madison pronounced the war officially over.

RESULTS OF THE WAR (Casualties, Costs, Consequences)

American: Official enlistment figures indicate that a total of 528,000 Americans served in the War of 1812—57,000 regular Army troops, 10,000 volunteers, 3,000 rangers, 458,000 militia, and 20,000 sailors and marines.

Those figures are probably misleading, as numerous militiamen were known to have enlisted as many as ten times over in order to gain sign-on bonuses. Had the United States used even half the number of troops recorded as enlisted, it would probably have won the war early on.

Casualties were generally well-documented on the American side. The official toll of deaths from battle was 2,260 men with another 4,505 wounded. Those figures do not indicate how many men later died from their wounds or from sickness or accidents in camps. In addition, at least 1,000 U.S. civilians died during the war, most of them killed during Indian attacks in the Northwest. The U.S. Army executed 205 men, mostly for desertion.

Financial costs to the American public were heavy. The cost of the war was $105 million, and most of the debt was owed to wealthy Americans, such as Stephen Girard of Philadelphia, who financed much of the government's needs during the war. After 1815, the United States government was able to rapidly pay the debts incurred, due to the prosperity of 1815–1818. Indeed, two decades after the war's conclusion, the U.S. government paid off its total bonded indebtedness for the first and only time.

Commercial costs were also significant. During the first year of the war, many American vessels were able to go to sea, but after June 1813 the British blockade was highly effective, and many commercial enterprises suffered greatly, particularly those in New England.

Territory was not an issue at the end of the war, since the peace treaty abided by the principle of *status quo ante bellum*. However, the Americans and the American government never lived up to Article IX of the Treaty of Ghent, which required the United States to restore to the Native Americans the land they had held in 1811. Instead, American settlers quickly swarmed into the areas wrested from the Shawnee in the North and the Creeks in the South. The United States also held West Florida, which Andrew Jackson had captured from the Spanish in 1814. Since there was no peace treaty with Spain, there seemed no reason to return the land, and in 1819, the Adams-Onis Treaty brought the rest of Florida under the American flag.

British: British losses were difficult to determine because Britain seldom released precise casualty figures. However, extrapolated from the lists that were gathered after the battles of Lundy's Lane and New Orleans, it seems likely that the British losses in the war probably exceeded those of the Americans.

When the war began the British had more than 8,000 regular army troops in Canada. By the end of the war, that number had risen to more than 30,000, and the cost of feeding, equipping, and supplying those troops had a large economic impact on the British taxpayer. The economic cost of the war to Britain was considerable. The British public debt was 451 million pounds in 1800; by 1815, it had risen to 840 million pounds (more than $3.7 billion). Much of that debt was due to the Napoleonic Wars and to the extreme cost of fighting in faraway North America. During 1814, British ships had to deliver 45 tons of supplies every day to the troops in Canada, and guns for the ships on the Great Lakes had to be shipped overland at great expense.

Commercially, the British also suffered considerable losses during the war. By the most careful recording, 1,334 British merchant ships were captured by American privateers. To give one example—in the first four months of the war, 600 American privateer ships captured 219 British merchant vessels carrying 574 guns and 3,108 men.

Territorial gains and losses were negligible. Just before the signing of the Treaty of Ghent, the British peace commissioners gained merely a few islands off the coast of Maine for Great Britain.

Canadian: It is nearly impossible to separate Canada's losses from those of Great Britain, since Canada was part of the British Empire. It is worth noting that the war triggered the growth of an independent Canadian militia, which performed well in some circumstances and badly in others. Regardless of their performance, their creation marked the beginning of a long process toward the growth of Canadian nationalism, and the War of 1812 made Canadians certain that they did not want to become part of the United States.

Indians: Native Americans were the biggest losers in the War of 1812. Tribes such as the Shawnee in the North and the Creeks in the South lost thousands of warriors in the war. Millions of acres of land were taken from the Indians in a number of treaties. The most significant of those were the second Treaty of Greenville (July 22, 1814) between the northern tribes and the U.S. and the Treaty of Fort Jackson (August 9, 1814) between the U.S. and the Creeks. Most important, the tribes east of the Mississippi River never rose again in a group to fight against the Americans, possibly because warrior-chief Tecumseh was dead and no leader rose to take his place.

MILITARY INNOVATIONS, TACTICS, EQUIPMENT

All four parties involved (American, British, Canadian, Indians) used traditional weapons, tactics, and strategies. The American armies were more adaptable than those of their enemies to the circumstances, as witnessed in Perry's building of unconventional ships and Jackson's employment of pirates.

American: The American forces used muskets and the Kentucky rifle, essentially the same weaponry that they had employed during the Revolutionary War. The Kentucky rifle could not be fitted with a bayonet, but it was highly accurate at a range of 300 yards.

Tactically, the American armies began the War of 1812 unprepared but improved as the war continued. In particular, the drilling and reorganization of regular Army units by Gen. Winfield Scott made at least certain units of the U.S. Army equal to, and sometimes superior to, their British counterparts. Scott's impressive performance during the summer of 1814 led to the development of a new fighting tradition for the regular U.S. Army. However, as historian Allan Millett and Peter Maslowski have noted, "New Orleans had a further importance. It enshrined the Kentucky and Tennessee squirrel hunters who had mowed down England's regular veterans and glorified the militian ideal at a time when the militian system was virtually dead." The myth of the American militia lasted even beyond the failures of American forces during the war, and in March 1815, Congress reduced the regular army to a strength of 10,000. Those two parallel military traditions, that of the homespun minuteman and that of the regular Army professional soldier, continued long after the war.

The American land forces used little new equipment, but the U.S. frigates, built in the 1790s, used heavier construction materials and employed a heavier weight of artillery than did those of their opponents.

British: The British army employed only a few innovations during the war. The most notable weapon introduced was the Congreve rocket (named for its inventor, William Congreve, 1772–1828), first used in the British attack on Havre de Grace, Maryland (May 1813). Although one American was believed to have been the only fatality caused by a rocket in the entire war, the rocket frightened and even panicked American militiamen at the Battle of Bladensburg, and its fearsome appearance led Francis Scott Key to use the words, "by the rockets' red glare" in the *Star Spangled Banner* (see Songs, p. 160).

Tactically, the British commanders proved to be rigid and almost simpleminded during the war. With a few notable exceptions, such as during the capture of Fort Detroit and the march on Washington, D.C., British commanders used the type of straight-ahead, line-by-line attack and defense that their predecessors had abandoned by the end of the American Revolution. Pakenham's attack at New Orleans was the worst error in this regard, and General Prevost's retirement from the Battle of Plattsburg was the most overly cautious move made by a British general during the war.

The British infantryman still used the brown Bess musket introduced at the start of the 18th century. The brown Bess was well-adapted for use with bayonets. The battle tactics and fighting equipment of the British army generally were dated, but given the success of British armies in Spain, there was little chance that tactics would be changed for the American war.

Canadian: There was no truly Canadian equipment; nearly all of it came from Britain. But the Canadian militia did develop the makings of a fighting style, one based on cautious and stubborn defense. This practice of digging in during battles with the Americans came about because the Canadians were not interested in advancing and taking new territory; they simply wanted to keep the Americans from taking their territory.

Indians: Indian equipment was a mixture of traditional tribal weapons (bows, arrows, tomahawks) and British small arms (Brown Bess muskets). The Indians proved to be excellent woods fighters, and in some cases their resistance on the battlefield put that of the British to shame (for example, at the Battle of the Thames). However, the Indian warriors were often fatalistic and easily discouraged by omens, bad fortune, and minor military setbacks. Like the American militia, the Indian fighters were unreliable in campaigns of long duration.

LEGENDS AND TRIVIA

The term **Uncle Sam** originated during the War of 1812. According to one widely accepted version, it referred to Samuel Means (1766–1854), a merchant and meat packer of Troy, New York, who packed crates of meat for the Army units that bore the stamp EAUS. Soldiers wondered what the initials stood for, and they were told in jest that the US stood for "Uncle Sam" Means. Means did not resemble the caricature figure that emerged; he was broad-shouldered, clean-shaven, and well-proportioned.

Johnny Appleseed came into greater prominence during the war. John Chapman (1774–1845) was born in Massachusetts. He arrived in Ohio around the start of the 19th century and began to give freely of his tree seedlings and the writings of the Swedish mystic Emmanuel Swedenborg. Known to settlers throughout Ohio as "Johnny Appleseed" and "Crazy Johnny," Chapman acted as the Paul Revere of the War of 1812, when he volunteered to run through the night from Mansfield, Ohio, to Mount Vernon, Ohio, warning many lonely settlers of the danger posed by Indian attacks.

Mother Bailey (real name Anna Warner Bailey, 1758–1851) was an American hero. She figured prominently in the American Revolution and in the War of 1812. When Groton, Connecticut, was attacked by British ships (1813), she stepped forward to offer her red flannel petticoat for use as cartridge wadding. The episode was celebrated in story and in song.

Laura Secord (born Laura Ingersoll, 1775–1868) was a Canadian war hero. She was born in Massachusetts. She went with her loyalist parents to Upper Canada at the end of the American Revolution. She married James Secord, a sergeant in the First Lincoln Militia. During the summer of 1813, American troops were stationed in her house in Queenstown, Ontario. Coming into possession of U.S. plans to make a surprise attack on Beaver Dams, she made her way through the U.S. lines and warned Lt. James Fitzgibbons in command at Beaver Dams. She became an immediate hero to British Canada.

One of the most repeated legends from the War of 1812 is that **Dolley Madison** fled with a rolled-up Gilbert Stuart portrait of George Washington before the White House was burned on August 24, 1814 (see p. 151). The facts are a bit different. As the British advanced on the capital, Dolley packed up some presidential papers and personal belongings and then ordered that the portrait be taken. The frame was screwed to the wall and she ordered it to be chopped apart and the canvas removed. Still on its stretcher, the picture could not fit in her carriage, so she entrusted it to two men who had come by to help, Jacob Barker, a prominent merchant-banker, and Robert de Peyster, a young New Yorker. They fled with the picture in a wagon to the Virginia countryside; later returned, the painting now hangs in the East Room of the White House.

NOTABLE PHRASES

Keep the guns going! Fight her till she sinks! Don't give up the ship!

Capt. James Lawrence's words on June 1, 1813, as he lay fatally wounded aboard his ship, the USS *Chesapeake*, have been hotly debated. It is not certain exactly which phrase he uttered that day. (Some sources report his words as "Tell the men to fire faster and not to give up the ship; fight her till she sinks." In any case, the expression "Don't give up the ship" was taken by Capt. Oliver Hazard Perry, who used it as his battle slogan on Lake Erie (September 10, 1813). Perry's phrasing has been used ever since by sailors of the United States Navy.

We have met the enemy, and they are ours.

Oliver Hazard Perry's words, written on the back of an old letter addressed to Gen. William Henry Harrison electrified the American public. Perry's victory on Lake Erie was the most complete and convincing that any naval force had ever handed to a British squadron. "We have met the enemy, and they are ours" became a statement of triumph used by American military leaders again and again.

The Almighty has been pleased to Grant us a Signal Victory on Lake Champlain in the Capture of one Frigate, one Brig and two sloops of war of the enemy.

Thomas Macdonough's message to the secretary of the U.S. Navy (William Jones) is much less well known than the statements of Lawrence, Perry, and Decatur, but at the time it caused a sensation equal to that of Perry's message after the Battle of Lake Erie.

By the Eternal! They shall not sleep on our soil!

Andrew Jackson was said to have uttered those words when he learned of the British advance on New Orleans. In its confident appeal to God and its biblical yet homely rhetoric, it was characteristic of the man, his times, and the type of men he led.

SONGS

Several songs came out of the War of 1812 but two stand out. One is the U.S. national anthem, "The Star-Spangled Banner" (although it was not officially adopted as such until 1931). The words were composed by Francis Scott Key, after he had observed the British artillery bombard Fort McHenry in Baltimore Harbor on the night of September 13–14, 1814 (see p. 151). He was on deck of a British ship, where he had conducted an exchange of prisoners, when the morning light revealed that the American flag was still flying over the fort. Taking an unfinished letter from his pocket, he wrote down the words. Some historians have doubted that he actually wrote all the words on that occasion, but he may well have written the first verse at that time. He went to Baltimore and finished his verses, then had them distributed on handbills the next day. He seems to have written the words to fit the music of an already popular English drinking song, best known for the version titled "To Anacreon in Heaven." (Anacreon was an ancient Greek poet known for his poems in praise of wine and love.) The music had been used for many songs, from a march to a political song during the Quasi-War with France ("Adams and Liberty")(see Songs, Quasi-War with France, p. 126).

The other well-known song inspired by the War of 1812 is "Hunters of Kentucky," words and music by Samuel Woodworth (although he probably adapted a traditional tune). Woodworth was well known in his day and long after for another ballad, "The Old Oaken Bucket." "Hunters of Kentucky" is a direct tribute to the riflemen who fought alongside Andrew Jackson at the Battle of New Orleans on January 8, 1815. Jackson claimed that the Kentuckians had "ingloriously fled," but his statement was challenged by their commanders. And Woodworth's ballad was immensely popular right up to the Civil War, probably because it paid tribute to the Kentuckians in terms that every American wanted to identify with:

We are a hardy freeborn race,
    each man to fear a stranger;
What'er the game, we join in chase,
    despising toil and danger;
And if a daring foe annoys,
    what'er his strength and forces,
We'll show him that Kentucky boys
    are alligator horses.

Woodworth also wrote a song commemorating the Battle of Tippecanoe, "Battle of Wabash," set to the same melody as "The Star-Spangled Banner." But it was another song, "Tippecanoe and Tyler, Too" that in 1840 became the campaign song of William Henry Harrison. The words were by Alexander Ross, set to the old melody of "Little Pigs."

There were many songs inspired by particular battles or incidents of the war, most long since forgotten: "Decatur's Victory," "Hull's Victory," "Perry's Victory," "Lawrence the Brave," "Battle of the Wabash," "Erie and Champlain," "Patriotic Diggers," "Brave General Brock." A song with broader implications was one that appeared in 1815—"Peace," which looked ahead to a future free from war:

From your father to son,
Every blessing you've run,
Unimpair'd to the last generation shall run
And no right will you yield,
Not an inch will retire;
If your charter's consumed,
In its flames you'll expire.

HISTORICAL PERSPECTIVES AND CONTROVERSIES

Historians have long debated a number of aspects of the War of 1812, centering around the following questions:

What drove the United States into the war? Were maritime concerns or western land hunger the primary motivation?

Historian Julius Pratt's work maintained that the primary cause of the War of 1812 was the desire for expansion, whether that expansion came from the maritime interests of New England or the land hunger of the western states. However, Pratt's thesis was later challenged by Bradford Perkins and Patrick White, who went back to the 19th-century view that maritime issues and the larger question of national honor led the United States into the war. Few historians have given much emphasis to the Indian question as a primary cause of the war.

What was the motivation of the delegates at the Hartford Convention in 1814–1815? Did they actually contemplate secession from the United States? Did they set a precedent for the later secessionist movement of the Confederate States of America?

The Hartford Convention was long seen as near treason and indeed as the reason for the complete disintegration of the Federalist Party. Samuel Eliot Morison presented his view that the Federalist leaders at the convention were moderate in their demands and conscious of the importance of national solidarity. Although some historians have declared that Morison was too generous to his New England forebearers, most detailed studies have come to a similar conclusion: The Hartford Convention was much more frightening in its implications and its potential than in its reality. Historians Henry Adams and George Dangerfield also took that view.

Why was the Treaty of Ghent so favorable to the Americans?

In 1815, the American public was jubilant about the terms of the Treaty of Ghent, but public opinion in Great Britain was mixed (with many British newspapers lamenting that the Americans had escaped a well-deserved thrashing). Even today, there is a general concurrence that "because of the clear headed determination shown by the American envoys at Ghent, the nation could at least claim that it had won the peace" (Donald R. Hickey). Bradford Perkins claimed that the Americans fared well at Ghent because of a natural rapprochement between Britain and the United States. Fred L. Engleman approached the treaty from a strictly American perspective and concluded that the American victories at Plattsburg were crucial in bringing on the peace. Samuel Flagg Bemis, long the dean of American foreign policy studies, credited John Quincy Adams's negotiating skill for forging the peace treaty.

What if the American armies had conquered Canada? Is it conceivable that the United States and Canada could have been united by the war?

That question is more an intriguing speculation than a historical debate. Could the United States have seized Canada during the war? A more disciplined and intelligent war effort on the part of the United States—a direct thrust against Montreal in either 1812 or 1813—might well have yielded that objective. Aside from the questions of whether the British would have sought to reconquer Canada or would have agreed to give it up at the peace table, one may ponder what the United States would have done to digest Canada, whose population mix of French Canadians, British, British Empire loyalists, and Scots Irish would have proved difficult to assimilate. Historians almost universally agree that the War of 1812 was instrumental in the formation of a new, stronger British-Canadian identity.

CIVILIAN AND MILITARY BIOGRAPHIES

AMERICAN

Armstrong, John W. (1758–1843)—U.S. secretary of war (1813–1814): John Armstrong was born in Pennsylvania. He served as an adjutant general in the Revolutionary War and was secretary of war for the United States during the height of the War of 1812. Although he improved the general condition of the Army, he was forced to resign after the burning of Washington, D.C. He retired to Red Hook, New York, and pursued his interest in agriculture and writing.

Brown, Jacob Jennings (1775–1828)—general: Jacob Jennings Brown was born in Pennsylvania. He was a pioneer settler in western New York State and founded Brownsville, New York. He became active in the state militia, and when the War of 1812 began, he was a natural choice for leadership. He repulsed British attacks on Lake Ontario in 1812 and 1813. In 1814, he led the American attack in the Niagara area, where his troops won the Battle of Chippewa. He became the senior officer of the U.S. Army in 1815 and held the post of commanding general from 1821 until his death.

Harrison, William Henry (1773–1841)—soldier, president of the United States (1841): William Henry Harrison was born in Virginia. He joined the U.S. Army in 1791. He was governor of Indiana (1800–1812). He led American forces to victory at the Battle of Tippecanoe (November 7, 1811) and the Battle of the Thames (October 5, 1813). He left the Army in 1814 and served in the U.S. House of Representatives (1816–1819) and in the U.S. Senate (1825-1828). He was also minister to Colombia (1828–1829). He won the presidency in 1840 but served only one month before he died from pneumonia, allegedly contracted while delivering his inaugural address in the bitter cold.

Jackson, Andrew (1767–1845)—soldier, politician, president of the United States (1829–1837): Andrew Jackson was born on the border between North Carolina and South Carolina. He became a judge, land speculator, and U.S. Congressman. He was always anti-British. He rose in the southern militia forces and won the key battles of Horseshoe Bend (March 27, 1814) and New Orleans (January 8, 1815); the latter made him a national hero. He ran for president three times, winning in 1828 and 1832. As president, he epitomized the hard, tough frontier ethic that he had grown up with and that he had employed to marshal his unruly army prior to the battle of New Orleans.

Laffite, Jean (1782–1854)—pirate: Jean Laffite was born in Port-au-Prince, Haiti. He arrived in New Orleans before 1803 and became the leader of the pirate colony of Barataria (situated on Grand Terre Island in southern Louisiana). Late in 1814, the British offered him $30,000 and a captaincy in the Royal Navy to help them capture New Orleans. Instead, Laffite offered his services (and those of his followers) to Andrew Jackson. After serving as skillful artillerists in the Battle of New Orleans, Laffite and his men were granted pardons for their piratical actions by President James Madison. But Laffite soon reverted to piracy. The park in New Orleans built to commemorate the Battle of New Orleans is called Jean Laffite National Historical Park.

Lawrence, James (1781–1813)—naval officer: James Lawrence was born in New Jersey. He entered the U.S. Navy as a midshipman in 1798 and served in the Tripolitan War. As a lieutenant, he won the impressive USS *Hornet*-HMS *Peacock* bout (February 24, 1813) and was promoted to captain. Transferred to command of the USS *Chesapeake*, he led his ship out of port and engaged in the furious *Shannon-Chesapeake* battle of June 1, 1813. In the 15-minute fight, Lawrence was mortally wounded. As he was taken below

decks he uttered something to the effect of "Don't give up the ship" (see Notable Phrases, p. 159). The ship did surrender, and Lawrence's body was taken first to Halifax, Nova Scotia, and then to New York City, where his funeral was attended by thousands. Even if the words were not exact (and debate still remains on that subject), "Don't give up the ship" became the rallying cry for U.S. sailors, replacing the earlier motto of "Free Trade and Sailors' Rights."

Macomb, Alexander (1782–1841)—general: Alexander Macomb was born in Detroit. He entered the U.S. Army in 1799 and was one of the first officers to train at West Point. He built coastal fortifications in North Carolina, South Carolina, and Georgia (1805–1812). During the land battle of Plattsburg, New York, he turned away a large British invading force. He became head of the Army Corps of Engineers in 1821 and served as commanding general of the entire U.S. Army from 1829 to 1841.

Macdonough, Thomas (1783–1825)—naval officer: Thomas Macdonough was born in Delaware. He entered the U.S. Navy in 1800 as a midshipman and fought in the Tripolitan War. As master commandant of the American ships on Lake Champlain (1812–1814), he directed the building of the American fleet. He fought and won the crucial battle of Lake Champlain (September 11, 1814). He received many honors, a captaincy, and the thanks of Congress. He died at sea, 600 miles from the American coast; his body was taken to Middletown, Connecticut, for burial.

Madison, James (1750–1836)—president of the United States: James Madison was born in Virginia. He served in the Continental Congress and was on hand to help to write the U.S. Constitution in 1787. A protégé of Thomas Jefferson, he followed Jefferson into the presidency in 1809. Never a warmonger, he was drawn by events into the War of 1812, and the phrase "Mr. Madison's War," popular in New England, was wholly inaccurate. He and his wife, Dolley, showed courage and firmness in restoring Washington, D.C., to its place as the capital of the United States after the British assault in August 1814. He left the presidency in 1817 and lived the life of a gentleman farmer in Virginia.

Perry, Oliver Hazard (1785–1819)—naval officer: Oliver Perry was born in Rhode Island. He was the older brother of Matthew Calbraith Perry, the naval officer who opened Japan to American trade (1854). Oliver Perry entered the U.S. Navy as a midshipman in 1799. In 1813, he built American ships at Erie, Pennsylvania, and sailed forth to win the Battle of Lake Erie (September 10, 1813), for which he was promoted to captain. In a move that displayed the flexible interservice movement of the times, he joined Gen. William Harrison's troops briefly and led a cavalry charge at the Battle of the Thames. He died of yellow fever while on duty in Venezuela; his body was taken to Newport, Rhode Island, in 1826.

Pike, Zebulon (1779–1813)—explorer, soldier: Zebulon Pike was born in New Jersey. He entered the U.S. Army and led several expeditions of exploration in the American West, finding the headwaters of the Arkansas and Red Rivers and spotting the peak that bears his name. Commissioned brigadier general in the War of 1812, he led an unsuccessful venture into Canada by way of Lake Champlain (1812), then commanded the successful American landing at York (Toronto) on April 27, 1813, where he was killed by an explosion of the British powder magazine.

Scott, Winfield (1786–1866)—general: Winfield Scott was born in Virginia. He studied law before joining the U.S. Army. Captured at Queenstown Heights (1813), he was soon exchanged and was promoted to brigadier general in 1814. In the Niagara area, he drilled his men in a manner similar to that of Baron von Steuben in the Revolutionary War. Scott's men enjoyed great success in the battles of Chippewa and Lundy's Lane, where they stood up to British regulars. As a drillmaster and tactician, his reputation was made by 1815. His brilliance as a strategist came to light during the Mexican War, when he led the campaign that captured Mexico City (1847). Replete with honors and fame, Scott ran unsuccessfully for president in 1852. He remained in the U.S. Army until the outbreak of the Civil War in 1861. At the start of the Civil War, he designed the Anaconda Plan to strangle the Confederacy.

Tompkins, Daniel D. (1774–1825)—governor of New York State (1808–1817): Daniel D. Tompkins was born in Scarsdale, New York. He took up law, then moved into politics. During his long tenure as New York's governor, he was intensely loyal to the Madison administration, even during the trying events of the Embargo Act and the War of 1812. As governor, he was commander in chief of the New York militia, which was the single largest militia contingent during the war. After the war's end, he was unable to account for all the money he had spent on the war effort; although his debts were settled in 1820, the experience left him a weary and cynical man. Tompkins served as vice president of the United States under James Monroe (1817–1825).

BRITISH

Brock, Sir Isaac (1769–1812)—general, Canadian hero: Sir Isaac Brock was born in England. Brock arrived as a soldier in Canada in 1802. He was promoted to major general in 1811. When the war broke out, he was the general on the scene in the western and Niagara theaters. He enjoyed great success on the western front, capturing Fort Detroit, then went to the Niagara front, where he was killed by an American sharpshooter at the Battle of Queenstown Heights, Ontario. Brock was known as a daring and resourceful commander. His image has remained untarnished in Canadian history; in 1964, Brock University in St. Catharines, Ontario, was named for him.

Cockburn, Sir George (1772–1853)—admiral: Sir George Cockburn was born in England. He went to sea at the age of 14 and fought in many of the important sea battles of the Napoleonic wars. Transferred to America (November 1812), he fought with equal relish against the United States. He conducted raids against American towns on Chesapeake Bay (1813–1814), and he was the guiding spirit behind the British march on Washington, D.C., in 1814; he persuaded a cautious Gen. Robert Ross to advance at key moments. After the war was over, Cockburn took the French emperor Napoleon I to the island of St. Helena (1815). He became a full admiral in 1837 and was elected three times to Parliament (1819, 1828, 1841).

Jenkinson, Robert Banks, Second Earl of Liverpool (1770–1828)—prime minister: Robert Jenkinson was born in London. He first entered Parliament in 1790. He rose to become the Tory prime minister (1812–1827) at the very start of the War of 1812. Known as plain and awkward in his manner, he relied on the military successes of the Duke of Wellington to enhance the stature of his ministry. Never truly an American hater, he nevertheless relished the thought of extracting territory from the United States, but was disappointed when this objective was not realized. Jenkinson remained in office for many years and was considered one of the most stable prime ministers of his era.

Procter, Henry (1763–1822)—general: Henry Procter entered the British army in 1781 and compiled a distinguished record prior to his service in the War of 1812. Commander on the western front after the death of Gen. Isaac Brock, Procter won the Battle of Raisin River in 1813. For the ensuing massacre of American captives by his Indian allies, he was court-martialed and suspended from the British army for six months without pay. His most costly failure was his inability to gain and hold the confidence of the Shawnee chief Tecumseh, something that General Brock had been able to do through the force of his personality.

Ross, Robert (1766–1814)—general: Robert Ross was born in England. He entered the British army in 1789 and served with distinction in Spain (1808–1814), where he won the respect of the Duke of Wellington. Transferred to the American war in 1814, Ross reluctantly led the British army to its capture of Washington, D.C. He was mortally wounded while riding at the head of his men during the night attack on Baltimore. He was buried in Halifax, Nova Scotia. A monument was raised in his honor in St. Paul's Cathedral.

Wellesley, Arthur (1769–1852)—general: Arthur Wellesley was born in Dublin, Ireland. He entered the British army in 1787. Through his victories over Napoleon's armies in India and in Spain and his climactic triumph at the Battle of Waterloo, he rose to become the foremost soldier in England, indeed in all of Europe. When offered the position of commander in chief in North America by Lord Liverpool, Wellington responded, "I confess that I think you have no right from the state of the war to demand any concession of territory from America" (November 9, 1814). This rebuttal led to a serious reevaluation of British policy and hastened the signing of the Treaty of Ghent. Wellington was known as the "iron Duke." He remained a legend in his own time. Ever a keen military observer, he kept a careful eye on the progress of the Mexican War in North America and on the capture of Mexico City in 1847. He declared that American general Winfield Scott was the greatest soldier of his time.

INDIAN

Tecumseh (c.1768–1813)—Shawnee chief: Tecumseh was born in the Ohio River valley. He fought as a young man against the Americans at the Battle of Fallen Timbers (1794). With his brother, known as the "Prophet," Tecumseh attempted to create a large Indian confederacy from the Great Lakes to the Gulf of Mexico. Intent upon resisting American encroachment, he allied himself with the British (and with Gen. Isaac Brock in particular) in 1812. Tecumseh was thrilled with Brock, but disappointed in Brock's successor, Gen. Henry Procter, but fought on gamely throughout the summer of 1813. When the British withdrew from Detroit in September, Tecumseh went with them reluctantly. He persuaded Procter to stand and fight at the Battle of the Thames (October 5, 1813). Tecumseh and his Indian warriors provided the stiffest resistance; he was reported killed in the battle, but his body was never found. Many Americans, including Richard Mentor Johnson, claimed to have killed Tecumseh.

Weatherford, William, Red Eagle (c.1780–1824)—Creek chief: William Weatherford was born to a white father and an Indian mother. He became the leader of the Red Sticks, the militant faction of the Creek nation. He led the attack on Fort Mims (1813) and was the foremost Indian leader during the Creek War. Following his defeat at the Battle of Horseshoe Bend, he surrendered to Gen. Andrew Jackson. Weatherford left his Indian lifestyle and lived among the white settlers of Monroe County, Alabama, for the rest of his life.

FURTHER READING

Barnes, James. *Naval Actions of the War of 1812.* New York: Harper & Row, 1896.

Bemis, Samuel Flagg. *John Quincy Adams and the Foundation of American Foreign Policy.* New York: Alfred A. Knopf, 1949.

Berton, Pierre. *Flames Across the Border: The Canadian-American Tragedy.* Boston: Little, Brown & Co. 1981.

(Continued on p. 165)

Everest, Allan S. *The War of 1812 in the Champlain Valley*. Syracuse, N.Y.: Syracuse University Press, 1981.

Guttridge, Leonard F., and Jay D. Smith. *The Commodores: The U.S. Navy in the Age of Sail*. New York: Harper & Row, 1969.

Greenblatt, Miriam. *The War of 1812: America at War*. New York: Facts On File, 1994.

Hickey, Donald R. *The War of 1812: A Forgotten Conflict*. Chicago: University of Illinois Press, 1990.

Horsman, Reginald. *The War of 1812*. New York: Alfred A. Knopf, 1969.

Jacobs, Major James Ripley, and Glenn Tucker. *The War of 1812: A Compact History*. New York: Hawthorn Books Inc., 1969.

Leckie, Robert. *The Wars of America*. New York: Harper & Row, 1969.

Lossing, Benson J. *The Pictorial Fieldbook of the War of 1812*. Somersworth, N.H.: New Hampshire Publishing Co., (1869, 1976).

Lord, Walter. *The Dawn's Early Light*. New York: W. W. Norton Co., 1972.

Mahon, John K. *The War of 1812*. Gainesville, Fla.: University Press of Florida, 1972.

Perret, Geoffrey. *A Country Made by War*. New York: Random House, 1989.

Peterson, Merril D. *The Great Triumvirate: Webster, Clay, and Calhoun*. New York: Oxford University Press, 1987.

Pratt, William Veazie, ed. *Journals of Two Cruises Aboard The American Privateer Yankee*. New York: The Macmillan Company, 1967.

Reilly, Robin. *The British at the Gates: The New Orleans Campaign in the War of 1812*. New York: G.P. Putnam's Sons, 1974.

Remini, Robert V. *Andrew Jackson and the Course of American Empire: 1767-1821*. New York: Harper & Row, 1977.

Roosevelt, Theodore. *The Naval War of 1812*. New York: Putnam's Sons, 1883.

Sugden, John. *Tecumseh's Last Stand*. Norman, Okla.: University of Oklahoma Press, 1985.

Tully, Andrew. *When We Burned the White House*. New York: Simon and Schuster, 1961.

Weigley, Russell F. *History of the United States Army*. New York: The Macmillan Company, 1967.

THE SEMINOLE INDIAN WARS

DATES OF THE WARS

November 1817–April 1818. December 1835–August 1842. December 1855–March 1858.

ALTERNATE NAMES

Some history texts treat the First Seminole War as merely a campaign and refer to the latter two as the First and Second Seminole Wars. Some historians group all those actions as the Florida Wars to emphasize that many other Indians besides Seminoles were involved.

SIGNIFICANCE

The Seminole Indian Wars, a relatively obscure series of wars, marked a major change in white Americans' dealings with Indians. It provided the first indication that the United States government was prepared to mobilize and coordinate its armed forces to expel virtually all Indians from lands east of the Mississippi River. In 1830, Congress passed the Indian Removal Act. This law forced the relocation of all the southwestern Indians to the Indian territory west of the Mississippi River. As such, the Seminole Indian Wars were the other side of the coin of the Removal Acts by Congress and removal actions by the U.S. Army: The Seminole Indian Wars signaled to all remaining Indian tribes what would happen if they chose to resist. Sheer perseverance would get the Indians nowhere: The Second Seminole Indian War (1835–1842) was the third longest war fought by the United States; the American Revolution and the Vietnam War were the first and second longest, respectively. Unlike the wars against the Indians of the trans-Mississippi west, moreover, the Seminole Indian Wars were fought against relatively small and powerless bands of Indians trapped in a dead-end territory, with the sea at their backs. And although not prominently noted at the time or since, much of the motive behind those wars came from white men who were determined to keep blacks enslaved.

BACKGROUND

The hostilities between white Americans and Seminole Indians were basically rooted in the pressures and demands applied by the white settlers in the Southeast to force the Indians off their lands in Florida. The Seminole Indians had not always lived in Florida; they were a group of Creek Indians who, in the early 18th century, had left the Creek homelands in Georgia and Alabama and moved into the territory of the Apalachee Indians. (The name, *Seminole* is based on a Creek word meaning "escapee" or "separatist.") In Florida, the Seminoles gradually absorbed the Apalachee and other Indians living there; in fact, by the early 19th century, the name *Seminole* came to be applied loosely to almost any Indian living in Florida. Equally important, the Seminoles allowed many blacks to live among them. Some blacks were slaves who had fled to Florida from elsewhere in North America, but they lived as free people because Florida was under the control of Spain, which did not allow slavery. But many blacks were slaves of the Seminoles, although the Seminoles tended to treat their slaves more as tenant farmers. There were entire "towns" or settlements in Florida composed entirely of blacks. There had also been so much intermarriage over the previous decades that there were many so-called black Seminoles, people of mixed race.

During the War of 1812, some Creek Indians in Georgia and present-day Alabama took advantage of the British war against the United States and tried to overthrow American rule in their territories (see War of 1812, pp. 149, 151), but the victory of Gen. Andrew Jackson at Horseshoe Bend in present-day Alabama (see War of 1812, March 27, 1814, p. 151) put an end to those efforts. Not all Seminoles, however, were content to live under the terms accepted by many of their fellow Creeks and other Indians. In fact, many Creeks, including Osceola (see Civilian and Military Biographies, p. 177), had come into Florida after their defeat in 1812–1814, and they joined the Seminoles in the Seminole Indian

Wars. Some Seminoles continued to resist U.S. efforts to first restrict them and suppress their communities, then to remove them to west of the Mississippi River. It was that persistent resistance that led to the series of wars known as the Seminole Indian Wars over some four decades.

CAUSES OF THE WARS

Each of the three Seminole Indian Wars had some incident or development that served as the immediate cause, but behind all the wars lay the simple determination of the U.S. to remove the Seminoles from Florida. Closely related to that determination was the desire of many whites to round up and enslave all blacks in Florida.

PREPARATIONS FOR WAR

In all three Seminole Indian Wars, the United States officially authorized military forces to move against the Seminoles; to that extent, the U.S. Army, state militias, and other service branches made the normal preparations for campaigns. Well before the federal government mobilized for war, however, many individuals along the frontier were preparing for battle against the Indians. (Andrew Jackson was one such individual.) At least some Seminole Indians were equally deliberate about undertaking war against the white man; unlike the Indians in other tribal conflicts with whites, the Seminoles did not just wander into the Seminole Indian Wars as the result of random incidents.

DECLARATIONS OF WAR

In none of the three Seminole Indian Wars did the president make a formal declaration of war or seek congressional approval. In all cases, the president simply instructed the appropriate civilian and military authorities to take action. Although individual congressmen disapproved of the actions taken, Congress invariably voted for the necessary funds to support the military and for other costs.

COMBATANTS

U.S. forces: A combination of regular U.S. Army, state militia, and occasional volunteer troops were the main combatants in all three Semi-

nole Indian Wars; at their peak strength, the U.S. could count on about 5,000 men in the field. About one out of ten enlisted men carried the newest rifles; the rest carried conventional muskets. Officers often carried pistols as well as swords; the enlisted men also tended to carry their favorite knives. Although the U.S. forces had some artillery pieces in a few actions, they provided little advantage in the kind of fighting in which the Indians engaged.

In the Second Seminole Indian War, U.S. Marines and the U.S. Navy also were utilized; about 460 marines saw some action, and the navy provided transport for troop movements along the Florida coast and even engaged in search-and-destroy missions along the Florida waterways.

The U.S. forces also utilized the services of at least 1,500 Creek Indians, who had for some time been friendly with white Americans and regarded the Seminoles as enemies.

Seminoles: At the outset of the Seminole Indian Wars, the Seminoles numbered only some 4,000, including women and children, and they declined in numbers with each war. Even at their peak, they could muster only some 1,400 warriors. However, they fought the wars with aid from Creeks who had come down from Georgia and present-day Alabama as well as aid from other Indian tribes in Florida. The Seminoles were also supported by at least several hundred black males who lived among them as either freemen or slaves; several of those blacks, in fact, played prominent roles, as they were multilingual and so could function as interpreters, emissaries, and spies. Including those allies, the Seminoles could never field more than a total of some 2,000 warriors. Along with their traditional weapons such as bows and arrows, knives, and hatchets, the Seminoles were well armed with rifles, most of which they had obtained from the Spanish over the years.

GEOGRAPHIC AND STRATEGIC CONSIDERATIONS

The Seminole Indian Wars were fought entirely within and for the territory of Florida which was controlled by Spain until 1819. The U.S. government had become convinced that it must own the entire southeastern corner of North America. It would not allow Indians independent possession of or control of that territory, nor would it permit a place of refuge for runaway black slaves on its borders. The United States sent its ground forces into Florida from adjacent states. As the wars dragged on, the U.S. continued to build and reinforce forts in Florida and to maintain its forces from a seemingly limitless storehouse of men and supplies. The Seminoles, however, were restricted to obtaining warriors and supplies from within Florida and eventually were pushed into a smaller and smaller area. At the same time, every inch of the forests, swamps, and Everglades, where the Seminoles made their last stands, were familiar to the Indians and favored their type of guerrilla warfare. The extremes of the climate in Florida proved to be a problem for the white forces: high temperatures in the summer and cold nights in the winter; drenching rains, then droughts, and insects and diseases. In the end, though, as the noose tightened around the Indians, they grew more and more desperate for food and other supplies and stood no chance against the overwhelming numbers of U.S. forces.

The First Seminole Indian War: November 1817–April 1818

CAUSES OF THE WAR

With the conclusion of the War of 1812 against Great Britain, the United States was free to devote its attention to various problems elsewhere. Among those was the continuing unrest among the Indians in the Southeast, who had still not accepted the conditions laid down as the cost of peace. For years, Indian parties from Florida had been moving across the borders with Georgia and present-day Alabama and harassing U.S. settlements, stealing corn and livestock, and, on occasion, killing settlers. Those Indians then retreated back into Florida, which was still a Spanish possession. Some Americans, in particular Southerners from nearby states, were offended by the fact that the Seminoles offered sanctuary to runaway slaves.

After the War of 1812 ended, the British abandoned a fort in eastern Florida on the Apalachicola River about 60 miles below the border with the U.S. It was known in the United States as "Negro Fort" because the free blacks, who had been living around that region for generations, had taken over the fort. The blacks

openly offered refuge to slaves who escaped from the United States. In July 1816, the U.S. Army, supported by two small Navy gunboats that came up from the Gulf of Mexico, sent an expedition along the Apalachicola River into Spanish-held Florida. When the blacks and Indians in the fort refused to surrender, the U.S. ships on July 27 fired on the fort and hit its powder stores; the explosion killed some 300 blacks and Indians. (Blacks who were captured were taken back to Georgia and returned to their owners.)

That incident aggravated the bad relations between white Americans along the U.S. border and the Seminoles and blacks in Florida, but the Spanish took no action. Throughout the rest of 1816 and most of 1817, individuals were killed in various incidents, but it was not until November 1817, when a U.S. force attacked a Seminole village in southern Georgia, that war commenced.

PREPARATIONS FOR WAR

Washington had been kept well informed of incidents in Florida throughout the years; various civilian and military leaders maintained a steady correspondence, and some (including President James Monroe, who was elected in 1816) made no secret of their desire to take over Florida from Spain. Although the U.S. military forces had been greatly cut back after the end of the war with Britain in 1815, there was a constant military presence along the frontier borders with Spanish Florida. Many men, including Gen. Andrew Jackson, army chief of the Southern district, were more than ready to go to war against Indians and to put an end to the refuge for runaway slaves. However, in his rush to attack the Indians, Jackson led his troops far ahead of their food supplies, and often his troops were on near-starvation rations.

DECLARATION OF WAR

There was no declaration of war. At a cabinet meeting on December 26, 1817, President Monroe authorized Secretary of War John C. Calhoun to order Gen. Andrew Jackson to raise a militia force to punish the Indians raiding Georgia.

COMBATANTS

In the aftermath of the War of 1812, the U.S.

government wanted to cut back on its military forces. By 1817, the regular Army had only 8,200 men; however, there were the state militias that could be mobilized when needed, and many men volunteered for the chance to fight Indians. In addition, some 1,500 Creeks friendly to the whites joined in the wars against the Seminoles. The main expedition under Gen. Andrew Jackson consisted of some 3,300 American troops plus the 1,500 Creeks. U.S. Navy ships also provided support on several occasions.

The Seminoles, their Creek allies from Georgia, their black allies, and other Florida Indians, including the Mikasuki and Tallahassee, could never count on more than 2,500 fighters.

GEOGRAPHIC AND STRATEGIC CONSIDERATIONS

Most of the brief First Seminole Indian War was fought in one small section of the Florida panhandle—between the Apalachicola River on the west and the Suwannee River on the east. At the very end, Jackson struck off westward to take Pensacola on the Gulf coast.

BATTLES AND CAMPAIGNS

November 21, 1817: Gen. Edmund Gaines, based at Fort Scott in southern Georgia, had summoned a Seminole chieftain from the nearby Seminole village of Fowltown. When the chief refused to come, Gaines sent a detachment of 250 U.S. troops under Col. David Twiggs to Fowltown to arrest him. When the chief resisted, the U.S. forces attacked and burned Fowltown; five Indians were killed.

November 30, 1817: In retaliation for the attack on Fowltown, an Indian band attacked a U.S. military supply boat on the Apalachicola River, killing some 30 soldiers and 10 dependent women and children.

January 6, 1818: Writing to President Monroe from Nashville, Tennessee, Gen. Andrew Jackson said he felt "that the possession of the Floridas would be desirable to the United States, and in sixty days it will be accomplished." Although Monroe never responded to that, Jackson later argued that Monroe's silence represented approval of his subsequent actions.

January 11, 1818: Jackson received his orders from Secretary of War Calhoun to go to Fort Scott and from there to the Florida panhandle to put an end to Seminole activities that affected the U.S. border territory. There were about 800 regulars at Fort Scott along with 1,000 Georgia militia; Jackson brought another 1,000 volunteers from Tennessee.

March 11–April 16, 1818: With about 2,500 men, Jackson marched into Florida from Fort Scott in southern Georgia. Ignoring potential diplomatic complications, Jackson crossed into Spanish territory and burned Seminole villages in his path. Along the way, Jackson's force was joined by some 1,000 friendly Creek warriors and another 500 militia volunteers. Within a few weeks, all Indian resistance west of the Suwannee River had ceased. The final battle was fought on April 16, along the Suwannee River itself, when about 300 Seminoles and their black allies put up the major resistance (because they feared being dragged into slavery); they and the Seminole Indians were totally outnumbered and outgunned, and, in the end, they retreated to east of the Suwannee River.

April 7–29, 1818: Jackson seized the Spanish fort at St. Marks, about midway between the Apalachicola and Suwannee Rivers. Almost the first thing he did was hang two Seminole chiefs who had been tricked aboard a U.S. Navy ship offshore; one was Hillis Haya, known as Josiah Francis, the Prophet. Shortly thereafter, Jackson's forces arrested Scottish trader Alexander Arbuthnot and English trader Robert Armbrister; Jackson accused them of inciting and aiding the Seminoles in their war. After returning from his expedition to the Suwannee River, Jackson had both men court-martialed; Arbuthnot was sentenced to death by hanging. Armbrister was sentenced to a lashing and imprisonment, but Jackson reversed the court's sentence and had him shot. Jackson was sharply criticized for those actions by many people in the United States, including some in Congress, but no formal action was ever taken against him.

April 23, 1818: A force of some 270 Georgian militiamen, on their way home from the Florida campaign, entered the Creek village of Chehaw in southwestern Georgia. Without any provocation, they killed at least ten men, women, and children before setting fire to the village. The young Georgian in charge of the militia, Obed Wright, was eventually threatened with a trial, but in July he fled, eventually ending up in Cuba. Jackson and others expressed great indignation at that atrocity, although in fact such incidents were not uncommon on the frontier.

May 23–28, 1818: On May 23, Jackson took Pensacola, the capital of Spanish Florida, without a shot. On May 28, after a brief exchange of fire with the Spanish defenders, Jackson's forces captured nearby Fort Barrancas. That effectively ended the First Seminole Indian War.

NEGOTIATIONS AND PEACE TREATY

The First Seminole Indian War had occurred so swiftly that Spain barely had time to protest before it was over. After several cabinet meetings during July, President Monroe agreed that the Spanish posts Jackson had seized should be returned to Spain. But Monroe insisted that the expedition had been simply an act of self-defense against the raids from hostile Indians and that if Spain could not control Florida, it should cede the area to the United States. Spain decided that it was no longer worthwhile to defend Florida against the many American incursions and agreed to negotiate its cession.

July 1818–February 1819: Monroe's secretary of state, John Quincy Adams, and Spain's ambassador to the United States, Luis de Onís, carried on a series of exchanges that linked the disposition of Florida to settling Spain's border with the United States.

February 22, 1819: The Adams-Onís Treaty was signed. In return for gaining all of Florida, the United States renounced its claim to Texas and recognized Spain's holdings in the southwest. The U.S. also agreed to pay $5 million in claims (about $250 million in 1990 dollars) by Americans against Spain.

February 22, 1821: After a long delay by Spain, the Adams-Onís Treaty was presented to the U.S. Senate for final ratification; Florida came under formal control of the United States.

RESULTS OF THE WAR (Casualties, Costs, Consequences)

U.S. military and civilian casualties during the hostilities were about 50; the Indians and their black allies lost at least twice that many. If losses suffered during episodes dating back to 1816 are included, the United States lost about 80 and the Seminoles and blacks lost about 500.

Even before the United States had taken full possession of Florida in 1821, white settlers from the U.S. began to stream into Florida, where they quickly moved to take over all the prime agricultural land. Some of them also began to seize as many blacks as they could—to enslave them either in the Southern states or on Florida plantations. Once the U.S. had gained sovereignty over the territory, the government decided to concentrate the Seminole tribes on reserved lands in central Florida, promising rations, farm tools, and annual cash payments. In 1823, representatives of the Florida Indians met with U.S. delegates at Moultrie Creek, Florida (south of present-day St. Augustine), and under pressure from the U.S., agreed to give up all claims to land in Florida except for a reservation north of the Charlotte River in southwestern Florida. The reservation land proved to be parched and infertile, however, and despite the government's promises, the Seminoles faced starvation not long after falling under U.S. jurisdiction. Once again, there were incidents involving killings by both the Indians and the whites.

The Second Seminole Indian War: December 1835–August 1842

CAUSES OF THE WAR

The Indian tribes remaining in the Southeast could see that their living conditions as well as their relations with white people had been deteriorating for years. For decades, the United States had talked about a solution to the "Indian problem": removal of the Indians to the trans-Mississippi west. Finally, Congress passed the Indian Removal Act of 1830, calling for the forced relocation of all the southeastern Indians to the vast Indian territory west of the Mississippi River (present-day Oklahoma and part of present-day Arkansas). Some of the southeastern Indian tribes accepted the terms offered, but the Seminoles resisted.

May 1–9, 1832: Meeting with friendly Seminoles at Payne's Landing, Florida (about 110 miles northeast of present-day Tampa on the Oklawaha River), U.S. agent James Gadsden presented the terms of a treaty that would remove all the Indians from Florida within three years. In return, each tribe would be given $15,400 plus a homespun shirt and a blanket for each member. (The United States would also pay up to $7,000 to individual Seminoles who could prove they had lost their black slaves because of the war.) Some of the Seminole delegates agreed to the terms of that treaty, but most of the Seminole bands repudiated the Treaty of Payne's Landing.

October 1832–March 1833: Seven Seminole chiefs and their interpreters traveled to the Indian territory to inspect the land. On March 28, at Fort Gibson in the Indian territory (present-day northeastern Oklahoma), the chiefs signed another treaty, agreeing to accept the land.

April 1833–October 1834: The Seminole chiefs returned to their people and reported on the land they were being offered; most Seminoles continued to resist relocation.

October 28, 1834: The United States had appointed a new agent to negotiate with the Seminoles, Wiley Thompson, a veteran of Indian wars and a general in the Georgia militia. At a meeting, Thompson informed the Seminoles that they must leave Florida, as called for under the Treaty of Payne's Landing (May 1–9, 1832). During the months that followed, the Seminole chiefs continued to resist, in part because they were being encouraged to do so by a young Creek Indian, Osceola, who had come to live with them after fleeing the Creek wars in present-day Alabama.

April 3, 1835: Thompson called the leading chiefs into council at Payne's Landing and presented a new resettlement treaty for their approval. Some of the Seminoles seemed willing to agree to the treaty, but Osceola stoutly resisted. (Legend has it that Osceola expressed his views on the matter by driving his hunting knife through the treaty document.) Thompson arrested Osceola, releasing him only after Osceola agreed to accept the treaty. Osceola had done so only to gain his freedom, and he immediately went into the forests and swamps to organize resistance (see Notable Phrases, p. 176).

October 1835: At an autumn council, Thompson learned that only around 400 Seminoles had agreed to resettlement in Arkansas Territory. He gave the tribes a deadline of January 1836 to be ready for the move. Some of the Seminoles began to prepare for the move, but Osceola and his followers prepared for war.

PREPARATIONS FOR WAR

By 1823, the regular U.S. Army had been reduced to only 6,000 men. As the number of inci-

dents involving Indians in the southeast and elsewhere began to rise, Congress authorized a buildup of the army to some 7,200. By late 1835, the governor of Florida had organized a militia of several hundred men, and he could count on militias from neighboring states. By that time, U.S. civilian and military authorities in Florida were well aware of possible confrontations with the Seminoles.

Osceola and his supporters among the Seminoles had begun to organize for their resistance as early as 1835. In addition to their Indian allies, they were counting on the many free and enslaved blacks living in Florida, who realized what their fate would be under the rule of whites.

DECLARATION OF WAR

Andrew Jackson, who had become president in 1832, had been a vigorous Indian fighter and was a staunch proponent of removing the Indians to the west. He never asked Congress for a formal declaration of war, but on January 21, 1836, he directed one of the country's leading soldiers, Gen. Winfield Scott, to mount a campaign to subdue the Seminoles (see War of 1812, Civilian and Military Biographies, p.163).

COMBATANTS

U.S. forces: The Army consisted of only some 7,200 men at the outset, but over the course of the Second Seminol Indian War, it grew to about 15,000; some 10,000 regulars and 30,000 militiamen saw service in Florida at some time during the war. At any one time, however, the largest number of men the U.S. had in the field was about 5,000 men, half regular Army, half militia.

The U.S. Navy consisted of some 5,500 men and 19 ships. The West Indies Squadron, commanded by Capt. Alexander J. Dallas, was assigned to support the Army in the war. The Navy had only five warships, but other smaller ships were used for transport. In addition, the U.S. Navy had a force of some 1,400 marines attached to it. On May 23, 1837, President Jackson, as commander in chief of the armed forces, ordered that all able-bodied marines were to be detached from their regular assignments with the Navy and sent to support the Army for the duration (see Notable Phrases, p. 177).

The United States also called on about 1,500

friendly Creek Indians to fight alongside the U.S. troops.

Seminoles: The Seminoles could count on some 1,200 to 1,600 warriors, including Creek and other Indian allies. Hundreds of blacks—freemen, slaves, and recently escaped slaves—also joined the Seminoles.

GEOGRAPHIC AND STRATEGIC CONSIDERATIONS

The Second Seminole Indian War was essentially a guerrilla war, conducted by the Seminoles out of the forests and swamps of north-central Florida. Osceola's main base was on the Withlacoochee River about 80 miles north of Tampa Bay; gradually, though, the resisting Indians retreated farther and farther south. The Indians concentrated on attacking small units and simply vanished when large U.S. forces appeared. That explains why the numerical superiority of the U.S. forces gave them little advantage and why the war dragged on for so long.

BATTLES AND CAMPAIGNS

December 18, 1835: The Second Seminole Indian War began with Osceola's attack on an Army supply train in which eight soldiers were killed and six wounded. That occurred near the town of Micanopy in north-central Florida.

December 26–27, 1835: Indians along the St. Johns River in northeastern Florida raided the sugar plantations in the area; they were then joined by some 400 black slaves.

December 28, 1835: A Seminole war party in north-central Florida, about 50 miles northeast of Tampa Bay (near present-day Bushnell), ambushed and wiped out two companies of U.S. soldiers, 108 officers and enlisted men under Maj. Francis Dade. Only three privates survived, and two of them died soon after from their wounds.

Osceola ambushed and killed his personal enemy, Indian agent Wiley Thompson, along with four other white people 50 miles to the north at Fort King.

December 29–31, 1835: Gen. Duncan Clinch, commander of the U.S. Army in Florida, decided to retaliate by attacking Osceola's hideaway in the swamps near the Withlacoochee River in northern Florida. Leading a force of some 250 regulars and 500 militia, Clinch set out on December 29 and arrived at the river on December

31. Unable to ford the river, the regulars crossed it a few at a time in a single canoe found there; before the militia could get across, the Indians opened fire on the regulars. They were in danger of being annihilated until they mounted bayonet charges. About 50 of the militia managed to cross the river and protect their route back to the river. Eventually, almost all the men crossed a crude bridge erected by the militia. The battle ended in a draw—the U.S. counted 4 killed and 59 wounded; the Indians claimed only 3 killed and 5 wounded. For long afterward, the regulars and militia accused each other of having failed to conduct themselves in a proper fashion.

February 22, 1836: Gen. Winfield Scott arrived in Florida to assume command of the U.S. forces.

February 27–March 6, 1836: Gen. Edmund Gaines, with a force of some 900 men, was preparing to cross the Withlacoochee River to make his way south to Fort Brooke (near present-day Tampa) when his force was trapped by Indians. The troops built a log breastwork, or a temporary fortification, but as each day passed, they grew short on food and ammunition. Finally, a relief column led by General Clinch arrived to drive off the Indians. Gaines's men counted 5 killed, and 46 wounded.

March 25–May 21, 1836: On March 25, some 4,500 U.S. regulars and militiamen moved out from several bases in northern Florida to start Scott's three-pronged operation to trap Osceola's men in their Withlacoochee stronghold. Through a combination of poor tactics, the difficult terrain, and the Indians' ability to evade the overburdened U.S. forces, Scott's elaborate strategy had little success; perhaps some 60 Indians were killed. After several weeks of inconclusive engagements, Osceola's warriors were able to continue their attacks on plantations and settlements. Scott spent much of his time arguing with other officers, and on May 21, he left Florida to take command of the fight against some Creeks in the Alabama Territory.

September–November 1836: Disease and summer heat had left the U.S. forces almost powerless. An autumn campaign under Florida's territorial governor, Robert K. Call, proved uneffective. His troops never managed to catch up to the warrior bands. Call launched one final offensive in November, but on November 21, it ended in near disaster at Wahoo Swamp across the Withlacoochee River. Call was soon removed from command.

December 1836–April 1837: In December, Gen. Thomas Sidney Jesup assumed command in Florida. With 4,000 regulars and 4,000 militia, Jesup took the field in January 1837. Jesup soon adopted unconventional methods to break Seminole resistance, including false truce flags and broken promises of safe conduct. Although the U.S. forces could not engage large numbers of Seminoles in any decisive battles, they did manage to kill several Seminole leaders. And the Army's systematic burning of Seminole villages kept the Indians on the run. With no opportunity to plant, famine loomed for the Seminoles.

January 27, 1837: In one notable encounter, a column commanded by Col. Archibald Henderson, commandant of the Marines, chased a party of Seminoles into Great Cypress Swamp northeast of Fort Brooke. The 500-man U.S. force included marines, regular Army infantry and artillery units, Georgia volunteers, and Creek scouts, but the force was unable to prevent the Indians from vanishing into the swampland.

May–October 1837: During the summer and autumn, the fighting eased. Some Seminoles tried to negotiate new terms with the U.S. Army and civilian authorities. Jesup adopted an unofficial armistice with the Seminoles and even allowed them to obtain food and ammunition for hunting weapons from the forts and trading stations. But Jesup never wavered in his goal of subduing the Seminoles and forcing them to emigrate.

July 31, 1837: Col. Zachary Taylor was given command of the U.S. military forces in Florida, freeing General Jesup to pursue his diplomatic negotiations with the Indians.

October 21, 1837: In his most successful subterfuge, Jesup invited Osceola to parley under a flag of truce. When the Seminole leader arrived at the meeting, Jesup arrested him. The U.S. forces escorted Osceola to Fort Moultrie, a military prison at Charleston, South Carolina.

December 1837: With 1,000 men, Colonel Taylor pursued the Seminoles deep into the wilderness country around Lake Okeechobee in south-central Florida. By the final conflict on December 25, Taylor claimed 150 prisoners taken and 600 cattle seized. U.S. casualties were severe: 26 killed, 112 wounded. By claiming a decisive victory, Taylor became one of the few officers whose reputation was enhanced by the war.

January 1838: Osceola became ill and grew steadily weaker in prison, but he refused medical treatment. On January 30, he struggled into his shirt, leggings, and moccasins; painted his face, throat, neck, and hands red; shook hands with a group of his captors and with his wives and children; and fell back on his pallet. The post surgeon, Dr. Frederick Weedon, recounted Osceola's final moments:

He then slowly drew from his war belt his scalping knife, which he firmly grasped in his right hand, laying it across the other on his breast, and a moment later smiled away his last breath, without a struggle or groan.

January–December 1838: Jesup's harsh methods and Taylor's exertions in the field achieved results: Nearly 3,000 Seminoles were captured and sent to the Indian territory during Jesup's command. Taylor pursued the Seminoles relentlessly, pushing them southward. One by one, the isolated bands began to submit to relocation. Jesup and many in the U.S. military in Florida were ready to stop the fighting so long as the Seminoles also stopped and agreed to be relocated, but white Americans in Florida insisted that the Seminoles surrender. Much of white Americans' motivation for continuing the war, in fact, centered around the disposition of the many blacks in Florida. Many white people were determined to enslave all blacks, whether or not they had formerly been slaves.

January 1839–August 1842: Gen. Walker K. Armistead succeeded Gen. Thomas Jesup and Col. William J. Worth succeeded Col. Zachary Taylor. Seminoles under Wild Cat (Coacoochee), Sam Jones (Arpeika), Tiger Tail (Thlocko-Tustenuggee), and other leaders were increasingly beleaguered. Beginning in 1840, the U.S. Navy began to send small ships along the coast and up the rivers and waterways of southern Florida to seek out and destroy the Seminole Indians; the squadron was known as the "Mosquito Fleet." By that time, many of the most belligerent Indians had retreated as far south as the Everglades, where U.S. forces pursued them. With so many of their villages and crops destroyed, the relatively few Seminoles still offering resistance faced starvation.

NEGOTIATIONS AND PEACE TREATY

February 5, 1842: Informal negotiations for

resettlement had been underway almost throughout the entire Second Seminole Indian War. There had hardly been a month when at least some Seminoles and U.S. representatives had not met to discuss terms; increasingly, those talks had led to Seminoles turning themselves in to be relocated to the Indian Territory. With only some 300 Seminoles at large in all of Florida, Col. William Worth wrote his superiors in Washington, D.C., recommending that the government call off the war. Especially in Florida, there was a protest from whites who insisted that the Indians be forced to accept a total surrender.

August 14, 1842: Colonel Worth had continued to send out small detachments to try to round up the last holdouts; men on both sides continued to be killed. Finally, on August 14, Worth issued Order No. 28, formally declaring an end to the hostilities.

October–December 20, 1842: The Second Seminole Indian War did not come to an abrupt end. Many U.S. troops were killed in minor battles between October and December. Colonel Worth returned from leave in November and directed the final negotiations and roundup. On December 20, the last of the Seminole bands, some 50 people led by Tiger Tail, was tricked into attending a negotiation session and captured. By that time, about 100 Seminoles who had not been relocated agreed informally to confine themselves to lands west of Lake Okeechobee.

RESULTS OF THE WAR (Casualties, Costs, Consequences)

Historians have calculated a cost of some $1 billion (in 1990 dollars) for the Second Seminole Indian War. The U.S. armed forces, regulars and militia, counted some 1,800 deaths during combat or from wounds and illness. The Seminoles lost perhaps 500 in the hostilities; other Indians on both sides also lost hundreds of their people.

Well before the war ended, thousands of white settlers had moved into Florida and had taken the land to raise crops and cattle. The Armed Occupation Act of 1842 allowed any head of a family to claim 160 acres. By 1843, there were 65,000 white people in Florida. As early as 1839, white Americans drew up a constitution for statehood; Florida was admitted to the union in 1845 as a slave state.

By the close of the Second Seminole Indian War, almost all Seminoles were either dead or had been moved to Indian Territory. About 100 Seminoles (along with some 200 other Indians) were allowed to stay in Florida but could live in a remote area of south Florida, about 2,000 square miles west of Lake Okeechobee. However, under pressure from the encroaching whites, most of the Seminoles retreated into the Everglades.

The Third Seminole Indian War: December 1855–March 1858

CAUSES OF THE WAR

Road building, surveying, and other white encroachments on the land promised to the Seminoles continued in the years following the Second Seminole Indian War in defiance of prior agreements. By the 1850s, Florida's Seminole population had increased slightly to about 500 people, only about 120 of them warriors. There were occasional incidents involving violence on both sides. Settlers resumed demands for complete removal of the Seminoles, and the U.S. government continued to try to persuade every last Seminole to go to the Indian territory: Under one plan, the government paid $800 for each warrior and $425 for each woman and child who emigrated. Tensions continued to build, climaxing in November–December 1855, with the encroachment of Army patrols and survey parties into Seminole territory. In December, when a U.S. detachment under Lt. George Hartsuff vandalized a banana grove belonging to Chief Billy Bowlegs (Holatter Micco), the Seminole leader decided to strike back.

PREPARATIONS FOR WAR

There were no special preparations on either side for the very limited Third Seminole Indian War. The U.S. Army and the Florida militia were more than strong enough to take on the relatively powerless Seminole Indians.

DECLARATION OF WAR

President Franklin Pierce did not make a formal declaration of war, but in January 1856 he authorized Secretary of War Jefferson Davis to accept the Florida militia units into federal service. Davis also ordered Col. John Munroe, who was in charge of military affairs in Florida, to mobilize the regular Army troops in south and central Florida.

COMBATANTS

U.S. forces: The U.S. began its operations with only a few hundred militia troops, but during the two years of intermittent action, the U.S. eventually deployed 800 regulars and 1,300 militia. As there were several rivers and waterways along the Florida coast, U.S. Navy ships assisted in some of the operations.

Seminoles: The Seminoles could count on only about 120 of their own warriors, but there were numerous other Indians living alongside them, and some of those Indians fought with the Seminoles.

GEOGRAPHIC AND STRATEGIC CONSIDERATIONS

The Third Seminole Indian War was fought at selected points throughout southern Florida: east of Lake Okeechobee, along the Gulf and Atlantic coasts of the peninsula, and on the edges of the Everglades. That was a relatively sparsely inhabited region, and much of the terrain was swampy. The relatively few Indians in that area would seem to have presented little threat to the growing white population, but there were enough incidents to convince at least some whites that all the Indians should be removed.

BATTLES AND CAMPAIGNS

December 20, 1855: With 35 warriors, Billy Bowlegs attacked Lt. George Hartsuff's small command and killed four men; Hartsuff withdrew with six wounded men. As word of the attack spread, settlers in southern Florida began to move into the Army's outposts.

January–September 1856: The Seminoles made a number of attacks on various isolated farms and homes of white people; on occasion, the Seminoles also attacked small militia units. Using the tactics of ambush and withdrawal, the Indians killed some two dozen white settlers and militiamen. On a few occasions, militia or regular troops engaged the Indians in skirmishes, but usually the Indians withdrew into the forests or the swamps.

September 1856–December 1857: Brig. Gen.

William Harney, a veteran of Indian wars, was appointed to command the federal troops in Florida. He tried to negotiate with the Seminoles, but when nothing came of the negotiations, he called for building a line of forts across southern Florida. He then launched an offensive in January 1857; by that time, there were some 800 U.S. regulars and 1,300 Florida militiamen in the field. In April, General Harney was transferred to Kansas and took with him about half of the regulars. Throughout 1857, small detachments of regulars and militia pursued the Indians around Lake Okeechobee and deeper and deeper into the Everglades and surrounding swamps, often using small flat-bottomed boats that could penetrate the shallow waterways. Although they killed only a few Indians, the U.S. forces burnt villages, destroyed crops, and took captives in a war of attrition that gradually wore down the Seminoles. The final engagement came in December 1857, when a troop of 90 volunteers attacked a village in the Big Cypress Swamp; they killed seven Indians at the cost of one of their own.

NEGOTIATIONS AND PEACE TREATY

January 1858: Starting in late 1857, the U.S. authorities had tried to use captured or surrendered Indians to persuade Chief Billy Bowlegs and other holdouts to surrender. On January 19, 1858, a group of 40 Seminoles and 6 Creeks from the Indian territory arrived in Florida to make one more effort to persuade the resisting Seminoles to move to the Indian territory. A niece of Billy Bowlegs was released from prison to join them, and the delegation then split into three groups and went into the interior to seek out Billy Bowlegs. One group succeeded in convincing the Seminole leader that it was fruitless to continue resistance.

March 15–27, 1858: At a meeting 35 miles east of present-day Fort Myers, Billy Bowlegs and three of his warriors accepted the terms offered for removal to the Indian territory. On the March 27, the full band of Seminoles agreed to the removal.

May 4, 1858: Billy Bowlegs, 122 warriors, women and children, along with 41 captive Seminoles, boarded ship for the trip to New Orleans; from there, they traveled overland to the Indian territory. There was no peace treaty (see Historical Perspectives and Controversies, p. 177).

RESULTS OF THE WAR (Casualties, Costs, Consequences)

U.S. military and civilian losses numbered some 40 dead and another 60 wounded; the Seminoles suffered fewer casualties because of their hit-and-run tactics.

With the end of the Third Seminole Indian War, Florida was almost totally cleared of Seminoles and other Indians, with only 100 Seminoles remaining in small enclaves in southern Florida.

RESULTS OF THE WARS (Casualties, Costs, Consequences)

The three Seminole Indian Wars together cost the U.S. some $1.5 billion (in 1990 dollars); at least 80 percent of that was for the second and most serious of the wars. The U.S. military (including militia) lost some 2,000 men in those wars, most in the second war and most from wounds and illness. (Conditions in the field were so bad that a number of men committed suicide.) The reward for such a high cost was total possession of the valuable territory of Florida.

The Seminole Indians lost virtually everything. Although some 3,800 were relocated in the west, some 100 remained in Florida, and they and other Indians were restricted to small reservations at Big Cypress Swamp and the Everglades. By the late 20th century, the Seminoles in Florida had increased to about 1,000.

MILITARY INNOVATIONS, TACTICS, EQUIPMENT

There were no important improvements in military weaponry during the Seminole Indian Wars; although a few men had the new (but still unreliable) Colt repeating pistols, most of the men on both sides fought with muskets or rifles that required muzzle-loading and flintlocks. But the U.S. military forces did gain valuable experience during the wars; in particular, the Army learned that it had to adopt new tactics when fighting Indians. In a few set battles, the Army's large units with supply trains and artillery gave the Army an advantage; but in most engagements, the U.S. Army learned that small mobile units were more successful. The Army also learned the value of using local scouts and guides.

In effect, the U.S. Army learned how to fight a guerrilla war. Another lesson learned was the usefulness of coordinating naval forces with army operations. Many of the men who gained experience in the Seminole Indian Wars went on to apply their knowledge in the Mexican War, the Trans-Mississippi Indian Wars, and the Civil War.

LEGENDS AND TRIVIA

Georgia militiaman Sgt. Duncan McKrimmon was captured in March 1818 in the vicinity of the old Negro Fort and taken to the village of a prominent Creek leader, Hillis Haya, then allied with the Seminoles (see April 7–29, 1818, p. 169). McKrimmon was tied to a stake and about to be executed when a teenage girl, Milly Francis, daughter of the chief, rushed forward and pleaded for him to be spared. McKrimmon was released and ransomed to the Spaniards, who freed him. Eventually, his story circulated as popular lore and was embellished in some versions. When the Seminole Indian Wars ended, one version claimed, McKrimmon returned to find Milly and her mother destitute and living near the old Negro Fort. He brought them a gift of money collected from his hometown in gratitude for Milly's action; he also asked Milly to marry him. She accepted the gift but refused to marry him. One thing that is certain is that she imigrated to Indian territory, married an Indian, and had many children. In 1842, Maj. Ethan Allen Hitchcock interviewed Milly; he spent two years persuading Congress to provide her an annual pension of $96 (about $4,000 in 1990 dollars).

NOTABLE PHRASES

The white man says I shall go, and he will send people to make me go; but I have a rifle, and I have some powder and some lead. I say we must not leave our homes and lands. If any of our people want to go west, we won't let them. And I tell them they are our enemies, and we will treat them so, for the great spirit will protect us.

Those were the words allegedly said by Osceola to the Seminoles after he had been released from prison by Wiley Thompson (see April 3, 1835, p. 171). Osceola was determined to organize a resistance to the planned relocation of the Seminoles.

Gone to fight the Indians. Will be back when the war is over.

One of the legends of the U.S. Marines Corps, those words are said to have been the notice that Marine commandant Col. Archibald Henderson tacked on his office door in Washington, D.C., in the summer of 1836, when he set off to command the Marines in the war against the Creeks and later the Seminoles. Although there is no evidence that such a note existed, it does express the special spirit of the Marines and the general attitude of civilian Americans at that time. For the Marines, it conveyed the jaunty attitude the corps is supposed to have had in the face of danger as well as the confidence that the Marines would succeed. For the civilian Americans, it conveys the condescending way white Americans regarded Indians—as little more than nuisances that had to be dealt with.

HISTORICAL PERSPECTIVES AND CONTROVERSIES

For generations, the Seminole Indians were the only major Native American tribe still technically at war with the United States. Because the Seminole Indian Wars simply ended, they did not involve formal surrender documents or peace treaties. Although many Seminole leaders did sign various treaties agreeing to terms set down by the U.S. government, they did so under extreme pressure. Those treaties were not surrender documents but land transfers. In particular, the last Seminoles who held out after the war that ended in 1858 did not sign any peace treaties. Technically speaking, their descendants could claim that they were still at war with the United States Thus, surviving Seminoles continued to press their claims for payments from the United States. It was not until April 30, 1990, that Congress passed Public Law 101-277, a last settlement bill for the land taken from the Seminoles. Although not all Seminoles have been happy with the bill, it may be said that the tribe, for now at least, has closed its account with the United States.

CIVILIAN AND MILITARY BIOGRAPHIES

Osceola (1804?–1838)—Seminole leader:

Osceola was born in Georgia. He is said by some sources to have been the son of a white man; by others, the grandson. It is also believed that he had some black ancestry. In any case, his Creek mother's second husband was named William Powell, and Osceola was widely known among white people as Powell. (His Indian name was Asi Yahola, the basis for Osceola.) He fled with his family after the Creek War of 1813–1814 and settled with a Seminole band in Florida. Although not a chief, he encouraged the Seminoles to reject land-giveaway treaties and to resist the whites. From 1835 to 1837, in the early stages of the seven-year Second Seminole Indian War, he carried out a highly effective guerrilla campaign against U.S. forces. Captured by a ruse in 1837, he died in prison at Fort Moultrie, South Carolina, early the following year.

FURTHER READING

Heidler, David S, and Jeanne T. Heidler. *Old Hickory's War: Andrew Jackson and the Quest for Empire.* Mechanicsburg, Pa.: Stockton Books, 1996.

Lancaster, Jane. *Removal Aftershock: The Seminoles' Struggles to Survive in the West, 1836–1866.* Knoxville, Tenn.: University of Tennessee Press, 1994.

Laumer, Frank. *Dade's Last Command.* Gainesville, Fla.: University Press of Florida, 1995.

Mahon, John K. *History of the Second Seminole War, 1835–1842.* Rev. ed. Gainesville, Fla.: University Press of Florida Press, 1991.

Sturtevant, William C., ed. *A Seminole Sourcebook.* New York: Garland Press, 1987.

Wickman, Patricia R. *Osceola's Legacy.* Tuscaloosa, Ala.: University of Alabama Press, 1991.

Wright, J. Leitch. *Creeks and Seminoles: The Destruction and Regeneration of the Muscogulge People.* Lincoln, Nebr.: University of Nebraska Press, 1986.

THE MEXICAN WAR

DATES OF WAR

April 26, 1846–February 2, 1848

ALTERNATE NAMES

The War with Mexico. The Great War for Empire. The War of American Aggression (Mexico's name for the war).

SIGNIFICANCE

Most historians agree that the United States fought the Mexican War for the simple goal of acquiring territory. The war increased the size of the United States by about 25 percent (40 percent of the territory of the Republic of Texas is also regarded as having been secured by that war). The war established that the United States would employ military force in pursuit of national goals and naked self-interest—just like the major nation-states of Europe. The Mexican War was the first war the American military fought with a proactive strategy conceived of by civilian and military leaders in Washington, D.C. Certainly, the Mexican War was one of the most one-sided wars the United States ever fought: From the first major engagement to the last, Mexico's troops proved no match for the increasingly professional U.S. military forces. In that sense, the Mexican War signified the coming of age of the United States, the passage from the nation's use of power to defend its ideals to its use of power to advance its interest. At the same time, many idealistic Americans openly proclaimed their opposition to the war on moral grounds, a phenomenon embodied in a major milestone in history: Henry David Thoreau's concept of civil disobedience, which inspired many people in the decades that followed (see Notable Phrases, pp. 205-206). In the short term, the significance of the split in Americans' attitudes toward the Mexican War was that it foreshadowed the greater divide that within a generation would result in the Civil War (see Civil War, Background May 1846–February 1848, p. 212).

BACKGROUND

American expansionism, Mexican independence from Spain, the "Texas question," and the intransigence of the governments of both the United States and Mexico set the stage for the Mexican War.

American expansionism had a long history. From the moment they first set foot in North America, European settlers pushed forward against the boundaries and peoples that seemed to fence them in against the eastern seaboard. In the decades that followed the establishment of the United States in 1789, Americans came up against two formal obstacles to expansion west of the Mississippi River: Spain, which held control of the vast territory that covered the entire southwest quarter of North America; and Mexico, which in 1821 replaced Spain as the ruler of that empire. As for the Native Americans, their claims to that land were regarded less as formal barriers than as temporary inconveniences.

The issue of expansion into the region west of the Mississippi River seemed to have been settled in 1819, when Secretary of State John Quincy Adams negotiated the Adams-Onís Treaty with Spain. Under the terms of that agreement, the United States gained Florida but yielded any claim it might have to the area west of the Sabine River (present-day Texas). The Mexican Revolution and the resultant Mexican independence changed the players but not the basic scenario. Since 1811, Mexicans had fought a war to win their independence from Spain. That process was aided by the Napoleonic Wars in Europe, which weakened Spain's ability to resist Mexico's revolt. Nonetheless, it was not until 1821 that Mexico actually won its freedom and established a government. That government began as an empire under a Mexican general, Augustín de Iturbide, but changed quickly into a federated republic, modeled to a large extent on the American form of government. By 1824, there were two sister republics in North America: the United States and Mexico. There seemed to be no obvious reason the two countries could not live in peace, but the troublesome dynamic of American expansionism and the assertiveness of various individuals remained.

The Texas question developed from the pioneering activities of Moses Austin, Stephen Austin, and the Americans who followed in their footsteps. In 1820, Moses Austin, who had made and lost a fortune mining in Missouri, negotiated with the Spanish government for the right to move across the Sabine River into Texas and set up a colony of Americans who would live under Spanish law and government. Moses Austin died in 1821, before he could move to Texas, but his son, Stephen, took up his mission. Because Spanish rule had been overthrown in 1821, Stephen Austin had his father's agreement reconfirmed by the new government of Mexico. Before the end of 1821, 300 American families moved into Texas. The next year, Stephen Austin established the colony's government at San Felipe de Austin.

During the next 15 years, some 30,000 Americans—often referred to as Anglo-Americans to distinguish them from their Mexican neighbors—followed Austin and settled in Texas. (Other Anglo-Americans settled in the Mexican territories that became the states of New Mexico and California.) In moving into Mexican territory, the Americans agreed to become Mexican citizens and to practice the Catholic faith, but many refused to change their religion and continued to think of themselves as U.S. citizens. One of the points of contention was slavery, which Mexico abolished throughout all its territory in 1829; some of the Americans had brought their slaves into Texas and did not want to give them up. That issue was aggravated when, in April 1830, Mexico barred any more U.S. immigrants from settling in Mexican territory. From that date on, a struggle emerged between the 30,000 Americans in Texas and the representatives of the Mexican government. Aside from the obvious cultural differences between the two peoples, the Americans believed that Mexico's federal system of government, like that of the United States, granted many liberties and privileges to the different Mexican states and that Texas should also enjoy those liberties and privileges.

There were even many prominent Mexicans who agreed that the central government in Mexico City was exceeding its powers. Independent of the American settlers in Mexican territory, some of the Mexican federalists in Texas and California by 1834 were carrying on a revolt of their own against the centralists. Emboldened by that challenge to Mexico's government, led by a virtual dictator, Gen. Antonio López de Santa Anna, a group of largely Anglo-American Texans held a meeting in San Felipe de Austin on November 3, 1835, and organized a temporary government of federalists. They sent a small force to overthrow the centralist government in San Antonio; when they succeeded, Santa Anna raised an army of 6,000 Mexican troops and moved north to attack the rebels in San Antonio.

Despite the warnings of some experienced observers, a group of mainly Anglo-Americans chose to remain in the Alamo, a walled Catholic mission in San Antonio. Santa Anna's troops isolated the Alamo on February 23, 1836; the defenders remained besieged until the final attack on March 6. The exact number of those who died at the Alamo is unknown, but most historians agree on 183 to 190; only a few women and children survived. Davy Crockett, James Bowie, and William B. Travis were among those who died when the Mexicans came over the walls and conquered the mission (see Songs, p. 206).

Three weeks later, on March 27, one branch of Santa Anna's army attacked the town of Goliad about 60 miles southeast of San Antonio. After the Texans surrendered, some 300 were executed by the Mexicans. Then, on April 21, Sam Houston led the Texas militia in a surprise attack on Santa Anna and a part of his army along the San Jacinto River (east of present-day Houston). The Texans suffered only 16 killed and 24 wounded. They killed or wounded some 630 Mexicans and took 730 prisoners, including Santa Anna.

In order to win his freedom, Santa Anna signed a treaty that yielded Texas to the Americans living there. As soon as he returned to Mexico, that treaty was abrogated by the Mexican government, and in the years that followed, tension built up along the Texas-Mexico border. The Anglo-Americans declared the independence of Texas on March 2, 1836, and during the next nine years, Texas was known as the Lone Star Republic. It had its own constitution, president, and legislature. (Sam Houston served as president of Texas from 1836 to 1838 and again from 1841 to 1844.)

Although some government leaders in the United States, especially in the South, considered annexing Texas, Presidents Andrew Jackson and Martin Van Buren held back from taking the step during their administrations, which covered the years 1829 to 1841. It was not only that both presidents did not wish to provoke a war with Mexico, but also that they were well aware that slavery was already a divisive issue in American society. Knowing that the annexation of Texas (a region committed to the right to hold slaves) might inflame the issue, both presidents declined to bring Texas into the Union. Americans' disagreements over slavery did in fact color many of the actions involved in the Mexican War.

CAUSES OF THE WAR

The Texas question was resolved in 1845. President John Tyler, who succeeded Martin Van Buren in 1841, tried to have Texas annexed by a treaty, but Northern senators denied him the necessary two-thirds majority. In one of the last acts of his presidency, Tyler evaded the usual routes to statehood by bringing the issue before the House and Senate as a joint resolution. Requiring the support of a simple majority of those congressmen present, the resolution passed on March 1, 1845. Tyler signed the measure on the same day, and on March 4 turned the issue over to his successor, President James K. Polk. Texas formally joined the Union on December 29, 1845, thus ending the debate, at least as far as most Americans and Texans were concerned.

Mexico refused to accept the U.S. annexation of Texas; in fact, Mexico had broken off diplomatic relations with the United States in March 1845. Knowing that it was futile to fight for all of Texas, the Mexicans drew the line at the Nueces River 150 miles to the north of the Rio Grande. Declaring that the Nueces River had always been the southern boundary of the Mexican state (or province) of Texas, Mexico strongly asserted its right to territory up to that line. Although there was considerable disarray within Mexico's government, which was facing a potential revolt in California, there were some in Mexico calling for war against the United States because it had annexed Texas.

The pride and intransigence of Mexico during that period was equaled by that of the United States. James K. Polk had won the presidential election of 1844 in a campaign that openly called for the annexation of both Texas and the Oregon

Territory up to 54° 40' north latitude. Although his campaign slogan, "Fifty-four forty, or fight!" referred only to a threat to fight the British over the disputed Oregon Territory (see Notable Phrases, p. 204), it was part of a broader expansionist spirit rampant in the United States. That spirit was labeled "manifest destiny" by John L. O'Sullivan, an editor-lawyer-activist, who defined it as meaning the United States was clearly fated to spread its power and people throughout the North American continent, from the Atlantic to the Pacific (see Notable Phrases, p. 204).

PREPARATIONS FOR WAR

Once in office, President Polk asserted that he was ready to fight for the southern boundary of the United States as well as for the disputed boundary in Oregon. In fact, realizing that he faced trouble with Mexico, Polk agreed in June 1846 to a treaty with Britain that fixed the Oregon boundary at the 49th parallel.

In December 1845, Polk had sent John Slidell as his delegate to Mexico City with an offer to buy the Mexican states of California and New Mexico if Mexico would accept the Rio Grande as the boundary of Texas and resolve the issue of money owed by Mexico to Americans. That latter issue, the long-outstanding debts to Americans, was cited by Polk as one of the major justifications for going to war against Mexico. Another justification cited by Polk (and endorsed by some historians since) was that Great Britain and to a lesser degree France were showing signs of wanting to seize or purchase California. In any case, in October 1845, Polk had sent secret instructions to his consul in California, Thomas Larkin, that he would support a movement there for separation from Mexico, but it was six months before Larkin actually received that notice (see California theater, April 17, 1846, p. 185).

As early as June 1845, Polk had ordered Brig. Gen. Zachary Taylor to take a detachment of U.S. Army troops and position himself "on or near the Rio Grande." By the end of July, Taylor had established his base camp on the Nueces River at Corpus Christi, the southernmost American settlement in Texas. By the end of October, Taylor's force had built up to some 4,000 men, including volunteers, Texas Rangers, and about half the regular U.S. Army. On January 12, 1846, Polk learned that Slidell's mission in Mexico was proving unsuccessful: Mexico would not negotiate the sale of any territory. On January 13, Polk ordered General Taylor to march across the disputed boundary all the way to the Rio Grande. It was early March before Taylor left Corpus Christi with 3,550 men, followed by 307 oxcarts and mule-drawn wagons. On March 28, 1846, they reached the northern side of the mouth of the Rio Grande; there, Taylor set up a camp that he called Fort Texas. About 25 miles away was the Mexican city of Matamoros, which lay inland on the southern side of the Rio Grande.

On April 11, 1846, Mexican general Pedro de Ampudia arrived at Matamoros with 3,000 Mexican troops. He promptly sent a message to Taylor ordering the Americans to withdraw from the area within 24 hours. Taylor refused. There were several incidents that cost both sides casualties. On April 23, Ampudia was replaced by Gen. Mariano Arista, who, the very next day, sent 1,600 cavalrymen north of the Rio Grande. That patrol met an American patrol of 56 cavalrymen, and on April 24–25, they engaged in a skirmish in which 16 Americans were killed or wounded; all the others were captured. When General Taylor learned of that disaster on April 26, he immediately put his men on a war footing and sent news of the encounter to Washington, D.C., adding that "hostilities may now be considered as commenced." Taylor then pulled most of his force back about 18 miles to Point Isabel, where his supply ships were waiting.

DECLARATION OF WAR

General Taylor's message about the fighting along the Rio Grande reached President Polk on May 9. By coincidence, John Slidell had returned from Mexico only the day before, confirming that the Mexican government would not negotiate new boundaries or the sale of any lands. On May 11, 1846, President Polk sent a message to Congress citing the fact that "Mexico has shed blood on the American soil" (see Notable Phrases, p. 205). On May 11, the House of Representatives approved Polk's request to pursue the Mexican War by a vote of 173 to 14; the next day, the Senate approved it by a vote of 40 to 2. (Some congressmen primarily objected to letting a president embark on a war before Congress declared war.) Those who voted against the war in the House of Representatives, all from the Northeast, called themselves the "Conscience Whigs"; in New England, they became known as the "Immortal 14." Mexico's president, Mariano Paredes, had actually proclaimed a "defensive war" against the United States on April 23, but Mexico did not make a full and formal declaration of war until July 1, 1846.

COMBATANTS

Americans: When the Mexican War began, there were 637 officers and 5,925 enlisted men in the regular U.S. Army, of whom around 3,000 were already in the boundary area between the Nueces River and the Rio Grande. During the course of the war, 1,016 officers and some 35,000 enlisted men joined the regular Army, bringing the total of those who served in the regular Army to about 42,585. In addition, 73,532 men had their names entered on the rolls of various volunteer militia units that were created during the Mexican War. Upon declaring war, Congress immediately authorized the expansion of the Army to 15,540 regulars and called for 50,000 volunteers to be recruited from all the states. Most states met their quotas without difficulty, although there was considerable resistance to the war in New England. Throughout most of the war, the volunteers were placed under the command of the regular Army, but there were some relatively independent units, such as the Texas Rangers. Although small in numbers at the start of the war, the troops of the regular U.S. Army were relatively well trained and well equipped. They had the advantage of an officer corps that had been trained at the U.S. Military Academy at West Point in New York; in particular, the artillery officers commanded some of the best weapons and most sophisticated units of any military establishment in the world. Conditions in the U.S. Army, however, were not ideal. Food, living quarters, hygiene, and medical treatment for the lower ranks were often of disgraceful quality. Many of the soldiers had volunteered simply to earn what they thought would be easy money; they soon became disillusioned, and there were incidents of undisciplined behavior and even mutiny. Thousands of men deserted, and hundreds went over to the Mexican side (see Legends and Trivia, pp. 203-204).

The U.S. Navy had gone into some decline since the War of 1812. Navy personnel was down to 7,500, and the Naval Academy at Annapolis, Maryland, had begun classes only in October 1845. Of the seven 74-gun vessels authorized by Congress in 1816, only three had been built, among them the USS *Pennsylvania*, which, with its 120 guns, was probably the largest warship in the world. Steam warships were just coming into use; the USS *Fulton* was a 700-ton steam-powered side-wheeler that proved valuable in shallow coastal operations. The Navy's limited number of ships were divided among several squadrons stationed off North American shores and in seas around the world, primarily to protect American commerce. When the Mexican War began in 1846, the Home Squadron had 3 frigates and 7 smaller, noncombat ships, and the Pacific Squadron had 3 frigates and 6 smaller, noncombat ships. By 1847, the Home Squadron had 2 frigates and 16 smaller, noncombat ships, and the Pacific Squadron had 2 frigates and 10 smaller, noncombat ships. The smaller ships—steamers, schooners, and brigs—proved most useful in the operations along Mexico's Gulf coast.

The U.S. Marines did not play a major role in the Mexican War in terms of numbers or engagements, but marines did participate in several important actions. Marines attached to the Navy's Gulf Coast Squadron made a series of landings at Mexican river and coastal ports to enforce the blockade that denied Mexico the importation of needed armaments and supplies. Other marines attached to the Pacific Squadron played a crucial role in the seizure of California. The U.S. Marine Corps numbered only about 42 officers and 1,000 enlisted men when the war began, but the commandant was allowed to recruit more; in August 1847, a special 375-man battalion of marines arrived to reinforce Gen. Winfield Scott's forces at Puebla, Mexico; they participated in the attack on the Mexican fort Chapultepec and in the final assault that took Mexico City. It was that last action at "the halls of Montezuma" that is alluded to in the "Marine's Hymn" (see Barbary Wars, Songs, p. 137).

***Mexicans*:** At peak moments during the Mexican War, the Mexican Army numbered about 30,000 men, but it was poorly organized and had a continual turnover. The Mexican Army was nourished by memories of its defeat of the Spaniards in Mexico's war for independence, but the material used by its soldiers had hardly changed or improved over 20 years' time. The Mexican

foot soldier was generally drafted, and his food rations were not only scanty but also often delivered late; his weapons and ammunition were often of poor quality. Despite those disadvantages, there was a general level of strong morale in the Mexican army at the start of the war. The Americans were believed to be poor soldiers, and many Mexicans, as well as many European observers of the Mexican War, believed that Mexico would prevail in the fighting because of its more experienced soldiers (see Historical Perspectives and Controversies, p. 207).

When the war began, Mexico had only two significant warships, the steamers *Moctezuma* and *Guadalupe*. Mexico transferred ownership of the vessels to British commercial captains in order to protect them from being captured. Smaller Mexican craft were in abundance on both the eastern and western sides of Mexico, but they were generally held in port by a highly effective American blockade. In fact, no Mexican naval vessel ever put to sea to challenge the American Navy.

GEOGRAPHIC AND STRATEGIC CONSIDERATIONS

When the Mexican War began in April 1846, most of the advantages seemed to lie with Mexico. The seat of the first phase of the war (along the Rio Grande) lay much closer to the Mexican army's sources of supply than to the American Army's. American troops and supplies had to be brought from the East Coast and from New Orleans all the way to Texas and then into Mexico when the fighting began in earnest and spread into the Mexican heartland. American commanders in the field were often cut off from Washington, D.C. and from each other. Those problems became even more severe when the war spread into New Mexico and California: American land forces and naval units were practically cut off from supplies from the East, and they had to conduct their operations with little or no communication from Washington.

By contrast, the Mexicans had an unimpeded route across northern Mexico for supplies and men. The apparent advantages of the Mexicans were, however, negated by several factors. First, the Mexican government and army were insufficiently organized to take advantage of their proximity to the battlefront. Second, the United States held an undisputed naval mastery on the Gulf of Mexico and the Pacific Ocean off Mexico and California. This naval supremacy allowed the Americans to transport many of their men and much of their supplies and weaponry by water, which was much faster and easier than transporting them by land; it also allowed the U.S. Navy to enforce an almost total blockade, cutting Mexico off from both exports and imports. Finally, when it came to the fighting in New Mexico and California, the Mexicans did not have any great advantages over the American forces in terms of obtaining supplies and reinforcements.

The Mexicans did possess one distinct geographical advantage. When the Americans marched from Veracruz to Mexico City in the summer of 1847 (along much the same route that Hernando Cortes and his Spanish conquistadors had taken in 1519–1520), they had to advance through hilly country that gave every advantage of defense to the Mexicans. The same was true when the Americans reached the perimeter of Mexico City, and the surprise of the American victory there led one Mexican officer to lament that "God is a Yankee."

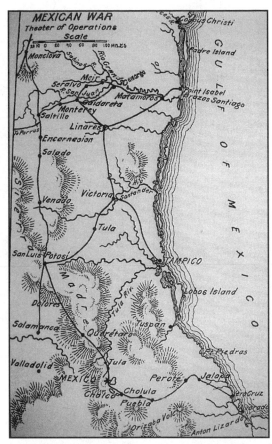

This map shows the locations of the main battles in Mexico during the Mexican War. Other battles occurred in Chihuahua, Mexico, to the northwest and in present-day New Mexico and California.

BATTLES AND CAMPAIGNS: 1846

There were four theaters of military operation during 1846: northern Mexico theater, California theater, New Mexico theater, and naval theater.

NORTHERN MEXICO THEATER

April 26, 1846: Gen. Zachary Taylor sent a message to Washington, D.C., declaring that "hostilities may now be considered as commenced." Without any official declaration of war, he called upon the governor of Texas for four regiments of volunteers to aid him in his defense of the Rio Grande boundary.

May 1, 1846: Taylor led the bulk of his troops to Point Isabel, leaving about 300 men to maintain and hold Fort Texas, just to the north of the Rio Grande across from Matamoros. Point Isabel was at the mouth of the Rio Grande, where supply ships could put in.

May 2–7, 1846: The Mexican Army of the North, led by Gen. Mariano Arista, began a siege of Fort Texas. Although the Mexicans bombarded the fort for several days, during which 2,700 rounds of ammunition were fired against

the fort, the garrison maintained its control and morale.

May 7, 1846: Taylor led his resupplied and reinforced American troops back from Point Isabel toward Fort Texas, seeking to lift the siege. In his orders for the day, he anticipated a battle and instructed his men to rely on their bayonets.

May 8, 1846 (Battle of Palo Alto): Taylor encountered the Mexican army of Arista drawn up in a defensive position along a stretch of open plain known as Palo Alto on the north side of the Rio Grande. Although facing an army that was twice as large as theirs, the Americans chose to attack. Following an exchange of artillery fire, in which the Americans gave much better than they received, the Mexicans sent their cavalry forces in an attack. They were repelled by a volley of fire from the Americans. By that time, the prairie grass had caught fire and smoke obscured the battlefield. But both sides continued to maneuver, and two attacks by Mexican troops were again repelled by American artillery. By dusk, the fighting had halted. The battle itself was indecisive, but the superiority of the American artillery was clearly demonstrated. When Arista withdrew his men the next morning, the Mexicans had suffered some 500 killed or wounded; the American loss came to only 5 killed and 42 wounded.

May 9, 1846 (Battle of Resaca de la Palma): Arista set up his troops in a defensive position near a ravine protected by trees. The Mexicans still outnumbered the Americans by at least two to one. Upon arriving at the scene, Taylor decided to attack at once. The crucial moment in the battle came when U.S. cavalrymen failed in their first attempt to capture the Mexican artillery that was holding back the Americans. Seeing that, Taylor commanded his men to "take those guns and by God keep them" (see Notable Phrases, p. 205). The Americans succeeded on the second try. The Mexican army was soon routed and Arista was among the first to flee; the survivors of the battle passed Fort Texas as they fled to the Rio Grande, where many drowned in their overcrowded small boats. By the end of the day, the Mexicans had suffered at least 450 men killed or drowned and almost as many wounded; American casualties were 33 dead and 89 wounded. The Americans were unable to pursue the Mexicans across the Rio Grande because they lacked boats or pontoon bridges.

May 17–18, 1846: On May 17, Arista sent a message to Taylor asking for an armistice, but Taylor replied that he would settle for nothing less than the total surrender of Matamoros. That afternoon, Arista began a two-day evacuation of Matamoros. Following the departure of the Mexican army, Taylor's men entered the city and proclaimed American control over the area. The Mexican Army of the North, having fled south to Linares, was decimated and demoralized; Arista was removed from command and replaced by Gen. Francisco Mejia.

June–July 1846: American volunteers from New Orleans arrived in Taylor's camp at Matamoros, swelling Taylor's total force to around 10,000. Conditions at Matamoros quickly deteriorated as the bored troops began to brawl, pillage, and rape. Moreover, the climate and poor hygiene led to disease and death among the troops. General Taylor realized that he must get his troops out of Matamoros and decided to relocate at Monterrey, the nearest large Mexican city. On June 15, Taylor sent Capt. Ben McCulloch with 40 of his Texas Rangers to scout the best route to Monterrey; for the next few weeks those Texas Rangers behaved in a most undisciplined way, offending and violating the Mexican communities they passed through.

July 6, 1846: Taylor led his men out of Matamoros and began a march up the Rio Grande; they headed first for Camargo, a city en route to Monterrey.

July 14, 1846: Taylor and his army occupied Camargo without having to fire a single shot. The Mexican Army of the North had withdrawn to Monterrey. Camargo proved to be as unhealthful as Matamoros was; hundreds of Americans died from disease due to the unsanitary conditions there.

August 19, 1846: Taylor commenced a march from Camargo and headed toward Monterrey, which had a civilian population of about 20,000.

September 19, 1846: The American Army, commanded by General Taylor, came within sight of Monterrey for the first time. The city was strongly defended by several forts around its perimeter: the Citadel (which the Americans called the "Black Fort"), Bishop's Palace, El Diablo, La Libertad, and Fort Soldado. Gen. Pedro de Ampudia, who had succeeded General Mejia as commander of the Army of the North, had around 7,000 regular troops and 3,000 volunteers with which to defend the city. Nonetheless, the Mexican confidence had been badly shaken by the battles of Palo Alto and Resaca de la Palma, and Ampudia found that he could not persuade his staff to fight offensively against Taylor; his generals were determined to fight within the impressive defenses of the city.

September 21–September 25, 1846 (Battle of Monterrey): Taylor determined that Bishop's Palace was the key to the defense of Monterrey. Therefore, he commenced a three-pronged attack on the city's defenses on September 21. Col. William Worth led a column that defeated a Mexican cavalry attack, then proceeded to take and hold the road to the Mexican city of Saltillo, the only route by which supplies could reach the defenders of Monterrey. Worth then led his forces in an attack on Federation Hill; they soon took Federation Hill and turned the captured Mexican cannon on the fleeing Mexicans. Other units took nearby Fort Soldado. On the same day, however, another of Taylor's columns spent itself in fruitless attacks that left 394 Americans killed or wounded. Taylor recovered from that setback and continued his encirclement of the Mexican position. On September 22, Worth's forces took Independence Hill and Bishop's Palace with only 32 casualties. During the night of September 22–23, the Mexicans abandoned the key defensive position of El Diablo. Worth and Taylor took up their attacks on the city itself, engaging in street fights. General Ampudia eventually realized that the American artillery was capable of bombarding the main plaza and the cathedral, in which the Mexicans had stored large amounts of munitions. By the evening of September 23, Ampudia indicated a willingness to negotiate. During September 24, the American negotiating team agreed to allow the Mexican forces to leave with their sidearms, their horses, and six pieces of artillery; the Americans also agreed not to pursue the Mexicans for eight weeks. The official surrender was signed in the early hours of September 25, and Ampudia led his forces out of Monterrey that morning. Taylor had taken that "impregnable" city in four days at the cost of 800 American casualties, but he knew that his forces, although victorious, were exhausted and needed some time to recuperate and get back to fighting strength.

September 26, 1846: Brig. Gen. John Ellis Wool set out from San Antonio with a force of 1,400, including regulars, volunteers, and Texas Rangers. During the following three months, they marched almost 800 miles, as they made their way south to join Taylor's forces.

November 13–16, 1846: Disobeying orders from Washington D.C., to hold his position at Monterrey, General Taylor decided to occupy the Mexican city of Saltillo, which he believed would provide a stronger means of defense against Mexican attack from the south. General Worth went ahead, and Taylor followed shortly after. By November 16, they had taken Saltillo.

December 22, 1846: General Wool arrived in Saltillo with his force of 1,400.

December 27, 1846: Gen. Winfield Scott arrived at Brazos at the mouth of the Rio Grande (see Home Front, November 18, 1846, p. 190). He began to assemble his Army for his campaign to take Mexico City; he ordered Taylor to turn over thousands of his regular troops to his command. Meanwhile, thousands of new volunteer units from the United States joined Scott. Because Scott's plan called for an amphibious assault at Veracruz, he also began to assemble a fleet of large ships and small landing craft.

CALIFORNIA THEATER

March 4, 1846: U.S. Army captain John C. Frémont and his company of some 60 Americans (a mixture of adventurers, mountainmen, and Indians) dug entrenchments on top of Hawk's Peak about 25 miles north of Monterey, California, and raised the American flag. They did that after having been ordered to leave California by Col. José Castro, Mexico's military governor in Monterey. Frémont had entered northern California late in 1845 as head of an expedition (guided by Kit Carson, the renowned scout and fur trader) authorized by the U.S. government. Officially, Frémont was to just make a survey of western lands, but he understood that he should keep an eye on events in California. American settlers had been moving into the Mexican state of California since 1841 and were hoping that vast territory would become part of the United States. President Polk wanted that, too, and when his plan to purchase California from Mexico failed (see Preparations for War, pp. 180-181), he did not hesitate to take steps that would provide support for the Americans in California.

March 9, 1846: Advised by the American consul, Thomas Larkin, to avoid hostilities, and fearing that Castro was about to attack with cannons, Frémont and his men retired northward from Hawk's Peak. Eventually they crossed the border into Oregon Territory, and by May 6, they were encamped near Klamath Lake.

April 17, 1846: Marine lieutenant Archibald Gillespie arrived in Monterey, California, bearing a secret dispatch from President Polk to consul Thomas Larkin. The gist of Polk's message was that if war broke out between the United States and Mexico (as it did within nine days), the Americans in California should use every resource to take and hold that area for the United States. Meanwhile, Larkin should serve as a secret agent and advance America's interests in California. Gillespie then set off to contact Frémont.

May 9, 1846: Gillespie finally caught up with

Frémont near Klamath Lake (on the same day that the battle of Resaca de la Palma was being fought). Exactly what Gillespie told Frémont has never been proved as Gillespie did not carry written orders from Polk to Frémont. Frémont set off for California with his band of men, and by the end of May, arrived close to Sutter's Fort (near present-day Sacramento), the main outpost of the Americans in northern California. Although Frémont claimed that he was simply starting the first leg of his journey back to the East, it was clear from his actions that he was determined to play a role in overthrowing the Mexican rule in California. He began to gather more men and even sent to an American naval vessel off San Francisco for ammunition.

June 8, 1846: Having just learned of the hostilities that had taken place the previous month along the Rio Grande, American commodore John D. Sloat sailed from Mazatlán on the west-central coast of Mexico with the Pacific Squadron. Sloat had standing orders from Washington, D.C., to occupy the principal ports of California in the event the United States and Mexico went to war.

June 14, 1846 (The Bear Flag Revolt): A group of American citizens living primarily in the Sacramento valley carried out a successful revolt against Mexican rule in that area of California. Mexican general Mariano Vallejo was captured at his home in Sonoma, California, by Americans, who informed him that there was to be a new order in California. The rebels seized the arms and ammunition at Sonoma, replaced the Mexican flag with one featuring a crudely drawn grizzly bear and a single star (in reference to Texas), and declared itself the Bear Flag Republic. Vallejo was taken to Sutter's Fort and imprisoned. It has never been clearly established just what role Frémont played in that revolt, but it appears he did not start it. However, by June 25, Frémont had taken his band of some 100 men to Sonoma and had put himself at the head of the Bear Flag rebels.

June 24, 1846 (Battle of Olompali): American Californians met Mexican Californians in the only engagement of the Bear Flag Republic, fought at a ranch in present-day Marin County, California. An exchange of gunfire between the two sides left two Mexicans killed and two wounded; the Americans suffered no casualties. The Mexicans withdrew, leaving the Americans in possession of the field.

July 1, 1846: Frémont led a small force of men to the ungarrisoned Mexican fort at San Francisco and spiked the guns to ensure that they could not be used.

July 4, 1846: With the encouragement of Frémont, now back at Sonoma, Californians who had overthrown the Mexican government in the northern part of California declared the Bear Flag Republic an independent nation. The next day, Frémont organized the "California Battalion," with marine lieutenant Archibald Gillespie as his adjutant, with the intention of meeting any Mexican challenge.

July 7, 1846: Comdr. John Sloat sent a force of 250 sailors and marines ashore to take Monterey, California, where they raised the American flag. A proclamation from Sloat was read stating that "henceforth California will be a portion of the United States." Sloat's proclamation promised that all residents, including Mexicans, would be treated as citizens of the United States and their persons, property, and rights would be respected.

July 9, 1846: U.S. Navy lieutenant Joseph Warren Revere (grandson of Paul Revere) raised the U.S. flag at Sonoma, thus ending the short-lived Bear Flag Republic. (The Bear Flag, which bears the legend California Republic, is today the state flag of California.) The "Bear Flaggers" agreed to support the U.S. occupation and rule of northern California. U.S. Navy captain John Montgomery took 70 men ashore at San Francisco and claimed it for the United States. Col. José Castro, seeing that he was outmanned, led his force south to Los Angeles.

July 23, 1846: Comdr. John Sloat, in poor health, transferred command of the Pacific Squadron to Comdr. Robert F. Stockton, who was young, vigorous, and politically ambitious. Stockton immediately accepted the California Battalion as a volunteer force under the U.S. Army, with Frémont as major.

July 26, 1846: Stockton sent Captain Frémont with his battalion on a ship south to San Diego to cut off retreating Mexicans.

July 29, 1846: Frémont arrived at San Diego with Kit Carson still at his side. In northern California, Stockton issued a proclamation in which he repudiated Sloat's promise to treat Mexicans as citizens of the United States and placed California under martial law.

August 6–7, 1846: Having sailed down the

coast of California, Stockton occupied San Pedro about 18 miles north of Los Angeles.

August 10, 1846: Stockton led American troops by land out of San Pedro, heading for Los Angeles, the last remaining stronghold of Mexican defiance in California. Realizing that they were outmanned and outgunned, Castro and other Mexican leaders fled to Sonora, Mexico.

August 13, 1846: Stockton, with his force of sailors and marines, and Frémont, with his band of civilian volunteers, entered Los Angeles, a city at that time of around 1,500 inhabitants.

August 17, 1846: Stockton issued a proclamation that placed the entire province of California under U.S. martial law. Mexicans who did not accept American rule were warned to quit the region. Within a few weeks, Stockton established a school and a newspaper and conducted municipal elections. Stockton divided California into a northern and southern district; he placed Frémont in charge of the northern district and Archibald Gillespie in charge of the southern district. Stockton then ordered Kit Carson, who had accompanied Frémont throughout his adventures in California, to go by horseback to carry word to Washington, D.C., of what had occurred in California. Frémont marched back to the Sacramento valley with his band of men.

September 22–23, 1846: A group of Mexican-Californians, led by José Maria Flores, revolted against the despotic rule of Archibald Gillespie. In Los Angeles, they isolated Gillespie and 50 men into a defensive position, then placed San Diego under siege.

September 29, 1846: Gillespie and his men surrendered to the leaders of the Mexican revolt in Los Angeles. Under the terms of the surrender, Gillespie and his men were allowed to march to San Pedro, where they boarded the merchant ship *Vandalia*. Prior to his surrender, Gillespie had sent John Brown north to alert the American forces in San Francisco Bay.

September 24–October 1, 1846: Brown made a remarkable ride of some 500 miles from Los Angeles to San Francisco, bringing the news of the Mexican revolt in the south to the American commander in the north, Frémont. (Brown's ride was every bit as inspiring and far more hazardous and strenuous than the well-known ride of Paul Revere in 1775.)

October 7–8, 1846 (Battle of the Old Woman's Gun): American troops marching from San Pedro toward Los Angeles were met by Mexican troops and one artillery piece (which the Mexicans had named the "Old Woman's Gun"). The Americans withdrew after suffering 12 men killed or wounded; the Mexican casualty figures are unknown.

November 17, 1846: Capt. John Frémont led 300 American soldiers out of Monterey and began a march southward to quell the Mexican rebellion in southern California.

December 1, 1846: Stockton reoccupied San Pedro and relieved the Americans under siege in San Diego.

December 6, 1846 (Battle of San Pasqual): One hundred American dragoons, led by Gen. Stephen Kearny, encountered a much larger Mexican force at San Pasqual 30 miles northeast of San Diego. Kearny's men, who had been making an arduous march from Santa Fe, New Mexico, since September (see New Mexico Theater, p. 188), recklessly charged the Mexicans and narrowly escaped disaster. The short but intense fight cost the Americans 22 dead and 16 wounded (including Kearny). During the battle, Kit Carson and two others slipped through the enemy's lines and walked (and occasionally crawled) some 30 miles for reinforcements from the Americans in San Diego. The Mexicans withdrew from the battlefield, thereby avoiding being caught in a vise between Kearny and other American troops hurrying from the north.

December 11, 1846: One hundred eighty marines arrived to reinforce Kearny and his battered force, who had been lying low at a ranch outside San Diego.

December 12, 1846: Accompanied by the marines, Kearny and his force of dragoons entered San Diego.

December 29, 1846: An American force of 607 men (drawn from Kearny's command, volunteers, and marines from the squadron of Commodore Stockton) left San Diego intent upon recapturing Los Angeles and ending the Mexican revolt in southern California.

NEW MEXICO THEATER

May 13, 1846: Having just signed the declaration of war against Mexico, President Polk sent a message to Col. Stephen Kearny, commander of the American forces at Fort Leavenworth, Kansas, ordering him to protect American caravans from Mexican attack and to organize a column of troops to march on Santa Fe, New Mexico. By the end of June, Kearny was promoted to brigadier general, and his new force was named the Army of the West.

June 22–30, 1846: Led by General Kearny, the Army of the West set out from Fort Leavenworth in stages. Including regulars and volunteers, it numbered some 1,600 men. It brought with it 1,556 wagons, 459 horses, 3,658 mules, and 14,904 cattle and oxen.

July 29, 1846: Kearny's Army of the West reached Bent's Fort in the southeastern corner of Colorado after a 537-mile march from Fort Leavenworth in circumstances that were described as miserable by most of the participants. Footsore and thirsty, the Americans settled down for a short rest at Bent's Fort.

July 31, 1846: Kearny issued a proclamation designed to divide the already weak Mexican resistance within New Mexico. Promising protection of religious and civil rights, Kearny called upon the Mexicans to yield peacefully to American occupation.

August 2, 1846: The Army of the West broke camp at Bent's Fort and moved south toward Santa Fe.

August 8, 1846: The Mexican governor of New Mexico, Manuel Armijo, summoned the population of the state to defend its territory against the oncoming Americans. Armijo positioned several thousand men, along the Apache Canyon, through which Kearny's force would have to pass to get to Santa Fe.

August 16, 1846: The soldiers who had been recruited by Governor Armijo showed no great will to defend Apache Canyon. Many Mexicans were discontented with their government; many were also convinced that the American force would be far too powerful to resist. When his force disintegrated, Armijo and his escort of cavalrymen rode off; they arrived in Chihuahua, a major city in northern Mexico, three weeks later.

August 17, 1846: While Kearny was considering the best way to approach Apache Canyon, he was informed by a Mexican that Armijo's defending force had abandoned the canyon.

August 18, 1846: Kearny's Army of the West entered Santa Fe, having reached and occupied the capital of New Mexico without having to fire a shot on their long march from Fort Leavenworth. Kearny raised the American flag in the central square and announced that he had taken possession of all New Mexico for the United States.

August–September 1846: Kearny built Fort Marcy outside the town of Santa Fe. Most of New Mexico, with an estimated population of 80,000 inhabitants, came under the control of Kearny's Army of the West. Kearny drew up a constitution, set up a civil government, and named Charles Bent, a trader (and cofounder of Bent's Fort in Colorado), governor. During the weeks at Santa Fe, Kearny's Army was reinforced by hundreds of regulars and volunteers. He chose to divide his force into three parts. A unit under Col. Sterling Price was to remain in Santa Fe to control the newly captured territory. A second unit under Col. Alexander Doniphan was sent to seize Chihuahua, Mexico (see December 16, p. 189). Kearny led the third force across to California, as he had been ordered to do by Washington, D.C., to support the Americans there.

September 25, 1846: Kearny left Santa Fe with 300 men, most of them dragoons, some of them mounted on mules. He did not know of the events during July and August that had led to Capt. John Frémont's and Comdr. Robert Stockton's taking California (see California Theater, pp. 185-187).

October 2, 1846: Colonel Price arrived at Santa Fe with an advance guard known as the "Mormon Battalion." The battalion was made up of a group of 397 Mormons recruited at Council Bluffs, Iowa, to improve the trail for Kearny's force en route to California. The Mormons were willing to do that because they assumed that if the United States won the war, they would have the support of the U.S. government at a time when they were intending to immigrate to the west to avoid persecution. But Kearny had not been sure of the whereabouts of Price and the Mormon Battalion, so he had left without them.

October 6, 1846: Near Socorro, New Mexico, Kearny's force of dragoons met scout Kit Carson and 19 men who were riding eastward with the welcome news that the Americans had succeeded in capturing California. Learning this, Kearny sent 200 of his men back to Santa Fe and proceeded with only 100 dragoons. He also persuaded Carson to accompany him on the westward march, knowing that he would need the scout's skills in order to make the journey easier.

November 22, 1846: After a grueling journey, Kearny and his men reached the junction of the Gila and Colorado Rivers almost due east of San Diego. Kearny learned from some Californians of the uprising in southern California that had overthrown the Americans' control there. Kearny decided he had to proceed to San Diego.

December 1846: Many Mexicans and Indians in Santa Fe and elsewhere in New Mexico were resentful of the American rule, and increasing numbers began to conspire to rebel.

December 6, 1846: Kearny and his men fought the battle of San Pasqual (see California Theater, p. 187), then proceeded to San Diego, arriving there on December 12.

December 15, 1846: Col. Sterling Price learned of the planned uprising against American rule in New Mexico. He arrested some of the leaders, but others fled to Mexico. Price and Governor Bent believed that the rebellion had been put down.

December 16, 1846: Col. Alexander Doniphan set off from New Mexico with 850 mounted riflemen, mostly volunteers from Missouri; that rowdy group of men was known as "the Roarers." Doniphan was headed for El Paso del Norte (present-day El Paso, Texas, and Juarez, Mexico), but his ultimate destination was a rendezvous with Gen. John Wool in or around Chihuahua, Mexico. Wool was leading a force of some 1,400 men south from San Antonio; his ultimate goal was to join Gen. Zachary Taylor's army at Saltillo.

December 16–25, 1846: In southern New Mexico, Doniphan's troops crossed the dreaded *Jornada del Muerto* ("Journey of the Dead"), 90 miles of a trackless desert basin at an altitude of 7,000 feet; much of the time, they were without water and sufficient rations.

December 25, 1846 (Battle of the Brazito): Emerging from the mountains, Doniphan's men met 1,200 Mexican troops where the Brazito River entered the Rio Grande about 30 miles north of El Paso del Norte. The Mexican commander, Lieutenant Colonel Ponce de Leon, sent his cavalry to attack the Americans; the poorly motivated Mexican horsemen were quickly routed by the sharpshooters of Doniphan's force. The Mexicans broke and fled, leaving 100 men killed or wounded on the battlefield; the Americans suffered a handful of wounded and no men killed.

December 27, 1846: Doniphan entered and occupied El Paso del Norte, which straddled the Rio Grande. With a population of between 10,000 and 12,000, El Paso del Norte was full of Mexican traders who initially welcomed the American takeover, but the Roarers' undisciplined behavior soon made them unwelcome.

NAVAL THEATER

April 12, 1846: Gen. Zachary Taylor ordered the U.S. Navy to set up a blockade at the mouth of the Rio Grande to prevent Mexican forces from obtaining any supplies via that route.

May 13, 1846: Secretary of the Navy George Bancroft sent instructions to Comdr. David Conner of the Home Squadron, ordering him to blockade the eight major ports of eastern Mexico: Matamoros, Cármen, Tampico, Soto la Marina, Tuxpan, Alvarado, San Juan Bautista, and Veracruz.

June 8–15, 1846: Comdr. John L. Saunders of the frigate *St. Mary's* made a series of abortive attacks against Tampico.

Summer 1846: Scurvy spread among the crew of several of the ships of the Home Squadron. The problem was resolved by initiating trade for citrus fruits with the Mexican state of Yucátan, which was in rebellion against the federal government of Mexico. Conner convinced Washington that Yucátan deserved to be recognized as a neutral in the war.

June 15, 1846: The Mexican congress authorized the use of privateers against American shipping. Despite the best efforts of Mexican skippers, the privateer effort did not get very far, due to the supremacy of the American fleet.

August 7, 1846: Commodore Conner led American ships and sailors in an unsuccessful attack against the port city of Alvarado.

August 10, 1846: The U.S. Congress authorized an increase in the wartime strength of the U.S. fleet; a strength of 10,000 sailors was authorized (up from 7,500 in peacetime), but due to the higher wages paid by the merchant marine ships, the Navy never had more than 8,100 sailors in uniform during the war.

September 14, 1846: With the Pacific Squadron, the USS *Cyane* entered the Mexican port at La Paz, Baja California, and captured two brigantines, five schooners, and one sloop.

October 15, 1846: Commodore Conner made a second unsuccessful attempt to capture the port city of Alvarado.

October 23, 1846: Capt. Matthew C. Perry captured the Mexican port of Frontera at the mouth of the Tabasco River and seized two brigs, two schooners, and one sloop. He then led a force 72 miles upriver to attack San Juan Bautista, the capital of the state of Tabasco; after shelling the city and seizing some ships, Perry withdrew.

November 14, 1846: In the first major success for the U.S. Navy on Mexico's Gulf coast, Commodore Conner captured the port city of Tampico, taking three Mexican navy gunboats and two merchant schooners as prizes. Tampico remained in American hands until the end of the Mexican War.

November 26, 1846: American sailors from the brig *Somers* rowed silently into the harbor of Veracruz in a small boat. Finding the blockade-running Mexican schooner *Criolla* tied to the walls of the fortress of San Juan de Ulúa, the Americans set the ship afire and escaped from the harbor in an action that resembled that of Stephen Decatur and his men at Tripoli in 1804 (see Barbary Wars, February 16, 1804, p. 131).

December 2, 1846: Captain Perry led four ships to the town of Cármen, a port on the edge of the Yucátan Peninsula, and occupied it.

HOME FRONT

June 1846: News of Gen. Zachary Taylor's victories at Palo Alto and Resaca de la Palma spread throughout the United States, and he was instantly regarded by many as a national hero. He was brevetted major general and named commander of the Army of the Rio Grande. Congress voted him two gold medals, and the Whigs began to talk of him as a presidential candidate. Volunteers rushed to enlist in the army in greater numbers than could be accepted.

July 1846: Henry David Thoreau, a writer and poet living in Concord, Massachusetts, was jailed for one night for failing to pay his poll tax. Thoreau was against the war, and he argued that to pay the poll tax would mean he supported the war, which in his opinion was being fought to extend slavery (see Notable Phrases, p. 205-206).

July 27, 1846: Secretary of State James Buchanan sent a diplomatic note to Mexico City, proposing that peace negotiations be opened.

August 2, 1846: President Polk sent to the Senate a copy of the peace overture that Secretary of State Buchanan had sent to Mexico. Polk went on to request the Senate to fund an undisclosed amount of money to forward the peace negotiations. When Buchanan was questioned by the senators, he intimated that the amount needed was $2 million.

August 6, 1846: The Senate agreed to open negotiations with Mexico and to fund the appropriation indicated by Buchanan.

August 8, 1846: President Polk requested that the House of Representatives appropriate $2 million in case negotiations with Mexico required the purchase of territory. Congressman David Wilmot (D–Pa.) offered an amendment to the bill. Known as the "Wilmot Proviso," the amendment required that any new land purchases be expressly restricted to being a free territory or state, no slavery allowed. Accepting Wilmot's amendment, the House passed the measure by a vote of 83 to 64, with Northerners and Southerners sharply divided. The Senate later considered the measure but didn't pass it.

October 1, 1846: Official word of the victory at Monterrey reached Washington, D.C.; as the news spread throughout the United States, Gen. Zachary Taylor was once again hailed as a hero. But President Polk and Secretary of State Buchanan as well as some army officers were unhappy with Taylor because he had not attacked and wiped out Ampudia's forces; they were more angry that Taylor had agreed to an eight-week armistice. The cabinet agreed to send a letter to Taylor ordering him to end the armistice.

November 18, 1846: Gen. Winfield Scott, hero of the War of 1812 and commander of the U.S. Army, had been trying from the outset of the Mexican War to be named by President Polk to lead the U.S. forces in Mexico. Unhappy with Taylor's conduct of the war, President Polk finally appointed Scott to lead the campaign to take Mexico City.

INTERNATIONAL DEVELOPMENTS

July 6–7, 1846: U.S. Navy commander Alexander Slidell Mackenzie (brother of John Slidell), serving as a confidential agent for President Polk, met twice with exiled Mexican general Santa Anna in Havana, Cuba. Santa Anna, who had been exiled from Mexico in January 1845, told Mackenzie that if he were allowed to return to Mexico, he would recognize the Texas border at the Rio Grande and work for a lasting peace with the United States. In their second conversation, Mackenzie indicated to Santa Anna that when he sailed from Cuba for Mexico, he would be permitted to slip through the American naval blockade. Santa Anna then told Mackenzie that once he became leader of Mexico, he might have to fight a few battles against the Americans to regain his standing with the Mexican people.

August 6, 1846: Mexican president Mariano Paredes resigned amid a storm of controversies over the events of the war, including Mexico's early losses along the Rio Grande.

August 8, 1846: Exiled Mexican general Santa Anna boarded the British steamer *Arab* in Havana, Cuba, bound for his homeland.

August 16, 1846: Santa Anna stepped ashore at Veracruz, Mexico, having been allowed to slip through the American naval blockade. Once ashore, the 51-year-old general and politician denounced the by-then-defunct government of Paredes but declared that he would fight against the Americans to the last. Santa Anna then retired to El Encero, his 90,000 acre cattle ranch above Veracruz, to await developments. Shortly thereafter, most factions in Mexico went along with Santa Anna's call for raising an army of 30,000, and he accepted appointment as commander of that "army of liberation." He then set off for San Luis Potosí, a small mining town about 250 miles south of Monterrey, to direct operations against General Taylor's Army.

BATTLES AND CAMPAIGNS: 1847

There were five theaters of military operations during 1847: Northern Mexico theater, Central Mexico theater, California theater, New Mexico theater, and naval theater.

NORTHERN MEXICO THEATER

January 1847: Leaving some of his forces at Saltillo, Mexico, Gen. Zachary Taylor moved his command post back to Monterrey, Mexico. Meanwhile, Gen. Antonio Santa Anna set up his central command post at San Luis Potosí, Mexico. There, Santa Anna gathered a large number of recruits and conscripts to collect an army of at least 18,000 (some said as large as 25,000) troops. Those men were far from being combat veterans, and the depth of their loyalty to the Mexican Republic was questionable, but Santa Anna used all his powers of persuasion to mold them into a fighting force. Aware that the Americans planned to land at Veracruz in the spring, Santa Anna decided that a quick and successful strike against General Taylor's army in the north would prevent an American attack from the east.

January 28, 1847: The leading units of Santa Anna's army moved out from San Luis Potosí and headed north, seeking to cover the distance between themselves and the American army in the north in the shortest possible time.

February 3, 1847: Taylor began to move the main body of his forces to the Agua Nueva valley, 18 miles south of Saltillo, with the intention of confronting Santa Anna's army there. Shortly thereafter, Santa Anna learned that Mexicans to the north had captured (and killed) an American bearing a message from Washington, D.C., that instructed Taylor to assign certain of his units to support Gen. Winfield Scott's planned invasion at Veracruz. Santa Anna mistakenly concluded that Taylor's force in the Agua Nueva valley was a small unit of reinforcements.

February 8, 1847: Col. Alexander Doniphan set out from El Paso del Norte, Texas, with 924 soldiers, a heavy artillery unit, 300 civilian traders and teamsters, and 312 military and merchant wagons. Having learned that Gen. John Wool's force had been deterred from going to Chihuahua, Mexico, Doniphan put the matter to his men; they voted in favor of going forward without Wool's force to capture Chihuahua.

February 17, 1847: The advance units of Santa Anna's army reached Encarnación, which placed them within striking distance of Taylor's men encamped in the Agua Nueva valley. When all Santa Anna's troops arrived at Encarnación, they found that nearly one-quarter of the total (around 5,000 men) had either died or deserted during the march.

February 21, 1847: Having learned of the proximity of the Mexican army, General Taylor consented to the advice of his second in command, General Wool, and ordered a move back about 10 miles to a place called the Narrows, an ideal defensive position near a hacienda (estate) called San Juan de Buena Vista. The road at Buena Vista was lined by steep gullies and ravines; Wool stationed soldiers and most of the 15 U.S. cannons on the plateau above the road, onto which he emptied wagonloads of boulders.

February 21–22, 1847: After finding the

American camp in the Agua Nueva valley empty, with some campfires still burning, Santa Anna ordered an immediate, headlong pursuit of the enemy. The result was that his men, already strained from their march northward, marched 50 miles in two days' time and arrived in front of the American position at Buena Vista.

February 22–23, 1847 (Battle of Buena Vista): On February 22, Santa Anna's advance cavalry realized they could not make it through the narrow road. Santa Anna sent about 2,500 of his cavalry on a wide circling movement in an attempt to come at Taylor's force from Saltillo. At that point, Santa Anna sent a message to Taylor: "You are surrounded by 20,000 men and cannot avoid being cut to pieces. I wish to save you this disaster, and summon you to surrender at your discretion and give you an hour to make up your mind." In some accounts, Taylor is said to have replied "Tell him to go to hell."

Santa Anna sent some 15,000 Mexican soldiers to move against General Taylor's 5,000 American troops. Nonetheless, the odds could not be calculated strictly by numbers, since the Mexicans had recently made a 50-mile march and had not enough food rations for a decent breakfast. (Santa Anna promised his men they would have a feast with the American provisions after they won the battle.)

Early in the morning of February 23, the Mexican army lined up after reveille, then attended a Catholic mass before the battle. Santa Anna had failed to intimidate Taylor, so he put into effect his plan to assault the Americans. Correctly perceiving that the American left wing was the most exposed and endangered element of the American position, Santa Anna threw in two divisions of Mexican troops. Although the American artillery fire halted one division, the other swept in and nearly smashed the entire left wing. At that critical moment in the battle, General Taylor returned (he had spent the night at Saltillo organizing its defenses). Seeing the danger his army was in, he sent Jefferson Davis's Mississippi riflemen to stem the tide. At the same time, a combination of American cavalrymen and artillerists was able to halt the Mexican advance. An hour later, Santa Anna sent another division against the extreme American left. That attack was met by the Mississippi riflemen and other units, who stopped it with an ingenious and courageous three-pronged defense that turned to offense

when the Mexicans were halted by the rifle fire. Taylor then took to the offensive and ordered an attack, which swiftly ran into trouble. Only the presence of the American field guns prevented greater casualties for the attacking Americans. It was 5 o'clock in the afternoon before the Mexicans finally began to withdraw.

When the battle and the day came to an end, the Americans had suffered 673 men killed or wounded; 1,500 others were unaccounted for.

February 24, 1847: Taylor and Wool had spent the previous evening preparing their forces to continue the battle in the morning. But scouts reported that the campfires burning in the Mexican area were untended and that Santa Anna had withdrawn his entire army during the night. Taylor and Wool were reported to have openly embraced one another; both men knew what a close call it had been for the American forces, and neither had been sure they could have withstood a second day of attacks as ferocious as the first day's. The Mexican casualties were about 2,100 men killed, wounded, or missing; Santa Anna and his officers had made little effort at an orderly withdrawal, and many of the Mexican wounded were abandoned in the retreat across the desert to San Luis Potosí.

February 25, 1847: Colonel Doniphan's troops reached Laguna de Encinillas, a shallow, 20-mile-long lake north of Chihuahua. They had crossed 200 miles of scorched desert and arid prairie in their march from El Paso del Norte. A prairie fire, started by their carelessness, put the Americans in peril. They drove some of their wagons into the water and lit backfires in order to save themselves from the flames that raged from 10 to 20 feet in height.

February 28, 1847 (Battle of Sacramento): Knowing that Colonel Doniphan was marching against Chihuahua, the Mexicans had made thorough preparations to resist him. Mexican general Garcia Conde, commanding 1,500 infantry, 1,200 cavalry, and 119 artillerymen manning 10 cannons, arranged his forces on a plateau just north of the Sacramento River. Strongly fortified by natural defenses and the Mexican use of the terrain, the Mexican camp lay astride the only passable road between El Paso del Norte and Chihuahua. Given the Mexican advantages in numbers and position, Conde felt confident that he could repel any American attack.

After reconnoitering the Mexican position,

Doniphan undertook the daring approach of taking his wagons off the road and making his way up a sharp incline and coming at the Mexican left over an escarpment. Seeing that flanking movement, Conde sent the Mexican cavalry against the Americans, but it was fended off by American sharpshooters. Once Doniphan had completed his turn of the Mexican left, his infantry and artillery advanced, defeating each segment of the Mexican army in turn. A final charge by the Mexican cavalry failed. The Americans gained a complete victory, opening the road to Chihuahua. The Mexicans suffered 300 killed and 300 wounded; the Americans suffered 1 killed and 8 wounded.

March 1, 1847: Doniphan entered and took formal possession of Chihuahua. As the residents of El Paso del Norte had done in December 1846 (see New Mexico theater, December 27, 1846, p. 189), many Mexicans in Chihuahua welcomed the Americans at first, but Doniphan's Roarers' rowdy conduct soon cost them all support.

March 9, 1847: Santa Anna arrived back at San Luis Potosí. Within a few days, the remnants of his army arrived in that town. Of the 20,000 Mexicans who had been recruited and sent north in late January, approximately 10,500 had lost their lives to battle wounds, hunger, fatigue, and disease. The Battle of Buena Vista was a catastrophe of major proportion, but Santa Anna sought to conceal that fact from the Mexican people, even claiming victory by producing some flags and guns he had captured during the battle.

April 28, 1847: Colonel Doniphan's troops began their march from Chihuahua, which they had occupied since March 1, to Saltillo, in compliance with General Taylor's order.

May 21, 1847: Doniphan's column arrived at Saltillo, concluding its march through the American southwest and northern Mexico; Doniphan's Missouri volunteers had marched more than 2,000 miles through inhospitable terrain and had won two significant victories against larger enemy forces. It was probably the most extensive march undertaken by any American military unit to that point in history. But General Taylor was upset by the Roarers' disgraceful conduct and by their ragged condition, so he immediately dismissed them and sent them by ship to New Orleans; there, most of them boarded riverboats and went up the Mississippi River to Missouri. Ironically, that marked the end of Zachary

Taylor's active role in the war, as all the American efforts became concentrated on General Scott's campaign to take Mexico City.

CENTRAL MEXICO THEATER

February 18–21, 1847: On February 18, Gen. Winfield Scott arrived with his expeditionary fleet and forces at Tampico along Mexico's Gulf coast north of Veracruz. Three days later, he moved his command post another 60 miles south to Lobos Island; ships and troops moved to join him during the next few days. Scott's orders, as enunciated by President Polk, were simple and straightforward. He was to lead his Army by ship to capture Veracruz, then march inland to Mexico City to compel the Mexican government to come to terms and end the war. Scott was supremely confident in his abilities and in those of his men.

March 2, 1847: The American fleet, commanded by Comdr. David Conner, sailed from Lobos Island carrying 10,000 soldiers of the Army of General Scott.

March 9, 1847: Scott and Conner commanded an amphibious landing by an American force 3 miles south of Veracruz. Scott's soldiers were carried by specially designed surf boats to within 100 yards of the shore; they then left the boats and waded ashore in heavy surf. The Mexicans, who might have inflicted a heavy toll on the invaders, chose not to resist the landings. By nightfall, almost 10,000 American troops were ashore, without the loss of a single life. It was the most ambitious amphibious landing by American troops and the largest until World War II.

March 16, 1847: Having made a careful survey of the area around Veracruz and its massive fortress, San Juan de Ulúa, General Scott completed his preparations for a siege and attack. American troops and artillery were positioned in an arc that ran for 7 miles around the city and fort, cutting off the Mexican garrison from any retreat or possible reinforcement by land.

March 22–26, 1847: Having completed his preparations for an artillery bombardment, General Scott issued a call for the surrender of Veracruz. Upon receipt of the refusal, he gave the order for the artillery bombardment to begin. With the aid of extra guns brought ashore from American navy ships (now under command of Comdr. Matthew Perry), a massive shelling ensued that lasted five days; one estimate was that

An engraving shows the amphibious landing of U.S. forces, led by Gen. Winfield Scott, at Veracruz, Mexico, on March 9, 1847.

500 shells fell on Veracruz and the fortress every 24 hours. U.S. Navy ships offshore also contributed to the bombardment.

March 23, 1847: General Santa Anna was named president of Mexico, ending months of total chaos in the government. Part of his popularity was based on his false claim that he had secured a victory at the Battle of Buena Vista (see Northern Mexico Theater, February 22–23, 1847, p. 192).

March 26, 1847: The foreign consuls in Veracruz sent messages asking Scott to stop the deadly fire. He replied that he would do so only when the Mexicans surrendered.

March 27–28, 1847: Scott stopped the bombardment on March 27 to demand a surrender by 6 A.M. the next day. The Mexicans surrendered on March 28.

March 29, 1847: Scott's forces entered the city of Veracruz and the fortress of San Juan de Ulúa. The 4,000-man garrison was permitted to leave Veracruz with the honors of war. Although the public property of the city was at the mercy of the Americans, Scott made sure the surrender agreement declared that private property be respected. The total siege had cost the Americans

19 dead and 63 wounded; Mexican casualties were more than 1,000 dead or wounded, most of them civilians.

April 5, 1847: General Santa Anna established his headquarters at El Encero, his ranch, preparing to meet the invading Americans at the narrow mountain pass of Cerro Gordo about 50 miles inland. The Mexicans believed that if they could block the American advance at that point, Scott could retreat only to the coast, where the dreaded *vómito* ("yellow fever") season was about to begin.

April 8, 1847: Scott also knew that the season for yellow fever was approaching, so he sent the first units of his Army up the road from Veracruz toward Mexico City 260 miles to the west.

April 12, 1847: Brig. Gen. David Twiggs, leading an advance force of Americans, arrived at the Cerro Gordo pass and chose to enter it despite warnings by his scouts. The Mexicans opened fire before too many of Twiggs's men were far into the pass, and he was able to extricate them. Twiggs decided to wait until General Scott arrived.

April 17–18, 1847 (Battle of Cerro Gordo): Santa Anna had drawn up his 10,000-man army in a strong defensive position, placing the artillery in strategic positions to fire on Scott's troops once they entered the pass. On April 17, a small skirmish was fought as the Americans tried to find a way around the Mexican's left flank. A reconnaissance by officers, including Capt. Robert E. Lee, the future Confederate general, found the best way, but it required that heavy 24-pound howitzers be dragged and even lifted by the men to get them into position. As Scott's men performed that epic move during the night of April 17, Twiggs mounted a diversionary attack elsewhere. The next morning, at 7 o'clock, the Americans struck, catching the Mexicans by surprise when the American artillery began firing from their flank. The battle lasted three hours. Despite heavy resistance at the outset, the American forces proved too mobile and too persistent; the final blow came when Americans seized the Mexican artillery and turned the guns on the Mexicans. Santa Anna and his staff fled, and by 10 A.M. the entire Mexican force at Cerro Gordo was in flight.

By mid afternoon on April 18, the Americans could assess the magnitude of their victory, won at a cost of 63 men killed and 368 wounded; Mexican dead and wounded were estimated at 1,000, and the Americans captured 199 Mexican officers and 2,837 enlisted men. In addition, the Americans captured Santa Anna's El Encero ranch, where, among other things, they found $20,000 in coins. Given the strength of the natural defenses and the size of the Mexican army, Cerro Gordo was one of the most impressive American victories of the entire war.

April 19, 1847: General Scott led his force into Jalapa, the next big city on the road west. He held his troops there to await supplies of food, clothing, and ammunition. Meanwhile, he faced two problems: Increasing numbers of his men were becoming ill from various ailments, and many of the volunteers' enlistments would end in June. Scott knew he had to keep moving.

May 11, 1847: Santa Anna arrived at Puebla, a city of 80,000 people to the west of Jalapa, and tried to reorganize his forces. Many Mexicans were disillusioned with his plans, and the best he could do was round up a force of some 2,000.

May 14, 1847: General Santa Anna rode out with 2,000 mounted troops to attack the Americans advancing on Puebla. The Americans quickly overpowered the Mexicans, and Santa Anna fled with his troops.

May 15, 1847: The American Army entered Puebla. Many American soldiers who drank the water and ate the local food found themselves deathly ill.

May 19–June 2, 1847: Santa Anna returned to Mexico City. Since the news of his defeat at Cerro Gordo had made him vulnerable to political opposition, he resigned the presidency on May 28. He withdrew the resignation on June 2 when it became apparent that no one else could organize an effective opposition to the oncoming Americans.

June 6–7, 1847: General Scott sent seven regiments back to Veracruz, where they were demobilized and sent home. Those were the 12-month recruits, who could not be trusted to reenlist, given the terrible conditions in the field. Their departure left Scott deep in Mexican territory with only about 7,000 men fit for duty.

June 8, 1847: American major general Gideon Pillow arrived at Puebla with 2,000 men who had been recruited in the United States. Pillow and his force had gone to Veracruz, but learning of Scott's shortage of manpower, they quickly left Veracruz to join Scott.

July 15, 1847: By July 15, President Santa Anna had put together an army of about 25,000 men to defend Mexico City. Though the quality of many of the troops was questionable, the Mexicans enjoyed significant advantages of terrain, as the valley surrounding Mexico City was protected by marshes, lakes, and lava formations, which would make it difficult for an invading army to concentrate its force on Mexico City.

August 6, 1847: Brig. Gen. Franklin Pierce arrived at Puebla with a force of 2,500 men. Scott's force now numbered some 13,000 (although about 2,000 were on the sick list).

August 7–10, 1847: General Scott supervised a gradual departure of the American Army from Puebla. As he headed for Mexico City, which he believed would be defended by 30,000 Mexican soldiers, Scott counted his force at 10,738 men.

August 11, 1847: Brig. Gen. David Twiggs, leading the advance guard of the American Army, had occupied the town of Ayotla 15 miles east of Mexico City. When Scott arrived with the full force, and his scouts described the terrain surrounding Mexico City, he decided not to attack Mexico City from the east but from the south.

August 17, 1847: Gen. William Worth entered

the village of San Augustin, completing a flanking movement by the Americans that brought them to the southern flank of Mexico City. Worth conducted a probe northward to the village of San Antonio, Texas, where he found significant Mexican opposition; Santa Anna had hastily redeployed much of his army to that area and was poised to meet the enemy.

August 19, 1847: While General Worth conducted a feint against the defenses of San Antonio, General Twiggs and General Pillow led the main body of American troops across a lava formation called the *pedgregal*, heading toward Contreras, a village directly to the south of Mexico City. They soon found themselves facing 5,000 troops and 22 guns commanded by Gen. Gabriel Valencia. When Santa Anna moved in with another large force from the northeast, the Americans were in serious danger. Scott sent a message to the Americans urging them to hold on until he could come to their rescue. Valencia convinced himself that the Americans were defeated and began celebrating that night. A cold rainstorm settled on the battlefield, further discouraging the American forces, who expected to be greeted by overpowering Mexican forces in the morning. However, Scott accepted the advice of several of his officers and planned an early morning surprise attack.

August 20, 1847 (Battles of Contreras and Churubusco): Starting about 3 A.M., some of General Pillow's troops made their way through the darkness. At 6 A.M., they sprang an attack on General Valencia's camp at Contreras. Some Mexican artillery got off a few wild shots, but within minutes the battle turned into a complete rout. The Americans reported capturing 7 generals, 800 enlisted men, 22 pieces of artillery, many horses and mules, and large amounts of ammunition; the Mexican dead or wounded numbered some 700; American casualties were 60.

Having vanquished Valencia's troops at Cortreras, Pillow's men almost immediately set off marching north; they were joined by the forces under General Worth and General Scott. The reunited American Army then turned its attention to the Mexican defensive position at Churubusco, 3 miles south of Mexico City. At Churubusco, the Mexicans had turned a convent and its thick walls into a fortress, and Santa Anna had gathered thousands of troops there to stop the American advance on Mexico City.

Shortly after noon, flush with enthusiasm from their early morning victory at Contreras, the Americans attacked the Mexican positions with abandon. There was fierce resistance by the Mexicans, particularly from the Mexican artillery manned by the American deserters who had formed the San Patricio Battalion. Several times during the fighting, Mexican troops hoisted a white flag of surrender, which was torn down by the San Patricios, who knew they could expect no mercy from their former comrades in arms (see Legends and Trivia, pp. 203-204). The outcome was settled late in the afternoon with a series of American bayonet charges. Santa Anna withdrew with his battered forces, and American mounted forces began to chase the Mexicans up the road toward Mexico City. By late afternoon, the battle had ended. It was one of the most deadly battles in which Americans had engaged. The Americans suffered some 900 casualties; the Mexicans lost 2,500 men.

Mexico City was within General Scott's reach, but he decided that he would first seek to come to terms with the Mexicans.

August 21, 1847: Santa Anna sent an emissary to General Scott with a request for a truce to allow for burial of the dead. Santa Anna also agreed to deal with Nicholas Trist, President Polk's official negotiator (see Negotiations and Peace Treaty, p. 199).

August 23, 1847: An armistice was signed. There were to be no hostilities within a 78-mile range of Mexico City. The armistice would hold as long as peace negotiations proceeded but could be terminated by either side with 48 hours' notice. Santa Anna interpreted the Americans' agreement as a sign that they were weak and in no position to make any demands.

August 27–September 6, 1847: American negotiator Nicholas Trist met several times with Mexican negotiators, seeking to find a way to bring the war to an end. General Scott moved his forces up to Tacubaya, just south of Mexico City.

September 6, 1847: Claiming that the Mexicans had refused the American demands and that Santa Anna appeared not to be negotiating in good faith, General Scott terminated the armistice. Two formidable defenses still remained before Mexico City could be taken: Molino del Rey (the "king's mill," which was used as a foundry) and the fortress of Chapultepec ("hill of the grasshoppers").

An engraving depicts the final assault of the U.S. forces on Mexico City on September 13, 1847.

September 8, 1847: The Americans made an early morning attack against Molino del Rey. There had been insufficient information and planning for the attack, and the Americans ran into withering artillery and musket fire. The position was finally taken after hand-to-hand combat but at a terrible cost: 116 dead and 665 wounded Americans and 2,500 Mexicans either killed, wounded, or taken prisoner. One American officer present at Molino del Rey called the operation "a sad mistake."

September 12–13, 1847 (Battle for Chapultepec): General Scott decided that the best way to enter Mexico City was through the western gates, which meant that the Americans first had to take the fortress of Chapultepec. It housed Mexico's military academy, and its high walls were well defended by artillery. The Americans bombarded the fort all day on September 12. The cannonade began again at about 5:30 A.M. on September 13. At 8 A.M., the troops of Generals Twiggs and Pillow made a ferocious assault on the walls of the fortress. By 9:30 A.M., the Mexican general surrendered and the American flag was raised over the fort. (American casualties numbered about 450; the Mexicans suffered some 1,800 dead, wounded, or captured.) Several units of the American Army proceeded

to the city walls, and after fierce fighting, the Belan and San Cosme gates were in American hands. Santa Anna's last desperate efforts to rally his troops failed, and by nightfall, Mexico City was taken by the Americans. Among the last Mexicans to continue to fight the Americans was a group of young officer-cadets; when they realized all was lost, six committed suicide; they have ever since been honored by all Mexicans as *los niños heroes*, "the child heroes."

September 13–14, 1847: Over 4,000 Mexican troops, led by Gen. Joaquin Rea, attacked Puebla, held by the American garrison led by Col. Thomas Childs. The initial attack failed, and Rea's men settled in for a siege of the city.

September 14, 1847: A Mexican delegation rode out to meet General Scott to surrender Mexico City. Scott and his military entourage entered the city and raised the American flag in the *Zocalo* ("Grand Plaza"). A state of terror pervaded the city for several days as Mexicans fired on Americans from ambush and Americans looted and raped.

September 22, 1847: General Santa Anna, having escaped before the surrender of Mexico City, arrived in front of Puebla with several thousand troops and volunteers he had gathered along the way.

September 27–October 1, 1847: The Mexican troops led by Santa Anna and General Rea made a series of attacks against Puebla.

October 12, 1847: An U.S. relief column of some 4,000, led by Gen. Joseph Lane, reached Puebla, and the Mexicans raised the siege.

CALIFORNIA THEATER

January 8, 1847: American troops met a force of some 450 Mexicans at Bartolo Ford 12 miles from Los Angeles on the San Gabriel River. A minor skirmish led to two Americans killed and nine wounded. The Mexicans withdrew in the face of the superior American force.

January 10, 1847: American forces led by Gen. Stephen Kearny and Comdr. Richard Stockton reoccupied Los Angeles, which had fallen to a Mexican revolt (see California Theater, September 29, 1846, p. 187).

January 13, 1847: Capt. John Frémont received the surrender of the remaining Mexican rebels in California under the terms of the Treaty (or Capitulation) of Cahuenga. The agreement called for the Mexicans to return to their homes and assured the Mexicans that their lives and property would be protected. The treaty effectively ended the resistance and fighting by Mexicans in California. In the months that followed, Stockton and Kearny feuded over who was in command in California. Frémont sided with Stockton, and when Kearny won the command, he had Frémont court-martialed. (Polk later overruled Frémont's dismissal from the Army, but Frémont resigned anyway.)

NEW MEXICO THEATER

January 19, 1847: Gov. Charles Bent, assuming that there was no more threat of a rebellion, visited relatives and friends in Taos, New Mexico. There, a different group of plotters, mostly Pueblo Indians and some Mexican supporters, early in the morning attacked and killed Bent, along with six other Americans (including an Army captain). As part of the same uprising, 13 other Americans were killed at other locales in central New Mexico.

January 23, 1847: Col. Sterling Price led a force of about 425 regulars and volunteers determined to find the center of the uprising in New Mexico.

January 24, 1847: Price met 1,500 rebels, who had hastily joined together in the revolt, north of Santa Fe. The rebels fled when they were charged by the Americans.

January 29, 1847: Continuing to pursue the rebels, Colonel Price, through a series of flanking movements, drove a large group of them from a strong position they had taken along the Embudo road.

February 3–4, 1847: The forces under Colonel Price fought a hard battle and eventually gained control of Taos Pueblo, the focal point of the uprising. The adobe walls were too strong for the American artillery, so Price's men used ladders and axes to breach the walls. The Americans counted 7 killed and 45 wounded. An estimated 150 Indians and Mexicans were killed in the fighting; Price quickly tried and executed another 25, including Pablo Montoya, the Mexican co-leader of the uprising. During the following few days, a few skirmishes were fought, but the action at Taos Pueblo ended most resistance to American rule in New Mexico. From that point on, Price imposed an extremely harsh regime on New Mexico.

NAVAL THEATER

January 22, 1847: Comdr. William Branford Shubrick replaced Comdr. Robert F. Stockton as commander of the Pacific Squadron. Because hostilities continued in east-central Mexico, the Pacific Squadron continued to carry on operations against the Mexicans along the Pacific coast.

March 21, 1847: Comdr. Matthew C. Perry took command of the Home Squadron off Mexico's east coast. He thus was in charge of the Navy during the bombardment that led to the taking of Veracruz (see Central Mexico Theater, March 22–26, 1847 through March 29, 1847, pp. 193-194). Shortly afterward, Perry initiated a series of amphibious operations, using sailors and marines to capture several Mexican ports along the east coast.

March 30, 1847: American sailors and soldiers (140 men in all) from the USS *Portsmouth* landed at and briefly occupied San José del Cabo at the southern tip of the Baja Peninsula.

April 14, 1847: Ninety U.S. sailors and marines landed at La Paz, a major port on the east coast of Baja California, and occupied the town.

June 16, 1847: Commodore Perry again led

an ambitious operation up the Tabasco River and captured San Juan Bautista, Mexico's last remaining major port. However, the American troops abandoned San Juan Bautista on July 22.

September 30, 1847: A U.S. landing party took and occupied Muleje near the midpoint of the east coast of the Baja Peninsula.

October 17–20, 1847: U.S. captain Elie A. F. Lavallette led three American ships in the capture of Guayamas, Sonora, the major Mexican port on the Gulf of California. The Americans withdrew soon after.

November 11, 1847: Comdr. William Branford Shubrick landed 750 men at Mazatlán, a major port on Mexico's Pacific coast. The 1,200-man Mexican garrison evacuated the city in the face of the American approach.

November 17, 1847: The USS *Dale* landed 65 marines and sailors on Guayamas. They held the port until June 24, 1848.

HOME FRONT

February 11, 1847: A large antiwar rally was held at Faneuil Hall in Boston, Massachusetts. Sen. Charles Sumner (D–Mass.) was one of the principal speakers. The rally sought to indicate the strength of the antiwar movement, but troops who heckled the speakers were more numerous than the dissidents themselves.

February 15–19, 1847: The House of Representatives approved a bill that allowed the U.S. to purchase territory from Mexico. The bill included the Wilmot Proviso (see Home Front, August 8, 1846, p. 190). The Senate took up the bill on February 19 and passed the main part but rejected the Wilmot Proviso. The House then accepted the Senate version. The issue of slavery in new territories was thus avoided.

November 1847: The results of the voting for members of the 30th Congress became available. The Whigs gained control of the House of Representatives (115-108), but the Democrats gained an additional five seats in the Senate, increasing their majority to 36 to 22. In general, the Whigs opposed the war in Mexico, but it was too late to do much to stop it.

December 14, 1847: Sen. Daniel S. Dickinson (D–N.Y.) introduced a resolution in the Senate to support *popular sovereignty:* The question of whether to allow slavery would be left to each territorial legislature. Everyone was aware that the territory most immediately affected was the territory about to be acquired from Mexico. Nothing came of that resolution, but if adopted as a policy, it would have set aside the Missouri Compromise of 1820. As the doctrine of popular sovereignty became increasingly more hotly debated, it contributed to the causes of the Civil War.

December 22, 1847: Whig congressman Abraham Lincoln, from Illinois, introduced the "spot resolutions" (see Notable Phrases, p. 205). He challenged the Polk administration to prove the exact spot on U.S. soil where Americans had first been attacked by Mexicans in 1846.

NEGOTIATIONS AND PEACE TREATY

Almost from the very start of the Mexican War, American president James Polk sought to end the conflict through negotiation—although always on his own terms (see Home Front, July 27, 1846, p. 190). When the attempt to end the war by allowing Santa Anna to slip into Veracruz failed (see International Developments, July 6-August 16, 1846, pp. 190-191), Polk returned to military efforts. The first opportunity for serious negotiation came in August 1847, after Mexico accepted an armistice in the wake of the disastrous Battles of Contreras and Churubusco (see Central Mexico theater, August 20, 1847, p. 196).

August 27, 1847: Four Mexican commissioners met with U.S. commissioner Nicholas Trist at Atzcapuzalco. The initial Mexican demands were unrealistic, given the military situation.

September 1, 1847: Trist met with the Mexican commissioners at Casa Colorado, near Tacubaya. The Mexicans saw that meeting as a sign of weakness by the Americans because Casa Colorado lay within Mexican military lines.

September 6, 1847: The Mexican commissioners presented a list of demands, including demands that the United States pay for Texas, that the U.S.-Mexico border be returned to the Nueces River north of the Rio Grande, and that the United States reimburse Mexican citizens for all war damages. Trist broke off the negotiations, and General Scott canceled the truce.

October 6, 1847: President Polk, blaming Trist for the failure to negotiate proper terms, issued an order recalling him. The order was not sent until October 20, and Trist did not receive it until November 16.

November 11, 1847: The Mexican legislature elected Gen. Pedro Maria Anaya interim president of Mexico. One of Anaya's first acts was to appoint Manuel Peña y Peña foreign minister.

November 16, 1847: President Polk's letter recalling Nicholas Trist reached Mexico City. Trist at first decided to accede to the order and prepared to return to Washington, D.C., General Scott informed Trist that no escort could be provided for him for several weeks and urged him to continue negotiating a peace. Meanwhile, Scott's army of occupation was attempting to maintain order in the capital and throughout much of northern Mexico. It did so but at considerable cost, as increasing numbers of Americans were ill and dying of various diseases. There was also an increasing breakdown in morale and discipline. At one point, Scott placed both Gen. Gideon Pillow and Gen. William Worth under arrest because they wrote letters to the Secretary of War in Washington, D.C., that personally attacked Scott.

December 4, 1847: Trist decided to disobey his order from President Polk and remain in Mexico City. He was persuaded to do so by General Scott, certain Mexican leaders, and British diplomats in Mexico City, who convinced him that his presence was essential and that if the negotiations were delayed for even a short time it would be impossible to effect a treaty.

December 6, 1847: Trist sent a 65-page letter to Secretary of State James Buchanan. Trist not only explained his reasons for remaining in Mexico City but also criticized Buchanan and Polk for failing to understand the situation in Mexico. Trist effectively defied his government and set himself up as an independent negotiator of peace terms.

January 2–8, 1848: Trist met with the four new Mexican commissioners. The Mexicans made initial demands for foreign arbitration that would guarantee any boundary lines that might be drawn. Trist firmly rejected those demands, but he showed a willingness to negotiate the line between Upper California and Baja California. For a week, Trist guided the Mexican commissioners step by step toward terms that he found acceptable; several of those were actually contrary to the terms he had been delegated to accept.

January 8, 1848: Pedro Maria Anaya's one-month term as interim president of Mexico came to an end. Manuel Peña y Peña became president of Mexico.

January 15, 1848: President Polk received Trist's 65-page letter explaining his reasons for failing to comply with his recall. Though furious, Polk saw that he could not alter the situation without completely unbalancing whatever progress had been made in negotiations.

January 29, 1848: After negotiations again seemed to stall completely, Trist threatened to cease all efforts to negotiate as of February 1, unless some type of agreement was reached by that time.

January 31, 1848: The Mexican commissioners agreed to a treaty draft that was forwarded to Mexican president Peña y Peña.

February 2, 1848: Having received the approval of President Peña y Peña, the Mexican commissioners and Trist signed the Treaty of Guadalupe Hidalgo (so named for the town just north of Mexico City in which the treaty was negotiated and signed). Under the terms of the treaty, the United States acquired the vast Mexican states of California and New Mexico, and Texas was recognized as U.S. territory all the way to the Rio Grande. In return for that land, the U.S. paid Mexico $15 million. In addition, Trist committed the United States to assume the long-standing debts of Mexico to American citizens (which eventually came to more than $7 million) and to pay the costs of claims by Mexican citizens against Indians from the United States (which eventually came to some $31 million). Trist also conceded certain rights to Mexicans living in what was to become U.S. territory; the Senate did not ratify that article, so those terms were never fully honored. In agreeing to the southern boundaries of New Mexico and California, Trist neglected to gain land for a good railroad route across the Southwest to the Pacific, and he also failed to gain an outlet for the United States on the Gulf of California. (That was taken care of by the Gadsden Purchase of 1853.)

February 19, 1848: James L. Freamer, a correspondent for the New Orleans *Delta*, arrived in Washington, D.C., with a copy of the Treaty of Guadalupe Hidalgo. Polk was furious with Trist and Scott for having agreed to such terms, but he saw no other option but to accept the treaty.

February 21, 1848: In the House of Representatives, a resolution was introduced proposing the awarding of medals to American officers who had served in the Mexican War. John Quincy Adams voted no and seconds later slumped over in his seat. He was carried unconscious to a chamber in the Capitol.

February 23, 1848: On the day that Polk submitted a copy of the treaty to the Senate, John Quincy Adams died in the Capitol, never having regained consciousness. Adams was a member of the "Immortal 14," members of Congress who had voted against the war in 1846, and he was unalterably opposed to the expansion of slavery. However, Adams had supported the annexation of the Oregon Territory and in general had been an expansionist in his middle years; his opposition to the war with Mexico was based entirely on his opposition to slavery.

February 28, 1848: The Senate resumed debate on the treaty after a short adjournment in respect for Adams.

March 10, 1848: The U.S. Senate ratified the Treaty of Guadalupe Hidalgo, with minor changes, by a vote of 38-14, with 4 abstentions.

March 17, 1848: Under orders from Washington, Trist was placed under arrest and escorted out of Mexico (see Civilian and Military Biographies, p. 208).

April 11, 1848: Nathan Clifford, United States attorney general, arrived in Mexico City with copies of the ratification of the Treaty of Guadalupe Hidalgo.

May 19–25, 1848: The Mexican Chamber of Deputies (the lower house of the Mexican legislature) ratified the treaty by a vote of 51-35. On May 25, the Mexican senate ratified the treaty by a vote of 34-4.

May 30, 1848: Delegates of both countries exchanged ratifications of the treaty at Querétaro, a town serving as temporary capital of Mexico.

June 12, 1848: The American flag was replaced by the Mexican flag in Mexico City. Newly elected president Jose Joaquin Herrera entered the city.

RESULTS OF THE WAR (Casualties, Costs, Consequences)

Only a small proportion of those in the military actually served on the battlefield; many of the militia units never saw combat. The Americans suffered 1,192 men killed in action; 529 died from battle wounds, 11,155 died from disease, 4,102 were wounded in action, 9,754 were discharged from service during the war, and 9,207 deserted. The total of 12,876 dead represented more than 10 percent of the total of both the regular Army and militia personnel combined (116,119). Although relatively few Americans were killed by Mexicans, the casualty rate was one of the highest in American history, largely due to the diseases that took their toll on so many American soldiers.

It has proved next to impossible to calculate the number of Mexican casualties. The best estimates are that Mexico suffered about 30,000 men killed and wounded during combat, apart from losses to disease.

The United States spent approximately $74 million for army expenditures and $27 million for naval expenditures, for a total of $101 million. The $15 million paid to Mexico under the peace treaty acquired 529,017 square miles of land (a price of 48 cents per acre), but the treaty also obligated the United States to pay another $38 million to settle claims and debts.

Mexico's monetary losses have been impossible to establish; the distinguished historian Justin H. Smith, who exhaustively combed the archives and records of both sides, made no determination of the financial cost to Mexico. Even allowing for the low wages and prices in Mexico at that time, the war cost Mexico many millions of dollars in today's terms. What can be said with certainty is that the cost was one that Mexico could not afford, that only through repeated borrowing from the Catholic Church could Santa Anna assemble and even partially supply the armies that he raised.

Mexicans lost a vast territory with mineral and other riches they could not have conceived of at the time. The war left their government in a shambles and their economy in ruins. Beyond that, in terms of morale and national pride, the war was devastating to Mexico, which began the conflict with hopes for victory and ended it in complete disarray. The loss soured Mexico's relations with the United States for many decades.

The first and most obvious result for the United States was the acquisition of the vast territory that became the states of California, New Mexico, Arizona, Nevada, Utah, and parts of Colorado, Wyoming, and Kansas. The mineral and agricultural riches of that land alone proved to be of an incalculable value; scenic and touristic resources also proved priceless. Less tangible but equally important was the fact that the United States emerged from the war as the dominant power in the Western Hemisphere. In acquiring California, with its several Pacific ports, the United States became a nation with a link to Asia. All that the United States gained encouraged Americans in their expansionist mode by confirming for many that the United States was indeed fated to become a world power.

There were also negative consequences of the war for the United States. Quite aside from what might be called the moral issue of taking land from Mexico, the United States soon found it was unable to absorb the new territories without provoking dissension between the states that permitted the holding of slaves and those that did not. The result was that the United States, fresh from its triumphs in Mexico, came to conflict within itself over the issues of slavery and states' rights. The Mexican War had demanded the services of many young officers who became famous during the Civil War: Robert E. Lee, Ulysses S. Grant, Ambrose E. Burnside, Braxton Bragg, George Meade, George McClellan, and Jefferson Davis were only the most notable of a host of officers who honed their skills during the Mexican War. (The war also produced two presidents—Zachary Taylor and Franklin Pierce—three if Jefferson Davis is included.) Furthermore, important innovations in armaments, transportation, and military tactics evolved during the Mexican War that would further be advanced by the Civil War.

MILITARY INNOVATIONS, TACTICS, EQUIPMENT

Since so many volunteers and irregulars carried their favorite weapons, there was considerable variety in the firearms used in the Mexican War. But it was during that war that the flintlock muskets and rifles that American soldiers had used for many decades began to give way to percussion-lock weapons. Flintlocks were unreliable due to worn flints or damp powder; there was also a slight but unsettling delay between the pulling of the trigger and the explosion of the propellant charge. In the percussion-lock system, a hammer fell directly onto a paper or thin-copper cap that caused an instant explosion of the propellant charge. Not only was hangfire time reduced but misfires were less frequent, and the reloading process was speeded up. In 1841, the percussion-lock musket had been ordered as

the standard U.S. infantry weapon. However, the conventional Springfield Model 1835 flintlock musket was actually used by most soldiers, mainly because Gen. Winfield Scott distrusted the new percussion mechanism. Some soldiers also carried the Remington-Jenks bolt-action, breech-loading rifles. The U.S. cavalry, however, was more progressive, and by the start of the Mexican War had adopted the Hall carbine Model 1841 (known as the "Mississippi rifle" or the "Yager"), which was breech-loading as well as percussion-firing.

In the later months of the war, some men—mostly officers and cavalry—used the new Colt revolvers. Samuel Colt's six-shooter, one of the first practical revolvers invented, had been manufactured since 1836, but the U.S. Army was slow to be convinced of its efficacy. When certain improvements were made, the U.S. Army ordered 1,000 in 1846. The first soldiers to use them found them so reliable that the Army ordered thousands more, and the Colt revolver became one of the most popular American firearms.

In was with artillery that the Americans made significant innovations, ones that gave them a consistent and lasting advantage over their Mexican foes. In 1840, Secretary of War Joel Poinsett (who, incidentally, had been the first U.S. ambassador to the Republic of Mexico, 1825–1829) had sent a board of officers to Europe to study the artillery systems of the major European powers. As a result of that survey, a completely new system of U.S. ordnance was adopted in 1841. The American artillery system rested heavily upon the horse-drawn 6-pounder fieldpiece (with a weight of 880 pounds and a range of 1,500 yards) and the 12-pound howitzer. Due especially to the former cannon, the U.S. forces were able to deploy light, or flying, artillery throughout the major battles of the Mexican War. At such battles as Resaca de la Palma and Buena Vista, a lieutenant or captain of artillery sometimes contributed just as much as a colonel or general of infantry to winning the battle, since deployment and use of the artillery was crucial to the edge that the American forces held over their enemy. So successful was the artillery that in 1847 Congress authorized the formation of four more artillery regiments.

It was in their more mobile and flexible tactics that the Americans proved to be the most advanced. Gen. Winfield Scott was quoted as saying that without the training provided by West Point for American officers, four times as many men as he commanded in September 1847 (40,000 men) would not have been able to penetrate the valley surrounding Mexico City and capture the Mexican capitol. Young officers such as Robert E. Lee showed initiative and daring that went far beyond the ordinary call of duty. Whether they were inspired by their West Point training or by an American social system that prized individual performance, junior American officers often provided the difference between victory and defeat for the American armies.

By contrast, Mexico fought with relatively backward weaponry. The muskets used by its infantrymen were handed down from the War of Mexican Independence against Spain, and the gunpowder used was markedly inferior to that used by the Americans. The Mexicans did not have the flying artillery that the Americans had, and the disparity in the quality of gunpowder meant that in some crucial battles (Palo Alto, for example). Mexican cannonballs actually dropped to the ground and rolled to the American lines while American cannon fire wreaked havoc on the Mexicans. In general, too, the Mexican officers fought with the more traditional tactics of fixed lines of battle.

LEGENDS AND TRIVIA

The unusual story of **Jane McManus Storms** (1800–1878) provides one of the most colorful, if least known, episodes of the Mexican War. Jane McManus Storms was born in upstate New York. She moved to Texas in the 1830s and became an outspoken advocate of manifest destiny. (Her personal life was rather flamboyant: She was involved in Aaron Burr's divorce and had a duel fought over her honor in Texas.) Even prior to the Mexican War, she urged such policy makers as Secretary of the Navy George Bancroft to work for the total annexation of Mexico. Once the war was under way, she attached herself to Moses Beach, editor of the *New York Sun*, in his effort to negotiate a peace settlement with Mexico. Traveling to Mexico City with Beach and his wife, Storms sent behind-the-lines dispatches to New York City. Storms was the only female reporter of the war and perhaps the only reporter behind the lines. She claimed to have met with Gen. Winfield Scott and proposed a different line of march to

Mexico City, but that has never been proven. She later became an outspoken advocate of annexation of Cuba, Nicaragua and Santo Domingo, and to the end of her life, she remained a controversial proponent of manifest destiny.

Among the more curious and controversial historical footnotes attached to the war concerns **the San Patricio Battalion**. From the earliest days of the U.S. encampment along the Rio Grande, there were desertions from the Army; both regulars and volunteers deserted. (The desertion rate during the war was eight percent, the highest of any in America's foreign wars.) Some of the deserters, for any number of motives, went over to the side of the Mexicans. Among the first to desert and join the enemy was John Riley, an Irish immigrant who had enlisted in Michigan; he went over to the Mexicans at Matamoros in April 1846. He was something of a natural leader, and the Mexicans made him a lieutenant. Soon he was in charge of a company of mostly American deserters. Within a few months, there were two companies of deserters, and they assumed the name San Patricio Battalion; Riley later took credit for naming it after St. Patrick, and it was true that a sizeable proportion (perhaps 40 percent) of the eventual 200 or so members were Irishmen. The battalion marched under a green flag; at some point, that flag had an Irish harp on it and the slogan "Erin go bragh!" ("Ireland Forever!") But although Irish Catholics may have been the largest single group in the San Patricio Battalion, there were many British, French, Germans, and others, and not all had been in the American Army. The battalion fought at several of the major battles—Resaca de la Palma, Buena Vista, Cerro Gordo—but their greatest moment came at Churubusco (see Central Mexico Theater, August 20, 1847, p. 196). Of the 72 members of the battalion captured after the fall of Churubusco, 70 were found guilty of desertion and treason by courts-martial. General Scott reviewed the sentences, however, and approved the execution of only 50; he pardoned 5 and sentenced 15 to 50 lashes and the brand of D (for deserter) on their cheek. Riley was among those pardoned because Scott ruled that he had deserted before the U.S. formally declared war. The San Patricios who had escaped from Churubusco and those who emerged from prison in June 1848 were taken as a unit into the Mexican army, but it was dissolved within two months. Riley stayed on in Mexico for another two years, then vanished from history. (Stories that he returned to the United States have proved unfounded.)

In addition to the myth that the battalion was entirely Irish Catholic, a related myth claimed that many of the San Patricio deserted because they saw the mostly Protestant U.S. soldiers mistreat Mexican Catholics and their church. In fact, at their courts-martial, none argued that in their defense. Some San Patricio said they disliked the discipline and hardships of Army life; some said they joined the Mexicans for the money, promotion, and land the Mexicans offered; some claimed they had been captured and forced to serve (and that they had never actually fired at Americans); some admitted they had been attracted to Mexican women; only a few said they had deserted because they disapproved of making war against Mexico. It should be said that many of those men were newly arrived immigrants in the United States and so did not have deep roots in or loyalty to the United States. In any case, the Mexicans appreciated the San Patricio and in 1959 dedicated a plaque with the names of 71 San Patricio members in the square of San Angel, a suburb of Mexico City.

When the Americans captured Santa Anna's El Encero ranch, among the items claimed to have been found was **Santa Anna's wooden leg**. Eventually, some volunteers from Illinois brought back a wooden leg to Springfield, claiming that it was Santa Anna's. The question of whether that leg was actually Santa Anna's never has been answered; but it is known that Santa Anna remained active after his ranch was captured and that he still had a wooden leg.

NOTABLE PHRASES

manifest destiny

John L. O'Sullivan was an influential American editor and an active proponent of American expansion in the middle decades of the 19th century. (He personally schemed to have the United States annex Cuba.) By 1845, the country was hotly debating the issue of the Oregon Territory when, in the July-August issue of the *United States Magazine and Democratic Review*, he attacked anyone who advocated "limiting our greatness and checking the fulfillment of our manifest destiny to overspread the continent allotted by

Providence for the free development of our yearly multiplying millions." That is regarded as the first appearance in print of the phrase manifest destiny. In fact, the editorial was not signed, but scholars have analyzed it and are sure O'Sullivan wrote it, especially as he was writing other pieces that used that phrase. It is also accepted that it was his later use of the phrase in an editorial in the more popular *New York Morning News* (December 27, 1845) that put the phrase into wider circulation. (The phrase was first used in Congress on January 3, 1846.) In any case, since the establishment of the United States, some Americans claimed that there was a kind of fate or even divine force that gave Americans the right, indeed the obligation, to take control of the North American continent from the Atlantic to the Pacific. (O'Sullivan even suggested that Canada should someday join the United States.) Often, there was a strong tinge of racism to that notion of manifest destiny, with its proponents suggesting that peoples such as the Indians and Mexicans were inferior beings who would profit from being "civilized" by Americans. Eventually the phrase took on an even broader suggestion, that the United States had some higher duty to spread its influence throughout the world.

Fifty-four forty, or fight!

In the early 1840s, the United States shared with the British the occupation of the vast, poorly defined Oregon Territory. In 1844, Sen. William Allen, an ardent expansionist Democrat from Ohio, is said to have made an impassioned speech on the Senate floor, calling for the United States to take and hold all the Oregon Territory up to 54° 40' north latitude, a line that ran from just below Alaska across British Columbia. Allen's speech electrified Democratic audiences around the country, and "Fifty-four forty, or fight!" became the slogan of the Democratic party in that campaign. In 1846, President Polk, who had to some extent been elected on the fervor created by Allen's speech, compromised and agreed to a treaty with Britain that drew the line at 49° north latitude. That left the United States with a territory that was eventually divided into the states of Oregon, Washington, and Idaho.

Mexico... has shed blood upon the American soil.

Those words of James K. Polk, included in the war message he sent to Congress on May 11, 1846, provoked controversy from the beginning of the Mexican War. No one in Congress had any way of knowing the exact details of the encounters that lay behind Polk's claim. The fact is that Mexico had always claimed the right to the land between the Rio Grande and the Nueces River, and when Polk ordered American armed forces into that disputed territory, he was clearly being provocative.

In any event, President Polk's assertion that "after repeated menaces, Mexico has passed the boundary of the United States, has invaded our territory, and has shed blood upon the American soil" was accepted by Congress, which passed the request for a declaration of war on May 12, 1846. But that by no means ended the national debate over America's right to challenge Mexico. The most famous challenge to the Mexican War came on December 22, 1847, when Polk submitted a request for more funds to pay for the war: A young, unknown, newly elected Whig congressman from Illinois, Abraham Lincoln, presented what came to be known as the "spot resolutions." Those were eight very specific queries to President Polk "to establish whether the particular spot of soil on which the blood of our citizens was so shed, was, or was not, our own soil at that time."

Take those guns and by God keep them!

Gen. Zachary Taylor is alleged to have shouted that command on May 9, 1846, at the battle of Resaca de la Palma. Knowing that artillery was the key to victory n the battle, Taylor watched as Capt. Charles May and his men captured a battery of Mexican cannons but were then forced to pull back as Mexican infantry surrounded them. General Taylor is said to have then turned to Col. William Belknap of the 8th Infantry and barked out his famous order, which was repeated in newspaper columns by the American press.

Scott is lost. He has been carried away by successes. He can't take the city, and he can't fall back on his base.

Learning that Gen. Winfield Scott had commenced his march from Puebla to Mexico City, the Duke of Wellington, Britain's great military hero of the war against Napoleon, made that comment on the American general. Although sympathetic to the American cause, Wellington thought it impossible that Scott should succeed, given the terrain and the numbers arrayed against him. However, when he learned that Scott and his small American Army had prevailed and had taken Mexico City, Wellington urged British junior officers to study the campaign and Scott's tactics in particular. Wellington then said of Scott: "His campaign was unsurpassed in military annals. He is the greatest living soldier."

I believe if we were to plant our batteries in Hell, the damned Yankees would take them from us.

Santa Anna was alleged to have said those words as he saw the American flag replace the Mexican flag over the walls of Chapultepec on the morning of September 13, 1847. Close to his side, another Mexican officer said simply, "God is a Yankee."

civil disobedience

Henry David Thoreau was a young, little-known author when in 1846 he was living in a cabin on Walden Pond near Concord, Massachusetts. In the summer of 1846, he received his poll tax bill. Although the money would not directly support the war, he decided to make a symbolic protest by refusing to pay the tax. Sometime in late July (probably July 23), he was taken to the local jail, but after only one night, he was released when a friend or relative paid the tax. It was 1848 before Thoreau gave two speeches in Concord that set forth his thoughts about his not paying the poll tax. Although opposed to the war against Mexico and to expansionism in general, he based much of his protest on his opposition to slavery, which he rightfully foresaw was the issue that would emerge from the war. In May 1849, *Aesthetic Papers*, a new magazine, published a version of the speech in an essay titled "Resistance to Civil Government." The essay never appeared in print again during Thoreau's lifetime, but in the years since, it has been reprinted countless times and in many languages. Beginning with a publication in 1866, the essay became known as "Civil Disobedience," although Thoreau never used that particular phrase. The essay is recognized as one of the most influential texts in history; the Indian nationalist leader Mahatma Gandhi was influenced by it, as was American civil rights leader Martin Luther King, Jr.

SONGS

Americans turned rapidly toward popular music in the second quarter of the 19th century; annual sales of pianos for home use rose from 2,500 in 1829 to more than 9,000 in 1851.

The fall of the Alamo inspired numerous songs, among them "Remember the Alamo" and "The Death of Crockett."

The Mexican War provided composers and singers with even more material. Capt. Samuel Ringgold's death at the Battle of Palo Alto was lamented in no less than six compositions. General Scott's troops sang "We Are Bound for the Shores of Mexico" prior to their debarkation at Veracruz. The famous English song "The Girl I Left Behind Me" was sung by many soldiers; it was also parodied as "The Leg I Left Behind Me," in reference to Mexican general Santa Anna and the battle of Cerro Gordo (see Legends and Trivia, p. 204).

There were numerous marching songs that were inspired by the Mexican War. Most notable among these were "The Soldier's Return," "General Taylor's Encampment Quickstep," "The Rio Grande Quick March," and "Matamoros Grand March." There was also "Buena Vista Quickstep," composed and published by William Cumming Peters, Stephen Foster's teacher and early publisher of his songs.

Toward the end of the war, songbooks came out in pocket size for the mass market. The songbooks made the war live vividly in the imagination of the American people. One such songbook, *The Rough and Ready Songster: Embellished with twenty-five splendid engravings, illustrative of the American victories in Mexico* (1848), contained only poems, "songs without music." Many of them openly expressed the manifest destiny chauvinism that lay behind the war with Mexico in such lines as: "The Mexicans are doomed to fall / God has in wrath forsook 'em," or "For Freedom's great millennium / Is working earth's salvation, / Her sassy kingdom soon will come / Annexin' all creation."

HISTORICAL PERSPECTIVES AND CONTROVERSIES

Several key questions have been discussed and debated by historians regarding the Mexican War. The most important have been:

Was it truly Mr. Polk's War, as some have claimed? Did the American president deliberately provoke war against a weaker neighbor, or did the Mexican government contribute to the tensions that led to war?

Disregarding the fact that the most distinguished American historian of the day, William Hickling Prescott, author of *History of the Conquest of Mexico* (1843), thought the war was immoral and unprovoked, most 19th-century American historians cited the Mexican political leadership as unrealistic and eager for war. To Americans puffed up with pride over their victories, it seemed only natural to attribute the war to Mexican intransigence, arrogance, and belligerence. (There was undeniably a strong streak of racism in some justifications for the war: Anglo-Saxon Americans assumed they were superior to the Mexicans.) President Polk's role in sending General Taylor to occupy the land between the Nueces River and the Rio Grande was dismissed by those historians as being peripheral to the decisions that had already been made in Mexico City. Some historians stressed the fact that Mexico had refused to pay the long-standing financial claims awarded to U.S. citizens by an arbitration panel. Even as late as 1947, Princeton historian Alfred Hoyt Bill (in *Rehearsal for Conflict*) argued that Americans were misled when they blamed the United States for fighting Mexico. He dismissed the Mexicans as a "backward and illiterate people"; extolled the "moderation, the patience and the restraint of the government at Washington"; and cast James Polk as virtually a martyr-hero for his great vision, "the expansion of his country to the Pacific Ocean."

Needless to say, Mexican historians never accepted North Americans' view of the war. Some of those Mexican voices can be heard in *The View from Chapultepec: Mexican Writers on the Mexican-American War* (translated and edited by Cecil Robinson). In North America, a revisionist view emerged during the 1960s, not coincidentally when the United States was involved in another controversial war: Vietnam. Historians during the 1960s emphasized such things as Polk's duplicity in claiming that blood had been shed on "American soil," when, in fact, the area between the Rio Grande and the Nueces River had long been claimed by Mexico. A generation of American scholars who witnessed the abuses of presidential power during the Vietnam War and Watergate were quick to point to the White House as the focal point for the start of the Mexican War (see Vietnam War, pp. 608-664).

Most histories of the Mexican War that have appeared since the 1970s, however, have attempted to present a more balanced approach to the origins of the war. Generally speaking, all scholars acknowledge the importance of the personality of James K. Polk, his determination to expand the boundaries of the nation, and his belief in manifest destiny. At the same time, those scholars point to the political chaos that existed throughout much of Mexico during 1845–1846 and the belligerent attitude of the Mexican government as factors that contributed to bringing on the war. In *North America Divided*, historians Seymour V. Connor and Odie B. Faulk go to some length to establish that internal Mexican politics had much to do with the events that developed in Texas and California. But few historians deny that President Polk bore the ultimate responsibility for declaring and directing the war against Mexico.

Given the fact that when the Mexican War began, European observers expected Mexico to win because of its large professional army, why was the United States able to win so many battles in such a convincing fashion while incurring relatively few casualties?

That question greatly disturbed the Mexican people during and after the Mexican War. Early predictions pointed toward a Mexican victory. The Spanish ambassador to the United States asserted, "There are no better troops in the world, nor better drilled and armed, than the Mexicans," and the more objective London *Times* declared that the Mexican soldiers "are superior to those of the United States." Remembering American performance on land during the War of 1812, an important British weekly, *Britannia*, asserted, "America, as an aggressive power is one of the weakest in the world...fit for nothing but to fight

Indians." All those early predictions turned out to be completely wrong; time and again, often outnumbered American soldiers defeated their Mexican counterparts.

Some early historians, such as Charles J. Peterson, boldly asserted that Americans were racially superior to the Mexicans, who, they postulated, were merely "degenerate Spaniards who inherited few of the virtues and most of the vices of their Iberian ancestors." As repellent as such an assertion is in the late 20th century, the notion was broadly accepted among Anglo-Americans in the 19th century. Justin H. Smith, another early historian, emphasized the superior quality of the American soldiers, who, he believed, were more highly motivated. Over the last 50 years, most historians have endorsed variations on that latter explanation. The West Point training of American officers and generally better training of the troops, the superior quality of American artillery, better equipment and supplies, and the higher morale of American soldiers are the factors that most historians today advance to explain the American victories.

CIVILIAN AND MILITARY BIOGRAPHIES

AMERICAN

Conner, David (1792–1856)—naval officer: David Conner was born in Pennsylvania. He entered the Navy in his youth. As commander of the Home Squadron during the Mexican War, he masterminded and led the brilliant amphibious landing near Veracruz that brought 10,000 American soldiers ashore in one day. (His plans for that action were later studied by American war planners during World War II.) He gave up his command just before the bombardment and capture of Veracruz.

Doniphan, Alexander William (1808–1887)—soldier: Alexander Doniphan was born in Kentucky. He made a name for himself as a brilliant lawyer. He led the Missouri volunteers on a remarkable march through New Mexico and northern Mexico that culminated in the taking of Chihuahua on March 1, 1847. He and his men were feted for their accomplishments, and the unit was called "Doniphan's Thousand" by the poet William Cullen Bryant, an obvious comparison to the march of 10,000 Greeks under

Xenophon during the Greek-Persian wars of antiquity. Doniphan returned to his law practice and took no part in the Civil War.

Frémont, John Charles (1813–1890)—soldier, explorer: John Chrales Frémont was born in Georgia. He became known as the "Pathfinder" during the 1840s for his series of government-sponsored explorations of the West. On his own initiative, he placed himself at the head of the Bear Flag Revolt, organizing his own force, known as the "California Battalion," and leading it in several actions against the Mexican Californians. Due to a conflict with Gen. Stephen Kearny, he was court-martialed in 1847 and discharged from the Army. Although President Polk overruled that sentence, Frémont resigned in 1848. He later served as a senator from California (1850–1851), and in 1856, became the Republican Party's first presidential candidate. Frémont would also serve in the Union army during the Civil War.

Kearny, Stephen Watts (1794–1848)—soldier: Stephen Kearny was born in New Jersey. He served in the War of 1812 and on the western frontier. Promoted to brigadier general, he was ordered by President Polk to capture New Mexico, which he did in 1846. Proceeding to California, he helped to subdue the Mexican revolt there in late 1846 and early 1847. He later served as military governor of Veracruz and Mexico City.

Polk, James Knox (1795–1849)—president: James Polk was born in North Carolina. He became prominent in the politics of Tennessee. A protégé of Andrew Jackson (thus sometimes called "Young Hickory"), Polk won the presidential election of 1844 as a dark horse candidate. A forceful and determined chief executive, he wanted to secure Texas, California, and the entire Oregon Territory for the United States. With the exception of his compromise with the British on the 49th parallel, he achieved his goals. He died three months after leaving office. Although sharply criticized by his contemporaries—many called the Mexican War "Mr. Polk's War"—modern historians tend to regard Polk as one of the most successful one-term presidents.

Taylor, Zachary (1784-1850)—soldier, 12th president of the United States: Zachary Taylor was born in Virginia. He entered the Army in 1806, saw service in the War of 1812, and rose slowly in the ranks. He was known as "Old Rough and Ready" to his men, whom he led to victory at Palo Alto, Resaca de la Palma, Monterrey, and

Buena Vista. Far from a brilliant general, he nevertheless inspired his men through his imperturbable countenance. He was lionized by the newspapers during the war, and in 1848, he sought and won the presidency. As president, he surprised his fellow Southerners by favoring the entrance of California to the Union as a free state. He died two years into his term in 1850.

Trist, Nicholas (1800–1874)—diplomat: Nicholas Trist was born in Virginia. He went to West Point and married the granddaughter of Thomas Jefferson. Trist entered the State Department in 1828 and became chief clerk in 1845. Sent to Mexico to negotiate a peace treaty, he was recalled by President Polk, who was angered by Trist's generous approach to Mexico. Disregarding the recall, he remained in Mexico and negotiated the Treaty of Guadalupe Hidalgo (1848). He returned to the United States under arrest for disobeying Polk's orders; he was never tried. He soon returned to Virginia to practice law. Due to President Polk's anger over his insubordination, Trist did not receive full pay and compensation for his expenses until 1871.

MEXICAN

Ampudia, Pedro de (1805–1865)—soldier: Pedro de Ampudia was born in Havana, Cuba. He rose slowly in the ranks of the Mexican army. He was known for his cruelty (in 1844 he ordered 14 captured rebels shot and their heads boiled in oil). He briefly held command of the Mexican army at Matamoros in 1846. He led the defense of the city of Monterrey and later participated in the battle of Buena Vista.

Arista, Mariano (1802–1855)—soldier: Mariano Arista was born in San Luis Potosí. He was one of the most respected generals in the Mexican army. Exiled briefly by Santa Anna prior to the Mexican War, he lived for a time in Cincinnati, Ohio. He took command of the Mexican army at Matamoros in 1846 and led his men at the battles of Palo Alto and Resaca de la Palma, both of which he lost to American general Zachary Taylor. Arista was court-martialed after those losses and dismissed from the army in June 1846.

Armijo, Manuel (?–1854)—administrator: Manuel Armijo was born to a poor family in New Mexico. He was self-educated. He rose to serve briefly as governor of Santa Fe in the late 1820s. He was reappointed governor and military commandant of New Mexico in 1837, removed in 1844, but returned to power in November 1845. When American troops under Gen. Stephen Kearny claimed New Mexico and threatened to take Santa Fe, Armijo mustered his militia and planned to stop the Americans at a mountain pass north of Santa Fe. His plans frustrated by a lack of commitment by his men, he retreated to Chihuahua (see New Mexico Theater, July 31-August 18, 1846, p. 188). He later returned to what had become the American territory of New Mexico.

Paredes y Arrillaga, Mariano (1797–1849)— politician: A leading member of the Mexican Centralist faction, Paredes led the overthrow of the Jose Joaquin Herrera government on December 29, 1845 (coincidentally the same day that Texas was accepted into the Union). An ardent nationalist, he ordered Generals Arista and Ampudia to commence hostilities against American general Zachary Taylor's men north of the Rio Grande and proclaimed a defensive war against the United States on April 23, 1846.

Santa Anna, Antonio Lopez de (1794-1876)— soldier, politician: Santa Anna was the son of a respected mortgage broker in Veracruz. He entered the army of New Spain but transferred his allegiance during the Mexican Revolution and became an ardent Mexican nationalist. He first became president of Mexico in 1833. He fought against the Texans (1836) and the French (1839) and was in exile in Cuba when the Mexican War began. Negotiating secretly with American president James K. Polk, he returned to Mexico and led the armies of Mexico. Following the disastrous losses of 1847, he went to the island of Jamaica but returned to Mexico and served another term as its president. He was the most controversial figure on either side during the war.

FURTHER READING

Bauer, K. Jack. *The Mexican War 1846–1848*. Lincoln, Nebr.: University of Nebraska Press, 1974.

——*Surfboats and Horse Marines: U.S. Naval Operations in the Mexican War, 1846–1848*. Annapolis, Md.: U.S. Naval Institute, 1969.

Bill, Alfred Hoyt. *Rehearsal for Conflict: The War with Mexico*. New York: Alfred A. Knopf Inc., 1947.

Brack, Gene. *Mexico Views Manifest Destiny, 1824–1846: An Essay on the Origins of the Mexican War*. Albuquerque, N. Mex.: University of New Mexico Press, 1975.

Chidsey, Donald Barr. *The War with Mexico*. New York: Crown Pub. Inc., 1968.

Connor, Seymour V. and Odie B. Faulk. *North America Divided: The Mexican War 1846–1848*. New York: Oxford University Press, 1971.

Crook, Philip St. George. *The Conquest of New Mexico and California*. Albuquerque, N. Mex.: Horn and Wallace, 1964.

Crutchfield, James A. *Tragedy at Taos: The Revolt of 1847*. Plano, Tex.: Republic of Texas Press, 1995.

de Castillo, Richard Griswold. *The Treaty of Guadalupe Hidalgo: A Legacy of Conflict*. Norman, Okla.: University of Oklahoma Press, 1990.

Eisenhower, John D. *So Far from God: The U.S. War with Mexico 1846–1848*. New York: Random House Inc., 1989.

Johannsen, Robert W. *To the Halls of the Montezumas: The Mexican War in the American Imagination*. New York: Oxford University Press, 1985.

Merk, Frederick. *Manifest Destiny and Mission in American History: A Reinterpretation*. New York: Alfred A. Knopf, 1963.

Miller, Robert R. *Shamrock and Sword: The St. Patrick's Battalion in the U.S.-Mexican War*. Norman, Okla.: University of Oklahoma Press, 1989.

(Continued p. 210)

Robinson, Cecil, trans. and ed. *The View from Chapultepec: Mexican Writers on the Mexican-American War*. Tucson, Ariz.: University of Arizona Press, 1989.

Ruiz, Ramon Eduardo, ed. *The Mexican War: Was It Manifest Destiny?* New York: Holt, Rinehart & Winston, 1963.

Schroeder, John H. *Mr. Polk's War: American Opposition and Dissent, 1846–1848*. Madison, Wis.: University of Wisconsin Press, 1973.

Singletary, Otis A. *The Mexican War*. Chicago: University of Chicago Press, 1960.

Weems, John Edward. *To Conquer a Peace*. Garden City, N.Y.: Doubleday, 1974.

THE CIVIL WAR

DATES OF WAR

April 12, 1861–June 2, 1865

ALTERNATE NAMES

The War of the Rebellion (the Union's name). The War between the States (the Confederacy's name).

SIGNIFICANCE

The Civil War resolved the question of American nationhood—specifically, of the American Union. The notion that one or more states could voluntarily exit the Union could not be sustained. The war's outcome guaranteed the survival of a grand experiment in nation building—"the last, best hope of earth," in Abraham Lincoln's words. Even though the states had their own rights and duties, they were nevertheless components of a greater and indissoluble whole.

The war also settled the vexed question of slavery. Lincoln stated that he believed a nation "half slave and half free" could not endure. It has become clear that secession and the firing upon Fort Sumter heralded the destruction of slavery in America. After four years of unprecedentedly costly warfare, a new nation arose. With the emancipation of slaves, encoded in 1865 in the 13th Amendment to the Constitution, the United States rededicated itself to the ideal of freedom and equality for all. The victory of the Union established the *federal* government as the guarantor of individual freedom.

The Civil War was the first of the world's modern wars, foreshadowing the terrible global conflicts of the 20th century. Mass armies met in titanic clashes that claimed appalling numbers of young lives. New, more powerful weapons and auxiliaries were introduced, improved upon, or converted to military use—ironclad warships and submarines, rapid-fire rifles and machine guns, the telegraph, the railroad, and hot-air balloons. Both sides marshaled their entire resources to wage war. In Gen. Ulysses S. Grant and Gen. William T. Sherman, the North found commanders who redefined the practice of war: In seeking to attack and destroy not just the Confederacy's military forces but its economy, social structure, and political will as well, Grant and Sherman introduced what later generations would know as total war.

BACKGROUND

May–September 1787: The framers of the Constitution crafted a torturous compromise on the issue of slavery during the summer of 1787. Fugitive slaves were to be returned to their owners; the slave trade would be allowed to survive for another generation, until 1808; and for the purpose of apportioning congressional seats on the basis of population, a slave—who had no political rights—would be counted as three-fifths of a white person. That compromise appeased several Southern states and led to the establishment of the federal Union; it also contained the mechanism for the Union's eventual rupture.

July 1787: In its final meeting under the Articles of Confederation, Congress passed the Northwest Ordinance to govern settlement of the vast territory that was eventually subdivided into the states of Ohio, Indiana, Michigan, Illinois, and Wisconsin. One clause stated that "there shall be neither slavery nor indentured servitude" in the territory. To many, that suggested a national free soil policy under which new territory would be off-limits to slavery.

January 1, 1808: The importation of slaves into the United States became unlawful. The buying and selling of slaves within the United States continued, however.

January–March 1820: The prospective admission of Maine as the 23rd state threatened to upset the delicate sectional balance of 11 free states and 11 slave states. To maintain the balance, the Senate approved a bill coupling Maine's admission as a free state with that of Missouri's as a slave state. The Senate also adopted a second compromise, an amendment barring slavery in the vast territory of the Louisiana Purchase north of latitude 36 degrees, 30 minutes. The House accepted the Senate bill; the Missouri Compromise, as it became known, muted the dispute over slavery for a quarter of a century.

November 1832–March 1833: A South Carolina state convention adopted an ordinance nullifying the tariff acts of 1828 and 1832—that is, asserting the state's right to set aside any federal law that it deemed violated the voluntary compact between the state and the Union. In opposing the tariffs, South Carolina senator John C. Calhoun articulated a theory of secession that was revived and tested in 1860–1861. President Andrew Jackson responded to the nullification crisis with a threat of force; when Congress approved a compromise tariff early in 1833, the crisis abated.

December 1833: In New York City, abolitionists Arthur and Lewis Tappan and others founded the American Anti-Slavery Society. The American Anti-Slavery Society demanded immediate, uncompensated freedom for slaves. The Tappans; William Lloyd Garrison, publisher of the *Liberator*; Theodore D. Weld; George G. Finney, and others campaigned tirelessly for abolition during the 1830s, 1840s, and 1850s, enlisting many prominent Northerners in the cause.

May 1846–February 1848: War with Mexico, touched off over American settlers' efforts to attach the Mexican territory of Texas to the United States, revived the slavery issue (see Mexican War, pp. 178–210). In a 16-month campaign, U.S. forces won ten major battles; on September 14, 1847, the U.S. Army raised the Stars and Stripes over Mexico City. In the Treaty of Guadalupe Hidalgo, which the United States signed in February 1848, Mexico ceded 500,000 square miles of territory from New Mexico west to California and north into parts of what became the states of Nevada and Utah (and parts of present-day Wyoming and Colorado). Southerners put up strong opposition to Northern attempts, most notably via the "Wilmot Proviso" (named for its sponsor, Pennsylvania representative David Wilmot, who first introduced it in 1846), to bar slavery in the new territories.

January–September 1850: As the controversy over the extension of slavery into the new territories heated up, Southern radicals again threatened to secede. In the Senate, Henry Clay, the Kentucky Whig, sought a compromise on slavery based on a series of proposals from Sen. Stephen A. Douglas of Illinois, a Democrat. The Compromise of 1850, as it became known, brought California into the Union as a free state. Settlers in Utah and New Mexico were granted the option to decide for or against slavery when their territories were ready for statehood. The compromise, actually a package of five bills, also abolished the slave trade in the District of Columbia but, as a sop to the South, included a strict fugitive slave law, under which federal magistrates and policemen were obligated to capture runaway slaves and return them to their owners. Some 330 runaway slaves eventually were so returned, some in highly publicized cases that fueled antislavery opinion in the North. Many Northerners found the law an affront and an outrage against morality, and, for the first time, widespread support for abolition began to build. "We went to bed one night old-fashioned, conservative, Compromise Union Whigs," wrote one Yankee, "and waked up stark mad abolitionists."

June 1851: The first serial installment of Harriet Beecher Stowe's novel *Uncle Tom's Cabin*, which dramatized the evils of slavery, appeared in the antislavery journal *National Era*. Published in book form in March 1852, *Uncle Tom's Cabin* sold 350,000 copies in the first year alone, and by the outbreak of the Civil War, more than a million copies were in circulation. ("So this is the little lady who made this big war," Abraham Lincoln said of Stowe when she called at the White House in November 1862.)

February 1854: In Ripon, Wisconsin, an antislavery meeting called to protest the Kansas-Nebraska Bill, which threatened the 1820 Missouri Compromise limiting the spread of slavery, recommended the formation of a new political party to express free-soil views. Throughout the following months, the Republican Party came gradually into being in a number of Northern states.

May 1854: Congress passed the Kansas-Nebraska Act, which Sen. Stephen A. Douglas conceived as part of a political bargain that would route the coveted transcontinental railroad through the Northern Great Plains. To win support from Southern congressmen, who favored a southern route, Douglas proposed to create separate territories of Kansas and Nebraska, with the implication that one would be slave territory and the other free, even though both lay north of the free-soil boundary the Missouri Compromise had established.

The measure also endorsed the notion of *popular sovereignty*, which meant that territorial voters had the authority to decide for or against slavery. In effect, the act repealed the hard-won Missouri Compromise. Douglas's initiative drew a fellow Illinois politician, Abraham Lincoln, out of a self-imposed five-year political retirement. In a speech at the Illinois State Fair on October 4, 1854, Lincoln delivered a passionate argument against the extension of slavery:

"Slavery is founded in the selfishness of man's nature, opposition to it in his love of justice. These principles are in eternal antagonism, and when brought into collision so fiercely as slavery extension brings them, shocks and throes and convulsions must ceaselessly follow. Repeal the Missouri Compromise, repeal all compromises; repeal the Declaration of Independence; repeal all past history—you still cannot repeal human nature. It will still be the abundance of man's heart that slavery extension is wrong, and out of the abundance of his heart his mouth will continue to speak."

March–November 1855: Thousands of proslavery Missourians—the Border Ruffians, they styled themselves—crossed into Kansas in March to vote a proslavery territorial legislature into office—a fraudulent election and the first exercise of Douglas's popular sovereignty. In July the legislature moved to expel antislavery members. In the autumn, free-soil Kansans converged on Topeka to adopt a constitution outlawing slavery. At the same time, the Topeka convention adopted a law barring all blacks from the territory. With rival legislatures claiming authority, Kansas found itself in a state of civil war, with both sides carrying on intermittent guerrilla campaigns of ambush, crop burning, and livestock rustling.

May 1856: The debate over slavery turned violent. Three days after Massachusetts senator Charles Sumner delivered a passionate antislavery speech, South Carolina representative Preston Brooks attacked Sumner savagely with a stick as he sat at his desk in the Senate. Sumner needed a full three years to recover his health.

In Kansas, a proslavery gang attacked the antislavery settlement of Lawrence, burning several buildings and killing one man. In retaliation, an abolitionist band led by John Brown murdered five proslavery Kansans on Pottawatomie Creek. Later in the year, an energetic new governor, John Geary, with the assistance of U.S. regular troops, restored order to what had become known throughout the North as "bleeding Kansas."

March 1857: In an infamous ruling known as the Dred Scott Decision, the Supreme Court declared that a slave was not a citizen of the United States and thus had no right to sue in a federal court. Dred Scott had sued for his freedom on the grounds that he had moved with his master onto the free soil of Illinois and Wisconsin. Denying Scott's claim, Chief Justice Roger Brooke Taney declared the Missouri Compromise a dead letter, on the grounds that Congress had no right to interfere with private property—a slave, in this case. The decision outraged Northern moderate as well as abolitionist opinion. "A judicial lie," one Republican newspaper termed it.

December 1857: A territorial legislature meeting in the town of Lecompton approved a proslavery constitution for Kansas. Early in 1858, Kansas voters rejected the Lecompton constitution; even so, President James Buchanan asked Congress to grant Kansas statehood under the Lecompton document. After intense debate, Congress passed a bill allowing for another popular vote in the territory. Kansans finally and decisively voted to ratify an antislavery constitution in October 1859.

June 1858: Illinois Republicans nominated Abraham Lincoln of Springfield to challenge Democrat Stephen A. Douglas for Douglas's seat in the U.S. Senate. Lincoln decided early on to make the election a test of anti-slavery conviction.

"A house divided against itself cannot stand," Lincoln said in his acceptance speech at the Republican convention. "I believe this government cannot endure permanently half slave and half free.... It will become all one thing, or all the other. Either the opponents of slavery will arrest the further spread of it, and place it where the public mind shall rest in the belief that it is in the course of ultimate extinction, or its advocates will push it forward till it shall have become alike lawful in all the states, old as well as new, North as well as South."

August–October 1858: In a series of seven debates, Lincoln and Douglas argued the slavery issue. Douglas did not actually defend slavery; he argued for the right of people to vote for or against it. Douglas accused Lincoln and the Republican Party of abolitionism. Lincoln argued strongly against slavery on moral as well as political grounds. He stressed, though, that his party would not interfere with slavery alone where it existed. The Lincoln-Douglas debates attracted enormous crowds throughout Illinois—10,000 people for the first one in Ottawa; 15,000 at Freeport; 12,000 at Charleston. Lincoln won the popular vote by a narrow margin, but state legislatures elected U.S. senators then, and there Douglas prevailed. The campaign, however, made Lincoln a rising figure among Republicans.

October–December 1859: Radical abolitionist John Brown, a veteran of the violent struggles in Kansas, vowed to carry the war against slavery into the enemy's country. On the damp, moonless night of October 16, Brown and his little army of 20 or so advanced on the U.S. arsenal at Harpers Ferry in present-day West Virginia. Brown aimed to seize rifles and ammunition stored there, arm Virginia's slaves, and touch off an uprising that would establish a slave-free territory.

A long-time abolitionist, deeply religious, Brown became more obsessed—and more radical—as he grew older. "Without the shedding of blood there is no remission of sin," he said, quoting the Old Testament Book of Hebrews, and he prepared to shed some blood. An advance party cut telegraph wires leading into Harpers Ferry. A patrol took a few hostages. Brown himself approached the main gate of the arsenal and told the lone night watchman posted there: "I came here from Kansas, and this is a slave state; I want to free all the Negroes in this state; I have possession now of the United States armory, and if the citizens interfere with me I must only burn the town and have blood."

Brown's band and the townspeople exchanged fire. Eventually, the locals gradually drove Brown and his men back into the armory firehouse. A detachment of U.S. troops under Lt. Col. Robert E. Lee arrived the night of October 17 and stormed the firehouse the next morning, capturing Brown and eight other survivors.

Virginia moved rapidly to try Brown for conspiracy and treason. He was found guilty in Charles Town in present-day West Virginia, and he was sentenced to hang. On December 2, 1859, on his way to the scaffold, Brown handed his escort a note. "I, John Brown am now quite certain that the crimes of this guilty land will never be purged away but with blood."

Brown's execution elevated him to martyrdom in the North, where church bells tolled and memorial sermons were preached. Southerners were aghast at the elevation of a man they considered a thief, killer, and traitor. "The Harpers Ferry invasion has advanced the cause of disunion more than any [other] event," a Richmond newspaper asserted. "Thousands of men who a month ago scoffed at the idea of a dissolution of the Union now hold the opinion that its days are numbered."

April–June 1860: The Democratic Party met to choose a presidential nominee on April 23 in Charleston, South Carolina. (The incumbent Democratic president, James Buchanan, did not seek re-election.) When the party refused to adopt a series of proslavery platform planks, Robert Barnwell Rhett, William Lowndes Yancey, and other Southern radicals—dubbed "fire-eaters"—persuaded a group of Southern delegates to bolt the convention. About 50 followed the fire-eaters out, leaving the convention short of a quorum.

The same issues arose when the party reassembled in Baltimore, Maryland, in June, and the same impasse resulted. Southerners again walked out; this time the convention went ahead and nominated Stephen A. Douglas. Southern Democrats, meeting separately, nominated Buchanan's vice president, Kentuckian John C. Breckinridge, to run on a proslavery platform.

May 1860: The Republicans, meeting in Chicago, nominated a dark horse presidential candidate, Abraham Lincoln, on the third ballot.

November 1860: In a four-way election, Lincoln won the presidency with 40 percent of the vote, defeating Democrat Douglas, proslaver Breckinridge, and John Bell of Tennessee, who ran under the banner of a party of former Whigs, the Constitutional Unionists.

The contest was purely sectional, Lincoln versus Douglas in the North, Breckinridge versus Bell in the South. Lincoln carried all the Northern states except New Jersey, whose electoral votes he and Douglas split. Breckinridge won 11 slave states. Bell captured the border states of Virginia, Kentucky, and Tennessee. Douglas received the second-highest vote total, but he carried only a single state, Missouri.

Southern radicals refused to accept the result. In secessionist South Carolina, the editor of the *Charleston Mercury* stigmatized the president-elect of the United States as a "free-soil Border Ruffian, a vulgar mobocrat, and a Southern hater."

CAUSES OF THE WAR

The immediate causes of the Civil War were the secession of seven Southern states and the determination of the national government to prevent the dissolution of the Union. Although many then and later contended that the principle of states' rights was the reason for the war, the deepest underlying cause was slavery and the intense sectional rivalry it engendered—"the irrepressible conflict," in the phrase of Republican politician William Seward.

The first Africans to reach America came ashore at Jamestown, Virginia, in 1619, and a system of slavery soon flourished in the Southern colonies. After the American Revolution, the Northern states gradually abolished slavery, though Northerners continued to profit from the slave trade and, later, from the goods that slave labor produced, particularly the cotton to feed New England's textile mills.

The census of 1860 counted some 4 million slaves. Slave populations and slave ownership were uneven throughout the South. Most Southerners owned no slaves at all; only one-quarter of Southern families, about 385,000 households, claimed human property. In South Carolina and Mississippi, half the families owned slaves; in Virginia, about a third; in Maryland and Missouri, only an eighth. And 90 percent of all slaveholders had fewer than 20 slaves.

The conditions of slavery varied. In many areas, the breakup of slave families was common. Corporal punishment could be savage. Many slaveholders, however, were careful of their slaves' welfare, if for no other reason than that which led them to take care of livestock or farm equipment or any other major capital investment. Still, slaves too often were overworked and undernourished. Fewer than five of every hundred slaves lived beyond the age of 60.

Slaves worked year-round, six days a week producing the South's cash crops: cotton and rice in the Carolinas, Georgia, and Florida; cotton in Tennessee, Alabama, Mississippi, and Arkansas; cotton and sugar in Louisiana.

The existence of slavery assured the parallel development of two increasingly distinct societies in the United States, Northern and Southern. By the 1850s, a dynamic new industrial system had reshaped the North and the Midwest. Northern farmers invested in the tools Yankee industry perfected—John Deere plows and McCormick reapers. Southern farmers, when they could afford them, invested in slaves and continued to depend on the traditional cash crops of cotton, rice, and sugar.

Increasingly, the South had become an economic dependency. "We purchase all our necessities from the North," an Alabama newspaper editor remarked. "Our slaves are clothed with Northern manufactured goods, have Northern hats and shoes, work with Northern hoes, plows, and other implements." So the two cultures drifted in opposite directions, the traditional ties—a common language and a broadly democratic political heritage (for white males)—becoming more frayed year by year, as the conflict over slavery persisted.

By 1860, many Southerners were willing to break from the Union—and risk war—in defense of what was euphemistically called the "peculiar institution." "On the subject of slavery," the *Charleston Mercury* asserted, "the North and the South are not only two peoples, but they are rival, hostile peoples." South Carolina, with the legacy of John Calhoun's theories of nullification and secession, led the way.

December 1860–January 1861: In Charleston, South Carolina, a state convention met to consider secession. Preceded by fireworks, parades, and bands, the convention on December 20 voted 169-0 in favor of an ordinance dissolving "the union now existing between South Carolina and the other states."

In Washington, D.C., Congress convened to attempt a compromise. Sen. John Crittenden, a Kentucky Democrat, offered a series of proposals, including a constitutional amendment restoring the Missouri Compromise boundary between free soil and slave territory.

During the night of December 26, Maj. Robert Anderson, commander of the two Federal forts in Charleston harbor, moved his entire small force from Fort Moultrie into the larger and more powerful Fort Sumter. President Buchanan, rejecting South Carolina's demand that all U.S. troops leave Charleston, announced that Fort Sumter would be defended. Buchanan then authorized a relief expedition to prepare to sail for Charleston. On January 2, 1861, Buchanan's cabinet ordered the reinforcement of the fort.

In Springfield, president-elect Lincoln tried to stay aloof from the crisis, except for one explicit comment: "Let there be no compromise on the question of extending slavery."

January–February 1861: Six states—Mississippi, Florida, Alabama, Georgia, Louisiana, and Texas—followed South Carolina out of the Union. During the first half of February, representatives of the seven states, meeting in Montgomery, Alabama, formed a provisional government and adopted a states' rights constitution closely modeled on the U.S. Constitution. On February 16, they inaugurated Jefferson Davis, a former Mississippi U.S. senator and war secretary, president of the Confederate States of America.

"The South is determined to maintain her position," Davis said, "and make all who oppose her smell Southern powder and feel Southern steel."

PREPARATIONS FOR WAR

January 1861: At Norfolk, Virginia, the USS *Brooklyn* made ready to sail for Charleston. On January 2, South Carolina forces seized the inactive Fort Johnson in Charleston harbor. On the same day, the U.S. Army commander, the aged Gen. Winfield Scott, named Col. Charles Stone to take charge of the defense of Washington, D.C. Over the following days, Georgia troops occupied Fort Pulaski at the mouth of the Savannah River, Alabama troops seized the forts guarding Mobile Bay, and Florida troops took over the Federal arsenal at Apalachicola and Fort Marion at St. Augustine.

January 5–9, 1861: After General Scott vetoed sending the *Brooklyn*, as too provocative a gesture, 250 U.S. regular troops embarked on the merchant steamer *Star of the West* and set sail from New York for Fort Sumter. On January 9, South Carolina troops opened fire on the vessel as it approached Charleston harbor; the master of *Star of the West* turned his ship around and headed back to New York.

January 1861: Singly or in groups, Southern congressmen withdrew from Washington, D.C., and headed home. Jefferson Davis's state voted to leave the Union on January 9. "I concur in the action of the people of Mississippi, believing it to be necessary and proper," Davis said in his farewell remarks on the Senate floor.

February 4, 1861: A Peace Convention, with 131 delegates from 21 states, gathered in Washington, D.C., to seek a way out of the impasse. Former president John Tyler presided over that effort to reach a compromise and avert disunion and war. No representatives of the seceded states attended, however.

In Montgomery, Alabama, the Provisional Congress of the Confederate States of America met for the first time.

February 20, 1861: The Confederate government established a Department of the Navy; the Provisional Confederate Congress authorized President Davis to contract for the purchase and manufacture of war matériel.

March 4, 1861: Abraham Lincoln was inaugurated the 16th president of the United States. In his inaugural address, he emphasized that he did not intend to interfere with slavery where it existed. He asserted that secession was unlawful, and he promised to use Federal authority to "hold, occupy and possess the property and places belonging to the government," and to collect taxes and customs duties. "In your hands, my dissatisfied countrymen, and not in mine, is the momentous issue of civil war," Lincoln said. "The government will not assail you. You can have no conflict without yourselves being the aggressors."

The president concluded the speech with an appeal to a common past and a peaceful restoration of the Union:

"I am loath to close. We are not enemies, but friends...Though passion may have strained, it must not break our bonds of affection. The mystic chords of memory, stretching from every battlefield and patriot grave to every living heart and hearthstone all over this broad land, will yet swell the chorus of the Union when again touched, as surely they will be, by the better angels of our nature."

March 1861: Dispatches from Maj. Robert Anderson, the garrison commander at Fort Sumter, suggested the 80-man garrison there would be forced to surrender if it were not resupplied. General Scott advised withdrawal, but Lincoln resisted.

March 6, 1861: The Confederate government authorized an army of 100,000 to serve for 12 months.

March 29, 1861: Lincoln announced that the government would send a force to resupply Fort Sumter.

March 31, 1861: Lincoln ordered troops to Florida to relieve the besieged garrison at Fort Pickens. Fort Bliss in Texas surrendered to pro-Confederacy Texas troops.

April 3–4, 1861: On April 3, Confederate batteries opened fire on the U.S. schooner *Rhoda H. Shannon* in Charleston harbor. The next day, Lincoln wrote Major Anderson that the relief expedition would go forward; he also gave him permission to use his own judgment on how to respond to a Confederate attack on the fort.

April 8–11, 1861: On April 8 and 9, three U.S. vessels left New York bound for Fort Sumter. On April 10, Confederate war secretary Leroy Walker ordered Gen. Pierre G. T. Beauregard, commanding Confederate forces at Charleston, to demand the surrender of Fort Sumter or to attack it.

On April 11, three Confederate messengers were rowed out to Fort Sumter to convey the surrender demand to Major Anderson. "If you do not batter us to pieces, we shall be starved out in a few days," Anderson replied. The Confederate delegation retired; when the delegation returned that night, Anderson informed them that he would be forced to evacuate by noon on April 15 unless he received new orders or supplies. Regarding that as too conditional a promise, Beauregard ordered the batteries into action against the fort.

DECLARATION OF WAR

The Confederacy did not declare war until May 6. The U.S. Congress never did formally declare war, leaving Lincoln to conduct it with his powers as chief executive and commander in chief of the armed forces. Moreover, a formal declaration of war would have provided European powers with a rationale for recognizing the Confederacy as a belligerent—the last thing Lincoln wanted.

April 12–14, 1861: Four years of war began around 4:30 A.M. April 12 when a 10-inch mortar shell arced a red trail through the sky, the signal for the opening of the artillery bombardment of Fort Sumter in Charleston harbor, South Carolina.

During the following 34 hours, 30 Confederate guns and 17 mortars poured 4,000 rounds into the 300-by-350-foot-fort. The Union garrison returned fire at around 7:30 A.M. on April 12. Ammunition soon began to run short, however, and by the afternoon of April 12 Anderson had only six guns in action.

Steady Confederate fire did little damage to Fort Sumter's 12-foot-thick, 40-foot-high walls, but heated round shot set buildings inside the compound on fire. The intensity of the heat and the thickness of the smoke gradually made the fort untenable. With the garrison low on food as well as ammunition and barely able to defend itself, Anderson decided to surrender at 2:30 P.M. on April 13.

The only Federal casualties were two men killed. A third soldier was wounded when Anderson fired off a ceremonial salute at the formal surrender on April 14. The garrison then boarded a steamer for the journey north to New York.

April 15, 1861: President Lincoln and his cabinet had learned of the fall of Fort Sumter on April 14. Referring to the crisis as an "insurrection" rather than a war, Lincoln issued a public proclamation and called for 75,000 volunteer soldiers. Northern states responded enthusiastically to Lincoln's call; the New York legislature voted to commit $3 million to the Union cause. The border states—Virginia, Maryland, Kentucky, and Missouri—were cool to the proposal; Kentucky, North Carolina, Tennessee, and Missouri refused the president's request for troops.

April 17, 1861: A Virginia state convention approved a secession ordinance by a vote of 88-55. In Montgomery, Alabama, President Jefferson Davis announced that the Confederate government would issue letters of marque, allowing licensed privateers to legally prey on Union commercial shipping.

Over the next few days, Virginia troops moved to seize the arsenal at Harpers Ferry and the Gosport Navy Yard near Norfolk.

April 19, 1861: President Lincoln ordered the blockade of all Southern ports, part of a strategy of encirclement and slow strangulation that Gen. Winfield Scott designated the Anaconda Plan. Close blockade was a job beyond the capacities of the U.S. Navy in the spring of 1861. To seal off ten major ports and patrol the 3,550-mile Confederate coastline, the navy had about 40 warships fit for service, manned by 9,100 officers and men. The Atlantic Blockading Squadron had only 14 warships to patrol more than 1,000 miles of coast from Hampton Roads, Virginia, to Key West, Florida. With the blockade order, Navy Secretary Gideon Welles set in motion a tremendous expansion of the navy.

The 6th Massachusetts, the first Northern militia regiment to respond to Lincoln's call for volunteers, reached Baltimore on April 19. Marching through the city to make a railroad connection, the regiment and a secessionist mob came to blows. The rioters heaved bricks and paving stones at the Bay State troops; the soldiers fired into the crowd. Twelve rioters and four soldiers were killed.

April 22, 1861: Arkansas governor H. M. Rector refused Lincoln's appeal for troops to support the Union. In North Carolina, state militia seized the U.S. arsenal at Fayetteville.

April 25, 1861: The 7th New York militia reached Washington, D.C. By the end of April, some 10,000 troops were available for the defense of the capital.

April 27, 1861: Still concerned about the security of Washington, D.C., President Lincoln suspended the writ of habeas corpus (that is, the right of anyone arrested to appear before a court to appeal the detention) for an area running south from Philadelphia to the capital. Lincoln took the action as a means of curbing anti-Union activity that had disrupted the movement of troops and supplies from the Northeast through Baltimore into Washington, D.C.

The Virginia Convention offered Richmond, the state capital, as the permanent capital of the new Confederacy.

May 6, 1861: Jefferson Davis approved a bill from the Confederate Congress declaring the existence of a state of war between the United States and the Confederate States.

COMBATANTS

The Union: The North entered the Civil War with substantial material advantages over the South. Most of the nation's heavy industrial capacity, including its weapons-manufacturing capacity, lay in the North. The loyal states were better served than those in rebellion, too, by the modern innovations of steam transportation and telegraphy. The North could arm and feed itself and move men and goods with far more ease and efficiency than could the South.

By 1860, 110,000 factories were turning out goods in the North; only 18,000 in the South. The industrial output of New York State alone doubled that of the South. More than 20,000 miles of the nation's 30,000-mile railroad network were in the North. The Northern states counted six times as many engineers as did the Southern states; three times as many merchants; and more doctors, educators, and artists.

The North maintained its advantage in available forces throughout the Civil War, with some 4,000,000 men between the ages of 15 and 40. At the outbreak of the war, the U.S. Regular Army mustered about 16,000 officers and men, most of them scattered in small detachments on the frontier. On May 3, as the three-month volunteer regiments were streaming into Washington, D.C., Lincoln issued a call for 42,000 three-year volunteers

and 22,700 regulars. Some 2,130,000 men served at some point in the Union Army; another 120,000 served in the Navy. By the last year of the war, the North had more than 1,000,000 men under arms.

The Confederacy: When the Civil War broke out, Southerners formed a disproportionate part of the U.S. Regular Army. More than 300 U.S. regular officers, close to a third of the total, resigned their commissions during the first months of 1861 and offered their services to the Confederacy. Robert E. Lee, generally regarded as America's most capable soldier, received offers from both armies. On April 18, Lee refused Lincoln's offer of command of the Union field Army. "I must side with or against my section," he wrote a Northern friend. "I cannot raise my hand against my birthplace, my home, my children." Lee submitted his resignation on April 20 and took command of the Virginia forces at the end of April. In May, he joined the Confederate service as a brigadier general. Many other talented former and present soldiers joined Lee, including several who rose to senior command in the Confederate army, including Thomas J. Jackson, James Longstreet, Joseph E. Johnston, and J. E. B. Stuart.

The Confederate army had its origin in Confederate congressional acts of February 28 and March 6, 1861. That legislation gave President Davis control of military operations and of the volunteer militia forces that formed the bulk of the Confederate army. By April, the president had called for some 80,000 troops, and on May 8, the Confederate Congress decreed that Confederate enlistments would last the duration of the war. But the inalterable fact was that the Confederacy could count on only some 1,140,000 white males between the ages of 15 and 40. At most, some 900,000 served at various times, and during the last year of the Civil War only some 200,000 were still under arms.

At the outset of the Civil War, the military balance seemed close to even, with a slight edge for the South in terms of capable military leaders. In the long run, however, the North's major advantages in manpower, industrial potential, and wealth overwhelmed the South's capabilities in these areas. Observant Southerners recognized this. A young Georgian, Edward Porter Alexander, resigned from the U.S. Army in the spring of 1861 and made his way home and eventually to Richmond via a roundabout route that took him through extensive regions of the North as well as through Tennessee, Georgia, and the Carolinas. In New York, Ohio, and Indiana, Alexander noted, "Every station was a town, & everywhere there were camps & soldiers in regiments & brigades. And they were all fine, healthy looking, with flesh on their bones & color in their cheeks, thoroughly well uniformed, equipped and armed."

In the South, he saw, there were fewer men under arms, and they were ill-clad and poorly equipped. "Then no one could fail to note a marked difference in the general aspect of the men," remarked Alexander. "Our men were less healthy looking, they were sallower in complection & longer & lankier in build, & there seemed too to be less discipline & drill among them."

Blacks: More than 180,000 blacks, most of them recently freed slaves, served in the Union Army, and another 30,000 served on Union ships. (Another 200,000 worked for the Union forces as cooks, laborers, nurses, and scouts.) Louisiana provided the largest contingent of black recruits, about 24,000 men; the first regiment was formed in Louisiana, after the capture of New Orleans, in September 1862. There were several well-known units formed of free (or escaped) blacks in the North—the first temporary brigade in Cincinnati, formed in September 1862, and regiments in Rhode Island, Kansas, and Massachusetts. Most black troops did not serve in combat, but some did. Those that did participated in some 190 engagements and battles.

The Confederates, desperately short of manpower, debated throughout the war whether to use their slaves in other than menial capacities in the military; not until the closing weeks of the war, in the winter of 1865, did the Confederate Congress authorize the enlistment of 300,000 slaves, but only a few companies were organized by the final days of the war at Appomattox.

Foreign-born: The United States was still a nation of immigrants, and inevitably tens of thousands of those who fought in the Civil War, North and South, had been born abroad. Some 200,000 German-born Americans fought for the Union, the most numerous of the foreign-born contingents. New York State alone raised ten largely German-speaking regiments; German-born Americans served in nearly every unit in the Northern Army.

Over 150,000 Irish-born men fought for the Union cause, but the Irish were also the largest single foreign-born contingent to serve the Con-

federacy. In one Alabama company, 104 of 109 enrollees listed themselves as Irish-born. New York raised five regiments of Irish-born immigrants. Massachusetts, Pennsylvania, Ohio, and Indiana each raised two regiments of Irish-born immigrants. The Irish Brigade of the 1st Division, 2nd Corps, Army of the Potomac distinguished itself at Antietam and at Marye's Heights, Fredericksburg. North or South, the Irish were usually held in high regard as attacking troops.

Norwegian-born immigrants were the norm in the 15th Wisconsin, with a few Swedes and Danes intermixed. One company of the 15th Wisconsin contained five men named Ole Olsen. Louisiana, with cosmopolitan New Orleans, supplied more foreign-born soldiers to the Confederate army than any other Southern state.

In addition to the above-mentioned foreign-born Americans, some 50,000 Canadians, 45,000 Englishmen, and thousands of Scots and Welsh volunteers also fought for the Union, with many of the British, at least, remaining after the war to settle in the United States.

GEOGRAPHIC AND STRATEGIC CONSIDERATIONS

The Civil War was a continental war, with operations from the Atlantic to the Pacific. In theory, geography gave the Confederacy the advantage of interior lines of communications, along which rebel commanders theoretically could move their forces into position against the Union faster than Union forces could counter the moves. But the South's inferior railroad network discounted that edge; in practice, the North, with better lateral communications, could move men and equipment faster than the South could.

The Confederacy also enjoyed the advantage of waging war on the strategic defensive. The South, in effect, could win the war by not losing. The North, on the other hand, had to conquer, pacify, and hold Southern territory in order to achieve victory.

As noted, the North had substantially the greater industrial potential. Among other things, that meant that adquate numbers of modern warships could be produced to enforce the strategic blockade of the Confederate coastline and to dominate the Mississippi, Cumberland, Tennessee, Red, and Arkansas Rivers in the West and the James and Potomac Rivers in the East, major lines of

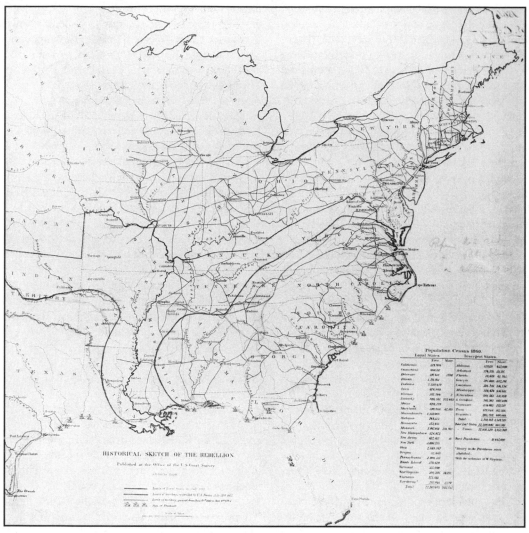

This map of July 1862, the work of the U.S. Coast Survey, is marked to show the progress of the "loyal states" from the early months of the Civil War in 1861 as they occupied increasingly more territory.

Union offensive operation during the war.

BATTLES AND CAMPAIGNS: 1861

With the outbreak of the Civil War, North and South faced urgent and immediate political and military problems. Each side moved swiftly to raise, train, and equip a large army. The Union attempted to prevent Virginia and other states from breaking away; loyalist and rebel joined the struggle for the critical border states of Maryland, Kentucky, and Missouri. Students of the Civil War traditionally divide the combat among three main land areas: eastern theater, western theater, trans-Mis-

sissippi theater. There was also some action in the naval theater.

In Washington, D.C., and in Richmond, Virginia, political leaders prodded the generals to fight a decisive battle that would assure an early end to the conflict.

EASTERN THEATER

May 24, 1861: Union forces occupied Alexandria, Virginia, across the Potomac River from Washington, D.C., encountering only token resistance from Virginia troops. The action produced one casualty, however, prominent volunteer E.

Elmer Ellsworth, colonel of the 11th New York. A Confederate sympathizer shot him as he removed a rebel flag from a tavern roof. The death of Ellsworth, 24 years old, gave the North a martyr and helped arouse war sentiment in the loyal states.

June 10, 1861: Confederates under Col. D. H. Hill repulsed a Federal attack at Big Bethel, Virginia, near the Union stronghold of Fort Monroe. Federal casualties were 76 killed, wounded, or missing from about 4,000 troops, mostly New Yorkers, engaged; the Confederates lost 11 of 1,400. Some historians consider Big Bethel the first land battle of the war.

July 1861: Under intense political pressure, Gen. Irvin McDowell prepared to commence offensive operations against Confederate forces near the railroad junction of Manassas, Virginia, some 30 miles from Washington, D.C. McDowell had argued for several weeks that his 34,000 troops, most of them short-term militiamen, were not ready to move against Gen. P. G. T. Beauregard's army of 23,000. "You are green, it is true," President Lincoln told McDowell, "but they are green, also; you are all green alike." So Lincoln's cabinet ordered McDowell to bring off a battle that might deal the rebellion a death blow.

As a preliminary, U.S. troops under Gen. Robert Patterson were directed to close on Gen. J. E. Johnston's Confederate forces in the Shenandoah Valley to prevent them from reinforcing Beauregard at Manassas. Patterson, with 18,000 men, moved on July 15, but failed to pin Johnston's 12,000 in place. On July 16, McDowell began his advance from Washington. He reached Centreville, near a sluggish stream called Bull Run, with about 30,000 men on July 18. The Confederates, meanwhile, ordered Johnston's little army to fall back to the Southeast and reinforce Beauregard. Johnston's troops traveled most of the way by train—the first instance in military history in which a railroad was used for strategic mobility.

July 18, 1861: Federal troops carrying out a reconnaissance bumped into two Confederate brigades drawn up at Mitchell's and Blackburn's fords on Bull Run. In a sharp action, the Confederates repulsed the attackers, inflicting about 80 casualties. (The Confederates called that encounter the First Battle of Bull Run.)

July 21, 1861: General McDowell's plan of attack for what the Federals called the First Battle of Bull Run (the Confederates styled it the First Manassas) was to send a turning column of 14,000

to cross Bull Run at Sudley Springs 2 miles north of the Confederate line, with orders to fall on the enemy's presumably unsuspecting left flank. As a diversion, another 10,000 Federals were to attack at the stone bridge that carried Warrenton Turnpike over the stream.

The flanking column, consisting mostly of inexperienced, poorly trained militia, turned up late, however. In any case, the Confederates spotted it in time for troops to be repositioned to meet the initial thrust. Col. Nathan Evans reacted quickly, shifting a small force from the stone bridge to contest the Union advance. Evans's few hundred troops held out for about an hour, sufficient time for Beauregard to rush two infantry brigades to the threatened point.

The Federal pressure intensified as the morning advanced. Two hours of hard fighting forced the rebels back across the Warrenton Turnpike and up Henry House Hill. At the stone bridge, meantime, Gen. Daniel Tyler's diversionary attack began to show results. By noon, some of Tyler's troops, joined by infantry from Gen. William T. Sherman's division, had crossed Bull Run and driven the defenders from the bridge. For a time, it looked as though the Federals would unhinge the enemy line and rout the tiring Confederates.

Beauregard, however, established on Henry House Hill a strong defensive line anchored by a brigade of Virginia infantry under Gen. Thomas J. Jackson. It was there that Jackson earned his sobriquet "Stonewall," for the stubbornness of his Virginians' stand (see Notable Phrases, p. 285). During the early afternoon, Jackson's regiments, firing largely concealed from the reverse slope, repulsed several Federal charges.

General McDowell launched a series of piecemeal attacks that accomplished little. In the midafternoon, he ordered two artillery batteries into the front line to pour close-range fire into the enemy. A charge of Virginia cavalry under J. E. B. Stuart caught the guns exposed. With infantry assistance, the batteries were broken up and knocked out of the action.

Beauregard then prepared to throw everything he had into a counterattack on the exposed, worn-down Federal right. At around 3:30, the rebels, among them Johnston's late-arriving troops from the Shenandoah Valley, came charging down the hill, howling furiously—the first recorded instance of the notorious, bloodcurdling rebel yell. The charge broke McDowell's line and sent the

Federals reeling back across Bull Run.

The retreat, orderly at first, soon became a rout. Hastily abandoned provisions, knapsacks, and weapons littered the road to Washington, D.C. "Both armies were fairly defeated," General Sherman remarked afterward. "Whichever had stood fast, the other would have run." The Confederates failed to pursue the beaten Yankees. Still, the Confederates could claim a decisive victory in what they considered the first great battle of the war, capturing 9 battle flags, 28 cannons, and 500,000 rounds of ammunition and inflicting around 2,600 casualties. Confederate losses were roughly 2,000 killed, wounded, or missing.

The defeat shocked and demoralized the North. "The fat is all in the fire now and we shall have to crow small until we can retrieve this disgrace somehow," John Nicolay, one of Lincoln's secretaries, wrote a few days after the debacle.

Southerners celebrated wildly, assuming that victory at Manassas would mean a quick end to the war. "The breakdown of the Yankee race, their unfitness for empire, forces domination on the South," a Richmond newspaper remarked. "We are compelled to take the sceptre of power."

July 27, 1861: In the aftermath of the defeat at Bull Run, President Lincoln removed McDowell and turned over command of the forces around Washington, D.C., to Gen. George B. McClellan, summoned from the Department of the Ohio, one of the Union Army's major administrative units. "I found no army to command, [but] a mere collection of regiments cowering on the banks of the Potomac, some perfectly raw, others dispirited by the recent defeat," McClellan wrote. "The city was almost in condition to be taken by a dash of a regiment of cavalry." Energetic and capable, McClellan, 34 years old, turned at once to the reorganization and training of the Army of the Potomac, a task he performed brilliantly and—or so the president complained—with an agonizingly deliberate thoroughness.

August 14–15, 1861: Citizen-soldiers in the 79th New York and the 2nd Maine carried out what amounted to a mutiny in protest of, among other things, the denial of furloughs. McClellan, a strict disciplinarian, reacted decisively. There were many arrests, and some 60 mutineers were sent to prison on Dry Tortugas, a small group of islands off Key West, Florida.

October 21, 1861: Confederates ambushed and broke up a Union raiding force under Gen. Charles Stone at Ball's Bluff on the Virginia bank of the Potomac River. Stone's command suffered more than 900 killed, wounded, or missing in that demonstration against Confederate positions guarding the Potomac fords near Poolesville.

Among the dead in the affray was the politically connected Col. Edward Baker, a former Oregon senator and a friend of President Lincoln's. Arrested early in 1862, allegedly for suspicion of treason at Ball's Bluff, General Stone was imprisoned without trial for six months. No charges were ever filed. Stone returned to service in 1863, but never held an important position; he resigned from the Army in September 1864.

Late October 1861: McClellan ordered the Army of the Potomac into winter quarters. Much to Lincoln's disappointment, the "Little Napoleon," as McClellan had been dubbed, decided that his army would be in no condition to launch a major offensive until the spring of 1862.

WESTERN THEATER

June 3, 1861: Federal forces under General McClellan routed a detachment of 1,500 Confederates in a night attack at Philippi, in what became the state of West Virginia, inflicting 15 casualties before the rebels beat a hasty retreat. That action, an early operation in McClellan's campaign to secure western Virginia for the Union, is regarded by some historians as the first battle of the Civil War.

July 11–13, 1861: A detachment of McClellan's army surprised and broke up a Confederate force at Rich Mountain, in present-day West Virginia. The beaten rebels retreated across difficult mountain terrain toward Laurel Hill, but some 500 officers and men were forced to surrender on the night of July 12–13. That, coupled with a success over a Confederate rear guard at Carrick's (also known as Corrick's) Ford on the Cheat River on July 12, largely cleared northwestern Virginia of Confederates, opened a potential invasion route into Virginia proper, and made a hero and idol of McClellan. Confederate commander Gen. Robert S. Garnett was killed in the action at Carrick's Ford.

September 10, 1861: McClellan's successor as commander of the Department of the Ohio, Gen. William Rosecrans, attacked strong Confederate positions at Carnifex Ferry in present-day West Virginia. Several Union assaults through thick woods achieved little at a cost of about 150 casualties, but the Confederates withdrew after dark.

September 10–15, 1861: In Gen. Robert E. Lee's first campaign of the Civil War, Confederate forces attempted to cut off and destroy a Union brigade defending Cheat Mountain in present-day West Virginia. Heavy rains impeded Lee's movements, and Federals under Gen. John J. Reynolds withstood attacks on September 11 and 12. Lee finally called off the operation on September 15. Federal casualties totaled 80; Reynolds claimed to have killed or wounded 100 Confederates.

November 1–6, 1861: As part of the maneuvering for Kentucky, Gen. Ulysses S. Grant launched operations to keep Confederates at Columbus, Kentucky, on the Mississippi River off balance. Moving south by river from Cairo, Illinois, with 3,100 troops, Grant threatened Confederate general Leonidas Polk at Columbus. On December 6, acting on a report of enemy troops moving from Kentucky into Missouri to reinforce Confederate forces there, Grant decided to attack Belmont, Missouri, opposite Columbus.

November 7, 1861: Grant's troops landed from their transports 3 miles above Belmont at 8:30 A.M. Grant pushed ahead through thick woods with a combined force of infantry, cavalry, and a six-gun battery and drove the rebels from their camps to the riverbank. While the Federals looted the abandoned camps, Polk ferried infantry across the Mississippi River in an attempt to cut off Grant from the transports. Grant withdrew hastily with spoils of the camps and a few prisoners, barely escaping a debacle. Confederate losses totaled about 640; Union casualties were about 600.

TRANS-MISSISSIPPI THEATER

July 5, 1861: In their continuing effort to control the critical border state of Missouri, Federal troops under Gen. Fritz Sigel attacked a larger prosecession force at Carthage, Missouri. Repulsing the attack, the rebels claimed victory. Losses were comparatively light, about 120 for the secessionists and fewer than 50 for the Federals.

July 25–August 1, 1861: In present-day New Mexico, U.S. regulars fought a brief skirmish on July 25 with a 250-man Confederate force advancing up the Rio Grande, then withdrew to the north, abandoning the Union stronghold of Fort Fillmore. On July 27, the Confederates captured 700 U.S. troops, together with 2 guns and 300 cattle, without a battle. On August 1, rebel commander John

Baylor appointed himself governor of the newly established Confederate territory of Arizona.

Early August 1861: Confederate forces in Missouri, totaling about 21,000 troops, combined for an intended advance on St. Louis. In Springfield, Federal general Nathaniel Lyon, whose prompt actions in the spring of 1861 had held Missouri for the Union, decided to go on the offensive against the advancing Confederates under Gen. Ben McCulloch and Gen. Sterling Price.

In two columns, Union troops moved on the Confederates at their camp at Wilson's Creek southwest of Springfield. By the night of August 9, they were within striking distance. Lyon directed Gen. Fritz Sigel's column to attack from south of Wilson's Creek; the main column under Lyon would strike from the north.

August 10, 1861 (Battle of Wilson's Creek): Lyon's column opened the Battle of Wilson's Creek at 4 A.M. By 6:30, a Federal attack had driven the rebels from their position on Oak Hill to the creek, where they re-formed for a counterattack. Sigel, meanwhile, had moved up from the south. McCulloch easily repulsed Sigel and drove off his infantry, which played no further part in the battle.

The Confederates then massed their full strength against Lyon's wing on Oak Hill. The Federals repulsed two Confederate attacks. Then, around 10:30 A.M., Lyon, already twice wounded, was killed. A third Confederate charge failed to dislodge the Federals, but Lyon's successor, fearing that the line could not withstand a fourth battering, ordered a withdrawal toward Rolla, Missouri. McCulloch did not pursue.

Union losses were 1,235 killed, wounded or missing from about 5,400 engaged. The Confederates, with 11,600 in the battle, reported 1,184 casualties.

September–October 1861: Gen. Sterling Price led a Confederate column north after the Wilson's Creek victory. In mid-September, Price's command laid siege to Lexington, Missouri, on the Missouri River. The 3,600-man Lexington garrison surrendered to Price on September 20. A Federal column recaptured Lexington on October 20.

NAVAL THEATER

May–December 1861: Union naval forces tightened the blockade of the Confederacy. On May 1, warships blocked the mouth of the James River in Virginia; they sealed off the Rappahannock

River on May 18. By May 26, the blockade had been established outside the Gulf coast ports of Mobile, Alabama, and New Orleans, Louisiana.

More than 800 ships penetrated the U.S. blockade during the first year of the war, but the number represented a sharp decline from the 6,000 vessels that had come in and out of Southern ports during the final year before the war.

As the Union Navy increased in size, the blockade gradually tightened. By the end of 1861, 76 old naval vessels had been reconditioned and returned to service, 136 ships had been purchased and put into commission, and 52 new ships had been built. Most of those vessels were put to work sealing off the Confederacy.

Union sailors found the duty tedious. But a lucky capture could fill a man's pockets, as the age-old rules of naval warfare were still in effect and allowed a captured ship's value to be divided among the victorious crew. The tug *Eolus*'s seizure of the blockade runner *Hope* earned its captain $13,000 and each crewman $1,000. An ordinary seaman's monthly salary was $16.

June–December 1861: On June 30, the Confederate commerce raider CSS *Sumter*, under Comdr. Raphael Semmes, slipped the blockade at New Orleans, Louisiana, and set out on a six-month cruise in search of U.S. vessels to capture, sink, burn, or otherwise destroy. Semmes abandoned the ship at Gibraltar after taking 18 prizes.

August 28–29, 1861: A combined Union Army-Navy expedition came ashore on Cape Hatteras, North Carolina, to capture and garrison two Confederate strong points, Forts Hatteras and Clark, that guarded Hatteras Inlet. The action, though minor, closed off an important route for rebel blockade runners.

November 7, 1861: In a combined operation, U.S. warships and troops seized Forts Walker and Beauregard guarding Port Royal Sound, South Carolina, about midway between Savannah, Georgia, and Charleston, South Carolina.

Flag Officer Samuel DuPont's heavy warships, carrying 155 great guns, described a circular course past the forts, firing broadsides as they glided by. The defenders endured that for a time, then fled. Federal troops landed and occupied the abandoned forts that afternoon and evening.

HOME FRONTS

May 10–11, 1861: In Missouri, a critical po-

litical battleground, Federal troops clashed with pro-Confederate militia. Capt. Nathaniel Lyon, an officer in the Regular Army, led a detachment of Federal troops to the militia encampment at Camp Jackson outside St. Louis; the state forces surrendered. In subsequent encounters between Federal troops and pro-Confederate mobs, 29 people were killed or mortally injured. The outbreaks continued, and seven more people were killed in skirmishes between Federal troops and civilians.

May–June 1861: On May 16, the Kentucky legislature proclaimed the state's neutrality in the developing North-South conflict. All the same, on May 28 the Union Army established the Department of Kentucky, a major administrative unit incorporating all of the state within 100 miles of the Ohio River, and assigned the command to Kentuckian Maj. Robert Anderson.

On May 20, a state convention at Raleigh, North Carolina, voted to secede from the Union. On May 23, Virginians approved secession by a vote of 97,000 to 32,000. On June 8, Tennesseans voted 104,913 to 47,238 for secession.

June 8, 1861: To improve health conditions in the Army camps and as an outlet for the overflowing energy of volunteers in the North, President Lincoln approved the creation of the United States Sanitary Commission. Among other duties, commission members coordinated volunteer programs to collect such items as food, blankets, and medical supplies for distribution to the troops. The commission also sent nurses into Army hospitals, established a home for discharged soldiers in Washington, D.C., and operated canteens at railroad depots for soldiers passing through.

June 19, 1861: A convention of western Virginians, strongly Unionist, elected Francis H. Pierpont governor of what became the state of West Virginia (June 20, 1863). On July 2, the breakaway legislature convened at Wheeling, with prompt Union recognition.

July 4, 1861: The first wartime session of the U.S. Congress convened. In a message to Congress, President Lincoln pledged that the United States would maintain "its territorial integrity, against its own domestic foes." The president asked Congress to authorize the raising of another 400,000 volunteers.

July 22, 1861: A Missouri state convention in Jefferson City vowed to keep Missouri in the Union, and moved to relocate the capital to St. Louis. Missouri's pro-Confederate governor,

Claiborne Jackson, responded that his administration remained the state's legal government.

August 2, 1861: To pay for the war, the U.S. Congress adopted the nation's first income tax and added various tariffs to imported goods, measures designed to raise some $500 million. The tax bill levied 3 percent on incomes in excess of $800 a year. Congress passed additional tax legislation in 1862 and 1864.

August 6, 1861: Congress passed the first Confiscation Act, a measure aimed at depriving the South the use of slaves in its war effort. The act decreed that all slaves used as laborers on fortifications or in the transport of stores and munitions would be freed. On August 30, Gen. John Frémont, in command in Missouri, took the matter a step further by issuing a proclamation freeing the slaves of all in the state who resisted the Union government. President Lincoln promptly revoked Frémont's proclamation, saying that political times were not ripe for emancipation.

August 16, 1861: In separate cases, the Brooklyn *Eagle*, the New York *Journal*, and other newspapers were hauled into Federal court to answer for alleged pro-Confederate sympathies. In Haverhill, Massachusetts, on August 19, a mob tarred and feathered an editor of the *Essex County Democrat*.

September 4, 1861: Kentucky's precarious neutrality came to an end with the movement of Confederate forces into Columbus on the Mississippi River. The Confederates acted, at least in part, because they suspected impending Union moves to secure the state. Within days, Gen. Ulysses S. Grant, commanding Union forces at Cairo, Illinois, occupied Paducah at the mouth of the Tennessee River and Smithfield at the mouth of the Cumberland River. Other Union troops occupied Louisville and Covington; Confederate forces moved on Bowling Green and took up positions along the Cumberland River.

September 18, 1861: Continuing its crackdown against newspapers regarded as subversive, the U.S. government denied the Louisville *Courier* the use of the mails. In a raid on the newspaper's office, Federal agents arrested several employees suspected of having pro-Confederate sympathies.

October 1861: After several weeks of discussion, Lincoln on October 24 moved to relieve Gen. John Charles Frémont of the Missouri command. In Washington on October 31, Gen. Winfield Scott,

enfeebled by age and exhausted by clashes with the young, ambitious, and energetic Gen. George B. McClellan, offered his resignation. The president accepted on November 1 and appointed McClellan in Scott's place as commander of the Union forces.

November 6, 1861: In a general election, the Confederate States chose the provisional president, Jefferson Davis, to fill a full six-year term. The balloting confirmed Alexander Stephens of Georgia as Davis's vice president.

November–December 1861: Union military operations along the South Carolina coast, particularly the capture of Port Royal south of Charleston on November 7 and the subsequent seizure of the nearby Sea Island, forced large-scale civilian evacuations of the low country.

Many planters burned their valuable cotton crops before they fled. The Charleston (South Carolina) *Courier* approved, saying that those voluntary acts of destruction would aid the Confederate war effort and deny the North "the extensive spoils with which they have feasted their imagination and the attainment of which was one of their chief objects."

November 28–December 4, 1861: On November 28, the Provisional Congress in Richmond formally admitted Missouri to the Confederacy. On December 2, the Federal government empowered Gen. Henry Halleck, commanding the Union Department of Missouri, to suspend the writ of habeas corpus in the state. Two days later, Halleck authorized the arrest of anyone aiding the pro-secessionist movement in Missouri.

December 9–10, 1861: On the recommendation of the U.S. Senate, Congress established the soon-to-be-powerful Joint Committee on the Conduct of the War.

December 11, 1861: A fire destroyed about half the city of Charleston, South Carolina, ravaging the city's business district and leaving many people homeless.

INTERNATIONAL DEVELOPMENTS

May 9–10, 1861: The Confederate government assigned naval agent James D. Bulloch, a Georgian, to negotiate warship purchases and outfitting with British firms. On May 10, President Davis authorized the purchase of arms and vessels from British sources.

November 8, 1861: Off Havana, Cuba, Capt.

Charles Wilkes of the sloop USS *San Jacinto* stopped the British mail steamer *Trent* and removed two Confederate commissioners bound for England, James Mason and John Slidell, from the vessel. The commissioners eventually were delivered to Boston, where they were held captive. The stopping of the *Trent* and the seizure of Mason and Slidell touched off a serious diplomatic crisis between the United States and Britain and encouraged Confederates to hope that the British would come to their support.

November 30–December 30, 1861: The British government sent word to its minister in Washington, D.C., Lord Lyons, of its displeasure over the *Trent* incident. British foreign secretary Lord John Russell sought a U.S. apology and the release of the diplomats Mason and Slidell to the British. The British Admiralty ordered the Royal Navy's North Atlantic Squadron on alert.

In Washington, President Lincoln urgently sought a solution. "One war at a time," he said. On December 4, the British stepped up the pressure by announcing a ban on shipments of vital war supplies to the United States. Britain's envoy argued for a tough stand: "I am so concerned that unless we give our friends here a good lesson this time, we shall have the same trouble with them again very soon," Lord Lyons wrote. "Surrender or war will have a very good effect on them."

Lord Lyons and William Seward, Lincoln's secretary of state, reached a settlement that seemed to satisfy both sides. Saying Captain Wilkes had acted without instructions, Seward, on December 26, ordered Mason and Slidell to be freed and allowed to resume their journey. On December 30, the U.S. released the diplomats to Lord Lyons.

BATTLES AND CAMPAIGNS: 1862

In 1862, the first full year of the Civil War, major campaigns were fought in Virginia and in the Mississippi River valley. Union forces recorded important gains in Kentucky and Tennessee. The Confederates, with Robert E. Lee, won victories in Virginia, but Lee's first invasion of the North proved a failure. In the trans-Mississippi theater, Missouri and Arkansas were key battlegrounds.

There were important developments in politics too in the North and the South, including Lincoln's Preliminary Emancipation Proclamation (see Home Fronts, September 22, 1862, p. 242). The Confederates bent their diplomatic efforts to attaining recognition from Britain and France.

EASTERN THEATER

January 27, 1862: In Washington, D.C., President Lincoln issued his General War Order Number 1 as a means of prodding the balky Gen. George B. McClellan into action against the Confederate army near Manassas. Lincoln and McClellan disagreed on the line of operations—Lincoln favored a direct approach to Manassas while McClellan favored an indirect movement on Richmond via the Virginia peninsula, the narrow, low-lying country between the York and James Rivers.

March–June 1862 (Peninsular Campaign): When Confederate general Joseph E. Johnston withdrew from Manassas to the Rappahannock River, Lincoln reluctantly approved General McClellan's shift of the 100,000- strong Army of the Potomac to the Virginia peninsula.

McClellan's Peninsular Campaign commenced on March 17 with the movement of 12 divisions by water to Fort Monroe at the tip of the peninsula. The advance toward Richmond began on April 4 but stalled on the following day, when the Federals bumped up against lightly held Confederate positions along the Warwick River near Yorktown. General McClellan, with a numerical superiority of close to four to one, paused to lay siege to the Confederate lines, a plodding, methodical approach that was to be characteristic of the entire campaign.

"No one but McClellan could have hesitated to attack," General Johnston said later. While McClellan wasted a month besieging Yorktown, Johnston shifted his army to meet the threat and strengthened Richmond's outer defenses. On May 3, the Confederates withdrew from Yorktown and abandoned the place to McClellan. Johnston's rear guard engaged advance elements of the Army of the Potomac at Williamsburg on May 5, inflicting 2,000 casualties, while Johnston's main body backpedaled to the safety of the Richmond defenses.

McClellan had expected two Federal corps on the outskirts of Washington, D.C., to reinforce his troops for the drive on Richmond. But with Confederate general Thomas J. Jackson's command on the move in the Shenandoah Valley, Lincoln refused to release the Federal corps—just the strategic diversion the Confederates had sought when they turned Jackson loose in late March.

March–June 1862 (Jackson's Shenandoah Valley Campaign): Preliminary to the Shenandoah Valley Campaign, Federal troops under Gen. Nathaniel P. Banks inflicted a sharp defeat on Jackson's corps at Kernstown, Virginia, on March 23. The engagement, however, turned Lincoln and war secretary Edwin M. Stanton cautious; they prevented Banks's corps and another corps under Gen. Irwin McDowell from joining McClellan. Washington also withdrew a division from McClellan and dispatched it to the Shenandoah Valley to oppose Jackson.

Jackson's aim was "always to mislead, mystify, and surprise the enemy." In the Shenandoah Valley Campaign, regarded as one of the most brilliant operations in military history, Jackson's 17,000-strong corps raced up and down the valley, outmaneuvering the 33,000 Union troops sent to destroy it.

In less than two weeks, Jackson's "foot cavalry" fought and won the Battles of McDowell (May 13), Front Royal (May 23), and Winchester (May 25). Federal efforts to trap Jackson only served to make further difficulties for McClellan. Jackson concluded his remarkable performance with twin victories over his pursuers at Cross Keys and Port Republic on June 8–9.

May 1862: While Jackson tore up the Shenandoah Valley, Union forces crept to within 8 miles of Richmond. Union gunboats, in the meantime, steamed up the James River toward Richmond, reaching Drewry's Bluff only 7 miles below the capital before they were repulsed on May 15. Toward the end of the month, the Army of the Potomac came to within earshot of the bells of Richmond's churches. One wing of the army, though, lay south of the rain-swollen Chickahominy River, out of touch with the main body and exposed to an enemy thrust.

May 31–June 1, 1862 (Battle of Fair Oaks/ Seven Pines): On May 31, Confederate general Johnston struck Union general McClellan's left wing, isolated south of the Chickahominy River. In the two-day battle, known as the Battle of Fair Oaks/Seven Pines, the Confederates stalled the advance on Richmond even though they failed to inflict a crippling defeat on McClellan.

The battle, fought in rain and mud, claimed more than 11,000 casualties, Union and Confederate. Among the wounded was Johnston. On June 1, Gen. Robert E. Lee replaced Johnston in command of what would soon be known as the Army of Northern Virginia. Lee broke off the Fair Oaks/ Seven Pines battle at once and pulled back into Johnston's defensive lines. There, summoning Jackson's corps from the Shenandoah Valley, Lee began to plan a counteroffensive.

June 1862: As he prepared his counterstroke, Lee ordered his cavalry commander, Gen. J. E. B. Stuart, to reconnoiter McClellan's right flank and rear. In what was dubbed "Stuart's first ride around McClellan," 1,000 Confederate troopers, on June 12–15, made a complete circuit of the Army of the Potomac. Before Lee could attack, though, McClellan struck. By the third week of June, McClellan had shifted all but one corps, the 5th Corps under Brig. Gen. Fitz-John Porter, south of the Chickahominy River for what McClellan hoped would be the final drive on Richmond.

June 25–July 1, 1862 (Battles of the Seven Days): In the opening engagement of the Battles of the Seven Days, McClellan attacked Confederate positions at Oak Grove. The Federals made minor gains during the day but broke off the battle at dusk. On June 26, Lee regained the initiative. Gambling that McClellan would remain frozen south of the Chickahominy River, where about 75,000 Federals faced 27,000 Confederates, Lee sent the bulk of his army, 60,000 men, including Jackson's command, against Porter's isolated 5th Corps at Mechanicsville, Virginia, north of the river.

Poor coordination, slipshod staff work, and tardiness doomed the Confederates' Mechanicsville initiative, even though McClellan reacted as expected—he did not attack south of the river. Lee's attack stepped off at 9 A.M. on June 26, a full six hours behind schedule. Uncharacteristically, Jackson seemed unsure of his role, turned up late, and failed to carry out his assignment. After a day's fierce fighting, Porter's corps retreated to stronger positions at Gaines Mill. Lee had missed the chance to destroy the 5th Corps.

Lee renewed the attack the next day. Again, Jackson turned up late and bungled his assignment. A final attack just before dark seemed to stagger the 5th Corps. Porter gave up the Gaines Mill positions after dark and retreated safely across the Chickahominy River.

Those setbacks led McClellan to give up the advance on Richmond and order a withdrawal to the James River. The Army of the Potomac had managed to parry Lee's counterthrusts, but its commander was a beaten man. Lee attacked McClellan's rear guard at Savage's Station and

White Oak Swamp on June 29 and 30, but the Federals managed an orderly retreat. On July 1, Lee's attempt to destroy McClellan came to grief on the slopes of Malvern Hill, where three Federal corps, strongly entrenched, repulsed the Confederates, inflicting heavy losses.

The Battles of the Seven Days were a strategic victory for the Confederates in spite of a series of tactical blunders. Lee, however, had hoped for more. "Under ordinary circumstances," he observed, "the Federal Army should have been destroyed." In fact, Lee had suffered 20,000 men killed, wounded, or missing from Oak Grove to Malvern Hill, a quarter of his army. Losses in the Army of the Potomac, larger than Lee's army and more easily able to replace its losses, totaled 16,000. The Army of the Potomac remained largely intact; it remained idle too, at rest in its camps at Harrison's Landing on the James River, until Lee launched his move on Washington, D.C.

June–July 1862: In the wake of the Federal debacle in the Shenandoah Valley, Lincoln and War Secretary Stanton combined the three separate forces there into one, designated the Army of Virginia. Lincoln and Stanton chose Gen. John Pope, a "western" general who had enjoyed success in Mississippi River operations, to command this new army.

July–August 1862 (Second Battle of Bull Run/Manassas): In mid-July, General Pope began a slow advance toward Gordonsville, Virginia. Lee, with McClellan's 90,000 on the James River and Pope's 50,000 approaching from the north, opted to leave a covering force to watch the Army of the Potomac and turn to confront the Army of Virginia. Those were the initial movements in the Second Bull Run Campaign.

As the Army of the Potomac prepared to board the transports at Harrison's Landing, Virginia, for a return to the Washington, D.C., area, Lee maneuvered in an attempt to destroy General Pope before McClellan could reach him. Lee assigned Gen. James Longstreet to hold the line of the Rappahannock River while Jackson attempted an enveloping movement. Marching 50 miles in two days, Jackson wrecked a Federal supply depot at Manassas deep in the rear of Pope's army, then vanished for two days.

Jackson found excellent cover on a wooded ridge 2 miles west of the first Bull Run battlefield and awaited the arrival of Lee's main body. Pope turned to meet the threat but could not locate Jack-

son. On August 28, Jackson showed himself, feinting at Pope in order to lure him into battle. The result was the Battle of Groveton, a fierce firefight that went on until midnight. Both sides suffered heavy casualties; in one Federal brigade, the midwestern "Black Hats" (later known as the "Iron Brigade"), one in every three fell. Overnight, Pope issued orders for a heavy attack on Jackson the following morning.

The Second Battle of Bull Run opened on the morning of August 29 with a series of frontal attacks on Jackson's positions. Though heavily outnumbered, Jackson held out, his lines wavering at times, until General Longstreet arrived. Longstreet reached the battlefield by midday but did not join the battle. The day's fighting ended in a draw. That night, Jackson pulled back slightly to a stronger defensive position. Mistaking the move for the beginning of a retreat, Pope telegraphed a victory message to Washington.

The Federals met ferocious resistance when they renewed the battle on August 30. Lee let Pope's attack develop fully, then launched Longstreet's powerful command into the Federal left flank. Caught between pincers, the Federals began to pull back. A stout rear guard defense on Henry House Hill allowed most of Pope's army to escape and begin a withdrawal toward Washington. Though he had won a smashing tactical victory, Lee had missed an opportunity to destroy the Army of Virginia.

September 1, 1862 (Battle of Chantilly): Lee attacked Pope's rear guard at Chantilly, Virginia, and in costly action, the Federals held on until nightfall, then joined in the general retreat. All told, the Second Battle of Bull Run cost the Union some 16,000 casualties of 65,000 engaged. Lee's losses were about 10,000 of 55,500. The battle also cost Pope his job. Lincoln merged Pope's command with McClellan's and banished Pope to Minnesota to quell an uprising of Sioux Indians. Overall command went to McClellan. "We must use what tools we have," the president explained.

September 1862: The events of spring and summer had reversed the fortunes of North and South. In a remarkable summer campaign, Lee had driven the Federals from the gates of Richmond to the shelter of the defenses of their own capital. Still, he refused to surrender the initiative. Declining to spend the Army of Northern Virginia on Washington's entrenchments, Lee decided to strike north of the Potomac River and force

McClellan to come to him. Such a move would give war-ravaged northern Virginia a respite, and Lee's pinched and hungry infantry could feed off the rich Maryland harvest. An invasion of the North might have political consequences too. A victory north of the Potomac might strengthen the antiwar movement in the loyal states, and it might finally persuade the British to recognize the Confederate states.

September 4–7, 1862: Lee's army began crossing the half-mile-wide Potomac River at White's Ford, some 30 miles north of Washington, D.C. Two days later, advance elements reached Frederick, Maryland. "They were the dirtiest men I ever saw," a local man recalled, "a most ragged, lean, and hungry set of wolves. Yet there was a dash about them that the Northern men lacked." On September 7, McClellan began a slow pursuit from Washington, D.C.

September 12-16, 1862: As at Bull Run, Lee gambled and divided his forces. He sent Jackson with six divisions south to Harpers Ferry in present-day West Virginia to capture the Federal garrison there and open up a supply line—and a line of retreat—from the Shenandoah Valley. Lee, Gen. James Longstreet, and the rest of the Army of Northern Virginia, three divisions, waited in Maryland, behind the loom of South Mountain, while Jackson went about his task.

On September 13, Lee's dispositions, spelled out in his Special Orders Number 191, fell into General McClellan's hands. Two Indiana soldiers found the orders in a field near Frederick, Maryland. By evening, McClellan knew everything. "Now I know what to do," he told himself. "Here is a paper with which if I cannot whip Bobbie Lee, I will be willing to go home." In McClellan's grasp lay the opportunity to destroy the Army of Northern Virginia.

Still, McClellan proceeded with caution. The Army of the Potomac did not move until September 14, some 18 hours after the Federal commander had seen Special Orders Number 191. Lee, meanwhile, discovered that McClellan had read his plans. Lee promptly sent forces to defend the South Mountain passes and ordered his army to concentrate near the little town of Sharpsburg, Maryland, in the valley of Antietam Creek, a mile or so from the S-bends of the Potomac River.

In sharp fights at the passes on September 14 (the Battles of Crampton's Gap and South Mountain), the outnumbered Confederates held off

McClellan's assault columns long enough for Lee's main body to fan out along the high ground overlooking Antietam Creek—tilled fields and meadows, with plenty of cover for the infantry; ravines and woodlots; expanses of tall corn, rock outcroppings, and split-rail fences. On September 15, Jackson forced the surrender of the 12,000-man Harpers Ferry garrison. Learning of this, Lee decided to stand and fight. Jackson left Gen. A. P. Hill's division in Harpers Ferry to collect the spoils and moved immediately to join Lee 17 miles distant at Sharpsburg.

After the battle at Sharpsburg, Lee's officers questioned his decision to risk his divided army there. The destruction of the Army of Northern Virginia could have meant the end of the Confederacy. Why did he choose to fight there, with his army backed up against the Potomac and with only one ford available for retreat in the event of disaster? Lee doubtless believed he could win.

"He found it hard, the enemy in sight, to withhold his blows," James Longstreet, one of Lee's generals, said.

McClellan, meanwhile, allowed September 15 to pass without a fight, failing to send out cavalry patrols to probe Lee's strength. McClellan held off through September 16 as well, even though by then he had some 60,000 troops in line, roughly double the number available to Lee. During the afternoon and evening of September 16, three Union Army corps massed on the Federal right for an advance next morning southward down the Hagerstown Turnpike. On the left, McClellan assigned a single corps to launch a diversionary attack on the southernmost of the four bridges that spanned Antietam Creek. The tactical plan left McClellan with two corps in reserve, to be used wherever the battle looked most promising.

September 17, 1862 (Battle of Antietam): The Battle of Antietam opened in the damp, murky dawn, when Union general Joseph Hooker's 1st Corps moved against the Confederate left, advancing along a half-mile-wide front astride the Hagerstown Turnpike. In this first phase of a distinct three-phase engagement, Hooker's three divisions aimed for the whitewashed meetinghouse of a sect of German Baptists—the Dunker church. The fighting soon spread outward into a cornfield and, a little later, into the woods that stretched away on either side of the turnpike.

In furious fighting, the 1st Corps drove General Jackson's just-arrived infantry from the cornfield and pressed on toward the Dunker church. Just as the Confederate line seemed to bend, Gen. John B. Hood's Texas Brigade poured out of the woods and, in a savage counterattack, drove the 1st Corps back through the cornfield.

At around 7 A.M., as General Hooker withdrew, the 12th Corps, under the command of Joseph Mansfield, moved up to try roughly the same line of attack. Mansfield was killed at the outset, but one of his divisions pushed ahead, chasing the Confederates out of the cornfield for the second time. The advance came within 200 yards of the Dunker church before Jackson, with reinforcements from the still-quiet Confederate right flank, stopped it.

At that point, McClellan fed a third corps, the 2nd Corps under Gen. Edwin V. Sumner, into the battle. One of Sumner's divisions, advancing through the West Woods, seemed to be on the verge of a breakthrough when yet another Confederate counterattack struck the division's flanks. Within a quarter-hour, the division suffered 2,000 men killed or wounded.

So, one after another, the Confederates, roughly 12,000 strong, stopped three Federal corps, totaling 31,000 men. By 9:30 A.M., some four hours into the battle, nearly 12,000 Union and Confederate soldiers had become casualties.

General Sumner opened the battle's second phase, launching his two surviving divisions into the Confederate center, anchored in a sunken farm track, soon to be dubbed "Bloody Lane," that ran between split-rail fences for half a mile. The second of Sumner's divisions spent itself trying to carry that nearly unassailable position. After a pause, Sumner sent in his third division. Confederates firing from behind stacked fence rails initially blunted that assault. Then, misinterpreting an order, a Confederate officer pulled his regiment out of the line. The Federals poured into the vacated spot and loosed volley after volley down the sunken lane. The defenders left in a rush, not stopping until they reached the outskirts of Sharpsburg.

So ended the fighting at Bloody Lane: 5,000 killed or wounded on both sides. The Confederate center had been pierced. The commander there, Gen. D. H. Hill, re-formed an improvised line and, with a mere 200 infantrymen, led a short-lived counterattack. Then he waited for the final Federal effort. For a while, it looked as though a decisive victory lay within McClellan's grasp. "We were

badly whipped, and were only holding our ground by sheer force of desperation," General Longstreet wrote later. But General Sumner's corps had been badly mauled, and he argued against pressing the attack. Concurring, McClellan decided against sending in his reserves to exploit the opportunity.

For the final phase, the scene shifted to the Federal left, to a graceful three-arched stone bridge over Antietam Creek. Ordered to mount a diversionary attack there, the 9th Corps commander, Gen. Ambrose E. Burnside, so bungled the job that Lee was able to withdraw troops all morning from Burnside's front to the Dunker church and Bloody Lane. A depleted brigade of about 550 Georgians repulsed several efforts to storm the bridge (later known as "Burnside's Bridge") before the Federals finally swept across in a rush an hour or so after noon.

By 3 P.M., Burnside had expanded his bridgehead on the other side of Antietam Creek and assembled two divisions, about 10,000 men. That offered a second chance for McClellan to destroy the Army of Northern Virginia. As Burnside advanced on the weakened Confederate right, a dust cloud appeared on the southern horizon. It gradually resolved itself into the van of Gen. A. P. Hill's Light Division coming up from Harpers Ferry.

Hill shook his 3,000 or so infantry into the line of battle and pitched into the left flank of Burnside's advance. This lunge stopped Burnside's attack cold, and the Federals began falling back toward the bridgehead. McClellan still had a fresh corps at hand, the 5th Corps, which he almost committed, but its commander, Gen. Fitz-John Porter, talked him out of it. "Remember," Porter said, "I command the last reserve of the last Army of the Republic."

As twilight descended on Antietam, Lee's lines were intact. Both armies ended up roughly where they had started at daybreak. Some 6,000 men lay dead or dying on the battlefield, and another 17,000 were wounded in what was the most costly single-day's fighting of the entire Civil War.

September 18, 1862: Burial details and stretcher parties went out under flags of truce to gather up the dead and wounded. General McClellan decided against renewing the battle after the expiration of the truce. After dark, Lee's army withdrew silently and recrossed the Potomac River into Virginia.

Tactically, the Battle of Antietam was a draw. Strategically, though, the Union could claim suc-

President Abraham Lincoln is here photographed on a visit to Union general George McClellan (facing Lincoln) and his staff at Antietam, Maryland, before the battle on September 17, 1862.

cess. The Federal victory—or at least the absence of defeat—proved to be a turning point of the Civil War. The outcome at Antietam won President Lincoln the opportunity to convert the war from a limited effort to restore the Union to a crusade to end slavery. Five days after the battle, the president issued the Preliminary Emancipation Proclamation (see Home Fronts, September 22, 1862, p. 242). After January 1, 1863, Lincoln pledged, people held in slavery would be freed.

October 1862: McClellan failed to pursue the Confederates after the Battle of Antietam. "He has got the slows," Lincoln complained of McClellan, who seemed to have lapsed into a state of military somnolence. McClellan did not cross the Potomac until October 26, by which time he had forfeited the president's confidence.

November 7, 1862: Lincoln replaced McClellan with Gen. Ambrose E. Burnside, an Indiana-born West Pointer. Although Burnside's ability was questionable, he had at least one attribute necessary in an army commander. "Burnside could and would fight, even if he did not know how," one of Robert E. Lee's officers remarked.

November 1862 (Fredericksburg Campaign): Burnside reorganized the Army of the Potomac, forming three large "Grand Divisions,"

each consisting of two corps. On November 15, he put the army in motion for Fredericksburg, Virginia, an old colonial center of 5,000 on a sharp southward bend of the Rappahannock River midway between Washington, D.C., and Richmond. Burnside's notion was to shift the line of operations east to Fredericksburg and make a dash for the Confederate capital from there.

Failures of execution hampered Burnside. He needed pontoons to cross the 400-foot-wide Rappahannock River. Through a mix-up, the bridge trains arrived late, giving Lee sufficient time to move the Army of Northern Virginia down the right bank and fortify the hills behind Fredericksburg.

By the end of November, Burnside's six corps, about 120,000 men, were massed opposite Fredericksburg. Lee had 78,000 men and a nearly unassailable position on the high ground commanding the Fredericksburg plain.

December 9–12, 1862: Troops of the Army of the Potomac were issued three days' cooked rations and 60 rounds of ammunition per man— the essential prelude to a battle. Before dawn on December 11, Burnside's engineers began throwing the pontoons across the Rappahannock River—building three bridges at Fredericksburg and another two a couple of miles downstream.

The effect of a 32-pound shell on a Confederate caisson and horses is inspected by Union forces at Fredericksburg, Virginia, May 3, 1863.

Burnside intended to make his main effort from his left, below the city, with two corps under Gen. William B. Franklin. Gen. Edwin Sumner, with another two corps, would make a secondary attack on Marye's Heights.

Lee decided not to contest the crossing, leaving only a brigade of Mississippi troops to harass the pontooniers. The Mississippi troops did their job with such skill that Burnside lost a full day trying to evict them so the bridges could be completed. A heavy cannonade set parts of Fredericksburg on fire. Finally, Federal infantry, using pontoons as assault boats, crossed the Rappahannock River and drove away the Mississippians. The delay allowed Lee to concentrate the right wing of his army under Gen. Thomas J. Jackson on Prospect Hill south of Fredericksburg, opposite Franklin.

The Federals crossed the Rappahannock in force and occupied Fredericksburg on December 12. Burnside spent the balance of the day completing preparations for his two-pronged attack on Lee's army in the hills.

December 13, 1862 (Battle of Fredericksburg): A thick fog blanketed the Fredericksburg plain at first light. As the rising sun burned the fog off, Franklin's infantry advanced on Jackson's front, aiming to storm the

ridge, turn right at the crest, and bowl Lee's entire army off the hills. In Fredericksburg, the first assault brigades spilled out of the city and headed for Marye's Heights.

Franklin scored some initial gains. Gen. George G. Meade's division struck a weak point in Jackson's line and broke through briefly before a Confederate counterattack sealed the breach. In Fredericksburg, General Sumner's troops had no success at all. Confederate riflemen, packed three and four deep behind a stone wall at the base of Marye's Heights, repulsed a series of brigade-strength frontal assaults, covering the snow-dusted plain with Federal dead and wounded.

In the late afternoon, a lull fell over the battlefield. With the failure of Meade's attack, Franklin suspended the battle on his front. His net gain: nothing, and at a cost of 4,800 casualties. Burnside persisted at Fredericksburg, where the Confederate defenses were even stronger. His infantry launched charge after suicidal charge at the stone wall. The 2nd Corps commander, Gen. Darius Couch, watched the unequal battle from the steeple of the Fredericksburg courthouse.

"As they charged," wrote Couch, "the artillery fire would break their formation, and they would get mixed; then they would close up, go forward, receive the withering infantry fire, and those who were able would run to the houses and fight as best they could; then the brigade coming up in succession would do its duty and melt like snow coming down on warm ground."

Gen. Winfield S. Hancock's Federal division lost more than 2,000 men—42 percent of its total strength, the heaviest divisional loss of the Civil War. Still the Federals came on, one brigade after another, until the fall of night mercifully ended the slaughter.

December 14–16, 1862: The Marye's Heights assaults cost Burnside 7,000 killed, wounded, or missing; the Confederates had 1,200 casualties. Overall, the Army of the Potomac lost 12,700 men. Confederate losses were about 5,300 men.

Burnside's corps commanders talked him out of renewing the battle the next day, and the day after. A storm of wind and rain blew through the Rappahannock River valley the night of December 15–16. Under its cover, the Federals withdrew across the river, taking up their pontoons behind them.

In Washington, D.C., the president was inconsolable. "If there is a worse place than Hell," Lincoln said when word of the disaster reached him, "then I am in it." As for Lee, he had hoped for more. "They went as they came—in the night," he wrote his wife. "They suffered heavily as far as the battle went, but it didn't go far enough for me."

WESTERN THEATER

January 1862 (Forts Henry and Donelson Campaign): From Cairo, Illinois, Gen. Ulysses S. Grant prepared a waterborne expedition into Kentucky and Tennessee, the first step in the Union's strategic penetration of the South. An advance down the Tennessee and Cumberland Rivers would open up invasion routes into the Southern heartland and turn the Confederates' lightly held 500-mile defensive line in Kentucky, forcing the Confederates to abandon the state.

Grant, with 15,000 men in three divisions, proposed to advance in company with a seven-gunboat flotilla under Flag Officer Andrew Foote. In the first phase of the campaign, Grant intended to capture Fort Henry on the Tennessee River, a half-finished strongpoint in Tennessee that guarded the river and a railroad trestle on the

Memphis & Charleston Railroad line.

February 5–6, 1862 (Fort Henry): The transports landed Grant's army a few miles north of Fort Henry. Heavy rains had turned the roads to mud and so swollen the Tennessee River that Grant asked Foote to attack with his gunboats before the infantry advanced.

At midday on February 6, Foote opened the bombardment from his flagship, the *Cincinnati.* Despite rising waters that threatened to flood the defenders, Fort Henry's 17 guns returned fire. But Fort Henry's guns made little impression on the armored carapaces of Foote's gunboats. After a two-hour exchange, a white flag was raised over the fort. Foote sent in a small boat to accept the surrender.

Most of Fort Henry's garrison escaped and marched overland 12 miles to Fort Donelson on the Cumberland River. The loss of Fort Henry forced the Confederate commander, Gen. Albert Sidney Johnston, to retreat southward from Bowling Green, Kentucky, to Nashville, the Tennessee capital. Johnston, however, decided to try to hold Fort Donelson. With reinforcements, he had some 12,500 men available for the task.

February 12–16, 1862 (Fort Donelson): Grant marched from Fort Henry on February 12. After launching a series of probing attacks on the outer Fort Donelson defenses on February 13, he decided to wait for Foote's gunboats, cut over to the mouth of the Cumberland River, then steam 50 miles up the Cumberland. The weather, from being bright and mild, turned miserable. The wind blew hard out of the north, bringing rain, sleet, and snow. Troops, who had discarded their overcoats and blankets during the warm spell, suffered keenly from the cold.

The gunboats arrived on February 14 to find Fort Donelson a much tougher proposition than Fort Henry was. Nine great guns dug into the high bluffs poured fire onto the flotilla. One after another, the gunboats were disabled or driven off. The *St. Louis* alone counted 57 hits. Ashore, Grant settled in for a siege.

Inside Fort Donelson, the senior Confederate officers, Gen. John Floyd, Gen. Gideon Pillow, and Gen. Simon Bolivar Buckner, resolved to try a breakout. The Confederates enjoyed initial success the morning of February 15, driving a wedge into the siege lines and opening a potential route of withdrawal southward. But the three commanders could not agree on how to

This engraving depicts the attack by Gen. Ulysses S. Grant's forces on Fort Henry in February 1862. With the capture of that fort at the Tennessee and Cumberland Rivers and the capture of nearby Fort Donelson, the Union forces were able to launch their campaign to open the Mississippi River to the Union fleet.

exploit the opening. Grant personally directed a counterattack that sealed off the escape route. By evening, the Federals had retaken all the lost ground.

On the night of February 15, Floyd, a former U.S. war secretary (1857–1860) who feared he would be tried for treason if captured, and Pillow turned over the Fort Donelson command to Buckner and escaped. The cavalry commander, Gen. Nathan Bedford Forrest, also made good his escape, with a small party of troopers and infantry.

Buckner and Grant had been friends in the prewar U.S. Army, and Buckner may have expected some show of generosity from the Union commander. However, Grant's reply to Buckner's request for surrender terms was stern. "No terms except unconditional and immediate surrender can be accepted," Grant wrote. "I propose to move immediately on your works." Buckner had no choice but to comply.

The February 16 surrender of the 13,000-man Fort Donelson garrison was the biggest Union victory of the war to date. The capture of Fort Donelson forced the Confederates to evacuate Nashville (which in late February became the first rebel state capital to fall), and Columbus, Kentucky, the Mississippi River stronghold. Johnston's army eventually retreated all the way to Corinth, Mississippi, a railroad junction a few miles below the Tennessee line.

March 1862 (Shiloh Campaign): By the third week of March, Grant's Army of the Mississippi had advanced southward to Pittsburg Landing on the Tennessee River 20 miles north of Corinth, Mississippi. There, Grant awaited the arrival of a second Union column advancing from Nashville under Gen. Don Carlos Buell. In Corinth, the Confederate army rested and made good its losses, while Gen. Albert Johnston and his new second in command, Gen. Pierre G. T. Beauregard, the hero of Fort Sumter and Bull Run, planned a counteroffensive to regain Tennessee. Johnston, with about 40,000 men, decided to attack Grant's army before Buell's slow-moving Army of the Ohio could arrive.

April 3–5, 1862: Johnston's army marched north out of Corinth during the afternoon of April 4. Johnston planned a surprise attack that would cut off Grant's army from the Tennessee River and pin it against Owl Creek, where it could be cut to pieces before General Buell turned up.

Outposts of Gen. William T. Sherman's division at Pittsburg Landing reported contact with enemy patrols on April 4 and 5, but Sherman dismissed that as trivial. "I do not apprehend anything like an attack on our position," he told Grant. Grant's five divisions lay exposed in their camps; Grant had decided not to order the men to entrench.

April 6–7, 1862 (Battle of Shiloh): The Confederates burst out of the woods near Shiloh church (in southwestern Tennessee) before dawn on April 6 and roared through Grant's Federal camps, driving hundreds of panicked Federals toward the Tennessee River. But Johnston's attack soon lost cohesion, and strong pockets of Union resistance began to form. Sherman managed to keep his division intact, and on the left center, Gen. Benjamin Prentiss's division resisted so fiercely that the Confederates dubbed his strong point the "hornet's nest."

Grant, who had been 9 miles downstream conferring with Buell when the battle exploded on his unsuspecting army, hurried back to Pittsburg Landing and at once made for the front. He found heavy fighting in progress along much of a 6-mile line that ran from the Tennessee River on the left to Owl Creek around to the right.

Grant ordered Prentiss, with 4,500 men, to hold his position at all costs. In one of the fiercest actions of the Civil War, Prentiss's command repulsed 11 distinct Confederate charges. By late afternoon, the Confederates had massed 60 field guns to blast the Federals out. The barrage blew in "like a mighty hurricane," an Iowa lieutenant recalled, "sweeping everything before it." The last charge overwhelmed Prentiss. His line collapsing around him, he surrendered the position and about 2,500 survivors at 5:30 in the afternoon.

But Prentiss's stand had given Grant's other four divisions time to fall back and regroup along a strong defensive line overlooking Pittsburg Landing. Grant expected an evening attack, but at around 6 o'clock Beauregard called off the battle. He had succeeded Johnston, who had bled to death on the battlefield earlier in the day after a stray bullet cut an artery in his leg.

Beauregard went to bed confident he had won the Battle of Shiloh. "I thought I had General Grant just where I wanted him and could finish him up in the morning," he wrote later. His optimism proved misplaced. Grant ignored suggestions from some of his officers that he withdraw. "Retreat? No," he said. "I propose to attack at daylight and whip them." The first of Buell's regiments had arrived in late afternoon. Grant spent a rainy, windy night planning his attack and reorganizing his forces, now augmented by 25,000 fresh troops.

Grant delivered his counterstroke at 7:30 A.M. on April 7, the blue infantry advancing over the dead and wounded of the day before. The advance carried past Bloody Pond, stained with the blood of the wounded who had crawled to its edge to drink, and through a peach orchard carpeted with shredded and blood-stained peach blossom petals. Heavy fighting boiled up around Shiloh church. By midafternoon, recognizing that reinforcements from across the Mississippi River in Arkansas would not reach him in time, Beauregard broke off the battle and retreated toward Corinth.

The Battle of Shiloh is known as a "soldier's battle"—one in which individual courage and initiative, rather than generalship, determine the outcome. Certainly, the ordinary soldiers of both sides suffered heavily. Federal casualties over the two days of fighting were more than 13,000 killed, wounded, or missing. Confederate losses were 10,600. Shiloh was a clear Union victory. Grant remained in possession of the battlefield; Beauregard fell back, leaving his wounded behind. And the Battle of Shiloh brought the Union another step closer to controlling the Mississippi River and splitting the Confederacy in two.

Grant's reputation temporarily plummeted after Shiloh. His army had been surprised; he had been miles away when the Confederates attacked; some said he had been drunk. In Washington, Lincoln heard the rumors and stood by Grant. "I can't spare this man," the president said. "He fights."

April–May 1862: Gen. Henry Halleck arrived to take command of the combined forces of Grant and Buell. Halleck's plan was to push southward toward Corinth, Mississippi. By the end of April, Halleck had 100,000 men under his command. As the Federals approached Corinth, skirmishing in the area grew fiercer and more frequent. At the end of May, Beauregard ordered Corinth abandoned and withdrew to Tupelo, Mississippi.

July 1862: After Shiloh and Corinth, General Buell's army moved on the Tennessee communications center of Chattanooga. Confederate cavalry general John Hunt Morgan's first Kentucky raid had the object of deranging General Buell's supply lines.

Morgan left Knoxville, Tennessee, with 800 troopers on July 4, struck Union garrisons and depots in several Kentucky towns, and returned to his base around August 1. In 24 days, Morgan's horsemen covered a thousand miles and captured (and swiftly paroled) 1,200 Federals. Morgan lost about 100 men. The raid shook Union morale and led to renewed criticism of Buell's generalship.

July 11, 1862: President Lincoln summoned General Halleck, who claimed credit for maneuvering the Confederates out of Corinth, to Washington, D.C., to become commander of the Union Army. In practice, Halleck functioned more as a chief of staff than as a warlord, and Lincoln's search for a winning general did not end until 1864, when Gen. Ulysses S. Grant came east (see Eastern Theater, March 1864, p. 257).

July 13–27, 1862: Confederate cavalry raider Gen. Nathan Bedford Forrest struck the Union depot at Murfreesboro, Tennessee, capturing most of the 1,000-man U.S. garrison and supplies valued at $1 million.

Forrest's operations were concurrent with Morgan's in Kentucky and wreaked even greater havoc in the Federal rear. Forrest's 1,000 troopers destroyed railroad bridges south of Nashville and put the Nashville-Stevenson Railroad out of action for a full week (July 20–27), further delaying Buell.

August–September 1862 (Bragg's Invasion of Kentucky): Two Confederate commanders, Gen. Braxton Bragg and Gen. Edmund Kirby Smith, arranged to cooperate in a counteroffensive against Union forces in Tennessee and Kentucky. The plan called for Bragg to maneuver Buell out of middle Tennessee and Smith to advance into eastern Kentucky, where Bragg would eventually join him.

Smith left Knoxville, Tennessee, on August 14 with three divisions, about 9,000 men. On August 30, he virtually annihilated an inexperienced Union force of about 6,500 at Richmond, Kentucky. Federal losses were more than 5,300, including 4,300 taken prisoner; Confederate casualties were 450 killed or wounded. The Union survivors retreated toward Louisville; Smith occupied Lexington on September 1.

Bragg launched his Kentucky invasion with two corps, roughly 30,000 men, on August 28. By mid-September he had reached Munfordville, Kentucky, astride Buell's lines of communication. Disposing his army around Bardstown later in September, Bragg turned to political matters and to recruiting among what he considered to be a strongly pro-Confederate population. On October 4 in Frankfort, the state capital, he appointed Richard Hawes provisional Confederate governor of Kentucky. As it happened, Kentucky declined to join the Confederacy, so Bragg did not gain many recruits.

Buell, meanwhile, withdrew northward through Nashville, reaching Louisville, Kentucky, on September 29, where he added some 40,000 new troops, many of them untrained, to his army. On October 1, Buell left Louisville to find and attack Bragg.

October 3–4, 1862 (Battle of Corinth): In northern Mississippi, Confederate forces under Gen. Earl Van Dorn opened the Battle of Corinth with a morning attack that drove the Federals under Gen. William Rosecrans back to their inner line of breastworks. After several repulses, Van Dorn broke off the engagement in midafternoon and withdrew to the west.

On October 4, Rosecrans set out in pursuit of Van Dorn. The Confederates managed to shake free, however, and reach the safety of Holly Springs. Van Dorn suffered about 4,200 killed, wounded, or missing from his army of 22,000 during the battle and retreat. Rosecrans's casualties were 2,500 of 21,000 engaged. Though Grant faulted Rosecrans for failing to destroy Van Dorn, Corinth proved to be a considerable strategic victory for the Union, allowing the important Vicksburg campaign to get under way.

October 8, 1862 (Battle of Perryville): After a morning's skirmishing, Confederate general Benjamin F. Cheatham opened the Battle of Perryville in Kentucky (also known as Chaplin Hills) at around two o'clock with an assault on the left flank of Buell's army. A green Federal brigade collapsed at first contact, but steadier troops stabilized the line.

A Confederate attack led by Gen. Simon B. Buckner sought to exploit a weak spot between two Federal corps. But Gen. Philip H. Sheridan's division held its ground and repulsed the attack. Then Sheridan delivered a counterattack that drove the Confederates back through Perryville.

To Sheridan's left, a two-brigade counterattack regained ground the Confederates had taken at the outset of the battle.

Though Buell's headquarters lay less than 3 miles away, an "acoustic shadow" (a phenomenon in which some unusual feature of the terrain or atmosphere prevents those close to a battle from hearing its noise) prevented him from hearing the sounds of the fighting. Buell thus lost an opportunity to commit overwhelming forces and achieve a decisive victory. Bragg retreated into eastern Tennessee, leaving his dead and wounded behind. Union casualties exceeded 4,200; Bragg's losses were about 3,400. Lincoln relieved Buell of command on October 24 for tardiness in pursuing Bragg, who managed a successful retreat from Kentucky.

October 1862: In the wake of Bragg's defeat at Perryville, Gen. John H. Morgan won permission for a second raid behind Union lines in Kentucky. On October 18, his 1,800 troopers routed Union cavalry at Lexington and took 125 prisoners. Morgan captured several minor Union outposts and burned many railroad bridges before returning to his base at Gallatin, Tennessee.

December 1862: Grant's long, arduous campaign against the Mississippi River fortress of Vicksburg, Mississippi, began with the overland march of some 40,000 men south from Corinth along the line of the Mississippi Central Railroad. At the same time, Gen. William T. Sherman, with 32,000 men, moved by river from Memphis to threaten Chickasaw Bluffs above Vicksburg.

Confederate cavalry under Generals Van Dorn and Forrest halted Grant's overland campaign by choking off Grant's supplies. Van Dorn's cavalry captured Grant's advance base at Holly Springs, Mississippi, on December 20, taking 1,500 prisoners and supplies worth more than $1 million. Meanwhile, Forrest's troops wrecked some 60 miles of railroad north of Jackson, Tennessee.

Sherman's waterborne expedition had no more success. Van Dorn's raids temporarily cut communications between Grant and Sherman, and Sherman went ahead with his attacks on the Chickasaw Bluffs strong point, not knowing Grant had turned back. The defenders easily repulsed Sherman's attacks of December 28 and 29, inflicting 1,700 casualties. "I reached Vicksburg at the time appointed," Sherman reported to his chief, "landed, assaulted, and failed."

December 21–31, 1862 (Stones River Campaign): After the Perryville defeat and the retreat from Kentucky, Bragg's army, styled the Army of Tennessee, concentrated near Murfreesboro, Tennessee. General Rosecrans, with the Army of the Cumberland, lay in camps at Nashville to the north.

General Morgan's third raid of 1862 aimed to disrupt Rosecrans's communications. With 4,000 troopers, Morgan left Alexandria, Tennessee, four days before Christmas, crossed into Kentucky, and struck the Louisville & Nashville Railroad near Munfordville, Kentucky. Eluding pursuit, Morgan returned to Columbia, Tennessee, arriving on the first day of the new year after taking nearly 1,900 prisoners and destroying property and supplies worth $2 million.

December 31, 1862 (Battle of Stones River): General Rosecrans took advantage of the absence of Confederate cavalry (Forrest and Morgan were both off on raids) to march on General Bragg. Learning of Rosecrans's move, Bragg concentrated his forces along Stones River near Murfreesboro and prepared to do battle.

The Battle of Stones River (also known as the Battle of Murfreesboro) opened at dawn on the last day of 1862, with a Confederate attack on Maj. Gen. Alexander McCook's corps on the right of Rosecrans's army. The battle surged back and forth inconclusively for several hours. By noon, though, the Federal right had been bent back, and Bragg called in fresh troops for what he hoped would be a knockout punch.

Fierce fighting boiled up during the afternoon in the Round Forest, a grove of oaks the Federals dubbed "Hell's half acre." Bragg made a last effort late in the afternoon of December 31, throwing four fresh brigades into the Round Forest. But the Union line held, and toward dusk a counterattack drove the Confederates back.

Rosecrans hesitated, then decided to hold the field overnight and to attack if Bragg did not hit him first. After a quiet New Year's Day, the battle resumed on January 2, 1863 (see Battles and Campaigns of 1863, pp. 247-248).

TRANS-MISSISSIPPI THEATER

February 21, 1862 (Battle of Valverde): The small Confederate Army of New Mexico under Gen. Henry Hopkins Sibley advanced up the Rio Grande early in 1862, threw itself athwart the

Union line of communications, and forced Gen. E. R. S. Canby's Federal garrison at Fort Craig to fight.

The battle opened about 8 o'clock in the morning with light skirmishing. By noon, the main event was well under way. Canby failed in an attempt to envelop Sibley's left, but the Federals repulsed a rebel counterattack. Shortly before sundown, Sibley's frontal assault routed the Federals. Canby lost some 260 men of 3,800 engaged. Sibley's losses were fewer than 200 of 2,600 in the battle.

February–March 1862: In Missouri, the Union Army of the Southwest under Gen. Samuel Curtis moved on Springfield and the winter camps of Confederate general Sterling Price. Price withdrew his 8,000-strong command into northwestern Arkansas, where he intended to unite with troops under Gen. Ben McCulloch. In early March, the overall Confederate commander, Gen. Earl Van Dorn, took charge of both contingents, totaling 17,000 men, and prepared to attack Curtis.

Curtis, meanwhile, learned from the scout "Wild Bill" Hickok that the Confederates were about to strike. Curtis took up a defensive position near Pea Ridge in northern Arkansas. By the night of March 6, Curtis's troops lay in line of battle on high ground facing south, toward the approaching enemy.

March 7–8, 1862 (Battle of Pea Ridge): A long march to Pea Ridge in cold, wet weather had tired the Confederates. Van Dorn began the operation at dawn on March 7. The Federals, though, quickly detected Van Dorn's complicated plan of battle, which involved a flank movement around Curtis's left. Curtis's infantry faced about and held off the Confederate thrust.

On the opposite end of the line, skirmishing broke out before 7 o'clock northeast of Elkhorn Tavern (the alternate name for the battle), where the Federals clashed with Texas troops and a contingent of several thousand Indians under Brig. Gen. Stand Watie. The fighting gradually built in intensity and continued, though inconclusively, for much of the day.

Though his plans had miscarried, Van Dorn decided to renew the battle on March 8. Overnight, Curtis determined to go on the attack. Two Federal divisions under Gen. Fritz Sigel struck from the left and drove the Confederates off the ridge. A second attack from the right completed the rout and sent Van Dorn in full retreat south-

ward to the Arkansas River. Federal casualties approached 1,400 of 11,250 in the battle. The Confederates lost about 800 men out of the 14,000 engaged in the battle.

March–April 1862 (New Madrid and Island No. 10): Union expeditions sought to capture the Confederate strong points at New Madrid, Missouri, and on Island No. 10 that blocked passage on the Mississippi River. On March 3, Gen. John Pope reached New Madrid with the newly formed Army of the Mississippi and began preparations for a siege. On March 13, the Confederate garrison of 5,000 withdrew across the river to avoid being cut off, leaving $1 million in military stores behind.

Pope decided to send his army across the river south of New Madrid, using a newly dug canal through the swamps to bypass Island No. 10's strong defenses. A brigade-sized force blocked the Confederate line of retreat south of the island on April 7. That forced the surrender of the entire garrison of some 3,500 Confederates, many of them ill.

Pope's operations opened a long stretch of the Mississippi River. His success brought him to the attention of President Lincoln, who summoned him to take charge of Union forces around Washington, D.C., in mid-1862. Pope's brief ascendancy ended with his humbling at the Second Battle of Bull Run in late August (see Eastern Theater, July-August 1862, p. 228).

March–May 1862: After the Battle of Valverde, Sibley continued his campaign to drive the Federals out of New Mexico. He took the U.S. depot at Santa Fe on March 23 and advanced eastward toward Fort Union 60 miles distant. Skirmishes at Johnson's Ranch and Glorieta on March 26 and 28 were inconclusive. Meanwhile, Federal forces were combining against Sibley. Determining that he lacked the strength to win, Sibley decided to withdraw. Canby, commanding the Union forces, did not pursue aggressively, and Sibley retreated with the remains of his small army all the way to San Antonio, Texas.

August 17–September 23, 1862 (Sioux Uprising): In the Minnesota Territory, Sioux Indian tribes, protesting living conditions on their reservation, rose in revolt. Over several weeks, insurgent Sioux killed more than 400 whites. By late September, U.S. troops under Gen. Henry Hastings Sibley had managed to quell the uprising and arrest the rebel leaders (see 19th Century

Trans-Mississippi Wars, Sioux Upsrising in Minnesota, pp. 310-313).

November 28, 1862: A 5,000-strong Union force under Gen. James Blunt surprised some 8,000 enemy cavalry at Cane Hill, Arkansas, and drove the Confederates southward into the Boston Mountains. Federal losses were about 40; Confederate casualties exceeded 400.

December 7, 1862 (Battle of Prairie Grove): In early December, a Confederate army of 11,000 under Gen. Thomas Hindman advanced north toward Cane Hill in search of Blunt's contingent. Blunt learned of the movement and sent out a call for help. As reinforcements under Gen. Francis Herron began arriving late on December 6, Hindman attempted to swing around Blunt and deal first with the relief column.

Hindman attacked at Prairie Grove at dawn on December 7, but soon broke off the battle and settled into a defensive position. Despite some desertions, the Confederates managed to repulse several Union assaults. During the afternoon, however, Blunt marched to the support of Herron and pitched into Hindman's left. The Confederates managed to hold their ground until nightfall, when they withdrew. Confederate casualties were about 1,300, including some who died of exposure. Federal losses were 1,250.

NAVAL THEATER

January 30, 1862: Swedish-born ship designer John Ericsson launched the revolutionary ironclad USS *Monitor* at Greenpoint, Long Island (now part of Brooklyn, New York). The vessel, with its two 11-inch great guns in a unique revolving turret, resembled nothing else afloat—it looked like "a cheese box on a raft," one observer said. The heavily armored vessel, 172 feet long and 1,200 tons, carried a crew of 58.

February–July 1862: A 65-vessel Union armada entered Pamlico Sound, North Carolina, on February 7, for the start of the amphibious operation known as Burnside's Expedition to North Carolina, named for the land forces commander, Gen. Ambrose E. Burnside.

The Navy opened the bombardment of the first objective, Roanoke Island, North Carolina, before noon on February 7. Burnside's troops landed on the island during the afternoon and evening. Burnside's infantry overwhelmed the 2,500 Confederates and captured the position the next day. On February 10, Union gunboats annihilated a Confederate flotilla at Elizabeth City, North Carolina.

Burnside then advanced on New Bern, North Carolina, which fell to the Federals on March 14. After a 15-day siege, Union forces captured Beaufort, North Carolina, on April 26. In addition, several inland expeditions were launched from New Bern. In early July, Burnside marched to Virginia with 7,500 men to reinforce McClellan's forces. A Federal occupation force of 7,500 settled in to hold and defend the territory gained in North Carolina.

March 8–9, 1862 (Monitor vs. Merrimack): The Confederate navy's ironclad *Virginia* (formerly the USS *Merrimack*, a captured and rebuilt U.S. Navy steam frigate) attacked a Union squadron of wooden-hulled vessels in Hampton Roads off the coast of Virginia. The *Virginia* destroyed the sailing sloop USS *Cumberland* and the frigate USS *Congress* with no harm to itself.

The newly built Union ironclad USS *Monitor* reached Hampton Roads during the night of March 8 and tied up alongside the wooden-hulled USS *Minnesota* early on March 9. "We thought at first it was a raft on which one of the *Minnesota*'s boilers was being taken ashore for repairs," one of the *Virginia*'s officers later said. In fact, the small warship was more than a match for the Confederate ironclad.

In history's first encounter between ironclad ships, the *Monitor* and the *Merrimack* (as the *Virginia* has become known in history) blasted each other for four hours, neither able to inflict any serious damage on the other. Finally, the *Merrimack* scored a lucky hit on her adversary's pilothouse, temporarily blinding her captain. The battle thus ended in a draw. But the *Merrimack* returned to Norfolk and did no further damage to the Federal fleet. Stranded in Norfolk by Union general George McClellan's advance up the Virginia peninsula, the *Merrimack*'s crew blew up the ship on May 11, 1862.

April–May 1862: Flag Officer David G. Farragut's flotilla of 8 steam sloops, 1 sailing sloop, 14 gunboats, and 19 mortar schooners prepared to move up the Mississippi River to attack the commercial and strategic center of New Orleans. By April 18, Farragut had his fleet over the sandbars and in the river just downstream of Forts Jackson and St. Philip 90 miles below the

The battle between the ironclad ships, the Confederate **Merrimack** *(left) and the Union's* **Monitor** *(right) on March 9, 1862 off Hampton Roads, Virginia, ended with no clear winner.*

city. From there, the mortar vessels commenced a week-long bombardment in which nearly 3,000 shells fell on the Confederate forts.

The mortar attack did little damage, however, and Farragut determined to run the ships past the forts. At 2 A.M. on April 24, he ordered the fleet to weigh anchor. Protected by chains hung overside to protect the engines and powder stores, with tubs of brown river water on deck to douse fires, the Union warships steamed ahead in single file, with Farragut's flagship USS *Hartford* in front. The Confederates returned a heavy fire from some 75 guns, but the fleet got through, though at a cost of 37 dead and 149 wounded.

The *Hartford* glided up to the quayside in New Orleans around one o'clock in the afternoon of April 25. Farragut sent two officers through the Crescent City's streets to city hall to demand surrender. The Confederate commander had withdrawn his 4,000 troops before the fleet's arrival; the city formally surrendered on April 29. On May 1, the first of 18,000 Federal troops arrived to occupy New Orleans.

May 10, 1862: At Plum Run Bend on the Mississippi River, Confederate gunboats attacked a stronger Union flotilla, sinking two ironclads. The better armed and armored Federal vessels regrouped, however, and their steady fire forced the Confederate squadron under Capt. James Montgomery to retreat downriver to the safety of Memphis, Tennessee.

May 15, 1862: As part of General McClellan's Peninsular Campaign, Union gunboats attacked the Confederate strong point of Drewry's Bluff on the James River below Richmond, Virginia. A heavy Confederate response turned back the flotilla, which included the USS *Monitor*.

May 16, 1862: Gen. Benjamin Butler, commanding the occupation forces of New Orleans found the citizens to be an unruly and rebellious lot. He acted swiftly to quell what he viewed as disloyalty. He issued his controversial Woman Order. It read, in part: "As the officers and soldiers of the United States have been subjected to repeated insults from the women (calling themselves ladies) of New Orleans…when any female shall…show contempt for the United States, she shall be regarded as a woman of the town plying her avocation."

May–July 1862: After taking New Orleans, Farragut set his sights on the Mississippi River fortress of Vicksburg, Mississippi. Steaming upriver virtually unopposed, Farragut shelled the fortress when the defenders rejected his surrender demand. A weeklong (June 20–27) bombardment by the mortar schooners failed to dislodge

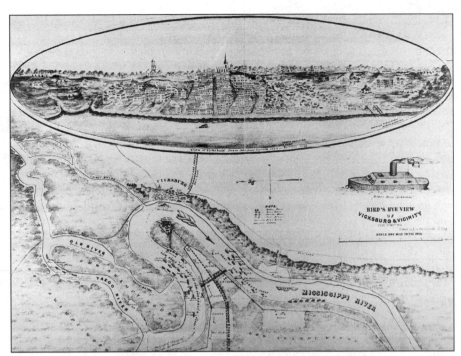

This map and view show Vicksburg, Mississippi, on July 15 and 16, 1862. That was at a time when Adm. David Farragut, fresh from his capture of New Orleans, brought his fleet up and was heavily bombarding Vicksburg. Although he inflicted some damage and casualties, the Confederates held out. A year later, a new Federal campaign took Vicksburg.

the Confederates. A second Federal river fleet, moving south from Memphis, Tennessee, linked up with Farragut for a second long bombardment (July 12–26). As the summer advanced, the water level in the Mississippi River dropped, threatening to strand Farragut's fleet. He called off the operation at the end of July and bumped back through the shallows to New Orleans.

June 6, 1862: Union gunboats advancing on Memphis, Tennessee, attacked and defeated Montgomery's heavily outgunned river flotilla. Only one Confederate vessel managed to escape the early-morning debacle. At noon, U.S. forces accepted the Confederate surrender of Memphis.

July 29, 1862: The Confederate raider *Alabama* sailed from Liverpool, England, despite U.S. efforts to detain it. The *Alabama*, Comdr. Raphael Semmes commanding, had orders to attack and destroy Union commerce on the high seas.

December 30, 1862: The USS *Monitor* sank in a storm off Cape Hatteras, North Carolina. Sixteen officers and enlisted men drowned; another warship, the USS *Rhode Island*, rescued 47 of the *Monitor*'s crew.

HOME FRONTS

January 1862: On January 11, President Lincoln accepted the resignation of his war secretary, Simon Cameron, who had been widely accused of incompetence, mismanagement, and graft—or at least of tolerating graft—in the administration of the War Department. On January 13, Lincoln appointed Edwin M. Stanton, a former U.S. attorney general, as Cameron's successor. The Senate confirmed Stanton's appointment on January 15.

February 18–22, 1862: In Richmond, Virginia, the First Congress of the Confederate States of America convened. The Provisional Congress, the rebel's legislative branch for nearly a year, had been dismissed on February 17.

On February 22, the Confederacy inaugurated Jefferson Davis as president. (He had governed as provisional president.) "We are in arms to renew such sacrifices as our fathers made to the holy cause of constitutional liberty," Davis said in his inaugural.

February–March 1862: In Richmond on

February 27, the Confederate Congress authorized President Davis to suspend habeas corpus. (Lincoln had authorized the same on July 2, 1861.) On March 1, Confederate authorities arrested former Virginia congressman John Minor Botts, who had claimed neutrality in the conflict, and others on charges of treason. One of those arrested, the Rev. Alden Bosserman, a Universalist minister, had prayed in public for an end to "this unholy rebellion."

March 1862: In Washington, President Lincoln initiated discussions of potential ways to end slavery. In a message to Congress on March 6, he asked for the states' cooperation in abolishing slavery. On March 14, he justified Federal compensation to slaveholders by arguing that it would be cheaper to buy slaves' freedom than to pay for "the indefinite prosecution of the war." On March 24, he wrote journalist Horace Greeley: "We should urge [emancipation] persuasively, and not menacingly, upon the South."

April 1862: On April 4, the U.S. Senate approved a bill to abolish slavery in the District of Columbia. On April 11, the House of Representatives passed legislation calling for gradual abolition in the district. On April 16, President Lincoln signed the measure prohibiting slavery in the capital region.

April 16, 1862: In Richmond, Virginia, President Davis approved a military draft in the Confederacy, North America's first conscription act. The bill made all males 18 to 35 liable for service. In conflict with the views of many Southerners, who were strong proponents of states' rights, the draft remained controversial throughout the life of the Confederacy. According to some estimates, fully half the draftees never reported for duty.

Summer 1862: Despite the absence of thousands of farmers, who were in the Army, the North produced more wheat in 1862 than the entire United States had produced in 1859, which had been a record year. Increasingly, women took the place of men who were fighting in the Civil War. "Our hired man left to enlist just as the corn planting commenced, so I shouldered the hoe," an Iowa woman wrote. "I guess my services are as good as his."

July 1, 1862: Lincoln signed a federal income tax into law. Unlike the 1861 tax measure, the new law actually took effect. To pay for the war effort, the tax law levied a tax of 3 percent on incomes from $600 to $10,000 and 5 percent on incomes greater than $10,000.

July 17, 1862: Lincoln signed the Second Confiscation Act, which provided for the freedom of runaway slaves coming into Federal jurisdiction from outside the Union.

July 22, 1862: The War Department empowered U.S. forces to employ anyone of African descent as paid laborers.

August 19, 1862: Horace Greeley, editor of the influential *New York Tribune*, published "The Prayer of Twenty Millions," his appeal for the end of slavery that sharply criticized Lincoln's policy. "All attempts to put down the Rebellion and at the same time uphold its inciting cause are preposterous and futile," wrote Greeley.

Three days later, Lincoln responded, saying his chief objective was to preserve the Union. "If I could save the Union without freeing *any* slave I would do it, and if I could save it by freeing *all* the slaves I would do it."

August 25, 1862: War Secretary Stanton authorized the recruitment and enlistment of as many as 5,000 black soldiers, including former slaves.

September 22, 1862: Lincoln issued the Preliminary Emancipation Proclamation, freeing all slaves held in areas still in rebellion, effective January 1, 1863.

September 24, 1862: In response to opposition to state drafts for militia service, President Lincoln suspended the writ of habeas corpus for anyone found guilty of "discouraging volunteer enlistments" and other "disloyal practices." That breach of civil liberties meant that anyone suspected of disloyalty could be arrested and held without trial for an indefinite period. Over a two-year period, Federal agents made 13,000 such arrests—including one man who was jailed for "hurrahing for Jeff Davis."

October 11, 1862: In Richmond, the Confederate government amended the draft law to exempt anyone owning more than 20 slaves from military service. That widely unpopular measure, aimed at protecting women and children at home on large plantations, gave rise among Southerners to the bitter view that the war had become "a rich man's war and a poor man's fight."

November 4, 1862: Democrats, some of whom called for a negotiated end to the war, made broad gains in midterm elections in the North. New Yorkers elected Democrat Horatio Seymour governor. Democrats made gains in New Jersey, Illinois, and Wisconsin as well. Republicans did, however, retain control of the U.S. House of Representatives.

December 1, 1862: In his address to mark the opening of the third session of the 37th Congress, President Lincoln discussed proposed constitutional amendments involving slavery, including one that would have compensated slaveholders. Lincoln said, "In *giving* freedom to the *slave*, we *assure* freedom to the free."

INTERNATIONAL DEVELOPMENTS

January 30–31, 1862: The Confederate commissioners Mason and Slidell, principal figures in the *Trent* affair, arrived in England to complete their interrupted voyage. On January 31, Queen Victoria again emphasized the British policy of neutrality in the American Civil War.

BATTLES AND CAMPAIGNS: 1863

In 1863, an eventful year, Union armies fought and won the two most decisive battles of the Civil War, Gettysburg in the eastern theater and Vicksburg in the western theater. By year's end, Confederate forces were everywhere on the defensive, though it would require another 16 months of bloodletting to bring the conflict to an end. The war also continued in the naval theater.

In 1863 too, Lincoln's Emancipation Proclamation took effect, and black troops saw extensive combat. In the South, shortages of food and other necessities were increasingly felt as the Union blockade clamped down.

EASTERN THEATER

January 1863: Only a month after his repulse at Fredericksburg, Virginia, Gen. Ambrose E. Burnside planned another Union offensive across the Rappahannock River in an effort to outflank Gen. Robert E. Lee's Army of Northern Virginia.

Union troops moved out on January 20, just as heavy rains set in, turning the roads to ooze. Burnside called off the march, dubbed the "Mud March" even in official reports, on January 23.

The episode further demoralized the Army of the Potomac. Lincoln dismissed Burnside and, on January 26, replaced him with Gen. Joseph Hooker, known as "Fighting Joe."

March 8, 1863: In a daring raid, Confederate irregulars under Capt. John Singleton Mosby captured Union general E. H. Stoughton in his bed at his headquarters in Fairfax courthouse in Virginia. Along with prisoners, Mosby's men seized 58 horses and quantities of arms and equipment.

March 17, 1863: A Federal cavalry division under Gen. William W. Averell, moving toward the vital Orange & Alexandria Railroad, clashed with some 800 Confederate troopers at Kelly's Ford on the Rapidan River in Virginia. Averell withdrew in the evening after a daylong inconclusive battle. He lost 78 men; Confederate casualties were 133 killed, wounded, or missing.

April–May 1863 (Suffolk Campaign): Lee sent Gen. James Longstreet with two divisions into coastal Virginia to block a possible Federal advance on Richmond from Fort Monroe. When the Federal offensive did not materialize, Longstreet surrounded Suffolk, Virginia, held by 15,000 Union troops. When reinforcements brought the Union troops in Suffolk to 25,000, Longstreet decided against attacking the town. Instead, he foraged the rich surrounding country for supplies.

Late April 1863 (Chancellorsville Campaign): With the arrival of spring, Gen. Joseph Hooker planned a complicated campaign that he predicted would achieve the destruction of the Army of Northern Virginia. "My plans are perfect," Hooker announced, "and when I start to carry them out, may God have mercy on Bobby Lee; for I shall have none." Hooker conceived a wide turning movement to pry Lee out of his powerful Fredericksburg defenses and into the open field.

On April 27, three corps of the Army of the Potomac broke camp and marched for the Rappahannock and Rapidan fords. On April 30, 70,000 Union troops arrived on Lee's flank and rear at the crossroads hamlet of Chancellorsville, Virginia, near the southern edge of the dark, forbidding 120-square-mile tangle of vine, briar, and second-growth forest known as the Wilderness. Two more Federal corps crossed the Rappahannock River below Fredericksburg, threatening Confederate positions there.

Lee, however, puzzled out Hooker's scheme in time to counter it, guessing correctly that the main effort would come from the north. Though still shorthanded after the detachment of Longstreet to Suffolk, Lee left 10,000 troops in

Fredericksburg and put the balance, about 45,000 men, in motion toward Chancellorsville.

May 1–6, 1863 (Battle of Chancellorsville): Advance elements of the two armies collided east of the Chancellorsville crossroads around noon on May 1. The initial contact seemed to deflate Hooker. He sent word at once for his lead divisions to suspend the advance and pull back to the hamlet. Hooker thus chose to fight on the defensive and let the initiative pass to Lee.

That evening, Lee and Jackson discussed how to attack the massive army in their front. "Show me what to do, and we will do it," Jackson offered. A cavalry patrol had reported the Federal right flank "in the air"—that is, unprotected by any natural barrier. Lee divided his army into a third segment, sending Jackson with 26,000 men on a wide swing through the Wilderness, with orders to fall on Gen. Oliver O. Howard's 9th Corps.

The 16-mile approach march consumed most of May 2. It was midafternoon before Jackson had his first view of the objective—Howard's line, facing south and exposed to an attack from the west. A little before 6 o'clock, the relaxed Yankees caught sight of large numbers of deer and smaller wildlife bounding out of the woods. Moments later, long lines of Confederate infantry emerged—Jackson's corps, advancing at a trot and shrieking the rebel yell.

Howard's line swiftly collapsed; Howard found himself powerless to stem the rout. "Push right ahead," Jackson called out to his brigade and regimental commanders. "Press them, press them!" By nightfall the advance had carried to within a mile or so of Chancellorsville and a reunion of two of the three wings of Lee's divided army.

A short time later, in the darkness, confused Confederate troops inadvertently opened fire on Jackson as he rode among the jumbled units to organize a night attack intended to cut off Hooker's retreat to the Rappahannock River. Seriously wounded, Jackson turned over command to Gen. A. P. Hill. Then Hill, too, fell wounded. By the time cavalry general J. E. B. Stuart arrived to take charge, the opportunity for a surprise attack had passed. Both armies settled down for the night.

Next day, May 3, the battle flared on two fronts. Stuart launched a dawn attack that drove the Federals out of Chancellorsville and into a defensive arc guarding United States Ford on the Rappahannock River. At Hooker's order, Gen. John Sedgwick went into action at Fredericksburg. Sedgwick's infantry stormed Marye's Heights and set out down the Orange Turnpike toward Lee's rear. But Stuart's early-morning success enabled Lee to turn and face Sedgwick. The Confederates stopped Sedgwick's advance late in the afternoon at Salem church 6 miles short of Chancellorsville.

All day on May 4, Lee searched for an opening to attack and destroy Sedgwick's command, while Stuart held off the inert Hooker's much larger force. But the late-day assaults failed. That night, General Sedgwick withdrew across the Rappahannock River.

Hooker, too, prepared to retreat. Rain began falling around noon Tuesday, May 5. By midnight, the Rappahannock River had risen 6 feet. The pontoon bridges held, though, and by midday of May 6 the army had safely recrossed the Rappahannock River.

Hooker had been thoroughly out-generalled in what is regarded as Lee's masterpiece battle. Though the Federals suffered 17,000 casualties, Hooker failed to bring a large part of his force to bear—thousands of bluecoats hardly had been engaged at all. Hooker offered no excuses. "For once I lost confidence in Joe Hooker, and that is all there is to it," he said.

The Confederates lost heavily as well—13,000 killed, wounded, or missing. Lee recognized, too, that, for all the brilliance of his victory, the Army of the Potomac had escaped largely intact, to fight again.

May 10, 1863: Jackson, badly wounded at Chancellorsville, slipped into a delirium, calling out commands throughout the day from his sickbed. "Pass the infantry to the front!" he shouted once. Late in the afternoon, Lee's incomparable general died. Jackson's final utterance: "Let us cross the river and rest in the shade of the trees."

June 1863 (Gettysburg Campaign): On June 3, keen to follow up his Chancellorsville success, Lee roused the Army of Northern Virginia out of its camps around Fredericksburg and sent it north for the Potomac River, the opening of the month-long campaign that culminated in the Battle of Gettysburg.

On June 9, Hooker's cavalry, searching for leading elements of Lee's army, surprised J. E. B. Stuart's cavalry corps at Brandy Station in Virginia, touching off the Civil War's greatest cavalry battle. Stuart's troopers recovered, however, and the fighting proved inconclusive. Confederate casualties were 523 killed, wounded, or missing; Federal losses approached 900.

From mid- through late-June, Lee's army of 75,000 marched north, through the Blue Ridge passes and up the Shenandoah Valley to the Potomac River, rekindling the old dream of winning the great battle on enemy soil that would fuel Northern antiwar sentiment and encourage the British and French to intervene on the side of the Confederacy.

The 90,000-strong Army of the Potomac followed Lee's forces, though Hooker seemed reluctant to give chase. First, he proposed attacking the tail of the advancing Confederates; then he turned about and suggested marching south, toward Richmond, while his adversary marched in the opposite direction, toward Washington, Baltimore, and Philadelphia.

Sensing that Hooker had lost his nerve, President Lincoln replaced him on June 28 with Gen. George Gordon Meade. On that day, the Army of the Potomac lay in and around Frederick, Maryland. Lee, characteristically, had divided his army. Longstreet's and A. P. Hill's corps were near Chambersburg, Pennsylvania. Forty miles or more to the northeast, Gen. Richard Ewell split his corps in two, sending part to Carlisle, Pennsylvania, and part to York, Pennsylvania.

But Lee had been advancing into the unknown. On June 24, Stuart had led his three cavalry brigades on a sweep to the east, depriving Lee of the "eyes and ears" of his army. Lee assumed the Federals were still in Virginia, until a scout caught up to him the night of June 28 to report the enemy across the Potomac River. Within a few hours, Lee had dispatched orders for his army to concentrate at the crossroads town of Gettysburg, Pennsylvania.

July 1–4, 1863 (Battle of Gettysburg): The threadbare Confederates found Pennsylvania a cornucopia. Shops and storehouses were full of clothing and other goods. Rumor reached one of A. P. Hill's division commanders, Gen. Henry Heth, of a warehouse full of shoes at Gettysburg. When Heth went off to empty the place, he touched off the greatest battle of the Civil War.

Three brigades of Federal cavalry awaited Heth just west of Gettysburg. The battle opened at 8 o'clock on the morning of July 1, Wednesday. Fighting dismounted with rapid-fire Spencer carbines, Gen. John Buford's troopers held off the Confederate infantry for more than two hours, just time enough for the 1st Corps under Gen. John Reynolds to reach the battlefield.

Reynolds sent word of the developing battle to Meade, still in Maryland 15 miles to the southeast, and summoned the two nearest formations, the 9th Corps under Gen. Oliver Howard and the 3rd Corps under Gen. Daniel Sickles. A Confederate marksman shot Reynolds dead as he directed his arriving infantry into line on a spur of high ground known as McPherson's Ridge.

The Federals held fast for several hours, but at great cost. One of the Union's hardest-hitting units, the Iron Brigade of five midwestern regiments, lost a full two-thirds of its strength, 1,200 men killed or wounded, in the fighting on McPherson's Ridge and on a parallel rise to the southeast, Seminary Ridge. Meanwhile, both sides fed fresh forces into the battle. Howard's corps took up position north of Gettysburg and prepared to meet the leading elements of Ewell's corps coming down from Carlisle and York.

By midafternoon, some 24,000 Confederates faced some 19,000 Yankees in a line curving from Seminary Ridge to Oak Ridge north of Gettysburg. Lee reached the battlefield just as Ewell's assault brigades were driving a wedge into Howard's front. Lee at once ordered a general advance. Howard's line melted away, and his troops fell back through the streets of Gettysburg in a panic. Howard's failure unhinged the right flank of the 1st Corps, which also began to withdraw. The remnants of both corps, about 7,000 men, kept going through the town to the commanding high ground to the south.

There, on Cemetery Hill and Culp's Hill, the Federals threw up rough defensive breastworks and awaited a renewed attack. A senior general, Winfield Scott Hancock, arrived to take charge, and three more Federal corps reached Gettysburg during the night. Meade rode in an hour or so before daybreak. By then, Hancock had fashioned a strong line, which had been likened to a fishhook: the barb at Culp's Hill, the hook curving westward to Cemetery Hill, the shank running southward down Cemetery Ridge to the eye, a rocky eminence called Little Round Top. The Confederates were arrayed just opposite, beyond the Emmitsburg Road a mile to the west on Seminary Ridge.

By midnight, it had become clear that Lee had lost the initiative. If he renewed the battle, it would be on Meade's terms. The third of Lee's corps commanders, Gen. James Longstreet, proposed a flanking movement to the left that would land the Confederates between the Army of the Potomac and Washington, D.C., and force Meade into the open. But Lee resolved to fight at Gettysburg.

"The enemy is there," he told Longstreet, gesturing toward Cemetery Ridge, "and I am going to fight him there."

Lee chose Longstreet to carry out the main assault, to be aimed at the left of Meade's fish-hook line. On July 2, the 3rd Corps commander, Gen. Daniel E. Sickles, created an outward bulge in the lower portion of the shank when he moved the corps a half mile forward onto higher ground west of a little stream called Plum Run, encompassing a peach orchard, a wheat field, and a jumble of boulders known as the Devil's Den. Behind the Devil's Den rose Little Round Top, a craggy hillock that commanded the entire length of Meade's line. Little Round Top had been left undefended for most of the day.

Longstreet, slow to move, was not ready to attack until 4 o'clock. When he finally advanced, some of the war's hardest fighting resulted. Longstreet's 15,000-man infantry overran Sickles and knocked the 3rd Corps out of the battle. And his right-hand brigades came agonizingly close to capturing Little Round Top.

Just in time, one of Meade's staff officers quick-marched a brigade to Little Round Top. The brigade's left-hand regiment, the 20th Maine, had barely settled into position before the first enemy infantry came charging up the slope. That regiment, under a 34-year-old colonel and former Bowdoin College professor named Joshua Lawrence Chamberlain, repulsed five successive Confederate assaults. Then, with more than a third of its complement killed and wounded, the Maine troops swept the attackers away for the last time in a bayonet charge.

As quiet descended on Little Round Top, the fighting spread down the line. Only the desperate charge of the half-sized 1st Minnesota prevented the Confederates from achieving a breakthrough on Cemetery Ridge. The charge blunted a division-strength assault just long enough to give General Hancock time to rush reinforcements to the front. The 1st Minnesota lost all but 47 of its 262 officers and enlisted men.

Toward sunset, the three-hour battle flared out. Two days of fighting had left a total of 35,000 men killed or wounded. The Union commanders agreed to stay on for a third day at Gettysburg. And Lee, who still believed he could achieve a victory, laid plans for the Confederate debacle that would be known as Pickett's Charge.

Having failed on the right and the left, Lee decided to test Meade's center. On July 3, Lee called for a massive opening bombardment that he hoped would stun the Federal infantry and disrupt the artillery long enough to give the 14,000-strong storming column under Gen. George C. Pickett a chance to cover the mile-deep no-man's-land and break the Federal line.

As the sun climbed, the day became hot and sultry. Near the objective point of the Confederate assault, an umbrella-shaped clump of trees on Cemetery Ridge, the Union troops lay as though in a daze, stunned by the heat. There had been fighting earlier on Ewell's front. But by midday, all had become still. Then, at a few minutes past 1 o'clock, the Confederate great guns opened fire, delivering the heaviest cannonade of the Civil War. Union gunners responded in a roaring artillery duel that could be heard as far away as Pittsburgh, 150 miles distant.

The battle went on for nearly two hours, causing havoc in the Federal rear, damaging some guns, but barely disturbing the front-line infantry. At 3 o'clock, Longstreet reluctantly signaled the advance. "I don't want to make this attack," he told one of his officers. "I believe it will fail. I do not see how it can succeed. I would not make it even now, but General Lee has ordered and expects it."

So the Confederates set out for the clump of trees on Cemetery Ridge, advancing on a mile-wide front. They made an easy target. The federal artillery tore great gaps in the slow-moving Confederate line. Federal infantry swung out on either flank to rake the attackers as they struggled through the high grass.

The fighting was soon over. A few hundred Virginians managed to breach the Union line; within minutes, all either were dead or captured. Everyone else—around half of those who had started out had been killed or wounded in the charge—streamed back toward Seminary Ridge.

Lee met them there. "It is all my fault," he called out, as he rode among the survivors. "It is

I who have lost this fight."

The Battle of Gettysburg left the Army of the Potomac too weak and shaken to mount a counterattack. The casualty totals were appalling: 23,000 Union and 28,000 Confederate soldiers were killed, wounded, or missing. A hard rain fell during the day. After dark on July 4, Lee began his retreat south to the Potomac River.

July 6–14, 1863: Meade chased the retreating Confederates halfheartedly. "The enemy pursued us as a mule goes on the chase of a grizzly bear—as if catching up to us was the last thing he wanted to do," the Confederate artillery commander Col. Edward Porter Alexander observed. On July 6, Lee's army went into line near Williamsport, Pennsylvania, on the Potomac to await Meade's attack.

The attack did not come. Lee's engineers built a new bridge, and the army crossed the Potomac River safely to the Virginia bank during the night of July 13–14. Lincoln was disconsolate at the escape. "Our army held the war in the hollow of their hand & they would not close it," he lamented.

Gettysburg, along with the Union victory at Vicksburg on July 4, (see Western Theater, pp. 249-250) seemed to leave the Confederacy at the edge of ruin. The invincible Lee had been beaten. The Northern Copperheads, too, toned down their calls for a negotiated peace that would leave Southern slavery intact. After Gettysburg, the chances of foreign intervention were virtually nil. Still, the South fought on; Lee's escape gave the rebellion nearly two more years of life.

July 10–18, 1863: As part of the effort to capture Charleston, South Carolina, Union forces moved on Morris Island in Charleston harbor. On July 10, Federal commander Gen. Quincy Gillmore sent a brigade from neighboring Folly Island to occupy the southern part of Morris Island. An assault on the island strongpoint, Fort Wagner, failed on July 11, with heavy losses—339 Union casualties, compared to Confederate losses of only 12.

On July 18, after a bombardment from siege guns, the 54th Massachusetts, the first black regiment to be raised in the North, led a second assault on Fort Wagner. In a much-praised action, troops of the 54th secured a foothold in the fort but were driven off before reinforcements could arrive. Again, the Federals suffered heavy casualties, 1,515 in all, with the brigade commander

and five of six regimental commanders either killed or wounded.

October 9–November 9, 1863 (Bristoe Campaign): In September, with Lee's Army of Northern Virginia weakened by the dispatch of part of Longstreet's corps to Tennessee, Meade advanced south to the Rapidan River. When Lee learned in early October that forces had been detached from Meade and sent west, he, in turn, went on the offensive.

In a month-long campaign, Lee tried and failed to turn Meade's flank from the west and cut the Army of the Potomac off before it could reach the comparative safety of the Bull Run defenses.

In the only significant action of the campaign, Union infantry withstood an attack from Gen. A. P. Hill's corps at Bristoe Station on October 14, driving off Hill, with heavy Union losses of about 1,900 killed, wounded, or missing. There were lesser fights at Buckland Mills on October 19 and at Rappahannock Bridge on November 7.

Though the campaign proved indecisive, the outnumbered Lee forced Meade to retreat some 40 miles and tore up the railroad that supplied the Army of the Potomac, putting Meade's army out of action for a month.

November 26–December 1, 1863 (Mine Run Campaign): In a bid to regain the initiative, Meade attempted to turn Lee out of his defensive line along the Rapidan River. Meade sent five corps across the river at Germanna Ford and headed west for Orange Court House. Confederate cavalry alertly detected the move, allowing Lee to take up position along Mine Run.

Judging the enemy's position too strong, Meade declined to attack and withdrew. On December 1, the Army of the Potomac went into winter quarters.

WESTERN THEATER

January 2–3, 1863 (Battle of Stones River): After resting and regrouping from the savage opening round of the Battle of Stones River on the last day of 1862 (see pp. 237-238), Confederate general Braxton Bragg renewed the action late in the afternoon of January 2, attacking strong Federal positions on high ground just east of Stones River near Murfreesboro, Tennessee. But Federal artillery, some 58 guns firing massed, broke up the Confederate attack, with Federal losses of 1,700 killed, wounded, or missing.

Union general William Rosecrans held his ground on January 3. Bragg withdrew during the night of January 3; Rosecrans did not pursue. Stones River has been judged a Confederate tactical victory and strategic failure, for Bragg failed to destroy the Union Army or to drive it into retreat.

January–May 1863 (Vicksburg Campaign): Two Mississippi River fortresses, Vicksburg, Mississippi, and Port Hudson, Louisiana, held the halves of the Confederacy together. Federal campaigns working south from Memphis, Tennessee, and north from Baton Rouge, Louisiana, sought to capture the strong-points and reopen the Mississippi River from the midwestern heartland to the Gulf of Mexico.

Vicksburg overlooked a long horseshoe bend of the Mississippi River from a chain of hills rising from a drowned landscape of swamps, river bottoms, and bayous. All but unassailable from three sides, that Confederate "Gibraltar of the West" commanded the river for miles in both directions.

Grant kept the Union Army gainfully employed during the wet early winter of 1863 with four offensive operations against Vicksburg, known as the Bayou Expeditions.

In the first effort, Federal engineers sought to cut a passage at Duckport to connect with a route through the swamps that would bypass the guns of Vicksburg. When that project proved a failure, Grant ordered an Army corps to clear a 400-mile route through west-bank creeks and bayous to a point on the Mississippi south of the fortress.

Grant abandoned this operation, known as the Lake Providence project, to pursue what he thought was a more promising alternative, an expedition through the Yazoo Pass north of Vicksburg. Engineers blew a hole in the Yazoo levee so troop transports could pass into the Yazoo River. Confederate defenses blocked the penetration 90 miles north of Vicksburg, and on March 17 the Union gunboats and troop transports withdrew.

Grant decided the fourth option, the Steele's Bayou Expedition, offered the greatest prospect for success. With 11 shallow draft vessels, Adm. David D. Porter attempted to cut a path through the 200-mile chain of creeks and rivers, bypass the strong-point of Haines Bluff, and land 10,000 of Sherman's troops in Vicksburg's rear.

The defenders ambushed Porter's flotilla on March 19 and came close to cutting off and destroying it. "Dear Sherman," Porter wrote. "Hurry up for Heaven's sake. I never knew how helpless an ironclad could be steaming around through the woods without an army to back her." Sherman's relief column, wading through swamps, reached Porter on March 20, and rescued the gunboats. "The game was up," Porter wrote later, "and we bumped on homeward."

With the failure of the Bayou Expedition, Grant decided to march his Army down the west bank of the Mississippi, cross the river south of Vicksburg, advance inland onto high, dry ground, and attack the fortress from the east.

In April, as a diversion, Grant sent a Union cavalry brigade under Col. Benjamin H. Grierson on a raid from LaGrange, Tennessee, deep into the Mississippi heartland. In a 16-day, 600-mile raid, Grierson's troopers won a series of skirmishes, tore up miles of railroad track, burned rolling stock, and destroyed hundreds of tons of Confederate supplies.

The main campaign opened on the moonless night of April 16, when a flotilla of Union gunboats and transports ran past the water batteries at Vicksburg and joined up with Grant's land forces on the Louisiana bank of the Mississippi River. By month's end, the entire Army had been ferried across the mile-wide river.

On May 1, Grant, against the advice of Gen. William T. Sherman and other senior subordinates, cut loose from his base and struck deep into enemy territory. The Federals moved swiftly, taking Jackson, the Mississippi capital, in a headlong assault on May 14. Leaving Sherman's corps behind to wreck Jackson, Grant sent the other two corps toward Vicksburg 40 miles to the west. On May 16, the Federals defeated a Confederate army under Gen. John Pemberton at Champion's Hill, Mississippi. The next day, the Yankees routed Pemberton at Big Black River and drove the Confederate remnants into the Vicksburg defenses.

In only 19 days, Grant's Army had crossed the Mississippi River, marched 180 miles, fought and won five battles, and sealed up the enemy's mobile forces.

On May 19, Grant ordered a frontal attack on Stockade Redan, one of Vicksburg's strong points. The defenders met the advance with a devastating fire. "The heads of the columns have been swept away as chaff thrown from the hand on a windy day," wrote Sherman after the repulse. Grant tried again on May 22, with similar results, this time at a cost of 3,000 killed, wounded, or missing.

June 7, 1863: A Confederate brigade attacked the largely black Union garrison at Milliken's Bend, Louisiana. The defenders repulsed several assaults. Before withdrawing, the Confederates murdered several black prisoners; others were later sold as slaves. Federal losses exceeded 600; the Confederates reported 150 killed, wounded, or missing.

June 23–30, 1863 (Tullahoma Campaign): To prevent Confederate general Braxton Bragg from sending reinforcements to besieged Vicksburg, General Rosecrans went on the offensive in central Tennessee. Rosecrans flanked Bragg out of his defensive position along the Duck River and drove the Confederates southeastward to Tullahoma, Tennessee. Heavy rains fell during much of the period, making movement difficult. Rosecrans called off the campaign on June 30, retiring behind the line of the Tennessee River to rest and refit.

May 23–July 4, 1863 (Siege of Vicksburg): On May 23, the Federals settled in for the five formal stages of a siege: investment, artillery bombardment, construction of parallel and approach trenches, initial breaching of the defenses, and final assault.

Throughout the year, the Confederates had prepared a formidable defensive system on the high ground around Vicksburg. The lines extended in a 7-mile semicircle north to south along the steep, wooded bluffs, forming a mutually supporting complex of forts, redoubts, and deep-dug trenches.

The Federals built similar fortifications, some as close as 50 yards from General Pemberton's lines. Grant had a three-to-one advantage in numbers, a secure supply line and supreme confidence in the eventual outcome. "The enemy are now undoubtedly in our grasp," he wrote Henry Halleck, the Union general in chief. "The fall of Vicksburg and the capture of most of the garrison can only be a question of time."

For his part, Pemberton thought that his 20,000 Confederates could hold out until a relief column reached Vicksburg. Northeast of Jackson, Confederate general Joseph E. Johnston assembled a 30,000-strong field force to attempt a move on Grant's rear. Communicating via messages smuggled through the siege lines, Pemberton begged Johnston to move as swiftly as possible to his assistance.

By mid-June, Grant had some 70,000 men in 16 divisions in line—nine divisions pressed up to Vicksburg, the remaining seven faced east in anticipation of Johnston's appearance. Opposite the Confederate works, the digging went on, day after day in the rising heat and humidity of the Mississippi high summer.

Inside Vicksburg, the Confederates were short of food, supplies, and ammunition. Pemberton put the garrison on half-rations, then quarter-rations. Vicksburg's bakers made their dough from a gritty compound of ground corn and dried peas. "The corn meal cooked in half the time the peas meal did, so the stuff was half raw," a siege survivor recalled. "It had the properties of india-rubber, and was worse than leather to digest." Mule meat, on the other hand, proved palatable to all but the most squeamish, though it was expensive at $1 a pound (about $30 a pound in 1990s terms).

Vicksburg's prewar population approached 3,500, and Grant's sudden appearance had trapped many civilians inside the fortress. They carved shelters out of the hillsides for protection against the Federal bombardments, a honeycomb of caves and dugouts the besiegers dubbed "prairie dog village." Though the cannonades were destructive of property, deafening, and nerve-racking, they caused surprisingly few civilian casualties, perhaps fewer than a dozen. It was the cumulative effect of hunger, fear, and unrelieved tension that inflicted most of the damage.

Wrote Vicksburg diarist Dora Miller Richards: "I have never understood the full force of these questions—what shall we eat? What shall we drink? And wherewithal shall we be clothed?"

Johnston, meanwhile, concluded he could do little for Vicksburg. On June 13, a two-week-old message from Johnston reached Pemberton. "I am too weak to save Vicksburg," Johnston wrote. "Can do no more than attempt to save you and your garrison. It will be impossible to extricate you unless you cooperate and we make mutually supporting movements. Communicate your plans and intentions if possible." A few days later, Pemberton replied that he could not hold out beyond the first few days of July.

Johnston suggested that Pemberton try to

escape across the Mississippi River. Pemberton did, finally, put his field force in motion for Jackson, setting out on June 29, a day after Pemberton received what amounted to a threat of mutiny in the form of a petition from "Many Soldiers" of the Vicksburg garrison. "If you can't feed us," it read, "you had better surrender."

On July 3, Pemberton sent an emissary to Grant under a flag of truce. Pemberton wanted to discuss terms; Grant replied, characteristically, that he would accept nothing short of unconditional surrender. After thinking it over, and after calculating the number of river transports that would be required to ship 20,000 prisoners north, Grant relented. He offered to allow the Confederates to go home on parole—a promise not to take up arms again until a similar number of Federal prisoners were turned over to the Union.

On the night of July 3, the troops observed an informal cease-fire. There were exchanges of news and gossip and family reunions through the short summer night. Pemberton surrendered at 10 o'clock in the morning of July 4, bringing the 48-day Siege of Vicksburg to a close.

May 26–July 16, 1863 (Port Hudson Campaign): In concert with Grant, the 19th Corps of Gen. Nathaniel P. Banks advanced on the Confederate river stronghold of Port Hudson, Louisiana, 240 miles south of Vicksburg. An initial assault on May 27 failed. The defenders repulsed successive attacks on June 11 and 14.

The Federals then settled down to a siege. Near starvation, the Port Hudson garrison surrendered five days after the surrender of Vicksburg. Together, the two Union successes cut the Confederacy in two and reopened the Mississippi River from source to mouth. On July 16, a merchant steamboat glided up to a levee in New Orleans after an uneventful trip downriver from St. Louis.

"The father of waters," President Lincoln exulted, "again goes unvexed to the sea."

July 2–26, 1863 (Morgan's Ohio Raid): In a diversion aimed at slowing Rosecrans's advance on Chattanooga, Tennessee, Confederate general John H. Morgan, with 2,500 men, set off on July 2 to raid Federal communications in Kentucky. Eluding some 10,000 Federal troops sent against him, he reached the Ohio River on July 6 and—against orders—crossed to the Indiana bank.

Turning east, with militia forces of two Union states in pursuit, Morgan passed through the outskirts of Cincinnati on the night of July 13–14. Strong Federal forces met Morgan at Buffington, Indiana, on the Ohio River, where he had intended to recross. In a fight on July 19, Morgan lost more than 800 men, including 700 taken prisoner. On July 26, Federal cavalry captured Morgan and what remained of his command, fewer than 400 troopers.

Jailed for a time, Morgan escaped in November 1863 and rejoined the Confederates, though his reputation never recovered from the disastrous Ohio raid.

August–September 1863 (Chickamauga Campaign): Rosecrans's Tullahoma Campaign had opened the route to Chattanooga, Tennessee, an important Confederate communications center. After a brief pause, his Army of the Cumberland resumed the advance, forcing Bragg's Army of the Tennessee to fall back through Chattanooga, across the Tennessee River, and into the Georgia hills.

Bragg halted in northern Georgia and, with substantial reinforcements in hand or on the way, including the 12,000-strong corps of Gen. James Longstreet from Virginia, prepared to reverse direction and lash out at the oncoming Federals.

Two Confederate attempts to pounce on elements of the divided Union Army miscarried. By the third week of September, Rosecrans had the Army concentrated in the wooded, vine-choked valley of Chickamauga Creek, Georgia, a dozen miles south of Chattanooga. The armies' outriders skirmished inconsequentially on September 18, setting the stage for a general engagement. On September 18, too, Longstreet's two divisions reached Bragg, making the armies roughly equal in size, each with about 65,000 men.

September 19–20, 1863 (Battle of Chickamauga): At daybreak on September 19, the Federal 14th Corps under Gen. George H. Thomas, Rosecrans's left wing, opened fire on probing Confederates near Jay's Mill just west of Chickamauga Creek.

The initiative lay with Bragg, who aimed his initial effort at Thomas. As the Federals fell back, Bragg's attack evolved into a series of individual encounters that defied central control. Smoke from the discharge of thousands of muskets rose into the forest canopy and hung there, trapped. Only rarely could the opposing infantry see more than a few yards ahead through the dense undergrowth and stinging smoke.

"There was no generalship in it," wrote Union colonel John T. Wilder of the first day of the Battle of Chickamauga. "It was a soldier's fight purely, wherein the only question involved was the question of endurance. The armies came together like two wild beasts, and each fought as long as it could stand up in a knock down and drag out encounter. If there had been any high order of generalship displayed, the disasters to both armies might have been less."

The fighting spread through the woods and ravines of the Chickamauga valley. Thomas's corps held, barely. After noon, Bragg shifted his main effort southward, against Rosecrans's center and right. The Federals withstood the onslaught there too. With the waning light, the battle sputtered out. As night fell, the sound of axes rang through the woods—Yankee troops throwing up log-and-brush breastworks against an expected renewal of the fight the following morning.

In a late-night war council, Rosecrans and his corps commanders decided to await events. On the other side of the line, Bragg reorganized his army into two wings, the right under Gen. Leonidas Polk, the left under Longstreet. Bragg directed Polk to open the proceedings at dawn.

On September 20, Polk's assault jumped off at 9:30 A.M., some four hours behind Bragg's schedule. On the extreme left, the Federals stopped the initial Confederate charge. The echelon attack rippled down the line. Thomas's corps stood its ground through the morning, aided by a steady stream of fresh troops drawn from Rosecrans's right.

Longstreet's turn came toward noon. Frequent comings and goings of troops created confusion in the Federal command. Someone reported, mistakenly, that one such shift had opened a gap in the center of the line. So Rosecrans put a frontline division in motion to fill the place, in fact creating a gap where none had existed before. Longstreet's storming column broke out of the woods and drove straight for the opening.

It was one of the Civil War's great strokes of fortune. Encountering slight resistance, Longstreet's infantry advanced a full mile into the Federal rear. On either side of the Confederate wedge, Federal units broke and ran, racing in panic for McFarland's Gap and the safety of the far slope of Missionary Ridge, in the Georgia mountains just south of Chattanooga.

The swelling roar of Longstreet's attack interrupted the catnap of the War Department observer, Charles Dana. When he looked up, he saw Rosecrans making the sign of the cross. "Hello," Dana said. "If the general is crossing himself, we are in a desperate situation." As the larger scene swam into focus, Dana saw that the entire Federal right wing had been blown away, "like leaves before the wind."

On the left, meanwhile, Thomas—who had held fast against Confederate pressure all day—pulled back to a shorter, stronger line on the rise of Snodgrass Hill, deployed scattered units from the right that had not set off in flight for Chattanooga, and fought on through the afternoon.

Later, Longstreet estimated that the Confederates launched 25 separate charges at Thomas, whose refusal to yield earned him the sobriquet of "the Rock of Chickamauga." Thomas's stand saved what remained of the Army of the Cumberland. At about 5 o'clock, an hour or so before sundown, he issued orders for a withdrawal. The first troops began pulling out of the line about 5:30. By nightfall, Thomas had disengaged the entire corps and set it on the road for McFarland's Gap.

The Confederates won a smashing victory, breaking up a Yankee army and taking 8,000 prisoners, 51 guns, and thousands of small arms. Longstreet and others pressed Bragg to organize a rapid pursuit toward Chattanooga. The commanding general refused. Confederate casualties were crippling—20,000 men killed, wounded, or missing over two days, roughly 30 percent of Bragg's army's strength.

The failure to follow up the victory of Chickamauga disgusted Bragg's chief subordinates. One of the most aggressive of those subordinates, cavalry commander Nathan Bedford Forrest, could barely contain his anger when he learned that Bragg intended to let the beaten and demoralized Army of the Cumberland escape. "What does he fight battles for?" Forrest growled.

September–October 1863: On September 22, Bragg's forces occupied the heights of Missionary Ridge, planted artillery on Lookout Mountain, and posted infantry at the Tennessee River crossings, essentially sealing off Chattanooga. Confederate command of the rail and wagon routes into the town left the defenders with only

During October–November 1863, Union forces, shown here in an encampment, fought the Confederate forces in and around Chattanooga, Tennessee, a strategic city along the Tennessee River.

one tenuous supply line, a rough mountain track over the Cumberland Plateau from the north.

In Washington, D.C., President Lincoln and his war secretary, Edwin Stanton, acted swiftly to contain the disaster. On September 25, two corps of the Army of the Potomac, the 11th and 12th under Gen. Joseph Hooker, were detached and sent west by railroad to replace Rosecrans's Chickamauga losses of about 15,000 killed, wounded, or missing. In addition, Gen. William T. Sherman and the Army of the Tennessee were en route to Chattanooga.

Stanton also made changes at the top. He relieved two of Rosecrans's corps commanders and considered removing Rosecrans as well. Defeat had paralyzed the commanding general. Rosecrans seemed, Lincoln thought, "confused and stunned, like a duck hit on the head." In mid-October, Lincoln named Gen. Ulysses S. Grant to command the newly created Department of the Mississippi, with headquarters in the field at Chattanooga. Arriving in Chattanooga on October 23, Grant promptly replaced Rosecrans with Gen. George Thomas.

Late October–November 1863 (Chatta-nooga Campaign): From October 26 to 30, Grant put in a series of operations that broke the siege

and opened the "cracker line"—so named for the Army's hard-bread staple food—into Chattanooga. Soon goods of all kinds were pouring in. Sherman arrived in Chattanooga in mid-November. With some 60,000 men and a now reliable supply line, Grant prepared to take the offensive against Bragg on Missionary Ridge.

The besiegers, it turned out, had been as hungry, cold, and demoralized as the besieged. "Nothing to eat, but we are well supplied with lice," a Florida soldier remarked wryly. Bragg's army had been weakened in early November by the detachment of Longstreet's corps, sent northeast to recapture Knoxville. Dissension wracked the senior leadership of the Army of Tennessee. To a man, Bragg's chief lieutenants despised him.

Grant's plan for the breakout battle gave the leading role to Sherman on the left, with supporting help from Hooker's two corps on the right, opposite Lookout Mountain. Grant assigned a minor part to the Army of the Cumberland; Gen. George Thomas's troops were merely to divert the Confederate center on Missionary Ridge.

November 24, 1863 (Battle of Lookout Mountain): While Sherman opened the attack from the north end of Missionary Ridge, Hooker with three divisions moved on the Confederate strong point of Lookout Mountain 1,100 feet above the Tennessee River. In a heavy fog, sharp fighting broke out at Craven's Farm around 10 A.M. The Confederates pulled back a few hundred yards and dug in. At midnight, they were ordered to withdraw. A Union detachment planted the Stars and Stripes atop Lookout Mountain on the morning of November 25.

November 25, 1863 (Battle of Missionary Ridge): Sherman resumed his attack at dawn, but it met stiff resistance through the morning from a Confederate division under Gen. Patrick Cleburne. Suspecting, wrongly it turned out, that Bragg had been borrowing troops from the center to strengthen Cleburne, Grant ordered Thomas to move on the Confederate advance line at the base of Missionary Ridge.

Thomas's assault, intended only to ease pressure on Sherman, in fact decided the battle. At 3:30, 23,000 troops of the Army of the Cumberland advanced on a 2-mile front and swept over Bragg's first-line rifle pits. The Confederates fell back to a second line midway up the ridge, where they began to pour an effective fire into the Yankees below. Faced with the choice of continuing uphill or dropping back, the attackers opted to resume the advance. From his command post on Orchard Knob, Grant watched anxiously.

"Thomas, who ordered those men up the ridge?" he asked.

"I don't know," Thomas answered. "I did not."

The Federal wave broke over the second line. Groups of infantry scrambled uphill, finding cover among the rocks and in slight dips of ground. The defenders fell back in disorder. Forty-five minutes after the bugles sounded the advance, the Federals reached the crest of Missionary Ridge. There, the Confederate front wavered, then collapsed. Bluecoats shouting "Chickamauga!" swarmed over the top of the ridge.

The outcome of that improvised assault seemed like a miracle—"as awful," in Charles Dana's words, "as a visible interposition of God." Bragg's army kept going southward, covering some 30 miles on the road to Atlanta, Georgia, before slowing to a halt around Dalton, Georgia. Bragg hardly knew what to make of the rout. "No satisfactory excuse can possibly be given for the shameful conduct of our troops," Bragg wrote President Davis. A week after the debacle, Davis accepted Bragg's resignation.

Told years later that the Confederates believed the Missionary Ridge line to have been impregnable, Grant thought for a moment, then replied: "Well, it *was* impregnable."

Union losses were about 5,800, roughly 10 percent of the total engaged. The 6,000 Confederate casualties, 14 percent of those engaged, included 4,100 men missing.

November 29, 1863 (Battle of Knoxville): Judging that he lacked the resources to mount a siege, Longstreet moved to carry Knoxville by assault, aiming for the strong point known as Fort Sanders in the northwest corner of the Knoxville defenses.

In an effort to achieve surprise, Longstreet dispensed with a preliminary bombardment. The assault infantry moved out at first light and soon reached a ditch in front of the fort. Longstreet's troops were not equipped with ladders, and the parapet proved slippery and too steep to scale. (Some historians claim that it was at the Battle of Knoxville that the Federal forces first used wire entanglements to foil the Confederates [see Battle at Drewry's Bluff, May 4–17, 1864, pp. 258-259]). Milling around at the base of Fort Sanders, the Confederate infantry took heavy casualties. Longstreet abruptly called off the attack, which cost him more than 800 killed, wounded, or missing. The defenders lost about 100 men.

December 1863: After Missionary Ridge, Grant sent Sherman northeast to relieve Gen. Ambrose Burnside at Knoxville. Learning of Sherman's advance, Longstreet withdrew on December 3 and 4. Sherman returned to Chattanooga, and Longstreet's corps took up winter quarters at Greenville in east Tennessee.

TRANS-MISSISSIPPI THEATER

January 4–12, 1863 (Arkansas Post Expedition): Union general John McClernand initiated a campaign to take the outpost of Fort Hindman 50 miles up the Arkansas River, from which Confederate gunboats could sortie into the Mississippi River to attack Union communications.

With 30,000 men, 50 transports, and 13 gunboats, the expedition landed 3 miles below Fort Hindman on January 9. By midmorning of January 10, Federal forces had enveloped the bastion from the landward side. A combined Army-Navy attack on the morning of January 11 quickly silenced the fort. Some 4,700 Confederates were taken prisoner. Union losses were about 1,000.

Grant, who had not authorized the expedition, ordered McClernand to withdraw immediately so that his forces could be used in the campaign against Vicksburg.

April–May 1863 (Red River Campaign): Gen. Nathaniel P. Banks decided to sweep away Confederate forces on the west bank of the Mississippi River as a preliminary to the Port Hudson (Louisiana) expedition.

Banks's army, 15,000 strong, advanced up Bayou Teche and the Atchafalaya River in early April. On April 13, Banks attacked a force of 2,700 Confederates under Gen. Richard Taylor at Fort Bisland, Louisiana. Taylor abandoned the fort during the night, struck at Banks's flank at Irish Bend during the morning of April 14, then withdrew with little challenge from Banks.

Banks continued his advance, capturing Alexandria, Louisiana, against light opposition on May 7. Two weeks later, Banks marched east to the Mississippi, crossed the river, and began operations against Port Hudson in cooperation with Grant's Vicksburg Campaign.

August 21, 1863: Some 450 Confederate bushwhackers under William Clarke Quantrill plundered and burned the strongly Unionist town of Lawrence, Kansas, killing 150 men and boys and destroying $500,000 worth of property.

August–September 1863: On August 10, Federal forces in Helena, Arkansas, under Gen. Frederick Steele began the advance on Little Rock. Steele's troops occupied the Arkansas capital without opposition on September 10.

September–November 1863 (Banks's Texas Coast Operations): With the reopening of the Mississippi River, Banks received reinforcements and orders to "raise the flag in Texas," in part to discourage the French troops, then active, in Mexico, from any notion of invading Texas.

On September 8, Banks sent 4,000 troops with a naval escort against the Confederates at Sabine Pass on the Texas-Louisiana border. Confederate fire quickly disabled two of the three attacking gunboats (they eventually surrendered), leading the Federals to abandon the attempt to gain Sabine Pass.

Banks then decided to land troops at the mouth of the Rio Grande and advance eastward from there. Federal forces captured several strong points before halting in front of the defenses of

Galveston in late November. Denied reinforcements, Banks chose to call off the operation, leaving garrisons behind in Brownsville and on Matagorda Island.

NAVAL THEATER

January 31, 1863: Two Confederate ironclads, *Chicora* and *Palmetto State*, steamed out of Charleston harbor to challenge the Federal blockade. In a short, fierce action, the gunboats extensively damaged two Union vessels. The blockade, however, remained unbroken.

March 14, 1863: Adm. David Farragut's gunboats bombarded the Mississippi River stronghold of Port Hudson, Louisiana, in an attempt to move upriver to attack Vicksburg in concert with Grant's land forces. Confederate fire drove the USS *Mississippi* aground and forced two other vessels to turn back. Farragut's flagship, *Hartford*, and a second vessel passed Port Hudson safely and continued on to Vicksburg.

April 7, 1863 (Fort Sumter): Union admiral Samuel DuPont, with eight monitors and a heavy ironclad, attempted to force the entrance to Charleston harbor in South Carolina and capture the city from the sea. Heavy fire from Confederate batteries in Fort Sumter and on Sullivan Island and a floating obstruction behind Fort Sumter forced DuPont to withdraw. The USS *Keokuk*, seriously damaged in the attack, sank the next day.

April 1863 (Vicksburg Campaign): On April 16, Adm. David Porter's flotilla of 12 gunboats, cooperating with Grant, ran the Vicksburg (Mississippi) batteries, with the loss of one ship. On April 22, 6 transports and 12 barges made the attempt. One transport and six barges were sunk; the rest delivered their cargoes of supplies to Grant's Army. On April 30, Porter's vessels covered the crossing of Grant's Army at Bruinsburg.

June 26, 1863: In a daring exploit, the Confederate raider *Archer*, Lt. Charles Read commanding, attempted to seize the U.S. revenue cutter *Caleb Cushing* at anchor in Portland (Maine) harbor. Alert U.S. naval forces destroyed the *Archer* and captured Read and his crew, ending a three-week escapade in which the raider had taken 21 Federal vessels.

August 29, 1863: The Confederate submarine *H. L. Hunley* sank on a test cruise in Charleston harbor, drowning five crewmen. Salvage teams eventually raised the experimental craft.

August–September 8, 1863: The Navy's last effort to capture Charleston, South Carolina, opened with a weeklong artillery bombardment that destroyed Fort Sumter's guns. In a nighttime landing on September 8, a party of 400 Union sailors attempted to surprise the garrison. The Confederates repulsed the attackers, with a loss of 125 men.

October 5, 1863: In a bid to pierce the Union blockade, the Confederate semisubmersible steamship *David* attacked the USS *New Ironsides* with a spar torpedo, seriously damaging the Federal warship. Two of the *David*'s four-man crew were captured after the attack. The remaining two managed to steer the unhandy vessel back to Charleston.

HOME FRONTS

January 1, 1863: President Lincoln signed the Emancipation Proclamation, freeing slaves in all parts of the United States still in rebellion. For the great majority of the South's 4 million slaves, the practical effects of the proclamation would not be felt until liberating Union military forces arrived in the South.

January 12, 1863: In Richmond, Virginia, the third session of the First Confederate Congress convened. In his address to Congress, Jefferson Davis emphasized his hopes for European recognition of the Confederacy.

January 27, 1863: Davis wrote Georgia governor Joseph Brown to urge him to spur his state to produce more food and less cotton. "A short supply of provisions presents the greatest danger to a successful war," Davis observed.

February 1863: The Confederate currency continued to shrink in buying power. On February 1, the Confederate dollar was worth about 20 cents. In Charleston, South Carolina, in February, a half-pound loaf of bread sold for $25, and flour went for $65 a barrel. The average family food bill increased tenfold during 1863, to $70 a week.

January 27, 1863: As part of a continuing crackdown on dissent, Federal agents arrested A. D. Boileau, editor of the Philadelphia *Journal*, on grounds that he had published anti-Union material.

February 19, 1863: Convalescent Federal soldiers in Keokuk, Iowa, ransacked the office of the *Constitution* newspaper, accused of publishing allegedly anti-Union views.

March 5, 1863: In Columbus, Ohio, Federal troops smashed the office of the newspaper the *Crisis*, also accused of taking an anti-Union stand.

March 3, 1863: In Washington, D.C., Congress passed the Enrollment Act (also known as the Conscription Act), which called for the three-year draft of all able-bodied males between the ages of 20 and 45. The act supplied about 170,000 draftees during all of 1863 and 1864.

March 10, 1863: President Lincoln proclaimed an amnesty for all U.S. soldiers absent without leave. Soldiers who did not return to their regiments by April 1 would be court-martialed for desertion.

March 13, 1863: An accidental explosion in the Confederate Ordnance Laboratory in Richmond, Virginia, killed or wounded 69 workers, 62 of which were women hired to work in the factory in place of men in military service.

April 2, 1863: In Richmond, hunger and frustration boiled over in a "bread riot" in which an estimated 100,000 people ransacked shops and warehouses for provisions. The rioters dispersed only when a column of troops—with President Davis at the head—threatened to open fire.

April 13, 1863: General Burnside, commanding the Department of the Ohio, issued a proclamation threatening to deport Southern sympathizers into the Confederacy. Burnside also announced that his department would impose the death penalty on those found guilty of aiding the rebellion.

April 24, 1863: In an effort to curb profiteering and to raise revenue to pay for the war, the Confederate Congress in Richmond approved a bill that heavily taxed agricultural products and profits made from the purchase or sale of most food and clothing. The measure also imposed a graduated income tax.

May 1863: In Dayton, Ohio, Burnside's troops, on May 1, arrested former representative Clement Vallandigham, a leading Copperhead who had been active in the antiwar Knights of the Golden Circle. On May 6, a military commission convicted Vallandigham of having uttered "disloyal sentiments and opinions" and ordered him imprisoned for the duration of the war.

Lincoln commuted Vallandigham's sentence to banishment to the Confederacy, and on May 25, Federal cavalry escorted Vallandigham through the rebel lines at Murfreesboro, Tennessee. The president stoutly defended this attempt to silence Vallandigham: "Must I shoot a simple-minded soldier boy who deserts, while I must not touch a hair of a wily agitator who induces him to desert? I think that in such a case to silence the agitator and save the boy is not only constitutional, but withal a great mercy," Lincoln said.

July 11–16, 1863: On July 11, Enrollment Act officials in New York City drew the first names for the draft. Some 1,200 conscripts were listed in the newspapers on July 12, along with the casualties from the battle of Gettysburg. Publication of the names touched off three days of rioting in the city.

On July 13, rioters sacked and burned the draft offices at Third Avenue and 46th Street. By the evening, the mob, 50,000 strong, stormed an armory and attacked an orphanage for black children. The 237 children managed to escape out the back before the building went up in flames.

Street fighting continued through June 14 and 15. By June 16, 4,000 troops had reached the city—including troops of the Army of the Potomac—and order largely had been restored. The rioting left 119 people dead and more than 300 wounded.

August 1, 1863: In Richmond, Virginia, President Davis offered amnesty to Confederate deserters who returned to their units within 20 days. In fact, desertion had become so common that many commanders treated it leniently, in hopes the men eventually would return. A Virginia general, finding most of his men "had all gone to their homes without leave," granted everyone in the command a 20-day furlough.

October 1863: In off-year elections, Republicans triumphed in a number of state elections, including Ohio, where the Copperhead Vallandigham, campaigning from exile in Canada, went down to defeat in the race for governor. Lincoln furloughed Ohio troops and granted home leave to Federal clerks so they could support the Republican candidate. "The people have voted in favor of the war," a disappointed Ohio Copperhead wrote after the election.

November 19, 1863: Before an audience of 15,000, Lincoln delivered a ten-sentence speech at the dedication of the military cemetery at Gettysburg, Pennsylvania. The crowd applauded unenthusiastically at the end of the oration; Lin-

coln himself regarded it a "flat failure." In time, though, the Gettysburg Address took its rightful place as one of the most significant and moving speeches in history.

December 8, 1863: In his annual message to Congress, Lincoln outlined his views on reconstruction. The president offered a full pardon for all Confederates except government officials, senior army officers, officers who had resigned from the U.S. military to join the Confederacy, and those found to have mistreated prisoners of war. And a rebellious state could be readmitted to the Union when one-tenth of its citizens forswore slavery and took an oath of allegiance.

December 31, 1864: The Confederacy prepared to enter the third year of the war amid widespread pessimism for the future. "Today closes the gloomiest year of our struggle," observed the Richmond *Examiner*, looking back on the great Union victories at Gettysburg, Vicksburg, and Chattanooga.

INTERNATIONAL DEVELOPMENTS

February 5, 1863: In an official statement on February 5, Queen Victoria said Britain had no plans to mediate between the Union and the Confederacy. Mediation, the queen said, would not be "attended with the probability of success."

February 6, 1863: U.S. Secretary of State William Seward rejected a mediation offer from the government of Emperor Napoleon III of France.

April 5, 1863: British authorities detained several Confederate vessels in the port of Liverpool, England, including the blockade runner *Alexandria*. The British eventually released the *Alexandria*, but the seizure gave an early sign of the British government's more favorable attitude toward the Union.

September 5, 1863: In response to U.S. protests, British authorities seized two newly built Confederate ironclads at the Laird shipyards in Liverpool. With the seizures, a great blow to the Confederate navy, what proved to be the last major diplomatic crisis between Britain and the United States evaporated.

BATTLES AND CAMPAIGNS: 1864

In hindsight, it is evident the Confederacy was doomed as 1864 dawned. Yet, some of the hardest fighting, heaviest casualties, and most widespread destruction of the Civil War were to come. In the eastern theater, Grant's spring offensive brought Union armies to Richmond's door, but at an appalling, unprecedented cost in lives and destruction. In the western theater, Sherman's Atlanta Campaign and March to the Sea set the stage for the Civil War's final, brief, and conclusive act.

Fending off dissidents in his own party, Lincoln won reelection, even as war-weariness crept over the North. In the South, hunger, loss, and despair prevailed. For millions of black slaves, Confederate defeat meant personal freedom. And by year's end, it had become clear that, at last, the long, cruel war would soon come to a close.

EASTERN THEATER

February 9, 1864: In the Civil War's most daring prison break, 109 Union officers dug their way out of the notorious Libby Prison on the banks of the James River in Richmond, Virginia. Forty-eight escapees were recaptured, 2 drowned, and 59 reached the Federal lines safely.

February 20, 1864 (Battle of Olustee): A cavalry clash touched off the Battle of Olustee, near Jacksonville, Florida. A Confederate attack led by Gen. Joseph Finegan routed two Union regiments before the 54th Massachusetts, of Fort Wagner fame, arrived to stabilize the line. Gen. Truman Seymour withdrew his troops after dark, with heavy losses—more than 1,800 casualties. Confederate casualties approached 1,000.

February 28–March 4, 1864 (Kilpatrick-Dahlgren Raid): On February 28, Union cavalry general Judson Kilpatrick crossed the Rapidan River northwest of Richmond, Virginia, with 3,500 troopers on a raid designed to penetrate Richmond's defenses, enter the city, spread alarm there, and free Federal captives at Libby Prison.

Confederates learned of the operation and were waiting for Kilpatrick, who judged the Richmond fortifications too strong to attack when he reached them on March 1. Withdrawing eastward, Kilpatrick's force regained the Federal lines on March 4.

Meanwhile, Col. Ulric Dahlgren, with a second, smaller Union column, tried to approach Richmond from the south. Misinformed about a fording place on the Rapidan River (he ordered the informant, a young black, hanged on the spot

for treachery), Dahlgren still managed to penetrate to within 2 miles of the Confederate capital before meeting stiff resistance from Confederate cavalry.

During the withdrawal, Dahlgren rode into a trap in which he was killed and most of his remaining men captured. Confederate authorities claimed to have found on his body papers indicating that the purpose of the raid had been to burn Richmond and kill President Davis and his cabinet. The papers may have been forged, but subsequent inquiry has been unable to resolve the matter.

March 1864: On March 1, President Lincoln nominated Ulysses S. Grant to become commander of the Union land forces, with the rank of lieutenant general. The Senate confirmed Grant's appointment on February 2. On February 8, Lincoln introduced Grant to official Washington during a reception at the White House. On February 9, Grant left the capital for his headquarters in the field, with the Army of the Potomac at Brandy Station, Virginia.

April 1864: Grant settled on strategic aims and began issuing orders for the 1864 spring campaigns. In the West, he instructed Gen. Nathaniel Banks to advance into Alabama and Gen William T. Sherman to move against the Army of Tennessee in north Georgia, with Atlanta as the objective. In Virginia, he laid out a three-pronged offensive: Gen. Fritz Sigel in the Shenandoah Valley, an important Confederate granary; Gen. Benjamin Butler along the James River toward Richmond; and Gen. George Meade along the Rapidan River, with the Army of Northern Virginia as his target. To Meade, with whom Grant would travel, went the chief assignment: "Lee's army is your objective point," Grant told Meade. "Wherever Lee goes, there you will go also."

April 27, 1864: Grant issued final orders and set dates for the opening of the spring offensive. He announced that he would advance with the Army of the Potomac on May 4. Sherman, he instructed, was to begin his move on Atlanta the following day.

May 4–5, 1864 (Wilderness Campaign): With the blooming of the dogwoods, the Union and Confederate armies returned to the old Wilderness (Virginia) battlefields. The 120,000-strong Army of the Potomac crossed the Rapidan River on schedule on May 4 and 5 and advanced south into the Wilderness.

Gen. Robert E. Lee, with barely half Grant's numerical strength, resolved at once to attack. He sent two of his three corps on parallel routes from the west, with a view to striking the Federals in the flank before they could clear the Wilderness tangle.

May 5–7, 1864 (Battle of the Wilderness): The action opened around 7 o'clock on the morning of May 5 when the Confederate 2nd Corps under Gen. Richard S. Ewell bumped into Union general Gouverneur Warren's 5th Corps in the thickets near Wilderness Tavern. The collision touched off a full day's blind, confused, and inconclusive struggle.

Ewell's battle died out around 3 o'clock. As soon as the guns fell silent, his infantry began digging in along both sides of the Orange Turnpike. To the south, the Federal 2nd Corps under Gen. Winfield S. Hancock struck Gen. A. P. Hill's corps across the Orange Plank Road. Here, as the long day waned, the Yankees pressed the Confederates nearly to the breaking point. Only the coming of darkness saved Hill's outnumbered, outgunned corps from collapse.

That night, Grant sent orders for Hancock to renew the attack at first light next morning. For his part, Lee passed word to Gen. James Longstreet, whose 1st Corps was still on the way to the battlefield, to be ready to pitch into Hancock as soon as he arrived. Hill, meanwhile, granted his frazzled troops a full night's rest, ignoring a recommendation from one of his division commanders to keep the men awake and at work entrenching.

On May 6, when Hancock struck, Hill's unfortified line gave way almost at once. Only the timely arrival of the first of Longstreet's infantry double-timing down the Plank Road prevented a rout. Longstreet's lead brigades drove the Federals back to their start lines and allowed Hill time to regroup. During the lull, Longstreet prepared his counterstroke.

Earlier, a Confederate staff officer had discovered an unfinished, overgrown railroad cut through which a flanking column could approach unobserved. Longstreet assembled four brigades and assigned them the task of moving up through the cut and pouncing on Hancock's unsupported left. The idea was to crumple the flank, then meet up with the rest of the corps and the rest of the army to make a great "wheel" that would hurl Grant back across the Rapidan River.

The initial assault overwhelmed Hancock's left. His end brigade broke, then the next in line broke, and so on. But Longstreet's great wheel never got rolling. As he pushed up to the front, jittery Confederate infantry opened fire on him. The wounding of Longstreet brought the attack abruptly to a standstill, much as Stonewall Jackson's wounding under similar circumstances had done at Chancellorsville the year before.

Fighting broke out again late in the afternoon, with Confederate lunges at both Union flanks. On Ewell's front, a brigade-sized attack managed a limited breakthrough and had the added effect of spreading alarm and despondency as far back as Grant's field headquarters. The first reports sounded dire; one unstrung officer claimed that Lee had turned the Union right and soon would sweep up the entire Union Army. For once, the usually imperturbable Grant lost his temper.

"I am heartily tired of hearing what Lee is going to do," he said. "Some of you always seem to think he is going to turn a double somersault and land in our rear and on both flanks at the same time. Go back to your command and try to think what we are going to do ourselves instead of what Lee is going to do."

The exhausted armies rested on May 7 and tallied their losses. The Federal totals were grievous—more than 17,000 killed, wounded, or missing over the three days. The Confederates lost 7,700 men. Brush fires spread through the woods, and stretcher parties fanned out, trying to save as many of the wounded as possible. Some 200 men were burned or suffocated to death in the smoking woods.

During the night, Grant began to disengage. For many in the ranks, the order to break contact came as no surprise: in the tradition of the Army of the Potomac, the generals would mismanage a battle, then retreat. "We had expected so much from General Grant," one private wrote, recording the prevailing view, "and now he was to be defeated as other generals before him had been." This time, though, there would be no turning back. Grant pulled away from Lee not to retreat but to continue the southward march. He put the Army on the road for Spotsylvania Court House, Virginia, 12 miles distant—and on the shortest and most direct route to Richmond.

May 4–17, 1864 (Battle of Drewry's Bluff): As part of Grant's overall strategy, Gen. Benjamin Butler began his advance up the James

River. Moving cautiously, he gave the Confederate commander, Gen. P. G. T. Beauregard, ample time to organize his defenses. Reaching the lines at Drewry's Bluff on May 15, Butler looked to his own defense first, using wire entanglements made from telegraph wire: Stretched between trees and stumps, it trapped the attacking Confederates. Some historians claim that this was the first time such wire was used in warfare, but others say such wire was first used at the Battle of Knoxville (see November 29, 1863, p. 253).

With three divisions, Beauregard, the defender, struck Butler, the attacker, early on the morning of May 16. Butler's troops generally fought well, and the lines held, but Butler decided to withdraw anyway. By the morning of May 17, Butler's army found itself "bottled up" (Grant's phrase) in the Bermuda Hundred cul-de-sac. The brief campaign cost the Federals some 4,100 casualties. Confederate losses were about 2,500.

May 8–20, 1864 (Battle of Spotsylvania Court House): Confederate cavalry reconnaissance tipped Lee to Grant's southeastward move, and advance units of the Army of Northern Virginia managed to reach Spotsylvania Court House, Virginia, on May 8 just ahead—literally, only a few minutes ahead—of the Federals. The Confederates withstood a series of piecemeal attacks during the day.

With the arrival of the rest of the Confederate army, Lee hunkered down in a strongly entrenched semicircle, with a prominent bulge (dubbed the "Mule Shoe" for its shape) in the center. From those fieldworks, the Confederates repulsed a series of full-scale assaults on May 10, inflicting heavy casualties on the attackers.

Grant took a day off to plan an all-out effort at the Mule Shoe for May 12, with General Hancock's 2nd Corps leading the way. Rain fell in torrents during the night, then slackened to drizzle before dawn. A little after 4:30 A.M., 20,000 Yankees came ghosting through the murk. The initial advance overwhelmed the defenders. Hancock's assault troops took 2,500 prisoners and 20 cannon in the first rush.

The Confederates regrouped and launched a furious counterattack that stopped the advance before it could cut Lee's army in half. The Yankee infantry settled into the enemy's trenches and thwarted all efforts to retake the salient, which became known as the "Bloody Angle."

Much of the fighting took place at arm's length, and in a cold, numbing rain. The volume of fire rose to an intensity never before experienced in the Civil War. Toward midnight an oak tree 22 inches in diameter, cut in two by gunfire, crashed into the Confederate lines.

Around midnight, some 20 hours after the Union 2nd Corps assault brigades loomed out of the fog, the Confederates finally abandoned the salient, falling back to a shorter line a few hundred yards to the rear. The combined casualties of the Mule Shoe fighting approached 13,000. For the next three days, the armies lay quiet. A final set of attacks on May 18 and 19 failed to break the stalemate.

The Federals, on the attack nearly all the time, suffered 35,000 men killed, wounded, or missing in the Wilderness, and at Spotsylvania Court House nearly twice the Confederate total. Still, Grant was undaunted. "I propose to fight it out on this line if it takes all summer," Grant wired President Lincoln.

May 9–24, 1864 (Sheridan's Richmond Raid): When Gen. Philip Sheridan complained to Grant about Gen. George Meade's use of cavalry, Grant gave Sheridan carte blanche to carry out a raid toward Richmond that would force the Confederate cavalry commander Gen. J. E. B. Stuart to give battle. Sheridan set out for Richmond May 9 with 10,000 troopers; Stuart moved at once in pursuit with 4,500.

Reaching Yellow Tavern early on May 11, Stuart took up position to block Sheridan's route to Richmond. The battle opened around eleven o'clock in the morning and continued with varying intensity—the fighting was sometimes hand-to-hand—through the afternoon. Around 4, heavy Federal attacks bent the left of the Confederate line. Riding over to investigate, Stuart was shot and mortally wounded. Stuart's cavalry withdrew during the night, and Sheridan had the victory he had promised Grant.

The Federal troopers did not reach Richmond, however. After a brief rest within the lines of Butler's Army of the James, Sheridan set out to rejoin Grant on May 17. His cavalry reached the Army of the Potomac on May 24.

Late May–early June 1864: After Spotsylvania, Grant persisted in trying to turn Lee's flank, this time in a series of operations along the North Anna River in Virginia. Again, however, the Army of Northern Virginia proved too nimble. After several days of skirmishing, Grant tried another turning movement, a wide swing 20 miles to the southeast of the North Anna River. His leading elements reached the crossroads of Cold Harbor on May 31. Lee kept pace, marching hard by day and digging by night. By June 1, the armies faced each other over several miles of trench lines. Grant ordered an attack for dawn on June 3.

June 3, 1864 (Battle of Cold Harbor): The Union assault troops seemed to know their assignment was hopeless. The evening before the Battle of Cold Harbor, many of the men had sewn little slips of paper with their names and addresses onto the backs of their coats, for they had resolved not to die anonymously.

The attacking brigades formed in the predawn darkness and stepped off at 4:30 A.M. In a half-hour, the fighting was essentially over. "It seemed like murder to fire on you," a Confederate officer told a New Hampshire prisoner. Still, the battle went on, charge after charge until noon, when Grant mercifully called it off. The Federals suffered 7,000 killed, wounded, or missing, against Confederate casualties of about 1,500. "I regret this assault more than any one I have ever ordered," Grant said that night.

June 1864 (Petersburg Campaign): The costly failure at Cold Harbor cured Grant, temporarily anyway, of launching frontal assaults on Lee's veterans. He put the Union forces in motion for the James River and aimed for the critical communications center of Petersburg, Virginia, just beyond Cold Harbor.

Four vital rail lines ran through Petersburg. With those communications severed, Lee's army could not be fed or supplied. Richmond, the Confederacy's political, industrial, and psychological heart, would have to be abandoned. "We must destroy this army of Grant's before he gets to the James River," Lee had told one of his officers at the outset of the spring campaign. "If he gets there, it will become a siege, and then it will be a mere question of time."

During the second week in June, in what Gen. Edward Porter Alexander, one of Lee's officers, later called "the most brilliant stroke in all the Federal campaigns of the whole war," Grant moved around Lee, oversaw the building of the 2,100-foot-long James River pontoon bridge in a day, and had the Union Army across the river and on the march for Petersburg.

June 15–18, 1864 (Petersburg Assaults): The Confederate commander at Petersburg, Gen. P. G. T. Beauregard, had the advantage of stout physical defenses, though he could call on only the scantiest of forces to man them. When the Federal van, the 18th Corps of Gen. William F. Smith with Gen. Winfield Scott Hancock's 2nd Corps close behind, approached Petersburg on June 15, Beauregard had but 2,500 old men and boys of the Home Guard and a few scattered cavalry units in line.

The defenders were drawn up behind fieldworks in a 10-mile arc covering Petersburg. Beauregard's first test came early in the evening of June 15, when Smith sent a full division—consisting of black troops seeing their first combat—against two strong points along the eastern curve of the arc.

The Yankees swiftly overran more than a mile of the Confederate entrenchments, capturing 7 bastions and 16 guns within an hour or so. Then Smith, turning cautious, broke off the battle. That turned out to be a fatal mistake. According to Beauregard, Smith and Hancock, who arrived later in the evening, could have marched into Petersburg practically unopposed that night.

The missed opportunity did not greatly trouble Grant. "I think it is pretty well," he said, "to get across a great river and come up here and attack Lee in the rear before he is ready for us." Indeed, Lee hesitated for several days, unwilling to believe the Federals were across the James River in force. As a consequence, he starved Beauregard of troops. On June 16, two more Union corps reached Petersburg, along with the Army of the Potomac's commander, Gen. George Gordon Meade. The new arrivals brought Grant's strength to some 75,000 soldiers against Beauregard's 14,000.

The Federals launched a series of uncoordinated assaults against the beleaguered Confederates on June 17. Toward evening, the attacking Federals captured a mile or so of Beauregard's outer works. Meade, in immediate command, failed to follow up that success, opting instead to order a full-scale assault along the entire line for dawn the next day.

With increasing urgency, Beauregard repeated his appeals for reinforcements. By the night of June 17, there could no longer be any doubt that Petersburg was the Union objective. Lee ordered the main body of the Army of Northern Virginia

Union troops huddle in trenches outside Petersburg, Virginia, during the long siege that began in June 1864, and lasted until the end of the war in April 1865.

on the road to Petersburg. Overnight, Petersburg's defenders quietly withdrew to a second, shorter line a mile to the rear.

The Federal advance began at dawn on June 17, on schedule. The assault troops found only empty entrenchments in their front. Beauregard's step backward confused Meade's officers. Hours were lost while they reconnoitered the new line and prepared new schemes of attack. Frustrated by the delay, Meade finally ordered his corps commanders to cease making plans and "attack at all hazards without reference to each other." In most cases, the troops merely went through the motions. They had learned all they needed to know about the Confederates' skill in building fortifications. Theodore Lyman, a Union staff officer, thought all the attacking troops went in grudgingly that day—the cumulative effect, he believed, of the Wilderness, Spotsylvania, and Cold Harbor. "You can't strike a blow with a wounded hand," Lyman said.

All along the line, the defenders easily repulsed the Federal attacks. The fighting of June 15–18 added another 12,000 names to Grant's casualty lists, which now totaled 66,000 killed, wounded, or missing since the opening of the campaign on the Rapidan River in early May.

Grant could see that further attacks would be profitless, and he abandoned the effort to take Petersburg. "Now we will rest the men, and use the spade for their protection until a new vein can be struck," he told Meade.

July–August 1864 (Early's Washington Raid): With the Army of Northern Virginia under extreme pressure, Confederate general Jubal Early launched the Shenandoah Valley offensive to draw off Federal strength from Lee's front. With 10,000 men in two corps, he marched north in early July, easily outmaneuvering Gen. Fritz Sigel, who had fumbled his part in Grant's spring offensive. Early crossed the Potomac River on July 5, and on the following day, Grant began detaching units to send north to meet Early.

On July 9, a Union force of 6,000 under Gen. Lew Wallace moved into position along the Monocacy River near Frederick, Maryland, directly in Early's path. In a series of assaults, Early's veterans routed this scratch Union force and pushed on toward Washington, D.C.

Early's column reached Silver Spring, on the outskirts of Washington, D.C., on July 11. After looking over the ground, he ordered an assault for July 12, then rescinded the order that night when he learned that the Federal 6th Corps had arrived in Washington from the Petersburg front. Early pulled back the night of July 12 and recrossed the Potomac at Leesburg on July 14.

Retreating into the Shenandoah Valley, Early abruptly resumed the offensive at Kernstown, Virginia, turning to strike the Federal pursuit under Gen. George Crook. After cavalry skirmishes on July 23, Early launched a general attack on July 24 and drove Crook from the town, with Confederate losses of more than 1,000.

Resuming the northward march, Early recrossed the Potomac River and sent his cavalry into the prosperous town of Chambersburg, Pennsylvania, early on July 30. In reprisal for Union property destruction in Virginia, Early demanded $100,000 in gold from the townspeople, on pain of destruction of the town.

Around 9 A.M. on July 30, Early ordered the 3,000 inhabitants out of Chambersburg and ordered his soldiers to set fire to the town. Some officers refused to carry out the order, but eventually the matches were struck and some two-thirds of the town was destroyed.

July 1864 (Siege of Petersburg): In front of Petersburg, Virginia, the two armies settled down to siege warfare. Toward the end of June, a Pennsylvania officer floated an unorthodox idea for breaking the deadlock. Lt. Col. Henry Pleasants of the 48th Pennsylvania proposed tunneling under the Confederates, rigging a mine, and blowing a hole in the works through which the Union infantry could pour. He offered his troops, mostly volunteers from the Schuylkill Valley (Pennsylvania) coalfields, for the job.

Gen. Ambrose E. Burnside, commander of the Federal 9th Corps, endorsed the project. Within a month, the industrious Pennsylvanians had burrowed a tunnel more than 500 feet long. Some 8,000 pounds of explosive powder was packed into lateral galleries 20 feet below the Confederate bastion. Burnside planned a four-division advance into the expected breach and assigned a division of black troops specially trained for the work to lead the advance.

July 30, 1864 (Battle of the Crater): Grant and Meade overruled Burnside's decision to give the starring role to the black troops. The interference demoralized Burnside, who lost interest in the operation. Still, the Pennsylvanians held up their end. The mine blew at 4:44 A.M. on July 30 with a thunderous roar, blasting a 400-foot-wide gap in the Confederate line.

The assault troops moved out before the dust had settled. But things went awry from the start. The explosion created a rubble-filled crater 60 feet across, 200 feet wide, and 10 to 30 feet deep. The awestruck attackers paused to gaze into the chasm; hundreds actually descended into it for a close-up look or to tend the enemy wounded buried in the debris.

The Confederates acted decisively to seal the breach. Survivors of the blast met the oncoming Federal infantry with a murderous fire. The pit rapidly filled with a milling mass of confused, panicked Yankees seeking cover from the enemy volleys. Counterattacking Confederates surged up to the rim of the crater and poured a point-blank fire into the crowd.

At 9:30 A.M., after nearly four hours of bloodshed, Meade ordered the distracted Burnside to suspend the attack. The cost: nearly 4,000 killed, wounded, or missing. Grant regretted the missed opportunity and the wasted lives. It was, Grant later said, "the saddest affair I have witnessed in this war."

August–September 1864: In early August, Grant sent Sheridan to the Shenandoh Valley to smash Early. With 48,000 troops of all arms, Sheridan had a powerful force with which to subdue Early's 23,000. During August and September, the two forces maneuvered, each looking for a vantage point for attack.

August–October 1864: Through the summer and early autumn, Grant carried out large-scale attacks on both flanks of the long Richmond-Petersburg line, costing Lee casualties he could not afford and forcing him to thin his defenses by extending the works westward to protect vital railroads.

On August 18, in heavy fighting, the Union 5th Corps got astride the Weldon Railroad near Globe Tavern south of Petersburg and tore up miles of track, leaving only the Southside Railroad to the west to supply the city.

On the other side of the line, Grant, in late September, ordered a surprise attack against Forts Harrison and Gilmer on Richmond's outer defenses. In heavy fighting on September 29, the Federals captured Fort Harrison but failed to carry Fort Gilmer. Lee counterattacked, but was unable to retake the lost ground. The two days' fight cost the Confederates 2,800 irreplaceable men. Union losses were roughly 2,500.

September–October 1864 (Sheridan's

Shenandoah Valley Campaign): On September 19, Sheridan found Early—from whom Lee had detached an infantry division and 12 guns to fill out his thinning lines—at Winchester, Virginia, and prepared to attack. Badly outnumbered, Early nevertheless managed to withstand the Union assault and withdraw to the south, with Sheridan's cavalry in pursuit.

Sheridan attacked again at Fisher's Hill (or Strasburg) on September 22, striking the Confederates, who occupied a strong natural position on a heavily wooded ridge, first on the flank, then in front. The gray line gave way, and the retreat quickly became a rout. Early lost some 1,200 men; Federal casualties were about 525.

With Early battered, Sheridan resumed his campaign to turn the Shenandoah Valley into a wasteland, stripping the country of food, forage, and livestock. "The people must be left with nothing," he said, "but their eyes to weep with over the war." On October 7, Sheridan reported to Grant that his troops had destroyed 2,000 barns and 70 grain mills and had taken 4,000 cattle and 3,000 sheep.

Early, however, managed to regroup. By mid-October, he had prepared a counterstroke for Sheridan's army in its camps along Cedar Creek near Middletown, Virginia. As it happened, Sheridan was in Washington, D.C. Returning on October 18, he stopped for the night at Winchester, Virginia, some 20 miles north of Cedar Creek. Sheridan awoke the morning of October 19, heard firing in the distance, and rode to the sound of the guns.

October 19, 1864 (Battle of Cedar Creek): Early had surprised the Federals asleep in camp and crumpled the left of their line. No less than four divisons turned and ran. Sheridan arrived just in time to stem the rout. As he rode down the road waving his hat, the troops began to cheer. "God damn you, don't cheer me," he shouted. "If you love your country, come up to the front. There's lots of fight in you men yet."

Thus was born one of the legends of the Civil War—Sheridan's ride. It took more, of course, than a promenade down the road. Sheridan and his staff labored two full hours to re-form the Federal line and prepare a counterattack. When it came, though, it bowled the Confederates right out of the captured camps and into headlong retreat. Sheridan took more than a thousand prisoners, and Early's career came abruptly to an

end. Sheridan resumed his thorough ransacking of the Shenandoah Valley.

December 18–27, 1864 (Fort Fisher Expedition): On December 18, transports carrying 6,500 Union troops under Gen. Benjamin Butler met Adm. David D. Porter's fleet off Hampton Roads and set sail for Fort Fisher, guarding the Confederacy's last open port, Wilmington, North Carolina.

Union troops landed on December 24 and 25 and captured the fort's outposts. Porter's vessels opened a heavy bombardment. Skirmishers approached to within 75 yards of the fort, supported by naval gunfire. But the commander on the spot, Gen. Godfrey Weitzel, determined an assault would be too costly, and Butler ordered a withdrawal. Federal losses were reported at 15 men; the Confederates lost 300 taken prisoner.

December 1864: By year's end, a greatly weakened Army of Northern Virginia held a nearly continuous 37-mile front, curving from the White Oak Swamp east of Richmond to Hatcher's Run southwest of Petersburg. Winter found the troops hungry, weary, and discouraged. "Some of the men have been without meat for three days," Lee wrote War Secretary John Breckinridge near year's end, "and all are suffering from reduced ration and scant clothing, exposed to battle, hail, cold, and sleet."

WESTERN THEATER

Early February 1864: On February 7, a Federal expedition landed at Jacksonville as part of an effort to secure Florida for the Union. Encountering no resistance, the Union commander, Gen. Truman Seymour, marched inland 20 miles to Baldwin, where a second Union column joined him. That set the stage for a clash between some 5,000 Union troops and a Confederate force of roughly equal size.

February 3–March 5, 1864 (Meridian Campaign): Partly to support a proposed Red River Campaign west of the Mississippi River, and partly to strengthen the Union hold on Vicksburg, Gen. William T. Sherman set out in early February to destroy communications and supplies in Confederate central Mississippi.

Sherman marched from Vicksburg at the head of 25,000 men toward Meridian, Mississippi. At the same time, 7,000 Union cavalry under Gen. William Sooy Smith left Memphis, Tennessee, bound for Meridian. Sherman fought several skirmishes en route to Meridian, which he reached on February 14. Over five days, his troops destroyed everything of military value in the town. Withdrawing slowly westward, the Federals fought several more skirmishes before safely returning to Vicksburg on March 5.

Smith, meanwhile, found the going slow. Heavy rains flooded the swampy countryside. Then Smith had the misfortune of encountering Gen. Nathan Bedford Forrest. The Confederate cavalryman's 5,000 troopers intimidated Smith's larger force at West Point, Mississippi, on February 21, and Smith ordered a withdrawal after a light skirmish. At Okolona, Mississippi on February 22, six hours of skirmishing ended in a rout of Smith's forces, which fell back some 9 miles to Ivey Hills before halting to make a stand. That debacle brought Smith's operation to an end.

February 27, 1864: The Confederate prisoner of war compound at Andersonville, Georgia, received its first Union captives. The prison grounds covered 16.5 acres (later enlarged), with a stream running through the middle. From the outset, prison housing, rations, and medical care were grossly inadequate.

March 17, 1864: Gen. Ulysses S. Grant, the newly appointed commander of the Union Army, and Sherman, who succeeded Grant as the senior commander in the West, met at Nashville, Tennessee, to plan the spring campaign against Gen. Joseph E. Johnston's Army of Tenesee in northern Georgia.

Early April 1864: The Confederate high command ordered Gen. James Longstreet's corps, which had wintered in east Tennessee, to rejoin Gen. Robert E. Lee's Army of Northern Virginia for the spring campaign.

April 12, 1864: Forrest's Confederate cavalry attacked the isolated Union garrison at Fort Pillow, Tennessee, overlooking the Mississippi River. The 500-strong garrison included more than 250 black troops. Forrest's 1,500 troopers took the fort with ease, but questions were raised about the extremely high proportion of Union battlefield deaths—231 killed, 100 seriously wounded. The Federals later charged that Forrest's men had cold-bloodedly murdered many black soldiers after they had surrendered.

May 7–June 26, 1864 (Atlanta Campaign): Sherman grouped his 100,000-man western command into three unequal wings: the Army of the

Cumberland under Gen. George H. Thomas, the Army of the Tennessee under Gen. James McPherson, and the small Army of the Ohio under Gen. James Schofield. Facing Sherman, well dug in around Dalton, Georgia, were Johnston's 62,000 Confederates.

Sherman decided to use Thomas's army, the largest, to pin the Confederates in their trenches while the two smaller, handier armies swung out on the Confederate flanks. Sherman resolved to force the pace to Atlanta, Georgia, nearly 100 miles to the southeast.

Sherman opened on May 7 by sending McPherson on a wide swing west and south toward Resaca, Georgia, 15 miles in Johnston's rear. McPherson failed to block the enemy's line of retreat, however, and Johnston withdrew safely into new lines around Resaca the night of May 12–13. "Well, Mac, you missed the opportunity of a lifetime," Sherman told the disappointed McPherson.

The two armies sparred near Resaca for three days. When Sherman threatened another turning movement, Johnston again pulled back, this time some 25 miles to Cassville. On May 19, he withdrew another 10 miles to strong positions at Allatoona Pass on the Etowah River in Georgia.

Still another flank march pried Johnston out of the Allatoona Pass stronghold. Once again, McPherson swung out wide to the west. From May 25–27 the armies tangled in the woods and ravines around Dallas, Georgia. During the first weeks of June, they gradually settled into fortified positions, moving in concert slowly southeastward toward Kennesaw Mountain. In less than two months, Sherman had covered half the distance to Atlanta at a comparatively light cost— about 10,000 casualties.

June 10, 1864 (Battle of Brice's Crossroads): Sherman, concerned about his communications, ordered a combined force of 8,000 cavalry and infantry to march from Memphis, Tennessee, in search of Gen. Nathan Bedford Forrest. With 4,700 men, Forrest struck the Federal cavalry advance at Brice's Crossroads in northern Mississippi. When Union infantry under Gen. S. D. Sturgis arrived, jaded from the severe heat, Forrest massed his forces for an attack on the Union center. Then, he followed up with sharp attacks on both flanks. The Federals soon gave way, confusion turning to panic.

Forrest pursued the beaten Federals all night

and into the next day. Sturgis's losses were about 2,200, including 1,600 taken prisoner. With a loss of fewer than 500 men, Forrest had defeated a force of twice his number and captured 18 guns and a 250-wagon supply train.

June 27, 1864 (Battle of Kennesaw Mountain): In late June, Sherman, suspecting that the campaign of maneuver had dulled his army's aggressive edge, decided to launch a frontal attack against Johnston's works on the slopes of Kennesaw Mountain.

At 9 o'clock in the morning, in near 100-degree heat, Thomas sent three divisions against the Confederate center on the mountainside. One division overran the enemy outpost line but could gain no further ground. A second assault suffered a sharp repulse. The third likewise failed to make any headway. Total Federal casualties were about 2,500 killed, wounded, or missing, a heavy toll for that campaign.

Sherman took the setback philosophically. "Our loss is small compared with some of those in the east," he told Thomas. "It should not in the least discourage us. At times assaults are necessary and inevitable."

July 1–17, 1864 (Atlanta Campaign): Sherman kept Thomas's troops in line on the Kennesaw Mountain slopes while he prepared new marching orders for McPherson's mobile forces. On July 1, McPherson moved toward the east; the turning movement once again compelled Johnston to leave a strong defensive position and fall back toward Atlanta. By July 9, Sherman's troops were across the Chattahoochie River and closing in on Atlanta from the north and east.

Johnston's backpedaling had increasingly worried President Davis. He urged his western commander to hold the city of Atlanta, with its arms factories and communications, at all costs. Its loss, he reminded Johnston, would "open the way for the Federal army to the Gulf on the one hand and to Charleston on the other, and close up those rich granaries from which Lee's armies are supplied." But the Army of Tennessee did not finally come to a halt until it reached Peach Tree Creek only 4 miles from Atlanta.

Davis, out of patience, replaced Johnston on July 17 with the aggressive Gen. John Bell Hood. Davis made the change against Lee's advice. ("All lion," said Lee of the brave but limited Hood, "and none of the fox.") Across Peach Tree Creek,

Sherman's officers welcomed the move. They expected and hoped that Hood would go on the offensive. "We were confident that a succession of attacks would soon destroy the Confederate army," one of Sherman's corps commanders recalled.

July 13–15, 1864 (Battle of Tupelo): Sherman continued to try new combinations for Forrest's destruction. After General Sturgis's failure at Brice's Crossroads, Sherman ordered Gen. A. J. Smith with 14,000 men to bring the Confederate "wizard of the saddle" to grief. The forces skirmished near Tupelo, Mississippi, on July 13, with inconclusive results. Over the following two days, Forrest launched a succession of unsuccessful assaults at the Union line.

Smith, however, decided to retreat, even though he had inflicted some 1,300 casualties to only around 700 of his own. For once, Forrest, who had been slightly wounded in the fight, had been repulsed, though not defeated and certainly not deterred from preying on Sherman's rearward communications.

July 20–September 1, 1864 (Battles around Atlanta): On July 20, in an action known as "Hood's First Sortie," Confederate forces under Gen. John Hood attacked Thomas's army astride Peach Tree Creek. Repulsed, Hood withdrew into the Atlanta defenses with heavy casualties, about 2,500, including 600 men dead on the field.

Sherman then sent McPherson on a flank march to the south and east. In an action dubbed "Hood's Second Sortie," Hood, on July 22, struck McPherson's exposed flank, while Confederate cavalry under Gen. Joseph Wheeler curled around to hit the Federal rear. McPherson, one of the Union's most promising young commanders, was killed in that fight. Failures of execution, especially on the part of Confederate general William Hardee's corps, doomed Hood's effort, however. The Confederates were stopped with heavy losses—about 8,000 killed, wounded, or missing to Sherman's 3,700.

By July 25, Sherman had closed in on Atlanta from the north and east. Two major operations— Stoneman's and McCook's Raids of July 26–31 and a move toward Ezra Church on July 28— failed, however, to cut Hood's railroad lifeline to the south. In an engagement at Ezra Church (also known as "Hood's Third Sortie"), the Confederates and Gen. Oliver O. Howard's Army of the Tennessee (Howard succeeded McPherson)

The railroad roundhouse in the foreground was among the many structures destroyed when Union forces took Atlanta, Georgia, in September 1864.

struggled for several hours through the afternoon of July 28 before Hood finally ordered a withdrawal into the Atlanta lines. Again, Confederate losses were heavy, about 5,000 killed, wounded, and missing.

Cavalry operations consumed most of August. Gen. Joseph Wheeler led Hood's cavalry on a month-long raid of Sherman's communications. Union general Judson Kilpatrick's Jonesboro (Georgia) raid of August 18–22 did not achieve its purpose of forcing Hood to pull out of Atlanta.

In late August, Sherman shifted the bulk of his forces to the south and west in a renewed effort to turn Hood's defenses. On August 31, Hood attacked Union positions at Jonesboro southeast of Atlanta but failed to drive the Federals off his supply line. On September 1, Howard struck Hardee's corps, isolated at Jonesboro, and destroyed a portion of it before the Confederate lines stablized. During the afternoon and evening of September 1, with the railroad approaches firmly in Sherman's control, Hood evacuated Atlanta. The first Federal troops entered the city the next day.

September 4–8, 1864: Union forces completed the occupation of Atlanta. "Atlanta is ours, and fairly won," Sherman telegraphed Washington, D.C.

With Hood's battered but still dangerous Army of Tennessee hovering off to the north and west, General Sherman ordered the evacuation of civilians in Atlanta to make the city easier to defend. When the mayor and city council protested, Sherman replied: "War is cruelty, and you cannot refine it. The only way the people of Atlanta can hope once more to live in peace and quiet at home is to stop the war. You might as well appeal against the thunderstorm as against these terrible hardships of war" (see Notable Phrases, p. 285).

September–October 1864: In hopes of forcing Sherman from Atlanta, Hood unleashed a series of strikes at the 140-mile Union supply line north to Chattanooga, Tennessee, the beginning of the ten-week Franklin and Nashville Campaign. Sherman pursued for a time, then began to plan an offensive that would take the Union Army through the heartland of Confederate Georgia.

"I could cut a swath through Georgia to the sea," he wrote Grant, "divide the Confederacy, and come up on the rear of Lee." Grant and Lincoln, however, still feared Hood. "Damn him," Sherman responded, "if he'll go to the Ohio River, I'll give him rations. Let him go north. My business is down south." When Sherman agreed to leave Thomas and the Army of the Cumberland behind to check Hood, Grant reluctantly approved Sherman's proposed march to the sea.

"I can make this march," Sherman exulted. "I can make Georgia howl."

November 1864: Hood decided to march his 40,000-strong army north toward Nashville, reasoning that an invasion of Tennessee would draw Sherman out of Georgia in pursuit.

Sherman, however, left Hood to Thomas. During November, Thomas's Cumberland army fell back from Pulaski to Spring Hill to Franklin, Tennessee, with cavalry actions and skirmishing along the route. By November 30, a wing of Thomas's army under Gen. John Schofield had entrenched in strong positions at Franklin, 15 miles south of Nashville.

November 15–December 12, 1864: Sherman's stripped-down army of 60,000, four infantry corps and a cavalry division, left Atlanta in flames on November 15. Rearguards fired railroad facilities, factories, warehouses, and other buildings of military value, burning some 200 acres of the city's heart.

The Union Army marched in two wings, one under Gen. Oliver O. Howard, the other under Gen. Henry Slocum, following parallel routes from 25 to 60 miles apart. Some 2,500 light wagons carried 200 rounds of ammunition per man, 20 days' rations, and a five-day supply of oats and corn for the animals. Georgia's farms and plantations were to provide the balance of the Army's needs.

The wide-front advance confused Confederate resistance that lay in its path, and the march took on something of a holiday air. "This is probably the most gigantic pleasure excursion ever planned," one Yankee officer observed early in the campaign. "It already beats everything I ever saw soldiering and promises to prove much richer yet." Once the Army cleared the picked-over Atlanta environs, the countryside provided plenty of food and forage.

For civilians in Sherman's path, the march was a cataclysm. "Like demons they rushed in," wrote Dolly Burge, a widowed plantation mistress. "To my smokehouse, my Dairy, Pantry, Kitchen and Cellar, like famished wolves they come, breaking locks and whatever is in their way. The thousand pounds of meat in my smokehouse is gone in a twinkling, my flour, my meat, my lard, my butter, eggs, pickles both in vinegar and brine, wine, jars and jugs, are all gone. My 18 fat turkeys, my hens, chickens and fowl, my young pigs, are shot down in my yard and hunted as if they were the rebels themselves."

Sherman encouraged such depredations, believing they would shorten the war by undermining the Confederate will to fight. "This may seem a hard species of warfare," he said, "but it brings the sad realities of war home to those who have been directly or indirectly instrumental in involving us in its attendant calamities."

The two wings converged at Milledgeville, then serving as Georgia's capital, on November 22. On December 1, the Union Army reached Millen, the site of an abandoned prisoner of war compound, where half-starved and sickly Federal captives had been forced to burrow into the ground for shelter. By November 12, Sherman's army, with its long tail of thousands of liberated slaves, had drawn up before the swamps and cypress groves outside Savannah, some 325 miles from Atlanta.

November 30, 1864: Around 3:30 in the afternoon, Hood, with 26,000 men, sent his infantry on a broad front over 2 miles of open ground toward Gen. James Schofield's 28,000 in their well-fortified lines at Franklin. Accurate Federal artillery pounded the Confederate assault columns. The Confederate units that managed to reach their objectives were bloodily repulsed. In six hours of unequal struggle, Hood suffered some 6,200 men killed, wounded, or missing, including six generals killed. Union losses were about 2,300.

That night, Schofield withdrew to join the balance of Thomas's army in the Nashville defenses. Hood and his bled-down army unwisely followed.

December 1864: Grant prodded the methodical Thomas to come out of the Nashville defenses and destroy the Army of Tennessee, barely half the strength of Sherman's army. Grant so lost patience with Thomas that he ordered him removed from command. But by mid-December, Thomas reported that he was ready to strike, and Grant stayed the order.

December 15–16, 1864 (Battle of Nashville): Hood had pulled up before the Nashville defenses with no particular plan in mind. Too weak to attack the stronghold, he awaited events. Early on December 15, Thomas struck both Confederate flanks, holding Hood's left in place while he tried to crush the right with his main effort. The Confederates barely held, then pulled back into tighter lines at the end of the day.

Thomas resumed the action on December 16. The pounding finally forced the Confederate line to give way. It collapsed from left to right; soon, more than 4,400 of Hood's veterans surrendered. The rest were in full flight southward.

Apart from captives, Confederate casualties in the Battle of Nashville were comparatively light—an estimated 1,500 killed or wounded. Thomas's losses were roughly 3,000.

December 12–21, 1864 (March to the Sea): Sherman prepared to lay siege to Savannah, Georgia, whose defenses were formidable though undermanned. His forces made contact with the Union fleet in Ossabaw Sound on December 13, sent out the first word of the success of Sherman's epic march through Georgia, and opened a reliable seaborne supply line. With assured food and ammunition supplies, Sherman prepared to attack Savannah.

On the foggy night of December 20, however, Savannah's garrison of about 10,000 slipped quietly out of the city, leaving it to Sherman without a fight. Federal troops entered Savannah early on December 21.

Sherman wired President Lincoln: "I beg to present you as a Christmas gift the city of Savannah, with 150 heavy guns and plenty of ammunition, also about 25,000 bales of cotton."

Almost at once, Sherman began to plan his next campaign. "I'm going to march to Richmond," he said. "I expect to turn north when the sun does—and when I go through South Carolina, it will be one of the most horrible things in the history of the world."

December 15–30, 1864: Union cavalry pursued Hood's remnants, about 20,000 men, into Alabama and Mississippi. Having all but destroyed the Army of Tennessee in a series of ill-advised offensive actions, Hood, at year's end, prepared to resign his command.

TRANS-MISSISSIPPI THEATER

March–May 1864 (Red River Campaign): Under pressure from President Lincoln, Gen. Ulysses S. Grant directed Gen. Nathaniel P. Banks

to extend Union control over interior Louisiana before turning to his preferred project for 1864, the capture of the Gulf of Mexico port of Mobile.

The Red River Campaign plan called for Banks with 17,000 men to link up with 10,000 troops from Vicksburg, Mississippi, under Gen. A. J. Smith and, eventually, another 15,000 under Gen. Frederick Steele advancing south from Arkansas. A powerful flotilla of 13 ironclads under Adm. David D. Porter would advance upriver with Banks's land forces.

Smith set out from Vicksburg in Porter's riverboats on March 10. He took Alexandria, Louisiana, on March 18 without opposition from the Confederate forces under Gen. Richard Taylor. Banks's column arrived a week later, and the combined force marched on the next objective, Shreveport, Louisiana.

Low water hampered Porter's flotilla, and Banks's columns were strung out on a narrow road through Louisiana wilderness. Massing his forces, Taylor struck Banks at Sabine Crossroads on the afternoon of April 8. Routed, the Federals withdrew 15 miles to Pleasant Hill. There, on April 9, they withstood a full-scale Confederate assault, then drove off Taylor's troops with a powerful counterattack. All the same, Banks withdrew to Grand Ecore that night. Taylor, meanwhile, turned north to deal with Steele coming down from Arkansas.

Confederate cavalry had harassed Steele from the outset, causing delays that had allowed Taylor to combine to thwart Banks before Shreveport. In mid-April, learning that Banks had failed to take Shreveport, Steele moved into the town of Camden, Arkansas, and awaited events. There, on April 25, a Confederate detachment attacked Steele's supply line and captured a 200-wagon train, forcing a retreat. Steele's expedition survived Confederate attacks at Jenkins' Ferry with heavy losses on April 29–30 and continued rearward to Little Rock, reaching the Arkansas capital, and ending a disastrous campaign on May 3.

Even though he had defeated Taylor, Banks, too, decided on retreat. Confederate skirmishers harassed the Union columns all the way to Alexandria, where low water in the Red River threatened to strand Porter's gunboats.

An ingenious engineer, Lt. Col. Joseph Bailey, came up with a solution: He built a series of wooden wing dams above the Alexandria rapids to raise the water level so the boats could resume their journey. The first Union vessel cleared the rapids on May 9; the others followed. Banks continued his harrassed retreat. By May 26, his army had reached the comparative safety of Donaldson, Louisiana, bringing the ill-starred Red River Campaign—as well as Banks's career as a commander in the field—to an inglorious end.

September–October 1864 (Price's Missouri Raid): With 12,000 men, Confederate general Sterling Price crossed from Arkansas into Missouri to carry out a hit-and-run campaign against Federal outposts in Missouri. Attacking Fort Davidson on the 27th, his forces were driven off with heavy losses—about 1,500, compared to only 200 for the defenders.

Continuing west, Price encountered growing resistance from Union forces. Gen. Alfred Pleasanton's cavalry roughed up Price at Westport on October 23 and again at Marais des Cygnes on October 25, forcing him to turn and flee into Arkansas. The raid, a signal defeat for Price, turned out to be the last Confederate operation in Missouri.

NAVAL THEATER

February 17, 1864: Armed with a marine mine, the hand-propelled Confederate submersible *Hunley* attacked the USS *Housatonic* on blockade duty off Charleston, South Carolina. The explosion sent both vessels to the bottom, the submersible with a loss of seven crewmen, the U.S. warship with a loss of five.

April 19, 1864: The Confederate ram *Albemarle* attacked and sank the gunboat USS *Southfield*, chased off a second vessel, and assisted in the Confederate capture of Plymouth, North Carolina.

June 19, 1864: In a rare Civil War ship-to-ship duel, the eight-gun sloop USS *Kearsarge* engaged the seven-gun Confederate raider *Alabama* off Cherbourg, France. Over a two-year career, the raider, Adm. Raphael Semmes commanding, had sunk, burned, captured, or destroyed 69 Union vessels. The action opened at 10:57 A.M., and in less than two hours, the *Kearsarge*, Capt. John Winslow commanding, sent the raider to the bottom. Semmes evaded capture and reached England as a passenger in a yacht that had stood just out of range to observe the sea fight.

August 5, 1864 (Battle of Mobile Bay): A Union fleet under Adm. David Farragut moved on Confederate defenses at Mobile Bay in Alabama, guarding one of the Confederacy's last open ports. At 6 A.M., Farragut's 14 wooden steam warships and four *Monitor*-class ironclads set a course for the harbor forts and, beyond, an enemy flotilla of three wooden gunboats and the powerful Confederate ironclad *Tennessee*.

Shortly after 7 A.M., the batteries at Fort Gaines and Fort Morgan opened fire. At 7:45, the USS *Tecumseh* struck a torpedo (the Civil War term for a submerged mine) and sank at once. Farragut shouted his famous battle cry: "Damn the torpedos—full speed ahead!" (see Notable Phrases, p. 285) The Union warships pushed past the forts and into the bay. At around 8 o' clock, the *Tennessee* moved to the attack. The Federal warships rammed it several times, and the monitors poured a steady close-range fire into its iron sides and exposed machinery.

Its steering damaged, the *Tennessee* surrendered at 10 A.M. Farragut's casualties were 319, including 93 sailors drowned in the *Tecumseh*. Confederate losses totaled 312. Though the city of Mobile remained in Confederate hands, by month's end, the harbor forts had fallen to Farragut, rendering the port unusable.

October 7, 1864: At Bahia, Brazil, the USS *Wachusett* captured the Confederate raider *Florida* and put to sea with its prize, over Brazilian protests. Brazilian diplomatic protests later led U.S. Secretary of State William Seward to condemn the *Wachusett*'s action as unlawful.

October 12, 1864: Rear Adm. David D. Porter, after Farragut the most distinguished naval commander of the Civil War, took command of the main Union fleet, the North Atlantic Blockading Squadron.

October 27, 1864: In a daring small boat attack, U.S. Navy lieutenant William Cushing and 15 men in a small launch ended the career of the Confederate ram *Albemarle*, sending the vessel to the bottom of the Roanoke River with a spar torpedo.

HOME FRONTS

January 4, 1864: In Richmond, Virginia, the Confederate government authorized Gen. Robert E. Lee to commandeer food supplies for the increasingly hungry Army of Northern Virginia. Virginia civilians, already deprived of many necessities by the effectiveness of the Union blockade, suffered increased hardships as the winter advanced.

January–February 1864: In North Carolina on January 18, protests erupted over the Confederate conscription law. Desertion had become a serious problem for the Confederate forces. At the start of the year, about 187,000 men, some 40 percent of the army's nominal strength of 465,000, were absent, either at home with their families or in hiding from Confederate provost authorities. On February 3, President Jefferson Davis recommended the suspension of habeas corpus for desertion, spying, associating with the enemy, and other forms of dissent. On February 17, the Confederate Congress adopted the recommendation. It also extended conscription to boys and men between the ages of 17 and 50.

February 1864: In Washington, D.C., President Lincoln struggled with military and political problems of his own. On February 1, he proposed a draft of 500,000 men for the Union Army. He also acted to fend off challenges from the Republican left—radicals impatient with his hesitations on emancipation. On February 22, Lincoln learned of the so-called Pomeroy Circular, a Radical Republican proposal to put Treasury Secretary Salmon P. Chase in Lincoln's place as the party's 1864 presidential nominee.

March–April 1864: Reconstruction proceeded in the rebellious states of Louisiana and Arkansas. On March 15, Union military authorities in Louisiana transferred power to a civil governor. In Arkansas, on March 18, a pro-Union convention ratified a constitution that abolished slavery in the state. In New Orleans, on April 6, Louisiana loyalists followed with a new constitution abolishing slavery.

March 28, 1864: A gang of Copperheads attacked Union soldiers in Charleston, Illinois, in the most serious antiwar eruption since the New York City draft riots of July 1863. Five people were killed and 20 wounded in the melee.

April 8, 1864: By a 38 to 6 vote, the U.S. Senate approved the 13th Amendment to the U.S. Constitution, which abolished slavery in the United States and all its jurisdictions.

April 17, 1864: Gen. Ulysses S. Grant announced that he would suspend prisoner-of-war exchanges with the South until the exchanges were numerically equal on both sides, a measure that worsened the Confederacy's growing man-

power problem. Some 145,000 Confederates were in Northern prison camps.

Grant also announced that the Union would permit no distinction to be made between white and black prisoners. Confederates generally treated captured blacks as escaped slaves and refused to exchange them.

May 4, 1864: Over Lincoln's objections, the U.S. House passed the Wade-Davis Reconstruction Bill, which called for punitive measures against the defeated South. The bill was in response to what Radical Republicans regarded as Lincoln's lenient policies on reestablishing civil government in the former rebel states of Louisiana, Arkansas, and Tennessee.

May 1864: Horace Greeley, editor of the influential *New York Tribune*, in an editorial on May 13, called for the Republican 1864 presidential nomination to go to someone other than Lincoln. On May 31, insurgent Radical Republicans met in Cleveland, Ohio, to nominate their presidential candidate, Gen. John C. Frémont.

June 7–8, 1864: In Baltimore, Maryland, the National Union Convention—Republicans with a sprinkling of Democrats—nominated Abraham Lincoln for a second term. With the president claiming neutrality on the question, the convention chose Tennessee politician Andrew Johnson, a prewar Democrat, as Lincoln's running mate. The party's platform called for pursuit of the Civil War to a successful end, reunification, and an eventual passage in the House of Representatives and state ratification of the constitutional amendment banning slavery that passed in the Senate in April 1864 (see Home Fronts, April 8, 1864, above).

July–August 1864: With Senate passage of the Wade-Davis Reconstruction Bill, the measure went to President Lincoln for action. Committed to his softer policies for readmitting seceded states, Lincoln on July 4 pocket-vetoed the bill, touching off a long struggle for control of reconstruction policy. On August 5, the bill's sponsors, Sen. Benjamin Wade and Rep. H. W. Davis, issued a manifesto that asserted their "right and duty to check the encroachments of the Executive on the Authority of Congress."

August 1864: On August 18, Grant refused a second Confederate request to exchange prisoners. The policy increased hardships for Union prisoners at such places as Andersonville, where facilities were overburdened and food and medicines in fatally short supply. Ultimately, many thousands died; there are more than 12,000 graves in the National Cemetery at Andersonville.

August 29-31, 1864: The Democratic National Convention opened in Chicago, Illinois, on August 29. Clement Vallandigham, returned from his Canadian exile, delivered the keynote address. On August 31, the Democrats nominated the former commander of the Army of the Potomac, Gen. George B. McClellan, who had been unemployed militarily since November 1862, to challenge Lincoln for the presidency.

September 2, 1864: Faced with a deepening manpower shortage, Gen. Robert E. Lee approached President Davis about replacing white army laborers, teamsters, and other noncombatants with slave labor. Lee also pressed the president for a more effective recruitment policy to offset battle losses and desertions.

September 5, 1864: Louisianans who had taken the loyalty oath went to the polls to ratify a new state constitution that abolished slavery and provided for the readmission of the state into the Union.

September 1864: On September 8, Gen. George B. McClellan by letter formally accepted the Democratic presidential nomination, but he rejected a clause in the party platform that declared the war a failure. "I could not look in the faces of my gallant comrades of the Army and Navy, who have survived so many bloody battles, and tell them that their labor and sacrifice had been in vain," he wrote.

On September 17, in the wake of Lincoln's political resurgence after Gen. William T. Sherman's capture of Atlanta, Frémont withdrew from the presidential race, saying he feared his candidacy might lead to a Democratic victory, a negotiated peace settlement, and the reestablishment of slavery.

October 19, 1864: A party of Confederate raiders swept down from Canada and attacked the northern Vermont town of St. Albans, robbing three banks of a total of $200,000. Eleven raiders escaped across the border, where they were arrested and later released when Canadian authorities decided that they lacked jurisdiction in the case.

November 6, 1864: Federal agents foiled an alleged Confederate/Copperhead plot to release Confederate prisoners at Camp Davis in Chicago on Election Day, November 8. The plotters had planned to seize polling places, stuff ballot boxes, and set fires in the city. Several of the alleged conspirators—100 were arrested—were heavily armed, and agents found a large cache of arms and ammunition at the home of one conspirator.

November 8, 1864: President Lincoln defeated George B. McClellan for a second term, winning more than 55 percent of the popular vote and carrying every loyal state but three, Delaware, Kentucky, and New Jersey. Soldiers on active duty overwhelmingly supported Lincoln. Of about 154,000 votes cast by soldiers, Lincoln won 119,000.

November 25, 1864: In an arson offensive, Confederate agents set fire to ten hotels and other buildings in New York City. None of the fires caused much damage, however, and all were quickly doused. One arsonist, R. C. Kennedy, was eventually arrested and executed for setting fire to P. T. Barnum's museum.

December 30, 1864: Maryland Union politician Francis P. Blair sent out peace feelers to Confederate officials in Richmond, Virginia. This led, within a few weeks, to the Hampton Roads peace conference in which President Lincoln met with Confederate Vice President Alexander Stephens (see February 3–5, 1865, p. 277).

INTERNATIONAL DEVELOPMENTS

April 4, 1864: In Washington, D.C., the House of Representatives passed a resolution stating the United States would not tolerate a monarchy in Mexico. In fact, the French—having invaded Mexico in 1862 to force payments of debts—had just imposed Maximilian, brother of the Austrian emperor, as emperor of Mexico. With the Civil War on its hands, however, the U.S. could do little or nothing to alter the situation.

BATTLES AND CAMPAIGNS: 1865

The last acts of the Civil War were swift and final. In February and March, Gen. William T. Sherman swept through the Carolinas against rebel Confederate opposition, leaving a trail of destruction behind him. Then Grant moved in late March, overwhelming Gen. Robert E. Lee's army. With the conclusion of those two campaigns, the Confederacy ceased to exist in the eastern theater, although there were a few holdouts in the western theater and the trans-Mississippi theater, and several months passed before all activities ceased in the naval theater.

In the North, President Abraham Lincoln's assassination tainted the joy of victory. Southern soldiers returned home to a ruined and defeated land, and Northern troops, many of them disabled, could take little satisfaction in having defeated their countrymen. Millions of freed slaves tested their new-won freedom. And with the passing of the smoke of war, the nation settled into an uneasy peace.

EASTERN THEATER

January 4–15, 1865 (Fort Fisher Expedition): After Gen. Benjamin Butler's failure in December 1864, Gen. Ulysses S. Grant assigned Gen. Alfred Terry to lead a second expedition to Fort Fisher in North Carolina. (Butler formally was relieved of command on January 7.) Terry's force of 8,000 left Bermuda Hundred, Virginia, on January 4, and embarked in transports. By late afternoon of January 12, shipborne troops and Adm. David D. Porter's naval armada had arrived off the Confederate strong point.

Porter opened the bombardment of Fort Fisher around midnight. Four hours later, the first troop landings were underway. Terry consolidated the beachhead and brought field guns ashore over the next two days. Porter's point-blank bombardment opened at 8 A.M. on January 15. After several hours of hard fighting, Union assault troops carried the fort in a rush. The last of the defenders surrendered at 10 P.M.

The Federals captured about 2,000 of Fort Fisher's garrison and reported losses of 1,300 killed, wounded, or missing.

January–March 1865 (Siege of Petersburg): At the New Year, Gen. Robert E. Lee had fewer than 60,000 undernourished and ill-clad troops to face Grant's well-fed, lavishly equipped Union Army of 124,000. As spring approached, President Jefferson Davis ordered Lee to try a breakout. Lee chose Fort Stedman east of Petersburg, Virginia, where the Confederate and Union lines lay only 150 yards apart.

In late February, Grant ordered Gen. Philip H. Sheridan with 10,000 cavalry to destroy what remained of Gen. Jubal Early's command in the Shenandoah Valley, and march on Lynchburg, Virginia, for a possible move to join Gen. William T.

Sherman advancing from the Carolinas.

Sheridan set out from Winchester on February 27, defeated Early's remnants at Waynesboro on March 2, took 1,600 prisoners, and reached Charlottesville on March 4. Deciding that he could not take Lynchburg, he sent one division to break up the railroad from Charlottesville to Lynchburg and a second to wreck the James River canal and the industries along its banks.

Following a roundabout route, Sheridan escaped Confederate infantry pursuing him and reached the Petersburg area safely toward the end of March.

March 25, 1865 (Battle of Fort Stedman): The initial assault, launched at 4 A.M., took the Union defenders by surprise and gained the fort and some positions beyond. A strong Federal counterattack drove the Confederates back into Fort Stedman, and Lee finally ordered a withdrawal and return to the start point. Confederate losses were about 3,500 killed, wounded, or missing in that last offensive operation of the Army of Northern Virginia.

March 29–April 1 (Appomattox Campaign): On March 29, Grant opened the last campaign of the Civil War by sending Sheridan with a combined force of cavalry and infantry on a wide swing around Lee's right in an operation designed to pry the Confederates out of their defenses and bring them to battle in open country.

Heavy rains slowed the initial advance. Then, on April 1, Sheridan's infantry routed the Confederates at Five Forks, an important road junction covering the South Side Railroad in Virginia. As the attackers overwhelmed the Five Forks defenses, the Confederates surrendered in droves. "We are coming back into the Union, boys," one rebel announced. Sheridan took some 5,000 captives and, more to the point, he turned Lee's right, making the Petersburg lines untenable. When news of Five Forks reached Grant, he ordered a general assault all along the line for first light on April 2.

Early on April 2, Lee informed President Davis in Richmond that he could no longer hold Petersburg. Grant's attack opened at 4:30 A.M. along the Jerusalem Plank Road. A little later, 6th Corps infantry punctured the Confederate line at Fort Fisher and rolled it up all the way to Hatcher's Run southwest of Petersburg. The 24th Corps attacked at Hatcher's Run and, in hard fighting, captured the strong points of Forts Gregg and Whitworth.

A heroic defense of Fort Gregg, in which a few hundred Confederates held off 5,000 Union attackers for more than two hours, bought just enough time for Lee's army to escape. The withdrawal westward, toward Amelia Courthouse and a hoped-for junction with Confederate forces in North Carolina, began at nightfall.

April 2–3, 1865: On Lee's advice, the Confederate government evacuated Richmond during the day on April 2. Overnight, retreating Confederates set fire to warehouses and arsenals, and looters helped themselves to such luxuries as remained in the shops. A brisk south wind spread the fires through the heart of the capital. Around 7 o'clock on the morning of April 3, the first Union troops entered Richmond—among the early arrivals, a regiment of black cavalry. The 80-year-old mayor of Richmond met the troops with the white flag of surrender.

April 3–8, 1865: On April 3, the beaten Confederates streamed west from Petersburg and Richmond, Union forces in relentless pursuit. Lee sought to push on to the Danville railroad, then turn south for a junction with Confederate forces in North Carolina. The Federals sought to overtake Lee's army, block its escape route, and end the war.

From a distance, the Confederates shuffling westward were mistaken for refugees. The troops were ragged, hungry, inexpressibly weary. The litter of retreat—broken-down wagons and exhausted mules, knapsacks, cooking implements, even arms and ammunition—lay heaped along the road, evidence of an army in disintegration.

By some bureaucratic misadventure, Lee found a trainload of ammunition at Amelia Courthouse on April 4, but no rations. He sent forage parties fanning out over the countryside in search of provisions. The delay allowed Grant's pursuing Federals to cut into the Confederate head start from Petersburg. A large force of cavalry and infantry under Sheridan raced in parallel and just to the south of Lee's army, straining to outrun the Confederates, turn, and confront them head on astride their line of retreat.

Sensing the end, Sheridan—the guiding spirit of the pursuit—abandoned all caution. By April 5, he had caught and passed his quarry, cut the Danville railroad, and blocked Lee's escape route to the south.

Lee changed direction, heading for Farmville on the upper Appomattox River. The Federals stepped up the pace. With forced marches at night, the Confederates maintained a slight lead. But the chase seemed to invigorate the Yankees. "They began to see the end of what they had been fighting four years for," wrote Grant. "Nothing seemed to fatigue them. They were ready to move without rations and travel without rest until the end."

On April 6, "Black Thursday" to the Confederates, Sheridan's cavalry with heavy infantry support isolated and destroyed Gen. Richard S. Ewell's corps near Sayler's Creek, removing at a stroke a full third of Lee's remaining strength. As the Federal infantry pressed Ewell's front, the cavalry tore into his flanks and rear. After a feeble effort, Ewell's line collapsed. The Confederate casualty total for the day reached 8,000—including as many as 6,000 men taken captive, among them Ewell himself.

The retreat continued after dark on April 6, a cold night with a biting wind and flurries of snow. Lee intended to cross the Appomattox River at Farmville, burn the bridges there, and put the river between himself and Grant. But Federal infantry managed to cross the partially burned High Bridge a few miles downstream. By dawn on April 7, two separate Union columns, each larger than the remnant of the Army of Northern Virginia, were marching alongside Lee: one north of the river, the other south, and both rushing to head off the Confederates at Appomattox Station. Late that afternoon, Grant sent a note through the lines calling on Lee to surrender.

Lee sent Grant a vague reply, and the pursuit continued on April 8. Sheridan's cavalry reached Appomattox Station and broke up a small Confederate force there, capturing 24 guns and 4 trainloads of rations and other supplies. By nightfall, the Federals held the place in strength. The troopers, with infantry on the way, were athwart the Lynchburg road, Lee's last line of retreat.

April 9, 1865 (Surrender at Appomattox Court House): Overnight, Lee issued orders for a final effort to clear the road to the west. The assault, launched at dawn that Palm Sunday, broke through the light crust of the cavalry lines, then ran headlong into advancing Federal infantry.

An aide carried word of the failure of the breakout to Lee. "Then there is nothing for me to do but go and see General Grant," he said, "and I would rather die a thousand deaths." Lee had asked to meet Grant between the lines at 10 o'clock in the morning. When the Union general failed to turn up, Lee sent another note through the lines, expressly offering to surrender. An informal one-hour truce went into effect. An aide galloped off to deliver Lee's message. Grant read it, then pushed his way to the front.

The two generals met at 1 o'clock in the parlor of the house of Wilmer McLean. Lee had turned out in full dress uniform, complete with sash and sword. Grant apologized for his mud-caked boots, spattered trousers, and unadorned coat. There was an awkward silence. Later, Grant, guessing at what must have been going through his adversary's mind, wrote:

"As he was a man of much dignity, with an impassable face, it was impossible to say whether he felt inwardly glad that the end had finally come, or felt sad over the result and was too manly to show it. Whatever his feelings they were entirely concealed from my observation; but my own feelings, which had been quite jubilant on receipt of his letter, were sad and depressed. I felt like anything rather than rejoicing at the downfall of a foe who had fought so long and valiantly, and had suffered so much for a cause, though that cause was, I believe, one of the worst for which a people ever fought."

Grant wrote out his terms for surrender. They guaranteed that ordinary soldiers would be immune for prosecution for treason. In the Confederate army, cavalrymen and cannoneers supplied their own horses. At Lee's request, Grant allowed those troops to keep their mounts. The animals would be useful, Grant acknowledged, for spring plowing. "This will have the best possible effect upon the men," Lee told him. "It will be very gratifying and will do much toward conciliating our people." Grant also offered to send three days' rations to feed the hungry Confederates.

Fair copies of the documents were drawn up and signed. At a few minutes before 4 o'clock, the Army of Northern Virginia passed into history. Lee left the McLean house, mounted his horse, Traveller, and rode slowly back to the Confederate lines. The telegraph flashed word of the surrender to Washington, D.C. The capital marked the occasion with the firing of a 500-gun salute. At Appomattox, though, Grant forbade such ostentatious celebration.

"The war is over," he said, "the rebels are our countrymen again."

April 12, 1865: The remnant of Lee's army stacked arms and surrendered its battle flags after a ceremonial march past Union troops at Appomattox. Gettysburg hero Maj. Gen. Joshua L. Chamberlain of Maine commanded the division that accepted the Confederate tokens and offered a "carry arms" salute in return.

WESTERN THEATER

January 3, 1865: Elements of Gen. Oliver O. Howard's wing of Gen. William T. Sherman's army moved from Savannah, Georgia, to Beaufort, South Carolina.

January 9, 1865: What remained of Gen. John Bell Hood's broken Confederate army reached Tupelo, Mississippi, after the long retreat from Nashville, Tennessee. President Jefferson Davis set in motion orders that brought some 4,000 Army of Tennessee infantry to South Carolina to reinforce Gen. William Hardee's forces there.

January 9–16, 1865: War Secretary Edwin Stanton met with General Sherman and reviewed the Army during a visit to Savannah. Among other things, Stanton undertook the trip to investigate charges that Sherman's troops were mistreating black refugees who followed the Army in the thousands. On January 12, Stanton met with 20 representatives of Savannah's black community, who testified that the freed people had great confidence in Sherman.

They also told Stanton that they regarded land ownership as the key for blacks in the transition from slavery to freedom. As a result, Sherman, on January 16, issued Special Orders Number 15, which set aside abandoned or confiscated plantation lands in a 30-mile-wide coastal belt for the exclusive use of black homesteaders.

February 1–17, 1865 (Carolinas March): After two weeks of rain delays, Sherman's Carolinas March got underway with 60,000 men, 2,500 wagons, and 600 ambulances. Howard's wing advanced north from Pocotaligo on the Charleston & Savannah Railroad. Gen. Henry Slocum's wing crossed into South Carolina from positions north of Savannah, Georgia, and moved north on a roughly parallel track.

Sherman arranged his dispositions in such a way that the Confederates could not be certain of his objective. Augusta, Georgia, and Charleston and Columbia, South Carolina, all seemed potential targets. Opposing Sherman were a total of 22,500 Confederate troops under P. G. T. Beauregard.

The Union advance proceeded against light

opposition, as the widely scattered Confederate forces fell back into interior South Carolina. Howard's troops reached the environs of Columbia, the South Carolina capital, on February 16. Howard's infantry entered Columbia on February 17, on the heels of Confederate general Wade Hampton's retreating cavalry.

Hampton's troopers had set a number of bales of cotton alight before they pulled out. A rising wind carried burning cotton aloft, touching off numerous fires. Union forces at first did little to contain the fires, and some drunken Federals contributed to the spread with arsons of their own. In the end, fully two-thirds of the city lay in ashes.

Hampton later charged that Sherman had burned Columbia to the ground "deliberately, systematically, and atrociously." Sherman replied that, on the contrary, his troops had labored to stamp out the fires Hampton's cavalry had set and had thus saved what little of the city survived the conflagration. But the Yankee general did not show any remorse over Columbia's destruction, then or later. "Though I never ordered it, and never wished it," he said after the war, "I have never shed any tears over it, because I believe it hastened what we all fought for—the end of the war."

February–March 1865 (North Carolina Coastal Operations): Federal forces under Gen. John Schofield carried out a series of subsidiary operations to protect General Sherman's flank and maintain supply and communication lines. On February 22, Union troops occupied Wilmington, North Carolina. By the end of February, Schofield had his 30,000-strong force in New Bern, North Carolina, preparing to march inland for a junction with Sherman.

Schofield advanced on Kinston, North Carolina, in early March. Near Kinston on March 8, Confederates under Gen. Braxton Bragg attacked the head of the Union column under Gen. Jacob D. Cox. Bragg's initial assaults were repulsed, and Schofield promptly reinforced Cox. Fighting flared up intermittently over the next two days. On March 10, Bragg, unable to overpower Cox, pulled back to Goldsborough, North Carolina, to join forces with Gen. Joseph E. Johnston's main body.

March 3–15, 1865: Slowed by heavy rains, Sherman's advance reached Cheraw, South Carolina, on March 3. After resting three days, the Union Army pushed on for Fayetteville, meeting only light resistance, and reached the North Carolina city on March 12.

The Confederate commander, Gen. Joseph E. Johnston (he had succeeded Beauregard, who became his second in command), struggled to concentrate his forces for an attack on one of the two columns of advancing Federals.

March 16, 1865 (Battle of Averasboro): Hardee's corps halted on a ridge south of Averasboro and offered battle in a bid to delay Slocum's advance. Sherman, traveling with Slocum, ordered a flank move to the right to complement Slocum's two-division frontal assault. When darkness ended the fighting, Slocum's infantry had overrun the Confederate first line. Hardee withdrew during the night toward Smithfield, North Carolina. Federal casualties were 678 killed, wounded, or missing. The Confederates reported losses of 865.

March 19, 1865 (Battle of Bentonville): Massing his forces at last, Johnston with 21,000 men struck Slocum's wing near Bentonville, North Carolina. Slocum, isolated, stood his ground and repulsed a series of assaults.

March 20–21, 1865: On March 20, Sherman with Howard's wing reached the battlefield at Bentonville. Sherman attacked on the morning of March 21, sending a division around Johnston in a bid to cut off his retreat. Alert to that danger, Johnston pulled back on March 21. Federal losses were about 1,600. Confederate casualties exceeded 2,600 killed, wounded, or missing. Bentonville proved to be Johnston's last major effort to stop Sherman's advance.

March 17–April 12, 1865 (Mobile Campaign): Two Union columns moved on Mobile, Alabama, in March. Gen. E. R. S. Canby with 45,000 troops, approached from the harbor forts that Adm. David G. Farragut's naval campaign had taken in August 1864. Gen. Frederick Steele advanced from northern Florida with 13,000 men.

Steele's column pushed back Confederate outposts near Blakely, Alabama, on April 1 and laid siege to the town. Five miles to the south, Canby's column closed up on Spanish Fort, another Mobile outwork, and captured it in a frontal assault on April 8. With the fall of Spanish Fort, Canby massed his entire force outside Blakely. In what generally is regarded as the last major infantry battle of the Civil War, 16,000 Federals attacked Blakely at 5:30 P.M. on April 9. Within 20 minutes, Blakely was captured.

The Confederate commander in Mobile, Gen. Dabney Maury, ordered Mobile evacuated on the night of April 11. Maury joined the remnants of his command, about 4,500 men and 27 guns, in a withdrawal toward Montgomery, Alabama.

Canby entered Mobile on the morning of April 12. Federal losses were around 1,400 for the campaign. Grant, in his memoirs, wrote of the Mobile operation, "I had tried for more than two years to have an expedition sent against Mobile when its possession by us would have been of great advantage. It finally cost us lives to take it when its possession was of no importance."

March 22–April 20, 1865: During the third week of March, Union general James H. Wilson struck out from northwestern Alabama for Selma, a Confederate stronghold and manufacturing center with an armory, factories, foundries, and warehouses.

Advancing in three columns, Wilson's corps cleared Montevallo, Alabama, on March 31 against light Confederate resistance, routing a cavalry force under Gen. Nathan Bedford Forrest just south of the town. Forrest withdrew into the Selma lines, which Wilson reached on April 2. Union forces carried the works on the afternoon of April 2, and Wilson entered the town that night.

Wilson's troops dismantled Selma's war industries before resuming their march through Alabama on April 9. Union cavalry captured Montgomery on April 12 and Columbus, Georgia, on April 20. Wilson learned at Columbus that the war had ended.

Wilson's reported losses were 725. He claimed to have killed or wounded 1,200 Confederates and taken prisoner some 6,800.

March 23–April 26, 1865: Sherman's army and Schofield's column marching north from Wilmington, North Carolina, reached Goldsborough, North Carolina, on March 23. With a massed force of 80,000, Sherman prepared to move on Raleigh, the North Carolina capital.

Sherman's army occupied Raleigh on April 13. Confederate resistance in the Carolinas essentially came to an end. On April 14, Johnston, recognizing the situation as hopeless, asked for an armistice. That Sherman granted, on terms Washington, D.C., swiftly rejected as too lenient. Charging that Sherman had overstepped his authority in making political arrangements that included an easy return of the rebel states to the Union, War Secretary Stanton rescinded the surrender agreement and ordered Sherman to resume operations against Johnston's remaining 30,000 men. There

was no more fighting, however, and Johnston formally surrendered on April 26, on terms nearly identical to those Grant had offered Lee.

May 10, 1865: A detachment of Gen. James H. Wilson's cavalry captured the fleeing Confederate president Jefferson Davis near Irwinsville, Georgia.

TRANS-MISSISSIPPI THEATER

May 12–13, 1865 (Battle of Palmitto Ranch): In the last significant encounter of the Civil War, Union forces attacked a Confederate encampment at Palmitto Ranch, Texas, on the Rio Grande. In the first day's fighting, the Federals overran the camp but withdrew at nightfall. Union troops recaptured Palmitto Ranch on May 13, then were driven off by a Confederate counterattack.

May 13, 1865: Confederate governors of Arkansas, Mississippi, and Louisiana met with Gen. Edmund Kirby Smith, commander of Confederate forces west of the Mississippi River, to discuss surrender arrangements. One of Smith's officers, cavalry Gen. J. O. Shelby, threatened to arrest Smith if he refused to carry on the struggle.

May 17, 1865: Gen. Philip H. Sheridan assumed command of the Federal Department of the Trans-Mississippi south of Arkansas. His responsibilities included overseeing the last Confederate surrenders and keeping watch on the French in Mexico, whose intrigues seemed to threaten Texas.

May 26–June 2, 1865: On May 26, Union and Confederate negotiators met to discuss the surrender of Gen. Edmund Kirby Smith's command. The terms were essentially those Grant gave Lee at Appomattox Court House. Smith approved the terms on June 2, and the last Confederate army ceased to exist. June 2 is generally regarded as marking the end of the Civil War. The last surrender of a large body of Confederate troops occurred on June 23 in the Oklahoma Territory, when the Confederate Cherokee general Stand Watie disbanded an Indian unit.

NAVAL THEATER

January 6, 1865: The French-built ironclad ram *Sphinx* sailed from Copenhagen bound for Quiberon Bay, France. Confederate agents in Denmark had secretly purchased the vessel, later renaming it *Stonewall.*

May 19, 1865: The *Stonewall* surrendered to U.S. officials in Havana harbor, Cuba.

May 22, 1865: President Andrew Johnson declared that all Southern seaports except four in Texas would be reopened to trade as of July 1. The declaration lifted the Union blockade that had been in effect since April 1861.

November 1865: The Confederate raider *Shenandoah* ended her long campaign against Union shipping, surrendering to British authorities at Liverpool, England. From September 1864 until August 1865, when *Shenandoah's* commanding officer, Capt. James Waddell, learned of the Confederate surrender, the raider captured or destroyed 36 vessels. The British later turned the vessel over to the United States.

HOME FRONTS

January 12–16, 1865: Francis P. Blair, a prominent Maryland Republican, met President Jefferson Davis in Richmond, Virginia, to sound out the possibility of a negotiated end to the war. Blair suggested to Davis that North and South combine to expel the French from Mexico, an expedition he believed would promote national restoration. Davis promised nothing more than to continue the discussion. In Washington, D.C., on January 16, Lincoln rejected Blair's scheme but agreed to meet with Confederate representatives.

January 16–19, 1865: In a challenge to President Davis's military authority, the Confederate Senate on January 16 approved a resolution advising Davis to name Gen. Robert E. Lee commander in chief of the Confederate army, restore Gen. Joseph E. Johnston to command of the Army of Tennessee, and give Gen. P. G. T. Beauregard overall command in Florida, Georgia, and South Carolina. On January 19, Lee reluctantly accepted appointment as commander in chief of the Confederate land forces.

January 31–February 1, 1865: On January 31, the U.S. House of Representatives, following the Senate's lead of the year before, passed the proposed 13th Amendment to the Constitution abolishing slavery. The next day, Illinois became the first of the required three-quarters of the states to ratify the amendment.

February 3–5, 1865: President Lincoln and Secretary of State William Seward met on February 3 with Confederate vice president Alexander Stephens and two other Confederates aboard the steamer *River Queen* at Hampton Roads, Virginia. No common ground could be found, however. The Southern negotiators sought an armistice first, with any discussion of reunion to come later. Lincoln insisted on the recognition of Federal authority as the essential starting point for talks.

Back in Washington, D.C., on February 5, Lincoln presented the cabinet with a proposal to pay $400 million in compensation to slaveholders if the rebellious states ceased resistance before April 1. The cabinet strongly objected to the scheme, however, and Lincoln allowed it to drop.

March 3, 1865: In Washington, Congress approved legislation that established the Bureau of Refugees, Freedmen, and Abandoned Lands—popularly, the Freedmen's Bureau. The measure charged the agency with assisting former slaves in the transition to freedom and with providing temporary assistance for freed people and others, white and black, dislocated by war.

March 4, 1865: President Lincoln took the oath of office for his second term. "Fondly do we hope—fervently do we pray—that this mighty scourge of war may speedily pass away," he said in his inaugural address. He went on to outline his hopes for a brighter future. "With malice toward none; with charity toward all; with firmness in the right, as God gives us to see the right, let us strive on to finish the work we are in; to bind up the nation's wounds…to do all which may achieve and cherish a just, and a lasting peace, among ourselves, and with all nations."

March 13, 1865: In Richmond, Virginia, the Confederate Congress sent President Davis a measure calling for the arming of slaves for service in the Confederate army. The implication was that slaves who served would be freed after the war. Davis signed the bill at once.

March 27–28, 1865: At City Point, Virginia, Lincoln conferred with Ulysses S. Grant, William T. Sherman, and Adm. David D. Porter. Sherman reported afterward that Lincoln discussed his views on reconstruction, which called for lenient treatment of the defeated South.

April 4, 1865: Traveling up the James River on one of Admiral Porter's gunboats, President Lincoln entered Richmond, Virginia, the day after Union forces occupied the Confederate capital. With an escort of ten sailors, he walked the streets of the city, leading his 12-year-old son, Tad, by the hand.

Freed slaves crowded around to catch a

glimpse of Lincoln. "Thank God I have lived to see this," he told Porter. "It seems that I have been dreaming a horrid dream for four years, and now the nightmare is gone."

On the same day, from Danville, Virginia, the fleeing Jefferson Davis issued a statement lamenting Richmond's fall but vowing to continue the fight for Confederate independence.

April 11, 1865: Lincoln, who had returned to the U.S. capital from Virginia on April 8, the day before Lee's surrender at Appomattox Court House, addressed a large crowd gathered outside the White House on April 11. In what proved to be his last speech, he told the crowd that he favored granting the vote to black Union Army veterans as well as to "the most intelligent of the race," but he also called for flexibility in reconstruction policies.

April 13, 1865: President Lincoln suspended the draft and ordered reductions in orders for war supplies.

April 14–15, 1865: President Lincoln decided on a favorite form of relaxation the evening of April 14, a visit to the theater. He chose Ford's Theatre and the English farce *Our American Cousin*, with the American actress Laura Keene. Joining the president were his wife, Mary Todd Lincoln, Clara Harris, a senator's daughter, and her fiancé, Maj. Henry Rathbone.

Just before 10 o'clock, actor John Wilkes Booth slipped into the unguarded presidential box at Ford's Theatre, shot Lincoln behind the ear, and leapt to the stage, where he shouted, *"Sic semper tyrannis!"* ("Thus be it ever to tyrants!"). Booth then limped out of the theater; he had broken his leg when he jumped to the stage.

The attack was the climax of several months of plotting on the part of Booth and a number of accomplices, among them Confederate deserters Samuel Arnold, Michael O'Laughlin, Lewis Paine and Confederate secret agents John Surratt and George Atzerodt. Booth had planned that he would kill the president; he had assigned Atzerodt to kill Vice President Andrew Johnson and Paine to kill William Seward, the secretary of state.

Atzerodt's courage failed him, and he did not attempt to carry out his part. Paine, however, broke into Seward's house and stabbed the secretary, seriously wounding him. Lincoln, carried unconscious from the theater to a boarding house across the street, died at 7:22 A.M. on April 15. At 11 o'clock that morning, Andrew Johnson was sworn in as the nation's 17th president.

April 1865: War Secretary Edwin Stanton took charge of the investigation into the assassination. Several hundred people were arrested on suspicion of conspiracy. Atzerodt, Paine, Surratt, and two other plotters were imprisoned at Fort Monroe near Norfolk, Virginia. Surratt managed to escape, eventually reaching Italy, where he joined the papal guards.

Lincoln's funeral service took place in the East Room of the White House on April 19. Two days later, the slain president's body was taken from the Capitol rotunda and placed aboard a special funeral train for the trip to Springfield, Illinois. Lincoln was buried there on May 4.

Meanwhile, Booth and a young accomplice, David Herold, fled into Virginia. On May 26, Federal forces cornered them in a barn on the farm of Richard H. Garrett near Bowling Green, Virginia. Herold heeded Federal calls to surrender; Booth remained in the barn, which the troops soon set alight. As Booth tried to flee the burning barn, a shot sounded, and he fell. He died shortly after.

April 27, 1865: The riverboat *Sultana*, carrying more than 2,000 recently freed Union prisoners of war, exploded and burned. At least 1,238 men died in the explosion, the worst accident on the Mississippi River.

May 10, 1865: In a formal announcement, President Andrew Johnson declared the armed rebellion against the U.S. government to be "virtually at an end."

On May 10, too, a detachment of the 4th Michigan Cavalry captured fleeing Confederate president Jefferson Davis and his entourage near Irwinville, Georgia. The prisoners were taken under heavy guard to Nashville, Tennessee; Davis was later moved to Fort Monroe, Virginia.

May 12, 1865: President Johnson appointed Gen. Oliver O. Howard, who had commanded a wing of Gen. William T. Sherman's army in the March to the Sea and the Carolinas March, to head the Freedmen's Bureau.

May 23–24, 1865: On May 23, Gen. George Meade's Army of the Potomac marched past President Johnson, other dignitaries, and thousands of spectators in Washington, D.C. On May 24, Sherman's western troops completed the two-day Grand Review of an estimated 150,000 men of the victorious armies. Over the next few week,s the volunteer Union Army was largely disbanded.

May 25, 1865: In Mobile, Alabama, 20 tons of

captured Confederate gunpowder went up in a tremendous explosion that destroyed many buildings along the city's waterfront. Some 300 people were killed or wounded in the blast.

May 27–29, 1865: President Johnson ordered the release of all those in U.S. military prisons, with a few exceptions. Jefferson Davis remained in custody at Fort Monroe, where he had been held since May 22.

On May 29, Johnson issued a proclamation offering a general amnesty to most Confederates who would swear a loyalty oath. Rebels who owned property worth $20,000 or more and high-ranking Confederate government or military officials were excluded, though they could apply directly to the president for pardons. Johnson granted pardons wholesale.

May–July 1865: On May 12, eight defendants charged in the Lincoln assassination conspiracy pleaded not guilty. On June 30, a military court in Washington, D.C., found all eight guilty. Four were sentenced to prison terms; four were sentenced to be hanged.

On July 7, Paine, Atzerodt, Herold, and Mary Surratt (John Surratt's mother, at whose boardinghouse Booth and accomplices had plotted) were hanged at the Old Penitentiary in Washington. O'Laughlin, Arnold, Edward Spangler (a Ford's Theatre scene-shifter and friend of Booth's), and Dr. Samuel Mudd (a Maryland physician who had set Booth's broken leg) received life terms in the Dry Tortugas off Key West, Florida. Mudd, Arnold, and Spangler were pardoned in 1869. O'Laughlin died in prison.

October 1865: President Johnson pardoned former Confederate vice president Alexander Stephens of Georgia and four other high-ranking Confederates who had been held in prison since the collapse of the rebellion. Jefferson Davis remained in prison. The U.S. government never brought him to trial and he was freed in May 1867.

November 1865: After a military trial, the U.S. government hanged Maj. Henry Wirz, commandant of Andersonville Prison in Georgia, for war crimes. That was the only such execution of the Civil War. The total number of deaths at Andersonville is unknown; over 12,000 Union prisoners are buried in the national cemetery there.

December 6, 1865: With ratification by 27 states, the 13th Amendment to the U.S. Constitution went into effect, formally abolishing slavery in the United States and all its dependencies.

INTERNATIONAL DEVELOPMENTS

February 13, 1865: The British foreign secretary, Lord John Russell, complained to U.S. officials about Union naval and military activities on the Great Lakes, which the United States shared with Canada. The United States justified the buildup as a response to Confederate raids launched from Canada.

April 7, 1865: The U.S. and Britain opened negotiations over damage claims involving the British-built Confederate raider *Alabama.* The raider destroyed or captured 65 vessels before the USS *Kearsarge* sunk it off Cherbourg, France, on June 19, 1864. The claims were settled in 1873.

HOME FRONTS

Information on home front developments are provided year by year in the preceding sections.

NEGOTIATIONS AND PEACE TREATY

Just as the Civil War did not begin with a formal declaration of war, it did not end with a negotiated agreement and a peace treaty. It ended with an overwhelming Union battlefield victory.

There had been abortive efforts to negotiate a peace early in 1865. On January 5, President Lincoln issued a pass through the lines to James W. Singleton, an Illinois lawyer who hoped for a breakthrough via unofficial channels. One week later, Maryland Republican Francis P. Blair met with Confederate president Jefferson Davis in Richmond, Virginia, to discuss possible avenues for peace between North and South.

The Blair-Davis session led to the Hampton Roads conference on February 3 aboard the steamer *River Queen.* (Hampton Roads was a stretch of water along the coast of Virginia.) But Lincoln, Secretary of State William Seward, and a three-member Confederate delegation headed by Confederate vice president Alexander Stephens found no common ground in four hours of talks. The Confederates insisted on independence; Lincoln on reunion. With Union forces everywhere triumphant, the Confederate government and the Confederate armies in the field had little or no negotiating power.

The generous surrender terms that Gen. Ulysses S. Grant offered Gen. Robert E. Lee at Appomattox Court House on April 9, 1865—Confederate troops were paroled, given leave to go home, and promised they would not be prosecuted for treason if they obeyed the law—were the model for the terms the two other large Confederate armies, Gen. Joseph E. Johnston's in North Carolina and Gen. Edmund Kirby Smith's in the trans-Mississippi theater, eventually accepted. On May 10, 1865, President Andrew Johnson declared the war "virtually at an end."

In North Carolina, Gen. Joseph E. Johnston asked for an armistice on April 14, five days after Lee's surrender. On April 17 and 18, Union general William T. Sherman offered Johnston terms that included a pledge of Federal recognition of all state governments whose leaders took an oath of allegiance. Such political clauses far exceeded Sherman's authority, and Union leaders in Washington, D.C. swiftly repudiated the provisional agreement. On April 26, Johnston surrendered his army on virtually the same terms Lee had been given in Virginia. General Smith surrendered the last Confederate army in the field on June 2, at Galveston, Texas, and it was June 23 before the Cherokee Confederate general Stand Watie disbanded an Indian unit in the Oklahoma Territory.

Minor skirmishes occurred in a few isolated places until all the Confederates surrendered. But there was never a single surrender or peace document that covered the entire Confederacy. What came, instead, was President Andrew Johnson's relatively generous plan for the former Confederate states, followed by the much harsher acts of Congress that became the Reconstruction period.

RESULTS OF THE WAR (Casualties, Costs, Consequences)

The Civil War claimed approximately 620,000 military lives—360,000 Union and 260,000 Confederate. Of those, approximately 200,000 occurred in combat—in one of the war's 10,000 actions, including 76 full-scale battles, 310 engagements, and 6,337 skirmishes. More than 400,000 men died of disease, accidents, and other causes. Hundreds of thousands of men were severely wounded, some suffering permanent disabilities.

The number of Confederate civilian war dead is indeterminable—certainly, many tens of thousands. Nor is it possible to calculate property losses (although estimates run to many billions of dollars in today's terms). Much of the South lay in ruins in 1865. Fires had burned the hearts of

Atlanta, Georgia; Columbia, South Carolina; and Richmond, Virginia. Sherman's armies had left a broad, charred swath of destruction through Georgia and South Carolina. The contending armies had stripped bare large areas of Tennessee, Georgia, and Virginia. The Southern transportation system, especially the railroads, had been thoroughly wrecked. If all such costs, plus veterans' pensions, interest on the national debt, and other indirect costs are included, the cost for both sides would be approximately $15 billion ($350 billion in 1990 dollars).

The chief results of the Civil War were the restoration of the American Union and the emancipation of 4 million enslaved persons of African descent.

The issue of secession is highly unlikely ever to arise again in the United States. Before the Civil War, the notion that a state or states might pull out of the Union seemed plausible, at least in theory. Indeed, up to that time, most people used the plural when speaking of the American arrangement: *these* United States. The war invalidated the idea of secession. After 1865, the nation truly was one, indivisible: *the* United States.

The Civil War produced the 13th Amendment to the Constitution, abolishing slavery in the United States and its dependencies. It also established the principle of the Federal government as the guarantor of individual freedom. In the aftermath of the war, the 14th Amendment defined American citizenship, prohibited the states from curtailing federally mandated rights, and explicitly extended citizenship to former slaves. The 15th Amendment guaranteed voting rights to every citizen regardless of race, color, or previous condition of servitude. Despite those amendments, the Civil War and its immediate aftermath did not provide or guarantee full freedom, equality, or justice to African Americans: Those were battles that were fought for many decades thereafter.

MILITARY INNOVATIONS, TACTICS, EQUIPMENT

With some exceptions—notably Robert E. Lee's invasions of the North in September 1862 and June-July 1863—the Confederacy stood on the strategic defensive. Tactically, though, Southern commanders often were bolder, at least in the earlier phases of the war, than their Union counterparts. Lee himself set the standard during the

Seven Days Battles, at Second Bull Run, at Chancellorsville and Gettysburg. The Southerners were especially effective in their dynamic use of cavalry troops: Men such as J. E. B. Stuart, John Hunt Morgan, and Nathan Bedford Forrest literally rode circles around the Union troops.

Although Lee has the reputation as the master tactician of the Civil War, historians have faulted his strategic vision. As strategists, Ulysses S. Grant and William T. Sherman were without peer. Their two most brilliant operations, Grant's Vicksburg campaign of 1863 and Sherman's march through Georgia and the Carolinas in 1864–1865, were decisive in that they brought about the Union's final victory.

Setting aside any differences or advantages either side demonstrated during the war, the strategies and tactics of the campaigns and battles of the Civil War, to this day, are studied throughout the world by those interested in military history. The Civil War is regarded as one of the first total wars—a war in which the resources of both sides were fully engaged and a war in which the combatants viewed war-making capacity, civilian as well as military, agricultural production as well as armaments, as a legitimate military target.

The contending armies used similar tools—weapons whose basic designs, in most cases, dated from the 1840s and 1850s. Percussion caps had made flintlocks obsolete; the widespread use of rifling greatly increased the capabilities of the standard smoothbore musket.

In both armies, the primary small arms were muzzleloader rifled muskets firing to an effective range of a thousand yards or so. Later in the war, breech-loading small arms were widely available, though they were used mainly by Union cavalry.

Most Civil War muskets began life as .69-caliber smoothbores, firing a round ball. With the appearance of the conically shaped minié ball (rifle bullet) in the 1850s, most smoothbores were rebored and rifled for greater range and accuracy. In 1861–1865, both armies used the .58-caliber Springfield, which fired the minié ball—officially, the United States Rifle Musket Model 1861. The Springfield (Massachusetts) Arsenal produced 1,200 rifles a year at the outset of the Civil War. By mid-1864, production had risen to 300,000 annually. Between January 1861 and December 1865, the Springfield Arsenal alone turned out nearly 800,000 Model 1861 and 1863 rifled muskets for the Union Army. Altogether, some four million

small arms were issued to Union troops during the war.

The Confederates could not keep pace. From 1864, when the blockade took full effect, the Southern forces were chronically short of small arms. Confederate blockade runners smuggled in some 100,000 English-made Enfield rifles. The Yankees, too, were a major supplier of Southern small arms. After Gen. Thomas J. Jackson's taking of Harpers Ferry on September 15, 1862, for instance, Confederate ordnance officers forwarded captured muskets and cannon to Lee in time for their use against their former owners at Antietam just two days later (see Battles and Campaigns, September 12–17, 1862, pp. 229-230).

The Civil War spurred the development of more efficient breech-loading weapons. One of the best breechloaders was the Sharps rifle, patented in 1848 by Christian Sharps of Philadelphia. The U.S. Ordnance Department purchased some 80,000 Sharps rifles during the Civil War, mostly for cavalry use.

Connecticut gunmaker Christopher M. Spencer patented the first effective breech-loading repeater carbine in 1860. It fired a quickly replaceable 9-cartridge magazine. The Union army bought some 77,000 Spencers and 60 million cartridges during the war. Union troops used them to great effect on the first day at Gettysburg, Pennsylvania, in July 1863, at Darbytown Road, Virginia, in October 1864, and at Franklin, Tennessee, in November 1864.

The 12-pounder Napoleon smoothbore muzzleloader served as the basic field artillery weapon of the Civil War, with rifled cannon in a lesser role, despite their greater range and accuracy. The most effective and versatile 12-pounder Napoleon fired both shot and shell, and so carried the designation of gun-howitzer.

North and South, the standard field artillery pieces, along with the 12-pounder gun-howitzer, were 6- and 12-pounder guns; 12-, 24-, and 32-pounder howitzers; 12-pounder mountain howitzers; 10- and 20-pounder Parrot rifles; and the 3-inch ordnance rifled gun. Maximum effective ranges were around 1,500 yards for smoothbores and 2,500 yards for rifles; rates of fire were two to three rounds per minute.

Union resources were more than adequate to supply the armies with sufficient numbers of cannon—more than 7,800 pieces were issued to Northern gunners from 1861 to 1866. Southern capacities, however, were limited. The Tredegar Iron Works in Richmond, Virginia, supplied most of the cannons manufactured in the South.

As for ammunition, solid shot and explosive shell were used for long-range work. Case shot (also called *shrapnel* after its inventor, Henry Shrapnel)—a hollow cast-iron projectile filled with lead bullets—scattered death and ruin over a wide area when it burst. Canister, a shorter-range version of case shot, broke apart on firing and sent musket balls toward an enemy with the effect of a large-scale shotgun blast. Grapeshot, usually a cloth bundle filled with lead shot, worked well only at close ranges.

Both armies experienced difficulties with unreliable fuses and defective ammunition, but such problems were far more severe in the Confederate artillery service. Badly fuzed shells bursting prematurely caused so many casualties among Confederate frontline troops at Fredericksburg, Virginia, the artillerist Edward Porter Alexander reported, that the gunners were ordered to use solid shot only when friendly infantry lay near.

Wartime demands also stimulated several invention. Battery guns were primitive rapid-fire weapons in which multiple rifle barrels were mounted on a wheeled carriage. One of the best known, the Ager Battery Gun, claimed a rate of fire of 100 rounds per minute. But Union ordnance officers were skeptical, and only about 50 were manufactured.

A Confederate officer, Capt. R. S. Williams, designed the first machine gun to see action in any war, the Williams gun; it was first used at the Battle of Seven Pines in Virginia on May 31, 1862, and the results were successful enough for the Confederates to order some two dozen before the Civil War ended. Northerner Richard J. Gatling developed the best-known and most effective machine gun, and named it after himself. A side crank turned the weapon's six barrels to provide a high rate of small-arms fire.

Gatling had difficulty penetrating the military bureaucracy, and his weapon saw only limited service during the Civil War. Union general Benjamin Butler spent $12,000 of his own money to buy a dozen Gatlings for use around Petersburg, Virginia, in 1864, and a few other Federal commanders ordered a small number for the infantry and for gunboat service. The U.S. Army adopted the Gatling for general use in 1866.

Civil War armies immeasurably advanced the art of field fortifications. Intricate systems of trenches and bombproof shelters, designed to give the defender overlapping fields of fire, ringed strategic objectives such as Vicksburg, Mississippi, and Petersburg, Virginia. Southerners, so often on the defensive after 1863, became especially adept at throwing up protective works quickly and with minimal tools—at times, little more than bayonets and tin cups.

Military uses were found for new combinations of steam, iron, and explosives. In 1861–1862, Indiana manufacturer James B. Eads built seven flat-bottomed, broad-beamed, armor-sheathed gunboats for river warfare. Gen. Ulysses S. Grant and the commander of the river flotilla, Flag Officer Andrew Foote, employed the steam-driven vessels to great advantage during the Cumberland-Tennessee Rivers Campaign in early 1862.

The Civil War's best-known ironclad, the USS *Monitor*, armed with two great guns in a revolving turret, was the Union's answer to the Confederacy's armored marauder, the *Virginia*, converted from the raised hull of the scuttled steam frigate USS *Merrimack*. In the world's first clash of ironclad ships, the *Monitor* and *Merrimack* fought to a draw at Hampton Roads, Virginia, on March 9, 1862 (see p. 239).

The Confederate navy experimented with submersible vessels as a potential means of piercing the Union blockade. The *David*, a steam-driven semisubmersible, approached the *New Ironsides* on station off Charleston, South Carolina, the night of October 15, 1863, and rammed its 14-foot-long spar torpedo into the Union warship's side. The blast nearly swamped the *David*, but did not cause sufficient damage to sink the target.

A fully submersible vessel, the *H. L. Hunley*, named after its builder, had greater success, but at a high cost. The submarine, driven by eight crewmen operating a crank that turned the propeller, attacked and sank the USS *Housatonic* off Charleston February 17, 1864. But the explosion sent the submarine to the bottom too. Many years later, divers found the wrecked hull of the *H. L. Hunley*, with the skeletons of the crew of eight inside.

Both sides made widespread use of technological innovations in communications. Confederate major Edward Porter Alexander, who served as an aerial observer during the Peninsula Campaign in 1862, communicated with ground forces by using black cambric balls suspended from the basket of his hot air balloon, varying their numbers as a code. The Federals took aeronautical communications a step further, rigging a telegraph to provide an air-to-ground signals link.

The Civil War saw the first extended use of the electrical telegraph and the first use of the field telegraph. George W. Beardslee developed a portable field telegraph, with a range of 10 miles, on which messages were composed via an alphabet dial and pointer. Union forces used it to effect at Fredericksburg, Virginia, in December 1862, where fog and battle smoke made visual communications across the Rappahannock River impossible.

Ponderous and vulnerable, the field telegraph saw little use in the latter part of the Civil War. Instead, the armies relied on faster, more powerful commercial telegraphy. In a 12-month period in 1862–1863, the Union's Military Telegraph System averaged 3,300 military messages a day. (President Abraham Lincoln kept in touch with events in the field by reading the telegraph messages in Washington, D.C.)

The Civil War was also the first war in which railroads played a major role, both in transporting supplies and in moving troops. The first instance in military history in which a railroad was used for strategic mobility was when Gen. J. E. Johnston moved his troops by train to fight at the First Battle of Bull Run (Manassas). Throughout the war, the railroads continued to play an important role, and here as elsewhere, the Union held an advantage.

Matthew Brady and others extensively photographed Civil War campsites and the aftermath of battles. Although pictures were made during the Crimean and Mexican wars, the Civil War was the first to be recorded photographically on a large scale. Brady and his assistants alone are said to have made some 3,500 photographs.

LEGENDS AND TRIVIA

Panic swept through the Union ranks during the first phase of withdrawal after the First Battle of Bull Run on July 21, 1861. Word of a ferocious troop of bloodthirsty Confederate horsemen helped turn retreat into a rout. "Black horse cavalry," fear-struck soldiers shouted. "The cavalry is on us!" There was no such thing as **black horse cavalry**; in fact, the Confederates, almost as disorganized as the beaten Federals, were unable to mount any sort of effective pursuit.

Johnny Clem ran away from home at age 9 in May 1861 and joined the 22nd Michigan as an unofficial drummer boy. The regiment's officers chipped in to pay Clem a $13 a month private's wage. In September 1863, at age 12, he shouldered a musket and became a legend as the "drummer boy of Chickamauga." After the war, President Ulysses S. Grant gave Clem a second lieutenant's commission. He served until 1916, when he retired with the rank of major general.

In an army rich in eccentrics, Confederate general **Richard Ewell** stood out for his oddness. Ewell rose to corps command in the Army of Northern Virginia. He was completely bald; had a long, sharp nose that gave him something of the look of a predatory bird; and cursed fluently. A martyr to ulcers, Ewell subsisted on an invalid's diet of hulled wheat boiled in milk with egg yolk and garnished with raisins.

Union forces captured Lookout Mountain near Chattanooga, Tennessee, after a sharp but brief fight on the foggy morning of November 24, 1863. Exaggerated postwar accounts turned that minor action into the romantically named **Battle above the Clouds**.

Mother Bickerdyke (Mary Ann Ball Bickerdyke) worked as a nurse and Sanitary Commission Agent in Gen. Ulysses S. Grant's, and later Gen. William T. Sherman's, Western Army. An imposing and much respected figure, Bickerdyke used her influence effectively on behalf of the sick and wounded. When one of Sherman's officers complained that Mother Bickerdyke, protecting her charges, had interfered with him on some sanitary matter, Sherman claimed that he lacked the authority to intervene. "She ranks me," he said.

An indeterminable number of women disguised their sex to serve in the ranks of both armies. **Sarah Seelye**, age 20, enlisted in the 2nd Michigan infantry in May 1861 under the name Franklin Thompson and served for nearly two years before she acknowledged her gender and left soldiering to become a nurse.

During the evening of July 1, 1863, the Union 5th Corps infantry approaching Gettysburg, Pennsylvania, heard the first rumors of a bloody battle fought there earlier in the day. Soon, men began repeating the story of a stirring sighting: Men had seen **George Washington** riding over the hills around Gettysburg, the sun setting behind him. "I half believed it myself," recalled one 5th Corps regimental commander, Maj. Gen. Joshua L. Chamberlain of Maine.

According to Bell I. Wiley, a historian of the common soldier of both armies, the Yankees seem to have originated the term **Johnny Reb**. It dated from early in the Civil War, when Federals called out across the lines, "Hello, Johnny." Common Confederate soldiers took at once to the nickname. **Billy Yank**, on the other hand, is of postwar coinage. For instance, Army of Northern Virginia veteran Alexander Hunter's memoir *Johnny Reb and Billy Yank* appeared in 1905.

Northern issues of **commissary whiskey** fueled many a soldier's drunk. Though they consumed it in quantity when available, most Union soldiers agreed it was vile stuff — a concoction, in one skeptic's words, of "bark juice, tar-water, turpentine, brown sugar, lamp oil, and alcohol." Another soldier left this account of a morning-after: "Got up this morning with severe bee hives in my head."

With the influx of Union troops and the wartime expansion of government activity, Washington, D.C., became a center of prostitution. As early as 1862, 450 bawdy houses were said to be in operation in the city; 7,500 prostitutes were working in the nation's capital in 1863. A frequent claim is that prostitutes have become known as *hookers* because they were particularly active among the troops commanded by Gen. Joseph Hooker. Knowledgeable students of language discount this etymology. Although it is in dispute, the origin of the word may simply come from the word hook, or catch.

Wilmer McLean's house was so badly damaged in the First Battle of Bull Run in July 1861 that he moved his family to another house some 110 miles to the southwest. It was in the parlor of that second house at Appomattox Court House that Gen. Robert E. Lee surrendered to Gen. Ulysses S. Grant on April 9, 1865.

Cavalry units and horses played such prominent roles in the Civil War that inevitably statues were erected throughout the U.S. showing military heroes on horses. To art historians, these belong to a particular genre of sculpture, what are known as **equestrian statues**. Many people have come to believe that all equestrian statues—or at least those within the long history of Western sculpture—adhere to a certain tradition or rule: namely, that if the subject died of natural causes, the horse's four feet are on the ground; if he died of wounds received in battle, one of the horse's front legs is raised; and if he died in battle, the two front legs are raised. In fact, a close look at just the statues of the Civil War heroes reveals no such pattern. One of the most famous (by Augustus Saint-Gaudens, in New York City) is of General Sherman: he died of old age and yet his horse has the left rear leg and right front leg off the ground—simply to convey motion. General John Logan is shown (in Washington, D.C.) with his horse's right front leg raised—yet he died of natural causes; meanwhile, another famous Saint-Gaudens sculpture (in Boston) shows Robert Gould Shaw with his horse's left front leg raised— yet Shaw died in battle. These inconsistencies can be seen in representations of military heroes from many times and lands: For every statue that appears to adhere to the tradition, there is another that does not. George Washington is portrayed on several equestrian statues—some with one leg raised, some with none raised. There is, however, one, somewhat related tradition that is said to be derived from an ancient Roman practice of depicting their leaders or heroes on a horse with a captive enemy under a raised front leg. The captive figure was eventually eliminated, but the tradition of the raised leg as a symbol of victory is still often followed, consciously or not.

NOTABLE PHRASES

I don't believe there is any North. The 7th Regiment is a myth. Rhode Island is not known in our geography any longer.

That was President Abraham Lincoln's anguished view on April 24, 1861, when Washington, D.C., seemed open to a rebel invasion and Northern militia forces had not yet been able to reach the city.

Yonder stands Jackson like a stone wall.

Those were South Carolinian Barnard Bee's admiring words on July 21, 1861, as he rallied his troops during a critical phase of the First Battle of Bull Run. Gen. Thomas J. Jackson was known to the world thereafter as "Stonewall" Jackson.

We can get along without anything but food and ammunition. The road to glory cannot be followed with much baggage.

Stonewall Jackson made that observation to

his officers at the outset of his brilliant Shenandoah Valley campaign in the spring of 1862.

No terms except an unconditional and immediate surrender can be accepted. I propose to move immediately upon your works.

Gen. Ulysses S. Grant dashed off those phrases in a note to the commander of besieged Fort Donelson, Tennessee. The Confederates surrendered the fort on February 16, 1862.

I can't spare this man. He fights.

President Lincoln made that retort to those who called for Grant's removal after the battle of Shiloh in April 1862.

He is an admirable engineer, but he seems to have a special talent for the stationary engine.

That was President Lincoln's exasperated response to Gen. George B. McClellan's defeat at the Battle of Antietam in September 1862. An able organizer and administrator, the plodding, cautious McClellan frustrated Lincoln's hopes for a quick end to the war.

It is well that war is so terrible, or we should grow too fond of it.

Gen. Robert E. Lee spoke those words in an aside to Gen. James Longstreet as he watched Union troops advance over the Fredericksburg, Virginia, plain on December 13, 1862.

It's a rich man's war and a poor man's fight.

That anonymous and widely quoted phrase conveyed the ordinary Southerners' disgust with Confederate conscription laws during the Civil War that exempted from service property owners with more than 20 slaves.

The world has seen its iron age, its silver age, its golden age and its brazen age. This is the age of shoddy.

That was a *New York Herald* editorialist's comment on the prevalence of the frayed clothes made from a cloth called *shoddy* (a byword for cheap), broken shoes, spoiled food, and defective weap-

ons that greedy contractors passed off on the Union Army.

Give them a chance. I don't say they will fight better than other men. All I say is, give them a chance.

Abolition leader Frederick Douglass made that plea in 1862 as part of an argument for the enlistment of black troops in the Union armies.

Home, boys, home. Remember, home is just beyond those hills.

Those were the words of an anonymous Confederate lieutenant urging his men forward during Gen. George Pickett's charge into a curtain of Union fire at Gettysburg on July 3, 1863.

The father of waters again goes unvexed to the sea.

That was President Lincoln's exultant reaction to news of Grant's entry into Vicksburg, Mississippi, on July 4, 1863.

I propose to fight it out on this line, if it takes all summer.

Grant wired that succinct summary of his campaign plan to Gen. Henry Halleck, the army chief of staff, from Spotsylvania Court House, Virginia, on May 11, 1864.

Damn the torpedoes—full speed ahead!

Adm. David G. Farragut responded to the threat of submerged mines in Mobile Bay with that memorable battle cry on August 5, 1864.

War is cruelty, and you cannot refine it.

Sherman offered that blunt reply to Atlanta mayor James Calhoun's protests against Union Army orders to evacuate civilians from the city in September of 1864.

There is nothing left for me to do but go and see General Grant, and I would rather die a thousand deaths.

Lee made that observation to aides at

Appomattox Court House, Virginia, the morning of April 9, 1865.

Git thar fustest with the mostest.

That phrase has long been attributed to Confederate general Nathan Bedford Forrest. Although the expression does reflect his genius for swift, no-nonsense tactics, his actual words of advice as reported by two of his fellow generals were "Get there first with the most men."

I went into the army worth a million and a half dollars and came out a beggar.

That was Gen. Nathan Bedford Forrest's lament after the collapse of the Confederacy in the spring of 1865.

Boys, it is all hell.

That was Gen. William T. Sherman's considered view of war, delivered before a Grand Army of the Republic convention in Columbus, Ohio, in 1881. The similar, more famous quote of "War is hell" was alleged to have been said in a speech by Sherman before a graduating class of the Michigan Military Academy in 1879.

Through our great good fortune, in our youth our hearts were touched with fire.

Oliver Wendell Holmes, a Civil War veteran who later became Chief Justice of the United States, uttered that evocative phrase as part of a Memorial Day speech in Keene, New Hampshire, in 1884.

SONGS

The Civil War could be set to music. Bands performed nightly concerts in camps. In camps and in the field, army buglers issued universally recognized calls to order. Regimental drummers beat time as the assault lines moved forward to the attack. The dead were buried to the mournful notes of taps. Each side had sheaves of marching songs. North and South, young soldiers were addicted to the sentimental ballads of the day.

In late 1861, Julia Ward Howe wrote the lyrics of "The Battle Hymn of the Republic," sung to the popular Union marching song "John Brown's Body" (one line of which began, "We'll hang Jeff Davis...."). "Dixie," composed by Dan Emmett, the son of an Ohio abolitionist, began life as a minstrel tune (and was said to be a favorite of Lincoln's). The Confederates appropriated it as a patriotic anthem, playing it at Jefferson Davis's inauguration in February 1861.

"Lorena" and "The Yellow Rose of Texas," songs about sweethearts and wives at home, were two of the great hits of the Civil War. There was, too, "The Girl I Left Behind Me." The ballad "The Vacant Chair" acknowledged loss. "When This Cruel War Is Over" expressed sadness, longing, and hope. "Tenting Tonight on the Old Camp Ground" captured the mood of the great encampments. Union marching tunes included the stirring "Battle Cry of Freedom":

Yes, we'll rally round the flag,
Boys, we'll rally once again,
Shouting the battle cry of Freedom.
The Union forever,
Hurray, boys, hurray.
Down with the traitor, up with the star;
While we rally round the flag, boys,
Rally once again,
Shouting the battle cry of Freedom!

Historian Bell Wiley says music was Johnny Reb's chief recreation. Like the Yankees, rebels took at once to "Lorena." "Who Will Care for Mother Now?" became popular. Like those of the North, Southern publishers produced pocket songbooks such as the *Stonewall Song Book* of 1863. Long a favorite in America, "Home, Sweet Home" was among the more popular of all the ballads sung by Southerners.

"The Bonnie Blue Flag" was said to have been the most widely sung Confederate patriotic song. A close second was "Maryland, My Maryland," belted out as Gen. Robert E. Lee's army crossed the Potomac for the 1862 and 1863 invasions of the North. The song ended this way:

I hear the distant thunder-hum
Maryland! My Maryland!
The Old Line's bugle, fife and drum,
Maryland! My Maryland!
She is not dead, nor deaf, nor dumb—
Huzza! She spurns the Northern scum!
She breathes—she burns!
She'll come, she'll come!
Maryland! My Maryland!

"I don't believe we can have an army without music," Gen. Robert E. Lee observed in 1864, at the end of a brass serenade.

HISTORICAL PERSPECTIVES AND CONTROVERSIES

Was it inevitable that the Civil War end in a decisive Northern victory?

Historians have been debating that question since the Civil War ended in 1865. Their conclusions may be grouped broadly into three main categories.

1. Northern manpower and economic superiority simply overwhelmed the South. The loyal states had a manpower advantage over the rebellious states of three-to-one—three times as many males of military age. During most of the Civil War, the Union Army had close to twice as many men under arms as their Confederate adversaries. The North had an even greater advantage in economic resources. From the start of the war to the finish, Union soldiers were better armed, better equipped, better clothed, and better fed than were Southerners. Northern industrial and agricultural capacity seemed boundless. Despite wartime labor shortages, Northern farms fed the nation and the army and at the same time managed to double agricultural exports to Europe. On the other side, the increasingly effective Federal blockade prevented Southerners from exporting cotton and importing arms, munitions, and other war matériel.

The Northern advantages negated the South's chief advantage: that of fighting on home ground, with interior lines of communication and the ability to win the war by not losing, by managing to survive, however precariously, as a national entity.

2. Some historians believe that internal divisions and lack of will to continue the fight doomed the Confederate cause. According to that argument, the very dogma that helped bring on the Civil War—states' rights—helped the South lose it. Conflicts between Richmond, Virginia, the Confederate capital, and the Confederate states vitiated the Confederate effort. Some states withheld men and supplies from the main armies at critical times. In North Carolina and elsewhere, politicians encouraged the desertions that weakened the Confederate field armies. And the South,

too, had a hostile population of 4 million enslaved blacks within its borders.

Critics of that interpretation point out that the North found itself equally beset by internal divisions and contradictions, if not more so, but managed to overcome them to achieve ultimate victory.

3. The North gradually developed superior civilian and military leaders. As the Civil War progressed, President Abraham Lincoln emerged as a far better war leader than Confederate president Jefferson Davis. The Confederate president failed to hold his new nation together; Lincoln succeeded in restoring the old Union. Lincoln learned quickly, too, to rid himself of incompetent battlefield commanders, such as Gen. George B. McClellan, Gen. Ambrose E. Burnside, Gen. Joseph Hooker, and Gen. William S. Rosecrans. And Lincoln recognized and rewarded the brilliance of Gen. Ulysses S. Grant and Gen. William T. Sherman, the Civil War's outstanding military figures.

The South, on the other hand, could not sustain its initial leadership advantage. Gen. Joseph E. Johnston, regarded by some as the most able general the Confederacy possessed, never actually won a battle on his own. Gen. Robert E. Lee's strategic shortsightedness limited the main Confederate effort to the Virginia theater at the expense of the West, where Grant and later Sherman dominated second-string Southern commanders such as Gen. John Pemberton, Gen. P. G. T. Beauregard, Gen. Braxton Bragg, and Gen. John P. Hood. The Union's winning of the Mississippi valley, Tennessee, and Georgia sealed the Confederacy's fate long before Lee's final collapse in Virginia.

Were there crucial turning points in the Civil War, or did it just drag on and end because of the Confederacy's weariness?

Most historians recognize four turning points in the Civil War. James M. McPherson summarized those critical junctures in his *Battle Cry of Freedom* (1988).

1. In the summer of 1862, Confederate counteroffensives in Virginia (the Battles of the Seven Days, the Second Battle of Bull Run) and in Kentucky (the invasions of Gen. Braxton Bragg and Gen. Edmond Kirby Smith) blunted Union momentum and suggested the possibility of a South-

ern victory, thereby assuring that there would be no quick end to the war.

2. In the autumn of 1862, the repulse of the Confederate offensives at the Battle of Antietam in Maryland (September 17) and the Battle of Perryville in Kentucky (October 8) forestalled European recognition of the Confederacy and decreased the likelihood of European-sponsored mediation of the conflict. Lincoln used the occasion of the Battle of Antietam to issue the Preliminary Emancipation Proclamation, which expanded Union war aims to encompass the liberation of slaves.

3. In the summer and autumn of 1863, the great Union victories of Gettysburg, Pennsylvania (July 1–3), Vicksburg, Mississippi (capitulation July 4), and Chattanooga, Tennessee (Missionary Ridge, November 25), punctured the myth of Confederate military superiority and resulted in lasting and decisive strategic gains for the North.

4. In the summer of 1864, the Confederacy had its last chance to reverse the course of events, fight the North to a stalemate, and secure independence. Gen. William T. Sherman's capture of Atlanta (September 1–2) and Gen. Philip H. Sheridan's victories over Gen. Jubal Early in the Shenandoah Valley (September 19–22) restored Northern morale and crushed Southern hopes. Lincoln's reelection in November 1864 assured the eventual Union victory.

CIVILIAN AND MILITARY BIOGRAPHIES

UNION

Barton, Clara (1821–1912)—nurse: Clara Barton was a farmer's daughter. She was born near Oxford, Massachusetts. She went to work as a schoolteacher at age 15 and later worked as a clerk in the government Patent Office in Washington, D.C. With the outbreak of the Civil War, she became one of the first volunteer nurses. She saw front-line service in Virginia in 1862 and at the siege of Charleston, South Carolina, in 1863. Barton carried her work to Fredericksburg, Virginia, during General Grant's Wilderness and Spotsylvania campaigns of 1864. She organized and became the first director of the American Red Cross in 1881.

Burnside, Ambrose Everett (1824–1881)—general: Ambrose E. Burnside was born and raised in Liberty, Indiana. Burnside's magnificent muttonchop side-whiskers were the source of the word "sideburns." He was an 1847 West Point graduate and rose rapidly to senior command after the outbreak of the Civil War. His fumbling performance in command of a corps at Antietam, Maryland, helped rob the Union of a decisive victory there. Placed in command of the Army of the Potomac, he presided over the disaster at Fredericksburg, Virginia, in December 1862. Removed early in 1863, he afterward commanded a corps at Petersburg, Virginia, where his mismanagement of the Battle of the Crater in July 1864 led to his final removal from authority.

Dix, Dorothea (1802–1887)—nurse and reformer: Dorthea Dix was born in Hampden, Maine. She taught school in Worcester, Massachusetts, and in Boston until a tubercular illness sent her abroad for treatment. On her return, Dix commenced a campaign to reform America's prisons, insane asylums, and alms houses. President Lincoln appointed her superintendent of nurses in June 1861. Dix oversaw the recruitment, training, and placement of 2,000 Union volunteer nurses from 1861–1865. After the Civil War, she resumed her work to improve conditions for the insane.

Douglass, Frederick (ca. 1817–1895)—abolition leader: Frederick Douglass was born a slave in Talbot County, Maryland. He escaped in 1838, settled in Massachusetts, and almost at once began speaking out for abolition. His famous *Autobiography* appeared in 1844. From the start, Douglass saw the Civil War as a crusade for freedom. He fought tirelessly for the enlistment of blacks in the Union Army; two of his sons served in all-black regiments. After the war, Douglass campaigned for full civil rights for freed slaves. He later served as U.S. ambassador to Haiti.

Farragut, David Glasgow (1801–1870)—naval officer: David Farragut was born in Tennessee. He was orphaned at an early age. He entered the Navy at age nine and saw service during the War of 1812. Given command of the Gulf Blockading Squadron in January 1862, he became a national hero with the capture of New Orleans, Louisiana, in April. His daring assault on Mobile Bay in August 1864 ended in the defeat of a Confederate fleet and the closing of the South's last major port. Farragut went into semiretirement in 1867.

Grant, Ulysses Simpson (1822–1885)—general: Ulysses S. Grant was born in Ohio, the son of a tanner. He graduated from West Point in 1843 and served ably in the Mexican War, but he failed to adapt to life in the peacetime Army. Bored, lonely, and increasingly addicted to drink, he resigned under pressure in 1854. The coming of the Civil War altered his fortunes overnight. Grant won his military reputation in the West, proving himself a bold strategist and a master of logistics. His list of successes mounted: capture of Forts Henry and Donelson in Tennessee in February 1862; recovery from near disaster and eventual victory at Shiloh in April 1862; and the brilliant overland campaign in the spring of 1863 that yielded one of the Civil War's decisive victories, the surrender of the Confederate fortress of Vicksburg, Mississippi. His victory at Missionary Ridge near Chattanooga, Tennessee, in November 1863 opened the invasion route to Atlanta, Georgia, and the Deep South. It led, too, to Grant's ascension as commander of all the Union land forces. In May 1864, he launched a relentless campaign against the Confederates. In a continuous battle from the Wilderness to Spotsylvania to Cold Harbor, he ground down Gen. Robert E. Lee's army. With great directness of purpose, Grant pursued his strategy to the end. Lee's army surrendered at Appomattox Court House, Virginia, on April 9, 1865. The other Confederate armies shortly followed. As the chief architect of victory, Grant found the greatest of America's prizes within his grasp: the presidency. He was elected in 1868 and again in 1872. His two terms were marred by scandal and corruption on a grand scale. Grant had one final triumph—the completion, just before his death on July 23, 1885, of his *Personal Memoirs*, widely regarded as a classic of Civil War literature.

Hooker, Joseph (1814–1879)—general: "Fighting Joe" Hooker was vain and self-applauding. He was the grandson of a Revolutionary War officer. Hooker graduated from West Point in 1837. He commanded a division on the Virginia peninsula and a corps at Antietam, Maryland, in 1862. In January 1863, he succeeded Gen. Ambrose Burnside, against whom he had schemed, in command of the Army of the Potomac. In May, he launched a campaign he boasted would destroy the Army of Northern Virginia. Instead, Hooker became the victim of the most brilliant of Gen. Robert E. Lee's victories, Chancellorsville. Removed from command on the eve of Gettysburg and transferred west, he led two corps under Gen. Ulysses S. Grant at Chattanooga, Tennessee, in November 1863. Passed over for command of one

of Gen. William T. Sherman's armies in 1864, Hooker asked to be relieved of duty and never returned to the field.

Lincoln, Abraham (1809–1865)—president: Abraham Lincoln was born in a Kentucky log cabin and raised in Indiana. The self-educated 16th president read law, established a modestly successful law practice, and entered politics in Illinois. He served a term in Congress in the late 1840s and ran unsuccessfully for the Senate—his debates in 1858 with Stephen Douglas were famous even in their time. By then, his free-soil principles were well developed. In 1860, the new Republican Party chose him as its presidential candidate, and he won election in a four-way race. One by one, the Southern states seceded. Lincoln made vigorous war against the rebellion, surviving inept military leadership and outmaneuvering his political enemies. He issued the Emancipation Proclamation on January 1, 1863. His choice of Gen. Ulysses S. Grant to lead the Union Army in 1864 proved decisive, and Lincoln won reelection later in the year. On April 14, 1865, five days after Gen. Robert E. Lee's surrender at Appomattox Court House, an assassin mortally wounded the president. He died the next day.

McClellan, George Brinton (1826–1885)—general: George B. McClellan was born into a prominent Philadelphia family. McClellan was second in his West Point class of 1846 and was a veteran of the Mexican War. By the age of 31, he was the president of a railroad. McClellan rose to command the Army of the Potomac after the disaster at Bull Run in July 1861. A brilliant organizer, he inspired devotion in the troops and transformed the Army of the Potomac. In the field, though, he lacked dash and aggressiveness. His brilliantly conceived Virginia peninsula campaign of the spring of 1862 was barren of result. At Antietam, Maryland, in September, he missed several opportunities to crush the Confederate army, though he claimed a strategic victory. Lincoln relieved McClellan after Antietam, and he never saw field service again. Running as a Democrat, he challenged Lincoln for the presidency in 1864, but carried only three states.

Meade, George Gordon (1815–1872)—general: The Union victor of Gettysburg, Pennsylvania, in 1863, Gen. George G. Meade grades as a solid if unspectacular commander, cautious and careful in the field despite his famously ungovernable temper. Meade was born in Pennsylvania. An 1835 West Point graduate, he performed capably as a division and corps commander at Antietam, Maryland, and at Fredericksburg and Chancellorsville. Praised for his efficient handling of troops at Gettysburg, he has been faulted for failing to pursue the wounded and vulnerable Army of Northern Virginia after the battle. Meade retained nominal command of the Army of the Potomac after General Grant came east in 1864. However, Meade played a secondary role to Grant's protégé, Gen. Philip Sheridan, in the pursuit to Appomattox in April 1865, the campaign that brought the long war to an end.

Pope, John (1822–1892)—general: John Pope was born in Kentucky. An 1842 West Point graduate, Pope rose swiftly to senior command in the West. By late winter of 1862, his success in clearing New Madrid and Island No. 10, Missouri, of Confederates had opened the Mississippi River almost to Memphis, Tennessee. Lincoln chose him in the summer of 1862 to replace the popular Gen. George B. McClellan in command of the Army of the Potomac. But Gen. Robert E. Lee humbled Pope at the Second Battle of Bull Run on August 29–30, 1862, and he was relieved of command the next day. Exiled to frontier Minnesota, Pope never again held a wartime field command.

Porter, David Dixon (1813–1891)—naval officer: David Porter went to sea at age 13 and later fought in the Mexican War. With the coming of the Civil War, he served under his foster brother, Adm. David G. Farragut, in the capture of New Orleans, Louisiana. Porter commanded the Mississippi River flotilla in largely successful operations on the inland waters in 1863 and 1864. In late 1864, he rose to command the 120-ship North Atlantic Blockading Squadron. In a joint operation with the Union Army, Porter commanded the naval forces in the successful taking of Fort Fisher, North Carolina, in January 1865. After the war, he headed the U.S. Naval Academy in Annapolis.

Sheridan, Philip Henry (1831–1888)—general: Philip Sheridan was the son of immigrants from County Cavan, Ireland. The short-tempered Sheridan survived a year's suspension for fighting and other deficiencies of deportment to graduate a few places from the bottom of his West Point class of 1853. He seemed born for the swirl of battle. Sheridan's aggressive handling of a Michigan cavalry regiment in 1861–1862 won him promotion and an eventual infantry command. He led the impulsive infantry charge that carried Mis-

sionary Ridge near Chattanooga, Tennessee, in November 1863. Coming east with General Grant in 1864 to take charge of the Army of the Potomac's cavalry, Sheridan commanded the Shenandoah Valley Campaign that laid waste to that Confederate granary. Sheridan's rout of the Confederates at Five Forks, Virginia, on April 1, 1865, turned Gen. Robert E. Lee out of the Petersburg defenses and sent him into a precipitous westward retreat. Sheridan, with cavalry and infantry, pursued without letup, trapping the remnants of the Army of Northern Virginia at Appomattox Court House a week later. Like Gen. William T. Sherman, Sheridan stayed on in the postwar Army. He organized a series of punitive expeditions against the Plains Indians in the 1870s and, in 1884, became second in succession to Grant as army commander.

Sherman, William Tecumseh (1820–1891)—general: Some authorities rate Gen. William T. Sherman the outstanding Federal commander of the Civil War. His masterly campaigns of 1864-1865 carried Union forces a thousand miles, from Chattanooga through Georgia and the Carolinas. Sherman was born in Ohio and orphaned at age nine. He graduated from West Point in 1840. Resigning from the Army in 1853, he had indifferent success in the business world. Sherman reentered the Army at the outbreak of the Civil War. He commanded a division under Gen. Ulysses S. Grant at Shiloh, Tennessee, in 1862, the beginning of the most successful military partnership of the Civil War. In March 1864, Sherman succeeded Grant as the senior Union commander in the West. Two months later, Sherman launched the grand offensive that, in combination with Grant's relentless pursuit of Gen. Robert E. Lee in Virginia, closed out the war in less than a year. Sherman's campaigns were noteworthy for their promiscuous destruction of property and their comparatively low casualty rates. He preferred maneuver to frontal assault and held that the war would end only when its realities were brought home starkly to the civilian population. Sherman succeeded Grant as commander of the Army in 1869, waged merciless war on the Plains Indian tribes, and resisted all entreaties to enter politics, for which he had a profound contempt.

Stanton, Edwin McMasters (1814–1869)—politician: Edwin Stanton was an Ohio lawyer. He became Lincoln's war secretary early in 1862. An efficient and honest administrator, he oversaw the recruitment and outfitting of a massive Union

Army. Abrasive personally, he made many enemies, civilian and military. Stanton was at the center of the Radical Republicans' impeachment attempt against President Andrew Johnson in 1868. He died only a few days after the Senate confirmed his appointment to the U.S. Supreme Court.

Thomas, George Henry (1816–1870)—general: George Thomas was born in Virginia but remained loyal to the Union when the Civil War broke out. He graduated from West Point in 1840, fought in Mexico, and participated in punitive campaigns against Indian tribes in Florida and on the Plains. His stout defense at Chickamauga, Georgia, in September 1863 made him a national hero and earned him the sobriquet of the "Rock of Chickamauga" and promotion to the command of the Army of the Cumberland. Thomas's troops launched the assault on Missionary Ridge in Tennessee in November 1863 that led to a decisive Confederate defeat at Chattanooga. Thomas checked the advancing Army of Tennessee at Franklin, Tennessee, in November 1864, and in December routed and nearly destroyed the Confederates at the Battle of Nashville.

Vallandigham, Clement Laird (1820–1871)—opposition leader: Clement Vallandigham was an Ohio journalist and politician. He stoutly opposed the war as a leader in Congress of the Peace Democrats—the so-called Copperheads. Lincoln exiled him to the South in 1863, but he returned via Canada to campaign against the president in 1864. Vallandigham later opposed Reconstruction policies but had little influence on postwar events.

CONFEDERATE

Beauregard, Pierre Gustave Toutaint (1818–1893)—general: P. G. T. Beauregard was born into a prosperous Creole family. He graduated from West Point in 1838. Beauregard directed Confederate forces in the bombardment of Fort Sumter in April 1861, the incident that touched off the Civil War. With Gen. Joseph E. Johnston, he led Confederate forces to their first significant battlefield victory at Bull Run in Virginia in July 1861. Never a favorite of President Jefferson Davis, Beauregard bounced from one command to another, serving at Shiloh at Charleston again (during the Union siege of 1863), and at Petersburg, where his skillful initial conduct of the defense saved the city for the Confederacy in 1864. Toward war's end, he served as second in command to Gen. Joseph E. Johnston in the Carolinas and surrendered there in April 1865.

Bragg, Braxton (1817–1876)—general: Braxton Bragg was born in North Carolina. An 1837 West Point graduate, he inspired indifference in the troops he commanded and widespread contempt, even hatred, in many of his senior lieutenants. Bragg's 1862 invasion of Kentucky ended in failure and retreat after the battles of Perryville, Kentucky, in October and Stones River, Tennessee, at year's end. His Army of Tennessee defeated Union forces at Chickamauga in September 1863, but he failed to follow up his success. In November, Gen. Ulysses S. Grant routed Bragg's demoralized army at Missionary Ridge, Chattanooga. Bragg served as President Davis's military adviser in 1864. Returning to the field near the war's end, he fought his last battle against Gen. William T. Sherman in North Carolina in March 1865.

Davis, Jefferson (1808–1889)—Confederate president: Jefferson Davis was born in Kentucky and grew up on a Mississippi plantation in what was then frontier country. He graduated from the U.S. Military Academy in 1828 and served in obscure frontier posts for several years. After some years as a planter in Mississippi, he turned to politics, winning election to Congress in 1845. Davis commanded a regiment of Mississippi volunteers in the Mexican War before claiming a seat in the U.S. Senate late in 1847. He served as secretary of war from 1853 to 1857. Quitting the Senate early in 1861, he followed Mississippi into the Confederacy. Davis became president of the Confederate States in February. His war leadership left much to be desired. From 1863 on, a majority in the Confederate Congress opposed him, and Davis never achieved wide popularity among Southerners. He failed, too, to obtain foreign recognition of the breakaway nation. Davis quarreled with some of his senior military commanders, notably Gen. Joseph E. Johnston, though he retained his faith in Gen. Robert E. Lee to the end. Arrested in Georgia in May 1865, he remained a prisoner of the United States for two years but was never tried. His two-volume *The Rise and Fall of the Confederate Government* appeared from 1878 to 1881.

Forrest, Nathan Bedford (1821–1877)—general: Nathan Bedford Forrest was born in Tennessee. He built a fortune as a cotton planter and slave trader in Tennessee. In 1861, he embarked on a career that eventually made him the best known and most feared Confederate cavalry commander of the Civil War. His raids on Union communications were so successful that Gen. William T. Sherman vowed to stop him "if it costs ten thousand lives and bankrupts the federal treasury." In April 1864, Forrest's command carried out the infamous massacre of surrendering black troops at Fort Pillow, Tennessee. After the war, he had a brief involvement with the Ku Klux Klan in Tennessee and is said to have served as its Grand Wizard for a time.

Hill, Ambrose Powell (1825–1865)—general: Ambrose Powell Hill was born in Virginia. He graduated from West Point in 1847 and fought in Mexico. Resigning from the U.S Army during the secession crisis, Hill joined the Confederate army. He quickly earned a reputation as one of the hardest-hitting division commanders of the Army of Northern Virginia. Following Gen. Thomas Jackson's death, Hill succeeded to corps command and fought at Gettysburg, Pennsylvania, and in a number of heavy engagements during the Petersburg siege of 1864–1865. Hill once remarked that he had no wish to survive the collapse of the Confederacy. Near Petersburg, Virginia, on April 2, 1865, advancing Union troops shot him dead as he rode toward the front to rally his broken command.

Jackson, Thomas Jonathan ("Stonewall") (1824–1863)—general: Thomas Jonathan Jackson survived a poverty-blighted childhood as an orphan in western Virginia to become the best known and most brilliant of Gen. Robert E. Lee's lieutenants. Educated at West Point, Jackson struggled in the peacetime Army and resigned in 1852 to teach mathematics. Joining the Confederate army early in 1861, he earned his nickname at the First Battle of Bull Run in July 1861, repulsing a Federal assault so conclusively that the world knew him ever afterward as "Stonewall." Austere, deeply religious and eccentric, Jackson fought with an intelligent slashing audacity that seemed to paralyze his opponents. His Shenandoah Valley operations of 1862 have been judged one of the great campaigns of maneuver in military history. Jackson distinguished himself at the Second Battle of Bull Run, at Antietam, and, most notably, at Chancellorsville, where his flank march and assault on the Federal right wing set up Lee's masterpiece victory. Jackson died on May 10, 1863, of wounds inflicted by his own

troops in the confused aftermath of the Chancellorsville battle.

Johnston, Joseph Eggleston (1807–1891)—general: Joseph E. Johnston was born in Virginia. He was in the 1829 class at West Point with Robert E. Lee. Johnston grades as one of the most skilled Southern commanders. With Gen. P. G. T. Beauregard, he led Confederate forces to a resounding victory at the First Battle of Bull Run in 1861. In sole command on the Virginia peninsula, Johnston dropped back steadily before McClellan's forces. Wounded near Richmond, Virginia, he yielded command to Gen. Robert E. Lee, and never returned to the eastern army. In command of the Army of Tennessee in 1864, Johnston retreated toward Atlanta, Georgia, before Gen. William T. Sherman's superior force. President Jefferson Davis relieved Johnston on July 17, charging he had failed to bring Sherman to battle. Johnston returned to the field in North Carolina in February 1865 and surrendered to Sherman on April 26. Johnston's partisans claimed, rightly, that he never lost a decisive battle; on the other hand, Johnston, a cautious commander, never actually won one on his own.

Lee, Robert Edward (1807–1870)—general: One of history's great commanders, Robert E. Lee led the Army of Northern Virginia from July 1, 1862, to the surrender at Appomattox Court House on April 9, 1865. For nearly three years, he fought the always larger, more powerful Union Army of the Potomac to a stalemate. Lee was born in Alexandria, Virginia, the son of an improvident Revolutionary War hero. He graduated from West Point in 1829, served in frontier garrisons, fought in Mexico and commanded the detachment that captured the insurrectionary John Brown at Harpers Ferry. With secession, his loyalties remained with Virginia. In mid-1862, with Union forces in sight of Richmond, Virginia, Lee succeeded Gen. Joseph E. Johnston in command of the Confederacy's main army. In the counteroffensive known as the Battles of the Seven Days, he drove the federals away from the capital. Lee followed the Battles of the Seven Days with a smashing success at the Second Battle of Bull Run. A few weeks later, his first invasion of the North, a bold move with political and diplomatic as well as military aims, came to grief in the Battle of Antietam in Maryland. Victory at Fredericksburg, Virginia, in December 1862 restored Lee's aura of invincibility. In May 1863, he conducted the brilliant battle of maneuver that yielded his greatest triumph, Chancellorsville in Virginia. Lee's second great gamble, the Pennsylvania campaign of June–July 1863, resulted in a decisive defeat at Gettysburg. From then on, the Confederates fought on the defensive. By mid-1864, the Federal commander, Gen. Ulysses S. Grant, had forced the once-nimble Army of Northern Virginia into static lines, covering Richmond and Petersburg. After a confused, desperate retreat in early April 1865, Lee surrendered to Grant at Appomattox Court House. Even in his day, Lee attained mythic stature. Handsome, courtly, unfailingly kind in manner, he inspired in his troops a near-absolute confidence and devotion. As a tactical commander, Lee had no peer. Critics have faulted him, however, for a strategic short sightedness that placed the defense of his beloved Virginia above all else. The U.S. authorities did not trouble Lee after the war. In the autumn of 1865, he accepted the presidency of Washington College (now Washington and Lee) in Lexington, Virginia. He died there on October 12, 1870.

Longstreet, James (1821–1904)—general: James Longstreet was Gen. Robert E. Lee's "Old War Horse," steady, reliable, and imperturbable. Longstreet was born in South Carolina and raised in Georgia and Alabama. He graduated from West Point in 1842. After an unremarkable career in the U.S. Army, he resigned in 1861 to accept a Confederate commission. A veteran of the First Battle of Bull Run and the Battles of the Seven Days, Longstreet found his true vocation as a corps commander under Lee—a methodical, precise, and hard-hitting complement to the elusive, fast-moving Gen. Thomas Jackson. Longstreet's corps launched the powerful counterattack that broke Gen. John Pope's army at the Second Battle of Bull Run and bore the greater share of the fighting at Fredericksburg. Stubborn and self-assured, Longstreet did not hesitate to challenge Lee, especially after Jackson's death. He vigorously opposed the Pennsylvania campaign of 1863 and tried to argue Lee out of attacking at Gettysburg on July 2 and 3. Longstreet was badly wounded in the Wilderness in the spring of 1864 but returned to duty in the autumn and served with the Army of Northern Virginia to the end. He became a deeply controversial postwar figure, not least because he embraced the Republican Party. Moreover, "lost-cause" diehards un-

fairly stigmatized Longstreet for the defeat at Gettysburg and its ultimate consequence, the collapse of the Confederacy.

Semmes, Raphael (1809–1877)—naval officer: Raphael Semmes was born in Maryland. He joined the Navy in 1826 and fought in the Mexican War in 1846–1847. In between sea assignments, he practiced law. Joining the Confederate service in 1861, Semmes commanded the successful commerce raiders *Sumter* and *Alabama*. The USS *Kearsarge* engaged and sank the *Alabama* off Cherbourg, France, on June 19, 1864. After the war, Semmes taught literature, edited a Memphis newspaper, and, eventually, resumed the practice of law.

Smith, Edmund Kirby (1824–1893)—general: Edmund Kirby Smith was born in Florida. He graduated from West Point in 1845 and saw action in the Mexican War. In the 1850s, he served on the frontier and later taught mathematics at West Point. He joined the Confederate army early in 1861 and rose, in February 1863, to command of the vast Trans-Mississippi Department, including Texas, Louisiana, and Arkansas. With Vicksburg's fall in July 1863, his domain became known as "Kirby Smithdom." Forces under his overall command disrupted the Federal Red River Campaign of 1864 and afterward turned back a Union offensive in Arkansas. He surrendered the last Confederate army at Galveston, Texas, on June 2, 1865. Smith was president of the University of Nashville from 1870 to 1875.

Stephens, Alexander Hamilton (1812–1883)—Confederate vice-president: Alexander Stephens was born in Georgia. He served in the U.S. House of Representatives from 1843 to 1859. Stephens was a strong defender of states' rights yet was also a firm believer in the Union. However, after his native Georgia seceded, he backed the Confederacy. For a time, he hoped to be president of the Confederacy but eventually accepted the position of vice president. As the war progressed, Stephens and President Jefferson Davis were increasingly at odds, especially over the issue of Davis's centralization of authority. He became increasingly frustrated that his advice was ignored. Stephens met with Abraham Lincoln in the fruitless Hampton Roads Peace Conference early in 1865. After the Civil War, he returned to Congress (1873–1882) and won election to the Georgia governorship in 1882.

Stuart, James Ewell Brown ("Jeb") (1833–

1864)—general: J. E. B. Stuart was born in Patrick County, Virginia, the son of a prosperous planter. "Jeb" Stuart graduated from West Point in 1854. He rose to prominence as the chief of Gen. Robert E. Lee's cavalry—the "eyes and ears" of the Army of Northern Virginia. Only his failure to keep Lee informed of Union movements during the Gettysburg campaign marred an otherwise distinguished war record. Stuart's plumed hats, red-trimmed capes, and flowing beard were legendary in the Confederacy. He was mortally wounded in a clash with Gen. Philip Sheridan's cavalry at Yellow Tavern near Richmond, Virginia, on May 11, 1864.

FURTHER READING

Alcott, Louisa May. *Hospital Sketches*. (Bessie Z. Jones, ed.) Cambridge, Mass.: Belknap Press of Harvard University Press, 1960.

Beringer, Richard E. et al. *Why the South Lost the Civil War*. Athens, Ga.: University of Georgia Press, 1986.

Boatner, Mark M. III. *The Civil War Dictionary*. New York: David McKay Co., 1988, revised.

Bowman, John, ed. *Encyclopedia of the Civil War*. New York: Dorset Books, 1992.

Catton, Bruce. *The Centennial History of the Civil War*: Vol. 1, *The Coming Fury*: Vol. 2, *Terrible Swift Sword*: Vol. 3, *Never Call Retreat*. Garden City, N.Y., Doubleday & Co., 1961–1965.

Chesnut, Mary Boykin. *A Diary from Dixie*. Boston: Houghton Mifflin Co., 1949.

Connelly, Thomas L. *The Marble Man: Robert E. Lee and His Image in American Society*. New York: Alfred A. Knopf, 1977.

Davis, William C. *Jefferson Davis: The Man and His Hour*. New York: Harper Collins, 1991.

Donald, David H. *Lincoln*. New York: Simon & Shuster, 1995.

———, ed. *Why the North Won the Civil War*. Baton Rouge, La.: Louisiana State University Press, 1960.

Fellman, Michael. *Citizen Sherman: A Life of William Tecumseh Sherman*. New York: Random House, 1995.

Foote, Shelby. *The Civil War: A Narrative*. 3 vols. New York: Random House, 1958–1874.

Golay, Michael. *To Gettysburg and Beyond: The Parallel Lives of Joshua Lawrence Chamberlain and Edward Porter Alexander*. New York: Crown Pub., 1994.

Grant, Ulysses S. *Personal Memoirs of U. S. Grant*. New York: Library of America, 1990.

Higginson, Thomas Wentworth. *Army Life in a Black Regiment*. New York: Collier Books, 1962.

Jones, Virgil Carrington. *The Civil War at Sea*. New York: Holt, Rinehart & Winston, Inc. 1960.

McFeely, William. *Grant: A Biography*. New York: W. W. Norton & Co., 1981.

McPherson, James. *Battle Cry of Freedom: The Civil War Era*. New York: Oxford University Press, 1988.

Morris, Roy Jr. *Sheridan: The Life and Wars of General Phil Sheridan*. New York: Crown Pub., 1992.

Royster, Charles. *The Destructive War: William Tecumseh Sherman, Stonewall Jackson and the Americans*. New York: Alfred A. Knopf, 1991.

Sherman, William T. *Memoirs of General W. T. Sherman*. New York: Library of America, 1990.

(Continued on p. 295)

Stampp, Kenneth M. *The Peculiar Institution: Slavery in the Antebellum South*. New York: Alfred A. Knopf, 1956.

Thomas, Emory. *Robert E. Lee: A Biography*. New York: W.W. Norton & Co., 1995.

Wiley, Bell Irvin. *The Life of Billy Yank: The Common Soldier of the Union*. Baton Rouge, La.: Louisiana State University Press, 1971 edition.

———*The Life of Johnny Reb: The Common Soldier of the Confederacy*. Indianapolis: Bobbs-Merrill Co., 1943.

Vandiver, Frank E. *Mighty Stonewall*. New York: McGraw-Hill Book Co., 1957.

Wilson, Edmund. *Patriotic Gore: Studies in the Literature of the American Civil War*. Boston: Northeastern University Press, 1984.

19TH-CENTURY TRANS-MISSISSIPPI
INDIAN WARS

DATES OF WARS

April 1832 (The Black Hawk War)—January 1891 (Ghost Dance Campaign of the Sioux War)

ALTERNATE NAMES

Not all the major conflicts between whites and Indians in the trans-Mississippi West during the 19th century have traditionally been called wars. And some that have been called wars were really not much more than a season's campaign or expedition. The conflicts that are treated in this chapter are:

The Black Hawk War (1832)
The Washington-Oregon Indian Wars:
    The Cayuse War (1847–1850)
    The First Rogue River War (1853)
    The Second Rogue River War (1855–1856)
    The Yakima War (1855–1858)
The Apache Wars (1861–1886)
Sioux Uprising in Minnesota (1862)
Navajo Conflict (1863–1864)
Plains Wars of the 1860s:
    Cheyenne-Arapaho War and the Sand
      Creek Massacre (1864-1865)
    Red Cloud's War (1866–1867)
    Hancock's War (1867)
    Cheyenne Winter Campaign (1868–1869)
The Modoc War (1872–1873)
The Red River War (1874–1875)
The Nez Percé War (1877)
The Ute War (1879)
The Sioux Wars:
    The Black Hills War (1876–1877)
    Ghost Dance Campaign (1890–1891)

SIGNIFICANCE

The 19th-Century Trans-Mississippi Indian Wars ended armed Indian resistance to the advance of white people across North America, a constant of life from the first years of European settlement. The wars' most obvious significance for white Americans was that they secured vast amounts of land and natural resources for settlement and development. For Indians, the significance of those wars was the opposite: a devastating loss of people, land, culture, and society. One of the more unusual aspects of the wars, in fact, was that they were not, in the final measure, won by the military. From 1866 to 1890, the last phase of U.S. settlement of the continent, U.S. regular troops fought in 24 operations officially classified as wars, campaigns, or major expeditions. During those years, soldiers and Indians clashed in some 1,000 combat actions from the Black Hills of South Dakota to the Texas plains, across the Southwest desert and in wilderness regions of northern California, Idaho, and Oregon. Yet, in the end, more so than soldiers, homesteaders, hunters, miners, railroad builders, even maverick adventurers, defeated the Native Americans of the West. That highlights the ultimate significance of the Trans-Mississippi Indian Wars: They cannot be separated from the broader theme of 19th-century U.S. history summed up under such names as "the westward expansion" or "the winning of the West."

BACKGROUND

By the 1840s, nearly all Indian resistance east of the Mississippi River had ceased. (For the most notable exception, see The Black Hawk War, pp. 300-303). The efforts of such leaders as Tecumseh (see The War of 1812, Military and Civilian Biographies, p. 164) and such tribes as the Creeks and Seminoles had failed, and the Indian Removal Act of 1830 put into operation the forced resettlement of many eastern tribes in the trans-Mississippi West. And by the 1840s, white Americans were poised, figuratively and literally, along the Mississippi River, ready to make the mass movement westward. During the 1840s and

1850s, white Americans, working out the nation's "manifest destiny" (see Mexican War, p. 204) to settle the continent, spilled across the Mississippi River into present-day Minnesota, Iowa, Missouri, Nebraska, and Kansas. Thousands more used the overland trails to reach the fertile valleys of the Oregon Territory and the gold and silver buried in the mountains and streams of present-day Colorado, Wyoming, Nevada, Montana, Idaho, and, above all, California. The United States triumph in the Mexican War of 1846–1848 opened vast new tracts of land inhabited by the Apache, Navajo, and other Southwest tribes to Americans. The Civil War somewhat slowed the great progression, although the Homestead Act of 1862 accelerated it. The Civil War was barely over when Americans turned their energies to spanning the continent: Four great transcontinental railroad lines were built from the 1860s to the 1890s. And throughout those decades, with each advance of the whites came the inevitable collision with the Native Americans. A major, but little-noted, turning point in the conflict between white Americans and Native Americans was the act passed by Congress on March 3, 1871, which ended the making of treaties with Native Americans. That meant the Indian tribes were no longer to be treated as independent nations. From that point on, the Indians were subject to the white people's laws though they were not citizens.

CAUSES OF THE WARS

Historians have isolated specific causes for most of the 19th-Century Trans-Mississippi Indian Wars. Always, though, the deepest cause lay in the inexorable advance of the whites: farmers, ranchers, and merchants; buffalo hunters, miners, and railroad builders; and the soldiers who came to protect them. The land they were taking was either owned by the Indians from time immemorial or was guaranteed them by treaties with the U.S. government. In nearly every case, the pressures from the whites—their demand for land, for boundaries, for rights of way, for minerals, for buffalo hides—touched off conflict. The cycle repeated itself endlessly: an advance guard of white settlers moving into Indian country, usually in violation of a U.S. government–Indian treaty; Indian attacks (often including arson, murder, and mutilation); a frantic call for protec-

tion and military reprisal; and a brief, bloody war that always, if not sooner than later, ended in an Indian defeat and another long step in the United States advance of the frontier.

PREPARATIONS FOR WARS

Although most of the Trans-Mississippi Indian Wars commenced with spontaneous, even accidental episodes, white Americans increasingly made more and more organized preparations for those conflicts. Wagon trains and small settlements had men assigned to protect them from attacks by Indians. As the white communities grew, the whites formed militias or territorial units; several of the most famous conflicts were fought by those volunteer forces. The U.S. government had assigned Regular Army units to support the movement westward from the outset. By the 1840s, a major proportion of the U.S. Army's personnel and resources was allocated to the western frontier; the Civil War temporarily disrupted that, but soon after that war ended, the U.S. Army mounted a major campaign to suppress the Indians of the West. For U.S. forces, supply issues were of utmost importance: making sure the punitive columns had adequate water, food, forage (many were cavalry units), and ammunition to carry out their mission. As the 19th century advanced, that task was supported by a major and costly infrastructure: permanent military posts across the western frontier; a network of trails and roads, in part due to the work of the U.S. Army engineers; several railroad systems (also made possible by generous government grants); and large boats that carried U.S. troops up and down the rivers of the West.

The Indians also made preparations for some of the conflicts, but for the most part, those preparations were sudden, short-term, and in response to the immediate situation. Some tribes, such as the Sioux, the Cheyenne, and the Apache, were accustomed to organizing for extended wars, but their preparations can not be compared to the resources mobilized by the U.S. government.

DECLARATIONS OF WAR

In the strict, legalistic sense, there were no formal declarations of war by Congress, but all the appropriate branches, departments, and agencies of the federal government, from the president on down, supported the Trans-Mississippi Indian Wars. In many cases, a government ultimatum served as notice that a state of war would exist after a certain date; for example, the Army ordered Sioux hunting and raiding parties to report to the reservation authorities by January 31, 1876, or consider themselves at war with the United States. In the broader sense, then, it can hardly be denied that the U.S. government declared war on the Native Americans simply by deciding to take over the land, in disregard of treaties and at whatever the cost.

COMBATANTS

Native Americans: By 1840, the Native American population west of the Mississippi River totaled about 350,000; those people were scattered, lacked communication, and were certainly not united. Furthermore, they were never able to field more than a relatively few thousand warriors. Estimates put the total population of the Plains tribes in 1865 at about 75,000, but not all of those tribes were willing or able to make war against the white people; the population of the seven warlike Teton Sioux tribes of the Northern Plains probably never exceeded 16,000, with perhaps 4,000 fighting men. Probably the largest Indian force assembled for a single engagement (at Little Bighorn) numbered 3,000 warriors.

The major tribes involved in the wars treated in this chapter included the Sauk and Fox, Sioux (Lakota), Cheyenne, Arapaho, Kiowa, Comanche, Apache, Navajo, Ute, Nez Percé, Modoc, Cayuse, Rogue River, Yakima, Paiute, and Bannock. Many smaller tribes, subtribes, and bands participated in the Trans-Mississippi Indian Wars with the United States at various times and places between 1832 and 1891. Sometimes Indian tribes formed alliances in their wars with the whites: Sioux and northern Cheyenne in the Dakota country, for example, and Cheyenne, Comanche, and Kiowas on the southern Plains. At any given moment, one tribe might be at war with a neighboring band of Indians, as well as with the local whites and/or with the U.S. government forces. U.S. forces often did not clearly distinguish between hostile and neutral Indians.

There were also some Indian tribes who aided and even fought alongside the white settlers. The most prominent of those were the Shoshone and Crow, Plains Indians who provided scouts and occasionally even small numbers of warriors for the U.S. Army in the latter's actions against other Indians. (Officially, the Army was limited to hiring 1,000 Indian scouts. One such scout was the Crow Curley, who led Custer to the Sioux encampment at Little Bighorn. However, Curley was not with Custer at the ensuing battle and so survived.) The Indians' reasons for aiding the whites usually were based on some long-standing enmity between themselves and the other Indian tribe, an enmity usually based on competition for the same territory and resources. The Shoshones, for instance, were enemies of the Cheyenne and Sioux; the Shoshones were also influenced greatly by their chief, Washakie, who chose to befriend the white settlers. The Crow were enemies of the Sioux and Blackfeet. In some instances, Indians who had fought against the U.S. military ended up fighting against fellow Indians; sometimes that was for simply mercenary motives, but it was also because young warriors were looking to do something more challenging than sit on reservations.

United States: By the mid-1850s, the U.S. Army numbered some 15,000, the majority deployed in the trans-Mississippi West. The post–Civil War Regular Army of some 54,000 men in 1867 was gradually reduced to about 25,000 by 1890. After the Reconstruction occupation of the former Confederacy ended in 1877, about 9,000 Army troops were assigned to the entire trans-Mississippi west, scattered in forts and outposts throughout the frontier. In general, infantry divisions were assigned to hold the forts and to defend the whites who moved between and around them. The cavalry units were sent on expeditions to seek out and challenge Indians; anticipating that, in 1866, the U. S. Army established four new cavalry regiments, the 7th through the 10th. The 9th and 10th Cavalry Divisions were primarily African-American troops led by white officers; they fought in many actions (see Legends and Trivia, p. 340).

In many of the conflicts, including the Black Hawk War and the Civil War-era clashes on the Great Plains, organized militia and/or special volunteer forces supplemented the regulars; as the number of white settlers in the West rapidly increased after the Civil War, the U.S. Army could provide increasingly larger and better-organized units, sometimes numbering several thousand.

Mexicans: Mexican forces fought raiding

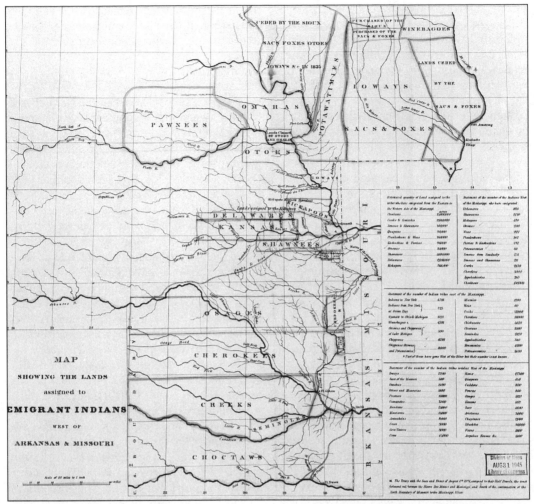

This map of 1836 shows the western lands set aside for what were here called "emigrant Indians"—in fact, the Native Americans displaced from their tribal lands to the east. In the decades to come, even those Indian territories were taken by white settlers and eventually became the states of Iowa, Nebraska, Kansas, and Oklahoma.

Apache bands south of the U.S.-Mexico border, sometimes in cooperation with U.S. forces.

GEOGRAPHIC AND STRATEGIC CONSIDERATIONS

At different times, the Trans-Mississippi Indian Wars were fought in an area of some 2 million square miles, from the Mississippi River to the edge of the Pacific Ocean, from Canada to Mexico. Enormous distances, extreme weather conditions, problems of transport and supply, and political considerations influenced United States conduct of the Trans-Mississippi Indian Wars. As settlements spread over the entire continent—from the Northwest across the Mississippi River and the Great Plains, over the Rocky Mountain spine and through the Great American Desert, over the Sierra Nevada and to the Pacific Coast, down into the old Spanish Southwest, up into the Black Hills—so, too, did military operations.

Indians, for the most part, fought on the strategic defensive; they were, after all, trying to hold on to their homelands. They knew their territory so much better than their white adversaries did that they could withdraw into inaccessible areas when threatened. Eventually, of course, they were trapped in dead ends. Most bands avoided set battles in favor of guerrilla tactics, hit-and-run operations, and assaults on lightly defended settlements or outposts. The Plains tribes were brilliant light cavalrymen, highly mobile, and extremely dangerous when fighting on their own terms. Most Indian warriors were excellent marksmen, whether with bows and arrrows or with rifles and pistols.

Although white American civilians were often on the defensive, the U.S. military forces after the Civil War were increasingly on the offensive. The Regular Army organized itself into small, widely scattered garrison detachments whose presence offered comfort to frontier settlers but who were slow and ponderous to combine for active operations. Experience clearly showed that large mobile columns were superior to small fixed outposts. With insistent settler demands for protection, however, the outpost system prevailed.

After the Civil War, the U.S. Army implemented the tactics of total war in most Indian conflicts. Villages, crops, and herds were considered as legitimate a target as bands of hostile warriors. Gen. William T. Sherman, Gen. Philip H. Sheridan, and other senior commanders deployed converging columns of cavalry and infantry to hem in the hostile bands, destroy their livelihoods, threaten their families, and, where possible, bring their war parties to battle. Increasingly, too, the Army turned to winter campaigns, when the tribes were most vulnerable and least mobile. But there was never a single master plan to defeat the Indians throughout the West; each expedition, campaign, battle, and war was simply fought to force the Indians onto ever-shrinking reservations.

The Black Hawk War:

DATES OF WAR

April–August 1832

SIGNIFICANCE

Strictly speaking, the Black Hawk War was not a Trans-Mississipi Indian War, but it is included here because it occurred as a direct result of the attempt to remove Sauk and Fox Indians to the west of the Mississippi River. It was a minor war, indeed, not much more than a summer campaign, but it attains significance from the fact that it closed out the Indian wars east of the Mississippi River and commenced the Indian wars west of the Mississippi River.

BACKGROUND

The Sauk and Fox Indians, allied tribes of the Illinois country, had a long history of actively resisting white people who intruded into their territory. They had fought the French and then the British. In a disputed 1804 treaty with U.S. agents, some Sauk and Fox agreed to cede their lands east of the Mississippi River. In the Sauk chief Black Hawk's view, however, the treaty permitted whites to only hunt the land in northern Illinois and southern Wisconsin, not to settle it. ("Had that been explained to me," Black Hawk said later, "I would have opposed it.") During the War of 1812, the Sauk and Fox split into two factions. A "peace party" under Chief Keokuk surrendered the Illinois lands without incident and resettled across the Mississippi River in Iowa. Black Hawk, having refused to accept the treaty, fought alongside Tecumseh and the British during the War of 1812; hence his faction became known as the "British Band."

With the end of the War of 1812, white settlers streamed into Illinois, crowding the Fox and Sauk from their villages, fields, and hunting grounds. In 1829, an aging Black Hawk (he was born in 1767) returned from a winter hunt across the Mississippi River to find whites settled in lodgers in his village of Saukenuk, including his own. (Saukenuk was near present-day Rock Island, Illinois.) Then, in 1831, the government land office, under the terms of a newly imposed treaty, offered Black Hawk's village and adjacent lands for sale; soon the white people were erecting fences and plowing fields. Black Hawk was forced to withdraw back across the Mississippi River.

CAUSES OF THE WAR

In early 1832, Black Hawk led some 1,500 Sauk and Fox back to their village of Saukenuk after wintering west of the Mississippi River. The white settlers issued a call for help.

PREPARATIONS FOR WAR

On April 16, Illinois governor John Reynolds issued a call for volunteers to "repel the inva-

This picture by M.R. Longacre, typical of the idealized portrayals that encouraged millions of well-intentioned whites to go West, shows them making a friendly visit to a tepee rather than forcing the Indians off their land.

sion" of the Sauk and Fox. Some 1,600 militiamen responded. Shortly thereafter, Gen. Henry Atkinson, at Jefferson Barracks near St. Louis and commander of the U.S. Army in the region, was authorized by the War Deparrtment in Washington, D.C., to organize an expeditionary force of regulars. Black Hawk had brought some 500 warriors with him when he returned to his village and was prepared to do battle.

DECLARATION OF WAR

There was no formal declaration of war from the U.S. government against the Sauk and Fox, but General Atkinson did give Black Hawk and his supporters an order to go back to Iowa. Black Hawk refused to obey it.

COMBATANTS

Black Hawk could call on only about 500 Sauk and Fox warriors. Some 150,000 settlers in Illinois could be called on to provide thousands of militia to supplement Atkinson's regulars; those militia were mobilized, but many never saw ac-

tion. The U.S. Army assigned some 500 regulars from Fort Jefferson to aid the militia. (Another force of some 1,000 regulars was sent from the East Coast via the Great Lakes, but they arrived too late to take part in any of the fighting; in any case, many of them were disabled by a cholera outbreak.)

GEOGRAPHIC AND STRATEGIC CONSIDERATIONS

The first phase of the brief Black Hawk War was fought in the relatively hilly northwestern corner of Illinois, a triangle formed by the Rock River and the Mississippi River. By July, Black Hawk's band, which included women and children, had moved into Wisconsin, and the final battles were fought in the southwestern corner of Wisconsin, a more rugged terrain backed against the Mississippi River. The Indians were somewhat more at home in that land than were the white troops, although the Indians had to move about so much that they had a hard time getting enough food for their party. Meanwhile, in the heat of summer and on the often swampy land, cholera spread among the white troops.

BATTLES AND CAMPAIGNS

Early May, 1832: Some 2,000 troops under Illinois militia commander Gen. Samuel Whiteside and Col. Zachary Taylor, a regular, took the field in search of Black Hawk's British Band.

May 14, 1832: A detachment of 275 militia under Maj. Isaiah Stillman cornered Black Hawk with 40 warriors on Old Man's Creek near the Rock River in northern Illinois. Badly outnumbered, Black Hawk decided to parley. When some militia opened fire at his emissaries, killing three, he changed his mind and ordered a charge. Stillman's command broke up in panic and ran. Militia losses in the derisively named Battle of Stillman's Run were about 50 killed, wounded, or missing.

May 15–21, 1832: Black Hawk went on the offensive, burning farms and killing settlers as he moved northward along the valley of the Rock River. The militia, reinforced by hundreds more volunteers, pursued Black Hawk's British Band.

May 22, 1832: A relief party investigating reports of a disturbance on Indian Creek in northwestern Illinois found the mutilated bodies of 15 white settlers. Word of the Indian Creek massacre spread terror through the settlements of northern Illinois and southern Wisconsin.

May 23–July 20, 1832: Black Hawk continued his northward course, with both Federal and militia forces in pursuit. The Indians moved into Wisconsin (then part of the Michigan Territory). Many of the American troops became ill with cholera. The Indians, constantly on the move, were becoming tired and hungry.

July 21, 1832: A militia force under Gen. James D. Henry caught up with Black Hawk's band at Wisconsin Heights on the Wisconsin River. In a well-managed rearguard fight, most of the Indians escaped across the river. Henry estimated the Sauk and Fox dead at about 40.

July 22–August 2, 1832: U.S. forces continued the chase, finally cornering the Sauk and Fox on the first of August with their backs to the Mississippi River at the mouth of the Bad Axe River in southwestern Wisconsin (opposite the present-day border of Iowa and Minnesota). The Sauk collected rafts and canoes to ferry themselves across the Mississippi River. On August 2, with the approach of the steamboat *Warrior,* however, Black Hawk sought a parley. Instead, the vessel opened fire on the party ashore with a 6-pounder cannon fitted in the bow.

August 3, 1832: In the early morning, some 1,300 militia attacked Black Hawk's band. Called the Battle of the Bad Axe, it was in fact a massacre because the troops simply refused to accept the Sauks' surrender. In the words of one witness, the Mississippi became "perceptibly tinged with the blood of the Indians who were shot in its margin and in the stream." Atkinson's regulars took only 39 prisoners, mostly women and children. Another 100 or so Indians managed to escape across the river, but there they were met by a band of Eastern Sioux, or Dakotas, allied with the Americans; the Sioux attacked the Sauk and Fox, killing most of them. Atkinson later estimated the Sauk and Fox dead at 300. Combined militia and regular casualties were 7 or 8 killed and about 20 wounded.

NEGOTIATIONS AND PEACE TREATY

After the Battle of the Bad Axe, Black Hawk fled with a small group northward into Winnebago Indian territory. A Winnebago band took him (and his two sons) captive and handed them over to the U.S. government for a reward of $100 and 20 horses.

Any Sauk and Fox left east of the Mississippi River were removed to Iowa. In the Black Hawk Purchase agreement of September 21, 1832, the Sauk and Fox ceded 6 million acres in eastern Iowa to the United States. The government reserved a 400-square-mile area (near Fort Des Moines, Iowa) for use of Keokuk's band, a reward for having kept out of the Black Hawk War (see Background, Black Hawk War, p. 300).

RESULTS OF THE WAR (CASUALTIES, COSTS, CONSEQUENCES)

The cost of the Black Hawk War to the United States has been roughly estimated at $3 million to $8 million (in 1990 dollars). About 70 whites were killed; about 450–600 Indians perished. The four-month war only briefly slowed the migratory flow into Illinois and Wisconsin. The terrible toll it had taken on the Sauk and Fox followers of Black Hawk made its point, for it was the last organized uprising by Indians east of the Mississippi River.

In what was little more than a display of an exotic trophy, the elderly Black Hawk was taken by U.S. authorities on a tour of the country, including a visit with President Andrew Jackson. Black Hawk's appearances drew large crowds, especially in the East. Black Hawk and his sons were kept at Fort Monroe (near Norfolk, Virginia) until late in 1833, when they were allowed to return to the remnant of their tribe in Iowa.

The Washington-Oregon Indian Wars

DATES OF WARS

The Cayuse War: November 1847–June 1850. The First Rogue River War: August–September 1853. The Second Rogue River War: October 1855–June 1856. The Yakima War: September 1855–September 1858.

SIGNIFICANCE

Unlike the situation in the eastern United States, there was no long-standing encroachment on Indian lands in the Northwest, no decades of vicious assaults by both sides, no history of broken treaties. Settlers had leapfrogged over the Great Plains in the mid-1800s and arrived in the Northwest. It might have been assumed or hoped that the new conditions would create new resolutions. It was especially discouraging, then, to find that relations between whites and Indians in the Northwest could deteriorate so rapidly and lead, as elsewhere, to war.

BACKGROUND

The vast territory that included what would later become the two states of Oregon and Washington was long disputed by the United States and Great Britain; it was only in 1846 that the boundary with Canada was set by treaty at the 49th parallel. White settlements began in Oregon when John Jacob Astor established his fur-trading post, Astoria, in 1811. That same year, Astor's people set up a fur-trading post at Fort Okanogan, in northeastern Washington. In 1834, Methodist missionaries from the East established the first permanent settlement in the Willamette valley in west-central Oregon. The first large influx of white settlers did not commence until 1843, when about 1,000 people came over the Oregon Trail to settle in the Willamette Valley. As the white migration into the Pacific Northwest increased, tensions built between the whites and the various local tribes.

CAUSES OF THE WARS

Each of the Washington-Oregon Indian Wars was triggered by specific incidents, the most unusual being the measles epidemic that caused the Cayuse War. But behind each incident lay the resentment of the Indians at the white people's seizing of their lands and resources.

PREPARATIONS FOR WAR

Neither side made any preparations prior to the incidents that led to the hostilities, although the white settlers, by organizing volunteer forces and calling on the U.S. Army, could be said to have prepared for war to a degree.

DECLARATION OF WAR

There was no formal declaration of war, but the Oregon territorial legislature did issue a call for volunteers to fight the Cayuse Indians.

COMBATANTS

The Indian warriors were mostly from the Cayuse, Rogue River, Shasta, and Yakima tribes; there were others from Palouse, Spokane, and Coeur d'Alene bands. The whites fought the Indians with territorial volunteers and a few hundred U.S. Regular Army forces.

GEOGRAPHIC AND STRATEGIC CONSIDERATIONS

The Washington-Oregon Indian Wars were fought in three distinct regions: the Cayuse War, in southeastern Washington; the Rogue River Wars, in southwestern Oregon; and the Yakima War, across a broader area of southern and eastern Washington. The Indians fought on familiar territory (see Geographic and Strategic Considerations, pp. 299-300).

THE CAYUSE WAR: 1847–1850

BATTLES AND CAMPAIGNS

In 1836, Presbyterian medical missionary Marcus Whitman established a mission outpost near Walla Walla in southeastern Washington. By the early 1840s, the native Cayuse had become increasingly hostile as the stream of white migration into the upper Walla Walla valley increased to a torrent. In 1846, the Indians began to be struck by measles. Most authorities claim that this disease was brought among the Cayuse by the white settlers in the immediate area; others claim that it was brought back from California by Walla Walla chief Pio-pio-mox-mox and his band, who had been to California in 1846, where they had fought for the Americans against the Mexicans. In either case, measles came from contact with white people. By 1847, almost half the Cayuse Indians, especially the children, were dying. Whitman and his fellow missionaries provided what medicine they could, but it did not prove helpful. Some among the Cayuse began to claim that they were being poisoned by the missionaries; other Cayuse believed that the white people had simply brought bad spirits with them.

November 29, 1847: Cayuse chief Tilokaikt appeared at the Whitman mission with a request for medicine. As Whitman prepared to oblige, the chief and a companion attacked him with a tomahawk. Warriors emerging from the woods joined Tilokaikt in the massacre of Marcus Whitman, his wife Narcissa, and 12 others. They burned all the buildings and took away 5 men, 8 women, and 34 children.

The Oregon territorial legislature raised a force of 550 volunteers to pursue the Cayuse. The British Hudson's Bay Company officials, meanwhile, tried to negotiate the captives' release. In return for freeing the hostages, the Indians were given 62 blankets, 63 shirts, 12 guns, 600 rounds of ammunition, and 37 pounds of tobacco.

February–March 1848: The release of the hostages did not satisfy the settlers. In early February, a volunteer force under Col. Cornelius Gilliam attacked the camp of a neutral Indian band, killing at least 20. That touched off a larger conflict. In March, a war party of 250 Palouse Indians attacked Gilliam's command, wounding ten.

June 1848: After an inconclusive campaign, Gilliam's volunteers returned to their homes. Thereafter, the war sputtered on, with no decisive engagements and few skirmishes.

Spring 1850: Chief Tilokaikt and the four other men most responsible for the Whitman massacre decided to surrender. They were tried, convicted, and sentenced to death.

June 3, 1850: Tilokaikt and his four accomplices were hanged, bringing the Cayuse War to an end. In the aftermath, Oregon authorities declared the Cayuse lands forfeited to settlers.

THE FIRST ROGUE RIVER WAR: 1853

Miners, settlers, and the Rogue River Indians of the river valley of that same name in southwestern Oregon were in frequent conflict in the early 1850s. In 1853, the cycles of incident and retaliation escalated into the brief, inconclusive First Rogue River War.

BATTLES AND CAMPAIGNS

August 1853: Settlers attacked a Rogue River Indian camp because they suspected the Indians of thievery; as it happened, the Rogues were innocent. They, in turn, sought revenge, attacking settlers. A small force of U.S. regulars and four companies of volunteers pursued the Rogue River band into the Cascade mountains of southwestern Oregon.

August 24, 1853: U.S. forces and 200 Rogue River warriors clashed in the high mountains. In the aftermath, the two sides agreed to a truce and a council.

September 8–10, 1853: The Treaty of Table Rock brought the short war to a close. By its terms, the Rogues agreed to cede all their territory and retire to a reservation.

THE SECOND ROGUE RIVER WAR: 1855-1856

The Table Rock settlement did not last. One of the Rogue River leaders, Old John, repudiated the treaty and continued to agitate for a general uprising against the whites. In the autumn of 1855, a new round of minor clashes led to the Second Rogue River War.

BATTLES AND CAMPAIGNS

October 8, 1855: Volunteer troops from Jacksonville, Oregon, a settlement on the southern end of the Cascades, attacked a camp of Rogue River Indians, killing 23 women, children, and old men.

October 9, 1855: A Rogue River war party

set out on a retaliatory raid in which homesteads were put to the torch and 27 settlers killed. Under Old John's leadership, 150 Rogue River and allied warriors retreated into the mountains to carry on the war from there.

October 15, 1855: Oregon governor George Curry called up two battalions of militia for service in the Rogue River country. The volunteers were given orders to conduct a take-no-prisoners campaign.

October 31, 1855: A combined force of 250 regulars and volunteers brought a war party of 100 Rogues to battle in the Cascade hills. In two days of fighting, 9 whites were killed and 25 wounded before the Indians drew off, carrying their dead and wounded with them.

Winter 1855–1856: Government forces patrolled the hill country through the winter, searching out Indian bands and burning their camps. "It has become a contest of extermination by both whites and Indians," noted the U.S. commander in the Pacific Northwest, Gen. John E. Wool.

With the approach of spring, the U.S. commander in the field, Lt. Col. Robert C. Buchanan, formed three separate columns for an offensive against the Rogues.

March–April 1856: Buchanan's columns fought several indecisive skirmishes with Rogue River bands, with little damage to either side.

May 21, 1856: Old John and other Rogue River leaders met with Buchanan in council. Some chiefs agreed to lay down their arms. Old John, however, vowed never to surrender.

May 27–28, 1856: A party of 200 warriors under Old John attacked a detachment of 85 infantry and cavalry under Capt. Andrew J. Smith at Big Meadows in southwestern Oregon. The fighting continued all day and into the night and resumed early the next day. On the afternoon of May 28, a relief column arrived to reinforce Smith's hard-pressed command, which had run low on water and ammunition and had suffered 9 killed and 17 wounded.

June–July 1856: The Battle of Big Meadows effectively ended Rogue River resistance. Government forces counterattacked and drove Old John's band into the mountains. In late May and early June, several allied bands surrendered. Finally, on June 29, 1856, Old John gave up, bringing the bitter nine-month war to a close.

During June and July, some 1,200 Indians were escorted from the Rogue River valley to the Coast Reservation in Oregon.

THE YAKIMA WAR: 1855–1858

Washington Territory had been separated from Oregon Territory in 1853, and 35-year-old Isaac Ingalls Stevens was appointed its governor and Indian commissioner. He wanted to get rid of the Indians' claims to the land, so in 1854–1855, he pushed through a series of treaties that "bought" 60,000 square miles of land from the Indians, leaving them a number of small reservations; the Indians knew they had been tricked by Stevens's tactics and resisted going to the reservation. Meanwhile, gold was discovered on the upper Columbia River, and miners began to stream into Washington. Pressured from all sides, Yakima chief Kamiakin formed an alliance of bands sworn to halt whites from encroaching onto the central plateau from the eastern flank of the Cascades.

September 1855: Yakima raiders murdered six whites. Kamiakin sent word that whites trespassing east of the Cascades could expect to be attacked in the same manner.

October 1855: A party of some 500 warriors forced an Army patrol from Fort Dalles in northern Oregon along the Columbia River to beat a hasty retreat from Yakima country. The Army suffered 5 killed and 17 wounded.

The Oregon militia joined the fray, provoking the Walla Walla tribe to hostility by murdering one of its chiefs at a truce parley. General Wool accused territorial governor Isaac I. Stevens and other local officials of fomenting war in order to plunder Indian lands.

Spring 1856: Col. George Wright took the field with 500 men in pursuit of Kamiakin and his allies. Wright found that the hostile bands had withdrawn far to the east, out of harm's way.

Summer 1856–Spring 1858: An uneasy truce prevailed through the rest of 1856 and 1857. By the spring of 1858, however, a new gold rush had stirred up the Indians in the Snake River country of eastern Washington and western Idaho. A U.S. column of 164 infantry and cavalry under Lt. Col. Edward J. Steptoe set out from Fort Walla Walla to protect the miners from hostile Yakima, Palouse, Spokane, and Coeur d'Alene bands. By mid-May, hundreds of warriors had gathered and were hanging on to Steptoe's flanks as he advanced. Steptoe, seriously outnumbered and facing annihilation, agreed to turn back.

May 17, 1858: The Indians attacked Steptoe anyway. After a running fight that lasted all morning, Steptoe hunkered down in defensive positions on a hilltop. By nightfall, his beleaguered force was down to three rounds per man. After a council with the Indians, Steptoe buried his dead and led the survivors quietly through the encircling Indians to safety.

Soon after, Gen. Newman S. Clarke, Wool's successor, assigned Colonel Wright to lead an expedition to subdue the Indians and avenge the Steptoe humiliation.

Late August 1858: Some 600 warriors gathered at Four Lakes at the edge of the Great Spokane Plain to contest Wright's advance.

September 1, 1858: In the Battle of Four Lakes (some 10 miles south of present-day Spokane), Wright's column inflicted a sharp defeat on the Indian alliance. Long-range rifle fire inflicted many casualties; then the cavalry charged, sending the Indians into retreat. The U.S. forces reported no one killed or wounded and claimed 60 Indian battle deaths.

September 5, 1858: Wright pushed out of the lake country south of Spokane and onto the plain, where an estimated 500–700 warriors reformed and offered battle. As at Four Lakes, the Battle of Spokane Plain turned out to be an unequal struggle. Wright's decisive victory broke all resistance of Kamiakin's Indian alliance.

September 1858: Wright refused to let the Indian bands drift out of the war. Moving from camp to camp, he seized resistance leaders and warriors suspected of murder or thievery. Wright hanged 15 Indians summarily. Kamiakin, wounded on the Spokane Plain, vanished into the mountains.

October 5, 1858: Wright's command returned in triumph to Fort Walla Walla.

RESULTS OF THE WARS (CASUALTIES, COSTS, CONSEQUENCES)

No historian has ever calculated the costs of the Washington-Oregon Indian Wars, but the costs would probably be some $10 million–$20 million in 1990 dollars. The white people's losses, including civilian settlers, volunteers, and regular troops, amounted to some 90 dead and at least that many wounded; Indian losses were estimated at about 130 dead and at least as many wounded.

The Cayuse War ended with that tribe's forfeiture of all its lands. Some 1,200 Rogue River Indians and their allies were resettled on the Coast Reservation in the aftermath of the two Rogue River Wars. Col. George Wright's final campaign in the Yakima War marked the end of Indian resistance in Oregon and Washington. The Indians were herded onto reservations; even the irreconcilable Kamiakin spent the balance of his days on a reservation.

The Apache Wars

DATES OF WAR

February 4, 1861–September 4, 1886

SIGNIFICANCE

Aside from being yet another series of wars that secured vast amounts of land for whites to settle on and develop, the Apache Wars were distinguished by the particular people whose way of life was totally crushed. The Apache had centuries-old traditions revolving around their independence, their seminomadic existence, their warriors, and their raiding parties. All that was epitomized in the persons of such war chiefs as Mangas Coloradas, Cochise, and Geronimo. But none of that, neither the societal culture nor the strong individuals, proved able to withstand the armed might of the United States. The Apache, like more peaceable and passive Indians, ended up confined on reservations.

BACKGROUND

The United States had inherited the country of Arizona and New Mexico as a result of the Mexican War of 1846–1848 (and then acquired another portion with the Gadsden Purchase of 1853). Among the several Indian tribes living there were the Apache, whose warriors were among the fiercest of all Indian warriors. For centuries, the Apache had been accustomed to attacking neighboring Indians as well as white people in search of cattle, horses, food, weapons, and captives. Some Apache had long been accustomed to making raids into what had become the country of Mexico, and they were soon alienated from the new authorities in the American Southwest who tried to stop them from raiding south of the international border. As always, too, encroaching white traffic and settlement, accompanied by the U.S. Army, played a major role in aggravating tensions between the Indians and whites.

CAUSES OF THE WARS

The more immediate cause of the Apache Wars came with the arrest of Cochise, the Chiricahua Apache chief, on February 4, 1861. He had been falsely accused of stealing cattle and kidnapping a child. When he arrived with his brother and two nephews at a stagecoach post at Apache Pass (in the Chiricahua Mountains in the southeastern corner of Arizona) to refute the charges, he and his relatives were arrested by an Army officer at the post, but Cochise managed to escape. He later seized three white men to exchange for his brother and nephews. When the offer was refused, he killed his hostages, so the Army killed Cochise's three relatives. That triggered the first phase of the Apache Wars.

PREPARATIONS FOR WAR

Shortly afer acquiring the vast territory from Mexico, the U.S. government established a number of Army forts and outposts in the region and put a territorial government in place. (Arizona Territory split off from New Mexico in 1863.) As the hostilities between the Apache and whites intensified after the Civil War, more Army troops were assigned to the region.

DECLARATION OF WAR

There were no official declarations of war, but there were continual orders from Washington, D.C., authorizing action against the Apache.

COMBATANTS

Various U.S. commanders and units were engaged during the quarter-century of intermittent Apache warfare; many of them were cavalry units, among them the all-African-American 9th Cavalry Regiment. By the final phase of the Apache Wars, there were several thousand U.S. regulars in the region. But it was also true that U.S. Army general George Crook, in particular, relied on Indians in their pursuit of the hostile Apaches. Many of those friendly Indians were young Apache males who had been moved to reservations and had accepted the assignment (and payment) in return for the chance to enjoy the freedom of movement and some action. Although they were classified as scouts, they often ended up fighting alongside white forces.

Not all the Apache of the Southwest engaged in the Apache Wars. Two of the more aggressive bands were the Chiricahua, led by Cochise and later Geronimo, and the Chihenne (the Warm Springs Apaches to whites), led by Victorio.

GEOGRAPHIC AND STRATEGIC CONSIDERATIONS

The field of combat of the Apache Wars extended across southern New Mexico and Arizona and down into the Sierra Madre of northern Mexico. For the most part, that region is mountainous terrain, but in southern Arizona and New Mexico, the mountains are interspersed with desert basins. Much of the land is arid and during the summer extremely hot. The Indians knew almost every inch of that land. Traveling with only their horses and light gear, living off the land, and stealing cattle and horses when they needed to, the Indians long eluded the large Army expeditions. Moreover, the Apache warriors had been trained from childhood for survival under conditions for which the average U.S. soldier was not prepared. Relying on stealth and mobility, the Apache had the advantage of withdrawing into the mountains when threatened. The U.S. authorities never did decide on a single strategy other than to move as many Indians onto reservations as possible and to pursue the others. What defeated the Apache warriors in the end was that the whites were able to call on ever increasing numbers of troops while the Apache numbers steadily declined.

BATTLES AND CAMPAIGNS

1861: After Cochise killed his white hostages and the Army retaliated by killing Cochise's captive relatives, Cochise joined his father-in-law, Chief Mangas Coloradas, in raiding white settlers and travelers in southeastern Arizona. Over several months, the Apache killed some 150 whites. They also sealed off the Apache Pass through the Chiricahua Mountains in the southeastern corner of Arizona, through which travelers passed on their way to California.

June–July 1862: A pro-Union force of 3,000 men, mostly from California, made its way across Arizona to the Apache Pass. Commanding the force was Gen. James H. Carleton, who was ruthless in his determination to remove Indians from their lands. In the pass on July 15, the troops were ambushed from above by 500 Apache led by Cochise and Mangas Coloradas, but the soldiers regrouped and came back with wagons carrying howitzers. The next day, the Apache attacked again, but they were driven off; 63 of their warriors were killed in the two days of fighting.

In the last skirmish, Mangas Coloradas was seriously wounded, and Cochise took him into Mexico for medical assistance.

January 1863: Mangas Coloradas reappeared in Arizona. Approaching the whites to work out a truce, he was seized and tortured by U.S. troops. He was then shot to death for "attempted escape," and decapitated.

1863–1865: Inflamed by the death of Mangas Coloradas, Cochise and his band of 300 warriors continued their raids. During the Civil War, in fact, the Apache virtually drove white settlers out of Apache lands and defied the Federal troops that could be spared to fight them. Whenever possible, whites took violent revenge on Apache, and calls for the virtual extermination of the tribe grew more insistent. As soon as the Civil War ended in April 1865, U.S. agents offered a truce to the Apache, but it required them to go to the Bosque Redondo Reservation in eastern New Mexico. Cochise and the other chiefs refused and stayed in the mountains.

April 1865–April 1871: The Apache generally avoided white settlements and Army posts. Occasionally, however, the Apache would sweep down to take cattle or horses. Calls for eliminating Cochise and his band once again intensified.

April 30, 1871: During April, there were two raids by Apache; in one, four whites were killed. A vigilante group of 148 people from the Arizona town of Tucson—mostly Papago Indians and Mexicans organized by American whites—decided to punish a large group of Apache living near Camp Grant, a small Army outpost near the confluence of the San Pedro River and the Aravaipa Creek about 50 miles east of Tucson. Positioned by dawn on April 30, the vigilantes began to fire on the unsuspecting Apache and in the course of 30 minutes carried out an orgy of murder, accompanied by rape and mutilation. Estimates of the number of Apache dead ranged from 90 to 150, and the vigilantes took 27 Apache children and sold them into illegal slavery. (The white organizers from Tucson were put on trial; they were found not guilty.)

September 1871: Cochise met with U.S. Army officers in the mountains of southwestern New Mexico in an effort to work out a truce. When he learned that the plan was to move his people to a reservation in Tularosa in south-central New Mexico, he fled back to the Dragoon Mountains of southeastern Arizona with 200 of his people; another 600 Apache joined him soon after.

September 1872: Rebellious Chiricahua and Chihenne bands remained at large, but they had pretty much stopped attacking whites. In a negotiation session with Gen. Oliver Howard, Cochise asked for land in his Apache Pass home country in return for his surrender. Howard acquiesced, and Cochise moved back to the Chiricahua Mountains, but other Apache continued raiding.

November 15, 1872–March 27, 1873: In the Tonto Basin (central Arizona) offensive against the Apache, Gen. George Crook claimed to have killed some 200 warriors. A fight at Turret Peak in late March 1873 temporarily broke Apache resistance in Arizona. By spring, most Apache were surrendering in large numbers and settling more or less quietly on reservations.

The Indian Bureau accelerated the concentration policy in 1875, ordering all Apache west of the Rio Grande to the large San Carlos Reservation in the barren Gila River valley of southeastern Arizona. By the late 1870s, more than 5,000 Apache had been concentrated there, but many of the Chiricahuas and Chihennes continued to resist for another full decade. Among them was a Chiricahua band led by the war chief Goyathlay, known to whites as Geronimo. He led his warriors into Mexico and continued his raiding there and in the United States.

September 2, 1877–Summer 1879: The Chihenne's leader was Victorio, who, after being moved to the San Carlos Reservation, broke out with some 300 of his followers on September 2, 1877. In February 1878, he turned himself in; during the summer of 1879, old charges of murder and horse-stealing were raised against Victorio, so he broke out again and fled to Mexico.

This photograph, taken on March 26, 1886, shows Gen. George Crook (foreground right) negotiating with Apache warrior Geronimo (center, facing).

September 4, 1879: When Chihenne warriors under Victorio attacked the camp of the African-American 9th Cavalry, U.S. forces launched what became a year-long pursuit. By the following autumn, Victorio's band, moving back and forth across the U.S.-Mexico border, was hungry and worn down from constant skirmishing.

October 14–15, 1880: Mexican forces attacked and destroyed Victorio's band in the two-day battle of Tres Castillos in the Sierra Madre, killing Victorio and 77 other Apache. That left Geronimo of the Chiricahua, Cochise's successor, as the last great resistant Apache chief.

September 1881: Geronimo led a band with about 70 warriors across the Rio Grande into Mexico, where they attacked Mexicans. The Mexican government sent a regiment of troops in pursuit, and they managed to isolate and kill most of the women and children.

April 19, 1882: Warriors under Geronimo attacked the San Carlos Reservation, killed four reservation policemen, and forced some 500 of the Chihennes settled there to flee with them.

July 1882: General Crook returned to Arizona with orders to quell the Apache uprising.

March 1883: Geronimo led Apache bands in a destructive raid through New Mexico and Arizona, then vanished south of the border into the vastness of the Sierra Madre.

May 1883: Under a new treaty with Mexico that allowed U.S. forces to pursue Indians across the border, Crook's Apache scouts tracked Geronimo and 200 of his warriors to a camp in Mexico. Crook attacked on May 15, and, after taking their women and children hostage, forced the Apache men to negotiate. In an talks that lasted a week, Geronimo and the other chiefs finally agreed to go to the reservation.

March 1884: Geronimo's band, the last to come in, reached San Carlos Reservation. At first, Geronimo took up cattle ranching, but soon grew restless under the white man's regulations.

May 1885: Geronimo led another breakout, with 40 men and 92 women and children. As before, when hard-pressed, he disappeared into the Mexican Sierra Madre, killing 73 civilians and soldiers on his way.

December 1885–January 10, 1886: General Crook organized another expedition (mostly of Indian warriors) and set off for Mexico. He caught up with Geronimo in the Mexican mountains again, but in a confusing exchange of fire, Mexican soldiers shot at the Americans; Capt. Emmett Cawford, commander of Crook's main column, was killed, along with others. Geronimo escaped.

NEGOTIATIONS AND PEACE TREATY

January–August 1886: The Apache, tiring fast, sent word that they wished to negotiate. In

March, Geronimo agreed to terms, but on his way back to the U.nited States, he fled (see Notable Phrases, p. 341). When he escaped that time, Crook was relieved of command by Gen. Philip Sheridan and replaced by Gen. Nelson Miles. Miles had a force of almost 5,000 troops and 400 friendly Apache but couldn't trap Geronimo and his 80 warriors.

When Geronimo carried out yet another raid in Arizona, General Miles responded by ordering the removal of all Chiricahua Apache at San Carlos to detention camps in Florida. He sent an emissary to try one final parley with the insurgent chief.

September 4, 1886: When they learned of the Apache's removal to Florida, Geronimo's brothers surrendered to General Miles at Skeleton Canyon in the extreme southeastern corner of Arizona. Geronimo then surrendered, bringing the quarter-century-long Apache Wars to a conclusive end.

RESULTS OF THE WARS (CASUALTIES, COSTS, CONSEQUENCES)

Historians have not attempted to calculate costs for the Apache Wars, but they estimate the cost at $1 billion in 1990 dollars.

Including civilian settlers, volunteer forces, and Regular Army troops, white people's casualties in the various hostile actions amounted to an estimated 2,000 dead and at least as many wounded.

Indians' losses are unknown but must have amounted to at least twice the whites' losses, not counting the many Indians who died from disease, famine, and general substandard conditions due to the disruptions caused by the wars. When Indians were abruptly removed from their native surroundings, for example, many died in captivity or on reservations.

The final campaigns of 1876–1886 subdued the Apache for all time. Joining the nearly 400 reservation Chiricahua forced into Florida exile, Geronimo and 34 of his warriors were imprisoned at Fort Marion, an old Spanish fortress at St. Augustine, Florida. All the Chiricahua Apache age 12 to 22 were sent to the Carlisle Indian School in Pennsylvania to learn the white people's ways. In 1894, Geronimo and the Chiricahua were resettled at Fort Sill, Oklahoma, but he was never allowed to return to Arizona.

Sioux Uprising In Minnesota

DATES OF WAR

August 18, 1862–November 5, 1862

SIGNIFICANCE

Although extremely restricted in duration and area, the Sioux Uprising in Minnesota stands out for its explosive ferocity. Indians and white settlers had been living at close quarters for several decades. Yet, this did not lessen the intensity of the hostilities. What also gave the uprising its special edge was that it came during the Civil War and roused many white people's worst fear: that the Indians across North America would take advantage of the crisis and mount a concerted attack. (President Abraham Lincoln at first thought the Santee Sioux uprising might be part of a conspiracy organized by Confederate sympathizers.) In the end, the Indians did not mount a concerted attack. The Indians had no such strategy and, in any case, were already too crippled to take on the United States.

BACKGROUND

The Santee (sometimes known as the Eastern Sioux), one of the major branches of the Sioux, lived in the woodlands and fertile fields of Minnesota. As white settlers pushed into their territory, the Santee signed treaties that stripped them of their land. One in particular, signed in 1851, ceded 1 million acres to the whites, leaving the Santee Sioux crowded on a relatively narrow strip of land (about 10 miles wide and 150 miles long) in the Minnesota River valley of southwestern Minnesota. The area proved to be poor in wild game and could barely sustain the tribe. The Indian agents and traders responsible for disbursing the money and selling food to the Santee were clearly holding back on them. (One trader, Andrew Myrick, when told the Indians faced starvation, was reported to have said, "Let them eat grass or their own dung.") To add insult, many of the white settlers, fairly recent immigrants, treated the Santee with unconcealed disgust.

CAUSES OF THE WAR

In midsummer 1862, a delay in the

government's annual $72,000 installment for the Santee homeland touched off rumors that the Civil War had emptied the U.S. treasury and that the Santee would no longer be paid. At the same time, the Santee were experiencing a second year of poor crops, yet government officials at the Redwood Indian Agency refused to turn over rations to hungry Sioux. On August 4, about 500 Santee surrounded a food warehouse and held off 100 soldiers while some of the Indians broke in and seized sacks of flour. Against that backdrop, four young Sioux returning to their village from an unsuccessful hunting trip attacked and killed five white settlers near Acton, Minnesota.

PREPARATIONS FOR WAR

Santee war and peace factions argued matters in a tribal council on the night the five white settlers were murdered. The war faction, arguing that the whites would retaliate harshly anyway, carried the day. Chief Little Crow, who favored peace over war, agreed grudgingly to lead the nation to war.

By late July, anticipating some unrest, Indian agents had called in about 100 armed troops, but the white settlers were caught off guard by the sudden violence of the uprising. The Civil War was on and many of their men had gone off to fight for the Union. Any concern about having enough soldiers to put down the uprising was soon allayed, however, by the quick deployment to the area of both militia and Federal troops.

DECLARATION OF WAR

There was no formal declaration of war, but the governor of Minnesota, Alexander Ramsey, mobilized the militia, and the U.S. War Department assigned Regular Army troops.

COMBATANTS

The Santee Sioux numbered some 4,000 and could count on only about 800 warriors.

There were some 150,000 white settlers in Minnesota when war broke out, and many able-bodied men took up arms. Beyond that, the white settlers were soon backed by some 2,000 regular and militia troops, mostly from the Minnesota regiments that had been organized for the Civil War.

GEOGRAPHIC AND STRATEGIC CONSIDERATIONS

The hostilities were confined to the southwestern corner of Minnesota, more specifically, to the area along the Minnesota River from New Ulm to the Yellow Medicine River. A gently sloping terrain, the area was heavily wooded, but settlers had begun to clear land for farming. Most of the settlers lived in isolated homesteads and small settlements, which left them exposed to the hit-and-run tactics of the Indians; those settlers quickly fled to the safety of Fort Ridgely and areas far from the Santee. Nothing about the terrain presented any special problems to the U.S. forces, but they did not know the land as well as the Indians. Although the Indians held the advantage in the first weeks, they lost that advantage once the Army moved in with its superior numbers and weapons.

BATTLES AND CAMPAIGNS

August 18, 1862: A Santee war party attacked the Redwood Agency, killing 20 whites; they took 10 women and children captive, took the food stores, and burned the buildings. Another war party attacked a detachment of the 5th Minnesota volunteer infantry, killing 23 soldiers.

August 20–22, 1862: Little Crow led some 400 warriors in the first day's attack and closer to 700 in the second day's attack on the 200-man volunteer infantry at Fort Ridgely some 13 miles downstream from the Redwood Agency. The fort's three howitzers saved both days for the garrison. After losing 100 warriors in the assaults, the sightly wounded Little Crow called off the operation. "With a few guns like that," one of the Santee remarked, "the Dakotas [Sioux] could rule the earth."

August 23, 1862: Another party of 350 Sioux attacked New Ulm. The citizen defenders were prepared, however, and despite heavy losses— 36 killed, 23 wounded—they managed to drive off the raiders. Before withdrawing, the Indians managed to burn many of the buildings of New Ulm.

August 28, 1862: Col. Henry Hastings Sibley was commander of the Minnesota volunteer regiments. Immediately after the first incident on August 18, he was authorized to organize a force composed of volunteers and Regular Army troops stationed in Minnesota. Advance ele-

On December 26, 1862, 38 of the Santee Sioux who had taken part in the uprising in Minnesota were hanged in a public spectacle designed to let all Native Americans know the fate that awaited them if they chose the same course.

ments of a larger relief column arrived to reinforce the shaken defenders of Fort Ridgely. With their arrival, Little Crow's main force began to withdraw northward; they took with them some 200 white captives, about half of them women and children who Little Crow intended to use as hostages. Bands of Indians had been rampaging through the valley since August 19, burning houses and farms and killing white settlers. They did not, however, go into the more densely settled areas of the Mississippi River valley to the east.

September 3, 1862: Little Crow was leading a small party on a reconnaissance when they met a detachment of some 75 soldiers. In the close-in fight that ensued, the Santee killed 6 and wounded 15 before the soldiers retreated.

September 5–6, 1862: At dawn on September 5, several hundred warriors attacked a 150-man volunteer detachment at Birch Coulee near the ransacked Redwood Agency. The first rush nearly overwhelmed the government troops; 22 were killed and 60 wounded, but they rallied and repulsed the attack. The Sioux pulled back, and the two sides exchanged long-range fire for the rest of the day. A relief column from Fort Ridgely, 16 miles downstream from Birch Coulee, lifted the siege on the afternoon of September 6.

September 6–13, 1862: Little Crow and Colo-

nel Sibley exchanged several messages regarding conditions for ending hostilities. Sibley demanded that Little Crow release all whites held captive but made no promises; Little Crow said that he would release the captives only if Sibley guaranteed that the Santee would not be wiped out. There was disagreement among the Santee about what to do, and nothing came of the communications between the two.

September 19–22, 1862: Colonel Sibley led 1,600 men of the 3rd, 6th, 7th, and 9th Minnesota infantry northwest along the Minnesota River in pursuit of Santee war parties. On September 22, the column halted for the night at Wood Lake where the Yellow Medicine River joins the Minnesota River. In a council that night, Sioux leaders agreed on a plan to throw 700 warriors into an ambush of Sibley's force the next morning.

September 23, 1862: At daybreak, some Santee attacked a forage party of the 3rd Minnesota Regiment, initiating a battle before all the Santee were in position. After some confusion, the troops rallied, formed a battle line, and brought artillery into play. The guns broke up the Sioux assault, and a spirited charge drove them from the field. The Army reported losses of 7 killed and 30 wounded; Santee casualties were estimated at 30 dead and dozens wounded.

NEGOTIATIONS AND PEACE TREATY

The battle at Wood Lake broke the Santee's resistance. Bands began to surrender, and on September 26, some 270 white hostages were released. By the end of October, 2,000 Sioux had given up. As males of fighting age came in, they were chained together and imprisoned in a log structure Colonel Sibley had erected. There were no negotiations or treaties; instead, Colonel Sibley set up a military court of five officers, who tried hundreds of the Santee leaders and warriors. On November 5, 1862, the last of 303 Sioux warriors tried were sentenced to hang for murder, rape, and other crimes against the settlers.

RESULTS OF THE WAR (CASUALTIES, COSTS, CONSEQUENCES)

The cost of the Sioux Uprising in Minnesota to the U.S. government and white settlers has been estimated at $10 million (in 1990 dollars). No one has ever put a price on the Indians' losses. Despite the uprising's brief duration, the casualties were high. The whites counted some 400 dead and some 200 wounded; the Indians counted 200 dead and about as many wounded.

Hoping to avoid responsibility for executing so many Indians, Colonel Sibley passed the decision of whether to hang the Indians on to Gen. John Pope, commander of the Military Department of the Northwest. Pope, in turn, passed the decision on to President Abraham Lincoln, who assigned lawyers to distinguish between those Indians who were true murderers and those who had simply acted as warriors. On December 6, Lincoln announced that he was approving execution of only 39. On December 26, 1862, at Mankato, Minnesota, 38 Santee Sioux (one was granted a last-minute reprieve) were hanged, the largest mass execution in U.S. history.

Little Crow fled north into Canada with a small band. Deciding to join the Sioux on the western Plains, he returned to Minnesota, hoping to obtain horses. While gathering berries in June 1863, he was shot and killed by a settler.

Some 30,000 white settlers fled their homes during the summer of 1862. It was some time before they felt it was safe to return. Some of the Santee returned to the reservation along the Minnesota River. Many fled westward and joined their relatives, the prairie Sioux, to oppose the whites' advance. By 1865, full-scale war had broken out in the Dakotas.

Navajo Conflict

DATES OF WAR

July 20, 1863–January 14, 1864

ALTERNATE NAMES

The Navajo Removal. The Long Walk.

SIGNIFICANCE

The Navajo Conflict was a long, simmering war, less known for its brief, violent explosions than for what happened after it ended: the infamous "Long Walk" of the Navajo people. The war had several other special aspects. For one, it occurred during the Civil War, and, to some degree, the Navajo were victims of a kind of hysteria that so often accompanies civil war.

BACKGROUND

The Navajo and the settlers of New Mexico Territory (which included present-day New Mexico and Arizona), Spanish and later American, had a long history of conflict—repeated cycles of raids and retaliation over two centuries and more. By the 1860s, the U.S. authorities had decided to resettle the Navajo, partly to stop the incessant raiding and sheep stealing that afflicted the Rio Grande settlements, partly to remove the tribe from land wanted by white settlers. The excuse given for the resettlement, however, was for the safety of the Navajo. Thus, the Army commander in New Mexico, Col. Edward R. S. Canby, reported in 1861: "There is now no choice between their absolute extermination or their removal and colonization at points so remote from the settlements as to isolate them entirely from the inhabitants of the territory."

CAUSES OF THE WAR

Any one of several incidents might be regarded as the beginning of the final escalation that culminated in the Navajo Conflict. In January 1860, soldiers at the newly established Fort Defiance at the mouth of Canyon Bonito (just inside Arizona at the border with New Mexico), killed horses and mules belonging to the Navajo because the animals were said to be straying on the Army's land. The Navajo retaliated by raiding the Army's horse herd and supply trains; the soldiers retaliated by attacking the Indians. In February 1860, the Navajo conducted a major raid on the horse herd of Fort Defiance, and then, on April 30, some 1,000 warriors attacked Fort Defiance itself. That led to a fruitless expedition to track down the Indians responsible. Finally, both sides agreed on a truce, which was signed in February 1861. On September 22, 1861, after a disputed horse race between the Navajo chief Manuelito and an Army officer at Fort Wingate (near present-day Gallup, New Mexico), the army began to fire on and bayonet the protesting Indians. After that incident (in which a dozen Indians were killed or wounded), the Navajo felt an implacable hostility toward the Army.

Then, in 1862, Gen. James Carleton arrived in New Mexico with his force of California volunteers. He spent much of 1862 rounding up the Mescalero Apache, relatives of the Navajos, and deporting them to the Bosque Redondo Reservation in the Pecos River valley in eastern New Mexico. That reservation was essentially a military compound dominated by Fort Sumner. Once he had succeeded in relocating the Mescalero, Carleton turned his attention to the Navajo.

PREPARATIONS FOR WAR

In April 1863, Gen. James Carleton informed the leading Navajo chiefs of his plans to deport the tribe onto the Bosque Redondo Reservation, along with the Mescalero Apache. Those of the 12,000 Navajo who refused to leave their home country would be treated as hostiles.

As in many tribes, there were war and peace factions among the Navajo, but all factions ignored the ultimatum and awaited events.

DECLARATION OF WAR

There was no formal declaration of war, but the War Department and other authorities in Washington, D.C., including President Lincoln, supported the goal of removing the Navajo. On June 23, 1863, General Carleton issued the formal ultimatum, giving the Navajo until July 20 to put themselves in motion for the Pecos River valley,

300 miles eastward. "After that day, the door now open will be closed," Carleton warned. Meanwhile, Carleton ordered troops to concentrate at Fort Wingate and prepare to "prosecute a vigorous war" on the tribe.

COMBATANTS

United States: For his main force, Gen. James Carleton turned to the 1,000-strong 1st New Mexico Volunteer Cavalry under the famous frontiersman Col. Kit Carson. Carson had already shown his willingness to support Carleton by assisting in the roundup of the Mescalero Apache. Carson also enlisted the aid of traditional enemies of the Navajo, in particular the Ute and Zuni.

Navajo: Mounted bands of Navajo warriors, accustomed to hit-and-run raiding and adept in the art of ambuscade, opposed Carson's troopers. Although the Navajo could muster as many as 1,000 warriors, they were little match for the better-armed military.

GEOGRAPHIC AND STRATEGIC CONSIDERATIONS

The home country of the Navajo was the Colorado Plateau, which lay across northern New Mexico and Arizona, a mix of mountainous terrain and upland valleys lined with river valleys and canyons. The Navajo's final stronghold was Canyon de Chelly, located on the edge of the Chuska Mountains in the northeastern corner of Arizona. At the outset, General Carleton pursued a "scorched earth" policy, sending Kit Carson and supporting troops on wide sweeps through Navajo country to destroy crops, burn hogans (the Navajo's traditional earth-covered shelters), and seize livestock. While Carson's raids undermined the Navajo will to resist, rival Indians—particularly the Ute and the Zuni—sought out and attacked Navajo bands.

BATTLES AND CAMPAIGNS

July 1863: Col. Kit Carson sent out a detachment under Maj. Joseph Cummings to burn the Navajo crops and bring in their livestock. The detachment was attacked by the Navajo, and Cummings was killed.

August–December 1863: With 400 men, Carson's mobile column crisscrossed Navajo country, carrying out the work of destruction. Patrols from Fort Wingate joined, as did civilian vigilante groups looking for revenge or plunder. General Carleton offered a bounty for any Navajo horses, mules, and sheep captured. Carleton also ordered that every Navajo male be killed or captured; if captured, he was to be deported to Bosque Redondo Reservation. In one attack by Zuni Indians in December, 17 Navajo were killed, 44 women and children were taken captive, and 1,000 sheep were stolen. By year's end, the Navajo's numbers had been reduced by 300 killed, wounded, and captured, and their wealth reduced by more than 5,000 horses, mules, goats, and sheep.

Navajo bands launched retaliatory raids on the white settlements. One party managed to rustle 38 of Carson's mules. With the onset of winter, the cavalry's summertime destruction began to tell, and with the first heavy snows, Carleton decided to attack the Navajo in their ancient, forbidding stronghold—Canyon de Chelly.

Sheer red sandstone walls soared 600 to 1,000 feet from the floor of the canyon in the northeast corner of the Arizona Territory. For generations, Navajo bands patrolling the canyon rim had made the canyon floor a safe place. Although narrow and rocky at points, elsewhere the canyon was several hundred yards wide, offering trees for fuel, sufficient land on which to farm and graze flocks, and adequate water. Carleton's orders were for Carson to march the canyon's 30-mile length, destroying everything in his path.

January 6–12, 1864: Carson paraded his troopers, 389 strong, at Fort Canby (Carson's name for Fort Defiance) on the present-day Arizona–New Mexico border and set out through heavy snow for Canyon de Chelly. Once at the west entrance, he encamped and sent out reconnaissance parties along the rim of the canyon. One patrol encountered Navajo and, in the ensuing fight, killed 11.

January 12–14, 1864: While Carson's main force combed the canyon's rim, two detached companies swung around to penetrate the canyon from the east. Under Capt. Albert H. Pfeiffer, they marched the entire 30-mile length of the valley, destroying as much of the Navajo's possessions, crops, and livestock as they could. They killed 3 Navajo and captured 19 women and children. They reached the western portal unscathed

on the evening of January 14 and joined forces with Carson's men.

NEGOTIATIONS AND PEACE TREATY

On the night that Capt. Albert Pfeiffer's and Col. Kit Carson's forces linked, several Navajo came to them under a truce flag; they were told that everyone must surrender by the following morning or be prepared to die. The following morning, about 60 Navajo surrendered. Carson ordered his troops to go back through the canyon and destroy everything they could find, including the Navajo's cornfields and peach trees.

The Canyon de Chelly expedition effectively ended the Navajo Conflict. Demoralized and hungry, large bands of Navajo streamed into Forts Wingate and Canby to surrender. Within three weeks of Carson's campaign, more than 5,000 Navajo had presented themselves for deportation to Bosque Redondo Reservation.

March–December 1864: In the incident that became known as the Long Walk, 3,800 Navajo slogged eastward some 300 miles to the Pecos River wasteland during the early spring. Some 210 perished on the way. During the summer and autumn, the Army efficiently conducted further removals, with at least another 110 dying on the march. By the end of 1864, 8,000 Navajo had been resettled at Bosque Redondo Reservation.

RESULTS OF THE WAR (CASUALTIES, COSTS, CONSEQUENCES)

Historians have not put a price on the Navajo Conflict, but it must have cost several millions in 1990 dollars if all the associated costs (such as the relocation of the Navajo) are included. In the hostilities alone, the U.S. military, with its overpowering force, counted only a few dead and wounded, and the Navajo suffered about 30 dead with as many wounded. But at least 320 died on the Long Walk. Altogether during the battles and forced marches of the 1860s, the Navajo losses are estimated at 2,500 people.

Several hundred Navajo under the hard-line Chief Manuelito at first refused to give up, withdrawing into the farthest western reaches of the tribal homeland, along the Little Colorado River. But by the autumn of 1866, with starvation at hand for his people, Manuelito, too, surrendered.

Though the Navajo Conflict ended, the colonization of Bosque Redondo Reservation proved to be a disaster. The Pecos River country could not support a large population; the grasslands were too sparse to sustain the Navajo herds. Disease was widespread, and frequent Kiowa and Comanche raids caused further misery.

The Navajo continued to protest and resist their enforced life at Bosque Redondo Reservation. In the spring of 1868, Manuelito and other chiefs were allowed to present their case to President Andrew Johnson in Washington, D. C. On June 1, 1868, the tribe won permission to return to its homeland. A new treaty set aside 3.5 million acres of reserved lands (since enlarged to include about 15 million acres) for the Navajo in present-day New Mexico and Arizona.

Plains Wars of the 1860s

DATES OF WARS

Cheyenne-Arapaho War and the Sand Creek Massacre: 1864–1865. Red Cloud's War: 1866–1867. Hancock's War: 1867. Cheyenne Winter Campaign: 1868–1869.

SIGNIFICANCE

Although some of the Plains conflicts of the 1860s are called wars, they were in fact more like a series of campaigns. Escalating from one incident to another or from one misunderstanding to another, the wars involved many of the themes that dominated warfare on the Great Plains. Behind all the wars was the long-standing decision by the U.S. government to remove the Indians from their lands; the new elements were the organized military force brought to bear and the sheer viciousness of some of the whites, such as Gen. Philip Sheridan. Although the Indians could boast that Red Cloud's War was one of the few defeats suffered by the United States, Sand Creek (1864) to Wounded Knee (1890) was essentially a straight line of descent for the Indians.

BACKGROUND

Under the terms of the first Treaty of Fort Laramie, 1851, many of the Plains Indians (see Combatants, p. 317, for a list of Plains Indians tribes involved in the wars) agreed to allow white people to travel through their lands (see Geo-graphic and Strategic Considerations, p. 317), to maintain the trails, and even to establish military posts. But under the terms of that treaty, the Indians did not give up their claims to the lands, their right to move or settle there and their right to hunt and fish there. Soon, the Indians began to realize that the travelers on the overland trails, the waves of homesteaders and miners, and the military posts and troops were threatening their way of life, even their very existence. The U.S. government quickly shifted from a policy of sharing the land with the Indians to one of concentrating the Plains tribes on reserved lands to the north and south of the Platte and Smoky Hill Rivers, establishing the great central belt of settlements, and building overland trails (and eventually railroad lines). When the tribes resisted, increased numbers of volunteers and U.S. regular forces were called on to restore order and, where necessary, carry out forcible removal of the Indians to the reservations.

CAUSES OF THE WARS

Although each of the Plains Wars of the 1860s was triggered by some incident, fundamentally each was caused by the growing pressures of westward expansion: increased traffic along the overland trails; homesteaders and miners; white people's exploitation of timber, grass, buffalo, minerals, and other Plains resources; the fencing off of lands and settlements; and, later, the building of the transcontinental railroad.

PREPARATIONS FOR WARS

The U.S. government had been sending armed expeditions through the Plains region since the early 1840s—since 1804, if the Lewis and Clark expedition is considered. With Congressional authorization in 1846, the U.S. Army began to build and garrison several forts on the Plains. Fifteen years later, with the Civil War under way, there was a heavy demand for troops elsewhere. But with the end of the Civil War in 1865, the U.S. Army was free to establish new military posts to guard the trails and to reinforce existing posts. An elaborate and expensive system of supplying those forces was put into operation, with a constant succession of overland wagon trains. At the same time, the governors of the territories (much of the land involved in

those early Plains Wars had not yet been organized into states) were able and willing to raise
volunteer units to fight Indians.

For the Plains tribes, for whom raiding, like
hunting, was part of their way of life, few formal
preparations for warfare were necessary.
Throughout the Plains Wars, much of their energy was spent robbing supply wagons, both
civilian and military, of food, horses and cattle,
and, above all, arms and ammunition.

DECLARATION OF WARS

There was no formal declaration of war at the
national level, but there was almost complete
support from Washington, D.C., from the presidents through Congress and the War Department, for the actions taken; only a small minority
spoke out against the actions against the Plains
Indians. The specific orders, threats, and dead-
lines were issued by those on the scene, such as
the territorial governors and Army commanders
in the field.

COMBATANTS

During the Civil War, the Colorado territorial
and Kansas state militias provided most of the
troops that fought the Indians, but after the Civil
War ended, the U.S. Army assigned about 5,000
men to the Plains region. In general, infantry
units were assigned to hold the forts and to protect whites in the immediate area, and cavalry
units moved out in large mobile columns to take
the offensive against the Indians.

The principal Native American tribes engaged in the series of Plains Wars were Cheyenne, Arapaho, Kiowa, Teton Sioux, and
Comanche. There were many thousands of warriors active at any given time over a vast territory, but only about 2,000 participated in particular engagements.

GEOGRAPHIC AND STRATEGIC CONSIDERATIONS

The Plains Wars of the 1860s began in a relatively small area of Colorado but quickly spread
across a vast part of the Great Plains—north to
Wyoming and Montana, east to Kansas, south
to Oklahoma. Although there were mountains
throughout much of that territory, most of the
fighting took place on the Plains, and even there

it tended to be confined to the river valleys. (It is
no coincidence that many of the most famous
battles are named after rivers.) The valleys of
many rivers—the Upper Platte, the Lower Platte,
the Powder, the Tongue, the Arkansas, the Smoky
Hill—provided convenient routes for travelers
and armies; the Oregon Trail, for instance, followed the North Platte River. The rivers also
provided natural boundaries that the U.S. government tried to impose on the Indians.

Getting to the remote areas of the Great Plains
in the 1860s meant weeks of overland travel from
the jumping off cities along the Mississippi River.
(The railroads did not begin to change things
until the 1870s.) Weeks of arduous travel and
months of supplies could be wiped out in minutes by an Indian raiding party. The Indians
traveled relatively light, with their horses and
ponies. They hunted buffalo, deer, and other
game and generally lived off the land, but they
also preyed on the whites' grazing cattle, stole
horses and ponies, and raided wagon trains. That
way of life had its limits: The Indian warriors had
to pull back for the severe winters—they had to
save their limited food and ammunition and they
had to worry about their families.

CHEYENNE-ARAPAHO WAR AND THE SAND CREEK MASSACRE: 1864–1865

The Cheyenne and Arapaho tribes of the
southern Plains generally had lived up to the
terms of the 1851 Fort Laramie Treaty (see Background, p. 316). Even when the Civil War began,
they tried to avoid contacts with the whites, hunting buffalo in areas devoid of white travelers,
settlements, and forts. Gradually, though, increasing numbers of pro-Union armed forces
moved throughout the region, ostensibly to put
down pro-Confederate actions. To command the
Colorado units, Colorado Territory governor John
Evans appointed Col. John M. Chivington. Governor Evans tried to persuade the Cheyenne to
deed over their hunting grounds in eastern Colorado in exchange for reservation lands. The Cheyenne declined to do so.

BATTLES AND CAMPAIGNS

May 16, 1864: A Colorado detachment
moved into west-central Kansas with no authority other than Colonel Chivington's order "to kill

Cheyennes whenever and wherever found." It came across a large band of Cheyenne led by Lean Bear and Black Kettle. The soldiers attacked without provocation; three Indians (including Lean Bear) were killed and several wounded; the soldiers suffered a similar number of casualties.

May–June 1864: There were two more incidents involving unprovoked attacks by Chivington's units on Cheyenne; there were also incidents involving attacks by Indians on white settlers. Black Kettle tried to prevent an escalation into war, but Governor Evans used these and several other incidents as an excuse for issuing a circular to the Indians. In the circular he declared that some Cheyenne and Arapaho were at war with the whites and that all friendly Cheyenne and Arapaho should report to Fort Lyon some 150 miles southeast of Denver, Colorado.

July–August 1864: Throughout the spring and early summer, there had been many raids by Indians on settlers, forts, and stagecoaches in the Platte Valley, well north of Denver. The Sioux were responsible for most, if not all of those, but the Cheyenne and Arapaho were blamed by those in Colorado determined to eliminate them. In August, Governor Evans issued a proclamation authorizing all citizens of Colorado to pursue all "hostile Indians" and to kill them. Hearing and fearing that, some chiefs—notably, the southern Cheyenne chief Black Kettle—sent word the Indians were prepared to negotiate.

September 28, 1864: Black Kettle and six other Indian chiefs met with Evans and Chivington near Denver. Black Kettle came away understanding that his people could have peace only by moving into the vicinity of a military post and submitting to military authority.

Early November 1864: Black Kettle's 600 Cheyenne made camp in the valley of Sand Creek in southeastern Colorado, 40 miles northeast of Fort Lyon. They had a clear understanding that they would not be bothered so long as they stayed there.

November 27–28, 1864: Colonel Chivington arrived at Fort Lyon with 600 Colorado volunteers. Although some of his staff opposed his plan to attack the Indians at Sand Creek (see Notable Phrases, p. 340), Chivington was determined to wipe out the Indians. He set out on November 28, on a night march to Sand Creek.

November 29, 1864: With his 600 volunteers plus 100 regular soldiers from Fort Lyon and four howitzers, Chivington moved on the Sand Creek encampment. Over Black Kettle's tepee flew the Stars and Stripes and a white flag. Chivington attacked anyway. In what became known as the Sand Creek Massacre, Chivington's troops slaughtered some 150 Cheyenne, two-thirds of them women and children; 9 chiefs were killed; Black Kettle managed to escape.

January–February 1865: As news of the massacre spread, most of the Cheyenne and Arapaho fled northward, and their chiefs vowed to take to the warpath. In January and February 1865, war parties raided settlements in the South Platte valley, killing 50 whites and destroying stage stations and telegraph lines. With the coming of spring, most of the tribes drifted still farther northward, raiding in the North Platte region; however, Black Kettle and some 400 of his southern Cheyenne chose to return south.

July 26, 1865: A thousand warriors attacked the military post at Upper Platte Bridge on the Oregon-California trail, destroying an Army supply train and killing some 20 soldiers.

August–September 1865: Gen. Patrick E. Connor sent three punitive columns, a total of 3,000 men, north to the region of the Powder and Tongue Rivers and into Montana. The campaign proved disastrous for Connor's troops, with some 100 dead and wounded; although they took as many Indian casualties, the U.S. forces expended or lost hundreds of horses and ponies and vast amounts of supplies of all kinds.

RED CLOUD'S WAR: 1866–1867

With the close of the Civil War, the white presence on the northern Plains increased in numbers and activities, intensifying the pressure on the Teton Sioux tribes of the Dakotas and eastern Montana. Although the U.S. Army was reduced from its enlargement during the Civil War to just 54,000 men, a large portion of its fighting force was concentrated in the western territories. To support the civilian traffic and the Army's needs, the U.S. forces built a string of outposts—including Forts Reno and Phil Kearny in Wyoming and Fort C. F. Smith on the Bighorn River in southern Montana—to guard the Bozeman Trail, which ran northward through eastern Wyoming to the Montana goldfields. Since the official policy was to remove all Indians to reservations, a conflict was inevitable.

BATTLES AND CAMPAIGNS

June 5–14, 1866: Government negotiators at Fort Laramie, Wyoming, sought a treaty with the northern Sioux, Brulé, and Cheyenne that would guarantee the security of the Bozeman Trail. Led by their chiefs, some 2,000 Indians gathered at Fort Laramie. The Indians immediately learned that the United States intended to build the forts and support the trail, treaty or not. "The Great Father sends us presents and wants us to sell him the road," observed Red Cloud, a leading chief of Oglala Sioux, one of the most powerful of the Teton tribes, "but White Chief goes with soldiers to steal the road before Indians say yes or no." Refusing to sign the treaty, Red Cloud and all the Indians left the Fort Laramie area, determined to deny use of the route to all whites, soldiers, and civilians.

July 13, 1865: Col. Henry B. Carrington, in command of an infantry regiment of 700 men, along with some of their wives and children, arrived near the fork of the Little Piney and Big Piney Creeks, some 20 miles south of Sheridan, Wyoming. The men immediately set about to build Fort Phil Kearny.

July–November 1866: Red Cloud, Sitting Bull, Gall, and other Sioux war chiefs harassed detachments of soldiers building the forts along the Bozeman Trail, stealing from grazing herds and attacking isolated wood-cutting parties. In particular, Sioux warriors virtually maintained a siege around Fort Phil Kearny. The siege was known as "the circle of death." It took the lives of some 70 soldiers during the first six months. Yet Colonel Carrington, in command at Fort Phil Kearny, chose a strategy of passive defense. One of Carrington's officers, Capt. William J. Fetterman, a veteran of Sherman's Georgia campaign, boasted that with 80 men he could ride through the entire Sioux nation. He badgered Carrington for permission to search out and destroy Sioux villages.

November 12, 1866: Gen. Philip St. George Cooke ordered Carrington to attack the Sioux in their winter camps in the Powder River country of southeastern Montana.

December 6, 1866: When a Sioux war party attacked a wood train west of Fort Kearny, Carrington sent Fetterman with 30 troopers to drive off the raiders. Carrington led another detachment of 25 men north up the Bozeman Trail to cut off the Indians' retreat. A party of 100 warriors turned on Fetterman's troopers, who panicked and ran.

December 21, 1866: A large Sioux force of 1,500–2,000 warriors concentrated at the site of the December 6 skirmish. The main body lay concealed in ravines along snow-covered Lodge Trail Ridge while a small party raided a wood train. Carrington again sent Fetterman to relieve the work detail. Exceeding his orders, Fetterman, with 51 infantry and 28 cavalry, all armed with fast-firing Spencer carbines, pursued the raiders up the ridge.

Soon heavy firing was heard in Fort Phil Kearny 3 miles distant. Carrington dispatched a detachment of 40 infantry and cavalry to Fetterman's support. As the relief party arrived, hundreds of warriors streamed away to the north. The Sioux had killed Fetterman's entire command—3 officers, 76 soldiers, and 2 civilians—then stripped and mutilated the bodies. For years to come, many whites would use the Fetterman Massacre as a justification for killing as many Indians as they could. The Indians called it the Battle of the Hundred Slain, a reference to their enemy's losses; they themselves counted some 200 dead or wounded.

Winter–Spring 1867: The Sioux hunkered down in their winter camps. While the army prepared to avenge the Fetterman disaster, politicians in Washington called for a peaceful settlement. In March, a congressional committee under Wisconsin senator James Doolittle (who had previously absolved Col. John Chivington of blame for the Sand Creek Massacre; see p. 318) blamed most of the Plains Indian troubles on white aggression and recommended a conciliatory policy. As a result, President Andrew Johnson appointed a peace commission to parley with the Indian tribes.

July 1867: The Sioux chiefs and their Cheyenne allies closed the Bozeman Trail to all but the most heavily guarded wagon trains and resolved to destroy the three forts.

August 1–2, 1867: A Cheyenne war party attacked a Fort Smith hay-mowing camp on August 1. Twenty soldiers and 12 civilians repulsed three Indian charges during the daylong fight, with losses of 3 killed and 2 wounded. The next day, defenders behind a corral of wagon beds near Fort Phil Kearny drove off a party of Sioux after a four-and-a-half-hour fight, suffering 6 killed and 2 wounded. Those engagements, known as the Hayfield Fight and the Wagon Box Fight (or Medicine Fight), cost the Indians an estimated 60 killed and 120 wounded.

Although the Indians withdrew, they continued to threaten the Bozeman Trail through the winter of 1867–1868.

HANCOCK'S WAR: 1867

In March 1867, Gen. Winfield Scott Hancock prepared a "show the flag" expedition to awe restless Cheyenne and Kiowa bands south of the Arkansas River in southwestern Kansas, the Oklahoma panhandle, and north Texas. The expedition touched off a short, sharp war that brought Lt. Col. George Armstrong Custer, the "boy general" of the Civil War, to prominence as an Indian fighter.

BATTLES AND CAMPAIGNS

April 7–16, 1867: Hancock's expedition of 1,400 men, including the 7th Cavalry, the 37th Infantry, and a battery of the 4th Artillery, set out from Fort Larned, Kansas, along the Smoky Hill. Hancock's announced intention was to negotiate with several Indian chiefs at their encampment at Pawnee Creek, west of Fort Larned. Fearing what that powerful force might do to their people, the Indians abandoned their camp; Hancock ordered his men to destroy the camp. That so enraged the Cheyenne and Sioux that they began a new series of raids—burning stagecoach stations, driving off ranchers' stock, and killing a number of settlers.

Early May 1867: Hancock ordered Custer to search out and destroy Sioux and Cheyenne bands between the Arkansas and Platte rivers.

May–June 1867: Indian raiders hit mail stations, stagecoaches, wagon trains, and railroad work parties on the Platte (Union Pacific) and Smoky Hill (Kansas Pacific) Rivers.

June 1–July 13, 1867: Custer, with 300 troopers of the 7th Cavalry, pursued the roving bands. He reached Fort Wallace on the western reaches of the Smoky Hill River in mid-July after weeks of inconclusive skirmishing.

July–October 1867: Hancock had launched the war, but he could not bring it to a victorious end. By late summer, Hancock's forces were withdrawn from the field and stationed at several forts

to await the outcome of Gen. William Sherman's negotiations (see pp. 321–322). Indian war parties continued to raid unchecked through early autumn, halting stage services and slowing construction of the Kansas Pacific Railroad.

CHEYENNE WINTER CAMPAIGN: 1868–1869

The Medicine Lodge Treaty (see Negotiations and Peace Treaty, pp. 321–322) promised the tribes government issues of guns and ammunition, presumably for hunting. But as the winter of 1867–1868 passed into spring and summer, the Indians who remained south of the Arkansas River found themselves increasingly short of food and without the promised guns and ammunition. Many Indians began to move northward back into their familiar hunting grounds. By the fall, there were increasing numbers of incidents involving frustrated Indians and edgy troops. When one aggressive band, the Cheyenne Dog Soldiers under Tall Bull (see Legends and Trivia, p. 340), raided a Kiowa village, the government withdrew the offer of arms. In response, parties of Dog Soldiers raided white settlements along the Saline and Solomon rivers in northwest Kansas, killing 15 men, raping 5 women, and burning homesteads. Gen. Philip Sheridan arrived on the scene and prepared a winter campaign in which three heavy columns would converge on the Indians' winter camps along the Canadian and Washita Rivers in Oklahoma.

BATTLES AND CAMPAIGNS

September 17–24, 1868: A band of Cheyenne and Sioux warriors trapped a party of some 50 soldiers and civilian scouts on a small island in the Arikaree River in northeastern Colorado. The white men called it the Battle of Beecher's Island, after Lt. Frederick Beecher, who was killed there; the Indians called it the Fight When Roman Nose was Killed, after the great Cheyenne war chief Roman Nose, one of some 30 Indians killed there.

November 27, 1868: Just before daybreak, Custer's 7th Cavalry column found a Cheyenne camp in the frozen, snow-covered valley of the Washita River, in western Oklahoma. Attacking the sleeping camp, the troops killed some 103 Cheyenne, slaughtered 900 Cheyenne ponies, and burned the tepees. When Arapaho warriors

In April 1868, Gen. William T. Sherman met with Sioux and other Indian leaders at Fort Laramie and signed a treaty that guaranteed the Sioux rights to certain territory in South Dakota and Montana.

from nearby villages came to the aid of the Cheyenne, they managed to trap a pursuing detachment of 19 of Custer's men and killed all of them. When Custer saw the increased number of warriors, he withdrew with losses of 5 killed and 14 wounded (in addition to the 19 previously killed).

The village turned out to be one of Black Kettle's, the peaceable chief whose people had been victims of the infamous Sand Creek Massacre in eastern Colorado almost exactly four years earlier. Black Kettle and his wife were killed during Custer's attack. Critics of U.S. Indian policy stigmatized the Battle of Washita as another Sand Creek, but General Sheridan congratulated Custer for "efficient and gallant services rendered."

December 25, 1868 (Battle of Soldier Spring): Another U.S. cavalry column attacked a Comanche camp on the north fork of the Red River in west-central Oklahoma. As the new year approached, winter storms drove the three U.S. Army columns back to their bases.

March 1869: Custer prepared to resume the offensive against the Cheyenne. On March 15, his scouts located two large villages on Sweetwater Creek in the Texas Panhandle. With the Indians holding two white women hostage,

Custer decided to parley. During the talks, he seized four chiefs, sending one back with word that he would hang the other three unless the women were freed. On March 18, the Cheyenne released their hostages and promised to return to the reservation and surrender.

July 1869: Only Tall Bull's Dog Soldiers failed to observe Custer's surrender terms. On July 11, a detachment of the 5th Cavalry, supported by friendly Pawnees, surprised Tall Bull's camp at Summit Springs in northeastern Colorado; within a half hour, practically all 200 Cheyenne, including Tall Bull, were killed. The Cheyenne who had refused to settle on the reservations in Kansas and Oklahoma now made their way north to join the northern Cheyenne and Sioux north of the Platte River. The wars on the Central Plains had effectively ended.

NEGOTIATIONS AND PEACE TREATY

There had been almost continual negotiations on some level throughout the entire series of wars with the Plains tribes; sometimes the negotiations involved little more than field commanders trying to come to terms with a local band or tribe, but on other occasions, the negotiations involved formal meetings between delegates sent out from Washington and the most powerful chiefs. Finally, in 1867 and 1868, two groups of U.S. peace commissioners from Washington imposed what they believed were final settlements, the first with the Southern Plains tribes that included the Cheyenne, Arapaho, Kiowa, Plains Apache, and Comanche, the second with the Sioux at Fort Laramie in Wyoming.

Some 4,000 southern Plains Indians gathered at Medicine Lodge Creek, Kansas, in October 1867. The chiefs of the Kiowa and Comanche signed a treaty on October 21, but it was October 28 before the chiefs of the Cheyenne and Arapaho tribes affixed their marks to the treaty. It set aside two large reserved areas southwest of the Arkansas River in western Indian Territory (present-day Oklahoma). White settlers were to be kept out. Government teachers would open schools, and the government would issue clothing and supply seeds, tools, and instructions in farming. In return, the tribes agreed to relinquish all claims to lands beyond the reservations.

To the north, Red Cloud made it clear that he would not settle until the Army abandoned the Bozeman Trail forts. Finally, in April 1868, meeting at Fort Laramie, the commissioners, headed by Gen. William Tecumseh Sherman, agreed to give up the outposts. The first Sioux chiefs signed the treaty on April 29. Others soon followed, but not Red Cloud. In August, the Army withdrew from Forts C. F. Smith, Phil Kearny, and Reno, and the Indians moved in and burned them. On November 6, 1868, Red Cloud appeared at Fort Laramie to put his mark to the settlement.

In the south, repeated violations of the Medicine Lodge Treaty led to renewed warfare. Not until Custer subdued Tall Bull in July 1869 (see p. 321) did an uneasy—and temporary—peace descend on the southern Plains.

RESULTS OF THE WARS (CASUALTIES, COSTS, CONSEQUENCES)

Historians have not tried to put a price on the Plains Wars of the 1860s, but it would amount to hundreds of millions of 1990 dollars. As for casualties, the whites lost some 2,000 civilians, volunteers, and regular troops directly to the hostilities, with at least as many wounded, and the Indians suffered probably twice that number killed and wounded.

Though several fierce outbreaks lay ahead, the Plains Wars of the 1860s essentially ended the independent existence of the central and southern Plains tribes. The U.S. concentration policy had succeeded in clearing the great belt of the central Plains of Indians, making the area safe for white settlement.

Although some voices were raised in protest against the U.S. government's policy toward the Indians, the particular incidents occurred so far from the settled regions of the country that most Americans simply went about their daily affairs. And when questions were raised, little came of them. A year after the massacre at Sand Creek (see November 29, 1864, p. 318), congressional and Army committees investigated the incident; the congressional committee recommended taking no action against Col. John Chivington, and although the Army board condemned Chivington, he had left the Army and could not be punished.

The Modoc War

DATES OF WAR

November 29, 1872–June 1, 1873

SIGNIFICANCE

The Modoc War turned out to be the last Indian resistance to white settlement of northern California. Although extremely limited in duration, numbers involved, and casualties, the Modoc War reflected the determination of whites once they had decided they wanted Indian land. It also holds the distinction of being the only Indian war in which a U.S. general lost his life.

BACKGROUND

The Modoc Indians lived in the Lost River valley in northern California on the border with Oregon. Starting in the 1850s, the grasslands there attracted white ranchers, and by 1864, under pressure of white settlement, the Modoc reluctantly consented to cede their homeland and resettle on the Klamath Reservation 25 miles north in Oregon. Things went badly from the start. The Klamath, traditional enemies of the Modoc, resented the Modoc. There were internal divisions within the Modoc tribe. And there were dissatisfactions with reservation life; in particular, the Modoc found it hard to support themselves. By the late 1860s, the leader of the Modoc, Kintpuash Captain Jack to the whites and most of the Modoc (there were only about 500) had moved back to their homeland. They were persuaded to go back to the Klamath Reservation, but in the spring of 1870, Kintpuash returned to his California homeland with about 225 Modoc. Although his father had been killed by white settlers, Kintpuash maintained a good relationship with white people.

CAUSES OF THE WAR

By 1872, white settlers in northern California were increasing the pressure on their government authorities to remove the Modoc. Finally, the Indian Bureau turned to the U.S. cavalry to carry out a forced removal of the band to the Oregon reservation.

PREPARATIONS FOR WAR

With little or no preparation for serious hostilities, the Army sent only a troop of cavalry from Fort Klamath, Oregon, to carry out the Indian Bureau's request to return the Modoc to the reservation.

COMBATANTS

Brig. Gen. Edward R. S. Canby, a Union Civil War hero, commanded U.S. forces in northern California and Oregon. His forces eventually built to 1,000 men. The rebellious faction of the Modoc consisted of about 75 warriors and 150 women and children.

GEOGRAPHIC AND STRATEGIC CONSIDERATIONS

The area in contention was largely fertile grassland in the Lost River valley around Tule Lake on California's border with Oregon. The Modoc had lived there for hundreds of years, and although there were never more than about 1,000 of them, they enjoyed a relatively stable way of life. When whites began to move onto their land during the 1850s, some of the Modoc actively fought them. Although the fighting stopped, some Modoc continued to steal cattle

and horses from the whites. Finally, the white settlers determined to get all the Modoc off the rich grazing lands.

BATTLES AND CAMPAIGNS

November 29, 1872: A troop of 38 cavalrymen, led by Maj. James Jackson, approached Kintpuash's camp at dawn. When Jackson insisted that the Modoc men turn over all their weapons, one of the warriors resisted. Shots were exchanged; one Indian was killed and seven wounded. The Indians fled, moving south. Jackson's troop came across another camp of Modoc and without provocation attacked it, killing a baby and an old woman, and wounding several men. That group of Modoc also fled south, raiding along the way to take revenge. They killed 12 homesteaders before joining Kintpuash's group in the fastness of the lava country below Tule Lake. The Modoc called that wilderness the Land of Burnt-Out Fires. The Army called it Kintpuash's stronghold. To round up the Modoc band, about 50 warriors, Canby sent a force under Lt. Col. Frank Wheaton; it included some 225 regulars and 104 California and Oregon volunteers.

January 16–17, 1873: By January 16, Wheaton's force had effectively trapped the Modoc. Some of the warriors, Kintpuash among them, felt that it was useless to resist, but the majority wanted to fight. On January 17, Wheaton's men fired their howitzers and then attacked through a heavy fog. The Battle of the Stronghold proved to be a mismatch from the start. Firing with deadly accuracy, the Modoc were able to remain hidden while keeping the soldiers pinned down. At sunset, Wheaton pulled back, counting 9 men killed and 28 wounded. (A contingent of soldiers returned the next day under a white flag and were allowed to recover the dead.)

March 1873: The U.S. government sent a peace commission to the Modoc and appointed General Canby to head it. In the negotiations that ensued throughout March, one of the main issues was the commissioners' insistence that the Indians who had killed the settlers in November 1872 would have to face trial as murderers. Again, dissension racked Kintpuash's band. The more aggressive chiefs wanted to kill the commissioners and continue the war. Kintpuash counseled patience but was overruled.

April 11, 1873: Ignoring warnings of treachery, the peace commissioners met with Modoc emissaries. When Kintpuash could not get Canby to promise to remove all the soldiers and to allow the Modoc to stay in California, he drew a pistol and shot Canby in the face. Then he stabbed him. (Edward R. S. Canby thus became the only U.S. general killed in the country's Indian wars.) Kintpuash's companions killed a second commissioner and wounded a third. The Modoc then went back to the stronghold.

April 26, 1873: A Modoc party of 22 warriors ambushed a 78-man U.S. detachment sent to remove the Modoc from the caves and crevices of the lava wilderness, killing 25 and wounding 16. The siege tightened as the Army's strength grew to more than 1,000. By mid-May, the Modoc, running short of food and water, were arguing among themselves; small parties began to scatter or surrender. Troops rounded them up, bringing the Modoc resistance to a close.

June 1, 1873: A cavalry patrol captured Kintpuash, his family, and the last three warriors to remain by his side.

NEGOTIATIONS AND PEACE TREATY

The negotiations that occurred in April 1873 had led to disaster, so when the fighting took up again, both sides realized that there would be no more negotiations. When Kintpuash and the other Modoc leaders were captured, Army commander Gen. William T. Sherman ordered Canby's killers tried for murder. They were tried at Fort Klamath in July and found guilty. On October 3, 1873, Kintpuash and three other Modoc leaders were hanged on the parade ground at Fort Klamath.

RESULTS OF THE WAR (CASUALTIES, COSTS, CONSEQUENCES)

Historians have not put a price on the Modoc War, but it must have cost the equivalent of a few million 1990 dollars. The whites counted 50 dead (including General Canby) and about an equal number of wounded; the Indians' casualties were about the same.

Gen. William T. Sherman ordered the surviving Modoc to be deported east, "so that the name of Modoc shall cease." The Army escorted the 155 surviving Modoc to new homes in Indian Territory. As Sherman had decreed, the Modoc, in effect, ceased to exist. Their brief rebellion turned out to be the last Indian conflict in the California-Oregon border region.

The Red River War

DATES OF WAR

June 27, 1874–April 23, 1875

SIGNIFICANCE

The conduct and outcome of the Red River War, really not much more than an intense campaign, signaled that the balance had tipped: The white people could now count on overpowering military force. The era of trade-offs, truces, and treaties was over.

BACKGROUND

The Cheyenne, Kiowa, Comanche, Arapaho, and Plains Apache Indians of the southern Plains did not adapt well to reservation life. Confined under the terms of the Medicine Lodge Treaty (1867) to the land southwest of the Arkansas River in Indian Territory (present-day Oklahoma), the Indians stubbornly resisted the transition to a sedentary farming life. War parties continually slipped away to carry on the custom of raiding. Bands hit travel routes and frontier settlements in Kansas, Colorado, Texas, and New Mexico. They also attacked peaceful Indian tribes. Most of all, they set out to attack white buffalo hunters who were decimating the buffalo herds. Buffalo hides were commanding good prices, and professional white hunters, skinners (known as "hide men"), and traders were flooding the Plains. Ignoring the terms of the Medicine Lodge Treaty (see pp. 321-322), they began to move into the Indians' hunting grounds south of the Arkansas River.

CAUSES OF THE WAR

In the years between 1867 and 1874, there had been an almost unending series of minor hostile actions in which either a few Indians or a few whites, often both, lost their lives. Yet neither side seemed willing to call for an all-out war.

Then, on June 27, 1874, a large party of mostly Comanche, but also some Cheyenne, Kiowa, and Arapaho, cornered a group of white buffalo hunters and traders at a trading post named Adobe Walls in northeastern Texas. (The leader of that war party was Kwahadi Comanche Quanah Parker, son of a Kwahadi chief and Cynthia Ann Parker, a white woman who had been kidnapped by a Comanche as a young girl.) The Indians held the 28 white hunters and traders under siege, but one of them escaped and rode to Dodge City, Kansas; reinforcements arrived ten days later and helped all the white men to escape. The Indians burned the Adobe Walls post, but 15 of their warriors died and many more were wounded; the white men lost only 2. The tribes scattered and set off the west, east, and north, raiding as they went. White people throughout the region immediately raised calls for punitive actions against the rebellious tribes.

PREPARATIONS FOR WAR

Gen. Philip Sheridan, commander of the Army's Division of the Missouri, planned a converging campaign against warrior bands camped along the Red River and its tributaries (along the Oklahoma–Texas border) and in the Indian stronghold of the Staked Plain (Llano Estacado) of west Texas, southeast New Mexico, and northwest Oklahoma. In August, Sheridan launched punitive columns from several points of the compass, two from Fort Sill, Indian Territory (Oklahoma), and one each from Kansas, Texas, and New Mexico.

DECLARATION OF WAR

There was no formal declaration of war, but Gen. Philip Sheridan requested and received authorization from the War Department to make war on hostile Indian bands. Permission reached him on July 27, 1874.

COMBATANTS

The five columns of U.S. Army regular troops—combined infantry and cavalry, with some artillery—totaled about 3,000 men. They were in search of 1,800 Cheyenne, 2,000 Comanche, 1,000 Arapaho, and 1,000 Kiowa. Together, the Indians could mount an estimated 1,200 warriors, but at no time were more than several hundred involved in one engagement.

GEOGRAPHIC AND STRATEGIC CONSIDERATIONS

The Red River War has been so named because the major engagements took place along or near the upper reaches of the Red River in northwestern Texas. Its alternate name, the Buffalo War, actually conveys better what the war was about: not disputed territory but the right of the Indians to maintain the buffalo herds of the southern Plains. The movements of the five major army columns out of their forts as distant as New Mexico, Oklahoma, and Kansas meant that a territory far beyond the Red River was affected. Basically, the war was a sweep of the southern Plains from northwestern Kansas across western Oklahoma and into the Texas panhandle, a campaign to round up the Indians who had refused to stay on the reservation in Indian Territory. At the outset, during the summer of 1874, the soldiers and Indians feinted and skirmished in conditions of extreme drought and heat, with midday temperatures often reaching 110 degrees. Constant military pressure, coming from all directions, soon began to wear away at the insurgent strength. On the run, forced to feed thousands of their women and children, and short of ammunition, the Indian warriors could not compete with a highly organized army. Finally, the harsh weather of the 1874–1875 winter broke the Indians' resistance.

BATTLES AND CAMPAIGNS

August 30, 1874: Col. Nelson A. Miles had left Fort Dodge in southwestern Kansas and moved into the Texas panhandle with his column of some 750 men. Two hundred Cheyenne attacked the advance guard west of Mulberry Creek at the edge of the Staked Plain escarpment in northwestern Texas. Miles deployed his full force and drove the Indians toward the Prairie Dog Town fork of the Red River. As the warriors fell back, Comanche and Kiowa bands reinforced the Cheyenne. The chase continued in intense heat and dust for 12 miles. Running short of supplies, Miles broke off the pursuit, allowing the Indians to escape. Before he withdrew, though, he destroyed villages and material the Indians had hurriedly abandoned.

During the second week of September, heavy storms broke the drought and turned the trails to rivers of mud.

September 9–14, 1874: Maj. William R. Price's New Mexico column skirmished with Kiowa and Comanche bands along the upper reaches of the Washita River in western Oklahoma. In rain and damp chill, war parties held off Price's troops long enough for their families to withdraw to safety. But the operation disheartened many, and soon small bands began turning up at the agencies to surrender.

September 20, 1874: A column of 475 men under Col. Ranald S. Mackenzie broke camp and marched north along the edge of the Staked Plain in northwestern Texas in search of the warrior bands that had escaped Colonel Miles.

September 26, 1874: Scouts brought Mackenzie word of a large Indian encampment in the Palo Duro Canyon in the Texas Panhandle. Mackenzie brought his force up to the edge of the canyon. After dark, a party of 250 Comanche attacked Mackenzie's corral; the warriors failed to stampede the horses, and Mackenzie's men drove off the Comanche after sunrise.

September 28, 1874: Mackenzie sent his troops into the canyon at daybreak. In several skirmishes as his column pushed up the Palo Duro Canyon, Mackenzie had only one casualty: a slightly wounded trumpeter. The Indians had only five dead, but Mackenzie inflicted a crippling blow anyway, burning several hundred lodges as well as food and equipment, and carrying off the Indians' entire herd of 1,500 ponies. The next day, Mackenzie's troops cut out the strongest ponies for themselves and slaughtered the rest—nearly 1,000 animals.

In the weeks that followed, Indians were on the run throughout the southern Plains; by then, there were so many different Army columns in the area that they could hunt down and capture the demoralized Indians with ease. By mid-October, with winter approaching and lacking food and clothing, Indians in increasing numbers were arriving at the agencies. With the onset of winter, the punitive columns returned to their bases, but their autumn war on the Indians' means of support—lodges, equipment, food stocks, ponies—had been a success.

January–May 1875: Hungry, cold, and without resources to continue the struggle, hundreds of Indians continued to stream into the agencies to give themselves up, including a band of 500 Kiowa under Lone Wolf, who came into Fort Sill, Oklahoma. On March 6, Cheyenne chief Grey Wolf surrendered with 820 members of his band at Fort Sill. Quanah Parker brought his Kwahadi Comanche to Fort Sill in May.

April 23, 1875: At Sappa Creek in northwest Kansas, a 6th Cavalry detachment cut off a band of 60 Cheyenne heading north for sanctuary with the Cheyenne and Sioux. The troopers wiped out half the band, including eight women and children. Two soldiers were killed at Sappa Creek, the last action of the Red River War.

NEGOTIATIONS AND PEACE TREATY

There were no negotiations during the brief Red River War. The Indians felt that white people had broken the terms of the Medicine Lodge Treaty of 1867; the white people felt that the Indians had defied its conditions. The war simply ended with the surrender of the Indians and their settling on the reservations of Oklahoma.

RESULTS OF THE WAR (CASUALTIES, COSTS, CONSEQUENCES)

Historians have not calculated a cost for the Red River War, but it would be equivalent to millions of 1990 dollars. If only the casualties of the ten-month war are counted, the whites' military losses came to some half dozen dead and twice as many wounded, and the Indians suffered some 50 dead and twice as many wounded. But if all the incidents and engagements (over the years 1867–1874) that contributed to that war are taken into consideration, white people could point to some 100 killed, and Indians to several hundred dead.

On March 13, 1875, President Ulysses S. Grant ordered the imprisonment of the ringleaders of Indian resistance. Altogether, 74 leaders—33 Cheyenne, 27 Kiowa, 11 Comanche, 2 Arapaho, and 1 Caddo—were arrested and, beginning on April 28, transported to Fort Marion, the old Spanish fortress-prison at St. Augustine, Florida. They were freed in 1878, and most returned to the reservations where their people had settled.

Not only would the Cheyenne, Kiowa, Comanche, Arapaho, and Plains Apache bands never again go on the warpath, but their way of life had been crushed by the Red River War.

The Nez Percé War

DATES OF WAR

June 13–October 5, 1877

SIGNIFICANCE

The Nez Percé War, which was essentially a four-month campaign with a foregone conclusion, has taken on an almost tragic status in American history for several reasons. One reason is the epic nature of the Nez Percé's 1,700-mile trek in their bid for freedom. Another is the Indian warriors' courage while inflicting heavy casualties on much stronger and better equipped U.S. Army troops. Finally, there are Chief Joseph's eloquent words at the time of his surrender (see Notable Phrases, p. 341). The sum of all those reasons is a war that has become an archetype of the Native Americans' doomed resistance to American expansion.

BACKGROUND

The Nez Percé inhabited the land on the border of what eventually became the states of Washington, Oregon, and Idaho. From the time the Nez Percé aided the Lewis and Clark expedition when it arrived in their territory in 1805, that tribe had lived in relative harmony with the whites who moved onto their lands. Like many tribes, however, the Nez Percé split into factions under the impact of white culture. From the 1850s on, many Nez Percé followed missionary teachings and became sedentary, learning to live by farming in ancestral homelands in Idaho reserved for them by terms of an 1855 treaty. But about a third of the Nez Percé, the band of old Chief Joseph, dissented.

When the Idaho gold rush of the early 1860s increased pressure on Indian lands, the U.S. government in 1863 negotiated a new treaty that relieved the Nez Percé of still more of their home country. Old Chief Joseph's faction refused to accept the treaty. For several years, the band lived undisturbed in the remote Wallowa River valley in Oregon across the Idaho line. Then, in the mid-1870s, by which time young Joseph had succeeded his father as chief, ranchers laid claim to even that valley for grazing lands. In response to increased agitation by settlers, the U.S. government forced young Chief Joseph and his band out of the Wallowa River valley and onto the Lapwai Reservation in Idaho.

CAUSES OF THE WAR

In March 1877, the Interior Department asked the army to carry out the forced removal of the faction of Nez Percé under young Chief Joseph. Gen. Oliver O. Howard was the U.S. Army commander in the Northwest, and it was his responsibility to remove Chief Joseph. Howard agreed that old Joseph had never ceded the Wallowa River valley and proposed his own solution: buy the valley lands before moving all the Nez Percé to the smaller Lapwai Reservation in Idaho. When the chiefs refused in councils of November 1876 and May 1877 to sell at any price, Howard issued an ultimatum: Chief Joseph and his band had 30 days to quit the Wallowa River valley or face expulsion.

The Nez Percé chiefs finally agreed to leave, but en route to the reservation in mid-June, rebellious and drunken warriors raided a white settlement, killing four settlers known to have mistreated Indians. Other warriors joined the raiding parties, in which another 15 settlers were killed. The Nez Percé War had begun.

PREPARATIONS FOR WAR

Gen. Oliver Howard had many months to anticipate the resistance by Chief Joseph and his followers and could count on some several thousand regular troops stationed in the several forts in the northwest.

DECLARATION OF WAR

There was no declaration of war, but the Interior Department and War Department, operating under the authority of President Rutherford B. Hayes, initiated the orders and ultimatum that General Howard delivered to the Nez Percé.

COMBATANTS

At the outset, General Howard's mobile column consisted of 400 infantry and cavalry. Three separate forces participated in later stages of the campaign, bringing the total U.S. forces to more than 2,000.

Chief Joseph's band counted 300 warriors, with 500 women and children in train.

GEOGRAPHIC AND STRATEGIC CONSIDERATIONS

The territory originally in dispute was the Wallowa River valley in the northeastern corner of Oregon.

BATTLES AND CAMPAIGNS

After the two incidents in which settlers were killed, Chief Joseph decided that he should take his people out of reach of the U.S. forces in Oregon, and he set out with his followers eastward on the Salmon River into Idaho.

June–July, 1877: On June 17, in the Battle of White Bird Canyon (in northwestern Idaho just over the border from Oregon), the Nez Percé drove off a detachment of 100 cavalry. The cavalry suffered heavy losses, including 34 killed. Three Indians were wounded; none were killed.

Gen. Oliver Howard's column set off in pursuit. Over the next two weeks, the Nez Percé band, skirmishing occasionally, managed to keep a step ahead of the soldiers. On July 3, a Nez Percé war party ambushed a patrol of ten troopers and killed them all. Finally, during the second week in July, the soldiers caught up with the Nez Percé, who were camped on a plateau above the south fork of the Clearwater River in north-central Idaho.

July 11–12, 1877 (Battle of the Clearwater): Howard's scouts found the Indian village on the Clearwater River around noon on July 11 and deployed for battle. For seven hours that afternoon, the two sides exchanged heavy fire. After an overnight lull, the battle resumed the next morning. A sudden charge unhinged the Nez Percé defenses, and a follow-up attack soon turned Howard's advantage into a rout. The Indians withdrew to the north in disorder. Howard's artillery harassed the fleeing band, but he did not aggressively pursue the Indians.

Army casualties were 15 killed and 27 wounded. Howard claimed to have counted 23 Nez Percé corpses; later, the Indians reported losses of only 4 killed and 6 wounded.

July 15, 1877: In council, after some argument, Joseph and the other chiefs decided on a hard trek over the Bitterroot Mountains to the buffalo plains of Montana. After a time, the argument ran, the trouble would pass and the Nez

Percé could return to their home valley.

Howard delayed for a day or two at the Clearwater River, giving the Nez Percé a head start. By early August, the band had crossed the mountain spine and descended into the Bitterroot River valley in western Montana. A pause for rest on the Big Hole River allowed a second U.S column, 200 riflemen of the 7th Infantry from Fort Shaw, Montana, under Col. John Gibbon, to surprise the Indians in camp.

August 9–10, 1877: Gibbon attacked the sleeping camp at daybreak, inflicting heavy losses. (The Army counted 89 Indian corpses.) Under war chiefs White Bird and Looking Glass, the Nez Percé rallied, however, and mounted a successful counterattack. Firing with deadly accuracy, they kept Gibbon's force pinned down for two days, allowing the women and children to escape. The warriors followed at the end of the second day, having inflicted losses of 71 dead or wounded on Gibbon's command.

The trek continued southward, across the corner of the recently established Yellowstone National Park, where Nez Percé raiders killed two tourists. Howard, reinforced to a total strength of 700, pursued. By early September the Nez Percé had slipped through an obscure pass in the Bitterroot Mountains and reached the plains of southern Montana.

September 13, 1877: Approaching from the east, troopers of the 7th Cavalry caught up with the Indians at Canyon Creek near the Yellowstone River in south-central Montana. The band held off the cavalry, killing or wounding 14 troopers, while the women and children once again slipped away. By that time, Chief Joseph and his council of chiefs had decided that their only hope lay in moving all the way to Canada, where they would join the Sioux led by Sitting Bull. They faced a journey of some 240 miles.

Meanwhile, another U.S. column under Col. Nelson A. Miles marched to the northwest from Fort Keogh in eastern Montana to intercept the Nez Percé before they could reach the border.

September 30, 1877: Miles's column found the Nez Percé camped on Snake Creek in the Bear Paw Mountains in north-central Montana only 40 miles south of the Canadian border. Swinging wide around the camp, a 2nd Cavalry detachment captured most of the band's pony herd. Miles's frontal assault with infantry failed, however, at a cost of 60 killed or wounded.

In council, Chief Joseph urged negotiation; White Bird and other war chiefs proposed to fight on. In the end, White Bird led part of the Nez Percé in a successful breakout; altogether, 98 warriors and about 200 women and children managed to reach Canada.

October 5, 1877: Chief Joseph and the 400 remaining Nez Percé surrendered on Miles's terms. General Howard had arrived the day before, and he handled the negotiations with Chief Joseph (see Notable Phrases, p. 341).

NEGOTIATIONS AND PEACE TREATY

When the U.S. Army caught up with Chief Joseph in October, there was no longer any chance for real negotiations. Generals Miles and Howard, however, promised the Nez Percé that they would be resettled on the Lapwai Reservation in Idaho. Chief Joseph later said that he would not have given up without that assurance, but, in fact, he and his people had no other options at that time.

RESULTS OF THE WAR (CASUALTIES, COSTS, CONSEQUENCES)

No historian has put a price on the Nez Percé War, but it cost the equivalent of several million 1990 dollars. The whites, including settlers and military, counted some 180 dead and 150 wounded. The Indians lost at least 120.

Immediately after Chief Joseph and his followers surrendered, Gen. William Sherman, commander of the U.S. Army, overruled the promise given by Generals Miles and Howard. Over Miles's protests, the Nez Percé were escorted to a reservation at Fort Leavenworth, Kansas, in the spring of 1878. The Nez Percé were never allowed to return to the Wallowa River valley. In 1885, Chief Joseph and 150 Nez Percé were resettled on the Colville Reservation in Washington; another 100 or so were moved to the Lapwai Reservation in Idaho. To the end of his life, Chief Joseph persisted in his efforts to return home, but he died on the Colville reserve in 1904.

The Ute War

DATES OF WAR

September 29–October 21, 1879

SIGNIFICANCE

The Ute War was so brief that it hardly warrants the label "war," but it owes its significance to the bitter ironies that underlay the bloody incidents. The Ute were a once-aggressive tribe that had pretty much settled down; their chiefs had signed treaties, and many Ute cooperated with white forces as mercenaries. Nathan Meeker, the head of the Indian agency at White River in northwestern Colorado, was an intelligent, even idealistic man who soon became rigid in his belief that he knew what was best for the Indians. Then, even as Ute chiefs and Meeker himself tried desperately to stop the course of events, those events escalated to a bloody showdown.

BACKGROUND

The Ute in the late 1600s had led a nomadic existence across the Great Plains. By the 1870s, seven Ute bands with a total population of about 4,000 occupied a large area of western Colorado and eastern Utah, lands reserved for the tribe by treaties of 1863 and 1868. Within a few years of the latter agreement, however, the discovery of silver brought thousands of miners onto the Ute lands. With the 1873 silver strike in the San Juan Mountains of southwestern Colorado, Ute bands were forced to surrender another 4 million acres. When Colorado won admission into the Union in 1876, local officials agitated for the complete removal of the Ute and the opening of reservation lands to settlement and development.

CAUSES OF THE WAR

Nathan C. Meeker, a journalist, had moved to Colorado in 1869 with the intent of establishing a cooperative agricultural colony. Then, in 1878, he became the head of the U.S. government's Indian agency at White River. He soon antagonized the local Ute Indians with his plans for raising them to an "enlightened, scientific, and religious stage."

The immediate issue was his insistence that the Ute reject their life of hunting and herding and turn to farming. By the summer of 1879, Ute chiefs Jack and Douglas were mobilizing the White River bands' resistance to Meeker, and the agent was asking for U.S. troops to enforce his farming schemes.

On September 10, 1879, a Ute medicine man, Johnson by name, went to Meeker's house to protest the plowing of Ute grazing lands. "You have too many ponies," Meeker told him. "You had better kill some of them." Furious, Johnson pushed Meeker, then left. On September 12, Meeker wired the Indian Bureau in Washington, D.C., that he and his employees were in danger.

PREPARATIONS FOR WAR

On September 16, Maj. Thomas T. Thornburgh, commanding at Fort Fred Steele, Wyoming, 150 miles northeast of the White River Indian agency, received orders to march on the agency. He set out on September 21 with some 200 infantry and cavalry, and a wagon train.

On September 26, Chief Jack and a delegation of Ute met Thornburgh's column 50 miles north of the agency and tried to persuade Thornburgh to turn back. When Chief Jack informed Meeker of the danger of violence if the soldiers appeared, Meeker became alarmed. He joined the Indians in asking Thornburgh to halt the advance and come ahead with only a small escort for a parley. Thornburgh agreed at first, then ordered his entire force to move to within supporting distance of the agency.

DECLARATION OF WAR

There was no formal declaration of war, but the Department of the Interior, which was responsible for the Bureau of Indian Affairs, and the War Department acted with the support of the president. Upon receiving Meeker's telegram, the War Department ordered Major Thornburgh to move out.

COMBATANTS

When the hostilities began, the U.S. Army assigned only some 200 men to confront the Ute, but within a few weeks, the Army had over 3,000 en route to attack the tribe.

The Indians, almost all Ute, never mustered more than some 300 warriors.

GEOGRAPHIC AND STRATEGIC CONSIDERATIONS

The land in dispute constituted about 12 million acres in northwestern Colorado, much of it grassland in a well-watered plateau ringed south and east by the Rocky Mountains. The Ute had been pushed back into that area only within the previous 20 years, but they could count on that grazing land for the horses and cattle on which they depended. White miners and settlers, who had moved into Colorado in large numbers, wanted to remove the Indians from that land so they could cultivate it. The two main incidents occurred within that northwestern corner of Colorado; most of the Army troops involved came down from Wyoming.

BATTLES AND CAMPAIGNS

September 29, 1879: At around noon, Maj. Thomas T. Thornburgh with 120 troopers forded Milk Creek at the northern border of the Ute reservation. Chief Jack with 100 warriors commanded the trail. When Thornburgh sent an officer forward to parley, someone—whether a Ute or soldier is unknown—fired a shot that touched off the Battle of Milk Creek.

The troopers fell back to the creek and took up defensive positions around the wagon train. When Thornburgh was shot and killed, command fell to Capt. J. Scott Payne, who managed to send out messengers with word of the fighting.

During the afternoon, another war party struck the White River Agency. Meeker and nine others were killed, and the agency buildings were set afire. Taking Meeker's wife, another woman, and three children captive, the warriors withdrew into the mountains.

The fighting went on intermittently for six days, with the Army's troops held down by the Indians' fire. The Indians were reinforced by another 200 warriors.

October 2, 1879: The 9th Cavalry (African-Americans, under white officers) arrived at Milk Creek to reinforce Payne and his men. At Rawlins, Wyoming, Col. Wesley Merritt received orders to march south to Payne's relief. That same day, Chief Ouray, a venerable Ute leader from the Los Pinos Reservation in southwestern Colorado who had long tried to cooperate with white people, sent a message to the chiefs at the White River Agency and told them to cease fighting.

October 5, 1879: With Merritt's approach at the head of a powerful column of four troops of cavalry and five companies of infantry, Chief Jack's war party retreated into the mountains.

The Milk Creek siege cost the army 13 dead and 48 wounded. Chief Jack reported that 23 of his warriors had been killed in the battle (but the Army claimed 37 killed).

October 11, 1879: Merritt's force marched to the ruins of the White River Agency and discovered the bodies of Meeker and his agents. Reinforcements were rushed to Merritt, and soon other columns converged on the agency—more than 3,000 troops altogether. Fearing for the captive hostages, Interior Secretary Carl Schurz called for a halt to military operations and sent a commission to negotiate with the insurgents.

NEGOTIATIONS AND PEACE TREATY

October 21, 1879: The negotiators—former Indian agent Charles Adams and Chief Ouray—persuaded the rebellious bands to give up their prisoners. The commissioners judged the Indians not culpable in the Battle of Milk Creek—they had not been looking for a fight—but they charged 12 Utes with the murders of Meeker and the others and ordered them brought to trial.

RESULTS OF THE WAR (CASUALTIES, COSTS, CONSEQUENCES)

Historians have not calculated the cost of the Ute War, but it must have cost the equivalent of a few million 1990 dollars. The total casualties for whites came to 23 dead and some 50 wounded; the Indians suffered 23 dead (though the army counted 37 dead) and perhaps as many wounded.

Because none of the 12 charged with the "Meeker Massacre" could be directly linked to the killings, they were never tried. Colorado authorities, however, pressed their claims on Ute lands through the winter and spring of 1880. On June 15, 1880, Congress approved a new treaty, taking away most of the land of the Ute in Colorado. By late summer of 1881, nearly all the White River Ute had been forced out of Colorado and onto the Uinta Reservation in Utah; a small number were allowed to stay on a small reservation in southwestern Colorado.

The Sioux Wars

DATES OF WARS

The Black Hills War: March 1, 1876–May 6, 1877. Ghost Dance Campaign: November 20, 1890–January 15, 1891.

ALTERNATE NAMES

The Ghost Dance Campaign is sometimes called the Messiah War.

SIGNIFICANCE

The Sioux Wars—actually two short, sharp campaigns separated by a long lull of comparative peace—were ostensibly for control of a remote and rugged area of the West. Underlying the conflicts, however, were such issues as the U.S. government's practice of ignoring treaties, forcing Indians onto reservations, and generally subduing them. The central events of each war were two of the most powerful and enduring episodes of American history: the annihilation of Custer's cavalry at the Battle of the Little Bighorn in 1876 and the massacre of Sioux Indians at Wounded Knee in 1890. What is often forgotten is that the second action was conducted by the same cavalry regiment that was decimated at the first.

BACKGROUND

The Fort Laramie Treaty of 1868 guaranteed the Sioux, Cheyenne, and Arapaho permanent and sole possession of a vast territory west of the Missouri River, including the region where South Dakota, Wyoming, and Montana meet. At the time of the treaty, the U.S. authorities considered that land relatively worthless. Within four years, however, gold was discovered in the Black Hills, located along the border of South Dakota and Wyoming, and prospectors began to infiltrate the Indians' territory. By 1873, railroad survey parties were pushing up the Yellowstone River in Montana to lay out a route for the Northern Pacific Railroad. The white people's advance touched off a war for control of the Black Hills, the dwelling place of Sioux gods and sacred country to the Teton Sioux tribes.

CAUSES OF THE WARS

In 1874, the U.S. Army sent a reconnaissance expedition into the Black Hills with the goal of selecting a site for a new fort. The fact that that action was a clear violation of the Fort Laramie Treaty of 1868 did not deter the government. Lt. Col. George Armstrong Custer was placed in charge of the expedition, and in the spring of 1874, he led his 7th Cavalry regiment, some 1,000 strong, into the Black Hills. Accompanying him were geologists looking for valuable minerals. Soon word was sent back that gold had been discovered and, by the spring of 1875, thousands of miners had poured into the region. When the miners discovered even richer deposits of gold, still more miners rushed into the Black Hills. At first, the Army told the miners they were violating the treaty— soldiers even removed a few of them—but there was no consistent effort to enforce the treaty, and often as not soldiers protected the miners from attacks by the Indians.

Then another commission was sent out from Washington, D.C. In September 1875, the commission met with representatives of the Sioux and other tribes at White River in southwestern South Dakota. With some 20,000 Indians encamped nearby, the commissioners made their proposal: The United States would pay a sum to allow whites to mine the Black Hills and another sum to acquire a vast tract of land to the west. When the Indians refused both offers, the commissioners went back east. During the next several weeks, the authorities in Washington, D.C., decided that the Indians should be forced to accept the offers. The word went out during December that all Indians should return to their reservation in South Dakota.

PREPARATIONS FOR WAR

As it became clear that the Indians were going to ignore the financial offers and the ultimatum that followed, Gen. Philip H. Sheridan, commander of the Department of the Missouri, began to organize a campaign for the winter of 1876.

In early 1876, Sioux war parties began to concentrate for battle. Thousands of Sioux left the reservations to join Sitting Bull, Crazy Horse, Gall, and the other war chiefs in the Powder River country. They were joined by the northern Cheyenne, Arapaho, and Indians of other tribes.

DECLARATION OF WAR

There was no declaration of war from Washington, D.C., but there was an official ultimatum

from the relevant authorities: All Sioux raiding and hunting parties were to report to a reservation agency by January 31, 1876, or consider themselves at war with the United States. On February 7, 1876, the War Department authorized Gen. Philip Sheridan to commence military operations against the hostile Sioux.

COMBATANTS

For the Black Hills War, Sheridan formed three powerful mobile columns: those of Gen. George Crook, Gen. Alfred H. Terry, and Col. John Gibbon. Crook was based in Fort Fetterman, Wyoming; Terry was based in Fort Abraham Lincoln in the Dakota Territory; and Gibbon drew on troops based in Fort Shaw and Fort Ellis in northern and central Montana. Those units totaled about 2,500 regular cavalry and infantry. They were also accompanied by some 315 Crow and Shoshone allies—some merely scouts, but many prepared to fight against their traditional enemy, the Sioux. During the next 15 years, sometimes as many as 10,000 troops were assigned to track down and fight the Indians.

There were an estimated 30,000 Indians roaming the northern Plains; most were Sioux, but there were also many northern Cheyenne and Arapaho. Estimates of the total number of warriors rose to as many as 4,000.

THE BLACK HILLS WAR

BATTLES AND CAMPAIGNS

March 1, 1876: With some 1,000 regulars and 250 Crow and Shoshone allies, Gen. George Crook marched north from Fort Fetterman, Wyoming, up the Bozeman Trail into unceded territory. For three weeks, in bitter cold, snow, and ice, Crook's patrols searched for Indians in the Powder River country of southeastern Montana.

March 17, 1876: In the Battle of Powder River, Crook's cavalry under Col. Joseph J. Reynolds charged an Oglala Sioux–Cheyenne village of 105 lodges. About 200 warriors and their women and children lived in the village. The Indians were caught off guard and had to retreat in order to save the women and children, so the cavalry destroyed the village and took away more than 1,200 ponies and horses. During the night, the warriors recaptured the pony herd and forced

This photograph shows a column of cavalry and artillery commanded by Lt. Col. George Custer on the 1876 expedition into the Black Hills of Dakota.

Reynolds to withdraw. Cavalry losses were four killed and six wounded; Indian casualties were thought to be few.

That inconclusive battle marked the end of the brief winter campaign. For summer operations, Gen. Philip Sheridan ordered General Crook and his 1,000-strong command to again move up from the south. Sheridan ordered Gen. Alfred H. Terry and some 1,000 men (including Lt. Col. George Armstrong Custer and his 7th Cavalry) to penetrate Indian country from the east and Col. John Gibbon with 450 men to approach from the west.

June 17, 1876: Crook's column halted at the head of Rosebud Creek. When scouts reported the approach of a large war party of Sioux and Cheyenne, the troops moved hastily into defensive positions, fanning out over the hilly, broken ground. In a six-hour battle along a line of 3 miles, the troops held off repeated Indian attacks. Most of Crook's tactical maneuvers misfired until, in one unplanned movement, a cavalry squadron found itself in the rear of the main Indian force. With that threat, the Sioux and Cheyenne broke off the battle.

Left in possession of the battlefield, Crook claimed a victory in the Battle of Rosebud Creek. But he had suffered heavy casualties—at least 10 killed, 21 wounded. He withdrew to his base,

refusing to take the field again until reinforced. Indian casualties were high as well—about 36 killed—but warriors newly arriving from the reservations more than made up the losses.

June 21, 1876: Unaware of the battle of four days before, Generals Terry and Gibbon met on a boat on the Yellowstone River at the mouth of Rosebud Creek. Scouts reported a large Sioux camp on the Little Bighorn River to the southwest, and the two commanders planned how they would bring the Indians to battle.

Terry ordered Custer to take his 7th Cavalry and push up Rosebud Creek, cross over to the Little Bighorn River and sweep south down the valley in search of Indians, driving them into the columns of Terry and Gibbon, which were to take up a blocking position to the south.

June 22, 1876: Custer set out with some 600 troopers and a pack train.

June 25, 1876 (Battle of the Little Bighorn): From high ground at dawn, Custer's scouts saw the Indian camp some 15 miles distant, and, at the same time, they detected signs of a Sioux war party close by. Figuring the Sioux would alert the village to scatter, Custer resolved to attack at once. In fact, 1,800 well-armed warriors, three times Custer's strength, were approaching. Custer divided his command, sending three troops of the 7th Cavalry, about 125 men, under Capt. Frederick Benteen off on a scout to the south. Moving up to the Little Bighorn, Custer then detached another three troops under Maj. Jesse Reno to cross the river and attack the village. Custer planned to come to Reno's support, striking the village from the north with his five troops. (About 100 of Custer's force were left in place as a supply column.)

The village turned out to be far larger than Custer had thought. Reno, with 175 men, soon found himself engaged in the fight of his life. Custer's 210 troopers were cut off in rough ground and unable to come to Reno's assistance. And Benteen had wandered too far off to the south to assist either detachment.

The Indians then turned north, toward Custer. A combined force of Cheyenne (led by Two Moon) and Hunkpapa Sioux (led by Gall) splashed across the Little Bighorn and charged the troopers. At the same time, Oglalas under Crazy Horse curled around to attack Custer in the flank and from behind. The two forces then moved in to overwhelm the five troops of the 7th

Cavalry. In less than an hour, Custer and his entire detachment were destroyed.

Meanwhile, Reno, 4 miles upriver, lost close to half his command—40 killed, 13 wounded, and 17 missing. Benteen rejoined Reno, and then the pack train turned up, boosting the strength of what remained of the 7th Cavalry to 368 officers and enlisted men. Benteen showed Reno a message from Custer's adjutant, delivered by Custer's trumpeter: "Be quick," it read. "Big village." Surrounded, the remnant of the 7th Cavalry fought off periodic attacks until nightfall, when a lull fell over the bloody ground.

June 26, 1876: The fight continued through most of the day. Firing from shallow trenches, Reno's troopers repulsed two heavy charges and sustained further casualties, for a two-day total of 47 killed and 53 wounded. Late that afternoon, the entire Indian village moved to the south, toward the Bighorn Mountains. The warriors soon followed, setting the prairie grass afire to cover the withdrawal.

June 27, 1876: Terry's scouts found Custer and his men scattered along the ridge overlooking the Little Bighorn River. Most of the corpses had been stripped; some had been scalped or mutilated. Custer had died from two bullet wounds and had not been scalped.

July–August 1876: Terry and Crook were quickly reinforced to a total of almost 4,000 infantry and cavalry, and they set off in pursuit of the Indian bands. Hectic and fruitless pursuits wore down the troops, and the weather turned demoralizingly foul. "It has reached beyond a joke that we should be kept out and exposed because two fools do not know their business," one junior officer wrote home. Throughout July and August, the troops failed to engage any Indians. Terry gave up the chase; Crook continued on, turning east, then south into South Dakota.

September 9, 1876: An advance party of Crook's force came across a Sioux village at the end of a ridge in northwestern South Dakota called Slim Buttes. Sending word back to Crook, the party of 100 men attacked the village at once. Most of the Indians fled, but about 20 were trapped in a cave. Crook arrived with his main force, and they fired on those in the cave, killing five and wounding about as many. While the Army was destroying the village, Sitting Bull and Gall arrived with about 600 warriors, but the sol-diers were able to hold them off and get away; the Army counted two dead, nine wounded.

The main Indian body remained at large, most of the Indians having gone to the north. After a rest and refit, Crook, in late autumn, headed up the Bozeman Trail with 2,200 cavalry, infantry, and artillery.

November 26, 1876: Crook's cavalry under Col. Ranald Mackenzie (and supported by mercenary Pawnee) surprised a large Cheyenne camp in a canyon in the Bighorn Mountains in northern Wyoming. The Cheyenne, led by Dull Knife, fled through the snow and cold, leaving behind some 30 to 40 dead as well as hundreds of horses and ponies; the Army's casualties numbered 6 dead and 26 wounded.

The main effect of Mackenzie's strike was to turn some 1,000 Cheyenne out into the winter wilderness without shelter and with little clothing and food. On the night after the battle the temperature plunged to 30 degrees below zero. After several days of desperate fighting, the Cheyenne joined Crazy Horse and his group of Sioux at Box Elder Creek on the Powder River.

With the end of Mackenzie's operation, Crook retired into winter quarters. Col. Nelson Miles, however, remained in the field. With a column of 500 men, Miles kept up the pursuit through the autumn and into the fierce Plains winter.

January 8–18, 1877: Colonel Miles caught up with a war party of more than 500 Sioux and Cheyenne at Battle Butte near the Wolf Mountains on the Tongue River in southeastern Montana. More than a foot of snow lay on the ground, and snow was falling steadily when the Indians attacked a little after daybreak on January 8. Miles's troops became trapped in a canyon, but the battle turned into a standoff as the storm blew into a blizzard. No deaths were reported, but several on both sides were wounded. The Indians withdrew toward the Bighorn Mountains as the blizzard intensified. By January 18, Miles had safely returned to his base.

Winter–Spring 1877: As the winter wore on, Sitting Bull led his Hunkpapa Sioux across the border into Canada. In the spring, the surviving Cheyenne surrendered to Colonel Miles at Fort Robinson in northwest Nebraska. Around the same time, many of the Sioux drifted south and surrendered at the Red Cloud Agency. Crazy Horse also made preparations to turn in his band of Oglalas, which was close to starvation.

May 6, 1877: With 1,100 Sioux and Cheyenne and 1,700 ponies, Crazy Horse approached Fort Robinson near the Red Cloud Agency. The chief and 300 Sioux warriors sang a peace song, and soon the women and the reservation Indians joined in. Crazy Horse had given up the warpath, bringing the Black Hills War to a close.

1877–1890: During this period, several government peace commissions and federal laws forced new agreements on the Sioux. Under the new terms, increasing amounts of land were withdrawn from the reserved lands, foreshadowing the end of the Sioux and Cheyenne as free peoples. The Indians found themselves forced onto smaller and smaller reservations.

Crazy Horse never adapted to reservation life. The government watched him closely as a potential insurgent and, in early September 1877, moved to arrest him. On September 5, in a scuffle with his guards, Crazy Horse was bayoneted and died a few hours later.

Sitting Bull continued his holdout. "So long as there remains a gopher to eat, I will not go back," he said. By 1881, though, even gophers were scarce. On July 19, his band down to 200, Sitting Bull came to Fort Buford in northwestern North Dakota and handed over his Winchester. "I wish it to be remembered that I was the last man of my tribe to surrender my rifle," he said.

The northern Cheyenne were deported to a reservation with the southern Cheyenne in the Indian Territory in present-day Oklahoma. Unhappy, hungry, and ill, about 300 Cheyenne led by Dull Knife and Little Wolf broke out in September 1878. During the next six weeks, as they made their way across 1,500 miles, they were pursued by as many as 10,000 troops. At the Platte River, they split, with Little Wolf's group heading north to the Tongue River. In late winter 1879, Little Wolf's group surrendered and was taken to Fort Keogh at the junction of the Tongue and Yellowstone Rivers. Dull Knife's group was captured in late October 1878 and imprisoned at Fort Robinson in northwest Nebraska. Conditions were so bad at Fort Robinson that on January 9, 1879, most of the Cheyenne tried to escape, but 64 were killed and 78 were recaptured. About 30 got away, however, and were allowed to remain in the Rosebud valley.

In many cases, if not most, the reservation system reduced the Sioux to a permanent condition of dull misery. Confinement destroyed the Plains peoples' two main vocations: hunting and raiding. During the late 1880s, a series of droughts reduced crop harvests. Then, the government moved yet again to deprive the Sioux of land, reducing the size of the six Dakota reserves. That was the backdrop for the last Indian uprising in the United States.

GHOST DANCE CAMPAIGN

With conditions on the reservations so demoralizing, it was no wonder that many Sioux listened to anyone who promised some relief. In 1889, word of Wovoka, a Paiute Indian prophet in Nevada, began to reach the reservations. Wovoka, mixing ancient Indian beliefs with elements of Christianity, revealed the mysterious and beautiful Ghost Dance. In the world of the Ghost Dance, long-dead loved ones would reappear on earth, the white settlers and soldiers would vanish, and buffalo would again be plentiful. There would be no poverty, no illness. There would be no war (see Notable Phrases, p. 341).

Wovoka's message spread quickly throughout the western reservations in 1889 and 1890. Some Sioux, however, amended Wovoka's teachings to claim that he called for a war on whites. Some Sioux also came to believe that there was a magical ghost shirt that would protect them from the white man's bullets. By November 1890, the Pine Ridge and Rosebud Reservations were in a state of near hysteria, with thousands of Indians dancing the Ghost Dance. Government agents could not agree on a response. Some wanted to allow the phenomenon to fade of its own accord; others wanted troops. "Indians are dancing in the snow and are wild and crazy," agent Daniel F. Royer wired Washington, D.C., on November 15. "We need protection and we need it now."

BATTLES AND CAMPAIGNS

November 1890: The first troops, infantry and cavalry, turned up at Pine Ridge and Rosebud Reservations. Sitting Bull, a resident of the Standing Rock Reservation and still the most respected leader of the Sioux, was not entirely opposed to the Ghost Dance, but he did not want to see it become an excuse for action by the troops. He encouraged Short Bull and Kicking Bear, the two Sioux leaders of the Ghost Dance movement, to take their hundreds of followers to locales removed from the Sioux reservations.

Despite Sitting Bull's restrained conduct, Gen. Nelson Miles, the army commander, endorsed a proposal to arrest him as a potential insurgent leader. In a near-farce, Miles sent William F. ("Buffalo Bill") Cody, who had employed Sitting Bull in his traveling Wild West show in 1885, to make the arrest. Higher authority in Washington, D.C., canceled Cody's assignment before he could carry it out.

December 15, 1890: A detachment of 43 Indian police surrounded Sitting Bull's cabin and took the chief captive. A crowd surrounded the posse and shots were fired; Sitting Bull fell to the ground dead. A melee ensued and eight Sioux were killed and six Indian police were killed.

December 28, 1890: Miles moved to arrest a second chief he regarded as subversive, the Miniconjou leader Big Foot. Fearing he might be in danger after the death of Sitting Bull, Big Foot had set out with several hundred of his people for the Pine Ridge Reservation. When he was stopped by a squad from the 7th Cavalry, he was ordered to take his followers and camp near the cavalry's encampment at Wounded Knee Creek. There were some 350 Sioux, 230 of them women and children. The officer in charge, seeing that Big Foot was suffering from pneumonia, had him transferred to an Army ambulance wagon.

December 29, 1890: The rest of the 7th Cavalry had gathered at the camp during the night, bringing their strength to 500 troops. They had also placed four Hotchkiss guns on the ridge overlooking the Indians. In the morning, the officers called the Sioux leaders out and told them that the Indians must turn in all their arms. As the troops began to rummage through the tents, forcing the Indians to remove their blankets so they could be searched, a Ghost Dancer began to dance, encouraging the Sioux to believe that the white men's bullets could not harm them. An accidental discharge of a rifle by a young Indian provoked a volley from the soldiers. In the close-range fight that immediately ensued, some of the Sioux had firearms they had been hiding, but most fought with their hatchets, clubs, and knives. Big Foot was shot dead as he watched from the ambulance. In due course, the troops pulled back to allow the heavy weapons to fire. The four fast-firing Hotchkiss guns opened up, and, in less than an hour, two-thirds of Big Foot's band was wiped out. Sioux deaths at Wounded Knee

totaled at least 200; another 50 were wounded, and many of those who fled into the wilderness soon froze to death. About 25 soldiers died (many from friendly fire) and about 40 were wounded.

December 30, 1890: A Sioux war party ambushed a 7th Cavalry detachment at Drexel Mission near Wounded Knee Creek, killing two troopers and wounding five. But Miles was moving toward Pine Ridge with some 3,500 troops. The chiefs met in council to decide what to do. Faced with overwhelming force, they advocated that all the Ghost Dance followers surrender.

January 1–14, 1891: Miles laid siege to an Indian encampment, with about 800 to 1,000 warriors, and sent out peace emissaries. By the second week in January, hundreds of Indians were streaming toward the Pine Ridge agency.

January 15, 1891: The last of the insurgent leaders, Kicking Bear, surrendered his rifle to Miles, concluding the Ghost Dance Campaign.

NEGOTIATIONS AND PEACE TREATY

Throughout the years spanning the Sioux Wars, there had been an almost continual series of negotiations, some conducted by commissioners sent out from Washington, D.C., others simply conducted by officers in the field. (Many individual officers were fairly sympathetic to the Indians' situation and offered generous terms that were overturned by their superiors.) Once backed by the congressional act of 1871 (see Background, pp. 296-297), white negotiators no longer felt the Indians had rights. The Indians simply had to accept the conditions laid down by whites. In effect, it was no longer a question of *what* was to happen to the Indians, only when and where. So although many agreements with Indians were signed in the ensuing years (74 between 1871 and 1902) and hundreds of special laws were passed, there was no final peace treaty with the Indians.

RESULTS OF THE WAR (CASUALTIES, COSTS, CONSEQUENCES)

Historians have not tried to assign a price to the Sioux Wars, but even counting only the most direct costs the sum would be equivalent to several billion 1990 dollars. The U.S. Army maintained a network of forts, thousands of troops, and an ambitious supply system. And thou-

The frozen body of the Sioux chief Big Foot was photographed after he had been killed at Wounded Knee on December 29, 1890.

sands of Indians who had been supporting themselves for centuries became wards of the U.S. government because they were deprived of their sources of food.

The casualties for both sides are difficult to pin down, primarily because so many white civilians were killed in isolated incidents, and Indian casualties have always been somewhat approximate. In recorded engagements, U.S. forces reported about 350 dead (most of those in 48 hours at Little Bighorn) and about as many wounded; the Indians' battle casualties were about the same (if the 200 killed at Wounded Knee are included), but many hundreds more died from starvation, cold, and generally harsh conditions while fleeing the pursuing troops.

Despite the Indians' victory at Little Bighorn, the hostilities of 1876 ended the military threat of the northern Plains tribes. The 1890 campaign ended the long history of white warfare against the Indians. Almost all Indians were now confined to reservations. The trans-Mississippi West was now available for white people to settle as they saw fit.

RESULTS OF THE WARS (Casualties, Costs, Consequences)

No historian or government agency has ever

attempted to add up the costs for all these 19th-Century Trans-Mississippi Indian Wars for either side. For white Americans, on one level the wars cost billions of dollars (in 1990 dollars), even considering only direct expenses for the military operations, everything from cavalry units' wages and the network of forts to armaments and the War Department in Washington, D.C. Beyond those costs, the costs to the civilians directly engaged (everything from their weapons to destroyed crops and property) need to be considered. That excludes indirect costs such as widows' and veterans' pensions. Meanwhile, white Americans' acquired a vast amount of land and resources, but there is really no way of calculating the net gains, from petroleum deposits to tourist attractions.

Likewise, there is no way of putting a dollar value on all that the Indians lost, even when only the literal expenses of the 19th-Century Trans-Mississippi Indian Wars are in question. Another item that must be considered are the great buffalo herds. When the white settlers began to move across the Mississippi River in the 1850s, there were an estimated 20 million buffalo; in 1889, by one count, only 551 buffalo could be located in the United States. No one can put a price on those buffalo (although their hides earned a large amount of money for white people) or what their near extinction cost the Indians. As for land, when the 19th century began, almost all the trans-Mississippi land belonged to the Indians (setting aside the claims of Spain, France, and other European nations); by 1900, the Indians were confined to about 130 million acres, approximately 9 percent of that land.

The question of casualties during the 19th-Century Trans-Mississippi Indian Wars is equally tangled and unknowable. Historians, in general, tend not to try to make such calculations; but just adding up the most obvious military casualties of the separate wars (from 1832 to 1891) and estimating the number of civilian deaths, some 5,000 white people were killed and at least twice that many wounded in the trans-Mississippi wars. Those were relatively low casualties, given the time and space involved and the ultimate outcome. Far more lives were lost in a few hours in the Civil War or when a single ship went down at sea in World War II than were lost in the worst single battle of the 19th-Century Trans-Mississippi Indian Wars, the Battle of Little Bighorn.

The Indian casualties are even more difficult to calculate. Estimates of how many Indians were living in the trans-Mississippi West around 1840 vary widely, but cluster around 350,000. By 1900, there were probably only some 220,000 Indians living in the trans-Mississippi West. During 1840–1900, the Indian population might well have doubled under peaceful conditions. But not all the attrition can be assigned to the wars with white people in the strictest sense: Most Indians died from new diseases, general deprivation and substandard living conditions, and organized or random attacks. The several infamous removals of Indians took the lives of thousands of Indians but are not generally labeled wars. The Indian population of California dropped from about 275,000 in 1800 to only 15,000 in 1900, yet nothing worthy of being called a war occurred there: brutal attacks simply killed off the Indians in scores of separate incidents.

For white Americans, the most tangible result of the 19th-Century Trans-Mississippi Indian Wars was the acquisition and securing of the millions of acres and vast amounts of natural resourecs that became available for exploitation. The land involved in those wars constituted some 1.35 billion acres, 70 percent of the total area of the present-day 48 contiguous states. In fact, white Americans had been living in many

parts of those lands for some years. But one by one, the 19th-Century Trans-Mississippi Indian Wars (as well as other episodes, such as the removals) pushed the Indians off the land and onto restricted reservations, and those vast territories became pacified. The white settlers were then completely free to do with the land as they pleased. They farmed, they mined, they built factories, they laid down roads and railroad tracks and built dams, they developed cities. Such activities disrupted Indian life as much as the wars did. And the sheer numbers of white settlers overwhelmed the Indians: In 1840, there were only some 20,000 white people living west of the Misissippi River; the 1890 census counted 8.5 million settlers on former trans-Mississippi Indian lands.

As their numbers increased, the whites organized governments, which eventually applied for and attained the status of states. The result, then, was the consolidation of the United States as a transcontinental nation. By the closing decade of the century, the United States had spanned the entire continent, subdued the Indians tribes and confined the indigenous peoples within the bounds of reservations. In 1889, the government opened the largest reservation, the area of the southern Plains designated Indian Territory, to white settlement. (That region, once the treaty-guaranteed preserve of Native Americans, eventually became, in 1907, Oklahoma, the 46th state of the Union.) There were a few minor episodes, or skirmishes, involving U.S. troops and Indians—Chippewa in Minnesota in 1898, Ute in Colorado and Utah in 1907, Navajo in 1913, and Ute in 1915—but the Indian wars effectively ended at Wounded Knee.

The results for the Native Americans were the opposite: The land and resources gained by the white settlers were lost by the Indians. The great buffalo herds that had sustained the Sioux and Cheyenne were a memory. Cattle grazed in the old Comanche strongholds of Texas. Miners scratched at the foothills of the Rockies without fear of visitation from Ute raiders. "In the short span of two decades, the final surge of the westward movement had overwhelmed all the tribes of the trans-Mississippi West," historian Robert M. Utley has written. "Their territory appropriated, their traditional food sources destroyed, they had yielded to military coercion and diplomatic persuasion and accepted the proffered substitute—reservations and government dole."

The outlines of the reservation system were in place as early as 1875. By the mid-1880s, 187 reservations totaling 116 million acres held 243,000 Indians. Reservation life undermined traditional Indian institutions and ways; poverty and misery were endemic; and the Department of the Interior's Indian Affairs Bureau, which administered the reserved lands, became a byword for corruption. Today, some 1.5 million Native Americans in the trans-Mississippi West live on about 54 million acres of state and federal reservations, or some 4 percent of that total area.

Beyond the loss of land and population, the 19th-Century Trans-Mississippi Indian Wars had a massive impact on the Indians' psyches, cultures, and societies. It is important, however, not to assume that conquest, confinement, and coercion resulted in total destruction. The western tribes continued to exist and, against the odds, they managed to preserve many of their beliefs and traditions. A century later, many of those tribes continue to nurture and take pride in their Indian heritage.

Another of the legacies of the wars is a less tangible, but no less far-reaching one: The "winning of the West" is one of the major themes of U.S. history and identity. Long before Hollywood discovered the power of western images, many myths, legends, tales, novels, poems, songs, paintings, and sculptures drew on those conflicts. And just a few random allusions—Custer's Last Stand, Wells Fargo, sodbusters, cowboys and Indians, gunslingers, Geronimo, "circling the wagons," Buffalo Bill, Frederic Remington, and Charles Russell—remind us to what extent those conflicts remain part of the basic mythology of American life.

MILITARY INNOVATIONS, TACTICS, EQUIPMENT

The wars against the Indians did not call for very sophisticated armaments, but the Civil War did spur the development of more lethal weaponry which were then used against the Indians. The older powder-and-ball muskets had been replaced during the 1840s by the percussion rifles. By the Civil War, breech-loading rifles were coming into use, including the smoothbore Hall carbine and the Sharps "Buffalo Rifle." Then, in 1873, the Army adopted the Springfield Allin

model, which fired metallic cartridges more accurately and at longer ranges than had earlier models; it remained the U.S. Army standard until 1892. As the whites, both civilian and military, came to acquire the breech-loading rifles, they gained a further advantage over the Indians. Many cavalrymen preferred to carry the rapid-fire Spencer seven-shot carbine. The Westchester repeater rifle also came into use, although it was not issued by the Army. The Colt .45 caliber six-shooter of 1872 (dubed the "Peacemaker") became the armed forces' sidearm of choice, but comparable Remington and Starr models were also common.

After the Civil War, the artillery regiments in the West were supplied with some of the newer weapons. Among them were the Hotchkiss 2-pounder mountain gun; relatively mobile and fast-firing, it was accurate up to about 4,000 yards. There was also the Gatling gun, an early form of machine gun, capable of firing 350 rifle rounds a minute; it was known to overheat and jam, though, and not all commanders utilized it. In any case, such weaponry was often of little help in the guerrilla engagements the Indians preferred.

From years of trading with whites throughout the West, many insurgent Indians had managed to arm themselves with relatively modern weapons; even during the wars with white Americans, Indians sometimes acquired new weapons from U.S. government stores under the claim they were needed for hunting. In the post-Civil War era, most tribes favored the legendary Winchester repeating rifle, when it could be obtained. Meanwhile, many Indians continued to rely on their bows and arrows, lances, and hatchets.

The 19th-Century Trans-Mississippi Indian Wars were very much cavalrymen's wars: Both the U.S. forces and the Indians covered long distances over trails and fought many engagements on horseback. Cavalrymen had been part of armies for thousands of years, and the U.S. cavalry was well trained. But the Indians' swiftness, agility, and mobility on their horses forced the U.S. Army cavalry to modify its tactics.

Tactically, most U.S. operations were off-the-cuff. "An Indian war is a chapter of accidents," one young officer, Lt. Lawrence Kip, wrote in 1859. More often than not, the Army relied on conventional responses to subdue an unconventional foe. The Indians could be brilliant tacticians. Chief Joseph's fighting withdrawal from

Idaho across the Bitterroot Mountains and north toward Canada is regarded as a tactical masterpiece; he surrendered in the end only because he felt he could not subject the children and women to brutally harsh winter conditions.

Cadets at West Point were taught little or nothing about unconventional warfare, nor did the Army's post-Civil War professional schools deal with the subject. Experience obviously taught the Army much—at least enough to be successful in the Trans-Mississippi Indian Wars.

The U.S. Army also could rely on three new technologies denied the Indians: the railroad, the steamship, and the telegraph. Although all were used at times by the Army for logistical support, none played a significant role in the Army's tactical moves in the field.

LEGENDS AND TRIVIA

Several American presidents became associated with the hostilities with American Indians: William Henry Harrison rode to fame as the victor over Tecumseh ("Tippecanoe and Tyler, Too!" became Harrison's and running mate John Tyler's 1840 campaign slogan); Andrew Jackson enforced his reputation by defeating the Creek and removing many other tribes; Zachary Taylor owed some of his fame to fighting Indians.

Of all the incidents in the Trans-Mississippi Indian Wars, the destruction of Custer's command at the Battle of the Little Bighorn in 1876 has made perhaps the greatest impression on Americans. The outlines of the disaster are well known, and few of the facts are in dispute (see Sioux Wars, June 25, 1876, p. 333). All the same, Americans seemingly never tire of debating Custer's actions—bravery? arrogance? stupidity? or of dissecting his complex character. Indeed, **Custer's last stand** has become one of the touchstone events for Americans.

Among the western Indian tribes, the Regular Army's African American regiments became legendary, particularly the 9th and 10th Cavalry, which fought in many post-Civil War Indian campaigns. Freed from slavery yet denied full opportunities to work within white society, many young African-Americans enlisted in the U.S. Army. Although they were put into segregated units and commanded by white officers, they enjoyed a certain level of freedom, respect, and adventure. Sgt. William McBrayar, who fought in the Indian Wars, was the first black soldier to win the Congressional Medal of Honor. To the Indians, the black troopers were known as **"buffalo soldiers."** Different sources for that name have been proposed, ranging from the claim that the Indians said they fought the way tough bufffalo fought, to the claim that the soldiers' hair reminded Indians of a buffalo's mane.

Whatever the origin of the term, assigning men an animal's name was by no means an insult in Indian culture. On the contrary, Indians took great pride in being associated with animals. The Plains tribes, for instance, had a legendary fighting formation, the **Cheyenne Dog Soldiers**. Dating from around 1837, the Dog Soldiers were the hard-charging elite of the southern Cheyenne bands, perhaps the most skilled and aggressive warriors of the Plains. In the post-Civil War era, the Dog Soldiers consistently opposed the efforts of the Cheyenne peace chiefs to reach accommodation with the whites.

Most of the great Indian chiefs either were killed in their prime or spent their final years confined to reservations. Some of the great chiefs, however, were put on public display in a way that both honored and humiliated them. The once-feared **Geronimo** was brought to Washington, D.C., in 1905 and paraded through the streets as part of Theodore Roosevelt's inauguration procession. A famous 1885 photograph shows the Hunkpapa Sioux chief **Sitting Bull** in full-feathered regalia, posing with Buffalo Bill Cody. Sitting Bull traveled with Cody's popular Wild West Show in 1885; Cody paid him $50 a week and also gave Sitting Bull an opportunity to present the Sioux case to the politicians in Washington, D.C.

NOTABLE PHRASES

Damn any man who sympathizes with Indians! I have come to kill Indians and believe it is right and honorable to use any means under God's heaven to kill Indians!

Col. John M. Chivington uttered these words when one of his officers, Lt. Joseph Cramer, suggested that an attack on Black Kettle's camp would be a violation of promises made to the Indians. Soon thereafter Chivington's Colorado volunteer troops carried out the infamous Sand Creek Massacre 1864.

The only good Indian is a dead Indian.

Gen. Philip H. Sheridan allegedly uttered that infamous phrase, but no one has come up with solid proof of when and where. Some sources claim that he said it to the Comanche chief Toch-a-way (or Tosawi) at Fort Cobb in Indian Territory in January 1869, when the chief identified himself as a "good Indian." Other sources claim that it was in 1870 in the aftermath of the Marias River massacre in Montana, in which regulars under Maj. Eugene M. Baker killed 173 Piegan Indians, a third of them women and children. Sheridan always disavowed the remark. The phrase has also been variously reported, according to Sheridan's biographer, Roy Morris Jr., as, "A dead Indian is the only good Indian" and "The only good Indians I ever saw were dead."

I will fight no more forever.

After eluding the pursuing forces of Gen. Oliver Howard for several months in 1877, in October Chief Joseph and his fellow Nez Percé were forced to surrender in northern Montana. He dictated his surrender speech to a translator, and it included the following words: "I am tired of fighting. Our chiefs are killed... The little children are freezing to death. My people, some of them, have run away to the hills, and have no blankets, no food... Hear me, my chiefs. I am tired. My heart is sick and sad. From where the sun now stands, I will fight no more forever."

Once I moved about like the wind. Now I surrender to you, and that is all.

Geronimo was reported to have used those words in a surrender discussion with Gen. George Crook near the Mexican border in March 1886. In fact, he escaped soon thereafter, but five months later, he gave himself up for the last time.

You must not fight. Do no harm to anyone. Do right always.

The Paiute Wovoka, prophet of the Ghost Dance religion that swept the western tribes in 1889–1890, was quoted as asking that of his followers. As those words suggest, his message was strongly rooted in Christianity; he even called himself the messiah. Still, the Ghost Dance religion greatly alarmed the Indian agents on the Sioux reservations in South Dakota. It was a confrontation there in late 1890 that escalated into the tragedy at Wounded Knee.

SONGS

In the 19th-century U.S. Army, music played a critical role as a means of communication and as a morale builder. Drum-and-fife music woke soldiers and called them to meals. Bugle calls alerted soldiers to all kinds of military routines and battle maneuvers. Soldiers sang on the march. After the Civil War, campaign favorites such as "Marching Through Georgia" became the norm. Music was part of punishment too: Deserters, when caught, were drummed out of the service to the "Rogue's March."

There were many songs inspired by the westward movement in all its variants—pioneers, gold seekers, cowboys, robbers—but relatively few referred explicitly to the hostilities. The one late-20th-century Americans are most apt to think of, "Round Her Neck She Wore a Yellow Ribbon," has a complicated history (see Songs, Gulf War, p. xxx). No longer known but once widely sung was "The Sioux Indians." It told of a wagon train that was attacked by a band of Sioux; the men killed six in the first attack, and then:

> We killed their bold chief at the head
> of his band.
> He died like a warrior with his gun in
> his hand.
> They, seeing their bold chief lying dead
> in his gore,
> They whooped and they yelled and we
> saw them no more.

Another old favorite was "The Texas Rangers," often with words that refer to the enemy as Mexicans—or even Yankees—but in one version, the enemy is Indians:

> When I saw the Indians coming and
> heard their awful yell,
> My feelings at that moment no tongue
> can ever tell.
> I saw their glittering lances, the
> arrrows seemed to fly;
> And I thought unto my sorrow, "Now
> is my time to die."

Inevitably, there were many songs about Little Bighorn. One such was "Custer's Last Charge," which described the end in some detail:

Our gang went down three hundred souls,
    three hundred doomed to die.
Those blood-drunk braves sprang on the
    dead and wounded boys in blue;
Three hundred bleeding scalps ran high
    above the fiendish crew.

One thing noticeable in all the lyrics is that the Indians were characterized as, if not bloody savages, certainly hostile aggressors, and the white people come out as innocent victims.

Music and dance had profound and pervasive ritual and religious significance for many Indian tribes. Sioux war parties, for example, engaged in war songs and chants before the onset of hostilities. There are many references in first-person accounts by white observers of Indians singing or chanting at moments of great stress in their dealings with white people. In the late-19th and early-20th centuries, ethnologists recorded some of that music on paper and phonograph records, and some tribes have kept those songs and dances alive to this day.

HISTORICAL PERSPECTIVES AND CONTROVERSIES

What was the government's main purpose in prosecuting the Indian wars? Was extermination of Native Americans a goal?

Few historians would argue that the official policy of the United States was to wipe out entire tribes. On the other hand, there is no doubt that many innocents—among them women, children, and old people—suffered from the Sherman-Sheridan strategy of total war, and there were many occasions in which Indian noncombatants were needlessly and brutally killed. The massacres at Sand Creek (see Plains Wars of the 1860s, p. 316), Washita River (see p. 320), and Wounded Knee (see December 29, 1890, p. 336), are merely the best known of those. Most federal authorities—in practice, the regular Army and the Indian Bureau—would have argued that they were acting to protect white settlement, further the economic development of the country, and absorb the Indian tribes into the larger cul-

ture. Rather than eradicate the Indians, those officials claimed, they wanted to educate and Christianize them and make them self-sufficient through sedentary farming rather than through hunting.

Were the conflicts and conquests necessary? Could a middle way have been found?

Given the nature of human beings and the thrust of history, it is difficult to imagine how all westward movement might have been stopped, or how all Indian societies and landholdings of the trans-Mississippi West might have been preserved intact. On the other hand, it is not impossible to imagine more respectful dealings with the Indians and a fairer disposition of Indian lands. Had warfare been limited to direct engagements with selected warriors, there might have been a more peaceful withdrawal onto reservations. Treaties might have been renegotiated rather than broken; reservations might have been more fairly set aside.

How did contemporaries view the 19th-Century Trans-Mississippi Indian Wars? Was there a dissenting view or movement?

Newspaper reporting, the memoirs of participants, and early histories often presented the Indian wars as a clash between civilization and barbarism. For example, the many adventure novels of Charles King, a veteran of the Apache Wars, purveyed that simple, romantic view to a mass audience. In those accounts, Native Americans were portrayed as savages—often noble, sometimes debased—standing in the way of progress; they were to be brushed aside or, where willing, converted to white ways. Soldiers were the advance guard of civilization, making the West safe for miners, farmers, and merchants, fulfilling American's manifest destiny to settle the continent.

There are also countless examples of a far more ugly view of Indians. Many individuals, in their diaries and letters and reports—and certainly in their actions—made no secret of the fact that they viewed the Indians as virtually subhuman. Those people may not have controlled U.S. policies toward the Indians, but their views were not totally distinct from official views: Andrew Jackson referred to Indians as wolves.

It was not until after the Civil War that some white Americans, many of them former abolitionists, began to campaign for fair treatment for the western Indians. While settlers pressed for the elimination of the Indian threat, humanitarians pressed for checks on the settlers. "I only know the names of three savages upon the Plains," abolitionist Wendell Phillips remarked in 1870, "Colonel Baker, General Custer, and at the head of all, General Sheridan." By the end of the 19th century, there were numerous ethnologists, social activists, and reformers who were speaking out on behalf of the Indians. But it must also be said that some of those humanitarian reformers took a rather condescending view of Indians, seeing them as childlike beings who needed to be in the care of white people.

How have revisionist historians changed Americans' views of the 19th-Century Trans-Mississippi Indian Wars and the treatment of Indians?

The view of Indians as anachronisms, bound to give way before the march of progress, long prevailed in American popular culture, in popular fiction and, as the 20th century advanced, in movies and eventually on television. But starting in the 1960s, a number of scholars and even some popular writers initiated a major reappraisal of the whole westward movement and its treatment of the Indians. Some writers simply called for a more balanced view. In *Frontiersmen in Blue* (1967) and *Frontier Regulars* (1973), for example, military historian Robert M. Utley chronicled the campaigns of the westward movement with sympathy for both sides. The Army, Utley concluded, "wrote a dramatic and stirring chapter of American history, one that need not be diminished by today's recognition of the monstrous wrong it inflicted on the Indian." In *The Patriot Chiefs* (1961), Alvin Josephy, Jr. expanded the historical record with thoughtful biographical studies of Indian leaders. The turning point came, however, with the 1971 publication of Dee Brown's *Bury My Heart at Wounded Knee*; its subtitle, *An Indian History of the American West,* announced that from then on the Indians' version of events could not be ignored.

Within the academic community, there emerged a group of mainly younger historians who insisted on a virtual reversal of the good guys-bad guys rules in the story of western expansion. Known as "the New Western historians," they indicted as criminal white Americans' treatment of the Indians, indeed of white peoples' treatment of the West, both in reality and in history books. Those historians included Richard Brown, Patricia Nelson Limerick, Clyde Milner II, Richard White, and Donald Worster. In her influential 1987 book, *The Legacy of Conquest*, Limerick challenged the popular explanation of Americans' westward flow as an instinctive expression of manifest destiny; in actuality, she argued, the white people were moving in to conquer alien territory, staking economic, social, and political claims to foreign soil. The New Western historian attacked whites for their violence and cruelty in dealing with each other as well as with the Indians and for greedy exploitation and destruction of the environment. Basically, these historians attacked the whole underlying myth of the independent, free-spirited frontier settlers.

Popular culture has not totally adopted the revisionist views of New Western historians, but there has been some change in the presentation of Indians. Ahead of its time was the 1950 movie *Broken Arrow*, in which Apache leader Cochise was portrayed sympathetically. Then, in the 1964 novel (and its 1971 movie adaptation) *Little Big Man*, U.S. Army Indian fighters were sketched as sociopathic killers. Twenty years later, the 1990 movie *Dances with Wolves* reversed another stereotype, portraying Indians as a wise and noble people living in harmony with nature. In some ways, that was a regression to another, romanticizing vision of the Indian as "noble savage."

CIVILIAN AND MILITARY BIOGRAPHIES

NATIVE AMERICAN

Black Hawk (1767–1838)—Sauk and Fox chief: Black Hawk was born Makataimeshekiakiak. He fiercely opposed the advance of white settlement into the northern Illinois country. He fought for the British in the War of 1812 and also with Tecumseh. Determined not to surrender his tribal homelands, he led Sauk bands in a fierce, bloody, and hopeless resistance to the whites in what became known as Black Hawk's War (1832). After he was captured and taken to meet President Andrew Jackson, he was brought back to Iowa.

Black Kettle (1803?–1868)—Cheyenne chief: Black Kettle was born Moketavato in the Black Hills of the Dakota country. He became a leading advocate of peaceful coexistence with the whites. All the same, his people were victimized in two of the worst slaughters of the western Indian wars: the Sand Creek Massacre in Colorado in 1864 and the Battle of the Washita in 1868. Black Kettle perished in the latter clash.

Cochise (1812?–1874)—Apache chief: Cochise was born in present-day New Mexico and raised a warrior. With the murder of his father-in-law, Mangas Coloradas, in 1863, he became the paramount chief of the Chiricahua Apache. Falsely accused of cattle thievery and kidnapping in 1861, Cochise escaped from custody and launched a long, bitter war against the United States. Cochise finally surrendered in 1871 and died three years later on the Chiricahua reservation.

Crazy Horse (1842?–1877)—Sioux chief: Crazy Horse was born Tashunka Witco in the Black Hills of Dakota country. He grew up a skilled hunter and warrior, attributes his Oglala Sioux tribe greatly valued. He fought in Red Cloud's War (1866–1867), later became supreme war and peace chief of the Oglalas, and led Sioux and Cheyenne warriors to victory at the Battle of the Little Bighorn in June 1876. U.S. forces pursued his band, and, with his people near starvation, he surrendered in May 1877. Crazy Horse was killed shortly thereafter during a jailhouse scuffle with soldiers.

Geronimo (1829–1909)—Apache chief: Geronimo was born Goyathlay in the Gila River valley of Arizona. He led Chiricahua resistance to the reservation system in a series of uprisings from the early 1860s until his final surrender in 1886. Confined in Florida and Oklahoma for many years after his surrender, he never again saw his Arizona homeland. Toward the end of his life, Geronimo converted to Christianity and became a successful farmer. In 1904, he was allowed to tour with a Wild West show and to appear at the St. Louis World's Fair. Unlike so many Indian leaders, he died of natural causes.

Joseph (1835?–1904)—Nez Percé chief: Chief Joseph was born Hinmaton Yalatkit in the Wallowa valley of Oregon. He led a peaceable band that white encroachment forced to the warpath in 1877. Chief Joseph, his war chiefs, and some 750 of their people carried out a remarkable fighting withdrawal through Idaho and Montana before U.S. troops brought them to bay near the Canadian frontier. There, in October 1877, Chief Joseph surrendered with most of his tribe . He passed the last years of his life promoting education for Native Americans and warning them about the dangers of liquor and gambling.

Red Cloud (1822–1909)—Sioux chief: Red Cloud was born Mahkpiya-luta in the Platte valley of Nebraska. He commanded the Oglala Sioux in Red Cloud's War of 1866–1868, which temporarily closed the Bozeman Trail to soldiers, miners, and settlers. Although he remained an opponent of U.S. Indian policy, he observed the treaty ending the conflict named for him and never again made war on the United States. In the late 1870s, Red Cloud and his tribe were confined to the Pine Ridge Reservation in South Dakota.

Sitting Bull (1831?–1890)—Sioux chief: Sitting Bull was born Tatanka Yotanka on the Grand River in South Dakota. He became chief and medicine man of the Hunkpapa Sioux and one of the great Native American leaders, revered for his courage, skill, and wisdom. With the Arapaho and Cheyenne, his Hunkpapa band resisted white penetration into the Black Hills in the 1870s; although he did not fight at Little Bighorn, he had helped to inspire the warriors' aggressiveness. Afterward he led part of the defeated band into exile in Canada from 1876–1881. He surrendered and was placed on the Standing Rock Reservation in South Dakota, leaving it in 1885 to appear in Buffalo Bill's Wild West Show. Arrested for supporting the Ghost Dance movement, he was shot and killed in a melee at the Standing Rock Reservation on the eve of the Battle of Wounded Knee in December 1890.

AMERICAN

Carson, Christopher (Kit) (1809–1868)—guide, Indian agent, soldier: Kit Carson was born in Madison County, Kentucky. He ventured into New Mexico and became a frontier scout (guiding two expeditions for Gen. John Frémont in the 1840s), trapper, and Indian fighter. Carson was agent for the Ute Indians of Colorado from 1853 to 1861. As a soldier, he forced the Navajos to make the "long walk" to the Bosque Redondo Reservation in 1864. He was appointed a brigadier general in 1865 and given command of Fort Garland, Colorado.

Cody, William F. (Buffalo Bill) (1845–1917)—frontiersman: Buffalo Bill Cody was a Scott County (Iowa) native. He rode for the Pony Express at age 12 and later worked as a trapper and wagoner. He served as a Union Army scout during the Civil War. A professional buffalo hunter after the war, he claimed to have killed more than 4,200 buffalo. In 1883, he organized Buffalo Bill's Wild West Show, which toured America and Europe for 30 years.

Crook, George (1829–1890)—soldier: George Crook was born near Dayton, Ohio. He graduated from West Point in 1852 and held important Union Army commands during the Civil War. Among the most effective of the Army's Indian fighters, he led campaigns against Cochise (1871–1873), Crazy Horse (1876), and Geronimo (1882–1883, 1885–1886). A hard but compassionate fighter, Crook respected his Indian enemies and, as one authority remarked, was "more prone to pardon than to punish."

Custer, George Armstrong (1839–1876)—soldier: George Armstrong Custer was an Ohio native and an 1861 West Point graduate. He became a flamboyant and successful commander of Union cavalry during the Civil War. Breveted to major general in the Civil War, he fought in the western campaigns as a lieutenant colonel. Hungry for fame, he continued to add to his notoriety on the frontier, where he led the 7th Cavalry against the Plains Indians. His attack on a Cheyenne camp on the Washita River, in which many women and children were killed, has been characterized as a second Sand Creek Massacre. On June 25, 1876, Custer perished with nearly all his command at the Battle of the Little Bighorn, one of the worst disasters of U.S. Army history.

Howard, Oliver Otis (1830–1909)—soldier: Oliver Otis Howard was born in Maine. An 1854 West Point graduate, Howard had a distinguished career during the Civil War: He fought at Gettysburg, lost his left arm at Fair Oaks, Virginia, and commanded Gen. William T. Sherman's left wing during the Georgia and Carolinas campaigns. After the Civil War, Howard headed the Freedmen's Bureau and helped found Howard University in Washington, D.C. Known for his piety, "Christian" Howard directed several campaigns against insurgent Indian tribes, including the Nez Percé campaign of 1877, in which his columns pursued Chief Joseph's band for 1,500 miles before forcing its surrender only 40 miles south of the Canadian border. Howard retired from the Army in 1894.

Mackenzie, Ranald Slidell (1840–1889)—soldier: Ranald Mackenzie was born in New York City. He graduated at the top of his West Point class in 1862 and fought in most of the major battles of the Virginia theater during the Civil War. Assigned to the Great Plains after the war, he became one of the Army's most skilled and successful Indian fighters. His adversaries, remarking on his loss of fingers to a Civil War wound, knew him as "Bad Hand." His physical and mental health failing, Mackenzie left the Army in 1884. He died five years later.

Whitman, Marcus (1802–1847)—physician, missionary: Marcus Whitman was born in New York State. He went west with his wife, Narcissa, and established a Presbyterian mission near present-day Walla Walla, Washington, in 1836. Blamed for the influx of white settlers into the territory and for a measles epidemic that killed many Indians, the Whitmans were murdered along with several others in the mission massacre that touched off the Cayuse War of 1847–1850.

FURTHER READING

Barnett, Louise. *Touched by Fire: The Life, Death and Mythic Afterlife of George Armstrong Custer*. New York: Henry Holt & Co. 1996.

Berger, Thomas. *Little Big Man*. New York: Dial Press, 1964.

Brown, Dee. *Bury My Heart at Wounded Knee*. New York: Holt, Rinehart, 1971.

Brown, Richard M. *Strain of Violence: Historical Studies of American Violence and Vigilantism*. New York: Oxford University Press, 1975.

(Continued on p. 346)

Carrington, Margaret. *Absaraka, Home of the Crows: Being the Experiences of an Officer's Wife on the Plains*. Lincoln, Nebr.: University of Nebraska Press, 1983 reprint.

Connell, Evan S. *Son of the Morning Star*. Berkeley, Calif.: North Point Press, 1984.

Custer, Elizabeth Bacon. *Boots and Saddles; or, Life in Dakota with General Custer*. New York: Harper & Brothers, 1885.

Dillon, Richard H. *Burnt-out Fires*. Englewood Cliffs, N. J.: Prentice Hall, 1973.

Eby, Cecil. *"That Disgraceful Affair," the Black Hawk War*. New York: W. W. Norton & Co., 1973.

Hampton, Bruce. *Children of Grace: The Nez Percé War of 1877*. New York: Henry Holt & Co., 1994.

Josephy, Alvin. *The Patriot Chiefs: A Chronicle of American Indian Leadership*. New York: Viking Press, 1961.

———et al. *The Native Americans: An Illustrated History*. Atlanta, Ga.: Turner Publishing Co., 1993.

King, Charles. *"Laramie"; or The Queen of Bedlam*. Philadelphia: J. B. Lippincott, 1889.

———*Campaigning with Crook: And Stories of Army Life*. New York: Harper & Brothers, 1890.

———*Starlight Ranch and Other Stories of Army Life on the Frontier*. Philadelphia: J. B. Lippincott, 1890.

Knight, Oliver. *Following the Indian Wars*. Norman, Okla.: University of Oklahoma Press, 1960.

Lavender, David. *Let Me Be Free*. New York: Harper Collins, 1992.

Limerick, Patricia Nelson. *The Legacy of Conquest*. New York: W.W. Norton & Co., 1987.

Martin, Joel W. *Sacred Revolt: The Muskogees' Struggle for a New World*. Boston: Beacon Press, 1991.

Miles, Nelson A. *Serving the Republic*. New York: Harper & Brothers, 1911.

Roberts, David. *Once They Moved Like the Wind: Cochise, Geronimo and the Apache Wars*. New York: Simon & Schuster, 1993.

Utley, Robert M. *Frontiersmen in Blue: The United States Army and the Indian, 1848-1865*. New York: Macmillan Publishing Co., 1967.

———*Frontier Regulars: The United States Army and the Indian, 1866-1891*. New York: Macmillan, 1973.

Utley, Robert M., and Whitcomb E. Washburn. *Indian Wars*. Boston: Houghton Mifflin Co., 1977.

Warren, Robert Penn. *Chief Joseph of the Nez Percé*. New York: Random House, 1983.

Welch, James, with Paul Stekler. *Killing Custer: The Battle of the Little Bighorn and the Fate of the Plains Indians*. New York: W. W. Norton & Co., 1994.

White, Richard. *"It's Your Misfortune and None of My Own": A History of the American West*. Norman, Okla.: University of Oklahoma Press, 1993.

Worster, Donald. *Rivers of Empire: Water, Aridity, and the Growth of the American West*. New York: Pantheon Books, 1985.

———*Under Western Skies: Nature and History in the American West*. New York: Oxford University Press, 1992.

THE SPANISH-AMERICAN WAR

DATES OF WAR

April 21, 1898–August 12, 1898

ALTERNATE NAMES

The War with Spain. The Spanish War. The Splendid Little War.

SIGNIFICANCE

The Spanish-American War marked the emergence of the United States as a world power. The United States acquired colonial possessions in the Caribbean and in the Pacific and assumed an important role in international politics. The two-ocean war increased pressure for an isthmian canal to link the Atlantic and the Pacific Ocean; work on the Panama Canal commenced in 1904. But the war and its aftermath also led to the emergence of a strong anti-imperialist faction in American politics. The direct heirs of the anti-imperialists—the isolationists—exerted a significant influence on American foreign policy for decades.

The fighting revealed deficiencies in American military and naval capabilities. On land, supply services were primitive and the artillery arm poorly employed. The sea battles exposed flaws in American ship design (by world standards, U.S. vessels were slow and too lightly armored) and especially in gunnery. Indirectly, the Spanish-American War fostered a major advance in public health. The U.S. Army Yellow Fever Commission, part of the postwar American occupying forces in Cuba, discovered the means of transmission of the deadly infection and oversaw its near-eradication.

For the Spanish, the Spanish-American War forced recognition of Spain's lost status as a world power. There were significant material losses as well: the independence or cession to the United States of Cuba, Puerto Rico, Guam, and the Philippine Islands—much of what remained of Spain's once powerful empire.

BACKGROUND

By 1898, the Caribbean island of Cuba was in turmoil that had started 30 years earlier, with social and political agitation centering on the issues of slavery and independence from Spain. The long-distance Spanish imperial relationship with Cuba began in 1492, with Columbus's first voyage of discovery to the New World. The first Spanish settlements were established on the 750-mile-long island in 1511. The newcomers quickly subdued the native Taino and within a few years began importing the first African slaves. Cuba became the richest and most populous of all the West Indian islands—"the Pearl of the Antilles," as the Spanish dubbed it.

Cuba's population approached 1.5 million by the end of the 19th century. The indigenous Taino had long since been destroyed or absorbed into the general population of roughly 200,000 Spanish-born, 500,000 descendants of African slaves, and 800,000 Cuban-born whites. The *peninsulares*—those Cubans born in Spain—were the island's dominant economic force; the Spanish in Madrid exercised near-absolute political authority. Cubans, white and black, had mounted occasional challenges to Spanish hegemony. The destructive, bitter Ten Years' War, 1868–1878, led to some concessions of political power from Madrid and, most significantly, to the emancipation of Cuba's slaves.

Spain, however, failed to keep most of the home rule promises of the Treaty of Zanjon (1878), which ended the Ten Years' War. By the mid-1890s, the Cuban rebels were again astir. Economic dislocation expanded the opportunities of the independence party. A steep U.S. import duty sent prices for sugar, Cuba's mainstay, plunging to historic lows. In reaction, the Spanish clapped high tariffs on American goods in Cuba. The trade war triggered a severe island-wide depression. Sensing an opportunity, the young, dynamic leader of the Cuban rebels, 42-year-old José Martí, in February 1895, issued a call for a second war for independence.

Martí's Cuban Revolutionary Party, established in 1892, lobbied the 20,000 Cuban émigrés in Tampa, New Orleans, Chicago, and New York for political and economic aid. Martí found important allies in American labor groups and in the American press. Though he sought American material support, he urged the Cubans to win independence for themselves and warned against courting American military intervention. "Once the United States is in Cuba," he asked, "who will get her out?"

On May 19, 1895, just a few weeks after the outbreak of an insurrection, a Spanish cavalry patrol killed Martí. Maximo Gomez, the rebels' military leader, pressed on. Gomez called for a merciless war on Spanish wealth on the island, particularly on the sugar industry, which accounted for three-quarters of Cuba's economy. His *insurrectos* burned cane fields and mills and carried out reprisals against field hands and factory workers who failed to cooperate in Gomez's scorched earth campaign.

"They live by marauding," a Spanish officer wrote of Gomez's rebels. "The country people feed them, and help them so far as they can, and where these insurgents don't find sympathy, the machete, the torch, and the rope are good arguments."

The Spanish responded by withdrawing into the cities and garrison towns. The Spanish commander, Arsenio Martinez Campos, constructed a series of fortified belts called *trochas*, designed to confine the guerrillas to the eastern end of the island. Gomez's cavalry penetrated the *trochas* with ease. Campos conceded failure and returned to Spain. His successor, Gen. Valeriano Weyler y Nicolau, inaugurated a harsh new policy called *reconcentracion*, in which thousands of Cubans were uprooted from their homes and resettled inside the Spanish fortified lines. Some 500,000 Cubans endured a miserable, hungry, and disease-ridden existence in Weyler's concentration camps. Thousands died.

The effects of the new policy were felt beyond the island. The rebels found a powerful propaganda tool that mobilized an important segment of American opinion in their favor. Only 90 miles south of the U.S. mainland, Cuba had long been of interest to American diplomats. As early as 1848, President James K. Polk proposed buying the island from Spain. Though the United States remained neutral during the Ten Years'

War, Cuban rebel leaders moved freely throughout the United States, raising money and arms for their cause. By 1895, U.S. support for Cuban independence was running deep.

American newspapers, led by the sensationalist tabloids known collectively as the yellow press (after a yellow-tinted comic strip in the New York *World* titled "The Yellow Kid"), campaigned aggressively on the *insurrectos'* behalf. Joseph Pulitzer's New York *World* and its bitter rival, William Randolph Hearst's *Journal*, produced a steady stream of Spanish atrocity stories, inspiring mass rallies in the United States for Cuban independence, fairs to raise money and supplies for the rebels, and, in many places, the burning in effigy of "Butcher" Weyler.

Pulitzer and Hearst dispatched their most prominent writers to Cuba and signed on popular authors and illustrators—most prominently, Richard Harding Davis and Frederic Remington—to report firsthand on the progress of the insurgency. Through it all, the government of President Grover Cleveland followed a policy of scrupulous neutrality. Still, the drumfire of advocacy journalism created a climate of opinion that eventually came to favor U.S. intervention in Cuba.

The Spanish regarded the Americans as meddlers, and Spanish positions hardened as the American newspaper headlines grew bolder. There were anti-American demonstrations in Madrid. In Barcelona, a mob stoned the U.S. consulate. The Spanish government of Antonio Canovas del Castillo concluded that any compromise over Cuba would provoke a right-wing backlash that could threaten the throne of the regent Maria Cristina, ruling on behalf of her son, the underage Alfonso XIII. An assassin's bullet claimed Canovas in August 1897, and his Liberal Party successor, Praxedes Sagasta, adopted a more conciliatory policy. He recalled Weyler and offered Cuba home rule under the Spanish flag.

But matters had gone too far. The insurgents rejected mere autonomy; they would not make peace without independence. And, in fact, the feared right-wing response did occur, though in Havana rather than in Madrid. *Peninsulare* mobs went on the rampage on January 12, 1898, ransacking the offices of several Havana newspapers that had editorialized in favor of home rule. The American consul feared a further outbreak might endanger Americans in Cuba. As a consequence, Washington ordered the battleship USS

Maine to Havana. On January 25, 1898, the American warship steamed past the Moro Castle and dropped anchor in the harbor of Havana.

CAUSES OF THE WAR

The proximate cause of war between the United States and Spain was the destruction of the USS *Maine* in Havana harbor during the evening of February 15, 1898. The detonation came just as the ship's bugler finished playing taps. A sudden shock and a deafening roar were followed by a second explosion. "Out over the bay the air was filled with a blaze of light," recalled Clara Barton of the American Red Cross, who had gone to Havana to direct aid programs for Cubans the war had displaced, "and this in turn was filled with black specks like huge specters flying in all directions. Then it faded away, the bells rang, the whistles blew, and voices in the street were heard for a moment; then all was quiet again." Within minutes, the warship settled to the bottom. More than 260 U.S. sailors were killed in the explosion and sinking.

Initial U.S. government reaction was cautious, but the pro-Cuban press concluded at once that the Spanish had blown up the *Maine*. A hastily convened court of inquiry ruled that a submerged mine had destroyed the vessel (see Historical Perspectives and Controversies, p. 366). The underlying causes of the U.S. move toward war were two elements threatened by the political uncertainty in Cuba: humanitarian concerns for the victims of the long insurgency and U.S. trade and business investments (some $50 million in direct investment in 1898) in the island. "Free Cuba would mean a great market for the United States; it would also mean a great opportunity for American capital; it would mean an opportunity for development of that splendid island," Massachusetts Republican Henry Cabot Lodge said. Lodge belonged to a powerful faction of political leaders—the imperialists—who promoted American interests abroad. Those politicians, along with the pro-insurrection press and the sensation-mongering yellow journalists, persuaded a growing number of Americans to favor the notion of direct U.S. intervention to break Spain's four-century-long hold on Cuba.

U.S. newspapers raised suspicions of Spanish responsibility for the *Maine* tragedy into certain guilt. "THE WARSHIP MAINE WAS SPLIT IN TWO BY AN ENEMY'S SECRET INFERNAL MACHINE," a headline in Hearst's New York *Journal* proclaimed.

PREPARATIONS FOR WAR

At the outbreak of the Spanish-American War, President McKinley issued a call for 125,000 volunteers to reinforce the Regular Army. Tens of thousands of young men responded, as well as elderly veterans of the Civil War, North and South. Theodore Roosevelt, the assistant Navy Secretary who had pushed for an aggressive policy against the Spanish, resigned to help raise a regiment of volunteer cavalry—the Rough Riders. The War Department began to plan for an invasion of Cuba and the neighboring Spanish-held island of Puerto Rico.

The volunteers streamed into training camps in Virginia, north Georgia, Florida, and Texas. Food and sanitation were poor; disease widespread. Supplies of all kinds were lacking; the troops drilled in Civil War era uniforms and with obsolete Springfield rifles. "Everything had to be extemporized," one volunteer officer wrote. By early May, though, the first volunteer regiments were en route for Tampa, Florida, the staging point for the invasion of Cuba.

With the breaking off of diplomatic relations between Spain and the United States (April 21), the Navy proceeded at once to its blockade stations off Cuba. Thousands of miles to the west, in British Hong Kong, Comdr. George Dewey's U.S. Asiatic Squadron steamed out to sea on the afternoon of April 27; its objective was the Spanish flotilla based in the Philippines.

A ramshackle Spanish naval squadron under Adm. Pascual Cervera y Topete sailed for North America from the Cape Verde Islands on April 29. Cervera's four armored cruisers and three destroyers put to sea short of coal and with defective guns and ammunition. Cervera, a veteran of nearly a half century of naval service, could not have been more aware of his shortcomings. "The best thing would be to avoid war at any price," he said.

By early May, Regular Army units and a few volunteer regiments were converging on Tampa, Florida. As the camps filled, the Army and Navy argued over how and when the expeditionary force, designated 5th Army Corps, would be used. Gen. Nelson A. Miles, the Army commander, declared the 5th Corps could not be ready to move before the end of June. By then, the rains and the yellow fever season would have commenced; Miles recommended delaying the invasion until the autumn. The Navy pressed for immediate action. President McKinley agreed, and War Secretary Russell Alger reluctantly promised, on May 2, that the Army would be in position to land 30,000 to 40,000 troops in Cuba.

The 5th Corps commander, Maj. Gen. Rufus Shafter, established his headquarters in the Tampa Bay Hotel on April 29. "Tampa lay in the pine-covered sand flats at the end of a one-track railroad, and everything connected with both military and railroad matters was in an almost inextricable tangle," wrote Theodore Roosevelt, who arrived from Texas with the Rough Riders in June. Rail cars arrived without bills of lading describing the contents. Rations were insufficient. Troops in the Tampa camps went short of clothing; a 15-car train loaded with uniforms sat for weeks on a sidetrack 25 miles away.

Still, Shafter and his staff gradually made some order out of the chaos. Word reached the camps the evening of June 7 to prepare to board the transports for Cuba. U.S. Navy pressure had forced the Army to act. Admiral Cervera's fleet had reached the harbor of Santiago on Cuba's south coast on June 3. The Navy pressed the Army to capture the city before Cervera could attempt a breakout. "Every consideration demands immediate army movement," Adm. William Sampson, commanding the blockading squadron, cabled Washington, D.C. In reaction, the War Department, on June 7, ordered Shafter to "sail at once" for Santiago.

The expeditionary force overwhelmed the primitive facilities of the port of Tampa. Only two vessels could load at a time; the rail lines ended short of the pier, so the stevedores had to manhandle stores across 50 feet of deep sand and up a steep ramp to the ships. Even so, 32 transports were loaded and ready to sail within 24 hours. They carried the largest military expedition ever to leave the United States up to then: 16,000 officers and enlisted men, 2,500 horses and mules, 114 six-mule wagons, 81 escort wagons, 7 ambulances, 16 field guns, 4 howitzers, 4 siege guns, 1 dynamite gun, 4 Gatling guns, and 8 mortars.

Fear of Cervera's ramshackle ships led to several postponements. The U.S. invasion fleet finally set sail on June 14 for the journey south and west to Santiago, Cuba, 1,000 miles distant.

DECLARATION OF WAR

"I don't propose to be swept off my feet by the catastrophe," declared President William McKinley. Yet, that is precisely what happened. The *Maine* disaster set off a train of political, diplomatic, and military events. The naval court of inquiry that convened aboard a U.S. tug in Havana harbor on February 21 concluded a mine had destroyed the *Maine*, though it did not fix responsibility for the planting of the device.

McKinley and his cabinet reviewed the court's finding on March 25 and used it to increase diplomatic pressure on Spain. The United States delivered an ultimatum to the Madrid government, demanding the revocation of *reconcentracion* and an immediate cease-fire between Spanish and Cuban forces. Then, under pressure from Congress, McKinley escalated the U.S. demand: full independence for Cuba and a complete Spanish withdrawal. The Spanish agreed to the armistice, but the concession came too late. McKinley submitted the matter to Congress on Monday, April 11. Eight days later, the House and Senate passed joint resolutions that recognized Cuban independence, called for Spanish withdrawal from Cuba, and authorized the president to use U.S. naval and military power to end the war in Cuba.

McKinley signed the resolutions on April 20. On April 21, diplomatic relations between the United States and Spain were broken off and the president ordered a naval blockade of Cuban ports. The Navy's North Atlantic Squadron—two battleships, four cruisers, and escorting vessels—arrived off Havana the afternoon of April 22. Congress approved the formal declaration of war on April 25, retroactive to April 21.

COMBATANTS

United States: The U.S. Regular Army numbered 28,000 men, much of them scattered in small detachments in the West. The Army lacked nearly everything necessary for an overseas campaign: arms, ammunition, transport, medical supplies. A full 30 years had passed since U.S troops had formed for brigade drill. As in the Civil War, volunteer troops raised in the states would supplement the regulars. The 13,000-man U.S.

Navy, however, could send to sea a relatively well-trained force of battleships, armored cruisers, and escort vessels, over 100 ships altogether.

Spanish: The Spanish military organizations were decrepit; few army units were battleworthy. Though Spain fielded thousands of troops in Cuba, more than 20,000 in the Santiago district alone, the forces were ill-equipped, badly led, and sickly. To defend Puerto Rico, the Spanish could call on some 8,000 regulars and 9,000 lightly armed militia. Spanish forces in the Philippines were hardly stronger than those in Puerto Rico. Spain's naval squadrons in Manila and the Cape Verde Islands consisted of obsolescent, slow, and undergunned warships.

Cubans: Several thousand Cuban *insurrectos* remained in the field in Cuba. Those bedraggled and poorly trained irregulars would look to the United States for arms, supplies, and leadership.

Filipinos: Emilio Aguinaldo claimed leadership of several insurgent groups challenging Spanish rule in the Philippines. A small but highly motivated Filipino army fought on Luzon island in an uneasy alliance with the American expeditionary force. Then, even before the treaty with Spain had been ratified by the U.S. Senate, Aguinaldo led his Filipino insurgents in an uprising against the United States that led to three years of war and many thousands of casualties.

GEOGRAPHIC AND STRATEGIC CONSIDERATIONS

For the United States and Spain, the major combatants, the distance between the homeland and the war theaters greatly influenced military operations. Even so, with a larger and more modern fleet and a substantial merchant marine, the United States enjoyed a major strategic advantage in its ability to move troops and supplies over vast expanses of sea.

Cuba, the main theater of operations, lay within a few hours' steaming time of the nearest American ports. To reinforce or resupply its troops in Cuba, the Spanish had to cross more than 3,000 miles of ocean commanded by squadrons of the U.S. Navy. The Philippine theater lay several thousand miles distant from the shores of either combatant. However, the advantage again went to the U.S., with its superior naval and merchant assets.

American naval theorist Capt. Alfred Thayer Mahan greatly influenced U.S. strategic thinking with his treatise *The Influence of Sea Power upon History* (1890). He argued that American prosperity depended on expanding overseas markets for U.S. products. Only sea power could guarantee access to those markets. The United States thus required a strong Navy and a network of coaling stations and bases to sustain it. In the specific context of the Spanish-American War, Mahan regarded naval power as decisive. "The issue of the war depended upon naval force," he wrote afterward. "A million of the best soldiers would have been powerless in the face of hostile control of the sea."

The Spanish strategy, born of necessity, was simple: Spanish forces everywhere, on land and at sea, would fight on the defensive.

BATTLES AND CAMPAIGNS

There were three theaters of military operations in the Spanish-American War: the Philippines, Cuba, and Puerto Rico; two of those theaters involved naval and land operations. After the war formally ended, its aftermath—the Philippine Insurrection (see p. 362)—continued to take its toll on the U.S. military and American society.

THE PHILIPPINES

From the first phase of the USS *Maine* crisis, Assistant Navy Secretary Theodore Roosevelt lobbied reluctant President William McKinley for aggressive action against the Spanish. Roosevelt later wrote: "I gave him a paper showing exactly where all our ships are, and I also sketched in outline what I thought ought to be done if things looked menacing, urging the necessity of taking an immediate and prompt initiative if we wished to avoid the chance of some serious trouble." Roosevelt also helped engineer the appointment of Comdr. George Dewey to the Pacific command, effective January 1898. Seizing the initiative while in temporary charge of the Navy Department in February 1898, Roosevelt ordered Dewey to be prepared, should war break out, to attack the Spanish fleet in the Philippines. In the White House, the president twirled the globe in search of the distant archipelago. "I could not have told where those darned islands were within 2 thousand miles," he admitted.

Dewey's Asiatic Squadron consisted of seven ships: Dewey's flagship, the armored cruiser USS *Olympia;* three other armored cruisers, the USS *Raleigh*, the USS *Baltimore*, and the USS *Boston*; two gunboats the USS *Petrel* and the USS *Concord*; and one revenue cutter the USS *McCulloch*. Dewey needed no prodding from Roosevelt to act with dispatch. He ordered the ships into their gray war paint and purchased two colliers (ships for transporting coal to fuel the fleet) to operate as fleet train. In March, the squadron steamed to Hong Kong, the British island off the South China coast. There, Dewey completed his outfitting. Like McKinley, naval intelligence knew little of the Philippines. Dewey sent ashore to a ship's chandlery for up-to-date charts of Manila Bay on Luzon, the most important of the Philippine Islands.

April 24, 1898: When the Spanish-American War started, the neutral British advised Dewey that he must take his warships away from Hong Kong. On April 24, the squadron steamed 30 miles north to the quiet anchorage of Mirs Bay to await orders; McKinley's authorization to attack Manila bore the date of April 24. "Commence operations at once, particularly against the Spanish fleet," Navy Secretary John Long cabled Dewey. "You must capture vessels or destroy. Use utmost endeavors." The warships' crews removed hatches, chests, paneling, and other objects that could splinter or burn. Coal bunkers were topped up.

April 27, 1898: During the afternoon, the Asiatic Squadron steamed out from Mirs Bay into the China Sea and shaped a course for Manila Bay. There, the Spanish squadron lay at moorings, six old, obsolete vessels: the cruisers *Reina Cristina*, and *Castilla* and four smaller warships. The Spanish ships mounted 31 great guns altogether, though none larger than 6.3 inches in caliber. The U.S. ships carried 53 guns of 5-inch caliber or larger. Still, the Spanish coastal defenses were strong, especially the big guns planted in the rocky island of Corregidor at the entrance to Manila Bay. And the channel leading down to the city of Manila was suspected of being mined.

April 30, 1898: Dewey's lookouts caught sight of the coast of Luzon before dawn. The *Olympia* paused first for a look into Subic Bay north of Manila. Dewey speculated, incorrectly, that the Spanish squadron would be lying under

protection of the coastal batteries there. The bay was deserted and the U.S. warships pressed on to the south. Dewey issued orders for the squadron to run past the fortress of Corregidor and search out the enemy in Manila Bay.

The sun set and darkness fell with tropical abruptness. The squadron steamed on in line astern, the *Olympia* in the lead. "Not a glimmer was to be seen aboard any craft in the fleet," wrote New York *Herald* correspondent Joseph Stickney aboard the flagship. "As I looked astern, I could just get a faint suggestion of a ghostly shape where the *Baltimore* grimly held her course." At 9:45, Dewey ordered the crews to battle stations. Just before midnight, the *Olympia* entered the broad channel to the south of Corregidor. Suddenly a white glare lit up the squadron: Soot in the *McCulloch*'s stack caught fire. But the Spanish guns remained silent, and the U.S. warships glided safely past, steering for Manila 25 miles distant.

May 1, 1898: Dewey ordered coffee and breakfast served to the crews at 4 o'clock in the morning. At first light, the *Olympia* approached to within a mile of the Manila waterfront; the flagship's sharp-eyed navigator counted 16 merchant vessels in port, but no warships. A few minutes later, a lookout aloft sighted the enemy 5 miles farther south, at anchor off the Cavite naval station.

The American squadron steamed for Cavite in close battle order at a steady, slow 8 knots, the *Olympia* leading the way. The shore batteries opened fire from Manila. "Two harmless fountains sprang up miles ahead of our columns, and it was plain that the defense was flurried," recalled Lt. C. G. Calkins on the flagship. At 5:41 A.M., at a range of 5,400 yards, Dewey turned to the *Olympia*'s captain and declared: "You may fire when ready, Gridley."

The flagship's 8-inch guns played on the *Reina Cristina* and the wooden-hulled *Castilla*, the most dangerous of Adm. Patricio Montojo y Pasaron's vessels. The American line steamed past the Spanish, turned, retraced its course, turned again, and steamed down the line a third time, firing all the while. Belowdecks in the battened-down American ships, the bluejackets worked in a steaming cauldron. "It was so hot our hair was singed," a stoker in the *Olympia* wrote. "The clatter of the engines and the roar of the furnaces made such a din it seemed one's head would burst. The soot and cinders poured down in clouds. Now and then, a big drop of scalding water would fall on our bare heads. We knew it meant sure death if the *Olympia* got a shot through her anywhere in our vicinity."

Lt. Bradley Fiske of the USS *Petrel* viewed the battle from his perch in a range-finding post 45 feet above the waterline. "The whole thing looked like a performance that had been very carefully rehearsed," he wrote. "The ships went slowly and regularly, seldom or never getting out of their relative positions, and only ceased firing at intervals when the smoke became too thick."

The *Reina Cristina* took several immediate hits, knocking a number of guns out of action and killing or wounding a score of sailors. Soon smoke was pouring from the Spanish ships. The *Reina Cristina* weighed anchor and headed defiantly into the bay, making for the *Olympia*. Dewey's ships concentrated a furious fire into the *Reina Christina* and drove it ashore. Montojo called out the order to scuttle the ship before her magazines exploded. In 1903, when salvagers raised the *Reina Cristina* from the muck, 80 skeletons were found in the sick bay.

With a report of ammunition running low, Dewey ordered a pause at around 7:30, not quite two hours into the battle. As the smoke cleared, it became obvious that the Spanish squadron had been all but destroyed. Dewey called the captains aboard the *Olympia* for a conference and ordered a second breakfast for the crews. "There were sardines, corned beef, and hard tack on a corner of the wardroom table, still encumbered by the surgeons' ghastly gear, which was all unstained, however," wrote Lieutenant Calkins. No Americans had been killed, and only six were wounded, all aboard the *Baltimore*.

On the Spanish side, the *Reina Cristina* and the *Castilla* were out of the battle. The four surviving vessels, trapped in the little harbor at Cavite, refused to give up, however, and at 11:15, Dewey signaled a renewal of the action. The Americans directed their fire into the cruiser *Don Antonio de Ulloa*, which shortly rolled over and sank in the shallow water of the inlet. Then, the gunboat *Petrel* steamed into Cavite harbor. One by one, the Spanish captains hauled down their flags. At 12:30 P.M. the gunboat *Petrel* signaled the flagship: "The enemy has surrendered." The Spanish lost 10 warships wrecked or captured; 400 Spanish sailors were killed.

The American squadron anchored just off the Manila waterfront. The Spanish commander refused Dewey's request to cable news of the victory home; Dewey ordered the cable dredged up and cut. He sent the *McCulloch* to Hong Kong with his official report, to be transmitted to Washington, D.C., from the British colony.

The victory at Manila Bay turned the obscure Commodore Dewey an instant hero. American cafes served "ices *à la* Dewey," carved in the shape of warships. Americans celebrated him, too, in doggerel verse:

Dewey! Dewey! Dewey!
Is the hero of the day!
And the *Maine* has been remembered
In the good old-fashioned way.

May 1–June 27, 1898: Since the U.S. Navy's victory over the Spanish squadron in Manila Bay on May 1, Commodore Dewey faced diplomatic problems involving the supposedly neutral Germans and the Filipino insurgent forces. Dewey was attempting to enforce a blockade of the Philippine capital, and German naval forces in the area to observe the Americans kept him in a high state of tension.

June 12, 1898: Emilio Aguinaldo, leader of the Filipino insurgents, proclaimed Philippine independence from Spain. The insurgents had done much preliminary work for the Americans, clearing Cavite province of the Spanish and pushing on toward the capital. Aguinaldo, the 29-year-old son of a clerk at the Cavite naval arsenal, claimed leadership of the insurgent groups challenging Spanish rule. Aguinaldo thought, too, that he enjoyed American support. And, in fact, Dewey had supplied his forces with arms, ammunition and encouragement. Dewey's superiors in Washington, D.C., however, warned him off making any commitment to the cause of Philippine independence. The islands, President McKinley decided, were to be treated as spoils of war.

June 20, 1898: The cruiser USS *Charleston* opened fire on the far Pacific Spanish outpost of Guam, then sent a party of sailors ashore to demand the island's surrender. The Spanish commander told the bluejackets he had no idea war had begun, for no ship had called at Guam since mid-April. The *Charleston* dropped off a small occupation force and, with the troop transports, steamed on westward toward the Philippines.

June 23, 1898: Emilio Aguinaldo appointed

himself head of the Philippine Islands' revolutionary government.

June–July 1898: Dewey's landward responsibilities were eased in late June with the arrival of the first contingent of the American troops on Philippine soil. Still, the German naval force continued to cause him trouble. By June 27, there were five German warships in Manila Bay; their officers more or less flouted the blockade and carried on discussions with the Spanish authorities ashore.

July 10, 1898: An exasperated Dewey threatened to open fire on the German ships; after a decent face-saving interval, the Germans withdrew, having no wish for a serious quarrel with the Americans over the Philippines.

July 29–30, 1898: Gen. Wesley Merritt, commanding the U.S. expeditionary force, had 11,000 men, most of them volunteers, ashore ready to advance on Manila. With Merritt's arrival, the United States prepared to replace the Filipino forces in the lines outside Manila. Aguinaldo's troops withdrew on the night of July 29, and the Americans moved in.

July 31, 1898: The Spanish responded to the American presence opposite their lines with a sharp cannonade and musketry. The 90-minute night action cost the United States 50 casualties, including 10 dead. There were minor exchanges of gunfire on successive nights.

August 6, 1898: In spite of the setback to his insurgent forces, Aguinaldo reissued his declaration of independence and called on European powers to recognize the Philippine Republic.

August 8, 1898: The Spanish commander, Gen. Fermin Jaudenes y Alvarez, signaled his intention to put up no more than a token defense of Manila, "to show a form of resistance for the sake of Spanish honor." Jaudenes set two conditions: The United States was to make the advance into the capital look like a battle, and under no circumstances were the insurgents to enter the city.

August 13, 1898: Dewey's warships opened the sham battle at 9:30 in the morning with a bombardment of the Spanish outwork of Fort San Antonio. "Jaudenes said his honor demanded that," Dewey later wrote, "so I had to fire, to kill a few people." When the shelling stopped, two infantry brigades pushed down the Camino Real, the main road into Manila. Six Americans were killed and 40 wounded in the "mock" battle. Fi-

nally, from the *Olympia*'s bridge, Dewey caught sight of a white flag above one of the Spanish forts. Then, Gen. Francis Greene, commanding one of the infantry columns, walked into the captain of the port's office, hauled down the Spanish flag and raised the Stars and Stripes.

The Americans scrupulously observed their agreement with Jaudenes. U.S. detachments met and detained rebel units outside the city. "Strong guards were posted," General Merritt wrote, "and General Aguinaldo was given to understand that no insurgents would be allowed to enter with arms." A few days later firm orders arrived from Washington, D.C.: There would be no joint American-Filipino occupation of Manila.

August 14, 1898: The Spanish formally surrendered Manila.

August 16, 1898: A dispatch boat brought word that the United States and representatives of Spain had declared a peace protocol in Washington, D.C., on August 12—the day before Dewey, Merritt, and Jaudenes "performed" the battle for Manila.

CUBA

June 20, 1898: During the morning, lookouts aboard the transports carrying the 5th Corps sighted the loom of the Cuban coast. "High mountains rose almost from the water's edge, looking huge and barren across the sea," recalled Theodore Roosevelt aboard the transport *Yucatan* with the Rough Riders. Maj. Gen. Rufus Shafter decided to land the troops on what looked like a deserted stretch of beach near Daiquirí 15 miles east of Santiago. Dreading the heavy costs of a frontal assault, he intended to maneuver his soldiers into position around Santiago and force the city to surrender.

June 22, 1898: The landings at Daiquiri began early in the morning, after a preparatory shelling from six of Adm. William Sampson's warships. After a few minutes, a troop of Cuban insurgent cavalry cantered onto the beach, signaling the Spanish had gone. "Soon the sea was dotted with rows of white boats filled with men bound about with white blanket-rolls and with muskets at all angles, and as they rose and fell on the water and the newspaper yachts and transports crept closer and closer, the scene was strangely suggestive of a boat race, and one almost waited for the starting gun," wrote corre-

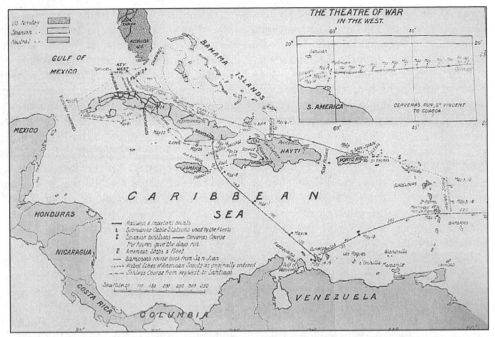

This map shows the sites of the main battles of the Spanish-American War in the Carib-
bean. The inset shows the "run" made by Adm. Pascual Cervera and his fleet from St.
Vincent in the Cape Verde Islands (off Africa) to Cuacoa (Curacoa) off Venezuela in
April–May 1898 before heading to engage the U.S. fleet in Santiago, Cuba.

spondent Richard Harding Davis. The boats landed through a heavy swell. Horses and mules were simply turned out of the ships and headed in the direction of Daiquiri beach. Many animals drowned; finally, someone suggested tethering them and towing large groups of horses ashore. The troops had less difficulty, though two troopers of the African-American 10th Cavalry drowned when their boat capsized in the surf. By nightfall, some 6,000 troops were safely ashore.

June 23, 1898: The route to Santiago ran westward to Siboney, then turned inland through a gap in the coastal hills. At dawn, a column of two infantry regiments moved up to Siboney and found the town deserted. By noon, troops were being landed in Siboney. The disembarkation continued deep into the night, the scene lit by the glare of the warships' searchlights. An advance column of dismounted cavalry, including the Rough Riders, pushed on beyond Siboney after dark, halting, finally, near Las Guásimas. There, the Spanish rearguards had entrenched. Brig. Gen. Joseph Wheeler, the former Confederate officer commanding Shafter's cavalry, ordered an assault for the next morning.

June 24, 1898: Wheeler sent a column of regulars down the main road toward the Spanish at sunrise, with the Rough Riders advancing on a parallel track that ran through deep woods. After a while, the Rough Rider commanding officer, Col. Leonard Wood, called a halt. Then, he ordered the men to fan out on either side of the track. Somewhere up ahead, firing had broken out. The volunteers advanced slowly and blindly through the dense growth. "It was like forcing the walls of a maze," Davis wrote. The firing grew heavier, and men began to fall. On the main road, the regulars advanced into a sharp fire. Suddenly the Spanish gave way, blurred figures pulling back in the direction of Santiago.

That first land action of the Spanish-American War cost the Americans 16 dead, 52 wounded; Spanish casualties were 10 dead, 25 wounded. Davis and the other journalists accompanying the U.S. columns reported the Las Guásimas skirmish in minute detail, with the effect of making national idols of the Rough Riders, particularly their lieutenant colonel, Theodore Roosevelt. Militarily, the clash cleared the road as far as San Juan Hill just east of Santiago, giving Shafter the opportunity to close in and commence the siege operations he favored.

June 25–30, 1898: Shafter paused for several days to consolidate his gains and stockpile food, ammunition, and other supplies. U.S. troops began to suffer in the tropical heat and dampness. Rations and tobacco were in short supply. "We did not get quite the proper amount of food," Roosevelt complained, "and what we did get, like most of the clothing issued us, was fitter for the Klondyke than for Cuba." Sick lists lengthened, with cases of tropical fever, dysentery, and heat exhaustion.

The Spanish, meantime, some 13,000 troops under Gen. Arsenio Linares, worked to improve their defensive lines on the hills around Santiago. The trench lines, with barbed wire and studded at intervals with blockhouses, curved north to south for 4,000 yards to cover the eastern approaches to the city. Trenches appeared along the tops of the high ground known as the San Juan Hills; a stone fort guarded the outlying hamlet of El Caney. The defenders trained their guns on the spot where the two jungle trails the Americans would use opened onto a grassy plain.

Shafter ordered an assault on the San Juan positions for the morning of July 1. He assigned a 5,400-man division under Brig. Gen. Henry Lawton to carry El Caney and ordered Brig. Gen. Jacob Kent's infantry division and the cavalry, 8,000 men, to cross the San Juan River and take the San Juan Hills.

July 1, 1898: The Americans opened fire on El Caney with four light cannon at 6:30 A.M. Spanish sharpshooters firing from trees, cottages, and blockhouses opened on the advancing infantry. Five hundred Spanish defenders held off ten times their number for several hours. Shafter suffered intensely from the heat and felt too ill to go to the front. From his tent behind the lines, he ordered the attack on the San Juan Hills to go forward, even though El Caney remained in Spanish hands. Kent's infantry and Wheeler's dismounted troopers filed down the jungle trails onto the plain into a hurricane of Spanish fire.

Within a few minutes, some 400 Americans were dead or wounded. The attacking troops staggered across the river and formed a line of battle at the base of two hills. Kent's infantry deployed to the left, below San Juan Hill. The troopers, including the Rough Riders, filed to the right, below an eminence dubbed "Kettle Hill" for the huge iron kettle used for sugar processing which was on the summit.

At the base of the two hills, the troops waited, pinned down under Spanish fire. Shafter seemed unable to reach a decision. Finally, one of his aides, Lt. John Miley, acted on his behalf. "The heights must be taken at all hazards," he told the cavalry commanders. The orders went out, and the dismounted troopers swarmed up the slope. Later, all the credit went to the Rough Riders. In fact, it was a joint effort. On the left, the African-American soldiers of the 9th and 10th Cavalry regiments kept pace with the Rough Riders.

The Americans reached the crest, where a large group of troopers found shelter behind the iron kettle. To the left, they could see Kent's infantry moving up San Juan Hill. With the infantry's success there, the advance pushed on across the valley to a second range of hills. "When we reached these crests," Roosevelt recalled, "we found ourselves overlooking Santiago." By 4:30 P.M., the firing had all but ceased. To the north, Lawton's troops had finally pushed the Spanish out of El Caney.

The attacks cost the Americans 205 killed, 1,180 wounded. Spanish losses were 215 dead, 376 wounded. The capture of the outlying positions set the stage for the siege of Santiago.

July 2, 1898: The U.S. Army's 5th Corps had sealed off the landward approaches to Santiago and settled into position in the hills overlooking the city. The U.S. Navy argued for an immediate assault that would seal the fate of Adm. Pascual Cervera's squadron in Santiago harbor. The Spanish, meantime, were beset with their own disagreements. The senior Spanish commander in Cuba, Gen. Ramon Blanco, urged Cervera to run the American blockade. Cervera demurred. "If we should lose the squadron without fighting, the moral effect would be terrible, both in Spain and abroad," Blanco persisted. Cervera finally agreed to make the attempt, though he felt certain it would end in absolute disaster.

July 3, 1898: Seven American warships—four battleships, 1 cruiser, and two escort vessels—were on station off Santiago. The flagship, the USS *New York*, was steaming eastward for Daiquirí, away from the squadron, carrying Adm. William Sampson to a conference with Maj. Gen. Rufus Shafter. Aboard the USS *Brooklyn*, flagship of the second in command, Comdr. Winfield Scott Schley, a lookout sighted smoke columns rising above Santiago harbor. "The enemy's ships are coming out," he reported.

U.S. ships are shown destroying the Spanish fleet of Adm. Pascual Cervera off Santiago, Cuba, on July 3, 1898.

Cervera's flagship, the cruiser *Maria Teresa*, cleared the harbor at a few minutes past 9 o'clock in the morning. The Spanish warship's captain ordered bugles blown to signal the start of the battle. The American ships swiftly cleared for action as the Spanish squadron emerged in single file: the flagship, then the cruisers *Vizcaya*, *Cristobal Colon*, and *Oquendo*; finally, the two destroyers, *Pluton* and *Furor*. "The Spanish ships came out as gaily as brides to the altar," wrote Capt. John Philip, commanding the battleship USS *Texas*. "Handsome vessels they certainly were, and with flags enough for a celebration." The Spanish squadron, slower than the Americans and far less powerfully armed, came out of Santiago at 5 knots, swung to the right, and steered for the *Brooklyn*.

The Spanish managed to get ahead of the Americans, and a pursuit on parallel tracks ensued. The *Maria Teresa* opened fire first, ineffectually. The heavier American ships replied. Within a few minutes, the *Maria Teresa*'s wooden decks were on fire. The *Iowa*, *Texas*, and *Brooklyn*, pouring on coal, soon caught up and began to batter the *Maria Teresa*. The trailing Spanish destroyers were destroyed almost as an afterthought. A large-caliber shell from the *Iowa* seemed to cut the *Furor* in two. Several hits drove the *Pluton* onto the rocks.

The *Maria Teresa* dropped out of the Spanish line, burning fiercely. Cervera ordered it run aground and abandoned. The U.S. ships began to pound the other Spanish cruisers. The fire drove the *Oquendo* ashore just west of Cervera's flagship. The *Brooklyn*, *Oregon*, and *Iowa* then overtook the *Vizcaya*. A 13-inch shell from the *Oregon*'s main battery struck the Spanish vessel, which seemed to shudder from end to end. The *Vizcaya*, too, ran aground and hauled down her colors.

That left only the *Cristobal Colon*, which by then had opened a 6-mile lead. The *Brooklyn* and the others gave chase. The *Oregon* opened from extreme range, around 10,000 yards, and continued firing deliberately. One 1,100-pound projectile struck just under the Spanish cruiser's stern. The *Colon* turned for shore and went aground, completing—as Cervera had foretold—the destruction of the Spanish squadron.

One of the American destroyers picked up Cervera and other survivors of the *Maria Teresa*. The futile action cost the Spanish 323 dead, 151 wounded, and 1,813 taken prisoner. The Americans reported a single fatality, a sailor on the *Brooklyn*.

"A glorious victory has been achieved," Schley signaled Sampson on the *New York*, which had not quite managed to catch up to the battle. The message touched off a long contest for recognition. Schley was the man on the spot. Sampson had issued the general tactical plan; the *New York* had been within sight of the battle, even though it had not taken part. Sampson believed his position as commander of the squadron entitled him to claim credit for the victory.

Schley sent an officer ashore to cable news of the victory to Washington, D.C., from Siboney. One of Sampson's aides intercepted the message and submitted the admiral's message. "The fleet under my command offers the nation, as a Fourth of July present, the whole of Cervera's fleet," Sampson said. Schley was bitter. "If the battle had miscarried," he said later, "there would have been no difficulty whatever about who was in command, or who would have had to bear the censure."

July 2–17, 1898: The Americans besieging Santiago, exposed in their lines, suffered under the burning Cuban sun. "If any one has discovered a more uncomfortable place to spend a hot day than in a 4-foot trench, I have yet to hear of it," wrote Trooper Frank Knox of the Rough Riders. "One had to sit all cramped up with no opportunity to move; just sit there and fry and boil and sweat under the blistering sun and drink muddy water and chew an occasional hardtack." Brig. Gen. Joseph Wheeler, meanwhile, scouted the inner Santiago defenses. He concluded they could be overcome but only at a high cost in casualties. For the time being, Shafter preferred to endure the discomforts—severe enough, but not so surely fatal—of the siege.

July 3, 1898: Inside Santiago, the Spanish commander, Gen. José Toral (he had succeeded Gen. Arsenio Linares, wounded on San Juan Hill), rejected Shafter's first surrender demand, sent in just before Cervera's cruisers dashed out of the harbor. Toral did agree to a brief cease-fire to allow women, children, and neutrals to leave before the Americans shelled the city.

July 4–6, 1898: Refugees poured out onto the El Caney road. Shafter agreed to extend the truce through the afternoon of July 6, delaying the bombardment. Thousands of evacuees streamed through the American lines.

"All day along the hot, dusty road leading from Santiago to El Caney passed the long, white line," Lt. John J. Pershing of the 10th Cavalry recalled, "frail, hungry women carried a bundle of clothing, a parcel of food or an infant, while weak and helpless children trailed wearily at the skirts of their wretched mothers." Some 20,000 displaced persons looked to the Americans for sustenance. By the end of the first week in July, El Caney had become, in the phrase of the novelist-war correspondent Stephen Crane, "a vast parrot-cage of chattering refugees."

Emissaries of Shafter and Toral continued to negotiate. Meanwhile, in the trenches, food and tobacco were in short supply. Roosevelt blamed his commanding general. "It is criminal to keep Shafter in command," he wrote his powerful political friend, Massachusetts senator Henry Cabot Lodge. "He is utterly inefficient; and now he is panic struck. The mismanagement has been beyond belief. We are half-starved; and our men are sickening daily."

Conditions were worse in Santiago, where the troops and remaining civilians were subsisting on a small amount of rice doled out each day. "Unfortunately, the situation is desperate," wrote Gen. Arsenio Linares. "The surrender is imminent, otherwise we will only gain time to prolong an agony."

July 6, 1898: Shafter renewed the surrender demand and extended the truce another three days to give Toral an opportunity to consult with his superiors in Havana and Madrid. Toral offered to evacuate Santiago if the Americans would let him march for Havana with all his arms and equipment. Shafter forwarded the proposal to Washington, D.C.; War Secretary Russell Alger and President McKinley rejected it out of hand. "What you went to Santiago for was the Spanish army," the president reminded Shafter. "If you allow it to evacuate with its arms you must meet it somewhere else. This is not war."

July 7–11, 1898: The shooting resumed, though without much conviction on either side. The 5th Corps reported three cases of yellow fever during the second week in July; malaria, dysentery, and other ailments were taking a growing toll on the soldiers.

July 11, 1898: General Shafter declared another truce and sent another surrender demand through the lines, with an offer to convey the Spanish forces back across the Atlantic free of charge.

July 15, 1898: Finally relenting, Toral told the Americans he had won approval from Madrid to capitulate. Toral agreed to surrender the troops defending Santiago together with all the scattered forces in his territorial command, some 12,000 men in several garrisons beyond the immediate reach of the Americans.

July 17, 1898: The commanding generals met for the surrender ceremony in a field beyond Santiago's walls. They exchanged courtesies, and the Spanish infantry presented arms. "The Spanish flag, which for three hundred and eighty-two years had floated over the city, was pulled down and furled forever," General Wheeler wrote. U.S. forces entered Santiago, a picturesque city of narrow streets and low stucco houses, and raised the U.S. colors over the governor's palace. After the firing of a 21-gun salute, the band of the 6th Infantry broke into "Hail, Columbia."

PUERTO RICO

Some 500 miles east of Cuba, lay Spain's other major possession in the Caribbean, the 108-mile-long, 40-mile-wide island of Puerto Rico, where Spain maintained some 8,000 regular troops, reinforced by 9,000 militia. Unlike Cuba, Puerto Rico had mounted no serious challenge to Spanish colonial control. In fact, Spain had moved to grant home rule to the island in 1897 as part of a broader package of reforms intended to pacify Cuba and end the insurgency there. Even so, the locals showed no great loyalty to the Spanish. Although the Americans expected to have to fight for the island, they anticipated the struggle would be fairly brief. With the Santiago campaign concluded, Gen. Nelson A. Miles, the commander of the U.S. Army, took personal charge of the campaign to seize Puerto Rico. Miles planned to land an expeditionary force near Ponce in the mountainous island's southwest corner and march overland for the capital, San Juan, along the 70-mile length of the military highway that linked the two cities.

July 25, 1898: As it happened, sailors from the USS *Gloucester* were the first Americans ashore. A party of bluejackets landed at Guánica west of Ponce and accepted the surrender of a detachment of Spanish police. American infantry, 2,000 men from the 6th Illinois and the 6th Massachusetts, landed from lighters later in the day. By evening, Miles's first contingents were securely ashore.

The troops camped along the edges of the single long street that led inland from the harbor. They found a peaceful little place—quiet, shady,

and disease-free. "To those of us who had just come from Santiago, the sight of the women sitting on porches and rocking in bent-wood chairs, the lighted swinging lamps with cut-glass pendants, and the pictures and mirrors on the walls, which we saw that night through opened doors, seemed part of some long-forgotten existence," correspondent Richard Harding Davis wrote. The Americans settled in for the night, prepared to begin the advance inland at first light.

July 26, 1898: General Miles's plan called for four separate columns to march on San Juan. Troops moving out from Guánica fought a skirmish at Yauco on the Ponce road, then advanced to the outskirts of Ponce to find the city undefended, with red, white and blue banners suspended from the balconies. "Long live Washington," one citizen called out.

July 27–August 5, 1898: Landing operations swelled the American invasion force to a total of 15,000 men.

August 6, 1898: Miles launched the first general movement in the four-pronged advance. There were short fights near Mayaguez and along the Ponce-San Juan road, but almost no other organized opposition. "This is a prosperous and beautiful country," Miles cabled War Secretary Russell Alger. "The Army will soon be in mountain region; weather delightful; troops in best of health and spirits; anticipate no insurmountable obstacles in future results." Rumors of an armistice circulated among the troops.

August 12, 1898: Miles learned that the United States and Spain had signed a peace protocol and an armistice. In response, he ordered a halt to offensive operations on the island, not much of a concession, as the Americans already held most of it. The six engagements of the short Puerto Rico campaign cost the U.S. forces 7 killed and 36 wounded. The Spanish reported some 450 casualties.

HOME FRONT

The short, decisive Spanish-American War affected ordinary Americans at home only in small ways. Few demands were made on civilians. There were some short-term price rises. Adm. Pascual Cervera y Topete's cruiser squadron caused a temporary scare along the U.S. East Coast. And for several hundred unfortunate American families, word came of a loved one killed in battle or, more often, dead of disease in one of the Army camps.

Alarmist newspaper headlines fueled the Cervera scare in May 1898. The governor of one eastern state refused to allow National Guard units to leave the state, expecting they would be needed to repel the Spanish. A congressman requested a warship to defend the resort of Jekyll Island, Georgia. Boston businesses sent cash and securities to bank vaults in inland Worcester, Massachusetts.

Maine senator William Frye, a strong supporter of intervention in Cuba, petitioned the government for protection of the Down East coast. "Senator Frye, who has been a blazing jingo, shouting for war, comes in with an appeal that a vessel be sent down," Navy Secretary John Davis Long complained. In response to Frye and other claimants, the Navy formed a fast squadron to patrol the coast northward from the Delaware capes to Bar Harbor, Maine.

The United States in 1898 had just emerged from an anxious period of economic recession, political instability, and social unrest. During the 1890s, the insurgent Populist alliance of farmers and laborers agitated for political and economic reforms, including government ownership of transportation, improved wages and working conditions, a graduated income tax, and the direct election of senators. Demonstrations sometimes turned violent. In Homestead, Pennsylvania, in 1892, striking workers fought street battles with the private police of the Carnegie Steel Company. When the financial panic of 1893 struck, hundreds of jobless men marched on Washington, D.C., with "Coxey's army." Banks collapsed; businesses folded; strikes multiplied.

Social divisions deepened, too, among America's 75 million people. Foreign-born urban dwellers made up an increasing share of the U.S. population—12 percent in 1898. The migration of large numbers of blacks from the rigidly segregated South to northern cities began. These movements focused attention on the contradictions between American ideals and American reality. For example, just as the U.S. went to war in the spring of 1898, white voters in Louisiana approved a new state constitution that effectively denied voting rights to African Americans.

Even so, the United States was rich and becoming richer. Conditions were improving for the majority of Americans. An upturn in the business cycle after 1896 brought nearly full employment. Rising prices for wheat eased farmer discontent in the last years of the decade. Technological advances led to near-revolutionary changes in styles of living: The vast rail network sped goods and people to all parts of the United States, the first automobiles appeared, and steam heat, electric light, elevators, and telephones were no longer novelties.

The return of prosperity came at a price: a steady rise in the cost of living after 1897. The outbreak of the Spanish-American War helped to fuel the increase. The cost of mules, still a mainstay in the rural United States, increased from $70-90 to $130-150 a head. And with Adm. Thomas Dewey's victory and the rush to volunteer, the price of bunting soared by 300 percent.

April–June 1898: Most Americans reacted to news of the war with patriotic enthusiasm. "In April, everywhere, flags were flying," wrote Kansas journalist William Allen White. "Trains carrying soldiers were hurrying to the Southland; and little children on fences greeted the soldiers with flapping scarves and handkerchiefs and flags." Newspaper sales shot up; Joseph Pulitzer's New York *World* circulated 1.3 million copies a day at the end of April.

Tens of thousands of young men signed enlistment papers and went off to training camps. Comparatively few of the 200,000 volunteers made it overseas, and boredom soon set in. The camps were deadly, too, especially those in north Georgia and Florida. "This park as a camping place is incurably infected," a government inspector wrote of Chickamauga, Georgia, the Civil War battlefield near the Georgia-Tennessee border.

July–August 1898: The war was over before it could greatly alter civilians' lives. For the 5th Corps in Cuba, victorious at Santiago and slowly disintegrating from sickness, it could not have ended soon enough. Yellow fever was the great dread, and malarial fevers were debilitating. By late July, 20 percent of the expeditionary force—more than 4,000 men—had fallen ill.

Maj. Gen. Rufus Shafter urged an immediate evacuation. "If it is not done, I believe the death-rate will be appalling," he cabled the War Department. Politically connected volunteer officers took matters into their own hands, outflanking the Army bureaucracy. Theodore Roosevelt drafted a round-robin letter, signed by a council of senior officers, calling for the withdrawal of the 5th Corps to healthy camps at home. "This army must be moved at once, or perish," Roosevelt wrote. Someone leaked the circular to the Associated Press, and it appeared in newspapers across the country on August 4. The letter raised a public opinion clatter and embarrassed the War Department, which, in fact, had already approved the evacuation. By August 8, the first 5th Corps troops were aboard transports en route to a quarantine camp at Montauk Point on Long Island, 125 miles east of New York City.

NEGOTIATIONS AND PEACE TREATY

August 12, 1898: Spain formally agreed to a peace protocol on U.S. terms: the cession of Cuba and Puerto Rico and an immediate Spanish evacuation of both islands and the American occupation of the "city, bay and harbor of Manila" pending a final peace treaty. At 4:30 in the afternoon, President McKinley and the French ambassador, Jules Cambon, acting for Spain, signed the protocol in a ceremony at the White House in Washington, D.C.

September 1898: Judge William R. Day, a political crony of President McKinley's, led the American Peace Commission to France in mid-September for treaty talks with the Spanish.

October 1, 1898: Peace negotiations opened in Paris. The diplomats fenced for weeks over the issue of U.S. assumption of Spain's Cuban debts. The Spanish proposed transferring $400 million in obligations; the United States refused.

The Philippine Islands were the greatest sticking point, however. McKinley and his chief policy makers had been leaning for several months toward American acquisition of the archipelago. In the president's view, the islanders were incapable of governing themselves; Spain, another European power, or the United States would have to be in control. "There was nothing left for us to do but take them all," McKinley concluded, "and to educate the Filipinos, and uplift and civilize and Christianize them, and by God's grace do the very best we could by them, as our fellow-men for whom Christ also died."

October 28, 1898: The president directed the American commissioners to demand all the Philippines in return for peace.

November 4, 1898: The Spanish rejected the demand, arguing that the U.S. actually had taken Manila after the signing of the peace protocol.

November 1898: In the United States, opposition to annexation began to mount. Newspaper king Joseph Pulitzer campaigned against acquiring the islands. The Anti-Imperialist League formed in Boston. Author Mark Twain, social worker Jane Addams, and former president Benjamin Harrison took up the anti-imperialist cause. "We insist that the subjugation of any people is 'criminal aggression' and open disloyalty to the distinctive principles of our government," the league proclaimed.

December 10, 1898: The American and Spanish peace commissions formally signed the Treaty of Paris. The American negotiators finally persuaded the Spanish with the offer of a $20 million payment for the Philippine Islands. The treaty obligated Spain to cede Cuba, Puerto Rico, and Guam along with the Philippines.

The McKinley administration faced a difficult ratification fight in the Senate, however. Senator George Hoar (R–Mass.) led the antiannexation forces. Taking the Philippines, he charged, would make the United States "a cheapjack country, raking after the cart for the leavings of European tyranny."

January 4, 1899: McKinley sent the treaty to the Senate. Passionate debate broke out at once. A poet of the press caught the public mood with these lines:

O Dewey at Manila
That fateful first of May
When you sank the Spanish squadron
In almost bloodless fray,
And gave your name to deathless fame;
O glorious Dewey, say,
Why didn't you weigh anchor
And softly sail away?

In the Philippines, Gen. Wesley Merritt flashed a note of warning. The Americans were underestimating the islanders. Emilio Aguinaldo's republic, Merritt said, had the support of 10,000 well-armed insurgents who were prepared to fight for their independence. The Philippines could thus end up costing the United States a lot more than the $20 million acquisition fee. Representative Thomas Reed (R–Maine), the cynical, sharp-tongued anti-imperialist Speaker of the House, put it this way: "We have bought ten million Malays at $2.00 unpicked, and nobody knows what it will cost to pick them."

February 6, 1899: The Senate ratified the treaty with Spain by a vote of 57–27. McKinley had attained the necessary two-thirds majority with only one vote to spare.

The Philippine Insurrection

February 4, 1899: While the U.S. Senate was debating the peace treaty with Spain, Emilio Aguinaldo's army launched a series of attacks on U.S. positions in the Philippines. The Americans repulsed the insurgents, but at a cost of 175 killed and wounded.

March 1899: Congress called for 35,000 volunteers to suppress the insurrection and authorized an additional 65,000 men for the Regular Army. A vocal minority of Americans strongly opposed efforts to subjugate Aguinaldo's forces. "It's a matter of congratulation that you seem to have about finished your work of civilizing the Filipinos," steel baron Andrew Carnegie sarcastically wrote New York *Tribune* editor Whitelaw Reid, a committed imperialist. "It is thought that about 8,000 of them have been completely civilized and sent to heaven." By the end of 1899, the U. S. had 65,000 troops in the Philippines.

April 28, 1899: Aguinaldo and his forces proposed negotiating peace terms but the U.S. demanded unconditional surrender. The adversaries continued to wage a furious propaganda campaign as well. Filipinos claimed the United States took no prisoners; insurgent casualty rates of five dead to every one wounded seemed to support the charge. The United States complained bitterly of the Filipinos' tactics of ambuscade and bushwhack.

November 1900: Aguinaldo had high hopes for the American presidential election of 1900, in which anti-imperialist William Jennings Bryan, a Democrat, challenged the incumbent Republican William McKinley. But the Philippine insurrection had no influence on the outcome; McKinley comfortably won the election. "We have failed to awaken the lethargic American conscience," Aguinaldo lamented.

March 23, 1901: American army general Frederick Funston and a group of officers, pretending to be prisoners, surprised Aguinaldo in his stronghold in the Luzon mountain village of Palanan and captured the insurgent leader.

April 19, 1901: Aguinaldo took an oath of allegiance to the United States, calling on his countrymen to end the rebellion and negotiate a peace with the U.S. and to work for eventual in-dependence. His followers fought on, however.

September 28, 1901: Filipino forces ambushed a 9th Infantry detachment and killed 48 Americans near the Samar Island village of Balangiga. President Theodore Roosevelt (he had succeeded to the presidency with McKinley's assassination earlier in September), ordered "the most stern policies" in reprisal. Gen. Jacob Smith, the U.S. commander on Samar, gave Roosevelt what he had asked for. Smith's troops faithfully carried out his instructions to convert the island into a "howling wilderness," excesses for which Smith ultimately faced a court-martial and a forced early retirement from the Army. Over the next year, the Americans gradually pacified the islands, and an American-run Philippine Civil Commission established effective local services throughout the archipelago.

July 1, 1902: Congress passed the Philippine Government Act, which provided for the Philippines to be governed by a commission appointed by the U.S. president. The inhabitants of the Philippines were to be treated as citizens of their own land, not of the United States. The United States effectively declared the insurgency at an end.

RESULTS OF THE WAR (Casualties, Costs, Consequences)

American: In the Spanish-American War, the United States suffered 379 battle deaths—10 sailors and 369 soldiers—but some 3,000 American servicemen died of other causes. Estimates of the monetary cost approached $250 million.

More than 500 American soldiers died of fever or other illness in Cuba, close to double the number of battle fatalities there. Another 250 died in the 5th Corps quarantine camp at Montauk Point on Long Island. At the Chickamauga training camp, more than 400 soldiers died after the fighting had ended overseas. And some of the survivors never regained their full health. "Many of them are wrecks for life, others are candidates for a premature grave," concluded Dr. Nicholas Senn, chief surgeon of the U.S. Volunteers.

The Philippine Insurrection turned out to be a far more costly venture for the United States: 4,234 deaths (from combat wounds or from disease), 2,818 wounded, and a cost estimated at $600 million.

Spanish: In addition to about 1,000 combat

U.S. Army troops are photographed in a trench during the 1899–1902 campaign in the Philippines that followed the Spanish–American War.

deaths (more than 700 sailors perished in the two naval actions alone), Spain lost possession of a significant portion of what remained of a once-glorious empire—Cuba, Puerto Rico, the Philippines, Guam—and all pretense to its status as a great power.

Cuban: The Spanish were gone from Cuba by the end of January 1899, and a U.S. Army of occupation settled in to rule, with the notion of preparing Cuba for eventual independence. There were, however, expressions of mistrust of American intentions. "The Americans have embittered the joy of the victors with their forcibly imposed tutelage," said the *insurrecto* leader Maximo Gomez. Still, most insurgent leaders were cooperative. The Cuban Constitutional Convention of 1900 granted the United States a long-term lease on the naval anchorage at Guantanamo Bay. It also recognized the U.S. right to intervene to protect Cuba's independence or to restore order.

Cuba attained independence in 1902 under the terms of the Platt Amendment, a U.S. law incorporated into the final Cuban independence treaty. The statute permitted close U.S. supervision of Cuban affairs; American troops returned briefly to Cuba in 1906. The Platt Amendment remained in force until 1934, when the Cuban government successfully pressed for its repeal.

The U.S. occupying force left one lasting mark on Cuba: the eradication of the scourge of yellow fever. The Army's Yellow Fever Commission, in 1900, led by Army surgeon Walter Reed and working from a theory developed by Cuban physician Carlos J. Finlay, proved that the bite of the female *Aedes aegypti* mosquito transmitted the infection. Gen. Leonard Wood, the former Rough Rider colonel who commanded the occupation force, oversaw the assaults on mosquito breeding grounds that all but wiped out the disease. In 1900, in Havana alone, 1,400 yellow fever cases were reported. In the following year, only 37 cases were reported in all of Cuba. In Cuba, in the United States, and elsewhere, the regular summer and autumn outbreaks of the disease gradually became a thing of the past.

Filipino: Many Filipinos lost their lives in the struggle against the Spanish rulers, but another estimated 20,000 Filipino insurgents were killed during the three years' war with the United States In addition, many thousands more Filipino civilians died directly or indirectly from famine or disease as a result of the fighting—estimates have ranged as high as 200,000.

MILITARY INNOVATIONS, TACTICS, EQUIPMENT

In Spain, the United States faced an extremely weak and demoralized enemy. There were thus few incentives to experiment with new tactics, and the short, one-sided war produced little in the way of tactical ingenuity or innovative developments in materiel and equipment.

The relatively new smokeless-powder rifle ammunition proved its value in the land battles. The U.S. volunteer regiments generally were issued with old rifles whose black powder discharges sent up puffs of smoke at which the enemy could aim an accurate fusillade. The 71st New York learned that lesson at a high cost below the San Juan Heights on July 1. The regiment suffered heavily from Spanish volleys poured into the telltale smoke cloud sent up by the troops' obsolete Springfields.

The U.S. Navy proved devastatingly superior to a decrepit opponent. Still, the sea battles revealed deficiencies in U.S. vessels and especially in U.S. gunnery. The American vessels were too slow and too lightly armored; the naval board that studied the Spanish wrecks off Santiago determined that Americans scored only 122 hits out of more than 9,400 rounds fired.

The Spanish-American War exposed major flaws in Army organization and supply. The postwar Dodge Commission, formed to investigate widespread charges of incompetence and fraud, concluded, in February 1899, that there had been no intentional dishonesty or neglect but plenty of mismanagement. The commission recommended that the War Department streamline its bureaucratic procedures, stockpile vital war supplies, and establish training schools to assure a steady supply of well-trained officers. In 1903, as a direct outcome of the Dodge recommendations, War Secretary Elihu Root established a general staff to plan for war, and Congress approved the Militia Act to standardize and improve the training of state troops.

LEGENDS AND TRIVIA

Exaggeration, embellishment and outright invention characterized American reporting—some would say overreporting—of the Spanish-American War.

In 1897, in a fairly typical example, **Richard Harding Davis** reported in William Randolph Hearst's *New York Journal* that Spanish authorities had subjected three attractive young Cuban female passengers aboard the U.S. steamer *Olivette* to a strip search. Frederic Remington's accompanying drawing showed three brutish Spanish policemen leering at a terrified naked girl. The women, embarrassed by the lurid illustration, came forward to assert that female officers had carried out the search in complete privacy and that they had been in no way mistreated.

Frederic Remington figured in one of the more enduring journalistic legends of the Spanish-American War. He had been sent to Cuba by **William Randolph Hearst** to provide illustrations of the war Hearst felt was imminent. Tiring of Havana café life in the months before the outbreak, Remington is alleged to have cabled Hearst for permission to return to New York.

"Everything is quiet," Remington supposedly wired Hearst. "There is no trouble. There will be no war."

According to legend, Hearst wired back: "Please remain. You furnish the pictures and I'll furnish the war."

Hearst denied the story, and no evidence (such as the actual telegrams) has been produced, but the story has been told for so long and so often that Hearst's reply has become a "quotation" with its own standing.

Remington and Richard Harding Davis also played a major role in the puffing up of the reputation of **Theodore Roosevelt and the Rough Riders**, a colorful band of Ivy Leaguers from prominent families, politicos, hunters and fishermen, adventurers, cowboys, and others animated by a sudden desire to avenge the USS *Maine*.

Roosevelt parlayed his renown as a Rough Rider into the governorship of New York and the vice presidency. And with McKinley's assassination in September 1901, Roosevelt became president. Legend and simplification (and a well-known painting by Remington) fashioned a popular image of Roosevelt leading the Rough Riders in a glorious pounding mounted charge up San Juan Hill. In fact, the objective was the twin eminence known as Kettle Hill. And the Rough Riders fought on foot, not on horseback, scrambling low-bent in small parties up the steep grassy slope. Roosevelt never shied from publicizing himself, but even he never claimed the charge as sole property of the 1st U.S. Volunteer Cavalry. Dismounted troopers of the 9th and 10th U.S. Cavalry—African-American regular soldiers under white officers—were as responsible as the Rough Riders for the successful outcome.

NOTABLE PHRASES

Remember the Maine!

Clearly an echo of the earlier "Remember the Alamo!" (and still earlier such slogans), no one has ever proved who cried that first. But it immediately became the rallying cry for the Americans in the Spanish-American War. The tabloid press, in particular, rushed to assign responsibility for the *Maine* disaster to the Spanish, and many Americans easily focused the emotion of the slogan against Spain.

You may fire when ready, Gridley.

As far as such statements can ever be proved, Adm. George Dewey seems to have said those words to the captain of the USS *Olympia* at the battle of Manila Bay. There were journalists aboard the ship, the words were reported in the earliest accounts of the battle, and it is just about what any commander would be expected to say. In any case, Admiral Dewey's celebrity after his victory at Manila Bay gave currency to his cool aside. (It is sometimes recorded as "You may fire when you are ready, Gridley.")

A splendid little war.

In the immediate aftermath of the Spanish-American War, John Hay, the American ambassador in London, wrote to his friend Theodore Roosevelt: "It has been a splendid little war, begun with the highest motives, carried on with magnificent intelligence and spirit, favored by that fortune which loves the brave." In the years since he wrote this, the phrase has been oft quoted—but usually with an ironic tone that Hay never really intended.

jingoism

Originally, "By jingo!" was merely a jocular oath—probably a variation of *by Jove!* in the same way that *gosh!* is a euphemism of God. But in the late 19th century, the phrase by Jingo was used in a British music hall song to evoke a person, according to Webster's dictionary, "who boasts of his patriotism and favors an aggressive, threatening, warlike foreign policy." The word jingoism then came to be applied to Americans' call for a showdown with Spain over Cuba, and though an import from overseas, it fit perfectly in the United States of 1898.

SONGS

The Spanish-American War was such a brief war that it would seem there was hardly time for anyone to write and popularize a song about it. But one songwriter, accustomed to turning out songs as fast as he could, did just that. Paul Dresser, known for his song "On the Banks of the Wabash Far Away," churned out a number of songs to capitalize on the "war fever": in 1898, there was "Our Country, May She Always be Right" and "We Fight Tomorrow, Mother"; in 1899, he wrote "Come Home, Dewey, We Won't Do a Thing to You"; then in 1903, when the U.S. troops were withdrawn from the Philippines and Cuba, he wrote "The Boys Are Coming Home Today."

Several other songs became popular during the Spanish-American War. The best known of those was "When Johnny Comes Marching Home," which had, in fact, been composed in 1863 by the well-known bandmaster Patrick Gilmore; it enjoyed some popularity during and after the Civil War (and its melody had been adapted by several serious composers), but it had a special revival during the Spanish-American War. "A Hot Time in the Old Town Tonight," although originally composed in 1886 to describe an actual fire, was adopted by Theodore Roosevelt's Rough Riders and then by many troops as a song celebrating their anticipated return home from their glorious victories.

Yet another was a sentimental ballad, "Break the News to Mother," composed some years before the war by Charles K. Harris in reference to the death of a fireman; by coincidence, Harris had converted the fireman to a soldier in 1897, and when the Spanish-American War began, the song became a big hit. And, finally, one of the best-known pieces of American music, John

Philip Sousa's "The Stars and Stripes Forever" was composed just in time—1897—to provide a rousing march.

HISTORICAL PERSPECTIVES AND CONTROVERSIES

The Spanish-American War inevitably gave rise to a number of controversies, some of which have been debated ever since.

Is it fair to blame individual military and political leaders for the various mistakes made and mishaps suffered by the U.S. Army during the war?

The first American accounts of the Spanish-American War generally were laudatory of U.S. motives and military performance, particularly naval performance. Richard Harding Davis's *The Cuban and Porto Rico Campaigns* (1898) is representative of the instant eyewitness histories that appeared in the war's immediate aftermath. Such works generally identified a number of villains as well: desk-bound War Department bureaucrats of the kind stigmatized in the Dodge Commission report of 1899, for instance, and profiteers such as those who sold old, inedible, and even tainted beef to the armed forces.

Maj. Gen. Rufus Shafter, commanding the expeditionary force in Cuba, came in for substantial criticism from journalists, particularly from Davis, who found him inert as well as lacking in style and dash. Roosevelt, too, sharply criticized Shafter in letters to his influential political friends. Gen. Nelson A. Miles, the Army commander, won more favorable reviews. Yet hardly anyone could be found to say a word critical of the admirals, though Comdr. Winfield Scott Schley came in for mild criticism, at the time and afterward, for failing to track down Admiral Cervera's cruiser squadron before it reached the comparative safety of Santiago.

Was the early enthusiasm and pride over the U.S. role in the Spanish-American War justified and sustainable?

Although the anti-imperialists were pushed aside by the larger thrust of American triumphalism, correctives to the early optimism eventually appeared. In *The Martial Spirit* (1931),

Walter Millis skewered the Imperialist movement and U.S. military pretensions, emphasizing cant, hypocrisy, bungling, and decidedly mixed American motives. Revisionist diplomatic historians of the 1950s and 1960s, most notably William Appleman Williams in *The Tragedy of American Diplomacy* (1959, revised 1962), argued that the United States had gone to war as part of a naked bid to snatch colonies, build markets, and keep pace with such rising economic and political powers as imperial Germany. However, as many historians have pointed out, many and perhaps most of U.S. business leaders (including Andrew Carnegie) opposed the war. Indeed, the exceptionally probusiness McKinley was a very reluctant warrior. Revisionists also have tended to emphasize the pathetic weakness of the Spanish military, thus casting the United States as a young, upstart bully.

Historians such as Frank Friedel in *The Splendid Little War* (1959) and Ernest May in *Imperial Democracy* (1961) present the Spanish-American War as the event that signaled the emergence of the United States as a world power. They do not deny economic motivations, such as substantial and growing U.S. business interests in Cuba, or the influence of imperialist theorists such as Alfred Thayer Mahan and his disciples, who argued the military, political, and economic necessity of U.S. overseas possessions. But historians also credit American humanitarian impulses, a genuine sympathy for the Cuban independence and a revulsion toward harsh Spanish methods of quelling the insurrection.

What actually happened to the USS Maine?

Controversy persisted over the immediate cause of the Spanish-American War, the sinking of the USS *Maine*. Salvage teams raised the rusted hulk from the mud of Havana harbor in 1911, and the reopened investigation confirmed the 1898 court of inquiry finding that a submerged mine had destroyed the warship. But in 1976, a team of American naval investigators, working with computer models, concluded that a fire on board touched off the *Maine*'s ammunition stocks. "The available evidence is consistent with an internal investigation alone," Adm. Hyman Rickover wrote. "The most likely source was heat from a coal bunker adjacent to the 6-inch reserve magazine."

CIVILIAN AND MILITARY BIOGRAPHIES

AMERICAN

Alger, Russell Alexander (1836–1907)—secretary of war: Russell Alger was born in Ohio. He was a Civil War veteran. Alger entered politics after the Civil War and won election as governor of Michigan in 1885. As war secretary from 1897 to 1899, he shouldered much of the blame—some of it unfair—for the Army's unpreparedness at the outbreak of the Spanish-American War.

Davis, Richard Harding (1864–1916)—journalist, author: Richard Davis was born in Philadelphia. A popular freelance newspaper and magazine writer and best-selling novelist, Davis also covered the Boer War and World War I. His *The Cuban and Porto Rico Campaigns* (1898) is an account of his experiences with U.S. forces in the Caribbean. The bulk of his work is today not well known or highly regarded.

Dewey, George (1837–1917)—naval officer: George Dewey was born in Vermont. He graduated from the Naval Academy in 1858 and saw service on the Mississippi River and on blockade duty during the Civil War. He took command of the Asiatic Squadron in January 1898 and led it to a decisive victory over the Spanish at Manila Bay on May 1, 1898. A national hero at the start of the Spanish-American War, his aura faded with the passing of time.

Hearst, William Randolph (1863–1951)—publisher: William Randolph Hearst was the son of a San Francisco newspaper proprietor. He moved east in 1895 to turn the struggling *New York Journal* into a powerhouse of the sensational press. Along with his rival, Joseph Pulitzer, he helped arouse public opinion against Spain in 1897–1898. He succeeded in developing one of the largest publishing empires in the United States but failed in his attempts at a political career.

Hoar, George Frisbie (1826–1904)—senator: George Hoar was born in Concord, Massachusetts. He became active in the antislavery movement and helped found the Republican Party in the mid-1850s. Elected to the Senate in 1877, he served in the upper chamber until his death. Splitting with his party and with the majority of his constituents, he passionately opposed U.S. acquisition of the Philippines in 1898–1899.

Mahan, Alfred Thayer (1840–1914)—naval officer: Alfred Thayer Mahan served on blockade duty during the Civil War but found his true vocation as a naval strategist and theorist. He taught at the Naval War College from 1885 on. His book *The Influence of Sea Power upon History* (1890) deeply influenced U.S. expansionists of the 1890s.

McKinley, William (1843–1901)—president: William McKinley was the 25th president of the United States (1897–1901). McKinley fought in the Civil War. He entered politics as a Republican in the late 1860s. His advocacy of a protective trade policy resulted in the high McKinley Tariff of 1890. As president, he proved unable to contain or deflect rising sentiment for military action against Spain and reluctantly led the nation to war in April 1898. Shot by an anarchist on September 6, 1901, he died eight days later.

Merritt, Wesley (1834–1910)—general: Wesley Merritt was a native of New York City. He graduated from West Point in 1860 and served in the cavalry during the Civil War. Postwar duty took him to the western frontier and eventually into the superintendency of the military academy (1882–1887). He commanded the U.S. force that captured Manila in August 1898 and was military governor of the Philippines in 1898–1899. He retired from the Army in 1900.

Miles, Nelson Appleton (1839–1925)—general: Nelson Miles joined a Massachusetts volunteer regiment early in the Civil War, saw extensive combat, and served as Confederate President Jefferson Davis's jailer in 1865–1866. He later fought Indians on the frontier. Becoming Army commander in 1895, he supervised troop training at the outset of the Spanish-American War and commanded U.S forces in the Puerto Rico campaign of July–August 1898. Miles retired in 1903.

Pulitzer, Joseph (1847–1911)—publisher: Joseph Pulitzer was born in Hungary. He arrived in the United States in 1864. He fought in the Union Army at the close of the Civil War. Going into journalism in St. Louis, Missouri, Pulitzer built that city's *Post-Dispatch* into a crusading newspaper of high reputation. In 1883, he took over the *World* in New York City and, in competition with Hearst in the 1890s, veered into increasingly shrill sensationalism. His will established journalism's most prestigious prizes, the Pulitzers.

Roosevelt, Theodore (1858–1919)—cavalry

officer, president: Theodore Roosevelt was a New Yorker from an established family. He was a sickly youth who turned to sports and the outdoors to rebuild his health and was a noted advocate for "the strenuous life." Service with the Rough Riders volunteer cavalry regiment in Cuba made him a national hero. From the governorship of New York (1899–1901), Roosevelt vaulted to the vice presidency (1901) and, with McKinley's assassination in September 1901, to the presidency. Drawing from his Spanish-American War experience, he built up the Navy and pressed for the building of the Panama Canal. He was re-elected president in 1904, but he chose not to run again in 1908. Roosevelt made an unsuccessful bid for the presidency as a third party candidate in 1912.

Sampson, William Thomas (1840–1902)—naval officer: William Sampson was born in Palmyra, New York. He graduated from the Naval Academy in 1861 and pursued a long naval career that culminated in commanding the U.S. North Atlantic Squadron in 1898. The squadron bottled up a Spanish flotilla in Santiago, Cuba, in June 1898 and destroyed it entirely in a running sea fight off the south coast of Cuba on July 3. Sampson and his second in command Winfield Scott Schley, later fell into a dispute over credit for the victory.

Shafter, William Rufus (1835–1906)—general: William Rufus Shafter is said to have been the first white child born in frontier Kalamazoo County, Michigan. He joined the volunteer Army during the Civil War and stayed on as a career soldier. Much criticized for his lethargy and poor battlefield management in command of the U.S. expeditionary force in Cuba, he nevertheless achieved his objective—the surrender of the Spanish army around Santiago, Cuba—without running up a heavy toll of casualties. William Shafter retired to a ranch in Bakersfield, California, in 1901.

SPANISH

Campos, Arsenio (1831–1900)—general: Campos led the Spanish to victory over the Cuban insurgents in the Ten Years' War of 1868–1878. In command in Cuba at the outbreak of the second independence war, he favored political reforms as a means of conciliating the rebels and balked at imposing the harsh measures he be-

lieved would be necessary to crush the uprising. He was recalled to Spain in 1896.

Castillo, Antonio Canovas del (1828–1897)—politician: One of the major political figures of 19th-century Spain, the conservative Canovas was a virtual dictator during the country's dynastic troubles of the 1870s. During the 1890s, he and liberal politician Praxedes Sagasta alternated the premiership; the Cuban crisis boiled up during Canovas's turn. He increased Spanish forces on the island and assigned the infamous General Weyler to subdue the rebels. An anarchist shot and killed Canovas in August 1897.

Cervera y Topete, Pascual (1839–1909)—naval officer: Carvera joined the navy at age 12 and, in 1898, commanded a cruiser squadron based at Cádiz, Spain. He led the warships across the Atlantic in late April 1898 and, after an odyssey of several weeks, found shelter in Santiago, Cuba. Under pressure from the authorities in Havana, he took the squadron to sea in a futile challenge to the Americans. Taken captive off his battered flagship, *Maria Teresa*, near Santiago, he was held prisoner briefly in the United States and enjoyed a short-lived celebrity there.

Sagasta, Praxedes (1825–1903)—politician: Trained as an engineer, Sagasta helped build Spain's first railroad before entering politics in the 1850s. He served the first of a half-dozen terms as premier in 1871. Succeeding Canovas in the autumn of 1897, Sagasta oversaw the Spanish military disaster of 1898. At the time of his death five years later, he had become one of Spain's most unpopular political figures.

Weyler y Nicolau, Valeriano (1838–1930)—general: Weyler was a hard-hearted officer who vigorously prosecuted the war against the Cuban insurgents in 1896–1897. He instituted the harsh resettlement program known as *reconcentracion*. That brought him a demon's reputation and the sobriquet "Butcher Weyler" in the American yellow press. Spain's liberal leader Sagasta recalled Weyler late in 1897, just before making an offer of local autonomy under the Spanish flag for Cuba.

CUBAN

Finlay, Carlos Juan (1833–1915)—physician: Carlos Juan Finlay was born in Camaguey, Cuba,

the son of a Scottish father and a French mother. He studied in France, in the U.S., and in Cuba before settling down to a medical practice in Havana. Long interested in yellow fever, his researches led him to conclude that the infection was mosquito-borne. Finlay worked with the U.S. Army Yellow Fever Commission in 1899–1900 in a fever control campaign that virtually eradicated the disease. In 1902, Finlay became chief public health officer for the Cuban government.

Martí, José (1853–1895)—revolutionary leader: Jose Marti was born in Cuba, the son of a Spanish soldier. He studied at the University of Saragossa in Spain and embarked on a career as journalist, essayist, and poet. Forced to flee Cuba in 1881 for his involvement in the autonomy movement there, he founded the Cuban Revolutionary Party in the United States in 1892 and mobilized American and Cuban émigré opinion against Spain. Returning to Cuba at the outbreak of the 1895 insurgency, he was shot and killed in a Spanish ambush on May 19 (see p. 348).

FILIPINO

Aguinaldo, Emilio (1870–1964)—insurgent leader: Emilio Aguinaldo was the son of a clerk at a Spanish naval base. He took up revolutionary politics as a young man and succeeded to the leadership of the Philippine insurgency upon the execution of insurgent José Rizal in 1896. Aguinaldo led Filipino independence forces against the Spanish (1896–1898) and against the Americans (1899–1900). Captured by the Americans in late 1900, he took an oath of allegiance to the U.S. and disappeared from political life for many years. In 1950, he became a member of the Council of State of the Philippine Republic.

FURTHER READING

Azoy, A. C. M. *Charge! The Story of the Battle of San Juan Hill.* New York: Longmans, Green, 1961.

Cashin, Herschel V., and others. *Under Fire with the Tenth U.S. Cavalry.* New York: Arno Press, 1969 reprint edition.

Churchill, Winston. *A Roving Commission: My Early Life.* New York: Scribner's 1930.

Crane, Stephen. *Prose and Poetry.* New York: The Library of America, 1984.

Davis, Richard Harding. *The Cuban and Porto Rico Campaigns.* New York, Scribner's, 1898.

Foner, Philip. *The Spanish-Cuban-American War and the Birth of American Imperialism.* New York: Monthly Review Press, 1972.

Friedel, Frank. *The Splendid Little War.* Boston: Little, Brown & Co., 1959.

Golay, Michael. *The Spanish-American War.* New York: Facts on File, 1995.

Jones, Virgil Carrington. *Roosevelt's Rough Riders.* New York: Doubleday, 1971.

Karnow, Stanley. *In Our Image: America's Empire in the Philippines.* New York: Random House, 1989.

Leech, Margaret. *In the Days of McKinley.* New York: Harper & Row, 1959.

Mahan, Alfred Thayer. *The Influence of Sea Power upon History.* Englewood, Cliffs, N.J.: Prentice-Hall, 1980 edition.

May, Ernest R. *Imperial Democracy.* New York: Harcourt Brace Jovanovich, 1961.

Morgan, H. Wayne. *America's Road to Empire: The War with Spain and Overseas Expansion.* New York: John Wiley and Sons, 1965.

O'Toole, G. J. A. *The Spanish War.* New York: W. W. Norton & Co., 1984.

Rickover, Hyman G. *How the Battleship Maine Was Destroyed.* Washington, D.C.: U.S. Government Printing Office, 1976.

Roosevelt, Theodore. *The Rough Riders.* New York: Scribner's, 1898.

Trask, David. *The War with Spain in 1898.* New York: Macmillan & Co., 1981.

Williams, William Appleman. *The Tragedy of American Diplomacy.* New York: Dell Publishing Co., 1962 edition.

WORLD WAR I

DATES OF WAR

July 28, 1914–November 11, 1918

ALTERNATE NAMES

The First World War. The Great War.

SIGNIFICANCE

Much of the historical impact of World War I stemmed from its sheer size: It was the largest war the world had ever fought up to that time, measured by the number of those engaged in combat and by those killed. In several European countries, so many young men died that there was a noticeable effect on marriage rates for a generation. Although not the longest war in duration, more than four years of intense fighting set new levels for the amount of arms, ammunition, equipment, and supplies of all kinds expended; great numbers of civilian lives and much property were also destroyed. And the battlefields were spread over greater distances around the globe than in any previous war.

Beyond such quantitative measures, World War I represented a qualitative change in the nature of warfare. In September 1914, French soldiers in brightly colored uniforms marched spiritedly in line formation to battle the Germans only to be mowed down by machine gun fire: If combat ever had an element of chivalry, World War I put an end to that. And no longer would it suffice, as it had throughout the 19th century, "to get there first with the most men" (as attributed to the American Civil War general Nathan Bedford Forrest). In World War I, the battlefields were clogged with men, yet embattled countries were hard-pressed to supply enough men and enough ammunition. Trench warfare became the signature attribute of World War I. The battlefields of World War I were marked by miles of man-made trenches, where soldiers remained cooped for weeks and sometimes months at a time. Gains in territory were not marked in miles but in yards and sometimes even in a few feet.

World War I was also the first war in which a combatant did not have to be anywhere near the enemy to kill him, thanks to long-distance artillery, bombs from the air, and clouds of poison gas. It was a war, too, in which the conduct of many generals was so vehemently attacked by civilians that their military careers and reputations were ruined. And although soldiers in other wars had deserted and otherwise avoided combat, World War I was one of the few wars in which thousands of troops (French) in the front lines actually mutinied to protest the inhumane conditions and senseless slaughter they faced (see May 27–June 1, 1917, p. 390). The horrific nature of the war also led thousands of soldiers to experience the phenomenon that became known as *shell shock* (see Military Innovations, Tactics, Equipment, p. 412).

The war's impact extended far beyond such conventional outcomes as the reshaping of nation-states, the toppling of dynasties and monarchies, and the destruction of economies. It changed the world view, the attitudes of an entire generation, and to some extent the attitudes of the generation that followed.

On the positive side, World War I prompted an important stage of a social revolution in Europe and in the United States that resulted in a redefinition of roles and an opening of new opportunities for women. So many millions of men were involved in fighting the war that women were welcomed into the workplace in positions in munitions factories and elsewhere that were previously barred to them.

In the cultural sphere, the destruction wrought by the war catalyzed international movements in art (such as dadaism) and literature (often summed up as modernism), in which artists and writers rejected traditional ideas and forms to reflect the war's negation of culture as it had been known. That was perhaps the war's most profound significance: The sheer numbers of the casualties, the blundering of civilian and military leaders of the "great powers," the ripping of the social fabric that occurred made World War I a war that forever changed people's view of war as some heroic enterprise and of Europe as a paragon of civilization.

BACKGROUND

At the beginning of the 20th century, Europe was dominated by the glittering royal families of Hapsburg (Austria-Hungary), Romanov (Russia), and Hohenzollern (Germany). Nobility and social class distinctions flourished even in the parliamentary democracy of Great Britain and the democratic republic of France. And Europe's thriving industrial economies generated imperialistic desires for colonies on the continents of Africa and Asia to serve as sources of raw materials for production of goods and as markets for those goods. That imperialism developed side by side with nationalism, strong feelings of patriotism or loyalty attached to a particular country or group of people with whom one shared an ethnic affinity.

Nationalism has benign and malignant features, but it was a disaster plain and simple for the Austrian emperor of the dual monarchy Austria-Hungary, which comprised several minority peoples, most of whom either wanted to be united with an existing country outside the empire or wanted to unite and form a country of their own. Serbia, which had become the first modern Slavic state (in 1878), became a magnet for the desire for unification among southern Slavs (in Bosnia-Herzegovina and elsewhere). But throughout Europe, underground and revolutionary movements were prepared to resort to terrorism to overthrow regimes they saw as oppressors.

In Germany, Kaiser Wilhelm's ambition was to establish a world empire comparable to those led by the other great colonial powers, Great Britain, France, and the Netherlands; Germany's colonies were little more than a few table scraps from those other nations' feasts. Germany's railway line, begun in 1899, reached from Berlin to Baghdad and Germany had plans to extend it from Baghdad to the Persian oil fields. The kaiser had made several friendly visits to Sultan Abdul Hamid of the Ottoman Empire (Turkey), regarded by most European states as an obstacle to realistic political arrangements. That concern for power and reputation made the kaiser one of the more dangerous leaders in Europe, since the perceptions on which he based his actions were colored by exaggerated fears of encirclement and

resentment over what he perceived as a lack of respect for Germany by other powers. Thus, one of the more unstable leaders of Europe was leading one of the militarily strongest and most industrialized countries in Europe.

The kaiser and the Germans, however, were by no means the only Europeans trying to promote their self-interest. The Europe of 1914, in fact, was very much a creation of the major powers—Britain, Austria-Hungary, Prussia, Russia, and France—who had met at the Congress of Vienna in 1814–1815 and divided Europe to their own benefit. Intent on preserving their spheres of influence and the "balance of power," they had shown little regard for the real identities and histories of the peoples who inhabited Europe. Not only were peoples such as the Poles and southern Slavs suppressed but also the major powers were breeding grounds of distrust, rivalry, and hostility. Even Great Britain was aroused from its "splendid isolation" when Germany challenged British supremacy on the high seas by building a heavy-duty navy.

There had not been a war on European soil since the early 1870s, when Germany took the territories of Alsace and Lorraine from France. The colonial conquests engaged in by Europeans were easily and quickly won, given their superior military strength compared to that of the native peoples. Therefore, most Europeans were ignorant of the destructive power of the new weapons that had been fashioned using the machinery and burgeoning technology of the industrial revolution. Although there were prophets of doom, others viewed any war that might break out as a high-spirited test of nationhood, of manliness, and of honor. That was the outlook that led many to battle with an expectation of adventure in what was called the Great War.

CAUSES OF THE WAR

Distrust among European diplomats of other countries' motives in seeking (often secret) alliances and fear of other nations' increasing military strength had peaked by 1914. There was a generalized fatalistic feeling among various governments and ruling circles that war was inevitable. In fact, many historians regard World War I as a textbook case of reaping the harvest of seeds that had been deliberately sown:

1. The Triple Alliance: In 1882, Germany,

through the office of Chancellor Otto von Bismark, made a *dreibund,* a "triple alliance," with Austria-Hungary and Italy that bound the countries to defend each other if one of them was attacked. However, Italy soon quarreled with Austria-Hungary and in 1902 made a secret treaty with France that negated Italy's obligations under the Triple Alliance.

2. The Entente Cordiale: In response to the Triple Alliance, France first formed a defensive alliance with Russia (1894), then a diplomatic agreement with Great Britain (1904); each was known as an *Entente Cordiale,* (or a "cordial understanding").

3. The Triple Entente: In 1907, when Russia and Great Britain signed an agreement, the arrangements between them and France became known as the *Triple Entente.* As a military alliance, it was not considered as binding as the Triple Alliance, but it did divide Europe into two hostile camps. (On September 5, 1914, once World War I had commenced, the British, French and Russians signed the Pact of London, pledging to make no separate peace.)

4. The Balkan Wars: Although not a direct cause of World War I, those wars exacerbated the intense nationalist tensions in the Balkans and irritated Germany's and Austria-Hungary's monarchs. Germany and Austria-Hungary found it irksome to have to deal with a small nation like Serbia, which in the first Balkan War (1912–1913), along with Bulgaria, Greece, and Montenegro, conquered most of the Ottoman Empire's European holdings. In the second Balkan War (1913), Serbia occupied Albania until Austria-Hungary insisted (with approval from Germany) that the Serbs evacuate Albania within eight days.

5. Restive populations: Austria-Hungary, itself a forced union, had a serious problem with its southern Slavic residents who wanted to leave the empire and join Serbia. Determined not to give up any of his access to the Adriatic Sea, Emperor Franz Joseph refused any changes.

6. Assassinations: Despite the unrest, Franz Joseph's designated successor, Archduke Franz Ferdinand, and his wife, Sophia, toured Sarajevo in the recently (1908) annexed territory of Bosnia-Herzegovina on June 28, 1914. Traveling in an open car with very little security, the pair avoided death once when a bomb lobbed their way bounced off the car and rolled into the street. Later that day, however, the driver made a wrong

turn onto a narrow dead-end street, and Gavrilo Princip, a Serb nationalist and a member of the Serbian nationalist terrorist group Black Hand, saw his chance. As the car slowly backed down the street, it passed by Princip, who shot and killed the royal couple.

7. A quick solution: Austria-Hungary chose to consider the assassinations as justification to declare war on Serbia and take care of the Slav question once and for all. Austria-Hungary's leaders hesitated only because Serbia was a client-state of Russia, and Russia had an ally in France. Then on July 5, Austria-Hungary received assurances from Kaiser Wilhelm of Germany's military support should Russia intervene on Serbia's behalf. Austria-Hungary then felt emboldened to declare war.

PREPARATIONS FOR WAR

A critical military planning issue throughout the late 19th century was how many full-time regular soldiers a nation could maintain and how many it could count on as reserves. Each country wanted to be able to call on a standing army for immediate action and then to be able to mobilize its reserves for long-term conflicts. Since full mobilization required time, the countries that expected to be involved in the Austro-Serbian conflict went on the alert during July 1914 in the wake of the assassinations of Archduke Franz Ferdinand and his wife. Serbia, in anticipation of Austria-Hungary's actions, called for a general mobilization of troops. Great Britain, while proposing more talks, delayed its fleet's planned maneuvers, and the German fleet was ordered to stand by at its base at Kiel.

July 23, 1914: Austria-Hungary delivered an ultimatum to Serbia; in it Austria-Hungary set terms that Serbia wouldn't accept, such as a strong implication that Serbia had officially sanctioned the assassinations and a demand that Austrian-Hungarian officials be allowed to go to Serbia to participate in the proceedings against the assassins.

July 25, 1914: Serbia sent a conciliatory reply, but Austria-Hungary refused to accept it as sufficient. Austria-Hungary had the excuse it wanted to make war against Serbia and began to mobilize its army.

July 28, 1914: Austria-Hungary declared war on Serbia, and Serbia declared war on Austria-

Hungary. Russia began a preliminary mobilization of its forces in anticipation of going to the aid of Serbia.

July 29, 1914: Austrian-Hungarian naval ships on the Danube River bombarded Serbia's capital, Belgrade, an act that astonished even the kaiser in its suddenness. In fact, the kaiser was having second thoughts about rushing into war, but his top generals and civilians in the government were determined to honor the alliance with Austria-Hungary. In Russia, Czar Nicolas II hesitated to authorize a mobilization because he felt he had the kaiser's promise that German policy toward Russia would be restrained. However, the Russian foreign minister had assurances of support from France, and so persuaded the czar to call for a partial mobilization.

July 29-30, 1914: Germany asked for Great Britain's neutrality should there be war; Britain responded by asking if Germany would respect Belgian neutrality. Germany did not respond; in fact, Germany had sent an ultimatum to Belgium on July 29, demanding the right to pass through Belgium in order to stop French forces from attacking Germany.

July 31, 1914: Germany delivered an ultimatum to Russia, ordering the military to stand down; instead, the czar's order for full mobilization went into effect. Austria-Hungary also called for full mobilization. Meanwhile, Germany inquired of France about its position in the case of a Russo-German war.

August 1, 1914: France ordered a general mobilization. The Germans mobilized within minutes of the French order and declared war on Russia. Russia declared war on Germany. Units of the German army began to move into Luxembourg late in the evening in order to seize crucial railway and telegraph lines.

August 2, 1914: The Germans issued an ultimatum to Belgium, claiming that since France was about to attack Germany by passing through Belgium, Germany had the right to pass through Belgium to attack France. The Germans completed their conquest of Luxembourg.

August 3, 1914: Belgium refused Germany's demand to move across its territory. Germany and France declared war on each other.

August 4, 1914: Great Britain, in response to Germany's refusal to respect the neutrality of Belgium (as set forth in the Treaty of 1839), declared war on Germany.

DECLARATION OF WAR

The dates on which the various nations declared war on at least one of the adversaries are listed in the table below.

The Allies:
July 28, 1914: Serbia
August 1, 1914: Russia
August 3, 1914: Belgium and France
August 4, 1914: Great Britain
August 5, 1914: Montenegro
August 23, 1914: Japan
May 23, 1915: Italy
June 3, 1915: San Marino
March 9, 1916: Portugal
August 27, 1916: Romania
April 6, 1917: United States
June 27, 1917: Greece
The Central Powers:
July 28, 1914: Austria-Hungary
August 1, 1914: Germany
October 14, 1914: Bulgaria
October 29, 1914: Turkey (Ottoman Empire)

Only six countries on the European continent did not declare war: Sweden, Norway, Denmark, Switzerland, the Netherlands (Holland), and Spain. (Luxembourg was occupied so quickly by Germany that it had no time to declare war.)

There was also an outer ring of countries—Italy, Portugal, Greece, Bulgaria, Romania, and Turkey—that essentially joined the conflict under pressure from the Allies or the Central Powers. There were also countries that declared war against at least one of the Central Powers only after the United States entered World War I in April 1917: Those included Cuba, Panama, Siam (Thailand), Liberia, China, Brazil, Guatemala, Nicaragua, Costa Rica, Haiti, and Honduras. Most countries that joined the war following its initial explosion in August did so only after extracting various promises for territorial booty. Although it was a distinction soon forgotten, the United States joined the conflict not as a formal Ally but as an Associate of the Allies.

COMBATANTS

The Allies: France mobilized an army of 1,650,000 men in 1914, but only by calling up its reserves; France had considerably fewer potential soldiers to call on than did Germany. The French army was also much less well equipped than the German army, and although the French spirit (*attaque, attaque, toujours l'attaque*) was formidable, French soldiers soon found that spirit was poor armor against machine-gun bullets. Great Britain, which had always relied on naval power, at the outset of World War I had only a small, though professionally trained army of 125,000 men with limited equipment. Both France and Great Britain relied on their colonial subjects to fill out their troop requirements; Britain also drew on many thousands of troops from Canada, Australia, New Zealand, and South Africa. Serbia and Belgium each had poorly equipped armies of fewer than 200,000 men. Russia, which eventually mobilized 12,000,000 men, had little else to offer beyond those numbers: The soldiers were poorly supplied and poorly armed, the army leadership was often in disagreement about direction and strategy, the military was riddled with corruption. In any case, Russia withdrew from the war in November 1917, as the country became embroiled in a revolution (see Battles and Campaigns, Eastern Front, p. 393).

The British, however, did have the largest navy of all the combatants, with 156 battleships and cruisers, 218 destroyers, and 55 submarines. Britain could also count on support from the French and the Japanese navies. Britain and France together had air power totaling 240 planes and 20 dirigibles.

The United States, which did not enter World War I until 1917, was the least prepared of all the Allies; its combined military forces, including reserves, totaled only about 200,000. In fact, in 1914, President Woodrow Wilson responded to stirrings in Congress to build a large Navy and a standing Army by saying in his State of the Union speech, "We never have had, and while we retain our present principles and ideals, we never shall have a large standing Army. We shall not ask our young men to spend the best years of their lives making soldiers of themselves." Even when the United States entered the war, the U.S. Army air corps had only about 55 obsolete airplanes, and the U.S. Navy was about one-quarter the size of Great Britain's.

Although 24 countries eventually declared war on the four nations that made up the Central Powers, only 12 of those countries actually fought in World War I. Those 12, with the numbers of soldiers at some point committed to the war, are listed here:

Belgium: 267,000
British Empire: 8,905,000 (in addition to Great Britain, this includes Canada, Australia, New Zealand, South Africa, India, and several other British colonies)
France: 8,410,000 (includes colonial troops)
Greece: 230,000
Italy: 5,615,000
Japan: 800,000
Montenegro: 50,000
Portugal: 100,000
Romania: 750,000
Russia: 12,000,000
Serbia: 707,000
United States: 4,355,000
Total mobilization of Allies and their associates: 42,189,000 soldiers

The Central Powers: Although starting with 2,700,000 men, Austria-Hungary's troops lacked training, and the army was not well run, with notable difficulties in staff and supply logistics. Another of Austria-Hungary's problems was a language barrier; German-speaking officers had trouble making themselves understood in an army in which only one in four soldiers could speak German.

By 1913, Germany's standing army numbered 661,000 troops, but Germany eventually mobilized many millions for its armed forces. In 1912, Germany added 15,000 men to its navy. Germany had 87 large warships, 142 destroyers, and 28 submarines (known as U-boats, from the German for submarine, *Unterseeboot*). In many ways, Germany's navy had superior technology compared to Great Britain's, but Germany's navy was smaller, and it represented the total naval force of the Central Powers. In terms of airpower, Germany again outclassed its allies, with 380 planes and 30 zeppelins. Germany was the most industrialized country of its allies, and although it lost its colonies early in 1914, its quick victories over Belgium and northern France in the summer of 1914 gave Germany the wherewithal to supply its allies with most of their ammunition needs.

Bulgaria and Turkey supported the Central Powers' efforts with men but had little to offer in terms of equipment.

The four Central Powers, with the numbers of soldiers at some point committed to the war, are listed here:

Austria-Hungary: 7,800,000
Bulgaria: 1,200,000
Germany: 11,000,000
Turkey: 2,850,000
Total mobilization of the Central Powers:
22,850,000 soldiers

GEOGRAPHIC AND STRATEGIC CONSIDERATIONS

World War I quickly spread to the Middle East, Africa, and even to Asia and the Pacific, but for the most part, the war was a European war fought along three fronts. The western front stretched some 600 miles from the Belgium coast on the English Channel across France to its border with Switzerland. The terrain was mixed, but, for the most part, relatively flat land, much of it wooded, much of it farmland, crisscrossed with many rivers, and studded with many villages, towns, and cities. The eastern front extended some 1,100 miles from Riga, Latvia, on the Baltic Sea down along the then eastern borders of Germany and Austria-Hungary to the shore of the Black Sea; the terrain was like that of the western front. The southern front ran from Switzerland's southeastern border with Italy around the edges of Austria-Hungary and down to Trieste on the Adriatic Sea; it was largely mountainous terrain. There was another segment of the southern front along the southern borders of the Balkans, also largely mountainous.

To the extent that the two main Central Powers, Germany and Austria-Hungary, were contiguous and controlled central Europe, they had an easier time in supplying their forces. Throughout World War I, the Allies faced greater difficulties in supplying their forces and maintaining communications among their various armies. (In the fighting outside Europe—with the exception of the fighting in the Middle East—the Allies were better positioned to maintain their forces than was Germany.) Gradually, the Central Powers' advantages in those matters declined: The Allies could call on far more men to fight and on virtually unlimited natural resources and industrial output; the British dominated the seas; the Central Powers became isolated; and finally, the United States tipped the balance.

Of all the combatants entering World War I during the eight days from July 28 to August 4, 1914, only Germany had an actual two-front plan of attack. Still famous in the history of military strategy, the plan was devised in the 1890s by German chief of staff Count Alfred von Schlieffen, with the specific goal of fighting a two-front war against Russia and France. The Schlieffen plan required swift mobilization, with troops marching through the Netherlands and Belgium to northwestern France, there capturing the channel ports (and isolating Great Britain), then moving to attack Paris and trapping the French against France's eastern borders. At the outset, a small number of troops would be sent east to Russia in defensive strength only; once France had capitulated, the Germans would shift troops to Russia and defeat the Russians. (Once in Russia, Germany would be free to move still farther into Asia.) The plan called for the entire war to be concluded in ten weeks. The Schlieffen plan was bold and risky. By 1914, it had been modified by Chief of Staff Count Helmuth von Moltke in response to changes in Russian strength and German industrial development. Moltke chose to avoid breaching Holland's neutrality and thus weakened the strength of the right-wing scythe-like attack (see Notable Phrases, p. 413).

Austria-Hungary assumed that its war with Serbia would be concluded before Russia fully mobilized. Unaware of Germany's strategy, Austria-Hungary also planned a joint maneuver in the salient formed by Russian Poland to protect East Prussia on the north and Austrian-Hungarian Galicia on the south.

The Russians had a front line of almost 1,100 miles, stretching from the Baltic Sea along East Prussia around the Polish salient, and along Austrian-Hungarian Galicia. As part of its overall strategy, the Russian military had a base in Warsaw, Poland, located in the center of the Polish salient. The Russians had also installed different railroad gauges to prevent German trains from transporting troops quickly into Russian territory. The Russian military had built up significant fortifications along the Galician border to protect against an attack from Austria-Hungary. By 1910, some of the Russian generals thought that if war began, Germany would first attack France. To take full advantage of that, those generals reasoned, an all-out offensive on East Prussia would be necessary. However, other generals insisted that the Galician border was vital for Russia's security. As events turned out, the Russians launched an invasion into East

Prussia, yet most of their fortification effort had been spent on the Galician border.

The French were the only army of the Allies to have a unified strategy for war. In 1913, Gen. Joseph Joffre drew up French War Plan XVII, which focused on liberating Lorraine by sending forces on either side of the Metz River. Joffre's plan assumed a Russian diversion of the Germans along an eastern front. The British expected to engage the Germans on the continent with their British Expeditionary Force (BEF), should the need arise, but had no concerted strategy for such an engagement. Serbia's strategy was completely defensive and included a planned retreat into the mountains.

Although the United States did not enter World War I until April 1917, its manufacturers had been supplying large quantities of war equipment to the Allies. Almost from the outset of the war, many individual Americans supported the Allies; private relief groups sent money and supplies to aid victims of the war; banks made loans to the Allies; Americans volunteered to serve in foreign armed services or ambulance groups (see Legends and Trivia, pp. 412); above all, American industry and transportation continued to supply the needs of the Allies despite the occasional attacks on American ships. Although some in the top levels of the U.S. government and the armed services were giving thought to the possibility of entering the war, they could take few direct steps. The result was that when the United States did declare war, it had to rush to enlarge and train its armed forces, to build ships and planes and other heavy equipment, and to manufacture weapons and other supplies needed in a modern war. And long after the first American military units appeared in Europe in May (Navy ships) and June (Army troops), they were essentially operating within the strategies and commands of the Allies. Only after some months in action did U.S. commanders begin to have a say in the strategic planning; throughout the first months, the U.S. army was greatly dependent on European weaponry and equipment.

BATTLES AND CAMPAIGNS: 1914

Since U.S. forces were not directly engaged in World War I until mid-1917, the battles and campaigns that occured prior to U.S. participation are not treated in detail.

WESTERN FRONT

August 1–2, 1914: As the first stage of their plan to invade France, German troops invaded Luxembourg and seized its railway system and telegraph lines.

August 4–20, 1914: German forces invaded Belgium and in the course of two weeks occupied much of that country.

August 7–9, 1914: As called for in their major strategic plan, War Plan XVII, the French under Gen. Joseph Joffre went on the offensive in Alsace, but had only limited success against the defending Germans.

August 12, 1914: Behind a protective shield of 19 battleships, 120,000 troops from the British Expeditionary Force (BEF) crossed the English Channel to France to help the Belgians defend against the invading Germans.

August 14–25, 1914 (Battle of the Frontiers): The French continued their offensive to reclaim the provinces of Alsace and Lorraine lost to Germany after the Franco-Prussian War (1870–1871); at that time they moved into Lorraine. The author of the Germans' main strategic plan, the late Count Alfred von Schlieffen, had counted on that, so the French were, in fact, walking into a German trap. By August 20, the Germans were turning the tide, and within the next few days, they forced the French to retreat to Nancy.

August 20, 1914: The Belgian army, led by King Albert, retreated to Antwerp in northernmost Belgium.

August 21–23, 1914: Along the northern sector of the Battle of the Frontiers, the Germans went on the offensive.

August 22–24, 1914: The BEF, in position at Mons to support the Belgians, was forced to retreat when the French withdrew their support from the BEF's southern flank. Informed of the heavy French casualties (an estimated 300,000), German commander Helmuth von Moltke, headquartered in Luxembourg far from the fighting, believed the western war was nearly won and dispatched some of his troops to East Prussia, by then under attack from the Russians. That has been considered the first of von Moltke's major mistakes.

August 25, 1914: A German zeppelin dropped several bombs on Antwerp, Belgium, killing ten civilians. German occupying forces in Belgium conducted vicious reprisals against civilians to quell sniper and other resistance efforts, which provided fodder for British and French propaganda to harden anti-German sentiment.

August 26, 1914: Exhausted soldiers of the BEF, in retreat from Mons, fought the Germans at Le Cateau in northern France. Although the BEF was defeated, its stand allowed a more orderly retreat of troops.

August 30, 1914: The Germans took Amiens, a major city on the Somme River, north of Paris. The Germans began their drive toward Paris.

August 31, 1914: Gen. John French, commander of the BEF, informed his superiors in London that he would take his soldiers and fall back behind Paris to leave the French soldiers to their fate. General Joffre immediately appealed to the French prime minister, and British field marshal Lord Horatio Kitchener brought General French back in line. The Anglo-French retreat continued toward the Marne River.

September 2, 1914: With German forces within 25 miles of Paris and moving closer, the Allies retrieved the knapsack of a dead German officer containing the German plan of attack. That gave the Allies some advantage in knowing where to position their forces.

The French government moved from Paris to Bordeaux, leaving behind the French Sixth Army. When the military governor of Paris, Gen. Joseph Gallieni, learned that the Germans were advancing on Paris, he ordered the French Sixth Army to move out to meet the Germans.

September 5–9, 1914 (Battle of the Marne): The Germans had crossed the Marne River to the northeast of Paris. French and BEF soldiers were under strict orders to gain ground against the Germans at any cost. To the west of the main action, the French Sixth Army attacked German soldiers at the River Ourcq with such force that the Germans had to send reinforcements. French colonial reinforcements were sent out from Paris in 2,000 requisitioned taxicabs. In all, 1,000,000 French soldiers (and colonials), 125,000 troops from the BEF, and 1,275,000 German soldiers fought in the Battle of the Marne.

On September 9, the Germans, exhausted from 33 days of advancing, and dangerously far from their supply lines, began to move back across the Marne, then across the River Aisne, for a total retreat of 60 miles. The Battle of the Marne, although no one realized it at the time, effectively signaled that the Germans could not win the war:

They spent the following four years trying to regain that lost territory.

The most immediate result of the Battle of the Marne was the so-called race to the sea—an attempt by the Allies and the Germans to outflank one another as their armies moved toward the coasts of Belgium and France along the English Channel and the North Sea. The Germans wanted to cut off the British; the Allies wanted to protect the supply line between Britain and France.

September 14, 1914: General von Moltke was removed for his failure to carry out the Schlieffen plan, as signified by his defeat at the Battle of the Marne, and replaced by Gen. Erich von Falkenhayn.

October 1–5, 1914: The Germans broke through two of the rings of forts outside Antwerp. In an attempt to keep the large port city from falling to the Germans, the British rerouted troops that had been ordered to support the French and British fighting the Germans in the race to the sea. Winston Churchill, in Antwerp as First Lord of the Admiralty, reported back to Britain that the situation was desperate. Eight thousand men from the Royal Navy, many of them new recruits, were sent to support the Belgians. An additional 22,000 trained BEF troops crossed the English Channel to Ostend, Belgium.

October 7–9, 1914: German howitzers, located almost 6 miles from the city proper, began bombarding Antwerp. Belgian troops fled the forts and, with no help coming from the French in Ghent, the BEF reinforcements remained at Ostend. After two days of German shelling, King Albert withdrew with his forces to a defensive enclave along the northern Belgian coast.

October 12–November 11, 1914 (First Battle of Ypres): The Germans launched an attack on Allied forces who were holding around the Belgian town of Ypres in an effort to cut them off from the coast. On October 20, in bitter and costly fighting, the Germans were finally stopped, and the Allies went on the offensive. That, too, failed, and the Germans launched a counteroffensive on October 29. Finally, the rains and snow forced the Germans to cease on November 11.

October 15, 1914: The Germans entered the Belgian port of Ostend. That put most of Belgium under German occupation.

October 26, 1914: Troops from India, a British colony, made their military debut on the western front. They attempted to fill a breach in the line at Neuve-Chapelle in northern France. The Germans first engaged in chemical warfare during that action, but the mild tear gas used then was hardly noticed by the troops (see p. 416).

November 11, 1914: With a final unsuccessful attack by the prestigious Prussian Guard, the first Battle of Ypres concluded. More than 10,000 soldiers were killed in the fighting in an area approximately 10 miles north to south and 5 miles east to west. Both sides then began to dig in for the long war of the trenches. Although it had no strategic value, German and Allied armies fought for control of the so-called Ypres salient for the next four years.

November 21, 1914: The British carried out the first Allied air raid of World War I by dropping bombs on German zeppelin sheds located on Lake Constance. The first French bombing group was formed two days later.

December 24–26, 1914: An informal armistice descended on several sections of the front. The truce was accompanied by an exchange of gifts, such as cigars, whiskey, and plum pudding. Soldiers used Christmas Day to bury their dead, sometimes with joint ceremonies.

December 31, 1914: After five months of fighting, the French dead numbered 350,000; wounded, captured, and missing totaled 600,000. German casualties were somewhat less. Those early battles between the French, British, and Germans succeeded in establishing a western front that barely moved 10 miles in either direction for the next two years.

EASTERN FRONT

July 31, 1914: Czar Nicholas II of Russia began mobilizing his troops for an invasion of East Prussia and Eastern Galicia, with the dual goal of honoring his promise to France and protecting the Russian-Polish salient.

August 10, 1914: The Austrians invaded Russian Poland, aiming for the city of Lublin.

August 17, 1914: Responding to pleas from France to distract the Germans, the First and Second Russian Armies, led by Gen. Paul Rennenkampf and Gen. Alexander Samsonov, respectively, invaded East Prussia. The Germans, led by Gen. Hermann von François, defeated Russian troops at Stalluponen just inside East Prussia and captured 3,000 soldiers.

August 18, 1914: Russian general Aleksei Brusilov invaded Austrian Galicia with 35 infantry divisions.

August 20, 1914: General Rennenkampf advanced his First Army farther into East Prussia, causing German commander in chief of East Prussia, Gen. Maximilian von Prittwitz, to panic as Rennenkampf's soldiers stopped a German counterattack. Russia was posing a greater challenge in East Prussia than Field Marshal Helmuth von Moltke had expected. General von Prittwitz was replaced by 67-year-old Gen. Paul von Hindenburg.

August 23–September 16, 1914: Poor reconnaissance made it hard for the Austrian and Russian armies to find each other on the Galician front. Gen. Nikolai Ivanov led two Russian armies in search of enemy contact. Austrian general Conrad von Hotzendorf was pressed by the Germans to engage the Russians so Germany could finish off France. General von Hotzendorf's First, Fourth, and Third (as well as part of the Second) Austrian Armies outnumbered the Russians when they surprised each other at Krasnik and Komorov. The Russian soldiers retreated after two days of fighting, but at the Battle of Gnila Lipa River, the Russians prevailed against the Austrians and forced a retreat. Austrian redeployment maneuvers opened a 40-mile-wide hole in the front, which the Russians took advantage of and forced an Austrian retreat into the foothills of the Carpathian Mountains. Russia then occupied most of Austrian Galicia; the cost to the Austrian army was 250,000 dead and 100,000 taken prisoner from fewer than 1 million soldiers.

August 27–30, 1914 (Battle of Tannenberg): At Tannenberg in southwestern East Prussia, the Russian 2nd Army fell into a trap and was encircled by the Germans; 30,000 Russians were killed and 125,000 were taken prisoner. Some 12,500 German soldiers were killed.

September 8–14, 1914: The Russian First Army under General Rennenkampf learned of the destruction of the Second Army at Tannenberg and dug in at the Masurian Lakes northeast of Tannenberg. Rennenkampf's southern flank was attacked by General François and forced into a well-executed retreat. However, the Russians launched a small counteroffensive that allowed most of their troops to get away. In the end, though, the Russians lost as many as 145,000 men to the Germans' 10,000 and were driven out of East Prussia.

September 28, 1914: The Germans attacked the Russian Polish salient with a combination of armies under Gen. Paul Hindenburg and Gen. Erich von Ludendorff. Using the German railway system, the army and supplies were transported 500 miles from East Prussia to near Kraków.

October 12–21, 1914: Within 12 miles of Warsaw, the German invasion, with its Austrian support, was repulsed by Czar Nicholas's troops, almost four times as many as the German-Austrian forces.

November 11–December 6, 1914 (Battle of Lodz): Two Russian armies continued their drive to capture the Silesian coalfields, a vital industrial area for Germany, but were stopped by the German Ninth Army at Lodz, a city southwest of Warsaw. In the ensuing battle, the Germans almost encircled the Russians. In the end, the Russians fell back and entrenched, and Lodz fell to the Germans. The Russian effort to take Silesia came to an end.

SOUTHERN FRONT

July 29, 1914: Austrian-Hungarian navy ships on the Danube River bombarded Belgrade, Serbia, the first shots fired in World War I.

December 1–15, 1914: By December 1, Austrian troops occupied Belgrade. Within two weeks, however, the Serbs recaptured their capital, seizing 133 guns and taking 40,000 Austrian soldiers captive. By December 15, the Austrian army was forced out of Serbia.

NON-EUROPEAN FRONTS

August 8, 1914: In Britain's initial attack on German East Africa (at Tanganyika), British battleships bombed Dar es Salaam, the main port.

August 20–25, 1914: French soldiers and a contingent of Belgian troops invaded the Cameroons (then divided between Nigeria and Cameroon) from the southeast and began an arduous 300-mile trek to the capital. On August 25, British troops crossed the border from Nigeria, but German troops drove them back in early September.

August 23–27, 1914: The Japanese declared war on Germany on August 23, and four days later, the Japanese navy invaded the islets off Kiauchow's main port, Tsingtao, from which the German Far Eastern naval squadron had escaped.

September–November 4, 1914: In German East Africa, German general Paul von Lettow-Vorbeck, leading an army comprised of 3,500 German and 12,000 African soldiers, launched a series of raids on the Allies across the borders of British East Africa and Uganda. General von Lettow-Vorbeck was so successful that by October his troops threatened the British port of Mombasa. For the rest of 1914, the Germans in East Africa continued to threaten British East Africa and Uganda.

September 11, 1914: The German possessions in the Bismark Archipelago surrendered to Australian soldiers with little fighting.

September 2–23, 1914: The Japanese army landed at Lungkow, Kiauchow, on September 2, but rains prevented it from overcoming the Germans. More Japanese troops landed on September 18, reinforced by British troops from Hong Kong on September 23. The combined forces began a campaign to take the port city of Tsingtao.

September 19–October 9, 1914: The British had assigned troops in the Union of South Africa to capture the adjacent German colony of Southwest Africa. On September 19 the first attack took the port of Lüderitz, but then the campaign halted on October 9 because two prominent officers chose to lead their Boer forces to support the Germans. The Boers were South Africans of Dutch origin who had long been resisting British rule of their land. The British had to assign troops to South Africa to quell the scattered uprisings of Boers. (The last of the rebellious Boers was suppressed in February 1915.)

September 26–27, 1914: In the Cameroons, French and British troops launched a successful joint amphibious attack up the Wuri River. On September 27, they captured the main town of Duala. The Allies continued to pursue the Germans deeper inland.

October 15–31, 1914: An Allied force of Japanese (30,000) and British (1,500) soldiers marched to within 5 miles of Tsingtao, and naval forces bombarded the port.

October 26, 1914: In the Cameroons, the British and French captured Edia, and the Germans fled to Yaoundé.

November 7–22, 1914: In Mesopotamia (Iraq), British and Indian soldiers landed at Fao on November 7. By November 22, the troops had reached the confluence of the Tigris and

Euphrates Rivers and occupied Basra, thus securing the British oil fields at Abadan.

December 1914: Russian and Turkish soldiers fought fiercely in mountainous terrain of eastern Turkey. Given the desperate nature of the Russian situation, Czar Nicholas begged Britain to divert the Turks. Thus the British War Council strategists, including Winston Churchill, again considered attacking the Dardanelles. One of their incentives was the increasing frustration of the stalemate along the western front.

December 9, 1914: Australian troops took the last of Germany's Pacific colonial possessions, the Solomon Islands.

December 17, 1914: Britain proclaimed that it was taking over Egypt as a protectorate.

December 25, 1914: Gen. Louis Botha had taken control of the South African army to support the British campaign in German Southwest Africa. On Christmas Day, he landed with 20,000 South Africans at Swakopmund and began to prepare for a march to the capital of German Southwest Africa, Windhoek.

NAVAL THEATER

August 10, 1914: Two German warships, the *Breslau* and the *Goeben*, were granted safe passage through the Dardanelles by Turkey. Since that would have been regarded a hostile act by Britain, and Turkey was not yet ready to join World War I, the Germans "sold" the ships to the Turks for a nominal sum, and the ships, renamed *Midilli* and *Javus Sultan Selim*, sailed through the Dardanelles under Turkish flags.

August 12, 1914: Great Britain set up a blockade to prevent cargo ships from reaching Germany's North Sea ports, and France set up a blockade to keep trading ships out of Austria's Adriatic ports.

September 22, 1914: The Germans intensified their submarine warfare around the British Isles. The *U-9* sank three British cruisers in one hour, resulting in the deaths of 1,459 men with only 837 saved.

October 1, 1914: Turkey closed the Dardanelles to maritime traffic.

October 13, 1914: The Russian Imperial Navy recovered a German navy signal book and sent it to British cryptographers in London. That gave the Allies an advantage in locating German warships and U-boats in the years ahead.

October 29, 1914: The two German warships that had been granted safe passage through the Dardanelles and into the Black Sea by Turkey, bombarded the Russian ports of Odessa and Nickolayev, mined Russian shipping lanes in the Black Sea, and then attacked three other Russian ports, setting fire to fuel storage tanks and granaries. Because the German ships were flying the Turkish flag while fighting, that effectively meant that the Ottoman Empire had joined the war on the side of the Central Powers.

November 1, 1914: In a serious setback to the British Royal Navy, German admiral Maximilian von Spee sank two British cruisers under Adm. Christopher Craddock at the battle of Coronel off Chile. Admiral Craddock and 1,500 sailors were drowned.

November 2, 1914: Charging that German mine-laying in the North Sea contravened the Second Hague Convention of 1907, the British declared the entire sea a military area. The British required all neutral ships to put into British ports to be searched as a condition of safe escort through the minefields and thus reinforced their blockade of food and goods entering Germany by sea.

November 3, 1914: In response to the "Turkish" bombardments in the Black Sea, the British attacked a Turkish minelayer. Russia also declared war on Turkey. British and French battleships bombarded the Turkish forts at the Dardanelles, hitting Sedd-ul-Bahr and destroying its powder magazine.

German battle cruisers bombarded Yarmouth and Lowestoft in Great Britain, the first time in 200 years the British homeland was attacked.

December 8, 1914: Off the Falkland Islands near Argentina, in an action that restored British morale, a British fleet sank four ships of Admiral von Spee's German Far East squadron, drowning 2,100 German sailors and officers (including von Spee and two of his sons).

December 16, 1914: German warships bombarded the British ports of Scarborough, Whitby, and Hartlepool; the raids killed 40 civilians and wounded hundreds more.

HOME FRONT

August 19, 1914: Having declared U.S. neutrality on August 4, President Woodrow Wilson sent a message to the Senate saying that the

"United States must be neutral in fact as well as in name....We must be impartial in thought as well as in action."

September 2, 1914: The Treasury Department established a Bureau of War Risk Insurance to provide up to $5,000,000 insurance for merchant ships and their crews.

September 5, 1914: President Wilson ordered that the U.S. Navy provide wireless stations for transatlantic communications; even German diplomats were allowed to use the stations for their encoded messages. Eventually, such a message helped bring the United States into World War I (see Home Front, March 1, 1917, p. 394).

October 15, 1914: The Wilson administration declared that it would not prohibit shipments of gold or extensions of credit to the belligerents.

November 3, 1914: Bethlehem Steel president Charles Schwab took an order from the British navy, for eight 14-inch guns; other U.S. companies took orders from the British navy for ships and from the French for other war materials.

INTERNATIONAL DEVELOPMENTS

August 2, 1914: Germany and the Ottoman Empire (Turkey) signed the Treaty of Berlin, a highly secret alliance, in Constantinople.

August 8, 1914: As part of a rounding up of suspected dangerous enemy aliens, Vladimir Lenin was arrested by Austrian police in Neumarkt, West Galicia. The head of the Austrian Social Democrat Party, which supported the war, argued that if Lenin were free, he would wage a vigorous propaganda campaign against the Czar, so Lenin was allowed to travel to neutral Switzerland.

August 15, 1914: The Panama Canal, under U.S. sovereignty, opened to traffic.

September 4, 1914: France, Russia, and Great Britain signed the Pact of London, agreeing not to negotiate a separate peace with the Central Powers.

October 1, 1914: The first Canadian troops, some 33,000, sailed for Great Britain.

October 13, 1914–January 8, 1915: Boers in South Africa opposed to their government's support of Britain in the war rebelled. Although the rebellion collapsed when its leader, Gen. Christiaan Beyers, drowned on December 14, the last rebels were not captured until January 8.

BATTLES AND CAMPAIGNS: 1915

WESTERN FRONT

January 19, 1915: The Germans launched their first bombing raid on Great Britain, using two zeppelins to bomb the Norfolk coast; four civilians were killed.

February 26, 1915: For the first time in modern warfare, the Germans used flamethrowers against the French in Verdun, with little effect.

March 1, 1915: The French lobbed the first grenades in warfare against a troop of Germans advancing behind armored shields. The Germans gave up the advance after half their number (35) were killed or wounded.

March 10–13, 1915 (Battle of Neuve Chapelle): In an attempt to break through German lines in northeastern France, the British, with the backing of reconnaissance airplanes, shelled German trenches for 35 minutes, using 342 guns. Four lines of German trenches were overrun along a 4,000-yard breach, with fierce hand-to-hand fighting by the British and Indian troops. Neuve Chapelle was recaptured by the Allies. Then the British made a mistake: Troops were ordered to attack a trench line in the northern sector that had not been shelled. Almost every soldier who participated in the attack, about 1,000 in all, was killed. The price for the three days spent in capturing a salient 2,000 yards wide and 1,200 yards deep was 11,200 Allied fatalities.

April 22–May 25, 1915 (Second Battle of Ypres): Preparing for a new offensive at Ypres, on April 22, the Germans fired 168 tons of chlorine gas from 4,000 cylinders against two French colonial divisions and an adjacent Canadian division over a 4-mile extension of the front line in the Ypres salient. The resulting panic caused a breach in the line, but the Germans were unable to advance. They repeated their gas attack on April 24. The BEF retreated to Ypres on May 1, and heavy fighting continued throughout much of May. British casualties totaled some 60,000; German losses were 35,000.

May 9–June 18, 1915 (Battle of Artois): The French and BEF launched simultaneous attacks at Souchez and Festubert, respectively. The British called off their attack because of a shortage of ammunition, increasingly a problem at the front. The French pushed the Germans back 2° miles at a cost of 100,000 casualties.

May 31, 1915: A German zeppelin dropped 90 incendiary bombs and 30 grenades over London, killing 7 and injuring 35.

September 25–November 6, 1915 (Second Battle of Champagne): The Allies had spent the summer preparing for a major offensive. After two days of heavy bombing, the French advanced only 5,000 yards. With encouragement from Gen. Joseph Joffre, the French fought on for several weeks, at a cost of 145,000 soldiers; the Germans lost 113,000.

September 25–October 30, 1915 (Third Battle for Artois): The offensive was launched by the BEF to draw off German troops from Champagne, France. The British used gas for the first time. The BEF captured Loos, although its goal was Lens.

EASTERN FRONT

January 3–4, 1915: Near Bolimov (southwest of Warsaw), the Germans lobbed shells with xylyl bromide, a tear gas, to support their assault on Russian forces. The Russians reported 1,100 dead from the gas.

February 7–21, 1915: In severe winter weather following a two-day blizzard, the Germans surprised the Russians in the Masurian Lakes region of East Prussia, encircling the 20th Russian Corps in the Forest of Augostów. The Germans advanced 70 miles, killing almost 100,000 Russians and capturing 110,000 as well as several hundred guns before they detoured to the south to help the Austrian offensive.

March 20–22, 1915: The Russians, under Gen. Aleksei Brusilov, continued pushing the Austrians back into the Carpathian Mountains. The Russians captured 1,400 heavy guns and other artillery pieces and 120,000 Austrian prisoners. Hundreds of wounded froze to death in blizzard conditions.

March 25, 1915: General Brusilov retook the Lupków Pass, and the Austrians appealed to the Germans for help in pushing back the Russians.

April 16, 1915: As part of a diversion, German soldiers attacked in the north and advanced into Lithuania before entrenching themselves along the River Dubissa. German troops were then sent south to join a major southern offensive to drive the Russians out of the Carpathian Mountains and back into Russia.

May 2–September 30, 1915: The Central Powers' offensive began with an intense early-morning bombardment in the Gorlice-Tarnów sector southeast of Kraków, Poland. Almost 1,000 guns delivered more than 700,000 shells, some of them containing gas, in a space of four hours. The overwhelmed Russians began to retreat, and after three days, the line broke. By June 22, the Austrians and Germans had advanced to the city of Lemburg; by August 5, they had taken Warsaw; by August 25, they had taken Brest-Litovsk on the western edge of the Pripet marshes. The Germans continued to push the Russians eastward, but by September 30, German general Erich von Falkenhayn halted the German advance within 100 miles of Minsk in Belorussia. His troops had outrun their lines of communication; the roads were poor; and the soldiers needed to prepare for winter. In four months, the poorly armed and poorly trained Russian soldiers had retreated 300 miles.

SOUTHERN FRONT

June 23–December 2, 1915: Having entered the war on the side of the Allies in May, Italy faced Austria along their shared border. Largely mountainous, broken by occasional passes, valleys, and rivers, the terrain offered few chances for either side to make large gains. However, at the far eastern sector, near the Isonzo River north of Trieste, the Italians launched 11 offensives before the war ended, the first of them on June 23. By December 2, the fourth battle of Isonzo had been fought, with nothing to show for the campaign except 66,000 dead Italians, 190,000 wounded, and 22,500 taken prisoner. (Austrian casualties totaled some 165,000.)

October 3, 1915: Allied troops landed at Salonika in northern Greece. Although neutral, the Greek government, headed by Elefuthérios Venizélos, did not put up a resistance. Pro-German King Constantine, however, forced Venizélos to resign on October 5.

October 12–23, 1915: Some 40,000 British and French troops landed at Salonika and set off to the northwest to aid the Serbs in their fight against the German-Austrian force that crossed into Serbia on October 6. By October 23, however, a Bulgarian army positioned itself north of the Greek border and cut off the Allied troops.

October 6–December 31, 1915: Along the Austrian-Serbian front, more than a quarter million German and Austrian troops were massed facing 200,000 Serbian troops, who had survived a recent typhus epidemic. The Central Powers crossed the River Sava (October 6), then the Danube (October 7); on October 9, they took Belgrade. On October 11, Bulgarian troops attacked Serbs from the east and cut off the advancing Allied troops from Salonika. By mid-November, the Serbian army was retreating southeastward through Montenegro and Albania to the Adriatic Sea. In January 1916, Allied ships carried some 150,000 Serb troops to the nearby Greek island of Corfu. The Serbs had suffered some 100,000 dead and wounded during the campaign, with another 160,000 taken prisoner.

NON-EUROPEAN FRONTS

January–December 1915: In German East Africa, sporadic fighting continued. Gen. Jan Christiaan Smuts, relieved from his South African duties by victory over the Germans in German Southwest Africa in July, moved his 20,000 troops to attack Gen. Paul von Lettow-Vorbeck from the south.

February 19, 1915–March 18 (Battle of Gallipoli): The British and French thought that the Turks would prove poor fighters and that by going through Turkey they could attack Austria-Hungary from the south and draw German troops from the western front. The strategy called for taking the Gallipoli Peninsula that guarded the northern side of the Dardanelles, then to move up Allied forces to take Constantinople. The Gallipoli campaign began with the bombardment of the outer forts guarding the entrance to the Dardanelles by the French and British navies. Then, on March 18, six English and four French battleships moved into the Dardanelles. A string of mines that had been laid by the Turks only ten days earlier sank three of the Allied ships; three others were badly damaged and forced out of action. With six ships down, the Allies called off the attack. The French abandoned the idea of seizing the Dardanelles, but the British proceeded with a land campaign.

April 25–26, 1915 (Gallipoli Campaign): Four British divisions, including Australian and New Zealand troops (Anzac) that had been training in Egypt, landed at two major points on the Gallipoli Peninsula. (French forces feinted a landing on the opposite coast.) The Anzac forces landed at Ari Buran on the northwest coast 1 mile north of their correct location under steep ridges. Shelling from the Turks didn't begin until midday; when they ran out of ammunition, they began to withdraw. Determined to hold the crest, Comdr. Mustafa Kemal ordered the Turks to prepare to attack with bayonets and, seeing the extent of the invasion, ordered more troops and guns into position.

Other British troops landed at Cape Helles, the southernmost tip of Gallipoli. Three beach areas were lightly defended. At the other two beaches, fighting was intense; the Turks had the advantage of holding the heights above the invading force. After two days, of the 30,000 Allied troops that were put ashore at both locales, 20,000 were killed or wounded. In the following weeks, the troops made only slight gains off their landing sites and took terrible casualties.

August 6–21, 1915 (Gallipoli Campaign): In an attempt to break the stalemate on the Gallipoli Peninsula, British troops landed at Suvla Bay just north of the Anzac sector. The British wasted valuable time after landing unopposed and were unable to take the heights. They were forced to dig trenches and, in the weeks that followed, were able to advance only a few miles.

November 25, 1915: In the continuing campaign to capture Baghdad, the British and Indian troops, led by Gen. Charles Townshend, had been fighting the Turks along the Tigris and Euphrates Rivers. When the Allies reached Ctesiphon, the Turks changed tactics, stood their ground, and counterattacked. Although only 22 miles from their goal, the British were 400 miles from the sea and reinforcements. They retreated to Kut, dug in, and were besieged by 80,000 Turks for 147 days (see non-European Fronts, April 29, 1916, p. 388). Reinforcements were unable to battle their way from Basra to help.

December 10, 1915–January 9, 1916 (Gallipoli Campaign): The Allies evacuated their troops from the beaches of Gallipoli.

NAVAL THEATER

January 24, 1915: A British squadron of five battle cruisers and several lighter cruisers intercepted four German cruisers near Dogger Bank, the region in the North Sea about midway between Britain and Denmark. In the ensuing fight, 192 sailors were killed on the German flagship, the *Seydlitz,* and 782 sailors were killed when the *Blucher* sank.

February 4–18, 1915: In response to a British warning that neutral ships carrying grain to Germany would be seized, Germany announced that the waters around the British Isles constituted a war zone. As of February 18, Germany reserved the right to conduct unrestricted warfare against neutral ships that entered the area.

March 11, 1915: The British declared a total blockade of all German ports. The United States protested the blockade on March 30, as did Germany on April 4.

March 28–29, 1915: Five battleships, two cruisers, and ten destroyers from the Russian Black Sea Fleet attacked Turkey's Bosporus forts. Fog on the second day and the loss of two destroyers forced the fleet's withdrawal.

May 1, 1915: Without warning, a German submarine sank the U.S. freighter *Gulflight*; Germany offered reparations in an effort to keep the United States neutral.

May 7, 1915: The Germans torpedoed and sank the British liner *Lusitania* off the coast of Ireland; 1,198 of the 1,959 civilian passengers were killed. Of those killed, 128 were Americans. The Germans claimed that the ship was carrying munitions, but the British denied that. In any case, that incident as much as any other turned U.S. opinion against Germany.

November 7, 1915: A German submarine sank the Italian liner *Ancona*; among the 272 who lost their lives were 27 Americans.

HOME FRONT

January 10, 1915: The Women's Peace Party (WPP), organized by Jane Addams, Lillian Wald, and Paul Kellogg, held its inaugural convention in Washington, D.C., with 3,000 attendees. The WPP developed a "program for constructive peace" that included a call for an immediate armistice, an international agreement to limit armaments, reduction of trade barriers, and a "Concert of Nations" to replace the militaristic balance-of-power mentality that had led to the arms buildup in Europe.

January 15, 1915: The U.S. investment firm of J. P. Morgan and Co. became the purchasing agent for Great Britain, then became one of the purchasing agents for France.

January 30, 1915: Col. Edward House, President Wilson's closest adviser, sailed for Europe to try to mediate a peace settlement. His efforts came to nothing because all parties felt that they could achieve their aims through military action.

February–August 1915: Under J. P. Morgan's auspices, the Allies ordered 4.4 million rifles, worth $194 dollars, from Remington and Winchester.

May 1, 1915: Several major New York newspapers published an advertisement sent to them by the German embassy in Washington, D.C., in which the embassy warned that Americans traveling on British or other Allied ships in the war zone around the British Isles did so at their own risk. That advertisement, placed next to an advertisement of the Cunard Line's sailing of the *Lusitania*, was considered fair warning by the Germans. It was one of many attempts by Germany to influence U.S. opinion and to keep U.S. money and munitions out of the hands of the Allies.

May 10–July 21, 1915: After the torpedoing of the *Lusitania* (see Naval Theater, May 7, 1915, above), the German ambassador to the United States apologized. On May 13, Secretary of State William Jennings Bryan sent a note to Germany demanding complete disavowal of such an action; however, he told the Austrian ambassador that the stern language of the note was only to "pacify excited public opinion." When word of that remark was leaked and Bryan, a pacifist, refused to sign a second strongly worded note to Germany, Bryan was forced to resign on June 8. On June 9, President Wilson sent a second note to Germany demanding reparations and other concessions in regard to the *Lusitania*. On July 21, Wilson sent a third note. In the end, Germany did nothing, and Wilson let the issue fade away.

June 1915: Ten submarines made by Bethlehem Steel were sent to England via Canada to avoid compromising U.S. neutrality.

June 17, 1915: The New York Peace Society organized a meeting attended by some 120 prominent conservatives at Independence Hall in Philadelphia to form the League to Enforce Peace. The conservative internationalist group elected William Howard Taft its president and advocated a world body (including the United States) prepared to use economic and military interventions to enforce international law and to appeal to international honor to keep world peace.

July 2–3, 1915: On July 2 Erich Muenter, a German instructor at Cornell University, exploded a bomb in the U.S. Senate reception room. No one was killed in the blast because it occurred late at night. The next day, Muenter shot and wounded J. P. Morgan because Morgan represented the British in war contract negotiations. Muenter was arrested and committed suicide in jail on July 6.

July 15, 1915: Dr. Heinrich Albert, head of the German propaganda movement in the United States, mistakenly left a briefcase on a New York City subway car. The briefcase was turned over to the Secret Service; it contained documents showing an extensive network of German espionage and subversive activities in the United States. The documents were released to the newspapers, further swinging U.S. public opinion to oppose Germany's position in the war.

August 10, 1915: A military training camp was established at Plattsburg, New York, the first of several "Plattsburgs," at which volunteers trained at their own expense, with the intention of joining the Allies and fighting under European commanders.

September 1, 1915: In response to threats from President Woodrow Wilson that he would break diplomatic relations with Germany because of submarine attacks on unarmed passenger liners without first seeing to the safety of the passengers, Germany met Wilson's demands and agreed to do that; that was known as the "*Arabic* pledge," after the British liner sunk (August 19, 1915) by German U-boats that resulted in two Americans being killed. Wilson was applauded for keeping the United States out of the war. Republicans like Theodore Roosevelt, who energized their crusade for military preparedness, were not satisfied.

December 4, 1915: Henry Ford, opposed to U.S. involvement in any war, outfitted a "peace ship," *Oscar II.* On December 4, Ford set sail from New York with some 150 fellow pacifists. His announced goal was "to get the boys out of the trenches by Christmas," but he was attacked from all sides and ridiculed. By the time the pacifists arrived in Europe, they were quarreling with one another. When the pacifists could find no neutral country willing to sponsor a peace conference, Ford sailed for the United States on December 24, leaving the whole venture in disarray.

December 7, 1915: President Wilson, responding to concerns about U.S. vulnerability given the war in Europe, presented to Congress a national defense program that would increase the size of the Army and Navy.

INTERNATIONAL DEVELOPMENTS

January 7, 1915: In a secret meeting in Constantinople, a Bolshevik Russian leader told the German ambassador that the Bolsheviks and Germans shared an aim: the total destruction of Czarist Russia. He said that without supporting the revolutionary effort in Russia, the Germans would never defeat that country.

March 20, 1915: The British signed a secret agreement with Russia that recognized each country's mutual interests in the Ottoman Empire (Turkey) and in oil-rich Persia (Iran). If Russia would support British interests in the Ottoman Empire and Persia, Britain would support Russian annexation of Constantinople, the Bosporus territory in Turkey, as well as Gallipoli.

April 1, 1915: German revolutionary Rosa Luxemburg led an antiwar protest in Berlin, Germany, for which she was arrested and imprisoned. Antiwar sentiments in Germany were spreading, at the front lines as well as at home.

April 8, 1915: Italy talked with Central Power officials about entering World War I on their side if Austria would cede certain territories. When Austria declined, Italy began negotiations with the Allies for an even larger territorial package from the Austrian-Hungarian Empire.

Incensed at the cooperation the Armenians were giving the Russians in the Caucasus region, the Turks rounded up tens of thousands of Armenian men and killed them.

April 15, 1915: The German ambassador to Turkey in Constantinople rejected an appeal for help from the Armenians in Turkey. Hundreds of thousands of women, old people, and children from the Caucasus region were rounded up and forced south to Cilicia and Syria in a tortuous death march across the desert.

April 19, 1915: In Turkey's easternmost province of Van, 50,000 Armenians were killed; the city of Van itself was surrounded for 30 days by Turkish soldiers until the Armenians were saved by Russian soldiers.

April 26, 1915: The Italians secretly signed a treaty with the Allied powers committing soldiers, supplies, and support in exchange for significant territory held by Austria-Hungary and Turkey.

April 26–30, 1915: The International Congress of Women, meeting at The Hague in the Netherlands, with 1,000 delegates from 12 countries, endorsed Jane Addams's Women's Peace Party platform and the idea of continuous mediation. Addams was authorized to present the platform to every European country and was received by leaders of the Allies, the Central Powers, and Pope Benedict XV. A group of German women attended the congress, but the British delegation was prevented from attending when Britain suspended ferry service to the Netherlands.

May 23, 1915: Italy declared war on Austria-Hungary.

May 26, 1915: Herbert Asquith, Britain's Liberal prime minister, formed a coalition government with Conservatives in an attempt to lessen the growing criticism of the progress of the war, from the western front to Gallipoli. Among those forced out was Winston Churchill, First Lord of the Admiralty; his Gallipoli campaign was beginning to look like a total disaster.

July 17, 1915: Bulgaria secretly signed a treaty with Austria and Germany that granted Bulgaria significant Turkish territory in Thrace, as well as portions of Macedonia, Serbia, and Greece, in exchange for helping the Central Powers attack Serbia.

October 11, 1915: Despite great international protest, Edith Cavell, an English nurse in Belgium, was executed by the Germans for aiding in the escape of Allied prisoners.

December 28, 1915: Britain instituted compulsory military service.

BATTLES AND CAMPAIGNS: 1916

WESTERN FRONT

February 21–December 18, 1916 (Battle of Verdun): The Germans attacked the fortress-ringed city of Verdun 137 miles east of Paris with a heavy bombardment that caught the French by surprise. French general Joseph Joffre had ignored warnings of a German attack and stripped the forts of their guns, putting them where he felt they could be of better use. On February 25, Gen. Henri Pétain rushed to Verdun with reinforcements, but he arrived too late to prevent the Germans from taking the outer fort at Douaumont.

On March 6, the Germans renewed their attack from both sides of the Verdun salient and fought into the summer, taking Fort Vaux on June 7. French reinforcements, however, were in position, and the Germans were unable to capture Fort Souville. By July 15, the Germans were forced on the defensive. During that operation, the Germans and the French occasionally used a new and more deadly gas, phosgene.

After small battles in the summer, the French took back Fort Douaumont (October 24), then Fort Vaux (November 3). The fighting around Verdun gradually faded away by mid-December, with both sides about where they had been in February. The longest in the war, the battle for Verdun consumed 23 million shells and the lives of 650,000 men.

July 1–November 18, 1916 (Battle of the Somme): Responding to French urgings, the British engaged Germans at the Somme River northwest of Paris. The assault began with an intense barrage of 250,000 shells, followed by the exploding of ten mines planted under German trenches. As the BEF troops advanced, at least 100 German machine guns fired at the advancing troops from enforced trenches that had withstood the barrage. From 7:30 A.M. until nightfall on July 1, more than 20,000 British out of a force of 100,000 were killed, including 1,000 officers, and 40,000 were injured. Both sides settled down to a battle of attrition.

August 28, 1916: Kaiser Wilhelm, concerned by the Russian advances, the entrance of Romania into the war on the side of the Allies, and the continued German casualties on the Somme Front, removed Gen. Erich von Falkenhayn as commander along the western front. Gen. Paul von Hindenburg came from the eastern front to replace him and brought along Gen. Erich Ludendorff as his chief of staff. General von Hindenburg was also made commander of all the armies of the Central Powers. Among his first orders were a resumption of unrestricted submarine warfare and an increase in production of munitions.

September 15, 1916: The British launched a major offensive along a 10-mile front, and for the first time in warfare, the British introduced tanks. At Flers Courcelette, several of the 49 tanks advanced more than 2,000 yards, but they were too slow and too few to take full advantage. On seeing their possibility, Gen. Douglas Haig, commander of the British forces in France and Belgium, requested 1,000 more tanks from the war department.

General von Hindenburg ordered 700,000 Belgian workers deported to Germany for work in the Hindenburg Industrial Program. That caused outrage in international diplomatic circles. President Woodrow Wilson protested that the deportations were a contravention of the Hague Conventions.

November 18, 1916: The battle of Ancre, the final phase of the Battle of the Somme, ended with the British still 3 miles short of what had been their first day's objective. Rains and mud brought an end to the offensive. For barely 7 miles achieved, the cost was 146,404 Allied dead, 164,055 German dead, and each side suffering another 500,000 wounded.

EASTERN FRONT

June 4-18, 1916: Russian general Aleksei Brusilov launched a major offensive to recover territory lost to the Germans and Austrians in the Polish salient and also to divert Austrian troops away from their front with Italy. Brusilov's offensive began with a 1,938-gun barrage along a 200-mile front from the Pripet marshes to Bukovina. Russian troops broke through the Austrian line and retook Lutsk in Ukraine, and pursued retreating Austrians all the way to Czernowitz in eastern Austria-Hungary. General von Hindenburg began to transfer German troops from the western front to aid the Austrians.

August 22, 1916: Still advancing successfully, though at great cost in human life, General Brusilov continued pushing the Austrians back into Galicia.

September 3, 1916: Romania, having declared war on Austria-Hungary on August 27, was invaded from the north and the south by Bulgaria, Germany, and Austria-Hungary.

September 20, 1916: Brusilov's offensive came to a stop, having advanced only about 50 miles westward. Although the territorial gains were insignificant, the impact was major: Each side suffered almost 1,000,000 casualties; Austria's army could no longer take the offensive; Germany transferred 15 divisions from the western front; and Russia's losses led to the collapse of morale and eventually to revolution.

December 6, 1916: German troops captured Bucharest, the capital of Romania, and added it to their list of conquered capitals (Luxembourg City, Brussels, Warsaw, Belgrade) with great celebration. Prior to the defeat, the British had blown up a fuel supply source, but with the conquest of Romania, Germany had a much needed source of grain.

SOUTHERN FRONT

January 8, 1916: After nine days of fighting with no help from the Allies, Montenegro surrendered to the Austrians.

August 6–November 4, 1916: The Italian army had continued its Isonzo campaign in northeastern Italy throughout 1916, with a fifth battle against the entrenched Austrians in March, and the sixth commencing on August 6. Heavy battlefield casualties were augmented by deaths from cholera and paratyphoid. By November 4, the Italians had completed a ninth battle with very few gains.

December 1, 1916: Greek forces loyal to the Allies again were defeated by King Constantine's army, thus maintaining Greek neutrality.

NON-EUROPEAN FRONTS

January 1, 1916: In the Cameroons, the British entered Yaoundé (followed within a few days by the French), still on the trail of elusive German soldiers. The garrison was empty. The Germans had evacuated to neutral Spanish Guinea.

January 9, 1916: The last of the Allied troops were removed from Gallipoli during the night. The casualties for the entire campaign were 50,000 Allied dead and another 150,000 wounded; the Turks counted 66,000 dead and 100,000 wounded. The Gallipoli Campaign stands to this day as one of the worst-conceived and worst-executed operations in military history.

January 1916: A relief force seeking to reach the British and Indian troops besieged in the city of Kut-el-Amara (in present-day Iraq) battled its way north against Turks commanded by German field marshal Kolmar von der Goltz. It failed to reach Kut-el-Amara and suffered 6,000 casualties. A second relief expedition in March also failed, costing the British some 3,500 casualties.

March–December 1916: In German East Africa, South African troops launched an offensive in March. They regained the Ugandan railway but operations dragged on, and by the end of 1916, Gen. Paul von Lettow-Vorbeck had still managed to elude his pursuers.

April 29, 1916: Despite offers of up to £2 million in gold from British officers, including T. E. Lawrence (Lawrence of Arabia), for the safe release of the British army in Kut, the Turks insisted on a British surrender. After some 9,000 troops surrendered, they were marched to prison in Anatolia, Turkey, in such appalling conditions of deprivation that 1,750 of the 2,500 British soldiers and 2,500 of the 6,500 Indian soldiers died from thirst, beatings, and starvation on the march and from the conditions in prison camps.

June 5–10, 1916: On July 5, Arabs led by Sherif Hussein, governor of the Ottoman Empire's Hejaz Province (the northwest region of present-day Saudi Arabia), revolted against the Turks in Medina, but they were repulsed by the larger force of Turks. On July 7, with counsel by British advisers including T. E. Lawrence, Hussein declared the independence of the Hejaz from the Turks. That was followed by a barrage on Turkish positions north of the port city of Jeddah from two British warships, aerial bombing by the British, and further attacks on Turkish soldiers by Arabs. On July 10, the Arabs took over Mecca, the Muslims' most sacred city.

NAVAL THEATER

March 22, 1916: The British introduced the depth charge into naval warfare by successfully destroying a German submarine off the coast of Ireland.

March 24, 1916: A French channel boat, the *Sussex*, was sunk. Although no Americans lost their lives, the 25 aboard were endangered. In response, U.S. Secretary of State Robert Lansing warned Germany that the United States would break off diplomatic relations unless Germany stopped such attacks.

May 31–June 1, 1916 (Battle of Jutland): In an attempt to break the blockade off the German coast, 29 major German warships (and almost as many smaller support ships) headed for the Norwegian coast. Off the island of Jutland, they were met on May 31 by 37 major warships (and more than 100 smaller ships) of the British Royal Navy. In the initial engagement between the scouting ships in late afternoon, two British battle cruisers were blown up, with a loss of 2,283

sailors; other ships on both sides were damaged. Then, about 6 P.M., the two main fleets engaged; as the ships maneuvered to gain advantage, they continued to fight until darkness, each side inflicting some damage. By 9 P.M, the British had managed to position many of their ships between the Germans and their base in Germany. Through a series of confusing encounters, the Germans were able to fight their way back to their home base, but at a loss of one battleship, four cruisers, and five destroyers. Early on the morning of June 1, the British headed back to their home base, having lost a total of three battleships, three cruisers, and eight destroyers. The Battle of Jutland remains one of the greatest battles (and most studied) in naval history, yet it was indecisive in its outcome. In any case, it was the last major surface battle of the war.

October 7–9, 1916: The German submarine *U-53,* located in international waters off Rhode Island, sank nine British merchant ships.

HOME FRONT

January 10, 1916: In protest against President Woodrow Wilson's recognition of the Mexican government of President Venustiano Carranza, members of Pancho Villa's revolutionary army removed 17 U.S. mining engineers from a train in Mexico and killed 16 of them.

March 9, 1916: Villa led 1,500 men on a raid into Columbus, New Mexico, and killed 17 Americans. Americans were outraged, and President Wilson ordered an expedition to capture Villa dead or alive.

March 15, 1916–February 5, 1917: Gen. John Pershing crossed into Mexico with 6,000 U.S. Army troops to capture Villa. The expedition chased Villa for almost a year without capturing him and finally abandoned the search in February 1917. Villa continued his activities in northern Mexico until 1920, when he negotiated a peace with the new Mexican government.

April 18, 1916: Following the surprise German torpedoing of the French *Sussex* in March, with a loss of 80 civilian lives (although none were Americans), President Wilson again threatened to sever diplomatic relations with Germany as a result of that country's breach of international law. Wilson insisted Germany follow the rules of warfare, requiring a warship to "visit and search" a ship to establish whether it was carrying war materials before attacking it. The resulting "*Sussex* pledge" from Germany was treated as a major gain by the Wilson administration.

May 27, 1916: By invitation, President Wilson addressed the conservative League to Enforce Peace and articulated a U.S. manifesto of three parts: (1) "every people has a right to choose the sovereignty under which they shall live," (2) small nations should be accorded the same respect with regards to sovereignty and territorial integrity as large nations, and (3) the world has a right to be free from aggressions that "disregard [the] rights of peoples and nations."

June 3, 1916: Congress passed the National Defense Act, authorizing a standing army of 175,000 and a National Guard that would number 450,000; it also provided for a reserve corps for both officers and enlisted men, the Reserve Officers Training Corps (ROTC), and for a volunteer army in case of war. In effect, that act provided the framework for U.S. Army forces that has persisted to the present day.

July 23, 1916: The United States commemorated the death of its first hero of World War I, Alan Seeger, who died on the western front. Seeger, a poet of 19th-century Byronic sensibilities, had joined the French Foreign Legion in 1914 for the "glory of it." He wrote rhapsodic verse about the war as the "supreme experience." His best-known poem was the oft-quoted "I Have a Rendezvous with Death."

August 29, 1916: Congress passed the "Big Navy Act," a ten-year plan to enlarge and improve the U.S. Navy.

September 7, 1916: Congress appropriated $50 million to purchase or build merchant ships under the United States Shipping Board Act.

October 8, 1916: After German U-boats sank five merchant ships off Nantucket Island, Massachusetts, President Wilson told the U.S. ambassador to Germany, who happened to be on a ship near the vicinity of the torpedoing, that he wanted to "keep and to make peace."

November 7, 1916: In a close contest, President Wilson was reelected; he defeated Republican Charles Evans Hughes, who had been identified with a pro-war stance, in part because of speeches supporting him by Theodore Roosevelt. Wilson had campaigned under the slogan, "He kept us out of the war." In fact, he was increasingly moving the country toward entering World War I on the side of the Allies.

December 18, 1916: President Wilson, on learning of Germany's interest in negotiating a peace with the Allies, issued a note to the fighting countries asking each to state its "precise objects" for making peace. Once more, nothing came of that because the Allies distrusted U.S. motives.

INTERNATIONAL DEVELOPMENTS

January 11, 1916: Discontent with the war and with overall conditions in Russia resulted in a strike by 10,000 workers in Nikolayev, a naval base on the Black Sea. The strife spread to Petrograd, where 45,000 dock workers went on strike.

February 22, 1916: Col. Edward House, as President Woodrow Wilson's emissary, met in London with British foreign secretary Edward Grey; they drafted the so-called House-Grey memorandum, which stated: Should the Allies accept the U.S. proposal to hold a conference to end the war and should Germany refuse it, the United States would probably enter the war against Germany.

May 1916: The British sent Sir Mark Sykes on a mission to Paris, where he and a French official, George Picot, secretly made the Sykes-Picot Agreement. Under it, Britain and France agreed to divide up the Ottoman Empire between their respective countries. When Italy learned of that agreement, it demanded its share, and on April 19, 1917, Britain and France promised Italy parts of the empire.

May 4, 1916: Concerned about the United States entering the war, Kaiser Wilhelm promised that U-boat attacks on merchant ships would not commence without sufficient warning to allow for saving civilian lives.

June 28–30, 1916: Protesters staged a three-day strike in Germany, an indication of growing antiwar feeling. Deaths by starvation as a result of the Allied blockade were a daily occurrence in Germany; such deaths had increased from 88,232 in 1915 to 121,114 in 1916. There were food riots in more than 30 German cities.

August 1916–June 27, 1917: Greece was practically torn by a civil war between the faction, led by King Constantine, that wanted to enter the war on the side of the Central Powers and the faction, led by Prime Minister Eleutherios Venizelos, that wanted to join the Allies. The

British and French stationed a fleet off Greece's main harbor of Piraeus near Athens. When fighting broke out between the two factions in Athens, 3,000 British, French, and Italian troops marched into Athens to bolster the Venizelists; the Allies withdrew under an armistice, but maintained a blockade around Greece. King Constantine left Greece on June 13, 1917, and on June 27, Venizelos brought Greece into World War I on the side of the Allies.

November 21, 1916: Austria-Hungary's emperor, Franz Joseph, died and was succeeded by his great-nephew, Archduke Karl.

December 12–30, 1916: On December 12, German chancellor Theobald von Bethmann-Hollweg, in a speech to the German parliament, announced that the German government was prepared to open peace discussions with the Allies in a neutral country. President Wilson, in a note of December 18, asked the warring powers to state their terms for peace. Suspicious that Wilson's approach favored the Central Powers, the Allies formally rejected the German chancellor's invitation on December 30.

December 29, 1916: The charismatic mystic Rasputin was assassinated by several highly placed Russians, fearful of his influence over the czar's family and several government officials. In the end, though, eliminating Rasputin did not save the czar or his government (see Eastern Front, pp. 392-393).

BATTLES AND CAMPAIGNS: 1917

WESTERN FRONT

February 3, 1917: The Portuguese Expeditionary Force joined the Allies in France with 50,000 troops.

February 4–April 5, 1917: After the fruitless Battle of the Somme in France, German troops withdrew about 25 miles to the east to a newly fortified, straightened (and thus shortened), and more strategically sound line, the so-called Hindenburg Line. (The Germans called it the Siegfried Line.) By April 5, the German front extended some 80 miles from Soissons in the south to Loos in the north.

April 9–May 3, 1917 (Battle of Arras and Vimy Ridge): East of Arras, near the northern end of the Hindenburg Line, the British launched an offensive. The British used tanks and a roll-ing artillery gun on wheels that advanced ahead of the attacking infantry to push through the Hindenburg Line's first two trenches. The tanks, however, were not generally successful due to the mud and mechanical problems. By the end of the first day, the Canadians had secured Vimy Ridge at a cost of thousands of men. But as the days passed, and German reserves came up, the offensive sputtered out.

April 16–May 9, 1917 (Second Battle of the Aisne): Gen. Robert Georges Nivelle replaced Gen. Joseph Joffre as commander of the French army. General Nivelle began the so-called Nivelle Offensive along the Aisne River, northwest of Reims and south of the Hindenburg Line. That battle was a complete failure. German machine guns mowed down the advancing French; many of the French tanks were destroyed. The advance, planned for 6 miles, was halted by the Germans at 600 yards. Although General Nivelle had pledged to halt the offensive within 48 hours if it failed, he continued to order attacks. At one point, the French did advance 2° miles, but finally the offensive was called off. (On May 15, General Nivelle was replaced by Gen. Henri Pétain.) The French suffered about 100,000 casualties, the Germans, 150,000. The dreadful conditions at the western front were leading to widespread mutinies by French troops (see May 27–June 1, 1917, below).

May 25, 1917: The Germans began using new long-range bombers, called Gothas, each of which could carry 13 bombs. Weather interfered with a planned raid on London, but two Gothas got through, killing 95 people and injuring 192.

May 27–June 1, 1917: In a major mutiny along the western front, approximately 30,000 French troops left their trenches. General Pétain responded with mass arrests; 23,385 French soldiers were court-martialed; 55 were executed, and another 357 were sentenced to death, but their sentences were commuted to life in prison in the colonies.

June 7–8, 1917: South of Ypres, the Messines Ridge was held by the Germans, which gave them a dominating position. After 18 months of tunneling under and mining the German positions on the high ground of the ridge, the British Royal Engineers were ready. At 3:10 on the morning of June 7, 19 mines were fired simultaneously. The Allies were able to take the high ground of the Ypres salient.

U.S. troops are photographed as they cross Westminster Bridge in London on September 5, 1917. They were among the first of the U.S. forces sent to fight in Europe.

June 13, 1917: German Gotha bombers dropped more than 100 bombs on London, killing 162 civilians.

June 26, 1917: The first U.S. infantry troops, 14,000 total, arrived in France at the port of Saint Nazaire. They were untrained, some unarmed, and not at all ready to fight. Gen. John Pershing's first tasks included establishing training schools and organizing supplies and communication networks.

July 12–17, 1917: At Ypres in Belgium, on July 12, the Germans fired 50,000 shells of a new chemical weapon, mustard gas, at the British; of the more than 2,000 soldiers who were affected, 87 died. On July 17, the British responded by firing 100,000 shells of chloropicrin; 75 Germans were killed.

July 31–November 6, 1917 (Third Battle of Ypres or Battle of Passchendaele): After much discussion among the Allies about whether to launch an offensive or wait for the Americans, British general Douglas Haig was allowed to proceed. A series of nine battles was fought mainly on the muddy, waterlogged "Flanders field" outside Ypres; men and mules actually drowned when they slipped into water-filled shell holes. In the last of the battles (October 26–November 6), the Canadians captured the village of Passchendaele, and because the offensive stopped there, it gave its name to the entire campaign. The battle cost the British some 250,000 soldiers to gain 9,000 yards. The German casualties were so high (also about 250,000) that Gen. Erich Ludendorff had to divert soldiers from the Isonzo front in Italy.

August 13, 1917: In France, General Pershing worked on setting up a communications system to link the ports, the bases, and the depots. Pershing also created the General Purchasing Board, which immediately ordered 5,000 airplanes and 8,500 trucks from the French, to be delivered by June 1918.

September 4, 1917: A German air raid on a British base hospital resulted in the deaths of four Americans, the first of the American Expeditionary Force (AEF) to die in World War I.

September 6, 1917: General Pershing moved the AEF's headquarters from Paris to Chaumont on the southern sector of the western front to be nearer to where U.S. soldiers were assigned to fight. On reviewing the troops with his chief of staff, Capt. George C. Marshall, and French president Raymond Poincaré, Pershing became convinced that U.S. troops needed further training.

October 3, 1917: General Pershing exploded in frustration at the lack of "experience, energy, [and] aggressive spirit" of the AEF troops after watching a demonstration of an attack on an enemy trench conducted by 1st Division major Theodore Roosevelt, Jr.

October 23, 1917: In a French attack on Germans at Chemin des Dames, U.S. soldiers operated one of the artillery batteries that preceded the attack.

November 2, 1917: A U.S. infantry battalion relieved French troops at Barthelémont, the first official AEF action. At an isolated outpost, the troops were subjected to a one-hour artillery barrage and a raid by a party of 213 Germans. The Americans were outnumbered four-to-one; 3 were killed and 12 taken prisoner. On learning of that, General Pershing was said to have wept.

November 20–December 7, 1917 (Battle of Cambrai): In what was the first major success in tank warfare, 324 tanks surprised the Germans and broke through the Hindenburg Line near Cambrai, east of Arras, in France. After the initial success, the British forces were stopped by German artillery, barbed wire, and tough fighting. On November 30, the Germans mounted a counterattack that drove the British back behind their starting line. The battle cost the British some 43,000 casualties and the Germans about 41,000.

EASTERN FRONT

January 1917: The battles and campaigns of the eastern front became subordinated to the civil turmoil engulfing Russia, which culminated first in the February Revolution (March), then in the October (or Bolshevik) Revolution (November). (Russia used the Julian calendar, so according to that calendar, the revolutions took place in February and October.) After the failure of the Brusilov offensive in September 1916, the Russian army effectively ceased operations. Morale was at a new low; ammunition, food, clothing, and other supplies were simply not available. Russia was on the verge of a revolution.

March 3–15, 1917: In Petrograd, workers at the Putilov munitions works went on strike, and bread riots broke out. The strike widened throughout Russia. Martial law was declared in Petrograd. On March 11, Czar Nicolas II tried to dissolve Russia's parliament, the Duma. On March 12, the revolution broke out in Petrograd

when 17,000 garrisoned soldiers joined others in the streets to demonstrate against the czar; police stations and law courts were set on fire. On March 14, a coalition of liberals and socialists formed a provisional government; the czar, who had been at the front lines and was making his way back to Petrograd, was stopped on his train and held captive. On March 15, Nicolas II abdicated (and he and his family were held prisoner). With Prince Lvov as its prime minister, a provisional government was formed, claiming that it would continue to support the war effort. A countergovernment, the Petrograd Soviet, appointed commissars to all military units; their job was to urge the units not to fight. Although nominally minister of justice, Alexander Kerensky, a liberal, was the actual head of the government, which effected some reforms but not enough to forestall a major revolution. (Kerensky became prime minister on July 22, 1917.)

April 3, 1917: As a sign of support for the revolution, 10,000 Russian troops surrendered to the Germans.

April 9–16, 1917: After the Czar abdicated, Vladimir Lenin, the leader of the radical Russian Communists (who was in exile in Switzerland), convinced the Germans that he would work to get Russia out of the war. Lenin and a small group of his fellow Bolsheviks were allowed to pass through Germany in a sealed train. They arrived at Petrograd's Finland Station. Lenin then set about organizing a new revolution.

May 15, 1917: The Petrograd Soviet issued a manifesto stating that "Socialists of all countries" should demand a peace without annexation or indemnity.

May 16–19, 1917: The Russian provisional government rejected any call for peace, including one offered by the German Reichstag. Kerensky appointed Gen. Aleksei Brusilov commander in chief and ordered an offensive.

July 1–19, 1917 (The Kerensky Offensive): General Brusilov launched an offensive in Eastern Galicia, during which a special Russian-Czech brigade persuaded Austrian-Czech soldiers to desert. Russian soldiers also refused to fight; Brusilov had to rely on Siberians, Finns, and Poles. After initial gains, the offensive turned into a rout when the Austrians broke through the Russian line, and the Russian soldiers fled or were taken prisoner. Prince Lvov resigned as prime minister, and Kerensky replaced him.

July 16–22, 1917: On July 16, armed workers and soldiers in Petrograd launched an uprising against the Kerensky government; 6,000 sailors at Russia's Kronstadt naval base revolted. Lenin's role was not clear, but he appeared to be taking control. When the revolt failed, Lenin fled to Finland on July 22, where he remained until October 21.

July 23, 1917: Polish soldiers refused loyalty oaths to the kaiser. In German-occupied Warsaw, Polish soldiers and their leaders chose prison over fighting the Russians.

September 1–3, 1917: The Germans conducted a bombardment with 100,000 gas shells, driving the Russians from the Baltic port of Riga.

September 15, 1917: Alexandr Kerensky declared a democratic republic in Russia.

November 6–7, 1917: Lenin had returned to Petrograd on October 21 and was awaiting the moment to lead a revolution. During the night of November 6, workers, soldiers, and sailors revolted; by the end of the day, Lenin, Leon Trotsky, and other Bolsheviks took command. The revolution still had many trials and battles ahead; Kerensky tried a counter-coup on November 10–12, then fled; and a civil war (1918–1920) broke out between the pro-Communist Reds and the anti-Communist Whites. The revolution is observed as the "October Revolution" because it occurred on October 24 in the Julian calendar.

November 17–19, 1917: On November 17, Leon Trotsky sent a telegram to the German government announcing that the new Soviet government wanted to make peace. On November 19, the Bolsheviks asked for an armistice on all fronts. Georges Clemenceau of France responded that his policy was "War, nothing but war."

December 2–5, 1917: Hostilities on the eastern front ended on December 2; on December 3, meeting at Brest-Litovsk in Belorussia, the new Bolshevik leaders of Russia began negotiations with the Germans over armistice terms. On December 5, German and Russian delegates signed an armistice at Brest-Litovsk. The armistice was broken in February after the Bolsheviks refused to agree to Germany's full demands but was finally implemented with a treaty on March 3, 1918 (see Negotiations and Peace Treaty, p. 406).

SOUTHERN FRONT

May 12–28, 1917: The Italians launched another offensive in the Isonzo River region, the tenth battle; it produced little except heavy casualties.

July 16, 1917: French troops fighting on the Salonika front in northern Greece mutinied over leave time.

August 19–September 12, 1917: In the 11th battle of the Isonzo, the Italians gained about 5 miles of mountainous terrain despite heavy casualties.

October 24–November 10, 1917 (Battle of Caporetto, or 12th Battle of the Isonzo): The Italians had suffered heavy losses during the 11 battles at the Isonzo River, and the Austrian army was near exhaustion. The Germans agreed to provide seven divisions to support the Austrians in what was to be a quick knockout blow against the Italians on the Isonzo front. The Germans launched the offensive near Caporetto north of Trieste on October 24, using gas as well as high-explosive shells. The Italian troops were not prepared and began to retreat in panic. By November 10, they had withdrawn all the way back to the Piave River just east of Venice; in this Battle of Caporetto, the Italians suffered some 320,000 casualties. Unexpectedly, though, that disaster strengthened the Italians' will to resist, and the Austro-German army during the next few weeks failed in its efforts to cross the Piave and encircle Padua, west of Venice.

NON-EUROPEAN CAMPAIGNS

January 1, 1917: T. E. Lawrence, assigned by the British to act as liaison for their support of the Arab struggle against the Ottoman Turks, joined Feisal, a son of Sherif Husein, for a campaign that ended in Damascus in October 1918.

January–December 1917: In German East Africa, Gen. Paul von Lettow-Vorbeck continued to elude his pursuers. On November 28, however, his principal force of 5,000 men was surprised and captured. General von Lettow-Vorbeck and a small force fled into Mozambique, a Portuguese colony to the south. For more than a year, the British and Portuguese pursued the small German force throughout Mozambique, back into German East Africa, and finally into northern Rhodesia, where General von Letto-Vorbeck surrendered on November 25, 1918.

March 11, 1917: After several battles against the Turks, British general Sir Frederick Stanley

Maude and a fighting force of some 120,000 men (about half of them Indian troops) entered Baghdad, Iraq.

March 26–April 19, 1917: The British launched two major attacks on Gaza, the city guarding the approach to Jerusalem—one on March 26, another on April 17–19. Both failed, with the British suffered some 10,000 casualties and the Turks about 4,000. Gen. Edmund Allenby was called from the western front to take command of the British forces in the Sinai-Palestine campaign.

October 31–November 7, 1917: The British, led by General Allenby, launched a major offensive against the Turks in Palestine at the city of Beersheba. The success of that operation was followed by an attack on Gaza in which a special Jewish unit, the 39th Battalion Royal Fusiliers, participated; Gaza fell on November 7. Turkish soldiers were forced from the coastal area, and Allenby's forces were on their way to Jerusalem.

December 9–30, 1917: The British took Jerusalem. The Turks tried to recapture it on December 26–30 but failed.

NAVAL THEATER

February 1, 1917: The German navy once again took up unrestricted warfare against neutral ships.

March 21, 1917: While in what its captain regarded as a special "safe zone" of Dutch waters, the United States tanker *Healdton* was sunk, and 20 crewmen were killed.

April 1, 1917: The *Aztec*, an armed U.S. merchant ship, was torpedoed by a German U-boat; 28 crewmen drowned.

May 4–June 5, 1917: Thirty-four U.S. destroyers arrived at Britain's naval base at Queenstown (now Cobh), Ireland; they were to operate as part of the antisubmarine fleet.

August 2, 1917: In a breakthrough for the British Royal Navy, an airplane not only took off from but also landed on an aircraft carrier.

HOME FRONT

January 22, 1917: President Woodrow Wilson delivered to Congress his "peace without victory" speech, in which he asked for a peace of compromise, not victory, because a victorious peace would leave vanquished nations with a burning desire for revenge. The speech also introduced his vision for a new world order, in which a "community of nations" would work out differences in a "League of Peace." Although many Americans were moved by that speech, it was not popular overseas, where the combatants were mired in a conflict they felt their side would win.

February 3, 1917: President Wilson broke off diplomatic relations with Germany as a result of its stated intention to resume unrestricted submarine warfare.

February 22, 1917: The U.S. Congress passed an arms appropriations bill, budgeting $250 million a sum intended as a signal that the United States was gearing up for war.

March 1, 1917: President Wilson allowed the State Department to publish the Zimmermann telegram, intercepted by the British on January 19 (see International Developments, p. 396). In the telegram sent by German foreign minister Arthur Zimmermann to the German ambassador in Mexico, Zimmermann introduced a scheme to incite Mexicans to take up arms against the United States. Initial reaction was that the telegram was a hoax; however, when Zimmermann himself declared it to be factual, U.S. public opinion was galvanized in opposition to Germany.

March 5, 1917: After the Germans again torpedoed several merchant ships, including the Cunard liner *Laconia* (February 25), in which four Americans were drowned, President Wilson refused to be provoked into war, insisting, "We stand fast on armed neutrality."

March 15, 1917: President Wilson called soldiers from the First Separate Battalion, District of Columbia National Guard, an African-American unit of about 1,000 soldiers and officers, to guard Washington's water supply, power plants, bridges, and public buildings from potential sabotage.

March 18–21, 1917: Four U.S. merchant ships were sunk by German submarines, putting almost irresistible pressure on Wilson to confront Germany. He announced that he would call a special session of Congress for April 2.

April 2, 1917: President Wilson announced to Congress, after two months of unrestricted submarine warfare and the deaths of many U.S. sailors: "There is one choice we cannot make, we are incapable of making. We will not choose the path of submission. The wrongs against which we now array ourselves are no common wrongs; they cut to the very roots of human life." In that famous speech (see Notable Phrases, p. 414), President Wilson asked for a declaration of war against Germany.

April 4, 1917: After two days of debate, the Senate voted in favor of war 82 to 6.

April 6, 1917: With a vote from the House of Representatives (373 to 50) in support of the Senate's declaration of war, the United States officially declared war on Germany. Among those who voted against the declaration was Representative Jeanette Rankin, the first woman elected to Congress in a country where only a few states had given women the right to vote.

The United States had only a small, poorly equipped standing Army of about 200,000 troops; the National Guard and militias added another 100,000. There existed a small Navy and 55 mostly obsolete "flying machines." The task ahead was enormous.

Ninety-one German ocean liners and merchant vessels that had been left in New York Harbor for safekeeping by the kaiser were seized by the United States. The German crews, acting on orders, wrecked the engines. However, the engines were repaired, and many of the ships were put to work for the Allied cause.

May 18, 1917: Over considerable objections, Congress passed the Selective Service Act proposed by President Wilson. The act required all able-bodied men between the ages of 21 and 30 to register for active duty. Automatically exempt from the call were some 2.5 million "nondeclared" alien males, men who didn't have preliminary citizenship papers. The age limits were later extended to include men from 18 to 45. Men reported to locally composed draft boards that had the power to issue deferments. Those called to serve had to remain in the military for the duration of the war.

May 19, 1917: Herbert Hoover, who had led the Commission for the Relief of Belgium, was named Food Administrator by President Wilson. He started voluntary "wheatless" and "meatless" days and advocated "Victory gardens" instead of a program of rationing so there would be more food to send to the Allies.

May 26, 1917: Brig. Gen. John Pershing was named commander of the American Expeditionary Force (AEF).

June 5, 1917: On the first registration day,

amid bands and other patriotic expressions, 9,660,000 men registered for the draft. The president was relieved that in the first draft since the Civil War there were no antidraft demonstrations.

June 13, 1917: Amid a stream of Allied visitors to the White House was Japanese viscount Kikujiro Ishii, who discussed Japanese interests in China with Secretary of State Robert Lansing. Ishii asked that the United States recognize Japan's "special interests" in China in return for an open-door policy between the U.S. and China. Lansing agreed, and the two exchanged notes to that effect on November 2, 1917.

June 15, 1917: The War Department announced that it would open an officer's training course for 1,250 black officer candidates in Des Moines, Iowa.

July 15, 1917: The Espionage Act passed Congress. It imposed fines and up to 20 years in prison for anyone found guilty of obstructing recruitment into the military or of supporting insubordination or disloyalty in the military. The act also gave the postmaster general the power to prohibit from the mails any materials that violated the act and that advocated or urged "treason, insurrection, or forcible resistance to any law of the United States." Two thousand cases were prosecuted under that act, and publications involving more than a million subscriptions, including the *Masses, American Socialist, International Socialist Review*, the *Milwaukee Leader*, and the *Jewish Daily Forward*, were either excluded from the mails or denied cheaper postage rates.

August 1917: Congress passed the Lever Food and Fuel Act, which legitimized the Food Administration and gave it powers and money to raise the price of wheat to encourage farmers to grow more. The war was not popular enough in the Midwest to spur farmers to voluntarily plant more acreage.

August 23, 1917: Angered by Jim Crow laws that required blacks to use separate facilities, African-American soldiers from the 24th Infantry ignored the laws in Houston, Texas, which were then enforced by the police. When one black soldier was arrested with unnecessary force, a riot broke out. Fifteen whites were killed 12 others injured. Sixty-seven of the black soldiers who participated in the riot were arrested and court-martialed by the Army; 13 were given the death sentence and executed, and 41 were sentenced to life imprisonment.

August 30, 1917: The United States Export Administration Board voted to withhold all licenses for exporting controlled commodities from the United States to reinforce the Allied blockade against shipments of grain and raw materials to Germany.

November 20, 1917: British prime minister David Lloyd George in a secret message to Col. Edward House, President Wilson's emissary, expressed dismay at the slow progress and lack of efficiency of the United States in preparing for war and doubted the U.S. promise to have a million armed troops in action in Europe by the summer of 1918.

INTERNATIONAL DEVELOPMENTS

January 19, 1917: German foreign minister Arthur Zimmermann sent a coded telegram to the German ambassador in Mexico with a scheme to involve Mexico in a war against the United States, in return for which Germany would help Mexico regain Texas, New Mexico, and Arizona. British intelligence intercepted the message but chose not to inform the United States, in part so as not to let the Germans know their code had been broken, in part to wait until the British felt the U.S. government would react as the British wanted (see Home Front, March 1, 1917, p. 394).

January 31, 1917: Germany issued its minimum requirements for peace coupled with an announcement that on February 1 it would resume unrestricted submarine warfare in the waters off the British Isles and in the Mediterranean, which Germany had declared war zones.

February 1917: In discussions with his Crown Council, Kaiser Wilhelm weighed the advantages of unrestricted submarine warfare. His advisers assured him that Britain would sue for peace within six months; one admiral assured the kaiser, "I will give Your Majesty my word as an officer that not one American will land on the Continent."

February 14, 1917: Negotiating secretly, French diplomats and representatives of Czar Nicholas reaffirmed their territorial objectives after victory: France would regain Alsace-Lorraine and the Saar Valley, and Russia would annex Constantinople and the Turkish Straits.

April 12, 1917: Austrian and Bulgarian diplomats inquired through Swiss diplomats under what conditions peace would be acceptable to the allies.

June 19, 1917: The British royal family—which had German ties from both the Hanover kings and the Saxe-Coburg-Gotha line of Victoria's husband, Prince Albert—renounced its German names and titles and adopted the family name of *Windsor*.

July 4, 1917: U.S. troops marched through Paris to the grave of the Marquis de Lafayette, the French aristocrat who had fought with the Americans against the British in the American Revolution (see American Revolution, Civilian and Military Biographies, p. 111). At a brief ceremony there, Col. Charles Stanton brought cheers from the gathered Parisians when he concluded his speech by saying, "Lafayette, we are here."

July 1917: The British tried to negotiate a separate peace with Turkey in Switzerland at a secret meeting between a British arms manufacturer and the Turkish war minister, Enver Pasha, who was offered a bribe of $1.5 million in gold. Pasha turned the bribe down.

July 19, 1917: The German Reichstag passed a peace resolution by a vote of 212 to 126, with 17 abstentions, urging the government to work on a peace by agreement and permanent reconciliation. The resolution was dismissed by Chancellor Georg Michaelis (who had replaced Theobald von Bethmann-Hollweg earlier in July).

July 20, 1917: The Pact of Corfu was signed after several weeks of negotiations on the Greek island of Corfu by representatives of various southern Slav constituencies. It established the desire of Serbs, Croats, and Slovenes to live as one nation, with linguistic and religious freedom. The Pact of Corfu, however, left undecided and in conflict whether the nation would be a greater Serbia or a unified Slav state.

October 2, 1917: The British discussed replacing Turkish rule in Palestine with a Jewish national home under British control. British intelligence spurred the discussions with the news that the Germans were negotiating with the Turks for a German-sponsored version of a Jewish homeland.

October 15, 1917: Mata Hari, the Dutch-born exotic dancer, Margerete Gertruida Zelle, 41, was executed in Paris for giving important information to German officers for money.

November 2, 1917: Arthur Balfour, foreign secretary in David Lloyd George's government, issued the so-called Balfour declaration, in which he committed the British government to aid the Jewish people in establishing a homeland in Palestine.

November 7, 1917: Meeting at Rapallo, Italy, representatives of the Allies, including the United States, agreed to establish a Supreme War Council, to be permanently established at Versailles, France. Consisting of political and military representatives from the major powers, the council would attempt to unify the procedures and strategies for pursuing the war; although never fully effective, it was better than the disparate and divisive ways that the Allies had been conducting the war.

November 16, 1917: Georges Clemenceau became prime minister and war minister of France.

BATTLES AND CAMPAIGNS: 1918

WESTERN FRONT

January 1918: Gen. John Pershing resisted pressure from Britain's prime minister to amalgamate U.S. troops into the Allied forces for less than a dire emergency. He did, however, agree to give Gen. Henri Pétain four African-American regiments (led by white officers), one of which was the 369th, the "Harlem Hellfighters." Those troops remained with the French for the duration of World War I.

January 18, 1918: The 1st American Division entered the front line at the Saint Mihiel salient south of Verdun, France; the division was to hold the line, not to take offensive action.

February 13, 1918: U.S. troops took part in a successful artillery barrage that broke the German line and allowed the French infantry to capture 150 German prisoners in Champagne, east of Reims.

February 24, 1918: U.S. soldiers volunteered to join a French raid on German trenches; 25 Germans were taken prisoner. Raiding was a new strategy developed by the French; it was more effective than rows of men launching themselves into a hail of bullets. In a raid, several small groups moved toward the target, one calling attention to itself while the others attacked.

February 26, 1918: The chief of staff of the U.S. 42nd Division (better known as the "Rainbow Division" because it was made up of men from all over the United States), Col. Douglas MacArthur, was the first American awarded the Croix de Guerre; he had joined a French raid and helped capture several German soldiers.

March 7–21, 1918: Gen. Erich Ludendorff, virtually in complete charge of Germany's strategy, decided he must mount a major offensive before U.S. troops got into the war in any numbers. With Russia's withdrawal from World War I, Ludendorff was free from fighting on the eastern front. Preparatory to launching their major spring offensive, the Germans intensified their artillery attacks along the western front. In one post, 19 Americans of the 42nd Division were killed; Alfred Joyce Kilmer, the American poet and a corporal with the 42nd Division, read a poem at the funeral service. (Kilmer was killed on August 2, in the Second Battle of the Marne.) The Germans launched a thousand tons of gas, both mustard and phosgene, between Ypres and Saint Quentin.

March 21–April 5, 1918 (Somme Offensive): The Germans opened their first major offensive on the western front in a year with five hours of shelling from more than 6,000 cannon and 3,000 mortars. The Germans then attacked a poorly prepared British Fifth Army and forced it to retreat. For the first week of the battle, the Germans pushed the British south of the Somme River toward Paris, but by March 28 the Allies were holding their ground, and the Germans were becoming exhausted. When the offensive stopped, the Germans had gained as much as 40 miles, inflicted some 200,000 casualties, taken 70,000 prisoners, and captured 1,100 guns. But the Germans had suffered an equal number of casualties and lacked fresh reserves to match the U.S. reinforcements joining the Allies.

March 23–April 5, 1918: During their Somme Offensive, the Germans shelled Paris from a distance of 74 miles with their Big Bertha cannons (see p. 411), killing 256 Parisians. Eventually, the French were able to knock out the cannons with their artillery.

March 26, 1918: During the Somme Offensive the lack of communication and coordination between the British and French hindered the Allies' efforts. Generals Haig and Pétain were constantly quarreling about their needs and strategies. Gen. Ferdinand Foch was named supreme commander of the Allied forces on the western front; however, Foch had neither the staff nor the authority to coordinate the Allies' effort.

April 2, 1918: President Woodrow Wilson decided to order General Pershing to assign some U.S. units to fight with British and French units and commanders. On receiving word from President Wilson, General Pershing agreed to assign as many Americans as available for the Somme Offensive, but he remained firm in his desire to hold back the bulk of the AEF as a separate army until it was ready.

April 9–29, 1918 (Battle of Lys): General Ludendorff went on the offensive near the Lys River south of Ypres. After a preliminary bombardment, mainly of gas shells, Germans attacked with 14 divisions along a 10-mile front. For the first few days, the Germans enjoyed considerable success in driving the British and Portuguese troops back, and by April 12, the British were desperately calling for reinforcements from the French. General Foch sent some French troops, and by April 29, the Germans were stopped. Once again, the Germans had achieved a tactical victory but at a tremendous cost: 350,000 casualties (to the Allies' 305,000).

April 20, 1918: During the Battle of Lys, two U.S. companies (655 men) assigned to the Allies at Seicheprey along the Saint Mihiel salient were caught in an attack by far superior and more numerous German troops (2,800 men). The Germans killed 81 Americans, wounded 187, and temporarily incapacitated 200 with gas.

May 1–2, 1918: At a meeting of the Supreme War Council of Allied Leaders, French premier Georges Clemenceau, British prime minister David Lloyd George, and General Foch tried to persuade General Pershing to reconsider his position on the assignment of U.S. troops. Pershing resisted all pressure, saying that he would not allow the American Army to be split up into small units and placed under the command of the British and the French. Pershing's only compromise was to allow the 130,000 troops arriving in May and another 150,000 arriving in June to be assigned as large units to the Allied lines. The rest of the troops, 650,000 of whom were in France, would not join the front line until they could do so as an individual army.

May 13, 1918: Pvt. Needham Roberts and Pvt. Henry Johnson held off 24 German soldiers despite serious wounds, and were honored with the Croix de Guerre. They were the first of many African-American soldiers decorated for bravery during World War I.

May 18, 1918: British aircraft bombed Cologne; the Germans retaliated the next night by bombing London. Although the air war was a minor factor in World War I compared to the air war in World War II, it had improved with practice and technology. Bombing raids by the Germans were continued and often effective, although the British and French had antiaircraft defenses.

May 27–June 6, 1918 (Aisne Offensive or Battle of Chemin des Dames): General Ludendorff decided on another major offensive in the Flanders sector but chose first to make a diversionary attack in the area known as Chemin des Dames, north of the road between Reims and Soissons. On May 27, 17 German divisions, backed by 4,600 guns, went on the attack; it was so successful that by May 30, the Germans were back at Chateau-Thierry on the Marne River (where they had been in September 1914). By June 1, the Germans were about 45 miles from Paris.

May 28, 1918: In the first U.S. offensive operation, 4,000 troops of the 28th Regiment, with air cover and preceding artillery support from the French, took Cantigny village, which had been an effective advance observation post for the Germans. Although they suffered more than 1,000 casualties, the Americans held Cantigny through seven counterattacks, thereby gaining the respect of the Germans and the Allies.

June 1–4, 1918: Although General Pershing still insisted that the AEF be maintained as a separate army, he heeded General Pétain's desperate request for reinforcements during the Aisne crisis. Pershing ordered the untried 2nd and 3rd Divisions brought by railway and vehicles to Chateau-Thierry on the Marne River northeast of Paris. For the next three days they resisted German attempts to cross the river. On June 3, at nearby Jaulgonne, the Germans managed to cross the Marne River using telescoping ladders; the U.S. 2nd Division (including a U.S Marine brigade) were brought up, and it attacked the Germans; 100 were taken prisoner and the rest forced to swim or boat back across the river.

June 6–26, 1918 (Belleau Wood): The U.S. Marine brigade assigned to the 2nd Division went on the offensive at Belleau Wood north of Chateau-Thierry and south of Soissons. At the end of the first day, the marines had 1,087 casualties. For the following three weeks, the Americans launched attack after attack; U.S. Army artillery was brought up, as were more marines, then U.S. Army troops. Determined not to let the Americans have a victory, the Germans also brought in reinforcements. Day after day, the Americans faced artillery, machine guns, and gas, as they tried to push the Germans from the forest. Finally, on June 26, the Americans prevailed, but at a price of some 5,200 casualties.

June 9–13, 1918: General Ludendorff decided to attack yet again, extending his salients from the north and northeast even closer to Paris, but the French were warned of a German surprise attack by a radio code breaker. Although the French were able to launch an artillery barrage ten minutes before the German attack, the Germans unleashed 15,000 tons of gas shells, which incapacitated nearly 4,000 French soldiers. The French retaliated by deploying mustard gas in a counterattack. The German infantry advanced about 7 miles through these few days, but they suffered heavy casualties.

July 1, 1918: U.S. troops attacked and took Vaux near Château-Thierry.

July 4, 1918: U.S. troops fought with the Australians at the Somme. For the first time, British airplanes supplied the troops at the front by dropping ammunition by parachute.

July 14–17, 1918 (Second Battle of the Marne): Ludendorff decided on a fifth offensive. The plan was to capture the city of Reims 50 miles west of Paris as a diversion, so that when the French brought their troops to Reims, the Germans could launch an all-out assault on the British in Flanders. The Germans renewed their Marne offensive at Château-Thierry, but again, intelligence allowed the French and Americans to prepare for the attack. More than a thousand Americans were incapacitated by gas from the initial barrage, but dummy trenches established by the French enabled Allied machine gunners to mow down oncoming German soldiers. American troops held their ground, and it was in that battle that the 3rd Division's 38th Infantry Regiment earned its nickname "Rock of the Marne" and the 28th Pennsylvania National Guard Division earned its nickname the "Iron Division." French airplanes and U.S. troops blew up every bridge the Germans built across the Marne. Not only did Ludendorff's plan fail, but from that point on, the Germans would be in retreat.

July 18–August 4, 1918 (Aisne-Marne Of-

fensive in the Second Battle of the Marne): With the failure of the latest German offensive, the French began a counterattack to remove the Germans from the Marne. It began with an artillery barrage and 400 tanks. The Germans were pushed back, an estimated 30,000 were killed, and by nightfall, Paris was again safe. The Allied counteroffensive, including 270,000 U.S. troops, continued pushing the Germans back to the north and east. In retaking the city of Soissons on August 4, the French pushed the Germans back to where they had been in May.

August 8–26, 1918: Gen. Ferdinand Foch launched another joint Allied offensive with the goal of pushing back the German salient that had threatened Amiens. On the first day, the Allies took 19 villages and advanced 9 miles; British tanks, although suffering high casualties, overran the German forces; the Allies seized 16,000 prisoners and 200 guns. General Ludendorff called that day the "black day" in the history of the German army. By August 23, the Allies were advancing along a 30-mile front; on August 26, the Germans began to retreat to the Hindenburg Line, to where they had started in March.

September 12–16, 1918 (Saint-Mihiel Offensive): General Pershing, in command of the independent U.S. Army, had been waiting to direct a U.S. offensive. After conferring with the British and French, he chose to take on the Germans' Saint Mihiel salient south of Verdun, which the Germans had held for four years. On September 12, Americans began their assault on that salient with 200,000 troops, supported by 48,000 French. The Allies opened with 100,000 shells of phosgene gas that incapacitated 9,000 Germans and killed 50. The offensive was supported by 1,483 planes from several Allied countries, including Brazil; Col. William "Billy" Mitchell commanded the air operation. There were also some 260 tanks, commanded by Col. George Patton, Jr. In less than 48 hours, 13,000 Germans were captured. The village of Saint Mihiel was liberated, and the salient collapsed in four days. The AEF had succeeded in its first large-scale independent operation.

September 26–October 31, 1918 (Meuse-Argonne Offensive): General Foch had planned for a general offensive along the entire western front; the collapse of the various salients since July persuaded him to initiate it. The offensive began on September 26, with an attack by U.S.

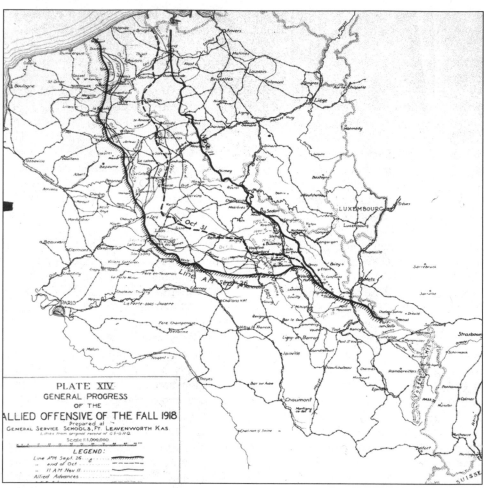

This map shows the situation along the western front before the Allied armies began their final offensive on September 26, 1918. From Verdun in the southern sector to the Belgian coast, the Allies pushed the Germans back 10 to 35 miles by the end of October, then made a final push that ended with the armistice of November 11.

and French forces on the southern sector between Reims and the Meuse River; the U.S. troops were to clear the German forces holding the Argonne Forest east of Verdun. The attack was preceded by mustard gas and phosgene shells; 700 tanks advanced at daylight after an all-night barrage. The Germans were pushed back 3 miles, and 23,000 prisoners were taken during the first few days. By October 1, however, the Germans were putting up some resistance, and what ensued was four weeks of brutal fighting by often disorganized U.S. forces against well-dug-in German troops. Things went so badly that French premier Georges Clemenceau suggested that General Pershing be removed; Foch, however, stuck by Pershing, who was close to

despair when he saw the casualties and disarray among his troops. Slowly but steadily, the Americans pushed the Germans back, until by the end of the month, the Germans were driven out of the Argonne Forest. In five weeks, the Americans had advanced only a little more than 10 miles.

September 27–October 31, 1918: The Allied offensive began along the middle section of the western front, with a massive attack by mostly British and French forces. It was so successful in the first two days that on September 28, General Ludendorff called on Field Marshal von Hindenburg to start armistice talks. By September 29, the British had breached the advanced positions of the Germans' Hindenburg Line, and by October 5, the Germans were pulling back

German prisoners taken by U.S. forces on the first day of the assault on Saint Mihiel in France are being marched to the rear in September 1918.

along the entire front. By the end of October, the entire Hindenburg Line had been breached, and the Germans were clearly nearing the end of any serious resistance.

September 28–October 31, 1918: As part of the general offensive, the British, French, and Belgians in the northern sector went on the attack between Armentières and the coast. In what was the fourth battle of Ypres, the Allies, supported by 500 aircraft, made a rapid advance and captured 4,000 Germans. The Germans simply lacked enough troops to mount a major resistance, but rain and transportation problems delayed the Allies' advance. By the end of October, however, the Germans were in full retreat across Belgium.

October 2–8, 1918 (The "Lost Battalion"): During the attack in the Argonne Forest, 505 men of the U.S. 77th Division under the command of Maj. Charles W. Whittlesey became trapped in a ravine. They held out for a week under often deadly fire from German machine guns, grenades, mortars, and rifles. Desperately short of food, water, and medical supplies, they sent their last carrier pigeon to tell the Allied artillery to cease firing on them. During the night of October 7–8, other U.S. troops finally relieved them, but 111

were dead and 199 wounded. They became known as the "Lost Battalion," even though they were much larger than a battalion and had never been lost.

October 8, 1918 (Meuse-Argonne Offensive): In the Argonne Forest, U.S. corporal Alvin York, stranded when his patrol was outnumbered, single-handedly killed 25 German soldiers and captured 132 others plus 35 machine guns.

November 1–10, 1918 (Final Offensive): The Americans and French launched a new offensive along the Meuse River. With mustard gas, an artillery barrage, and bombers to support the soldiers' advance, more than 1 million men (although by no means all in combat positions) moved forward; it was the largest U.S. military force ever sent into battle. They quickly sent the Germans in retreat; by November 10, the Americans and French had moved up to the Meuse River and taken the valuable rail centers of Sedan and Mézières. But by the time the fighting in that sector stopped, the U.S. counted some 25,000 dead and another 100,000 wounded since September 26.

During that same period, Allied forces to the north also went on the offensive, pushing the Germans out of northern France and out of

Flanders in Belgium. Canadian troops played a prominent role in that offensive, liberating Mons just hours before the armistice.

November 11, 1918: The fighting on the western front formally stopped at 11 A.M. as a result of an armistice signed between Germany and France, which represented the Allies, including the United States (see Negotiations and Peace Treaty, pp. 407-408). Men went on fighting right up to the final minutes, and some even continued for a while afterward because they had not been informed of the armistice.

EASTERN FRONT

February 10–27, 1918: Vladimir Lenin had taken charge of the Russian negotiations with the Germans at Brest-Litovsk. Trying to avoid agreeing to Germany's terms for peace, on February 10 Lenin simply declared that Russia was withdrawing from the war. The Germans were angry and on February 18 launched an offensive. Meeting no resistance from the Russians at first, the Germans continued along a broad front, sweeping into the Ukraine in the south and toward Petrograd in the north. As they approached the town of Narva across the border from Estonia, some 90 miles from Petrograd, a Bolshevik regiment put up some resistance. On February 27, the Germans bombed the Fontana Embankment in Petrograd and entered Mogilev, the former Russian military headquarters.

February 28, 1918: Treaty talks resumed at Brest-Litvosk, since the Germans refused to stop fighting until a treaty had been signed. On March 2, the Germans entered Kiev in the Ukraine.

March 3, 1918: On signing a peace treaty with Germany (see Negotiations and Peace Treaty, p. 406), Russia withdrew from the war.

SOUTHERN FRONT

March 4–9, 1918: In separate events, Austrians bombed four Italian cities, including Venice and Padua; and a German airship bombed the Naples (Italy) naval base and steel plant.

September 15, 1918: In the final offensive on the Salonika front, the Allies advanced on the Bulgarian town of Uskub, where there was an important railway junction. The Bulgarian troops surprised the Germans conducting the defense when they quit fighting and said they were go-

ing home to bring in the harvest.

September 29, 1918: Bulgaria signed an armistice with the Allies and withdrew from World War I.

October 24–November 3, 1918 (Battle of Vittorio Veneto): Ever since the retreat from Caporetto in November 1917, the Italians had been holding a defensive line against the mainly Austrian forces along the Piave River north of Venice and westward across the mountains to Lake Garda. Supported by some British and French troops, the Italians went on the offensive on October 24; by October 30, the Austrians were in retreat, their forces decimated by 50,000 bombs and strafed with machine gun fire by Allied planes. On November 3, the Austrians signed an armistice with the Allies.

NON-EUROPEAN FRONTS

February 21, 1918: Gen. Edmund Allenby's army drove the Turks from Jericho and reached the northern end of the Dead Sea. He was then forced to pause as many of his troops had been reassigned to the western front.

September 19–21, 1918 (Battle of Megiddo): General Allenby's troops routed the Turks out of Megiddo and Nazareth. Two columns of Turks were bombed as they fled; the Turkish army was at the point of disintegration.

September 25, 1918: New Zealand and Australian soldiers crossed the Jordan River and entered Amman.

October 1, 1918: General Allenby's cavalry and the Australian 3rd Light Horse Brigade entered Damascus with little resistance. By October 26, Allenby's troops were at Aleppo, and the Turks had retreated farther north.

October 30, 1918: Turkey signed an armistice with the British and French forces and withdrew from the war.

November 3, 1918: The British forces took Mosul, a major city in northern Mesopotamia. British and Indian troops lost some 19,000 men in combat or to disease in that campaign to keep the Mesopotamian oil fields from falling into German hands.

November 25, 1918: German general Paul von Lettow-Vorbeck surrendered in Abercorn, Northern Rhodesia, after hearing of the armistice in Europe. After four years of guerrilla fighting covering vast areas of East Africa, his losses

A U.S. gun crew is shown firing a 37mm gun during an advance against German entrenched positions in a battle during the autumn of 1918.

were 100 German troops and 3,000 African troops to battle or disease. For the Allies and their African supporters, total casualties were about 12,500, and deaths from disease amounted to an estimated 500,000.

NAVAL THEATER

1918: Since the Battle of Jutland (May 1916), Germany's surface ships had ceased to challenge Britain's navy on the open seas. However, the German fleet continued to guard access to the Baltic Sea (and by cutting off trade to Russia, contributed to its revolution), and German U-boats continued to sink merchant ships. The Allies, meanwhile, had developed the convoy system for holding off the U-boats: large fleets escorted on the perimeters by destroyers and submarine chasers, armed with such new devices as depth charges and contact mines. The convoys and those devices cut down on the U-boats' effectiveness during the last year of World War I. Moreover, between June and October 1918, the United States and Great Britain placed some 70,000 antisubmarine mines across the North Sea between Scotland and Norway, effectively isolating Germany from sea traffic.

November 21, 1918: The first of 183 ships of the German navy—eventually to include 10 battleships, 17 cruisers, 50 destroyers, and 102 submarines—sailed into the British naval base at Scapa Flow in the Orkney Islands north of Scotland. They did so because the armistice signed on November 11 required the Germans to turn their ships over to the Allies. But on June 21, 1919, acting on orders from the commander of the German navy, the captains of all the ships ordered the seacocks to be opened; 179 of the ships sank in Scapa Flow.

HOME FRONT

January 8, 1918: President Woodrow Wilson addressed a joint session of Congress to outline his Fourteen Points for establishing peace in the postwar world. The Fourteen Points were crucial in the shaping of the Treaty of Versailles: (1) open covenants and the abolition of secret treaties; (2) freedom of the seas, except to enforce internationally arrived at covenants; (3) removal of trade barriers and establishment of equality for trading conditions; (4) reduction of national arms to levels consistent with domestic safety; (5) adjustment of colonial claims to observe the principle of self-determination; (6) evacuation of Russian territories with the purpose of allowing self-determination in that country's political outcome; (7–13) points that dealt with specific countries and territories, such as Belgium and Alsace-Lorraine; (14) establishment of a League of Nations.

April 1918: Max Eastman and John Reed were prosecuted under the Espionage Act for their involvement in antiwar editorials published in the *Masses* during 1913–1917. The trial ended in a hung jury, as did a second trial. In St. Louis, the excesses of "100 percent Americanism" were revealed when a crowd of 500 self-styled patriots grabbed German-born Robert Prager, stripped him, bound him in an American flag, and dragged him through the streets before lynching him. At the trial, the defense counsel called it "patriotic murder," and the jury verdict was not guilty. Prager had been turned down by the draft for medical reasons.

March 4, 1918: President Wilson established the War Industries Board, with Bernard Baruch at its head, and gave it great powers to lead the war production effort, which, in effect, gave government increasing power over free enterprise.

May 16, 1918: Congress passed the Sedition Act, which extended the Espionage Act to cover anyone who obstructed the sale of U.S. bonds or uttered "disloyal or abusive language" about the government, the Constitution, the flag, and even military uniforms.

June 5, 1918: A second draft registration was held, with 920,564 responding; 44 percent of U.S. men were either in the Army or alerted for military service. That increased the need for women to move into the workforce, serving in munitions factories, in businesses, and as traffic police. A third draft was planned for September 12 as worried government officials looked ahead to 1919.

July 4, 1918: In addition to the usual parades and festivities of Independence Day, the Shipping Board celebrated by launching 95 ships.

August 1918: Yielding to intense pressure from the British, President Wilson agreed to send 5,000 U.S. troops to Archangel in northwestern Russia and 10,000 to Vladivostok on Russia's Pacific coast. The stated rationale for such a move was that the troops were to guard the supplies that had been sent to Czarist Russia when it was fighting with the Allies; the latter troops were also supposed to help keep the Siberian

railroad open so a group of Czech soldiers fighting their way across Russia could escape. Many of Wilson's supporters from the progressive-internationalist camp felt betrayed because that decision was interpreted as violating his own Fourteen Points.

August 5, 1918: A new shipyard opened in Hog Island, New York, where the workers had their own bank, post office, and weekly newspaper, as well as 50 construction bays instead of the usual 5. Shipbuilding was booming, with 16 yards in coastal cities such as Seattle, San Francisco, Newport News, Newark, and Portland.

September 3-6, 1918: Since March 1918, the Justice Department, aided by police and patriots belonging to the American Protective League, had been conducting "slacker raids": The raiders moved into ball parks, theaters, restaurants, union halls, and other public locales (and occasionally into private residences), where they seized draft-age looking males; if the latter could not produce selective service papers, they were detained at centers until their registration or classification status was established. Most such raids were conducted in large cities, and on these days in September the biggest series took place in New York City. These proved to be the climax of such raids because the war was winding down and protests against "slacker raids" were coming from many Americans who regarded them as violations of civil law. During the seven months of detaining several hundred thousand men, some 40,000 draft evaders were caught; only a few were found guilty of committing a crime, and most were simply drafted.

November 7, 1918: Americans were startled to learn that an armistice had been signed. Church bells rang, newspapers put out extra editions, but the celebration was premature, the result of a mistake by United Press reporter Roy W. Howard.

November 11, 1918: Word of the armistice reached Americans as they began to go about their daily activities and led to an eruption of public celebrations.

December 4, 1918: President Wilson sailed for Europe and the Paris Peace conference, accompanied by a large contingent of historians, political scientists, geographers, and economists.

INTERNATIONAL DEVELOPMENTS

January 1918: Austria and Germany were

disrupted by strikes, as the citizens grew impatient with the leaders who had been conducting World War I.

March 3, 1918: Germany and Russia signed the Treaty of Brest-Litovsk, named after the city in southwestern Belorussia where the delegates had been negotiating since December 1917. The new Bolshevik government under Lenin—under tremendous pressure from counterrevolutionary forces within and from the advancing German army—had little choice but to sign the treaty, under which Russia ceased fighting against the Germans and also recognized the independence of Finland, the Baltic States, the Ukraine, and much of Poland. The treaty freed the German army from fighting Russians, although it instantly set about to take over some of the lands given up by Russia, such as those in the Ukraine.

April 1918: The Congress of Oppressed Nationalities met in Rome, where Czechs, Poles, Yugoslavs, and Romanians denounced the Hapsburg monarchy. In Pittsburgh, Pennsylvania, the Czechoslovakia National Committee, led by Thomas Masaryk, called for the independence of Czechoslovakia from Austria-Hungary. That request was met sympathetically by the Allies, including the United States.

May 1918: The Bolsheviks and their supporters in Russia were besieged from all sides. Germans took over the Ukraine and supported the Finns in making war against the Russians. In Russia itself, various groups rose up against the Reds and launched a civil war that did not end until November 1920. Georgians proclaimed their independence. Czech nationalists saw a chance to gain their independence and began to shift their loyalties; a contingent of Czechs who had been fighting alongside the Russians set off across Russia to make their way eastward to Vladivostok. Meanwhile, the British and French governments opposed the Bolsheviks and soon were sending troops to fight against the Red Guards; by April they had already sent troops to Vladivostok, Russia's port on the Sea of Japan; other units were sent to northwestern Russia (see May 23, 1918, below). The British, French, and U.S. governments argued that they had agreements with the Czarist government about loans, supplies, and post-war territorial assignments.

May 23, 1918: The first 600 British troops landed at Murmansk in northwest Russia (another 500 landed at nearby Archangel in August); the announced goal of the troops was to guard British and other Allied military supplies from falling into the hands of the Germans. Eventually, that so-called North Russia Expeditionary Force was joined by French, U.S., Italian, and Serbian troops, and they began to openly resist the Bolsheviks.

May 26, 1918: The Turks defeated the Armenians in the battle of Karakilise, and 5,000 Armenians escaped through the Caucasus Mountain passes into Georgia, where they declared their independence on May 28. However, Tartars near Tiflis killed hundreds of Armenians, and the invading Turks killed more than 400,000 civilians as the Turks marched to the Caspian Sea.

June 28, 1918: The Czech force, after making its way across Siberia, seizing Russian cities and the Trans-Siberian Railroad, reached and seized control of Vladivostok.

July 16, 1918: Czar Nicholas II, his wife, and their five children were executed by Bolsheviks at Ekaterinaburg in the Ural Mountains. Although for decades there were claims that at least one of the children survived and escaped, those claims have been disproved.

August 14, 1918: At a meeting of the German Crown Council in Spa, Belgium, Gen. Erich Ludendorff and King-Emperor Karl advocated immediate peace negotiations, a condition that was echoed by most of the Central Powers' high command. The Allies, however, convinced they could attain total victory on the battlefield, continued to make plans to continue the war in 1919.

September 11, 1918: In Archangel on Russia's northwest coast, 4,500 U.S. troops landed; others soon landed at the nearby port of Murmansk. The Allied efforts to fight the Bolsheviks were called off in northwest Russia in June 1919 and in Vladivostok in 1920, but not before 174 Americans had been killed as a result of combat in Russia's civil war.

October 12, 1918: Germany and Austria declared their intent to withdraw from all invaded territories as a preliminary to an armistice.

October 14, 1918: President Woodrow Wilson wrote that there would be no negotiations with the kaiser and that all armistice conditions would be arranged through the military commanders in the field.

October 27, 1918: Ludendorff persisted in thinking that German forces along the western front could hold up the Allied advance long enough to win better armistice terms. Most members of the Reichstag, Gen. Paul von Hindenburg, and the kaiser were opposed to Ludendorff's strategy, resulting in his resignation.

October 28–November 13, 1918: Germany and the Austrian-Hungarian Empire were in total disarray. On October 28, Kaiser Wilhelm was stripped of all powers and the Reichstag began to rule Germany. The Czech National Council in Prague declared itself the government of a Czechoslovakia independent of Austria. On October 28, the Serbs reentered Belgrade and declared a Serbian National Council at Sarajevo. In Hungary, soldiers seized the government, and on October 31, Count Michael Karolyi became prime minister and began a series of reforms. On November 3, German sailors at the northern German port of Kiel mutinied and seized the city government; soon uprisings occurred in other German cities, and workers and servicemen began to set up revolutionary councils. On November 12, Emperor Karl I abdicated the throne of Austria and, on November 13, the throne of Hungary.

NEGOTIATIONS AND PEACE TREATY

At various times during World War I, diplomats for the Allies signed secret agreements in an effort to control the disposition of territory and trade routes once the war ended; those had little effect on the war itself, but they did affect the peace negotiations after the war ended. During much of the war, President Woodrow Wilson's government made a determined effort to keep out of the conflict and avoid taking sides, but Germany's submarine attacks made it hard for Wilson to maintain U.S. neutrality. In addition, two international movements developed in the United States: one progressive (liberal reformers and socialists) and one conservative (Republicans and capitalists). Each believed that the United States should be a champion of democracy and world peace.

As in many long wars, various individuals tried throughout much of World War I to bring the warring parties together. President Wilson offered to mediate a peace on several occasions; despite German provocation and intense pressure from the British and French, he insisted that the United States had a calling to "moderate the results of the war by counsel as an outsider."

Nothing came of those various peace efforts until 1918, when one by one different nations began to come to terms with one another.

March 3, 1918: The Bolsheviks signed the treaty of Brest-Litvosk with Germany. The treaty gave up Russian claims to the Baltic provinces, Poland, Belarus, Finland, Bessarabia, the Ukraine, and the Caucasus.

March 5, 1918: Romania signed a peace treaty with Germany.

September 1918: Austria asked the United States, Great Britain, and France for a noncommittal discussion of peace to see if an agreement was possible. The request was turned down by all three countries.

September 29, 1918: Bulgaria signed an armistice with the Allied powers that required immediate demobilization of Bulgarian troops and the return of certain territories occupied since 1916 (see Treaty of Neuilly, p. 408). The armistice also allowed French general Franchet d'Esperey to push his Allied troops through Bulgaria in an attempt to isolate the Turks from their Central Power allies.

Gen. Erich Ludendorff proposed approaching President Wilson to discuss a German armistice. Gen. Paul von Hindenburg agreed and insisted on speed. Meanwhile, the Allies were considering asking Gen. Douglas Haig to pull back and save his troops for 1919.

October 5, 1918: Newly appointed German chancellor Prince Max of Baden wrote President Wilson requesting an armistice based on The Fourteen Points, which Prince Max, in the name of Germany, accepted.

October 8, 1918: President Wilson's reply to Prince Max relayed further questions and a requirement that Germany withdraw from invaded territories as a sign of good faith.

October 10, 1918: When a German U-boat sank a passenger ship in the English Channel, killing hundreds of people, including women and children, President Wilson took a harder line; he told the Germans that they would have to deal with the Allied military leaders to work out terms for an armistice.

October 30, 1918: Turkey signed an armistice that required its armies be demobilized and opened the Dardanelles to Allied ships.

November 4, 1918: The Allies signed an armistice with Austria-Hungary.

November 7, 1918: When Germany began to

slip into a state of chaos, the kaiser appointed a new chancellor, Friedrich Ebert, who immediately appealed to President Wilson for an armistice. When word of that leaked out on November 7, a rumor spread throughout the world that Germany had signed an armistice.

November 9, 1918: In what was in effect a revolution, Germany's Social Democrats declared Germany a republic. German chancellor Friedrich Ebert promised the German Army command that it would retain its power.

Meeting at Gen. Ferdinand Foch's headquarters in the Forest of Compiègne north of Paris, German representatives began negotiating the conditions for a cease-fire. The armistice called for a blockade of Germany by Allied forces to make certain that there would be no return to war until the peace treaty could be signed. The blockade was continued throughout the delays in the peace treaty (and resulted in near famine for the German people).

November 10, 1918: Kaiser Wilhelm II abdicated and left for exile in Holland. The German government accepted armistice terms that required immediate evacuation of Belgium, France, Luxembourg, and Alsace-Lorraine. All citizens of the territories were to be repatriated.

November 11, 1918: The armistice was signed at 5 A.M., but it did not take effect until 11 A.M.— the 11th hour of the 11th day of the 11th month of 1918. The signing took place in a railroad car on a siding at Compiègne. (Adolf Hitler used the same car for France to sign its surrender to Germany on June 22, 1940; see p. 437.)

With the fighting ended, only armistices were in effect; true peace treaties remained to be negotiated and signed, and those took several years. Most Americans know of the Treaty of Versailles, but there were actually five major treaties that concluded World War I. Those treaties (known collectively as the Peace of Paris and named for various areas of the city) came about after separate and unconditional armistices were signed by the conquered to establish a cease-fire. The treaties were not negotiated between Allies and Central Powers as entities; instead, the Allies negotiated terms among themselves and then presented them to the losing nations on a take it or leave it basis. Each victor had an agenda involving territorial acquisition and strategic considerations, and the conflicts between those agendas required significant negotiations. One of

the chief sticking points for the Allies was President Wilson's Fourteen Points, which had been embraced popularly and, by the losers at least, diplomatically. Although lip service was paid to Wilson's ideals by the victors, few of the ideals actually were enforced.

Negotiators established a system of "mandates" for redistributing Germany's colonial holdings and other national interests. Those mandates, which were to be under the authority of the League of Nations to distinguish them from simple colonial imperialism, were the result of President Wilson's insistence on the principles of sovereignty and self-determination.

Of all the treaties, the most difficult to write was the Treaty of Versailles; the Germans initially refused to sign the treaty because of Article 231 (see Treaty of Versailles, p. 408) and did so only on threat of an invasion from the Allies. The Treaty of Sèvres was never implemented because Turkey's Mustafa Kemal fought and defeated the Greeks and forced negotiation of a treaty much more favorable to Turkey: the Treaty of Lausanne.

Delegates from the Allied and associated countries met on January 18, 1919, at the Palace of Versailles outside Paris. That number was winnowed to a Supreme Council of Ten (the heads of government and foreign ministers of Great Britain, France, Japan, Italy, and the United States), and then to four prime negotiators: Prime Minister David Lloyd George of Great Britain, President Georges Clemenceau of France, Premier Vittorio Orlando of Italy, and President Woodrow Wilson of the United States.

Much has been written about the Treaty of Versailles and its effect on the developments in Germany that led to World War II. In the view of many historians, the Allies came to the table with agendas that encompassed much more than establishing peace. Italy had a specific list of spoils; France, with its historically bitter relations with Germany, desired revenge; Great Britain's agenda was initially indistinguishable from that of France's, but Lloyd George had a change of heart when he returned from a retreat and appeared to weigh the consequences of the proposed treaty more heavily. President Wilson's position and his overwhelming international popular support were well established by the time he sat down at the table. After six months of difficult negotiations, a treaty was arrived at.

TREATY OF VERSAILLES

Signed June 28, 1919, between Germany and the Allies:

1. Germany relinquished all territory it had seized in Belgium, Czechoslovakia, Denmark, and France (including Alsace-Lorraine). It gave up all its overseas territories. And it gave up another one-tenth of its prewar territory to the newly independent state of Poland.

2. Germany gave control of the coal fields in the Saar Valley to France for 15 years.

3. Germany effectively eliminated its navy and greatly limited the size of its standing army.

4. Germany was required to give up munitions, livestock, and other goods to Allies and had to pay a reparations bill of $33 billion (about $650 billion in 1990 dollars).

5. Finally, Article 231 of the treaty required Germany to accept the responsibility of itself and of the Central Powers "for causing all the loss and damage [on the Allies] as a consequence of the war imposed upon them by the aggression of Germany and her allies."

TREATY OF ST. GERMAIN

Signed September 10, 1919, between Austria-Hungary and the Allies:

1. The independence of Hungary was recognized.

2. The territory of Austria-Hungary was reduced by more than two-thirds:

   A. Italy received South Tyrol, Istria, part of Dalmatia, and Austria's Adriatic Islands.

   B. Romania received Bukovina.

   C. Yugoslavia, a newly formed country, received Slovenia, Croatia, and much territory from Dalmatia, Bosnia, and Herzegovina.

   D. The independence of Poland was recognized, and Poland was given Western and Eastern Galicia.

   E. The independence of Czechoslovakia was recognized, and Czechoslovakia was given the provinces of Bohemia, Moravia, and the German-populated Sudetenland.

3. A reparations bill was figured for Austria, its army was reduced to no more than 30,000 soldiers, and its air force was eliminated.

TREATY OF NEUILLY

Signed November 27, 1919, between Bulgaria and the Allies:

1. Greece obtained Thrace, Bulgaria's only outlet to the Aegean Sea.

2. Romania received South Dobrudja, land along the Black Sea.

3. Yugoslavia received Strumica and Tsaribod, as well as 50,000 tons of coal a year for five years.

4. Bulgaria was allowed a volunteer army of 20,000 and agreed to greatly reduce all its armaments.

5. Bulgaria agreed to a long-term schedule of payments of reparation to those countries against which it had conducted hostilities.

TREATY OF TRIANON

Signed June 4, 1920, between Hungary and the Allies:

Hungary's treaty process was stalled by the upheaval and terrorism caused by Béla Kun's installation of Communist rule.

1. Czechoslovakia acquired Slovakia and Ruthenia.

2. Romania acquired Transylvania.

3. Yugoslavia acquired the Banat region.

4. Hungary's army was reduced, and Hungary's access to the Adriatic Sea was eliminated.

TREATY OF SEVRES

Signed August 10, 1920, between the Ottoman Empire (Turkey) and the Allies:

1. An independent Armenia was established under the leadership of Boghos Nubar Pasha and under the mandate of the United States. A section of Armenia in Russia was designated to become part of Armenia, with President Woodrow Wilson assigned to arbitrate the exact borders.

2. An independent state was to be established for the Kurds in the mountainous region where Turkey, Iraq, and Iran meet.

3. Syria became a French mandate, and Palestine and Mesopotamia (Iraq) became British mandates. Palestine was divided (as set forth by the Balfour declaration) to include a Jewish national homeland in the western part of Palestine and an exclusively Arab territory (Trans-Jordanian) in the eastern part of Palestine.

Before 1920 ended, Russia and Turkey had divided up Armenia, and the Kurds never did get their homeland.

The Ottoman sultan, who ruled Turkey, was losing his power, and the harsh terms of the Treaty of Sèvres brought about his final collapse. Mustafa Kemal, a revolutionary and a war hero, led the Turkish military in driving the Greeks out of western Turkey and the sultan from power. In

1923, Kemal set up the Republic of Turkey, but even before he did that, he persuaded the Allies to sign a new treaty with Turkey. That was negotiated in Lausanne, Switzerland.

TREATY OF LAUSANNE

Signed July 24, 1924, between Turkey and the Allies:

The Treaty of Lausanne recognized Turkish sovereignty in Anatolia, as well as European Turkey, including Constantinople and the Dardanelles. Mustafa Kemal agreed that the military cemeteries on the Gallipoli Peninsula would remain open in perpetuity for anyone who wanted to visit the soldiers' graves.

RESULTS OF THE WAR (Casualties, Costs, Consequences)

In 1920, the Carnegie Endowment for International Peace estimated that World War I cost the world nearly $338 billion dollars ($337,980,579,560) in direct and indirect costs to all involved; in 1990 dollars, this would be about $6.5 trillion. However, along with traditional costs such as armaments, property damage, and other expenditures, that estimate included a valuation of human lives (an American life was worth $4,720, and a Russian life was worth $2,020). Aside from the fact that that kind of calculation has not been made for other wars, it is rejected by historians on many grounds. Not counting that questionable valuation of human lives, World War I still would have cost some $6 trillion in 1990 dollars. The direct cost to the United States has been estimated at some $48 billion in 1990 dollars.

At least 9 million soldiers died in battle; another 21 million were wounded. Of the many wounded, perhaps as many as 250,000 suffered mental disabilities, primarily shell shock from the never-before-encountered (or imagined) brutality of extended trench warfare (see Military Innovations, Tactics, Equipment p. 412). Disease, particularly influenza, but also typhus, cholera, and malaria, killed millions of soldiers, laborers, and other civilians. In addition to the battle casualties, 62,500 Americans died from the influenza pandemic of 1918 or from other diseases.

Civilian deaths are hard to calculate with accuracy; estimates range from 5 million to 10 million. It is estimated that about 80 percent of the civilian deaths were from disease, starvation, or exposure. In some countries, civilian deaths outnumbered the military's: Serbia had 82,000 civilians killed in the war, while 45,000 soldiers were listed as war dead. The number of German civilians who died as a result of disease and starvation as a consequence of the Allied blockade of Germany has been estimated at more than 750,000. Although not directly attributable to the war, more than 1 million Armenians were massacred by Turkish soldiers between 1914–1918.

The figures in the table below are limited to military personnel killed in action and those who died from wounds received in action.

THE ALLIES	
NATION	ESTIMATED DEAD
Belgium	13,716
British Empire (including colonials)	908,371
France (including colonials)	1,357,800
Greece	5,000
Japan	300
Italy	650,000
Montenegro	3,000
Portugal	7,222
Romania	335,706
Russia	1,700,000
Serbia	45,000
United States	50,500

THE CENTRAL POWERS	
NATION	ESTIMATED DEAD
Austria-Hungary	1,200,000
Bulgaria	87,500
Germany	1,773,700
Ottoman Empire (Turkey)	325,000

The most obvious result of World War I was the breakup of so many of the world's political entities. The Austrian-Hungarian Empire and the Ottoman Empire were broken up into various nation-states. From Austria-Hungary came three new states: Austria, Hungary, and Czechoslovakia. Poland was carved out of the territory that had been taken by Russia, Germany, and Austria-Hungary. Yugoslavia was created out of Serbia, Montenegro, as well as parts of Bulgaria and Hungary. Romania doubled in size by taking land from Austria-Hungary. Greece and Italy also gained some land. Estonia, Latvia, Lithuania, and Finland all declared their independence from Russia in 1917–1918. The Ottoman Empire was splintered, with the heartland remaining as Turkey; Britain took over Mesopotamia (Iraq) and Palestine (Jordan and Israel) as mandates; France took over Syria and Lebanon as mandated territories. Germany lost all of its colonies in Africa and the Pacific; other powers took them over as mandates.

The mandated territories were assigned under the supervision of the League of Nations, another of the major results of World War I. The League of Nations was formed to maintain peace and security in the post-World War I world. The League of Nations which was a result of the Paris Peace conference and President Woodrow Wilson's initiative. However, the United States was never a member of the League of Nations because Congress never approved U.S. membership. The concept of mandated territory as opposed to a colony was that the country assigned to govern the mandated territory agreed to prepare it for self-government. Eventually, that was done, but in some cases, not for another 60 years, by which time several mandated territories had passed under United Nations trusteeship. That was telling, for the fact was that the League of Nations failed in its goals of preventing war. Whether or not U.S. participation would have prevented the league's failure has been extensively debated and can never be conclusively resolved. Already weakened by the withdrawal of Japan and Germany in 1933, the league collapsed following its refusal to take action against Italy in 1935 when it invaded Ethiopia. The league's greatest legacy was as a cautionary tale for the world's powers after World War II.

One of the legacies of World War I was the disarray and disillusionment that fostered the emergence of communism, fascism, and Nazism. In Russia, for example, the disarray caused by lack of leadership and massive destruction provided fertile ground for the revolution led by Vladimir Lenin and for the civil war and triumph of Bolshevism that followed. Benito Mussolini rode the wave of popular disaffection with Italian government and society to establish his Fascist dictatorship. Mutinies, uprisings, and general turmoil in Germany forced the kaiser to flee, but the Weimar Republic that eventually replaced him gave way in just 15 years to the Third Reich

of Adolf Hitler. The course of events in post-World War I Germany is often attributed directly to the terms laid down by the Versailles treaty, and most historians agree that imposing such vindictive terms was a major mistake; the only consolation was that such terms were not repeated at the end of World War II.

Some of the results of World War I came about less from mistakes committed than from decisions not made. Because the United States neither ratified the Treaty of Versailles nor joined the League of Nations, it weakened all the powers' sense of responsibility for enforcing many of the treaty's terms. Thus, although Armenians had been promised their own nation, no one intervened to protect Armenia when the Turks and the Russians reconquered and repatriated the territories. Independent Armenia ceased to exist within a year of its creation.

World War I and its outcome had repercussions far beyond politics. Almost every sphere of human activity was affected. The influenza pandemic that started in September 1918 and raged for several months spread more swiftly and intensely because of the many soldiers and others crowded together at the front lines. Although it probably began in China, the disease was identified as influenza at Fort Riley, Kansas, and given the name Spanish Flu because it came from soldiers on a Spanish freighter. Before the disease subsided, it killed some 20 million men, women, and children in many parts of the world.

Another result of World War I was the famine that devastated several nations, including Belgium and Russia. Civilians in every country had sacrificed considerably so their soldiers would have sufficient rations. Whole economies were reorganized to make the billions of shells, guns, vehicles, and equipment of war. Livestock was killed; crops were not planted; and harvests went uncollected during the war.

In the end, the chain of poor decisions made during and after the war by victors and vanquished alike led to the great economic depression that devastated the world in the early 1930s. The ruinous reparation payments demanded of the Central Powers were only the most tangible contributor to that depression. The world's political leaders and electorates also shared responsibility. While the dictatorships armed themselves and began to take over territory they coveted, the world's democracies did nothing.

MILITARY INNOVATIONS, TACTICS, EQUIPMENT

Most experts agree that the major development in weaponry in World War I was the modern machine gun; it completely changed the balance of power in combat and forced a rethinking of battlefield tactics. (Among other things, it made the horse cavalry obsolete.) Trench warfare led to the development of weapons such as hand grenades and trench mortars. The Germans experimented with flamethrowers, though their efficacy was minimal. Bullet design was changed— the blunt end of the projectile was replaced by a point, making the projectile more stable, accurate, and deadly. New artillery such as the French 75mm proved to be highly effective. Heavier artillery also was developed to fire more shells across farther distances. In particular, the Germans made two long-range guns, each known as Big Bertha (named after the wife of the head of the Knapp firm, which made the guns). The first was used against Liège, Belgium, in 1914; a still larger one was used to fire on Paris from 75 miles away. Antiaircraft artillery also was used for the first time.

World War I was the first war in which motor vehicles of all kinds played a major role—from motorcycles to ambulances. In particular, the tank made its first appearance when in 1916 the British first used their "Big Willie" tank (see September 15, 1916, pp. 386-387). It was the French 15-ton Schneider, however, that became the prototype for further tank development.

The telegraph and the train, technologies that had been around for 75 years, played important roles in World War I. Poison gas also was developed and used during World War I (see Historical Perspectives and Controversies, pp. 415-416).

Britain and Germany enlarged and refined their naval fleets throughout World War I. Technological developments in depth charges, mine-laying, and minesweeping kept pace with the newer naval equipment. But the most important development was submarine warfare: The Germans did not invent the submarine, but they developed the modern submarine and turned it into an instrument of strategic warfare. The typical U-boat was 214 feet long, and could carry 35 men as well as 12 torpedoes. A German U-boat could run underwater for 2° hours. Although the German U-boat fleet fell short of its goal to isolate and starve Britain, it did take a terrific toll on Allied shipping and provided the model that Germany improved upon in World War II.

More than a development, more like a revolution, was air warfare. The airplane itself was barely ten years old when World War I began. At first, the small planes were used only for reconnaissance, and throughout the war, many planes were used for photographing enemy positions, directing artillery, and dropping propaganda leaflets. The early fighter planes had no fixed guns; pilots simply fired their pistols at each other. The Germans were the first to use Dutch engineer Anthony Fokker's machine gun, which was synchronized to the propeller so that the pilot could shoot at the enemy without destroying the propeller or himself. Similar advances were made with bombs; in early bombing runs, the pilot or a passenger had to manually drop the bombs over the side; by 1917, planes could carry up to about 4,000 pounds of bombs and drop them mechanically. By the end of the war, the airplane had developed significantly and became a major factor in warfare.

The Germans also used lighter-than-air craft they called *zeppelins* (after the German who first made them in 1890–1900, Count Ferdinand von Zeppelin) for observation and bombing raids. Kept aloft by helium gas, Zeppelins were slow and not very maneuverable.

The most important strategic lesson learned from World War I was how *not* to conduct a modern war on land. The previous strategy—simply getting the most men into the front lines—proved disastrous in 1914. Behind that strategy lay the notion that the way to defeat the enemy was through one decisive battle. In World War I, that led to trench warfare, and trench warfare proved to be war by attrition. The typical trench was 7 feet deep and 3 feet wide, supported by wooden beams or sandbags. Soldiers shared their quarters with whatever the elements delivered (water, snow, mud, frogs, rats, mice, and other vermin). An attack began with an artillery barrage, sometimes including toxic gas, to "open the line," and the soldiers were commanded to go "over the top": get through their own barbed wire, cross "no-man's-land" (the middle ground that neither side held), get through the breach in the enemy line that hopefully had been made by the initial barrage, and take the opposing army's trench, hill, village, or patch of woods—whatever the order of the day listed as the object of the attack. Unfortunately, the enemy's order of the next day called for reversing that action, and often the reversal succeeded. The result was that hundreds of thousands of men on both sides became bogged down in the trenches on several fronts throughout Europe. Most armies vowed never again to become involved in that kind of futile warfare, which amounted to slaughter.

There were astonishing advances in medicine as a result of the desperate needs presented to doctors and nurses by wounded soldiers. Additionally, the American Red Cross developed an efficient inventory tracking system that used supply tables developed by the U.S. Army War College, in anticipation of America's entrance into the war, to tell what supplies were needed and where they were needed. The advances in all phases of medicine resulted in only 6.1 percent of the wounded dying during the World War I as opposed to the 14 percent mortality rate during America's Civil War (1861–1865) and the Franco-Prussian War (1870–1871).

With a clearer understanding of the body's healing process, doctors learned to treat deep wounds to avoid the kinds of infections that had previously caused death. Those new treatments included using an antiseptic solution called Dakin's compound, more extensive excision of dead or damaged skin (debridement), and delaying closing deep wounds until all signs of infection had been eliminated. World War I was also the first war in which X-rays were used to locate bullets and shrapnel and to determine the extent of internal injuries.

In 1915, U.S. doctors discovered that adding sodium citrate to blood kept it from coagulating. That simple advance helped save thousands of lives by making the transport of blood and use of transfusions much easier and more reliable.

Plastic, or reconstructive, surgery was developed and refined during World War I as a result of the numbers of disfiguring facial injuries doctors had to treat. The steel helmets worn by soldiers protected them from head wounds that might have killed them, but the projectiles were often deflected onto their face, causing terribly disfiguring wounds. Specialists also developed prosthetic devices, not just limbs but also masklike prostheses that used artistic techniques to sculpture missing facial parts, such as eye sockets or noses, which could be attached to eyeglasses.

Due to the pioneering research of British neuropathologist Frederick Walker Mott (1853–1926), the medical establishment came to a new diagnosis of a war injury called shell shock, a state of nervous exhaustion manifested by symptoms as various as tics, spasms, stuttering, catatonia, stupor, loss of muscle control, and other physical manifestations. Some men in previous wars had obviously suffered from shell shock, but it was the extraordinary trauma of extended trench warfare that led to the quantity and severity of cases in World War I.

For the soldiers who were wounded in gas attacks, there was little medicine could do; the extent of injury depended on what kind of gas was used and how long the victim was exposed to it. Thousands of men spent the rest of their (often shortened) lives suffering from the effects of having been gassed.

LEGENDS AND TRIVIA

Before the United States was ready to join in World War I, many individual Americans wanted to aid the Allies. Some, for instance, joined the **Royal Canadian Air Force**—among them, an aspiring young writer, William Faulkner (although the war ended before he could be sent overseas). The most famous of the volunteer military units was the **Lafayette Escadrille**, a privately funded group of U.S. pilots, including James R. Doolittle, who went on to become a famous aviator in World War II. The Lafayette Escadrille was integrated into the French military service in March 1915. It had 199 confirmed kills (according to French rules, which required two independent witnesses). Other Americans, anxious to be of service before the United States joined the war, preferred to volunteer for ambulance units; those volunteer units particularly attracted students and graduates of Ivy League and other prestigious schools as well as people from the world of arts. More than 1,000 college graduates volunteered for ambulance service prior to 1917. In 1914, the Norton-Harjes Ambulance Service was formed by Richard Norton, son of Harvard president Charles E. Norton; known as the **American Ambulance Service**, it counted among its volunteers John Dos Passos and e. e. cummings. Ernest Hemingway drove an ambulance for the American Red Cross.

World War I was also a time when women

began to take up tasks and to enter jobs that had been closed to them. There had long been military nurses, of course, but the **U.S. Army Nurse Corps** grew from 400 nurses prewar to 21,000 nurses by 1918. Those women were graduates of hospital training schools and were between the ages of 21 and 45, unmarried, U.S. citizens, and white. Although a few African-American nurses eventually were admitted in July 1918, none was sent abroad. Some U.S. women were employed in factory work, but not to the extent that British and French women were; hundreds of those women were exposed to terrible working conditions and dangerous chemicals that took a toll on their health and even shortened their lives.

As in all modern wars, **propaganda** was a major concern for governments. Every country had a department or agency whose job was to engage citizens physically, emotionally, and mentally in the war, arousing enthusiasm for their part in their country's heroic efforts and hatred for the enemy. In the United States, unlike in the European countries, the war was far away, so the task of the government was more difficult. The propaganda campaign's first task was to eliminate any question about America's purpose in World War I and who the enemy was. George Creel (1876–1953) headed President Woodrow Wilson's Committee on Public Information (1917–1920). His campaign was spearheaded by 75,000 **Four-Minute Men**, who made brief (thus the *four-minute*) patriotic speeches before the feature in local movie theaters. The campaign also involved posters and movies to stir love for liberty and valor and all that was American. The national propaganda effort extended into the public education system, with programs intended to portray war as a "glamorous adventure filled with deeds of patriotism, heroism, and sacrifice." Other successful efforts that Creel's office helped launch were Liberty Bonds (to help fund the war) and Victory gardens (to save food for soldiers).

France's **Foreign Legion** (*Légion Etrangère*) was founded in 1831 to aid in France's wars outside Europe. Made up of foreign mercenaries (officially, no Frenchmen were allowed to join, although many did under false identities), the legion offered adventure and cachet to men. Since it had been allowed to fight in France during the Franco-Prussian War in 1870, it was called on again in 1914 to fight in France. Based in North Africa at the time, the French Foreign Legion began recruiting new units in August 21, 1914; the response was overwhelming, and before the war ended, some 45,000 legionnaires fought against Germany, including 1,000 Germans and at least 100 Americans. Their units, which, suffered some 32,000 dead, wounded, or missing in action, were among the most decorated French units of World War I.

Among the many slang and novel terms that arose during the war was **ace**, a term used to designate the success of a war pilot, an allusion to the ace in a deck of cards being the highest in its suit. For German pilots, the requirement was downing ten enemy planes; French and American pilots had to down five or more planes to become aces; British pilots did not adopt the ace system (see Civilian and Military Biographies, Eddie Rickenbacker, p. 418, and Manfred von Richthofen, p. 422).

NOTABLE PHRASES

Keep the right wing strong!

Those were said to have been Count Alfred von Schlieffen's dying words in 1913. They referred to his strategy for Germany's quick defeat of France, in which he called for a swift "end run," or flanking movement, across the Netherlands and into France. The strategy was watered down by Field Marshal Helmuth von Moltke.

The lamps are going out all over Europe; we shall not see them lit again in our lifetime.

Sir Edward Grey, Viscount of Fallodon, Britain's foreign secretary during World War I, is said to have uttered those words on August 3, 1914, as he was standing at a window in his office and looking out at a lamplighter turning on the streetlights.

Our daily query is now—"Who has declared war today?"

Hugh Gibson, a U.S. diplomat in Brussels, Belgium, wrote those words in his diary on August 15, 1914, after having read in the newspaper of France's declaration of war against Austria-Hungary and Montenegro's intention of "wiping Austria off the map."

414 FACTS ABOUT THE AMERICAN WARS

The world must be made safe for democracy.

President Woodrow Wilson spoke those words in his speech to Congress on April 2, 1917, in which he asked for a declaration of war against Germany.

President Wilson and his Fourteen Points bore me—even God Almighty has only ten!

Those words are attributed to Georges Clemenceau, the president of France, when he heard of Wilson's Fourteen Point Plan for the postwar world. The words sometimes vary—"Fourteen? The good Lord had only ten." is one version; another is, "God had his ten Commandments. Wilson has his Fourteen Points. We shall see." In fact, no one has ever been able to pin down the exact occasion when Clemenceau said those words.

The war to end all wars.

That slogan, or expression, is often attributed to President Woodrow Wilson. Phrases he did coin—"peace without victory" and "the world must be made safe for democracy"—may seem to echo the sentiment, but, in fact, Wilson is not known to have ever said anything exactly like the above words. The closest anyone came to them was the well-known English novelist H. G. Wells, who, in 1914, published the book *The War That Will End War*. David Lloyd George, the British prime minister, is also said to have observed in a somewhat cynical mood, "this war, like the next war, is a war to end war."

SONGS

By the time of World War I, professional songwriters—based in what was known as Tin Pan Alley in New York City—were churning out an endless stream of music for popular consumption. Inevitably, those pros turned their hand to writing war songs, some of which continued to be sung for decades after many people forgot the origins of the songs. "Pack Up Your Troubles in Your Old Kit Bag and Smile, Smile, Smile" (1915, words by George Asaf and music by Felix Powell) is among those at least older Americans still sing today. Lyricists paid tribute to the efforts of the

Red Cross nurses in "The Rose of No Man's Land" (1918, words by Jack Caddigan and music by Joseph Brennan). Other songs included "I Didn't Raise My Boy to Be a Soldier" (1915, words by Alfred Bryan and music by Al Piantadosi), "How Ya Gonna Keep 'Em Down on the Farm?" and "Hello Central! Give Me No Man's Land" (words by the team of Sam M. Lewis and Joe Young and music by Walter Donaldson and Jean Schwartz, respectively). One of the most popular songs has never been traced to a single lyricist or composer: "You're in the Army Now."

As in all wars, soldiers sang many songs and parodies containing offensive language, but one that was mildly titillating and yet acceptable to a wider public was "Mad'moiselle from Armentières" (also known as "Hinky Dinky, Parley-Voo"):

Mademoiselle from Armenteers,
Hasn't been kissed in forty years,
Hinky dinky, parley-voo.

When the song appeared about 1915, its words were attributed to an Englishman, Edward "Red" Rowley, but the tune and the structure of the lyrics were based on an older British army song composed by Alfred James Walden.

One of the most famous American war songs, "Over There," was written by George M. Cohan on April 7, 1917, immediately after reading in the newspapers that the United States had declared war on Germany and that the Yanks would be going over to France. The song, with its catchy line, "And we won't come back till it's over over there," sold millions in sheet music and recordings (including a recording by the great operatic tenor Enrico Caruso). Cohan gave all his royalties for that song to war charities, and for that and for his other patriotic efforts, Cohan later received a Congressional Medal of Honor, presented by President Franklin D. Roosevelt.

Irving Berlin was already a well-known composer of popular music when he was drafted into the Army in 1918. On June 26, 1918, Berlin was asked to write and produce a show to raise money for a service center on his base. Berlin's show, *Yip! Yip! Yaphank*, opened in New York City on July 26, 1918, and was a rousing hit with such songs as "Oh, How I Hate to Get Up in the Morning!" After its initial success in New York City, the show went on tour to Boston, Philadelphia, and Washington, D.C., and made close to $200,000 for the armed forces.

Of all the regimental bands to entertain the troops, none was as remarkable as the Jim Europe Band of the "Harlem Hellfighters," the all-black 369th Regiment of the 93d Division. Lt. James Reese Europe, an African American who had made a name for himself conducting jazz orchestras in New York City, volunteered for service and put together a regimental band that gave a ragtime, or syncopated, touch to the songs it performed, including marches familiar to the troops. The band went to France in November 1917 and was extremely popular both on and behind the front lines. On February 17, 1919, it became the first African-American band to march in a Fifth Avenue parade, when it was allowed to join in the celebration of the returning U.S. soldiers. (A few months later, Europe was killed by a drummer in the band.)

HISTORICAL PERSPECTIVES AND CONTROVERSIES

Who should be "blamed" for World War I?

The question of blame for a war inevitably starts and ends in controversy. In the aftermath of World War I, locating a guilty party was treated as a necessary step toward attaching responsibility and sending a bill. Although it was not openly stated in the formal treaties, assigning blame had a moral subtext derived from a need to scapegoat in order for many people to resume orderly, righteous lives. So it was that Article 231 of the Treaty of Versailles (see Negotiations and Peace Treaty, November 11, 1918, pp. 407-408) attached blame for the war on Germany.

Germany has always vigorously resisted assuming sole responsibility for World War I. Shortly after the Treaty of Versailles was signed, in an effort to refute the charges of Article 231, the Germans published a voluminous collection of documents from their foreign office covering the period 1871 to 1914. Responding to that challenge, other governments also published documents. The result, according to Dwight E. Lee, has been a bottomless pit in which historians may plumb the origins of World War I.

In his study of World War I, *The Outbreak of the First World War*, Lee has excerpted historians' contributions to the question raised by Article 231. The debate was current in the 1920s; by the mid-1930s, it had receded in importance but was revived again by the events that took place in Germany preceding World War II. One of Lee's points in his introduction is that singling out one country for blame is not particularly relevant or helpful. In fact, the more pressing questions have changed from Who was guilty? to What were the conditions that made war possible? and Why did that war happen at that time when other controversies had been peacefully settled in earlier years?

The other point that becomes clear through the progression of essays on World War I, and that is most often reflected in discussions about the cause of the war today, is that there was enough responsibility/blame for every country that participated to take a portion. For one, even if there were devious warmongers among the Allies, as was suggested of French president Raymond Poincaré and Russian foreign secretary Aleksandr Izvolsky, they, like their counterparts among the Central Powers, had no idea of the cost that would be attached to such an adventure. The wreck of Europe wrought by the war was not within human experience or imagination.

Following World War II, two groups of professors, French and German, met for two sessions in 1951 to eliminate one-sided interpretations of history in an attempt to relieve tensions between the two countries. In "Agreement on the Origins of the First World War" (excerpted by Lee), those historians set aside as false the premise that *any* country in Europe had a premeditated desire for war and declared false the notion that President Poincaré followed a policy that inevitably led to war. The historians methodically enumerated the origins of World War I as coming from distrust among the rulers fatalism about the inevitability of war; unclear communications of diplomatic intent; excessive concerns to preserve the balance of power; and the possible duplicity of several governments, either for the purpose of manipulating their populace or for attaining a desired advantage.

Were the Germans the only ones to use poison gas in World War I?

To this day most U.S. histories of World War I tend to ignore the fact that the Allies, including the United States, used poison gas on the enemy during World War I. Nor did the Germans invent chemical warfare. The idea of using poison gas to overcome an enemy has been traced by military historian Ian Hogg back to the Crimean War, when several British admirals discussed the release of sulphur fumes during the Crimean War to overcome the defenders of Sebastopol; the admirals dismissed the idea as being a dishonorable way to conduct combat. The French, meanwhile, had developed a rifle grenade that carried a small quantity of tear gas, which was actually used in 1912 by French authorities to control a domestic gang.

There is no denying, though, that the Germans were the first to introduce poison gas into modern warfare and that they used it more often than did any other country. They first tried it in October 1914 at Neuve Chapelle, France, when they used some small tear-gas canisters inside shrapnel shells; the gas was not even noticed by the French troops. Then, on January 3–4, 1915, the Germans lobbed shells with xylyl bromide, also a tear gas, to support their assault on Russian forces at Bolimov along the eastern front; that did not have nearly the impact expected (although it killed some 1,100 Russians) because the gas froze in the cold weather instead of evaporating and spreading through the air. The first major and successful use of lethal gas came when the Germans released chlorine against the French at Ypres (see April 22–May 25, 1915, p. 381), and the Germans continued to use it more frequently than did other combatants.

But immediately after experiencing the first poison gas attacks from the Germans, the British and French also began to develop and use poison gases. As the war dragged on, the British and French used poison gases in numerous engagements. The excuse for using poison gas was that it was supposed to reduce the enemy's ability to respond; thus it was said to move the war forward and ultimately save lives. That rationale for chemical warfare has since been rejected by most nations. But in the final two years of World War I, the Germans, British, and French increased their use of poison gas, and had the war not ended when it did, they were all geared up for even heavier usage. Most experts agree, however, that despite its horrible effects, poison gas was not a decisive factor in the outcome of World War I.

What was the role of the U.S. forces? Just about the time the United States formally entered World War I, in April 1917, the United States launched a project to make poison gas; by May, 118 chemists in 127 college and university, industrial, and government laboratories were involved. Various units within the U.S. Army, both in the States and in Europe, soon began to prepare for gas warfare, although much of that preparation involved defensive work, such as procuring and distributing gas masks. Not until May 1918, however, did the U.S. government establish a Chemical Warfare Service to unify all chemical warfare activities. Eventually, the United States produced 5 tons of lachrymators (types of tear gas); 5,500 tons of acute lung irritants (cyanogen bromide as well as others); and 170 tons of vesicants (mustard gas, so named because the burning sensation it causes on contact with the skin is similar to that caused by oil from black mustard seeds), which produced blisters. Only a small amount of those poison gases was ever released, but the fact remains that the United States did use poison gas. Although the U.S. high command was not in favor of gas warfare, by the summer of 1918, the American Expeditionary Force did have a gas unit with 3,400 American soldiers assigned to oversee the firing of poison gas.

As for casualties, the experts agree that it is impossible to come up with absolutely reliable figures because of the diffferent ways in which casualties were recorded. The best estimates are that some 600,000 servicemen on all fronts were casualties of poison gas attacks; of those, some 4.5 percent, or 27,000, died. (Another 4,000 civilians were gassed either at the front or in accidents in factories; about 100 died.) Of the total casualties, some 73,000 were Americans; since they had better medical treatment by 1918, only some 2,000 died. However, any U.S. veterans, like thousands of servicemen throughout the world, suffered for the rest of their lives from the effects of gassing.

Did the United States emerge from World War I with any gains?

Although U.S. industrial power had been recognized by the early 1900s, the United States was regarded as a second-string player on the world stage when World War I began. By the time it ended, President Woodrow Wilson was regarded as practically the world's savior by millions of people who welcomed his progressive internationalism with its principles of self-determination and sovereignty (see Civilian and Military Biographies, pp. 418-419). Although the United States had considerable adjustments to make when the war ended, its stature had risen to that of a major power—principally through the combination of a fresh and invigorating presidential vision and the U.S. ability to muster industrial production and military might.

Meanwhile, within the United States, there were many changes in society that took significant energy from the war. Two of those changes were items carried over from the agenda of the 19th century and resulted in amendments to the Constitution. By exploiting the propaganda that portrayed Germans as bestial and linking that to alcohol consumption, the crusaders of the Women's Temperance Union and others were able to persuade Congress to pass the 18th Amendment that banned the manufacture, sale, importation, and transportation of "intoxicating liquors" in the United States. That was ratified by 36 states by January 16, 1919, and went into effect with the passage of the Volstead Act by Congress in 1920. Prohibition was repealed in 1933. A second outcome of World War I was the 19th Amendment to the Constitution which granted women the right to vote. Suffrage was not supported by President Wilson initially. But in 12 states of the Union, women could vote, and in Wilson's reelection of 1916, the majority of women who voted voted for him. So in 1918, he told the Senate that an amendment ought to be proposed to the states for ratification so all women could vote.

African Americans did not benefit from World War I; if anything, their situation worsened. Young black men were drafted the same as other young men, but that is where the similarities stopped. Eighty percent of black draftees were assigned to units of the Services of Supply (SOS), which built barracks, cleaned the mess, cooked, and otherwise did support work. SOS men also reburied the dead; black SOS units reburied the American dead in the Meuse-Argonne cemetery, the largest of the American cemetaries, containing 14,000 graves. Jim Crow laws went to the front with the American soldiers and were enforced by white American officers. There were no rest areas for African-American soldiers rotating off the front line as there were for white soldiers. African-American soldiers were not allowed to fraternize with French citizens. In spite of all that, some African Americans did see combat, and many were recognized for their bravey under fire.

CIVILIAN AND MILITARY BIOGRAPHIES

AMERICAN

Baruch, Bernard M. (1870–1965)—financier, public servant: Bernard Baruch was a self-made multimillionaire. He befriended U.S. presidents from Woodrow Wilson to Dwight D. Eisenhower and devoted himself to public affairs (and never took a salary). In 1917, Wilson appointed Baruch to head the War Industries Board; Baruch was credited with firing up U.S. industrial capacity to supply U.S. war needs. He also served on the president's war council, and after the war, he advised Wilson at the Versailles peace conference.

Creel, George (1876–1953)—journalist, public official: George Creel was born in Missouri. He became a journalist and magazine writer who openly advocated progressive social policies. Based in New York City in 1912, he helped a progressive Citizens Party defeat the Republicans and Democrats but after a brief term as police commissioner (1933), returned to his magazine writing. He had meanwhile worked for the Democratic National Committee, and his admiring book, *Wilson and the Issues* (1916) gained him Wilson's personal friendship. Right after the U.S. went into the war in April 1917, Wilson appointed Creel chairman of the Committee on Public Information and he proceeded to work zealously both to promote America's image abroad and to boost support for the war effort at home (see Legends and Trivia, p. 413). He was so successful in convincing Americans that the Germans were despicable, according to the noted historian Samuel Eliot Morison, that it backfired and led Americans to reject the idea of a just peace and a League of Nations that would include the Germans; others charge that Creel's zeal in enforcing patriotism led to the anti-Communist crusade after the war. Creel remained a friend of Wilson, and later served under President Roosevelt but in his final years he repudiated the New Deal and became an outspoken foe of communism.

Debs, Eugene V. (1855–1926)—socialist, activist: Eugene Debs started as a railroad fireman. He became the American Socialist Party leader and presidential candidate (1900, 1904, 1908, 1912, 1920). In 1918, he spoke out against the trials being conducted under the 1917 Espionage Act against people who opposed World War I. At his own trial under that act, he electrified the courtroom by saying, "While there is a lower class I am in it, while there is a criminal element I am of it; while there is a soul in prison, I am not free." Sentenced to ten years despite his age and poor health, he ran for president from prison in 1920. His sentence was commuted in 1921 by President Warren G. Harding.

House, Edward Mandell ("Colonel" House) (1858–1938)—presidential adviser: Edward House was a wealthy Texas government official ("Colonel" was an honorific). He worked to get Woodrow Wilson elected and became his closest adviser. House served as Wilson's private ambassador, particularly in trying to end World War I through mediation, then in dealings with the Allies. He helped the president articulate the famous Fourteen Points for Peace. But when House encouraged President Wilson to compromise somewhat on his plan for the League of Nations, Wilson cooled toward him, and House retired from public life.

Mayo, Henry T. (1856–1937)—admiral: Henry T. Mayo gained prominence in 1914 by leading the U.S. Navy in its seizure of Veracruz, Mexico, in retaliation for the arrest of U.S. sailors. He was named commander of the U.S. Atlantic Fleet and from 1916 to 1919 was in charge of the U.S. naval forces in the Atlantic and European waters. He also represented the U.S. Navy at the Allied naval conference in London (1917).

Palmer, (Alexander) Mitchell (1872–1936)—government official: Mitchell Palmer was a lawyer and former representative from Pennsylvania. He served as Alien Property Custodian (1917–1919); in that capacity, he confiscated millions of dollars worth of property from resident noncitizens. As attorney general (1919–1921), he conducted what were called "Palmer raids" to expose and deport aliens and radicals.

Pershing, John J. (1860–1948)—general: John Pershing was a West Point graduate. He served on the frontier and in the Spanish-American War. He gained prominence in leading the expedition in pursuit of Pancho Villa (1916–1917). In May 1917, he was made commander of the American Expeditionary Force. He insisted on making sure his troops were properly trained in France and kept his troops independent despite intense pressure from the British and the French to allow Americans to be integrated into their commands. Although the first Americans fought under the French in October 1917, it was not until September 1918 that Pershing led the AEF in the offensive that led to the collapse of the Germans and the ultimate end of World War I. His memoir, *My Experiences in the World War*, won a Pulitzer Prize in history.

Rickenbacker, Eddie (1890–1973)—ace aviator: Eddie Rickenbacker was a race-car driver from Columbus, Ohio. He served as Gen. John Pershing's chauffeur, then joined the Army's air force. In seven months, he shot down 22 enemy planes (and 4 balloons), earning the Congressional Medal of Honor and the nickname "Ace of Aces."

Schwab, Charles M. (1862–1939)—industrialist, public servant: Charles Schwab was director general of the U.S. Emergency Fleet Corporation and head of Bethlehem Steel. His company was one of several U.S. manufacturers that built ships for the Allies before the United States entered World War I. After April 1917, he led a massive naval build-up that involved establishing 16 shipyards on both coasts to double the U.S. Navy in two years.

Wilson, Woodrow (1856–1924)—president: Woodrow Wilson was born in Staunton, Virginia. In 1890, he joined the faculty of Princeton University, from which he graduated in 1879. He served as president of Princeton from 1902 to 1910 before becoming governor of New Jersey in 1911. A Democrat, he became the 28th U.S. president in 1912 and won reelection in 1916 by pledging to keep the United States out of World War I. Barely five months later, he and the country were drawn into the conflict. Germany asked for a peace based on Wilson's famous Fourteen Points, but at Versailles, Wilson's idealistic goals were diluted by the other powers. His dream of a League of Nations was defeated by Congress, at least in part because of what has been characterized as a "stiff-necked" attitude toward compromise by some and moral high-mindedness by others. Yet, he was a moral hero and a voice for millions of citizens in Europe and the United

States, as evidenced by the extraordinary acclaim and tributes given to him by millions of people when he traveled overseas to represent the United States at Versailles. He was awarded the Nobel Peace Prize in 1920. Illness left him almost incapacitated in his final two years in office.

York, Alvin (1887–1964)—soldier: Alvin York was initially a pacifist on the grounds that the Bible says, "Thou shalt not kill." He eventually made peace with the contradiction between the Bible and the war. That personal conflict resolved, he became a marksman and a hero; he was the greatest American hero of World War I. On October 8, 1918, York killed 17 Germans with 17 rifle shots, and another 8 with his pistol; as a result, 132 Germans surrendered to him. He was awarded a Congressional Medal of Honor for this. After World War I, he was a founder of the American Legion. York was immortalized by Gary Cooper in the 1941 movie *Sergeant York*.

AUSTRALIAN

Fisher, Andrew (1862–1928)—prime minister: Andrew Fisher was a Scottish coal miner who immigrated to Australia. He rose through the union movement to become a politician and finally prime minister (1908–1915). He committed Australia fully to World War I, promising support "to the last man and the last shilling."

AUSTRIAN

Ferdinand, Franz (Francis) (1863–1914)—archduke of Austria-Hungary: Franz Ferdinand was a nephew of Austrian emperor Franz Joseph. He would not have been the heir except that Franz Joseph's only son, Rudolph, killed himself in 1889. After he became heir presumptive, he began to gather around him a group of men who looked forward to re-organizing the Austrian-Hungarian Empire, and he often found himself in conflict with the Emperor. His ideas of reorganization, however, did not include independence for the people of Bosnia and Herzegovina, which had belonged to Austria since 1878; he simply wanted to tighten the central authority of the empire. Appointed inspector general of the empire's armed forces in August 1913, it was in this capacity that he decided to tour Bosnia with his wife in June 1914. He was assassinated by Serbian nationalist Gavrilo Princip on June 28, 1914.

BELGIAN

Albert Leopold I (1875–1934)—king: As leader of the Belgians, he refused the Germans' demand to move their troops through Belgium. He withdrew from Brussels but maintained Belgian resistance around Ypres throughout World War I. He then led Belgian and French forces in the final offensive in Belgium in 1918. At the war's conclusion, he helped his country rebuild and restabilize its industries and economy.

BRITISH

Bayly, Sir Lewis (1857–1938)—admiral: As a British admiral, Sir Lewis Bayly commanded the U.S. warships at the beginning of the United States' entry into World War I. Called "Uncle Lewis" by U.S. officers, he helped warm the relationship between the United States and Great Britain.

Churchill, Winston (1874–1965)—cabinet minister: Winston Churchill was the son of an American mother and an English father of a distinguished titled family. He attended England's officer school, Sandhurst, rather than a university. He saw action in India and the Sudan and achieved a reputation for his books about the campaigns he participated in. Resigning from the army in 1899 to pursue a political career, he entered the House of Commons in 1901 and rose quickly through several government posts. In 1911 he was appointed first lord of the admiralty, the British equivalent of the U.S. secretary of the navy, and was credited with building up the British navy so that it was ready to take on the German navy in World War I. But he also was one of the major promoters of the Gallipoli operation that ended in such disaster (see Non-European Fronts, 1915, p. 383) and was forced to resign from the cabinet in May 1915. He joined the army and served briefly in France, but in July 1917 the new prime minister, David Lloyd George appointed him minister of ammunitions, in which position he played a major role in promoting tank warfare. He spent much of his time between 1919 and 1940 writing books and painting. His new career began in 1940 (see World War II, Civilian and Military Biographies, p. 513)

French, John (1852–1925)—general: Chief of the Imperial General Staff (1911–1914), John French was made commander of the British Expeditionary Force in 1914. He directed operations on the western front until November 1915 and his failure in northeastern France.

Grey, Sir Edward (1862–1933)—foreign secretary: As Britain's foreign secretary (1905–1916) Sir Edward Grey consolidated the Triple Entente and was an important member of the London Peace Conference (1912–1913), at which the Balkan War problems were negotiated. He resigned in 1916 because of ill health and served as a special emissary to the United States to facilitate the peace process in 1919.

Haig, Douglas (1861–1928)—field marshal: Douglas Haig was a Scottish soldier who had served Britain in Egypt, South Africa, and India. He succeeded General John French as commander in chief of the British Expeditionary Force in December 1915. It was his task to preside over the years of attrition along the western front, and he was widely blamed for many of the decisions and actions of those years. By August 1918, however, he led the final offensive that resulted in the Germans' call for an armistice.

Kitchener, Herbert (1850–1916)—general, public official: Herbert Kitchener had a long army career, which culminated in being named Secretary of State for War (1914). Before conscription could be introduced, he formed what became known as "Kitchener's armies" or "Pals' battalions": groups of British volunteers who shared some aspect of their life, such as a Stockbrokers Battalion, the Liverpool Pals, and the Tramways Battalion. He was widely respected by the British people for his strength and stability, although he had come to be seen as ineffective by the British government. He drowned when the HMS *Hampshire*, on a mission to Russia, was torpedoed by a German U-boat in the North Sea.

Lawrence, Thomas Edward ("Lawrence of Arabia") (1888–1935)—scholar, adventurer: T. E. Lawrence was working as an archeologist along the Euphrates River when the war began. He first served with British Intelligence in North Africa (1914–1916) but then transferred to the Middle East to aid the Arabs in their revolt against the Turks (1916–1918). When the war ended, he attended the peace conference at Versailles and worked with the British Colonial Office (1921–1922), but he retired when he felt unable to get for his Arab friends all that he felt they had been promised by the British. He described his experiences during the war in *Seven Pillars of Wis-*

dom (first privately printed in 1922 under the name of T. E. Shaw).

Lloyd George, David (1863–1945)—prime minister: David Lloyd George was a Welshman and a reformist politician. He had been a pacifist until the Germans invaded Belgium. Appointed war secretary in the cabinet of Herbert Asquith, he forced Asquith out and served as prime minister (1916–1922), governing with a commanding style. He initially sided with the French in their punitive approach at Versailles, but after making a religious retreat, he softened his attitude and sought more conciliatory terms.

FRENCH

Clemenceau, Georges (1841–1929)—premier: Georges Clemenceau was a physician (who had lived in the United States from 1865 to 1869). He became a politician and went on to serve as premier of France (1906–1909, 1917–1920), leading France through some of the most difficult months of World War I. His nickname was "the Tiger," an appellation well earned by his hatred of the Germans. He represented the French at the treaty negotiations at Versailles.

Foch, Ferdinand (1851–1929)—general: As commander of a French army corps at the beginning of World War I, Ferdinand Foch cooperated with Gen. Joseph Joffre in the strategy that turned back the Germans at the Battle of the Marne in September 1914. Foch directed the spring and autumn offensives in Artois (1915) and the action at the Somme (1916), and their failure led to his being relieved of command in December 1916. He was given a staff job with the War Ministry, but in April 1918 he took over as supreme commander of all the Allied armies on the western front and led them, first in stopping the Germans, then to the Allies' final victories in November.

Joffre, Joseph Jacques (1852–1931)—general: Joseph Jacques Joffre was chief of staff of the French army when World War I broke out. Joffre planned the operations in the Battle of the Marne that set back the Germans advance in 1914. He became commander in chief of the French armies from 1915 to 1916, but he resigned after the disaster at Verdun in 1916.

Pétain, Henri Philippe (1856–1951)—general: Henri Pétain was born the son of peasants. He attended France's elite military academy, St. Cyr. Yet by the time World War I began, he had achieved no great victories, was only a colonel, and at age 58 was near retirement. As the war proceeded along the western front, he gained a reputation for fighting in a way that did not waste his soldiers' lives; in particular he was regarded as a hero for his defense of Verdun in the winter of 1916. In May 1917 he was made commander in chief of a French army approaching chaos; although he endorsed the execution of 55 army mutineers, he also took steps to improve conditions. When Foch took command of all Allied armies in April 1918, Pétain directed the French army in the offensives that led the Germans to seek an armistice. That November he was named a Marshal of France. During the next 12 years he served France in several military and civilian offices, but it was his conduct in World War II that forever blackened and destroyed his reputation (see World War II, Civilian and Military Biographies, p. 515)

Poincaré, Raymond (1860–1934)—president: Raymond Poincaré was president of France throughout World War I (1913–1920) and emerged with the reputation of a leader of spirit and oratory who fought defeatism in France's most difficult days.

GERMAN

Bethmann-Hollweg, Theobald von (1856–1921)—chancellor: Theobald von Bethmann-Hollweg was a lawyer who served Prussia and the German Empire. He became chancellor in 1909. He is best remembered as being surprised that Britain would go to war with Germany over "that scrap of paper," referring to the treaty establishing Belgian neutrality that had been signed by a host of countries, including Germany, in 1839. He was forced out of office in 1917.

Hindenburg, Paul von (1847–1934)—field marshal: Paul von Hindenburg was born in Posen, Prussia (now Poznan, Poland). He entered the Prussian army at age 11, fought in the Franco-Prussian War (1870–71), and by 1911 had retired from the army. When the Russians invaded East Prussia in August 1914, he was activated and placed in command of the army that faced the Russians. With Erich Ludendorff as his chief of staff, he led the Germans in defeating the Russians all across the eastern front. In August 1916 he was chief of the German supreme command and transferred to direct the German forces

on the western front. From that point on, he and the military commanders effectively made the major decisions for Germany's conduct of the war, including the fateful decision to recommence unrestricted submarine warfare that brought the United States into the war. After the failure of the final German offensives in the west, Hindenburg faded into the background and retired in 1919. In 1925 he was elected president of Germany, and in this position he appointed Adolph Hitler as chancellor in 1933.

Ludendorff, Erich (1865–1937)—general: Erich Ludendorff was born near Posen, Prussia. He entered the Prussian army in 1882 and spent most of his career as a staff officer. In the opening days of the war, he became a hero with the army's quick successes in Belgium, and by August 21, 1914, he was transferred to the eastern front as chief of staff to General Hindenburg. Widely regarded as the "brains" behind Hindenburg, he followed him to the western front in August 16, 1916, with the title of first quartermaster general. He was also responsible for the unrestricted submarine offensive in 1917 that brought the United States into World War I. He negotiated the treaty of Brest-Litovsk with the Russians in March 1918 and then commanded Germany's offensives on the western front that spring and summer. Although he himself recommended negotiating an armistice with the Allies, he later adopted Hitler's claim that the German command had been "stabbed in the back" and participated in the failed Beer Hall *Putsch* in November 1923. He was the Nazi party candidate for president in 1925, but thereafter played little role in Hitler's plans.

Moltke, Count Helmuth von (1848–1916)—general: As chief of staff of the German army, Helmuth von Moltke modified the plan of his predecessor, Alfred von Schlieffen, for a rapid invasion and takeover of France. When the war bogged down after the first six weeks, von Moltke was replaced by Gen. Erich von Falkenhayn (who was replaced in 1916 by the team of Gen. Erich Ludendorff and Gen. Paul von Hindenburg).

Rathenau, Walter (1867–1922)—industrialist, public servant: Walter Rathenau made his fortune in his family's electrical utilities firm. During World War I, he headed the War Raw Materials Department, which gathered the raw materials needed for supplies. He also oversaw development of synthetic methods for manufacturing some of the materials and sponsored the idea of importing thousands of Belgians to work in the war munitions factories. As minister of reconstruction after the war, he was in charge of German reparations; appointed foreign minister in 1922, he was assassinated by nationalists who hated him for being a Jew and for trying to fulfill the Versailles Treaty's obligations.

Richthofen, Baron Manfred von (the "Red Baron") (1892–1918)—ace aviator: A cavalry officer originally, von Richthofen switched to the air force. As commander of a unit known as "Richthofen's Flying Circus," he was credited with downing 80 planes and killing more than 87 men. He had the date and type of each aircraft he shot down engraved on a silver cup. He died when he was shot down in 1918 in the Second Battle of the Somme.

Schlieffen, Count Alfred von (1833–1913)—military strategist: A Prussian officer, von Schlieffen served as chief of general staff (1891–1905). By 1895, he had devised the so-called "swinging door" plan by which the Germans would defeat France by a massive flanking movement of German troops through the Netherlands, thus cutting the French off from the sea.

Tirpitz, Alfred von (1849–1930)—admiral: As state secretary of the Imperial German navy, Alfred von Tirpitz was credited with building it up in the years before World War I. By 1911, he was a grand admiral. Named commander of the German navy in August 1914, he promoted the policies of submarine blockade and unrestricted submarine warfare that helped draw the United States into World War I. He resigned over policy disagreements in March 1916.

Friedrich Wilhelm Viktor Albert, Kaiser Wilhelm II (1859–1941)—emperor: Kaiser Wilhelm II was a grandson of Queen Victoria. As Emperor of Germany and King of Prussia, he worked to industrialize Germany, expand its colonial empire, and build up its navy. During the war, he was little more than a figurehead for the military commanders. By late 1918, with German army and navy units beginning to mutiny and the country on the verge of revolution, he fled to Holland, where he lived out his years.

RUSSIAN

Bloch, Ivan (or Jean de) (1836–1902)—railroad magnate, financier: Ivan Bloch was the au-

thor of a seven-volume work, *The Future of War in its Economic and Political Relations: Is War Now Impossible?* (1899). In the book, he argued that modern war would be too terrible and expensive in its consequences to be engaged in as a means toward a diplomatic solution. Although his work was generally ignored at the time, many of his predictions of the consequences of war have proved accurate.

Izvolsky, Aleksandr Petrovich (or Iswolski) (1856–1919)—diplomat: Aleksandr Izvolsky was a professional diplomat and statesman who served as Russia's ambassador to France from 1910–1917. He conferred with President Raymond Poincaré about an alliance with France that would serve mutual strategic interests against Germany and Austria-Hungary. He resigned after the Russian Revolution and died in Paris.

Lenin, Vladimir (1870–1924)—Communist revolutionary: Vladimir Lenin embraced Marxism in 1889. He was exiled to Siberia in 1895 and spent five years there. He spent many of the years between 1900 and 1917 outside of Russia. In April 1917, after Czar Nicholas II was overthrown, Lenin was in Switzerland; the German government allowed him to pass through Germany in a sealed train, with the expectation that he would work to take Russia out of the war. That October, he led the Bolshevik Communists in their revolution and brought about the Russian withdrawal from the Allied war effort. Lenin became chairman of the Council of People's Commissars in 1917 and was soon dictator. He suffered a stroke in 1922 and a second, more serious stroke in 1923. He died on January 21, 1924.

Nicholas II (1868–1918)—czar: Czar Nicholas II was of the Romanov dynasty. He was the last emperor of Russia. He was open to some reforms but could not keep pace with the thrust of history. During World War I his leadership was characterized by insufficient preparation and lack of decisiveness. He was forced to abdicate in March 1917 and, with his wife and five children, was imprisoned until they were all murdered in July 1918.

Sazonov, Sergei (1861–1927)—foreign minister: Sergei Sazonov was the Russian foreign minister who promoted an alliance with Great Britain and defeated all attempts to have Russia make a separate peace with the Central Powers. At the time of the Bolshevik Revolution, he fled the country.

SERBIAN

Princip, Gavrilo (1895–1918)—revolutionary: Princip was a 19-year-old Serbian nationalist, a member of the terrorist organization, the Black Hand, when he shot Austrian archduke Franz Ferdinand and his wife, Sophia, at Sarajevo. Captured at the crime scene, he was tried and found guilty, but because of his age, he could not be executed under Austrian law. He was imprisoned in Austria, where he died in April 1918. A plaque was placed over footprints in cement marking the spot where Princip stood during the assassination; it read: "Here, in this historic place, Gavrilo Princip was the initiator of liberty…the 28th of June, 1914." The memorial was destroyed by Bosnian Muslims and Croats in the 1992 civil war.

TURKISH

Ataturk, Kemal (Mustafa Kemal) (1881–1938)—soldier, revolutionary, leader of Turkey: As an army officer, Mustafa Kemal commanded the Turkish soldiers at Gallipoli (1915), in the Caucasus (1916–1917), and in Palestine (1918). He organized the Turkish Nationalist Party in 1919 out of his strong opposition to the terms of the peace treaty forced on Turkey. By driving the Greeks out of Asia Minor (1922) and threatening to attack the British at Istanbul, he gained Turkey a more generous treaty than the one offered the Ottoman Empire (see Negotiations and Peace Treaties, Treaty of Lausanne, p. 409). Although dictatorial at times, he turned the Republic of Turkey into a modern, secular nation during his rule (1923–1938).

FURTHER READING

Bosco, Peter. *World War I*. New York: Facts On File, 1991.

Churchill, Allen. *Over Here! An Informal Re-Creation of the Home Front in World War I*. New York: Dodd, Mead & Co., 1968.

Gilbert, Martin. *The First World War: A Complete History*. New York: Henry Holt and Co., 1994.

Haber, Ludwig Fritz. *The Poisonous Cloud: Chemical Warfare in the First World War*. New York:Oxford University Press, 1986.

Henri, Florette. *Bitter Victory: A History of Black Soldiers in World War I*. Garden City, N.Y.: Zenith Books, Doubleday & Co., Inc, 1970.

Hogg, Ian. "Bolimow and the First Gas Attack," *Marshall Cavendish Illustrated Encyclopedia* (1984) pp. 609–611.

Lee, Dwight E., ed. *The Outbreak of the First World War: Who Was Responsible?* Boston: D.C. Heath, 1963.

Kennedy, David M. *Over Here: The First World War and American Society*. New York: Oxford University Press, 1980.

Knock, Thomas J. *To End All Wars: Woodrow Wilson and the Quest for a New World Order*. New York: Oxford University Press, 1992.

Naythons, Matthew, M.D., and Sherwin Nuland, M.D., *The Face of Mercy: A Photographic History of Medicine at War*. New York: Random House, 1993.

Stokesbury, James L. *A Short History of World War I*. New York: William Morrow & Co., Inc., 1981.

WORLD WAR II

DATES OF WAR

September 1, 1939–August 15, 1945

ALTERNATE NAMES

The Second World War. The Great Patriotic War (the Soviet Union's name for the war).

SIGNIFICANCE

Simply stated, the world was never the same after World War II—so widespread, all-encompassing, intense and profound and pervasive was that war. The millions of people who experienced the war at its most immediate, most tangible level found their lives changed forever. Decades after its formal end, many places, peoples, and situations around the world were still responding to forces released by the war. So World War II's primary significance was its sheer impact on human lives and society—quite probably the most devastating, most disruptive event for such a brief period of recorded history.

World War II was the second phase of the historical phenomena that had produced World War I. The armistice and treaties that ended World War I left many problems and quarrels unresolved and exacerbated others. Conflicts over territorial claims, national boundaries, and colonial rivalries were only partially or temporarily resolved by the Treaty of Versailles which ended World War I. Some of those issues—the fate of the feuding nationalists occupying the Austro-Hungarian Empire, the resolution of the border between France and Germany, and the size and very existence of Poland—had been festering for centuries. World War II largely settled those issues.

World War II also marked the beginning of the end of the great empires of Western European nations: those of Britain and France, in particular, but also those of Spain, Portugal, and the Netherlands. Despite some repossession of colonial holdings—the French in Indochina and the Dutch in the East Indies—one by one, the former colonies, inspired by the Allied democra-

cies' fight against the Axis powers, gained their freedom. When World War II ended, the newly founded United Nations had 50 members; when the UN celebrated its 50th anniversary in 1995, it had 185 members. Most of the nations added since 1945 had been colonies when World War II ended, and although long-term historical trends probably would have led many of those nations to gain their freedom, the currents released by the war made it possible for so many to attain independent status within those 50 years.

The Holocaust—the systematic killing of millions of Jews, gypsies, and other selected groups by the Nazis—also had a profound effect on world history. The prime lesson of the Holocaust—the horrifying consequences of state-supported race hatred—has in some respects come to be the prime lesson of World War II.

World War II was also distinguished by its escalation of new, more sophisticated, more powerful weapons of destruction, vehicles, tactics, and strategies. Strafing by the rapid-firing guns on swift fighter planes, ballistic missiles aimed at civilians, saturation bombing or carpet bombing, of cities are but three examples of the many innovations, but undeniably the most portentous were the two atomic bombs dropped on Japan by the United States. Setting aside for the moment the debate over the need and justification for resorting to those bombs (see Historical Perspectives and Controversies, p. 508), their use made such a terrifying impact on the consciousness, if not the conscience, of the world that no atomic bomb has been used in a theater of war since the end of World War II. Indeed, many historians and students of world events are inclined to believe that the example of those two bombs was a major factor in keeping the world from engaging in another major war in the decades that followed.

The use of atomic bombs on the Japanese cities of Hiroshima and Nagasaki also highlights another aspect of World War II: that it was in every sense a truly total war. On one level, that meant that, not only because of aerial bombing but also because of powerful and long-range artillery, civilians often suffered more casualties from weaponry than did military personnel. Beyond that, so completely were the world's economies and societies mobilized that hardly any civilians were allowed to lead normal lives during the war's six years' duration. Shortages of food and raw materials, conscription of vast numbers of people for military or industrial service (never before had women played such a direct and prominent role in the machinery of war), disruptions of movements and contacts, imposition of taxes and economic controls, and various other demands made on people's resources and energies brought the war home by affecting every aspect of society—science and technology, industry, education, entertainment, even psychology—so that total war was a literal description, not a figure of speech.

The concomitant of that total warfare was the insistence that those military and civilian leaders who began and led World War II had to answer for their actions. That resulted in the Nuremberg trials of Germans and the Tokyo trials of Japanese. Similar trials continued off and on, even up to 1997, when former German officers and officials were tried for their war crimes. Although that concept of holding individuals responsible for war crimes has not been easy to enforce, it has been attempted subsequently in several instances, including the Bosnian-Serbian-Croatian hostilities of the 1990s. It remains to be seen if that concept is a lasting and meaningful legacy of World War II and if its significance can be converted into action.

The United States went into World War II as a relatively insular, isolationist nation, one generally convinced that its culture and fortunes could be separated from those of the rest of the world. The United States emerged from the war realizing that it could no longer claim to be moving along its own path of history. Aside from choosing internationalism as a national policy, the United States simply slipped over into that new attitude through the irresistible forces unleashed by the war. Moreover, the United States was not the only country that readjusted its arrangements with the world at large. The irrefutable lesson of World War II was that there was no hiding: In the post-1945 world, all nations (with a few special exceptions) sooner or later accept that their present conditions and future prospects were inextricably linked.

BACKGROUND

The background to World War II is best understood if laid out on three planes. In the farthest distance, the war was rooted in various situations that had been festering throughout the world for centuries—national rivalries, territorial conflicts, social and economic factions, even personal emotional/psychological factors. Thus, beyond and beneath any immediate historical developments were such deep-seated tendencies most easily classed as *-isms*—imperialism, nationalism, militarism, chauvinism, racism, anti-Semitism—that motivated all kinds of dangerous actions. Equally deep-rooted but more specific causes also factored. France and Germany had been fighting over the territory known as Alsace-Lorraine since A.D. 350. In a more immediate time frame, Germany had long been resentful of Britain's and France's worldwide empires, and Japan had come to feel that it was not given the recognition and respect, let alone the reward, due it as a major power.

In the middle distance lay World War I and its aftermath—the Peace of Paris, more commonly known as the Treaty of Versailles (see World War I, Negotiations and Peace Treaty, p. 408). World War I was supposedly fought to resolve many of the issues regarding the assignment of European territories and even some outside Europe. It did break-up certain empires (the Austro-Hungarian, the Ottoman), create a number of new nation-states within Europe and elsewhere (Yugoslavia, Czechoslovakia, Iraq), and reassign a number of colonial possessions (Germany's in Africa and the Pacific). Unfortunately, some of those rearrangements aggravated long-standing grievances and created many artificial boundaries which led to new stresses and strains.

Perhaps most immediately and tangibly, the Treaty of Versailles punished Germany, effectively treating it as solely responsible for World War I; stripping it of land, population, and resources; abolishing its navy and reducing its army; occupying its industrial regions. Above all, the treaty imposed massive reparation payments on Germany, starting with livestock, transport vehicles, coal, and other materials and extending to $33 billion in cash payments. Those terms were greatly resented by the Germans and gave Adolf Hitler a receptive audience. Emerging from World War I as a wounded and decorated veteran, Hitler was quick to take up the notion that Germany had been "stabbed in the back" by its craven politicians. When the Weimar Republic government of Germany in the 1920s proved to be ineffectual, Hitler and his newly formed National Socialist German Workers' Party (Nazis) further exploited German discontent with liberal-democratic government, with the Treaty of Versailles, and with Communism.

Hitler's first attempt at seizing power—the Beer Hall Putsch of 1923—failed, and he was briefly imprisoned, but he turned that failure to his advantage, writing *Mein Kampf*, or "My Struggle." Upon its publication (1925–1927), it was largely ignored by most people, both Germans and foreigners. Yet, it is by any definition a remarkable document. On its pages, a penniless, powerless individual sets forth a plan to dominate the world and eradicate his enemies. It is actually the blueprint Hitler followed so closely that within 16 years he came perilously close to achieving his goal.

The world at large failed to act on the lessons that were supposed to have been learned from World War I. The League of Nations proposed by U.S. president Woodrow Wilson was rejected by the U.S. Senate. Although the league was set up, it was too weak to stand up to any threat. Despite a series of disarmament conferences, conventions, and peace treaties with high-minded resolutions during the 1920s, armed forces were once more being built up. On August 27, 1928, 15 nations (including Germany, Italy, and Japan) signed the Kellogg-Briand Pact, outlawing war as an instrument of public policy. Only four months after the signing, Japan simply occupied much of China's Shantung Province. The Japanese evacuated China, but from that point, disillusionment, distrust, and deception pervaded international relations.

Economically, the world was divided into camps during the 1920s. The United States insisted on payment of war debts from its former allies, and the former allies insisted that Germany pay war reparations. The value of the German currency plummeted, and inflation escalated. Tariffs and quotas smothered international trade. With the crash of the American stock market in 1929, the already shaky international stock, credit, and banking structures began to collapse. Unemployment spread. By 1932, the world was in a deep economic depression, with 30 million unemployed in the industrialized world alone.

Hitler saw that the pervasive personal unhappiness and economic depression in Germany could be exploited, and he made his second bid for power in 1932. In January 1933, he had himself appointed chancellor, and within a few months he began to crack down on opposition parties, trade unions, Communists, Jews—everyone and everything he saw as obstacles to his total dictatorship. In addition, Hitler was not alone in such aspirations. Benito Mussolini had been ruling Italy as a dictator since 1922 and was beginning to flex his military muscles. Joseph Stalin was consolidating his absolute power in the Soviet Union, forcibly collectivizing farms and sending millions to death camps or labor camps. In Japan, high ranking military officers were slowly but inexorably moving to take over the government to advance their ambitions for conquest.

All these actions set the scene for the third and frontmost plane of the background to World War II—a series of actions by some nations using brute force to gain their ends while other nations proved incapable of acting.

September 18, 1931: Using the excuse that the Chinese had set off a bomb on railroad tracks near Mukden, the capital of Manchuria—thus endangering Japanese troops stationed there to guard a Japanese-owned railway—the Japanese army moved quickly to seize the entire province of Manchuria.

June 1934: Mussolini ordered his navy to Albania as a show of force. Soon the Italians controled the Albanian army, were granted the right to colonize parts of Albania, and gained various other privileges.

December 5, 1934: Italian troops clashed with Ethiopian troops on the disputed Ethiopia-Somaliland border. Using that incident as an excuse, Italy invaded Ethiopia on October 2, 1935. By May 9, 1936, Italy had formally annexed Ethiopia, joining it to Eritrea and Italian Somaliland.

March 7, 1936: Hitler ordered German troops to reoccupy the Rhineland, which, according to the treaties signed after World War I, was to have remained demilitarized.

July 17, 1936: The Spanish Civil War began with the proclamation by Spanish army units in Morocco of a revolution against the Leftist Popular Front government in Madrid. The uprising spread the next day to many military units on the Spanish mainland and soon engulfed all of Spain in a bloody civil war. Hitler and Mussolini sent aid and men to support Gen. Francisco Franco and his cause.

November 1, 1936: Mussolini proclaimed that his and Hitler's governments had agreed on a common foreign policy and thus established the Rome-Berlin axis, which suggested that all other nations of Europe revolved around Italy and Germany. That was the origin of the phrase "Axis Powers."

November 24, 1936: Germany and Japan signed the Anti-Comintern Pact, a loose agreement to oppose the Soviet Union and the spread of Communism. Italy signed the pact a year later on November 6, 1937.

The lesson of those actions was clear: Sheer military force could prevail. The League of Nations proved powerless to stop that military force. The world's democracies protested but were unable or unwilling to act, as pacifism continued to exert its appeal after the slaughter of World War I. (On February 12, 1933, England's Oxford Union took its famous vote as to whether young men would be willing "to fight for [their] King and country": They voted no, 275 to 153.) When Emperor Haile Selassie of Ethiopia pleaded before the League of Nations (on July 4, 1936) that it take action to expel the Italians, the league refused and collapsed as a force of peace. Instead of acting together, the countries of the world divided into contesting blocs through interlocking pacts, treaties, and agreements. In the United States, isolationists—both from the Left and the Right—were, if not dominant, at least powerful in Congress and in public discourse.

CAUSES OF THE WAR

The deeper causes of World War II have been set forth in the Background (see pp. 425–427). The more immediate, or proximate, causes came down to the determination of the German and Japanese leadership to resort to force to right what they perceived as wrongs against their nations, specifically by gaining access to raw materials and markets from which they felt they had been unfairly cut off. (Historians generally conceded that Mussolini and the Italians would not have gone much further without the lead of Hitler and the Germans.) In response to the willingness of the Axis powers to use force to back up their demands and fulfill their ambitions, Britain and France adopted a policy of appeasement, designed to placate the militarists by accommodating some of their demands. Conferences were called, concessions were made, pacts were signed, but countries such as Great Britain and France seemed demoralized and irresolute. The series of events or decisions that caused World War II began long before 1939, but the immediate chain of events that made it unavoidable began in early 1937.

January 30, 1937: In a speech before the Reichstag, the German parliament, Hitler disavowed the provision of the Treaty of Versailles that made Germany responsible for World War I—effectively announcing to the world that Germany would no longer adhere to the restrictions of the Treaty of Versailles.

1937: The Japanese intensified the fighting in China, taking Beijing (July 28), Shanghai (November 8), and Nanjing (December 13). By the end of 1938, the Japanese controlled most of eastern China, including all its major ports.

December 12, 1937: The Japanese bombed and sank the U.S. gunboat *Panay* in China's Yangtze River. Japan apologized on December 14, agreed to pay compensation, and promised to avoid such incidents.

March 12–13, 1938: After several years of threats and interference in Austrian affairs, Hitler ordered the German army into Austria. On March 13, Hitler proclaimed Austria a province of the German Reich—thereby completing the *Anschluss*, or "annexation."

July 1938: In an incident barely noticed in the West, Japanese troops in Manchuria provoked a clash with Soviet border forces.

April–September 1938: A crisis developed in Czechoslovakia in which the German-speaking residents of the regions known as the Sudetenland demanded looser ties with the central government and closer ones with Germany. As the months passed, the French and British tried to get the Prague government to compromise, but each time Hitler upped the ante, finally demanding immediate cession of some of those regions to Germany and plebiscites in others. By September 23, Czechoslovakia had called for mobilization, and war seemed imminent, but Mussolini called for a meeting of European powers in Munich, Germany.

September 29, 1938: At the meeting in Munich, Hitler, Mussolini, British prime minister

Neville Chamberlain, and French prime minister Edouard Daladier agreed on the cession of the Sudetenland to Germany, with an international commission to set the boundaries. The agreement was signed on September 30, over the protests of the Czechoslovakians. Chamberlain flew home and announced the conference had guaranteed "peace in our time," but many people soon had their doubts, not only people in Britain but also those in other countries as well.

October 1–10, 1938: After the Germans annexed the Sudetenland, Hungary and Poland also seized parts of Czechoslovakia. By March 1939, Czechoslovakia was totally divided up, most of it taken by Germany. Slovakia became an independent republic but was under German control.

November 3, 1938: Having effectively gained control over much of China, Japan announced the New Order for East Asia, under which Japan would dominate the economies of the area and allow Western nations limited access to trade and resources.

April 7, 1939: Italy effectively conquered Albania. On June 3, Italy installed a Fascist government there.

May 22, 1939: Hitler and Mussolini signed a ten-year political and military alliance—the Pact of Steel, which called for increased technical and military cooperation.

May–August 1939: In another little-noted episode, Soviet and Japanese forces clashed along the border of Manchuria and USSR-controlled Outer Mongolia. By August 31—coincidentally the night that Hitler was preparing to invade Poland—the Soviets had scored a decisive victory, and the Japanese were forced to back down.

July 26, 1939: To express disapproval of Japan's war in China, the United States abrogated its 1911 commercial treaty with Japan. Japan interpreted that as an illegal and biased act.

August 23, 1939: In a sudden and unexpected reversal of their national policies, Germany and the Soviet Union signed the Nonaggression Pact in Moscow. In addition to that public pact, the former archenemies signed a secret agreement to divide between them certain "spheres of influence" in Europe. Each nation took about half of Poland; Germany gained control of Lithuania, and the Soviet Union gained Finland, Estonia, and Latvia. (Later, Germany traded Lithuania to the Soviets for more of Poland.)

August 25, 1939: The Anglo-Poland treaty of mutual assistance was signed, clearly warning Germany and the Soviet Union that Britain would intervene if they moved against Poland. Hitler had planned to attack Poland on August 25 but delayed the invasion when he learned of the treaty and that Mussolini was not prepared to join him in a war.

August 26–30, 1939: A flurry of diplomatic activity in Europe's capitals attempted to forestall hostilities from breaking out over Poland.

August 31, 1939: At noon, Hitler signed the order to attack Poland, and German forces moved to the frontier. At 8 P.M., in carefully staged attacks on a radio station and on a few other minor installations on the German side of the Polish border, German SS men wearing Polish uniforms staged a phony invasion of Germany, leaving behind some dead concentration camp inmates also in Polish uniforms to serve as "evidence of Polish aggression." (The SS, from its German name, *Schutzstaffel* ["protective force"], was Hitler's brutal, private army, headed by Heinrich Himmler. The SS men who conducted the operation were later executed.)

PREPARATIONS FOR WAR

Most of the major participants in World War II began preparing for war for years before the start of the war. After World War I, some of the treaties set limits on the military forces of various countries, and some countries reduced their armed forces in the interest of economy. But the series of disarmament conferences held in the 1920s and 1930s only served to reveal that each nation was basically committed to looking out for its own interests. In November 1921, the major naval powers met in Washington, D.C., to discuss limits on their armed forces, but because the French refused to negotiate on the size of their army, the conference settled for limits on naval forces. The Japanese, forced to limit their naval tonnage to only 60 percent of that of the United States and Britain, left feeling that the Western powers had treated them unfairly. Then in April 1930, the London Naval Treaty set a limit on naval ships, with no new battleship construction allowed before 1937, but that restriction was soon ignored (and various countries found ways to build ships that stayed only technically within the limits). Between February and July 1932, 60 nations met in Geneva, Switzerland, for a disarmament conference. Again, the French became an obstacle, refusing to cut back until a system of international policing was set up. At a follow-up meeting in Geneva that began in February 1933, proposals to limit European armies ran into the Germans' insistence that Hitler's storm troopers should not be included in their quota and that Germany should be allowed to acquire "defensive" weaponry at once. By March 1934, Hitler had assumed dictatorial powers over Germany, and, on October 14, the Germans withdrew from the Geneva disarmament negotiations and announced they would withdraw from the League of Nations on October 23. From that point, the arms race was on; the United States refused to join the race for some years.

April 12, 1934: The U.S. Senate established a committee to investigate the manufacture and sale of munitions during World War I. The hearings went on until 1936 and ended bolstering the isolationist and neutralist elements in the United States, as they had long argued that wars were fought to profit arms manufacturers and traders, or "merchants of death."

December 29, 1934: Japan announced that by December 1936 it would withdraw from all agreements made under the Washington Naval Treaty of 1922 as well as the London Naval Treaty of 1930.

March 16, 1935: Adolf Hitler denounced the terms of the Treaty of Versailles that required German disarmament. He also reinstated conscription of young men and declared that he would enlarge the German army to 36 divisions. His excuse was that other nations had been ignoring agreements to limit armed forces—and in that he was correct.

June 18, 1935: In a surprise move, Hitler signed an agreement with Britain to limit Germany's navy to 35 percent of Britain's tonnage. In return, he gained de facto acceptance of his plan to build up Germany's army—and created dissension between France and Britain. He renounced the agreement in April 1939.

August 31, 1935: President Franklin D. Roosevelt signed the First Neutrality Act. It forbade U.S. entities or individuals to ship arms and munitions to any and all belligerents once a state of war existed.

January 15, 1936: The Second London Naval Conference attempted once again to limit naval forces; Japan withdrew from the talks, soon followed by Italy.

February 29, 1936: The U.S. Congress passed the Second Neutrality Act, extending the first through May 1, 1937, and adding a prohibition barring loans and credits to belligerents.

March 3, 1936: Britain raised its defense budget on the grounds of increasing international tensions.

March 30, 1936: Britain announced plans to build 38 new warships, its largest naval construction project since World War I.

August 7, 1936: The U.S. government proclaimed a policy of nonintervention in the raging Spanish Civil War. Germany, Italy, and the Soviet Union supplied armed forces and weapons to assist the different sides.

October 5, 1937: President Roosevelt, in a speech in Chicago, attacked the isolationists. He proposed that the United States take the lead with peace-loving nations and place war-making nations under quarantine.

January 28, 1938: President Roosevelt called on Congress to increase appropriations for building up the armed forces, especially the U.S. Navy. On May 17, 1938, Congress adopted the Naval Expansion Act, funding a ten-year program to build up a two-ocean navy.

December 1, 1938: Britain instituted a voluntary register for war service. As part of its military rearmament program, it ordered aircraft from the United States.

January 12, 1939: President Roosevelt requested an additional $525 million to upgrade air and naval forces.

April 27, 1939: Britain instituted conscription to add 300,000 men to its armed forces.

July 14, 1939: Roosevelt asked Congress to repeal the arms embargo specifically so that the United States could aid Britain. On July 18, he asked for a similar revision of the Neutrality Act.

August 1939: The major European powers had begun to devote large proportions of their industrial output and economies to military spending. They were stockpiling scarce resources, building up large military forces, and expanding their industrial and other sectors, convinced that war was imminent. Although many nations were on a war footing, the Axis powers were making the most aggressive moves. During August 1939, for instance, Germany sent 14 U-boats to patrol the North Atlantic, and two pocket battleships, the *Graf Spee* and the *Deutschland,* also went out to sea.

August 2, 1939: Upon the urging of fellow scientists (particularly Leo Szilard), Albert Einstein wrote a letter to President Roosevelt to inform him that a powerfully destructive "nuclear chain reaction" in uranium might be harnessed to make "extremely powerful bombs," and that Germany might well try to make such a device. Through a mutual friend of Szilard and Roosevelt's, the letter was hand-carried to the president later in August.

August 16, 1939: Polish intelligence turned over to British and French intelligence services models of the Germans' most advanced code machine, known as Enigma.

August 24, 1939: Britain and Poland signed a treaty of mutual assistance—in essence, a warning to Hitler that Britain would come to Poland's defense if Germany attacked.

January–February 1940: Building on work already done by Polish cryptographers, a joint English-French effort cracked one of the new and more complex German ciphers used in January. In February, a British minesweeper sank a German submarine and then recovered rotors, or cipher keys, used in the Enigma machine for naval communications. In the months ahead, the British and then the Americans were able to read many of the coded messages of the Germans and by the most discreet use of that information—which came to be referred to as Ultra—the Allies gained tremendous advantages in dealing with German actions. The Germans never realized their codes were compromised.

DECLARATIONS OF WAR

Hitler's attack on Poland on September 1, 1939, is usually accepted as the beginning of World War II. Because he ran Germany by decree, Hitler proceeded to attack country after country without any declarations of war, often by surprise, often claiming some excuse. Likewise, Japan, the Soviet Union, and Italy simply proceeded to attack those countries they coveted. As a result, many of the countries attacked by those aggressors never got around to declaring war, as they simply found themselves engaged in war by surprise attacks.

September 3, 1939: Britain declared war on Germany. Australia and New Zealand also de-clared war. By that afternoon, France also declared war on Germany.

September 5, 1939: South Africa declared war on Germany.

September 10, 1939: Canada declared war on Germany.

June 10, 1940: Italy declared war on France and Britain.

December 7, 1941: The Japanese proceeded the same way as Hitler had in Poland; Japan launched a surprise attack on Pearl Harbor, a U.S. naval base on Oahu, Hawaii.

December 8, 1941: The United States and Britain declared war on Japan. Australia, New Zealand, the Netherlands, the Free French (French forces in exile led by Charles de Gaulle), and Yugoslavia soon thereafter declared war on Japan. China declared war on Japan, Germany, and Italy.

December 11, 1941: Germany and Italy declared war on the U.S. The U.S. Congress immediately declared war on Germany and Italy.

The many other dates of formal declarations of war are listed under Combatants below.

COMBATANTS

The Allies: The Allies and the dates on which they entered World War II are listed below. In general, those countries that entered after 1942 did not play an active role—several, in fact, joined in only when they saw which side was winning. On the other hand, some countries—China and Ethiopia, for example—that did not enter officially until the dates given below were actually among the earliest victims of Axis aggression.

Argentina: March 27, 1945
Australia: September 3, 1939
Belgium: May 10, 1940
Bolivia: April 7, 1943
Brazil: August 22, 1942
Canada: September 10, 1939
Chile: April 11, 1945
China: December 8, 1941
Colombia: November 26, 1943
Costa Rica: December 8, 1941
Cuba: December 9, 1941
Czechoslovakia: December 16, 1941
Dominican Republic: December 8, 1941
Ecuador: February 2, 1945

Egypt: February 24, 1945
El Salvador: December 8, 1941
Ethiopia: December 14, 1942
France: September 3, 1939
Great Britain: September 3, 1939
Greece: October 28, 1940
Guatemala: December 9, 1941
Haiti: December 8, 1941
Honduras: December 8, 1941
India: September 3, 1939
Iran: August 25, 1941
Iraq: January 17, 1943
Lebanon: February 27, 1945
Liberia: January 27, 1944
Luxembourg: May 10, 1940
Mexico: May 22, 1942
Mongolian People's Republic: August 9, 1945
Netherlands: May 10, 1940
New Zealand: September 3, 1939
Nicaragua: December 11, 1941
Norway: April 9, 1940
Panama: December 7, 1941
Paraguay: February 7, 1945
Peru: February 12, 1945
Poland: September 1, 1939
Soviet Union: June 22, 1941
San Marino: September 21, 1944
Saudi Arabia: March 1, 1945
South Africa: September 6, 1939
Syria: June 8, 1941
Turkey: February 23, 1945
United States: December 8, 1941
Uruguay: February 15, 1945
Venezuela: February 15, 1945
Yugoslavia: April 6, 1941

The main combatants among the Allies were clearly Great Britain and the Commonwealth nations, the Soviet Union, China, and the United States. Members of the British Commonwealth that contributed greatly in terms of manpower and materiel were Australia, Canada, India, South Africa, and New Zealand. The main combatants not only sent large armed forces into battle but also provided support of all kinds for the forces and operations of other countries: An example of the latter was the many British and American airdrops of materiel (food items, munitions, radio devices, etc.) and secret agents to support partisan and resistance groups in Axis-occupied countries.

The French played a somewhat ambiguous role during World War II. By surrendering early to the Germans, the French leaders saved their county from destruction but left about half of France under direct German occupation and the other half under the Vichy government (although that part also was seized by the Germans in 1942). Thousands of French fled France—mostly for North Africa or Britain—and many joined the Free French movement under Gen. Charles de Gaulle, who had his headquarters in London, and formed a small but important military force.

Similar to the Free French force were certain other Allied military units comprising men who fled their occupied homelands to join national units established and armed by the Allies. Those units, such as those of the Poles and the Greeks, were under the national authority of governments in exile. The Polish army in exile formed the fourth largest military force among the Allies. It included not only refugees from Hitler's Europe but also Poles who had immigrated to other lands, as well as many thousands freed from Soviet Union prison camps, where they had been held after Stalin invaded Poland in 1939. Thousands of Norwegians, Czechs, Belgians—even some anti-Nazi Germans—also fled their countries and joined Allied military units. There were also numerous guerrilla, partisan, maquis, underground, and resistance groups in countries occupied by the Germans and Italians. Among those were the many Jews who managed to escape from the "roundups" by the occupying authorities and their collaborators. These groups fought in the underground and played an invaluable role, not just because of the losses they inflicted on the Axis in terms of casualties and materiel, but also because they diverted and tied down Axis resources far out of proportion to their own numbers. But they suffered disproportionate casualties. Relatively small bands of guerrilla fighters in places like the Greek island of Crete or in Yugoslavia forced the Germans and Italians to station sizable occupation armies in those lands. However, some of those partisan groups ended up feuding, even fighting among themselves. For example, in Yugoslavia and in Greece, one partisan army was composed of Communists, or Leftists, and another was made up of Centrists, or Rightists (in some cases monarchists, and even quasi Fascists). Those rival armies then competed for support from the Allies and on some occasions even fought against one another.

The most extreme example of that was in China, where, almost simultaneous with the Japanese invasion in 1931, the Chinese Communists under Mao Tse-tung launched a civil war against the Nationalists led by Chiang Kai-shek. Not until 1937 did the two warring factions agree to focus on a joint war against the Japanese. From about 1938 on, the Chinese military units were totally dependent on supplies brought in from the Soviet Union and from Burma. The Chinese Communists and Nationalists competed for that aid and retained a somewhat wary stance against each other throughout the war against Japan. In October 1945, they returned to their postponed civil war.

The Axis: The Axis powers and the dates they formally entered the war were:

Albania: June 15, 1940
Bulgaria: March 1, 1941
Finland: June 25, 1941
Germany: September 1, 1939
Hungary: April 10, 1941
Italy: June 11, 1940
Japan: December 7, 1941
Romania: November 23, 1940
Thailand: January 25, 1942

The main Axis combatants were Germany, Japan, and Italy. Several of the countries listed above—Albania, Bulgaria, and Thailand, for example—joined the Axis only because Italy, Germany, or Japan had imposed puppet governments on them. (The Allies did the same thing in Iraq and Iran, where the Allies were determined not to let the Axis have access to their rich oil supplies.) Bulgaria and Romania switched sides in late 1944, when they felt free to defy the Germans. Finland was not so much pro-Axis as anti-Soviet Union. Croatia split from Yugoslavia and had a pro-German puppet government. In virtually all the German-occupied countries, nationals formed special units that fought alongside the Germans. Many of those individuals were motivated by their hatred of Communists and/or Jews. (The Germans were even able to enlist a small number of British prisoners of war to fight against the Communists.) Thus, many Ukrainians and Cossacks from the USSR fought on behalf of the Germans, as did thousands of Dutch. The dreaded *Waffen SS*, in fact, ended up with a high percentage of non-Germans in its ranks. One of the least known such groups was the so-called Indian National Army, formed by an Indian Nationalist leader, Subhas Chandra Bose, who enlisted Indians, Malays, Burmese, and other Asians from Japanese prison camps and formed an army that eventually numbered some 40,000. Bose persuaded them to fight for the Japanese by appealing to their dislike of the British and other Western imperial powers.

Although Austria is not listed as an Axis power because it had technically been annexed to Germany in 1938, it certainly supported the Axis cause with many troops. Indeed, Austria supplied the Axis with its leader—Adolf Hitler.

Neutrals: Many countries—such as Morocco, Algiers, Tunisia, and Libya—that were colonies of either Allied or Axis powers were drawn into the war even though they never made formal declarations of war. Moroccan troops, for example, fought bravely alongside the French, and many Africans from British colonies fought and died in combat in Europe. A number of European countries—Sweden, Switzerland, Spain, Portugal, Ireland—remained explicitly neutral. Sweden allowed Jews and others to escape through its territory but continued to trade with Nazi Germany. Formally neutral, Switzerland played a crucial role as a refuge for many fleeing from Germany and Italy and as the headquarters of the International Red Cross; the Spanish dictator, Francisco Franco, kept his country formally neutral but sent "volunteers" to fight alongside the Germans on the eastern front. The Republic of Ireland, still nursing an animosity against its former British masters, chose to remain outside the war, although thousands of Irish volunteered to fight alongside the British. Not until the 1990s was it revealed that Swiss banks had been holding large sums of money deposited by European Jews and never returned to their heirs.

Comparative Military Strength: During the 1930s, the Axis powers ignored the various disarmament treaties and agreements and proceeded to build up their armed forces. Perhaps just as important as the numbers of personnel in the military was the fact that the industrial sectors of the Axis powers were already organized around military needs. The Axis powers also developed more advanced weaponry such as the Germans' magnetic mines and torpedoes, which took a heavy toll in the early months of the war. By September 1939, Germany had 106 divisions ready for combat, with the latest tanks, many vehicles, and powerful artillery. Germany also had some 4,000 military airplanes, and although its total naval tonnage was only about 20 percent that of the Allies, Germany had a large, well-trained submarine fleet (containing at least 235 submarines, or U-boats, by 1943). Although Italy's armed forces did not perform impressively during the war, Japan built a well-disciplined though poorly supplied military machine. During the six years of the war, the Axis mobilized some 30,000,000 people in their armed forces.

At the outset of World War II (September 1939), the Allied military forces were not as large, as well-trained, or as well-equipped as those of the chief Axis powers. Nor were their industrial plants yet organized for war production. The Allies did have about the same number of military aircraft as the Germans had (3,700), and their combined navies were larger than those of the Axis powers, but the Allies had to be prepared to fight across all the world's seas. During the first months of the war, Britain lacked sufficient anti-aircraft guns and aircraft to protect itself from a major air attack. But the Allies had far greater reserves of people to call on; during the war, they mobilized an estimated 62,000,000 in their armed forces. The Allies' industrial sectors also far outstripped those of the Axis in the production of materiel.

GEOGRAPHIC AND STRATEGIC CONSIDERATIONS

World War II was truly a world war, the first fought in so many places—on or near six of the seven continents if naval battles are included. Therefore, the geography of the entire Earth was a factor in the war. Relatively few countries did not participate in the hostilities in some way, and even so-called neutrals were indirectly drawn into the war. Eventually, too, the war was fought in every possible environment, including vast plains, domesticated farmlands, great cities, tiny villages, oceans and seas, deserts, mountains, islands, Alaska, parts of Africa, remote Manchuria, Pacific atolls, and the Middle East.

The sheer distances involved affected the conduct of the war, especially in the Pacific. To the extent that Japan was operating out of its home base, the United States and Britain were at a disadvantage because they had to move their forces and supplies many thousands of miles, even allowing that they used Australia, New Zealand, and India as bases. Because the Allies' war in Europe became heavily dependent on materiel supplied by the United States, the Allies faced tremendous logistical challenges, such as moving massive amounts of personnel and equipment across the submarine-infested oceans.

Because of the geographic spread and diversity, climate and weather played a major role in World War II. (For one thing, the war was fought from the depths of the seas to the stratosphere.) Special uniforms, gear, fuels, and other supplies were designed and issued for the winter cold or summer heat. (Supplies did not always arrive in time, as the German army in the Soviet Union and American soldiers in the Battle of the Bulge discovered (see December 16, 1944–January 27, 1945, p. 470). Campaigns literally bogged down in mud, major operations were postponed because of fog or rain, and individual soldiers suffered greatly from extreme conditions. All kinds of exotic diseases, infections, and other ailments—malaria being the most pervasive—had to be dealt with as a result of those diverse environments.

To a large extent, World War II was fought for control of natural resources and won by competing logistical and industrial capacities. The war required so many natural resources—petroleum, metals, minerals of all kinds, rubber—that maintaining access to those essentials played a major role. Petroleum supplies, in particular, were a crucial factor at the beginning of the war and in its conduct. The Germans began the war by seizing the most important oil field in Europe—the Ploesti fields in Romania. Germany's chances of winning the war collapsed when it lost access to those oil fields and the oil fields in Hungary. Japan undertook its war in part to ensure itself of supplies of oil from the East Indies. Many countries made synthetic substitutes for such essentials as rubber and oil.

Initially, the aggressors gained an advantage in control over natural resources by quickly seizing what they could. Germany moved so decisively in its *Blitzkrieg* (lightning warfare) that, by November 1942, it controlled one of the largest empires in history. Japan soon dominated much of Asia. Italy to a lesser extent dominated part of the Mediterranean and North Africa. The natural resources the Axis powers obtained in those occupied territories enabled them for a time at least to challenge the Allies.

But as World War II dragged on, the Axis powers found themselves short not only of petroleum but also of important minerals, food, and other essential resources. Under the circumstances, the Germans and Japanese were able to produce surprisingly substantial resources until the final phase of the war. After the war, it was shown that despite the incredibly heavy Allied bombings, German factories had kept producing supplies until the very end.

Although the Allies constantly disagreed over certain substrategies—such as whether to invade North Africa or when to invade France— they did agree on the overall strategy, namely, to defeat Germany first and then go after Japan. On the other hand, the Axis never had a truly unified overarching strategy. Hitler wanted to occupy most of Continental Europe and at least intimidate Britain into becoming a neutral; he also wanted to control enough territory in the Middle East to ensure oil supplies. Mussolini had few illusions about dominating the world but simply wanted some land around the Mediterranean. Japan wanted to dominate Asia and the Western Pacific but had no intention of invading North America. For the first three years of World War II, the Axis seemed to be succeeding. But in the end, slowly and inexorably, the Allies gained the upper hand over Germany and Japan, as the Axis' initial strategic advantages evaporated.

Hitler made the greatest strategic blunder of World War II when, in June 1941, he suddenly turned against the Soviet Union and invaded it, stretching German human and physical resources to fight a two-front war. In a fundamental sense, the invasion of the Soviet Union was the inevitable outcome of Hitler's personal grand strategy. From the outset of his public career, he had made it clear that he was determined to rid the world of Communisim. Hitler's decision to invade the Soviet Union was opposed by many in his military, but his blind faith in his own military "genius" and contempt in the judgment of military professionals exasperated his generals to literally the last days of the Third Reich. Hitler's subsequent demand that the German army stay in place in the Soviet Union and confront the Soviets through the dead of winter planted the seeds of his defeat.

Likewise, the Japanese decision to attack Pearl Harbor and bring the United States into World War II sealed their fate as well as Germany's. Hitler is reported to have greeted the news with great satisfaction, but his judgment on such fundamental geopolitical questions was driven more by emotion than by rational calculation. Whether through hubris or plain miscalculation, taking on the Soviet Union and the United States —potentially the two strongest world powers—proved to be Hitler's and Japanese premier Hideki Tojo's downfall.

BATTLES AND CAMPAIGNS: 1939

In the opening months of World War II, military activity was limited to the European theater and the naval theater.

EUROPEAN THEATER

September 1, 1939: At 4:45 A.M., 53 German army divisions invaded Poland without declaring war. Although they said it was in retaliation for supposed Polish attacks on German installations the previous night (see p. 428), the Germans had long been preparing for the invasion under the code name *Fall Weiss* ("Plan White"). As many of the German units were armored and mobilized, they moved quickly against the smaller, poorly equipped, and less prepared Polish forces. The Germans also had great superiority in the air. The German navy moved against Polish ships and bases but several Polish ships managed to escape. By the end of the day, it was clear the Poles were going to be overwhelmed.

September 4, 1939: The Polish army was in retreat at almost every point. Britain's Royal Air Force began its first raids but confined them to German warships. Chamberlain later claimed in Parliament that the British could not bomb German industry because it was private property.

September 10, 1939: The first major units of the British Expeditionary Force landed in France. Before the month was over, some 160,000 British troops were sent to France.

September 16, 1939: German troops had surrounded Warsaw, and the Polish forces along the entire front retreated.

September 17, 1939: Soviet forces invaded Poland from the east and met little resistance as the Poles were heavily engaged with the Germans to the west.

September 27, 1939: After two days of heavy bombardment, Warsaw surrendered.

October 3, 1939: The last major resistance by the Polish military collapsed. Polish casualties were heavy, and the Germans lost 10,000 dead and 30,000 wounded. Many thousands of Poles escaped to the West, where eventually some 100,000 fought alongside the Allies.

October 9, 1939: Hitler issued a directive to his military forces that they should be prepared to invade Holland and Belgium as part of his plan to drive the British and French back. Some German commanders considered that decision foolish, but they proceeded to work on *Fall Gelb* ("Plan Yellow"), the plan for the operation.

November 30, 1939: After weeks of futile negotiations, the Russo-Finnish War began with the Soviets' invasion of Finland and the bombing of Helsinki. Although the Soviet forces were larger and better equipped, they were ineffective against the stubborn and resourceful Finnish defense of their homeland.

NAVAL THEATER

September 3–4, 1939: A German U-boat torpedoed and sank the British liner *Athenia* off the coast of Ireland—112 lost their lives, including 28 Americans. The Germans claimed they thought the *Athenia* was a warship and temporarily imposed strict controls over U-boats. Still, the Germans sank 41 Allied ships during September. On September 4, Secretary of State Cordell Hull announced that Americans' travel to Europe would be limited to "imperative necessity."

December 13–17, 1939: A British naval squadron in the River Plate between Argentina and Uruguay drew the German battleship *Graf Spee* into combat. In a two-hour battle, three British ships were damaged, but so was the *Graf Spee*. The German commander Hans Langsdorf brought his ship into the harbor of Montevideo, Uruguay, and for several days, the British deceived him into believing that a large British fleet had him trapped. He removed his crew and prisoners, then scuttled the ship outside the port as thousands watched. Shamed by his defeat, Langsdorf committed suicide on December 20.

HOME FRONT

September 8, 1939: President Roosevelt pro-

claimed a limited national emergency, which gave him the power to act quickly, without awaiting congressional approval on many issues of national security.

October 2, 1939: Secretary of State Cordell Hull stated that the United States did not accept the partition of Poland by Germany and the Soviet Union and would recognize the Polish government in exile.

October 21, 1939: Acting on the advice of Albert Einstein and other scientists, President Roosevelt called the first meeting of the Advisory Committee on Uranium to explore the possibility of an atomic weapon.

November 4, 1939: The U.S. Congress passed a modification of the Neutrality Acts, effectively repealing the embargo on arms by allowing any country at war to buy arms from private U.S. manufacturers so long as they paid cash and transported them on non-American ships. In effect, because of the British blockade of Germany, that really meant supplying the British and French with arms.

INTERNATIONAL DEVELOPMENTS

September 1, 1939: Britain and France demanded that Germany withdraw from Poland.

September 2, 1939: The British and French presented an ultimatum to the Germans to withdraw from Poland by September 3. Mussolini declared that Italy would remain neutral and called for a peace conference.

September 3, 1939: When the British ultimatum expired, Prime Minister Neville Chamberlain declared war on Germany at 11:15 A.M. Australia and New Zealand immediately followed suit. France declared war on Germany at 5 P.M.

September 5, 1939: The United States proclaimed its neutrality in the war.

September 10, 1939: Canada declared war on Germany.

September 28, 1939: The German-Soviet Boundary and Friendship Treaty was signed, effectively dividing Poland and the Baltic States between the two powers. The Soviet Union gained the larger share of Poland's land, but Germany gained more of the population and industrial centers. Hitler agreed to the division only to appease the Soviet Union while he turned against Western Europe.

October 1939: The Soviet Union continued

to force the Baltic States (Estonia, Latvia, and Lithuania) and Finland to concede various rights and even territories to the Soviet Union. Only the Finns were able to mobilize for resistance against the Soviets.

October 2, 1939: The Inter-American Conference, meeting in Panama City, issued the Declaration of Panama, which closed off zones in the seas of the Western Hemisphere to all belligerents' naval activities. All the countries at war ignored the declaration.

October 6, 1939: Hitler gave a speech in which he claimed he wanted only peace with England and France, and that Germany's actions were solely aimed at correcting the unjust terms of the Versailles Treaty. He called Winston Churchill and his supporters warmongers and called for a European conference to settle differences. Prime Ministers Chamberlain and Daladier rejected Hitler's peace attempt, or feeler, within a week. In truth, Hitler already was planning to attack France and England.

December 9–14, 1939: The League of Nations considered Finland's request of December 2 to intervene in the Soviet invasion and agreed to do so. When the Soviets refused to accept that, they were expelled from the league on December 14.

December 28, 1939: The British began meat rationing. During the next few months virtually every consumer item in Britain was rationed.

BATTLES AND CAMPAIGNS: 1940

Areas of activity in the first full year of World War II were European theater, Mediterranean/ African theater, Asian theater, and naval theater.

EUROPEAN THEATER

January 16, 1940: Hitler postponed the German attack in the west for several reasons: His military commanders generally resisted such an action; the weather was poor, and two German officers carrying plans for the attack were captured by the Belgians.

January 29, 1940: The Soviets began diplomatic exchanges with Finland via Sweden signaling a willingness to negotiate an end to hostilities with the Finnish government. But during the following five weeks, the Soviets made advances against the Finns to harden Soviet terms.

March 11–13, 1940: The Finns acceded to most of the Soviet conditions and agreed to an armistice. The treaty was signed in Moscow on March 13. Although Finland lost some territory, it retained its independence. Finnish casualties numbered 25,000 dead and 45,000 wounded, and the Soviets lost 48,000 dead and 158,000 wounded. When Hitler heard of the Soviet losses in men and equipment, he concluded that the Soviets could be defeated by the Germans.

April 7–9, 1940: A German invasion force set off for Norway accompanied by much of the German navy. The British navy was aware of that massive movement and moved to cut it off but failed to find and engage the main invasion fleet. The British and French canceled their plans to send a military expeditionary force to Norway.

April 9, 1939: The first German troops went ashore at various points along the Norwegian coast. They were joined by airborne units. Although the Germans lost some ships to coastal batteries and the British navy, they succeeded in the first phase of the operation. The Germans also invaded Denmark and took Copenhagen within 12 hours.

April 10–June 10, 1940: The British joined the Norwegians in putting up a fierce resistance to the Germans in Norway. The first British troops went ashore on April 14, but they were eventually overpowered by the Germans. The naval war along the coasts and fjords of Norway proved costly to both sides—the British lost the carrier *Glorious*, as well as two cruisers and 9 destroyers. The Germans lost three cruisers and ten destroyers. Military casualties included some 6,100 for the Allies and 5,600 for the Germans.

May 10, 1940: The Germans launched their attack in the west, crossing into Belgium, Holland, and Luxembourg. Although the Allies had a slight advantage in manpower, the Germans had superior airpower, a more unified command, and the advantage of being organized for mobilized warfare—the *blitzkrieg*. The British and French forces responded quickly, but the Dutch and Belgian forces were ill prepared to hold the line against the Germans.

British troops landed on Iceland to prevent it from falling into German hands and to use it as a naval and air base for protecting convoys between America and Britain.

May 12, 1940: The German army invaded France by simply out-flanking the northwest corners of the famed Maginot Line of fortification that the French had constructed to defend their border against the Germans.

May 14, 1940: The Germans, having moved quickly through Holland, bombed the undefended city of Rotterdam before the German surrender demand expired. The Dutch capitulated the next day.

May 17, 1940: German troops entered Brussels and Antwerp, effectively signaling the end of Belgium's resistance. The Germans were then free to concentrate their forces on France.

May 26, 1940: The Allied forces, having been pushed back to the Atlantic coast by the Germans, began Operation Dynamo—a total evacuation from the beach of Dunkirk (or Dunkerque), on the Belgian coast.

May 27–June 4, 1940: The British evacuated some 338,226 troops (of whom 112,000 were French) from Dunkirk. About 40,000 Allied troops were left behind and captured. Virtually all heavy equipment was left behind, and the British and French lost some 80 merchant and naval ships.

June 5–June 22, 1940: The Germans swept through France, taking Paris on June 14. On June 22, the French signed an armistice at Compiègne, France, in the same railroad car in which Germany had signed the armistice in 1918. The French were allowed to retain a puppet state in about half of France, to be headed by Marshal Henri Pétain, with its capital at Vichy.

July 10, 1940: The German air force began to step up its air attacks on Britain by bombing docks in South Wales. That was the commencement of the Battle of Britain. During the months that followed, the Germans launched massive bombing raids on British civilian, military, and industrial targets. The Germans also flew thousands of fighter-plane sorties, with the intention of knocking out the Royal Air Force (RAF) to pave the way for an invasion of Britain. The Battle of Britain lasted until October 31, by which date the Germans accepted that they had failed in their goal to knock out the RAF. They put Operation Sea Lion, their plan to invade Britain, on hold. The Germans continued their bombing raids on British population centers in a campaign the British referred to as "the blitz."

October 7, 1940: German troops invaded Romania, on the pretext that they wanted to help organize Romania's army. Actually, Germany wanted control of Romania's rich oil fields.

October 28–December 28, 1940: Although Mussolini had promised Hitler he would not invade Greece, the Italians crossed the Albanian border in the early morning of October 28 and moved into northern Greece. The Italians also bombed the Greek city of Patras. Within days, the Italians were stopped and the Greeks, with help from the British air force, began to push the Italians back. By November 16, the Greeks had chased the Italians back into Albania, and on December 28, the Greeks stopped their advance. Hitler was furious over Mussolini's attack on Greece, but he agreed to send troops to aid the Italians in the spring of 1941.

December 18, 1940: Hitler issued Directive 21, informing his military commanders to prepare for the invasion of the Soviet Union—code-named Barbarossa.

MEDITERRANEAN/AFRICAN THEATER

June 12, 1940: British ships shelled the Italian base of Tobruk, Libya. An Italian submarine sank a British cruiser off the Greek island of Crete and the RAF bombed Genoa and Turin. Those events spread the war to the Mediterranean, which became a theater of operations during the ensuing years.

September 13, 1940: Having driven the British out of East Africa, the Italians crossed the Egyptian border from Libya, their colony, and forced the British to pull back. The ultimate Italian objective was to capture the Suez Canal.

September 23–25, 1940: Free French and British forces tried to take Dakar, a major port on the West African coast and the main city of the French colony of Senegal. Ships loyal to the Vichy government damaged the Allied ships, and British prime minister Winston Churchill ordered that the operation be abandoned.

December 9–17, 1940: The British conducted a counteroffensive against the Italians in Egypt. By December 17, the British had driven the Italians back inside Libya.

ASIAN THEATER

March 30, 1940: The Japanese installed a puppet government in China, headed by a Nationalist politician, Wang Ching-wei.

August 9, 1940: The British government announced it was pulling its forces out of Shanghai and Tientsin Province.

September 22, 1940: After negotiating with the Vichy government in France, the Japanese moved troops into Indochina. The Japanese claimed their only goal was to keep supplies from reaching China.

October 18, 1940: The Burma Road—an overland route from Burma to China—was reopened so that supplies could be carried to Chiang Kaishek's forces. The British had closed it on July 18 because they were not prepared to challenge the Japanese.

NAVAL THEATER

January–December 1940: In what became known as the Battle of the Atlantic, German U-boats, armed merchant cruisers, and warships took a terrible toll on Allied shipping—a total of 1,059 warships and civilian transports were sunk. However, the Allies managed to sink 22 U-boats. After this, the German navy never had the chance to build its U-boat fleet to the level hoped for by its admirals.

April–June 1940: In the battle for Norway, the German navy suffered heavy losses, including 13 major warships and 4 submarines, with another 10 seriously damaged. The British navy also lost a number of ships (13 sunk) but had more in reserve and eventually was joined by the U.S. Navy.

May 16, 1940: The British government closed the Mediterranean to normal British merchant shipping, which included a ban on the much-needed convoys that carried troops, arms, and supplies. Those convoys had to go around the cape of Africa and up to Suez—some 20,000 miles—but the British navy could no longer provide safe passage, given the level of the Italian and German forces active in the Mediterranean.

July 3, 1940: The British were determined that the French navy's many ships not fall into the hands of the Germans. They seized 11 French warships tied up at English ports and tried to negotiate the surrender of a French fleet at Oran, Algeria. When the French admiral did not comply promptly, the British sank one French battleship and damaged two other ships. However, six others sailed to Toulon, France.

July–October 1940: July through October were known to the German U-boat crews in the Atlantic as *die glückliche Zeit* ("the happy time")

because of the high rate of success they had against Allied ships. Their success, however, prompted the British to take such measures such as increasing convoy escorts.

August 17, 1940: Hitler declared a total blockade of the British Isles, warning that even neutral ships would be sunk on sight.

November 11–12, 1940: Aircraft from the British carrier *Illustrious* made a daring attack on the Italian naval base at Taranto and seriously damaged five Italian ships.

HOME FRONT

May 25, 1940: President Franklin Roosevelt set up the Office of Emergency Management to coordinate planning for converting the U. S. home front to a wartime economy and society. Roosevelt was signaling that he was anticipating an active role in World War II.

May 31, 1940: Roosevelt introduced a "billion-dollar defense program," which greatly increased U.S. military forces.

June 3, 1940: The U.S. War Department agreed to sell Britain millions of dollars worth of surplus or outdated armaments and aircraft.

June 10, 1940: Prime Minister Paul Reynaud of France appealed to Roosevelt to intervene in the war in Europe, but Roosevelt was unable to act due to lack of domestic support for U.S. intervention and the forthcoming presidential election. Roosevelt did, however, deliver a speech in which he admitted that U.S. policy was moving from neutrality to "non-belligerency." By that, he meant that the U.S. would openly support the Allies but would not go to war against the Axis.

June 13, 1940: Congress passed the Military Supply Act, which included $1.8 billion for military projects. A large shipment of surplus artillery and rifles left the United States on a British ship. Although they were clearly government arms, President Roosevelt got around the Neutrality Act by first selling them to a private steel company.

July 19, 1940: Roosevelt signed the Two-Ocean Navy Expansion Act which provided for a greatly expanded Navy—on both the Atlantic and the Pacific.

September 16, 1940: The Selective Service Bill became law; it permitted induction into the armed services of all healthy males aged 21–35. The first draftees were selected on October 29.

September 26, 1940: The U.S. placed an embargo on the export of scrap iron and steel to Japan. Japanese leaders later used that embargo as an excuse for proceeding with their plans to declare war against the United States.

November 5, 1940: Franklin Roosevelt defeated Wendell Willkie for an unprecedented third term as president.

December 10, 1940: Roosevelt announced further limits on the export of iron ore and iron and steel products. Those embargoes deprived Japan of much needed materials.

December 17, 1940: President Roosevelt, in a press conference, announced his plan to extend aid to Great Britain and for the first time labeled it Lend-Lease. That term referred to the fact that the United States lent war equipment to Britain and Britain leased parts of its possessions in the Western Hemisphere to the United States for naval and air bases. Eventually, the term covered the whole program of providing weapons, equipment, and food to any nation that aided in the war against the Axis.

December 29, 1940: In a fireside chat radio broadcast, Roosevelt said that he wanted the United States to serve as the "arsenal of democracy" by providing aid to Britain in its war against the Axis powers.

INTERNATIONAL DEVELOPMENTS

February 1940: The Germans began construction of a concentration camp at Auschwitz, Poland.

February 5, 1940: The British and French Supreme War Council agreed to intervene in Norway and send aid to Finland. In the end, the help was too little too late.

May 10–13, 1940: The Germans invaded Luxembourg, Belgium, and Holland on May 10. Prime Minister Chamberlain lost support in the British House of Commons, where a debate over his conduct of the war, particularly the Norwegian campaign, had been under way for several days. Somewhat reluctantly, the Conservatives chose Winston Churchill as the new prime minister, and he immediately took office. On May 13, the first of Churchill's many inspirational speeches was broadcast to his country. In that speech, he declared, "I have nothing to offer but blood, toil, tears, and sweat" (see Notable Phrases, p. 503).

May 15, 1940: Churchill sent the first of many communications to President Roosevelt; he signed himself "Former Naval Person." He openly courted U.S. support in the war and even presented a shopping list of warships and arms.

June 10, 1940: Having seen how successful the Germans were, Mussolini declared war on Britain and France. The Italians brought a decent navy but a poorly trained army to the Axis, and the Italian people and economy were ill-prepared for war.

June 12–22, 1940: The Soviet government issued ultimatums to three Baltic states (Estonia, Latvia, and Lithuania), demanding installation of pro-USSR governments. All three states acceded, and on July 21, they were formally annexed by the Soviet Union.

June 16–17, 1940: France asked Britain to be released from its promise not to make a separate peace with the Germans. On June 17, Marshal Henri Pétain took over from Paul Reynaud as prime minister and immediately announced that his government was seeking an armistice with the Germans. On July 11, Pétain became president of France.

June 18, 1940: Gen. Charles de Gaulle, not very well known to even the French, broadcast from London, urging his countrymen to continue to fight.

June 27, 1940: Representatives of Britain and Australia met with Secretary of State Cordell Hull and asked that the United States take a more active role in blocking Japan's aggressive moves in the Pacific. Hull could not promise to do so, as he felt most Americans were not ready to become involved in the war. On September 4, however, the U.S. government warned Japan against taking aggressive action in Indochina.

June 28, 1940: The British government recognized Charles de Gaulle as the "leader of all free Frenchmen."

July 25, 1940: The United States announced that it was prohibiting the export of oil and metal products to countries outside the Western Hemisphere—except Britain. The Japanese government regarded that as an anti-Japanese step, as they needed both oil and valuable metals, and began seeking access to the valuable oil and raw materials in Malaysia and in the Dutch East Indies. On November 13, the Japanese concluded agreements with the major oil companies in the Dutch East Indies, allowing for the purchase of

1,800,000 tons annually.

August 1, 1940: Japanese government leaders announced that their goal was a "new order in Greater East Asia," led by Japan and extending throughout much of the Pacific. That became known as the policy, or goal, of the Greater East Asia Co-prosperity Sphere. In part, that policy was aimed at countering the economic activities and pressures from the United States and other Western countries, but it also expressed Japan's goal of imposing its domination over Asia.

September 2, 1940: The United States and Britain ratified an agreement under which the United States obtained the right to construct naval and air bases in Bermuda and in British colonies in the West Indies. In return, Britain obtained 50 old U.S. destroyers. This has generally been regarded as a move by Roosevelt to bring the American people to accept increasing involvement in the war.

September 27, 1940: Germany, Italy, and Japan signed the so-called Tripartite Pact, in which each promised to declare war on a third party that joined in war against one of them.

November 26, 1940: Describing the action as a "health measure," the Germans began to force the Jews of Warsaw, Poland, into a ghetto.

BATTLES AND CAMPAIGNS: 1941

There were several areas of military activity in this second full year of World War II: European theater, Mediterranean/African theater, Middle East theater, Asian theater, and naval theater.

EUROPEAN THEATER

January–May 11, 1941: The German air force kept up its blitz, bombing British cities and inflicting serious damage on many. The night of May 10–11 was one of the worst, at least for London, with the Houses of Parliament among the buildings damaged. Then, suddenly, the blitz ceased (for almost three years) as the German air force regrouped for other operations—in particular, the invasion of the Soviet Union on June 22.

January 4–April 6, 1941: The Greeks began a new offensive against the Italians in Albania. The Italians later counterattacked, and for several weeks the advantage seesawed until, finally,

Hitler had his forces launch a major invasion of Yugoslavia and Greece.

March 4, 1941: British commandos carried out a raid on the Lofoten Islands off the northwest coast of Norway. They returned with 215 Germans and Nazi collaborators and 300 Norwegian volunteers, but, in reprisal, the Germans killed many Norwegian civilians.

April 6–9, 1941: German forces invaded Yugoslavia and Greece with combined mobilized armored groups and air strikes. The Yugoslavians were in such disarray that they could do little to stop the Germans. The Greeks were reinforced by troops from Britain, Australia, and New Zealand, but the Germans had the advantage in armored units and airplanes.

April 12–17, 1941: Belgrade, the capital of Yugoslavia surrendered, and Yugoslavia fell to the Germans. King Peter and his government fled to Athens on April 14–15. On April 16, the Croat Republic broke away under its own Fascist-like Ustase government and in the ensuing months, proceeded to execute thousands of Orthodox Serbians and Jews. On April 17, Yugoslavia signed an armistice. The Germans conquered Yugoslavia at a cost of only 200 dead.

April 14–23, 1941: The Germans advanced so rapidly across Greece that the British canceled plans to bring Australian and Polish reinforcements from Egypt. Greek prime minister Alexander Korizis committed suicide on April 18. The King of Greece and his government were evacuated to Crete on April 23.

April 24–29, 1941: British, Australian, and New Zealand troops began to evacuate to Crete, a Greek island south of Greece, and Egypt from points along the coast of Greece. German planes bombed the British and other Allied ships and sank some 15, with the loss of about 15,000 men. By the morning of April 29, some 50,000 Allied troops had been evacuated. Although Hitler had conquered Yugoslavia and Greece in less than a month, the campaign had tied up units that might have been used to invade the Soviet Union. The postponement of that exercise had serious consequences in the following winter.

May 20–June 1, 1941: After several days of bombing, the Germans began their invasion of Crete. The Germans dropped parachute troops— some 23,000 in the first couple of days—and also brought in gliders with troops and equipment. The Germans landed at several points along the north coast and at first met heavy resistance from the Allied and Greek armies as well as from some Cretan civilians, but by the end of the second day the Germans had gained effective control of a crucial airfield on the far west of the island. From that moment on, the Germans were able to fly in reinforcements and steadily push back the Allies. By May 26, Allied troops began to move toward the south coast of Crete, and during the next few days, some 18,600 were evacuated to Egypt. Throughout the entire battle for Crete, German planes took a heavy toll on British ships off Crete: In total, three cruisers and six destroyers were sunk and several other warships were damaged. Although the Germans finally secured Crete, it was with such high casualties (7,000) that Hitler decided against any such large-scale airborne operations in the future. Moreover, Cretan guerrillas (aided by British agents) tied down fairly large German and Italian units on Crete during the next three and one-half years.

June 22, 1941: The Germans commenced Operation Barbarossa—the invasion of the Soviet Union. Hitler had been anticipating the invasion for years, but the actual military planning had been underway for only several months, and, despite their massive forces, the German military was not fully prepared for what lay ahead. The Germans, for instance, relied heavily on horse-drawn transport of supplies and artillery, and those horses eventually proved unsuited to the mud, snow, and cold of Russia. The Germans enjoyed early success, however, because the Soviet military was far less prepared—in part, because Stalin refused to believe his own and Allied intelligence reports of the German buildup along the Soviet border.

June 23–October 1, 1941: The mobilized German forces, aided by superior airpower, allowed the Germans to advance rapidly through the USSR. They were joined by units from Romania and Hungary, as well as by volunteers from Spain. More important, Finland declared war on the Soviet Union on June 26, with the intention of gaining back the land it had lost in March 1940, and Finnish troops put great pressure on the Soviets. Losses on both sides were horrific—several hundreds of thousands of Soviets were killed, wounded, or taken prisoner. German casualties were lighter but still punishing.

July 7, 1941: U.S. forces landed on Iceland to take over the garrisoning from the British. From

that point on, the United States took over the responsibility of guarding the nearby sea routes from German submarines.

September 1–15, 1941: The Germans began what they regarded as their final push toward Leningrad. By September 15, they had effectively isolated the city. Leningrad remained under siege until January 27, 1944. During that time, its citizens suffered from a lack of food as well as other necessities.

October 2–30, 1941: Operation Typhoon, the name for the German campaign to capture Moscow, officially began. After heavy bombings on October 16, foreign diplomats and many government offices were moved to Kuibyshev. Stalin remained in Moscow, however, and announced that the city must be defended. By the end of the month, the Germans were forced to call a temporary halt to their campaign because the winter weather and muddy ground was hindering the gradually weakening German forces.

November 15–December 5, 1941: The Germans renewed their offensive against Moscow on November 15, advancing against increasing resistance. On December 2, small German units reached the suburbs only 20 miles from the Kremlin. By December 5, even Hitler accepted that the offensive should be halted for the winter. On December 6, the Soviets began a counteroffensive against the Germans threatening Moscow.

December 31, 1941: Although they enjoyed some successes against the Soviets, the German armies hunkered down for the winter. On December 19, Hitler assumed direct responsibility as commander in chief of the army and continued to order his forces in the Soviet Union not to retreat. At first, that made him look like a bold strategist, but for the German troops in the Soviet Union the winter turned out to be one of the fiercest on record. The Soviet army had to deal with an estimated 5,000,000 casualties, plus the loss of thousands of tanks and guns.

MEDITERRANEAN/AFRICAN THEATER

January 3–22, 1941: The British began their drive across Libya to take Tobruk. By January 9, some 25,000 Italian troops were trapped there. On January 21, Australian units began the final assault, and the Italian garrison of 27,000 surrendered Tobruk to the British on January 22. The British wasted no time in pursuing other Italian forces across Libya.

January 19–July 3, 1941: British forces in East Africa (aided by Indian units and some Free French troops) campaigned to push the Italians out of Eritrea, Ethiopia, and Italian Somaliland. Gradually, the Allies pushed the Italians back, taking scores of prisoners. Emperor Haile Selassie returned in January, and on May 5, he entered his capital of Addis Ababa. By July 3, Italian resistance had effectively ended.

February 9, 1941: The British arrived at El Agheila (or Al Uqaylah) on the coast of Libya and called a halt to their drive across North Africa because they had run out of supplies and because some troops were sent to Greece. By that time, the British had taken 130,000 Italian prisoners (at a cost of barely 2,000 casualties).

February 12–24, 1941: Gen. Erwin Rommel arrived in Tripoli to take command of the German Afrika Corps that Hitler planned to send to resist the advancing British. The first German troops landed on February 14, and the first small skirmishes between the Germans and British occurred on February 24.

March 24–December 31, 1941: With Rommel in command, German and Italian units pushed the British out of El Agheila. On March 31, the Axis forces went on the offensive, pushing the British eastward. By April 11, thousands of British troops were isolated in Tobruk, and others fled into Egypt. An attempt in mid-June to relieve the siege failed. The besieged British forces, including many Australian units, received needed supplies by ships making night runs. At times, fresh troops were brought in and veteran troops removed by those ships. On November 18, the British launched an offensive from Egypt in an effort to draw Axis forces away from Tobruk. In the ensuing days, British and German tank and armored units fought a series of classic battles, with neither side gaining a decisive victory. Gradually, however, the British (including New Zealand units) pushed Rommel's forces back, and on December 10, the siege of Tobruk was lifted. On December 16, Rommel had pulled back his forces to El Agheila. The German units retreated in an orderly fashion and continued to inflict heavy casualties on the British.

MIDDLE EAST THEATER

April 1–3, 1941: In Iraq, Rashid Ali, a Na-tionalist politician, and army officers led a coup in opposition to the British presence in their country. The British immediately organized their forces in the Middle East and India to deny the Axis access to Iraq's oil.

April 19–May 1, 1941: British landed troops in Iraq. The Iraqis, aided by the Germans and supplied through Syria, then under the control of Vichy France, began to fight back on May 1.

May 15, 1941: The British began to bomb airfields in Syria.

May 31, 1941: The Iraqi government signed an armistice with the Great Brtain, under which the British were allowed to maintain troops in Iraq and the Iraqis agreed not to aid the Axis. In the next few days, the British effectively took over Iraq.

June 6–July 11, 1941: British and Free French forces invaded Syria. Most of the German forces had left, but the Vichy French put up considerable resistance. On July 11, the commander of the Vichy French forces accepted the Allies' terms for an armistice.

August 25–September 1, 1941: British and Soviet forces moved into Iran to deny the Axis access to Iran's oil. Resistance ended on August 29, and the final terms of the armistice were settled on September 1. British and Soviet forces occupied a number of strategic points but stayed out of Tehran, the capital.

September 16, 1941: Convinced that the Shah of Iran had not done enough to expel the Axis, the British and the Soviets moved into Tehran, forced the Shah to abdicate, and installed the crown prince, Mohammad Reza Pahlavi. The Allies then controlled all the oilfields in the Middle East.

ASIAN THEATER

July 28, 1941: After an ultimatum to the government of Vichy France demanding bases in Indochina, the Japanese began to occupy former French installations there.

November 26, 1941: A Japanese carrier force left its base and sailed across the North Pacific toward Pearl Harbor. U.S. intelligence was secretly decoding virtually all Japanese military and diplomatic messages, and on November 27, the U.S. government issued secret warnings to U.S. military commanders overseas.

December 1, 1941: The British received reliable reports of movements by Japanese military forces that suggested imminent attacks on Malaya and the East Indies.

December 2, 1941: Japanese naval headquarters sent a coded message to the Japanese ships of the carrier force: "Climb Mount Niitaka." That was the signal to carry out the planned attack on Pearl Harbor.

December 6, 1941: Japanese forces set off from Palau, one of the Caroline Islands in the western Pacific, to attack the Philippines.

December 7, 1941: At 7:55 A.M. (Hawaii time, 12:55 P.M. Eastern Standard Time), the first wave of Japanese aircraft appeared over the U.S. naval base at Pearl Harbor and began to bomb the ships and airfields (see Historical Perspectives and Controversies, pp. 506-507). As it was Sunday morning, the U.S. Army and Navy forces at Pearl Harbor were caught off guard, with most top officers away from duty stations. Airplanes were lined up wingtip to wingtip and antiaircraft ammunition was locked up (and no keys available). Taking off from six carriers about 200 miles north of Oahu, a total of 423 Japanese planes attacked in two waves. All eight U.S. battleships in port were damaged, with five sunk—the *Arizona* was a total loss; the *Oklahoma* was raised but scrapped; the *California*, *Nevada*, and *West Virginia* were raised and rebuilt. Three cruisers and three destroyers were also sunk. The Japanese lost 29 planes; 188 American airplanes were destroyed on the ground. American and Hawaiian casualties came to some 3,700. The Japanese commander of the carrier force decided at the last moment not to send in a third wave and thus failed to inflict much damage on the oil storage tanks and other harbor installations. Fortunately for the Americans, all three carriers assigned to the U.S. Pacific Fleet were out to sea. On the same day, Japanese planes raided U.S. installations on the island of Guam and Wake, and Japanese destroyers shelled Midway.

December 8, 1941: The United States declared war on Japan. About midday, the Japanese began air attacks on U.S. bases in the Philippines. The Japanese again caught most of the U.S. aircraft on the ground and destroyed about 100—crippling U.S. forces in the ensuing battle for the Philippines. That morning, a small Japanese force landed on Bataan Island, north of Luzon and overran a small garrison. Although Gen. Douglas MacArthur had a force of 130,000,

*After the attack on Pearl Harbor on December 7, 1941, the flagship of the Pacific fleet, the USS **Pennsylvania**, sits only slightly damaged, but in the foreground are the wrecked USS **Downes** (left) and USS **Casin** (right).*

110,000 of those were poorly trained and poorly equipped members of the Philippine army.

Earlier in the morning, large Japanese forces landed in Malaya and Thailand, and Japanese planes bombed Singapore. The British had been expecting such an attack but were unprepared to defend the landing zones. The Japanese also launched an attack on the British colony of Hong Kong and on the international sectors of Shanghai. In Shanghai, the small U.S. garrison was quickly overwhelmed.

December 10–31, 1941: Japanese forces moved quickly throughout the Pacific—Guam, defended by only 300 U.S. troops, fell to the Japanese on December 10. Japanese forces invaded Borneo and Burma and pushed the British forces back. The Japanese also advanced in Malaya and Thailand. The U.S. troops on Wake Island surrendered on December 23, and Hong Kong fell on December 25. In the Philippines, Manila was declared an open city on December 27.

NAVAL THEATER

January–December 1941: Fierce battles

raged across the Mediterranean Sea as the British sought to keep the sea-lanes from Gibraltar to Egypt open to their convoys. The German air force—and eventually the German navy—as well as various Italian naval and air units attacked relentlessly. Malta, the main British base in the Mediterranean, was particularly hard hit by the Axis, and the British took heavy losses in ships and personnel to protect Malta and the sea-lanes. The British, on the other hand, were able to choke off most of the supplies being sent to the Axis in North Africa.

The Battle of the Atlantic continued unabated. German U-boats took a heavy toll on the Allies—hundreds of ships, thousands of seamen, hundreds of thousands of tons were lost—but the convoys with their escort ships and radar were beginning to overwhelm the German U-boat fleet. Several of the leading German U-boat commanders were either killed or captured, and although the German navy had some 200 U-boats, at any given time, only a small percentage were on active patrol, and many of those were sunk. The Germans also sent out battleships, other warships, and armed merchant ships (often known as "raiders") to attack convoys; four battleships and heavy cruisers—the *Bismarck*, the *Gneisenau*, the *Prinz Eugen*, and the *Scharnhorst*—operated out of Scandinavian and French ports and continually played a cat-and-mouse game with the British. The British were aided in their struggles by their ability to read the German naval code (see Military Innovations, pp. 499-500).

March 1, 1941: The U.S. Navy formed a Support Force for the Atlantic Fleet. In the ensuing months, the United States was increasingly open in its support of the British navy and their convoys. New bases were opened in Bermuda, and the British were allowed to bring damaged ships into U.S. bases for repairs. U.S. naval and air forces were assigned to protect Allied ships of any nationality sailing to and from Iceland.

March 28–29, 1941: The British and Italian fleets fought a major naval battle off Cape Matapan, one of the southernmost peninsulas of the Greek mainland. The British lost only two airplanes, and sank an Italian cruiser and two destroyers, but the damaged Italian battleship *Vittorio Veneto* escaped.

May 21, 1941: A German U-boat sank the U.S. merchant ship *Robin Moor* off the coast of Brazil. That occurred inside the security zone that Roosevelt had proclaimed on April 11 as off limits to the Axis, but aside from diplomatic protests, the United States took no action. That was the first American ship lost in World War II.

May 23–27, 1941: British ships engaged the German battleship *Bismarck* and the heavy cruiser *Prinz Eugen* in the Denmark Strait between Greenland and Iceland. In the first engagement, the British cruiser *Hood* was sunk, with the loss of 1,413 men. The British ships, joined by others from nearby convoys, continued to follow the German ships, as the damaged *Bismarck* set off for the French port of Brest. On May 26, British aircraft and destroyers began to make direct hits on the *Bismarck*. The next day, as more British ships joined in the attack, the *Bismarck* was sunk.

September 4, 1941: The U.S. Navy in the Atlantic was allowed to escort convoys comprised of ships of any nation so long as at least one U.S. merchant ship was in the convoy. A German submarine attacked the U.S. destroyer *Greer*, mistaking it for a British ship. The *Greer* was not damaged, but President Roosevelt, citing that incident as an example of German aggression, on September 11 ordered U.S. warships to "shoot on sight" ships that endangered "American defense."

September 24, 1941: The first German U-boat entered the Mediterranean; many more entered in the next few months. Among their greatest successes were the sinking of the British aircraft carrier *Ark Royal* (November 14) and the sinking of the battleship *Barnham* (November 25).

October 16–17, 1941: In a convoy battle, a German U-boat torpedoed the U.S. destroyer *Kearny*. The ship did not sink, but 11 American sailors were killed.

October 31, 1941: While serving as a convoy escort, the U.S. destroyer *Reuben James* was sunk by a U-boat. One hundred American sailors were killed. That was the first U.S. warship sunk in World War II.

December 10, 1941: The British battleships *Prince of Wales* and *Repulse* were attacked in the South China Sea by Japanese planes and were sunk.

December 13–19, 1941: British and Italian fleets clashed in the Mediterranean, as each side attempted to get convoys through to its forces in Malta and North Africa, respectively. Both sides suffered heavy losses, but the worst came when, on December 18, three Italian midget submarines penetrated the British fleet's anchorage at Alexandria, Egypt, and sank two British battleships. The British lost a cruiser and a destroyer to Axis mines on the same day.

HOME FRONT

January 6, 1941: In his State of the Union speech, President Roosevelt asked Congress to extend lend-lease aid to all the Allies. It was in that speech that Roosevelt first referred to the "four essential human freedoms" (see Notable Phrases, p. 504).

January 10, 1941: The Lend-Lease Bill was presented to Congress. Although there was considerable opposition from isolationists, the bill passed both houses, and Roosevelt signed it into law on March 11. Hailed by some as an act of unprecedented generosity, the bill required the British to pay cash as long as they could. That meant that the British would have to sell many of their assets in the United States. The bill also forbade the British to export any items made from materials supplied through lend-lease. That cut greatly into Britain's trade.

February 4, 1941: The United Service Organization—the USO—was set up to serve the social, welfare, educational, and religious needs of those in the U.S. armed forces and defense industries. The USO became best known for the clubs set up throughout the world where service personnel could relax when off-duty.

April 11, 1941: Roosevelt established the Office of Price Administration, which was assigned to control prices and profits; it played a major role in the U.S. domestic economy during the following four years.

May 15, 1941: Roosevelt denounced the French who collaborated with the German occupation forces and ordered that all French ships in U.S. ports be seized. Among them was the luxury liner *Normandie*. It burned at its dock in New York harbor in 1942.

June 14–16, 1941: On June 14, Roosevelt froze all German and Italian assets in the United States. On June 16, he ordered all German and Italian consulates in the U.S. closed. (Germany and Italy took reciprocal action on June 19.)

July 21, 1941: Roosevelt asked for a service extension from one year to 30 months for men drafted into the military. The extension passed the Senate on August 7 and the House of Representatives on August 12.

September 27, 1941: The first hulls of a new type of freighter—the so-called Liberty ships—were launched at several shipyards. Made using innovative new methods that allowed for quick and economic construction, the ships were constructed at a rapid rate in the months ahead. The first ones took 244 days to build. Later, the average time dropped to only 41 days. Eventually, more then 2,000 were built.

November 6, 1941: Roosevelt announced a loan of $1 billion to the Soviet Union for the purchase of Lend-Lease supplies.

November 13, 1941: Congress passed changes in the Neutrality Laws to allow U.S. merchant ships to be armed and to enter war zones.

December 8, 1941: At a joint session of Congress, Roosevelt referred to December 7, 1941 as "a date which will live in infamy" and called for a declaration of war against Japan (but not against Germany and Italy). Congress voted to do so (with only the pacifist representative from Montana, Jeannette Rankin, voting against it). Britain's Parliament also declared war on Japan.

December 11, 1941: After Germany and Italy declared war on the United States, Congress voted to declare war on those two nations.

INTERNATIONAL DEVELOPMENTS

January 27–March 29, 1941: British and American representatives held secret talks in Washington, D.C. They agreed that if the United States entered into the war against Germany and Japan, Allied policy would be to work for the defeat of Germany first. That agreement was known as the ABC-1 Plan. In March, the Americans went to Britain to select sites for military bases should the United States enter the war.

February 19–March 2, 1941: Germany pressured Turkey and Bulgaria to sign a friendship agreement, primarily so that Turkey would agree to let the Germans move troops through Bulgaria. Bulgaria joined the Tripartite Pact (with Germany, Italy, and Japan) on March 1, and Germany began moving troops into Bulgaria on March 2.

March 25, 1941: Under pressure from Germany, Yugoslavia was forced to join the Tripartite Pact.

April 13, 1941: Japan and the Soviet Union signed a five-year neutrality agreement. Stalin did so in order to be free to move troops to the USSR western frontier, and Japan wanted to free troops to move into the East Indies.

May 11, 1941: Rudolf Hess, deputy leader of the Nazi party, flew a small plane to Scotland and landed by parachute. He claimed he wanted to contact the Duke of Hamilton (whom he had met at the 1936 Olympics) with the goal of persuading elements in Britain to join Germany in a war against the Communists in the Soviet Union. He was immediately disowned by German authorities and imprisoned by the British, who treated him as mentally unbalanced.

June 10, 1941: A German-Turkey treaty of friendship was signed in Ankara, Turkey. Germany achieved its goal of ensuring that Turkey did not join the Allies.

July 2, 1941: A top-level meeting of Japanese government and military leaders informed the Japanese Emperor of their plans to take bases in Indochina. The U.S. learned of that decision because it had deciphered the Japanese codes.

July 3, 1941: Joseph Stalin made his first broadcast to the Soviet Union since the German invasion. He defended his earlier pact with Germany on the grounds that he had hoped for peace. He exhorted his people to engage in total war, including a scorched-earth policy and guerrilla warfare in the face of German advances.

July 8, 1941: Germany and Italy formally announced their plans to divide Yugoslavia.

July 26, 1941: The United States and Britain froze Japanese assets in their countries. Japan retaliated on July 28. Japanese assets in the Dutch East Indies were also frozen. Japan retaliated against the Dutch on July 29. That meant that almost 75 percent of Japan's foreign trade and 90 percent of its oil supplies were cut off.

August 1, 1941: Roosevelt forbade the export of oil and aviation fuel from the United States except to Britain, the British Empire, or nations in the Western Hemisphere. That cut off Japan from virtually all supplies of oil.

August 9–12, 1941: Roosevelt and Churchill met on British and American warships in Argentia (or Placentia) Bay, Newfoundland, to discuss policies regarding the war in Europe and the situation in Asia. They issued a statement of eight principles, or goals, that became known as the "Atlantic Charter." Although it was not formally binding, it was signed by 15 Allied nations (including the Soviet Union) on September 24 and served as a basic blueprint for the United Nations.

August 17, 1941: The United States formally warned Japan not to move against British or Dutch possessions in Asia. In the ensuing weeks, the Japanese government made some efforts at conciliation, but, in fact, it was planning for war against the United States. The Japanese did not accept the two major demands of the Allies— that they get out of China and repudiate the Tripartite Pact with Germany and Italy.

September 6, 1941: The head of the German security service (the SD), Reinhard Heydrich, ordered all Jews over the age of 6 throughout occupied Europe to wear a yellow Star of David. That was one of the milder forms of inhumanity planned by the Nazi hierarchy for all the Jews of Europe.

October 16, 1941: War Minister Hideki Tojo took over as prime minister and the office of home affairs minister. He effectively served as dictator of Japan for almost three years.

November 17, 1941: The Japanese ambassador to the United States and an envoy began negotiations with the U.S. State Department in Washington, D.C.; they were under instructions to defend Japan's dominant role in Asia.

Alfred Rosenberg, one of Hitler's old comrades in the Nazi Party was appointed to head the new Reich Ministry for Occupied Eastern Territories. Among his duties was to rid those territories of "undesirable elements"—a license to murder Jews, Slavs, Communists, partisans, and others the occupying Germans and their collaborators regarded as enemies and inferiors.

November 27–December 1, 1941: On November 27, President Roosevelt and Secretary of State Hull presented the Japanese with final terms, among them that the Japanese leave China and Indochina. In return, the United States would negotiate new agreements on trade and raw materials. On November 29, the Japanese rejected those terms. On December 1, Tojo informed Emperor Hirohito of the decision to go to war. Hirohito did not object.

December 1941: The German Gestapo throughout Europe was authorized to arrest and hold anyone judged to be a danger to German security. That became known as the *Nacht und Nebel* ("Night and Fog Decree") because it meant that many people would be taken away at night without any warning and vanish forever.

December 6, 1941: Roosevelt made a final appeal to the emperor of Japan to avoid war, but there was no reply from the Japanese. Instead, by the end of the day, the Japanese started transmitting their final message to the U.S. government. The first 13 parts were intercepted by the U.S. code-breaking service, quickly translated, and conveyed to Roosevelt. He and his aides recognized that war was imminent, but they failed to notify the U.S. military command.

December 7, 1941: The 14th part of the Japanese message reached Washington, D.C., early in the morning and was decoded by about 9 A.M. It told the Japanese diplomats they were to break off relations with the United States. At 10 A.M., the Japanese diplomats were told to deliver the message at 1 P.M. That message was also decoded by the Americans. Some authorities realized that 1 P.M. was early morning in Hawaii and in the Pacific, but efforts to warn the American military there were perfunctory. The Japanese in Washington, D.C., were slow in translating the 14-part message, and they did not see Secretary of State Hull until 2:30 P.M. By that time, he not only knew the contents of their message but also of the attack on Pearl Harbor.

December 22, 1941–January 7, 1942: Roosevelt, Churchill, and their principal military and political aides met in Washington, D.C., for what was called the Arcadia Conference. There were two major results: confirmation of their previous agreement to concentrate on defeating Germany before turning to Japan and agreement to establish the combined chiefs of staff to direct the Allied military efforts. The meeting also established the basis for communication and cooperation between the American and British political and military leaders that, despite many strains, survived to lead the Allies to victory.

BATTLES AND CAMPAIGNS: 1942

There were several areas of military activity in this third full year of World War II: European theater, Mediterranean/African theater, Asian theater, and naval theater.

EUROPEAN THEATER

January–December 1942: In the air war, the British continued to bomb German cities and military targets in France as well as in Germany. In February, Air Marshal Arthur Harris was appointed to lead the RAF Bomber Command, and he immediately committed the RAF to "area bombing," in which large fleets of bombers dropped their bombs and incendiaries on a general area, rather than attempting precision strikes on selected targets. That proved to be a controversial strategy because it focused on destroying civilian housing and morale, but during 1942, the bombing attacks provided the British with one of their few opportunities to hurt the Germans. Those raids continued throughout the year, with often devastating results over an ever-widening series of targets across German-occupied Europe. The German Luftwaffe forces were stretched to the breaking point by the simultaneous operations in the Soviet Union and the Mediterranean. However, almost as fast as the bombing raids destroyed German industrial plants, they were rebuilt and restored to production.

January–March 1942: In the Soviet Union, the German army was no longer in control or on the offensive. Instead, the Soviet forces were slowly pushing the Germans back. The Germans simply weren't prepared for the hard winter— the troops weren't properly clothed or fed, tank and truck engines froze, and German supply lines were blocked. The Soviet counteroffensive around Moscow that began on December 6, 1941, not only removed the threat to that city but also pushed the Germans back 50 to 100 miles along a wide front. Although German resistance began to stiffen by the end of January, the Soviets kept the pressure on. Both sides literally bogged down when the spring thaw began in March. The German high command estimated that German casualties in the Soviet Union had reached 1.5 million by April. Hitler had taken over virtually all the planning and decisions for the German army in the Russian campaign. His frequent dismissal of generals he felt weren't aggressive enough only contributed to the lessening morale of the troops in the Soviet Union.

January 26, 1942: The first American troops (as opposed to planning and staff units) arrived in Great Britain.

February 13, 1942: The German High Command, with Hitler's agreement, was forced to permanently cancel Operation Sea Lion—the planned invasion of Great Britain.

March 28, 1942: British commandos raided the French naval installation at Saint Nazaire, damaging a dock used to repair large German battleships. The British suffered heavy casualties during the operation.

April 1942: With their own forces bogged down across the Soviet Union, the Germans received reinforcements from some of their allies—Italy, Romania, Hungary, Slovakia, and Spain.

April 24, 1942: The Luftwaffe bombed the historic English city of Exeter, the first of the so-called Baedeker Raids, named after the guidebook series. In retaliation for the RAF's raid on the old German port city of Lübeck (March 28), the Germans had literally selected a group of similar historic British cities from a Baedeker guide and bombed them.

May–July 1942: With the end of the spring thaw, the Germans resumed their campaigns in the Soviet Union. At first, they enjoyed considerable success. The Soviets then launched a major offensive near Kharkov in the Ukraine, but the Germans succeeded in pushing the Soviets out of Kerch. That last engagement cost the Soviets some 150,000 casualties. During May, the Germans also encircled Soviet units west of the Donets River, costing the Soviets another 250,000 casualties. By July, the Germans had advanced toward Rostov and along the Don River; Rostov fell on July 25.

May 30–31, 1942: In the largest raid of the war to date, the RAF sent 1,046 bombers over Cologne, Germany—only 40 bombers were lost. The city's value as a military or industrial target was debatable; some 45,000 Germans were made homeless by the raid. The RAF conducted a series of 1,000 raids on German cities in the following few weeks.

July 4, 1942: After being under siege since November 1941, Sevastopol, the main Russian-Crimean city and port on the Black Sea, fell to the Germans.

For the first time, U.S. Air Force planes joined the British in a bombing raid over Europe, with German airfields in Holland as the target.

August–October 1942: The Germans continued to advance in the Soviet Union, particularly in the Caucasus and against Stalingrad (now Volgograd). By September 1, German units were into the suburbs of Stalingrad. Hitler decided that Stalingrad should be the main target and, in mid-October, called off virtually all other offensive

operations by German units. The fighting around Stalingrad became extremely intense, as the Germans managed to gain control of large parts of the city, at a cost of heavy casualties.

August 17, 1942: Bombers of the U.S. Eighth Air Force struck Rouen, France, in the first American-only raid over Europe.

August 19, 1942: A commando force of some 6,000 men, mostly British and Canadian troops but with some Americans and Free French forces, raided the port installations of Dieppe, France. The raid was a disaster. Almost none of the targets was destroyed, and the Allies lost 3,600 men along with 106 aircraft, a destroyer, 33 landing craft, and 30 tanks.

November 11, 1942: Field Marshal Friedrich von Paulus launched what was to be the last German attack to take Stalingrad, but winter was closing in and the German troops were becoming weak and weary. Despite some small victories, the Germans could not drive the Soviet forces from the city.

November 19–December 31, 1942: The Soviets began a counteroffensive along the Don River, after amassing large numbers of vehicles and more than 500,000 infantry. The Germans were quickly pushed back at several points during the first day's fighting, making November 19 the high-water mark for the German advances in the Soviet Union. By November 23, Soviet troops around Stalingrad had surrounded several hundred thousand German, Romanian, and Italian troops. The Romanians and Italians began to surrender within days, but Hitler insisted that the German troops remain in place, promised by Luftwaffe commander Hermann Göring that the surrounded troops could be supplied by air. That did not happen. Although a German counterattack begun on December 12 recaptured some territory, by December 23, it stalled. Von Paulus was ordered by his superior, Gen. Fritz Erich von Manstein, to try to break out of the pocket where he was surrounded, but Hitler ordered von Paulus to remain in place. Soviet forces also drove the Germans out of other cities along the front.

November 27, 1942: German Panzer troops occupied Toulon, a major Vichy French port on the Mediterranean, but French admiral Jean de Laborde ordered the French ships there scuttled rather then let them fall into the hands of the Germans. Three battleships, 7 cruisers, 16 submarines, and 46 other craft were sunk.

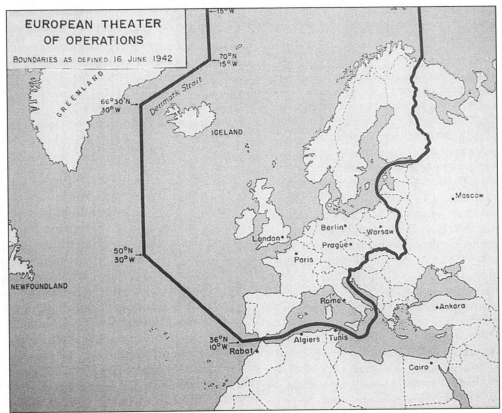

EUROPEAN THEATER
OF OPERATIONS

BOUNDARIES AS DEFINED 16 JUNE 1942

This map shows the European theater of operations as officially defined by the U.S. military in June 1942. Engagements fought to the west of the boundary were in the North Atlantic theater, and those to the south were part of the North African theater.

December 4, 1942: In the first U.S. raid on mainland Italy, U.S. Ninth Air Force planes attacked Naples.

MEDITERRANEAN/AFRICAN THEATER

January–December 1942: The German and Italian navies and air forces continued to take a heavy toll on British military and merchant forces. Malta remained the focal point of the air and naval fighting because the British needed that small island as a staging post. The Axis subjected the island to constant bombing raids. (On April 16, King George VI of Britain awarded the island of Malta the George Cross in recognition of the heroism of the entire populace in the face of the Axis onslaught.) Throughout 1942, the British continued to make costly runs with ships to supply the besieged island and to bring in new fighter planes to make up for the heavy losses caused by the German air force.

January 6–February 6, 1942: Rommel's German Afrika Corps stopped their retreat just west of El Aghelia, Libya. With new tanks, Rommel immediately regrouped and planned a counteroffensive. On January 21, Rommel launched his attack, catching the British off guard. The Germans advanced rapidly along the coast, and by February 6, their forces had pushed the British all the way back to a line just west of Tobruk. In addition to suffering many casualties, the British 8th Army was demoralized by Rommel's swift campaign.

May 26–June 21, 1942: Rommel began a new offensive, with German and Italian troops and tanks pitched against the British, Free French, and South Africans. Although the Allies had the superior forces at the outset, the British failed to exploit their advantages. On June 20, Rommel retook Tobruk, taking not only 30,000 prisoners but also 500,000 gallons of gasoline and vast amounts of food rations. The British again suffered terrible losses in both men and tanks. Although the original German plan had been for

Rommel to hold up and let the Axis concentrate on destroying Malta, he obtained permission to pursue British forces retreating toward the Egyptian border.

June 23–July 22, 1942: Rommel's first units set off eastward toward disorganized British forces. On July 23, some Germans crossed into Egypt. Gen. Claude Auchinleck took control of the British forces and ordered them to withdraw to El Alamein, a small rail station along the coast about 75 miles west of Alexandria, Egypt. By June 30, the British were preparing their defensive position at El Alamein. The German and Italian forces reached that line on July 1, but their attacks on July 2–4 ended in a stalemate. Auchinleck ordered some small counterattacks, which took a heavy toll on Axis troops and tanks. On July 21, Auchinleck ordered a major counteroffensive. The next day, both sides paused to rest and regroup. The Axis supply line was badly overtaxed, leaving its forces short of gasoline and other essentials.

August 15, 1942: The first Battle of El Alamein was a British victory of sorts, but Churchill and other British leaders were unhappy about the conduct of the 8th Army. General Bernard Montgomery replaced Auchinleck as commander. Immediately, he prepared to take the offensive.

August 30–September 6, 1942: Rommel began a major offensive intended to drive the British out of Egypt. But he ran into better-prepared British ground forces, aided by minefields in the desert, strong artillery, and the RAF. The German attack soon came to a halt at the Alam Halfa Ridge, in the desert southeast of El Alamein. By September 2, Rommel was ordering his troops to withdraw, and by September 6 they were back to the positions they had left the week before.

October 23–November 4, 1942: Montgomery launched a major attack against the German and Italian units dug in on a perimeter to the west of El Alamein. The Axis had been preparing for the attack with barbed wire, booby traps, and minefields, but Montgomery had also taken great pains to prepare his forces. Although they outnumbered the Axis in men and tanks, the British ran into heavy opposition during the first 48 hours. Rommel, who had been in Germany for medical care, returned on October 25 and immediately rallied his forces to launch counterattacks, but by November 3, the Axis had lost so many tanks that Rommel ordered his forces to begin to withdraw. Although Hitler countermanded that order, the Axis losses were so heavy that they had no alternative but to retreat on November 4. During the next few days, the Germans fled westward in uncharacteristic disorder, but Montgomery did not immediately pursue them. British and Commonwealth troops suffered 13,500 casualties; German losses were even heavier.

November 7–23, 1942: Montgomery's army pursued Rommel's forces along the coast, from Egypt and across Libya to El Aghelia. Montgomery called for a halt at that point to reorganize his forces.

November 8–13, 1942: The Allies began the invasion of French North Africa—code-named Operation Torch. Most of the assault troops were American. In what was the first major commitment of U.S. troops to the war in Europe, Gen. Dwight D. Eisenhower was the Allied commander, in part to reassure Americans that the nation's soldiers were not being sent to battle under European commanders. Landings took place at three sectors: around Casablanca on Morocco's Atlantic coast; near Oran on Algeria's Mediterranean shore; and near Algiers, also on Algeria's Mediterranean coast. There was some resistance from the Vichy French—especially in the Casablanca and Oran sectors—but there were less than 2,000 Allied casualties. Oran fell to the Allies on November 10. Admiral Darlan, one of the leaders of the Vichy government, was in Algiers, and negotiations began at once to persuade him to use his influence to stop all resistance from the Vichy forces in North Africa. On November 10, Darlan broadcast orders to all French forces in North Africa to stop fighting the Allies. On November 11, the French authorities in North Africa signed an armistice, and Casablanca was occupied by the Allies. On November 13, Darlan was formally recognized by the Allies as the head of civil government in North Africa (although Gen. Charles de Gaulle claimed that the Free French did not recognize Darlan).

November 11–15, 1942: Allied forces in Algiers were moved eastward toward Tunisia to trap the Germans fleeing from Montgomery's troops coming from the east. Under orders from Hitler to hold on to as much of North Africa as possible, the Germans flew reinforcements into Tunisia and by November 15 had 10,000 troops there. Allied paratroopers moved into several positions inside Tunisia.

December 1–8, 1942: The Germans in Tunisia launched a series of attacks against the advancing Allies and exacted considerable casualties. On December 8, the Germans took the important Tunisian port city of Bizerta.

December 11, 1942: Montgomery's forces began to advance again from their positions in Libya.

December 24, 1942: Admiral Darlan was assassinated by a French fanatic. Two days later, Gen. Henri Giraud took over his post, but, like Darlan, he was not accepted by De Gaulle and his Free French adherents.

December 25–31, 1942: The fighting in Tunisia and the advance from Libya slowed because of bad weather and a shortage of supplies on both sides.

ASIAN THEATER

January 1–25, 1942: The Japanese continued to push the British forces down the Malay Peninsula. By January 25, the British had retreated to the island of Singapore.

January 2–23, 1942: On January 2, the Japanese occupied Manila, as the American and Filipino forces withdrew to the Bataan Peninsula. A week later, the Japanese moved against the Allies in Bataan. By January 23, the Allies had fallen back to their second line of defense. The Japanese kept the pressure on for several weeks but did not launch a major offensive until April 1.

January 11–March 12, 1942: The Japanese began to invade the Dutch East Indies. By March 12, the Dutch forces had surrendered. Although that gave the Japanese access to the oil denied them by the Allies' embargo (see July 25, 1940, p. 439), they never managed to extract and refine as much as they had anticipated.

January 15–May 15, 1942: The Japanese moved into Burma and slowly pushed the Allied forces back into smaller and smaller areas. Rangoon, Burma's only major port, fell on March 7. In the following two months, British, Indian, Chinese, and other Allied forces retreated out of Burma, leaving China cut off from land routes. By May 15, the Japanese controlled all of Burma. The British and their Allies—in particular the Indian troops, known as Chindits, led by Gen. Orde Wingate—continued fighting the Japanese without making any major advances.

January 23, 1942: The Japanese landed at Rabaul on New Britain Island, on Borneo, on New Ireland, and on Bougainville in the Solomon Islands. One by one, those and other Pacific islands fell to the Japanese.

January 31, 1942: The last of the British and Australian forces withdrew from the Malayan mainland to Singapore, the most important British base in southeast Asia.

February 8–15, 1942: The Japanese made landings at several points on the island of Singapore. The Allies resisted, but they lacked ammunition and water so were forced to surrender a week after the Japanese invasion. (Contrary to press reports of the time, the large naval guns at Singapore were able to fire inland, but their armor piercing shells were of little value against advancing infantry troops.) Total British and other Allied casualties were about 9,000 dead or wounded. Thousands of the 130,000 taken prisoner died in captivity. That was regarded as the worst disaster in British military history.

February 19, 1942: Carrier-based Japanese aircraft attacked Darwin in northern Australia, sinking several warships and damaging the harbor installations. That was the most serious raid on Australia during the war.

March 11, 1942: Under orders from Washington, D.C., Gen. Douglas MacArthur left the Philippines (see Notable Phrases, p. 504) to go to Australia to take command of the Allied forces in the Southwest Pacific. He left Gen. Jonathan Wainwright in command of the American forces on Bataan. During the next few days, U.S. troops began to arrive in Australia.

April 1–9, 1942: The Japanese began major attacks on Bataan. By April 3, the exhausted British troops were being driven back. By April 7, General Wainwright was withdrawing as many troops as possible to the island fortress of Corregidor in Manila Bay. On April 9, the 12,000 American and 63,000 Filipino troops on Luzon surrendered to the Japanese. Wainwright continued to hold out on Corregidor, and some small American and Filipino units still held out elsewhere in the Philippines.

April 18, 1942: In a daring, technically difficult, and totally unexpected raid, 16 B-25 Mitchell bombers took off from the USS *Hornet* some 650 miles off the coast of Japan. Led by Lt. Col. James Doolittle, they dropped their loads on Tokyo and several other targets and then flew on to China. (Three of the bombers crash-landed; one went down in Soviet territory, and the crew was held prisoner; two crashed in Japanese-occupied China, where three of the eight crew members were executed.) The actual damage to Japanese installations was slight, but the raid was of immense value to Americans as a morale-booster. More important, the raid caused the Japanese to assign large numbers of aircraft to defend their home islands instead of using them to attack the U.S. Navy.

May 6, 1942: On Corregidor, Wainwright surrendered his 15,000 American and Filipino troops. The next day, he broadcast an appeal to all remaining Allied troops in the Philippines to surrender. Most did so within the next few days.

June 3–4, 1942: Planes from a Japanese naval force attacked the U.S. base at Dutch Harbor in the Aleutian Islands off Alaska. Although the Japanese heavily damaged the military base (and the local Russian Orthodox church), they did not drive the Americans from the island. The Japanese action was a diversionary tactic to aid their assault on Midway Island (see Naval Theater, June 3–6, 1942, p. 454).

June 6–7, 1942: In the Aleutians, the Japanese landed on Kiska Island on June 6 and on Attu on June 7. Encountering little resistance, they soon took the islands over.

July 21–December 31, 1942: On July 21, the Japanese landed on New Guinea, determined to drive Australian forces from that pivotal island. In the ensuing weeks, the battle swayed back and forth at various points on the island. Reinforced by American troops, the Australians began to push the Japanese back by September, and by November 13, the Japanese controlled only relatively small beachheads. The Japanese were reinforced by thousands of fresh troops from mid-November on, and during December, there was fierce fighting, with heavy casualties on both sides.

August 7–October 20, 1942: In what was the first step in the long march to Tokyo, U.S. Marines landed on Guadalcanal in the Solomon Islands. They met little opposition during the first days and easily overran a Japanese airstrip, which they renamed Henderson Field. The Japanese had more success in fighting the supporting U.S. naval forces offshore, and both navies fought hard to keep the supply lines to their troops open. On August 24, in what became known as the Battle of the Eastern Solomons,

planes from the two nations' carrier groups fought a brief battle, in which a Japanese carrier was lost and the USS *Enterprise* was damaged. Then on August 27, another U.S. carrier, the *Saratoga*, was damaged by a Japanese submarine. That left the USS *Wasp* as the only operational U.S. carrier in the Pacific (until it, too, was sunk on September 14). The Japanese were forced to bring in troops and supplies during night runs. On October 11–12, a major sea battle was fought in Cape Esperance off Guadalcanal. Although both sides lost several ships in the battle, both also managed to get reinforcements and supplies ashore.

October 21–27, 1942: The Japanese on Guadalcanal, numbering 20,000 men, launched a series of attacks. To support that offensive, the Japanese had four battleships and four aircraft carriers. On October 26, a major battle took place off the Santa Cruz Islands (east of Guadalcanal), and the USS *Hornet* was sunk. Several Japanese ships were damaged, but, more important, the Japanese lost so many aircrews that they were unable to launch an attack on Henderson Field. Having suffered heavy casualties, the Japanese called off their offensive on October 27.

November 1–December 31, 1942: U.S. Marines on Guadalcanal launched a counterattack on November 1, but by December 9, there had been little gain and the troops were exhausted. The Japanese continued to make constant night runs with their ships to supply their troops: The Americans dubbed that operation the "Tokyo Express." On November 13–15, a large Japanese fleet made up of warships escorting transports loaded with reinforcements came up against a smaller U.S. fleet. Both sides took heavy losses during the so-called Battle of Guadalcanal. On the night of November 30–December 1, another fierce naval battle, known as the Battle of Tassafaronga (for the nearby point on the north coast of Guadalcanal), was fought. The U.S. Navy suffered the more serious losses (one cruiser sunk), but the Japanese were stopped from delivering supplies that night. The United States gained effective control of the seas around Guadalcanal, and for awhile, the Japanese were forced to employ submarines to supply their troops, but by mid-December the Tokyo Express was back in operation. Unknown to the U.S., on Decemeber 31, the Japanese had decided to evacuate their forces from Guadalcanal.

A Japanese bomb splashes near a U.S. carrier during the Battle of Santa Cruz near Guadalcanal in the Pacific on October 26, 1942.

NAVAL THEATER

January–December 1942: In the Battle of the Atlantic, German U-boats (aided by a few Italian submarines) continued to take a terrible toll on Allied shipping and personnel, from the Arctic waters down to the Caribbean and off the South American coast. (Brazil declared war on the Axis on August 22 after the sinking of several Brazilian ships.) German surface ships also continued to destroy their share of Allied ships, and the several German warships based in Norway remained a major threat. The U.S. Navy became fully active in the war against the Germans in the Atlantic, although most of its heavy ships were assigned to the war in the Pacific. Among the several convoy routes that had to be protected were those to the ports of Murmansk and Archangel on the northwestern coast of the Soviet Union. Although the British and Americans had learned how to organize convoys with destroyer escorts and had acquired new methods of detecting and destroying submarines, many hundreds of Allied merchant ships were sunk, many thousands of lives were lost, and the U-boat threat remained throughout 1942. Among the various technologies the Allies employed during 1942 were improved radar and sonar, high-frequency direction finding (for reading German radio traffic), blimps, and depth charges (see Military Innovations, Tactics, Equipment p. 500). In September, the Allies established the first support groups, specially trained groups of escort vessels to assist convoys under attack and stayed on the scene to track down U-boats.

The sea war in the Mediterranean raged throughout 1942, as the Italian and German navies—supported by the German air force—fought to keep British and, occasionally, U.S. ships from supplying their armed forces and civilian outposts, particularly those in Malta. British losses in support of Malta were punishing, and at times, the situation on the island was desperate. The Axis powers were determined to keep the sea routes to their forces in Africa open, and they generally succeeded until September, by which time the British naval and air forces began to crack down on Axis shipping.

In the Pacific, the Japanese navy began 1942 with considerable numerical advantage over the American and British navies, and for several months, Allied losses of warships and merchant vessels were heavy. One advantage the British had, however, was that they had radar-equipped planes. Soon, modern naval battles depended on aircraft as much as on ships, and with the Battle of Midway in June, the Allies began to gain the advantage.

January 13–July 19, 1942: In a maneuver code-named *Paukenschlag* (or "Drum Roll"), German U-boats began to operate along the east coast of North America. At first, the U.S. Navy and merchant marine were unprepared and failed to take even the most basic precautions; lights were left on and radio messages were not coded. Gradually, U.S. ships began to adopt the protective measures urged on them by their more experienced British allies. By July 19, the last two German U-boats were assigned elsewhere because of the improved convoy defensive system. German U-boats remained in the Caribbean and off South America for several months.

February 27–March 1, 1942 (Battle of the Java Sea): An Allied squadron of 5 cruisers and 11 destroyers tried to stop a Japanese fleet bound for Java. In the battle, the Allies lost ten ships.

March 1942: With 80 U-boats assigned to the Atlantic, the Germans enjoyed great success against Allied shipping. The Germans sent out their first *Milch Kuh* ("milk cow"), a submarine tanker that provided fuel and supplies to cruising submarines, thus greatly extending the U-boats, distances and time they could stay at sea.

April 1–10, 1942: In the Indian Ocean, Japanese warships and planes from aircraft carriers attacked and sank a number of British warships and merchant ships (including the British carrier HMS *Hermes*). On April 10, the British chose to withdraw their fleet from Ceylon and send it to the Persian Gulf.

April 20, 1942: The U.S. carrier *Wasp* made its first run to Malta to carry much-needed Spitfire fighter planes to the beleaguered island.

May 2–8, 1942: The Japanese had concentrated a large fleet in the Coral Sea, south of the Solomon islands and southeast of New Guinea, to prepare for an amphibious landing on the southeastern coast of New Guinea to take Port Moresby. But the Americans had broken the Japanese codes and by May 2 also were moving naval forces into the area. On May 3–4, aircraft from the USS *Yorktown* attacked the Japanese forces; the next engagement did not take place until May 7. The major battle was fought on May 8. The fighting was often chaotic, with American planes dropping bombs on their own

fleet and Japanese planes trying to land on American carriers. The USS *Lexington* was so badly damaged, it was abandoned and then sunk by an American destroyer. The *Yorktown* also was heavily damaged. The Japanese lost only one small carrier, but they lost so many of their aircraft that they abandoned their planned invasion. That was the first major naval battle in history fought without visual contact between the main units of the opposing forces.

May 25–June 2, 1942: Two Japanese light carriers and two cruisers left port to carry out diversionary raids in the Aleutian Islands. The raids were meant to draw U.S. forces away from the main Japanese fleet, which was heading for Midway Island some 1,300 miles northwest of Hawaii, where the U.S. Navy maintained a valuable base and radio signal station. The Japanese intended to capture Midway to use as a base to wipe out the U.S. Navy in the Pacific. During the next few days, a Japanese carrier fleet and invasion force set out for Midway, believing that the U.S. Navy did not have enough ships to engage them. But, U.S. intelligence was able to read the Japanese naval codes, and three U.S. carriers (*Yorktown*, *Enterprise*, and *Hornet*), with 250 planes and many other U.S. warships—among them were 25 submarines—moved toward Midway. By June 2, that large naval force was in position northeast of Midway Island.

June 3–6, 1942: On June 3, U.S. bombers from Midway attacked some Japanese ships with little effect. On June 4, the battle was fully joined, with the Japanese bombing the American defenders on Midway and American planes attacking Japanese carriers. In a second wave of attacks, U.S. dive-bombers hit three Japanese carriers packed with bombs and airplanes preparing to take off. However, planes from a fourth Japanese carrier were able to critically damage the USS *Yorktown*. Later that afternoon, planes from the *Enterprise* and *Hornet* damaged that fourth Japanese carrier. Within 24 hours, all four Japanese carriers were sunk or were scuttled. A Japanese submarine sank the *Yorktown* on June 7. That, the Battle of Midway, turned out to be one of the most crucial of the war, as it cost the Japanese so many of their carriers, planes, and trained pilots. From that point on, the initiative in the Pacific shifted to the Allies.

July 9, 1942: Ships from the convoy designated PQ-17 began to straggle into Soviet ports.

That was one of the more disastrous convoy runs of the war; 24 ships were lost to German submarines and warships. Those ships carried 3,350 vehicles, 430 tanks, 210 aircraft, and 96,000 tons of other equipment. The Germans lost only five airplanes.

September 14, 1942: A Japanese submarine sank the U.S. carrier *Wasp* in an engagement that also saw an American destroyer sunk and the battleship *North Carolina* damaged.

September 24, 1942: The Liberty ship *Stephen Hopkins*, armed with only one 4-inch gun, fought the more powerful German raider *Stier*. Both ships sank.

October 7–November 13, 1942: A group of four German U-boats operating off the coast of South Africa sank 170,000 tons of Allied shipping, demonstrating just how widely spread the naval war had become.

December 30–31, 1942: A small fleet of heavy German warships set off from Norway to attack a large Allied convoy in the Barents Sea (part of the Arctic Ocean off Spitsbergen Island) north of the Soviet mainland. The convoy was well protected by British warships, and in the ensuing battle, a British destroyer was sunk and the large German force lost a heavy cruiser and a destroyer.

HOME FRONT

January 14, 1942: President Roosevelt ordered all aliens in the U.S. to register with the government. Although that was aimed at Germans, Italians, and Japanese, the effects of the action were felt solely by the Japanese. Already some in the government were planning to move American-born Japanese (known as *nisei*) to internment camps.

January 26, 1942: The Board of Inquiry, established to investigate the U.S. military's performance at Pearl Harbor, published its findings. It found Adm. Husband Kimmel (then commander of the U.S. Pacific Fleet) and Gen. Walter Short (then commander of the Hawaiian Department) guilty of dereliction of duty. Both already had been dismissed from their posts; both retired shortly after the inquiry.

January 28, 1942: The Office of Civil Defense was established. It was charged to coordinate various tasks that civilians would take on, such as enforcing blackouts, manning plane-spotting stations, and preparing for air raids.

February 9, 1942: To save electricity, clocks were turned ahead one hour to Daylight Saving Time all across the United States. The United States remained on that plan throughout the war.

The French liner *Normandie* burned and capsized at a dock in New York harbor, where it was undergoing conversion to a troop ship. Although sabotage was suspected, it was determined that careless workmen had caused the fire.

February 20, 1942: Roosevelt formally authorized the removal of Japanese Americans from their homes and lands in the Pacific Coast states and Arizona to internment camps in Colorado, Utah, Arkansas, and a few other inland locales. The actual relocation of some 110,000 Japanese Americans and Japanese aliens began in March. The reason given for the interment was that they might provide aid to the enemy. That episode was one of the more shameful in American history, yet at the time, few Americans protested. Japanese Americans and Japanese aliens had never shown signs of disloyalty, and, in fact, thousands of young Japanese Americans (including many in Hawaii) volunteered to join the Army. Usually assigned to segregated units, they fought with great distinction in the campaigns through Italy and France.

February 23, 1942: A Japanese submarine shelled an oil refinery near Santa Barbara, California—the first of a few incidents during World War II when the continental United States was attacked by the Axis. (The Oregon coast was shelled on June 21.)

April 8, 1942: The War Production Board stopped all production not essential to the war.

April 28, 1942: Along a 1500-mile zone down the entire Atlantic coast, a blackout or dimout went into effect each night to deny aid to Axis submarines, ships, or planes approaching American shores.

May 15, 1942: Gasoline rationing was introduced in 17 states, with a weekly ration of three gallons for nonessential vehicles. On December 1, it was extended to all states.

Roosevelt signed the act establishing the Women's Army Auxiliary Corps (WAAC)—later the Women's Army Corps (WAC). On July 30, Congress established the women's naval reserves, known as the WAVES.

June 13–17, 1942: Eight Germans landed from submarines off the coasts of Long Island, New

York, and Florida. They were all quickly apprehended, and after a trial by a military tribunal, six were executed and two were imprisoned.

September 17, 1942: All atomic research in the United States was placed under military control, with Gen. Leslie Groves directing the program, code-named the Manhattan Project.

November 1, 1942: President Roosevelt, under the Stabilization of the Cost of Living Act passed by Congress on October 2, assumed the power to control wages, salaries, and agricultural prices.

November 12, 1942: The draft age for American males was reduced from 21 to 18.

November 21, 1942: The Alcan International Highway, a 1,523-mile road from Alberta, Canada, to Alaska, opened. It played a role in supplying the U.S. forces that eventually recaptured the Aleutian Islands seized by the Japanese.

December 2, 1942: The first human-made, self-sustaining chain reaction was achieved at an atomic "pile" of uranium at the University of Chicago. It was primarily the work of Enrico Fermi. That achievement encouraged those with the Manhattan Project to race ahead to make an atomic weapon.

INTERNATIONAL DEVELOPMENTS

January 1, 1942: Representatives of 26 Allied countries met in Washington, D.C., to endorse the principles of the Atlantic Charter (see International Developments, August 9–12, 1941, p. 446). That is sometimes regarded by some historians as the first step toward establishing the United Nations.

January 13, 1942: Allied representatives meeting in London announced that Axis war criminals would be punished after the war.

January 20, 1942: At a conference held at Wannsee, on the edge of Berlin, Reinhard Heydrich, the Nazi governor of Czechoslovakia, presented to Hitler and other Nazi leaders a plan titled "Final Solution of the Jewish Problem." It called for the transportation of all Europe's Jews to concentration camps. Hitler approved, and the SS was delegated to oversee the project. Adolph Eichmann was placed in charge of the operation.

February 6, 1942: The first meeting of the Combined Chiefs of Staff took place in Washington, D.C. (That was called for by the Arcadia Conference that opened on December 22, 1941.)

February 16, 1942: General Tojo outlined Japan's goals to the Japanese Diet, or parliament, in which he referred to a "new order of coexistence and co-prosperity on ethical principles in Greater East Asia."

March 1942: Large-scale transportation of Jews to Nazi concentration camps began. The most notorious of those camps was Auschwitz in Poland. Polish Jews were the main victims in the first months.

April 14, 1942: Pierre Laval formed a new pro-German government in Vichy, France. Marshal Pétain remained as the figurehead president.

May 27–June 9, 1942: On May 27, Czech resistance fighters shot Reinhard Heydrich; he died of his wounds on June 4. On June 9, SS troops moved on the Czech village of Lidice and obliterated it, killing all its residents. (On June 24, another village, Levzasky, also was destroyed; altogether 1,000 Czechs were killed in reprisal.)

June 18, 1942: Churchill arrived in Washington, D.C., for talks with American leaders about plans for a second front (to aid the Soviets on the first front). They agreed that there could be no invasion of France in 1942 but discussed an invasion of North Africa. They also discussed work on atomic weapons, and Roosevelt agreed that Americans should share their findings with the British. However, Americans working on the project were not forthcoming, and on December 28, President Roosevelt, on the urging of certain advisers, ordered that no information about atomic research be given to the British unless it affected an area in which British scientists were directly involved. The British were unhappy with that decision.

July 2, 1942: Prime Minister Winston Churchill defeated a motion of censure in Parliament on his direction of the war by a vote of 476 to 25; the main criticism was that he had taken on too much by trying to run both the war and the civilian government.

July 29, 1942: The combined British and American Production and Resources Board was established in London to oversee allocations of materials and industrial priorities.

August 12–15, 1942: Churchill and U.S. representative W. Averell Harriman visited Moscow to explain to Stalin why there could be no second front in 1942.

October 6, 1942: An expanded Lend-Lease agreement was signed in Washington, under which the United States agreed to provide 4.4 million tons of supplies to the Soviet Union during the following ten months.

October 7, 1942: President Roosevelt would announce a plan to set up a United Nations Commission for the Investigation of War Crimes after the war. The intent was to let the Axis know that certain actions would not be excused as conventional acts of war.

BATTLES AND CAMPAIGN: 1943

There were several areas of military activity in the fourth full year of World War II: European theater, Mediterranean/African theater, Asian theater, and naval theater.

EUROPEAN THEATER

January–December 1943: The British and American air forces increased their attacks, dropping many thousands of tons of bombs on targets in Germany and German-held sites throughout Europe. U-boat facilities in France and elsewhere along the Atlantic coast held an especially high priority, along with the great industrial centers in Germany's Ruhr region. With each passing month, the Allies added to the numbers of bombers available and the numbers of sorties flown; they also benefited from increasingly sophisticated navigational aids. However, the Germans were able to repair most of their industrial plants after the bombing raids.

January 3–March 26, 1943: The Soviets intensified their offensive in the Caucasus, retaking one city and town after another. However, Gen. Fritz Erich von Manstein counterattacked and, on March 2, recaptured Kharkov. Within a few weeks, the onset of the spring thaw forced both sides to halt their activities.

January 8–February 2, 1943: On January 8, the Soviets called on the Germans besieged in Stalingrad to surrender, but Gen. Friedrich von Paulus refused to do so. On January 10, the Soviets went on the offensive against Stalingrad. On January 21, the last of the airports held by the Germans fell to the Soviets, and the Germans were completely cut off from supplies. On January 24, General Manstein asked Hitler's permission to order Paulus to surrender, but Hitler refused. On January 25, Soviet forces attacking from several directions met in the center of Stalingrad. On

January 31, Paulus surrendered the German forces in the southern area, and on February 2, the last German troops in Stalingrad surrendered. Altogether, some 90,000 Germans were taken prisoner (of whom only some 5,000 lived to return to Germany); 147,000 Germans died during the entire battle; the Luftwaffe lost some 500 transport planes and massive amounts of other equipment.

January 11–27, 1943: On January 11, the Soviets opened a narrow corridor into Leningrad, but it was so exposed to German firepower that it was known as the "corridor of death." After a week, the Soviets secured the corridor, and by January 27, Leningrad was finally free of the siege that had begun on September 15, 1941. Hundreds of thousands of Soviets had died of starvation and other causes directly attributed to the siege.

January 27, 1943: The U. S. Army Air Force made its first air raid in Germany, bombing the city of Wilhelmshaven. The success of that raid encouraged the Americans to believe that their Flying Fortress and Liberator aircraft were able to defend themselves in unescorted daylight raids and that they could hit specific targets with some accuracy. Those beliefs were questioned in the months to follow.

February 17–March 18, 1943: On February 17, Hitler visited General Manstein's headquarters in the southeast Ukraine and approved plans for a counteroffensive, which was launched on February 22 in several sectors, including the Caucasus. Although outnumbered, the Germans were successful in driving the Soviets back on several fronts. After March 18, however, the German advances began to halt because the spring thaw prevented movement, and the Germans had lost 1 million men in the Soviet Union during the previous four months. Both sides remained relatively inactive for the following four months as they built up their forces.

February 28, 1943: A team of Norwegian soldiers parachuted into the Norsk Hydro power station near Ryukan, Norway, and damaged the facility, which Allied intelligence had learned was being used by Germans to produce heavy water for atomic research.

May 16–17, 1943: During the night, a special RAF squadron of 19 planes attacked the dams believed to produce much of the electricity supply to the Ruhr. Eight of the 19 planes were lost, and the dams were quickly repaired.

May 27, 1943: Marshall Tito's partisans in Yugoslavia resisted one of the most serious of several attacks from the Germans, Italians, and Bulgarians. Previously, the British had supported the Cetniks, led by Draza Mihailovic, but there were increasing reports that the Cetniks were cooperating with the Germans. British officers parachuted into Yugoslavia to rendezvous with Tito, shifting Allied support to his partisans.

June 10, 1943: The Joint Chiefs of Staff issued the Pointblank Directive to the commanders of the British and American heavy bomber forces in Europe. While setting forth aims and priorities, it essentially allowed the British and Americans to follow separate strategies: The British would continue their area bombing at night, and the Americans would continue to conduct pinpoint bombing during the day. Neither approach produced the results their advocates promised.

July 5–23, 1943: Since March, the Soviets had occupied a salient, or pocket, that included the city of Kursk. Based on intelligence that the Germans were planning an offensive against that salient, the Soviets built up in-depth lines of defense. By early July, some 2 million men, 6,000 tanks, and 5,000 aircraft had been brought up to confront each other. The Germans began their attack on July 5, with tank units moving from both the north and south, trying to pinch off the salient. However, the Soviets had more and better tanks than in previous battles, and their air force was also much improved. The Germans experienced problems with their new Panther tanks and large Elefant assault guns. What was the largest tank battle in history raged near Prokhorovka south of Kursk for six days until it ended in a stalemate, with both sides having lost hundreds of tanks. The battle around the Kursk salient continued for another ten days, but by July 23, most of the German forces were back in their original positions. Although Soviet losses were greater than German losses, from that point on the Soviets held the strategic advantage over the Germans. A Soviet offensive to the north of Kursk and the Germans' need to shift tanks and personnel to Italy allowed the Soviets to start a counteroffensive along the entire eastern front.

July 24–August 3, 1943: The RAF, aided by some U.S. Air Force sorties, made four major night raids on Hamburg, Germany, killing some 50,000 civilians and leaving another 800,000 homeless.

The attack on the night of July 27–28 dropped so many incendiary bombs that for the first time in warfare a firestorm was raised (see Military Innovations, Tactics, Equipment, p. 498). And during those raids, the RAF for the first time used *windows*—strips of metal foil dropped from aircraft to confuse the German radar by producing false echoes.

August 2–23, 1943: The Soviets began their counteroffensive on the Germans around the Kursk salient, driving the Germans northwest and southwest. By August 23, the Soviets had retaken Kharkov from the Caucasus and Crimea to the border of Finland. The Germans were in retreat along the entire eastern front from August onward.

October 14, 1943: The ball-bearing works at Schweinfurt, Germany, was attacked by 291 Flying Fortresses (a follow-up to a similar raid on August 17). Although some damage was done, 60 planes were lost and 140 damaged—most of the planes were lost on the stretch between Aachen and the target, when the bombers were beyond the range of fighter escorts. The losses were so drastic that the U.S. Air Force abandoned its long-range, unescorted daylight attacks for some time.

November 6, 1943: The Soviets retook Kiev, at that time the third largest city in the USSR. Stalin made a special radio broadcast to observe the achievement. Almost all German forces escaped, however, and the very next day, the Soviets took up their pursuit along the entire front. During the rest of 1943, with occasional and temporary setbacks in some sectors, the Soviet forces continued to push the Germans back.

MEDITERRANEAN/AFRICAN THEATER

January 15–23, 1943: Field Marshal Bernard Montgomery took the offensive against the Germans on the Libyan coast; by January 22, the Germans had withdrawn from Tripoli after destroying its port facilities. The British 8th Army entered Tripoli early on January 23, and by February 1, they had the port in operation again, and the first British units crossed into Tunisia.

February–December 1943: In February, Allied bombers based around the Mediterranean began to raid Italian cities and military installations; the raids intensified as the months passed. With the ejection of the Axis from North Africa, the Axis attacks on Malta finally ended. By mid-1943, the Axis threat in the Mediterranean was virtually eliminated, although the Germans mounted various attacks on shipping and occupied certain Greek islands that had been occupied by the Italians. On November 26, a German glider bomb sank a British troop transport off Algeria, with the loss of more than 1,000 men.

February 14–25, 1943: Although the Germans and Italians in Tunisia to the east were in retreat, the Germans facing the advancing Allies from Algeria in the west were enjoying some success. The American forces were inexperienced, and an attack on February 14 by the Germans, barreling through Tunisia's Kasserine Pass with their powerful Tiger tanks armed with 88mm cannon, cost the Americans more than 100 tanks and some 5,270 casualties. The Americans fell back 50 miles over several days, and on February 22, the Germans were only 12 miles from the Allied supply depots at Tebessa, Algeria. But by February 25, the Allies had regrouped and stopped the Axis. A major result of that disaster was a change in the American command, with Gen. George Patton taking over in North Africa.

March 6–29, 1943: On March 6, the Germans and Italians mounted a major attack against the British and New Zealanders facing them along the Mareth Line in eastern Tunisia, but the New Zealanders began a major counterattack on March 20, and by March 28, the Germans and Italians had retreated to Wadi Akarit. Field Marshall Rommel left Africa on March 9, never to return; he tried to persuade Mussolini and Hitler to withdraw their forces from North Africa while there was still time, but both leaders rejected his advice.

April 5–14, 1943: Montgomery began a new attack on the Axis at Wadi Akarit, while at the same time, Patton's forces were pressuring the Axis from the west. By April 14, the Axis had fallen back to the ring of hills around Bizerta and Tunis, their final defensive position against the approaching Allied forces.

April 22–May 13, 1943: The Allies began their main attack against the Axis line in Tunisia on April 22. The Germans were trying to resupply their forces, but many of their transport planes were shot down. Hill by hill, the American and British forces pushed back the Germans until, on May 7, they made a sudden breakthrough and took both Bizerta and Tunis. Axis forces began to surrender in large numbers by May 10; the formal surrender took place on May 13. Some 250,000 Axis troops were taken prisoner in the final days. The defense of North Africa had cost the Axis powers hundreds of thousands of troops and vast numbers of tanks and other equipment.

April 30, 1943: As part of an elaborate plan (code-named Operation Mincemeat) to deceive the Axis, a British submarine off Spain released the corpse of a Englishman wearing the uniform of a British major and carrying what appear to be letters from the Allied high command to commanders in the Mediterranean describing plans for an invasion of Greece—code-named Operation Husky. (In reality, Operation Husky was the planned invasion of Sicily.) As intended, the body washed ashore, and the letters were found and sent to the German high command. As a result, the Germans reinforced their units in Greece and remained uncertain about the true objective of Operation Husky.

June 11–14, 1943: Four small Italian islands off Sicily—Pantelleria, Lampedusa, Linosa, Lampione—were captured by the Allies.

July 9–10, 1943: On the night of July 9, American and British paratroopers and gliderborne troops descended on the southern coast of Sicily. Because of strong winds, the landings were scattered, and many of the gliders came down in the sea. But at dawn on July 10, thousands of American and British troops came ashore and, meeting little resistance from demoralized Italian troops, soon captured several southern Sicilian cities.

July 11–22, 1943: Within the first three days, the Allies had 150,000 troops ashore in Sicily, backed up by increasing numbers of tanks and artillery pieces. The Germans, however, moved troops into position to challenge the Allies along their front in Sicily and stopped the British on their advance up the southeastern coast. American and Canadian forces, however, moved swiftly into the northwest and central parts of the island, and on June 22, the Americans—under the command of Gen. George Patton—entered Palermo, the island's capital.

July 19, 1943: Some 500 U.S. bombers raided selected targets in and around Rome; special care was taken to avoid all structures with historical, religious, or artistic significance. (Only one church near a railroad yard was damaged.) The intention was to show the Italian people that they should give up—before more serious bombing raids were conducted.

July 23–August 17, 1943: The Americans chased the retreating Axis forces along the north coast of Sicily, launching several amphibious landings in an attempt to cut off the Germans. Although the Germans eluded those efforts, the Americans continued to advance quickly. Meanwhile, the British—commanded by Field Marshal Bernard Montgomery—moved up Sicily's east coast against resistance. The goal of both armies was to trap the Axis forces in the northeast corner—near the main city of Messina—before they could escape to the Italian mainland. Montgomery understood the British would be allowed to enter Messina first; instead, Patton's troops entered Messina a few hours ahead of the British. Although more than 100,000 Italian troops were taken prisoner, the Axis had managed to ferry 100,000 troops, along with many tanks and guns, over to the mainland.

September 3, 1943: Field Marshal Montgomery's 8th Army landed on the Italian coast opposite Messina and met virtually no resistance. That was by arrangement with the Italian forces who had arranged to secretly surrender to the Allies; in the hope of forestalling the Germans' reaction to the surrender, it was not announced until September 8.

September 8, 1943: The Italian surrender was publicly announced. By arrangement with the Allies, many of the remaining ships of the Italian navy left their ports in Italy to surrender to the Allies. The Germans then became the enemy and occupiers of Italy.

September 9, 1943: While the British continued their advance up the "toe" of Italy, the Allies launched an amphibious invasion at Salerno on the coast just south of Naples—with a supporting invasion at Taranto on the "heel" of Italy. The latter operation succeeded quite easily, but the landings at Salerno met heavy resistance from the Germans. The Germans sank one of the Italian battleships trying to flee to Malta. In Rome, the Italian government fled from the Germans.

September 10–17, 1943: The British forces on Italy's heel continued to advance, but the Germans mounted such stiff resistance to the Americans and British outside Salerno that by September 13 some American units were considering evacuation. Air support and bombardments from offshore ships as well as airborne reinforce-

ments saved the Allied forces, and by September 17, the Allies began to advance beyond their beachheads.

September 10–November 20, 1943: With the Italian surrender, the Allies and Germans raced to take control of the Dodecanese (held by the Italians since the end of World War I) and other Greek islands in the eastern Aegean. The British and Germans both rushed in troops, but the Germans were able to drive the British from most of the islands.

September 13–22, 1943: German troops moved onto the Greek Ionian island of Cephalonia off the northwest coast of Greece and seized it from its Italian occupiers. The Italians resisted but, after losing 1,500 men, surrendered. The Germans then massacred some 5,000 Italian troops and deported the rest to labor camps.

September 16–October 1, 1943: The Allies moved against the Germans in several sectors in southern Italy. Patrols from Montgomery's force coming from the south made contact on September 16 with forward units of the Salerno force. By September 25, the combined armies established a front across Italy south of Naples. On October 1, Naples fell to the Allies.

October 12–December 31, 1943: On October 12, the Germans withdrew in the face of the advancing Allies but established a defensive line (the so-called Volturno Line, named after the river that marked the boundary) across Italy north of Naples. On the night of October 12, the Allies mounted a major offense against that German line. During the first few weeks, the Allies slowly drove the Germans northward, but by mid-November the advance had stalled. On November 28, a new offensive was launched. New Zealanders, Canadians, and French-Moroccan units fought with the Americans and British. Although the Allies made some gains, 1943 ended with the Allied forces bogged down and facing stiff German resistance.

ASIAN THEATER

January 1–December 31, 1943: On New Guinea, the Americans and Australians continued to advance against the Japanese. By January 22, the last Japanese left Papua, the southeastern end of the island. The Japanese lost some 7,000 dead in that campaign, and the Allies about 3,500 dead. But throughout 1943, the fighting continued to rage elsewhere on New Guinea, and the Japanese made air attacks against the Allied forces on and around the island.

January 2–February 9, 1943: On Guadalcanal, American forces continued their attacks on the Japanese defending Mount Austen. The Japanese, unable to hold out much longer against the increasingly superior American forces, began to withdraw on January 20. The Japanese completed the evacuation of their forces on February 9. Guadalcanal was an American victory—with the Japanese losing some 10,000 dead to the Americans' 1,600—but the intensity of the Japanese resistance foreshadowed what awaited the Allies across the Pacific.

April 18, 1943: Using flight plans gleaned from decoded secret Japanese messages, U.S. fighters shot down a plane carrying Adm. Isoroku Yamamoto, commander of the Japanese fleet and chief planner of the attack on Pearl Harbor, over the island of Bougainville north of Guadalcanal. In order not to reveal that they had broken the Japanese code, the Allies pretended not to know who was in the plane, allowing the Japanese to announce his loss in May.

May 11–30, 1943: U.S. forces landed on Attu Island in the Aleutians. The Japanese put up stiff resistance but were defeated by May 30. Hundreds of Americans became very ill, and some died, from the extreme cold during that campaign.

June 30–August 25, 1943: U.S. forces landed on several islands in the New Georgia group of the Solomon Islands north of Guadalcanal. On July 25, they invaded New Georgia, and by August 25, the Japanese abandoned New Georgia. In the following weeks, the Allies continued to push the Japanese off several of the smaller Solomon Islands.

August 15, 1943: After some weeks of bombarding Kiska Island in the Aleutians, U.S. and Canadian troops went ashore. What they did not know was that the Japanese had evacuated most of their forces at the end of July. However, in the invasion, the United States lost a destroyer and 75 men to a Japanese mine offshore, and 21 ground troops were killed by friendly fire.

November 1–December 31, 1943: U.S. forces landed on Bougainville, the largest of the Solomon Islands; by the end of the first day, some 14,000 men were ashore. In the days that followed, there were major battles involving air and naval forces around Bougainville. Simulta-

neously, the Americans carried out fierce air and naval attacks on the adjacent island of New Britain, with heavy losses on both sides. The fighting raged through the end of 1943.

November 20–23, 1943: U.S. marines landed on Tarawa Island and Makin Island in the Gilbert Islands in the central Pacific. Although the landings had been preceded by heavy bombardment, the Japanese were able to maintain a murderous crossfire as the marines went ashore: Of the first 5,000 marines to go ashore at Tarawa, some 1,500 were casualties. By November 23, though, the Japanese on Tarawa and Makin were wiped-out. The U.S. casualties—1,100 killed, 2,100 wounded—made that operation the most costly operation in U.S. military history in proportion to the forces engaged.

December 26–31, 1943: After a diversionary invasion of the offshore island of Arawe, U.S. marines landed on New Britain, the island off New Guinea's northeast coast. With a relatively easy operation, the Allies ended 1943 in possession of the Japanese airfield at Cape Gloucester on New Britain.

NAVAL THEATER

January 1–December 31, 1943: In the Battle of the Atlantic, the German U-boat fleet continued to take a heavy toll on Allied shipping. The month of March 1943, with 72 ships in North Atlantic convoys lost to U-boats, was one of the most disastrous for the Allies. But the British and Americans began to improve their convoy support by using escort carriers and air operations to close the air-cover gap in the mid-Atlantic, where most of the sinkings occurred. The result was that by late May, losses of U-boats were becoming so high that Adm. Karl Dönitz, commander of the German navy, called off the attacks on the Allied convoys in the North Atlantic. Most of the U-boats were reassigned to the Bay of Biscay (on the French Atlantic coast), to around the Azores and the waters off West Africa, and to the Caribbean and the waters off South America. In September, Dönitz reassigned some U-boats equipped with more advanced technology—radar, acoustic homing torpedoes, antiaircraft guns—to the Allies' North Atlantic convoy routes. But even these U-boats could not regain the upper hand over the convoys; in November and December, 78 convoys crossed the

U.S. Coastguardsmen on the cutter Spencer, *protecting a convoy in the Atlantic, watch the explosion of a depth charge that blasted and sank a German U-boat on April 17, 1943.*

North Atlantic without losing a ship. Meanwhile, the German tanker fleet that supplied and refueled the U-boats was also being decimated.

In the Pacific, the Allied fleets—particularly the U.S. Navy—were continually involved in support of ground operations. There were heavy losses of ships and personnel in such operations as bombarding islands, escorting invasion forces, and providing planes to attack land facilities. In one minor operation, the invasion of Makin Island in the Gilbert Islands, the escort carrier USS *Liscombe Bay* was sunk (November 23), with the loss of more than 600 men. There were few outright naval battles in the traditional sense. And U.S. submarines were taking an increasingly heavy toll of Japanese shipping.

March 2–4, 1943: In the battle of the Bismarck Sea off the coast of New Guinea, a Japanese convoy transporting reinforcements to New Guinea was attacked by Allied planes and PT boats: Eight Japanese transports and four destroyers were sunk, with the loss of 3,500 Japanese. The Japanese also lost 25 planes (to the Allies' five). That was a major setback to Japanese plans for New Guinea.

August 2, 1943: Shortly after midnight, U.S. PT boats attacked Japanese destroyers off the Solomon Islands. One of the PT boats, PT-109, was rammed and cut in two; 11 of its crew survived, and after several days of a grueling ordeal, were rescued. Their commander, who took the lead in managing their survival, was a young Navy lieutenant and future president of the United States, John F. Kennedy.

September 6–December 26, 1943: The German battleships *Tirpitz* and *Scharnhorst* bombarded the island of Spitsbergen on September 6–9. On September 22, British midget submarines attacked the *Tirpitz* in its port and put it out of action until March 1944. On December 26, the *Scharnhorst* was out in the Arctic Ocean searching for British and American convoys when it ran into a British covering force of three cruisers. The ships began to battle, then the *Scharnhorst* broke off and began to sail back to Norway. The British battleship *Duke of York* unexpectedly came up opposite the *Scharnhorst* and a terrific duel began. The *Scharnhorst* was soon destroyed by the bombardment and torpedoes and sank; only 36 of the crew of 2,000 were saved.

HOME FRONT

February 7, 1943: Shoe rationing began throughout the United States; each civilian was limited to three pairs of leather shoes annually.

March 6, 1943: President Roosevelt appointed a committee to look into the manpower problems threatening the U.S. war industry.

April 8, 1943: To combat inflation, Roosevelt issued an order forbidding certain wage and price increases. He also ordered workers in certain industries not to change jobs unless the job change would benefit the war effort.

May 27, 1943: Roosevelt established the Office of War Mobilization to coordinate the nation's war efforts. He also ordered that all government contracts with war industries forbid racial discrimination.

June 1–June 7, 1943: More than 500,000 coal workers went on strike. Most returned to work on June 7, when talks resumed. (Another strike began on June 21, but most returned to work by early July.)

June 20–22, 1943: In Detroit, Michigan, white people, protesting the employment of African Americans in decent paying jobs, clashed with African Americans; by the time federal troops put down the riot, 34 people were dead.

August 14, 1943: New regulations for the draft came into force: The list of essential occupations was revised, and dependents became crucial in any deferments. (On December 10, Roosevelt signed a further revision that specified that men who were fathers before Pearl Harbor would be the last to be drafted.)

September 21–November 5, 1943: On September 21, the House of Representatives passed the Fulbright Concurrent Resolution; it called for participation in a world organization to support peace. On November 5, the Senate passed the Connolly Resolution supporting the same goal.

October 28–November 1, 1943: On October 28, another strike by coal miners began to gain momentum, and within a few days, some 530,000 miners were out on strike. On November 1, Roosevelt ordered Harold Ickes and the Solid Fuels Administration to take over the operation of the country's coal mines.

INTERNATIONAL DEVELOPMENTS

January 14–24, 1943: Franklin Roosevelt and Winston Churchill met at Casablanca, Morocco, with their top military advisers. Tension over priorities had been growing: The Americans felt the British weren't pulling their weight in the Pacific, and the British complained that the Americans weren't committing their full energies to defeating the Germans in Europe. The differences were worked out and priorities agreed on. On January 24, at a press conference at the conclusion of the meetings, President Roosevelt stated that the Allied leaders were "determined to accept nothing less than the unconditional surrender of Germany, Japan, and Italy." Churchill endorsed that position.

April 12, 1943: The Germans announced that they had discovered mass graves in the Katyn Forest in the Soviet Union (northwest of Smolensk); eventually, some 4,100 bodies were counted, most of them Polish army officers. After accusations on both sides, it has been determined that the bodies were those of people killed by the Soviets in 1939 when the Soviet Union turned on Poland.

April 19–May 16, 1943: The Jewish population in the Warsaw ghetto rose up against the Germans. Originally some 500,000 Jews were forced into the ghetto; as a result of the "final solution," only about 60,000 were left. On April 24, the Germans began their all-out attack on the Jews in the Warsaw ghetto, moving from street to street blowing up every building. Many Jews took to the sewers to carry on the fight. Some escaped to the Christian sections of the city (but most were later apprehended). In the final act, the Germans blew up the synagogue. The Jews killed some 300 Germans, but virtually all 60,000 Jews eventually were killed.

May 12–25, 1943: Winston Churchill met with President Roosevelt in Washington, D.C., for what was known as the Trident Conference. Some of the same strategic disagreements discussed at Casablanca in January resurfaced, but compromises were reached. In particular, the Americans persuaded the British to schedule an invasion of the French coast across the English Channel for 1944.

May 18–June 3, 1943: A United Nations Food Conference was held at Hot Springs, Virginia; the conference concluded with a resolution calling for fairer distribution of resources in the postwar world.

June 3–22, 1943: At a meeting in Algiers,

Gen. Charles deGaulle and Gen. Henri Giraud agreed to share the joint presidency of the Committee of National Liberation—an umbrella organization of the various French resistance and Free French groups. On June 22, the generals agreed that Giraud would retain command of the French forces in North Africa and DeGaulle would lead all other French forces. That was a crucial step in deGaulle's effectively taking control of the entire Free French movement and forced the Allied leaders to deal with him.

July 16, 1943: Roosevelt and Churchill issued a joint statement calling on the Italian people to overthrow Mussolini and surrender. In fact, some Italian leaders were already planning a coup.

July 20, 1943: Roosevelt issued an order that the United States atomic research program share its information with Great Britain; that order was formalized at the Quebec Conference in August 1943. That was a return to the original cooperation that Americans had ceased to extend in late December 1942.

July 24–26, 1943: On July 24, two days after the fall of Palermo, Sicily, to the Allies, the Fascist Grand Council in Rome called on King Victor Emmanuel to take over the government. On July 25, the king summoned Mussolini and dismissed him. Mussolini was arrested as he left the meeting. On July 26, Marshal Pietro Badoglio assumed control of the Italian government.

August 13–24, 1943: Roosevelt and Churchill joined the British and American military leaders meeting at Quebec City, Canada, to decide on various policies, strategies, and command plans for forthcoming military operations. Churchill agreed that the supreme commander of the invasion would be an American.

August 26–27, 1943: The Allied leaders gave conditional recognition to the French Committee of National Liberation, further consolidating deGaulle's power.

August 28–29, 1943: Denmark had been under German occupation since April 1940, but its government had managed to maintain a certain independence. On August 28, Denmark's government rejected a German ultimatum to resign. The German commander took over and, on August 29, declared martial law.

September 3–8, 1943: On September 3, the Italian military signed a surrender document in Sicily, but no public announcement was made until September 8. The Allies and the Italians agreed that the formal armistice agreement would be signed on September 29 by General Dwight D. Eisenhower and Marshal Pietro Badoglio.

September 12–23, 1943: Mussolini was being held at an isolated hotel in the Abruzzi Mountains. In a rescue operation code-named Operation Oak, Capt. Otto Skorzeny, a German commando, led a force of 90 soldiers in gliders and a small plane that landed on the edge of the mountain and seized Mussolini. After first being flown to Vienna, Mussolini was then flown to Hitler's headquarters at Rastenburg in East Prussia. On September 15, Mussolini proclaimed that he was resuming power; on September 23, he proclaimed the formation of the Italian Social Republic, with its headquarters in northern Italy, but he ceded real control to the Germans.

October 13, 1943: Italy, led by Marshal Badoglio, declared war on Germany.

November 22–25, 1943: Roosevelt, Churchill, and Chiang Kai-shek met at Cairo, Egypt, to discuss plans for pursuing the war in China and Burma.

November 28–December 1, 1943: Roosevelt, Churchill, and Stalin met at Tehran, Iran, with their staffs: That was the first time those three leaders met. There was agreement on invading southern France (Operation Anvil) as well as on making the cross-channel invasion. Stalin also agreed to join in the war against Japan after Germany was defeated.

December 24–29, 1943: In a series of command appointments announced in Washington, D.C., and in London, it was revealed that General Eisenhower would be the Supreme Allied Commander for the invasion of Europe.

BATTLES AND CAMPAIGNS: 1944

Throughout the fifth full year of the war there was military activity in many areas: European theater, Mediterranean/African theater, Asian theater, and naval theater.

EUROPEAN THEATER

January 1–December 31, 1944: In the air war in Europe, many hundreds of thousands of tons of bombs were dropped on German cities, industrial plants, military installations, and communications and transportation centers. Targets in France, Italy, and the Balkans also were heavily

bombed. Among the major targets were any facilities involved in oil production; by May, the
Germans were experiencing a serious shortage
of fuel. In addition to the strategic bombings, the
Allies used their air forces tactically—in support
of ground forces. During 1944, the Germans suffered tremendous losses in planes and personnel; by the end of the year, the Luftwaffe had
effectively ceded control of the air to the Allies.
That did not mean that the Luftwaffe did not
inflict serious damage in certain situations; the
Luftwaffe, too, had radar, for instance, and could
send up fighter planes at night, which took heavy
tolls on occasion. The Germans attempted a so-
called little blitz of London in February (18–25)
but could not sustain such raids. Although the
Germans introduced the first turbojet fighter—
the Me 262 Swallow— in July, they could never
produce enough of the fighter planes to present
a major threat.

January 1–May 12, 1944: Along the eastern front in the Soviet Union, the Soviet army
continued to push the Germans steadily westward. In the southern Ukraine, advance units were
inside former borders of Poland by January 6. In
the north, the blockade of Leningrad was totally
lifted by January 27. The spring thaw slowed
down the advance at times, but in March the
Soviets went on the move again; many German
units put up stiff resistance, but others were
forced to flee to avoid encirclement. Hitler's response to the inevitable retreat was to replace
his generals. By the end of March, the Soviets
had moved into Romania. Early in April, the Soviets took Odessa (April 10). By April 20, the
Soviets had pushed so far ahead of their supply
lines that they called a temporary halt to their
offensive, except in the Crimea. The Germans there
withdrew their troops by May 12; some 8,000
Germans, however, lost their lives as some of the
ships on which they were escaping were sunk
by Soviet planes and ships.

February 20–27, 1944: In a series of bombing raids known as Big Week, hundreds of U.S.
planes attacked targets in the German aircraft industry. U.S. losses were heavy (65 bombers of
800 on one raid).

March 6–8, 1944: Hundreds of U.S. bombers and fighter support planes made the first raids
by U.S. air forces on Berlin.

June 1, 1944: The BBC transmitted a coded
message (based on a poem by French poet Paul
Verlaine) to the French resistance, stating that
the invasion of France was imminent. The Germans understood the intent of the message and
alerted some units, but they failed to bring up
enough forces.

June 4, 1944: Operation Overlord—the
transchannel invasion of France—was scheduled for June 5, and the first convoys were already at sea on June 4 when bad weather forced
Gen. Dwight D. Eisenhower and his advisers to
call them back. They decided, however, that the
invasion would definitely proceed at dawn on
June 6; the tide would be low along the Normandy
coast at that time. Meanwhile, the poor weather
had led the Germans to relax their guard. Gen.
Erwin Rommel went to Germany to celebrate his
wife's birthday.

June 5, 1944: Allied convoys with landing
ships left Britain for France during the evening
and just before midnight airborne units set off,
thus beginning the largest combined sea, air, and
land operation in history. Some 3 million men
were under the Allied command (although only
some 150,000 were actually on French soil during the first day). The invasion force included
more than 13,000 aircraft, 1,200 warships, 2,700
merchant ships, and 2,500 landing craft. Immense
amounts of equipment were required, including
landing craft and land vehicles specially designed
for the operation. Among the most unusual
equipment were the two Mulberry Harbors that
the British had designed. Those were gigantic
floating ports made of old ships, concrete, and
steel. In the preceding days, there had been intensified bombing raids on targets in France, carefully chosen to avoid giving away the planned
landing zone. Elaborate deceptions, in fact, were
an integral part of Operation Overlord. Two fictional army groups were created, using the names
of real commanders and staff (Gen. George Patton
commanded the U.S. force); dummy equipment
was displayed on the ground; false radio traffic
and "leaks" from double agents were concocted.
The idea was to mislead the Germans into believing that the invasion was aimed at Calais, France,
and/or Norway. Even after the Allied forces went
ashore at Normandy, Hitler and some of his generals believed it was a diversionary attack. The
Germans had let up on their aerial and naval reconnaissance of the Channel, but they had by
no means neglected to construct strong defenses
along the beaches at Normandy.

U.S. soldiers left their landing boat and waded through the surf to the French coast on D-Day, June 6, 1944.

June 6, 1944: Between 1 A.M. and 2 A.M., some 13,000 men of three airborne divisions (the U.S. 101st and 82nd and the British 6th) began to drop inland on the flanks of the Normandy landing beaches. Because of the normal disarray that accompanies most complex military operations, the men came down in far more scattered groups than intended. Although they were not able to achieve all their goals, they distracted the Germans enough to tie down valuable forces.

The first units in their landing craft began to approach the beaches in the light of early dawn, and, about 6:30 A.M. the U.S. First Army, commanded by Gen. Omar Bradley, landed on Normandy beaches code-named Utah and Omaha; slightly later, the British Second Army went ashore at beaches code-named Gold and Sword, and a Canadian division went ashore at a beach code-named Juno. The British and Canadians at their beaches and the Americans at Utah Beach established secure beachheads relatively easily. Although they were unable to attain their full goals, by the end of the day, some units were as much as 6 miles inland. On Omaha Beach, however, the Americans came close to disaster. The troops found the beaches raked by German

artillery and machine-gun fire; the amphibious tanks were swamped by the heavy seas; soldiers were trapped behind the metal obstacles that the Germans had set into the surf, thus preventing the engineers from blowing them up; those who got ashore were stalled behind a concrete seawall. By noon, however, scattered groups of Americans were fighting their way off the beach, and by the end of the day, they had extended the beachhead to about 1 mile inland.

About 3 miles west of Omaha Beach, at a 100-foot-high cliff known as Pointe du Roc, a U.S. Ranger battalion was in even more serious trouble. Only about one half of the force even made it onto the beach; about 200 then fired their grappling hooks with ropes to the top of the cliff and began to climb up in the face of terrific German resistance. Once the rangers reached the top, they drove off the Germans, but the Americans were trapped there for two days. Before they were relieved, some 110 of the 200 Rangers were dead or wounded.

The day's toll at Omaha Beach was some 1,000 Americans dead; at Utah Beach, 200 Americans died; the British and Canadians counted another 800 dead at their beaches. But by midnight on June 6, some 150,000 Allied troops were in Normandy, and they held about 80 square miles. Among the many factors that had contributed to the Allies' success was the fact that the Luftwaffe had proved to be virtually powerless: They had shot down only one Allied aircraft.

June 7–30, 1944: Although the Allied forces in Normandy were taking longer to reach their goals than planned, they began to move steadily forward in all sectors. By June 11, all five invasion forces had linked up, and they proceeded to take the French towns they had targeted—Bayeux and Carenten—and Cotentin Peninsula. By June 27, American forces had captured Cherbourg, which gave the Allies a major port. By June 30, the Allies had landed 630,000 men, 600,000 tons of supplies, and 177,000 vehicles at a cost of 62,000 dead or wounded. German resistance varied from point to point, but German strategy, dictated as usual by Hitler, was based on contesting every yard, which prevented the Germans from regrouping for a counterattack.

June 10–September 10, 1944: On June 10, the Soviets launched an offensive against Finland. The Germans could not provide much support, and on September 4, a cease-fire between the Finns and Soviets was announced. The formal armistice between Finland and the Soviet Union was signed on September 10; it provided for the restoration of the 1940 frontiers, and for Finland to pay reparations. The Germans withdrew their forces to Norway and the Baltic ports.

June 14, 1944: The Germans launched the first V-1 flying bombs toward England: of ten launched, only four made it across the channel, and only one landed on London, killing six civilians. The bombs were launched from sites in Belgium and northern France. As the Allies advanced, the launch sites were pulled back. Eventually, 9,200 V-1 rockets were launched against Britain, of which 5,000 reached their targets. Antwerp became another major target after its capture by the Allies (see Military Innovations, Tactics, Equipment, pp. 500-501).

June 22–December 31, 1944: On the third anniversary of the German invasion of the Soviet Union, the Soviets began their summer offensive along four fronts, from the Baltics in the north through Belorussia in the center to the Ukraine in the south. The offensive had been preceded by partisans' blowing up the railroad lines to the west, which the Germans needed for transporting supplies. The Soviets had a force of some 1.7 million troops, and immense numbers of trucks, tanks, planes, guns, and artillery. Within the first week, 38,000 Germans were killed and 116,000 were taken prisoner, and the Germans were in retreat all along the front. Minsk, Belorussia, fell on July 3. Vilna, the capital of Lithuania, was captured on July 13. On September 22, Tallinn, the capital of Estonia, fell to the Soviets. On October 15, Riga, the capital of Latvia, fell. Although a pocket of Germans held out until the end of the war, the war in the Baltic states was effectively over. By December 31, the Soviets had pushed the Germans back to a line that stretched from East Prussia down through Czechoslovakia, Hungary, and Yugoslavia.

July–August 1944: After a difficult drive, U.S. forces took Saint- Lô, a crucial junction, on July 18. The British faced stiff resistance in their attempt to take Caen, but by July 12 they had taken most of it. On July 18, the British launched a massive raid by RAF bombers in an effort to break out beyond the city. On July 25, U.S. forces to the west, launched Operation Cobra with massive bombing raids. The Americans then moved out to the southwest, with the goal of cutting off the Germans in Brittany. The Americans then swung east to move into the heart of France. At Hitler's insistence, the Germans counterattacked on August 7, but they were soon isolated around Falaise. Many got away, but when the "Falaise gap," or "pocket," was closed on August 20, 10,000 Germans had been killed and 50,000 captured. The Americans moved steadily eastward, taking Orleans on August 17, and by August 20, they had established the first bridgehead across the Seine only 30 miles west of Paris. By August 23, French resistance forces had almost liberated Paris. And after several days of bitter fighting, the U.S. 4th Division accompanied by a Free French division entered the city. Ignoring Hitler's orders to destroy the city, the German commander surrendered. On August 26, Gen. Charles de Gaulle marched in a parade down the Champs d' Élysées. By the end of August, the British and Canadians were also advancing northward toward the port of Le Havre and Belgium, and the Germans were in retreat all along the western front. The Germans suffered some 300,000 dead or wounded and 200,000 taken prisoner.

August 1–October 2, 1944: The Soviet forces advanced to within 100 miles of Warsaw and expected to capture the city. But the Polish Home Army (AK) began an uprising within the city. The Home Army had ties with the exile government in London and was generally anti-Communist. Within a week, the Home Army seized control of much of Warsaw. But the Germans also mounted an attack on the Polish Home Army, during which various SS, police, and punishment battalions dealt brutally with the Poles. The Soviets, meanwhile, stopped their advance. They later claimed they had stopped not because of the Home Army's political leanings but because they needed to restore and re-supply their own units. The British and Americans asked the Soviets to let them drop much-needed supplies to the Home Army; the Soviets agreed but refused assistance. In the only such attempt (on September 18), only about one-fifth of the supplies dropped fell into territory held by the Home Army. By October 2, the uprising in Warsaw came to an end. At least 200,000 Poles were killed, much of central Warsaw was destroyed, and the Germans razed even more under Hitler's orders.

August 15, 1944: In what was known as Operation Dragoon (originally, Operation Anvil), Allied forces landed along the Mediterranean coast of France between Toulon and Cannes. Most of the force consisted of Americans, but there were also many French troops. The invasion was supported by heavy air cover and naval bombardment from British as well as American units. There was almost no resistance—the Allies took only 183 casualties.

August 16–28, 1944: Meeting little resistance, the French and American forces in southern France moved swiftly to take all the major cities. The U.S. forces moved north up the Rhone valley and took Grenoble on August 24, and Avignon on August 25. The French moved westward along the coast and by August 28, captured Toulon and Marseilles.

August 26–October 28, 1944: The Bulgarian government tried to take that country out of the war, but the Soviets quickly rejected that attempt. The Soviets proceeded with their advance, and on September 16, Sofia, Bulgaria, fell to the Soviets. On October 28, the Soviets signed an armistice with Bulgaria and placed the Bulgarian troops under Soviet command.

August 28, 1944–February 13, 1945: Hungary's government announced on August 28 that it wished to negotiate with the Soviets,

but the offer was rejected. On October 15, Adm. Nikolaus Horthy broadcast a request to make an armistice with the Soviets. He was arrested by German SS troops and taken to Germany. After stiff resistance by the retreating Germans, the Soviets finally trapped the Germans in Budapest by December 26; the last surviving 62,000 German troops surrendered on February 13, 1945.

August 30–31, 1944: As the Soviets advanced into Romania, many Romanians fighting with the Germans surrendered. On August 30, the Ploesti oil fields in Romania fell to the Soviets. From that point on, the Germans were desperately short of oil for their war machine. On August 31, Bucharest fell to the Soviets.

September 1944: On September 1, Gen. Dwight D. Eisenhower established his headquarters in France, where he had to deal with a bitter debate among the Allied generals. Eisenhower and his supporters favored a broad front advance across the entire western front, with a sharing of supplies and less risk for all; but others—led by British Field Marshal Bernard Montgomery—argued for a thrust on one narrow front, specifically a drive through Belgium and Holland that would isolate the Ruhr, the industrial heart of Germany. In the end, there was a compromise, with the American forces pushing eastward to the Rhine and Montgomery's forces pushing northward. In any case, the Allies desperately needed a major port to handle the incredible volume of material required by their armies. The first British forces entered Antwerp, Belgium, on September 4, but it was the end of November before the Allies controlled Antwerp's seaward approaches and had that great port fully operational. American forces moved quickly across eastern France and through Luxembourg and actually reached German territory north of Trier as early as September 12, but they had to halt there to wait until the rest of the U.S. forces could pull up.

September 3–15, 1944: On September 3, a Free French force took Lyons. On September 12, at Catillon-sur-Seine, units of the Free French 2nd Corps coming from the south linked up with other French units attached to the U.S. 3rd Army that had come from the north. On September 15, the French and U.S. forces that had come from the south were placed under the command of General Eisenhower and became part of the overall movement against Germany.

GERMANY:

This map shows the international boundaries of Germany (and Austria) in 1938—before Hitler began expanding Germany's territory—and the boundaries of Germany (and Austria) that the Allies were prepared to assign in 1944. The map makes clear that Germany was going to have to give up much territory to the east to Poland.

September 8–December 16, 1944: The Germans fired the first V-2 rockets on London on September 8. Eventually, some 1,115 V-2 rockets were launched against Britain, causing some 2,750 deaths. V-2 rockets were also used against Antwerp. On December 16, a V-2 rocket hit a movie house, killing 567 people—296 of them Allied servicemen. Altogether, some 3,752 Belgian civilians and 731 Allied servicemen were killed by V-2 rockets in Antwerp (see Military Innovations, Tactics, and Equipment, pp. 500-501).

September 17–25, 1944: General Montgomery persuaded General Eisenhower to allow him to conduct Operation Market Garden. In that plan, United States and British airborne troops were dropped across German lines in Holland where they were to seize several bridges and canal lines. They were supposed to be reinforced by quickly advancing ground forces to force a collapse of German resistance and allow the entire front to rush into Germany. The U.S. 81st and 101st Airborne Divisions achieved their goals, but the British assigned to take the farthest bridge, the one at Arnhem over the lower Rhine, met more resistance than anticipated. Then the reinforcement columns began to meet stiff resistance and could not aid the paratroopers as quickly as planned. Finally, on September 25, about 2,400 troops were evacuated across the river, but they left 6,400 behind as prisoners; 1,100 had been killed.

October–December 15, 1944: As the Allies approached the German frontiers, German forces began to stiffen their resistance all along the western front. Canadian forces continued their hard fighting along the Schelde estuary to free the approaches to Antwerp, British forces continued their slow drive into northern Belgium and Holland, and U.S. forces fought to take the German city of Aachen, which surrendered on October 21. On November 8, U.S. forces began an offensive to take the French city of Metz and the Saar River region; Metz fell on November 22. The first Allied convoy finally reached Antwerp on

November 28. In two months, the Allies had advanced along the western front, only a few miles at many sectors and 80 miles at the farthest point.

October 20, 1944: Tito's partisans combined with Soviet army units and completed the liberation of Belgrade, Yugoslavia. German troops from Greece, Albania, and southern Yugoslavia fled by every possible route to avoid being trapped.

October 25, 1944: Soviet troops entered Norway in the far north across the border from Finland.

December 16, 1944–January 27, 1945: The Germans launched a major offensive in the Ardennes forest in southeastern Belgium. Hitler's goal was to split the British and American armies, drive on to Antwerp, and hope that the discouraged Allies would join the Germans in their war against the Soviet Union. The Germans had assembled 24 divisions for that offensive, and it took the Allied intelligence completely off guard. In the first days, the Germans penetrated the American front, despite reinforcements for the inexperienced and exhausted American units. On December 17, 72 American soldiers were captured at the town of Malmédy; they were lined up in a field and shot. Twelve soldiers managed to get away and hid in a café, but the Germans set the café on fire, then shot the Americans as they fled. By December 24, the Germans had pushed the American line back by a large "bulge" (thus, the Battle of the Bulge, as that action is best known), with the 101st Airborne Division and part of the 10th Armored Division encircled in the town of Bastogne. On December 22, when the Germans demanded that the Americans surrender, the American commander, Gen. Anthony McAuliffe, simply replied, "Nuts!" (see Notable Phrases, p. 504). By December 24, the German advance had come to a halt, and by December 26, Bastogne was relieved by elements of Gen. George S. Patton's 3rd Army. On December 30, the Allies launched a counteroffensive; it was another month before the Allies regained all the territory they gave up in the Ardennes offensive. The Battle of the Bulge delayed the Allies for about a month, but the German army paid dearly for that delay.

MEDITERRANEAN/AFRICAN THEATER

January 22–May 23, 1944: In Italy, the Germans dug in across the so-called Gustav Line, stretching across the entire peninsula about 75 miles south of Rome. On January 4, U.S. and British forces launched an offensive from south of the line. Then, on January 22, as part of a coordinated plan called Operation Shingle, Allied forces landed around Anzio, a port on the coast north of the line but south of Rome. Because the German forces were focused on defending the Gustav Line, the first day of the offensive went easily, with only 13 Allied casualties. The beachhead was slowly expanded, and by January 29, the Allies had some 69,000 men ashore. But significant German reinforcements including air support, stopped the Allies' attack by February 2. German air attacks took a heavy toll of Allied ships offshore. On February 16, the Germans launched a major attack on the Anzio beachhead and pushed the Allies back in places. At that point, the U.S. commander, Gen. John P. Lucas, was replaced by Gen. Lucian Truscott, but Truscott accomplished little more than Lucas had. The Germans launched a second attack on February 28. Although it failed to drive the Allies off their beachhead, it kept them trapped there and subject to intense air attacks and artillery bombardment from the surrounding hills. At the end of May, the Allies at Anzio went on the offensive and pushed the Germans back.

February 15–March 26, 1944: The Allied forces south of the Gustav Line had been moving ahead in some sectors, but they were unable to capture a hill and town named Monte Cassino with a medieval monastery on its crest. On February 15, the New Zealand commander called in a major bombing raid that totally destroyed the monastery; he thought, erroneously, that the Germans were based in the monastery. After the bombing, the Germans did set up their artillery in the ruins. New Zealand and Indian troops attacked the hill but initially with little success. On March 15, the Allies launched a major attack on both the town and hill, preceded by a heavy bombardment from planes and artillery. By March 26, the weather, the German artillery, and the heavy Allied casualties combined to force the Allies to call off that offensive and regroup.

May 11–June 5, 1944: The Allies launched a major offensive all along the Gustav Line. By May 15, the Germans began to give way. The Germans withdrew from Monte Cassino on May 18, and the Allies moved in. On May 23, the Allied forces at Anzio joined in the offensive and began to break out. Against stiff resistance, the Allies slowly advanced in all sectors, and by June 1, the Germans began to withdraw to a line north of Rome. After a truce between the Germans and Italian resistance fighters, Rome was declared an "open city," and the Germans were allowed to leave. On the evening of June 4, the first units of U.S. troops entered Rome, and on June 5, the Allied forces pushed through Rome in pursuit of the Germans.

June 21–December 31, 1944: After moving quickly up the Italian peninsula north of Rome, the Allies reached the Germans' new defensive positions at the so-called Albert Line, south of Florence, by June 21. On August 4, South African units entered Florence, and the city was completely captured by August 12. The Germans withdrew to form a defensive line (the Gothic Line) across the peninsula north of Florence. On August 30, the Allies began their drive against the Gothic Line and pushed the Germans back. By early November, however, the offensive stalled as winter weather set in. In the remaining weeks of 1944, the Allies advanced at several points, but essentially they waited until April 1945 to launch a major offensive.

October 4–December 12, 1944: On October 4, Allied forces landed near Patras, Greece, on the western coast of the Peloponnesos; other landings were made by the Allies, including Greek exile forces, on other Greek islands in the Ionian and Aegean Seas. On October 12, Allied paratroops landed at the Athens airport as the Germans began to flee Greece from the port of Piraeus. On October 18, the exiled Greek government returned to Athens. On October 31, the Germans evacuated Thessalonike, Greece's second largest city. Many Germans were stranded on Greek islands and in pockets throughout Greece; some managed to escape, but many surrendered.

ASIAN/PACIFIC THEATER

January–July 30, 1944: In the Solomon Islands (Bougainville), the Bismarck Archipelago (New Britain and New Ireland), and New Guinea, American and Australian forces continued to advance against the Japanese but with considerable casualties. On March 8, the Japanese launched an attack on American positions on Bougainville, but within five days, the Americans had pushed the Japanese back, and by

March 24, significant Japanese resistance on the island had ceased. Some small Japanese naval and air bases on New Britain and New Ireland were left cut off until the end of the war. On New Guinea, U.S. forces made a series of landings along the north coast from April to July, which increased the pressure on the Japanese but failed to force their collapse. The small offshore island of Biak, for instance, was captured after only two months of hard fighting, during which the Americans suffered 2,550 casualties. Of a Japanese garrison of nearly 5,000, only 220 lived through the battle; they were taken prisoner. With the capture of the town of Sansapor, the New Guinea campaign effectively ended.

January 31–April 22, 1944: The campaign to take the Marshall Islands in the central Pacific began on January 31 with a landing on Kwajalein Island; by February 7, Japanese resistance had ended; American casualties were 370 dead and some 1,500 wounded. Eniwetok Atoll was the next target, and landings began there on February 17. The fighting on Eniwetok ended on February 23; Americans counted some 300 dead and 750 wounded; of the original Japanese force of 3,400, only 66 surrendered. The rest of the Marshalls were taken by April 22. That was the first territory captured from the Japanese that they had owned before the war.

February 3, 1944: U.S. warships shelled the Kurile Islands of northern Japan, the first attack by ships on the Japanese homeland.

February 17, 1944: American ships and planes attacked the Japanese naval base at Truk in the Caroline Islands and inflicted heavy damage on Japanese warships, merchant shipping, and airplanes.

February 23, 1944: U.S. carriers carried out the first attack on the Mariana Islands.

February 27–May 18, 1944: On February 27, U.S. airplanes attacked some Japanese installations in the Admiralty Islands, preparing for the February 28 invasion of Los Negros Island. The Japanese mounted considerable resistance, but by March 9, the Americans had taken over the airfield on Los Negros. The American forces moved on to seize other of the Admiralty Islands, including Manus. Although most Japanese opposition in those islands ceased by April 1, the campaign did not officially end until May 18. U.S. losses were 1,400 dead or wounded; the Japanese lost 3,820 dead and only 75 taken prisoner.

March 8–August 4, 1944: After months of continual harassing attacks by British, Indian, Chinese, and American units in Burma, on March 8, the Japanese launched a major offensive. Their goal was to isolate the American and Chinese forces in China and push the British and Chindits (Indian units) back into India, thus cutting off any transport routes between the two countries. The advantage shifted back and forth, but by April 18, the British had relieved the siege at Kohima and by June 22, another siege at Imphal. By August 4, Mogaung and Myitkyina had fallen to Chinese troops and Merrill's Marauders (American rangers commanded by Col. Frank Merrill). From that point on, the Japanese in Burma were in retreat, but due to bad weather during the monsoon season, it was fall before the Allies drove the Japanese out of Burma.

March 30–April 1, 1944: A U.S. Navy task force took up the assault on the Caroline Islands by first attacking Palau Island, then Woleai Island. The U.S. Navy inflicted heavy damage on Japanese shipping.

April 29–May 1, 1944: A U.S. Navy task force sent airplanes and warships against Truk and other islands in the Carolines, inflicting heavy damage on Japanese ships, planes, and shore installations.

May 22–23, 1944: U.S. ships and planes bombarded Wake Island.

June 11–July 9, 1944: Airplanes from U.S. carriers attacked Saipan, Tinian, and other islands in the Marianas and inflicted heavy losses on Japanese shipping. By June 14, U.S. Navy ships were bombarding those islands preparatory to landing. The Japanese sent a large fleet to defend the Marianas, but failed to prevent the U.S. landing on Saipan that began on June 15. There was fierce fighting, day after day, as the Americans ground their way across Saipan. On July 6, seeing the end, the two senior Japanese commanders committed suicide; the remaining 3,000 Japanese mounted a desperate attack on July 7, but all organized Japanese resistance on Saipan ended on July 9. In that bloody action, the United States counted 3,400 dead and 13,000 wounded; the Japanese lost an estimated 27,000 dead; 1,780 were taken prisoner.

June 15, 1944: The first raid on the Japanese mainland by U.S. B-29 "Superfortresses," flown from a base in eastern China, marked the beginning of an increasingly intense series of destructive bombing raids on Japanese cities and military installations.

July 21–August 10, 1944: In the Marianas, U.S. forces invaded Guam, meeting little resistance on the first day. On July 24, U.S. forces invaded Tinian in the same group; they met strong resistance and used napalm for the first time in the Pacific. Japanese resistance on Tinian effectively ended on August 1. The United States counted some 390 dead and 1,800 wounded; the Japanese lost 6,000 dead and 250 taken prisoner. Fierce fighting on Guam continued until the last serious Japanese opposition ended on August 10. U.S. casualties totaled 1,300 dead and 5,700 wounded, and the Japanese toll was some 9,900 dead and only 100 taken prisoner.

July 26, 1944: In Hawaii, President Roosevelt met with Gen. Douglas MacArthur and Adm. Chester Nimitz, the top commanders in the Pacific, to discuss the strategy for the final defeat of Japan. MacArthur wanted to take the Philippines, and Nimitz argued that U.S. forces could by-pass those islands and go straight to Formosa. That dispute bedeviled American military planning almost to the end of the war, and, in effect, each side pursued an independent strategy.

September 9–October 19, 1944: On September 9, airplanes from U.S. carriers began to attack Japanese installations on Mindanao and other islands of the Philippines, preparing for the invasion of Japan. They launched another series of raids on September 21–24, and a still more powerful series against Leyte on October 16–19.

September 15–October 21, 1944: U.S. forces landed on Morotai Island in the Moluccas Islands and on Peleliu Island in the Palaus; the opposition on the latter was especially strong. During September, U.S. forces landed on other islands in the Palaus. By the end of the month, most Japanese forces in the Palaus were wiped out, but some heavy fighting continued until October 21. The United States counted 265 dead and 1,355 wounded in the taking of the Palaus; Japan lost 1,300 dead and 45 taken prisoner.

October 12–14, 1944: In its first raids on the island of Formosa, the United States lost 71 aircraft. Three Allied warships were damaged.

October 20–December 31, 1944: On October 20, the first U.S. forces went ashore at two points on the east coast of Leyte in the Philippines. The Japanese put up minimal opposition on the beach; General MacArthur landed a few

U.S. Marines churn through the sea, headed for the beaches of Tinian Island near Guam in July 1944. They are in an amphibious landing vehicle known as a "water buffalo."

hours after the assault and broadcast a message to the Filipino people on his promised return (see Notable Phrases, p. 504). As the U.S. forces slowly advanced, week after week, against increasing Japanese opposition, there was intense action in the air and offshore, with heavy losses on both sides. It was during that operation that the Japanese kamikaze ("divine wind") pilots began to dive their planes directly into Allied ships (the first attack was on an Australian ship on October 21). In the first week (October 24–November 1), those attacks sank one U.S. escort carrier and a destroyer and damaged another 14 ships (at the cost of 53 kamikaze pilots). During the entire Philippines campaign, kamikaze pilots sank 16 U.S. vessels and damaged another 87, at a cost of 378 kamikaze planes. By the last day of 1944, although the Japanese were still launching some counterattacks, U.S. forces had effectively driven the Japanese off Leyte. American casualties were some 15,500 dead or wounded, and the Japanese counted almost 70,000 dead.

NAVAL THEATER

January 1–December 31, 1944: Although the German navy was worn down by the sheer numbers and technical superiority of the Allied forces, the U-boat threat was far from over; it received a boost from the introduction in 1944 of the *Schnorchel* breathing tube used by submarines to allow them to remain underwater for long periods. And the Germans had developed a method of making submarines from prefabricated sections; that meant that U-boats could be quickly assembled at ports without being exposed to bombing raids.

In the Pacific, the U.S. Navy (and other Allied navies, most especially the British and Australian) engaged in a variety of actions that went far beyond what had traditionally been known as naval warfare—supporting a series of island-hopping invasions, attacking Japanese supply convoys, bombarding Japanese-held islands, providing support for air battles. In addition to the more renowned battles and operations between fleets, U.S. warships, submarines, and mines also took a continual toll of Japanese ships in isolated encounters. American naval (and other Allied forces) losses were heavy compared to those suffered in previous wars, but Japanese losses were more staggering still. By the end of

1944 the Japanese navy was reduced to a fraction of its former size, was running short of fuel, and could barely man its carriers with adequately trained pilots.

May 14, 1944: A German submarine sank a British merchant ship in the Mediterranean; that was the last sinking by a U-boat in that sea.

June 19–20, 1944: In the Philippine Sea between the Marianas and the Philippines, a large U.S. naval force gathered to protect the U.S. invasion of the Marianas was attacked by Japanese carrier aircraft on June 19. Before the battle ended—in what became known as the "Great Marianas Turkey Shoot"—the Japanese lost 240 airplanes in the air (and another 50 were destroyed on the ground at the Japanese base at Guam), and the United States lost only 29 planes; the Japanese also lost two aircraft carriers. On June 20, the U.S. sank another Japanese carrier, damaged several other warships, and shot down several more Japanese planes; 20 U.S. planes were shot down, and an additional 72 crashed while trying to land on their carriers in the darkness. The Japanese withdrew during the night, but the Battle of the Philippine Sea had decimated the Japanese naval air capacity.

October 23–26, 1944: The Japanese sent massive naval forces to the Philippines, with the goal of disrupting the U.S. invasion of Leyte, but the Americans outnumbered the Japanese in most categories of ships and more so in planes and experienced pilots. On October 23, as a squadron of Japanese ships approached Leyte Gulf, American submarines sank two cruisers (at the cost of one submarine). On October 24, Japanese planes from Luzon put the U.S. carrier *Princeton* out of action, but U.S. planes sank a Japanese battleship and forced a cruiser to flee. For the next eight hours, both fleets maneuvered but engaged in little combat. Between midnight and dawn on October 25, part of the Japanese fleet tried to sneak through the Surigao Strait (off southern Leyte), but it was attacked first by U.S. PT boats and destroyers, then by cruisers and battleships: The Japanese lost two battleships, two cruisers, and three destroyers and were forced to withdraw. Meanwhile, another part of the Japanese fleet had passed through the San Bernardino Strait (north of Leyte), and on the morning of October 25, off Samar, their ships and planes launched an aggressive attack on the American ships. Both sides suffered heavy losses in ships and personnel, but after several hours, the Japanese fleet turned away. A third section of the Japanese fleet had remained off the northeast coast of Luzon, well away from the main action, to decoy American ships; Adm. William "Bull" Halsey had pursued those ships, and almost simultaneously with the battle off Samar, his carrier group engaged the Japanese; four Japanese carriers, a cruiser, and two destroyers were sunk by Halsey's planes. On October 26, U.S. airplanes sank another three cruisers of the retreating Japanese squadrons. The Battle of Leyte Gulf all but eliminated the Japanese navy as a threat, not only because of the loss of so many ships (24 large warships) but also because so many irreplaceable pilots were lost.

November 12, 1944: The German battleship *Tirpitz*, based in a fjord in Norway, played hide-and-seek with the British navy in the Arctic Ocean throughout much of 1944. The British tried several attacks that came to nothing; on September 15, some 25 British bombers managed to land only one bomb on the ship. Finally, on November 12, another squadron of British bombers made enough direct hits to capsize the *Tirpitz*.

HOMEFRONT

January 19, 1944: Railroads in the United States, under the authority of the U.S. government since December 27, 1943, to prevent strikes, were returned to private ownership after the unions accepted the terms proposed by Roosevelt to establish labor peace.

February 1944: A Victory ship, the first of the new class of freighters, was delivered. Faster, larger, more efficient than Liberty ships, Victory ships were mass produced. By November 1944, 82 were commissioned.

March 14, 1944: In the New Hampshire presidential primary, Roosevelt topped the Democrats; Wendell Willkie, the Republicans' defeated candidate of 1940, won his party's poll. But after he lost the primary in Wisconsin on April 4, he withdrew from the race.

March 29, 1944: The U.S. Congress approved a resolution authorizing up to $1.35 billion for the United Nations Relief and Rehabilitation Agency. That marked the start of the massive effort to aid millions of people whose lives had been disrupted by the war.

May 4, 1944: The United States removed

meat from rationing, except for steaks and certain cuts of beef. However, rationing of all beef products was restored on December 24, 1944.

June 22, 1944: Roosevelt signed the Servicemen's Readjustment Act, better known as the G. I. Bill, which established a number of financial-aid programs to meet the education, housing, and other needs of returned veterans.

June 28, 1944: Thomas Dewey, the governor of New York, won the Republican nomination for president.

July 11, 1944: At a press conference, Roosevelt said that he would run again for president if nominated: "If the people command me to continue in office...I have as little right as a soldier to leave his position in the line." On July 21, he was nominated; Harry S. Truman, a senator from Missouri, was nominated for vice president.

September 1944: A special bomber unit was established to drop an atomic bomb; work at Los Alamos had proceeded to the point that such a weapon seemed practical.

November 7, 1944: Roosevelt defeated Thomas Dewey in the presidential election, winning 36 states with 53 percent of the popular vote.

December 15, 1944: Congress established the new rank of General of the Army—better known as a five-star general. The rank was immediately conferred on George Marshall, Dwight D. Eisenhower, Douglas MacArthur, and Henry "Hap" Arnold.

INTERNATIONAL DEVELOPMENTS

January 27–31, 1944: The United States, Britain, and Australia formally protested against the ill treatment of their prisoners of war by the Japanese. The Allies promised that after the war they would put those responsible on trial.

June 17, 1944: Hitler went to Soissons, France, to meet with his top commanders on the western Front, Gen. Gerd von Rundstedt and Gen. Erwin Rommel. Hitler rejected their advice that the German troops withdraw to better defensive positions and went into a rage, accusing the German army of cowardice. He insisted that Germany's V-1 bombs and jet aircraft would soon turn the tide against the Allies.

June 24–30, 1944: Based on reports from Jews who had escaped from Auschwitz, telegrams describing the gas chambers at the extermination camps were sent from neutral Switzerland to the governments in London and Washington, D.C. Winston Churchill supported the bombing of the rail lines but was overruled by his Air Ministry. In Washington, Assistant Secretary of War John McCloy instructed his staff to "kill" such a plan.

July 1–22, 1944: At Bretton Woods, a resort hotel in New Hampshire, an international monetary conference (representing 44 countries) established various policies and institutions for the postwar world. Among the most important policy was an agreement to stabilize national currency values based on a gold standard; among the institutions were the International Monetary Fund and the International Bank for Reconstruction and Development.

July 18, 1944: General Hideki Tojo, the principal architect of Japan's war policies, resigned his posts as prime minister and chief of staff as part of a major shake-up in the Japanese government. The new leaders felt that they were signaling the Allies their desire to negotiate an end to the war, but they failed to send an explicit message to that effect.

July 20, 1944: At a meeting attended by Hitler and some of his military commanders at his headquarters at Rastenburg in East Prussia, a bomb exploded under the table. It had been placed there in a briefcase carried into the meeting by Col. Klaus Philip Schenk von Stauffenberg, one of the leading members of a conspiracy to assassinate Hitler. When von Stauffenberg excused himself and left the room, someone moved the briefcase behind a leg of the table. Although greatly shaken, Hitler was only slightly wounded; indeed, he received Mussolini at his bombed headquarters only four hours later and, after showing him around, sat and took tea with the deposed Italian dictator. Von Stauffenberg believed Hitler had been killed and set in motion the plans to seize the government in Berlin, but the various conspirators in Berlin did not move quickly enough, and within hours, it was clear that Hitler had survived. At once, some of the conspirators turned against others, and just before midnight, von Staffenberg and several other leaders were executed. Within the ensuing days and weeks and months (and as late as April 1945), several thousand Germans alleged to have conspired to kill Hitler were executed.

July 23, 1944: In Moscow, it was announced that a Polish Committee of National Liberation had been formed. The Polish government in exile in London denounced it as "the creation of a handful of unknown Communists."

August 21–October 7, 1944: At Dumbarton Oaks, an estate in Washington, D.C., representatives of the United States, Britain, the USSR, and Nationalist China met to discuss setting up an international organization to be called the United Nations. In addition to calling for such branches as the assembly, the security council, and the International Court of Justice, the delegates laid great stress on finding ways to peacefully resolve international disputes and to enforce the organization's decisions. Most of the proposals were incorporated into the UN charter.

August 29, 1944: The Soviets and Polish Communists revealed evidence that the Germans had murdered as many as 1.5 million people (mainly Jews, but also Polish anti-Nazis and Soviet prisoners) at a concentration camp at Majdanek, Poland. Photographs of the corpses provided the West with the first visual evidence of the Nazi "final solution."

August 30, 1944: Charles de Gaulle established his provisional government in Paris; from that point on, he effectively took over the governing of France. On October 22, the Allied governments gave formal recognition to de Gaulle and his provisional government.

September 5, 1944: The governments in exile of Belgium, the Netherlands, and Luxembourg announced they would form a Benelux customs union after the war. That announcement was one of the first steps toward establishing the European Community.

September 11–16, 1944: Roosevelt and Churchill met at Quebec City, Canada, for the second time, this time for the so-called Octagon Conference. They reached general agreement on the strategy to end the war in Europe and in the Pacific.

October 9–20, 1944: Churchill and his foreign minister, Anthony Eden, visited Moscow for talks with the Soviets on postwar political arrangements in Eastern Europe. Stalin insisted that Poland, Bulgaria, and Romania be under Communist control, and that Hungary and Yugoslavia be under Soviet as well as British influence. In return, he agreed that Greece be under British influence.

October 14, 1944: On Hitler's orders, two generals appeared at Gen. Erwin Rommel's home

and informed him that there was testimony implacating him in the July assassination attempt on Hitler. They had poison with them and said that if he took it, his death would be announced as caused by his injuries, he would be given a state funeral, and his family would not be bothered in any way. Rommel told his wife and son of the agreement, then got in a car with the generals, and about a mile from his home took the poison. Hitler wired Rommel's widow his "sincerest sympathy," and Rommel was given the promised state funeral at which he was lauded as a hero.

October 18, 1944: The German government announced that all males from 16 to 60 were liable for conscription into the home-defense force.

December 16–31, 1944: In Greece, the two major guerrilla groups—one basically Communist, the other anti-Communist—openly turned against each another. On December 3, a demonstration in Athens sponsored by the Communists was fired upon by the police; the next day, martial law was declared. On December 5, British tanks and warships were brought in to support the anti-Communist elements; the British were then engaged in a virtual war against the Communist guerrillas. On December 12, the out-fought Communists asked for terms for a cease-fire. On December 16, British general Ronald Scobie, who had been appointed the Allies' military commander in Greece, reminded the Communist guerrillas that they had agreed to work with the exile government, now moved to Athens. On December 25, Churchill and Eden arrived in Athens for talks with the government; it was decided that Greece should be ruled by a regency until elections determined the kind of government Greeks wanted. On December 31, Prime Minister George Papandreou resigned and Archbishop Damaskinos was sworn in as regent.

BATTLES AND CAMPAIGNS: 1945

There was military activity in several areas in this sixth and final year of World War II: European theater, Mediterranean theater, Asian/Pacific theater, and naval theater.

EUROPEAN THEATER

January 1, 1945: In a surprise raid, some 800 Luftwaffe airplanes attacked Allied airfields in northern France, Belgium, and Holland. Although the Allies lost some 300 planes—most of them on the ground—and the Germans only 200, the Allies were able to replace their losses immediately. For the Germans, the raid was a futile and last, desperate gesture, as many of the German pilots were totally inexperienced.

January 1–31, 1945: In the Ardennes, the Allies continued to push the Germans back, out of the bulge. German losses would have been less had Hitler accepted the advice of his generals that, in the face of obviously superior Allied forces, the troops be withdrawn. By the end of the month, the Allies had not only recovered all the German gains of mid-December but had also begun to move into Germany along that center sector. Meanwhile, in the southern sector of the western front, the Alsace region of France, the Allies met considerable resistance but were slowly advancing.

January 1–May 3, 1945: In the air war over Europe, the Allies effectively controlled the skies. The strategic bombing raids continued to devastate German cities, military installations, transportation centers, factories, ports, and every possible target; many thousands of sorties dropped hundreds of thousands of tons of bombs. Allied planes based in the Mediterranean also raided Germany and German-held targets. Meanwhile, tactical flights supported the swiftly advancing Allied troops. With a few exceptions, the Luftwaffe was almost powerless to resist those overwhelming forces. In the final months of World War II, the Germans lacked not so much planes as fuel and trained pilots; many of their airfields were also bombed out of commission by the end of March. The final raid by Allied planes on a German target came on the night of May 2–3. During the last weeks of May, Allied planes were used to drop food to starving people and to evacuate prisoners of war from places recently liberated from the Germans.

January 12–31, 1945: On the eastern front, the Soviets launched a major offensive all along the front from the Baltic Sea to the Carpathian Mountains. The Soviets had superiority in numbers and in all classes of equipment, and the German lines were soon broken. On January 17, Warsaw was finally relieved by the Soviets, but the city was devastated. The Russians continued advancing across East Prussia; by January 25, the German forces in East Prussia were effectively isolated and began to evacuate from the

sea. During the following weeks, they suffered heavy losses, as many of the ships were hit by mines and attacked by submarines. Meanwhile, the Soviets advanced across Poland. By January 31, Soviet units had reached the Oder River less than 50 miles from Berlin.

February–March 1945: By the start of February, on the western front, the Allies had their armies drawn up along a long line stretching from the south—at the Rhine River just north of Strasbourg—along the western border of Germany's Saar region, through Luxembourg and Belgium and the Netherlands, and up to a point near the lower Rhine. By early March, the Allies had reached or crossed the Rhine at almost every point north of Cologne, Germany; a few days later, other units reached the Rhine from Koblenz to Mannheim. Several large German pockets remained for another two weeks, but by the end of March, they had been pushed back, and the Allies crossed the Rhine along almost its entire length, pushing large salients into parts of central Germany.

On the eastern front, the Soviets briefly halted their advance into Germany until they could bring all their forces up to a line roughly along the Oder and Neisse Rivers. Meanwhile, they had to wipe out some pockets of resistance to their rear, although others were isolated, as in the major Polish city of Breslau. On February 13, in Budapest, Hungary, where the Soviets had had the Germans trapped since late December, the last 62,000 Germans surrendered. By February 20, major Soviet units were on the move again, forcing the Germans to retreat all along the front. On March 6, German forces in Hungary launched a counteroffensive (code-named Spring Awakening), but after two weeks, the Soviets pushed them back again. By the last day of March, on the northern end of the front, Danzig on the Baltic fell to the Soviets, and on the southern end, the Soviets advanced into Czechoslovakia and Austria. The Soviets were then poised to make the final drive to Berlin.

February 13–15, 1945: In one of the most controversial Allied operations of World War II, the RAF carried out a massive bombing raid on Dresden on the night of February 13–14; U.S. planes followed up with daytime raids on February 14 and 15. The combination of explosive and incendiary bombs caused a firestorm that killed an estimated 70,000 Germans and devastated a

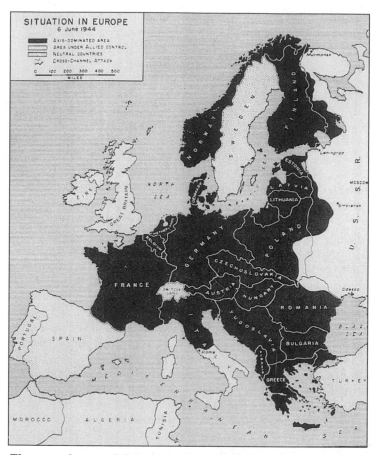

The map above and the map on the following page contrast the extent of the German domination of Europe before D-Day, June 6, 1944, with the situation on January 15, 1945. German-controlled territory is in black, the area under Allied control is white; neutral nations are shown lightly shaded.

large part of the central city (see Military Innovations, Tactics, Equipment p. 498). The bombing was controversial because Dresden had little importance as a military target, and the raid appeared to be motivated principally by a desire to punish German civilians. (There were also many Allied prisoners of war in the city, among them Kurt Vonnegut, who depicted the event in his 1969 novel *Slaughterhouse Five.*)

March 7–17, 1945: On March 7, tanks of the U.S. III Corps reached the Rhine opposite Remagen and found the Ludendorff Bridge there still standing. Troops and vehicles were immediately rushed across. (Hitler was so furious that he fired Gen. Gerd von Rundstedt as commander of his forces in the west.) German planes tried to take out the bridge, but the Allies continued to move their forces across and expand the beach-

head on the other side. Finally, on March 17, the bridge collapsed (killing 25 U.S. soldiers) from the strain of its heavy use and from artillery and bomb damage. By that time, however, U.S. Army engineers had erected other bridges nearby.

March 15, 1945: In a raid on the Bielefeld aqueduct in Germany, the RAF dropped for the first time, the most powerful bomb (until the atomic bombs) to be used in World War II, the 22,000-pound "grand slam."

March 27, 1945: The Germans fired the final V-2 rockets from the last remaining launching site (near The Hague, the Netherlands); one landed in England that afternoon and for the last time in World War II, a British civilian was killed. Two days later, the V-2 crews retreated eastward, taking 60 unfired rockets with them.

April 1945: On the eastern front, the Soviets

continued to advance. Vienna, after fierce street battles, fell to the Soviets on April 13. On April 16, Soviet forces along a wide front launched their final drive on Berlin, with the ultimate goal being the river Elbe to its west, previously agreed-upon with the British and Americans as the boundary of their postwar occupation zones. Although the Germans still had about 1 million troops, they were no match for the 2 million Soviet troops with their many artillery, tanks, and planes. As early as April 21, some advance Soviet tank units were in the eastern suburbs of Berlin; by April 25, the two main Soviet armies had converged, and Berlin was completely encircled. On April 25, too, other advance Soviet troops met up with the American troops at Torgau on the Elbe River some 65 miles south of Berlin. Although there were hundreds of thousands of German troops still fighting desperately all along the front, the Soviets advanced into Czechoslovakia and Austria to the south and all across northern Germany. By April 28, Berlin was defended by only about 30,000 troops, and the So-

viets had advanced to within a mile of Hitler's bunker in the center of the city. During the next four days, there was bitter house-to-house fighting, as the Soviets inexorably closed in on Hitler's bunker, or subterranean command center.

On the western front, by early April, the German forces in the Ruhr, the great industrial region of northwestern Germany, were effectively trapped and surrendered in large numbers. Meanwhile, the Americans concentrated their forces in a drive into the southern part of Germany; Eisenhower feared that the Germans were intending to make a last stand in a heavily fortified "National Redoubt" in the Alps, and he decided to try to block any such move. Eisenhower informed the Soviets of this plan, thereby effectively conceding to them the capture of Berlin and most of Eastern Europe. That was opposed by Churchill and the British, who feared that the Soviets would thereby gain control of much of Germany and Eastern Europe, as, in fact, they did, but the Americans stuck by their strategy, thrusting toward Stuttgart in the southwest, into

By March 1945, Germany was near total ruin and close to surrender, as testified by this view of Lunebach, where a U.S. Army column makes its way across a portable bridge.

Nuremberg and Munich in south-central Germany, and then into Austria and into western Czechoslovakia. Not all American forces went south, however; some units pushed directly east toward Dessau, Magdeburg, and Leipzig, and still others went to the northeast, taking Hanover, then pushing still farther north toward the Elbe River. Meanwhile, British and Canadian forces pushed across the Netherlands and into northwestern Germany.

April 4, 1945: U.S. troops entered a Nazi concentration camp at Ohdruf, near Gotha, Germany. That was one of the first such camps liberated by Americans, and the horrific sights that greeted them caused total revulsion. General Eisenhower visited the camp and personally telephoned Churchill to report what he had seen; he then sent photographs to Churchill, who distributed them to his cabinet.

April 11–15, 1945: On April 11, U.S. troops entered the concentration camp at Buchenwald; among those liberated at the camp was a young Romanian Jew, Elie Wiesel, who, in 1986, won the Nobel Peace Prize for his writings on the Holocaust. On April 15, British troops entered the camp at Belsen.

April 18, 1945: Some 325,000 German troops trapped in the Ruhr pocket surrendered. On April 21, Field Marshal Walter Model, who had commanded that sector, committed suicide.

April 25, 1945: Units of the U.S. First Army met Soviet troops at Torgau on the Elbe River.

April 29, 1945: American forces entered the concentration camp at Dachau, north of Munich. The Americans were so repulsed by the sight of the rotting corpses and the emaciated living that within a few hours of arriving they executed the German commandant and some 500 of his troops. Although such an incident was not publicized at the time, accounts of that execution and numerous such executions were later revealed.

April 30–May 2, 1945: On April 30, with the Soviets only a few blocks away from his bunker under the chancellery in Berlin, Hitler committed suicide. On May 1, Joseph Goebbels, Martin Bormann, and Gen. Hans Krebs tried to negotiate terms with the commander of the Soviets in Berlin, Gen. Vasili Chuikov, but he refused anything less than unconditional surrender. That evening, Goebbels and General Krebs committed suicide; Bormann tried to escape but was either killed or committed suicide not far from the chancellery. On May 2, the Soviets entered the chancellery and found the charred corpses of the Nazi leaders.

May 1–3, 1945: In northeastern Germany, U.S. troops had been ordered not to advance beyond the Elbe and the Mulde Rivers, so they halted to allow the Soviets to take Berlin. The British continued northeastward, taking Hamburg on May 3. Soviet troops then made contact with the British and Americans all along the Elbe River. In the south, American troops pushed into Bavaria and Austria, taking Innsbruck on May 3. The only major German forces still resisting the Soviets were those in Latvia on the Baltic and those in Austria and Czechoslovakia.

May 4–5, 1945: Adm. Karl Dönitz sent envoys to Gen. Bernard Montgomery at Luneburg Heath in northwestern Germany to arrange for the surrender of all German troops in Holland, Denmark, and northwestern Germany. The surrender took effect at 8 A.M. on May 5.

May 5–8, 1945: On May 5, Czech resistance forces rose up against the Germans remaining in Prague. On May 7, as the fighting was going on, three U.S. Army vehicles arrived in the city, but the Soviets, who were also fighting there, insisted that the agreement called for the Americans to leave Prague to them. The Americans returned to Pilsen. Early on the morning of May 8, the Germans in Prague surrendered.

May 6, 1945: Units of Gen. George Patton's U.S. Third Army took Pilsen, Czechoslovakia, but Patton was under orders to advance no farther and to allow the Soviets to take over the rest of that country.

May 7–9, 1945: On May 7, at 2:41 A.M., Gen. Alfred Jodl signed the document surrendering all German forces on all fronts; the surrender, however, did not take effect until 11:01 P.M on May 8; the surrender would be formally ratified in Berlin about midnight on May 8–9 (see Negotiations and Peace Treaty, p. 490).

May 8–15, 1945: Almost all troops in Germany stopped fighting by May 9, but some small German units in Latvia, Czechoslovakia, and Yugoslavia held out for a few days. Throughout Europe, small isolated groups of German troops also surrendered—from the Aegean islands to Denmark and Norway—including a besieged garrison in Dunkirk. On May 15, the last German troops to surrender were some 150,000 troops in Yugoslavia.

MEDITERRANEAN THEATER

January–March 1945: In Italy, the Allied forces essentially halted their offensive operations along a line that ran from above Ravenna on the Adriatic Sea north of Florence to the Tyrrhenian Sea near Pistoia. There were occasional minor engagements, but the cold and wet weather and the need to concentrate troops and materiel for the drive across France limited the Allies' capabilities.

April 9–26, 1945: The Allies began a spring offensive in Italy, driving first toward Ferrara to the east and Bologna in the center. On April 21, Polish units were the first to enter Bologna. By April 23, advance units pushed a salient to the Po River. Ferrara fell on April 24, and Allied forces began to move across the Po almost at will. The Allies, then on an open plain, began to move at great speed against the totally outmanned and outgunned Germans. Some Allied units headed east toward Padua and Venice; others headed north to Verona and Milan; others set off west to Genoa and Turin. Italian partisans had by then emerged as a major force against the retreating Germans and actually took over Genoa before the first American troops arrived on April 26.

April 29–May 2, 1945: On April 29, German representatives at Caserta in southern Italy negotiated the surrender of the German forces in Italy to the Allies. It was May 1 before Gen. Heinrich von Vietinghoff, commander of all German forces in Italy, approved the surrender, which went into effect May 2. Sporadic fighting occurred during the following few days, as the Allies pushed to the northernmost borders of Italy.

May 7, 1945: Tito's Yugoslavian partisans took the city of Trieste on the Adriatic; Italy and Yugoslavia later disputed possession of the city.

ASIAN/PACIFIC THEATER

January–August 1945: In the air war in the Pacific, except for their kamikaze planes, the Japanese found themselves almost powerless to inflict serious damage from the air. The Allies inflicted a crescendo of strategic bombing raids on military installations and cities in Japan, on Japanese installations in China, on Japanese-held islands, and on merchant ships. Tactical air operations supported all the operations, and as the Allies gradually drove the Japanese out of the various islands and lands they had occupied, the Allies seized more and more airfields for their own operations and further restricted the Japanese capability to respond. By mid-March, Gen. Curtis LeMay, commander of the bomber forces based in the Marianas, shifted from daytime raids over Japan to night raids; incendiaries were increasingly used in firebombing Japanese cities. With the capture of Okinawa in late June, the Allies were poised for even more punishing air raids on Japan. And it was, in fact, airplanes that delivered the knockout punch to Japan—the two atomic bombs.

January 2–31, 1945: A large Allied task force set off from the Philippine island of Leyte to invade the island of Luzon. For the first week, the Allied ships suffered heavy losses from Japanese submarines, surface ships, and kamikaze planes, but the Allies' overwhelming forces finally pushed the Japanese back. On January 9, the first Allied troops went ashore on the northwestern coast of Luzon. The Japanese chose not to contest the invasion on land, but their planes attacked the ships. While Allied reinforcements streamed ashore, the Japanese began to intensify their resistance on land and from the air. The Japanese strategy called for making their stand in the interior mountains. By January 25, U.S. troops occupied Clark Field north of Manila. On January 29, American troops went ashore north of Subic Bay, west of Manila. On January 31, other troops went ashore at Nasugbu, southwest of Manila. By the end of the month, the Allies were secure on Luzon, but the Japanese showed no signs of abandoning the fight.

Fighting also continued on the adjacent island of Mindoro, but by January 24, Japanese resistance there effectively ended.

January 3–May 3, 1945: In Burma, the Allies continued their offensive, launching attacks at numerous points. By January 27, the Ledo Road, the major supply route from India to China, was cleared. Fighting raged week after week, but, gradually, the Allies advanced, and the Japanese evacuated. By the time the Allies carried out a seaborne landing (Operation Dracula) near Rangoon on May 2, most Japanese had left Burma. With the fall of Rangoon on May 3, the long, obscure, Burma campaign effectively ended, although mopping-up operations continued for several days and a few Japanese units held out until September, the final unit not surrendering until October 25.

February 1945: On Luzon in the Philippines, the Japanese put up stiff resistance against the advancing Allies, but by February 4, some Allied units reached the outskirts of Manila. By February 13, the Japanese forces on Bataan Peninsula were cut off, and the U.S. Navy operated freely in Manila Bay. As other Allied units landed at other points around Luzon, a relatively small Japanese force continued to defend Manila. On February 26, the island of Corregidor, so significant to the Americans at the start of the war, was captured: There were some 5,000 Japanese dead and 19 taken prisoner (U.S. casualties were around 1,000).

February 19–March 26, 1945: After heavy bombardment from offshore ships and raids by airplanes, U.S. marines invaded the island of Iwo Jima. The Japanese garrison numbered only about 21,000, but they had prepared an elaborate system of tunnels, trenches, and strongpoints, and the Americans knew that the 8-square-mile island would be a hard nut to crack. Kamikaze planes took a terrific toll on the supporting ships. On February 23, marines raised the U.S. flag on Mount Suribachi, the 600-foot-high peak that dominated the tiny island. That flag raising was captured in one of the most famous photographs of World War II (and was replicated for the U.S. Marine Memorial in Washington, D.C.). In the days that followed, U.S. forces slowly advanced but only by using massive firepower and taking heavy casualties. By March 3, U.S. forces controlled all three of the airfields on the island. As the Americans began to push the Japanese into a corner, the Japanese launched suicide attacks; the final one was on March 26, and the last few hundred Japanese troops were wiped out in one last desperate attack. With that, the resistance ended. There were only some 200 prisoners of the original force of about 21,000; American casualties included more than 6,000 dead and 17,200 wounded. The capture of Iwo Jima was regarded as necessary to provide airfields from which fighter planes could take off to protect bombers from more distant islands and where those bombers, in turn, could land if they were not able to make it back to their bases after raids on Japan.

March 1945: On March 3, after a month of bitter fighting, Japanese resistance in Manila ended. About 20,000 Japanese died, and the city was devastated. Fighting continued on Luzon

In February 1945, U.S. Marines fire a steady barage of shells from the black-sand beach of Iwo Jima onto well-emplaced Japanese positions.

and on other Philippine islands. Filipino guerrillas played an increasingly crucial role in attacking the Japanese.

March 9–10, 1945: Some 300 U.S. Superfortresses raided Tokyo during the night, dropping almost 2,000 tons of incendiary bombs. As Tokyo was then largely a city of wood (and paper) homes, the raid caused a massive firestorm (see Military Innovations, Tactics, Equipment p. 498). The bombing raid left at least 100,000 Japanese dead—the most destructive single bombing raid of the war, excluding the atomic attacks on Hiroshima and Nagasaki.

April–July 5, 1945: On Luzon and on other Philippine Islands, fighting continued, week after week. The Allies brought in reinforcements, and, one by one, began to take some of the smaller islands but the Japanese continued to hold out on Luzon. Gradually, the Allies pushed the Japanese back into smaller and smaller enclaves. On June 28, MacArthur announced that offensive operations on Luzon were finished. Fighting continued here and there on Luzon and on other Philippine islands (in some locales, the Japanese held out until the very end of the war), but by July 5, MacArthur announced that the Philippines were completely liberated.

April 1–June 22, 1945: U.S. forces began their invasion of Okinawa, the largest such operation yet in the Pacific, with 450,000 Army and Marine troops in 1,200 transports. The Japanese defenders numbered some 130,000 (but there were also some 450,000 civilians living on that island). The Japanese did not contest the landing but concentrated their forces in the southern end of the island, so the Americans advanced fairly easily during the first three days. On April 4, resistance began to stiffen, and offshore, the kamikaze pilots continued their deadly attacks. Throughout April, the battle raged on land and on the seas around the island. American reinforcements arrived, and by April 20, most of the northern part of the island was captured, but the Japanese still held out behind the Shuri Line in the south. During the night of May 3–4, the Japanese launched a counteroffensive, but it failed to break the Americans' front and ended on May 6. Meanwhile, Japanese artillery forces had revealed their positions and were subjected to attack from ships and planes. By May 21, the Japanese were withdrawing from their Shuri Line. However, the Japanese continued to make the

Americans pay for every bit of land they gave up. In the final stage, the Japanese were isolated in the Oruku Peninsula; many Japanese soldiers, believing that surrender was shameful, committed suicide. On June 18, Gen. Simon Bolivar Buckner, commander of the U.S. forces on Iwo Jima, was killed by Japanese artillery. On June 22, the fighting ended. The Japanese lost 120,000 soldiers and 42,000 civilians, but almost 11,000 surrendered; the Americans counted 12,500 dead and 35,000 wounded. The Allies also lost 36 ships, and another 368 were damaged—mostly by kamikaze attacks. The Japanese lost many ships, including a battleship and some 7,000 airplanes, compared to the Allies 763. That was one of the bloodiest battles in history. With the capture of Okinawa, the Allies prepared for the invasion of the Japanese home islands. The plan called for invading the southern island of Kyushu in November 1945, and Tokyo's island of Honshu in March 1946.

May 1–August 15, 1945: The British navy had maintained a presence in the Indian Ocean for much of the war, a constant threat to the Japanese forces that had occupied Indonesia and Malaysia. On May 1, British and Australian troops invaded Borneo. In the ensuing weeks, more British troops went ashore at various points on Borneo and on nearby islands. By the end of July, the Allies had taken most of the strategic points on the island, but scattered resistance continued until the Japanese surrender. Even then, the final Japanese garrison on Borneo did not surrender until October 6.

August 6, 1945: The first atomic bomb was dropped on Hiroshima by a U.S. B-29 piloted by Col. Paul Tibbets; he had named his plane the *Enola Gay*, after his mother. The 9,000-lb. bomb (code-named Little Boy) was a uranium fission weapon that exploded some 1,850 feet above the center of the city about 8:15 A.M. It set off a blast with the force of 13,000 tons of TNT, but at least as damaging as the explosive power was the radioactivity it released. Some 60 percent of the city (about 4 ° square miles) was destroyed in the blast and firestorm, and about 92,000 people were killed or missing; at least as many were horribly burned or became ill from the effects of radiation and died at an early age. The firebombing raid on Tokyo on March 9–10 had killed more people, but this atomic bomb forever changed the way people thought about conducting war.

August 9, 1945: A second atomic bomb was dropped, this time on the city of Nagasaki. It was a plutonium fission device (code-named Fat Man) that weighed 10,000 pounds; it exploded about 1,650 feet above the city at 11:02 A.M. It destroyed about 1 ∫ square miles of the city and left at least 40,000 dead or missing and as many injured. Immediately after this, President Truman broadcast a message threatening Japan with destruction by more atomic bombs, though none was actually ready.

That same day, Soviet forces launched a massive offensive against the Japanese in Manchuria. The Japanese were completely overwhelmed by the superior numbers and equipment of the Soviets. The Soviet's entering the war against Japan had been agreed to by the Allies at the Yalta conference in February 1945, but at least some American leaders hoped to bring the Japanese to surrender before the Soviets could contribute enough to the war effort to justify claims on Japanese territory.

August 9–15, 1945: In addition to dropping the atomic bombs, the Allies continued their bombing raids on and bombardment of Japanese cities and installations. The Japanese could do little to counter those, but they did launch some final kamikaze attacks. On August 12, a Japanese submarine sank two U.S. warships east of Okinawa. In Manchuria, the Soviets continued to push back the Japanese.

August 15, 1945: After days of negotiating with the Allies and much internal wrangling (see Negotiations and Peace Treaty, p. 491), the Japanese government surrendered to the Allies. Emperor Hirohito broadcast the surrender to his people, and the Allies celebrated V-J Day. Some Allied planes were in the air at the time and did not hear the recall and so bombed military installations in Tokyo after the announcement.

August 16, 1945: The new Japanese premier transmitted Emperor Hirohito's cease-fire order to all Japanese troops. Not all Japanese forces received the message immediately, so sporadic fighting occurred for several days in several locations. It also took several days before word got through to some of Japan's more remote prisoner of war camps in places like Thailand and Burma. In particular, the Japanese in Manchuria continued to put up some resistance to the swiftly advancing Soviets, but on August 22, the Japanese army in Manchuria surrendered;

on August 25, the Soviets took over the southern half of Sakhalin, the island off Siberia that they had shared with Japan since 1905; on September 1, the Soviets took control of the Kurile Islands, a chain north of the Japanese home islands. Japanese on some of the more remote Pacific islands formally surrendered several days later: September 4 for the Japanese garrison on Wake Island, September 7 for garrisons on some of the smaller Ryukyu Islands, October 21 for the garrison on Sumatra. In some of the more isolated jungles and mountainous regions, it was not until March 1946 that the Japanese found Allied units to which they could surrender.

NAVAL THEATER

January–May 1945: In the Atlantic, the Germans managed to keep about 150 U-boats at sea during the first months of 1945, but they could do little damage to the Allies' convoys with their sophisticated defensive systems. The U-boats, however, were equipped with the *Schnorchel* air tube that allowed them to remain beneath the surface longer and so elude aircraft. The U-boats continued almost to the final days of the war in Europe to strike at ships as they approached the ports of Europe, but the destruction of construction and weapon facilities for U-boats and the massive loss of crews left the German navy powerless by the end of the war.

January–August 1945: In the Pacific, the now dominant Allied fleets moved pretty much where they chose, although by no means free of deadly attacks. The Japanese navy had essentially been eliminated as a threat in surface engagements; the Japanese relied more on its carriers and airplanes, especially planes used in kamikaze attacks. Allied carriers served as bases for planes that attacked targets in support of the advancing invasion forces, and Allied battleships and other heavy ships conducted massive bombardments of various islands, including Japan's home islands. Allied ship-based planes flew thousands of sorties, sank hundreds of thousands of tons of shipping, and shot down hundreds of airplanes. At least as important as the destruction of the Japanese navy was the virtual elimination of Japanese transport shipping, so that in the closing months of the war the Japanese were practically cut off from fuel and other supplies.

February 23, 1945: In the Atlantic, the USS *Henry Bacon* was sunk by German bombers, the last Allied merchant ship sunk by German aircraft in World War II.

March 18–21, 1945: Planes from U.S. carriers conducted a series of attacks on Japan's home islands and inflicted considerable damage. But kamikaze planes also did great damage, hitting six American carriers, the *Intrepid, Yorktown, Enterprise, Franklin, Essex,* and *Wasp* (a new carrier with that name). The 832 dead on the *Franklin* was the highest number of casualties ever on a U.S. warship.

March 23–31, 1945: In preparation for the forthcoming invasion of Okinawa, the large island south of Japan, hundreds of Allied ships mounted a massive bombardment and air attacks on the island. Kamikaze planes took a heavy toll on the ships. Those kamikaze attacks continued throughout the weeks that it took to capture Okinawa, and the Allied navies suffered heavy losses of ships and personnel: Some 10,000 Allied sailors were killed or wounded during the three-month campaign to take Okinawa.

April 7, 1945: U.S. carrier-based planes sank the Japanese carrier *Yamato* before it could get to Okinawa.

April 29–May 2, 1945: In the North Atlantic, the final convoy battle was fought between 14 German U-boats and 25 warships (escorting 24 merchant ships). One escort ship was hit and two U-boats were sunk, but all the merchant ships got through.

May 3–29, 1945: Kamikaze planes carried out a series of attacks on Allied ships supporting the Okinawa campaign. They damaged the U.S. battleship *New Mexico* and several carriers and sank several destroyers.

May 7, 1945: A German submarine sank two merchant ships off the east coast of Scotland, the last victims of U-boats in the war.

May 15–16, 1945: In the Malacca Strait between Malaya and Sumatra, British navy ships intercepted a Japanese convoy trying to get through with supplies to their forces on the Indonesian islands. Torpedoes from British destroyers sank the Japanese cruiser *Haguro* in what turned out to be the last action of the war involving major surface warships.

July 10–18, 1945: A large task force of American and British ships, including 15 carriers and 8 battleships, conducted a series of air attacks, bombing raids, and bombardments of Japanese cities and industrial plants. Because the Japanese were unable to mount much of a defense in the air or on the sea, the Allied ships were able to move relatively close to shore and bombard specific plants.

July 24–30, 1945: Ships and planes of the American and British naval task force continued their operations against the Japanese islands. They damaged several of the remaining large ships of the Japanese navy and shelled industrial plants.

July 29–August 2, 1945: The U.S. cruiser *Indianapolis*, which had delivered the first atomic bomb to the U.S. bomber base at Tinian in the Marianas and was on its way alone to Guam, was torpedoed and sunk by a Japanese submarine during the night of July 29. In the explosion and sinking, some 350 of its crew went down with the ship; another 850 were left adrift in the sea—50 of those drowned during the night; in the morning sharks attacked many of the survivors. At Guam, no one realized that the ship had been hit because there had been no time to put out a distress signal; and although U.S. naval intelligence had intercepted the submarine commander's radio message of his success, they assumed he was exaggerating the size of his victim. The survivors were by chance spotted by a reconnaissance plane on August 2. They had been in the water for 84 hours, 318 survivors were rescued, all the rest had drowned. The loss of some 880 men was the greatest loss at sea in the history of the U.S. Navy.

September 2, 1945: In the final contribution by and tribute to the Allied navies, the U.S. battleship *Missouri*, anchored in Tokyo Bay, was the site of the formal surrender of Japan.

Home Front

April 12, 1945: While vacationing at Warm Springs, Georgia, President Franklin Delano Roosevelt was having his portrait painted when he complained of a headache; at 4:35 P.M. he was declared dead of a massive cerebral hemorrhage. At 7:00 P.M. that evening, Vice President Harry S. Truman was sworn in as the 33rd president. Although regarded as a decent and competent man, he had none of the stature of Roosevelt as a world leader. Roosevelt and his circle of war leaders had not kept Truman fully informed of the details of their policies. In particular, it was

only in the next few days that he was briefed on the work underway toward an atomic bomb.

April 16, 1945: At a joint session of Congress, President Truman assured Americans that he would continue the foreign and domestic polices of President Roosevelt. Congress extended the Lend-Lease Act to its Allies for an additional year. On August 20, however, Truman ordered a halt to lend-lease aid.

May 5, 1945: A bomb released from a Japanese balloon fell on Bay, Oregon, killing a woman and five children. The Japanese had been releasing such balloons for some time, but that was the only one that took American lives.

May 8, 1945: President Truman proclaimed May 8 V-E Day, as the nation celebrated the news of Germany's surrender the day before. A nationwide dimout was lifted.

May 10, 1945: The secretary of war announced the adoption of a point system to guarantee a fair yet swift discharge of military personnel. Military personnel would be assigned points on the basis of time in service, time in combat, and such factors.

June 29, 1945: President Truman approved the plans to invade Japan, with the initial invasion scheduled for November 1.

July 16, 1945: After years of secret research, the Manhattan Project detonated the first atomic bomb at Alamogordo, near Los Alamos, New Mexico. It was kept a total secret from the world, including from those living in that region, who were told that there had been an accident at a military ammunition dump.

July 19, 1945: Congress ratified the Bretton Woods agreements that provided the foundations for the postwar international economy.

July 28, 1945: The U.S. Senate approved the United Nations Charter by a vote of 89 to 2.

August 14, 1945: The War Manpower Commission lifted controls on the disposition of the labor force.

August 15, 1945: With the formal announcement of Japan's surrender, Americans joined millions of people around the world in celebrating V-J Day. The United States also ended gasoline and fuel rationing.

August 20, 1945: The War Production Board removed most controls over manufacturing activity. That led to a quick conversion to consumer-oriented manufacturing and a boom in the postwar economy.

INTERNATIONAL DEVELOPMENTS

January 6, 1945: Winston Churchill personally asked Joseph Stalin to order the Soviet forces to go on the offensive in Poland to relieve some of the pressure on the Allied armies in the Ardennes. Stalin agreed to ask his army to do so as soon as possible.

January 20, 1945: The Hungarian provisional government concluded an armistice with the Soviet Union, the United States, and Britain. The Hungarians agreed to pay reparations and to join in the war against Germany.

January 30–February 2, 1945: Roosevelt, Churchill, and their advisers met on Malta to discuss their forthcoming meeting with Stalin at Yalta, a popular Soviet resort town on the Black Sea.

February 4–11, 1945: Roosevelt, Churchill, Stalin, and their senior military and political staffs met at Yalta. When the meeting ended on February 11, they issued a statement about their agreements to set up occupation zones in Germany, to establish a freely elected government in Poland, to hold a conference in San Francisco to form the United Nations, and to reendorse the Atlantic Charter (see August 9-12, 1941, p. 446). Only later did it come out that Roosevelt and Churchill had also agreed that, in return for the Soviet's entering the war against Japan two to three months after Germany surrendered, Stalin was promised the right to take over the Kurile Islands and the southern half of Sakhilin Island (all islands long disputed with Japan). Stalin did not allow free elections in Poland or in the other East European countries, and he used other elements in the Yalta agreements to his own ends.

March 5, 1945: Germany announced that it was calling up 15- and 16-year-old boys to serve in the army.

March 19, 1945: Hitler issued a general order that all military, industrial, transportation, and communication installations, as well as all storehouses of materiel be destroyed in order to prevent them from falling intact into the hands of the enemy. Albert Speer, Germany's minister of armament and war production, had anticipated that order and because he was put in charge of overseeing it, took the lead in preventing it from being carried out. A number of high ranking army officers also disobeyed Hitler's scorched earth policy.

April 21, 1945: The Soviet Union concluded a mutual assistance agreement with the Lublin-based provisional government of Poland; that was the Communist-dominated group and thus indicated that Stalin had little intention of honoring his agreement at Yalta to hold free elections in Poland. Britain and the U.S. chose to recognize the Polish government-in-exile that had been based in London throughout the war.

April 25–June 26, 1945: Delegates from 50 nations met in San Francisco, California, to draw up the charter for a United Nations organization. The text of the charter was completed on June 23 and signed by all 50 participating nations on June 26. The major issues had been the smaller nations' opposition to allowing the major powers to have a greater say in world affairs and the Soviet's fear that the Soviet Union would be outvoted in the Security Council; in the end, the smaller nations conceded the greater power to the Security Council, but the Soviets won the provision that a single member of the council could veto any action.

April 28–29, 1945: On April 28, Italian partisans caught Mussolini and his mistress Clara Petacci, near Lake Como as they were trying to flee to Switzerland; they were shot (along with 15 members of Mussolini's entourage). On the morning of April 29, Mussolini's and Petacci's bodies were taken to Milan and hung upside down outside a garage.

June 5, 1945: The Allied Control Commission met for the first time in Berlin and announced that it was assuming the government of Germany.

July 17–August 2, 1945: Truman, Churchill, and Stalin met at Potsdam, outside Berlin, to discuss more details for dealing with Germany and the former occupied countries. Stalin revealed that the Japanese had been trying to treat the USSR as a neutral power to negotiate peace with the Allies, but the Japanese proposal did not seem to be specific enough to open discussions (see Negotiations and Peace Treaty, p. 490). Stalin also confirmed his agreement to join in the war against Japan. On July 17, Truman was notified by a coded message that the atomic bomb test at Los Alamos had succeeded (on July 16); he immediately informed Churchill, but it was July 24 before they chose to inform Stalin that they possessed that potentially devastating weapon. (It was later revealed that Stalin knew about the bomb from his espionage organization.) It was also on July 24 that Truman gave his final approval for using an atomic bomb against Japan.

July 26, 1945: The British delegation returned to Great Britain on July 25 to await the results of the national election. On July 26, it was revealed that the Labor Party had won a majority; Clement Attlee replaced Winston Churchill as prime minister. On July 26, a broadcast from Potsdam beamed expressly to Japan repeated the demand for unconditional surrender. Although it also promised that the Japanese would be extended many rights and would be allowed to restore their economy, it said nothing about the status of the emperor; that so-called Potsdam Declaration was later blamed by some historians for prolonging the war with Japan.

July 28–August 2, 1945: With Clement Attlee and his Labor advisers now representing Britain in Potsdam, the final agreements were reached. The main agreement allowed Poland to transfer its western boundary to the Oder and Neisse Rivers and moved the Soviet's borders westward into what had been the eastern regions of Poland. Another agreement provided for the removal of all Germans from Poland, Czechoslovakia, and Hungary.

August 8, 1945: The Soviet Union declared war on Japan. It had agreed to do so at Yalta, but there was suspicion among some Allied leaders that it was rushing in to have a say in the terms to be dictated to a defeated Japan.

NEGOTIATIONS AND PEACE TREATY

In the months following Hitler's invasion of Poland, there were numerous attempts to broker a peace—some involving the major adversaries' representatives, some involving neutral governments, some simply involving private citizens. Scandinavian businessmen, Pope Pius XII, the Duke of Windsor, the Turkish government, Francisco Franco of Spain, the Japanese foreign minister, among others, tried to arrange terms, but it soon became apparent that Hitler was not going to be content with anything less than imposing his "new order." With the German invasion of Denmark and Norway in April 1940 and France in May 1940, all such negotiation efforts became meaningless, although they did continue. Some disaffected Germans, including such prominent figures as Adm. Wilhelm Canaris and diplomat Franz von Papen, tried to deal secretly with the British and Americans, but the Allies' declara-

tion on January 24, 1943, that they would accept only the "unconditional surrender" of the Axis essentially put an end to such negotiations. Throughout the war, however, there was distrust between Stalin and the Anglo-American leaders, and there were numerous secret meetings between their governments' agents and German agents to make sure that neither side made some "deal" with Hitler. The Soviets feared that the Great Britain and the United States would join with Germany to turn on them, the Communists; the British and Americans feared that Stalin would return to his previous alliance with Hitler to divide up Eastern Europe.

ITALY SURRENDERS

Although Mussolini certainly had his own scheme of conquest, he never really gained Italians' support for Hitler's grandiose plans to conquer the world. After losses suffered by the Italians at Stalingrad in December 1942, the Italian foreign minister, Count Galeazzo Ciano (Mussolini's son-in-law), suggested to Hitler that they strike an armistice with the Soviets. Hitler dismissed that, as he would a similar suggestion by Mussolini after the terrible losses in North Africa in April 1943. Ciano and others then tried secretly to strike a separate peace with the British and Americans, and Mussolini considered simply withdrawing from the war. With the invasion of Sicily in July 1943, Italy's situation worsened, and on July 25, Mussolini was forced out of office. The new Italian leader was Marshal Pietro Badoglio, who immediately began secret negotiations with the Allies. The Italian surrender was signed at Cassibili, Sicily, on September 3, but was not announced until September 8. Immediately, the Germans turned from being an ally of Italy to an enemy occupying force.

GERMANY SURRENDERS

Hitler may have been paranoid, but he was right to suspect that many of his subordinates were trying to negotiate terms with the Allies behind his back. Some of those were members of the military, particularly the *Abwehr* (or intelligence section) who were primarily interested in getting rid of Hitler and negotiating a separate peace with Britain and the United States. The various attempts on Hitler's life, culminating in the bomb explosion at a conference on July 20, 1944, would presumably have led to some sort of negotiations, but all the attempts failed. With the end of the Third Reich clearly inevitable by the end of 1944, various Germans tried to negotiate a peace, but always one that would leave Germany—as well as themselves—unpunished for aggression.

January 19, 1945: Heinrich Himmler met secretly with Count Folke Bernadotte, vice chairman of the Swedish Red Cross, to negotiate the release to the Swedish Red Cross of the small number of Jews still alive in concentration camps. In fact, few Jews actually benefited from that. Himmler was more interested in promoting himself to the Allies as a viable alternative to Hitler.

February 1945: With the Soviets, British, and Americans having crossed Germany's borders, the German foreign minister, Joachim von Ribbentrop, (with Hitler's knowledge) tried to approach the British and Americans with an offer to join a Nazi-led Germany in its war against the Communist Soviet Union, but nothing came of that proposal.

April 20, 1945: Himmler attended Hitler's birthday party in Hitler's underground bunker in Berlin, then later in the day met secretly with Swedish representatives of the World Jewish Congress. Still trying to promote himself as an honorable successor to Hitler, he agreed to send several thousand women—about half of them Jewish—to Sweden from the Ravensbrück concentration camp.

April 23–27, 1945: Through further contacts with Count Folke Bernadotte, Himmler offered a secret peace with the Allies, independent of the Soviet Union; the Allies, in return, were to join Germany in fighting the Soviets. The Western Allies rejected that offer on April 27 and reported the discussion to Stalin. Meanwhile, on April 23, Hitler had received a telegram from Hermann Göring, announcing that he was ready to take over since Hitler had lost "freedom of action." Hitler was furious and demanded that Göring resign all offices, and Hitler's assistant, Martin Bormann, ordered the SS to arrest Göring.

April 28, 1945: Hitler learned of Himmler's secret negotiations (reported on a BBC broadcast) and gave orders for him to be arrested. Himmler avoided capture and went into hiding. Disguised as a private in the German army, he was captured by the British on May 21, but he committed suicide two days later, before he could be brought to trial as a war criminal.

April 29–30, 1945: After marrying his longtime mistress, Eva Braun, on April 29, Hitler dictated his final political testimony. He expelled Göring and Himmler from the Nazi Party and all state offices and named Adm. Karl Dönitz, commander of the German navy, to succeed him as president of the Third Reich. The next day, about 3:30 P.M., Hitler and Eva Braun committed suicide (he shot himself, she took poison). Their bodies were taken into a courtyard, doused with gasoline, and burned.

April 29–May 2, 1945: On April 29, German representatives at Caserta in southern Italy negotiated the surrender of German forces in Italy to the Allies. It was May 1 before the German commander in Italy approved the surrender, which went into effect on May 2.

May 1, 1945: Joseph Goebbels and his wife, after poisoning their six children, committed suicide; their bodies were also burned.

May 2, 1945: Soviet Gen. Vasili Chuikov accepted the surrender of Berlin. Soviet troops moved into the chancellery and into Hitler's underground bunker.

May 3–4, 1945: Two high-ranking German military officers arrived at the headquarters of British field marshal Bernard Montgomery in northwestern Germany. On behalf of Admiral Dönitz, they offered to surrender the German forces then facing the Soviets to the east (hoping, thereby, that those forces would be taken prisoner by the Western Allies instead of by Soviet forces). Montgomery told them that they would have to surrender those troops to the Soviets, but advised them to surrender the German forces in Holland, Denmark, and northwest Germany—the forces then facing the British. The officers reported that to Dönitz in the nearby city of Flensburg, and on May 4, they returned to surrender those forces, effective May 5.

May 3–6, 1945: Various German military forces from Holland to southern Germany continued to surrender to commanders in the field.

May 5–7, 1945: Adm. Hans von Friedeburg, commander of the German navy, flew from Flensburg to Gen. Dwight D. Eisenhower's headquarters at Reims, France, to try to negotiate a surrender of only the German forces facing the Western allies. On May 6, Gen. Alfred Jodl, head of the German general staff, joined him at

Reims. Eisenhower insisted that the Germans surrender all units, including those facing the Soviets. Jodl radioed that demand back to Dönitz in Flensburg. After having been authorized by Dönitz, on May 7, at 2:41 A.M., Jodl and von Friedeburg signed a final surrender of all German forces everywhere. Gen. Walter Bedell Smith signed for the Allied Expeditionary Force, Gen. Ivan Susloparov signed for the Soviet Union, and Gen. François Sevez of France signed as a witness. The surrender took effect at 11:01 P.M. on May 8.

May 8, 1945: V-E Day was observed in Great Britain and the United States. (The Soviets observed May 9 as Victory Day.) In Berlin, about midnight, the surrender document was ratified by representatives of the German military and witnessed by Allied military leaders. Scattered fighting, surrenders of German units, and suicides by high-ranking Germans continued in parts of Europe for another week.

JAPAN SURRENDERS

The Japanese had barely begun their war of conquest in the Pacific when some high-ranking Japanese military and government officials put out feelers to negotiate an end to hostilities. In September 1943, some officials had Emperor Hirohito's approval to deal with representatives of Chiang Kai-shek to end the fighting in China, but Prime Minister Hideki Tojo stopped that peace initiative. Tojo was removed from office in July 1944, and the co-premier, Adm. Mitsumasa Yonia, initiated efforts to seek peace. He wanted to hold onto Formosa and Korea, however, and the Allies had called for "unconditional surrender." In August and September 1944, the Japanese tried to persuade Germany to make peace with the Soviet Union so that the Western Allies would have to concentrate all their forces on the war in Europe; neither the Germans nor the Soviets were prepared to make a deal. By March 1945, a Japanese naval aide in Switzerland had contacted the American Office of Strategic Services (OSS) to begin negotiations, but nothing came of those discussions. (Japanese naval officers, who had seen virtually their entire navy destroyed, were more ready to seek peace than were army officers.) In April 1945, Kantaro Suzuki took over as prime minister and prepared to negotiate peace; many individuals in Japan's high-

est echelons had come to recognize the hopelessness of their struggle. However, the Japanese peace seekers had to deal with the fact that leaders of the army were determined to fight on; the peace faction further confused the issue by attempts to negotiate separate arrangements with the Soviet Union.

As late as July 21, 1945, Japanese agents in Moscow were still trying to negotiate terms with the Soviet Union; only then did the Japanese give a clear sign that they were willing to discuss a mediated peace with all the Allies. On July 26, the Potsdam Declaration was broadcast to Japan, reaffirming the requirement of unconditional surrender and setting forth generally reasonable terms after that surrender. The declaration was intentionally vague about the status of the emperor: Maintaining the emperor was the one condition that even the most dedicated Japanese peace seekers would insist upon.

Meanwhile, on July 17, President Truman and Prime Minister Churchill, in Potsdam for a conference with Stalin, were informed of the successful explosion of a nuclear device in New Mexico. That changed Truman's thoughts on such issues as the need to negotiate with Japan and the desirability of bringing the Soviet Union into the war with Japan. When Japanese Prime Minister Suzuki held a press conference on July 28 and reported that he would pay no attention to the Potsdam Declaration, Truman became more convinced than ever that the United States should use the new atomic weapon to bring the Japanese to accept surrender. The first atomic bomb was dropped on Hiroshima on August 6. Despite the horrific death and destruction visited upon Hiroshima, the Japanese leaders continued to resist surrendering. A second atomic bomb was dropped on Nagasaki on August 9.

August 9, 1945: The Supreme War Direction Council met in Tokyo, but it remained split over whether to surrender.

August 10, 1945: Emperor Hirohito called a second meeting that met in the early hours of August 10, and flatly called for the acceptance of the Potsdam Declaration—"with the understanding that said Declaration does not compromise any demand that prejudices the prerogatives of His Majesty as a sovereign ruler." That acceptance was forwarded to the Japanese ambassadors in Sweden and Switzerland; they immediately forwarded it to the Allies.

August 10–12, 1945: Negotiations between the United States and Japan continued to be conducted through neutral powers. The U.S. argued for the survival of the emperor but stated that "the authority of the emperor and the Japanese government to rule the state shall be subject to the Supreme Commander of the Allied Powers." Meantime, hostilities continued, especially in Manchuria; the Soviet Union had entered the war against Japan on August 8, and Soviet forces were taking a terrible toll on Japanese forces.

August 14, 1945: Hirohito called another meeting of the Supreme War Direction Council and flatly ordered that the war end. He recorded a message—to be broadcast the next day—calling on the Japanese people "to bear the unbearable." The Allies were informed that the Japanese were accepting unconditional surrender, and word of that began to circulate around the world. During the night, some 1,000 Japanese army officers attacked the Imperial Palace with the intention of seizing the emperor's recorded message before it could be broadcast, but they were repulsed by the palace guards.

August 15, 1945: A Japanese radio announcer asked that listeners stand "respectfully" in front of their sets; the Japanese national anthem was then played, followed by the emperor's recording. (It was the first time the Japanese had ever heard their emperor's voice.) The Allies celebrated V-J Day.

August 16, 1945: The new Japanese premier called on all Japanese military forces to cease fire. A week later, the last Japanese surrendered to the Soviets in Manchuria.

August 28, 1945: The first Americans—a task force of about 150 men—landed in Japan flying into an airfield near Yokohama to prepare the way for Gen. Douglas MacArthur. He landed in Japan on August 30.

September 2, 1945: In Tokyo Bay, on the battleship USS *Missouri*, the new Japanese foreign minister, Mamoru Shigemitsu, and the chief of staff of the Japanese army, Gen. Yoshijiro Umezu, signed the surrender document; General MacArthur signed on behalf of all the Allies, Adm. Chester Nimitz signed for the United States and Adm. Bruce Fraser signed for Great Britain.

September 12, 1945: In Singapore, Lord Louis Mountbatten of Great Britain accepted the formal surrender of all Japanese forces in Southeast Asia.

OTHER AXIS POWERS SURRENDERS

September 10, 1944: Finland signed an armistice with the Soviets, agreeing to pay reparations and to return to its 1940 boundaries. The Germans began to leave Finland, and many Finns joined the Soviets in fighting the Germans.

September 13, 1944: The Romanians signed an armistice with the Allies; the terms had essentially been set by the Soviets and called for reparations as well as the cession of territory to the Soviet Union.

October 28, 1944: Bulgaria signed an armistice with the Soviet Union. Among other provisions, it placed Bulgarian troops under the Soviets command.

January 20, 1945: The Hungarian Provisional Government signed an armistice with the United States, the Soviet Union, and Great Britain. The Hungarians also agreed to join the war against Germany.

PEACE TREATIES

All the documents described above were surrender documents. The peace treaties required many international conferences spread out over many months (many years, in some instances). They were as follows:

The Allies signed peace treaties with Bulgaria, Finland, Hungary, and Romania in Paris on February 10, 1947. (The U.S. did not sign one with Finland, as the two had never formally been at war.) The treaties established reparations, limits on armed forces, as well as other conditions.

The Allies also signed a peace treaty with Italy in Paris on February 10, 1947. In addition to agreeing to reparations and limits on its armed forces, Italy gave up its African colonies of Libya and Tunisia, gave some borderlands to France and Yugoslavia, gave the Dodecanese Islands to Greece, and recognized the independence of Albania, Ethiopia, and the city of Trieste.

Under the terms agreed to at Potsdam in July and August 1945, the Allies divided Austria and Germany—and Berlin separately—into four occupation zones, one for each of the major Allies: the Soviet Union, the United States, Great Britain, and France. Germany gave the northern part of East Prussia to the Soviet Union; the city of Danzig (Gdansk) and the southern part of East Prussia, Silesia, and Pomerania went to Poland;

some territory was also given to Belgium, Czecho-slovakia, and France. Germany was forced to make reparations. Austria was granted its inde-pendence on May 15, 1955. The three zones of Germany occupied by the United States, Britain, and France were combined as the Federal Re-public of Germany on September 21, 1949, and a civilian commission replaced the military occu-pation, but the United States did not formally end hostilities with Germany until October 19, 1951. It was May 5, 1955, before all the Western Allies signed a treaty recognizing Germany as an independent state. The Soviet Union did not sign that treaty, and Germany and Berlin remained divided into Western and Eastern entities until the Soviet Union began to come apart; the two Germanys were reunited on October 3, 1990.

Representatives of 52 countries met in San Francisco in 1951, and on September 8 of that year, 49 (including the United States and Great Britain) signed a peace treaty with Japan. (Czechoslovakia, Poland, and the Soviet Union would not accept the terms of that treaty; the USSR did not sign a treaty with Japan until De-cember 1956.) The treaty set reparations, forced Japan to give up all former possessions outside its home islands, and limited its right to arm itself only for self-defense. The treaty did not take effect until April 28, 1952, at which time the Al-lied occupation officially came to an end.

RESULTS OF THE WAR (Casualties, Costs, Consequences)

Most sources give the total number of those who died because of World War II (military and civilian) as 50 million but many who have stud-ied the subject closely believe that the truer fig-ure is higher—up to twice that number. Since it is virtually impossible to assign exact numbers—even for military forces (although those of cer-tain nations are probably fairly accurate)—listed here are only rounded-off numbers for the re-ported dead. (Not even the most scholarly sources agree on these figures.) Tens of thou-sands of military personnel who died or were missing in combat went unreported simply due to the chaos of battle, and many millions of civil-ians died without their deaths being recorded: One certain fact is that more civilians than mili-tary personnel died in World War II. Millions more were left homeless by the war: An estimated

50 million Chinese were left homeless. In Eu-rope, millions of people were forced to take flight and became refugees, or "displaced persons" in the euphemism of the period.

The following table:

(1) includes the many military personnel and civilians who died of diseases—in particular, ty-phus and malaria—that, it is assumed, they would never have contracted except for the war. By some estimates, almost half the civilian deaths were due to diseases.

(2) attempts to separate by countries of ori-gin those Jews killed in what is known as the Holocaust. But it was not always clear whether Jews who died during the war were killed be-cause they were Jewish: When German occupa-tion forces moved into Poland and the Soviet Union, for example, they wiped out thousands of people almost indiscriminately, and it is hard to say whether they selected their victims because they were Poles or Slavs or Communists or Jews.

(3) includes under Civilians (wherever pos-sible) those killed in bombings and other military actions, reprisals, and executions, and those who died from starvation, privation, illnesses and other hardships directly attributable to condi-tions of war.

(4) makes no attempt to tally the wounded (who recovered) or the missing. (Military experts generally assume that about five times more people are wounded in combat than are killed.) Many of the wounded survived the war but died prematurely as a result of their wounds. Hun-dreds of thousands, perhaps millions, of the wounded lived their entire lives suffering from their injuries and disabilities.

(5) excludes millions of deaths that might well have been prevented had the war not been rag-ing: One of most dramatic examples is the 1.5 million Bengalis who died in a famine in 1943; it is believed that many would have survived had shipping and railroads been free to carry food.

THE ALLIES

NATION	ESTIMATED DEAD
African Military	3,600
Australian Military	29,000
Australian Civilian	12,000

(Continued on p. 493)

NATION	ESTIMATED DEAD
Belgian Military	11,000
Belgian Civilian	78,000
Canadian Military	42,100
Chinese Military	2,500,000
Chinese Civilian	10,000,000
Czechoslovakian Military	250,000
Czechoslovakian Civilian	90,000
Danish Military	4,400
Dutch Military	34,000
Dutch Civilian	170,000
French Military	250,000
French Civilian	350,000
Greek Military	80,000
Greek Civilian	400,000
Indian Military	25,000
Luxembourg	5,000
Moroccan Military	500
New Zealand Military	12,300
Norwegian	10,000
Philippine Military	40,000
Philippine Civilian	100,000
Polish Military	200,000
Polish Civilian	2,000,000
South African Military	7,000
United Kingdom Military	398,000
United Kingdom Civilian	91,000
U.S. Military	406,000
U.S. Merchant Marine	5,600
U.S. Civilian	2,000
*Soviet Military	10,000,000
*Soviet Civilian	9,000,000
Yugoslavian Military	305,000
Yugoslavian Civilian	1,000,000

*Includes Ukrainians, Belorussians, Lithuanians, Latvians, Estonians, and others living in the Soviet Union. The Soviet Union gave various figures on how many of its citizens lost their lives in the war, but a total of 20 million—including those of Jewish origin—is the accepted figure.

THE HOLOCAUST**

NATION	ESTIMATED DEAD
Polish Jews	2,700,000
Soviet Jews	1,250,000
Hungarian Jews	300,000
Czechoslovakian Jews	200,000
German Jews	160,000
Jews Elsewhere in Europe	1,390,000
Gypsies***	250,000

(All figures are estimates.)

** Here restricted to the two groups of people who were systematically rounded up and executed by the Germans because they were regarded as members of an "impure race"—indeed, virtually outside the human race. In fact, many hundreds of thousands of others died in concentration camps, mass executions, and other situations for no other reason than they were Slavs, homosexuals, subversives or some other category that the Germans thought should be eliminated. Those people are counted among the civilian deaths of their respective lands, to the extent that their numbers are known.

*** The official Nazi policy regarding gypsies was never clearly defined or carried out. At times, there was some attempt to spare those who were "pure" and settled gypsies and kill only those of "mixed" blood and a vagrant lifestyle. In the end, though, most gypsies were eventually labled "asocials" and rounded up and killed in concentration camps.

THE AXIS

NATION	ESTIMATED DEAD
Austrian Military	240,000
Bulgarian Military	32,000
East European Civilians*	2,000,000
Finnish Military	80,000
German Military	4,000,000
German Civilian	1,400,000
Hungarian Military	140,000
Italian Military	160,000
Italian Civilian	250,000
Japanese Military	2,200,000
Japanese Civilian	2,000,000
Romanian Military	200,000
Spanish Volunteers	4,500

* This figure is a rough estimate of East European Civilians other than Jews who died during World War II.

Arriving at the exact total cost of World War II is literally impossible and almost no authorities attempt to do so. About $40 trillion (in 1990 dollars) is the best estimate that can be offered. Even attempting to break down the cost into special categories is impossible. It might seem that the direct outlays in national budgets for military costs could be calculated—and some scholars have tried to do so, but they have never come up with the same figures because none can agree on just what those costs should include or exclude. For example, should military costs include the medical bills for veterans with serious wounds and disabilities?   If those costs are included, should the many other payments to veterans, such as pensions, also be included?   By some calculations, the United States alone has spent about as much on its World War II veterans as it spent on the war itself.

What about the costs to resettle refugees in the aftermath of the war? Should reparations by the losers be counted as costs of the war? If so, should they cancel out losses sustained by those who received payments? What about costs incurred in financing underground and resistance movements—sums that were secret at the time and that remain virtually unknown.

There were the costs—in terms of units and value—of the destruction of private dwellings, public buildings, factories, and farms. There are some fairly authoritative figures for the number of private dwellings destroyed: 3 million in the Soviet Union, 2.25 million in Japan, 510,000 in Poland, 450,000 in Great Britain, 255,000 in France, and 2.5 million in Germany. But no one can do much more than assign the most general averages to the monetary value of those homes. Then there were the great public structures—cathedrals, historic buildings, government offices, private institutions, museums—that had values beyond calculation. And the infrastructures of so many lands—highways, railroads, docks, water delivery systems, electric and phone systems—lay in waste. That does not take into account the immediate damage to the industrial fabric of much of the world—estimated at up to 50 percent for countries such as France and Japan. Only the vaguest of values can be assigned to the total of property damage, but $240 billion is one figure that has been used.

Several of the consequences of World War II have been discussed under Significance (see pp. 424-425)—the redrawing of boundaries of former states, for example, the liberation of former colonies, even the formation of new nations. At least two of the European countries that were assigned new boundaries—Yugoslavia and Czechoslovakia—came apart in the 1990s, but by and large, the new boundaries have held up. The liberation of so many former colonies was arguably the most important single consequence of the war. Primarily in Africa and Asia, but also in the Middle East, some of those lands had been dominated by foreigners for centuries. Although by no means did all gain instant freedom—many had to fight their former dominators—most can point to the end of World War II as the turning point in their history. Not exactly in the same class as those colonies were such lands as Korea, which gained its freedom from Japan, or the Dodecanese Islands, which went to Greece after many centuries of foreign occupation. Not all these new arrangements have proved to be peaceful: The establishment of the state of Israel, directly resulting from World War II, is perhaps the most obvious example. Whatever the consequences since, World War II redrew the political map of much of the world.

The establishment and growth of the United Nations has also been recognized as one of the most significant outcomes of World War II. Despite its flaws, many see the UN as the best alternative to World War III, and, in a profound sense, the UN has been held together by the knowledge that the failure of the League of Nations led to World War II. Beyond that global political organization and its several units (UNICEF, World Health Organization, and others), various regional organizations emerged from World War II, also inspired by the recognition that it was time to end the centuries of regional friction. Perhaps the most notable example of that is the European community that has progressed by stages, building on the vision of Europeans who were determined to put a stop to the wars that had ravaged Europe for so long. Many other regional pacts, cooperative efforts, and international arrangements can also trace their origins back to World War II: monetary arrangements, trade treaties, the World Bank, disarmament pacts—those and others were in large measure motivated by the experience of World War II.

The new striving for more cooperative international relations also manifested itself in an acceleration of trade, transportation, communication, and tourism throughout the world, in turn leading to a general rise in the standards of living. By no means have all people prospered, but many have: World War II released a burst of productivity stifled by the Great Depression of the 1930s and by various age-old traditions. Ironically, among the nations that profited most from the new internationalism were the two chief aggressors (and chief losers) of World War II—Germany and Japan. Had there been no war, they might still have emerged at the end of the century as economic superpowers, but certainly they profited from being able to "wipe the slate clean" after World War II. Freed from the need to maintain military forces and assume international responsibilities and with their antiquated factories in ruins, Germany and Japan turned their talents and energies to their domestic economies and civilian products. Fifty years after the end of World War II, their economies and societies seem to be among the war's chief beneficiaries.

One nation that clearly emerged from the war as an economic powerhouse was the United State. (It was the only major warring power that did not end up as a debtor.) After several years of a major depression, with effectively no damage to its domestic plants and with the enforced savings of the war years, the American production machine, which had geared up during the war to levels never before known, took off. New consumer products, new homes, new cars and roads—Americans wanted them all, and now they could afford them. Beyond the basics, Americans began to demand new materials, new devices, new services, new designs, new ways. There was a new energy, a new style, a new confidence in the American way of life.

It was not just in the economic and material spheres that Americans suddenly came to be so expansive. Although much of the rest of the world needed some time to recover from the disasters of World War II, Americans were on the go, traveling everywhere, trying everything, buying everything. On the most literal level, millions of American service personnel, business people, and government officials and their families were stationed around the world and exposed to other cultures in ways that would affect them subtly: They acquired a taste for foreign foods, saw different ways of doing things, married foreigners, came to realize that other people could make good

radios and cars. To cite just one specific result linked to World War II, the Fulbright scholarships (originally financed by the sale of American war materials abroad) sent thousands of Americans to study and teach in foreign lands. Not everyone became sophisticated and cosmopolitan, but millions of Americans certainly came to some better understanding of the different ways of the world.

This new "internationalization" of the world had another side to it: a homogenization of culture. For if Americans took in the rest of the world, the converse was also true: The rest of the world took up America as never before. The popularity of GIs—with their chocolate and cigarettes, their ready smiles and open manner—carried over to the popularity of many things "Made in the U.S.A."—clothing, movies, popular music. Some of that might well have occurred just due to the passage of time, but World War II undeniably accelerated that phenomenon. For better or worse, the world has been moving toward a global village ever since.

Many nations trace fundamental social and cultural rearrangements and shake-ups of the last half of the 20th century to World War II; those have involved everything from socioeconomic classes, ethnic groups, and population movements to more internalized traditions, customs, and restrictions. The United States, in particular, experienced a major social revolution in the postwar years with the breakup of the segregation of its African-American citizens. During the war, black troops had fought alongside white troops—for the most part in segregated units but on a few occasions side by side. When the war ended, many African Americans questioned why they should go back to second-class status when they had just risked their lives to open the world to democracy. It was no coincidence, then, that President Truman officially eliminated segregation in the armed forces in 1948. Likewise, it was no coincidence that after the war Jews began to be accepted into the mainstream of American life. The war had forced many people to reexamine many preconceptions and prejudices.

Meanwhile, because it emerged as the only country to have prospered from World War II, the United States found itself taking on a new role as an international superpower. In particular, the U.S.—having learned from its failure to support the League of Nations—became as committed as any nation to the United Nations. Through its financial support and activism, the United States, for better or worse, became the world's "policeman." From Korea (see Korean War pp. 570-607) and Berlin and Vietnam (see Vietnam War pp. 608-664) to the Persian Gulf (see Persian Gulf War, pp. 700-720) and Haiti and Bosnia, the United States seemed to be applying the lessons it had ignored after World War I.

The context to that activism by the United States and some of its allies, however, was the almost 50-year struggle between the Communist and non-Communist worlds that was known as the Cold War (see Cold War, pp. 525-569). Although the confrontations between the Communists, particularly those based in the Soviet Union, and the many opposed to Communism began even before World War I ended, continued through the 1920s, and became even more overt in the 1930s, World War II put that issue on hold—or more aptly, temporarily suppressed it. However, even before the formal peace treaties were signed, that deep conflict began to surface again in various parts of the world. Within a few years, many of the world's nations had realigned themselves into Communist and anti-Communist blocs; in several instances—Berlin, Korea, Vietnam—the dividing line was drawn right through a people. If World War II did not cause or start that confrontation, the war's outcome certainly moved the confrontation into a higher gear. Proof of that is that only with the end of the Cold War in the 1990s are some of the still-lingering issues and problems of World War II (indeed, of World War I) finally being resolved. (For example, it was the 1990s before Estonia, Latvia, and Lithuania regained the full freedom they had been promised after World War I.) Whatever its precise causes, whoever shares the blame, the Cold War was one of the most pervasive, enduring, and costly results of World War II. Hovering over the Cold War, too, was the threat of nuclear war. Only with the end of the Cold War has that threat also begun to recede: In that sense, the immediate consequences of World War II may finally be coming to an end.

MILITARY INNOVATIONS, TACTICS, EQUIPMENT

There were so many innovations, inventions, firsts, and novelties used by the various partici-

pants in World War II that only the most important ones can be singled out here.

Virtually every type of firearm was improved during the war: pistols, rifles, hand grenades, automatic weapons, machine guns, mortars, artillery, and many more. All tended to be made more efficient, more powerful—more deadly. Many other weapons that had been invented before World War II came into widespread use during the war: antipersonnel and antitank mines, flamethrowers, antiaircraft weapons, and self-propelled guns. Among the several true inventions was the rocket launcher known as the bazooka, a shoulder-fired recoilless weapon that gave U.S. soldiers a portable weapon against Axis tanks and armed vehicles. (The name came from the crude homemade trombone used by comedian Bob Burns as a prop; he named it as early as 1905. The Germans copied the U.S. bazooka and came up with a better model, the *Panzerfaust*, or "armored fist.") Above all, the volume of firepower—massive artillery bombardments before and during operations—intensified the level of destruction beyond anything previously known.

Tanks were made far stronger, faster, more maneuverable, and, above all, more deadly during World War II. The heavy tanks that evolved by the end of the war—the British Matilda II, the American Pershing, the Soviet Joseph Stalin, and the German Tiger—raised tank warfare to a level hardly conceived of when the war began.

On another level, the U.S. Army needed a general purpose vehicle, soon known by the pronunciation of its acronym, GP—the Jeep. The Willys Motor Company developed that amazingly versatile (and enduring) vehicle. The Germans also had their own all-purpose vehicle, made by the company that had begun to make Hitler's "people's car," or Volkswagen.

Then there was the U.S.-developed amphibious vehicle known as the DUKW (an acronym formed from the army's code: D=design year, U=amphibian, K=all-wheel drive, W =dual rear)—pronounced "duck." A more powerful amphibian was the LVT (landing vehicle, tracked), a landing vehicle that carried personnel and heavier armor across the sea and onto a beach.

Beyond the many new weapons and vehicles, new tactics distinguished World War II. The Germans not only developed new tanks and armored personnel vehicles and motorcycles and self-propelled guns, they also used those in a swift maneuver that caught opponents off guard—the *Blitzkrieg*. Even aside from the surprise of their early invasions, the Germans changed the pace of battle—from the North African campaign to their final gasp at the Battle of the Bulge—with the dynamic tactics of their highly motorized and mobile units. (The Germans used literally millions of horses and mules for hauling artillery and supplies; they also used mounted cavalry in various combat operations, as did the Soviets, the Italians, and several other forces. The U.S. military used mounted cavalry units for reconnaissance and guard patrol.) The Allies soon changed their tactics and adopted similarly dynamic units and operations. Battles were fought over extended distances and with constantly changing front lines in ways never before witnessed.

Amphibious warfare also moved into an entirely new dimension: small armed units had been going ashore in boats for centuries, but there had never been anything comparable to the massive amphibious operations conducted in World War II—first by the Axis, then on a still larger scale by the Allies. The series of landing operations that cleared the Japanese from Pacific islands, one by one, redefined amphibious warfare, and in the sheer size of the forces, equipment, and materiel involved, the invasion of France on D-Day (see June 6, 1944, pp. 466-467) was like nothing ever imagined or experienced in the history of warfare. Among the many innovations that played an important role in that operation were the two so-called Mulberry Harbors. Those were large floating docks made of old ships, concrete and steel blocks, and metal roadways that were floated across the English Channel from England and put into place along the coast of Normandy to create instant artificial harbor installations. Another innovation that played a crucial role in amphibious landings was the U.S. Navy's LST (landing ship, tanks), which, as its name suggests, allowed for tanks (and other heavy vehicles) to be brought onto a beach.

The navies of the major powers also were enlarged and improved in almost every aspect, raising ocean warfare to new heights of ferocity. Battleships, which in some ways symbolized the very origins of the war—the "Great Powers" race to own more and bigger ones paralleled their competition for power and territory—were made close

to obsolete by aircraft carriers and their planes. Battleships were effective in bombarding various shore defenses and islands before invasions, and there were several major sea battles involving battleships. Yet, the whole nature of naval warfare was changed when—as at the Battles of the Coral Sea (see May 2–8, 1942, p. 454) and Midway (see June 3–6, 1942, p. 454)—major battles were fought by aircraft that left their carriers hundreds of miles away: Relatively small and inexpensive aircraft sank large expensive ships—with a comparably disproportionate level of casualties.

The most extreme example of this came with the Japanese introduction of *kamikaze* (or "divine wind") pilots in the closing months of World War II: Japanese pilots sworn to sacrifice themselves simply dove their bomb-laden aircraft straight at Allied ships. Between April 6 and July 29, 1945, the Allies lost 83 ships (including 13 destroyers) to those suicide pilots; 350 others were damaged. The Japanese lost about 3,900 aircraft (and thus pilots) in those attacks, but the attacks cost the U.S. Navy alone some 4,900 dead and another 4,800 wounded: although often dismissed as a freak episode of the war, those *kamikaze* attacks were, in fact, a serious threat and might have been far more serious had the Japanese introduced them earlier in the war.

Another type of armed vessel that gained a glamorous reputation in World War II was the PT boats (patrol torpedo boats) of the U.S. Navy and their equivalent in other navies, MTBs (motor torpedo boats). Those swift attack craft dashed in where larger ships could not go and fired torpedoes that sank many larger ships. In retrospect, though, naval warfare experts have concluded that they were not all that effective or crucial in major engagements.

The far less glamorous Liberty ships—and their successors, Victory ships—made significant contributions to the Allied victory. Those merchant ships were constructed in U.S. shipyards in record-breaking time by using new construction techniques such as prefabricating large sections, moving them into place by cranes, then welding the parts together (see p. 445). Although the basic design of the ships was British, most were built in U.S. shipyards. Those and the thousands of other Allied merchant ships—and the bravery of their crews—affected the entire logistics and strategy of the war.

Submarines were as influential as aircraft carriers in the conduct of the war. They had already shown their potency in World War I, but they truly came into their own in World War II. The Germans were in the forefront in designing submarines that were not just faster and more powerful but also far more sophisticated in their equipment and capabilities than were earlier versions. In the years 1940–1943, German U-boats exacted a terrible toll on Allied shipping. Gradually, the Allies developed not only their own submarine fleets but also anti-submarine warfare based on new ships, new detection devices, new weapons, and new tactics. Indeed, submarine warfare in World War II was a striking example of what total war had become: Technology (the Germans' electric homing torpedo and the Allies' radar), tactics (the Germans' wolf pack approach and the Allies' use of aircraft to spot enemy submarines), manufacturing potential (the Axis powers' declining as the Allies' increased), and other factors played major roles in the submarine warfare that raged almost independent of the land campaigns.

There were so many advancements made in aircraft both by the Axis and the Allies during World War II that it is fair to say that the airplanes of 1945 bore little resemblance to the airplanes of 1939. New materials, special designs, powerful engines, deadly armaments, navigational aids, and aiming devices and bombsights transformed aerial warfare. Two of the more revolutionary developments, the helicopter and the jet plane, saw only limited service in the war. The development of the helicopter had begun during the 1930s, with the Germans taking an early lead. During World War II, Germany, Britain, and the United States made some use of helicopters—especially for light transport and observation and communications—but the full potential of the helicopter as a military vehicle was realized only after the war. Jet-powered airplanes had also been developed by the late 1930s, but the first practical turbojet airplane was a British plane flown in 1941. The Germans, however, put the first jet-propelled fighters, the Messerschmitt Me-262, into action in 1944. The Germans were nearing defeat by this time, and the speed and firepower of those planes gave only a glimpse of what lay ahead in future air wars.

One of the most controversial books published early in World War II (1942) was Alexander de Seversky's *Victory Through Airpower,* which claimed that future wars were going to be fought and won almost entirely by air forces. (De Seversky was not the only person nor the first to make such a claim.) Although that proved an exaggeration, there is no denying that aircraft played a decisive role in many instances: The British victory in the Battle of Britain prevented an invasion, the Japanese practically wiped out the U.S. Navy in the Pacific with relatively few cheap airplanes at Pearl Harbor, the British-American bombing raids helped turn the tide against the Germans, and the U.S. Air Force's devastating raids on Japanese cities that saved the Allies a costly invasion of the Japanese home islands.

It must also be recognized that studies during the war (but generally kept secret) and after the war showed that the so-called strategic bombing of Germany by the Allies did not prove nearly as effective as promised. Strategic bombing was based on the belief that saturation bombing of industrial and population centers could so undermine the enemy's productive capacity and morale that land armies would be needed only for mopping up. It did not work that way in Germany, although similar bombings did bring Japan to its knees. In both countries, in addition to the toll of buildings and human lives taken by conventional air raids, a hitherto unknown phenomenon also played a major role: firestorms in cities saturated by incendiary bombs and regular bombs sucked up all the oxygen and created hurricanelike howling winds, and a virtual ocean of fire that destroyed everything—and everyone—in its path.

Air power was also enlisted to make infantry more mobile than ever before. For example, the German invasion of the island of Crete (see May 20–June 1, 1941, pp. 440-441) was accomplished by the use of gliders and paratroops. Paratroops (and gliders) also played a role in other operations, most notably in the Allied invasion of France (see June 6, 1944, pp. 466-467), but in general, parachuting large units often proved very risky, and many airborne units spent most of their time fighting as conventional ground troops.

Another way that airpower transformed warfare was through the use of aircraft for observation, communications, control of artillery, and coordinating movements of armies and navies. The U.S. Army in particular developed a sophisticated control of artillery by sending forward observers in airplanes to radio back the necessary information about the location of targets and where the shells had landed. That meant that the Germans and Japanese usually confronted withering fire wherever they moved. Ultimately, almost all the major invasions, operations, and campaigns relied heavily on airplanes.

Although hardly an invention of World War II, guerrilla and underground units seldom had played such an active, pervasive role in a war. (Guerrilla is here used to refer to individuals—often also known as partisans—engaged in military type of activities, usually in the countryside; underground is used to refer to those more involved in gathering intelligence, aiding escapees, and maintaining morale—often in more urban settings.) Comprised mostly of civilians but often supported by military forces, those units sprang up in virtually every country occupied by the Germans and Italians, and to a lesser degree in certain lands occupied by the Japanese. At first, they were usually spontaneous, civilian-organized units in occupied lands; sometimes they would be joined by isolated military personnel, downed fliers, or escaped prisoners of war; eventually, the Allies—particularly the British, Americans, and French—sent civilians (including many women) and military personnel into the occupied lands to join those groups and provide special skills. Communication was maintained by radio (using coded messages); airdrops of food and weapons (and money to finance purchases) were made. Eventually, there was some coordination between the internal guerrilla actions and external military operations. For example, a guerrilla group blowing up railway lines and bridges behind enemy lines could facilitate an invasion or campaign. Partisan groups performed many valuable services, from publishing materials that helped boost morale to tying down large enemy military forces. There were countless tales of bravery and cunning by the resistance, but one of the more legendary feats was the capture of the German commandant on Crete by a combined Cretan and British guerrilla force; after days eluding the Germans, the guerrillas transferred the general to a British boat offshore and took him to Egypt. In that and in many other incidents, however, these underground operations often brought swift and disproportionate reprisals: the occupiers—particularly the Germans—often destroyed complete villages and

killed ten or more civilians for each one of their personnel lost. All in all, though, the guerrilla and underground forces contributed significantly to the Allied victory.

Intelligence gathering, spies, deceptions, tricks, codes, and other covert or unconventional methods had always been part of warfare, but never before World War II had they been used to such an extent, with so many resources and personnel devoted to them, with so many variants, with so much sophistication. The major Allied and Axis powers maintained conventional intelligence units, civilian and military, to keep track of what the enemy was doing by closely reading every possible scrap of information: Neutral cities from Ankara, Turkey, to Lisbon, Portugal, were hotbeds of agents from both sides. Spies within the enemy camp contributed somewhat to intelligence gathering, but they were usually caught: all the German spies in Britain were "turned" and became double-agents, working for the Allies, sending cleverly deceptive information (but much of it correct, in order to maintain their credibility) back to the Germans.

The Allies, particularly the British, carried out numerous tricks and deceptions, such as forming "paper units" to confuse the enemy and lighting fires on the ground to mislead German bombers. One of the most famous (Operation Mincemeat) involved dropping a dead Englishman off the coast of Spain; he wore an air force uniform and carried various official documents, including what seemed to be top secret plans for the forthcoming Allied invasion of Greece. The Spanish passed the documents on to the Germans who diverted forces to protect Greece. The Allies then executed their plan to invade Sicily. On a much grander scale was the creation of dummy invasion forces in Britain, one poised to go ashore in France well north of the actual landing beaches, another poised to invade Norway. Using everything from the names of real officers (including Gen. George S. Patton) and mock vehicles, the Allies' maintained radio traffic and activities that kept the Germans expecting those and several other invasions even after the invasion of Normandy.

Undoubtedly, the most amazing achievement of the secret war was the Allies' ability to read many of the Axis powers' coded military and diplomatic communications. The Germans and Japanese also read some of the Allies' coded messages. However, their failure to realize that the Allies were reading virtually all theirs allowed the Allies to send out much misleading information. The United States had broken the Japanese code even before Pearl Harbor and continued to read Japanese communications throughout World War II. Known as Magic to the Allies, this code and its information played a crucial part in the conduct of the war in the Pacific (although the significance of one of the most important messages on December 6, 1941, hinting at an attack on Pearl Harbor, was not recognized until it was too late).

Even more crucial was the Allies' ability to read the Germans' coded communications based on their Enigma machine, a complicated device for coding messages at one end and then decoding them at the other. Polish and French intelligence operatives had been the first to break those codes during the 1930s, but by 1939, the new and more complex Enigma machine and codes made it difficult to keep up with the messages. The Poles brought British and French intelligence into the operation by August 1939, but after the fall of France, the main work was done at Bletchley Park, an estate about 50 miles northwest of London, with hundreds of experts engaged in the processing of the secret information. That operation was known to the Allies by the code name Ultra. (Ultra also included information from other sources, including the machine code-named Purple, used by the Japanese, and the Italian coding machine, C38m.) U.S. intelligence services began intensive cooperation with the British shortly after Pearl Harbor, and throughout the war, the British and Americans were able to read (and share with whomever they deemed reliable) much of the Axis powers' radio traffic. The full success of the Ultra operation, however, rested on the Allies' willingness to *not* use certain information in order to deceive the Axis. By and large, the Axis never mastered that kind of sophisticated covert warfare.

World War II also served as a spur to the invention or at least development of a number of items that had even greater use and value in peace time. For example, a shortage of certain raw materials, such as rubber, forced the chemical industry to develop synthetic substitutes. (Much of the world's natural rubber came from countries that fell under Japanese domination.) Chemists had been trying long before World War II to make a good substitute for natural rubber. In fact, it was the Germans who, just before the war began, came up with the best synthetic rubber up to that time, a form trademarked Buna rubber. During the war, U.S. chemists improved on that and began the large-scale manufacturing of synthetic rubber, which has since become essential to civilian industry. Nylon, an invention of the Du Pont Chemical Company, had been first used in a commercial product in 1938; during World War II it turned out to have several highly useful applications as a substitute for silk, which was needed for parachutes. Perhaps its most publicized use was to make women's stockings.

Another area in which the war spurred important developments was in medicine and in health products that would save thousands of lives during the war and millions of lives after the war. Penicillin had been discovered in England before the war, but the first large-scale production of that invaluable antibiotic was developed in the United States during the war. Likewise, blood plasma had been separated from whole blood before the war, but it was not until the war that the modern system of banking large quantities of plasma was developed. Finally, DDT had been identified as an insecticide by a Swiss scientist, Paul Mueller, in 1939, but it was not until it was used by the U.S. Army to fight an epidemic of typhus fever in Naples, Italy, in 1944 that its full significance was realized.

There were at least three inventions that were to completely transform warfare as it had been practiced for centuries.

(1) Modern electronic warfare really began during World War II. Although some of the basic inventions—radio, radar, sonar—had existed before the war, they were improved and/or utilized beyond recognition, often by both the Allies and the Axis. The many electronic devices used included improved variants of radar (ground-mapping, for example), detectors of enemy radar, airborne navigation devices, jammers and disrupters of radio and radar signals. Subsequent wars have intensified the reliance on those and related devices.

(2) The pilotless rocket-powered missiles developed by the Germans and fired with such devastating results—mostly on London but also on a few other targets—were truly revolutionary. (The "V" used to designate those weapons came from the German word *Vergeltungswaffe*, "ven-

geance weapons," but that was not the official name of the weapons.) The initial version (known to the Allies as the V-1 but to the Germans as the FZG-76) was a ram jet powered missile that could travel about 600 miles with its warhead of 1,870 pounds, before falling from the sky. The Germans launched some 9,200 of those missiles against Britain; about 2,400 hit targets, most of them in London, killing some 6,200 people. The second German missile (known to the Allies as the V-2 but to the Germans as the A-4) was a liquid fuel powered missile. Although its warhead was only slightly more powerful than that of the V-1, its supersonic speed made it all but impossible to intercept. About 4,000 were fired at targets on the Continent (most of them at targets in Belgium, especially Antwerp), and another 1,115 were sent against England, killing some 2,750 people and wounding another 19,000. Only the forced withdrawal by the Germans from launching sites within range of England kept those weapons from having a far greater impact on the outcome of the war.

(3) The final invention of World War II, which foreshadowed the future was just that—the final weapon used and the final word in destructive weaponry, the atomic bomb. The bomb was developed in a secret project code-named Manhattan Project. The official name of the project was the Manhattan Engineer District of the Corps of Engineers. The Manhattan Project eventually drew on the talents of thousands of individuals from many countries. Ironically, some of the most talented scientists were refugees from Hitler's Germany, scene of some of the pioneer work in understanding the atom. The Manhattan Project leaders thought they were in a race with the Germans, but it turned out that the Germans never came close to developing a nuclear weapon.

LEGENDS AND TRIVIA

World War II inevitably produced many heroes, but surprisingly few have survived as national legends. One near legend for a while in the U.S. was **Audie Murphy**, a fresh-faced young soldier from Tennessee, son of a poor sharecropper, and barely 21 when the war ended. During combat in North Africa and Europe, he gained a battlefield promotion to lieutenant and became the most decorated U.S. soldier in World War II; included among his many medals was the Con-

gressional Medal of Honor. He went on to act in numerous Westerns and war movies, but his personal and professional life took a turn for the worse in the late 1960s. He went into bankruptcy, faced a charge (but was cleared) of attempted murder (for beating up a man in a barroom brawl), then died in an airplane crash in 1971.

A variation on this fate befell **Ira Hayes**, one of the five U.S. Marines photographed raising the U.S. flag on Mt. Suribachi, Iwo Jima (see February 19–March 26, 1945, p. 482). Hayes was a Pima Indian from Arizona. He came home to a hero's welcome but then could not get his life together; he became an alcoholic. He died in 1955 at age 33 from hypothermia, a result of falling asleep in the cold outdoors.

Native Americans of the **Navajo** tribe were the source of a different sort of legend. Since their language was totally unknown to the Germans and Japanese—indeed, was said to be known by only about 28 non-Navajo Americans—they were recruited by the U.S. Marine Corps to serve as special "code-talkers." They transmitted important military messages to each other in their native language without the need for any coding. Eventually, some 420 Navajos were code-talkers in the marines, and many of them held positions of great responsibility and risk as the Marines advanced across the Pacific. Those code-talkers had to take special training to master the many military words not otherwise in their language and to make sure they all agreed on the precise vocabulary they would use (the Navajo language has many dialects). One reason the Navajos were selected for that job—as opposed to other Native Americans—was that the Bureau of Indian Affairs determined that they were one of the few Indian tribes that had not been closely studied by German anthropologists, linguists, and artists. Before the war ended, however, Indians from several other tribes were also employed by different units to communicate secret messages in their native languages.

In addition to heroes and villains, every war turns up some dubious characters, and among those in World War II were the various individuals from the Western Allied countries who chose to lend their talents to the Axis—particularly as broadcasters. Among the most notorious were **Lord Haw-Haw** and **Tokyo Rose**. The former was William Joyce, who was born in Brooklyn, New York, in 1906, to an English father and Irish mother.

He settled in England in 1921 but went to Germany in 1939. First heard on September 18, 1939, he broadcast regularly from Berlin throughout the war, constantly telling the British that their cause was doomed. (It was his nasal tone that earned him his sobriquet.) Arrested by British soldiers in May 1945, he was tried, then hanged in January 1946.

Tokyo Rose was a U.S. citizen of Japanese parentage—Mrs. Iva Ikuko Toguri d'Aquino. (During World War II, there was much speculation about who she was—with some claiming she was the missing aviator Amelia Earhart.) She had graduated from UCLA and was in Japan on a visit at the time of Pearl Harbor; she stayed on and turned to broadcasting to the American troops in the Pacific, trying to demoralize them by mixing popular music with claims that their womenfolk at home were consorting with other men. Although she later denied any anti-American motivation for her broadcasts, Tokyo Rose was sentenced to ten years in jail; she served only six years and was pardoned in 1977.

Still more scandalous in his way was **Ezra Pound**, the noted American poet, who remained in Italy during World War II and made occasional broadcasts in which he promoted his pro-Fascist and anti-Semitic views. Arrested for treason after the war, he was judged insane (with the help of influential literary friends) and so allowed to spend 12 years in a Washington, D.C., mental hospital. Released in 1958, he returned to Italy and only obliquely tried to explain his behavior.

Another broadcaster was the popular English author, **P. G. Wodehouse**. He differed from the others in that he had been arrested on the Continent by the Germans, and his broadcasts were rather innocuous, but it took many years for him to clear his reputation.

There is some dispute as to exactly when and why and by whom the **V sign**—both as indicated by the upheld fingers and by the Morse code (...-)—was introduced during World War II. But the conjunction of three elements seemed to contribute to the use of the V sign: The word Victory in English and in French begins with v; the Morse code is internationally understood; and Beethoven's Fifth Symphony begins with four notes (the "Fate" motif) that have the same beats—three short notes and one long one. The British Broadcasting Corporation (BBC) had for some years been introducing its programs using the Morse code for v as its call sign when, on July 19, 1941, a special BBC broadcast urged the people of occupied Europe to organize resistance forces and use the slogan "v for victory." Following that broadcast, the V sign came to be painted on walls and German posters throughout occupied Europe. Even before this, however, Winston Churchill took to visiting bombed-out sites in London during the blitz of 1940 and raising his fingers to make the V as a sign of encouragement. All those—the scrawled letter, the hand sign, the code, and the musical phrase—came together to provided the British and Americans with their symbol of victory.

Baseball played a special role for Americans during World War II and generated some wartime legends of its own. President Roosevelt wrote the commissioner of baseball, Kenesaw Mountain Landis, on January 15, 1942, that major league baseball should continue, as it was good for the nation's morale. It did, although 60 percent of the major leaguers, including some of the most famous, went into military units, where some played on service teams. It was because of the shortage of young men that the All-American Girls Professional Baseball League was established in 1943. At its peak, the league had ten teams in midwestern cities. (It survived until 1954.) Among other things, the league was the inspiration for the 1992 movie *A League of Their Own*. Many all-star and other special games were played to raise large amounts of money for various war-related causes. Scrap-metal savers were admitted free to a game in New York's Polo Grounds on September 26, 1942—and cost the Giants a forfeit when they swarmed out on the field. During the war, fans were asked to return all balls hit into the stands so that they could be sent to service teams. In Japan, where *besuboru* had already gained considerable popularity, the game was renamed *yakyu*, and some elements in Japan tried to squelch the game as a foreign intrusion. There were stories about Japanese soldiers in the jungle who were able to fool American guards when asked to name the player of a position on a particular team. In a variation on that, American soldiers claimed they would hear Japanese soldiers crying "F—Babe Ruth!" as they rushed into battle; others tell of victorious Japanese fighting over copies of the *Sporting News* and of Japanese prisoners asking for the results of the World Series. Shortly after taking command in Japan, Gen. Douglas MacArthur gave the order to refurbish the Tokyo Giants Stadium; within months, many teams were reorganized. Limited professional baseball began in 1946. According to some authorities, Moe Berg, a well-educated man who had been a major league catcher from 1923 to 1939, was sent to Japan on an all-star team in 1934—not because he was such a great player but to photograph Tokyo for the U.S. Army intelligence; his photographs, it has been claimed, were used in planning the bombing raids of Tokyo during the war.

A surviving legacy of World War II is **Spam**. Regular meat was strictly rationed—only so many ounces per person—so there were various efforts to find substitutes. One such substitute was a canned product with the brand name Spam. It was chopped scraps of beef, ham, and pork shoulder pressed into a 12 ounce loaf and placed in a can about half the size of a brick. Because Spam did not require ration stamps and was relatively cheap, it became a staple for many people. It also became the butt of endless jokes and cartoons. Thus, GIs were said to have prayed:

Now I lay me down to sleep
And pray the Lord the Spam don't keep.

In fact, servicemen were probably not eating true Spam, but the name had been extended to apply to all kinds of processed canned meats; true Spam is a trademarked product of the Hormel meat processing company (then as now based in Austin, Minnesota); it was developed by Jay Hormel and first went on sale in 1937.

NOTABLE PHRASES

I have nothing to offer but blood, toil, tears and sweat.

Winston Churchill spoke those words on May 13, 1940, in his first statement to the House of Commons as prime minister. Several other authors—including John Donne and Lord Byron—had written phrases much like that. For that matter, Churchill wrote a very similar phrase in a book published in 1931. But in the context of his new role, those words were fresh and stirring—so stirring that Churchill would repeat that phrase in several subsequent speeches to the British. On that first occasion, Churchill's speech was not recorded, but the BBC wanted to broadcast it. Since Churchill was totally preoccupied by the disasters then engulfing the Continent, the BBC had an actor read the speech to the radio public. Churchill's subsequent speeches were either recorded or delivered live by Churchill himself.

We shall not flag or fail. We shall go on to the end. We shall fight in France, we shall fight on the seas and oceans, we shall fight with growing confidence and growing strength in the air, we shall defend our island, whatever the cost may be, we shall fight on the beaches, we shall fight on the landing grounds, we shall fight in the fields and in the streets, we shall fight in the hills; we shall never surrender.

On June 4, 1940, the British had completed their narrow escape from the beach at Dunkirk (see p. 437). Churchill addressed the House of Commons and, with those simple but direct words, managed to inspire all the foes of the Axis to go on with the fight.

Never in the field of human conflict was so much owed by so many to so few.

Winston Churchill spoke those words in an address to the House of Commons on August 20, 1940, in paying tribute to the British (and some foreign) pilots who were then engaged in fighting the Germans in the Battle of Britain.

Our boys will never leave these shores.

Those words were attributed to President Franklin D. Roosevelt and often repeated by those opposed to his policies of every kind. Did he say them? In fact, if he did not say those precise words, he said many things close to them during the late 1930s, when he judged the temper of the nation to be inclined toward neutrality. But perhaps the closest he came to those words on a public occasion was during his campaign for reelection in 1940. France had fallen, Britain was fighting for its survival against German bombing raids, and Italy had just invaded Greece when on October 30 FDR said to an audience in Boston; "And while I am talking to you mothers and fathers, I give you one more assurance. I have said this before, but I shall say it again and again and again: Your boys are not going to be sent into any foreign wars."

In the future days, which we seek to make secure, we look forward to a world founded upon four essential human freedoms. The first is freedom of speech and expression—everywhere in the world. The second is freedom of every person to worship God in his own way—everywhere in the world. The third is freedom from want...everywhere in the world. The fourth is freedom from fear...anywhere in the world.

In his message to Congress on January 6, 1941, President Franklin D. Roosevelt, without actually calling for the United States to abandon its neutrality, set forth goals that were clearly not those of the Axis. They quickly became known as the Four Freedoms (and Norman Rockwell painted four famous paintings capturing those freedoms). The Four Freedoms were also incorporated in the so-called Atlantic Charter, jointly issued on August 10, 1941, by Roosevelt and Churchill after their meeting aboard a U.S. warship in Argentia Bay, Newfoundland (see August 9–12, 1941, p. 446).

Remember Pearl Harbor!

No one knows who was the first to use that phrase, but it appeared in the newspaper headlines across the land on the morning of December 8, 1941, and instantly became the nation's slogan. It was clearly an echo of at least two other such events in U.S. history: "Remember the Alamo!" and "Remember the Maine!"

I shall return.

By early March 1942, it was clear that the Japanese forces were going to overrun the U.S. forces in the Philippines (see March 11, 1942, p. 451). It was decided in Washington, D.C., that the U.S. commander, Gen. Douglas MacArthur, should get out while he could so that he could direct the Allied forces from Australia. On March 11, 1942, MacArthur was flown off the island of Luzon to Australia; on March 30, he gave a prepared speech at a press conference and spoke those words. He did return to the Philippines on October 20, 1944 (see pp. 473–472), and within his first hours there, he made a broadcast and declared: "People of the Philippines, I have returned. By the grace of almighty God, our forces stand again on Philippine soil." MacArthur was criticized by some for using the first person singular pronoun because other great military leaders had used we, but it has been pointed out that he knew that the Philippine people had, in fact, placed their greatest trust in him personally, not in the U.S. forces.

Nuts!

On December 16, 1944, the Germans launched a counteroffensive in the Ardennes Forest in Belgium, beginning what became known as the Battle of the Bulge (see p. 470). By December 22, several thousand U.S. soldiers of the 101st Airborne Division were trapped under siege in the town of Bastogne. Their commander was Maj. Gen. Anthony McAuliffe. The Germans sent a delegation with a written request that the Americans surrender; it was carried to McAuliffe, and because he was preoccupied, he simply muttered, "Nuts!" Shortly thereafter, he realized he must send a formal response, and, with his subordinates' encouragement, he sent a typed reply:
To the German Commander:
Nuts!
From the American Commander.
That message was carried to the German delegation, and the American officer who sent the delegation on its way volunteered that, if the Germans wondered what the message meant, it was "Go to hell!'" Bastogne was freed on Dec. 26, and McAuliffe became an instant legend.

Kilroy was here.

That phrase—suggesting that some ordinary guy always got to someplace before anyone else—began to appear as early as 1939, usually scrawled on docks and ships, so it has been assumed that it originated with someone in the United States Navy or Merchant Marine. During World War II, the phrase began to appear wherever U.S. servicemen were stationed—especially in places where someone might assume no American had yet been. Often, it was accompanied by the drawing of the top of a head—bald and wide-eyed—apparently peering over a fence, with the nose and fingers showing. (That same drawing appeared with the British equivalent of Kilroy, Chad.) Although there have been countless claims for who the original Kilroy was, none can be proved: One of the leading candidates was James J. Kilroy, an inspector in a Massachusetts shipyard, who claimed he used to chalk "Kilroy was here" when he approved work. But no one has ever been able to establish who started the fad, and no one knows why the name Kilroy was chosen. To some, the name is synonymous with an inveterate wanderer, others see Kilroy as the eternal outsider, and still others see Kilroy as a Chaplinesque little guy mocking the conventional world.

Gremlin and Snafu

A war as extensive and pervasive as World War II inevitably introduced many new words into the language. Two somewhat related words that emerged among military personnel were gremlin and snafu. The former was first used by British pilots, possibly as early as World War I. In the 1920s, at least some British pilots used it to describe junior officers who made problems for their superiors. By 1941, gremlin had been adopted by American pilots, who used it to refer to some invisible gnomelike creature that caused mechanical problems in airplanes. The word was soon used by other service personnel to explain the causes of mishaps in all kinds of equipment and situations. The exact origin of the word has never been proved, but it is agreed that it clearly is based on the goblin of medieval folklore, an elfin creature that worked mischief or evil. The word snafu, appeared first among U.S. servicemen in 1941 and was explicitly an acronym for "situation normal—all fouled [in polite usage: in the military, it was f—d] up." Snafu was used with a tone of resignation in the face of the chaos and ineptitude that accompany military operations. Both words survived the war to become widely used for explaining situations in which things go wrong.

SONGS

Naturally, there were many popular songs that came and went during the years of World War II, several of them dealing explicitly with the war: "Let's Remember Pearl Harbor," "Praise the Lord and Pass the Ammunition," "Comin' In on a Wing and a Prayer," "When the Lights Go On Again," "This is the Army, Mr. Jones." But, the most popular songs with American military personnel, at least, were those with sentimental, roman-

tic, or nostalgic themes. Irving Berlin's "White Christmas" (1942) became immensely popular. (At the request of the government, Berlin also wrote two eminently forgettable songs, "Any Bonds Today" and "I Paid My Income Tax Today.") Another of the more memorable songs was "The White Cliffs of Dover" (1941), a typical American pop song (although also very popular in Britain as sung by Vera Lynn), with its oblique but optimistic allusions to England's wartime situation: "There'll be bluebirds over, the white cliffs of Dover, tomorrow, just you wait and see." It remained on the hit parade for 17 weeks.

On the home front, many Americans learned the words to the hymns of the four armed services. The Navy's was "Anchors Aweigh." Originally titled "Sail, Navy, Down the Field," it was composed in 1906 as a marching song for the Naval Academy in Annapolis. "The Army Air Corps Song" ("Off we go, into the wild blue yonder....") was composed in 1939 but didn't come into its own until World War II. The closest to an Army song was "The U.S. Field Artillery March," ("Over hill, over dale, we will hit the dusty trail, as the caissons go rolling along"). Composed in 1918 by then Lt. (later Brig. Gen. Edmund L. Gruber, it was revised in 1956 and retitled "The Army Goes Marching Along," when it finally became the official U.S. Army song. Best known of all was "The Marine Corps Hymn," ("From the halls of Montezuma to the shores of Tripoli"). No one knows for sure who wrote the words (Henry C. Davis is one candidate, L.Z. Phillips another), but, in 1919, they were paired with music based on a song from an opera by Jacques Offenbach, Geneviève de Brabant (1859-1875). Millions of Americans could and did sing those service songs with great gusto and pride.

Ironically, perhaps the most moving and enduring song to come out of World War II was a German song, "Lili Marleen" ("Lili [or Lily or Lilli] Marlene" in the English version). In German, it was also known as "My Lili of the Lamppost." The song originated as a poem written in 1915 (some sources say as late as 1923) by Hans Leip, a German soldier in World War I, telling of a soldier in some distant combat zone who is thinking of the woman at home he used to meet "underneath the lamppost, by the barracks gate." There were various musical settings, but it was Norbert Schultze who in 1939 composed the musical setting known today. (Schultze was popular with the Nazis for writing such songs as "Bombs on England" and "The Panzers Are Rolling in Africa.") It was recorded in 1939 by a Swiss singer, but did not become popular among Germans until a German armed forces radio station in Yugoslavia featured a version by German singer Lala Anderson in 1941. Beamed to the German troops in North Africa, it was also enjoyed by the British troops. American troops in North Africa also took it up, and it became even more popular when Marlene Dietrich—a German actress/singer who had settled in the United States and become an outspoken anti-Nazi—recorded it (with English and German lyrics) in 1944. (The same year, she appeared in a movie with the same name, which was loosely based on the words). The song was translated into many languages and has retained some popularity among Germans.

HISTORICAL PERSPECTIVES AND CONTROVERSIES

Not unexpectedly, the debates and controversies generated by World War II are nearly endless, in terms of both their quantity and their duration. Only a few of the most important and provocative issues can be addressed here.

The "moral lesson" (vs. the morality) of the agreement reached at Munich in 1938 (see September 29, 1938, pp. 427-428) has been debated ever since. On one side are those who argue that the lesson of the Munich agreement is clear: There must be instant and clear opposition to any acts of open aggression. (For example, President Harry S. Truman entered the Korean War and President George Bush resisted Iraq in the Persian Gulf War in part because of the importance of the "lesson" of Munich.) There are those who argue that there are few analogies in history and that the real lesson is that we must pay close attention to events, individuals, deeds, words—then act appropriately. In that view, not all aggressive acts are equally dangerous, and not all foreshadow a series of future aggressive acts.

That debate can never be finally resolved: The lesson of Munich will always be perceived in different ways by different viewers. At first glance, it seems fairly clear-cut: The infamous "appeasement" by Neville Chamberlain and Edouard Daladier (and silently accepted by most of the rest of Europe) convinced Hitler that Britain and France lacked the will to resist his demands. Had even a few European states actively resisted Hitler at that point, they might have saved the whole world from the eventually devastating war. But the true question is how do we know today that what we are confronting is directly analogous to Munich 1938. How often in history have all the elements of Munich been replicated? Vietnam was one of many instances during the Cold War in which the specter of "another Munich" was raised to assert that the use of U.S. military was not only justified but essential to prevent another world conflagration.

How much and how soon did President Franklin D. Roosevelt know about the planned attack on Pearl Harbor, and did he, in fact, deliberately allow it to occur to bring the United States into World War II?

That debate began soon after the last bomb fell on Pearl Harbor and has continued ever since. Over the years, evidence has emerged that the U.S. government and military authorities did indeed have many warnings about a forthcoming Japanese attack. U.S. intelligence could read virtually all Japanese coded messages, and by November 1941, several high-ranking government officials had even expressed concern about the vulnerability of Pearl Harbor. But various other high-ranking government and military officials were equally concerned about other U.S. facilities in the Pacific: There was no specific warning that the Japanese planned to attack Pearl Harbor. By November 27, President Roosevelt and his advisers realized that the Japanese were on the verge of starting a war; the War Department telegraphed Gen. Douglas MacArthur in the Philippines: "Hostile action possible at any moment. If hostilities cannot be avoided, United States desires that Japan commit the first overt act." Taken out of context, that kind of message has been made to sound as though Roosevelt was seeking to "trick" Americans into a war with Japan. In fact, no one really knew exactly what the Japanese had planned, and President Roosevelt was surely right in not wanting to give the Japanese an excuse to start a war. Undoubtedly, though, Roosevelt and his advisers might have given more explicit orders to bring U.S forces to a state of combat readiness.

On the morning of December 6, an alert cryptographer in Washington, D.C., translated a series of Japanese secret messages asking for reports about the U.S. Navy's ships at Pearl Harbor; her superior said that they would pursue that on Monday, December 8. Meanwhile, although the commanders of the U.S. Army and U.S. Navy forces in Hawaii had been warned to keep their units in a state of alert, they were undoubtedly too lax on Sunday morning. Then came two notorious gaffes early on the morning of December 7: First, an experimental Army radar station picked up approaching planes on its equipment, but an officer decided they must be American planes en-route from California. Second, a Japanese midget submarine was sunk at the entrance to Pearl Harbor, but the significance of its presence was not realized or acted upon by naval officers.

As Gordon Prange, one of the leading historians of Pearl Harbor, has put it in *Pearl Harbor: The Verdict of History*, "There's enough blame for everyone." Incompetence, rather than a conspiracy (led by Roosevelt) seems to have been the cause of the U.S. failure at Pearl Harbor.

How soon did the Allies know of Hitler's concentration camps, and did the Allies do as much as they might have to help save the Jews of Europe from the Holocaust?

The Holocaust evolved through several stages, or phases. During the first phase, from the time of Hitler's accession in 1933 until his invasion of Poland in September 1939, the ever increasing mistreatment of the Jews was apparent to the outside world: the Nuremberg Decrees (1935), which clearly supported the persecution of the Jews, and *Kristallnacht* (or "the night of [broken] glass," November 9–10, 1938), when Jewish shops and other property throughout Germany were destroyed. Although there were some official and unofficial protests, other countries had no basis under international law for directly intervening in domestic German affairs. Nor, of course, were other nations free of anti-Semitism or other racist doctrines, even if their manifestations were less virulent than those in Germany.

Many Jews fled Europe during the years before World War II (it has been estimated that some 250,000 got out of Germany), but many more might have been encouraged to do so had not many Western nations made it clear that Jewish refugees were unwelcome. One of the most shameful incidents involved the liner *St. Louis*, carrying some 900 German Jews. When the *St. Louis* arrived in Havana on May 30, 1939, Cuban authorities turned it away on the grounds that the German Jews' visas were not valid. In the ensuing days, no other Latin-American nation would let them land. The United States and Canada were similarly inhospitable (the United States even sent a Coast Guard ship to make sure the *St. Louis* didn't make landfall). The liner went back to Europe, where many of the passengers dispersed to various countries. Some survived the war, but many others died in the Holocaust. Most authorities agree that even if other nations had opened their doors to Jewish refugees, it is unlikely that millions of Jews would have given up nearly everything they owned to flee their homelands.

The second phase in the persecution of the Jews extended from the conquest of Poland (September 1939) until the end of 1940. During that relatively brief period, almost all the Jews who were slaughtered fell under control of Germany or its allies (including at that time the Soviet Union). From that point on, it was virtually impossible for most Jews to get away. Again, we now know that certain officials in the American and British governments knew more about the harsh treatment of the Jews in the occupied lands than did the general public. The Allies could have done more—raised louder alarms, helped more Jews—but it would have been difficult to save large numbers of European Jews at that point. Hitler was never one to give in to public outrage, and he was determined to wipe out the Jews. Britain was already at war, and many thousands of Jews from occupied Europe were enlisting in the fight or were going underground.

Then came the third phase—what is known as the "Final Solution," the Germans' attempt to eliminate all Jews from Europe. For many years, it was accepted that the first solid information about the concentration camps did not reach the West until August 8, 1942, when a representative of the World Jewish Congress in Geneva, Switzerland, sent a telegram about the extermination campaign to embassies and Jewish leaders in London and New York. We now know (particularly because of David S. Wyman's *The Aban-*

donment of the Jews, 1984) that reports of the execution of Jews had gotten out well before that. (By August 1942, at least 1 million Jews had been executed.) Beyond that, Wyman and others have shown that the British and American governments had made numerous decisions that rejected any help for the Jews.

Might not the Allies' military have been directed at least to adopt some tactics designed to disrupt the rail lines and the camps? Many experts now believe the Allies could have and should have; even if many Jews were killed in the process, they were doomed anyway, and the attacks might have opened up other possibilities. On the other hand, much more sophisticated equipment and weapons have demonstrated over and over that there are limits to what can be accomplished by bombs. The issue of whether the Allies could have done more to help the Jews cannot be resolved in a few paragraphs; many historians continue to wrestle with it.

Why were the atomic bombs dropped on two Japanese cities? Was it to send a message to the Japanese—or to the Soviets? Was it even necessary to drop the bombs at all?

Most historians of the period believe that President Harry S. Truman and his closest advisers, such as Secretary of War Henry L. Stimson, genuinely believed that an invasion of Japan would cost many hundreds of thousands of American lives: Historians and others may dispute the figures, but what matters is how many Truman thought would be killed. (Taking just the small island of Okinawa had cost the United States some 12,500 dead (See April 1–June 22, 1942, pp. 483-484). Was Truman influenced by the prospect of the Soviet Union's jumping into the war against Japan and then demanding a say in the occupation of Japan? Historians seem to agree that that played at least some role in Truman's thinking.

By August 1945, was not Japan practically on the verge of surrendering anyway? Some argue that that was clearly the case: Gar Alperovitz (*The Decision to Use the Atomic Bomb*, 1995) is the most prominent of such critics. Others contend that there would almost certainly have to be at least one major Allied ground assault on the Japanese home island, and that assault would have cost many Japanese as well as Allied lives.

The conventional bombing raids on Japan were actually taking a higher toll than the two atomic bombs would. The kamikaze attacks had revealed the lengths to which the Japanese were willing to go: In less than one year, kamikaze pilots took the lives of some 15,000 Allied sailors. Even after the atomic bombs had been dropped, many in the Japanese military tried desperately to block the surrender process.

The argument then shifts to whether the atomic bombs should have been dropped on "demonstration" areas or, at least, on more strictly defined military targets. The objection to that theory is that there were only the two bombs and, if they failed to convince the Japanese, the conventional war would have continued. Moreover, no one really knew whether the bombs would work nor what the extent of the destruction would be.

That leaves still another point of contention: Did the Allied insistence on "unconditional surrender" prolong the war because of the Japanese devotion to preserving the emperor? Alperovitz and others have contended that some prominent Japanese were sending signals at least by the summer of 1945 that they would be willing to surrender so long as some understanding about the emperor's status could be reached. Others argue that it was not until after the dropping of the atomic bomb on Nagasaki that the Japanese sent such an unequivocal message to the Allies: As soon as they got that message, the Allies, in fact, did quietly accede on that point. With 20-20 hindsight, it can be argued that the Allies might have signaled something to that effect earlier, but there was little indication at the time that Japan was willing to negotiate peace terms that reflected its overwhelming defeat in the war.

Did the Allies win only because of their superior material resources, despite the fact that they were often out-generaled and out-fought?

Many students of World War II have argued that the German army, at least, was superior in its combat capabilities to the Allied armies: Martin Van Creveld (in *Fighting Power: German and U.S. Army Performance, 1939-1945*) so argues. Certainly in the early years of World War II the German military was a superior fighting machine—its intensity, intelligence, commitment, daring, and sheer doggedness allowed it to overpower far larger forces. Others contend that the German military's downfall came about not because of bad generalship or poor soldiering but because Hitler insisted on dictating strategics and tactics right to the end. Some evidence supports that theory. Right until the end—and certainly including the Ardennes offensive of December 1944—the Germans in the field proved tough opponents. The same must be said of the Japanese: their willingness to sacrifice all kept them a threat until the final days of the war.

When World War II started, Germany and Japan had access to plenty of material resources, but once the United States entered, the balance was tipped. Eventually, the output of the U.S. industrial machine overwhelmed what the Axis powers could produce. For example, by 1943, the Ford Motor Company was providing more war material than was the entire country of Italy. Both Germany and Japan were literally running out of petroleum in the final weeks of the war, and they had long ceased being able to manufacture the planes and tanks and ships they needed because of relentless bombing raids and shortages of material and manpower. Indeed, the wonder was that they kept producing as long as they did.

Yet, it is simplistic to claim that the Allies won only by throwing more hardware at the Axis. Some of the Axis hardware, in fact, was decidedly superior to that of the Allies, but for one reason or another the advantage could not be fully exploited. For example, German tanks were excessively complex for the rigors of the Soviet campaign and required expert mechanics to keep them repaired. Moreover, at times, the German military seemed overly cautious; at other times too rash. Both the Germans and the Japanese in the field were often outbluffed by the Allies, and, in many equal contests, they were just plain outfought. (When Allied troops were rushing ashore at Normandy or on some Pacific island, the comparative production rates of, say, airplanes or trucks seemed irrelevant. Neither the Germans nor the Japanese ever seemed to run out of ammunition in battle.) Perhaps it came down to a certain rigidity in their cultures or at least in the totalitarian systems for which they fought, but the Axis military seemed unable to call on that extra element of imagination, improvisation, and initiative that finally won the day.

After all, despite numerous plots not a single German officer was able to assassinate Hitler during all those years.

Was World War II really fought for ideals, or was it just another act in the age-old drama of power politics? In other words, was it a truly "just war"?

Long-standing geopolitical issues undoubtedly played some role in World War II: The desire to control natural resources and for *Lebensraum* (living space) was certainly not limited to the Axis, and they had some legitimate gripes about the way the old European colonial and commercial powers were running the world. But nothing that the future Allies did in the 1920s or 1930s quite matched in ruthlessness the attacks on China, Ethiopia, Albania, and Czechoslovakia and Poland: from September 1939 on, it seems fair to say, the Allies had to fight a war, whatever their past failings. Although it had nothing to do with the start of the war, the Germans' treatment of the Jews certainly justifies viewing World War II as a contest between good and evil.

Paul Fussell (in *Wartime*, 1989) argued that Americans and British, at least, have never had a very realistic view of the true horrors of the war they engaged in, but nothing he says proves that World War II was ultimately wrong. Whatever the legitimacy of some of their claims, Germany, Japan, and Italy were undeniably aggressors, and it finally boils down to whether the world was going to acquiesce to their aggression or resist it.

CIVILIAN AND MILITARY BIOGRAPHIES

AMERICAN

Arnold, Henry (1886–1950)—general: As a young Army officer, Arnold learned to fly with the Wright brothers and became an early advocate of airpower. Before there was a separate air force, he became chief of air staff in the U.S. Army in 1938 and chief of the U.S. Army air forces in 1941. He was responsible for getting the aircraft industry to increase production and the Army Air Corps to step up training. After the United States entered World War II, he oversaw basically every aspect of the U.S. air war. He also served on the Combined Chiefs of Staff Committee of the Allies and generally enjoyed good working relations with his British counterparts. He did, however, disagree with the British approach to strategic, or area bombing—favoring precision bombing of specific targets. When the U.S. Air Force became an independent service in 1947, Arnold became a five-star general.

Clark, Mark (1896–1984)—general: Mark Clark served in World War I and then at a succession of Army posts during the 1920s and 1930s. Clark was Dwight D. Eisenhower's deputy during the invasion of North Africa. Clark played a major role in negotiating with Adm. Jean François Darlan to get the French forces to cease resisting. As commander of the 5th Army, in September 1943, he led the invasion at Salerno on the Italian mainland, then through the battle of Monte Cassino, and finally into Rome in June 1944. Clark continued to battle the Germans all the way up the Italian peninsula, accepting their final surrender in April 1945.

Clay, Lucius (1897–1977)—general: Lucius Clay supervised several major engineering projects for the Army during the 1920s and 1930s. He was made the U.S. Army's deputy chief of staff in 1942 and oversaw the massive production and procurement efforts for the Army. In November 1944, he went to Europe to command the Normandy base and the port of Cherbourg, key entry points for military supplies, and he continued to supervise the provision of materiel for the Army's drive across France and Germany. In April 1945, he became Eisenhower's deputy, charged with setting up the military government in Germany, and from 1947–1949, he was the military governor of the U.S. zone of occupation.

Donovan, William (1883–1959)—intelligence chief: William Donovan was a decorated veteran of World War I and a lawyer by profession. He was sent on several observing missions by Secretary of the Navy Frank Knox and President Franklin D. Roosevelt before the United States entered World War II. In June 1942, he was named to head the newly formed Office of Strategic Intelligence (OSS). Based on the older British model, the OSS recruited many people from the more prestigious U.S. colleges and universities. At its peak during the war, the OSS employed some 13,000 Americans as well as countless foreign agents abroad. The OSS gathered intelligence from every possible source, which it fed to the appropriate military and civilian leaders. It also engaged in many clandestine espionage and military operations, often in conjunction with foreign resistance groups that it supported. Donovan retired from the OSS at the end of World War II.

Doolittle, James (1886–1993)—air force officer: James Doolittle was a member of the Army Air Corps in the 1920s. He pioneered instrument landing techniques and won the Harmon Trophy in 1930 for that and other contributions to early flying. He left the service to work for Shell Oil but was recalled to active duty in 1940; he was first assigned to convert the automobile industry to aircraft production. He burst onto the world scene when he personally led the 16 B-25s that flew from the deck of the USS *Hornet* to bomb Tokyo (see April 18, 1942, pp. 451-452). He commanded the 12th Air Force in the North African campaign (1942–1943) and the 15th Air Force in Italy (1943), then commanded the 8th Air Force in the strategic bombing of Germany (1944–1945). In 1945, he brought his 8th Air Force to the final bombing efforts in the Pacific. He retired to private industry after World War II.

Eisenhower, Dwight D. (1890–1969)—general, Supreme Allied Commander in Europe: Dwight D. Eisenhower was an obscure brigadier general, when in 1941, Gen. George Marshall brought him to Washington, D.C., to join the Army's War Plans Division. In June 1942, he was advanced over 366 higher ranking officers to command all U.S. forces in Europe. He was promoted to command the Allied invasion of North Africa (November 8–13, 1942, see p. 450), then of Sicily (July 1943, see p. 459), and Italy (September 1943, see p. 460). Because of his demonstrated ability to get the often adversarial Allied officers to cooperate, in December 1943, Eisenhower was sent to London as Supreme Allied Commander of the invasion of France. He succeeded in achieving that enterprise but soon found himself having to arbitrate an ongoing quarrel between Field Marshal Bernard Montgomery and Gen. George Patton, each of whom wanted to push ahead on his own "narrow front." Again, Eisenhower's manner and diplomatic skills managed to get the Allied forces to accept his "broad-front" strategy. Eisenhower went on to serve two terms as president (1953–1961). (See his biography in the Cold War, pp. 564-565.)

Groves, Leslie (1896–1970)—army engineer: Leslie Groves was a West Point graduate and an engineer. He worked on various projects (including the Pentagon) during the 1930s and early 1940s. In 1942, he was appointed to head the Manhattan Engineer District, (the Manhattan Project) for the development of an atomic bomb. He supervised the construction of facilities for the development, testing, and production of the first atomic bombs.

Halsey, William (1882–1959)—admiral: William Halsey sailed the world on the U.S. Navy's famous White Fleet (1907–1909) and fought in World War I. By 1940, he was a vice admiral, and after Pearl Harbor, he was given command of some of the first American offensives in the Pacific. He escorted the USS *Hornet* in the bombing raid on Tokyo (April 1942) and fought in major naval battles off Guadalcanal. Based on his experiences in those operations, he made important innovations in night-flying techniques. From 1943 on, he played a major role in the island-hopping campaign across the Pacific. In October 1944, off the coast of Leyte in the Philippines, he received word of the sighting of a large Japanese carrier fleet and in a bold move went after it and sank much of it (see October 20–December 31, 1944, pp. 472–473). His reputation for aggressive and even risky actions earned him his nickname, "Bull."

King, Ernest (1878–1956)—admiral: After serving in the Spanish-American War and World War I, Ernest King took flight training and became chief of the Navy's Bureau of Aeronautics (1933–1938). Shortly after Pearl Harbor, he was named commander of the U.S. fleet; in March 1942, he was also named Chief of Naval Operations. Those posts brought him onto the U.S. Joint Chiefs of Staff and the Allies' Combined Chiefs of Staff. As chief strategist of the U.S. Navy throughout the war and as President Roosevelt's naval adviser, he was clearly the premier U.S. naval figure of the war.

MacArthur, Douglas (1880–1964)—general: After a relatively colorful career with the U.S. Army, Douglas MacArthur was appointed a military adviser to the Philippine government in 1935. In July 1941, he was recalled to active U.S. Army service with instructions to prepare the Filipino forces for war. MacArthur was among those who underestimated Japan's readiness to attack, and Filipinos and the small U.S. Army units on the Philippines were quickly overwhelmed by the Japanese (see April 1–9, 1942, p. 451). In March 1942, MacArthur was ordered to escape to Australia. From that point on, he was determined to recapture the Philippines. As commander of the U.S. armed forces in the Southwest Pacific, he often found himself at odds with many in the U.S. military, including the top command in Washington, D.C., and the U.S. Navy in the Pacific. In the end, he got his way, and after a long and costly campaign of island hopping, he returned to the Philippines on October 20, 1944 with an invasion force (see p. 482). In April 1945, he was named commander of all American forces in the Pacific but he actually played little part in the final advance toward the Japanese mainland. His contention that the Japanese would fight to the last man influenced President Harry S. Truman's decision to use the atomic bombs. MacArthur accepted the formal surrender of the Japanese on the USS *Missouri*, then served as virtually the supreme ruler of Japan (1945–1951). (See his biography in the Korean War chapter, p. 605.)

Marshall, George (1880–1959)—general: George Marshall served as an aide to Gen. John Pershing in World War I. By 1939, he had risen to become Chief of Staff of the U.S. Army. In the following two years, he doubled the Army's size and reorganized it for modern warfare. After Pearl Harbor, he became chairman of the new Joint Chiefs of Staff, and in that position, he was President Franklin D. Roosevelt's major adviser on strategy and supervisor of the Army's worldwide operations. In addition to having good relationships with Roosevelt and his civilian advisers, Marshall was able to work well with the other Allied leaders; likewise, he managed to give his field commanders a maximum of freedom to fight World War II as they saw fit. He was universally admired for his judgment and integrity; it was no coincidence that after the war he became secretary of state (1947–1949). Because of his advocacy of aid to Europe (known as the Marshall Plan), he was awarded the Nobel Peace Prize in 1953.

Nimitz, Chester (1885–1966)—admiral: Chester Nimitz had served with the U.S. Navy in World War I, and shortly after Pearl Harbor he was named commander of the Pacific fleet. Charged with rebuilding the fleet after the disaster at Pearl Harbor, he quickly brought it back to victories at the naval battles of Coral Sea (see

May 2–8, 1942, p. 454) and Midway (see June 3–6, 1942, p. 454). In 1942, he was named commander of all U.S. forces in the Central Pacific and was responsible for the leapfrogging strategy that took the U.S. forces across the Pacific islands, closer and closer to Japan. Throughout that time, he was often in competition with Gen. Douglas MacArthur for resources and support from the Joint Chiefs, but at the end, Nimitz's flagship, the USS *Missouri*, was chosen as the site of the Japanese surrender, and Nimitz signed for the United States.

Patton, George (1885–1945)—general: Service in the new tank corps in World War I convinced George Patton that mobilized warfare was the wave of the future. By April 1942, he was commander of the 2nd Armored Division, and that October he led an armored corps in the invasion of North Africa (see November 8–13, 1942, p. 450). In July 1943, he was in command of the U.S. 7th Army that invaded Sicily (see July 9–August 17, 1943, pp. 459–460). He became notorious, first for beating the British in the race to take Palermo, and then for slapping two American soldiers hospitalized for combat fatigue (which Patton saw as cowardice). When word of the incidents got out, he was temporarily stripped of command. Sent to Britain, he was given command of the 3rd Army and led it in the crucial breakout from Normandy in July–September 1944. Like his British rival Field Marshal Bernard Montgomery, Patton was convinced that he could make a quick end to the war if he were allowed to race to the heart of Germany, but Eisenhower's strategy did not allow that. As it was, Patton's units did perform great feats, saving the besieged U.S. troops in the Battle of the Bulge (see December 16, 1944–January 27, 1945, p. 470), then crossing the Rhine and driving quickly to Czechoslovakia. As a staunch anti-Communist, Patton openly called for turning Allied forces against the Soviet Union as well as for putting Nazis back into positions of responsibility. That led to his removal from command. In December 1945, he died from injuries in an automobile accident.

Roosevelt, Franklin Delano (1882–1945)—president: When Franklin D. Roosevelt was inaugurated president for the first time in March 1933, he made no mention of foreign policy: He had been elected to lead the United States out of the Depression. As the 1930s developed, he found himself increasingly drawn into foreign affairs because of the aggressive actions by Germany and Japan. He gradually became convinced that sooner or later the United States would have to join in the fight against the Axis powers. Once the United States entered World War II, Roosevelt assumed the role of coordinator and inspirer. One of his greatest contributions was to sign on competent people, then to let them do their jobs. That was especially true of his relations with the military leaders: He interfered with his commanders far less than did Churchill (much less than did Hitler, who constantly interfered with his military subordinates). When it came to summit dealings with his fellow Allied leaders, he was probably overly idealistic, trusting Britain to give up its colonial empire and the USSR not to impose its system on Eastern Europe. Throughout World War II, to much of the world, Roosevelt was a symbol of a democratic society that was worth fighting for.

Spaatz, Carl (1891–1974)—air force general: Carl Spaatz had shot down three German planes in World War I. After World War I he rose slowly in rank. By July 1941, he was chief of air staff to Gen. George Marshall. A year later, he was sent to England to set up the 8th Air Force's strategic bombing program; he favored precision bombing in daytime raids. He was then given command of the U.S. bombing forces assigned to the North African and Sicilian campaigns. In January 1944, he was recalled to Britain where, as Commanding General of the Strategic Air Force, he directed the bombing raids that prepared for the invasion of Germany, then the invasion itself, and, finally, the destruction from the air of German industrial and transportation systems. In July 1945, he was assigned to command the Strategic Air Force in the Pacific. Spaatz directed the final destructive raids on Japan, including those on Hiroshima and Nagasaki.

Truman, Harry S. (1894–1972)—president: Harry S. Truman volunteered to serve in the army in World War I. In 1935, he became a U.S. senator from his home state of Missouri. Early in 1941, he was assigned to head the senate committee to investigate the National Defense Program, looking for possible misappropriation of funds and misallocation of contracts in the burgeoning war industry, a task he handled with tact and integrity. He was selected as a compromise between the liberals and conservatives to run as Franklin D. Roosevelt's vice president in

1944, but even those who knew the true condition of FDR's health never expected Truman to succeed him so soon. During his few months as vice president, Truman was informed of very little about plans for World War II—including the atomic bomb—but as president he moved quickly to take the helm of power, threw his support behind the United Nations, negotiated at Potsdam with Churchill and Stalin, and made the crucial decision to use the atomic bombs. It was that last decision that forever linked him with World War II. Although his motives may be debated, it was typical of Truman that he acted decisively.

BRITISH

Alexander, Harold (1891–1969)—field marshal: Harold Alexander was sent to France in 1940 with the British Expeditionary Force and was one of the last to leave Dunkirk. In January 1942, he was sent to command the British forces in Burma, but all he could do was to withdraw them to India. In August 1942, he was placed in command of the Middle East, and he directed the campaign in North Africa that led to the defeat of the Afrika Corps. He became Gen. Dwight D. Eisenhower's deputy in the Allied campaigns in Sicily and Italy, and when Eisenhower was called to London in December 1944 to serve as Supreme Commander for the invasion of France, Alexander became Supreme Allied Commander in the Mediterranean and led the campaign that ended with the surrender of the Germans in Italy in April 1945. Like General Eisenhower, Alexander was respected for his ability to get cooperation from often adversarial officers.

Auchinleck, Claude (1884–1981)—field marshal: Claude Auchinleck made his reputation before World War II with the British army in India and was recalled in 1939 to serve various commands. In June 1941, he was named Commander in Chief, Middle East, to replace Gen. Archibald Wavell. Alexander achieved some success against Field Marshal Erwin Rommel's Afrika Corps, but Auchinleck finally had to surrender Tobruk on June 21, 1942. Churchill blamed Auchinleck and replaced him with Gen. Harold Alexander. Auchinleck went back to India to command the British forces there.

Churchill, Winston (1874-1965) Prime Minister: Winston Churchill had served as first lord of the admiralty as well as briefly spending time in the British army during World War I (see World War I, Civilian and Military Biographies, p. 419). Churchill was far from a respected or beloved figure in British public life when he took over as prime minister on May 10, 1941. However, from his early words to Parliament, which were broadcast to the nation at large, he was able to rally the British and then sustain their morale throughout World War II with his oratory and upbeat image. He left many of the administrative details of the civilian sector to assistants and devoted himself to military strategies and tactics; his meddling in many military decisions often frustrated, even infuriated, his own military commanders (several of whom he removed). He also introduced considerable tension into his generally good relations with President Franklin D. Roosevelt and the U.S. military because of his insistence on plans that seemed designed to protect Britain's colonial interests. In the various summit conferences with Roosevelt and Joseph Stalin, he remained suspicious of Stalin, but in the end he traded off Eastern Europe to the Soviet Union in return for concessions in the Eastern Mediterranean designed to shore up the British Empire. When his Conservative Party lost the election in July 1945, it came as a tremendous shock to the world. Churchill later returned as prime minister and never lost his reputation as one of the great leaders of the 20th Century.

Harris, Arthur (1892–1984)—air chief marshal: When World War II began, Arthur Harris was in command of a bomber group. In February 1942, he was named head of the Royal Air Force Bomber Command. In that post, he committed the British air force almost entirely to area bombing, as opposed to precision bombing, which called for massive bombing attacks on large areas, such as cities. No arguments or statistics could change his mind, and, as a result, he became increasingly controversial, especially for devastating raids on cities such as Dresden. Called "Bomber Harris" by critics and supporters alike, he remained in his command until the end of the war.

Montgomery, Bernard (1887–1976)—field marshal: Bernard Montgomery fought in World War I. Despite a reputation for arrogance, he rose to the rank of general by 1939. He commanded a division of British troops that had to be evacuated at Dunkirk. In 1941, he was assigned command of the British 8th Army in North

Africa. After building up morale and fighting abilities, he spearheaded the offensives that led to the victory at El Alamein and the Axis surrender in Tunis. Those victories made him a hero to the British and increased his egotism. He led the British forces in the campaign for Sicily, then moved up the Italian peninsula. He was recalled to Britain in January 1944 to take command of the Allied ground forces under Gen. Dwight D. Eisenhower's supreme command of the invasion of Normandy. Going ashore after D-Day, he proved to be one of the more able Allied generals, although he often seemed too cautious to some American military leaders, with whom he was often in conflict over competition for supplies. His Operation Market Garden (see September 17–25, 1944, p. 469) to seize a number of bridges in Holland was a disaster, but he came through at the Battle of the Bulge (see p. 470), and he played a crucial role in crossing the Rhine. Even after World War II, he continued to be a controversial figure.

Tedder, Arthur (1890–1967)—air chief marshal: In 1941, Arthur Tedder was named commander in chief of the Royal Air Force in the Middle East and, in that post, directed the air war against Field Marshal Erwin Rommel's forces. By the end of the campaign, Tedder had demonstrated the value of close relations between the air force and ground operations. Named Dwight D. Eisenhower's deputy in the Mediterranean, Tedder was responsible for coordinating the Allies' land and air operations for the campaigns in Sicily and Italy. In 1944, he joined Eisenhower in Britain as his deputy for the invasion of Normandy; Tedder was responsible for coordinating the Allies' strategic air war with their tactical operations.

Wavell, Archibald (1883–1950)—field marshal: After a long and distinguished career with the British army—in the Boer War, at the Indian frontier, in Palestine—Wavell was commander in chief of the British force in the Middle East when the war broke out. He helped defeat the Italians in Ethiopia, but by April 1941, he had been defeated by Field Marshal Erwin Rommel in North Africa. Churchill lost patience with Wavell and had him assigned to India where he was expected to direct the Allied forces in defending Malaya and the Dutch East Indies from the Japanese. Once again, he had little chance against overwhelming forces. He planned an offensive on

Burma that began in December 1942, but when that stalled, Churchill kicked him upstairs by appointing him to the political post of British viceroy in India (1943–1947).

CHINESE

Chiang Kai-shek (1887–1975)—general, political leader: As a young officer, Chiang Kai-shek fought to bring about the revolution in China in 1911; then in the 1920s, he took the lead in forcing the unification of China. He also took the lead in opposing the role of Communists in China, and from 1928 on, he was the effective ruler of the Nationalist government. Throughout the 1930s, Chiang found himself fighting two wars—one against the Japanese and another against the Chinese Communists. By 1942, he had appointed U.S. Gen. Joseph Stilwell as his chief of staff, but he continued to try to direct all operations. He was almost totally dependent on U.S. aid for maintaining his military operations against the Japanese, and he diverted much of that aid to support his fight against the Communists. During World War II, he was treated by the Allies as one of the major leaders (along with Winston Churchill, Franklin Roosevelt, and Joseph Stalin). Part of his status, at least in the United States, rested on the appeal of his American-educated wife, Soong Mei-ling, widely known as Madame Chiang Kai-shek. Shortly after the end of the war, the Communists launched their offensive that sent Chiang Kai-shek and his Nationalists fleeing to Taiwan in 1949.

FRENCH

Daladier, Edouard (1884–1970)—politician: A leader of the French radical socialists throughout the 1930s, Edouard Daladier became prime minister in 1938 and signed the Munich pact that sacrificed Czechoslovakia to Hitler's ambitions. Strongly criticized for failing to prepare France for the obvious threat from Germany, he resigned in March 1940 but remained in the government, first as war minister, then as foreign minister. With the fall of France, he fled to Algiers, but he was arrested there, brought back to Vichy, and tried for failure to organize France for war. Sent to a German concentration camp, he survived and was released in 1945.

Darlan, Jean François (1881–1942)—admiral: Jean François Darlan was commander in chief of the French navy when France fell to the Germans. He personally met with Churchill and agreed not to let this navy fall into German hands. He sent the ships to French colonial ports in North Africa, then accepted the post of minister of the navy in Henri Pétain's Vichy government, becoming vice premier in February 1941. Later, Darlan was made head of the French armed forces and high commissioner in French North Africa. He happened to be in Algiers when the Allies invaded there in November 1942. The Americans wanted to negotiate with Darlan as to the disposition of French military forces, but the British were reluctant to deal with a member of the Vichy government. That dilemma suddenly vanished on Christmas Eve when Darlan was assassinated by a young French monarchist.

de Gaulle, Charles (1890–1970)—general, statesman: Based on his service in World War I, Charles de Gaulle became an advocate of the new tactics coordinating airpower and armored units but he won little support from his fellow army officers. With the fall of France in June 1940, he escaped to England, where he proclaimed himself the leader of the "Free French." During the following year, he failed to deliver the French colonies to the Allies but gradually rallied many French to his cause. Throughout the war, his prickly, arrogant manner often put him at odds with other Allied leaders—especially with the Americans. But by 1943, he had gained recognition as the only possible leader of those French prepared to take up arms against the Germans. He returned to France on June 14, 1944, entered Paris on August 26, and soon became the president of the Committee of National Liberation.

Juin, Alphonse Pierre (1888–1967)—general: Alphonse Juin was a graduate of France's St. Cyr Military Academy. Juin saw service in World War I. With the German invasion of France, he commanded the First French Army and was captured. Pétain won Juin's release and appointed him military governor of Morocco. Disliking the Vichy government, Juin joined the Allies in November 1942 when they were fighting in Tunisia and distinguished himself in North Africa and in Italy. In 1944, he became chief of staff of the French National Defense Committee. De Gaulle later promoted him to Marshal of France, but the two fell out over de Gaulle's policies in Algeria in the 1960s.

Leclerc, Philippe (1902–1947)—general: As an officer in the French army, Leclerc was captured twice by the Germans during the invasion of 1940, but he escaped each time. On the second occasion, he joined de Gaulle in England. He went to Africa to hold some of the sub-Saharan French colonies for the Free French. In December 1942, he led a Free French force across the Sahara to join with the British Eighth Army in Libya. He led the French Second Armored Division at the Normandy invasion and received the formal surrender of the Germans in Paris in August 1944. He died in an airplane accident shortly after the war.

Pétain, Henri Philipe (1856–1951)—marshal: Henri Pétain emerged from World War I a hero and marshal of the army. During the 1930s, he promoted the Maginot Line as France's best defense. When the French government collapsed in 1940, he took over as head of the government from Paul Reynaud (June 16, 1940) and negotiated a surrender that left France divided in two— one part occupied by the Germans, and one he governed from Vichy. But Pétain was 84 by then, and the true power in Vichy France soon gravitated to Pierre Laval, an opportunistic politician. The Germans took over Vichy France in November 1942, and in August 1944, Pétain went to Germany. In 1945, he was arrested by the French and put on trial; although found guilty of treason, his death sentence was commuted to life imprisonment by de Gaulle. Pétain died in prison a few years later.

GERMAN

Canaris, Wilhelm (1888–1945)—admiral: Wilhelm Canaris was a U-boat commander in World War I and retired from active duty with the navy in 1934. Although he disliked the Nazis, in 1939, he accepted the post of chief of the *Abwehr*, the intelligence service of the high command of the armed forces. For the following few years, Canaris was an ambiguous figure, for the *Abwehr* provided valuable intelligence to the Nazi leaders and served as both a channel for leaks to the Allies and as a center for many plots against Adolf Hitler. It may never be known just what Canaris's true role was, but after the July 1944 plot to assassinate Hitler, Canaris was arrested and sent to a concentration camp. He was hanged there in April 1945.

Dönitz, Karl (1891–1980)—admiral: Karl Dönitz joined the German navy after World War I and became a U-boat officer. He argued that the submarines could win the war for Germany by themselves. For the first three years of World War II, it seemed they might do just that: U-boats sank many hundreds of thousands of tons of Allied shipping. After March 1943, the Allied convoy escorts began to prevail, but the U-boats remained a constant threat almost to the end of the war. Dönitz replaced Raeder as commander of the German navy in 1943, but German naval power was in decline. Hitler, however, admired and trusted Dönitz and just before committing suicide—passing over all the other leading Nazis and high officers—named him his successor as head of state. On April 30, Dönitz assumed command and set about negotiating the surrender of Germany to the Allies. Tried at Nuremberg, he was sentenced to ten years in prison.

Goebbels, Joseph (1897–1945)—politician: Joseph Goebbels was kept from military service in World War I by a deformed foot. He earned his Ph.D. and wrote a novel. He joined the Nazi party in 1924 and edited its newspaper attacking Communists, Jews, and capitalists. When Hitler came to power in 1933, Goebbels became the minister of propaganda and "popular enlightenment," a post he used to control virtually all the information and entertainment Germans had access to. During the early years of World War II, he found it easy to maintain Germans' morale, but from 1943 on, he had a hard time putting a positive spin on events. Increasingly, he appealed to German fears of what would happen if the Soviet Communists conquered Germany. By 1944, he was named Plenipotentiary for Total War and, calling for even more drastic sacrifices from the German people, effectively ran the country while Hitler concentrated on the war. Goebbels remained loyal to Hitler to the end. After witnessing Hitler's marriage to Eva Braun in the bunker, he poisoned his six children and then had himself and his wife shot by an aide.

Göring, Hermann (1893–1946)—military and political leader: Hermann Göring was a flying ace in World War I. He joined the Nazi Party in 1922. As president of the Reichstag from 1928 on, he helped bring Adolf Hitler to power. After Hitler took power, Göring became one of the most unscrupulous of Hitler's henchmen, founding the Gestapo, setting up concentration camps, and murdering longtime comrades. His greatest achievement was to build up the *Luftwaffe*, or German air force. By 1939, Hitler had named him Marshal of the Third Reich and appointed him his successor. By 1940, Göring was basically the economic dictator of Germany. Although German pilots achieved some impressive feats, Göring was an erratic manager, made several miscalculations in ordering the type of aircraft needed, and frequently promised Hitler more than he could deliver. After the failure of the Germans to bomb Britain into submission and the defeat of the German forces in the Soviet Union, Hitler relied less and less on Göring, who retreated into a private life of drugs and art collecting. Near the end of World War II, he proposed that he take power if Hitler died or was captured. Hitler's response was to order Göring arrested. But Göring was captured by Americans and tried at Nuremberg. He committed suicide just before he could be executed.

Guderian, Heinz (1888–1954)—general: Heinz Guderian was a professional soldier. He published *Achtung! Panzer!* in 1937, laying out his theories about how fast-moving mobilized units should be utilized. Essentially, that was the blueprint for the *blitzkrieg*. He proved his theories in the invasions of Poland and France. He then led his armored units in the invasion of the Soviet Union, but after initial successes, he was dismissed by Adolf Hitler for failing to follow his battle plans at Moscow. In February 1943, Guderian was recalled to build up the armored corps, but his plans were dashed at the battle of Kursk in July. After the July 1944 plot against Hitler, Guderian was named Chief of General Staff but Hitler ignored all his advice and finally dismissed him on March 28, 1945.

Hess, Rudolf (1894–1987)—Nazi politician: Rudolf Hess was a student at the University of Munich when he fell under Hitler's spell and joined the Nazi Party. Sentenced for participating in the Beer Hall Putsch in 1923, he was imprisoned with Hitler (and took down much of *Mein Kampf* which Hitler dictated). By 1934, Hess was the deputy leader of the Nazi Party and, in 1939, was named the second in line (after Göring) to succeed Hitler. Because he was always pictured at Hitler's side, it came as a major shock to the world when, in May 1941, he flew alone to Scotland, parachuted to the ground, and announced he had come to negotiate a peace between Germany and Britain. (He was totally disowned by the German authorities.) Eventually judged mentally disturbed, he was nevertheless tried at Nuremberg and sentenced to life imprisonment. He was held at Spandau prison in Berlin with other war criminals, and from 1966 to his death, he was the sole prisoner there.

Heydrich, Reinhard (1904–1942)—Nazi leader: In 1931 Reinhard Heydrich was dismissed from the German navy for "compromising" the daughter of an important shipbuilder. He joined the newly formed SS. He soon became Heinrich Himmler's deputy. Heydrich arranged for the incident at the Polish border that Hitler used as the pretext for invading Poland. After the invasion of the Soviet Union, Heydrich took charge of the *Einsatzgruppen*, the special extermination squads assigned to murdering thousands of Jews, Slavs, and other "undesirables" in the occupied territories. It is generally believed that he drafted the proposal for the "Final Solution of the Jewish Problem" that was adopted by the Wannsee Conference in January 1942. He was appointed the governor of occupied Czechoslovakia. In June 1942 he was assassinated by Czech partisans. In reprisal, the Germans obliterated the town and population of Lidice.

Himmler, Heinrich (1900–1945)—Nazi leader: Heinrich Himmler was a poultry farmer outside Munich. He marched in the Beer Hall Putsch of 1923. When Adolf Hitler was released from prison, he made Himmler chief of the Nazi SS (*Schutzstaffel*, or "protective force"), which Himmler built into a large private army. He then directed the Gestapo, or secret police, first within Germany and then in the conquered countries, moving from espionage and deportation and torture to mass executions and eventually to the systematic liquidation of whole populations. As much as any single individual, he was responsible for overseeing the "Final Solution" on behalf of Hitler. After the failed attempt on Hitler's life (see July 20, 1944, p. 475), Himmler was made commander in chief of the home forces, but he saw the end coming and early in 1945 began secret negotiations to surrender to the Western Allies—hoping to align them in a war against the Soviet Union. He was captured shortly after World War II ended but took poison to avoid a trial for war crimes and almost certain execution.

Hitler, Adolf (1889–1945)—dictator: Adolf Hitler was born in Austria. He was drawn to Germany, studying art in Munich, then volunteering for service with the German army in World War I. He was wounded and awarded a medal. He turned his energies to building a small National Socialist German Workers' Party, with its appeal based heavily on blaming politicians for a "stab in the back" by signing the armistice and the Versailles Treaty after World War I. His first attempt at seizing power—the Munich Beer Hall Putsch of 1923—led to his being jailed, which gave him time to set down his agenda in *Mein Kampf*. He exploited divisions among the German political parties and frustrations among the electorate. He was appointed chancellor in January 1933. He wasted no time in suppressing all opposition, unions, free speech, Communists, and Jews and took absolute power. He then began to build up German military strength. By the late 1930s, he had effectively discarded the Versailles Treaty. With the invasion of Poland (see September 1, 1939, p. 434), he openly launched his campaign to conquer Europe. At first he appeared to be an invincible strategist, but he made a fundamental blunder in invading the Soviet Union in June 1941 and compounded his error by micromanaging his forces in the Soviet Union. Indeed, Hitler's constant meddling with the decisions of his field commanders contributed immeasurably to Germany's defeat. Not content with waging a cataclysmic war, he authorized the Holocaust and other policies aimed at eliminating vast numbers of civilians.

Jodl, Alfried (1890–1946)—general: Alfried Jodl was an artillery officer in World War I. By 1939, he had become chief of staff (under Wilhelm Keitel) in the OKW, the organization that the Nazis set up to replace the War Ministry and the High Command. In that role, Jodl attended the twice-daily conferences at which Adolf Hitler laid down the strategies and tactics that Jodl then translated into operational orders. Although outranked (and outpositioned) by many others, he was regarded as a major contributor to Germany's military operations. He advocated the terror bombing of British cities and ordered the killing of prisoners of war. Tried at Nuremberg, he pleaded that he had only been following orders as a soldier, but he was found guilty and hanged.

Keitel, Wilhelm (1882–1946)—field marshal: Wilhelm Keitel was an officer in World War I. He became a devoted Nazi in the 1930s, and by 1938, he had become the chief of the OKW, the supreme command of the armed forces. Throughout the war, he was one of Hitler's most trusted military advisers—primarily because Keitel never disagreed with Hitler. (His nickname among those in the know was *Lakaitel—Lakai* being the German word for "lackey.") Keitel was one of the German signers of the full surrender in May 1945. Tried at Nuremberg for war crimes, he was found guilty and hanged.

Kesselring, Albrecht (1885–1960)—field marshal: Albrecht Kesselring was an artillery officer in World War I. He transferred to the Luftwaffe in 1933 and played an important role in the German air force's campaigns in Poland, France, and the Battle of Britain. In 1941, he became Commander in Chief, South. From his headquarters in Rome, he tried to coordinate the air war with Gen. Erwin Rommel's ground campaign in North Africa. After the loss there, Kesselring directed the Germans' hard-fought campaigns in Sicily and up the Italian peninsula. By the time Hitler transferred Kesselring to command the German forces along the western front in March 1945, it was too late. He was tried for war crimes and was imprisoned until 1952.

Manstein, Erich von (1887–1973)—field marshal: Erich von Manstein was chief of staff to Gerd von Rundstedt by the time of the invasion of Poland. He became legendary for his willingness to challenge his superiors. He personally converted Hitler to his plan for invading France and was rewarded with a major command in the invasion of the Soviet Union, where he achieved equally daring results. Even he, however, was unable to save Friedrich von Paulus at Stalingrad, (see November 19–December 31, 1942, p. 448), and thereafter he was effectively leading an army in retreat. Because Hitler refused to accept any withdrawal whatever the circumstances, von Manstein was dismissed from command in March 1944 and spent the rest of the war on his estate. Arrested in 1945, he was imprisoned as a war criminal until 1953. He is still regarded as one of the major exponents of modern warfare.

Paulus, Friedrich von (1890–1957)—field marshal: Friedrich von Paulus was a staff officer during the invasions of Poland, Belgium, and France. He was responsible for much of the planning for the invasion of the Soviet Union. As a tank officer, he was given a field assignment to lead the German Sixth Army in its drive toward Stalingrad. By November 1942 he penetrated the city, but was short of supplies and his exhausted troops were facing winter. Hitler ordered him not to withdraw, and because von Paulus obeyed, Hitler named him a Field Marshal on January 30, 1943—but the next day von Paulus surrendered, one of some 90,000 German soldiers captured at Stalingrad (see p. 457). By 1944 he was making broadcasts from Russia urging Germans troops to surrender; he settled in Russia after the war and appeared as a witness for the Allies at the Nuremberg war trials.

Rommel, Erwin (1891–1944)—field marshal: Erwin Rommel was a decorated officer in World War I. Between the wars, Rommel wrote an influential book on infantry tactics. He was also an open supporter of the Nazis, commanding Adolf Hitler's headquarters' guard in the late 1930s. Rommel was in command of an armored division in the invasion of France and in February 1941, was given command of the Afrika Corps and sent to North Africa, originally to save the Italian army in Libya. For the following two years, he carried on one of the most dramatic campaigns in military history, constantly threatening the Allied forces and even in retreat making them pay dearly for every inch of ground. His canny tactics earned him the sobriquet "The Desert Fox" and the respect of even enemy soldiers. Brought back to Europe in March 1943 before the collapse of the Afrika Corps, he was placed in charge of the German preparations against an Allied invasion of France. Had he been able to position his forces as he wanted without interference from Adolf Hitler, he might have made the invasion even costlier to the Allies than it was. On July 17, 1944, Rommel was wounded when a British fighter plane strafed his car, and he was evacuated. After the assassination attempt on Hitler's life three days later (July 20, 1944, p. 475), Rommel fell under suspicion; two emissaries from Hitler visited him at his home and offered him the choice of a trial or suicide. Rommel went with them and swallowed the poison they offered, but it was announced he died of his wounds and was given a state funeral (see October 14, 1944, p. 476).

Rundstedt, Gerd von (1875–1953)—field marshal: Gerd von Rundstedt was from the traditional Prussian military caste. He was "purged" from the army in 1938 for expressing his negative opinions of Adolf Hitler. Eventually, he was reinstated and given command of the German army's *blitzkrieg* invasions of Poland, then of

Belgium and France. In France he made a crucial error in halting the attack on the British troops at Dunkirk, thus allowing many to escape (see May 27–June 4, 1940, p. 437). In 1941, he was in command of a major army group during the invasion of the Soviet Union, but when he did not act as aggressively as Hitler desired, he was removed from command. He was reinstated in 1942 as Commander in Chief, West, which meant that he was responsible for defending against the invasion of France. He and Field Marshal Erwin Rommel disagreed over the best plan, but Hitler imposed his own plan. Rundstedt was removed from command on July 1 but reinstated in September. The Ardennes Offensive (Battle of the Bulge) was Hitler's idea, but von Rundstedt carried it out. After its failure, von Rundstedt once again lost his command (in March 1945). Ill health saved him from a trial at Nuremberg.

Speer, Albert (1905–1981)—Nazi official: Albert Speer was a young architect and party member when he caught Hitler's fancy and, in 1934, was named the chief designer/architect for the grandiose ceremonies and sterile buildings that Hitler favored. In 1942, Speer was made minister of armaments and proceeded to show an amazing talent for organizing the war industry. Despite the heavy bombing and shortages of materials, Speer managed to maintain the output until the final months of World War II. Tried at Nuremberg, he was found guilty of using slave labor in the factories and sentenced to 20 years in prison. After his release, he published two historically interesting but self-serving books. Although he did oppose Hitler toward the end of the war and showed some contrition for the evils of Nazism, he never fully explained why he, such an evidently intelligent man, had worked so hard for Hitler for so many years.

Stauffenberg, Klaus von (1907–1944)—colonel: Klaus von Stauffenberg served in Poland, France, and North Africa. In the North African campaign, he was severely wounded by a strafing airplane. Back in a German hospital, he came to believe that he and his fellow high ranking officers should take action to stop Hitler. Assigned to a high staff position, he soon was at the center of a group of officers who agreed that Hitler should be eliminated. By June 1944, von Stauffenberg was attending briefing sessions with Hitler. On July 20, he carried a briefcase containing a bomb into a meeting. Excusing himself before it was timed to explode, he left for Berlin as soon as he heard the explosion. But the briefcase had been moved, and Hitler was only slightly wounded (see July 20, 1944, p. 475). Arriving in Berlin, von Stauffenberg tried to assure his fellow conspirators that Hitler was dead, but as soon as that proved otherwise, Gen. Friedrich Fromm had him arrested, court-martialed, and executed (July 21). Von Stauffenberg was eventually regarded as a martyr, but some still question his motives and tactics.

HUNGARIAN

Horthy, Nikolaus (1868–1957)—admiral, dictator: An admiral in the Austro-Hungarian Empire, Nikolaus Horthy took the lead after World War I in putting down a Communist regime in Hungary and in restoring the Hapsburg monarchy in 1920. He had himself named regent and effectively ruled as a dictator. He brought Hungary into World War II on the side of the Axis but tried to walk a narrow line that maintained some independence from Adolf Hitler. He tried to stop the persecution of Hungary's Jews and limit the role of Hungary's troops in World War II. In October 1944, he broadcast an appeal for an armistice with the Allies, but Hitler sent a German force that kidnapped Horthy's son and forced Horthy's surrender. Horthy was taken to Germany and imprisoned there until freed by American forces in May 1945.

ITALIAN

Badoglio, Pietro (1871–1956)—military and political leader: Pietro Badoglio was an Italian hero of World War I. He commanded the Italian army that conquered Ethiopia (1935–1936), then became its viceroy. Named army chief of staff when Italy entered World War II (1940), he resigned that December after the failure of the Italian invasion of Greece. He had long disliked Mussolini and took the lead in his overthrow in July 1943. Badoglio then became prime minister and signed the armistice with the Allies in September. He resigned from the government in 1944.

Borghese, Prince Valerio (1906–1974)—naval commander, politician: Valerio Borghese directed Italian naval operations that sank many thousands of tons of Allied shipping in the Mediterranean. In December 1941, he commanded the raid on the British fleet in the harbor of Alexandria, Egypt, in which three midget submarines crippled two British battleships. By 1943, he was in charge of the Italian naval operations assigned to thwart the Allied invasion at Anzio in January 1944. He could do little and, when Italy surrendered in September 1944, he joined Mussolini in northern Italy. Borghese fought the anti-Fascist and anti-Nazi partisans. He was arrested after the war as a Nazi collaborator. He retained his fascist beliefs and, in 1973, was linked to a neo-Fascist plot to overthrow the Italian government, but, by then, he had fled to Spain.

Ciano, Count Galeazzo (1903–1944)—diplomat: Galeazzo Ciano married Mussolini's daughter, Edda. He became the foreign minister in 1936. At first, he supported Mussolini's policies, but as he saw that disaster loomed he tried to curb Mussolini's excesses. Ciano resigned as foreign minister in February 1943. As a member of the Fascist Grand Council, he voted for the removal of Mussolini that July. Tricked by the Germans into placing himself in their hands, he was tried and executed with his father-in-law's approval.

Mussolini, Benito (1883–1945)—dictator: Although grouped with Hideki Tojo and Adolf Hitler in the Axis Big Three, Mussolini was a more prominent figure than the former and a lesser villain than the latter. He was a journalist before he seized power in 1922. He earned some respect as the man who "made the trains run on time." Although he conquered Ethiopia and Albania, he soon lost Hitler's respect. He had to get aid from the Germans to take over Greece. His armies were decimated in Tunisia and Russia, and with the fall of Sicily imminent, he was deposed and imprisoned in July 1943. In September he was released in a daring operation by German commandos and headed a phony government in northern Italy until he was captured and executed by Italian partisans, who hung his body upside down in Milan.

JAPANESE

Hirohito (1901–1989)—emperor: As a young man, Hirohito was more interested in marine biology than in the political and military concerns of his position. Although he was revered by most Japanese as the "Imperial Son of Heaven," Hirohito actually exerted little power over the Japanese government. Basically, he gave his assent to decisions reached by the government. Personally he was opposed to the militarists. Still, the invasion of China, the preparations for a greater war in the Pacific, the attack on Pearl Harbor, and the subsequent pursuit of World War II were conducted in his name. Only when Japan seemed in danger of being invaded did he give his support to those who wanted to negotiate an end to the war. And in the war's very final days, he at last spoke out, first telling his cabinet that he did not want the status of the emperor to be used as an obstacle to peace, then recording the broadcast to his nation in which he told his people they must "accept the unacceptable, endure the unendurable." Gen. Douglas MacArthur wanted Hirohito to facilitate the transformation of Japanese society but forced him to declare his nondivinity in January 1946.

Homma, Masaharu (1881–1946)—general: Masaharu Homma was an obscure intelligence officer in the Japanese army until he was chosen to lead the invasion of the Philippines in December 1941. He landed in Luzon and, finding little opposition, advanced quickly to Manila. In January 1942, he then moved to capture the U.S. and Filipino forces who had retreated to Bataan. When he became stalled, he was removed from true command in February, but he remained at his post. After some 76,000 U.S. and Filipino troops surrendered in April 1942, they were forced to undergo the infamous Bataan death march, during which some 20,000 died due to the inhumane treatment by the Japanese. After the war, Homma was arrested and charged with responsibility for that inhumanity; tried and found guilty, he was executed by a firing squad.

Konoye, Prince Fumimaro (1891–1945)—political leader: A member of an old aristocratic family, Prince Konoye was a moderate. As prime minister in 1937, he compromised with the emerging militarists and allowed the invasion of China. He left office but returned as prime minister in 1940 and tried to negotiate with the United States over their differences in Asia. The militarists forced him to resign in October 1941. He remained in the wings until the fall of Hideki Tojo in July 1944, when he reemerged as an advocate for negotiating an end to the war. Hirohito authorized Konoye to go to Moscow in July 1945, but the Soviets weren't interested in negotiating. After Japan's surrender, he committed suicide when he was named as a potential war criminal.

Nagumo, Chuichi (1887–1944)—admiral: A torpedo specialist by training, Chuichi Nagumo was assigned command of the carrier strike force that attacked Pearl Harbor (see December 7, 1941, p. 443). Because of his lack of experience with naval-air warfare, he was overly cautious and canceled the third wave of planes that might have truly shut down the U.S. fleet in the Pacific. At the Battle of Midway (see June 3–6, 1942, p. 454), his inexperience and caution also led to a crucial victory for the American forces. After two more unsuccessful naval battles (Eastern Solomons and Santa Cruz Islands), Nagumo was relieved of command of the carrier force and assigned to defend the island of Saipan. On July 6, 1944, when Saipan was about to fall to the Americans, he committed suicide.

Suzuki, Kantaro (1867–1948)—political leader: Kantaro Suzuki had served in Korea and in the Russo-Japanese War, retiring in 1927. In 1929, he was made grand chamberlain, merely an advisory post to the emperor, but he also served on the supreme war council. He was personally opposed to the Japanese military aggression of the ensuing 15 years but was powerless. Not until the fall of Hideki Tojo (July 1944) did Suzuki begin to re-enter public life, and when the government fell in April 1945 after the invasion of Okinawa, he was named prime minister. He faced a difficult job of balancing the demands of the still assertive military against (as he saw it) the threat of total destruction of his country. His policies in the ensuing months may not have always been the best, but in the end, he took the bold step of allowing the emperor to surrender.

Tojo, Hideki (1884–1948)—general, prime minister: As an army officer in the 1930s, Tojo came to the fore by promoting Japan's aggression in Manchuria. More important, he became the leader of those in the military who opposed the democratic civilian government. By 1938, he had a special dispensation to hold both military and cabinet posts. By 1940, he was minister of war and he played a major role in negotiating the Tripartite Pact with Germany and Italy. Becoming prime minister in October 1941, he moved quickly to occupy French Indochina, then authorized the attack on Pearl Harbor. From that point on, he effectively ruled Japan and ran the war. When Japan's fate was irretrievably sealed with the fall of Saipan in July 1944, he was forced to resign. Tojo failed at a suicide attempt after

Japan surrendered, was tried for his war crimes, and hanged in December 1948.

Yamamoto, Isoroku (1884–1943)—admiral: Isoroku Yamamoto studied at Harvard (1917–1919) and was naval attaché at the Japanese embassy in Washington, D.C. (1926–1928). As vice minister of the navy (1936–1939) and commander in chief of the Combined Fleet (1939–1943), he built up the Japanese navy and naval air force. He opposed taking on the United States in a war, but when war seemed inevitable he argued and planned for the surprise attack that led to Pearl Harbor. Determined to wipe out the U.S. fleet, he planned the extremely ambitious operation designed to take Midway Island, but instead the Japanese lost four carriers in the battle (see June 3–6, 1942, p. 454). Yamamoto was shocked by this loss and subsequent defeats of his naval forces, but he continued to direct their offensive operations. Because the U.S. forces could read the Japanese naval code, they learned of his planned tour of the Western Solomons in April 1943 and were able to shoot down his plane on April 18. That was a major blow to Japan's military morale, for Yamamoto was a bold strategist of naval warfare.

Yamashita, Tomoyuki (1885–1946)—general: After fighting in China in 1939, Tomoyuki Yamashita was sent on a military mission to Germany. He returned to advise that Japan should not become involved in a war with Britain and the United States. When his superiors ignored his advice, however, he led the Japanese forces that overran Malaya and took Singapore (earning the sobriquet "Tiger of Malaya"). He then took charge of the final campaign against the Filipino and U.S. forces trapped on Bataan and Corregidor. For some reason, Hideki Tojo then assigned Yamashita to command a training division in Manchuria. Only with Tojo's fall in July 1944 did Yamashita get a combat command, to defend the Philippines against the U.S. invasion. Although the Japanese were effectively defeated by the end of June 1945, Yamashita remained to direct resistance until he was informed of his country's surrender in September 1945. Arrested and tried as a war criminal, he was executed in February 1946.

NORWEGIAN

Quisling, Vidkung (1887–1945)—politician:

A onetime army officer, then a diplomat, Vidkung Quisling founded the Norwegian equivalent of Adolf Hitler's National Socialist party in 1933. He visited Hitler in December 1939 to explain his plan for seizing power in Norway, but Hitler preferred to invade Norway. Quisling was made head of the puppet government, but he was forced out that September. The Germans installed him again as a puppet minister president in February 1942. He surrendered to the Allies in May 1945, and although he presented himself as one who had dealt with the Nazis only for the good of his country, he was executed as a traitor in November. His name remains synonymous with all politicians who collaborate with an enemy, as he did.

SOVIETS

Chuikov, Vasili (1900–1982)—general: As a Red Army volunteer in 1918, Vasili Chuikov fought against the White Russian army. He rose in rank and fought in Finland in the "Winter War" (1939–1940) and in the invasion of Poland in 1939. He was then assigned as the Soviet military attaché to China. But in 1942, he was recalled and put in command of the Soviet forces that successfully defended Stalingrad. He then led his forces on the counteroffensive through the Ukraine, Belorussia, and Poland, all the way to the capture of Berlin. He was a staunch Communist and a respected general. In 1960–1961, he served as supreme commander of the land forces of the Soviet Union.

Konev, Ivan (1897–1973)—general: When the Germans invaded the Soviet Union in June 1941, Ivan Konev was in the Smolensk sector, but from October 1941 throughout 1942 he commanded the Kalanin front that delayed the German advance on Moscow. He then became one of the principal commanders in the counteroffensive that drove the Germans out of the Ukraine, encircling ten German divisions at Korsun-Sevchenovsky in February 1944. He was promoted to marshal in February 1944 and, along with Gen. Georgi Zhukov, led the offensive that pushed the Germans all the way back to Berlin. After joining the U.S. forces at the Elbe, he continued on southward to enter Prague in May 1945.

Rokossovsky, Konstantin (1896–1968)—general: Konstantin Rokossovsky had been arrested during Stalin's purging of the military in 1938 but was reinstated at the outbreak of World War II.

After the German invasion, he saved the inexperienced armies trapped at Smolensk from encirclement by the Germans. He played a crucial role in the defense of Moscow, then led the breakthrough at Stalingrad. At the Battle of Kursk in July 1943 (see July 5–23, 1943, p. 458), he commanded the front that resisted the German onslaught, then led the counteroffensive. In June 1944, he commanded the offensive against the Germans in Belorussia and, by August, had advanced to near Warsaw. With an uprising by the Polish Home Army then underway, Rokossovsky held back the Soviet forces for two months until the Germans effectively wiped out the Polish Home Army; the Soviets defended that inactivity as based on their need to regroup and resupply. He started his new offensive in January 1945, taking Warsaw, then moving up to East Prussia and joining the British in May.

Stalin, Joseph (1879–1953)—dictator: During the 1930s, Joseph Stalin consolidated his power by getting rid of anyone in the Soviet Union—including military leaders—whose loyalty he suspected. By 1939, however, realizing that his forces were not strong enough to resist the Germans, he made a nonaggression pact with Adolf Hitler, then proceeded to annex part of Poland and invade Finland. When Hitler invaded the Soviet Union in 1941, Stalin continued to manage the military but finally had to rely on men like Gen. Georgi Zhukov. Unlike the other Allied leaders, who had to deal constantly with domestic opposition, Stalin had total power to dictate everything—ordering a scorched-earth strategy in the face of the German onslaught, moving the factories eastward, concentrating the entire economy on the war. He also interfered with his generals and their operations. Because of the undeniably heroic role of the Soviet people in World War II, Stalin was elevated by many to the status of a respectable Allied leader. Meanwhile he continually pressured the other Allies to open up a second front—even threatening to make a separate peace with Hitler. By 1944, with the Allied forces, including his own, converging on Germany, he turned his attention to the postwar role of the Soviet Union; at the Yalta (see February 4–11, 1945, p. 487) and Potsdam (see July 17–August 2, 1945, pp. 487-488) conferences, he managed to get Franklin Roosevelt, Winston Churchill, and Harry Truman to concede to him virtual control of Eastern Europe. He died as the

Cold War was moving into high gear (see Cold War, Civilian and Military Biographies, p. 567).

Timoshenko, Semyon (1895–1970)—general: An old comrade of Joseph Stalin's, Semyon Timoshenko had fought in the Russo-Finnish War. In May 1940, he was made a marshal and was placed in charge of training and reorganizing the Red Army. When the Germans invaded the Soviet Union, he was placed in command of the Western Front, and although he could not stop the German advance, he delayed their arrival at Moscow until the winter. Transferred to the southwestern front, he again failed, and the Germans took the Crimea. His counteroffensive at Kharkov in May 1942 miscalculated the Germans' strength, and after the Soviets were routed, he was transferred to the northwestern front.

Vasilievsky, Alexander (1895–1977)—general: As the Chief of General Staff of the Armed Forces through most of World War II, Alexander Vasilievsky was the Soviet Union's major strategist, responsible for coordinating operations on all fronts. He is credited with such operations as the offensive that freed Stalingrad, the battle at Kursk, and the final Soviet offensive against Germany. He remained near the front lines and communicated with Stalin back in Moscow. After the death of Gen. Ivan Chernyakhovsky, Vasilievsky assumed command of the campaign in East Prussia. With the surrender of Germany, he was sent to command the Soviet forces in the Far East and led his troops across the Manchurian border when the atomic bombs were dropped.

Voroshilov, Kliment (1881–1969)—general: Kliment Voroshilov had fought alongside Stalin in the Russian revolution and by 1934 was appointed commissar for defense charged with mechanizing the Red Army. After the invasion by Germany, he was named to the State Defense Committee that directed the mobilization of Soviet resources as well as the overall conduct of the war. Given command of the armies of the northwest front, he lacked the experience and troops to save Leningrad. Relieved of his command, he spent the rest of World War II in staff positions and on diplomatic assignments.

Zhukov, Georgi (1896–1974)—general: Georgi Zhukov first came to prominence by defeating the Japanese in Mongolia in 1939. The victory over Japan led to his appointment as chief of staff of the Red Army in 1940. From that point on, he was one of the major commanders of the Soviet army, leading it through several of its greatest moments—lifting the siege of Moscow, taking the offensive at Stalingrad that led to the surrender of Paulus's Sixth Army, fighting the great tank battle at Kursk, sweeping across the Ukraine, taking Warsaw, and capturing Berlin. On May 8, Zhukov signed for the Soviet Union the surrender of the Germans in Berlin. Among his other achievements was his ability to hold the support of Joseph Stalin, who was notoriously distrustful of successful generals.

YUGOSLAVIAN

Tito (Josip Broz) (1892–1980)—guerrilla and political leader: While serving in the Austro-Hungarian army in World War I, Josip Broz, as Tito was then known, was captured by the Russians; he became a Communist and served in the Russian Revolution. He had little success in advancing Communism in Yugoslavia during the inter-war years but when the Germans and Italians invaded and took over Yugoslavia in 1941, he quickly organized partisans that conducted minor sabotage and major campaigns against the Axis. Until late in 1942, the Allies gave most support to the rival Yugoslavia partisans, led by the anti-Communist general Draza Mihailovic, but once the Allies realized that Mihailovic was doing little to oppose the Germans, they threw their support to Tito. By early 1944, Tito commanded an army of some 250,000 men, was able to tie down large Axis forces, and controlled much of Yugoslavia. By October 1944, he had taken Belgrade. When the Communists won the first elections in 1945, they abolished the old monarchy, and Tito took over, ruling Yugoslavia until his death in 1980.

FURTHER READING

Alperovitz, Gar. *The Decision to Use the Atomic Bomb and the Architecture of an American Myth*. New York: Knopf, 1995.

Barnett, Correlli. *The Desert Generals*. Bloomington, Ind.: Indiana University Press, 1982.

De Seversky, Alexander. *Victory Through Airpower*. New York: Simon & Schuster, 1942.

Dallek, Robert. *Franklin D. Roosevelt and American Foreign Policy, 1932–1945*. New York: Oxford University Press, 1979.

Dunnigan, James E., and Albert A. Nofi. *Dirty Little Secrets of World War II*. New York: William Morrow, 1994.

Eubank, Keith. *Munich*. Norman, Okla.: University of Oklahoma Press, 1963.

Fussell, Paul. *Wartime: Understanding and Behavior in the Second World War*. New York: Oxford University Press, 1989.

Gilbert, Martin. *The Second World War: A Complete History*. Rev. Ed. New York: Henry Holt, 1991.

Irons, Peter. *Justice at War: The Story of the Japanese American Internment Cases*. New York: Oxford University Press, 1983.

Keegan, John. *The Second World War*. New York: Penguin Books, 1990.

Marras, Michael R., ed. *The Nazi Holocaust: Historical Articles on the Destruction of European Jews*. 9 Vols. Westport, Conn.: Meckler, 1989.

Miller, Edward S. *War Plan Orange: The U.S. Strategy to Defeat Japan, 1897–1945*. Annapolis, Md.: U.S. Naval Institute, 1991.

Morison, Samuel Eliot. *The Two Ocean War*. Boston: Little, Brown, 1963.

Overy, R. J. *The Air War: 1939–1945*. New York: Stein and Day, 1981.

Palmar, Norman and Thomas B. Allen. *World War II: America at War, 1941–1945*. New York: Random House, 1991.

Perrett, Geoffrey. *There's a War To Be Won: The United States Army in World War II*. New York: Random House, 1991.

Prange, Gordon R., with Donald M. Goldstein and Katherine V. Dillon. *At Dawn We Slept*. New York: McGraw Hill, 1981.

———*Pearl Harbor: The Verdict of History*. New York: McGraw Hill, 1986.

Ready, J. Lee. *Forgotten Allies*. 2 Vols. New York: McFarland, 1985.

Rhodes, Richard. *The Making of the Atomic Bomb*. New York: Simon & Schuster, 1986.

Rystad, Goran. *Prisoners of the Past: The Munich Syndrome and Makers of American Foreign Policy in the Cold War*. Lund, Sweden: CWK Gleeerup, 1982.

Shirer, William L. *The Rise and Fall of the Third Reich*. New York: Simon & Schuster, 1960.

Stouffer, Samuel A. et al. *The American Soldier: Studies in Social Psychology in World War II*. 2 Vols. Princeton, N. J.: Princeton University Press, 1949.

Van Creveld, Martin. *Fighting Power: German and U.S. Army Performance, 1939–1945*. Westport, Conn: Greenwood Press, 1982.

Watt, D. Cameron. *How War Came*. New York: Pantheon, 1989.

Wyman, David. *The Abandonment of the Jews: America and the Holocaust*. New York: Pantheon, 1984.

THE COLD WAR

DATES OF WAR

October 2, 1945–November 19, 1990

Starting and ending dates for the Cold War are bound to be especially arbitrary and potentially controversial. Most sources agree on the years, but the pivotal events, and thus the months and days, remain in dispute.

The beginning date used here is that of the last meeting of the major powers' Council of Foreign Ministers, which ended with a deep split between Western nations and the Union of Soviet Socialist Republics (USSR). The date was chosen because it reflects the multinational and diplomatic/political nature of the Cold War as opposed to singling out one nation or event with a military cast.

Although the Cold War was to all intents and purposes over by the end of 1988, the key events of 1989–1990 in European politics are so important and so symmetrical to those of 1945–1946 that the ending date selected here is that of the meeting in Paris of the NATO and Warsaw Pact nations (see Negotiations and Peace Treaty, pp. 555-556). Some might consider the Cold War not to have ended until December 31, 1991, when the Soviet Union, the United States' chief adversary in the Cold War, officially ceased to exist.

ALTERNATE NAMES

The Soviets also adopted the Russian words for "the Cold War" although the Soviets had a slang term meaning "the pushbutton war."

SIGNIFICANCE

The history of the Cold War is a global story of perceptions and judgments as well as of events, all profoundly shaped and distorted by ideology. For 45 years, the U.S. government evaluated virtually all its policy decisions in light of their probable effects on the Soviet Union and the Communist bloc. The Communist leaders of the Soviet Union were equally dedicated to basing their policies and practices on analyses of U.S. behavior and response. And although the United States and the Soviet Union were the two main antagonists, many other countries joined in with considerable commitment and zeal. In fact, it is almost impossible to overstate the impact that the Cold War had on the daily lives of people on every continent.

The importance of post–World War II treaty and territorial settlements was greatly magnified by the geopolitical demands of the emerging Cold War blocs. The United States and the Soviet Union struggled to control the rebuilding and economic integration of Europe; the development of newly independent nations in the Middle East, Africa, and Southeast Asia; and the revolutionary changes from Cuba to China. The United States tended to see itself as having a mission as the world's "policeman" to protect vulnerable new governments for the "free world" and a free market economy, and the Soviets sought to realize the Marxist destiny of a socialist/Communist world domination.

Superpower rivalry magnified the importance of nationalist movements and indigenous Communist parties and gave new Third World nations enormous leverage, which was increased by the United Nations (UN) rule of one country, one vote in the General Assembly. The United States, despite its role as leader of the free world, found itself supporting bloody dictators and corrupt governments solely because they were anti-Communist; the Soviets supported almost any government that proclaimed allegiance to or sympathy for Communism.

Nations were able to exploit the rivalry between the United States and the Soviet Union, even though their own situation had little or nothing to do with the Communist-anti-Communist conflict. Perhaps the most notable was the situation in the Middle East involving Israel and its neighbors, a conflict played out against the background of the threat of Soviet intrusion in the Arab world, even though the Arabs by and large had no liking for Communism. The result was that the United States provided generous aid not only to Israel but often to Jordan and Egypt, too, longtime adversaries of Israel.

For four peacetime decades, the superpowers supported wartime levels of defense spending to equip and maintain huge military and intelligence establishments. Client states required enormous infusions of foreign aid. The sheer cost of the Cold War skewed national budgets and economies all over the world, particularly those of the Soviet Union and the United States. The Soviet leaders were able to prop up what appeared to be a superpower economy, capable of maintaining a massive military machine but only by depriving their people of many of the amenities taken for granted elsewhere in the world: In effect, the Soviets did without cars so they could have tanks. Although the United States economy seemed to be able to provide both guns *and* butter, it was fueled to some extent by the government's spending for the Cold War: The "military-industrial complex" (see Notable Phrases, p. 561) employed millions, drew on massive resources and production, and generally paid good wages.

The great ideological struggle between Communism and free-market capitalism had a profound effect on the daily lives of Americans. McCarthyism, denoting the anti-Communist persecutory methods employed by Sen. Joseph McCarthy (R–Wis.), and the "Red scare" (and "blacklists") of the 1950s destroyed many careers, including that of J. Robert Oppenheimer, the father of the atom bomb. (The crusade against Communism also made the careers of many, Richard Nixon being one of the most notable.) The Federal Bureau of Investigations (FBI), the Central Intelligence Agency (CIA), and the Defense Department all abused the rights of U.S. citizens with illegal surveillance; secret drug and chemical and nuclear weapons tests on civilians and military personnel; and infiltration of universities, religious groups, unions, and the media. U.S. national policies in education, trade, social programs, and the space program—to name but a few of the areas pervaded by Cold War imperatives—were formulated in light of superpower rivalry and to some degree affected the lives of millions of ordinary Americans.

BACKGROUND

The deep roots of the Cold War reach back at

least to 1917, when Vladimir Lenin led the Russian Revolution. In Lenin's ideological formulation, the Communist state he created was the engine of an international movement; he saw the spread of the Communist system and war with capitalism as historically inevitable. His view was to some extent validated when the United States joined Great Britain in sending troops to fight the Reds in the Russian civil war (1918–1920) (see World War I, May 1918, p. 405) and then refused to recognize the Soviet Union until 1933. Many people had reason to fear the Communists, who appeared to stop at nothing to gain their ends, especially after Soviet dictator Joseph Stalin emerged in the late 1920s. Millions of peasants starved to death in the 1930s under forced collectivization of their farms; during the purges of 1936–1938, millions of Soviets were murdered or imprisoned for little more than suspicion of being less than 100 percent pro-Communist.

By World War II, then, two mutually exclusive and competing systems were already in place. President Harry S. Truman called them "two ways of life," and it is fair to say that they had become so. The two sides were destined to misunderstand and miscalculate each other's aims and strategies, to accuse each another of bad faith while practicing deception, and to base policies large and small on assumptions of doubtful validity. The Soviet-German secret nonaggression pact of 1939, for instance, assured Moscow's control over the Baltic republics and parts of Poland and Romania, reanimating Soviet dreams of empire. But when Adolf Hitler's Germany invaded the Soviet Union in 1941, Joseph Stalin was forced to attach the Soviet Union to the European security system. Stalin's wartime alliance with the United States and Great Britain was uneasy from the outset; even before hostilities ended, the Western powers were worried by Stalin's expansionism and unreliability. It is generally accepted that the U.S. hoped to conclude the war with Japan before the Soviet Union became involved in the Pacific theater, where it would have wanted a say in the postwar occupation of the defeated island nation.

Once they had defeated their common enemy, the Soviet Union and most of the Allies lost their shared purpose and resolve. President Franklin D. Roosevelt had pulled most Americans through World War II's alliance with the Soviet Union by fudging on divisive issues, but as the war was winding down, the United States and the Soviet Union were forced to acknowledge their differences. The Soviets opted out of the international economic order established by delegations from 44 nations at the Bretton Woods (New Hampshire) Conference in July 1944. A more contentious and yet essential question was the postwar territorial and political settlement required in much of the world. The Western leaders agreed to deals at Yalta (February 1945) and Potsdam (July-August 1945), acknowledging a Soviet sphere of influence in Eastern Europe in return for a Western European/U.S. sphere of influence in various other parts of the world. They also agreed on the joint postwar occupation of Germany, which was certain to become confrontational (see World War II, Negotiations and Peace Treaty, pp. 488-492).

The end of World War II left a power vacuum in Europe and the Far East. Germany was destroyed and powerless. Great Britain was finished as an imperial power; France, too, was weakened. Japan was not only physically destroyed but also demilitarized by the postwar settlement imposed by the victorious Allies. The Soviet Union reportedly suffered some 20 million fatalities; the country was devastated by war. But the Soviet Union was nearly ready to test its own atomic bomb, and it had an avowedly aggressive ideology opposed to liberal democracy and the capitalist system; the Soviet leaders were not about to abandon their ambition of bringing as much of the world as possible into the circle of Communism.

Americans had little experience of Great Powers diplomacy and were focused in 1945 on demobilizing their armed forces. Yet, with its military strengthened by war and its industries producing fully half of the world's goods, the United States emerged from World War II as the only true global superpower. That concentration of power was perceived by some nations as a potential threat. The Communists feared that the United States and its allies might reimpose the old colonial, imperial, capitalist order. French reentry into Indochina, for example, and the United States' abrupt cancellation of aid to the Soviet Union in 1945 reinforced the Soviets' apprehension. No one knew whether the United Nations, established in 1945, would be able to fulfill its promise of sustaining world peace, the national right to self-determination, and the equality of member states. Meanwhile, Americans became the guarantors of the Western democracies' security and, as such, the main challenger to the competing Soviet system. The stage was set for years of peacetime conflict.

Compounding their ideological differences, the United States and the Soviet Union saw their national security needs in very different terms. The advent of nuclear weaponry played a major role in the Cold War. At the end of World War II, the U.S. nuclear monopoly increased the Soviet Union's sense of insecurity, which contributed to an atmosphere of growing distrust, fear, and instability. Conflicting proposals from both sides, whether to limit nuclear power to peaceful uses or to bring it under UN or other international control, foundered. The Soviets meanwhile developed their own atomic bomb, beginning the arms race that proved one of the Cold War's most lasting legacies.

CAUSES OF THE WAR

Given the nature of the Cold War, there is no clear line that can be drawn between its background and its causes: Events tended to meld into one another. Certainly, no single incident caused the Cold War. The question of whether the Soviet Union or the United States "began" the Cold War is still debated by historians and political scientists (see Historical Perspectives and Controversies, pp. 562-563). Whether or not the Cold War was inevitable is a question upon which historians and political scientists will probably always disagree. The consensus today, however, tends to be that structural weaknesses in the post–World War II international system were exposed and exacerbated in the early years of the peace and before the world's powers were willing or able to negotiate their differences.

But there were two pressure points that come close to qualifying as what historians call the proximate, or most immediate, causes of the Cold War: Germany and Eastern Europe. The conferences at Yalta and Potsdam had failed to resolve the question of Germany's future; indeed, it proved to be insoluble in the short term. The United States saw the reconstruction of Germany as the centerpiece of European recovery. The Soviet Union, however, sought to eliminate any possibility that Germany might reemerge as a European power. The division of Germany and of Berlin into East and West sectors was essentially an unstable solution; Berlin in particular became the scene of several Cold War confrontations between 1945 and 1990.

Potsdam negotiators also failed to address Soviet expansionism in Eastern Europe. The Red Army's wartime occupation of Eastern Europe and the Soviet absorption of territories from the 1939 Stalin-Hitler pact left the Soviet Union in position to impose Communist governments over a vast region after World War II. The Soviets viewed that region as an essential buffer between the Soviet Union and its historical enemy, Germany. British prime minister Winston Churchill had met with Joseph Stalin in Moscow in October 1944 and had agreed to allow Poland, Bulgaria, and Romania to stay in the Soviet "sphere of influence," in return for allowing Greece to remain in Britain's; the Soviet Union and Great Britain would "share" influence in Hungary, Czechoslovakia, and Yugoslavia. The Yalta Conference (February 1945) solidified those arrangements, and even before the Potsdam Conference (July 17–August 2, 1945), the Soviets were busy making sure that Communists were in positions to take over in Eastern Europe, even though they had said they would support free elections in Eastern Europe. In particular, the Soviets moved into Poland, and as early as July 5, 1945, they installed a puppet regime; by including a few token pro-Westerners and non-Communists, the Soviets persuaded the U.S. and Great Britain to extend diplomatic recognition to that government.

In the interests of presenting a united front to Germany and Japan, the United States and the Western Allies agreed to certain arrangements with the Soviet Union for the post–World War II world. It was not long before relations between the two sides began to cool, and the Cold War was under way.

PREPARATIONS FOR WAR

Just as with the causes, the preparations for the Cold War cannot be pinned down to any simple time frame. The creation of spheres of influence and the development of Cold War military strategy occurred gradually during the immediate post–World War II years. Eastern and Western blocs solidified as the United States and the Soviet Union cemented military, trade, and social alliances by means of various pacts and treaty organizations. By 1955, the division of the world into two camps was complete.

The U.S. strategy of "containment" called for encircling the Soviet Union with U.S. allies. The Western bloc was constructed with the Latin-American Treaty of Rio (September 1947), the North Atlantic Treaty Organization (NATO, April 1949), the Australia-New Zealand-United States (ANZUS), treaty, a defense treaty with Japan (September 1951), the South East Asian Treaty Organization (SEATO, September 1954); and the Near Eastern Baghdad Pact (February 1955), later Central Treaty Organizatin (CENTO). Massive foreign aid reinforced these alliances: Between 1948 and 1951, the United States spent $12 billion (easily equivalent to $100 billion in 1990 dollars) on the Marshall Plan, formally known as the European Recovery Program and named after Secretary of State George Marshall.

The Soviets responded with parallel treaties formalizing the Eastern bloc: The Communist Information Bureau (Cominform, October 1947); the Council for Mutual Economic Assistance (Comecon, January 1949); and, finally, the Warsaw Pact (May 1955).

Military planners needed to accommodate two wholly new realities: Their field was now worldwide and the nuclear age had begun. The adoption of National Security Council Memorandum 68 (NSC-68) committed the United States to rearmament, which in the new equation meant a nuclear arms race (see Chronology, April 7, 1950, p. 535). The Soviets followed suit. The result was the continuation in both countries of huge defense economies and the development in the 1950s of new generations of hydrogen bombs and long-range missile-delivery systems.

DECLARATION OF WAR

There were no formal declarations of war between the superpowers during the Cold War, but early speeches on both sides acknowledged the existence of conflict. President Harry S. Truman's Navy Day speech on October 27, 1945 set out 12 points of foreign policy that included the right of national self-determination and a willingness "to use force if necessary to insure peace." On March 5, 1946, in his famous "iron curtain" speech, Winston Churchill called on the United States and Great Britain to lead the fight against Communism (see Notable Phrases, p. 560). Although the Soviets did not issue any ultimatums, their actions—from Albania and Bulgaria in Europe to Azerbaijan Province in Iran and Mongolia in the Far East—showed that they were prepared to exercise power to install puppet regimes. And it was on February 9, 1946, that Joseph Stalin called for a fourth Five-Year Plan, which committed the Soviet Union to a military and industrial buildup and a declared technology race with the West, in particularly with the United States.

COMBATANTS

Anti-Communists: The United States led the anti-Communist bloc, whose primary members were Great Britain and the British Commonwealth (including Canada, Australia, and New Zealand) and the nations of western and southern Europe. (Eventually, Japan became part of that bloc.) At the height of the Cold War in 1960, the combined population of those countries was about 560 million. In addition, post–World War II treaties put most of Latin America, Turkey, Iraq, Pakistan, South Korea, and South Vietnam in the U.S. camp.

At the end of World War II, the U.S. military cut its personnel within about one year from 7 million to 1.1 million. In addition, the military sold, abandoned, or destroyed vast amounts of weapons and equipment, including nearly 30,000 airplanes. Hundreds of ships went to scrap metal yards or were sold to other navies, used to store grain, mothballed, and often used for target practice in testing new weapons. (In one atomic bomb test on the island of Bikini in 1946, 73 surplus warships were used as targets.)

Despite the cutbacks, the United States had a far more powerful military force than it had ever contemplated, and soon the United States was rebuilding its military with still more advanced weapons. Equally important, the United States did not withdraw its forces to the continental United States but left many of them in position throughout the world—250,000 in West Germany alone. It was that worldwide network of bases that challenged the Soviets at every turn.

In addition to U.S. military forces, the West could draw on the large forces of many other nations: Great Britain and its Commonwealth, France, and the other NATO nations—including Greece and Turkey, and, eventually, West Germany and Italy—maintained military forces that totaled 1.5 million by the mid-1960s. The level of their commitment may have varied, but those forces presented a major obstacle to Soviet expansionism.

Communists: The Soviet-led Communist bloc was anchored by Warsaw Pact signatories: the Soviet Union, East Germany, Poland, Czechoslovakia, Hungary, Romania, and Bulgaria. In 1960 their combined population was about 320 million. Other Communist countries, such as Cuba, Mongolia, North Korea, and North Vietnam, were either Soviet client states or were accepting Soviet aid, and a few independent Communist nations, such as Yugoslavia and, after 1968, Albania, could also be counted on as allies in an ultimate showdown with anti-Communist nations.

The Communist bloc also encompassed smaller nations with Communist leaders or revolutionaries whose identities changed over the years as coups and counterrevolutions washed over them. In addition, Communist parties in the Western bloc collaborated with the Soviets; French and Italian Communists figured prominently in elections immediately after World War II and in the 1980s, for example. Again, the domestic Communists were not able to mount military forces, but they were a constant irritant to their homelands' policymakers.

Mainland China, Communist since 1949, split ideologically from the Soviet Union in 1961 and afterward headed a rival Communist power bloc, acquiring nuclear capability, energetically pursuing Third World client states, and unsettling superpower relations. China was economically backward, but its population of some 650 million (growing to more than 1 billion by the end of the Cold War) made it a "sleeping giant," feared as a potential enemy and desired as a potential ally by both superpowers.

The Soviets and Chinese had an average of 2.5 million and 2 million men, respectively, under arms. The Chinese military lacked advanced equipment, but its sheer numbers could tip the balance, as proved in the Korean War; the Soviet Union devoted a large portion of its economy to the development of advanced weapons. After 1961, significant proportions of their military establishments faced each other across a troubled border, but there was never any question that separately or together they were prepared to turn their forces against the anti-Communist bloc. The Warsaw Pact nations' military forces provided another 1 million men.

GEOGRAPHIC AND STRATEGIC CONSIDERATIONS

The aim of both the Western bloc and the Communist bloc during the Cold War, whether stated or not, was world domination. Virtually every point of land and mile of sea was regarded as valuable and worth contesting for one reason or another; of the world's continents, only Antarctica was out of bounds. A major strategic consideration of both sides was control of natural resources (especially oil and minerals) and shipping routes. Recruiting allies had a moral and propaganda value, too. That was largely a numbers game, hence the rapid consolidation of Eastern and Western blocs after World War II. The wave of decolonization in the Middle East, Africa, and Southeast Asia in the 1940s and 1950s opened vast areas to Soviet-American rivalry. Bordering on Europe, the Middle East, and Asia, the Soviet Union was ideally sited for that intercontinental struggle. To that extent, the United States had to expend far more energy and resources to confront Soviet expansionism.

The global reach of that geopolitical enterprise demanded tremendous military capability on both sides. Nuclear weapons, cheaper to maintain than were large standing armies and intercontinental in range, proved to be the weapons of choice. The superpower arms race and the proliferation of nuclear capability were perhaps the most distinctive and dangerous features of the Cold War. The U.S. "strategic triad" eventually involved thousands of land-based intercontinental ballistic missiles (ICBMs) of varying power and range, submarines patrolling the seas, and Strategic Air Command bombers in flight 24 hours a day. Nuclear strategies like "massive retaliation," "flexible response," "mutual assured destruction" and "counterforce" required huge arsenals and relentless technological advances. Nuclear strategy was an arcane art, but the underlying doctrine was deterrence: The larger and more powerful the arsenals, that doctrine went, the lower the risk that anyone would actually use them. However, by the 1980s, President Ronald Reagan and Soviet president Mikhail Gorbachev finally faced the fact that nuclear war was unwinnable and were spurred to negotiate major arms reductions.

Geopolitical strategy encompassed concepts of expansionism and containment. Each side aimed to control, directly or indirectly, as much of the world as possible while minimizing the other's sphere of influence. NATO and the Warsaw Pact were the superpowers' core alliances; Europe was central geographically and strategically. Pacts such as SEATO and CENTO enlarged the Western bloc. Far-flung allies were useful in hosting military forces or missiles, extending the superpowers' geographical reach. Aside from the massive military establishment it supported in Western Europe, the United States maintained bases at various times in Japan, the Philippines, Iran, and Turkey and sited missiles in Turkey as well as in Western Europe. Soviet troops were stationed in Warsaw Pact countries throughout the Cold War years; the Soviet Union sited missiles in Eastern European satellites aimed at western Europe; both the Soviets and the United States had military advisers in many countries at different times. The Soviets' only attempt to locate missiles in the Western Hemisphere resulted in the Cuban Missile Crisis (see Chronology, October 1962, pp. 541-542).

Speaking about the Cold War, Joseph Stalin once said, "In this war, each side imposes its system as far as its armies can reach," and at its most coercive, containment involved direct military intervention. Immediately after World War II the Soviet Union occupied Eastern Europe and was removed from Iran only with difficulty. The Soviet Union invaded Hungary (see Chronology, October 24–November 4, 1956, p 538-539), Czechoslovakia (see Chronology, August 20, 1968, p. 543), and Afghanistan (see Chronology, December 27, 1979, p. 548) to maintain Communist regimes, and the threat of Soviet invasion hung over all of its client states. On the other side, one study indicates that the United States intervened militarily 215 times between 1946 and 1975, justified on the grounds that it did so to resist Soviet expansionism.

Superpower sponsorship of revolutions and coups was common. During the Cold War, the Third World was politically fluid and particularly vulnerable to that kind of interference. The Soviet Union supported revolutions in Greece, Indonesia, Malaya, and the Philippines, among other places. The United States sent military advisers to support anti-Communist insurgencies in Nicaragua and elsewhere. Both sides sponsored coups, the Communists in Czechoslovakia, Ethiopia, Afghanistan, and elsewhere; the

U.S. in Iran, Ecuador, Guatemala, Cuba (a failure), Chile, and Nicaragua. Occasionally, as in Angola and Ethiopia, the United States and Soviet Union armed opposite sides in regional proxy conflicts or civil wars.

The idea on both sides was to avoid direct confrontation, and for the most part, they did avoid active military involvement in the innumerable regional wars during the Cold War. The two notable exceptions were the Korean War (see pp. 570-607) and the Vietnam War (see pp. 608-664); in both wars, the United States ended up taking an active role and the Soviet Union managed to limit its military involvement. The Soviet Union's major military adventure during the Cold War was in Afghanistan, where there was no involvement of U.S. troops (although the United States did provide arms to the anti-Communist side).

Much superpower activity during the Cold War, particularly during the 1950s–1960s, was covert. The CIA specialized in secret operations, employing them, for example, in Iran, Indonesia, Syria, and Nicaragua; the agency also tried to assassinate foreign leaders, notoriously making several attempts on the life of Cuban leader Fidel Castro. Military and economic intelligence was an extremely important—and expensive—strategic requirement. The Soviet intelligence service, the KGB, is said to have had a half-million-strong staff in the mid-1970s. Cold War history is replete with stories of spies being exposed, caught, and swapped for captured enemy counterparts. Propaganda ranged from disinformation released by governments on both sides to the very public efforts of Radio Free Europe and the Voice of America.

Economic aid was a potent superpower weapon. The U.S. foreign aid budget largely served national security interests, and the economic viability of many Communist client states, such as Cuba, was dependent on Soviet funding. The Cold War also spilled over into superpower competition in science and technology (especially in space exploration), economic development, social welfare, and cultural affairs. The Cold War relied heavily on economic subversion, threats, and posturing, supported on both sides by sophisticated propaganda machines. The Cold War was an ideological, political, economic war conducted under the ever-present threat of nuclear confrontation.

CHRONOLOGY

1945–1946:
BREAKDOWN OF THE GRAND ALLIANCE

September 11–October 2, 1945: The first meeting of the Council of Foreign Ministers (the United States, the Soviet Union, Great Britain, China, France) met in London to draft World War II peace treaties with the former Axis powers. After three weeks, the meeting ended with a clear split between the Soviet Union and the other nations; the ministers could not even agree on procedural matters, as the Soviet Union insisted on exercising a veto power and then used that to prevent France and China from having a say in the treaties. U.S. secretary of state James F. Byrnes did his best to put an optimistic face on events by insisting that there were general areas of agreement and that the peace conference would resume after the Soviet Union foreign minister Vyacheslav Molotov had further instructions from Moscow. In fact, the meetings, seven in all, went on intermittently through June 1949, and were marked by constant dissension, particularly over the future of Germany.

October–November 1945: In postwar elections, Communists made gains in France and Communist Parties rigged elections to take control of Yugoslavia and Bulgaria. Western nations recognized a Communist government in Albania. The Hungarian Communist Party was defeated at the polls. In December, Austrian Socialists joined a coalition government.

October 24, 1945: The United Nations charter went into effect. In November, former U.S. secretary of state Cordell Hull won the Nobel Peace Prize for his role in creating the UN.

November 16, 1945: A Communist uprising broke out in the Soviet-occupied Azerbaijan Province in Iran; the Soviets supported the uprising and tried to create an autonomous state.

January 10, 1946: The UN General Assembly held its first meeting in London. Fifty-one nations attended, with the aim of "not just the negation of war, but the creation of a world which is governed by justice and the moral law."

January 11, 1946: The recently elected Communist government of Albania declared Albania a people's republic.

February 9, 1946: Joseph Stalin declared that the world was divided into "two camps" and claimed that wars were inevitable as long as capitalism survived.

March 5, 1946: At exercises in which he was awarded an honorary degree by Westminster College in Fulton, Missouri, former British prime minister Winston Churchill delivered his iron curtain speech, urging the U.S.-British military alliance to oppose the Soviet Union (see Notable Phrases, p. 560).

March 21, 1946: The U.S. Strategic Air Command (SAC) was created with the mission of undertaking long-range operations anywhere in the world at any time.

March 24, 1946: In the first test of containment, the Soviet Union yielded to U.S. diplomatic and military pressure and announced that it would withdraw its troops from Azerbaijan Province, Iran. On June 13, the province was returned to Iranian control, leaving Iran in the Western sphere of influence.

May 26, 1946: A minority election victory allowed Communists to form a coalition government in Czechoslovakia.

June 14, 1946: The Baruch Plan, so named after its chief framer, Bernard Baruch, was unveiled to the recently formed U.S. Atomic Energy Commission. The plan proposed sharing atomic energy technology with other countries and destroying U.S. nuclear weapons. The Soviet Union, which backed a nuclear weapons ban, rejected it.

July 4, 1946: The United States granted the Philippines independence, retaining rights to military bases there. U.S. aid subsequently helped the Philippine government fight an eight-year Communist rebellion.

July 25, 1946: The first underwater nuclear bomb test was conducted on the Bikini atoll by the United States.

August 7, 1946: The Soviet Union proposed joint control with Turkey over the strategically important Dardanelles. Western powers rejected the proposal.

September 1, 1946: Greeks voted overwhelmingly to retain their monarchy; within days, Greek Communists, backed by neighboring Communist states, started a civil war. The Communist insurgents lost after three years of fighting.

September 20, 1946: President Harry S. Truman fired commerce secretary Henry Wallace for urging peace with the Soviet Union and UN control of nuclear weapons.

October 3, 1946: Greece complained to the Security Council of the UN that Communist rebels were being trained and supported by its Communist neighbors; the Soviet delegate said that the Western powers were intervening in Greece more than the Communists. After a series of escalating incidents which occurred during the preceding months, a full-scale civil war spread through much of Greece, with as many as 25,000 armed Communists in the field against the Greek army. Under the Truman Doctrine (see March 12, 1947, below), the United States supplied financial aid, military equipment, and many "advisers" to the Greek government to help put down the Communists, who fought on until October 16, 1949 (see p. 535).

October 27, 1946: Rigged elections put the Communists in power in Bulgaria.

November 4, 1946: The United States and China signed a five-year treaty of friendship.

November 19, 1946: Rigged elections In Romania put the Communists in power. Romania's king abdicated in December 1947, and the government declared Romania a people's republic.

November 23, 1946: The first Indochina War began with the French bombardment of Haiphong, Vietnam.

December 2, 1946: The United States and Great Britain merged their zones of occupation in Germany into an economic bizone.

1947–1953:
CONTAINMENT, THE KOREAN WAR,
THE BEGINNING OF THE ARMS RACE

January 19, 1947: Joseph Stalin broke his pledge to allow non-Communist moderates a role in the Polish government, and rigged elections installed a Communist regime in Poland.

February 10, 1947: The Allies signed World War II peace treaties in Paris with Hungary, Italy, Bulgaria, Romania, and Finland (see World War II, Negotiations and Peace Treaty, pp. 491-492).

March 12, 1947: At a nationally broadcast joint session of Congress, President Harry S. Truman presented the Truman Doctrine, calling for American defensive assistance to "free peoples." Aid to Turkey and Greece, totaling $400 million, to support anti-Communist efforts was accordingly approved by Congress in May; it replaced aid to those countries that had been recently canceled by war-poor Britain.

June 5, 1947: At Harvard College to accept an honorary degree, Secretary of State George C. Marshall proposed a European Recovery Program (which became known as the Marshall Plan) for the economic and financial reconstruction of Europe. Sixteen European nations submitted an economic recovery plan to the United States in September. The Soviet Union and its Eastern European satellites declined to participate. From 1948 to 1951, the United States would furnish Western Europe with $12 billion in Marshall Plan aid.

July 1947: Under the pseudonym "X," Soviet expert George F. Kennan published an analysis of the evils of Communism and the rationale for containment in *Foreign Affairs*. His argument dominated U.S. foreign policy until the 1970s; Kennan later claimed that he meant that the United States should employ diplomatic and political means of containment but many interpreted the containment policy as requiring military action.

July 26, 1947: Truman signed the National Security Act, creating the United States Air Force, a unified Department of Defense, the National Security Council (NSC), and the Central Intelligence Agency (CIA).

August 15, 1947: India gained independence, ending 200 years of British domination.

August 31, 1947: In a contest forced by the Soviet ouster of Hungary's prime minister, Communists rigged elections to take power.

September 2, 1947: The United States and 18 Latin American nations signed the Treaty of Rio, calling for mutual defense of the Western Hemisphere.

September 18, 1947: The Soviet deputy foreign minister accused the UN of "warmongering" and seeking "world domination." In November, Secretary of State Marshall advised the Soviets to stop their anti-U.S. propaganda. Superpower exchanges of accusations, threats, and counterthreats became a Cold War fixture.

October 5, 1947: The creation of the Communist Information Bureau (Cominform) to coordinate nine European Communist Parties under Moscow's control was announced. The manifesto railed against the "imperialist camp" led by the United States. Cominform lasted until 1956.

October 20, 1947: The House Un-American Activities Committee (HUAC) opened hearings on Communist subversion in government,

academia, and Hollywood. The hearings were nasty and divisive; Ronald Reagan, who testified later called HUAC "a pretty venal group."

October 30, 1947: The General Agreement on Tariffs and Trade (GATT), designed to stimulate international trade by sweeping reductions in tariffs, was signed by 23 nations and took effect in January 1948. Czechoslovakia was the sole Eastern European signatory.

December 4, 1947: Bulgaria became a people's republic.

February 23–25, 1948: A coup ordered by Joseph Stalin replaced the Czech government, which had tried to accept Marshall Plan aid. On March 10, the body of pro-Western foreign minister Jan Masaryk was found below his apartment house window; it would never proved whether he committed suicide or was pushed, but his death was widely assumed to have been a politically motivated murder.

February 23–March 6, 1948: Having reached an impasse with the Soviets, representatives of Great Britain, France, and the United States met at the London Conference to discuss Germany's future. On March 20, the Soviet Union quit the Allied Control Council governing occupied Germany.

March 17, 1948: The signing of the Brussels Treaty formalized a 50-year mutual defense and economic alliance of France, Britain, and the Benelux countries (Belgium, the Netherlands, and Luxembourg), creating the basis for the later Council of Europe (1949) and the Western European Union (1954).

April 2, 1948: Congress passed an unprecedented $6 billion foreign aid bill, providing aid for Greece, Turkey, and China, as well as for the Marshall Plan. The bill's aim was to combat Communist expansion.

April 20–June 1, 1948: Despite Soviet opposition, the London Conference agreed to the formation of a separate West Germany and to its participation in the Marshall Plan.

April 30, 1948: The United States joined the 20 Latin American republics at the Bogotá (Colombia) Conference in founding the Organization of American States (OAS). That regional security alliance became a strong anti-Communist force in the Western Hemisphere.

May 14, 1948: The Jewish state of Israel was proclaimed at midnight. Arab League nations invaded Israel the next day; fighting ended in

January 1949, with Israel having secured its borders. As the first nation to recognize Israel, the United States forged a special alliance that often became entangled with Cold War events.

June 18, 1948: The U.S. Air Force announced the deployment of jet fighters and bombers to Great Britain and Germany.

June 24, 1948: After several months of obstructing surface access, the Soviet Union blockaded the divided city of Berlin, located well inside what became East Germany, hoping to dislodge the Allies from Germany. In a massive airlift to 2 million residents of the Western section of Berlin, the United States and Britain landed 277,264 planeloads of supplies during the months that followed. The lifting of the blockade in May 1949 was a major victory for the West.

June 28, 1948: Denouncing Yugoslav leader Josip Tito as a "deviationist," Cominform expelled Yugoslavia. Tito was the first Communist leader to oppose Joseph Stalin and retain his office; he pursued an independent Communist path, accepting Western aid and staying outside the Warsaw Pact.

August 15, 1948: South Korea proclaimed its independence.

September 5, 1948: Wladyslaw Gomulka, leader of the Communist Polish Workers' Party and deputy premier of Poland, was forced to resign as party leader because of his "deviations" and "nonappreciation of the decisive role of the Soviet Union." In 1951, he was arrested and imprisoned, but he was released in 1954 and restored to power on October 19, 1956 (see October 19–20, 1956, p. 538).

November 1, 1948: In the Chinese civil war, Communists took Mukden, the capital of China's northern province of Manchuria.

December 5, 1948: Social Democrats decisively won West Berlin elections boycotted by the Communists.

December 9–10, 1948: The UN General Assembly adopted a convention against genocide and a nonbinding declaration on human rights.

January 22, 1949: Chinese Communists captured Beijing, the capital of China.

January 25, 1949: In a Communist counterpart to the Marshall Plan, the Council for Mutual Economic Assistance (Comecon) to promote economic cooperation in the Eastern bloc was announced in Moscow.

March 2, 1949: U.S. Communist Party leaders joined other international Communists in declaring their allegiance to the Soviet Union in the event of war.

March 13, 1949: The Benelux countries (Belgium, the Netherlands, and Luxembourg) agreed on an economic union. On March 26, France and Italy signed their intention to enter the same union.

April 4, 1949: The North Atlantic Treaty Organization (NATO) was created with the signing of the North Atlantic Treaty in Washington, D.C., by the United States, Canada, and ten Western European nations. Greece and Turkey joined in 1952. NATO members agreed to regard an attack on one member as an attack on all; President Harry S. Truman termed NATO a "shield against aggression." The United States guarantee of European security underpinned that pivotal military alliance throughout the Cold War.

May 5, 1949: Ten Western European democracies signed the Council of Europe statute creating a European consultative assembly. The original ten signatories were: Belgium, Denmark, France, Great Britain, Ireland, Italy, Luxembourg, the Netherlands, Norway, and Sweden; Greece, Iceland, and Turkey subsequently joined. The Council of Europe proved a strong unifying force through initiatives such as the European Court of Human Rights.

May 23, 1949: The Federal Republic of Germany (West Germany) was formally established, although it did not become a sovereign nation, free from Western occupation, until 1955 (see May 5, 1955, p. 538).

August 5, 1949: The United States withdrew its support of Chiang Kai-shek's Nationalists in the Chinese civil war, making their defeat by Mao Tse-Tung's Communists inevitable. Chiang retreated to Taiwan, where he formed a government in December.

August 29, 1949: The Soviet Union tested its first atomic bomb.

September 21, 1949: Mao Tse-Tung proclaimed China the People's Republic of China, the largest Communist state in the world.

October 6, 1949: President Truman signed two major bills promising arms and economic aid to Western European allies.

October 7, 1949: The Communist German Democratic Republic was proclaimed in East Germany.

October 14, 1949: After a ten-month trial, 11

American Communist Party leaders were convicted of conspiring to overthrow the United States government.

October 16, 1949: Greek Communist rebels, after three years of fighting a civil war in which they gained some victories but gradually lost ground, declared a "temporary end" to military operations to save Greece "from total destruction." Although there were "incidents" involving Communists in Greece in the following decades, the organized insurgence never revived.

October 24, 1949: At the dedication of the UN's permanent headquarters in New York City, President Truman pleaded for an international agreement controlling nuclear arms.

January 4, 1950: In his State of the Union address, President Harry S. Truman announced a Four-Point Program of technical assistance to developing countries; he later called it his long-term answer to Communism. The program ran until 1953.

January 12, 1950: Secretary of State Dean Acheson accused the Soviet Union of grabbing China, but defended Truman's policy of not intervening militarily. He defined a U.S. "defense perimeter" in the Pacific, from Japan through Okinawa to the Philippines, that the United States would fight to defend.

January 21, 1950: Alger Hiss was found guilty of perjury, effectively upholding the charge that he spied for the Soviet Union during the 1930s, even though he was not actually tried for espionage. Sentenced to five years in prison, Hiss served three years and eight months of his sentence.

January 31, 1950: President Truman authorized U.S. development of a hydrogen bomb.

February 9, 1950: Sen. Joseph McCarthy claimed that the State Department staff had been infiltrated by Communists, launching a four-year Red scare.

February 10, 1950: Klaus Fuchs, a top British atomic physicist who had worked on the Manhattan Project, confessed that he had supplied the Soviets with U.S. bomb designs for seven years in the 1940s. He was sentenced to 14 years in jail, of which he served 9.

February 14, 1950: The Soviet Union and Communist China signed a 30-year treaty of friendship and economic cooperation.

April 7, 1950: NSC-68, a secret U.S. National Security Council document prepared by State Department official and hard-liner Paul Nitze, proposed countering the Soviet threat with a military buildup large enough to respond to Communist aggression anywhere in the world. That seminal document governed America's overarching Cold War security strategy and virtually ensured an arms race.

June 15, 1950: West Germany joined the Council of Europe.

June 25, 1950: North Korea invaded South Korea, starting the Korean War. The war formally ended in July 1953, but it resulted in 20 years of Sino-American hostility, major U.S. rearmament, and the permanent deployment of U.S. forces in Korea (see Korean War pp. 570-607 and Vietnam War, pp. 608-664).

July 1950: Radio Free Europe made its first broadcasts into Eastern Europe, immediately becoming an important U.S. propaganda tool. The same nonprofit corporation that sponsored Radio Free Europe also started Radio Liberty in 1951 to broadcast in several languages to the Soviets.

September 23, 1950: Congress overwhelmingly overrode President Truman's veto to enact the controversial Internal Security Act, requiring Communist organizations in the United States to register with the government and supply membership lists.

October 7, 1950: China invaded Tibet; in May 1951, China formally annexed Tibet. Western powers declined to intervene.

October 19, 1950: The UN General Assembly passed the Acheson Plan for UN peace enforcement.

March 29, 1951: Julius and Ethel Rosenberg were convicted of passing wartime nuclear secrets to the Soviets. Over strong domestic and international protests, they were executed in June 1953, the first U.S. civilians ever executed by the United States for spying.

April 2, 1951: Supreme Headquarters, Allied Powers in Europe (SHAPE) was activated in Paris, with Gen. Dwight D. Eisenhower as the first commander of NATO forces.

May 26, 1951: Guy Burgess and Donald MacLean, British diplomats and spies, fled to the Soviet Union with the aid of their colleague Kim Philby.

September 1, 1951: A day after signing a mutual defense treaty with the Philippines, the United States, Australia, and New Zealand signed a mutual defense pact (ANZUS), forming an anti-Communist alliance that survived for over 35 years.

September 8, 1951: A treaty ending World War II with Japan was signed by Japan and 49 non-Communist nations in San Francisco. The Soviet Union and its satellites boycotted the final session and refused to sign the treaty. A separate bilateral treaty authorized the continuance of U.S. military bases in Japan, barring the Soviets from influence in Japan.

November 7, 1951: The Big Three (the United States, Great Britain, and France) and the Soviet Union presented competing nuclear disarmament plans to the UN.

March 1, 1952: The Congress Party headed by Jawaharlal Nehru was the overwhelming victor in India's first national elections.

March 10, 1952: In Joseph Stalin's famous "peace note," the Soviet Union unexpectedly proposed German reunification, rearmament, and neutrality in a futile effort to keep West Germany from being partitioned and joining NATO. Stalin's sincerity in making that offer was one of the most lingering and controversial questions of the entire Cold War.

May 27, 1952: In signing the Treaty of Paris, West Germany, France, Italy, Belgium, Holland, and Luxembourg established the European Defense Community (EDC), a coordinated European army. (The French scuttled the creation of the EDC in August 1954.) The Soviets threatened to initiate another Berlin blockade.

October 1952: Stalin's *Economic Problems of Socialism in the Soviet Union* was published; it claimed that war between capitalists and Communists was not inevitable.

October 2, 1952: An Asian and Pacific Peace Conference opened in Beijing; 37 nations attended to organize "an extensive mass movement" to combat "American aggression" in the Far East.

October 3, 1952: Britain tested its first atomic bomb off Australia, becoming the world's third nuclear power.

November 1, 1952: The United States tested the world's first hydrogen bomb at Eniwetok Atoll in the Pacific.

November 27, 1952: Eleven former Communist officials were condemned to death in Czechoslovakia in the largest Communist purge in Eastern Europe to date. Similar show trials had been staged in Bulgaria, Hungary, and Albania; none

came close to persecuting the number of people that Stalin's party purges did during the late 1930s.

December 12, 1952: A Soviet-sponsored World Peace Congress of Communists met in Vienna to promote the Soviet line on West Germany and nuclear arms control.

January 21, 1953: In the fourth such mass trial in the United States, 13 "second string" American Communist Party leaders were convicted in New York of conspiring to overthrow the government. Prosecution of Communists and harassment of Communist organizations continued in the United States throughout the 1950s.

March 5, 1953: The death of Joseph Stalin set off a power struggle in the Soviet Union. His successor, Nikita Khrushchev, became first secretary of the Communist party in September 1953; he did not assume the additional post of chairman of the Council of Ministers (premier) until March 1958.

April 16, 1953: In a major foreign policy speech broadcast internationally, President Eisenhower challenged the Soviets to build peace and free the world from "fear and force."

April 20, 1953: The American Communist Party was ordered to register with the Justice Department as a Soviet-controlled organization.

June 16–17, 1953: In East Berlin, anti-Communist protests against labor conditions turned into countrywide riots and were crushed by the Soviet army, dashing Eastern bloc hopes for liberalization in the post-Stalin era.

July 4, 1953: Reform Communist Imre Nagy became prime minister of Hungary and, citing the riots in East Berlin, introduced an anti-Stalinist "New Course" of political and economic liberalization measures.

July 27, 1953: The Korean War ended, leaving Korea divided (see Korean War, p. 596).

August 12, 1953: The Soviets tested their first hydrogen bomb.

October 1953: The Eisenhower administration adopted National Security Council document NSC-161/2, directing that nuclear weapons should be regarded as "available" for use the same as any other weapons. Known as the "New Look" policy, NSC-161/2 also set out to limit the costs of maintaing U.S. ground forces internationally as a means of containment.

December 8, 1953: In his "Atoms for Peace" speech at the UN, President Eisenhower proposed an International Atomic Energy Agency

(IAEA) to develop peaceful uses of nuclear technology and reduce the threat of nuclear war. The IAEA was created in 1957.

1954–1962:
WESTERN AND EASTERN BLOCS, THIRD WORLD CAMPAIGNS, THE SPACE RACE, THE STRUGGLE OVER GERMANY, THE CUBAN MISSILE CRISIS

January 12, 1954: United States secretary of state John Foster Dulles introduced the strategy of "massive retaliation," calling for the United States to meet any Soviet use of nuclear weapons with an immediate counterstrike by the entire U.S. nuclear arsenal. Massive retaliation, soon adopted by Britain and the Soviet Union, was regarded as a nuclear deterrent and remained the favored nuclear strategy for nearly ten years.

January 21, 1954: The world's first atomic-powered submarine, the USS *Nautilus,* capable of circling the Earth without refueling, was launched.

January 25–February 18, 1954: A four-power meeting of foreign ministers in Berlin, the first in five years, ended without agreement on German and European security. The Soviets proposed to restructure European security without the involvement of the United States. Great Britain and France rejected the proposal.

March 1, 1954: At a meeting in Caracas, Venezuela, the OAS condemned Communism in the Western Hemisphere.

March 31, 1954: The Soviet Union offered to join NATO in exchange for Western European abandonment of the EDC, a proposal promptly rejected by Western nations.

April–July 1954: The four-power Geneva Conference negotiated the end of the first Indochina War but failed to agree on the situation in Korea. Secretary of State John Foster Dulles pointedly refused to shake Zhou Enlai's hand at the meeting.

April 5, 1954: In a radio and television address, President Dwight D. Eisenhower promised no first use of the hydrogen bomb and called the danger of nuclear war exaggerated.

May 17, 1954: The leader of an eight-year-long Communist rebellion finally surrendered in the Philippines.

June 27, 1954: A CIA-sponsored coup replaced Guatemala's Soviet-supported, but democratically elected, regime with a pro-U.S. government. The United States would continue to support right-wing Guatemalan governments and their military forces, who would kill (or "disappear," as this word is used in the Latin American context) an estimated 140,000 of their own citizens—many of them of Mayan descent—and displace another million during a 36-year civil war that raged until December 1996. Although seemingly far removed from the main line of the Cold War, this was only one of many such "civil wars" that persisted throughout the world because successive U.S. governments were determined to stamp out anything that was tinged with Communism.

June 29, 1954: President Eisenhower and British prime minister Winston Churchill issued the Potomac Charter, an eight-point declaration of world peace, freedom, and security.

July 20, 1954: Vietnam was divided by the Geneva Accords at the 17th parallel into Communist North Vietnam and non-Communist South Vietnam.

August 24, 1954: Eisenhower signed an act outlawing the American Communist Party.

September 1954: China bombarded the Taiwanese islands of Quemoy and Matsu and threatened Taiwan. The United States signed a mutual defense pact with Taiwan in December. Eisenhower briefly considered using nuclear weapons against China; the Chinese backed down, but intermittent hostilities continued until spring 1955.

September 3, 1954: Eisenhower authorized the death penalty for peacetime espionage.

September 6–8, 1954: The Manila Conference agreed on the creation of the South East Asian Treaty Organization (SEATO) and the Pacific Charter. Signatories included the United States., Britain, France, the Philippines, Thailand, Pakistan, Australia, and New Zealand. Although largely ineffectual, SEATO would survive until 1976.

October 23, 1954: Nine nations signed agreements in Paris, creating the Western European Union, replacing the defunct EDC and opening the way for West German NATO membership. In protest, the Soviets canceled their wartime treaties with Great Britain and France in May 1955.

November 29–30, 1954: A security conference of Soviet satellite nations in Moscow called for an Eastern European military bloc.

February 24, 1955: Pro-Western Iraq and Turkey signed the Baghdad Pact. Within the year, Pakistan, Iran, and Great Britain joined, containing the Soviets' long Near Eastern border. The Baghdad Pact was renamed the Central Treaty Organization (CENTO) in 1959. That alliance proved weak, but lasted until 1979.

March 16, 1955: At a press conference, Eisenhower backed the tactical use of nuclear weapons in warfare.

April 14, 1955: Hungarian prime minister Imre Nagy was ousted.

April 17–27, 1955: Two thousand delegates from 29 Asian and African nations represented more than half the world's population at a major international conference in Bandung, Indonesia. Under the influence of China's Zhou Enlai and India's Jawaharlal Nehru, the Bandung Conference adopted the "five principles of peaceful coexistence" and condemned colonialism and bloc politics. The conference increased China's influence in the Third World.

May 5, 1955: The Western powers' occupation of West Germany formally ended, and West Germany became a sovereign nation. The Western European Union (WEU) also took effect, and within the week, West Germany joined the WEU and NATO.

May 14, 1955: The Warsaw Pact was signed by the Soviet Union, East Germany, Poland, Czechoslovakia, Hungary, Romania, Bulgaria, and Albania. (The Warsaw Pact essentially replaced Cominform, dissolved in April 1956.) Mirroring NATO and the Western European Union, the Warsaw Pact integrated the Eastern bloc militarily and politically; it would survive until 1991.

May 15, 1955: Independence was restored to a neutral Austria with the four-power signing of the Austrian State Treaty. That triumph for NATO and Western diplomacy forced the Soviets to withdraw eastward, raising hopes that their military occupation of Eastern Europe might be ended.

July 18–23, 1955: The first East-West summit since World War II was held in Geneva. Eisenhower sprang his "open skies" proposal to exchange complete military information and allow unrestricted aerial reconnaissance by both sides. Western nations refused to recognize the Soviet sphere of influence, and the Soviets continued to disagree over various policies of the Western powers, but the "spirit of Geneva" did lead to cultural and technical exchanges. Harold Macmillan, Britain's foreign defense minister, summed it up by proclaiming, "There ain't gonna be no war."

August 8, 1955: The Geneva "Atoms for Peace" Conference opened; 72 nations met to discuss peaceful uses of nuclear energy.

January 16, 1956: As part of an international effort that had included sending technical advisers to China, the Soviet Union offered diplomatic relations, trade, and technical assistance to all Latin American nations.

February 24–25, 1956: At the 20th Soviet Communist Party congress, Nikita Khrushchev denounced Stalin's tyrannical and bloody rule in a four-hour "secret" speech, launching a period of de-Stalinization. Khrushchev's call for "peaceful coexistence" and acknowledgment of diversity among international Communists raised hopes for liberalization in Soviet satellite nations.

June 28-30, 1956: Two months after the release of 30,000 Polish political prisoners, labor riots erupted in Poznan, west of Warsaw. Polish army and security forces quashed the anti-Communist riots with tanks and full-scale military weaponry. The government claimed that only 28 had been killed, but independent observers estimated the dead at closer to 250.

July 18–19, 1956: Josip Tito of Yugoslavia, Jawaharlal Nehru of India, and Gamal Abdel Nasser of Egypt, the most influential leaders of the Third World, met and reaffirmed the Bandung principles without formalizing a neutral bloc.

July 26, 1956: Nasser nationalized the internationally owned Suez Canal, precipitating a six-month international crisis. Egypt retained control of the canal after botched Anglo-French military intervention, destroying the last claims of British imperial power. The Soviet Union threatened to launch nuclear strikes; the U.S. Strategic Air Command was placed on full alert. Soviet Union support of Nasser ensured future Soviet participation in Middle East politics.

October 19–20, 1956: Amid continuing unrest, Khrushchev visited Warsaw. Reformer Wladyslaw Gomulka, purged eight years previously, was rehabilitated and reinstalled as Poland's Communist leader. Over the following weeks, the crisis was defused as economic reforms were allowed, Polish cardinal Stefan Wyszynski was released from prison, and Poland's Soviet defense minister was dismissed.

October 24–November 4, 1956: After four days of pro-democracy demonstrations in Hungary, the reformist Imre Nagy resumed the premiership of Hungary on October 24. Bowing to popular pressure, he withdrew Hungary from the Warsaw Pact, declared neutrality, and introduced anti-Stalinist reforms. On November 4, the Soviet army invaded, attacking Budapest; during ten days of resistance, 3,000 Hungarians were killed. Nagy had been replaced as prime minister and seized by the Soviets, who hanged him in June 1958. Embroiled in the Suez crisis, the West did not intervene. The suppression of the Hungarian revolution continued, as thousands of Hungarians were imprisoned or executed during the following five years.

January 1–4, 1957: In the wake of the invasion of Hungary, Eastern bloc leaders at a meeting in Budapest affirmed the principle of Soviet intervention.

January 5, 1957: In Congress, President Dwight Eisenhower announced the Eisenhower Doctrine, pledging military assistance to Middle Eastern states threatened by "overt armed aggression." Absorbed in its own deep-seated conflicts, the Middle East remained largely free of outright superpower confrontation.

March 25, 1957: The European Economic Community (EEC) and the European Atomic Energy Community (Euratom) were created with the signing of the Treaties of Rome by France, West Germany, Italy, and the Benelux countries (Belgium, the Netherlands, and Luxemburg).

August 26, 1957: The Soviets announced the successful test-launch of the world's first intercontinental ballistic missile (ICBM).

September 19, 1957: The United States conducted its first underground nuclear test at the Nevada proving grounds.

October 2, 1957: At the United Nations, Polish foreign minister Adam Rapacki proposed a Soviet plan for a central European nuclear-free zone to include both Germanies. Western nations rejected the plan, which was aimed primarily at removing U.S. tactical nuclear weapons from West Germany.

October 4, 1957: Sputnik, the first artificial satellite, was launched by the Soviet Union, shaking Americans' confidence in their technological superiority. A month later *Sputnik II* carried a dog into space.

December 17, 1957: The United States conducted its first successful test-launch of a limited-range ICBM. The first full-range test occurred in December 1958.

January 31, 1958: The United States launched its first successful artificial satellite, *Explorer I.*

May 12, 1958: The United States and Canada reached final agreement on the North American Air Defense Command (NORAD), a coordinated air reconnaissance and defense force.

July 1, 1958: The United States, Britain, and the Soviet Union began trilateral talks on a nuclear test ban. From the outset, progress was thwarted by Soviet refusal to allow on-site inspections, but an informal moratorium on testing lasted from October 1958 to August 1961, and negotiators met periodically until 1963, when a test ban treaty was finally achieved (see July 15–August 5, 1963, p. 542).

July 29, 1958: The National Aeronautics and Space Administration (NASA) was created to coordinate the U.S. space program.

September 2, 1958: A U.S. C-130, flying top secret missions along the Turkish-Soviet border (near the Black Sea and then Soviet Armenia) was shot down by Soviet fighter planes; all 17 U.S. Air Force personnel died. (Only six bodies were ever returned.) The plane was part of an ongoing mission to monitor Soviet radio transmissions, so the U.S. Air Force simply reported that the plane had crashed. No charges were made against the Soviets because the United States did not want to admit to flying such missions. This was not the first nor the last incident in the Cold War in which U.S. personnel were killed by the Soviets, and over which the United States chose not to make an issue.

November 10, 1958: Two months after the West rejected talks on Germany, Nikita Khrushchev provoked a second Berlin crisis with an ultimatum on a Berlin settlement. Four-power talks (May–August 1959) ended without agreement, but they reduced tension.

January 2, 1959: Communist guerrilla leader Fidel Castro took over the Cuban government after the flight of U.S.-backed dictator Fulgencio Batista.

March 5, 1959: The United States signed bilateral defense pacts with Baghdad Pact signatories Turkey, Iran, and Pakistan.

June 9, 1959: The United States launched its first nuclear-armed submarine, the USS *George Washington.*

July 23, 1959: Vice President Richard Nixon

arrived in Moscow on an 11-day visit to the Soviet Union, where he debated the virtues of capitalism versus Communism with Soviet premier Nikita Khrushchev at a trade show in Moscow. That became known as the "kitchen debate" because the two debated in the kitchen of a model of an American home (see p. 559).

September 15–27, 1959: Nikita Khrushchev made an unprecedented tour of the United States "with open heart and good intentions," helping to de-escalate the Berlin crisis. The first-ever U.S.-Soviet summit included talks on disarmament. Addressing the UN, Khrushchev appealed for complete world disarmament.

December 1, 1959: In the first sign of progress on arms control, 12 nations including the United States declared Antarctica a scientific preserve, free of all military activity.

December 3–23, 1959: President Eisenhower made a world tour to promote peace, the first U.S. head of state to visit Asia.

January 7, 1960: In his State of the Union address, President Eisenhower attributed improved East-West relations to "recent Soviet deportment."

January 14, 1960: The Soviets proposed a 1.2 million troop reduction in light of their nuclear weapons capability.

January 19, 1960: A mutual security pact was signed by the United States and Japan. Riots in Japan over the treaty's provision for a permanent U.S. military presence in Japan forced the cancellation of Eisenhower's visit.

February 10–March 5, 1960: Khrushchev toured neutral south Asian nations.

February 13, 1960: France conducted its first nuclear test, in the Sahara, becoming the world's fourth nuclear power.

February 22–March 3, 1960: Eisenhower made a Latin American goodwill tour.

May 1, 1960: A U.S. U-2 spy plane was shot down over central Russia, and its pilot, Francis Gary Powers, was captured. After initial denials, Eisenhower admitted on May 7 that the United States had been spying. A long-awaited four-power summit meeting in Paris collapsed after the first session on May 16 when Khrushchev demanded an apology from Eisenhower.

June 30, 1960: The former Belgian colony of Congo gained independence. In the ensuing civil war, the superpowers armed opposing factions. UN troops restored peace in 1963. The Congo

would change its name to Zaire in 1971 and changed it back to the Congo in 1997.

September 14, 1960: In Baghdad, Iraq, the Organization of Petroleum Exporting Countries (OPEC) was established by Iran, Iraq, Kuwait, Saudi Arabia, and Venezuela.

September 19–October 13, 1960: At Khrushchev's urging, the 15th annual UN General Assembly session, attended by thousands of delegates, was held as an international summit on major world problems, including East-West relations, colonialism, and disarmament. In one memorably boisterous session, Khrushchev threatened a Philippine delegate and banged his shoe on the podium.

December 14, 1960: The United States, Canada, and 18 European nations signed the charter for the Organization for Economic Cooperation and Development (OECD), an economic development body.

December 19, 1960: After months of Soviet-U.S. saber rattling over U.S.-Cuban relations and two months after a U.S. embargo on Cuban trade, Fidel Castro adopted Soviet-style Communism and declared support for Western Hemisphere Communist revolutions.

January 1961: The United States broke diplomatic relations with Cuba. In a public endorsement of "wars of national liberation," Khrushchev took the opportunity to attack Communist China.

January 20, 1961: Having called for a more aggressive U.S. anti-Communist stance during his campaign, President John F. Kennedy delivered an inaugural speech promising that the United States would "pay any price, bear any burden" to ensure the security of democratic principles.

March 1961: In two major Third World initiatives, President Kennedy announced the creation of the Peace Corps and the Alliance for Progress; the latter contributed $18 billion during the 1960s for social and economic reform in Latin America. A warning to the Soviets about arms shipments to Laos resulted in negotiations later in the spring.

April 17–20, 1961: The United States suffered a major humiliation in the Bay of Pigs, a failed invasion of Cuba by 1,400 Cuban exiles recruited and financed by the CIA. The failure was at least in part due to Kennedy's last-minute refusal to call in U.S. airplanes to support the faltering troops. It would be December 23-25, 1962, and only after long and frustrating negotiations, before Castro released the 1,113 surviving Cuban invaders (and 1,000 of their relatives). He did so only after the Cuban community raised $2.9 million demanded by Castro for the medical expenses incurred by the 60 previously released wounded invaders, and U.S. private industries and organizations promised to send Cuba $53 million worth of food, pharmaceuticals, and agricultural materials.

May 25, 1961: Clearly challenging the Soviet space program, President Kennedy announced a project to land Americans on the moon, a goal realized in July 1969.

June 3–4, 1961: Nikita Khrushchev tried to bully the young and inexperienced President Kennedy at a bilateral summit in Vienna and delivered another ultimatum on the demilitarization of Berlin and Western recognition of East Germany. The Western allies pledged to defend their rights in Berlin, and Kennedy pointedly predicted a "cold winter."

July 8, 1961: Citing the German issue and Western arms buildup, the Soviet Union canceled troop cutbacks and increased its military budget. In a major address on July 25, President Kennedy reiterated U.S. support for West Berlin, "an isle of freedom in a Communist sea," and announced a major military buildup.

August 13, 1961: To halt the mass flight of its citizens to the West (3 million East Germans had emigrated since 1945), the East Germans sealed all roads between East and West Berlin. On Khrushchev's orders, they first erected a barbed wire barricade between East and West Berlin, then ten days later began to build a 29-mile, 9-foot-high wall of cement and barbed wire between the two sectors. Traffic between East and West Berlin was greatly restricted (in 1971, the Communists relaxed the rules somewhat). Western powers could do nothing about the Berlin Wall; it stood as the most powerful tangible symbol of the Cold War until its demolition in 1989. The Soviets and East Germans also erected an extraordinary barrier along most of the 850-mile border between East and West Germany: high fences, barbed wire, minefields in the cleared land on both sides, guard towers, floodlights, dogs, and armed guards authorized to shoot at anyone attempting to escape. (Some 200 East Germans were killed trying to escape during the ensuing 28 years.)

August 31, 1961: Breaking their three-year moratorium on nuclear tests, the Soviets exploded a hydrogen bomb. An Anglo-American proposal to ban atmospheric tests was rejected; the United States resumed underground nuclear testing. Atmospheric nuclear tests resumed in April 1962.

September 30, 1961: The North American station of the U.S.-Canadian Ballistic Missile Early Warning System (BMEWS) was activated in Clear, Alaska. Others were constructed in Greenland and Great Britain.

October 6, 1961: President Kennedy urged every American family to build a fallout shelter. Kennedy and Soviet foreign minister Andrei Gromyko held unsuccessful talks on Berlin. Later in the month, when a U.S. official refused to show his passport, U.S. and Soviet tanks faced off at Berlin's Checkpoint Charlie, the single point for Western traffic into East Berlin.

October 17–31, 1961: The depth of the Sino-Soviet split was revealed at the Soviet Communist Party conference. China thereafter became an active competitor for leadership of Third World Communists.

January 12, 1962: The State Department barred U.S. Communists from foreign travel.

January 30–31, 1962: The OAS suspended Cuba's membership on the grounds of its newly avowed Marxism.

May 1962: Defense Secretary Robert McNamara outlined a new U.S. nuclear "counterforce strategy." That strategy of deterrence was based on achieving the capability of fighting a limited, protracted nuclear war that would target military and industrial installations and avoid civilian casualties.

May 6, 1962: The United States tested its first submarine-launched nuclear warhead in the central Pacific.

October 1962: The Cold War reached a dangerous climax as the Cuban missile crisis occasioned two weeks of nuclear brinkmanship. On October 14, U.S. spy planes photographed Soviet missile sites and bombers in Cuba. President Kennedy made a tense nationwide address on October 22, blockaded Cuba, and reminded Khrushchev that any attack on Berlin was tantamount to an attack on the United States; the U.S. military was placed on its highest ever alert during the Cold War. Khrushchev backed away from his threat of nuclear war and agreed on October 28 to withdraw Soviet offensive weapons in exchange for an American guarantee not to invade

Cuba. U.S. missiles were later quietly removed from Turkey, fulfilling a secret geopolitical bargain. Khrushchev's humiliation in that crisis ended his foreign adventurism.

December 18–21, 1962: The United States agreed to provide Polaris missiles to Great Britain as part of a unified Western nuclear force.

1963–1973:
THE VIETNAM WAR AND DETENTE

March 13, 1963: Soviet reconnaissance planes flew over Alaska in the first such overflight of U.S. territory.

May 25, 1963: The Organization of African Unity (OAU) was formed in Addis Ababa, Ethiopia.

June 10, 1963: In a speech at American University, Kennedy called for an end to the arms race and a peaceful exit from the "dangerous cycle" of the Cold War.

June 26, 1963: President John F. Kennedy, in a ringing assurance of continuing U.S. support, told a huge crowd in West Berlin, "*Ich bin ein Berliner*" ("I am a Berliner") (see Notable Phrases, p. 561).

July 15–August 5, 1963: The United States, Great Britain, and the Soviet Union forged a treaty in Moscow banning nuclear tests in the atmosphere, in outer space, and underwater; more than 100 nations (but not France and China) eventually signed.

August 30, 1963: Chastened by the fact that the Cuban missile crisis had nearly resulted in a nuclear war, the United States and the Soviet Union opened an emergency "hot line" between the Kremlin and the White House.

October 9, 1963: Kennedy announced the first-ever U.S. sale of wheat to the Soviet Union in a $250 million deal.

November 12, 1963: Eastern bloc diplomats were barred from 355 U.S. counties, officially because of concerns for national security but also in retaliation for restrictions placed on U.S. diplomats in Eastern bloc countries.

November 22, 1963: President John F. Kennedy was assassinated in Dallas, Texas. Lyndon Johnson assumed the presidency. When the alleged assassin, Lee Harvey Oswald, was revealed to have identified himself as a Communist and to have spent time in the Soviet Union, the Soviets went to great lengths to assure U.S.

authorities that they had absolutely no role in the assassination.

December 17, 1963: Addressing the UN General Assembly, President Johnson reaffirmed Kennedy's foreign policy and said the United States "wants to see the Cold War end... once and for all."

January 27, 1964: In his annual "defense posture" briefing to Congress, Defense Secretary Robert McNamara advocated a "damage-limiting" strategy, the creation of a nuclear force large enough to destroy the Soviet Union, China, and the Soviet satellites. That deterrence strategy, later known as *assured destruction*, dominated U.S. military planning. When the Soviet arsenal caught up, the strategy was renamed Mutual Assured Destruction (MAD). The "balance of terror" that resulted led to the arms control agreements of 1972.

May 9, 1964: The State Department revealed that electronic listening devices had been embedded in several places within the U.S. embassy in Moscow since 1953.

August 7, 1964: The U.S. Congress passed the Gulf of Tonkin Resolution, paving the way for years of U.S. military involvement in Vietnam. Although neither the Soviet Union nor China contributed more than financial aid and military supplies (and some military advisers) to the Communist side, U.S. leaders saw that conflict as one that tested the resolve of the free world in standing up to international Communism (see Vietnam War, Home Front, August 7, 1964, p. 615).

October 14–15, 1964: Nikita Khrushchev was ousted, a victim of his failed agricultural and economic policies; Leonid Brezhnev replaced him as Communist Party leader.

October 16, 1964: China conducted its first nuclear test, making it the world's fifth nuclear power.

April 28, 1965: U.S. Marines were sent to the Dominican Republic, officially to protect U.S. citizens and prevent a Communist takeover in a civil war (see Dominican Republic Intervention, pp. 665-676). Reinforced by OAS troops, the marines stayed until September 1966, when a right-wing elected government was securely in power. On May 2, 1965, in a national broadcast, President Johnson announced the Johnson Doctrine: "the American nations will not permit the establishment of another Communist government in the Western Hemisphere."

October 1965: The Chinese fomented an unsuccessful coup in Indonesia; it was later put down and avenged with the execution of 300,000 Communist supporters.

March 12, 1966: Indonesian president Achmed Sukarno surrendered power to Lt. Gen. Thojib Suharto after the armed forces issued an ultimatum. Suharto immediately banned the Communist Party and ordered the arrest of all leftist politicians. Sukarno was left as a figurehead until 1967.

July 1, 1966: France withdrew its armed forces from NATO, which transferred its headquarters to Casteau, Belgium. On September 7, France announced it would cease paying its share of NATO expenses, with some exceptions, at the end of 1966.

January 27, 1967: The United States, Great Britain, and the Soviet Union were among 60 signatories of an agreement pledging to keep outer space free of nuclear weapons. France and China did not sign.

February 14, 1967: Fourteen Latin American nations declared Central America, South America, and the Caribbean a nuclear-free zone in the Treaty of Tlatelolco.

June 17, 1967: China successfully tested a hydrogen bomb.

June 23–25, 1967: President Lyndon Johnson and Soviet prime minister Alexei Kosygin met at Glassboro, New Jersey, in a mini-summit, the first superpower summit since 1961. Major agenda items: the Middle East, Vietnam, and the arms race.

June 30, 1967: The United States and 45 other nations signed the accord for the Kennedy Round of General Agreement on Tariffs and Trade (GATT) tariff cuts, covering 75 percent of world trade.

September 18, 1967: Defense Secretary Robert McNamara announced deployment of the Sentinel antiballistic missile (ABM) system to counter China's nuclear threat.

December 13, 1967: The United States announced plans to develop a missile equipped with multiple independently targeted warheads (MIRV), which allowed multiple warheads carried by the same booster to be guided to separate targets. MIRV technology was introduced in 1970.

December 13–14, 1967: NATO ministers agreed to closer political consultation to promote détente. NATO adopted a flexible response strategy, allowing for a broad range of conventional and nuclear responses to meet any level of aggression.

January 23, 1968: Amid tensions on the Korean peninsula, the USS *Pueblo*, a navy intelligence ship, was seized by North Koreans off their coast. The vessel and crew was held until December, when the U.S. apologized.

July 1, 1968: The Nuclear Non Proliferation Treaty was signed in Geneva by 61 nations, including the United States and the Soviet Union, after four years of negotiations. It took effect in March 1970. Several would-be nuclear powers—including India, Pakistan, and Israel—refused to sign, but eventually, more than 130 nations signed the pact.

August 20, 1968: After standing by as reinstated Czech Communist leader Alexander Dubcek effected major reforms, including democratization and free speech, during the "Prague Spring," the Soviet Union and neighboring Warsaw Pact armies invaded Czechoslovakia. The Czech leadership was purged and replaced with a puppet regime.

November 12, 1968: In a speech to the Polish Communist Party Congress, Leonid Brezhnev unveiled the Brezhnev Doctrine, asserting the "limited sovereignty" of Communist states and Moscow's right to intervene in states threatened by "counter-revolution." The doctrine remained in force in the Eastern bloc until the late 1980s. One of its consequences was that Chinese leadership, anxious at the possibility of invasion by the Soviets, began to open to the Western bloc.

January 20, 1969: In his inaugural address, President Richard Nixon adopted a pragmatic tone toward the Soviet Union, anticipating an "era of negotiation" and stating, "Our lines of communication will be open." *Realpolitik* (diplomacy based on realism) would dominate his presidency.

March 2, 1969: Troops clashed along the Sino-Soviet border. Clashes continued for six months; the Soviets deployed nuclear weapons and consulted the United States about a nuclear strike in case of war between the Soviet Union and China. The two major Communist powers opened negotiations in October but did not settle their border dispute until 1988.

April 15, 1969: North Korea downed a U.S. EC-121 spy plane over the Sea of Japan.

July 20, 1969: The U.S. *Apollo 11* crew landed on the moon.

July 26, 1969: Nixon announced a policy that accompanied his policy of "Vietnamization" of the Vietnam War. The United States would continue to protect friendly Asian nations with economic and military aid but would no longer send troops, saying, "Asian hands must shape the Asian future."

November 17, 1969: Preliminary Strategic Arms Limitation Talks (SALT) between the United States and the Soviet Union, delayed after the Soviet invasion of Czechoslovakia, began in Helsinki, Finland. Seven rounds of talks would be held before the signing of the first set of agreements in May 1972 (see May 22–30, 1972, p. 545).

March 19, 1970: West German and East German leaders Willy Brandt and Willi Stroph met for the first time since Germany's partition to discuss normalization of relations. A week later, the first four-power talks since 1959 opened on the status of Berlin.

June 27, 1970: In the wake of a NATO foreign ministers' conference, Warsaw Pact ministers put forward yet another plan for a European Security Conference that for the first time included the United States and Canada.

August 3, 1970: The first successful underwater launch of a Poseidon missile was made by the USS *James Madison.*

August 12, 1970: Willy Brandt's *Ostpolitik* (that is, a reaching out by West Germany to promote closer relations with the "East"—the Communist Eastern bloc) bore fruit, as the Soviet Union and West Germany signed a nonaggression treaty. A similar pact with Poland was signed in December; a limited agreement on Berlin was reached in September 1971.

September 4, 1970: Salvador Allende of Chile became the world's first democratically elected Marxist leader.

September 25, 1970: U.S. aerial reconnaissance discovered a strategic submarine base under construction in Cienfuegos, Cuba, in apparent violation of the 1962 Cuban missile crisis settlement. After a U.S. warning, the Soviet Union pledged not to complete the base in exchange for a renewed U.S. guarantee of Cuban sovereignty.

October 8, 1970: Soviet dissident novelist Aleksandr Solzhenitsyn, whose works had been banned in the Soviet Union, won the Nobel Prize for literature for *The First Circle* (1968), *The Cancer Ward* (1968, 1969), and for other novels and short stories. The Soviet Writers Union called the award "deplorable."

December 7, 1970: In signing the Treaty of Warsaw with Poland, West Germany recognized the Oder-Neisse border as Poland's western frontier, resolving one of the knottiest territorial disputes left over from World War II.

December 15, 1970: Poles in Gdansk and other cities began a week of demonstrations and riots in protest against food price increases mandated by economic reforms. Polish troops put down the riots, which resulted in several hundred deaths. On December 20, Polish Communist leader Wladyslaw Gomulka was replaced by hard-liner Edward Gierek to forestall Soviet intervention; economic reforms were withdrawn.

February 11, 1971: The United States and the Soviet Union were among 63 signatories to an agreement banning nuclear weapons from the seabeds. France and China did not sign.

April 1971: A U.S. table tennis team played in China, thereby initiating what was dubbed "Ping-Pong diplomacy" and signaling a thaw in relations between the United States and Communist China. Western journalists, barred since 1949, were allowed into China to cover the event. On April 14, President Richard Nixon ended the 20-year U.S. trade embargo of China.

July 15, 1971: In a surprise announcement to the nation, Nixon declared that he would visit China to discuss normalization of relations.

July 27–29, 1971: At a Comecon summit, Eastern bloc nations tried to counter the growing strength of the EEC by agreeing to greater economic integration.

August 9, 1971: India and the Soviet Union signed a friendship treaty.

August 15, 1971: Without consulting its allies, the United States abolished the gold standard, ending the postwar international exchange system. That move strained the Western alliance but forced the Allies to share the economic burdens sustained by the United States since World War II.

October 20, 1971: West German prime minister Willy Brandt won the Nobel Peace Prize for his pursuit of *Ostpolitik*, détente with the Eastern bloc.

October 25, 1971: In a major defeat for the United States, the UN General Assembly overwhelmingly voted (76-35, with 17 abstentions) to give the single China seat on the UN Security Council to Communist China and to expel Taiwan from the council.

December 3–16, 1971: India and Pakistan fought each other in the Bangladesh war of independence. The conflict cemented U.S.-Pakistan-China and USSR-India alliances.

February 21–28, 1972: Nixon's historic trip to China opened the way for a profound Cold War geopolitical realignment. Diplomatic relations were not established until 1979, but the United States used its "China card" to revive U.S.-Soviet talks on Berlin and arms control.

April 10, 1972: The United States and the Soviet Union were among more than 70 signatories of a ban on biological weapons.

May 22–30, 1972: Nixon became the first U.S. president to visit Moscow, holding his first summit with Leonid Brezhnev. On May 26, they signed the SALT I and ABM treaties; other agreements covered space and technological cooperation and 12 "basic principles" of détente.

May 26, 1972: The signing of a West German-East German treaty eased cross-border goods traffic and visits. A week later, 27 years after the end of World War II, the four powers signed a final protocol on Berlin.

July 8, 1972: Nixon announced a three-year, $750 million grain deal with the Soviet Union. Another major trade accord signed in October offered the Soviet Union most-favored-nation trading status.

November 21, 1972: SALT II talks opened in Geneva. A final treaty would be signed in June 1979.

December 21, 1972: In a highlight of *Ostpolitik,* West Germany and East Germany signed the Basic Treaty, recognizing "two Germanies in one nation." Both countries joined the UN in 1973.

January 1, 1973: Great Britain, Ireland, and Denmark formally joined the EEC (later renamed the European Community, or EC, and finally the European Union, or EU), the primary engine for economic growth, political integration, and democracy in Europe. During the 1980s, Greece, Spain, and Portugal joined the alliance.

January 27, 1973: The Paris peace accords were signed, ending United States involvement in the Vietnam War (see Vietnam War, January 27, 1973, p. 647).

May 18–22, 1973: Brezhnev became the first Soviet leader to visit West Germany.

June 16–25, 1973: Agreements signed at the second Nixon-Brezhnev summit in Washington, D.C., included principles for starting the SALT II negotiations.

July 3, 1973: After many years of planning, the 35-nation Helsinki Conference on Security and Cooperation in Europe opened in Finland. The United States, Canada, NATO countries, Warsaw Pact countries, and nonaligned countries reached a final accord in July 1975.

September 11, 1973: With covert CIA aid, a military junta headed by Gen. Augusto Pinochet staged a coup against Chile's elected Marxist president, Salvador Allende (who was killed on the spot). The Pinochet dictatorship, characterized by mass arrests, tortures, and murder, survived until 1990.

October 6, 1973: The Yom Kippur War began in the Middle East, as Egypt and Syria attacked Israel (during the holy days of Yom Kippur). In protest against U.S. support of Israel, OPEC raised oil prices and embargoed U.S. oil sales. In late October, the U.S. and the Soviet Union undertook separate diplomatic efforts; U.S. troops were placed on alert, and Brezhnev threatened Soviet military involvement. Despite the signing of a cease-fire on November 11, the war represented a serious breakdown of détente and the most serious East-West confrontation since the Cuban missile crisis in 1962.

October 30, 1973: NATO and Warsaw Pact representatives opened Mutual and Balanced Force Reduction Talks in Vienna. Ten years of talks produced no agreement, but they opened a dialogue later fulfilled by the Conventional Forces in Europe Treaty.

November 7, 1973: In the wake of the Vietnam War, Congress passed the War Powers Act, limiting the president's powers to commit U.S. troops overseas. Congress continued to press for more influence on foreign policy, passing legislation controlling the export of weapons, and restricting the president's authority to make executive agreements with foreign powers.

1974–1984:
THE WEAKENING AND END OF DÉTENTE

February 13, 1974: The Soviets expelled Aleksandr Solzhenitsyn, the writer whose 1974 book, *The Gulag Archipelago*, openly exposed the Soviet Union's brutal system of detention camps.

May 18, 1974: India tested its first nuclear bomb, becoming the world's sixth nuclear power.

June 19, 1974: NATO foreign ministers agreed on the Ottawa Declaration on Atlantic relations. Its 14 points articulated principles of "common destiny," recognizing the potential of a larger geographical sphere of influence and calling for a common European defense.

June 27–July 3, 1974: The third Nixon-Brezhnev summit was held in Moscow. Nixon's position was weakened by the unfolding Watergate scandal, but agreement was reached on cuts in ABM levels.

August 9, 1974: Nixon resigned as president after months of Watergate revelations and the threat of impeachment. Vice President Gerald Ford succeeded Nixon.

September 12, 1974: Ethiopian Emperor Haile Selassie was dethroned after a 58-year reign in a Soviet-backed military coup. Soviet and Cuban military aid would later help Ethiopia repel a provincial rebellion and a Somali invasion; the U.S. mishandled the crisis and lost regional influence.

November 23–24, 1974: The SALT II treaty was the major agenda item at a Ford-Brezhnev summit in Vladivostok. That Soviet-U.S. summit, the last until 1979, temporarily derailed the new United States-China relationship.

January 3, 1975: The U.S. Trade Reform Act was signed with the controversial Jackson-Vanik amendment, which made trade concessions to the Soviet Union contingent on freer Jewish emigration. In retaliation, the Soviets rescinded the 1972 U.S.-Soviet trade agreement, and both Soviet-U.S. trade and Jewish emigration levels fell off markedly. Human rights, however, now took a permanent place on the U.S. Cold War agenda.

March 1975: Civil war broke out in Angola soon after Portugal announced its independence. Three governments claimed power: one Marxist, one pro-Chinese, one pro-Western. The CIA helped fund the pro-Western faction, but the Soviet-backed group declared Angola a people's republic in November; Cuban troops remained to fight in a years-long civil war. The U.S. Senate ended covert U.S. aid in 1976.

March 18, 1975: Under the Freedom of Information Act, the FBI released documents detailing its harassment of the American Socialist Workers Party throughout the 1960s. That was typical of the kind of conduct condoned by the government on the grounds that the United States was engaged in a Cold War.

April 16, 1975: Under the leadership of Pol Pot, the Maoist Khmer Rouge took over the Cambodian government after a five-year civil war and began a ruthless program of repression and genocide. One-fifth of the population, 1.2 million Cambodians, were killed in the holocaust (1975–1979).

April 30, 1975: With the fall of Saigon, the South Vietnamese government surrendered to Communist North Vietnam and all U.S. personnel were evacuated (see Vietnam War, April 30, 1975, p. 646).

June 5, 1975: The Suez Canal opened for the first time since the 1967 Six-Day War.

June 10, 1975: The Rockefeller Commission reported on extensive illegal domestic surveillance of antiwar activists by the CIA during the Vietnam War. The CIA came under further censure in November, when a Senate report disclosed that the CIA had plotted to assassinate foreign leaders.

July 17–19, 1975: In the first U.S.-USSR space mission, Apollo and Soyuz craft linked.

July 30–August 1, 1975: After two years of negotiations, the United States, Canada, the Soviet Union, and 32 other European nations from both blocs signed the Helsinki Accords, a monument to the architects of détente. The nonbinding agreement assured European security by confirming post–World War II borders, the division of Germany, and the principle of noninterference; provided for trade, technical, and cultural cooperation; and established the Conference on Security and Cooperation in Europe (CSCE) as a permanent organization to oversee and advance the provisions. Significantly, too, signatories agreed to respect human rights, opening a door to reform in the Soviet Union and Eastern Europe.

October 9, 1975: Andrei Sakharov, a dissident physicist and human rights activist, became the first Soviet citizen to win the Nobel Peace Prize.

November 20, 1975: Spanish fascist dictator Gen. Francisco Franco died after a 36-year rule. King Juan Carlos was recalled to the throne and together with Premier Adolfo Suárez set about restoring democracy in Spain. The first elections in 40 years were held in 1977, ending a long embarrassment to Western Europe's claim to be a bastion of democracy.

December 1–5, 1975: During a visit by President Ford to China, the Chinese government repeated its disapproval of détente. En route home from his Asian trip, the president unveiled a new Pacific Doctrine, calling for strategic reliance on Japan and normalization of relations with China.

December 3, 1975: The Communist Pathet Lao took over the Laotian government and declared Laos a people's republic.

May 28, 1976: The United States and the Soviet Union signed a pact limiting the size of underground nuclear tests for peaceful purposes. The Soviets for the first time acceded to on-site inspections.

June 29–30, 1976: Twenty-nine West and East European Communist Parties meeting in East Berlin endorsed "EuroCommunism," the right of national parties to pursue courses independent of Moscow. The conference occurred in a context of significant electoral gains for socialist and Communist parties in Italy, France, and Spain.

September 9, 1976: Mao Tse-tung, the sole ruler of China since 1949, died.

October 6, 1976: In a TV debate between the two presidential candidates, President Gerald Ford and Jimmy Carter, Ford made an unsettling gaffe when he insisted that there was "no Soviet domination of Eastern Europe." Within days, he claimed that he had meant that the United States did not *accept* the Soviets' role in Eastern Europe, but the damage to his reputation had been done.

January 6, 1977: "Charter 77," a manifesto signed by 240 Czech intellectuals opposing their government's suppression of human rights, was published in Western newspapers. Czech government objections were met with a second manifesto bearing 300 signatures. Charter 77 activists, including Václav Havel, were convicted of passing subversive literature abroad, and in October, many were sentenced to prison.

January 18, 1977: Leonid Brezhnev dismissed as "noisy and idle talk" growing Western claims that the Soviets were aiming for military superiority, not parity.

January 20, 1977: After a campaign strongly critical of the Nixon and Ford administrations' pursuit of détente, President Jimmy Carter delivered an inaugural speech stressing the centrality of human rights in U.S. foreign policy. Early in his term, he made public overtures to prominent Soviet dissidents and he cut aid to governments committing human rights violations.

March 18, 1977: U.S. travel restrictions to Vietnam, North Korea, and Cambodia were lifted by the U.S. government.

March 26–30, 1977: President Carter's new secretary of state, Cyrus Vance, visited Moscow amid an escalating row over the new U.S. human rights stance. Andrei Gromyko rejected U.S. interference in Soviet internal affairs. Fresh SALT II talks began on March 28.

May 10–11, 1977: Addressing a NATO ministers meeting, Carter called for closer coordination of NATO weapons and strategy to counter the Soviet military buildup in Europe.

June 3, 1977: The United States announced a new diplomatic exchange with Cuba.

June 30, 1977: Citing its high cost, Carter canceled production of the B-1 bomber.

July 7, 1977: The United States announced that it had tested a neutron bomb, which was designed to detonate in the air, killing people but leaving buildings and roads intact.

October 4, 1977: The CSCE convened in Belgrade in its first review conference since the signing of the Helsinki Accords (see July 30–August 1, 1975, p. 546) and disagreed on the centrality of human rights.

April 7, 1978: Carter deferred production of the neutron bomb.

April 27–30, 1978: A bloody coup backed by the Soviets put a Communist regime in power in Afghanistan.

May 18, 1978: Yuri Orlov, founder of a group monitoring Soviet compliance with the Helsinki Accords, was sentenced to 12 years in prison for "anti-Soviet agitation."

June 7, 1978: President Carter accused the Soviets of subverting Third World non-alignment by encouraging Cuban proxy wars in Angola and Ethiopia and said the Soviets must "choose either confrontation or cooperation."

July 1975: Anatoly Scharansky and Alexander Ginsburg received long sentences in the most heavily publicized of many Soviet dissident trials.

September 6–17, 1978: Under President Carter's sponsorship, Anwar Sadat of Egypt and Israel's Menachem Begin forged a historic agreement at Camp David; they signed a peace treaty at the White House in March 1979. Egypt was expelled from the Arab League.

November 3, 1978: Vietnam and the Soviet Union signed a 25-year treaty of friendship.

December 15, 1978: President Carter announced the initiation of full diplomatic relations with China and severance of ties with Taiwan on January 1, 1979. The formal addition of the "China card" to U.S. foreign policy set back détente with the Soviet Union as SALT II talks stalled in Geneva a week later.

January 16, 1979: After nearly a year of unrest and strikes in Iran, the United States lost its staunchest ally in the Muslim world when the Shah of Iran abdicated; a fundamentalist Islamic dictatorship formed under Ayatollah Ruhollah Khomeini replaced the Shah with a regime extremely hostile to the West.

January 28–February 5, 1979: On the first official visit to the United States by a top Chinese leader, Deng Xiaoping signed cultural and scientific agreements. Further indicating its westward tilt, China refused in April to renew a 1950 treaty of friendship with the Soviet Union. In July, the United States granted China most favored nation trading status.

May 1979: Conservative Margaret Thatcher became Great Britain's prime minister.

June 8, 1979: The White House announced full-scale development of the MX missile.

June 18, 1979: Carter and Brezhnev signed SALT II in an atmosphere of mutual distrust and weakening détente.

July 17, 1979: After months of unrest, U.S.-backed Nicaraguan dictator Antonio Somoza was overthrown by the pro-Communist Sandinistas. The CIA secretly financed and trained anti-Communist Contra guerrilla rebels until 1984.

October 3, 1979: The United States and the Soviet Union agreed on a record grain sale.

October 6, 1979: Brezhnev offered to reduce Soviet troops in East Germany and medium-range missiles in the western Soviet Union in exchange for a NATO guarantee not to deploy U.S. missiles in Europe. Carter spurned the proposal.

November 4, 1979: With Ayatollah Khomeini's blessing, Iranian revolutionaries took U.S. diplomats and others hostage in the U.S. embassy in Tehran. (In related violence in November and December, Islamic mobs attacked the U.S. embassies in Islamabad, Pakistan, and Tripoli, Lybia.) An attempted rescue by the U.S. government in April 1980 was a disaster. The

American hostages were held until January 1981.

December 12, 1979: NATO committed to deploy U.S. cruise and Pershing missiles in Western Europe by 1983; those would be the first European-sited nuclear missiles within range of the Soviet Union. The Soviets threatened to abandon arms control negotiations unless that decision was reversed.

December 27, 1979: After factional Communist fighting in Afghanistan risked a Muslim insurgency, the Soviet Union staged a full-scale invasion of Afghanistan and installed a puppet regime. Abandoning détente, President Carter imposed trade restrictions on the Soviet Union, boycotted the 1980 Moscow summer Olympics, and scuttled SALT II ratification (but announced his intention of adhering to its terms). During the civil war that followed, the United States and China armed the rebel *muhajadeen*, and Afghanistan became the Soviet Union's "Vietnam," as Soviet troops fought on for ten years.

January 23, 1980: In his State of the Union address, President Carter expounded the Carter Doctrine, promising to use force, if necessary, to defend vital U.S. interests in the Persian Gulf.

January 22, 1980: Soviet Nobel laureate and human rights activist Andrei Sakharov was charged with subversion and forced into internal exile in Gorky.

August 14, 1980: Polish workers took over the Gdansk shipyard amid widespread strikes protesting price increases; two weeks later, the Poles won the right to form independent unions. On September 24, Solidarity, a national organization of independent trade unions, was registered under the leadership of Lech Walesa.

January 20, 1981: President Ronald Reagan, elected in large part because of popular disaffection with Carter's indecisive diplomacy (particularly in his handling of the Iran hostage crisis) promised a tougher foreign policy in his inaugural address (and requested increased defense spending in February). The U.S. hostages in Iran were freed moments after the inauguration.

April 24, 1981: President Reagan lifted the ban on Soviet grain shipments imposed after the 1979 Afghanistan invasion.

June 16, 1981: In a major policy reversal, the U.S. agreed to sell weapons to China.

August 10, 1981: Secretary of Defense Caspar Weinberger announced that Carter's 1978 policy had been reversed and production of a neutron bomb had already begun.

September 2, 1981: President Reagan repeated that verification was nonnegotiable in any arms control talks and said the alternative was "an arms race they can't win."

September 22–24, 1981: At the UN, Soviet foreign minister Andrei Gromyko blasted the U.S. military buildup and adventurist foreign policy. On September 24, the United States and the Soviet Union announced talks on limiting intermediate nuclear forces (INF) in Europe.

October 2, 1981: The United States announced a program to modernize and strengthen the U.S. strategic nuclear arsenal, restructuring MX deployment and resurrecting the B-1 bomber cancelled in 1977.

October–November 1981: Both superpowers positioned themselves before the start of INF talks in Geneva on November 30. The Soviets denied Reagan's accusation that they were planning to wage nuclear war; Western European allies were alarmed by Reagan's claim that a limited nuclear war could be fought in Europe; Reagan put the "zero option"—the total elimination of INF weapons—on the table for the first time.

December 13, 1981: After a year of unrest and Solidarity strikes in Poland and concurrent large-scale Soviet military maneuvers along their common border, Polish Communist leader Wojciech Jaruzelski declared martial law, effectively forestalling a Soviet invasion. President Reagan imposed some economic sanctions on the Soviet Union.

February 1, 1982: The United States committed to aid the Salvadoran army, which was fighting a three-year civil war against leftist guerrillas in El Salvador.

February 24, 1982: Speaking to the Organization of American States, Reagan announced the Caribbean Basin Initiative, an Alliance for Peace–like aid program to counter growing Soviet and Cuban influence in the islands. He called it a "defense of freedom."

April 6, 1982: In a speech redefining nuclear strategy, Secretary of State Alexander Haig defended deterrence via an arms buildup and "flexible response," the strategy of maintaining a broad range of military options. He refused to commit to a "no first use" policy.

June 1, 1982: After 20 months of work, an independent international commission on disarmament called for the immediate reversal of the "arms spiral."

June 29, 1982: Strategic Arms Reduction Talks (START) opened in Geneva. In proposing those talks in May, President Reagan called for mutual one-third cuts in nuclear arsenals, observing, "We've given up on SALT."

October 8, 1982: The Polish government banned Solidarity and all other existing trade unions in Poland.

November 22, 1982: New Soviet leader Yuri Andropov pledged to continue détente in his first major policy statement; President Reagan coincidentally proposed a $27 billion deployment of MX missiles. The Soviet Union declared the MX in violation of SALT agreements.

March 23, 1983: Citing the Soviet military buildup, President Ronald Reagan went on national television to call for the development of the Strategic Defense Initiative (SDI), the so-called Star Wars antiballistic missile system (see Notable Phrases, "Evil Empire," pp. 561). The Soviet Union declared SDI in violation of the 1972 ABM treaty, but the Reagan administration insisted on interpreting the treaty to allow SDI. Strategically and technically problematic, SDI was tremendously controversial at home and abroad, but billions of dollars were committed to its development, and it proved a useful bargaining chip in arms talks.

March 30, 1983: Reagan proposed to reduce deployment of missiles in Europe in exchange for cuts in Soviet intermediate-range nuclear weapons in Europe and Asia. The Soviets rejected the proposal.

April 1–4, 1983: Tens of thousands of Western Europeans demonstrated against the planned U.S. missile deployment.

April 11, 1983: A bipartisan presidential commission headed by U.S. national security advisor Brent Scowcroft recommended a strategic mix of silo-based MX missiles and single-warhead ICBMs. The U.S. Congress funded the MX later in 1983.

August 25, 1983: The United States and the Soviet Union signed a new five-year grain deal, ending the 1979 embargo.

September 1, 1983: A South Korean commercial airliner strayed into Soveiet airspace and was shot down by a Soviet fighter plane, killing all 269 people aboard, including a U.S. congressman. The United States responded with token sanctions.

October 5, 1983: Lech Walesa, founder of the outlawed Polish Solidarity union, won the Nobel Peace Prize.

October 25, 1983: U.S. Marines, together with a small Caribbean force, invaded Grenada a week after a Marxist coup and restored order within a few days. A moderate government was elected in free elections in 1984.

October–December 1983: Imminent deployment of U.S. cruise missiles in Western Europe antagonized the Soviets (who again proposed INF cuts) and prompted antinuclear demonstrations by more than 2 million Europeans on October 22–23. The first U.S. cruise missiles arrived in Great Britain on November 14. A week later, West Germany voted to deploy cruise and Pershing missiles. The Soviets walked out of INF talks in protest; a START round of talks ended December 8 without a date for resumption being set.

January 11, 1984: The bipartisan Kissinger Commission reported serious threats to U.S. security from Soviet and Cuban activity in Central America and recommended long-term economic aid to the region.

January 16, 1984: President Reagan called for "realism, strength and dialogue" in the U.S.-Soviet relationship.

January 21, 1984: The U.S. Air Force tested an antisatellite missle.

April 26–May 1, 1984: Visiting his first Communist country on a "journey for peace" to China, President Reagan signed cultural, technical, and economic agreements.

May 7, 1984: The Soviet Union withdrew from the Los Angeles Olympics, citing a U.S. anti-Soviet campaign. Eastern bloc countries joined the boycott.

September 28, 1984: Reagan held his first talks with a Soviet leader, foreign minister Andrei Gromyko, at the White House. That conciliatory gesture opened the way to a more cooperative U.S.-Soviet relationship.

October 3, 1984: Richard Miller, an FBI counterintelligence agent, was charged as a Soviet spy. His first trial ended in a mistrial on November 1985; retried, he was convicted on June 19, 1986, and sentenced to life in prison.

October 15, 1984: News reports revealed that CIA training manuals for the Nicaraguan Contra rebels included instructions on political assassination.

1985–1991:
The End of the Cold War

January 7–8, 1985: At a Geneva meeting, Secretary of State George Schultz and Soviet foreign minister Gromyko agreed on terms for resumption of arms control negotiations.

February 4, 1985: President Ronald Reagan's budget proposed sharply higher defense spending. New Zealand turned away the U.S. nuclear-capable destroyer *Buchanan* in the first of a series of incidents leading to New Zealand's being forced out of the 1951 ANZUS alliance (see June 27, 1986, p. 551).

March 11, 1985: Mikhail Gorbachev became general secretary of the Soviet Communist Party; he was the first Soviet leader to come of age after the post–World War II generation.

April 7, 1985: Gorbachev froze Soviet INF missile deployments.

April 26, 1985: The Warsaw Pact extended the Warsaw Treaty for 20 years.

May 1, 1985: The United States embargoed trade with leftist Nicaragua, accusing it of exporting revolution. Moscow pledged Nicaragua aid. On May 8, Washington confirmed the Reagan Doctrine: the U.S. would aid anti-Communist revolutions.

June 8, 1985: Hungary held the first multicandidate elections in the Eastern bloc.

June 11, 1985: Blasting Leonid Brezhnev's economic policies, Gorbachev called for reforms to end Soviet stagnation.

July 23, 1985: The United States signed an agreement to sell nonmilitary nuclear technology to China.

August 6, 1985: The South Pacific Nuclear Free Zone Treaty was signed in the Cook Islands.

August 21, 1985: The State Department accused the Soviets of tracking U.S. diplomats in Moscow with a chemical dust.

October 3, 1985: On a trip to France, Gorbachev proposed halving the U.S. and Soviet nuclear arsenals. His flurry of arms control proposals during 1985 included calls to eliminate chemical weapons from central Europe and to hold separate arms negotiations with France and Great Britain. All were rejected.

November 19–21, 1985: At a summit in Geneva, the first since 1979, President Ronald Reagan and Mikhail Gorbachev made progress on arms control. They established a personal rapport; Reagan called it a "fresh start."

January 1, 1986: In New Year's television broadcasts to each other's countries, Ronald Reagan and Mikhail Gorbachev expressed their desire for world peace.

January 15, 1986: Gorbachev accepted the zero option in Europe (that is, Reagan's proposal to eliminate intermediate-range nuclear weapons) and proposed the elimination of nuclear weapons within 15 years. A blizzard of arms control proposals and counterproposals over the following two years called for ever deeper cuts.

February 1, 1986: Nine European Community members signed the Single European Act, a revision to the Treaty of Rome, agreeing to a completely free international market.

March 12, 1986: In an unprecedented referendum, Spain voted to stay in NATO but continued its ban on nuclear weapons.

April 18, 1986: Gorbachev told an East German Communist Party congress, "We offer the West not the clenched fist, but an open hand."

June 27, 1986: Ruling for the first time on an international military conflict, the World Court ruled the United States in violation of international law and Nicaraguan sovereignty for seeking to overthrow the Sandinista government and mining harbors.

To express its displeasure with New Zealand's refusal to allow U.S. nuclear ships in its harbors, the United States canceled its agreement with New Zealand under the ANZUS treaty. The United States, however, retained the agreement with Australia.

October 11–12, 1986: The second Reagan-Gorbachev summit in Reykjavik, Iceland, on arms control negotiations fell apart over "Star Wars" and ended with angry exchanges.

November 25, 1986: The admission that the U.S. government illegally diverted Iranian arms sales profits to fund the Nicaraguan Contra rebellion created the most serious crisis of Reagan's presidency. Direct funding for the Contras continued until 1989.

December 23, 1986: Dissident Soviet scientist Andrei Sakharov and his wife, Yelena Bonner, returned to Moscow after 17 years of internal exile, signaling Gorbachev's relaxation of political repression.

January 27, 1987: Mikhail Gorbachev opened the Communist Party central committee meeting by calling for radical political reform and "democratization."

February 1, 1987: Ethiopian voters approved a constitution establishing a Soviet-style Communist government. On February 22, Lt. Col. Mengistu Haile Mariam, the ruler since Haile Selassie was overthrowin in 1974, declared the new name of the country to be the People's Democratic Republic of Ethiopia.

February 14–16, 1987: The Soviet Union hosted 80 nations at an international peace forum in Moscow. An address by Gorbachev linked Soviet economic and political reforms to arms control efforts. In February and March, the Western press reported that Eastern bloc countries were generally wary of Soviet reforms, despite cautious support by Poland, Czechoslovakia, and Hungary.

March 25, 1987: At a National People's Congress, Chinese premier Zhao Ziyang backed economic reforms including foreign investment and free markets for China. The reforms were affirmed by a party congress in October.

May 28–29, 1987: A summit meeting of the Warsaw Pact in East Berlin called for the first-ever direct talks with NATO.

June 12, 1987: President Reagan, in a speech at the Brandenburg Gate in West Berlin, dramatically invited Gorbachev to "open this gate...tear down this wall."

June 25, 1987: Gorbachev proposed radical reforms, introducing competition and decentralization to the Soviet economy.

June 26, 1987: In the wake of highly publicized charges of espionage by U.S. Marine guards at its Moscow embassy, the State Department reported that the new U.S. embassy under construction in Moscow was riddled with Soviet eavesdropping devices. Construction halted and was not resumed for another decade.

August 7, 1987: The presidents of Nicaragua, El Salvador, Guatemala, Honduras, and Costa Rica signed a comprehensive Central American peace plan calling for ceasefires and democratic reforms brokered by Oscar Arias Sanchez of Costa Rica.

November 29, 1987: In the first free referendum in Poland in 40 years, voters rejected proposed economic and political reforms offered by Communists; the proposals were denounced as "purely propaganda" by Solidarity.

December 8–10, 1987: In a Washington summit, their third, Reagan and Gorbachev signed the bilateral INF Treaty, the first agreement to reduce nuclear arsenals. The first Soviet missiles were withdrawn from East Germany and Czechoslovakia in February 1988.

January 29, 1988: A Bulgarian Communist Party conference endorsed economic reforms.

March 2–3, 1988: The first NATO summit in six years made conventional force reduction in Europe a priority and deferred a decision on tactical nuclear weapons.

March 16, 1988: Weeks after Congress ended aid to the Nicaraguan Contras, the United States sent troops to Honduras to repel an anticipated Nicaraguan attack on Contra bases there. U.S. forces stayed only 12 days. On March 23, the Sandinista government signed a cease-fire with the Contras, ending the seven-year civil war.

April 14, 1988: Admitting defeat, the Soviet Union signed agreements to end its eight-year occupation of Afghanistan. The last Soviet troops left in February 1989.

May 14, 1988: An independent trade union was founded in Hungary, the first in the Soviet bloc since Solidarity. On May 22, Hungarian Communist Party leader Janos Kadar was replaced after 32 years amid growing calls for sweeping reform.

May 29–June 2, 1988: Reagan visited the Soviet Union for the first time for his fourth and final Gorbachev summit; he pushed Gorbachev on human rights.

June 28–July 1, 1988: Perestroika (economic restructuring) topped the agenda in Moscow at a national Communist Party conference.

July–November 1988: Nationalist and ethnic unrest seized the Soviet republics. The Baltic republics (Latvia, Estonia, Lithuania) held independence rallies in August and in October created nationalist political organizations.

August 1988: In Poland, the widespread strikes of April and May erupted again as the deteriorating economy prompted the worst unrest since 1982. The Polish government resigned in September.

August 17, 1988: The United States and the Soviet Union conducted their first joint nuclear test, in Nevada.

August 21, 1988: Protesters in the Soviet Union and Soviet bloc demanded the removal of Soviet troops from Eastern Europe.

October 10, 1988: The Czech pro-reform government resigned, a defeat for liberalization.

October 17, 1988: The United States and the Philippines renewed their 1947 pact permitting U.S. military bases in the islands, despite substantial public opposition in the island nation.

November 14, 1988: Spain and Portugal joined the Western European Union; the WEU pledged closer cooperation on defense.

November 15, 1988: The United States, Cuba, Angola, and South Africa signed accords on Angola-Namibia. Cuban troops began their withdrawal from the region in January, after 14 years of involvement.

December 6–8, 1988: Gorbachev met with Reagan and president-elect George Bush in New York City. In a historic UN address, Gorbachev announced a unilateral cut of half a million Soviet troops, the unconditional withdrawal of troops from Eastern Europe, and a strategic Soviet shift to a defensive military posture.

January 7–11, 1989: In Paris, a 149-nation conference on chemical weapons condemned the use of chemical weapons and urged an international ban. The Soviets unilaterally pledged to destroy their stockpile.

January 19, 1989: The CSCE ended its third formal review of the 1975 Helsinki Accords. The Vienna Concluding Document was a historic international accord on human rights; it named specific rights—such as tolerance of all religions, gender equality, and the right to travel—and spelled out certain mechanisms to ensure those rights.

February 11, 1989: Independent political parties were legalized in Hungary.

March 6, 1989: Conventional Forces in Europe (CFE) talks opened in Vienna between NATO and the Warsaw Pact nations.

March 26, 1989: In the first nationwide multicandidate parliamentary election in the Soviet Union, various non-Communists (populists, liberals, radicals, ethnic nationalists) defeated many of the Communist Party candidates. In the runoffs in the weeks that followed, the trend continued, but in the end, the Communists maintained a majority of the seats in the 2,250-member Congress of People's Deputies.

April 5, 1989: After two months of roundtable talks, Solidarity and the Polish government reached agreement on independent trade unions and broad economic and political reforms; Lech Walesa lauded "the beginning of the road for democracy and a free Poland." The United States offered Poland a large aid package.

April 9, 1989: After a week of unrest, nationalist demonstrations in the Soviet republic of Georgia were put down by Soviet troops, with heavy casualties. Similar unrest occurred during the spring in other Soviet republics; in May, hundreds of thousands of proindependence demonstrators gathered in Georgia, Azerbaijan, and the Baltic republics.

April 25, 1989: Soviet troops began promised cutbacks in Eastern Europe.

May 2, 1989: Hungary took down the barriers along its Austrian border, becoming the first Soviet-bloc country to open a Western frontier.

May 12, 1989: In a speech at Texas A&M University, President George Bush declared that it was "time to move beyond containment" and renewed President Dwight Eisenhower's 1955 "open skies" proposal.

May 15–18, 1989: The Soviet Union and China normalized relations at their first summit in 30 years, an event marked by growing pro-democracy demonstrations in Beijing.

May 29–30, 1989: At NATO's 40th anniversary summit, Bush unveiled a detailed plan for deep cuts in U.S. forces in Europe.

June 4, 1989: Tens of thousands of troops attacked a massive pro-democracy demonstration by Chinese students and workers in Tiananmen Square, Beijing. Hundreds were killed, thousands injured. The action launched a government crackdown on dissidents.

In Poland, Solidarity swept the first national elections in more than 40 years. The Communist government resigned in August, and in a democratic transfer of power, Solidarity formed a government in September.

July 6–8, 1989: At the Council of Europe in Strasbourg, France, Gorbachev indicated his abandonment of the 1968 Brezhnev Doctrine, declining to intervene as Poland and Hungary undertook reform.

At a Warsaw Pact summit in Bucharest on July 7–8, Gorbachev called for "independent solutions [to] national problems;" the final communique stated, "there are no universal models of socialism." The Eastern bloc was deeply divided over reform.

July 9–12, 1989: President Bush toured Poland and Hungary and offered U.S. aid.

July 17, 1989: The U.S. Air Force conducted the first test flight of the B-2 Stealth bomber.

August 17, 1989: A Politburo policy statement offered the 15 Soviet republics limited autonomy. On August 23, a million citizens of the Baltic republics would form a human chain in support of independence.

September–October 1989: U.S. Federal Reserve chairman Alan Greenspan visited the Soviet Union to discuss free markets. The United States offered to send economic advisers to the Soviet Union to help with *perestroika*. The United States and European Community guaranteed $2 billion in emergency aid to Poland and Hungary, whose economies were struggling to adjust to rapid free-market reforms.

September 11–14, 1989: A refugee crisis began as 13,000 East Germans streamed into West Germany via Hungary and Austria. East Germany filed a protest, but tens of thousands more fled the country.

September 19, 1989: After three months of roundtable talks, Hungary became the second Warsaw Pact state to commit itself to democratic multiparty elections, scheduled for March 1990. At a party congress in October, the Hungarian Communist Party would renounce Marxism in favor of democratic socialism; the Hungarian National Assembly renounced the Communist Party's "leading role." On the October 23 anniversary of the 1956 uprising, Hungary declared itself a free republic.

September 22–23, 1989: Soviet Foreign Minister Eduard Shevardnadze agreed to delink "Star Wars" from START negotiations in a major Soviet policy shift that removed the final obstacle to further arms control talks. A few days later, Shevardnadze and President Bush agreed in separate speeches at the UN that chemical weapons should be eliminated.

October 6–7, 1989: Widespread pro-democracy demonstrations coincided with Gorbachev's 40th-anniversary visit to East Germany, one of the most repressive Eastern bloc states; he urged the government to reform. The East German exodus to West Germany continued.

October 25, 1989: A Soviet foreign ministry spokesman joked that in Poland and Hungary the Brezhnev Doctrine had been replaced by the "Sinatra Doctrine," a reference to Frank Sinatra's trademark song, "My Way."

October 28, 1989: Police broke up a pro-democracy demonstration in Czechoslovakia.

November 9, 1989: At the end of a momentous week in East Germany, during which a million pro-democracy demonstrators gathered in East Berlin and the government was replaced by reformers, East Germany opened its borders. East and West Germans gathered to dance on the Berlin Wall, and on November 11 they began to tear the Berlin Wall down. Within a month, 130,000 East Germans moved to West Germany.

November 17, 1989: Antigovernment demonstrations gathered momentum in Czechoslovakia. The resignation of the Politburo a week later failed to head off a general strike. A non-Communist coalition government was formed on December 10. Elections in December made Alexander Dubcek parliamentary chairman and dissident writer Václav Havel president. By the end of November, the "leading role" of the Communist Party was rejected, and the border with Austria was opened.

November 18, 1989: The European Community (EC) pledged aid to newly democratic Eastern European nations. In December, the EC and the Soviet Union signed their first-ever trade agreement.

November 28, 1989: West Germany's chancellor Helmut Kohl outlined a plan for a German confederation, but East Germany and the Soviet Union rejected it. Kohl was simply too quick and independent; a year later, his plan was accepted.

December 2–3, 1989: At their first summit, on the island of Malta, Bush and Gorbachev agreed to expedite arms control and acknowledged the end of the Cold War.

December 21–31, 1989: A month after the Romanian Communist Party congress reaffirmed the "golden dream of Communism," Communist leader Nicolae Ceausescu was overthrown and executed amid riots and street fighting; the regular army joined the rebellion. The Romanian Communist Party was outlawed in January 1990.

January–February 1990: Bowing to Eastern bloc pressure, the Soviet Union announced that it would remove its troops from Hungary. Czechoslovakia, Poland, and East Germany demanded the same. Soviet troops began their pullout in February.

January 10, 1990: The Comecon summit, in Bulgaria, adopted free-market trading policies.

January 15, 1990: A month after the resignation of Todor Zhivkov, Bulgaria's Communist Party leader for 35 years, the Bulgarian parliament ended the "leading role" of the Communist Party and began round table talks. The Communists, however, won the first free elections since World War II, held in June.

January 31, 1990: In his State of the Union address, President Bush foresaw a "new era in the world's affairs" and proposed deep cuts in European military forces.

February–March 1990: In an atmosphere of growing discontent with Soviet rule, nationalists won republic-level elections throughout the Soviet Union. Lithuania declared independence on March 8; Latvia and Estonia did the same on August 20, 1991. Gorbachev's constitutional efforts to hold the Soviet Union together ultimately failed; one by one, the former republics achieved independence with the breakup of the Soviet Union in late 1991.

February 4, 1990: A massive pro-democracy rally was held in Moscow.

February 11–13, 1990: An unprecedented meeting of foreign ministers of NATO and the Warsaw Pact convened in Ottawa, Canada. They agreed on a German reunification process and superpower troop levels in Europe and discussed President Bush's "open skies" proposal.

March 13, 1990: The Soviet Congress of the People's Deputies renounced the Communist Party's "leading role."

March 18, 1990: Conservative, pro-unification Christian Democrats swept the first free elections in East Germany. The East German and West German economic union, agreed to in May, took effect July 1.

March 25, 1990: Hungarian center-right parties won the first free elections since World War II. In June, the new parliament voted to leave the Warsaw Pact.

May 20, 1990: In the first free elections in Romania since World War II, the provisional government's National Salvation Front won in a landslide.

May 23, 1990: The Soviet Union unveiled a major economic reform program leading to free-market capitalism and called for a national referendum.

May 31–June 3, 1990: At the second Bush-Gorbachev summit, in Washington, D.C., the superpowers agreed on large cuts in their nuclear arsenals and destruction of half their chemical weapons.

June 22, 1990: Checkpoint Charlie, the single

crossing for Big Four military personnel between East Berlin and West Berlin, was ceremonially dismantled.

July 5–6, 1990: In a major strategy shift, NATO leaders renounced the first use of nuclear weapons and voted to seek a nonaggression treaty with the Warsaw Pact.

August 2, 1990: The Persian Gulf crisis began with the Iraqi invasion of Kuwait. Bush and Gorbachev held a summit in Helsinki on the crisis on September 9, and an unprecedented international alliance including both superpowers soon formed to combat Iraq's aggression (see Gulf War, pp. 700-720).

September 12, 1990: World War II formally ended with the four-power signing of a final German settlement. The next day, Germany and the Soviet Union signed a 20-year treaty of friendship.

October 3, 1990: Germany was reunified, becoming the Federal Republic of Germany.

October 15, 1990: Gorbachev won the Nobel Peace Prize.

November 19, 1990: Delegates from all 22 NATO and Warsaw Pact nations at the second CSCE summit in Paris, France, signed the Conventional Forces in Europe (CFE) Treaty (see Negotiations and Peace Treaty, below).

NEGOTIATIONS AND PEACE TREATY

Just as there was no formal declaration of war, so it ended without a peace treaty. Superpower summits played an important role in the ongoing dialogue that ended the Cold War; arms control treaties marked the stages by which the United States and the Soviet Union slowly reached accord.

The historic SALT I and ABM treaties, signed at the May 1972 summit, were among the achievements of Richard Nixon's presidency. SALT I was the first treaty ever to limit offensive nuclear weapons. The development of spy satellites made verification possible without on-site inspections, to which the Soviet Union was implacably opposed. SALT I failed to restrict the number of warheads and the development of new weapons, however, and thus failed to forestall a significant Soviet arms buildup. The 1972 ABM Treaty permanently limited the number of sites and missiles for fixed, land-based defensive systems. Both treaties remained in force as of 1997.

SALT II, finalized after more than seven years of negotiations, was signed at the Carter-Brezhnev summit on June 18, 1979. It set stricter ceilings on strategic missile launchers—including intercontinental ballistic missiles (ICBMs), submarine-launched ballistic missiles (SLBMs), and bombers—aiming at parity between the United States and the Soviet Union. Restrictions were placed on MIRVs, "heavy" ICBMs, and the deployment of new missiles. The U.S. Senate has never ratified SALT II; ratification, initially derailed by the Soviet invasion of Afghanistan, was shelved in the 1980s era of weakening détente. Both sides have essentially conformed to its provisions, however.

The Intermediate Nuclear Forces (INF) Treaty was signed at the Washington, D.C., summit on December 8, 1987, and stands as a monument to the Reagan-Gorbachev era of détente. That was the first agreement to actually reduce nuclear arsenals; it called for the destruction of all intermediate- and short-range missiles in Europe within three years and, in an enormous concession by the Soviets, allowed for on-site inspections. The INF Treaty (still in force in 1997) sparked negotiations for deeper cuts. By the end of the Cold War, Strategic Arms Reduction Talks (START) were nearing agreement on reductions in strategic nuclear weapons. START, limiting the United States and the Soviet Union to 6,000 nuclear warheads each, was signed in July 1991 after nine years of talks. START II, signed in January 1993, cut nuclear arsenals to one-third of levels at that time. START II remains unratified by the Russian government.

Various events are regarded as signifying the end of the Cold War, but the closest thing to formal treaties would be those signed in Paris in November 1990. On November 19, delegates from all 22 NATO and Warsaw Pact nations at the second CSCE summit in Paris signed the Conventional Forces in Europe (CFE) Treaty. It enumerated steep reductions in military equipment to bring NATO and the Warsaw Pact into parity, allowing each side 20,000 European-based tanks, 20,000 artillery pieces, 30,000 armored vehicles, 6,800 planes, and 2,000 helicopters. Then, on November 21, delegates from the United States, Canada, and 34 European nations (all except Albania) signed the Charter of Paris for a New Europe (Paris Accords), which disbanded the Eastern and Western blocs and called for a united

Europe sharing the values of security, economic liberty, and social justice. The signatories stated the Paris Accords signified the end of "the era of confrontation and division in Europe" and affirmed their "steadfast commitment to democracy based on human rights and fundamental freedoms." At the signing on November 21, President George Bush said, "The Cold War is over. In signing the Treaty of Paris, we have closed a chapter of history."

RESULTS OF THE WAR (Casualties, Costs, Consequences)

It is impossible to estimate the number of casualties of the Cold War. Twenty-one million people around the world are estimated to have died in wars between 1945 and 1990, most of them in Third World countries; even accepting the Korean War and the Vietnam War as part of the Cold War, most of these deaths were unrelated to the struggles between its major antagonists (although it might be argued that many of them were killed by weapons supplied by the two sides). Casualties from some specific Cold War actions are known. For example, over the years, more than a hundred East Germans trying to breach the Berlin Wall were killed by East German border guards; hundreds were injured. There were occasional "incidents" in which U.S. service personnel were killed deliberately or accidentally by Communist forces. But the Cold War claimed countless other victims in diverse circumstances. On both sides, pilots of spy planes were shot down over foreign territory; spies were executed at home (including Julius and Ethel Rosenberg in the United States); the shooting down of the Korean Air Lines Flight 007 in September 1983 was one of the last major casualties of that spy mentality. Many U.S. civilians and military personnel suffered the effects of radiation exposure in nuclear tests in Nevada and Utah. Tests of new military hardware and spacecraft also claimed lives.

The costs of the Cold War are similarly difficult to pin down, for governments all over the world on both sides of the ideological divide devoted huge sums to the military, intelligence, and foreign aid budgets necessary to the continuance of the Cold War. One index of the costs of the Cold War is the percentage of the U.S. budget and the gross national product (GNP)

that went for defense: In 1947, defense was 37 percent of the federal budget and 5.8 percent of the GNP; in 1953, at the height of the Cold War, those figures increased to 69.4 percent and 14.5 percent, respectively; by 1979, they had decreased to 23.1 percent and 4.7 percent; under President Ronald Reagan, they rose again to 27.6 percent and 6.5 percent respectively. By 1996, the figures were falling again, to 18 percent and 4.5 percent respectively. (Some of the costs were completely hidden in the budget, charged to national security, and so can perhaps never be known: Even in the mid-1990s, the secret operations of the CIA and the National Security Agency were still costing as much as $25 billion annually.) Although outlays for defense never literally took over the nation's spending, the U.S. economy and society were unquestionably skewed by the decades in which defense spending soared and spending for domestic programs declined. Huge federal budget deficits accumulated without long-term investment in national infrastructure and industrial development; the United States owes a large part of its multi-trillion-dollar national deficit to its defense spending. Other Western nations may not have committed as much of their budgets to defense, but several, such as Great Britain and France, spent significantly high percentages. The Soviet Union and its allies spent similarly large sums and percentages, and there are grounds for claiming that the Soviet Union literally went bankrupt from its spending on the Cold War. Whatever the truth of that claim or the actual sums spent by any and all nations, there is no denying that the world's governments spent a large part of their budgets on the Cold War.

The consequences of the Cold War may not be as elusive as the casualties and costs, but they are no less far-reaching. For instance, the Cold War left thousands of stockpiled nuclear weapons. Some have been destroyed under terms of arms control agreements, but enough remain to blow up the planet. The specter of nuclear war still hovers over major regional conflicts; India has refused to sign international arms control treaties, including the Comprehensive Nuclear Test Ban Treaty approved by the UN in September 1996. Dangers remain of the threat of further proliferation to rogue nations such as Iraq and Libya and the possible leakage of nuclear materials (particularly from newly independent republics in which Soviet missiles were sited) and their use by terrorists. In December 1996, more than 60 retired generals and admirals from a dozen countries acknowledged those dangers in publicly calling for the complete elimination of the world's nuclear weapons.

The Cold War literally changed the face of the world. In Europe, the heart of the struggle, the "German question" was the central and apparently insoluble issue between the United States and the Soviet Union in 1945. Fittingly, German reunification in 1990 closed the Cold War. The collapse and breakup of the Soviet Union in 1990 and 1991 created 15 new nations from the former Soviet republics. European security was finally achieved (again with the redrawing of some national borders) when the Soviet bloc was dismantled; the eastern European nations sought military and economic integration in Europe by applying for membership in the European Community and NATO. By mid-1997, in a development that would have been unimaginable only ten years earlier, the Czech Republic, Hungary, and Poland were expected to be offered NATO membership.

The failure of Communism was everywhere apparent, as former Soviet satellites and Russia itself embraced democracy and free-market economies. The transition was not smooth. The post–World War II generation who grew up in those countries had no experience of an open economy, free enterprise, and financial responsibilities; unemployment, corruption and crime, and the lack of capital, financial institutions, and modern industrial infrastructure dogged most of those economic transitions. Russia had, in addition, to deal with domestic unrest, including a long rebellion in the province of Chechnya. The initial rush of international corporations eager for a commercial foothold in the former Communist nations proved insufficient to guarantee their economic strength.

Economics has become the driving force of geopolitics. Japan, the European Union, and the economies of the Asian "mini dragons" (such as Singapore, Taiwan, Hong Kong) have become formidable global powers, and analysts forecast the development of major trading blocs based on the dollar, mark, and yen. China, also implementing free-market reform, is hovering in the wings as the largest market in the world.

The superpower rapprochement stranded Third World nations. Russia found itself in need of foreign aid. The United States lost its strongest incentive to send economic assistance to developing nations and began to debate how much of the world's security burden it is willing to bear. American voices for isolationism and protectionism were once again being raised.

The Cold War may have been dangerous, but its rules were known. In its aftermath, foreign policy and military strategy have had to be reformulated in a world in which the rules are unclear and doctrines untested. Future military conflicts are considered likely to be small, localized confrontations arising from ethnic, political, or social unrest. The Gulf War was the first major test of the "new world order." Although an unprecedented ad hoc international coalition, led by the United States, succeeded in its mission in that case, it seems that regional alliances and international organizations such as the UN will need to take on more responsibility for mediating crises within and among member nations.

MILITARY INNOVATIONS, TACTICS, EQUIPMENT

Both the United States and the Soviet Union devoted enormous resources to military research and technological development in their efforts to "win" the Cold War. The arms race, nuclear weaponry, and global defense requirements resulted in a steady stream of new and improved bombs and delivery systems—bombers, submarines, and missiles.

Long-range, or strategic, bombers were defensively important, since they can be launched before incoming enemy missiles struck. The U.S. B-52 bomber and the Soviet intercontinental Bison bomber were operational by the mid-1950s. B-52s formed the basis of the Strategic Air Command, a U.S. nuclear force that was in the air 24 hours a day. Their intended replacement, the B-1 bomber, proved prohibitively expensive and technically flawed; the B-1 was abandoned by President Jimmy Carter in 1977. By the mid-1970s, the Soviets deployed the Tupolev-22M "Backfire" bomber, capable of reaching the continental United States.

Submarines were at a premium in nuclear planning; safe from attack underwater, they provided vital retaliatory capability. The development of nuclear-powered submarines produced vessels capable of circumnavigating the globe without resurfacing or refueling. Submarine-launched ballistic missiles (SLBMs) further advanced naval power; U.S. Polaris and Poseidon SLBMs were deployed in the 1960s; Tomahawk cruise missiles, in the mid-1970s.

Missiles are classified by range: short (300–600 miles), intermediate (300–3,400 miles), strategic, or long-range (more than 3,400 miles), intercontinental ballistic missiles (ICBMs). U.S. INFs included the Pershing II and cruise missiles developed for deployment in Europe in the early 1980s. The Soviet equivalent was the SS-20, developed in the 1970s and deployed against Western Europe, the Middle East, South Asia, and China. Mounted on wheeled transports, it was nearly invulnerable to attack.

U.S. ICBMs included the early Titan and its replacement, the Minuteman. Ground-based ICBMs are vulnerable to an enemy first strike, and in 1968, the United States froze long-range missile development in favor of cheaper technological improvements to existing systems. Multiple re-entry vehicle (MRV) systems enabled a single missile to deliver several warheads to the same target. In a further advance, multiple independently targeted reentry vehicles (MIRVs) were developed to counter the Soviet arms buildup of the 1960s. Those missiles carried separately targeted bombs; the biggest Soviet MIRVs could carry up to 30 warheads. The primary U.S. MIRV system was the Peacekeeper, a very accurate generation of missiles. Another important advance in ICBM design was the so-called heavy missile, one with superior throw weight, or nuclear power. Development of the American MX, an accurate and extremely powerful first-strike heavy missile, was controversial throughout the 1980s because of its high cost and problematic deployment. Soviet heavy missiles included the giant SS-18 and SS-19, deployed in the early 1970s.

U.S. defense secretary Robert McNamara created the U.S. "strategic nuclear triad" of strategic bombers, intercontinental ballistic missiles (ICBMs), and submarine-launched ballistic missiles (SLBMs) in the 1960s. The U.S. military is still preeminent in MIRVs, submarines, and bombers. The Soviet Union relied more heavily on conventional forces and land-based missiles and maintained an edge throughout the Cold War in ICBMs (especially in heavy ones), intermediate nuclear weapons, and antiballistic (ABM) missiles systems. Generally, Soviets had a larger arsenal and bigger weapons, but lagged behind the U.S. technologically.

Nuclear weaponry dominated Cold War military technology. The United States had, of course, already used atomic bombs against Japan in World War II. Much more powerful hydrogen fusion bombs (H-bombs) were developed in the early 1950s and became the primary nuclear weapons of both sides. In the mid-1970s, the United States designed a neutron bomb for deployment in Europe. That "enhanced radiation weapon" was a small hydrogen bomb that detonated in the air and was intended to produce maximum radiation and minimum blast. Nicknamed the "capitalist's bomb" by critics because it killed people and left buildings and infrastructure intact, the neutron bomb was canceled by President Carter, who found it morally abhorrent. President Reagan reauthorized its development, but the Cold War ended before it could be deployed.

Advances in design, materials, and microtechnology made stealth, or radar-evading, weapons, possible in the 1970s. U.S. cruise missiles were small, self-propelled missiles that evaded detection by hugging the ground. The most controversial application of that technology was the B-2 Stealth bomber, a long-range aircraft with a price tag approaching $1 billion. B-2 appropriations have been a politically charged issue since the late 1980s, and the program has continued with limited funding. The F-117A Stealth fighter plane, however, saw action in Panama and the Gulf War.

Defensive technology has also provoked controversy because of its cost, impracticability and strategic implications. Early antiballistic missile (ABM) systems were developed by both sides in the arms buildup that followed the Cuban missile crisis. The Soviet system, *Galosh*, was positioned around Moscow, and the U.S. Sentinel system (later renamed Safeguard) was designed to encircle 15 U.S. cities. Worries that complex ABM systems would invite a first strike by enemy forces eager to disable them led to the 1972 ABM Treaty (see May 22-30, 1972, p. 545), which sharply limited numbers and locations of those missiles. President Reagan brought defensive technology to the fore again in the 1980s with his sponsorship of the Strategic Defense Initiative (SDI), nicknamed "Star Wars" by its critics. Reagan foresaw a space-based shield of high-tech laser and particle weapons capable of destroying incoming missiles before their MIRVs deployed. Development promised to cost many billions of dollars, most scientists regarded the SDI as infeasible, and for years the Soviets made its abandonment a condition of arms talks. After years of political wrangling, Congress appropriated limited funding for its development.

Intelligence gathering was revolutionized by Cold War technology. Both military and intelligence services needed intercontinental reconnaissance capabilities and were beneficiaries of the superpowers' space race. By the mid-1950s, the United States had U-2 spy planes, lightweight craft that flew above air defenses. (It was in a U-2 that U.S. pilot Francis Gary Powers was shot down over the Soviet Union in 1960. See p. 540.) By the 1960s, satellites such as the CIA's Discoverer were providing data; the verification capability allowed by high-resolution satellite reconnaissance was instrumental in concluding the 1972 arms control treaties, since the Soviets refused to allow on-site inspections. Microelectronics also facilitated intelligence-gathering on the ground, as the Soviet agents who bugged the new U.S. embassy in Moscow during its construction in 1987 undoubtedly discovered.

LEGENDS AND TRIVIA

Amid many highly publicized cases of Cold War espionage, spies seized the American imagination. The **spy thriller** genre flourished in literature, on television, and in the movies, reaching its peak in the 1950s and 1960s. Ian Fleming's James Bond, a suave British secret agent, appeared in a series of novels, including *From Russia with Love* (1957). In contrast, John Le Carré's George Smiley, a British master spy, operated in a decidedly squalid, unglamorous milieu in novels like *The Spy Who Came in from the Cold* (1963). The filmed versions of both series have been enduringly popular. Television spy series *I Spy*, *Man from U.N.C.L.E.*, and *Mission: Impossible* all appeared in the 1960s. Although not spy thrillers in the strictest sense, there was also a long line of "atmospheric," or paranoid, Cold War movies, such as the classic *The Third Man* (1949), starring Orson Welles, and *The Manchurian Candidate* (1962), starring Frank Sinatra.

The late 1950s, too, saw the height of popular **fear of atomic war**, as the effects of radiation became more widely understood. A number of movies reflected that anxiety, most notably *On the Beach* (1959), *Fail Safe* (1964), and Stanley Kubrick's black comedy *Dr. Strangelove; or, How I Stopped Worrying and Learned to Love the Bomb* (1963). In 1957, the Gaither Committee report on U.S. defense recommended a huge national program to build nuclear shelters. Bomb shelters became a staple of U.S. home shows and backyards. Children practiced frequent civil defense drills in schools, diving under their desks when sirens wailed. In retrospect, it is easy to ridicule those naive efforts, but the fact was that the superpowers were stockpiling enough nuclear weapons to destroy the world. The Cuban missile crisis in October 1962 proved exactly how real and justified public fears were.

Quite aside from popular culture, the Communist menace was examined by many important writers of the era. Among the best known of those was the British author **George Orwell**, who, although a socialist who fought in the Spanish Civil War, denounced Communism in two modern classics, *Animal Farm* (1945) and *1984* (1949). **Arthur Miller**, the American playwright, took a different slant in *The Crucible* (1953), in which he used the Salem witch trials of the 1690s to attack McCarthyism.

Ronald Reagan returned the Communist threat to the national spotlight in the 1980s. The television miniseries *Amerika* (1986), depicting the United States ten years after a Soviet takeover, was widely attacked as anti-Soviet propaganda. John Adams's opera *Nixon in China* (1987) took a surprising turn as a heroic drama based on the president's historic 1972 China trip and featured the Nixons, Mao and his wife, and Zho Enlai in their bedrooms.

In real life, high politics sometimes became low comedy, as in the Khrushchev-Nixon **"kitchen debate"** in Moscow in 1959 (see July 23, 1959, pp. 539-540). As vice president, Nixon was showing Khrushchev around a U.S. exhibition, the Soviet leader attacked U.S. policy while the news cameras were rolling. Nixon staffers arranged for a second exchange in a "typical American home" exhibit, where the leaders traded finger-jabs while comparing their countries' washing machines and relative standards of living. Columnist and language expert William Safire, present as the press agent promoting the display, takes credit for dubbing it a "kitchen conference," but says that Harrison Salisbury of the *New York Times* probably gave it currency as the "kitchen debate."

The **Berlin Wall** was without question the most powerful icon of the Cold War. To those in the Western bloc it signified the forcible denial of the most basic freedoms to citizens of Communist countries. It was little wonder that one U.S. president after another used the Wall or Berlin as the backdrop for speeches about freedom and democracy, and that among the most moving images of the end of the Cold War were the televised scenes of East and West Germans celebrating together and pulling down the Wall by hand in November 1989. By the time the Berlin Wall was officially demolished, the Cold War was history. Perhaps fittingly, as the post–Cold War world would be based on economics, fragments of the Berlin Wall immediately found a market as souvenirs and museum exhibits.

NOTABLE PHRASES

The Cold War

As a term referring to the post–World War II political-ideological conflict chronicled here, the term Cold War is generally credited by U.S. sources to a speechwriter for economist Bernard Baruch, Herbert Bayard Swope, a well-known journalist of his day. Swope claimed to have coined the term in the spring of 1946 for the draft of a speech Baruch was to give about U.S.-Soviet relations; Baruch thought it too strong at that time, but on April 16, 1947, he did use it in a speech he gave at Columbia, South Carolina: "Let us not be deceived—we are today in the midst of a cold war." The term was quickly taken up in the press, and when others seemed to be credited with it—in particular, the distinguished journalist Walter Lippmann—Swope wrote Lippmann to set the record straight. Swope claimed that he had actually used the term in personal letters in the early 1940s to describe the United States' ambiguous situation before Pearl Harbor; he also said he had used it in a speech in 1945.

The *Oxford English Dictionary,* however, shows a somewhat different genealogy for the term. It credits the well-known British author George Orwell with first using Cold War in its current sense in a newspaper column on October 19, 1945; the dictionary then cites a second use by Orwell in another British newspaper, the *Observer,* on March 10, 1946. So, although Swope may have thought of the term on his own, it appears Orwell independently came up with it and gave it currency in England before it was given currency in the United States. In any case, the term also gave rise to "cold warrior" to describe someone who advocated especially strenuous action against Communists.

iron curtain

Borrowing a figure of speech in use since at least the early 1900s, Winston Churchill immortalized that term on March 5, 1946, in an address at Westminster College, in Fulton, Missouri. He acknowledged the division of the Allies' wartime alliance into two enemy camps, observing: "From Stettin in the Baltic to Trieste in the Adriatic, an iron curtain has descended across the Continent." It has since been shown that Churchill actually first used the term in a letter to President Harry S. Truman on May 12, 1945.

That symbolic barrier between the Eastern and Western blocs of Europe was effectively removed with the demolition of the Berlin Wall in November 1989.

We will bury you.

The belligerence of Nikita Khrushchev's alleged boast to Western diplomats on November 18, 1956, caused an uproar. (He evidently said it at a reception at the Polish Embassy in Moscow.) He tried for several years to explain that he had been referring to the inevitable outcome of historical process rather than military aggression, but some Americans remained firmly convinced that those were fighting words from a leader eager for an opportunity to invade the United States. It has been suggested, however, that a fairer translation of his boast is, "We shall be present at your funeral," meaning that Communism would outlast capitalism.

better dead than Red

Around 1960, the slogan of Great Britain's Campaign for Nuclear Disarmament, adapted from British philosopher/pacifist Bertrand Russell's writings, was "better Red than dead." Cold War hawks, contemptuous of a position they judged cowardly, inverted the words to form the phrase quoted on p. 560. That more militant version tapped more deeply into public fear and defiance of the Communists and became a popular American slogan. A variation of this is one that still appears on the license plates of New Hampshire: "Live Free or Die." In turn, that New Hampshire state motto is a direct descendant of the protest attributed to Patrick Henry, "give me liberty or give me death!" (see American Revolution, Notable Phrases, p. 105).

military-industrial complex

President Dwight D. Eisenhower had not expressed much concern in public for the economic and political dangers inherent in a large standing defense establishment. But in his farewell address on January 17, 1961, he said: "We must guard against the acquisition of unwarranted influence, whether sought or unsought, by the military-industrial complex. The potential for the disastrous rise of misplaced power exists and will persist." It has been claimed that Eisenhower originally intended to refer to the "military-industrial-scientific complex," but his science adviser, James Killian, persuaded him to drop the word *scientific*.

hawks vs. doves

At the time of the Cuban missile crisis in 1962, that became a convenient and catchy contrast of those who advocated a more aggressive, even military response to opponents of the United States, and those who advocated conciliation. Both words have distinguished ancestries. To begin with, a *hawk* is a bird of prey, and its name has long been applied to people who behave in an aggressive or combative way. Thomas Jefferson, is said to have coined the term *war hawk* (in a 1798 letter to James Madison) and applied it to Federalists, who wanted to go to war with France. *War hawk* was revived in 1810 and applied to those who seemed itching to go to war against England (see War of 1812, Causes of the War, p. 141). A dove, however, has been the symbol of peace at least since ancient Greece and Biblical times. Although the term was used at least once in print in 1930 in this sense of a peace-lover, its modern revival may be traced to

Pablo Picasso's painting of a dove, which was adopted in the 1950s by the international Communist movement as a symbol of peace. The *hawks vs. doves* analogy was then revived by journalists during the debate over the Cuban missile crisis in October 1962 and again during the Vietnam War.

Ich bin ein Berliner

Addressing a large crowd at the Rudolph Wilde Platz outside the city hall in West Berlin on June 26, 1963, President John F. Kennedy said, "All free men, wherever they may live, are citizens of Berlin. And therefore as a free man, I take pride in the words '*Ich bin ein Berliner*.'" ("I am a Berliner.") It was later claimed that Kennedy had committed a gaffe because a "Berliner" to Germans referred to a jelly doughnut, but a German authority on the German language has said that, in its context, the phrasing was perfectly acceptable. Perhaps the best way to understand the issue is to imagine a foreigner addressing a crowd in any one of several cities in the United States named Hamburg and proudly saying, "I am happy to say I'm a Hamburger." The speaker would be understood, but there would be a touch of humor.

evil empire

Ronald Reagan used the occasion of a speech to the National Association of Evangelists on March 8, 1983, to attack the immorality of the Soviet Union. In characterizing the Cold War as "the struggle between right and wrong, good and evil," Reagan called the Soviet Union an "evil empire." Its melodrama and science fiction overtones made that phrase an instant American catchphrase. As with so many such memorable presidential phrases, this one was credited to a speechwriter, Anthony R. Dolan, but it appears to have been an echo if not a direct allusion to *The Empire Strikes Back* (1980), the sequel of the immensely popular movie *Star Wars* (1977). That latter movie, in turn, lent its name to the highly complicated and expensive technological defense system that Reagan proposed on March 23, 1983; Reagan called the defense system the Strategic Defense Initiative and complained when the media quickly dubbed it "Star Wars," but the label stuck.

SONGS

Setting aside the songs inspired by the Korean War and the Vietnam War (see Songs, Korean War p. 601, and Vietnam War, p. 654-655), the Cold War did not appear to inspire any popular music. At least not in the United States: Presumably, people in lands most directly affected by the Cold War—Germany, Poland, Cuba, as well as others—had many popular songs about events and moods. The only songs that might be characterized as "Cold War" music were those of Tom Lehrer, the Harvard mathematics instructor who in the mid-1950s attained a small but devoted audience for his satirical and black humor songs. Eventually, he recorded many of his songs, accompanying himself on the piano, but they never gained much of a following beyond college campuses. Many of his songs were about current events, but two that came close to being Cold War songs were the "MLF Lullaby" (1964) and "Wernher von Braun" (1965). In the former, a satiric look at the multilateral forces (MLF), he sang:

> We've got the missiles, peace to determine,
> And one of the fingers on the button will
> be German.
> Hail to our loyal ally!
> MLF
> Will scare Brezhnev.
> I hope he is half as scared as I.

And in the latter, he took potshots at the German who converted from making rocket bombs for the Nazis to making rockets for the U.S. space program:

> You too may be a big hero,
> Once you've learned
> To count backwards to zero.
> "In German oder English,
> I know how to count down,
> Und I'm learning Chinese,"
> says Wernher von Braun.

HISTORICAL PERSPECTIVES AND CONTROVERSIES

Who began the Cold War?

The origin of the Cold War is the subject of many books and much scholarly disagreement. In the early years of the Cold War, most Americans took it for granted that Stalin in particular, and the Soviet Union in general, were to blame. The Soviets' post–World War II annexation of Eastern Europe and incursions into the Near East and Mediterranean were evidence of an aggressively expansionist ideology. Traditionalist historians such as Adam Ulam asserted that the United States bravely and responsibly shouldered the burden of countering Stalin's global challenge. Some historians of that school suggested that President Franklin D. Roosevelt's conciliation toward Stalin at Yalta and U.S. withdrawal from the Chinese civil war helped to entrench the Cold War, but historians now recognized that Winston Churchill bore at least as much responsibility for conceding Communist control of Eastern Europe to Stalin.

American revisionist historians in the 1960s and 1970s, disillusioned by the U.S. adventure in Vietnam, began to reassess the relative contributions of the United States and the Soviet Union to the Cold War. In the view of Stephen Ambrose, Walter LaFeber, Daniel Yergin, and other revisionist scholars, Stalin was simply pursuing limited and reasonable security aims; U.S. actions triggered the Cold War. U.S. open door diplomacy after World War II served the needs of what was essentially capitalist imperialism and, along with the abrupt withdrawal of lend-lease aid to the Soviet Union, was perceived as hostile by the Soviets. President Harry S. Truman was the real aggressor in those narratives. Those analysts point out that the Soviets could hardly claim superpower status in 1945: Their population and infrastructure had suffered terrible losses, and world domination was an unlikely goal, given the Soviet's economic weakness.

The opening of Soviet archives in recent years and the declassification and release of early Cold War documents in the West have allowed contemporary post-revisionist historians (John Lewis Gaddis is the most prominent) to take a more rigorous look at the early post–World War II years. A less ideological, more realistic picture is emerging, in which both sides are seen to have been pragmatically pursuing their own interests and ensuring a geopolitical balance of power. Historians of that school recognize that the United States had no coherent foreign policy immediately after World War II and that Europe and to some extent Asia were political vacuums. Washington and Moscow each had complex motivations and constraints without the benefit of mutual trust or understanding or accurate information about each other's policymaking. In other words, both sides share responsibility for the Cold War.

Did either side win the Cold War? If one side won, how did it do so? What does victory in such a conflict mean?

On the surface, at least, it seems that the United States and its allies were the ideological, economic, and political victors in the Cold War. Ample proof was afforded by the spectacle in the 1990s of former Warsaw Pact nations and Soviet republics rushing to implement free-market and democratic reforms and clamoring for admission to NATO and the European Union. The huge military forces and nuclear arsenals that had bankrupted the Soviet economy had not sold its people on Communism as an ideology. It turned out that nothing was holding the Soviet Union and Warsaw Pact together except the Red Army. The Poles, Hungarians, and Czechs had repeatedly rebelled against the Communist governments imposed on them after World War II. The Red Army suppressed those uprisings, but ultimately, as William Hyland has noted, "freedom was stronger." The far-flung Soviet system was completely dismantled; Russia lost its empire.

If it seems clear that the West won, then how did it do so? Some argue that, in the simplest terms, the Cold War ended when the Soviet economy imploded from years of military spending and financial overcommitments to its overseas empire. In that scenario, the Soviet Union unilaterally lost the struggle because of contradictions inherent in its system: After years of overwhelming military budgets, heavy foreign aid commitments, and failed economic reforms, centralized Communist planners were simply unable to supply their people with food and basic commodities. (Related to that explanation is the claim that Mikhail Gorbachev's opening the doors to social freedoms only exposed the economic failures.) But against that view is the argument that the Soviet Union was defeated by the West's pressures of containment, nuclear deterrence, and, more specifically, the Reagan administration's

arms buildup of the 1980s. If it is accepted that the Soviet Union's version of Communism was inherently expansionist-imperialistic-militaristic, then clearly it had to be combated by military might.

The complexities of this subject continue to occupy historians. The essays in Michael Hogan's *End of the Cold War* offer a variety of perspectives on the scholarly debate. They range from Arthur Schlesinger's sunny assessment (democracy won the political war; free-market capitalism, the economic war) to a provocative analysis by the Soviet historian Alexei Filitov. Filitov argues that although the Soviet Union certainly lost the Cold War, the United States can hardly be said to have won. Overriding national security requirements led the U.S. government to compromise democratic principles and political rationality; Americans suffered from the psychological insecurity and economic distortion engendered by the nuclear doctrine of mutual assured destruction. Filitov argues that if anyone won the Cold War, it was Germany and Japan, which did so by building strong civilian economies. In the final analysis, however, he believes that the Cold War was essentially an arms race and was, therefore, by definition unwinnable.

Why did Khrushchev deploy missiles to Cuba in 1962?

According to the memoirs of Nikita Khrushchev and his close advisers, Khrushchev's paramount reason was to defend Fidel Castro from further CIA plots and Cuba from what Khrushchev regarded as almost certain invasion by the United States. Almost incidentally, he acknowledged his desire to address the strategic imbalance created by the long-standing placement of U.S. military bases around the globe and the more recent siting of U.S. nuclear missiles in Turkey, Great Britain, and Italy. The story is told at length in Michael Beschloss's *The Crisis Years*.

Most historians dismiss Khrushchev's Cuban defense rationale. Instead, they stress what he treated as incidental: Soviet nuclear inferiority galled Khrushchev, and the imbalance of power was intolerable to him. Khrushchev had failed to get the United States out of Europe, to prevent the creation of West Germany, and to dislodge the United States from West Berlin. By mid-1962, talks on Germany's future were stalemated. William Hyland and other historians point out that installing Soviet nuclear missiles in the Western Hemisphere might not only have forced the U.S. to conclude a German agreement but might also have been used to bargain for the removal of U.S. missiles in Turkey.

Those close to Khrushchev have claimed he intended to reveal the presence of the missiles in Cuba after the 1964 presidential elections. He clearly expected President John F. Kennedy to accept their presence as a fait accompli (as had happened with the Berlin Wall the previous year), for the missiles were sited in permanent installations. Instead, U.S. intelligence discovered the warheads, and President Kennedy threatened war unless they were removed.

Historians are unanimous that Khrushchev misjudged Kennedy's strength of purpose and willingness to risk nuclear war. The Cuban missile crisis did, however, gain Khrushchev one important strategic concession, negotiated in secret: U.S. missiles were quietly removed from Turkey in 1963.

CIVILIAN AND MILITARY BIOGRAPHIES

AMERICAN

Acheson, Dean (1893–1971)—diplomat, secretary of state: Dean Acheson was born in Middletown, Connecticut. He brought to the Cold War the impeccable credentials of the U.S. Establishment: Yale College, Harvard Law School, private secretary to Supreme Court Justice Louis Brandeis (1919–1921), and after a successful law practice, posts with the State Department from 1941 on. As undersecretary of state (1945–1947), Acheson became a staunch proponent of the policy of containment of the Soviet Union and Communism; to that end, he promoted the Marshall Plan (rebuilding Europe) and the Truman Doctrine (intervention in Greece and Turkey). Then as President Harry S. Truman's secretary of state (1947–1953), he played a crucial role in creating NATO, reconstructing Germany, fighting the Korean War, and isolating Communist China. Acheson left the government under Dwight D. Eisenhower but served as an occasional adviser to Presidents John F. Kennedy

and Lyndon B. Johnson; only when Vietnam was clearly a disaster (in March 1968) did he become one of the "wise men" who advised getting out. Expressive of how tangled the Cold War was, Sen. Joseph McCarthy tried to blame Acheson for "coddling" Communists in the State Department and for "losing" China to the Communists, but most historians regard Acheson as a loyal if low-key cold warrior.

Carter, Jimmy (1924–)—president: Jimmy Carter was the son of a Georgia peanut farmer. He was elected governor of Georgia in 1970; he came out of nowhere to win the 1976 Democratic presidential nomination and then the presidency. Although he enjoyed some success, such as the signing of the Camp David Accords and the SALT II Treaty, his administration was plagued by a series of crises with which he seemed ill-prepared to deal. The Iran hostage crisis and the Soviet invasion of Afghanistan, both in 1979, led many to question Carter's ability to manage foreign affairs. One of Carter's final foreign policy acts as president was initiating a U.S. led boycott of the Summer Olympic Games in Moscow.

Dulles, Allen (1893–1969)—CIA director: Allen Dulles was the brother of John Foster Dulles. Allen Dulles was a foreign service officer and lawyer. He became the first civilian director of the Central Intelligence Agency (1953–1961). He authorized covert operations in Iran, Guatemala, and elsewhere, which became extremely controversial and set a pattern for future CIA operations. He resigned after the Bay of Pigs debacle (1961) in Cuba.

Dulles, John Foster (1888–1959)—secretary of state: John Foster Dulles was born in Washington, D.C. He was a distinguished international lawyer. As President Dwight Eisenhower's secretary of state (1953–1959) Dulles was a rigid anti-Communist and the chief architect of the U.S. Cold War strategy of aggressive containment. He encircled the Soviet Union through a network of regional alliances, including SEATO and the Baghdad Pact, presided over an arms buildup designed for "massive retaliation," and engaged in geopolitical brinkmanship with the Soviets. (In an interview with *LIFE* magazine in 1956, Dulles boasted of daring "to go to the brink" of war with the Soviet Union.)

Eisenhower, Dwight (1890–1969)—president: Dwight D. Eisenhower emerged from World War II as a relative moderate on matters to do with the

Soviet Union and Communism. Even as head of NATO, designed to counter a potential Soviet threat in Europe, he was not one for saber rattling. Elected president in 1952, he set to work to negotiate an end to the Korean War. Asked to intervene to help fight the faltering French in Vietnam he offered only financial aid. He dealt calmly with the Soviet leaders, but there was never any doubt as to where he stood in his opposition to Communism. On the home front of the Cold War, he was no rabid anti-Communist, but he refused to save Julius and Ethel Rosenberg from execution (see March 29, 1951, p. 535), and he was slow to defend his former comrade George Marshall from McCarthy's charge (see George Marshall, below). Among the ranks of cold warriors, Eisenhower would probably be known as a strong-but-silent type.

Hiss, Alger (1904–1996)—government official: Alger Hiss was a lawyer by training. He was an influential State Department official (1936–1947), accompanying President Franklin Roosevelt to Yalta. While serving as the president of the Carnegie Endowment for International Peace (1947–1949), Hiss was accused in 1948 of spying for the Soviets in the 1930s by Whittaker Chambers, a confessed Communist courier and perjurer. Hiss became a major target of the House Committee on Un-American Activities, and after denying Chambers' charges, he was convicted of perjury in 1950. (Because of the statute of limitations, Hiss could not be charged with anything more serious.) He spent nearly four years in jail, then devoted the rest of his life to clearing his name; he was never able to prove his innocence conclusively, and at least some disinterested scholars believe that he did pass some documents, whatever their value, to the Soviets.

Kennedy, John Fitzgerald (1917–1963)—president: After his naval service in World War II, Kennedy represented his native Massachusetts in the U.S. House of Representatives (1947–1953) and in the U.S. Senate (1953–1961). As president (1961–1963), he balanced liberal domestic programs with a tough anti-Communist foreign policy: He greatly increased U.S. military spending, and after the failed Bay of Pigs invasion of Cuba in 1961, faced down Nikita Khrushchev during the Cuban missile crisis (1962). In more peaceful reinforcements of U.S. influence, he established the Peace Corps and Alliance for Progress (see Civilian and Military

Biographies, Vietnam War chapter, p. 662).

Kissinger, Henry (1923–)government adviser, secretary of state: Henry Kissinger came to the United States as a young refugee from Nazi Germany. He spent his career fighting a different form of tyranny, Communism. He earned his Ph.D. at Harvard (1954) and while still an obscure academic, attracted some attention with the realistic observations in his book *Nuclear Weapons and Foreign Policy* (1957). He was an occasional adviser on foreign policy to presidents Dwight Eisenhower, John Kennedy, and Lyndon Johnson, but he only gained real influence when President Richard Nixon appointed him national security adviser and then secretary of state. Kissinger was a staunch opponent of Communism, but as a pragmatic politician, he worked hard to negotiate an end to the Vietnam War and to aid Nixon in the "opening" of China. The common theme throughout his career as a cold warrior was a dispassionate realpolitik.

Marshall, George (1880–1959)—secretary of state, secretary of defense: As chief of staff during World War II, George Marshall played a crucial if undramatic role in the Allies' victory. Named secretary of state by President Harry S. Truman in 1947, Marshall announced the plan to aid Europe's economic recovery (what became known as the Marshall Plan), widely credited with stopping the spread of Communism in Europe. He also helped to lay the groundwork for NATO. He resigned because of ill health in January 1949, but in September 1950, after the Korean War began, he became Secretary of Defense; he served in that post until September 1951. Never one for rhetorical statements or actions, he was clearly a foe of everything Communism stood for, so it came as a shock when in 1951 Sen. Joseph McCarthy accused Marshall of having been "soft" on Communism.

McCarthy, Joseph R. (1909–1957)—senator: Joseph McCarthy was a judge in his native Wisconsin before being elected to the U.S. Senate (1947–1957). In 1950, he charged that the State Department was riddled with Communist infiltrators. His televised Senate hearings on Communist influence in U.S. government agencies contributed greatly to the "Red scare" of the Eisenhower years. Most observers have since concluded that the hearings were based on Republican partisanship, unsubstantiated allegations, and a form of psychosis (both McCarthy's and the nation's), but the hearings destroyed the careers of many of those charged. A censure by the Senate in 1954 finally neutralized McCarthy's power, but "McCarthyism" entered the American lexicon as a synonym for a modern-day witch-hunt.

McNamara, Robert (1916–)—secretary of defense: First in the U.S. Air Force in World War II and then with the Ford Motor Company, Robert McNamara gained a reputation as a whiz kid, a genius for solving complicated problems by strictly "objective" analyses. President John F. Kennedy appointed McNamara secretary of defense in 1961, with the goal of introducing cost effeciency methods to the military establishment. With Kennedy's passing, McNamara put his expertise to work for President Johnson's policies in Vietnam.

Nixon, Richard Milhous (1913–1994)— congressman, vice president, president: Richard Nixon was born in Yorba Linda, California. In many respects, he was the archetypal cold warrior: Much of his political career was associated with the fight against Communism and the Soviet Union. He gained a national reputation as an anti-Communist, in particular while serving in the House of Representative (1947–1951) on the House Un-American Activities Committee during the Alger Hiss spy case. As Dwight Eisenhower's vice president (1953–1961), Nixon often played bad cop to Eisenhower's good cop by stridently attacking international and domestic Communists. After losing his presidential bid to John F. Kennedy in 1960, Nixon returned in 1968 to defeat Hubert Humphrey for the presidency with a promise to end the Vietnam War. Reelected in 1972, Nixon enlarged and increased the U.S. role in Indochina until negotiating a withdrawal in 1973. His obsession with the antiwar elements in the government eventually led to the Watergate break-in of 1972, which in turn led Nixon in 1974 to become the first U.S. president to resign.

Reagan, Ronald Wilson (1911–)—president: Ronald Reagan was born in Illinois. He became a popular film actor and governor of California (1967–1975). His two-term Republican presidency (1981–1989), marking a conservative shift in U.S. politics, began with intemperate attacks on the Soviet "evil empire"; he sent U.S. troops into Lebanon, Grenada, and Honduras; he increased defense spending on new weap-

ons, including the controversial Star Wars system. He developed a genuine rapport with Mikhail Gorbachev, and arms control agreements were major achievements of his administration.

Truman, Harry S. (1884–1972)—president: Harry S. Truman inherited the task of closing down World War II. It also fell to him to initiate the United States' role in the Cold War. From his first conference with Joseph Stalin at Potsdam in July 1945, Truman took a hard line against the Soviets and Communism. By sponsoring the recovery plan for Europe (the Marshall Plan) and committing the U.S. military to prevent the spread of Communism in Greece and Turkey (the Truman Doctrine), he set the pattern for the United States in the Cold War for the next 40 years: economic aid for anti-Communists, military operations against pro-Communists. On the home front, he was resolutely anti-Communist but he avoided the excesses of McCarthyism. Truman's conduct of the Cold War was like so much that he did, not an eloquent ideological crusade but a down-to-earth resistance to the unacceptable.

SOVIETS

Brezhnev, Leonid (Ilyich) (1906–1982)—political leader: Leonid Brezhnev assisted the Stalinist purges in the 1930s, became a military commissar, and succeeded Nikita Khrushchev in 1964. During his long tenure, Brezhnev oversaw the huge military buildup that made the Soviet Union a true superpower. The Brezhnev Doctrine mandated military intervention to preserve other Communist regimes; he ordered the invasions of Czechoslovakia (1968) and Afghanistan (1979) and cultivated Third World client nations. At the same time, he and foreign minister Andrei Gromyko aggressively sought détente and achieved major arms agreements.

Gorbachev, Mikhail S. (1931–)—political leader, Soviet president: Mikhail Gorbachev was trained as a lawyer. He was a Communist Party activist from his student days and advanced steadily through the party ranks. Through his position as general secretary of the Communist Party (1985–1991; he did not become president of the Soviet Union until 1990), he developed a close working relationship with Ronald Reagan, whose vehement anti-Communism was disarmed by Gorbachev's relaxed charm and energetic pursuit of détente. His domestic reforms of *perestroika* (economic restructuring) and *glasnost* (openness) took on an unanticipated momentum of their own, leading to the democratization of Eastern Europe and the end of the Cold War. He was awarded the Nobel Peace Prize (1990) for those achievements, but the attendant political unrest in Russia forced his resignation as the Soviet Union disintegrated.

Gromyko, Andrei (1909–1989)—diplomat: Andrei Gromyko was born in Minsk, Belorussia. After studying agriculture and economics, in 1939 he joined the staff at the Soviet embassy in Washington, D.C., becoming ambassador to the United States in 1943. In 1946, he became the Soviet Union's permanent delegate to the UN, and for over a decade, he stood firm at the UN and at other international conferences as the Soviets' main representative to the international community, casting a veto 25 times to stop UN actions the Soviet Union disapproved of. In 1957, he became the Soviet Union's foreign minister, and for two decades, he seemed to personify Soviet Communism's cold war—with his icy demeanor and implacable defense of Soviet policies. By the late 1970s, he began to relax somewhat as part of Soviet Union's new policy of détente, and by the time he retired in 1985, he had become a cooperative, if not genial, worker in thawing the Cold War.

Khrushchev, Nikita S. (1894–1971)—political leader: A committed Communist Party member from 1918, Nikita Khrushchev successfully negotiated Joseph Stalin's purges to become the party's first secretary (1953–1964) and Soviet premier (1958–1964). He committed the Soviets to "rocket diplomacy" by creating a nuclear arsenal and actively extended the Cold War to Third World countries such as Cuba, the Congo, and Indonesia. Although he maintained a working relationship with the West, he was unpredictable, crude, and pugnacious: He miscalculated American intentions during the Cuban missile crisis (1962). His failed economic and agricultural reforms prompted his removal from office by the Politburo.

Stalin, Joseph (1879–1953)—political leader: A Bolshevik activist and protégé of Vladimir Lenin, Joseph Stalin took control of the Communist Party and the Soviet government in 1928. His 25-year dictatorship endured by means of a relentlessly enforced personality cult, a brutal secret police force, and the elimination of political opponents: an estimated 20 million Russians were killed in purges, executions, and labor camps; millions more were imprisoned. After leading the Soviet Union through World War II, Stalin presided over the division of his wartime alliance into opposing Cold War blocs and the heavy industrialization and early nuclear armament of the Soviet Union.

OTHER NATIONALITIES

Adenauer, Konrad (1876–1967)—West German political leader: The Nazis removed Konrad Adenauer from the mayoralty (1917–1933) of his native Cologne. Returning to politics after World War II, he founded the centrist Christian Democratic Union and drafted West Germany's democratic constitution. As West Germany's first chancellor (1949–1963), Adenauer was a staunch anti-Communist and strong proponent of NATO and the Western Alliance. He adroitly used Western aid in overseeing West Germany's economic recovery.

Brandt, Willy (1913–1992)—West German leader: Willy Brandt was born Karl Herbert Frahm. He changed his name as an expatriate anti-Nazi activist in Scandinavia (1933–1945). As mayor of West Berlin (1957–1966) and West German foreign minister (1966–1969) and chancellor (1969–1974), he was the architect of *Ostpolitik*, a successful strategy of engagement with the Eastern bloc that won him the Nobel Peace Prize (1971). In later years he championed development aid to the Third World.

Castro, Fidel (1927–   )—revolutionary, leader of Cuba: Fidel Castro is the son of a prosperous sugar planter. He studied law and briefly practiced, but from student days on he plotted to overthrow Fulgencio Batista, the dictator of Cuba. Castro's first attempt in July 1953 failed, and he spent almost two years in prison. He fled to Mexico after his release from prison and organized the invasion and uprising that led to his triumphant entry into Havana in January 1959. As dictator of Cuba in the decades that followed, he exploited the Cold War by, for instance, getting the Soviet Union virtually to subsidize Cuba's shaky enonomy by buying overpriced Cuban sugar and selling underpriced Russian oil. Castro weathered various crises—the Bay of Pigs invasion, the Cuban missile crisis, mass exoduses of Cubans—and maintained considerable popular support for his social reforms. But with the end of the Cold War and the loss of Soviet support, by the mid-1990s Castro found himself presiding over a country that gave signs of approaching the end that marked most of the other Communist countries.

Nasser, Gamal Abdel (1918–1970)—Egyptian political leader: Nasser became a passionate nationalist in his youth and led the overthrow of King Farouk (1952). As Egypt's charismatic prime minister (1954–1956) and president (1956–1970), he was lionized for nationalizing the Suez Canal in the face of British and French military intervention (1956) and for modernizing Egypt through such grand projects as the construction of the Aswan High Dam.

Nehru, Jawaharlal (1889–1964)—Indian political leader: Nehru was educated in England. As a young lawyer in India, he was repeatedly jailed during the nationalists' struggle for independence. He was the first prime minister of independent India (1947–1964). A reform socialist, Nehru sought to mold his country into a secular industrialized state, using aid from both the Eastern and Western blocs. As the moving force behind the 1955 Bandung Conference of nonaligned nations, he tried to effect a reconciliation or at least improved relations between the two sides in the Cold War.

Philby, Kim (Harold Adrian Russell) (1912–1988)—British double agent: While a student at Cambridge in 1933, Philby was recruited as a Soviet spy. During his 30-year career as a British intelligence officer, he supplied the Soviets with top-secret British and American security information. He arranged the escape of British double agents Guy Burgess and Donald MacLean in 1951; he defected in 1963 to Moscow, where he joined the British section of the KGB.

Sukarno (Kusno Sosro) (1901–1970)—Indonesian political leader: Following local custom, Sukarno dropped his first two names in childhood. A nationalist leader, he collaborated with the occupying Japanese during World War II. After declaring Indonesia's independence from the Dutch, he was its first president (1949–1967). His "guided democracy" was, in fact, a corrupt dictatorship, and Sukarno flouted his declarations of non-alignment by cultivating ties with the Soviet Union and China. He lost public support after murdering 300,000 political opponents and was overthrown by General Suharto in 1966.

Thatcher, Margaret (1925–   )—British prime minister: Margaret Thatcher studied chemistry at Oxford but went on to London to become a lawyer. Elected to Parliament in 1959, she rose quickly in Conservative Party and became its leader in 1975, the first woman to become party leader in British history. As prime minister (1979–1990), she was opposed to everything Communism stood for; she became one of Ronald Reagan's most overt supporters, even when she did not always go along with his methods in dealing with the Soviets. She established good relations with Mikhail Gorbachev in the interest of promoting better relations between the Soviet Union and the West. She fell from power, at least in part because of her resistance to integrating Great Britain within the European Community.

Tito (1892–1980)—Yugoslavian political leader: Tito was born Josip Broz. After fighting in the Russian Revolution, he returned home to organize Yugoslavia's Communist Party in 1920; "Tito" was his party name. He led the partisan resistance during the Nazi occupation of Yugoslavia (1941–1945). As prime minister (1945–1953) and president (1953–1980) of Yugoslavia, Tito broke with the Soviets over his unique brand of socialism, which incorporated free-market forces and other elements intolerable to Stalin.

Walesa, Lech (1943–   )—reformer, president of Poland: Lech Walesa was an electrician in the Lenin Shipyard of Gdansk (1966-1976) when he became active in the union movement. Fired in 1976 for his open protest of government policies, he was reemployed in 1980 and thereafter helped to organize an independent trade union called Solidarity. During 1980–1981, he organized a series of strikes that forced the Communist Polish government to agree to some reforms, but in December 1981 he was arrested and Solidarity was outlawed. Walesa was released in November 1982, by which time he had become an international symbol of courage in the face of totalitarianism; he was awarded the Nobel Prize for Peace in 1983. By 1988 he had forced the Polish Communist government to re-legalize Solidarity and to establish a somewhat more liberal "socialist democracy." In 1990, he became president in Poland's first direct presidential election but did not to have the temperament for handling the compromises and challenges of democratic government and in 1995 he lost his bid for a second term and retired to private life.

FURTHER READING

Allison, Graham T. *Essence of Decision: Explaining the Cuban Missile Crisis*. Boston: Little, Brown & Co., 1971.

Ambrose, Stephen E. *Rise to Globalism: American Foreign Policy since 1938*. New York: Penguin Books, 1993.

Beschloss, Michael R. *The Crisis Years: Kennedy and Khrushchev, 1960-1963*. New York: Edward Burlingame Books, 1991.

Beschloss, Michael R. and Strobe Talbott. *At the Highest Levels: The Inside Story of the End of the Cold War*. Boston: Little, Brown & Co., 1993.

Bundy, McGeorge. *Danger and Survival: Choices about the Bomb in the First Fifty Years*. New York: Vintage Books, 1990.

Caute, David. *The Great Fear: The Anti-Communist Purge under Truman and Eisenhower*. New York: Simon & Schuster, 1978.

Freedman, Lawrence. *The Evolution of Nuclear Strategy*. New York: St. Martin's Press, 1989.

Gaddis, John Lewis. *The Long Peace: Inquiries into the History of the Cold War*. New York: Oxford University Press, 1987.

————*Russia, the Soviet Union, and the U.S.* New York: McGraw Hill, 1990.

Halle, Louis. *The Cold War as History*. London: Chatto & Windus, 1967.

Hogan, Michael J. *The Marshall Plan: America, Britain and the Reconstruction of Western Europe, 1947–1952*. Cambridge and New York: Cambridge University Press, 1987.

————, ed. *The End of the Cold War: Its Meaning and Implications*. Cambridge and New York: Cambridge University Press, 1992.

Hyland, William G. *The Cold War: Fifty Years of Conflict*. New York: Times Books, 1991.

Inglis, Fred. *The Cruel Peace: Everyday Life in the Cold War*. New York: Basic Books, 1991.

Jervis, Robert. *The Illogic of American Nuclear Strategy*. Ithaca, N.Y.: Cornell University Press, 1984.

Kennan, George. *Memoirs*. Boston: Little, Brown & Co., 1972.

Levering, Ralph B. *The Cold War: A Post-Cold War History*. Arlington Heights, Ill.: Harlan Davidson, 1994.

Paterson, Thomas G. *Meeting the Communist Threat: Truman to Reagan*. New York: Oxford University Press, 1988.

————and Robert J. McMahon, eds. *The Origins of the Cold War*. Lexington, Mass.: D. C. Heath, 1991.

Rhodes, Richard. *The Making of the Atomic Bomb*. New York: Penguin Books, 1988.

Whitfield, Stephen. *The Culture of the Cold War*. Baltimore, Md.: Johns Hopkins University Press, 1996.

Yergin, Daniel. *Shattered Peace: The Origins of the Cold War and the National Security State*. Boston: Houghton Mifflin, 1990.

THE KOREAN WAR

DATES OF WAR

June 25, 1950–July 27, 1953

ALTERNATE NAMES

Korean Conflict. Korean Police Action.

SIGNIFICANCE

At one point in September 1950, it appeared that the fighting in Korea would be little more than a footnote in history, a limited military operation aimed at restoring the status quo before the hostilities. Instead, the war dragged on for three years, with high losses on both sides: The Korean War is the United States' fifth most costly war in terms of casualties.

Arguably the greatest significance of the Korean War is that the two great superpowers, the United States and the Soviet Union, avoided a direct military confrontation. At the same time, the war demonstrated that the United States was willing to use military forces to "contain" the spread of Communism.

The Korean War was also significant because it was the first test of the ability of the United Nations (UN) to resist international aggression. The UN had been set up in the glare of World War II and in the shadow of the League of Nations, which had failed to resist naked aggression in the 1930s. Beyond that, the UN's action in Korea showed that the organization's effectiveness in international crises would depend largely on U.S. leadership, commitment, manpower, money, and material.

Finally, the Korean War was significant because it established the security of South Korea and Japan behind a U.S. military shield. That enabled those Asian nations to grow into economic powerhouses within decades.

BACKGROUND

The Korean War's immediate origins date back to 1945, when in the wake of World War II,

Korea was divided into two antagonistic states. In a deeper sense, the roots of the Korean War reached far back into the long history of Korea, which began in the third millennium B.C.; the nation's recorded history began in the second century B.C. By the seventh century A.D., the modern boundaries of Korea had been fairly well established, but during the ensuing centuries, Korea was usually dominated by whoever ruled China—the various Chinese dynasties, the Mongols, the Manchurians. Korea was often caught in the middle of the struggles between China and Japan and, eventually, the struggles between Japan and Russia. The Sino-Japanese War of 1894–1895 was fought over Korea, as was to some degree the Russo-Japanese War of 1904–1905. (Russia wanted to divide Korea at the 39th or 38th parallel and take over the northern part.) Japan won both these wars and was thus emboldened simply to annex Korea as a colony in 1910.

The ensuing 35 years of the Japanese occupation of Korea were harsh and exploitative. In keeping with U.S. president Woodrow Wilson's promise of "self-determination" after World War I (see Negotiations and Peace Treaty, World War I, pp. 406-409), the Korean Provisional Government was established in Shanghai, China, in April 1919; its president was Syngman Rhee, then in exile in the United States. But the Japanese suppressed any efforts by Koreans to gain independence; instead, during the 1930s the Japanese turned Korea into an industrial and military base from which to dominate Manchuria and China.

During World War II, Franklin D. Roosevelt, Winston Churchill, and Chiang Kai-shek, the leaders of the United States, Britain, and China respectively, met at Cairo, Egypt, in December 1943, and declared that Korea should be "free and independent" after the war. That was reaffirmed by the Allied leaders—including the Soviet dictator Joseph Stalin—when they met at Potsdam, Germany, in July 1945.

In the closing days of World War II, anticipating that the Soviets would soon enter the war against Japan, the U.S. military and political leaders realized that the Soviets would most certainly move across all Korea if not stopped at some point. A line was drawn beyond which the Soviets should not pass; they would, however, be responsible for taking the surrender of all Japanese troops north of that line. On August 11, 1945, some U.S. Army officers, with little knowledge of Korea's history or geography, looked at a map of Korea and picked an easily defined line—the 38th parallel. That dividing line fulfilled several criteria that the Americans desired: In particular, it ensured that the American zone of occupation contained Seoul, Korea's capital; Inchon, an important port on Korea's western coast; and Pusan, Korea's main port.

On August 8, 1945, the Soviet Union declared war on Japan and began to move its troops into Manchuria. On August 11, Soviet troops also crossed into Korea (with which the Soviet Union shared an 11-mile border along the eastern coast). The Soviet troops were virtually unimpeded as they moved southward, taking the surrender of Japanese troops they came across. By August 15, when Japan surrendered, the Soviet forces were pulling up to the 38th parallel.

The 38th parallel did not relate to any of the historical, administrative, political, or economic conditions of Korea; above all, it in no way reflected the geographical features of the peninsula. For instance, the 38th parallel cut right across the Ongjin peninsula jutting out from the west coast, isolating the southern part of that peninsula below the 38th parallel. The 38th parallel was and would remain an arbitrary and inconvenient line on a map.

At the time, that seemed of little consequence. The United States assumed that the boundary was only temporary—that, eventually, there would be free elections leading to a united Korea. Instead, the Soviets almost immediately set about to consolidate tighter control over Korea north of the 38th parallel. On October 3, 1945, the Soviet Union introduced the leader of their occupation zone, Kim Il Sung, a Korean Communist who had served in the Soviet army in World War II. By December 1945, the Soviets were erecting fortifications at points along the boundary. They soon turned the 38th parallel into virtually a national border and began to restrict traffic in and out of northern Korea. In addition, they made sure that the only people in northern Korea who had any dealings with the southern Koreans and the Allies were Communists or Communist sympathizers.

As 1946 passed, U.S. military and civilian leaders showed little interest in Korea; their attention was focused on the occupation of Japan and Germany. In Korea, however, the North and South were becoming polarized. In November 1946, the Communist-dominated Korean National Democratic Front tightened its grip on North Korea. A month later, the right-wing supporters of Syngman Rhee gained dominance over the legislative assembly in South Korea. The U.S. State Department accepted this and there was no national debate on the issue. Meanwhile, relations between the Soviet Union and the United States—as well as between North Korea and South Korea—had become so tense that the U.S. brought the issue of Korean independence before the UN General Assembly on September 17, 1947. The UN General Assembly voted on November 14, 1947, for an all-Korea election and named the nine-nation UN Temporary Commission on Korea to oversee it. Eight members of the commission met in Seoul with the intention of putting the election machinery into operation. Subsequently, the Soviets simply refused to allow the election to take place in North Korea; they even refused to let commission members into North Korea. At that point, the commission went back to the United Nations for support.

The UN Interim Committee passed a resolution on February 26, 1948, reaffirming the call for the commission to proceed with the election in as much of Korea as was accessible. The UN commission set the election for May 10, 1948.

The Communist-run People's Committee in North Korea held a conference about unification in Pyongyang, the capital of North Korea, on April 22–23, 1948. The conference, which was attended by some 360 delegates from South Korea, most of them moderates and leftists, ended by issuing a call for the withdrawal of all foreign troops from Korea and for allowing Koreans to settle their own affairs. The U.S. military commander in South Korea, Lt. Gen. John R. Hodges, called the conference a Communist plot.

The only result of the conference was to polarize still further the political situation in Korea. Moderate and leftist Koreans in the south feared that the UN-sponsored election would only freeze a divided Korea in place, and they urged everyone in South Korea to boycott the election. That allowed the rightist party headed by Syngman Rhee to run virtually unopposed.

In the elections held in South Korea on May 10, 1948, the conservatives and rightists won by a large majority and chose the 73-year-old Rhee as their leader. On August 15, 1948, a day deliberately chosen to commemorate the surrender of Japan in 1945, Rhee was inaugurated president of the Republic of Korea (ROK). The U.S. occupation of South Korea came to an end, and U.S. troops began to be withdrawn; the last combat unit left in June 1949.

The Democratic People's Republic of Korea was proclaimed on September 9, 1948, with 30-year-old Kim Il Sung as premier. By the end of December, the Soviets withdrew all their troops beyond the Korean-Soviet border (but left behind hundreds of military advisers).

Korea was now split into two totally polarized and antagonistic states. Some historians have argued that both the Soviet Union and the United States were at least partially at fault for the way they backed the more extreme elements in their respective Koreas. But others have contended that the fault lay entirely with the Soviets, because they never would have allowed truly free elections to take place. Noting that the Soviets had a longtime and deliberate policy of seeking to dominate Korea and establish it as a buffer state between its Far Eastern provinces and Japan, still other historians have characterized the U.S. entry into the Korean labyrinth in the aftermath of World War II as somewhat accidental. Those historians have stated that the United States was anxious to extricate itself.

CAUSES OF THE WAR

Even before the Korean election of 1948 and the formal recognition of the two Koreas, there had been occasional hostile encounters along the 38th parallel between elements of the two countries. In addition, North Koreans had secretly moved into the mountainous regions of South Korea; from there they mounted terrorist actions against southern forces. Kim Il Sung openly boasted of that. (Many thousands of Koreans were killed during what was effectively a civil war between 1945 and 1950.) Syngman Rhee, meanwhile, was openly calling for war against North Korea, with the goal of uniting Korea under his rule.

Both North Korea and South Korea were led by autocratic leaders, and both had managed to build up fairly large military forces—North Korea with the support of the Soviets, South Korea with the support of the United States. The Korean peninsula was becoming contested ground in the Cold War which was just then moving into full gear. At points all across the world, the Soviet Union and the United States were moving into confrontation. In Asia, the United States found itself on the defensive against the Communists, who under Mao Tse-tung had taken over control of China in September 1949.

After taking over the Chinese mainland, which became known as the People's Republic of China, the Communist Chinese soon threatened to invade Taiwan (then known as Formosa), the large island-province off China's southern coast. Chiang Kai-shek, his Nationalist government, remnants of the Nationalist army, and many of their followers had fled to Taiwan in the closing days of their struggle against the Communists. In December 1949, the Nationalists officially moved their capital to Taipei, Taiwan. From their island bastion, which then became know as Nationalist China (formally the Republic of China), the Nationalists insisted they were still the legitimate government of all China.

Meanwhile, the Soviet Union argued that the Communist government was entitled to China's seat in the United Nations. On January 13, 1950, the Soviet delegate to the UN, Jacob Malik, proposed a resolution expelling the Nationalist Chinese from the UN. It was defeated by the 11-member Security Council, 6-3 (Britain and Norway abstained). Malik immediately walked out of the Security Council and said that the Soviet Union would boycott the UN until the Nationalist Chinese were expelled. That eventually had a fateful effect on the UN's actions on Korea.

About the same time, two U.S. government leaders made statements that had a profound effect on events in Korea. On January 5, 1950, President Harry S. Truman announced that the United States had no intention of establishing military bases on Taiwan or in any way becoming "involved in the civil conflict in China." Then, exactly a week later, on January 12, 1950, Secretary of State Dean Acheson gave a speech at the National Press Club in Washington, D.C. He stated that the "defensive perimeter"—in effect, the border that the United States would be prepared to defend against Communism—ran from the Aleutians to Japan, then along the Ryukyu Islands (which included Okinawa) down to the Philippine Islands. He went on to say that "it must be clear that no person can guarantee [other] areas against military attack."

Acheson was later widely criticized for having made that statement, but he was simply repeating the established U.S. policy at the time. Not that many years removed from the casualties and costs of World War II, most Americans had little desire to become involved in a war in Asia. But the Communist Chinese and the Soviets—and the North Koreans—presumably noticed that neither Taiwan nor Korea fell within the "defensive perimeter." Kim Il Sung, the ruler of North Korea, must have also believed that either Communist China or the Soviet Union, possibly both, would come to his aid if he ever got into trouble with the United States. It was long thought that Stalin gave little or no support to Kim's plan to invade the South, but documents discovered in the Soviet files in the mid-1990s reveal that Stalin did in fact give full support and that he later sided with North Korea in persuading China to join in the fight. Most scholars, however, have contended that Stalin did not put Kim Il Sung up to the invasion of South Korea but simply told him to proceed as he saw fit (see Historical Perspectives and Controversies, pp. 601-602).

Whatever his motives and thoughts may have been, Kim Il Sung looked to South Korea and undoubtedly saw a country that had superior agricultural land as well as most of the best cities and ports; he evidently wanted to absorb that competitor and decided that with a surprise attack he could probably do so. He knew, too, that the aging Syngman Rhee had lost popularity, that many South Koreans wanted a change in government, and that most Koreans longed for a united country. His error lay in believing that they would be willing to welcome him as ruler of a united Korea.

PREPARATIONS FOR WAR

In the years since the division of Korea at the 38th parallel, the North Koreans had built up a fairly strong army—well-trained, well-disciplined, and relatively well equipped by the Soviets with everything from tanks and artillery to fighter

planes. In the weeks preceding the Korean War, the North Koreans concentrated their forces in the approaches to the three major invasion corridors to the south. Two North Korean divisions were poised for offensive action.

The South Korean armed forces were smaller and less well equipped than those of North Korea; in particular, they lacked combat planes as well as tanks and antitank weapons. When the Korean War broke out, only four of South Korea's eight divisions (and one regiment) were anywhere near the 38th parallel; the other four were spread out over South Korea. Even the units near the 38th parallel were under strength. And on the day war broke out, many South Korean soldiers were on weekend passes or back in their villages for the harvest.

The U.S. military since World War II had greatly declined not only in numbers but in readiness. Most of the U.S. armed forces were committed to Europe, where the Soviet Union was seen as the main threat to world peace. In the Pacific, the U.S. armed forces were concentrated in Japan, but there they lived the life of garrison troops, with little physical conditioning. Some of the noncommissioned officers and officers had experienced combat in World War II, but even they were not trained to fight in the mountainous terrain of Korea. On the day the Korean War broke out, the United States had no combat units in South Korea, only a 500-man Korean Military Advisory Group (KMAG). The United States did have powerful naval and air forces in the area, which established complete domination of the air and sea from the time that U.S. forces were committed. But when 90,000 North Korean troops, supported by Soviet-supplied tanks, crossed the 38th parallel on June 25, 1950, the U.S. military was caught completely unprepared for a war in Korea. By the end of that first day of war, the ill-equiped South Korean forces were in retreat (see Ground War, June 25, 1950, p. 578).

DECLARATION OF WAR

None of the principals actually declared war in the formal sense. North Korea simply claimed that South Korean forces had attacked North Korea and that their action was only a response. South Korea simply called out its military to respond to the attack from the north (see Ground War, June 25, 1950, p. 578).

The United States effectively relied on a statement by President Truman to the American people and subsequent legislation passed by the U.S. Congress that supported the military's needs. Although there was some grumbling about Truman's refusal to seek a formal declaration of war, he was able to ignore that because many of those who were most critical were staunch anti-Communists.

The only formal declaration involved in the war was what came about through the decisions taken by the United Nations. That proceeded in a fairly compressed time frame:

Word of the June 25, 1950[*] invasion first reached officials in Washington, D.C., on Saturday at about 8 P.M.. (Several hours had passed in Korea before Washington, D.C., realized the attack was an invasion rather than a border skirmish.) Secretary of State Dean Acheson immediately informed President Truman (who was spending the weekend at his home in Independence, Missouri), and together they agreed that they should ask for an emergency meeting of the UN Security Council. Trygve Lie, the UN secretary general, agreed and called the meeting for Sunday afternoon.

At the emergency meeting held on June 25, 1950, the Security Council approved a U.S. resolution calling for "immediate cessation of hostilities" and the withdrawal of North Korean forces to the 38th parallel. The vote was 9-0, with Yugoslavia abstaining. Because the Soviets were boycotting the Security Council (see Causes of the War, pp. 572-573), they lost the chance to veto that crucial resolution.

That same afternoon and evening, President Truman (having flown back to Washington, D.C.) presided over a meeting with his diplomatic and military advisers. Secretary of State Acheson completely reversed his earlier position that the U.S. defensive perimeter did not include Korea (see Causes of the War, pp. 572-573), and Truman made it clear that the United States was not going to stand by and do nothing. However, at that time, since the Security Council's resolution had not called for any direct military action, Truman only ordered the transfer to the South Koreans of U.S. arms and military equipment stored in Japan, and he authorized the use of U.S. military units to protect the evacuation of U.S. nationals from Korea. Another important step Truman took was to tell the U.S. 7th Fleet in Japan to stand by

in case it was needed to protect Taiwan from invasion by the Chinese Communists. Truman also ordered Gen. Douglas MacArthur, the U.S. commander in Japan, to send a survey team to Taiwan to appraise the situation there.

News from Korea on June 26, 1950, made it clear that the North Koreans had no intention of obeying the Security Council's resolution. That evening, Truman presided over another meeting with his top policy advisers. Before the meeting was over, Truman had taken three important steps. First, he removed restrictions on U.S. air and naval forces and allowed them to attack North Korean forces below the 38th parallel at will. Second, he authorized the 7th Fleet to stop any hostilities initiated by either Communist China or the Nationalists on Taiwan. Third, he directed that the U.S. present a new resolution to the Security Council the next day seeking international sanction for direct intervention by the U.S. military.

On June 27, 1950, Truman released to the nation and world a statement of the decisions that he and his advisers had reached the night before—effectively announcing that he was committing the United States to the defense of South Korea in order to stem the spread of Communism. It was in that statement, too, that Truman set forth his view that the security of Taiwan was linked to the situation in Korea, contending, in effect, that Communist China was a threat to both. Although he had no hard evidence for his position, Truman was suggesting that China, as well as the Soviet Union, was behind the North Koreans' invasion of South Korea.

On the same day, the U.S. House of Representatives voted (315-4) a one-year extension of the draft and authorized the president to call up reservists. The Senate approved (70-0) those same measures the next day.

Meanwhile, the UN Security Council met on June 28, 1950, to consider the U.S. resolution that called on all UN members to "furnish such assistance to the Republic of Korea as may be necessary to repel the armed attack and to restore international peace and security to the area." That was hotly debated until just before midnight when the council approved the resolution 7-1. (Yugoslavia alone voted against it, but that vote did not constitute a veto because Yugoslavia was not a permanent member; India and Egypt abstained.) Once again, the Soviet Union,

---

[*]Korea is 14 hours before Eastern Standard Time, so that 4 A.M. on a Sunday in Korea is 2 P.M. on Saturday in Washington, D.C.

which as one of five permanent members might have vetoed such an action, was boycotting the Security Council. U.S. government leaders interpreted the Soviet Union's absence as a signal that it would not intervene in Korea.

The implications of that resolution were clear to all those in the Security Council: It was effectively a declaration of war by the UN against North Korea. But having voted for that, the UN took no position on how the "assistance" was to be rendered. Again, the implications were clear: Implementation was to be left to the United States.

On being informed by his military advisers that General MacArthur had requested permission to send a U.S. regimental combat team at once to help the crumbling South Korean forces, President Truman gave his approval early on the morning of June 30. Later that morning, Truman gave MacArthur full authority to use all ground forces he had under his command in the Far East. President Truman also approved a naval blockade of North Korea.

The UN Security Council recommended on July 7 that all forces provided by UN member states be placed under the command of the United States military. The Security Council also requested that the U.S. designate a UN commander and that the U.S report "as appropriate" to the UN. In effect, the United States was authorized to act as the executive agent of the UN in fighting North Korea.

COMBATANTS

North Koreans: North Korea had been building up its army with the aid of the Soviets and, by 1950, had some 130,000 men under arms. Although not all North Korean forces were fully trained for modern warfare, about 35,000 had served with the Communist Chinese in their war that drove out the Nationalists, so they had far more combat veterans than the South Korean army had. Moreover, the North Koreans held back only about 5,000 of their troops for headquarters and service units, as they expected virtually all their troops to be prepared for the hardships of battle.

North Korea not only had three times as much artillery as South Korea had, but also most of its artillery outranged the South Koreans artillery. The greatest advantage the North Koreans had

in the early weeks of the Korean War were Soviet tanks: some 150, 32-ton T34s, among the best medium tanks in the world, with heavily armored plate and carrying high velocity 85mm guns.

The North Koreans had an air force that numbered about 42 combat aircraft and another 70 attack and ground-support aircraft—all Soviet made. The North Koreans had no true navy, only some small ships in their coast guard.

Chinese Communists: In October 1950, the Chinese Communists entered the Korean War against the UN forces. The Chinese called their forces the Chinese People's Volunteers, as though they were not part of the Chinese army, but no one was fooled. In the first weeks after they entered the Korean War, Chinese troops numbered about 130,000; eventually there were some 300,000 Chinese Communist troops in the field at a time. The Chinese Communists also assigned fighter planes in November 1950, and in the months that followed, they committed hundreds of fighters (most Soviet MiGs) and light bombers (Soviet IL-28s). Most of the Chinese planes were based in Manchuria, and because the UN air forces were ordered not to fly across the Yalu River, the Chinese pilots could always retreat back to that safe haven.

Soviets: Although at the time there was a constant threat of Soviet forces becoming involved in the war, the Soviet Union never sent in ground combat units. There were, however, as many as 3,000 individual Soviet "advisers" attached to North Korean units (and battle plans written in Russian were captured by UN forces). Many North Korean soldiers had fought in the Soviet military during World War II, and the Soviets supplied much of the military hardware used by the North Koreans and later by the Chinese Communists—from the T-34 tanks to the MiG fighter planes. Although they denied it at the time, it was suspected (and was later confirmed by the Soviets themselves) that Soviets did pilot many of the MiGs that shot down U.S. and UN planes; one Soviet ace, it has been revealed, was secretly honored for shooting down 11 U.S. planes.

South Koreans: With the aid of the United States, the South Koreans had also been building up their military. Their army numbered a total of 98,000 men in uniform, but under the influence of their U.S. sponsors, they assigned about one-third of those to headquarters and service units. Most of the Republic of Korea (ROK) troops were not well trained. In fact, the United States had a deliberate go-slow policy in military assistance to ensure that the ROK army did not become strong enough to embolden Syngman Rhee's aggressive ambitions.

Most crucial, the ROK army was poorly armed compared to the North Korean army. The ROK army had no tanks—and virtually nothing in its arsenal to stop the modern North Korean tanks. The ROK army did have 89 short-range 105mm light howitzers, but they were not deployed in the north when the first North Korean tanks came rushing across the 38th parallel. The best the ROK army had were 57mm antitank guns and old 2.36-inch rocket launchers (better known as bazookas). Both weapons were obsolescent U.S. army remainders from World War II, and neither could pierce the armor of the North Korean tanks. However, new 3.5-inch "super bazookas" were rushed to Korea in those early weeks of the Korean War, and they soon proved to be effective in stopping the North Korean tanks. Initially, the South Koreans had no antitank land mines: The first ones did not arrive in South Korea until June 30, six days after the invasion. The South Koreans also had no combat aircraft, only 12 unarmed liaison planes. They had only a small coast guard with no effective warships.

Americans: Since the end of World War II, the United States had deliberately and drastically cut its military forces all around the world. At the time of the North Korean invasion of South Korea, the U.S. military in South Korea consisted of only the 500 members of the Korean Military Advisory Group (KMAG); the first U.S. combat troops did not arrive from Japan until July 1. There were four Army divisions serving on duty in Japan, but those were greatly under strength, especially in combat-ready units. In essence, there was no shortage of cooks, clerks, and drivers, but there were relatively few riflemen. Eventually, the U.S. deployed eight infantry divisions and three regimental combat teams to South Korea to form the U.S. 8th Army, the main element of the UN forces in Korea. On June 30, 1950, Congress authorized the call-up of all reserve units of the armed forces, as well as National Guard units; the first reserve units were activated on July 19, and in the ensuing weeks and months, President Truman called up many more reserve and National Guard units. (Thousands of World War II veterans who had joined the reserves

never expecting another war in their lifetime soon found themselves back at duty stations.) With the extension of the draft in June 1950, thousands of conscripts per month were eventually sent to Korea.

The U.S. Marine Corps dispatched the First Provisional Marine Brigade from California in July; it was joined in the weeks that followed by units that formed the First Marine Division; those marines played a crucial role in many of the major actions in Korea.

When the Korean War began, the KMAG had only ten Mustang fighter planes in Korea, but those were soon joined by the full might of the U.S. Fifth Air Force. In addition, the other service branches—the U.S. Marines and the U.S. Navy—had their own air forces. There was considerable coordination of those various air forces as well as with those provided by other UN member states, especially those of Britain and the Commonwealth nations.

British: The United Kingdom was the first nation, after the United States, to provide ground troops for the war in Korea; in late August, the 1,600 men of the British 27th Brigade arrived in Korea. At their peak, the British ground force totaled about 14,000 troops. The Royal Navy was also active from the earliest days of the conflict; eventually, the British navy supplied many large warships and naval air units. The Royal Air Force was also active.

Canadians: Canada supplied the third largest (after the United States and the United Kingdom) foreign military force to Korea. At their peak, a total of 26,790 Canadians fought in Korea in the army, navy, and air force, with some 6,150 on the ground. Numerous Canadian ships were assigned to Korea, and Canadian pilots flew many combat missions.

Australians: The Australians were among the first, after the United States, to join in combat against the North Koreans; in early July, they committed a squadron of F-51 Mustang combat planes. Ships of the Australian navy also arrived in early July. The first Australian ground troops arrived in late September. At their peak, Australian ground troops in Korea numbered some 2,280.

Other nations: Numerous other UN member states supplied smaller military units of one kind or another. Belgium provided a volunteer infantry battalion and several air transport planes.

Colombia furnished a frigate and an infantry battalion. Ethiopia, the only African nation to contribute to the Korean War, provided an infantry battalion. France assigned a frigate and an infantry battalion to the war in Korea. (At that time, France was fully engaged in its war in Vietnam.) Greece assigned air transport planes and an infantry battalion. The Netherlands assigned several warships and an infantry battalion. New Zealand supplied a frigate and a field artillery unit. The Philippines assigned a 1,500-man infantry battalion combat team, with its own tank company and a howitzer battery. Thailand assigned an air transport unit, two frigates, and an infantry battalion. After the United States, the United Kingdom, and Canada, Turkey provided the largest number of ground troops to the Korean War. At their peak, the Turkish forces numbered some 5,450.

GEOGRAPHIC AND STRATEGIC CONSIDERATIONS

Korea, a country with an area approximately the size of Minnesota, is a largely mountainous land, with the north-south watershed closer to the eastern coast, leaving the more gradual slopes, longer rivers, and larger floodplains on the western part of the peninsula. Korean people have always lived mostly in the coastal plains. Only about 20 percent of the land is suitable for cultivation. Korea extends some 650 miles from north to south and about 320 miles at its widest point. Parts of Korea experience extreme cold in the winter, between 30 and 40 degrees Fahrenheit below zero, and extreme heat in the summer, over 100 degrees Fahrenheit. There are more than 3,000 small islands and islets, most of them uninhabitable, around the southern and western coasts of Korea.

If Korea were divided naturally into two parts, the division would be at the natural depression that cuts across the mountains on a northeast to southwest line, from Wonsan to Kaesong. The 38th parallel, which was imposed with no regard for geographic features, left South Korea with a smaller area—some 37,000 square miles (a little larger than Maine)—but with a larger population (21 million) than North Korea. South Korea has the best agricultural land, the traditional capital (Seoul), most of the big cities, the two best ports (Inchon and Pusan), and a small amount of light industry. It is not especially rich in minerals, except for tungsten.

North Korea has an area of 48,000 square miles (about the size of New York State), but its population in 1950 was only 9 million. Its land is mostly mountainous, with little land available for cultivation, but North Korea has a fair amount of valuable mineral deposits, particularly graphite and magnesium. At the outbreak of the Korean War, North Korea did have a certain amount of relatively heavy industry, but only because the Japanese had built that industry during their decades of occupation.

At the time of the Korean War, most people in both Koreas were peasant farmers who lived in small villages and spent their lives close to nature. They had little experience in or taste for waging modern war and had for years lived as virtual vassals of their Japanese conquerors.

The Korean peninsula had served as a buffer between China and Japan for centuries, although that rested as much on perception and politics as on actual objective features. Korea shares an 850-mile border with China (and an 11-mile border with Russia), and its southern tip is only 120 miles from the Japanese home islands of Honshu and Kyushu. The Sea of Japan separates Korea and Japan, the Yellow Sea lies between Korea and China. North Korea's border with China is defined for almost 500 miles by the Yalu River, which played a crucial role in the war.

Although U.S. planners until early 1950 had explicitly ruled out Korea as being strategically important, as soon as the Korean War broke out, they chose to see Korea as worth defending. In effect, the United States subscribed to the concept of a "buffer state." On one level, it was difficult to argue that the Korean peninsula had anything to do with the security of the United States. But once U.S. policy makers and politicians decided that if the Communists controlled that peninsula they would represent a threat to Japan (the key to U.S. control over the Western Pacific), South Korea began to seem of strategic importance to the United States. South Korea did have a port, at Pusan, that could be of use to the U.S. Navy, but Pusan had never really figured in U.S. military planning. South Korea had no particular raw materials that could not be obtained elsewhere (although its tungsten deposits were valued). The U.S. decision to defend South Korea was based on three strategic objectives: to protect the security of U.S.-occupied Japan; to demonstrate to the Soviet Union that the United States was prepared to fight to prevent Communist expansion; and to check the advance of Chinese Communist power and influence in the aftermath of their victory over the Nationalists, which had widely been perceived as a defeat for the United States (see Cold War, August 5, 1949, p. 534).

Battles and Campaigns: 1950

Ground War

June 25, 1950: At 4 A.M., some 90,000 troops of the North Korean People's Army launched an invasion of South Korea by crossing the 38th parallel in six separate columns. The Republic of Korea (ROK) forces were caught completely off guard; aside from being greatly outnumbered, they lacked weapons to stop the North Koreans' Soviet tanks. At a few points, the ROK army was able briefly to hold back the North Korean forces, but by the end of the day, the ROK troops were for the most part in retreat.

June 26, 1950: As the North Korean forces continued to advance in all sectors, the ROK chief of staff ordered a counterattack along two roads leading to Seoul, the South Korean capital, which was only 30 miles from the 38th parallel; only one attack was launched, and it soon collapsed. Early in the morning, American families in Seoul and elsewhere in South Korea began to be evacuated by ship; within four days, the United States evacuated some 2,000 persons.

June 27 1950: The ROK army headquarters moved south of Seoul. During the day, Gen. Douglas MacArthur ordered the head of the U.S. Korean Military Advisory Group (KMAG) to remain in Seoul; the head of the KMAG then persuaded the head of the ROK army to return his headquarters to Seoul. Syngman Rhee, however, relocated the government in Taejon about 95 miles south of Seoul. Thousands of ROK forces and civilian refugees streamed southward, many headed for Seoul, located on the Han River. Late that night, the American KMAG officers learned that the ROK army had mined the bridges on the Han near Seoul and were planning to blow them up. The Americans persuaded the ROK command to postpone that until more ROK troops and refugees crossed the river.

June 28, 1950: At 2:15 A.M., a ROK general arrived at the Han River to order the delay, but just then the main bridge was blown up. It was packed with thousands of soldiers and civilians; an estimated 500–800 people died. It was particularly catastrophic because there were still some six hours before the first North Korean units would have reached the bridge. Meanwhile, thousands of ROK troops were left north of the river; although many made their way across at other points. Masses of valuable equipment and arms were abandoned to the North Korean forces. By noon, the northern forces were moving into the center of Seoul and the ROK army was in total disarray, with most soldiers in flight across the entire peninsula.

June 29, 1950: Gen. Douglas MacArthur made a quick visit to Korea in his personal plane (the *Bataan*). Meeting with several top American officials and President Syngman Rhee, MacArthur was briefed on the desperate situation of the ROK forces. To the dismay of some of his advisers, he insisted on making a personal inspection of the front lines. After about seven hours on the ground, he flew back to Tokyo, and, within 16 hours, he called Washington, D.C., to ask for the immediate commitment of U.S. ground forces. Some ROK units were putting up resistance against the North Korean forces poised to cross the entire Han River, but, in general, the ROK army was proving powerless against the North Korean army.

June 30, 1950: MacArthur's advance commander in Korea asked for U.S. combat troops to reinforce the faltering ROK forces. The American military advisers left their headquarters at Suwon airfield about 20 miles southwest of Seoul and moved another five miles south to Osan.

July 1–4, 1950: On July 1, the first U.S. combat troops were flown from Tokyo into Pusan, the main port at the southeastern tip of South Korea. Commanded by Lt. Col. Charles "Brad" Smith, the 1st Battalion, 21st Infantry Regiment, 24th Division, consisting of 406 officers and enlisted men, became known as Task Force Smith. During the next four days, the force made its way by train and trucks to points a few miles north of Osan. Meanwhile, the North Korean forces crossed the Han River, and ROK forces were again in flight. In the ensuing chaos, U.S. and Australian planes ended up strafing and bombing ROK forces, and ROK forces shot down UN planes.

July 5, 1950: Task Force Smith, now reinforced by 134 men of the 52nd Field Artillery Battalion, took its stand on high ground above the main highway to Osan from the north. Early in the morning, some 33 North Korean tanks passed by them; the Americans were able to stop only four of the tanks. Shortly thereafter, a column of some 5,000 North Korean troops along with several tanks and many vehicles approached from the north. Colonel Smith held fire until they were only 1,000 yards away. In the ensuing firefight, the Americans were hopelessly outnumbered and outgunned, and after about three hours, they began to pull back, all the while taking terrible casualties. Over the next several days, the survivors made their way back to the American lines; of the 540 men in Task Force Smith, 181 had been killed, wounded, or were missing.

July 6–7, 1950: By July 3, Gen. William Dean, commander of the 24th Division, had set up his headquarters in Taejon about 80 miles south of Osan. He had assigned two battalions to stop the advancing North Korean forces, but on July 6, the battalions were quickly dispersed by North Korean attacks and withdrew all the way to Ch'Únan. General Dean ordered the battalions back into action the next day, but they were routed and took high casualties in their retreat. By the night of July 7, the North Koreans had overrun Ch'Únan.

July 8–13, 1950: The U.S. command decided to pull back to establish a defensive line at the Kum River in west-central Korea some 25 miles south of Ch'Únan and 15 miles north of Taejon, the headquarters of the UN forces. Although several U.S. and ROK units fought bravely against the North Korean forces, they were eventually overwhelmed and forced to retreat to the southern side of the Kum River. Other North Korean forces to the east threatened to move down and execute a converging attack. On July 13, Gen. Walton Walker, commander of the 8th Army and General MacArthur's designated commander of the forces in Korea, relocated the UN forces' headquarters to Taegu, 75 miles southeast of Taejon. His new plan called for a major stand against the North Korean forces at the Naktong River, just north of Taegu.

July 14–20, 1950: U.S. Army engineers had destroyed the bridges across the Kum, but the North Korean forces made their way across on barges at various points, overran the U.S. defensive positions, and gradually pushed the U.S. forces back. American forces, under strength, exhausted from two weeks of steady combat, and lacking experience and the proper equipment, suffered high casualties as they retreated from the North Korean forces. On the evening of July 20, the U.S. command had to flee from Taejon; it was during this retreat that Gen. William Dean became separated from his men (see Civilian & Military Biographies, pp. 604-605). The sacrifices made by the troops at the Kum and Taejon, however, gave Walker time to move recently arrived U.S. forces into defensive positions along the Naktong River.

July 21–August 3, 1950: Holding off numerous attacks and thrusts by North Korean forces on several fronts, U.S. and ROK troops made their way from various sectors and across the Naktong River; the river formed the western boundary of the new defensive line; the northern border ran eastward through mountainous terrain to the Sea of Japan. Some 100 miles north to south and 50 miles west to east, this line was known as the *Pusan Perimeter*; its main goal was to keep Pusan, the major port on the southeastern corner of Korea, from falling to the North Korean forces. If that occurred, all U.S. ground forces would be forced out of South Korea.

August 1950: As the fighting continued at various points along the Pusan Perimeter, the UN forces began to build up their strength. New U.S. units joined the original battle-weary troops, other UN units (such as British units) joined the battle, and an ever-increasing flow of military equipment and supplies arrived in Pusan and were brought to the front by rail. Meanwhile, the North Korean forces were far removed from their supply bases, and their units, despite having pushed back the U.S. and ROK forces, were now under strength and exhausted.

August 7–13, 1950: On August 7, U.S. forces launched their first counteroffensive along the southwestern edge of the Pusan Perimeter; they had superiority in numbers of personnel, tanks and vehicles, and artillery, along with total dominance in the air and on the seas offshore. Even so, they ran into fierce opposition; on August 12, two U.S. artillery battalions were overrun by North Korean tanks and troops. In what became known as the Battle of Bloody Gulch, U.S. forces lost all their howitzers and sustained 90 killed, 140 wounded, and 30 missing. In that first offensive, the U.S. forces were defeated and turned back by the sheer doggedness of the North Korean soldiers.

August 17–24, 1950: Since August 5, North Korean forces had been crossing the Naktong River along a broad front opposite Taegu, then serving as the temporary capital of Syngman Rhee's government. Although Rhee had been forced to move the capital to Pusan on July 18, U.S. commanders were determined to hold Taegu, and on August 17, they launched a major counterattack. U.S. and ROK troops, with heavy support from the air and artillery, decisively beat back most of the North Korean troops. In one particularly intense engagement north of Taegu, the North Koreans tried for seven nights (August 18–24) to move a tank column south along a road hemmed in by mountains. Each night the United States hit the tanks with bazooka and artillery shells, and the sound of guns and detonations made such a noise bouncing off the narrow corridor that the GI's called the road the "bowling alley." Although suffering horrendous losses of tanks and personnel, the North Koreans tried to outflank the U.S. forces by going around them through the mountains. The North Koreans achieved a temporary success on August 22, but by August 23, they were driven back. The Battle of the Bowling Alley proved extremely costly to the North Korean army.

August 23, 1950: Almost from the day that Seoul fell to the North Korean army, General MacArthur began planning an amphibious landing at Inchon, the port on the northwestern coast of Korea due west of Seoul. From the start, his plan was opposed by the members of the Joint Chiefs of Staff in Washington, D.C., and most of his fellow commanders in the Far East and on the ground in Korea. They did not oppose an amphibious flanking movement per se, but they objected to making it at Inchon—in part, because the entrance to the harbor was narrow and guarded and tides allowed only a brief window for the landing. MacArthur essentially ignored their arguments for choosing other landing points and continued to build up his forces for the Inchon landing. On August 23, he held a meeting in Tokyo with many of the top service chiefs, and in a 45-minute speech swept aside all objections. Not all the service chiefs were persuaded, but in the end, President Truman backed MacArthur's plan. MacArthur's planned inva-

sion was scheduled to proceed on September 15.

August 31–September 7, 1950: By the end of August, the North Korean forces had effectively lost the ability to threaten the Pusan Perimeter, but Kim Il Sung, the North Korean leader, could not accept that. On August 31, he ordered a major counteroffensive along much of the western and southwestern sectors of the perimeter; in the first few days, the North Korean forces once again were able to breach the UN lines along the Naktong. By September 6, however, the U.S. forces regained the offensive, and by September 7, the North Korean troops were in retreat. Both sides suffered heavy casualties, but the North Korean forces were overwhelmed by superior U.S. firepower.

September 15, 1950: At 6:33 A.M., the first U.S. marines went ashore on Wolmi, a small island in Inchon harbor; by 7:50 A.M., they had secured the island, which was connected to the mainland at Inchon by a causeway. That first force had to wait until high tides again that afternoon for the main invasion forces to come ashore about 5:30 P.M. Although they met some resistance, there was never any serious threat to their succeeding, and by 7:30 P.M., they had effectively sealed off Inchon.

September 16–28, 1950: Supported by vastly superior firepower, airpower, and manpower, the U.S. forces began to move toward Seoul less than 25 miles to the east of Inchon. The North Korean forces began to mount increasing resistance, but they could not stop the advance. By September 22, marines were on the outskirts of Seoul, and by September 28, the city was completely controlled by U.S. troops. The next day, General MacArthur led Syngman Rhee back to his seat of government.

September 16–30, 1950: In coordination with the Inchon landing, U.S., ROK, and British forces along the Pusan Perimeter went on the offensive. They had anticipated that the North Koreans would withdraw many troops to counter the Inchon landing; but, in fact, the North Koreans forces put up a stiff resistance. Not until the 23d did many North Korean units begin to retreat in panic or to surrender. In some places, the U.S. armored columns moved so quickly that they passed right through retreating North Korean forces. As the North Koreans proceeded to withdraw all across South Korea to the 38th parallel, they massacred thousands of South Korean ci-

U.S. marines storm over a seawall at the amphibious landing at Inchon, the port of Korea's northwest coast, September 15, 1950.

vilians and prisoners of war; the ROK military and South Korean police had also began executing thousands of South Korean civilians charged with being Communists. By September 30, about half the 100,000 North Korean troops thought to have been in South Korea had crossed above the 38th parallel. Some ROK troops also crossed the parallel on that day; they were under orders from President Syngman Rhee to proceed no matter what the UN Command said.

October 9, 1950: Ever since the U.S. had committed its forces to Korea, there had been a debate within the U.S. government as to whether the U.S. troops should stop when they reached the 38th parallel or invade North Korea with the goal of uniting the two states. On September 27, President Truman authorized MacArthur to move across the 38th parallel. On October 9, U.S. forces crossed the 38th parallel and headed for Pyongyang, the capital of North Korea.

October 10, 1950: ROK forces captured Wonsan, the port city on the east coast of North Korea some 110 miles north of the 38th parallel. MacArthur meanwhile was organizing an ambitious amphibious operation to take Wonsan; the first U.S. troops did not go ashore at Wonsan

until October 20.

October 14–20, 1950: Communist Chinese troops began to secretly infiltrate into North Korea.

October 19, 1950: U.S. and ROK troops captured Pyongyang, the capital of North Korea. Premier Kim Il Sung moved his capital to Sinuiju on the Yalu River on the western border with Manchuria.

October 20–23, 1950: ROK, U.S., and other UN troops pushed retreating North Korean forces back on all fronts. The retreating North Korean troops killed hundreds of American POWs they had taken in earlier battles; tales of such atrocities inevitably influenced other American prisoners, many of whom were held for years in Communist POW camps (see pp. 603-604).

October 24–November 1, 1950: Without fully clearing his decision with military and civilian leaders in Washington, D.C., MacArthur canceled an order restricting all but ROK forces from a 30- to 40-mile-wide strip south of the Manchurian border and ordered UN troops to pursue the North Korean forces all the way to the border. On October 26, ROK troops reached the Yalu River at Chosan in north-central Korea; that turned out to be the only point at which ROK or UN forces actually reached the Korea-China border. By November 1, U.S. troops were at a village 18 miles south of the Yalu River; that was the closest U.S. forces came to the Chinese frontier.

October 25–November 6, 1950: Chinese Communist troops launched their first attack against advancing ROK units. That was the first proof that the Chinese had entered the Korean War. The ROK were routed by the Chinese, and in the next few days, increasing numbers of Chinese troops became more and more of a factor in the war, shattering even more ROK units. U.S. units were sent forward to reinforce ROK units around Unsan. During November 1–2, the Americans were also routed by the Chinese, often in hand-to-hand combat; many wounded were abandoned when the U.S. troops fled through the hills. By the time the last stragglers made it back to the American lines, the U.S. had suffered more than 600 casualties.

November 6–7, 1950: The Chinese abruptly broke off all contact with ROK and UN forces and withdrew into the mountains. It appeared that the Chinese were trying to signal that they would be willing to break off hostilities if the U.S. and UN forces withdrew from North Korea.

November 10–23, 1950: U.S. and ROK units in the eastern part of North Korea took advantage of the Chinese withdrawal and continued to move northward; they met only slight resistance from North Korean troops. U.S. Marine units moved into the hills and high plateau around the Chosin (Changjin) Reservoir in the central part of North Korea. Winter was settling into North Korea, bringing snow and bitter cold.

November 24–December 2, 1950: General MacArthur's planned attack—dubbed the "home-by-Christmas offensive"—began in the western sector, along the Chongchon River. In the first hours, the battle went well, but on November 25 the Chinese launched their own offensive; within a few days ROK forces, U.S. forces, and other UN forces were in full retreat along the entire front. Casualties were heavy. By December 2, the forces in the west had withdrawn to a line around Pyongyang. By mid-December, the UN forces in the western part of North Korea had withdrawn to the Imjin River north of Seoul and along the 38th parallel.

November 27–December 11, 1950: U.S. marines in the hills above the Chosin Reservoir

found themselves cut off by Chinese Communist forces. Relief forces, including British marines, failed to break through the overwhelming Chinese forces. Casualties mounted; many UN troops were taken prisoner. Only airdrops of supplies and air attacks on the Chinese kept the U.S. marines from total annihilation. Units began to disintegrate as individual soldiers sought to make their way to Hagaru, a village just south of the reservoir, where the U.S. marines had established medical facilities. By December 4, the U.S. marines made it to Hagaru, but thousands had been left behind or were dead, wounded, or missing in action. With the temperatures around zero degrees Fahrenheit, thousands of men suffered from frostbite; they were evacuated by airplane along with thousands of other wounded. On December 6, about 10,000 U.S. marines, Army troops, and some British marines and ROK forces set forth on a march of about 50 miles to the eastern coast. They faced some Chinese attacks, but on December 7, they joined another 4,000 men at Koto. Meanwhile, the Chinese had blasted a 16-foot gap in the only road to the coast; large sections of prefabricated bridge were air-dropped by special heavy-duty parachutes. The next phase of the retreat began on December 8; the bridge sections were installed and the column proceeded. The military was joined by thousands of civilian Korean refugees fleeing the Chinese Communists. By midnight on December 11, the last of the 19,000 survivors of the military units involved in the Chosin Reservoir campaign arrived at Hungnam, a port on the east coast; some 6,000 men had been killed, wounded, or captured.

December 11–24, 1950: A large fleet of ships assembled at Hungnam and evacuated some 105,000 UN troops and 98,000 South Korean civilian refugees, along with 17,500 vehicles and 350,000 tons of cargo. Another 3,600 soldiers were evacuated by airlift. That marked the beginning of the end of the attempt to conquer North Korea.

December 23, 1950: Gen. Walton Walker, commander of the U.S. 8th Army, which controlled most of the UN ground forces in Korea, was killed when his jeep was struck by another vehicle. Walker was succeeded by Gen. Matthew B. Ridgway.

December 31, 1950: The Chinese, along with some reorganized North Korean forces, launched a major offensive against the UN forces along the western front. Along the western sector, poorly disciplined ROK troops retreated in panic, but the UN forces made a more orderly retreat.

NAVAL WAR

June 28, 1950: The British placed their naval forces in Japanese waters under control of the United States Far East Command in order to coordinate the UN's naval activities against the North Koreans.

June 29, 1950: President Harry S. Truman authorized a blockade of the Korean coast by U.S. naval forces. The USS *Juneau,* a light cruiser, fired the first naval shore bombardment of the Korean War at Mukho, on the east coast of North Korea.

July–August 1950: Throughout the summer, U.S. and other UN ships often supported land operations by bombardments and air attacks. The North Koreans did not have a navy to resist those operations.

September 1–14, 1950: The UN command assembled a fleet of more than 200 ships that converged on Inchon to support the invasion.

September 13–14, 1950: U.S. and British ships bombarded the island of Wolmi, guarding the entrance to Inchon harbor, and destroyed several mines leading to the landing site.

AIR WAR

June 26, 1950: While protecting American civilians being evacuated on ships, U.S. jet fighters engaged in their first air battles with North Korean airplanes.

June 29, 1950: The United States Air Force sent 18 B-26 Invader light bombers against the airfield at the North Korean capital city of Pyongyang. Twenty-five enemy aircraft were reported destroyed on the ground, and one YAK fighter was shot down.

July 3, 1950: In the first carrier-based air strike, U.S. and British airplanes attacked airfields in North Korea.

July 9–10, 1950: U.S. fighter bombers and fighter planes attacked North Korean columns of tanks, vehicles, and troops along the roads leading in and out of Ch'Ŭnan and destroyed massive amounts of equipment and personnel. Those raids established that the UN held superiority in the air and forced the North Korean army to adopt new tactics to move their vehicles and forces.

July 13, 1950: U.S. B-29s bombed the railroad yards at Wonsan, North Korea.

July 30–August 2, 1950: U.S. B-29s bombed the chemical plants around Hungnam, North Korea.

August 16, 1950: In a plan conceived by General MacArthur, 98 B-29 Superfortresses carpet-bombed a 26-square-mile area northwest of Taegu, where MacArthur believed a large force of NK troops were concentrated. Although the planes dropped some 850 tons of bombs (the equivalent of 30,000 rounds of heavy artillery)— the largest use of airpower in support of ground forces since the Normandy invasion (see World War II, European Theater, June 6, 1944, pp. 466-467)—a follow-up investigation could not prove that a single North Korean soldier or vehicle had been harmed by that raid. Bombers were not used in that way again during the Korean War.

September 26, 1950: U.S. B-29s bombed a major hydroelectric plant in North Korea. That campaign to destroy North Korea's power capacity was then put on hold.

November 1950: Up to the entry of the Communist Chinese, the UN air forces completely outclassed the North Korean air force, with its propeller-driven Yakelov, or YAK, fighters. With the Chinese came the jet-propelled MiG-15s, which at first enjoyed certain performance advantages over the UN planes. The United States soon introduced the F-86 Sabrejet and F-84 Thunderjet, and although even those were outclassed by the MiGs in some performance characteristics, the skills of U.S. and other UN pilots were superior and could generally give them an advantage in combat.

November 5, 1950: Without asking for official authorization, MacArthur ordered an ambitious series of bombing raids on the Yalu River bridges and all factories, transportation facilities, and cities and villages between the UN lines and the Yalu River. The bombings began on November 8 and continued for ten days.

November 8, 1950: The first aerial battle between jet aircraft took place when a U.S. F-80 Shooting Star shot down a MiG-15 near the Yalu River. Seventy-nine B-29 Superfortress bombers struck the Yalu River bridges near the temporary North Korean capital of Sinuiju.

HOME FRONT

February 7, 1950: Sen. Joseph McCarthy (R–Wis.) charged in a speech to a women's club in Wheeling, West Virginia, that the State Department was harboring Communists. That was the launching of what became known as "McCarthyism," the making of accusations of political disloyalty or even subversive and traitorous conduct without sufficient evidence. McCarthy and his supporters would attack the Truman administration's conduct throughout the Korean War.

July 19, 1950: The Marine Corps called up its Organized Reserve units to immediate active duty.

July 20, 1950: To cope with the anticipated demands of the war in Korea, President Harry S. Truman asked Congress to pass a $10 billion rearmament program and to approve a partial mobilization of U.S. resources.

August 4, 1950: The U.S. Army called up 62,000 reservists.

September 11, 1950: President Truman gave his full approval to the plan (known as NSC- 81) of his civilian and military advisers to move the UN troops across the 38th parallel with the aim of unifying both Koreas.

October 15, 1950: President Truman, accompanied by numerous high-ranking civilian and military leaders, flew to Wake Island, the tiny U.S.-owned atoll some 2,300 miles west of Hawaii, to meet Gen. Douglas MacArthur. MacArthur assured Truman that North Korean resistance would collapse by the end of the year and that there was little chance of intervention by China or the Soviet Union. MacArthur's stature was such that he influenced Truman, but, as MacArthur himself later argued, the decision to continue the war across North Korea finally was Truman's responsibility.

November 6–21, 1950: When word of the Chinese withdrawal and MacArthur's planned bombing raids reached Washington, D.C., Truman and his civilian and military advisers discussed the options. Influenced by MacArthur's overly optimistic claims about the small numbers of Chinese troops in Korea and about the effectiveness of the American bombing raids, they gave him the authority to do what he saw fit to drive the Chinese back to the Yalu River.

November 30, 1950: With the new offensive by the Chinese Communists and the retreat of the UN forces from the Yalu River under way, President Truman held a press conference at which he said that the United States would use every weapon at its disposal as needed to "meet the military situation in Korea." When a reporter asked if that included the atomic bomb, Truman replied: "That includes every weapon we have." When pressed whether that meant that the United States was actively considering such use, Truman said there had "always been active consideration of its use." That claim by Truman provoked an outcry throughout the world, including expression of concern by many of the UN allies. Prime Minister Clement Attlee of Britain was so unsettled by that that he traveled to Washington, D.C., to get clarification.

December 8, 1950: President Truman announced a ban on U.S. shipment of any goods to Communist China.

December 16, 1950: Realizing that the war in Korea had taken a turn for the worse, President Truman declared a national emergency; that gave Truman greater latitude in deploying the nation's military forces and also marshaling its production capacities.

INTERNATIONAL DEVELOPMENTS

February 15, 1950: After two months of negotiations, the Soviet Union and Communist China signed a 30-year friendship and mutual defense pact in Moscow. Among other terms, it called for the two nations to unite in repulsing an attack by Japan or any other state.

June 29, 1950: The Soviet Union claimed that the UN's decisions on Korea were illegal and refused to take any role in trying to stop the North Koreans. In fact, during the following weeks and months, various Soviet diplomats made efforts to resolve the crisis.

October 3, 1950: The United States government received word through diplomatic channels that Communist Chinese would intervene in Korea if U.S. troops crossed the 38th parallel. Meanwhile, U.S. intelligence was aware that the Chinese Communist had massed some 450,000 troops in Manchuria on the border with North Korea. U.S. leaders regarded those moves as bluffs.

October 7, 1950: With the United States taking the lead, the United Nations General Assembly passed a resolution instructing the United

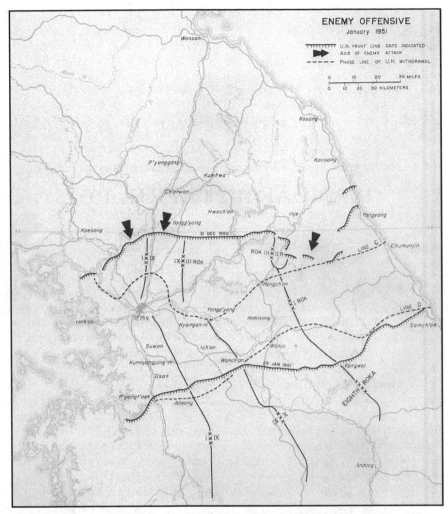

This map shows the UN positions between the end of December 1950 and the end of January 1951. UN troops pushed the North Korean forces north of the 38th parallel during the Fall of 1950, but when the Chinese entered the war at the end of October, the UN troops were forced to retreat. After the Chinese offensive of January 1951, the UN forces were again forced to abandon Seoul and move to a point 35 miles south of the city.

Nations Command to "ensure conditions of stability throughout Korea." South Korean troops had already moved across the 38th parallel a week before, but that resolution provided the license for General MacArthur to take the war into North Korea.

October 21, 1950: Communist Chinese forces invaded Tibet and drove the 16-year-old Dalai Lama into exile. By May 1951, the Chinese were in control of Tibet. Such an action only increased the U.S. desire to fight on in Korea.

December 14–19, 1950: On December 14, the UN General Assembly passed a resolution

calling for a cease-fire, but five days later Communist China rejected it.

BATTLES AND CAMPAIGNS: 1951

GROUND WAR

January 1–15, 1951: As the Chinese Communist offensive continued to push southward, on January 4, Seoul was abandoned by UN forces. On January 5, Inchon was abandoned. There was more resistance in the central and eastern sectors, but Gen. Matthew Ridgway ordered all UN forces to withdrew to a defensive line about 35 miles south of Seoul. By mid-January, most contacts between the two sides ceased, as the Communist forces stopped to build up their forces and supplies.

January 25–February 10, 1951: General Ridgway launched Operation Thunderbolt, a counteroffensive aimed at pushing the Communist forces north of Seoul. UN forces moved out along the entire front; at points, they encountered fierce resistance from the Chinese, but at other points, the Chinese simply vanished.

February 11–16, 1951: Chinese Communists launched a counteroffensive in central Korea. A major battle centered around the town of Chipyong-ni, where U.S. and French units met almost fanatical assaults by the Chinese. The UN forces held, costing the Chinese some 5,000 casualties. By February 16, the Communist offensive had been repelled, although many guerrillas remained in the mountains behind the lines.

February 21–March 1, 1951: UN forces launched Operation Killer, a new offensive designed to keep the Communists from building up their forces. In general, the Communists offered only token resistance as they pulled back to await a break in the spring rains. In particular, the Chinese were withdrawing their forces into what became known as the Iron Triangle, a mountain-flanked area north of the 38th parallel in the center of the Korean peninsula.

March 7–14, 1951: UN forces launched a new offensive, Operation Ripper. Meeting little more than delaying resistance—and muddy roads—the UN troops moved along a broad front. By March 14, they had retaken an abandoned Seoul.

March 27–31, 1951: UN forces pulled up to the 38th parallel in many sectors.

April 5–21, 1951: On April 5, General Ridgway launched Operation Rugged, with the intention of seizing the commanding ground north of the 38th parallel. By April 9, the operation was so successful that Ridgway called for a further advance to the western sector. The Communists were mostly concentrated in the Iron Triangle. It was during that period that Gen. Douglas MacArthur was removed from command; Ridgway was promoted to take over MacArthur's posts in Tokyo and was replaced in Korea by Gen. James Van Fleet (see Home Front, April 11, 1951, p. 589)

April 22–30, 1951: Chinese Communist forces launched their spring offensive with some 300,000 men along a 40-mile front north of Seoul. The fighting was extremely fierce at various points. One of the bloodiest battles was fought on April 23–25 at a hill (known as Gloucester Hill) along the Imjin River commanding a route to Seoul; there, men of Britain's Gloucestershire Regiment fought desperately against overwhelming numbers of Chinese. Isolated, out of ammunition, lacking artillery, the British finally retreated; their casualties were 63 dead, some 190 wounded, and some 450 taken prisoner. Although the UN forces had to retreat from their advance positions, they were able to hold a line north of Seoul. By the end of April, the Communist Chinese offensive had paused.

May 16–20, 1951: The Chinese launched a new offensive and in the first days advanced almost 20 miles in some sectors. UN air support and artillery, however, stopped the Chinese, and by May 20, their advance was halted.

May 21–June 24, 1951: UN forces counterattacked, and by May 30, the Communists had been driven out of South Korea once again to a line north of the 38th parallel that had been abandoned in early April. With another offensive that began on June 1, UN forces drove the Communists still farther north. The Communists dug emplacements with bunkers and underground rooms and occupied as many high points in the mountains as they could. Unless they were prepared to start a whole new level of warfare and take heavier casualties, the UN forces faced a stalemate. General Ridgway cabled the Joint Chiefs of Staff in Washington, D.C., that he thought the UN forces could hold that line for another 60 days and that it was a good time to proceed with diplomatic negotiations. In fact, the move toward an armistice and peace negotiations was already under way (see Negotiations and Peace Treaty, p. 594).

June 24–July 10, 1951: Military operations essentially ceased as negotiations for a conference on an armistice and peace proceeded on various levels. The sessions began on July 10. During the next few weeks, the UN forces made limited attacks at points along the battle line in an attempt to keep pressure on the Communists. For the following two years, the war in Korea became much like the Western Front during World War I—entrenched armies fighting a war

Marines take cover behind a tank as it advances, firing on Communist troops in the Hongchon area, May 22, 1951.

with no significant ground gains but very significant casualties.

August 18–September 5, 1951: Gen. Van Fleet received permission to seize three hills above the upland circular depression known as the Punch Bowl, just north of the eastern sector of the line. The North Korean forces there were able to observe the UN forces below and direct artillery fire on them. Republic of Korea (ROK) and U.S. troops attacked in force on August 18, but they met terrific resistance from the North Korean forces, which were protected by minefields and bunkers. Even the heavy artillery fire from U.S. units failed to dislodge the North Korean troops, and it took close-in fighting before the UN forces took control. The area and battle was dubbed Bloody Ridge because of the heavy casualties on both sides—some 3,000 UN troops and an estimated 15,000 Communists. The Communists simply withdrew to another set of hills less than a mile to the north—which soon became known as Heartbreak Ridge.

September 13–October 15, 1951: Having secured Bloody Ridge, the United States decided its forces should also take the hills just to the north. The North Korean forces had dug bunkers and artillery positions and camouflaged them, so when the U.S. forces began their assault on September 13, they met unexpectedly stiff resistance. Over the following two weeks, U.S. troops were able to take two of the hills, but North Korean forces managed to regain one. The casualties were so high that a new plan was adopted. Starting on October 5, the U.S. troops, aided by a French battalion, mounted a new attack on a broader sector with the goal of forcing the North Korean troops to spread out. Tanks were brought in, and by October 15, UN forces were in control of Heartbreak Ridge. UN casualties numbered some 3,700, and the North Korean casualties were an estimated 25,000.

October 3–19, 1951: Five UN divisions advanced to the Jamestown Line along the west-central sector of the main battle line; after 17 days of fighting, which cost them some 4,000 casualties, they had pushed the line back about 5 miles.

November 27, 1951: An agreement was reached at Panmunjom to accept the existent line of contact as the line of demarcation if a general truce agreement were reached in 30 days. During that period, which became known as the "Little Armistice," both sides took the occasion to strengthen their defensive positions. Since the cease-fire talks had begun in July, the UN forces had suffered about 60,000 casualties, more than 22,000 of them American; the North Korean and Chinese casualties were estimated at 234,000.

NAVAL WAR

February 16, 1951–July 27, 1953: Task Force 95, the UN Blockade and Escort Force, instituted a blockade of Wonsan harbor, North Korea's major port, on the eastern coast on the Sea of Japan. The blockade stayed in effect until the armistice was signed.

AIR WAR

May 9, 1951: The U.S. Air Force (USAF) launched a 300-plane strike on North Korea's temporary capital of Sinuiju on the Yalu River—the largest air raid of the war to that date.

May 20–June 30, 1951: The Far East Air Force launched Operation Strangle—an air interdiction campaign designed to break up the Communist supply system. That operation involved hundreds of sorties against transportation facilities.

USAF captain James Jabara became the first jet air ace; flying his F-86 Sabrejet, he shot down his fifth enemy plane.

July 30, 1951–March 1, 1952: After taking a break to analyze the effect of the raids in May and June (and because the armistice talks had begun), U.S. airplanes (occasionally supported by naval bombardments) took up Operation Strangle, concentrating on railroad lines and bridges in North Korea. Although they achieved considerable success, U.S. military commanders realized that the North Koreans were able to repair and restore the facilities quickly.

October 24, 1951: Chinese pilots in their MiGs were taking a considerable toll of U.S. bombers as they raided North Korean facilities. On this day 150 MiGs destroyed four B-29s and seriously damaged three others over Namsi airfield, the largest single- raid loss by the United States in the air war. That raid resulted in the suspension of daylight B-29 raids over northwest Korea.

POW SITUATION

Problems and disputes involving prisoners

of war taken by both sides came to assume a major and unique role in the Korean War. From the beginning, many North Korean forces tended to treat prisoners with considerable brutality—force-marching them under terrible conditions, starving and beating them, and on occasion simply slaughtering them. The South Korean troops did not always behave much better, and U.S. troops in the field killed prisoners in violation of the Geneva conventions. (The Geneva conventions—named for Geneva, Switzerland, where they were negotiated—are a series of agreements, begun in 1864 and adhered to by most nations, which call for humane treatment of prisoners and the wounded in wartime.) POWs in North Korean camps suffered far worse conditions and treatment than those in South Korean camps, although it cannot be denied that the Communist POWs also suffered. When the Communist Chinese entered the Korean War and took many of the prisoners to Manchurian camps, treatment did improve, at least for the UN troops. (In general, though, almost 40 percent of the UN soldiers known to have been taken prisoner died in captivity.)

As the UN and ROK forces began to take tens of thousands of prisoners, various problems began to arise. The main camp in South Korea was at Kuje-do, a large island just off the southern coast, and by January 1951, it was already holding five times its capacity.

February 1–8, 1951: When a number of high-ranking North Korean officers were transferred to Kuje-do, they imposed a new discipline over their fellow prisoners. They organized a hunger strike to protest the camp's rules, which escalated into a near riot. When a rock was thrown at the American camp commander, he fired his pistol; that was followed by machine gun fire. Two prisoners were killed and three wounded, but the POWs were subdued.

July 10–August 31, 1951: After the armistice negotiations began on July 10, the disagreement over what to do with the POWs soon became one of the most contentious issues. To begin with, the United States insisted that matters involving POWs be resolved before a cease-fire, but the North Koreans and Chinese Communists wanted a cease-fire first. Beyond that agenda dispute were more substantive disagreements; one in particular, the United States insisted that all POWs be allowed to choose whether they wanted to be repatriated, and the North Korean and Chinese Communists insisted that all POWs be sent back to their original side. As much as any single issue, that disagreement extended the war for almost two years.

September–December 1951: The POWs in the Kuje-do camp had split into two warring factions—the Communists and the anti-Communists. They carried out beatings, fights, and kangaroo courts; those latter even handed out death sentences. Fifteen anti-Communist POWs were sentenced to death, and three POWs were killed in riots. The U.S. Army attempted to impose more control by bringing in hundreds of additional guards, but by December, there were only 9,000 U.S. and ROK soldiers to guard 100,000 POWs. On December 18, a rock fight between the two factions led to rioting; by the time the guards restored order, 14 POWs were dead and 24 wounded.

December 19–20, 1951: One of the most immediate results of the agreement on a line of demarcation (see November 27–December 21, 1951, p. 595) was a change in the treatment of certain prisoners of war. Gen. William Dean, who had been captured by the North Koreans on August 25, 1950, was interviewed and photographed on December 21 by an Australian journalist, Wilfred Burchett, in an effort to show the world that he was not being mistreated.

HOME FRONT

March 24, 1951: Gen. Douglas MacArthur, knowing of a growing call for an offer of a cease-fire, issued a statement effectively threatening to invade Communist China unless it asked for peace. That was quite different from the approach that President Harry S. Truman was planning, and it thoroughly incensed the president. MacArthur was informed that he must clear all statements with Washington, D.C.

April 5, 1951: The Republican leader in the House of Representatives, Joseph W. Martin of Massachusetts, read a letter from MacArthur that advocated using Nationalist Chinese troops to invade China (see Notable Phrases, pp. 600–601).

April 11, 1951: President Truman dismissed MacArthur from all his posts—the U.S. Far East Command as well as the UN Command. Gen. Matthew Ridgway was named to succeed MacArthur, and Gen. James Van Fleet was named to replace Ridgway as commander of the U.S. 8th Army in Korea. Truman was immediately subjected to a torrent of attacks, particularly from Republicans and conservatives, many of whom called for his impeachment.

April 17–20, 1951: General MacArthur arrived in San Francisco and experienced the first of several hero's welcomes. (He had not set foot in the United States since before World War II.) On April 19, he addressed Congress (see Notable Phrases, p. 601). On April 20, he was given a ticker-tape parade in New York City.

May 3–June 27, 1951: The Senate Armed Services and Foreign Relations Committees held hearings over the conduct of the war in Korea and the Asia policy in general. Although intended to support General MacArthur's positions and embarrass the Truman administration, the hearings ended by revealing that no one in the highest echelons of the military supported MacArthur.

June 19, 1951: President Truman signed the Universal Military Training and Service Act, extending Selective Service to July 1, 1955; it also lowered the draft age from 19 to 18 and increased the term of service from 21 months to 24 months.

October 1, 1951: Although integration of military units had been taking place throughout the U.S. Army since 1948, especially in combat conditions in Korea, only on this day did the U.S. Army formally order the end of African-American units in Korea, distributing members of the African-American 24th Infantry Regiment and 129th Field Artillery Battalion throughout the U.S. 8th Army.

INTERNATIONAL DEVELOPMENTS

January 11–February 1, 1951: A UN committee charged with finding a solution to the war in Korea presented a six-step program for peace on January 11, but Communist China rejected it on January 17. Taking advantage of that rejection, the U.S. delegate presented a resolution calling for "additional measures" to meet Chinese aggression.

BATTLES AND CAMPAIGNS: 1952

GROUND WAR

June 6–September 23, 1952: Along the front

in west-central Korea near Chorwon was a line of hills, stretching from White Horse Hill and Arrowhead Hill in the northeast to Pork Chop Hill (named for its shape; its official name was Hill 225) and Old Baldy Hill in the southwest. On June 6, the U.S. Army commander at the front, having decided to keep the enemy from establishing its artillery and observation points on these high points, launched a series of attacks. The hills were taken fairly easily, but the Chinese mounted some counterattacks. Fighting on Old Baldy was especially tough. The Chinese launched a major counteroffensive on June 27, but that was finally repulsed, as was another Chinese attack in early July. During those actions, the U.S. suffered some 350 casualties, and the Chinese suffered an estimated 1,100. In mid-July, the Chinese managed to retake Old Baldy. On July 22, six days of heavy rain interrupted the battle, but the battle recommenced on July 28. By August 1, U.S. forces were back on Old Baldy. In mid-September, the Chinese regained control briefly, but by September 21, the U.S. took it back. The struggle for that hill continued intermittently throughout the autumn of 1952 and into 1953 (see March 23–July 11, 1953, p. 593).

September 1952: The Communists launched a series of small but often costly attacks in an effort to improve their positions before winter and the peace negotiations cut them off.

October 6–13, 1952: Chinese Communist forces began some diversionary forays and opened the floodgates of a small reservoir in order to divert the UN forces from their attack on White Horse Hill some five miles northwest of Chorwon. The Communist attack itself began on October 7 and although they persisted, they were driven back by ROK units, which were assisted by heavy U.S. artillery and airplanes. After a week, the Communists pulled back, but they had suffered an estimated 23,000 casualties to the ROK forces' 3,500.

October 14–November 18, 1952: Gen. James Van Fleet, claiming that he could seize the hills to the east of the Iron Triangle with only a couple hundred casualties, launched Operation Showdown. As part of that operation, to distract and lure the North Korean forces from the main operation, the 8th Cavalry Regiment faked an amphibious landing at Kojo on the east coast, about 25 miles south of Wonsan. The main operation then bogged down in fierce fighting and ended

with the UN having improved its position only slightly, at a cost of some 9,000 U.S. and ROK casualties and 19,000 Communist casualties.

October 16, 1952: Gen. Mark Clark, who replaced Gen. Matthew Ridgway as supreme commander of the U.S. forces in the Far East, had been advocating an increasingly more aggressive strategy against the Communists. He submitted to the Joint Chiefs in Washington, D.C., an operational plan (Oplan 8–52), in which he called not only for amphibious, airborne, and enveloping assaults on the Communists in Korea but also for air and naval attacks on targets in China and Manchuria, as well as for a naval blockade of China. In his accompanying letter, Clark also asked that consideration be given to using atomic weapons. The Joint Chiefs told Clark that they would consider his views. With the victory of Dwight D. Eisenhower in the presidential election, however, they came to accept that the Korean War would be settled by political means (see Home Front, October 24, 1952, p. 592).

NAVAL WAR

(See Naval War, February 16, 1951–July 27, 1953, p. 588.)

AIR WAR

March–May 1952: In a variation on Operation Strangle, a new operation, Operation Saturate, began, with U.S. airplanes now assigned to massive blanket bombing of selected transportation sectors. When the North Koreans again showed an ability to repair destroyed facilities within a brief time, the operation was halted. Risking million-dollar planes and highly trained pilots in order, for example, to put a short stretch of track out of operation for perhaps only a few hours made little sense. Since its inception in July 1951, Operation Strangle had cost the UN 343 aircraft and had damaged another 290.

June 23–25, 1952: U.S. Air Force (USAF) and Navy planes bombed hydroelectric generating stations and transformer stations on the Yalu River that provided much of the electric power for North Korea. At the end of those raids, North Korea had lost almost 90 percent of its electrical power capacity. Those attacks drew an outburst of criticism from around the world, including some from the U.S. allies in Korea.

July–August 1952: The USAF conducted a series of bombing raids over North Korea, particularly damaging to the former capital of Pyongyang. On August 29, in the largest single air raid of the Korean War, Pyongyang was virtually leveled. Other air raids struck along the Yalu River and in one instance planes bombed an oil refinery only eight miles from Soviet territory.

POW SITUATION

As the Korean War and negotiations dragged on, POWs began to experience more difficult conditions and to create more stressful problems for the guards. Some 170,000 Communist POWs were being held in camps, about 80,000 of them on Kuje-do Island. The American and ROK guards could do little except try to guard the outer perimeters. Inside the compounds, the Communists had set up their own organizations, instilling discipline, encouraging resistance, and plotting breakouts; they even had radios with which they could communicate with the Communist leaders in North Korea. Meanwhile, the U.S. was insisting that all POWs be allowed to decide whether they wanted to return to their homelands.

February 18, 1952: A Communist-dominated compound at Kuje-do refused to let its residents be polled, but the ROK teams were determined to do so, and U.S. Army troops were assigned to help them. With fixed bayonets the Americans charged the compound early in the morning; they were met by some 1,500 POWs (most of them civilian Communists) armed with knives, axes, and various other improvised weapons. The troops opened fire and after the riot was subdued, 55 inmates were dead, 22 more died in the hospital, and 140 were wounded; one American was killed and 38 others were wounded.

March 13, 1952: In another incident at Kuje-do, a group of Communist POWs began to throw stones at anti-Communist POWs walking by with their ROK guards. The ROK soldiers began firing at the Communists; 10 were killed at once, 2 died later, and 26 were wounded. (A U.S. officer was killed accidentally.)

May 7–11, 1952: After the incident at Kuje-do prison in February, a new commandant was assigned there, Brig. Gen. Francis T. Dodd. On May 7, Dodd went to a compound to discuss grievances with Communist POWs, and they seized him. As negotiations for his release proceeded, he was replaced by Brig. Gen. Charles Colson. On May 9, Colson demanded Dodd's release, but since he was waiting for a tank company and other troop reinforcements, he made no move against the POWs. Instead, he allowed the Communists to put General Dodd on trial. The tanks and reinforcements arrived during the night, but before they were ordered to attack, the POWs sent out a document listing their demands for releasing Dodd; these included "ceasing of barbarous behavior...stopping of so- called illegal and unreasonable volunteer repatriation... recognition of the POW Representative Group." Colson signed a reply that agreed to several of the demands and even admitted that there had been "instances of bloodshed in which many POWs have been killed and wounded by UN forces." Dodd was released at 9:30 P.M. that evening. Colson's statement was very soon repudiated by the U.S. government, but the damage had been done; the international Communist movement flaunted its propaganda victory. Both Dodd and Colson were reduced in rank to colonel (which effectively ended their careers in the Army). A new commandant, Brig. Gen. Haydon Boatner, was assigned to Kuje-do along with another 5,000 UN guards.

June 10, 1952: In the weeks after he took over at Kuje-do, General Boatner gradually imposed discipline on the POWs and increased the military installations and armaments around the camp. Finally, though, he decided that he would no longer put up with the behavior of some of the more defiant POWs. Armed with tear gas and concussion grenades, U.S. troops attacked the most recalcitrant compound. In the fighting that ensued, the U.S. troops did not fire their rifles, but 31 POWs were killed and 139 wounded; one American was killed and 14 wounded. After all the compounds within the camp were subdued, thousands of homemade weapons were found (as well as the bodies of 16 POWs who had been murdered, presumably by their ideological enemies). Boatner's operation was attacked by many throughout the world, but it did put an end to the more extreme acts of defiance by the Communist POWs at Kuje-do.

December 14, 1952: Communist civilian internees on the South Korean island of Pongam near Kuje-do staged an uprising. By the time the ROK guards put down the uprising, 85 internees were dead and 113 wounded. The Soviet Union tried to get the UN to condemn the United States for that "mass murder" at Pongam; although the motion failed (45-5), ten nations abstained, indicating the world's general uneasiness with the POW situation.

HOME FRONT

April 17, 1952: President Truman signed Executive Order 10345, extending all enlistments in the armed forces for nine months, regardless of how long an enlistee had already served.

October 24, 1952: In the closing days of the U.S. presidential campaign, Dwight D. Eisenhower, the Republican candidate, gave a speech at Detroit in which he promised to bring the Korean War "to an early and honorable end... That job requires a personal trip to Korea. I shall make that trip....I shall go to Korea."

November 4, 1952: Eisenhower won the presidential election with 55 percent of the popular vote; the Democratic candidate, Adlai E. Stevenson, governor of Illinois, won 44 percent.

December 2–5, 1952: Accompanied by several high-level military and civilian leaders, President-elect Eisenhower visited Korea. He toured the combat zone and other areas. Although he endorsed the enlargement of the ROK army and removed the prohibition on the use of Nationalist Chinese troops, he did not support the expansion of the Korean War as some military leaders had urged.

INTERNATIONAL DEVELOPMENTS

February 1952: On February 2, Jacob Malik, the Soviet delegate to the UN, charged in Paris that the UN forces had been using "toxic gases" in Korea. On February 22, the North Koreans and Communist Chinese charged the UN with conducting germ warfare by dropping bacteria-carrying insects onto their troops. The UN delegates countered that if the Communist troops were becoming sick it was because of lack of proper food, medicine, and services. The Communists continued to make that charge throughout the rest of the Korean War (see Historical Perspectives and Controversies, pp. 602-603).

May–August 1952: On May 27, Syngman Rhee declared martial law and arrested some members of South Korea's National Assembly. He hoped to change the constitution and win reelection by popular vote. In July, he forced members of the assembly to amend the constitution as he wished, and on August 5, he won reelection by a landslide.

November 12, 1952: At a UN session in New York City, in an effort to break the deadlock at the stalled armistice talks in Panmunjom, India's delegates presented a plan that called for a four-nation Repatriation Commission to screen those prisoners who did not want to return to their homelands. That proposal was rejected by Communist China on December 14.

December 19, 1952: At Geneva, Switzerland, the executive committee of the League of Red Cross Societies voted 5-2 (the Soviets and Chinese opposed) that both parties in the Korean War immediately repatriate sick and wounded prisoners as a "goodwill gesture." Gen. Mark Clark encouraged Washington, D.C., to accept the recommendation. The United Nations did not accept the recommendation until February 22, 1953.

BATTLES AND CAMPAIGNS: 1953

GROUND WAR

January 20–25, 1953: United States Air Force and Navy planes had made so many wrong strikes in 1952 (either on "friendly units" or on the wrong enemy targets) that Gen. James Van Fleet organized a demonstration of the new and improved coordination of Air Force bombing techniques and ground forces—Operation Smack. The demonstration began on January 20 with a massive artillery attack into what was known as the T-Bone complex near Chorwan. Then on January 24, the Air Force dropped 136,000 tons of bombs onto T-Bone Hill. The full-scale operation began on January 25, with a strike by eight F-84 Thunderjets, followed by strikes by a total of 48 Thunderjets, each carrying two 1,000-pound bombs. That was followed by diversionary tank movements, then by more sorties by planes dropping napalm and smoke screens. That was followed by more artillery, mortars, and automatic weapons. Finally, the attack was launched on Spud Hill by three platoons from the 7th Division. Despite all that support (a total of 224,000 pounds of bombs, 8 tanks of napalm, 150,000 rounds of ammunition, plus all the supporting tanks, artillery, mortars, and other weapons), the U.S. forces failed to take T-Bone Hill. The U.S. losses were 3 dead, 61 wounded; Chinese casualties were 13 known dead, another estimated 25 dead, and an unknown number wounded. What had been set up as a demonstration of the advanced U.S techniques (with a six-page, three-color "program" handed out to the visiting generals and the press sitting in a heated bunker) had ended with little gain. When reports reached the United States suggesting the operation had been staged to impress high-ranking officers and the press, several congressmen demanded an investigation, but General Van Fleet convinced everyone that the operation had followed standard procedures.

March 23–July 11, 1953: The Chinese launched a major attack on Old Baldy Hill and nearby Pork Chop Hill, which the United States controlled. By March 26, the Chinese had regained Old Baldy. At that point, the U.S. command, deciding that the hill was not essential, called off any further attempts to take it. However, the U.S. decided to defend Pork Chop Hill. On April 16–18, a battle for the hill ensued, with many thousands of artillery rounds from both sides leaving the hill virtually barren. The U.S. forces (supported by other UN troops, including those from Colombia and Ethiopia) remained in control. For the following ten weeks, the Chinese continued to pound the hill with artillery and mortar rounds. Then on July 6, the Chinese launched a major attack with far larger forces. The U.S. command, knowing that an armistice was imminent, withdrew on July 11. Barely two weeks later, Pork Chop Hill was part of the demilitarized zone between North Korea and South Korea. The battle for Pork Chop Hill came to symbolize the futility of the Korean War in the final stages of that war.

July 13–20, 1953: Communist Chinese forces launched a major assault against six divisions of ROK and U.S. forces. In the first days of fighting, many ROK and U.S. outposts and large amounts of equipment were abandoned. The attacks were finally stopped at the Kumsong River line, with heavy casualties on both sides, but the Communists had made their point: They still had fight in them.

July 27, 1953: The armistice was signed at about 10 A.M. at Panmunjom, and the cease-fire went into effect at 11 P.M. In the final hours of the Korean War, both sides exchanged some-times deadly artillery and mortar barrages.

NAVAL WAR

(See Naval War, February 16, 1951–July 27, 1953, p. 588.)

AIR WAR

May 10–20, 1953: In an effort to force the Communists to negotiate seriously, the USAF conducted some of the most intensive bombing raids of the Korean War on North Korean targets, including a major dam, several reservoirs, and many irrigation dikes.

June 10–16, 1953: To support the ROK forces being pushed back by the Chinese, U.S. and UN air forces mounted some of the most intensive air attacks of the Korean War, which were aimed at destroying the Communist supply lines as well as their best frontline troops.

July 1953: Up to the final day of the Korean War, UN airplanes conducted sorties against the Communists, with the goal of establishing that the UN controlled the skies and would continue the air war if the negotiations failed.

POW SITUATION

April 20–26, 1953: A major exchange of POWs, the so-called Little Switch, took place at Panmunjom: The UN turned over 5,194 North Korean soldiers, 1,030 Chinese soldiers, and 44 civilians. The North Koreans and Chinese turned over 684 sick and wounded UN POWs, 149 of them Americans.

June 18, 1953: President Syngman Rhee, in an effort to sabotage the armistice agreement, ordered his forces to release some 27,000 North Koreans who did not want to be repatriated to their homelands. Rhee was denounced by many, including some American leaders.

August 5–September 6, 1953: Operation Big Switch, the final exchange of POWs, took place. There were 12,773 UN POWs repatriated, including 3,597 Americans, 945 Britons, 229 Turks, 140 other UN soldiers, and 7,862 ROK soldiers. Some 75,823 Communist POWs (North Koreans and Chinese) were repatriated.

September 23–24, 1953: On September 23, the UN turned over to the Neutral Nation Repatriations Commission (NNRC) some 22,604 POWs (mostly Chinese who had been forced into the Communist army) who did not want to be repatriated, and the next day, the Communists turned over 359 nonrepatriates, including 23 Americans. As called for in the armistice agreement, the NNRC retained custody of those individuals for 120 days, then released them; two of the 23 Americans chose to return to the United States but the rest went to Communist countries. Some 630 of the former POWs in UN camps changed their minds and returned to their Communist homelands. But most of the remaining 22,000 who had been POWs in UN camps chose to settle in South Korea or Taiwan: In one sense, the last two years of the Korean War had essentially been fought over their right to do so.

HOME FRONT

January 20, 1953: Dwight D. Eisenhower was inaugurated the 34th president of the United States.

June 18, 1953: President Eisenhower sent a message to Syngman Rhee, president of South Korea, accusing him of violating the UN's agenda by releasing thousands of North Korean POWs from camps earlier in the day.

INTERNATIONAL DEVELOPMENTS

February 22, 1953: The U.S. government announced it was accepting the invitation of the Red Cross (see International Developments, December 19, 1952, p. 592) to exchange sick and wounded prisoners.

March 5, 1953: Joseph Stalin, premier and dictator of the Soviet Union, died in Moscow. Almost immediately, there was speculation that the Soviet Union would be more willing to negotiate an end to the war in Korea.

April 18, 1953: The UN General Assembly, aware that the two sides were close to a compromise on the POW issues, adopted Resolution 705 (VII), which called for a reconvening of the armistice sessions at Panmunjom.

NEGOTIATIONS AND PEACE TREATY

The Korean War was unique in that the negotiations for an armistice consumed more time than the war itself—indeed, more days of combat (and more casualties) occurred during the armistice negotiations than had occurred before

the negotiations began.

March 19, 1951: At the request of President Harry S. Truman, top U.S. civilian and military officials began circulating a draft proposal for a cease-fire offer to the Chinese Communists. The United States hoped the proposal would lead to an end to the fighting and to a political solution for Korea's reunification.

June 1, 1951: UN Secretary-General Trygve Lie announced that a cease-fire near the 38th parallel would be acceptable to the UN forces. Top-level U.S. officials agreed, but preferred to carry on negotiations with the Soviets behind the scenes. In the weeks that followed, the U.S. civilian leaders became convinced that the Soviets would also agree to that and would bring their Chinese and Korean allies to accept the 38th parallel.

June 23, 1951: Soviet UN delegate Jacob Malik broadcast a proposal for discussing a cease-fire in Korea. The U.S. government soon accepted that the proposal represented Soviet policy.

June 30, 1951: After receiving the text from Washington, D.C., Gen. Matthew Ridgway, who had replaced Gen. Douglas MacArthur as commander of the UN forces in Korea, broadcast a request to the commanders of the North Korean forces to meet to discuss an armistice. But what Ridgway was offering, on instructions from Washington, D.C., was strictly a military cease-fire along the present battle line—not a return to the 38th parallel or a solution to territorial and political questions.

July 1, 1951: The North Korean and Chinese commanders issued a joint statement agreeing to meet with representatives of the UN forces at Kaesong along the 38th parallel; they also proposed to suspend all military operations at once and throughout the negotiations. General Ridgway was convinced that the Communists would take advantage of a cease-fire to build up their armed forces and recommended to officials in Washington, D.C., that the UN agree only to meeting the Communists to discuss an armistice.

July 2, 1951: With the concurrence of Washington, D.C., Ridgway informed the Communist leaders that the United Nations would meet at Kaesong but that armistice terms would have to be worked out there before cessation of hostilities.

July 10, 1951: U.S. Vice Adm. C. Turner Joy,

the chief UN negotiator, and several other high-ranking U.S. and South Korean military officers, attended the first meeting with representatives of the Communist forces at Kaesong. (The character of the negotiations, which dragged on for two years, was foreshadowed by two minor episodes: Admiral Joy placed a small UN flag on the table, and later a slightly larger North Korean flag appeared beside the UN flag. Admiral Joy, noticing that his chair was closer to the floor than that of North Korea's chief negotiator, demanded that all chairs be the same height.) Because each side had its own goals, disagreements surfaced immediately. The United States wanted a demilitarized zone along the existing battle line (which was, at that point, north of the 38th parallel) and an armistice commission with the right to monitor compliance with an end to military buildup. The Communists wanted a restoration of the 38th parallel as the boundary between the two Koreas and the withdrawal of all foreign troops, including the Chinese forces and the UN forces.

July 11–August 4, 1951: Several meetings produced few results as the two sides insisted on their own goals. Meanwhile, President Syngman Rhee was furious with the United States for its willingness to negotiate any compromises or terms with the Communists.

August 10, 1951: After a six-day break because of the U.S. protest over the presence of armed Chinese soldiers in the conference area, talks resumed. But when the Communists insisted on discussing a return to the 38th parallel as an armistice line, the two sides sat in total silence for two hours and ten minutes before departing.

August 11–23, 1951: Talks continued in the form of the trading of insults. On August 22, a bomber flew overhead and dropped some bombs near the area. Each side accused the other of having called in an air strike; most authorities later agreed that it was a U.S. bomber that had made a mistake in its target. The next day, the Communists broke off the talks.

October 7, 1951: After weeks of hurling charges and countercharges at each other, the two sides agreed to move the conference site to Panmunjom, a tiny village a few miles southeast of Kaesong.

October 25–November 26, 1951: The delegates met at the new conference site, but the two sides continued to argue over the location of a demarcation line and a demilitarized zone. Behind the scenes, journalists from the United States and other UN countries grumbled about their lack of access to the UN delegates. Meanwhile, the top-level U.S. military negotiators were being pressured by Washington, D.C., to concede to some of the Communist demands in order to get the talks moving. On November 26, the UN delegates acceded to the Communists' request to draw a military line of demarcation that included Kaesong in Communist territory. U.S. forces suffered some 22,000 casualties in the weeks that had passed since July 10.

November 27–December 21, 1951: A 30-day agreement on the line of demarcation was reached. That 30-day period became known as the "Little Armistice." But as negotiations proceeded, both sides became deadlocked over several issues. The UN shifted to demanding an exchange of information about and visits to prisoners of war. The Communists asked for the immediate release of all prisoners within 30 days after an armistice was signed. Meanwhile, the judge advocate general of the 8th Army issued a report charging that the Communists had killed at least 5,500 U.S. prisoners. Finally, on December 18, the Communists agreed to provide data about the POWs in their camps.

December 1951–January 25, 1952: The issue causing the greatest disagreement in the negotiations revolved around the insistence by the United States that the North Koreans not be allowed to rebuild airfields capable of handling jet aircraft. As they could come to no agreement on that issue, the delegates agreed to set it aside temporarily and move on to other issues. At the end, the United States gave in on that point.

January 2–May 22, 1952: The UN delegates proposed that all POWs be allowed to choose whether they wanted to return to their homelands. The Communists rejected the proposal, and negotiations over the ensuing weeks deadlocked over that issue. The Communists did, however, agree to issue a declaration of amnesty to all Communist POWs, and that allowed the UN to interview all the prisoners as to their wishes. On April 20, the UN delegates announced that 70,000 of the 132,000 Communist prisoners did not want to be repatriated. The Communists insisted that all 132,000 had to be sent back, and the negotiations remained deadlocked. On May 22, Adm. C. Turner Joy wrote a long letter to the

Communist delegates that chastised them for their behavior; he also announced his resignation as the chief UN negotiator; he was replaced by Maj. Gen. William K. Harrison.

May 23–October 8, 1952: General Harrison took up negotiations where Admiral Joy left off, but there was no progress on the POW issue. After several days, Harrison walked out of the conference and thereafter met only after frequent recesses. Meanwhile, the events at the Koje POW camp, where the new U.S. commandant had mounted an attack on the buildings held by the more extreme Communist POWs, had led to worldwide criticism of the U.S. treatment of their prisoners. Taking advantage of that and their charges that the UN had resorted to germ warfare (see Historical Perspectives and Controversies, pp. 602-603), the Communists held fast to their demand that all POWs be repatriated. On October 8, General Harrison said that the UN would take a recess, and the talks ceased. Harrison returned to Tokyo, and efforts to revive the negotiations shifted to the UN in New York City.

March 5–April 26, 1953: On March 5, Joseph Stalin, the leader of the Soviet Union, died. Ten days later, his successor as chairman of the Council of Ministers, Georgy Malenkov, issued statements that indicated he was willing to use Soviet influence to get the peace negotiations moving.

March 28, 1953: The first sign of a change in Communist policy came when North Korean and Chinese commanders accepted the offer of an exchange of sick and wounded prisoners. They went a bit further by stating that the exchange should lead to resolving the POW issue.

March 30, 1953: China's Premier Chou En-lai proposed a compromise on the repatriation of POWs: All POWs who wanted to be repatriated would be allowed to do so after an armistice, and those who did not would be handed over to a neutral state. That was essentially the plan put forth by the Indian delegate at the UN (see International Developments, November 12, 1952, p. 592). The Soviet Union endorsed that proposal, but the United States remained cautious, not certain what was meant by "a neutral state."

April 26–June 4, 1953: Formal negotiations commenced again and immediately bogged down over many of the same issues. Meanwhile, the United States intensified its bombing of North Korean targets. On May 25, General Harrison agreed to the Chinese proposal to release to certain neutral countries the POWs who rejected repatriation. By June 4, the Communists and the UN negotiators were in agreement on all except a few minor conditions.

June 19, 1953: When word of the "escape" of some 25,000 POWs held in South Korean camps reached the Communist negotiators at Panmunjom and their leaders in their home capitals, they refused to accept that Syngman Rhee had released the POWs without the connivance of the United States. In fact, the United States had been caught off guard, and President Eisenhower was among the first to scold Rhee. All the Communist leaders denounced the United States and South Korea, and negotiations were broken off at once.

July 10–25, 1953: The meetings at Panmunjom resumed, and after some final negotiations over the demarcation line, agreement was announced on July 25.

July 27, 1953: At the specially constructed Peace Pagoda at Panmunjom, General Nam II, the chief delegate of the North Koreans, and General Harrison, the chief UN delegate, signed the armistice in silence shortly after 10 A.M. The cease-fire did not go into effect for another 12 hours, but the Korean War was officially over.

October–December 12, 1953: The first meetings of the political conference called for in the armistice were held at Panmunjom. After several futile sessions, the U.S. representative walked out on December 12. In the years since, occasional meetings between the various parties have been held at Panmunjom, and although charges and countercharges have been traded, the meetings continue with few concrete results. The original military demarcation line and demilitarized zone remain in place, with no sign of ever being eliminated.

April 26–June 15, 1954: Representatives of North Korea and South Korea, the United States, China, the Soviet Union, Britain, and France met at Geneva, Switzerland, to negotiate a permanent peace plan for Korea. After weeks of charges and countercharges, they were unable to agree on any terms, let alone on a plan to unify Korea. As of 1997, no peace treaty has ever been signed.

RESULTS OF THE WAR (Casualties, Costs, Consequences)

There have never been fully accepted official

figures for North Korea's casualties, but the United States military estimates that North Korea's military losses were 215,000 dead, 304,000 wounded, and 102,000 missing (and presumed dead). Another 1 million North Korean civilians were probably killed (many of them by the South Korean troops during their occupation of North Korea).

Although no official casualty figures were ever released by Communist China, U.S. military estimates place their losses at 400,000 dead, 490,000 wounded, and 21,000 missing (and presumed dead).

South Korean military casualties are reliably estimated at some 47,000 dead, 160,000 wounded, and 66,000 missing (and presumed dead). Probably another 1 million South Korean civilians were killed (many of them by North Korean troops during their occupation of South Korea).

The United States reported 54,246 dead (33,629 killed in combat and another 20,617 who died from accidents, diseases, and other noncombat causes). There were 103,284 wounded, and 12,939 missing (and presumed dead).

The United Kingdom, Australia, Canada, and New Zealand suffered considerable casualties: an estimated total of 1,263 killed, 4,817 wounded, and 1,000 missing (and presumed dead).

Other UN forces (contingents from Belgium, Colombia, Ethiopia, France, Greece, the Netherlands, the Philippines, South Africa, Thailand, and Turkey) had an estimated 1,800 dead, 7,000 wounded, and 1,000 missing.

Exact dollar values have never been assigned to the costs and material losses in the Korean War. North Korea lost most of its industrial and transportation infrastructures, and its arable land was temporarily devastated. The devastation in South Korea was almost as bad as that in North Korea. In today's terms, the destruction in Korea would add up to several billion dollars. U.S. Air Force general Emmett O'Donnell, drawing on his firsthand observations of the scene, stated: "I would say that the entire, almost the entire Korean peninsula is just a terrible mess. Everything is destroyed. There is nothing standing worthy of the name." And he said that at the Senate hearings in May 1951—two years before the Korean War ended.

Because the Korean War did not spread into China (except for the odd airplane raids into Manchuria), it did not destroy Chinese civilian

property, but it proved very costly for China to maintain and equip the hundreds of thousands of troops they fielded. The Soviet Union lent China money and military equipment, but then not only demanded repayment but also charged China interest. The Soviet Union also effectively equipped and supplied the North Korean armed forces throughout the war, and that must have run to several billion dollars in today's terms.

The United States spent an estimated $70 billion (in 1990 dollars) on the Korean War, and the other UN nations spent about a quarter of that. Quite aside from the massive costs for equipment, arms, transportation, and other direct outlays, there were costs associated with personnel (including such secondary expenses as medical expenses, insurance payments, and veterans pensions).

The most immediate outcome of the Korean War was that it left Korea as it was before the war: split in two. The difference was that the demarcation line ran for the most part somewhat north of the 38th parallel, so that South Korea gained 1,500 square miles of territory. In addition, there was a buffer, or demilitarized, zone 2.5 miles wide along the battle line.

Both sides agreed not to increase their military strength, but in the years that followed, both sides inevitably ignored that agreement: North Korea and South Korea long supported large military forces, each well equipped by one of the super powers (the Soviet Union in the case of North Korea, the United States in the case of South Korea).

The truce called for a political conference to negotiate a final peace settlement, but that goal has never been achieved (at least through 1997). The issue of reunification of Korea kept being postponed. The United Nations Commission for Unification and Rehabilitation of Korea was abolished in 1972, with the idea that the two parts of Korea could work out reunification by themselves, but that has not happened.

The Military Armistice Commission was established to enforce the truce terms, and that has continued to meet periodically at Panmunjom in the decades since the Korean War. Over the years, there have been various "incidents" at or near the demarcation line, some involving the killing of military personnel.

Because unresolved tensions and even the threat of war hung over the two parts of Korea, it was easy for the leaders to assert virtual dictatorial control over their countrymen. In South Korea, Syngman Rhee remained in office until April 1960, when he was forced by student demonstrations to resign. His successor, Gen. Park Chung Hee, seized power in 1961 and gradually became a dictator as well. In 1968, about 30 North Koreans made a raid into Seoul and tried to assassinate President Park. Although that attempt failed, he was assassinated by the director of the Korean Central Intelligence Agency in 1979.

Kim Il Sung remained in firm control of North Korea until his death in 1994; he was succeeded by his son, Kim Jong Il, who gave some signs of slightly relaxing the rigidity and isolation of North Korea. In general, though, South Korea prospered greatly by taking up modern manufacturing and entering into trade with the West; North Korea isolated itself, and its economy and standard of living went gradually downhill in the decades after the Korean War.

The demarcation line in Korea outlasted the Berlin Wall as a symbol of the schism between the Communist and non-Communist worlds, and relations between North Korea and the non-Communist world have remained particularly hostile across the decades. By the same token, the willingness of the United States in particular and its allies in the United Nations in general to send so many personnel and so much equipment to defend a minor state seemed to have given considerable pause to the leaders of the Soviet Union and Communist China. It can never be proved, but President Truman's swift and bold moves in going to the aid of South Korea may have deterred the Communist countries from risking direct military challenge to the Western allies elsewhere in the world during the long decades of the Cold War. On the other hand, the Americans most closely involved with the Korean War, including the major military leaders, emerged convinced that the United States should avoid becoming engaged in a land war in Asia. Yet, little more than a decade after the armistice in Korea, the United States began to commit military forces to Vietnam.

MILITARY INNOVATIONS, TACTICS, EQUIPMENT

The use of airplanes, both fighters and bombers, in support of ground operations had been developed in World War II, but it was brought to a higher state during the Korean War. That came about not only through better communications equipment but also through the adoption of U.S. Marine Corps procedures. At least one trained individual, known as the Tactical Air Control Party (TACP), was assigned to each Marine battalion; the TACP then maintained close contact with the air-support plane (usually a Corsair) flying overhead; that plane then called in the fighters and/or bombers and directed them in such a way as to avoid inflicting casualties on their own personnel (a major risk when airplanes operated close to frontline units).

Although jet fighters had appeared near the end of World War II, it was not until the Korean War that they came to play a significant role. As it happened, it was the Communist Chinese who introduced them first. In November 1950 the Chinese appeared with their Soviet-built MiG-15s, which at once became a serious threat to the U.S. propeller-driven F- 51 Mustangs. By December 15, however, the first U.S. F-86 Sabrejets began to appear; those were eventually replaced by the F-84 Thunderjets and F-80 Shooting Stars. The MiGs remained a versatile opponent, but U.S. pilots tended to be more skilled and in general held the advantage. In their speed and maneuverability and firepower, jet fighters changed forever the nature of air combat.

One of the major military innovations of the Korean War was the use of helicopters by UN forces (principally by the United States) for a variety of purposes. One was for battlefield observation. The U.S. Marine Corps pioneered that use when it sent the first operational helicopter unit in military history, the Marine Observation Squadron Six (VMO-6), to Korea in August 1950. Those helicopters served to report enemy troop movements and to provide information helpful to artillery units and other operations. Another role played by helicopters was to transport personnel and supplies to frontline units; with that swift means of deploying troops came the concept known to the U.S. military as vertical envelopment. Closely related to that was the more frequent use of helicopters for transporting cargo—everything from emergency medical supplies to ammunition and food rations—to the front lines.

Perhaps the most revolutionary uses of helicopters, however, were air-sea rescue missions and evacuation of the wounded. The former involved mostly downed pilots. The latter involved moving wounded soldiers and marines from frontline positions either to rear-area hospitals or to hospital ships offshore. In December 1951, the USS *Consolation* became the first hospital ship to receive wounded soldiers flown by helicopter directly from a battlefield. (Regular transport planes flew the seriously sick and wounded to Japan or to the United States.)

Closely related to the use of helicopters and airplanes for evacuating and transporting the wounded was the establishment of the Mobile Army Surgical Units, the MASH units later popularized by a novel, movie, and TV series (see Legends and Trivia, p. 600). Staffed by surgeons and other doctors, nurses, and support personnel, these units were designed to move quickly to stay close to combat operations. After those needing immediate surgical care had been treated in a MASH unit, the patients were evacuated to hospitals elsewhere. In the course of the Korean War, MASH units and other military hospitals pioneered several medical innovations, including peripheral vascular surgery (which greatly reduced the need for amputations), the identification of a clotting defect in the seriously wounded, and the use of plastic bags for blood and intravenous solutions.

The difference between the medical statistics for the U.S. military in World War II and the Korean War tell much of the story. In World War II, an average 12–15 hours were needed to evacuate the wounded by hand-carried litters and ground vehicles; in the Korean War an average 6–10 hours were needed. Whereas in World War II the development of gas gangrene in wounds was 0.7 percent, with a fatality rate of 31 percent, in the Korean War, it dropped to 0.08 percent, with no reported fatalities. The mortality rate for hospitalized wounded in World War II was 4.5 percent but only 2.5 percent in the Korean War; and although 28 percent of all U.S. military wounded died in World War II, only 22 percent died in the Korean War.

A minor but important innovation of the Korean War was the issuing of body armor, or armored vests, to combat troops. The vests were made of pads of woven nylon and plates of a plastic known as *doron*; they were capable of stopping a .45 caliber bullet, fragments of a hand grenade thrown from a distance of three feet, the full thrust of a bayonet, and 75 percent of the

fragments of a 81mm mortar. There were only 40 of those vests available for testing in the spring of 1951, but by the spring of 1952 the vests were being used by many Army and Marine troops.

LEGENDS AND TRIVIA

Although many American military personnel performed heroically in Korea, the war gave rise to no widely popular folk heroes. There was one such hero, though—**Marguerite Higgins**, a journalist. She first came to prominence for her reporting from Germany at the end of World War II and during the early years of the Cold War. When the Korean War broke out, she was a correspondent in Tokyo for the New York *Herald Tribune*. On June 27, she flew to South Korea and immediately began to report from the front lines. Some U.S. Army officers in the field were bothered by the petite woman who seemed impervious to falling shells and palpable danger; several of them persuaded Gen. Walton Walker that she should not be allowed in Korea, and on July 12, he forced her to fly to Tokyo. However, there was such an international outcry (a Soviet newspaper's cartoon, captioned "MacArthur's First Victory," showed MacArthur kicking Higgins out of Korea) that MacArthur ordered that she be allowed to return. Within days she was back in Korea, where she continued to file dramatic and engaging stories from the front lines. In 1965, she went off to report on the war in Vietnam, where she contracted a rare tropical disease, which took her life in 1966. To the end, Marguerite Higgins remained the epitome of a true war correspondent at a time when women were a rarity in a male-dominated profession.

In general, the Korean War did not inspire much in the area of culture. Although Harvey Kurtzman did a series of comic books about the war that enjoyed considerable popularity with boys at home and troops in the field, there was no memorable literature that came out of the war. But it did inspire a number of **movies**, starting with Samuel Fuller's *Steel Helmets* (1951) and *Fixed Bayonets* (1951). Then came several others: *Retreat, Hell!* (1952, directed by Joseph H. Lewis), *Battle Zone* (1952, directed by Lesley Selander), *One Minute to Zero* (1952, directed by Tay Garnett), *Mission Over Korea* (1953, directed by Fred F. Sears), *Sabre Jet* (1953, directed by Louis King), *The Glory Brigade* (1953, directed by Robert D. Webb). After the war ended, more ambitious movies were made. One of the most popular was *The Bridges at Toko-Ri* (1955, directed by Mark Robson), based on James Michener's novel; *Pork Chop Hill* (1959, directed by Lewis Milestone) gained some serious appreciation for its stress on the psychological aspects of the Korean War; *All the Young Men* (1960, directed by Hall Bartlett) dealt with race relations among the Marines in Korea. *The Manchurian Candidate* (1962, directed by John Frankenheimer) dealt with brainwashing and the Communist threat. One of the true curiosities was *Prisoner of War* (1954, directed by Andrew Marton), in which Ronald Reagan's character volunteers to be captured in investigate the conditions of the POWs in the Communist camps.

Although the Korean War inspired very few popular images, perhaps the best known was *M*A*S*H*. Inspired by the Mobile Army Surgical Hospital units, which were known by their acronym, MASH, *M*A*S*H* was the title and subject of a novel by Richard Hooker published in 1968. Although the novel enjoyed mild success as a gently comic look at the Korean War, it was not until Robert Altman made it into a movie in 1970 that it reached a really broad public. The success of the movie then led to a TV series, which began in 1972 and ran until 1983; its final episode drew one of the largest audiences ever for a regularly scheduled show on American TV. During the early years of the series, the United States was involved in the Vietnam War, which is why much of the attitude, humor, and social commentary of that Korean War–based sitcom looked suspiciously like events in Vietnam; moreover, the resonance of the show reflected the 1960s legacy of an antiwar and antiauthority culture.

NOTABLE PHRASES

Would it be correct to call this a police action under the United Nations?

On Thursday, June 29, 1950, two days after he had committed U.S. forces to resisting the North Koreans, President Harry S. Truman held a press conference in Washington, D.C. At one point, he insisted, "We are not at war," and he encouraged the press to quote those very words. Shortly afterward, he referred to the North Koreans' invasion as a raid by "a bunch of bandits."

Then a reporter asked Truman the question quoted above. Truman replied that that was exactly what it was, and for some time thereafter, in at least some situations, the war in Korea was called a police action. The U.S. military, meanwhile, continued to refer to it officially as the Korean Conflict until 1958. But most Americans recognized from early on that the United States had gone to war in Korea.

This is not retreat. This is an assault in another direction.

By the first days of December 1950, UN forces around the Chosin Reservoir were threatened with virtual annihilation by the Chinese (see November 27–December 11, 1950, p. 582). The UN forces decided that they must break out and pull back to the east coast. Col. Raymond Murray, commander of the 5th Marine Regiment, called his officers together on a snow-swept field and told them, "At daylight, we advance to the rear." Seeing their dismay at what lay ahead and what that meant to the tradition that Marines never retreated, he reiterated his claim with the words above. Although the phrase is often quoted in an ironic tone, Murray intended to let his men know that they faced a real battle to get away alive.

In war there is no substitute for victory.

Almost from the outset of the war in Korea, Gen. Douglas MacArthur took public positions that often embarrassed and sometimes contradicted U.S. civilian and military leaders. Although U.S. leaders were trying their best to limit the war to Korea and keep Communist China out of the war, MacArthur openly declared that he should be allowed to bomb Manchuria, blockade the Chinese coast, and make use of thousands of Nationalist Chinese troops offered by Chiang Kai-shek. Inevitably, many opposed to President Harry S. Truman's policies sought to exploit the differences between MacArthur and the Truman administration. Joseph W. Martin, the Republican minority leader of the House of Representatives, wrote to MacArthur asking if Nationalist Chinese troops should not be used to open up a second front on China's mainland. MacArthur replied, and Martin read the letter on the floor of the House on April 5, 1951. In a typical

MacArthur flourish, the letter stated that Martin's proposal "is in conflict with neither logic nor...tradition." MacArthur concluded his letter with the words quoted above, clearly a slap at Truman and those who were restraining MacArthur from carrying out what he regarded as a sure plan for victory.

I still remember the refrain of one of the most popular barracks ballads of that day, which proclaimed most proudly that "Old soldiers never die; they just fade away." And like the old soldier of that ballad, I now close my military career and just fade away—an old soldier who tried to do his duty as God gave him the light to see that duty. Goodbye.

After being dismissed by President Harry S. Truman on April 11, 1951, Gen. Douglas MacArthur returned to the United States and received a tumultuous hero's welcome, made even more pronounced by the fact that he was one of the great heroes of World War II and that he had not returned to the United States at the end of that war. Inevitably, he became a rallying point for many who opposed President Truman and his policies. On April 19, 1951, MacArthur addressed a joint meeting (not a session, which would have signified a formal state function) of the U.S. Congress. After a speech delivered in his customary magisterial manner, he concluded with the words quoted above. The song MacArthur referred to was a British army song from World War I. There was a small push to get him the Republican nomination for president in 1952, but that honor went to his old rival, Gen. Dwight Eisenhower, after which MacArthur did in fact "just fade away."

The American who has never known defeat in war does not expect to be again sold down the river in Asia. He does not want that kind of betrayal. He has had betrayal enough. He has never failed to fight for his liberties....He is fighting tonight, fighting gloriously in a war on a distant American frontier made inglorious by the men he can no longer trust at the head of our affairs.

Sen. Joseph R. McCarthy (R–Wis.) burst onto the broader public scene in February 1950 by charging that the U.S. State Department had been infiltrated by Communists. In the months that followed, he maintained his position as the leader of those who blamed Communists for many of the problems in the United States and in the world at large. Among the charges made by McCarthy and many of his supporters was that the Democrats had "lost China" through a combination of liberal wishy-washiness and almost traitorous leftist inclination. When the war in Korea came along, McCarthy exploited it to further his own agenda. The short excerpt quoted here is from a speech he made in the Senate on June 14, 1951, and is typical of the rhetoric that he used so deftly to create the phenomenon known as "McCarthyism."

SONGS

Popular music, often a good gauge of what Americans are thinking about, turned a deaf ear to the Korean War. During the early 1950s, Americans sang Irving Berlin's "I Like Ike" and a popular patriotic song, "This Is God's Country," but neither of those was inspired by the war. The same held true for the popular revival of "She Wore a Yellow Ribbon" in 1950: Its sentiment might seem to have been related to the troops in Korea, but neither its origins nor its lyrics really had anything to do with the war (see Gulf War, Songs, p. 716).

American Donald Erb composed "God Loves You Now," a setting of Thomas McGrath's "Ode for the American Dead in Korea," for chorus and instrumental ensemble; coincidentally, perhaps, that was not published until 1973, by which time the Vietnam War had come to dominate Americans' consciousness. Another strange coincidence was the appearance of a country music song, "Bonaparte's Retreat" by Pee Wee King, on the Hit Parade in the late autumn of 1950: Although its lyrics had nothing to do with the Korean War, its allusion to Napoleon's retreat from Moscow during a bitterly cold winter was apparently a chance premonition of the imminent retreat of U.S. forces in the snow of Korea.

HISTORICAL PERSPECTIVES AND CONTROVERSIES

Was either the Soviet Union or Communist China directly involved in the initial decision to attack and the actual attack by the North Koreans on South Korea?

That question, which seemed so crucial at the time of the Korean War, has never been absolutely resolved in all the years since. The tendency of the times, in the United States at least, was to see the Soviet Union as dominating and masterminding everything that went on in the international Communist movement. In the decades since, historians have recognized that the international Communist movement was far less monolithic than it seemed at the time. As for the Soviet's literal involvement, much rests on Nikita Khrushchev's claim (not revealed until 1970) that, in fact, North Korean premier Kim Il Sung visited Joseph Stalin in 1950 and had set forth his intention of invading South Korea. According to Khrushchev, Stalin discussed that with Mao Tse-tung, then, convinced that Kim Il Sung could carry it off, encouraged Kim to go ahead. Documents discovered in the mid-1990s in Soviet files reveal that Stalin did give verbal support to Kim's plan to invade the South. But the initiative came from Kim Il Sung.

One argument for the claim that Stalin assumed that the North Koreans could carry out a quick conquest without international intervention on either side was the fact that he did not send his UN delegate, Jacob Malik, to the Security Council sessions where he could have used the Soviet veto to bring an abrupt halt to the UN "police action" (see Declaration of War, pp. 573-574). Some historians have claimed that Stalin's real goal was to distract the United States by the disturbance in Korea and so weaken the U.S. commitment in Europe.

When, in the fall of 1950, Stalin saw how committed the United States had become and that the North Koreans were threatened by total defeat, some historians have contended—and secret Soviet documents discovered in the mid-1990s support this—that he encouraged Mao Tse-tung to bring his Chinese forces into the fray. The Soviets provided large quantities of arms and equipment to the Chinese, but when the Korean War ended, the Soviets billed the Chinese for those supplies. The Chinese suffered horrendous casualties in the war and allegedly came to feel that they had been used by Stalin—in effect, weakened so as to eliminate them as a potential rival to the Soviet Union. Although some historians have traced the Sino-Soviet split of the 1960s back to that issue, it is impossible to prove one way or the other.

The consensus, then, is that neither the Soviets nor the Communist Chinese were the instigators of the attack by the North Koreans, but that they were supporters. In any case, most students of the Korean War agree that there was no coordinated Sino-Soviet strategy for Korea.

Did the United States employ chemical and/ or bacteriological weapons during the Korean War?

The U.S. Army's Second Chemical Mortar Battalion, which was manned by personnel of the Chemical Corps, was equipped with 4.2-inch heavy mortars that were designed to fire toxic-gas shells. In fact, toxic-gas shells were never fired; the battalion spent the Korean War firing regular mortar shells in support of infantry operations. After the charges that the United States was either using or about to use chemical weapons reached a peak, the battalion was disbanded in October 1952, and its mortars and personnel were reassigned to regular infantry units.

As the war in Korea dragged on, the world at large tended to lose interest, but Communists, both in North Korea and abroad, tried at times to gain attention and sympathy by accusing the UN forces—the United States in particular—with resorting to chemical and bacteriological weapons. On February 2, 1952, Jacob Malik, the Soviet Union's delegate to the United Nations, repeated an earlier North Korean charge that the "Anglo-American bloc" had been using bullets filled with a "toxic gas." North Korea and Communist China went beyond that charge and claimed that U.S. bombs and artillery shells carried "germs"—specifically, beetles, lice, flies, ticks, snails, and rodents—that spread typhus, the bubonic plague, and other diseases. The Communists prepared fake exhibits, coerced some U.S. prisoners of war into supporting the charges, and conducted an investigation under the auspices of the Communist-dominated World Peace Council. (The Communists rejected offers by the Red Cross and the World Health Organization to investigate those charges.) Although no reliable evidence was offered at the time, the charge of germ warfare was taken up not only by the international Communist movement but also by some respected individuals, such as the noted British biochemist and historian of science, Joseph Needham.

In the years since, most objective investigators have concluded that although the United States did develop and maintain this capacity, and may even have considered using nerve gas and/or insect vectors as delivery systems for germs, the United States never did employ chemical or bacteriological weapons in the Korean War.

Did U.S troops, in combat and as prisoners of war, conduct themselves in a manner that lived up to the proclaimed standards of the U.S. military?

In the case of combat performance, starting from the earliest battles in the Korean War, United States forces came under some criticism for their failure to hold the line against the advancing North Koreans. There were tales of soldiers abandoning their posts and equipment, running away from the front lines and combat—in other words, cowardice, desertion, and total disarray, both in the ranks and among officers. When the United States regrouped and went on the offensive after the Inchon landing in September 1950, such accusations temporarily vanished, but when the U.S. forces began to retreat again in November–December 1950, and those accusations resurfaced.

That there was disarray and desertion is not disputed, but the consensus today is that such behavior came about because the U.S. troops were not properly trained, equipped, or led. Decisions made by numerous American leaders, civilian as well as military, left the frontline troops completely exposed, especially in the early months of the war. Furthermore, thousands of young Americans were thrown into Korea with no real understanding of why they were expected to fight to the end in that remote land and obscure struggle; it was perhaps inevitable that some retreated or fled in the frenzy of battle. The fact remains that some 33,700 Americans gave up their lives in combat.

Part of the controversy involves the alleged behavior of certain African-American units. Much of the Army was still segregated, and it had been suggested that at least some of those units did not behave well in combat. Again, though, objective students of that notion have concluded that those African-American units behaved no differently than the all-white units; the behavior of the African-American troops had much to do with the poor leadership of their white commanders. Clay Blair, author of one of the most highly regarded accounts of the Korean War, has said that "the bottom line is that the 24th [Infantry Regiment, an African-American unit] didn't do any worse" than other army units. And the official history of the regiment prepared by the Army's Center of Military History concluded, "Although the 24th Infantry clearly faltered in Korea, the race of its people was not the reason."

The case of U.S. prisoners of war is somewhat more complicated. There were numerous individuals (many of them officers) who did indeed give in to the constant indoctrination and propaganda campaigns they were subjected to in the POW camps: It was no coincidence that the term "brainwashing" gained wide currency during the Korean War. Some American prisoners, including several officers, confessed to conducting germ warfare or made broadcasts praising their captors. And 21 Americans refused to be repatriated at the end of the war, preferring instead to remain in the Communist world. But all that must be understood in the full context of the POW camps: Physical conditions were often atrocious, with prisoners being denied food, heat, medicine, and clothing. Treatment, especially from the North Koreans (the Chinese were better), was often barbaric. American POWs were young men, totally isolated from their familiar world, never sure why they had been thrown into the war; if it was a matter of death or survival, some prisoners felt they might as well cooperate to live. Hundreds of Americans died during the forced marches to the POW camps. Why would a young soldier not cooperate a bit in order to be fed properly once he made it to a camp? (It has been reliably reported that some of the so-called collaborators were killed by their fellow POWs on the trip to the prisoner exchange in August 1953. And the U.S. Army court-martialed 14 former POWs for collaborating with the enemy.)

All that said, serious issues were raised in the years after the Korean War when the story of the behavior of Americans in the POW camps came out (in such books as Eugene Kinkead's *In Every War but One*, 1959). It was revealed that young men of other countries, including Turkish soldiers, behaved differently: The Turks banded together, took care of one another, and survived in greater proportion. British soldiers, officers and enlisted men, also resisted their captors' attempts at indoctrination better than did their American counterparts. Many young Americans were vulnerable to the combination of grueling physical conditions and constant propaganda efforts. Their comfortable upbringing and/or their psychological bent toward individualism left the middle-class youths unprepared for improvising the kinds of support provided by prisoners from other countries. Other American servicemen were vulnerable because they came from economic, social, or racial backgrounds that led to some resentment of U.S. policies or at least to a failure to understand what they were doing in Korea.

Why did the Korean War become America's "forgotten war" or "unknown war" and its veterans virtually ignored?

During the first weeks of the Korean War, most Americans supported the position that their government took in Korea; some Americans began to lose their confidence after Communist China entered the fray in October 1950; many more lost all sense of commitment after the war bogged down at the negotiating tables in July 1951 and then dragged on for month after month. But unlike the Vietnam War, there was little overt antiwar activity; most of the protest was through articles in publications that did not receive wide circulation. The mass of Americans found it quite easy to ignore the war; television did not yet play the part in Americans' lives that it would in the Vietnam War. Meanwhile, although the casualties were mounting—and affecting many American families because of the use of reserves and National Guard troops—there simply wasn't much publicity given to those casualties. Moreover, the majority of Americans at that time were more passive, more accepting, more resigned to things as they were.

As a result, when the Korean War finally wound down in July 1953, there were no celebrations, no parades, no heroes. What had initially been characterized as an idealistic effort to restore the peace and security of a small defenseless nation became a long, confusing, costly war. Americans elected Dwight D. Eisenhower president in part because he promised to end the war, and that he did. They then turned their backs on everything associated with the whole episode,

including the veterans. (In great contrast to Americans' reaction to the Vietnam War, there was little attention given to the thousands of U.S. servicemen missing in action or to some 390 reliably known to have been POWs and never repatriated or accounted for.) There were few welcoming committees in any communities and fewer memorials. Although an Unknown Soldier of the Korean War was buried in a crypt beside the nation's Tomb of the Unknown Soldier at Arlington National Cemetery on May 30, 1958, it was not until 1986 that Congress authorized a national memorial in Washington, D.C., to the veterans of the Korean War. The memorial was not dedicated until July 27, 1995, the 42nd anniversary of the signing of the armistice.

CIVILIAN AND MILITARY BIOGRAPHIES

AMERICAN

Acheson, Dean (1893–1971)—secretary of state: Dean Acheson was born in Middletown, Connecticut. He graduated from Yale University in 1915 and served in the Navy during World War I. He earned his law degree from Harvard in 1918. He served as undersecretary of state from 1945 to 1947 before returning to private practice in the summer of 1947. In January 1949, Truman nominated Acheson to replace George Marshall as secretary of state. When the war in Korea broke out, Acheson was immediately attacked by Republicans and others for promoting policies that weakened the U.S. position in the world. In fact, he became a staunch proponent of pursuing the war in Korea to resist Communist aggression there and to send a message that the United States was prepared to resist it elsewhere. Acheson later served as an adviser to Presidents John F. Kennedy and Lyndon B. Johnson.

Dean, William (1899–1981)—general: William Dean was born in Carlyle, Illinois. He had seen service in World War II and afterwards briefly held command of a U.S. Army division in Korea. When the war broke out in Korea, he was in Japan, commanding the African-American 24th Infantry Division, the first American ground combat unit to be sent to Korea. He arrived in Korea on July 3, 1950, and took horrendous casualties against the overpowering North Korean forces. Dean was a hands-on general who personally went out to attack North Korean tanks. On July 20, on the retreat from Taejon, he and a small group came under North Korean cross-fire and crawled to the side of the road to await darkness. Attempting to make his way to a river below to get water for the wounded men, he fell down a slope and was knocked unconscious. By the time he regained consciousness, his men had lost contact with him and had moved on. He spent the next 36 days wandering behind enemy lines before he was captured by North Koreans on August 25. Taken to a prisoner of war camp, he spent the following 16 months in isolation. Not until late December 1951 did he suddenly begin to receive certain privileges and comforts befitting his status as the highest-ranking prisoner. He was not released until September 4, 1953. He was awarded the Congressional Medal of Honor for his actions.

MacArthur, Douglas (1880–1964)—general: Douglas MacArthur was born in Little Rock, Arkansas. He was one of the most controversial military men in U.S. history. MacArthur graduated first in his class from the U.S. Military Academy in 1903 and served as a colonel, then brigadier general during World War I. He served as superintendent of the U.S. Military Academy from 1919 to 1922 and Army Chief of Staff from 1930 to 1935. He retired from the Army in 1937 but was recalled to active duty when the United States entered World War II in 1941 (see World War II, Civilian and Military Biographies, p. 511). When the war in Korea broke out, he was the commander of all U.S. military in the Far East and was soon named commander of the United Nations Command in Korea. He proceeded to build up U.S. forces in Korea and to devise the strategy that led to the fallback to the Pusan Perimeter. Then, with great resistance from virtually all other U.S. military men, he planned the risky landing at Inchon. However, his actions soon became more and more questionable. He did not take advantage of the Inchon landing but allowed the North Korean troops to escape up the east side of the peninsula. When he did get moving, he went too far—all the way to the Yalu River; then he was caught off guard by the entry into the war of Communist China. In the end, though, it was not his decisions as a general that did him in but his intrusion into U.S. government policy decisions. He was dismissed by President Truman in April 1951.

Ridgway, Matthew (1895–1993)—general: Matthew Ridgway was born in Virginia. He served in a variety of posts before World War II, where he became a fearless and famed commander of the 82nd Airborne Division. He jumped with his men during the Sicily invasion in 1943 and again during the Normandy invasion in June 1944. In the first months of the Korean War, he was on the U.S. Army's planning team in Washington, D.C. With the accidental death of Gen. Walton Walker in December 1950, Ridgway was sent to Korea to command the 8th Army. He arrived to find an Army that had just gone through a dispiriting retreat, but within weeks, he was leading it on the offensive. He received high marks not only for his successes against the Chinese forces but also for inspiring his troops with his presence and words. When MacArthur was dismissed in April 1951, Ridgway was named to fill all MacArthur's posts, including command of the UN forces in Korea. In May 1952, he was sent to Europe to replace Dwight D. Eisenhower as commander of Allied forces and NATO.

Truman, Harry S. (1884–1972)—president: Harry S. Truman was born in Lamar, Kansas. He assumed the presidency in April 1945 after the death of Franklin Delano Roosevelt. Whatever historians have since decided about his decisions in the final months of World War II, it is generally acknowledged that he had little space in which to maneuver (see World War II, Civilian and Military Biographies, pp. 512-513). The Korean War, however, was very much his war. He is widely praised for his decisiveness in committing U.S. forces to save South Korea from being overrun by the North Koreans. But many historians question subsequent decisions, in particular, his allowing U.S. troops to pursue the war across the 38th parallel and his insistence, when the armistice talks began, on settling the POW issue before agreeing to a cease-fire. Those decisions cost many thousands of American lives (and the lives of hundreds of thousands of others). Truman's defenders have argued that his tough stands signaled to the Communists that the United States was prepared to do whatever it took to resist their threats.

Walker, Walton (1889–1950)—general: Walton Walker was born in Belton, Texas. He was a soldier's soldier, serving along the Mexican border in 1916, fighting in World War I, then in World War II. He earned the hard-won respect of Gen. George S. Patton as an aggressive leader. When the war in Korea broke out, Walker was in command of the U.S. 8th Army in Japan, and he soon moved his headquarters to Korea. During the following five months, he took a direct role in the withdrawal to the Pusan Perimeter—the offensive that pushed the North Koreans all the way up to the Yalu River—then in the retreat southward. On December 23, 1950, he was killed in a vehicle accident at Uijongbu. Although Walker had presided over two massive retreats, students of military history consider him to have been a superb commander.

SOUTH KOREAN

Rhee, Syngman (1875–1965)—president: Syngman Rhee was a not unfamiliar example of a national asset who eventually became a liability. He was born in what became North Korea. As a college student, he was active in a student movement demanding an independent Korea; in 1897, he was jailed and tortured by the Japanese for his activism. He converted to Christianity in jail. On his release, he went to the United States, where he earned a B.A. from George Washington University, an M.A. from Harvard University, and a Ph.D. from Princeton University. He returned to Korea in 1910 as the Japanese were seizing control and soon had to flee. In exile (usually in Hawaii), he was elected president of the Korean Provisional Government from 1920 to 1941. After the Japanese were removed from Korea in 1945, the United States brought Rhee back to Korea, and by August 15, 1948, he was president of the newly formed Republic of Korea (ROK). From that point on, his chief goal was to preside over a united Korea, and he did not hesitate to scold anyone, including American diplomats and military leaders, who did not seem dedicated to that goal. Once the armistice talks began in July 1951, he resisted any compromises with North Korea; his most outrageous act was to plan the nighttime "escape" of some 27,000 North Korean POWs who did not want to be repatriated (see p. 593). He was forced to accept the terms of the armistice but never really dropped his goal of uniting Korea. As president of the ROK, however, his increasingly dictatorial rule led to a coup in April 1960 and his flight back to Hawaii.

NORTH KOREAN

Kim Il Sung (1912–1994)—president: Little is known about Kim Il Sung beyond what is published in his official biography, and most experts suspect that was doctored to give him the proper credentials. Kim Il Sung was born near Pyongyang, later North Korea's capital. He was the son of a teacher who allegedly took the family to Manchuria to escape the Japanese occupation. He became a Communist in his teens and is said to have fought with the Chinese in their struggle against the Japanese during the 1930s. He is said to have served in the Soviet army during World War II, at one point commanding Korean units at the battle of Stalingrad in 1942. (The unofficial version claims that he was more like a bandit chieftain and never held high command in the Soviet army.) One thing is agreed on: When the Soviets moved into Korea in 1945, they brought Kim along and imposed him as the leader of North Korea. By 1948, he was the nation's premier. When the Korean War broke out, he appointed himself supreme military commander of the North Korean People's Army. It is believed that he persuaded Stalin that he could conquer South Korea in a few weeks, but when the war dragged on and China had to intervene, he had to hand over control of all Communist military forces to the Chinese. Until his death, he ruled North Korea as the "Great Leader," presiding over an increasingly dictatorial regime; on his death, he was succeeded by his son, Kim Jong Il.

FURTHER READING

Alexander, Bevin. *Korea: The First War We Lost*. New York: Hippocrene Books, 1993.

Blair, Clay. *The Forgotten War: Americans in Korea, 1950–1953*. New York: Times Books, 1987.

Cummings, Bruce. *The Origins of the Korean War*. Princeton, N. J.: Princeton University Press, 1981.

Goulden, Joseph C. *Korea: The Untold Story of the War*. New York: McGraw-Hill, 1982.

Hastings, Max. *The Korean War*. New York: Simon & Schuster, 1987.

Higgins, Marguerite. *War in Korea*. New York: Doubleday, 1951.

Isserman, Maurice. *The Korean War*. New York: Facts on File, 1992.

Kinkaid, Eugene. *In Every War but One*. New York: W. W. Norton & Co., 1959.

———. *Why They Collaborated*. New York: Longman, 1960.

MacDonald, Callum A. *Korea: The War before Vietnam*. New York: Free Press, 1986.

Manchester, William. *American Caesar: Douglas MacArthur, 1880–1964*. Boston: Little, Brown & Co., 1978.

Rovere, Richard, and Arthur Schlesinger, Jr. *The General and the President and the Future of American Foreign Policy*. New York: Farrar, Straus, 1951.

Spanier, John W. *The Truman-MacArthur Controversy and the Korean War*. New York: W. W. Norton, 1965.

Stokesbury, James L. *A Short History of the Korean War*. New York: William Morrow, 1988.

Toland, John. *In Mortal Combat: Korea, 1950–1953*. New York: William Morrow, 1991.

White, William L. *The Captives of Korea*. New York: Scribner's, 1957.

THE VIETNAM WAR

DATES OF WAR

August 5, 1964–April 30, 1975

There has never been an officially agreed upon date for the start of U.S. participation in the Vietnam War; the date given here is based on the first independent and overt military operation by the United States, a bombing raid following the Gulf of Tonkin incident. (For purposes of veterans' benefits, the Veterans Administration dates the start of the Vietnam War to February 28, 1961, when U.S. "advisers" first accompanied South Vietnamese troops.) For the Vietnamese people, the war began long before that: at least by 1957, Communist guerrillas were carrying on a war of sabotage and assassination within South Vietnam; in the fall of 1957, 13 U.S. officials in South Vietnam were wounded in terrorist bombings. U.S. military "advisers" were participating and dying in the Vietnam War from the early 1960s.

The end date of the Vietnam War is also debatable. Some historians prefer January 27, 1973, the day the peace agreement between the United States and North Vietnam was signed. Others prefer March 29, 1973, the date the last U.S. combat troops were withdrawn from Vietnam and U.S. POWs were released from North Vietnamese prisoner of war camps. But in recognition of the realities of this conflict—the fact that it never was a simple war and that U.S. involvement did not actually come to an end in 1973—we have chosen April 30, 1975, as the end date for the war. It was on this day that Saigon fell and the last U.S. military personnel were evacuated.

ALTERNATE NAMES

The Vietnamese Conflict. The Second Indochina War. The Ten Thousand Day War (1945–1973). The American War (the name used by the Vietnamese).

SIGNIFICANCE

The Vietnam War was the United States' long-est war, lasting at the very least from 1964 to 1973, counting only the time U.S. combat forces were directly involved: The sheer length of the Vietnam War explains Americans' declining commitment to it. The Vietnam War was the first major war the United States lost—at least in the sense that the United States walked away from the war without attaining its goal. Most historians have agreed that although the United States forces may have been victorious in every major battle during the Vietnam War, the nation suffered the worst military defeat in its history. The Vietnam War was also the first war, too, brought into American homes on television; many historians agree that this fact played a major role in the eventual withdrawal of U.S. troops from the Vietnam War.

The Vietnam War was the most divisive conflict for Americans since the Civil War. Set against a global backdrop of the Communist versus the Free World, at home the war in Southeast Asia was echoed in a protracted struggle between competing visions of America's role in international affairs. Those who opposed the war and those who supported it appealed to some of the highest, noblest motives in U.S. traditions; neither side was willing to concede any good intentions on the other's part; in the end, about all both sides would agree on was that the war had been mishandled.

The war in Vietnam took place during and contributed to one of the major eras of cultural upheaval in the history of the United States. Many U.S. personnel in Vietnam were exposed to drugs, and drug use extended beyond the war to become a pervasive domestic problem. The Vietnam War not only accelerated and exacerbated social change, it also contaminated U.S. public life by creating mistrust between the American people and their political and military leaders. Subsequent U.S. political leaders became wary of any foreign involvement for fear of becoming "mired in another Vietnam." The impact of the Vietnam War on U.S. social, economic, and political policies is still an issue at the end of the 20th century.

BACKGROUND

The Vietnamese, who emerged as an ethnically identifiable group during the first millennium B.C., entered the second half of the 20th century with a 2,000-year history of battling for independence against a series of foreign nations, including China, France, and Japan. The burning of the capital of Nam Viet—as Vietnam was then known—in 111 B.C. marks the beginning of the recorded history of Vietnam. During the following 1,000 years of direct Chinese rule, the Vietnamese retained only their language and a fierce determination not to be assimilated. *Doc Lap*, the Vietnamese spirit of independence and resentment of foreign control, became a permanent feature of Vietnamese life. The heroes of Vietnamese history are those who rebelled against invading armies from the north.

After 1,000 years of resistance, Vietnam expelled China in A.D. 939. For the following 900 years, Vietnam expanded southward, achieving roughly its modern-day boundaries. In 1427, it again expelled China after a 20-year reoccupation. Beginning in 1535, the Vietnamese resisted colonization by the Portuguese, Dutch, English, and French, but lost their independence to the French in 1893.

In 1919, at the Versailles Peace Conference following World War I, Nguyen Ai Quoc ("Nguyen the Patriot"), later known as Ho Chi Minh, with other Vietnamese living in Paris, presented an eight-point plan for Vietnamese independence from France to President Woodrow Wilson. The major powers ignored the Vietnamese, but that rebuff spurred Nguyen Ai Quoc and other Vietnamese nationalists to begin looking beyond the end of foreign domination to the creation of a new social and political order. Within the next decade, several Vietnamese independence movements emerged; many of the leaders, but not all, were Communists. It did not help matters when the French installed Bao Dai as a puppet emperor in 1932.

In 1940, the Vichy French government, under the control of Nazi Germany, acquiesced in allowing Vietnam to become a Japanese colony. The Vietminh (or Vietnam Independence League), chaired by Ho Chi Minh, most of whose leaders were Communists, formed a united front with all interested Vietnamese nationalist parties. Backed by Chinese and U.S. funds, the Vietminh rescued downed U.S. and Allied fliers and wrested a provisional independence from the Japanese.

In 1945, at the end of World War II, Bao Dai abdicated. Then, with U.S. Office of Strategic Services (OSS) officers at his side offering assurances of Allied support for an independent Vietnam, Ho Chi Minh read from the U.S. Declaration of Independence and proclaimed the Democratic Republic of Vietnam (DRV). The United States urged its French ally to accept Ho as the leader of an independent state, but France, with British assistance, almost immediately began trying to retake its old colony.

After eight years of bitter fighting, the Vietminh brought the French to their knees in May 1954, after the French outpost at Dien Bien Phu was overrun; the United States, which had supported France morally since 1945 and with military aid since 1950, stopped just short of direct military intervention. Fearing the spread of Communism, President Dwight D. Eisenhower contemplated sending U.S. troops to Dien Bien Phu and even employing a nuclear strike, but he was dissuaded by Britain's Winston Churchill.

That first Indochina War ended on July 20, 1954, with a peace treaty signed (at Geneva, Switzerland) by France and the Vietminh proclaiming Vietnamese sovereignty. At the same time, a Final Declaration of the Geneva Conference, unsigned but given general support by the international community, left Vietnam "provisionally" divided at the 17th parallel into North and South Vietnam, pending reunification or other permanent settlement to be achieved through nationwide elections in July 1956. It was that international acceptance of a partitioned Vietnam that sealed its subsequent history.

It must also be recognized that what is called simply the Vietnam War actually involved a concurrent, similar, and related war in the adjacent country of Laos. Laos, also a former French colony but an independent country since 1949, was torn by a civil war since 1960; one of the main antagonists was the Communist movement known as the Pathet Lao. From 1963 on, the Pathet Lao was supported by North Vietnamese troops as well as by Soviet and Chinese military advisers; the Laotian government was supported by troops from South Vietnam and Thailand as well as by military advisers from the United States. Once the United States entered the war in Vietnam, it began to bomb the Ho Chi Minh Trail and other locales in Laos where the North Vietnamese forces were believed to be operating. In 1971, South Vietnamese troops, supported by U.S. planes, invaded Laos to attack the North Vietnamese supply routes.

The Vietnam War also spilled over into Cambodia, with early events not unlike those in Laos. Throughout the 1960s, the Vietcong and North Vietnamese used Cambodian territory adjacent to Vietnam as a sanctuary; in fact, by 1969, the North Vietnamese had major bases in Cambodia. In March 1969, President Richard Nixon authorized the secret bombing of the North Vietnamese bases in Cambodia; at the end of April 1970, South Vietnamese and U.S. troops attacked the Communist bases in Cambodia. U.S. bombings in Cambodia continued through August 1973, which contributed to the civil war there. The Cambodian civil war culminated in Pol Pot's reign of terror (1975–1979), during which millions of Cambodians lost their lives.

CAUSES OF THE WAR

During the period beginning with France's attempt to reconquer Vietnam in 1945, two Vietnamese governments were emerging. The first, the Democratic Republic of Vietnam (DVR) was based in the more populous North and took the lead in resisting the French; the second, based in Saigon in the South, was the French-backed government that eventually became the Republic of Vietnam (RVN). The French even brought Bao Dai out of retirement in 1949 and set him up as a figurehead emperor.

In January 1950, China and other Communist countries recognized the DRV as the legitimate government of all Vietnam; in February, the United States and Great Britain recognized the state of Vietnam headed by emperor Bao Dai as the legitimate government. By then, the United States was supplying substantial military aid to the French for their war in Indochina; in addition, the U.S. Military Assistance Advisory Group (MAAG) Indochina, sent its first 35 soldiers to South Vietnam to teach its army how to use U.S. weapons. After the Geneva treaty partitioned Vietnam in July 1954, Ho Chi Minh and the Vietminh took over North Vietnam; in South Vietnam, Ngo Dinh Diem took power and moved to suppress all opposition. The United States began at once to channel aid directly to Diem in Saigon; China and the Soviet Union began to provide aid to Hanoi, the capital of North Vietnam. In 1955, Diem held a referendum between himself and Bao Dai which Diem won with more than 98 percent of the votes. Diem proclaimed the establishment of the Republic of Vietnam (RVN), with himself as its first president. Diem then refused to participate in nationwide elections, set for 1956 by the Geneva agreement, which he and his government would almost certainly have lost to Ho Chi Minh and his supporters.

The DRV, frustrated by repeated failed attempts to resolve the situation politically and by growing foreign influence, determined to overthrow Diem. Despite reservations about Diem, the United States gave ever more support to the RVN because of the U.S. policy of containment of Communist expansion. And there was no denying that China was supplying military aid to the Communist Vietnamese. In 1957, the Hanoi government began to help organize Communist guerrillas in South Vietnam; by 1959, North Vietnam was sending trained cadres into South Vietnam and providing supplies and personnel for a Communist insurgency. By the end of 1960, Hanoi had openly proclaimed support for a National Liberation Front for South Vietnam (NLF). Each of those steps was inevitably perceived as a direct threat to U.S. interests.

On July 8, 1959, Maj. Dale R. Buis and Sgt. Chester Ovnand were killed when Communist guerrillas struck a MAAG compound at Bienhoa only 20 miles northeast of Saigon. Although it took five more years before Americans realized their country was involved in a war in Vietnam, from that point on the United States became increasingly more committed to supporting the Saigon government.

PREPARATIONS FOR WAR

Although President Dwight D. Eisenhower had avoided becoming directly involved when the French were on the verge of losing their war in Vietnam, as early as December 1954, he was quietly authorizing direct aid to Ngo Dinh Diem's government. By April 1959, Eisenhower made a firm public commitment to maintain South Vietnam as an independent state. By the end of 1959, U.S. military advisers in Vietnam numbered 350; by the time Eisenhower left office in January 1961, U.S. military advisers numbered 900.

After John F. Kennedy succeeded Eisenhower as president, he renewed Eisenhower's pledge to South Vietnam and called for vastly increased military spending and enlarging the armed forces. Eisenhower's Cold War approach had relied on the threat of "massive [nuclear] retaliation" to deter the Soviet Union from supporting "wars of national liberation." Kennedy favored a "flexible response," using conventional and unconventional, especially "counterinsurgency," tactics to fight limited war. He authorized creation of the Special Forces, or Green Berets, an elite unit designed to combat insurgent irregulars. Above all, though, Kennedy authorized sending more U.S. military advisers to train the South Vietnamese army. Within 18 months of taking office, President Kennedy increased the U.S. advisers in Vietnam to 3,200, about 2,000 of whom served in battle areas with South Vietnamese forces and were authorized to return fire if fired upon.

Meanwhile, Diem was finding it increasingly difficult to hold power. He was under attack by a variety of opponents, including Buddhist monks and military officers. By August 1963, the new U.S. ambassador in Saigon, Henry Cabot Lodge, was letting some dissident officers know that the United States would not oppose their overthrowing Diem. That they did on November 1; the following day, they assassinated Diem and his brother Nhu, greatly disliked for his suppression of all opposition. Although individual agents of the Central Intelligence Agency (CIA) in Vietnam may have known of the plot to overthrow Diem, there is no evidence that the effort depended on CIA support. Before the Kennedy administration had time to sort out where to go next, Kennedy was assassinated on November 22; by that time, there were some 16,500 U.S. military advisers in Vietnam. During 1963 alone, 76 Americans were killed and another 400 wounded in the hostilities in Vietnam. The government in Saigon remained in constant turmoil throughout 1964, but President Lyndon Johnson, who succeeded John F. Kennedy, gave no sign of cutting back on U.S. support.

Preparations for the undeclared war against Communism in Vietnam increased as the U.S. commitment deepened. The United States supplied $3.5 billion in aid to the French war effort in Vietnam from 1950 to 1954. By 1956, South Vietnam was receiving $270 million per year, more U.S. aid per capita than any other country, except Laos

and South Korea, received. The United States, primarily through the CIA, was also conducting covert operations within Laos and Vietnam from 1956 on. By the end of 1962, more than half a billion dollars was being funneled annually to Saigon, along with vast amounts of materiel— helicopters, planes, tanks, boats, weapons, ammunition, communications equipment—for use by U.S. forces and the Army of the Republic of Vietnam (ARVN). After Congress passed the "Tonkin Gulf Resolution" on August 7, 1964, the tempo of overt and covert U.S. military engagement greatly quickened.

DECLARATION OF WAR

The United States never formally declared war on Vietnam, and unlike the Korean War, there was never a UN resolution supporting the Vietnam War. U.S. policies that led to involvement in the Vietnam War date from 1946, when President Harry S. Truman acquiesced in France's reconquest of its former colony; each succeeding U.S. president made further commitments that narrowed the choices for his successor. The closest thing to a declaration of war was the so-called Tonkin Gulf Resolution (see Home Front, August 7, 1964, p. 616) occasioned by alleged North Vietnamese attacks on U.S. ships in the Gulf of Tonkin (see Naval War, 1964, p. 615). Later, there were serious questions as to whether those attacks actually occurred. (The resolution was repealed by Congress in 1970.) President Richard Nixon, elected in 1968, continued involvement in the war under that same resolution. The U.S. Congress gave its support by continually passing the various finance and other bills necessary to prosecute a war.

COMBATANTS

The two groups of combatants in the Vietnam War, whatever their various origins or formal allegiances, really were organized around their desire either to overthrow or to support the Saigon government of the Republic of Vietnam (RVN). That split in turn signified a pro-Communist versus anti-Communist commitment. But because of the border that arbitrarily divided the main proponents of the two causes, the war was usually presented as one between North Vietnam and South Vietnam.

The Vietcong: The name *Vietcong* was applied by the pro-Saigon establishment to those in South Vietnam who opposed the government in Saigon; a short version of "Vietnamese Communists," the name was intended to label all such opposition as Communists. Numbering 25,000–30,000 at their peak, the Vietcong originated in the 5,000–10,000 Vietminh soldiers who remained in the south after the partition of 1954. There were regular Vietcong units of up to regimental strength and many small, part-time units in villages under Vietcong control. The Vietcong infrastructure also consisted of a party secretary; a finance and supply unit; and information and cultural, social welfare, and proselytizing sections; the last-named sought recruits from among civilians and soldiers in the Army of the Republic of Vietnam (ARVN). There were undoubtedly many Vietcong sympathizers in South Vietnam, people who never enlisted and never wore a uniform but who were willing to do whatever it took to advance the Vietcong cause.

North Vietnamese: In 1964, the North Vietnamese Army (NVA) consisted of about 250,000 soldiers organized into 15 divisions armed with World War II-vintage small arms, mortars, and artillery. As the Vietnam War proceeded, North Vietnam organized all available citizens for service. By 1974, the NVA comprised some 570,000 regulars organized into 18 infantry divisions, 2 training divisions, and 10 artillery divisions. The NVA had 4 armored regiments, 20 independent infantry regiments, 24 antiaircraft artillery regiments, and 15 SAM (surface-to-air missile) regiments. The North Vietnamese regular army at first supplemented, then absorbed the Vietcong's mission, especially after the Vietcong were decimated during the Tet Offensive of 1968.

The tiny North Vietnamese Navy (NVN), comprising about 80 torpedo boats, minesweepers, and small coastal and riverine patrol boats given them by the Soviet Union and China, could not stack up in any way with the powerful U.S. Navy assigned to the waters and waterways of Vietnam. North Vietnamese ships engaged the United States at sea only once, during the Gulf of Tonkin incident in 1964.

North Vietnam had no fighter aircraft until 1964; at peak strength in 1972, the North Vietnam Air Force numbered 93 MiG-21s and 113 MIG-15s, 17s, and 19s (mostly subsonic), all used exclusively for defense. The North Vietnamese also had a few Soviet bombers, but they played no part in the war. The North Vietnamese pilots had trained in the Soviet Union and many proved quite skillful and aggressive; all told, the North Vietnamese shot down a total of 92 U.S. bombers and fighter planes.

South Vietnamese: The South Vietnamese Armed Forces (SVNAF), formally the Republic of Vietnam Armed Forces (RVNAF), originated with the Republic of South Vietnam in 1955. Financed and equipped with U.S. funds and trained under U.S. Military Assistance Advisory Group Vietnam (MAAG-Vietnam) and later the U.S. Military Assistance Command Vietnam (MACV), the SVNAF comprised five components under the command of the SVNAF Joint General Staff: the Army of Vietnam (ARVN), the Air Force (VNAF), the Marine Corps (VNMC), the Navy (VNN), and the irregular home guards of the Territorial Force—the Regional Forces (RF) and the Popular Forces (PF). Numbering more than 550,000 at the end of 1964, by January 1973, when it completely collapsed, the SVNAF had more than 1.1 million soldiers.

The South Vietnam navy had never been asked to do much more than patrol the rivers of the Mekong Delta and the coastal waters; most of its boats were motorized junks. As the United States began to commit more and more personnel and equipment to the Vietnam War, the South Vietnamese navy also grew. From 1969 on, under President Richard Nixon's policy of "Vietnamization" (see March 1969, pp. 635-636), the U.S. Navy began to turn over more and more of its ships (although nothing larger than a destroyer escort). By the end of 1972, as the United States was pulling out, the South Vietnam navy was one of the largest in the world in terms of ships and personnel—some 700 of the former and 40,275 of the latter.

The South Vietnamese had their own air force, one totally armed and trained by the United States. It grew from some 29,000 members in mid-1969 to 42,000 in December 1972. The fighter pilots flew mainly F-5As, F5-Es, and A-37s; there also were transports, helicopters, and gunships. When the United States left the war in 1973, the South Vietnamese air force had 2,075 aircraft, the fourth largest air force in the world.

American: Between 1964 and 1975, almost 3.5 million U.S. military personnel served some time in Southeast Asia. Most of those were in the U.S. Army, but many U.S. Marines also served. In fact, it was the landing of 3,500 marines near Danang in early March 1965 that marked the first clear presence of U.S. combat troops in Vietnam (see March 8–12, 1965, p. 617). At their peak strength in 1969, the U.S. ground forces in Vietnam totaled about 543,400.

The United States hardly needed the full force of its navy during the war, but the 7th Fleet, positioned at "Yankee Station" in the Gulf of Tonkin, played a major role in the war. The navy faced no opposition at sea. Some of its ships were assigned to enforce a blockade of North Vietnam, but most of the navy's forces were engaged in providing support for the war on land. Cruisers, and even the battleship *New Jersey*, fired massive shells onto targets well inland. Surveillance planes provided information for land-based operations. Ships with special radar air-defense systems helped detect North Vietnamese MiGs for Air Force and navy pilots. U.S. Navy carriers provided a constant force of planes for air strikes and reconnaissance, and eventually carrier-based planes played a major part in the air war against North Vietnam. The U.S. Navy also conducted a river war in the Mekong Delta, sometimes merely trying to see which of the 50,000 Vietnamese junks operating there were helping the Vietcong, other times conveying troops on combat missions. No U.S. ship was ever hit by a North Vietnamese plane or ship.

The U.S. Air Force brought an immense amount of its power to bear in Vietnam; at its peak in 1968, there were some 170,000 men and 2,100 planes in the Pacific air forces, not all assigned constantly to the war in Vietnam, but all readily available. The planes the Air Force used included powerful bombers, such as the B-52 Stratofortress; giant transports, such as the C-47, the C-124 Globemaster, and the C-130 Hercules; swift and powerful air support planes, such as the F-100 Super Sabre; fighter-bombers such as the F-105, the F-4 Phantom, and the F-111; and a whole family of helicopters (see Military Innovations, Tactics, Equipment, pp. 651–652).

Other Nationals: In addition to the United States, several other nations provided some personnel to support the South Vietnamese. At peak strength, those forces numbered 7,672 Australians; 48,869 South Koreans; 11,568 Thais; 552 New Zealanders; 1,576 Filipinos; 29 Taiwanese; and 10 Spaniards. They were assigned for the most part to 31 infantry battalions; the Royal Australian Air Force, however, did provide a bomber squadron.

GEOGRAPHIC AND STRATEGIC CONSIDERATIONS

When the United States became involved in the Vietnam War, few Americans knew where Vietnam was located, let alone any details about its geography. Yet that geography was a significant factor in determining the nature and conduct of the war for both sides.

Located on the eastern extremity of the Indochina peninsula in Southeast Asia, Vietnam comprises 128,052 square miles, slightly larger than New Mexico, somewhat smaller than Montana. Its coastline stretches 1,400 miles, roughly the distance between Boston, Massachusetts, and Miami, Florida, and longer than the coastline of California. Its population in 1965 was some 35 million. (By 1995 it was 72 million making it the 13th most populous nation in the world, ahead of Italy, Great Britain, and France.)

Vietnam is bordered on the north by China; on the west by Laos, Cambodia, and the Gulf of Thailand; and on the south and east by the South China Sea and the Gulf of Tonkin. It has a tropical monsoon climate, with warm, dry winters in the south and cool, damp winters in the north. About one-third of the total land area is tropical evergreen and subtropical deciduous forest. Americans in Vietnam came to know well the hot, humid climate and thick forests.

Vietnam can be divided into five regions, four of which played a distinctive role in the Vietnam War. (The fifth, the Northern Highlands bordering China, remained untouched by the war.)

(1) The rugged and densely forested Annamite Range (Truong Son in Vietnamese) extends north to south along west-central Vietnam, with peaks of more than 6,000 feet, and covers two-thirds of the total land area. In southern Vietnam, the Annamite Range forms a plateau area, the sparsely settled Central Highlands, of about 20,000 square miles, and a number of major battles were conducted in that region. The north-south ridges of Vietnam's mountain chain had historically isolated Vietnam from the cultural and political influences of the rest of Southeast Asia; during the Vietnam War, however, the North Vietnamese took advantage of that isolat-

ing factor by withdrawing into the adjacent countries of Cambodia and Laos, thus leading to the extension of the war into those two nations.

(2) The Red River Delta (4,259 square miles), extending inland from the Gulf of Tonkin in the north, is the densely populated original seat of Vietnamese civilization; it is intensely cultivated. Its waterways are vital to irrigation and local freight transportation. Bombing raids in and around Hanoi were aimed at crippling the region.

(3) The Mekong River Delta (15,600 square miles), covering the southern extremity of Vietnam, is one of the richest rice-growing areas of the world. An almost distinct war was fought along the waterways of that region.

(4) Finally, north of Saigon and along the east-central coast of Vietnam, lie the narrow fertile coastal lowlands, broken into "enclaves" formed by the east-west spurs of the Annamite Range. Much of Vietnam's population has always lived there, and that was the scene of much of the most publicized fighting.

The Ho Chi Minh Trail, down which flowed the steady stream of troops and materiel upon which the North Vietnamese war effort depended, extended some 600 miles from north of the 17th parallel down to Tayninh north of Saigon. It was not just a single road but a network of trails through mostly heavily canopied forest. The Ho Chi Minh Trail had initially served as the communications-liaison line that linked Vietminh bases up and down the Annamite Range during the Indochina War; it was not expected to be used by anything much more than pack-carrying pedestrians. Starting around 1964, the Ho Chi Minh Trail was relocated to the western flank of the mountains inside Laos and Cambodia, and the North Vietnamese began to assign major resources to build it into a road (with bridges) that could support truck traffic; in addition to the road, was the immense support system—barracks for personnel, repair shops, medical facilities, fuel depots—as well as an antiaircraft defense system to protect the trail from the relentless U.S. air attacks.

From the beginning of the Vietnam War, North Vietnamese strategy consisted of two parts: "political struggle" and "armed struggle." They were never mutually exclusive. Until 1964, political struggle was so effective in undermining the unpopular South Vietnamese government that the United States was forced to either intervene or abandon the anti-Communist regime. From 1965, when the United States made the decision to intervene with its full ground and air support, until the 1968 Tet Offensive, the North Vietnamese concentrated on armed struggle. The political struggle was reemphasized until the Eastertide Offensive of 1972, then returned to predominance until the brief armed struggle of 1975 won the war for North Vietnam.

The United States, too, had its versions of a political strategy and an armed struggle. The political strategy was formulated by the Kennedy administration and emphasized diplomatic maneuvering on the world stage and "counterinsurgency" in Vietnam (see Preparations for War, pp. 610-611). Counterinsurgency meant carrying the war to the guerrillas in more than just military terms. Through covert and overt means, the United States hoped to fight a "special war" for the "hearts and minds" of the Vietnamese people with U.S. troops in the background. The result was overinvolvement in South Vietnamese internal affairs combined with a failure to develop policies that addressed the realities of life in Vietnam.

When the "special war" failed, U.S. strategy moved to that of limited war which, instead of trying to overwhelm the enemy, sought only to teach it lessons. However, the search-and-destroy missions, pacification campaigns, body counts, and other statistical measures of that limited war looked much like wanton destruction of civilian property to many people, especially to the Vietnamese whose hearts and minds were supposed to be won by a U.S. presence. The limited war failed, and that led to massive bombing operations, further disenchanting the American public. Short of resorting to atomic weapons, the United States had committed much of its armed might to the Vietnam War and still could not bring the North Vietnamese to their knees. In later reappraisals of U.S. strategy, some suggested that things might have gone differently in Vietnam had the United States, instead of gradually escalating its responses, made a total commitment of its armed forces at the very outset. But others contend that the sophisticated weapons and massive firepower were largely irrelevant in a war where one side was willing to accept huge losses and simply wait for its enemy to become discouraged and go away in what ultimately became a war of attrition.

BATTLES AND CAMPAIGNS: 1964

SOUTH VIETNAM

January 4, 1964: An offensive that began on December 31, 1963, when ten ARVN battalions set out to crush two Vietcong battalions in Bensuc 40 miles west of Saigon, ended when the Vietcong forces withdrew. Two Vietcong and 15 ARVN were killed. U.S. advisers described the operation as a failure.

January 5, 1964: In Long An 25 miles southwest of Saigon, a 500-man Vietcong battalion escaped an ARVN encircling movement. Fifteen U.S. planes were hit by ground fire; five Americans were wounded, nine ARVN were killed, and 60-70 Vietcong were casualties.

January 17, 1964: Five U.S. helicopter crewmen were killed and three wounded while supporting an ARVN attack on Communist bases in the Mekong Delta.

January 30, 1964: Maj. Gen. Nguyen Khanh seized power in Saigon, arresting the four ruling junta generals but allowing Gen. Duong Van Minh to remain as figurehead chief of state.

April 1964: Regular North Vietnam Army (NVA) units began infiltrating South Vietnam.

June 20, 1964: Gen. William Westmoreland replaced Gen. Paul Harkins as commander, U.S. Military Assistance Command Vietnam (MACV).

July 2, 1964: Gen. Maxwell Taylor replaced Henry Cabot Lodge as U.S. ambassador to South Vietnam.

July 6, 1964: At Nam Dong in the northern highlands, a 500-man Vietcong force attacked a U.S. Special Forces training camp. After a five-hour battle, the Vietcong retreated, having lost an estimated 40 dead and an unknown number wounded, but they had killed 57 North Vietnamese, two Americans, and one Australian.

October 30, 1964: Vietcong mortars shelled the U.S. air base at Bien-hoa only 12 miles north of Saigon; they killed five U.S. servicemen and destroyed six U.S. B-57 bombers. President Lyndon B. Johnson rejected a proposal for retaliatory raids against North Vietnam; he was accused by some of doing so because of the upcoming presidential election.

November 1, 1964: After months of political turmoil, Tran Van Huong became premier of South Vietnam.

December 24, 1964: Vietcong bombed U.S. billets in Saigon. Two Americans were killed; 70 were wounded.

December 31, 1964: U.S. military personnel in Vietnam totaled 23,300, but they were still designated as "military advisers." SVNAF strength increased to 265,000 (with another 290,000 in militia and paramilitary forces). During 1964, the U.S. lost 38 fixed-wing aircraft and 24 helicopters and suffered 140 dead, 1,138 wounded, and 11 missing in action.

AIR WAR

August 5, 1964: In response to reported attacks by North Vietnamese boats on U.S. ships in the Gulf of Tonkin, F-8 Crusaders, A-1 Skyraiders, and A-4 Skyhawks from the aircraft carriers *Ticonderoga* and *Constellation* flew 64 sorties over North Vietnam along the Gulf of Tonkin; they attacked torpedo boats and their bases, an oil storage depot, and antiaircraft installations. Two U.S. planes were shot down; the pilot of one, Lt. Everett Alvarez, became the first U.S. airman taken prisoner (and was not released until after the cease-fire agreement in 1973). As the first overt and independent U.S. military operation against North Vietnam, that incident could be regarded as the United States' entry into the war.

NAVAL WAR

July 30–31, 1964: South Vietnamese naval forces raided islands along the North Vietnam coast on the Gulf of Tonkin.

August 2, 1964: U.S. sailors on the destroyer USS *Maddox,* in the Gulf of Tonkin to monitor radio and radar signals from North Vietnam, reported that they were under attack by three North Vietnamese torpedo boats. The *Maddox* called in U.S. crusader jets from the USS *Ticonderoga* but claimed to have sunk one of the boats and crippled the other two before the jets arrived.

August 3–4, 1964: South Vietnamese PT boats conducted two more clandestine raids against North Vietnamese installations on the Gulf of Tonkin.

August 4, 1964: During the evening, some crewmen on the *Maddox* and another U.S. destroyer, the *C. Turner Joy*, believed that the ships were being attacked by North Vietnamese torpedo boats; they called in air support from the

On Christmas Eve 1964, an explosion in the parking area of a U.S. officers' quarters in Saigon killed 2, wounded 70, and destroyed much of the building and several vehicles in the area.

carrier *Ticonderoga* and fired into the darkness. Shortly afterward, the captain of the *Maddox* communicated that he had decided that the radarscope blips were "freak weather effects" and that the reported torpedoes were probably due to an "overeager" sonar operator. The captain's superiors in Honolulu and then the Joint Chiefs of Staff in Washington, D.C., ignored that opinion and planned a retaliatory air strike. (Although it would never be established absolutely, most experts who have studied the Tonkin Gulf incidents believe that the one on August 2 was a real attack but that the one reported on August 4 actually did not occur.)

CAMBODIA/LAOS

March 16, 1964: The Cambodian village of Chantes was bombed by the South Vietnamese.

May 27, 1964: The second Lao coalition government collapsed. The Communist Pathet Lao retook the Plain of Jars.

June 6–9, 1964: Two U.S. Navy jets flying target reconnaissance missions over Laos were shot down by Pathet Lao groundfire. The U.S. response was to order armed jets to accompany future reconnaissance flights; by June 9, those planes were attacking Pathet Lao positions.

December 24, 1964: The U.S. Air Force began Operation Barrel Roll by striking targets in northern Laos in support of forces of the Royal Lao Army and Meo tribesmen.

HOME FRONT

August 7, 1964: By a vote of 88-2 in the Senate and 416-0 in the House, Congress passed the Tonkin Gulf Resolution (Public Law 88-408), giving President Lyndon Johnson extraordinary powers to act in Southeast Asia and "to take all necessary steps...to prevent further aggression." The two senators who voted against it were Wayne Morse (D–Oreg.), and Ernest Gruening (D–Alaska).

November 3, 1964: Lyndon B. Johnson was elected president. He defeated the Republican candidate, Barry Goldwater, in part by portraying Goldwater as too ready to involve the United States in a war overseas.

December 14, 1964: A survey revealed that 25 percent of Americans did not know there was fighting going on in Vietnam.

INTERNATIONAL DEVELOPMENTS

October 14, 1964: Soviet premier Nikita Khrushchev was ousted and replaced by Leonid Brezhnev as party chief and Aleksey Kosygin as premier.

October 16, 1964: China announced that it had detonated its first atomic bomb.

BATTLES AND CAMPAIGNS: 1965

SOUTH VIETNAM

January 2, 1965: Six days of fighting in and around Binh Gia village ended in an ARVN defeat despite its use of tanks, artillery, and helicopters unavailable to the Vietcong. Two hundred ARVN troops were killed; 300 were wounded. Five Americans were killed and three were wounded—the highest U.S. casualties in a single battle to date.

January 3, 1965: South Vietnam's crippling political crisis was aggravated when thousands of antigovernment demonstrators clashed with police and marines in Saigon; rioting in Hué also highlighted opposition to Premier Tran Van Huong.

February 7, 1965: The Vietcong attacked the U.S. helicopter base at Camp Halloway and blew up the U.S. military advisers' barracks at Pleiku; 8 Americans were killed, 126 wounded, in those attacks. Gen. William Westmoreland and Ambassador Maxwell Taylor advised President Johnson to initiate air retaliatory raids, which Johnson did.

February 10, 1965: A Vietcong bombing at the Qui Nhon billet killed 23 U.S. soldiers.

February 18, 1965: Dr. Phan Huy Quat formed a new government in South Vietnam; General Khanh left the country.

March 8–12, 1965: On March 8, two U.S. Marine battalions went ashore near Danang, the first U.S. combat units openly assigned to Vietnam; during the next few days, a total of 3,500 marines went ashore at Danang. Although they had the limited mission of defending the airfield at Danang, the assignment of those marines signaled an escalation of the U.S. commitment.

April 6, 1965: President Lyndon Johnson authorized U.S. ground combat troops to engage in offensive operations in South Vietnam.

May 3, 1965: The U.S. Army's 173rd Airborne Brigade began landing in South Vietnam.

June 1965: The First Battalion Royal Australian Regiment was deployed to Vietnam for combat operations.

June 11, 1965: Air Vice Marshall Nguyen Cao Ky took over as prime minister of a military regime in Saigon; his cabinet was the ninth since November 1963.

June 26, 1965: The American command in Saigon reported that Vietcong units put five ARVN combat regiments and nine battalions out of action in the previous months.

June 27–30, 1965: Three thousand members of the U.S. 173rd Airborne Brigade launched the first major offensive by U.S. forces. With 800 Australian soldiers and an ARVN unit, they moved into an area some 20 miles northeast of Saigon. At the end of the inconsequential operation, one American had been killed, and nine had been wounded.

July 1965: New Zealand deployed a field artillery battery to Vietnam for combat operations. The total number of U.S. service personnel in Vietnam by now exceeded 50,000.

July 28, 1965: With 18 U.S. combat battalions already in Vietnam, President Johnson approved General Westmoreland's request for 44 more battalions.

August 13, 1965: ARVN forces scored a major victory in the Mekong Delta. More than 250 Vietcong were killed, the ARVN suffered only light casualties.

September 18–21, 1965: U.S. troops, in one of the largest engagements to date, killed 226 guerrillas at Ankhe.

October 27–November 20, 1965: U.S. troops launched a month-long operation, Silver Bayonet, in the Ia Drang valley in the central highlands. It involved helicptering in some 2,000 U.S. 1st Air Cavalry Division and ARVN troops; B-52s gave bombing support for the ground troops. Between November 14–20, in the bloodiest battle of the war to date, the NVA engaged in its first action of the war against massive U.S. military might. When the Ia Drang campaign ended, the U.S. claimed 1,770 NVA casualties and victory; some 300 Americans were killed and another 500 were wounded.

December 31, 1965: U.S. military personnel in Vietnam totaled some 184,000; General Westmoreland received assurances from President Johnson of an additional 250,000 troops and more if requested. American dead totaled 1,350, with 5,300 wounded in 1965. SVNAF strength remained at 514,000; other military forces supporting South Vietnam stood at 22,240.

AIR WAR

February 7–11, 1965: Operation Flaming Dart, a tactical air reprisal on military targets in North Vietnam for attacks against U.S. bases in South Vietnam, got under way.

February 24, 1965: The U.S. acknowledged that U.S. pilots were flying on operational missions against the Vietcong.

March 2, 1965: Sustained U.S. bombing of North Vietnam, called Operation Rolling Thunder, began with the first raid on North Vietnam that was not a retaliation for assaults against U.S. installations.

June 18, 1965: B-52 bombers from Guam made their first strikes of the Vietnam War on targets in South Vietnam.

July 24, 1965: For the first time, a U.S. plane was brought down by a Soviet-supplied SAM over North Vietnam.

August 13, 1965: Five U.S. Navy planes were downed over North Vietnam by conventional antiaircraft artillery fire.

September 3, 1965: U.S. and South Vietnamese planes flew a record 532 missions in one day.

December 25, 1965: President Lyndon Johnson suspended the bombing of North Vietnam as an inducement to the North Vietnamese to negotiate.

NAVAL WAR

May 1965: The U.S. Navy began Operation Market Time to seize or destroy enemy craft in South Vietnam's coastal waters.

CAMBODIA/LAOS

April 1965: The U.S. Air Force began Operation Steel Tiger to strike targets in Laos near its border with North Vietnam, to interdict troop and supply movements.

HOME FRONT

March 24, 1965: Classes at the University of Michigan, Ann Arbor, were canceled and stu-

dents and faculty held special seminars and rallies to protest the Vietnam War. That was the first so-called teach-in, a tactic that was adopted by many U.S. colleges.

July 8, 1965: Henry Cabot Lodge was reappointed U.S. ambassador to South Vietnam, replacing Maxwell Taylor.

August 6, 1965: Indicative of the dilemma that President Johnson found himself facing, a group of Republican congressmen charged him with preparing for a "coming surrender" because he had been showing a willingness to negotiate a peace with North Vietnam.

August 12, 1965: The Reverend Martin Luther King, Jr. criticized what he considered President Johnson's failure to negotiate with the Vietcong to end the war and pledged to appeal personally to Communist leaders, even if it meant breaking federal law.

October 15, 1965: At a pacifist rally, David Miller became the first U.S. war protester to burn his draft card and was arrested by the FBI.

November 1965: Widespread antiwar demonstrations took place.

December 14, 1965: A poll showed only 20 percent of Americans believed that the United States should withdraw from Vietnam.

INTERNATIONAL DEVELOPMENTS

April 7–8, 1965: In a speech at Johns Hopkins University, President Johnson offered Ho Chi Minh participation in a Southeast Asia development plan in exchange for peace. The following day, North Vietnam's premier Pham Van Dong rejected Johnson's proposal, maintaining that any settlement must be based on the Vietcong program.

July 24, 1965: Soviet leaders in Moscow announced that the Soviet Union would give defense aid to North Vietnam.

September 1965: Chinese defense minister Lin Biao, in a speech titled "Long Live the Victory of People's War," indicated that China would not intervene directly in Vietnam. China's Great Proletarian Cultural Revolution preoccupied China for the following three years. In fact, Chinese soldiers were already present in Vietnam, aiding the North Vietnamese in noncombat tasks and on December 5, China signed a pact agreeing to provide material aid to North Vietnam.

October 16, 1965: Demonstrators protesting American policy in Vietnam marched in London, Rome, Brussels, Copenhagen, and Stockholm; similar protests occurred in 40 U.S. cities. Premier Eisaku Sato of Japan announced that Japan would not send troops to Vietnam even if requested to do so by the United States.

BATTLES AND CAMPAIGNS: 1966

SOUTH VIETNAM

January 6, 1966: The Vietcong used 120-mm mortars for the first time in an attack at Khesanh in Quangtri Province. After a five-day siege, Vietcong troops overran the outpost at Conghoa.

January 24–March 6, 1966: Operation Masher/White Wing/Thang Phong II, involving the U.S. 1st Air Cavalry, ARVN, Korean, and eventually U.S. Marine troops, swept through Binh Dinh Province—the largest search-and-destroy operation to date, the U.S. reported some 350 of its troops killed, another 2,000 wounded, and 2,389 enemy casualties.

February 23, 1966: The allied mission in Saigon reported that ARVN desertions in 1965 totaled 90,000, double those for 1964, or about 14 percent of the total troop strength. Vietcong desertions in 1965 were estimated at below 20,000.

March 9–11, 1966: The U.S. Special Forces camp at Ashau near the Cambodian border was wiped out following two days of savage fighting; 5 U.S. Green Berets and some 200 ARVN were killed.

April 1, 1966: In Saigon, Vietcong commandos set off 200 pounds of explosives at a hotel housing U.S. troops. Three Americans and four South Vietnamese were killed, and the hotel was heavily damaged.

April 12, 1966: Vietcong guerrillas launched a mortar attack against Tansonnhut Air Base that killed 7 U.S. soldiers and South Vietnamese civilians, injured 160, and damaged 23 helicopters and 3 planes.

May 15–June 22, 1966: South Vietnam's Buddhists had opposed most of the government's leaders and policies for several years, and when Premier Nguyen Cao Ky sent troops to Danang to quell a rebellion, Buddhists began a new round of violent demonstrations. On June 20, Ky signed an agreement promising elections in September for a new civilian government, but his troops took control of the last remaining Buddhist stronghold.

July 15–August 3, 1966: Eleven thousand U.S. Marine and ARVN troops launched Operation Hastings, a massive drive through Quangtri Province to oust a similar number of NVA troops. The U.S. reported some 300 dead, 1,500 wounded, and 824 NVA killed.

September 14, 1966: The South Vietnamese village of Lienhoa, reportedly hostile, was burned by U.S. troops; a military spokesman said the burning resulted from air strikes and artillery fire, but reporters who had been present insisted U.S. troops set the village afire with matches.

October 16–November 12, 1966: Operation Attleboro, the largest U.S. operation to date, was conducted in Tayninh Province near the Cambodian border. At its peak, some 20,000 U.S., ARVN, and other allied troops were involved, supported by 2,500 air sorties, including 225 by B-52s. U.S. officials reported some 1,100 Communists killed. U.S. dead numbered about 400.

October 21, 1966: A mine exploded in Traon in the Mekong Delta, killing 11 and wounding 54 Vietnamese.

November 1, 1966: Two guerrilla attacks in the center of Saigon resulted in at least eight Vietnamese fatalities.

December 31, 1966: U.S. military personnel in Vietnam totaled 280,000, plus 60,000 Americans on ships off Vietnam. There were 35,000 U.S. personnel in Thailand. More than 5,000 U.S. servicemen were killed, and 30,093 were wounded in Vietnam in 1966. SVNAF strength reached 750,000. There were approximately 1,138,000 total in the allied forces, bolstered by the addition in 1966 of 25,000 South Koreans, 550 Australians, 180 Thais, 150 New Zealanders, and 1,500 Filipinos. Desertions from South Vietnamese forces in 1966 numbered 116,858, or about 20 percent; the United States reported about 20,000 Vietcong desertions.

AIR WAR

January 31, 1966: The U.S. resumed the bombing of North Vietnam after a 37-day pause.

April 12, 1966: For the first time, B-52s bombed targets in North Vietnam, attacking near Mu Gia Pass.

April 23, 1966: In the first major air battle over North Vietnam, U.S. aircraft shot down two MiG-17s.

May 31, 1966: In the largest raid since air attacks began in February 1965, U.S. aircraft inflicted heavy damage on the Yenbay munitions complex 75 miles northeast of Hanoi.

June 29, 1966: U.S. aircraft bombed oil depots near Hanoi and Haiphong.

August 9, 1966: U.S. Air Force jets mistakenly attacked two villages 80 miles southwest of Saigon, killing 63 and wounding 100.

December 31, 1966: Operation Rolling Thunder flew 148,000 sorties in 1966, dropped 128,000 tons of bombs, and lost 318 aircraft.

NAVAL WAR

April 1966: The U.S. Navy began Operation Game Warden to interdict NVA and Vietcong bases and lines of communication on inland waterways.

August 23, 1966: The U.S. freighter *Baton Rouge Victory* struck a mine and, partly submerged, blocked traffic in the sea channel linking Saigon to the sea. Seven crewmen were killed and one was injured.

October 25, 1966: Two U.S. destroyers launched operations against enemy junks attempting to land supplies along South Vietnam's coastline.

October 26, 1966: A fire broke out on the hanger deck of the U.S. aircraft carrier *Oriskany* stationed in the Gulf of Tonkin; before it was quelled, 43 servicemen were killed, 16 were wounded, and 4 jet bombers and 2 helicopters were destroyed.

October 31, 1966: U.S. Navy patrol boats and helicopters sank a Vietcong flotilla of 35 junks and sampans trying to cross the Mekong Delta near Mytho.

CAMBODIA/LAOS

July 1966: U.S. officials in Saigon reported an average of 100 air attacks a day in Laos to interdict the Ho Chi Minh Trail.

July 31–August 13, 1966: Cambodia accused the United States of bombing villages bordering Vietnam and killing its citizens. The United States at first denied the accusations, then admitted it had bombed the villages, expressing "regret." Cambodian chief of state Prince Norodom Sihanouk canceled a September meeting to discuss U.S.-Cambodian diplomatic relations.

HOME FRONT

January 1, 1966: Senator Strom Thurmond (R–S.C.) declared that the United States should use nuclear weapons in Vietnam if victory could not be achieved otherwise.

January 4, 1966: Democratic senator George McGovern of South Dakota, recently returned from Vietnam, announced that U.S. peace proposals were doomed because the administration refused to recognize that the conflict was primarily a civil war between Saigon and the National Liberation Front (NLF) and that talks that excluded either party could not succeed.

January 19, 1966: President Johnson requested an additional $12.8 billion from Congress for the war in Vietnam.

February 4, 1966: The Senate Foreign Relations Committee began televised hearings on the Vietnam War.

March 1, 1966: The Senate rejected a bill to repeal the Gulf of Tonkin Resolution.

March 2, 1966: Defense Secretary Robert S. McNamara released data showing that the Vietcong were able to fight with an average daily flow of only 12–30 tons of supplies from North Vietnam, while the U.S. forces required 1,000 times that much. That statistic eventually said much about the ability of the Vietcong to hold out against the might of the U.S. military.

McNamara also announced that American forces in Vietnam totaled 215,000 with another 20,000 en route.

March 16, 1966: Democratic congressman Clement Zablocki of Wisconsin, reporting on his visit to Vietnam, claimed that six civilians were killed for every Vietcong soldier killed in search-and-destroy missions.

July 11, 1966: A Harris survey showed 62 percent of Americans favored the air raids on the Hanoi-Haiphong area, 11 percent opposed, and 27 percent were undecided.

September 6–9, 1966: Three army privates were court-martialed at Fort Dix, New Jersey, for refusing to deploy to Vietnam after their argument that the Vietnam War was illegal and immoral was rejected (see Historical Perspectives and Controversies p. 656-657).

INTERNATIONAL DEVELOPMENTS

January 14, 1966: Moscow pledged increased military aid to Vietnam and reiterated support for Hanoi's peace demands.

February 8, 1966: President Lyndon Johnson and South Vietnamese leaders, meeting in Honolulu, Hawaii, issued a communique emphasizing the "Other War": providing the South Vietnamese rural population with security and economic and social programs that were designed to win their support.

September 1966: French president Charles de Gaulle, on a visit to Cambodia, called for U.S. withdrawal from Vietnam.

December 31, 1966: In his New Year's message, UN Secretary General U Thant called for unconditional cessation of U.S. bombing of North Vietnam.

BATTLES AND CAMPAIGNS: 1967

SOUTH VIETNAM

January 8–26, 1967: In the largest offensive of the Vietnam War to date, 16,000 U.S and 14,000 ARVN troops began Operation Cedar Falls, an attack to destroy the base of insurgent operations near Saigon. The 3,800 inhabitants of Bensuc, a village regarded as hostile, were resettled in a camp 20 miles to the south, and their village burned. More than 700 enemy were reported killed and 488 captured. The U.S. reported some 100 dead and 600 wounded.

January 28–29, 1967: During an operation in the Mekong Delta, U.S. helicopter gunships accidentally killed 31 and wounded 38 civilians as they crossed a river after curfew.

February 2–21, 1967: A U.S. force of 6,000–8,000 troops undertook a major offensive, Operation Gadsen, near the Cambodian border to divert the enemy from the forthcoming Operation Junction City.

February 16, 1967: Enemy groundfire downed 13 U.S. helicopters.

February 22–April 15, 1967: Some 27,000 U.S. and ARVN troops conducted Operation Junction City, which was supported by tactical air strikes, helicopter units, and even a parachute assault. The objective was to eliminate the Vietcong's stronghold in War-Zone C near the Cambodian border and ease pressure on Saigon. On March 1–4, the 1st Infantry Division suffered heavy casualties in Tayninh Province but reported 150 enemy dead. The 173rd Airborne was

ambushed near the Cambodian border and also suffered heavy casualties. On March 11, 1st Division troops reported killing 210 NVA troops in one of the heaviest battles of the operation. Then on March 21, U.S. forces killed 606 Vietcong, with 60 U.S. casualties. Gen. William Westmoreland described that as "one of the most successful single actions of the year." The operation ended with some 600 U.S. dead and 2,000 wounded. The U.S. claimed 2,000 Communist casualties, but the enemy forces had effectively avoided a major showdown.

February 27, 1967: The Vietcong shelled the U.S. air base at Danang, killing 12 Americans. Thirty-five South Vietnamese civilians died in the fire in the adjacent village of Apdo.

March 2, 1967: The village of Langvei, 15 miles south of the demilitarized zone (DMZ), which separated North Vietnam and South Vietnam, was accidentally hit by U.S. bombs, which killed more than 83 civilians and wounded 176.

April 6, 1967: About 2,500 Vietcong and NVA troops carried out four closely coordinated attacks on Quangtri City 15 miles south of the DMZ, resulting in 125 ARVN troops killed and 180 wounded and 4 Americans killed and 27 wounded. South Vietnam charged that the raid's success was attributable to aid and information supplied by disloyal ARVN troops.

April 24–May 5, 1967: U.S. Marines defeated NVA troops in fierce fighting on three hills near the airstrip at Khesanh less than 10 miles from the Laotian border. The marines lost 160 men and 746 were wounded.

May 1, 1967: U.S. military strength in Vietnam reached 436,000. Ellsworth Bunker replaced Henry Cabot Lodge as U.S. ambassador to South Vietnam.

June 2, 1967: Thirty miles southwest of Danang, fighting erupted when a U.S. Marine battalion came under fire from a 2,900-man NVA regiment. The U.S. Marine 5th Regiment reported 540 NVA troops killed, 73 marines killed, and 139 wounded.

July 15, 1967: Fifty rounds of rocket fire struck the U.S. air base at Danang. Twelve Americans were killed and 40 were wounded in a 45-minute attack.

August 2, 1967: U.S. helicopters returned fire against a group of Vietcong soldiers in a village 60 miles south of Saigon, killing 40 civilians and wounding 36.

Troops of the 1st Cavalry Division jump from a UH-1D Iroquois helicopter hovering over a ridge line during Operation Oregon, April 24, 1967.

September 3, 1967: Gen. Nguyen Van Thieu was elected president of South Vietnam. Gen. Nguyen Cao Ky was elected vice president.

September 29, 1967: Thailand's Queen's Cobras Regiment arrived in Vietnam for combat operations.

October 4, 1967: Four thousand troops of the U.S. 1st Cavalry Division, Airmobile, flew to two of South Vietnam's northernmost provinces to relieve pressure on U.S. Marines fighting in Quangtri, Thauthien, and Quangngai.

October 29–November 3, 1967: The 273rd Vietcong Regiment attacked the U.S. Special Forces camp at Locninh. Reinforced by 1,400 troops from the U.S. 1st Infantry, in fierce house-to-house fighting, the Americans drove the Vietcong from Locninh, reporting more than 900 Vietcong killed. U.S. casualties were reported as 11 dead and 66 wounded.

December 27, 1967: U.S. Marines and NVA troops battled in the village of Thonthamkhe on the borders of Quangtri and Thauthien Provinces. Forty-eight marines were killed and 81 were wounded.

December 31, 1967: U.S. forces in Vietnam totaled about 500,000 at the end of 1967—600,000 if Americans stationed in Thailand and Ameri-cans in the 7th Fleet were included. Official U.S. service personnel fatalities for 1967 totaled 9,353 and 99,742 wounded; 16,021 U.S. military personnel had been killed in action since 1964. SVNAF strength rose to 798,000, with 60,428 killed in action since 1964. Other allied military personnel in Vietnam totaled 59,300. Since February 1965, the U.S. and South Vietnamese air forces had dropped more than 1.5 million tons of bombs on North Vietnam and South Vietnam. The U.S. lost 328 airplanes over North Vietnam in 1967.

AIR WAR

January 2, 1967: In the biggest air battle of the Vietnam War since 1964, U.S. Air Force F-4 Phantom jets, flying cover for F-105 Thunder-chiefs attacking SAM sites in the Red River Delta, downed seven MiG-21s.

January 8–26, 1967: U.S. planes flew 1,229 sorties in support of Operation Cedar Falls.

January 15, 1967: U.S. planes resumed air strikes against the Hanoi area for the first time since December 1966.

January 25, 1967: U.S. pilots were ordered by the Joint Chiefs of Staff not to bomb within a 5-mile radius of the center of Hanoi. That came in response to mounting criticism that U.S. planes were hitting civilian facilities in and around Hanoi, even though the United States claimed to be targeting only military installations.

February 27, 1967: U.S. planes dropped nonfloating mines in rivers in southern North Vietnam.

March 10–11, 1967: In the first bombing raid on a major industrial installation, U.S. planes bombed the Thainguyen iron and steel complex 38 miles north of Hanoi. U.S. sources in Saigon acknowledged that the bombing constituted an escalation of the war.

April 20, 1967: For the first time, U.S. planes bombed Haiphong, port city of Hanoi, attacking two power plants inside the city.

May 2, 1967: U.S. pilots reported heavy damage after bombing MiG bases at Kep and Hoalac within 40 miles of Hanoi.

June 29, 1967: According to Soviet and North Vietnamese reports, U.S. planes hit foreign ships in Haiphong harbor, including the Soviet merchant vessel *Mikhail Frunze.*

August 2, 1967: U.S planes flew a record 197 missions over North Vietnam, the highest single-day total since October 1966.

September 17, 1967: U.S. planes bombed the Thatkhe highway bridge 7 miles from the Chinese border.

October 7, 1967: U.S. planes, striking 30 miles west of Hanoi, destroyed six Soviet-built helicopters on the ground. That marked the first time Soviet helicopters had been bombed and destroyed.

November 6, 1967: U.S. Air Force planes from Korat Air Base in Thailand bombed the Giathuong storage complex, a previously restricted target 3 miles from the center of Hanoi.

December 2, 1967: Thailand reported that it had received U.S. missiles for protection against potential retaliation for permitting U.S. air raids against North Vietnam to originate in its territory.

December 14, 1967: U.S. planes bombed the rail yards 6 miles east of Hanoi at Yenvien. North Vietnam reported that homes in northeastern Hanoi were destroyed in the attack.

NAVAL WAR

February 26, 1967: Cruisers and destroyers of the U.S. 7th Fleet shelled North Vietnamese supply routes along a 200-mile stretch between the DMZ and Thanhhoa.

June 19–20, 1967: U.S. Navy river assault boats and 800 U.S infantry on the Rach-hui River 19 miles south of Saigon killed 169 Vietcong troops and lost 28 of their own, with 126 wounded.

July 29, 1967: In the United States' worst naval disaster in a combat zone since World War II, fire swept the aircraft carrier *Forrestal* in the Gulf of Tonkin. One hundred thirty-four crewmen were killed and 62 were wounded; 21 of the carrier's 80 planes were destroyed, and 42 were damaged.

September 15–16, 1967: On the Rachba River in the Mekong Delta a flotilla of the U.S. Navy's River Assault Task Force was attacked by the Vietcong. Twenty-one Americans and 69 Vietcong were reported killed.

CAMBODIA/LAOS

September 26, 1967: Laotian premier Souvanna Phouma expressed opposition to extending "McNamara's Wall," a projected 25-mile barrier along the northern border of South Vietnam, into Laos. He said that extending the barrier into Laos would "enlarge the Vietnam conflict at a time when we are trying to limit and contain it."

November 19–24, 1967: After Associated Press correspondents George McArthur and Horst Faas filed stories from Phnom Penh that they had visited a Vietcong base in Cambodia, Prince Sihanouk announced that "from now on the door of Cambodia is hermetically sealed to all American journalists."

December 26, 1967: Laotian premier Souvanna Phouma reported that North Vietnamese troops had begun a general offensive against government forces in southern Laos. On December 29, North Vietnam denied that its forces had begun a drive in Laos.

December 27, 1967: A note sent by the U.S. State Department to Cambodia, assuring Phnom Penh that the United States had "no hostile intentions toward Cambodia," was made public after Cambodia broadcast a reply that Cambodia was not being used as a base for Communist forces involved in Vietnam. Cambodia accused the United States and South Vietnam of "flagrant violations of international law through daily incursions into Cambodian territory for purposes of sabotage and assassination." The United

States said that it had no intention of expanding the Vietnam War. Cambodia's Prince Sihanouk warned that if U.S. troops invaded Cambodia in search of North Vietnamese or Vietcong forces, he would ask China, the Soviet Union, and "other anti-imperialistic powers" for new military aid.

HOME FRONT

January 10, 1967: In his State of the Union address, President Lyndon Johnson asked for a 6 percent surcharge on personal and corporate income taxes to help support the Vietnam War.

March 2, 1967: Sen. Robert Kennedy (D–N.Y.) proposed a three-point plan to end the Vietnam War, including suspension of bombing of North Vietnam. Secretary of State Dean Rusk rejected the plan.

July 7, 1967: The Congressional Joint Economic Committee reported that the Vietnam War created "havoc" in the U.S. economy in 1966 and predicted that in 1967 the war would cost $4 billion to $6 billion more than the $20.3 billion requested by President Johnson. Expenses for the Vietnam War for the fiscal year ending June 1967 totaled $21 billion.

August 25, 1967: Secretary of Defense Robert McNamara, testifying before a Senate subcommittee, acknowledged that bombing North Vietnam had been ineffective. He said that it had neither reduced the flow of supplies into South Vietnam, nor significantly damaged the North Vietnamese economy.

September 29, 1967: In a speech delivered in San Antonio, Texas, President Johnson said the United States was willing to stop all bombing if the halt would promptly result in negotiations.

October 1967: Public opinion on the Vietnam War shifted; for the first time, polls showed that there were more Americans who opposed the war than there were who supported it.

October 16–21, 1967: Demonstrations against the draft were held throughout the United States.

October 21–23, 1967: On October 21, more than 50,000 people demonstrated in Washington, D.C., against U.S. policy in Vietnam. The demonstrators marched to the Pentagon for a rally and a vigil that lasted into the morning of October 23. Ten thousand troops surrounded the Pentagon. The antiwar protest was paralleled by demonstrations in Japan and Europe.

November 21, 1967: In a speech to the National Press Club, Gen. William Westmoreland, exuding optimism, claimed that the end of the war was in sight (see Notable Phrases, p. 653).

December 18–19, 1967: About 750 antiwar demonstrators attempted to block the armed forces induction center in Oakland, California; 268 demonstrators were arrested.

INTERNATIONAL DEVELOPMENTS

January 1, 1967: In a New Year's message, French president Charles de Gaulle called on the United States to end its "detestable intervention in Vietnam" by withdrawing its troops.

January 10, 1967: UN Secretary General U Thant urged an unconditional halt to the U.S. bombing of North Vietnam.

January 18–26, 1967: In a tour marked by violent antiwar demonstrations, South Vietnamese premier Nguyen Cao Ky visited Australia and New Zealand to thank the leaders of the two countries for their support in the war.

January 28, 1967: North Vietnamese foreign minister Nguyen Duy Trinh said that the United States must stop bombing North Vietnam before peace talks could begin.

March 9, 1967: For the first time, Thailand acknowledged that U.S. planes used Thai bases for air raids on North Vietnam.

March 21, 1967: President Johnson ended a two-day meeting on Guam with South Vietnam president Nguyen Van Thieu and Premier Ky.

June 23–25, 1967: President Johnson and Soviet prime minister Aleksey Kosygin met at Glassboro, New Jersey, for talks on world issues. Chief among the issues was Vietnam.

July 6, 1967: A four-day conference on Vietnam arranged by the Swedish Society for Peace and Arbitration and other organizations of the international peace movement began in Stockholm.

December 29, 1967: North Vietnamese foreign minister Trinh said that North Vietnam would talk once the U.S. bombing ended.

BATTLES AND CAMPAIGNS: 1968

SOUTH VIETNAM

January 20–April 6, 1968 (Siege of Khesanh): The 76-day siege of the U.S. Marines

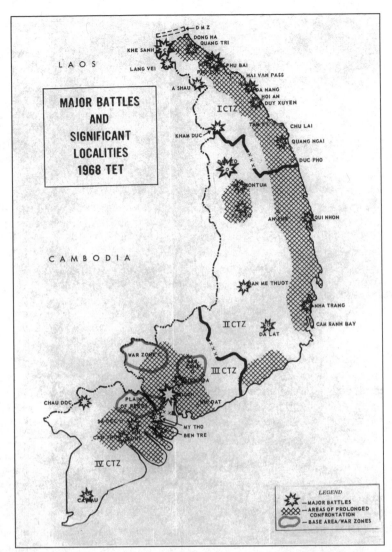

MAJOR BATTLES
AND
SIGNIFICANT
LOCALITIES
1968 TET

The Tet Offensive of January 1968—its major battles and confrontations are marked here—was the turning point of the Vietnam War. It was not that the U.S. and South Vietnamese forces suffered major military defeats but that the unexpected numbers and ferocity of the Communist attacks forced Americans to realize that the war was far from being won.

staging area at Khesanh, one of the most publicized and controversial battles of the Vietnam War, was viewed by both sides as a America's potential "Dien bien phu," a reference to the French outpost that, when lost in 1954, marked the end of France in Indochina (see Background, p. 609). Seized by U.S. Marines a year earlier, Khesanh was 6 miles from the Laotian border and 14 miles south of the DMZ. It was used as a staging area for forward patrols. In the first two days, NVA forces overran Khesanh village and

shelled the base with long-range artillery. The main ammunition dump was hit, detonating 1,500 tons of explosives, and the marines were pinned down by incessant fire. Lt. Gen. Robert Cushman, reluctant to send more troops to a base that could only be resupplied by air, relied on artillery and air strikes for relief. U.S. planes dropped 5,000 pounds of bombs a day during the siege. Gen. William Westmoreland contended that if the base fell, NVA forces would be able to flank marine defenses along the DMZ. President Lyndon

Johnson, informed by the Joint Chiefs of Staff (JCS) that Khesanh might become another Dien Bien Phu, demanded formal assurances that it would not be lost. Operation Pegasus, to relieve Khesanh, began in early April. The First Air Cavalry Division and an ARVN battalion approached the base from east and west, and the First Marine thrust westward to reopen Route 9. On April 6, the cavalrymen linked up with the ninth Marine south of the airstrip, and the siege was lifted. U.S. casualties at Khesanh included 471 dead and 2,744 wounded.

January 31–February 25, 1968 (Tet Offensive): On the first day of the traditional Tet (lunar new year) truce, the Vietcong, supported by NVA troops, launched the Tet Offensive, the heaviest and most coordinated Communist offensive of the Vietnam War. Strengthened by increasing numbers of NVA troops, the Vietcong attacked more than 30 provincial capitals and a number of U.S. and South Vietnamese airfields and bases from the DMZ to the Mekong Delta. The cities of Hué, Dalat, Kontum, and Quangtri were taken by the Vietcong during the first few days; all five provincial capitals in the north were overrun. Heavy fighting raged in the principal Mekong delta cities of Mytho, Cantho, Bentre, and Soctrang; Mytho, a city of 70,000, was nearly destroyed by allied ordnance. Most of the 50,000 Vietcong and NVA troops in South Vietnam were committed to the offensive. The bloodiest battles centered in Saigon and Hué. After almost a month of fierce house-to-house combat Hué, the former imperial capital, was regained. In Saigon, Vietcong forces took the police station and, for a few hours, occupied the U.S. embassy. Heavy fighting by 11,000 U.S. and South Vietnamese troops against a force of at least 1,000 Vietcong continued in Saigon and its suburbs through February 5. The total number of refugees in the battle areas reached 700,000; at least 5,000 civilians were killed, and 15,000 were wounded. Record casualties were suffered on both sides: An estimated 21,300 Vietcong and NVA troops had died in the fighting; about 2,000 U.S. (including 32 U.S. civilians) and allied troops also lost their lives, and about 10,000 were wounded. The Tet Offensive, coming as an almost complete surprise to South Vietnam, ended in a military disaster for North Vietnam that all but wiped out the Vietcong, but it dealt a fatal strategic blow to the United States. False expectations had been raised in the States that the Vietnam War was virtually won. The majority of Americans had been disenchanted with the war since October 1967, and the Tet Offensive proved to be the turning point that cost the military and the government the confidence of the American people. U.S. involvement in Vietnam continued for another five years, but the support of the American people was lost after the Tet Offensive. After January 30, 1968, the problem became not how to win the war but how to disengage.

February 7, 1968: NVA troops employing the latest Soviet model PT-76 light tanks overran the U.S. Special Forces camp at Langvei near Khesanh after an 18-hour siege, killing more than 300 allied troops, including eight U.S. soldiers.

February 10–17, 1968: U.S. casualties for the week, at 543 killed and 2,547 wounded in action, reached an all-time high.

February 25, 1968: After 26 days of fierce house-to-house fighting, U.S. and South Vietnamese troops recaptured Hué, the former capital in central Vietnam, with 5,113 known enemy casualties. That was the last major engagement of the Tet Offensive, although it was not officially declared over for another week. At the end of April, the U.S. embassy in Saigon reported that the NVA and Vietcong forces, during their occupation of Hué, had executed more than 1,000 civilians and buried them in mass graves; later investigations reported closer to 4,000 people had been executed by the Communists.

March 2, 1968: In one of the costliest ambushes of the war, 48 U.S. troops were killed and 28 were wounded 4 miles north of Tansonnhut Air Base.

March 11–April 7, 1968: Operation Quyet Thang, comprising 22 U.S. and 11 ARVN battalions, the largest operation to date, began in the area of Saigon and five surrounding provinces. When it ended, there were 2,658 enemy casualties; the United States suffered 105 killed, and 920 wounded.

March 14, 1968: For the first time, NVA troops are sighted in the Mekong Delta.

March 16, 1968: In what became known as the My Lai Massacre, a platoon from Charlie Company, First Battalion, 20th Infantry, Americal Division, led by Lt. William Calley, slaughtered 300–500 unarmed villagers in the hamlet of My Lai-4. (My Lai was a hamlet in the village of Songmy, the name sometimes given to the massacre.) Although it was reported to higher echelons in the Army, no one took decisive action. Not until November 12, 1969, did the Army publicly announce it was pressing charges against those responsible (see Home Front, November 12–19, 1969, p. 636).

April 10–12, 1968: U.S. troops recaptured the Special Forces camp at Langvei, lost it again to NVA forces, then retook it a second time in three days of intense fighting.

April 19, 1968: Operation Delaware/Lam Son 216 was begun in Ashau Valley to preempt enemy preparations for another attack on Hué.

May 5–13, 1968: The second major enemy offensive of 1968 began with the simultaneous shelling of 119 cities, towns, and military barracks. Heavy action continued for a week, especially in Saigon, the enemy's principal target. Allied sources reported that 5,270 North Vietnamese, 326 South Vietnamese, and 154 U.S. troops were killed during the fighting.

May 25–June 4, 1968: The Vietcong launched their third major attack of 1968 on Saigon. The heaviest fighting, during the first three days of June, centered on Cholon, where helicopters, tanks, and fighter bombers were used to dislodge entrenched Vietcong infiltrators.

June 10, 1968: South Vietnam's information minister Ton That Thien characterized the American impact on Vietnamese politics, culture, and religion as "devastating" and "disintegrating." General Westmoreland turned over command of U.S. forces in Vietnam to Gen. Creighton Abrams. In his assessment of the war, Westmoreland claimed that Washington's ban on ground attacks to interdict enemy infiltration through Laos precluded military victory.

July 5, 1968: U.S. forces completed the evacuation and abandonment of the military base at Khesanh.

August 18, 1968: In the heaviest fighting in three months, Vietcong and NVA forces attacked 19 allied positions throughout South Vietnam, all but four of which lay in Tayninh and Binhlong provinces, northwest of Saigon near the Cambodian border. Six hundred Vietcong infiltrators were driven out of the Tayninh provincial capital in fierce house-to-house fighting.

August 22, 1968: The first rocket attacks on Saigon in two months killed 18 people and wounded 59.

August 23, 1968: Heavy rocket and mortar

attacks hit numerous cities, military installations, and provincial capitals, especially the cities of Hué and Quangtri, Danang airfield, and the U.S. Special Forces camp at Duclap near the Cambodian border. More than 1,200 NVA troops assaulted Duclap following the attack. Two days later the NVA troops were driven out, leaving 643 troops dead.

September 11–16, 1968: About 1,500 Communist troops entered the city of Tayninh following rocket and mortar attacks on neighboring military bases. Four days later the local garrison, supplemented by 2,000 ARVN troops, drove the attackers out of the city, quashing the second assault on Tayninh in less than a month. Allied military sources predicted fighting in the area would remain heavy due to increased enemy infiltration from Cambodia.

September 13–October 1, 1968: In the largest sustained allied drive into the DMZ to date, U.S. and ARVN troops, supported by armor, artillery, planes, and U.S. Navy ships, drove two miles into the buffer zone to relieve enemy pressure on allied bases along South Vietnam's northern border and to preempt an anticipated attack by two NVA divisions operating in the DMZ. B-52 strikes and an additional 6,000 U.S. Marines were added as the drive progressed. Seven hundred forty-two NVA troops were killed; 65 U.S. troops were killed and 77 wounded.

October 5, 1968: U.S. Marines reoccupied the abandoned base at Khesanh to secure a hill for two artillery batteries.

October 26, 1968: An enemy force of 500–600 stormed a U.S. first Infantry base in Tayninh Province 59 miles north of Saigon near the Cambodian border in the first major ground assault in a month.

November 1, 1968: The U.S. mission in Saigon initiated Operation Phoenix, conducted under the auspices of the CIA. Set up to gather intelligence about the Vietcong infrastructure, it became one of the most controversial operations undertaken by the United States in Vietnam because it resorted to torture and assassination of suspected Communist leaders and sympathizers.

November 15, 1968: According to U.S. reconnaissance pilots, NVA troop movements north of the DMZ had quadrupled since the bombing halt, and the bombed-out bridges between the 17th and 19th parallels had been repaired.

November 20–December 19, 1968: The U.S.

ninth Marine, operating 10 miles south of Danang cordoned off an area believed to contain 1,400 enemy troops and moved in to kill them. Reported enemy casualties totaled 1,210; the U.S. forces had 107 killed and 523 wounded.

December 31, 1968: In 1968, 14,592 Americans were killed in Vietnam, bringing the total U.S. war dead since January 1961 to about 30,700 and the total U.S. wounded to about 200,000. SVNAF combat dead numbered 20,482 in 1968, and allied personnel casualties numbered 978. Vietcong and NVA combat deaths were estimated at 35,774 for 1968, with a total of 439,000 estimated killed since January 1961. Although the accuracy of enemy body counts was debatable, hundreds of thousands of Vietnamese, civilian and military, had died in the war. The Vietnamese countryside was being devastated. U.S. military personnel in Vietnam totaled 536,100, and allied military forces totaled 65,000; SVNAF strength reached 820,000, and 88,343 SVNAF had been killed in action to date.

AIR WAR

February 14, 1968: U.S. planes bombed targets near Hanoi in the heaviest assault against North Vietnam in six weeks.

March 19, 1968: Two NVA defectors reported that North Vietnam intelligence provided as much as 24 hours advance notice of U.S. B-52 raids.

April 26, 1968: After three weeks of grounding to check for suspected mechanical malfunctions of the planes, F-111 raids resumed.

July 1, 1968: U.S. B-52 bombers resumed raids north of the DMZ.

August 17, 1968: According to the Defense Department, since February 1965, U.S. planes had flown 117,000 combat missions over North Vietnam and dropped 2,581,876 tons of bombs and rockets.

September 2, 1968: Concerned that North Vietnam might celebrate its annual National Day with another assault on the capital, the U.S. command ordered heavy bombing along infiltration routes into Saigon.

October 3, 1968: U.S. planes destroyed 45 supply craft and 31 trucks and severed roads in the heaviest raid over North Vietnam since July.

November 8–9, 1968: U.S. B-52s conducted heavy raids against a suspected enemy concen-

tration of 35,000 troops in Tayninh Province about 5 miles from the Cambodian border.

December 12–13, 1968: U.S. B-52s pounded targets north of Saigon in an effort to disrupt an expected enemy offensive.

NAVAL WAR

January 1968: The U.S. Navy began Operation Clearwater to interdict enemy bases and lines of communication on inland waterways.

September 30, 1968: The USS *New Jersey*, the world's only active battleship, arrived in Vietnamese waters and began shelling NVA positions in the DMZ.

CAMBODIA/LAOS

January 4, 1968: Cambodia, repeating claims that it felt threatened by the United States, announced that it had accepted military aid from China.

January 12, 1968: After talks between U.S. emissary Chester Bowles and Prince Norodom Sihanouk, Cambodia and the United States announced agreement on measures designed to isolate Cambodia from the war.

January 13, 1968: A combined North Vietnamese-Pathet Lao force defeated Royal Laotian troops to capture Nambac, a government supply center 60 miles north of Luang Prabang, the royal capital.

January 18, 1968: Cambodia charged that allied forces entered 200 yards into its territory and killed three Cambodians. The United States acknowledged the incursion and expressed regret.

January 22, 1968: Prince Sihanouk and Yugoslavian president Josip Tito in a joint communiqué expressed full support for the NLF and North Vietnam.

January 25, 1968: NVA troops, strengthening their position in the northwest corner of South Vietnam, captured an outpost inside the Laotian border 9 miles west of Khesanh.

April 13, 1968: From Vientiane, capital of Laos, U.S. officials reported that a North Vietnamese-Pathet Lao offensive had succeeded in encircling the southern provincial capitals of Saravane and Attopeu.

June 28, 1968: Prince Souvanna Phouma of Laos declared that until the North Vietnamese agreed to withdraw all their forces from Laos, the

United States should reject Hanoi's demand for a bombing halt.

July 8, 1968: Cambodia charged in a formal complaint to the UN that allied helicopters had killed 14 Cambodians working in rice fields more than 6,000 yards from the border.

August 2, 1968: Three captured U.S. pilots were released in Laos. Ambassador-at-Large Averell Harriman announced five days later the release of 14 North Vietnamese seaman and expressed hope for further prisoner exchanges.

November 17, 1968: Cambodia charged that 12 Cambodians were killed and 12 wounded when South Vietnamese patrol boats shelled Prekkoeus, a village in Kampot Province.

HOME FRONT

January 3, 1968: Minnesota senator Eugene McCarthy announced his candidacy for the Democratic presidential nomination.

January 29, 1968: President Lyndon Johnson, in his annual budget message, asked for $26.3 billion to continue the Vietnam War and announced a tax increase.

March 10, 1968: The *New York Times* disclosed that Gen. William Westmoreland had requested 206,000 more troops for Vietnam. The leak heightened public concern with developments in Vietnam.

March 16, 1968: New York senator Robert Kennedy announced his candidacy for the Democratic presidential nomination.

March 25–26, 1968: The Senior Advisory Group on Vietnam, which became known as the "Wise Men," a panel of distinguished formal government officials, deliberated with and advised President Johnson against troop increases and urged a negotiated peace in Vietnam.

March 31, 1968: President Johnson, under fire from all sides since the Tet Offensive, announced the de-escalation of the war, including cessation of the bombing of North Vietnam, except near the DMZ. Then, in a complete surprise to all except a few of his closest advisers, Johnson announced that he would not run for reelection in November.

April 1, 1968: Clark Clifford succeeded Robert McNamara as secretary of defense.

April 4, 1968: Dr. Martin Luther King, Jr. was assassinated in Memphis, Tennessee.

April 22, 1968: In the first public announcement of the policy that would become known as "Vietnamization" under the Nixon administration, Secretary of Defense Clark Clifford declared that the South Vietnamese had "acquired the capacity to begin to insure their own security [and] they are going to take over more and more of the fighting."

April 26, 1968: In New York City 200,000 people demonstrated against the war.

June 5, 1968: After winning the California primary for the Democratic presidential nomination, Sen. Robert F. Kennedy was assassinated in Los Angeles.

July 2, 1968: Congress passed a $6 billion supplemental appropriations bill for the war effort in Vietnam.

July 13, 1968: Republican presidential candidate Gov. Nelson Rockefeller of New York revealed a peace plan that he argued could end the Vietnam War in six months.

August 5–8, 1968: At the Republican National Convention in Miami, Florida, a Vietnam plank was adopted, emphasizing the need for an honorable negotiated peace and "progressive de-Americanization" of the war. Richard Nixon received the Republican presidential nomination.

August 26–29, 1968: At the Democratic National Convention in Chicago, Illinois, impassioned debate between antiwar factions led by Senators Eugene McCarthy and George McGovern and those supporting the Johnson administration's policy reflected events outside the convention hall. On August 28, a week of mounting tensions and sporadic violence erupted into full-scale rioting between antiwar demonstrators and police and National Guardsmen on the streets of Chicago.

October 11, 1968: In San Francisco, more than 7,000 protestors, including 200 soldiers, 700 veterans, and 100 reservists, marched through the downtown area in the first antiwar demonstration organized and led by soldiers.

November 5, 1968: Richard Nixon was elected president of the United States, and Spiro Agnew was elected vice president. Nixon promised a gradual troop withdrawal from Vietnam.

December 2, 1968: Nixon selected Henry Kissinger as his national security adviser.

December 16, 1968: In a suit brought by 57 reservists, the Supreme Court refused to review the government's right to send reservists to Vietnam despite the absence of a declaration of war.

December 17, 1968: A Gallup poll showed that the majority of Americans were ready to let South Vietnam take over the fighting and lead the peace talks.

December 18, 1968: Henry Kissinger proposed in *Foreign Affairs* magazine that the United States and North Vietnam should arrange for mutual withdrawal of their forces in one set of negotiations and that South Vietnam and the NLF should arrange a political settlement in separate discussions. Although written before Kissinger held a formal appointment in the Nixon administration, the proposal influenced subsequent North Vietnamese demands.

INTERNATIONAL DEVELOPMENTS

January 4, 1968: The Soviet Union charged that a Soviet merchant ship had been damaged by U.S. planes during raids on Haiphong. The United States expressed regrets, adding that it was impossible to eliminate such risks.

January 23, 1968: The USS *Pueblo*, an intelligence vessel, allegedly violated North Korean waters and was seized by North Korean patrol boats in the Sea of Japan.

April 28, 1968: As part of an antiwar strike organized by the Student Mobilization Committee, students throughout the world cut classes to protest the war in Vietnam.

May 27, 1968: Thai premier Thanom Kittikachorn announced that he had agreed to President Johnson's request to send an additional 5,000 Thai troops to Vietnam.

July 18–20, 1968: President Lyndon Johnson and President Thieu met in Honolulu to discuss relations between the United States and South Vietnam.

September 26, 1968: UN Secretary-General U Thant, in his annual report to the UN General Assembly, characterized the Vietnam War as a nationalist struggle and declared that the major powers should "let the Vietnamese themselves deal with their own problems." He urged a total bombing halt, reunification of Vietnam, and neutrality for the Indochinese peninsula.

October 27, 1968: An estimated 50,000 persons marched in London, England, to protest the Vietnam War.

October 31, 1968: In a televised speech, President Johnson announced that he had ordered a cessation, effective the following day, of all bombing raids over North Vietnam in response to recent developments in Paris. He further disclosed that Hanoi and Washington had agreed to allow South Vietnam and the National Liberation Front (NFL) to participate in the peace talks.

November 1, 1968: Officials in Washington, D.C., disclosed that there would be a three-fold increase in air strikes along the Ho Chi Minh Trail in Laos. President Johnson reportedly approved those stepped-up attacks to obtain support from the military for terminating air strikes against North Vietnam.

BATTLES AND CAMPAIGNS: 1969

SOUTH VIETNAM

January 10, 1969: A nine-man U.S. patrol near Dongtam was wiped out in a Vietcong ambush. Vietcong mortar attacks on towns and bases killed at least 17 and wounded 155.

January 14, 1969: U.S. forces beat back an attack on a supply convoy northwest of Saigon, killing 112 enemy troops. U.S. casualties totaled seven dead and ten wounded.

January 18, 1969: President Thieu confirmed that he had made a request for the withdrawal of some U.S. troops in 1969.

January 22–March 18, 1969: Operation Dewey Canyon conducted by the U.S. ninth Marine Regiment north of the Ashau Valley in Quangtri Province reported 1,335 known enemy casualties. U.S. dead totaled 125, with some 600 wounded

January 25, 1969: After a six-day battle, a U.S. force of 800 succeeded in expelling 200 enemy troops from a village they had occupied 7 miles northwest of Quangngai.

February 15, 1969: Allied troop strength, including 539,000 U.S. soldiers, reached an all-time high of 1,610,500.

February 22, 1969: As the Tet cease-fire ended, enemy forces hit Saigon and about 70 other cities and military installations with rocket and mortar fire. Raids throughout South Vietnam killed 28 Americans and 8 South Vietnamese civilians, and 128 Americans and 81 South Vietnamese civilians were wounded. Attacks continued in what were known as the "post-Tet" offensive on hundreds of military bases, towns, and cities for another three to four weeks. Altogether, more than 10,000 enemy troops and about

Troops of the 11th Armored Cavalry advance against an enemy position on February 23, 1969.

500 Americans were reported killed during the offensive, and tens of thousands of civilians were rendered homeless. U.S. positions just south of the DMZ also came under heavy attack, resulting in the highest U.S. losses in a single battle in almost six months.

March 5, 1969: Rocket fire hit Saigon, killing at least 22 civilians and wounding scores.

April 10–11, 1969: Vinhlong, a provincial capital 60 miles southwest of Saigon, received heavy mortar fire as 45 targets were hit by enemy rocket and mortar attacks. Increased ground fighting was reported in the Mekong Delta and areas northwest of Saigon.

April 14, 1969: Repelling a massive enemy attack against an infantry camp 33 miles northwest of Saigon, U.S. troops killed 198 enemy soldiers; 13 Americans were reported killed, and 3 wounded.

April 27, 1969: U.S. forces turned back an attack by 300 enemy troops as heavy fighting erupted near the Cambodian border for the second consecutive day. Ten American and 100 enemy soldiers were reported killed.

April 30, 1969: The number of U.S. military personnel in Vietnam peaked at 543,400.

May 1–July 16, 1969: Operation Virginia Ridge, conducted by the U.S. ninth Marine Regiment, third Marine Division, in northern Quangtri Province along the DMZ, reported 560 enemy casualties. The U.S. casualties were 131 dead and some 700 wounded.

May 9, 1969: U.S. Marines, with air support, reported killing 129 enemy soldiers, 18 miles southwest of Danang. Six Americans were killed, and 12 wounded.

May 10–20, 1969: The bloody battle of "Hamburger Hill"—Apbia mountain (Hill 937) 1 mile east of the Laotian border—ensued as part of the 2,800-man allied sweep through the Ashua Valley called Operation Apache Snow. After air and artillery strikes and ten infantry assaults, the stronghold was captured on the 11th assault by 1,000 U.S. and 400 ARVN troops. U.S. officials reported 597 NVA troops killed; 56 Americans were killed, and 420 were wounded. The allied goal was to limit infiltration from Laos that threatened Danang to the southeast and Hué to the northeast. U.S. troops abandoned Hamburger Hill on May 28.

May 11–12, 1969: In the largest number of attacks since the 1968 Tet Offensive, Communist forces shelled 129 targets throughout South Vietnam, including Saigon and Hué. Terrorist attacks near Saigon killed 14 and wounded about 100.

May 18, 1969: More than 1,500 enemy troops

attacked U.S. and ARVN camps near Xuanloc 38 miles east of Saigon. In five hours of intense fighting, 78 enemy soldiers were killed and nine were captured; 14 Americans were killed, and 39 were wounded.

June 11, 1969: Two U.S. bases south of Danang sustained heavy ground attacks. At Tamky 35 miles south of Danang, 16 Americans and 62 enemy soldiers died in hand-to-hand combat.

June 16, 1969: Thailand's Black Panther Division, supported by U.S. firepower, repelled a force of 500 Vietcong that three times assaulted their base 20 miles east of Saigon. Six Thais were killed and 7 were wounded; 212 Vietcong were reported killed.

June 17, 1969: U.S. intelligence reported that about 1,000 NVA troops had reoccupied Apbia mountain (Hamburger Hill).

June 17–21, 1969: In increased fighting south of the DMZ, 250 enemy troops were reported killed; 30 Americans were killed, and 71 were wounded.

July 7, 1969: The withdrawal of U.S. troops from Vietnam began with the exit from Saigon of a battalion of the U.S. Ninth Infantry Division.

July 21–September 25, 1969: Operation Idaho Canyon, conducted by the U.S. Third Marine Regiment in Quangtri Province, reported 565 enemy casualties.

August 3–9, 1969: Ninety-six Americans were killed during the week, the lowest weekly U.S. death toll since August 12, 1967.

August 13, 1969: Allied military sources reported 1,450 enemy casualties during the previous 24 hours in the heaviest fighting in three months. Enemy forces had attacked more than 150 targets the previous day. In Danang, NVA commandos fought their way to the U.S. First Marine Division Headquarters before they were driven back.

August 17–26, 1969: At least 650 NVA troops and more than 60 U.S. troops were killed in a fierce battle in the Queson Valley 30 miles south of Danang.

August 28, 1969: More sharp fighting in the Danang area resulted in 18 enemy killed; 13 U.S. Marines were killed and 42 were wounded.

August 29, 1969: The 25,000-man withdrawal announced by President Richard Nixon on June 8 was completed.

September 13, 1969: A heavy attack on a village near Quangngai was repulsed; 113 en-

emy soldiers and 8 civilians were killed; 260 houses were destroyed.

September 16, 1969: Seven civilians were killed and 17 wounded when a U.S. helicopter gunship mistakenly opened fire in the Mekong Delta. Twenty-five U.S. Marines were killed, and 63 wounded in fighting with NVA troops south of the DMZ. Eight Americans were killed and 10 wounded in an explosion 33 miles northwest of Saigon.

September 17, 1969: Twenty-three U.S. Marines and 23 NVA soldiers were killed in assaults on two marine outposts just below the DMZ.

September 26, 1969: A U.S. helicopter killed 14 when it mistakenly attacked a group of civilians near Tamky.

October 3, 1969: In Saigon, U.S. military planners reported shifting their primary emphasis from battlefield support to military and technical training as part of the program of Vietnamization, turning the war effort over to the South Vietnamese armed forces.

October 21, 1969: Forty-six enemy soldiers were reported killed in six short battles north and west of Saigon. Seven Americans were killed, and 20 were wounded. Two more Americans died when their spotter plane was brought down by groundfire.

October 24, 1969: Blackhorse Base, 38 miles northeast of Saigon, headquarters of the U.S. Army's 11th Armored Cavalry, was turned over to the ARVN's 18th Division for use as a base and training center.

November 4, 1969: Supported by U.S. planes and artillery, ARVN troops, in the biggest battle in four months, clashed with NVA troops for ten hours near the Cambodian border. Eighty NVA soldiers were reported killed; 24 ARVN soldiers were killed and 38 wounded.

November 7, 1969: For the first time since May 1968, Saigon's outer defenses came under heavy attack as an estimated 100 enemy soldiers fired on two government police posts.

November 18, 1969: In the first major action in the northern Mekong Delta since the U.S. Ninth Division was withdrawn, 60 ARVN troops were killed or wounded, and 14 NVA troops were killed.

November 25, 1969: U.S. troops shielding bases near the Cambodian border came under stepped-up attack. Ten Americans were killed, and 70 wounded; 115 enemy soldiers were reported killed. The NVA destroyed more than a

In an action on October 6, 1969, U.S. troops prepare to move out behind the cover of an M-113 armored personnel carrier as a UH-1D Iroquois helicopter passes overhead.

dozen tanks and tons of ammunition at a U.S. base near the Cambodian border.

December 7–8, 1969: One American was killed and four wounded as enemy forces launched 44 attacks throughout South Vietnam. Eighty-eight NVA troops were killed in two clashes near Tayninh.

December 9, 1969: At a national police training center in Dalat, 13 police were killed and 25 wounded during a Vietcong attack.

December 27, 1969: U.S forces reported killing 72 of 250 NVA soldiers in a fierce battle near Locninh about 80 miles northwest of Saigon.

December 28, 1969: An explosive charge thrown into a U.S. field camp near Laikhe 25 miles northwest of Saigon killed seven and wounded five Americans of the 25th Infantry Division.

December 31, 1969: U.S. combat deaths in Vietnam totaled 9,414 in 1969 (down from 14,592 in 1968), bringing total U.S. servicemen fatalities in the Vietnam War to about 40,000, with 260,000 wounded and 1,400 captured or missing. President Richard Nixon's withdrawal of forces reduced the number of U.S. troops in Vietnam from a peak of 543,000 in April to about 479,000, the lowest number in two years. U.S. forces in Thailand were also being withdrawn, but still num-

bered 46,000. Australia and the Philippines began to withdraw their forces; South Korea and Thailand, whose 12,000 troops were fully funded by the United States, did not. Under Vietnamization, SVNAF strength rose from about 850,000 to more than 1 million, and vast quantities of U.S. materiel, including 1 million M-16 rifles, were turned over to the South Vietnamese. During 1969, some 6,000 South Vietnamese civilians were killed by terrorist actions alone. The continuing carnage coupled with the knowledge of U.S. troop withdrawals began to seriously demoralize U.S. combat troops. Drug use and attacks on officers (fragging) increased, and 1969 saw 117 U.S. Army convictions for "mutiny and other acts involving willful refusal" to follow orders, as opposed to 82 such convictions in 1968.

AIR WAR

January 10, 1969: North Vietnam reported the downing of an unmanned U.S. reconnaissance plane over Thaibinh Province.

March 18, 1969: The U.S. Air Force began the secret bombing of Cambodia.

April 8, 1969: Five waves of U.S. B-52s raided enemy camps near the Cambodian border.

April 19, 1969: The U.S turned over 20 of 60 jet fighter-bombers promised to the South Vietnamese air force.

April 24–25, 1969: One hundred B-52s based in Thailand and Guam dropped close to 3,000 tons of bombs on a border area 70 miles northwest of Saigon in two days of the heaviest bombing raids of the Vietnam War.

June 5, 1969: In retaliation for the shooting down of a reconnaissance plane, U.S. aircraft made their first raids against North Vietnam since the bombing halt of November 1, 1968. Such retaliatory strikes recurred from time to time throughout the year.

June 13, 1969: The total number of bombing sorties by U.S. planes rose to 242,000 in 1969. B-52 missions over the Ho Chi Minh Trail in southern Laos rose to 5,567, up 2,190 from 1968, as planes generally idled by the bombing halt over North Vietnam were diverted to Laos and, in secret, to Cambodia.

August 1, 1969: Twenty-seven U.S. planes were lost in the previous week, bringing the total number of U.S. planes lost since the fighting in Vietnam began to 5,690.

October 31, 1969: U.S. B-52s carried out heavy bombing against NVA troop concentrations along the Cambodian border in the Central Highlands to protect U.S. Special Forces camps at Duclap and Buprang.

NAVAL WAR

January 5, 1969: The U.S. Navy announced it had established the final link of water patrols involving more than 100 vessels interlocking along a 150-mile stretch of the Cambodia-South Vietnam border.

February 1, 1969: The U.S. Navy turned over 25 heavily-armed riverboats to the South Vietnamese navy.

February 7, 1969: The U.S. Navy announced that its operation on Cape Batangan, Quangngai Province, had succeeded. The navy reported 200 enemy killed and 251 captured since January 13.

June 25, 1969: The U.S. Navy turned over 64 river patrol gunboats worth $18.2 million to the South Vietnamese navy in the largest single transfer of military equipment to date. The transfer brought the total number of boats in the South Vietnamese navy to 600.

October 10, 1969: In the largest single turnover of naval equipment since the Vietnam War began, the U.S. Navy transferred 80 river-patrol boats to the South Vietnamese.

CAMBODIA/LAOS

January 11, 1969: Cambodian antiaircraft gunners shot down a U.S. helicopter that Prince Sihanouk later charged had intruded into Cambodian territory; one of the four crew members was killed.

March 6, 1969: Cambodia, protesting violations of its airspace, announced it would release four U.S. fliers captured when their plane was downed on February 14.

March 8, 1969: U.S. military sources reported an incursion of about 100 marines into Laos. South of Dongha, a dozen hilltops were seized as part of Operation Dewey Canyon.

March 18, 1969: Operation Menu, the secret bombing of Cambodia, ordered by President Richard Nixon on March 15 and hidden from the U.S. public and the Congress, was begun by U.S. Air Force B-52s raiding eastern Cambodia to a depth of 5 miles beyond the Vietnam border. A total of 3,630 sorties dropped 110,000 tons of bombs on Cambodia over a 14-month period through April 1970.

April 16, 1969: Cambodia reestablished diplomatic relations with the United States after a four-year break.

June 13, 1969: For the first time, Laotian premier Souvanna Phouma acknowledged publicly that U.S. planes carried out regular bombing raids in Laos. He said the raids would continue as long as North Vietnam used Laos for bases and infiltration routes.

September 10, 1969: Cambodian Prince Norodom Sihanouk expressed support for the "just stand" of North Vietnamese and called on the United States to withdraw from Vietnam.

October 7, 1969: President Richard Nixon, meeting with Premier Phouma at the White House, gave assurances that the United States would insist on the withdrawal of North Vietnamese forces from Laos and Cambodia as part of a peace settlement.

October 8, 1969: Souvanna Phouma requested increased U.S. aid to counter increasing Communist pressure in Laos.

November 16–17, 1969: NVA artillery positions inside Cambodia that had shelled camps at

Buprang and Duclap were attacked by allied artillery and bombers. The U.S. command called the raids "an inherent right of self-defense against enemy attacks."

HOME FRONT

January 15, 1969: President Lyndon B. Johnson's final budget called for $25.733 billion for Vietnam war-related expenditures for fiscal year 1970, including, for the first time since the United States entered the Vietnam War, a reduction ($3.5 billion) in war spending.

January 20, 1969: Richard Nixon was inaugurated as President of the United States. William Rogers replaced Dean Rusk as secretary of state; Melvin Laird became secretary of defense, replacing Clark Clifford; and Henry Kissinger replaced Walt Rostow as national security adviser.

March 1969: Melvin Laird, secretary of defense, coined the term "Vietnamization" to describe U.S. troop withdrawals.

March 20, 1969: A federal grand jury indicted eight persons on charges of conspiracy to incite riot during the 1968 Democratic convention in Chicago. Eight Chicago policemen were also indicted, seven on charges of assault.

March 22, 1969: Five Roman Catholic priests and four others were arrested after ransacking the offices of Dow Chemical Corporation, one of the manufacturers of napalm, in Washington, D.C. (see Military Innovations, Tactics, Equipment, pp. 651-652).

April 5–6, 1969: Thousands of demonstrators marched in New York City, demanding that the United States withdraw from Vietnam. A weekend of antiwar protests ended with parades and marches in many cities, including San Francisco, Los Angeles, and Washington, D.C.

May 9, 1969: After an accurate description of the secret bombing in Cambodia was reported in the *New York Times* by Washington military correspondent William Beecher, Henry Kissinger, presidential assistant for national security affairs, asked FBI director J. Edgar Hoover to help him discover the source of the leak. Over the next two years, Kissinger and aide, Alexander Haig, relayed names of reporters and national security staff members to the FBI for wiretapping. Their conduct laid the groundwork for the crackdown on antiwar elements that led to Watergate and cost Richard Nixon the presidency (see Home Front, August 9, 1974, p. 645).

May 20, 1969: Calling the battle for Hamburger Hill "senseless and irresponsible," Sen. Edward Kennedy (D–Mass.) attacked the military tactics of the Nixon administration. His Senate speech was seen as part of a growing outcry over U.S. military policy in Vietnam.

July 11, 1969: In Boston the U.S. First Circuit Court of Appeals reversed famed pediatrician Dr. Benjamin Spock's 1968 conviction on charges of conspiracy to counsel draft evasion.

August 14, 1969: The Department of Defense, in response to congressional criticism, conceded that the number of U.S. troops in Vietnam had actually increased since President Richard Nixon took office.

September 16, 1969: President Nixon revealed a plan to withdraw an additional 35,000 troops from Vietnam.

September 19, 1969: President Nixon announced a 50,000-man reduction in draft calls for the remainder of 1969.

September 23, 1969: The eight antiwar activists known as the "Chicago Eight" went on trial in Chicago as more than 1,000 antiwar protesters demonstrated outside. On November 5, Bobby Seale, a Black Panther leader, had his trial separated from the others because of his unruly behavior in the courtroom. (That is why the defendants are sometimes referred to as the "Chicago Seven.")

September 25, 1969: Sen. Charles Goodell (R–N.Y.) proposed legislation that would mandate the withdrawal of all U.S. troops from Vietnam by the end of 1970 and would cut off congressional funds for U.S personnel in Vietnam after December 1, 1970.

October 1, 1969: President Nixon allowed draft deferments for graduate students.

October 8, 1969: Forty demonstrators were arrested when members of the Students for a Democratic Society (SDS) clashed with Chicago police at a demonstration during the trial of the Chicago Eight. The next day, the National Guard was called out as demonstrations protesting the trial continued.

October 11, 1969: A Gallup poll reported that 57 percent of Americans said they would like to see Congress mandate a total U.S. troop withdrawal from Vietnam by the end of 1970.

November 3, 1969: In an attempt to blunt the renewed vigor of the antiwar movement and gain support for his Vietnam policies, President Nixon delivered a report on the Vietnam War before a nationwide television audience. In that, his second major and by far most expansive statement on the Vietnam War, Nixon conjured up visions of the disasters that would follow a Communist victory in Vietnam and appealed to the "silent majority" for support.

November 12, 1969: The federal government began assembling 9,000 troops in the Washington, D.C., area to augment the 1,200 National Guardsmen and 3,700 police already preparing for the massive protest demonstrations planned for November 14 and 15.

November 12–19, 1969: On November 12, the U.S. Army announced that it was charging Lt. William Calley with crimes against civilians in Vietnam on March 16, 1968 (see Battles and Campaigns, South Vietnam, March 16, 1968, pp. 626-627). On November 17, the *New York Times* published reporter Seymour Hersh's article setting forth the full story of the incident for which Calley was charged: the My Lai massacre of March 16, 1968. On November 19, the Cleveland *Plain Dealer* published photographs taken by a U.S. combat photographer at My Lai, further stunning the American public.

November 13, 1969: The second antiwar moratorium began with mass demonstrations in San Francisco and Washington, D.C. In Washington, 46,000 marchers, headed by relatives of servicemen killed in Vietnam, walked in a "March Against Death" from Arlington National Cemetery past the White House.

November 15, 1969: In the largest antiwar demonstration in U.S. history, more than 250,000 protestors gathered in Washington, D.C. Following a massive march down Pennsylvania Avenue and a rally at the Washington Monument, 6,000 radical protestors led by the Youth International Party (Yippies) and supporters of the Chicago Eight split off to march on the Justice Department. Nearly 100 demonstrators were arrested when the crowd, which was throwing rocks and bottles and burning American flags, was repelled with tear gas.

December 1969: Texas billionaire Ross Perot generated publicity for American POWs imprisoned in North Vietnam with his unsuccessful attempt to land two planes filled with gifts, food, and medical supplies in Hanoi.

December 15, 1969: President Nixon announced the withdrawal of an additional 50,000 U.S. troops from Vietnam by April 15, 1970.

December 18, 1969: Congress prohibited the use of existing Department of Defense appropriations for the introduction of ground combat troops into Laos and Thailand.

INTERNATIONAL DEVELOPMENTS

January 10, 1969: Sweden announced its intention to establish full diplomatic relations with North Vietnam.

March 17, 1969: Sen. George McGovern (D–S.D.) accused President Richard Nixon of continuing the "tragic course" of the Johnson administration. Cuba established diplomatic relations with the NLF.

May 14, 1969: With U.S. troop strength in Vietnam at 543,000, President Richard Nixon called for the withdrawal of "all non-South Vietnamese forces" and announced that U.S. troops would be gradually withdrawn.

June 8, 1969: President Nixon, meeting with President Thieu on Midway Island, announced the withdrawal of 25,000 U.S. troops. Both men emphasized that the U.S. forces would be replaced by South Vietnamese forces.

July 25, 1969: At a stop in Guam, President Nixon unveiled a policy that was promptly dubbed the "Nixon Doctrine": Following the conclusion of the war in Vietnam, the United States would have primary responsibility for defense of its Asian allies against nuclear attack, but each nation would be responsible for its internal security and for defending itself against conventional attack.

August 4, 1969: Hanoi announced the release of three American prisoners of war to the custody of a pacifist group led by Rennie Davis, one of the Chicago Eight, then under federal indictment for having conspired to incite disorder at the 1968 Democratic National Convention in Chicago.

September 3, 1969: Ho Chi Minh died in Hanoi at age 79.

September 30, 1969: The U.S. and Thai governments announced a plan to withdraw 6,000 Americans, mostly airmen, from Thailand.

November 15, 1969: Major antiwar protests timed to coincide with the moratorium in Washington, D.C., and San Francisco (see Home Front, November 13, 1969, above) were held in Frankfurt, Stuttgart, West Berlin, London, Paris, and 42 French cities. In Paris, 2,651 protestors were arrested.

December 12–20, 1969: The Philippine army's 1,350 noncombatant contingent, in Vietnam since September 1966, was withdrawn.

December 21, 1969: Thailand announced plans to withdraw its 12,000-man contingent from South Vietnam. South Korea planned to keep its 48,000-man force in South Vietnam.

BATTLES AND CAMPAIGNS: 1970

SOUTH VIETNAM

January 2, 1970: The U.S. command in Saigon reported that 65 Americans died in action during the preceding week.

January 8–9, 1970: U.S. troops supported by air strikes, artillery, and armor reported killing 109 enemy soldiers near Tayninh. Two Americans were killed and 10 wounded.

January 26, 1970: Enemy forces shelled 29 targets throughout South Vietnam, killing nine Americans and wounding five. Seventy-five enemy casualties were reported.

January 31–February 1, 1970: Rocket, mortar, and ground attacks hit more than 100 bases and towns from the Mekong Delta to the DMZ, killing 19 Americans and wounding 119. ARVN losses were 11 killed and 86 wounded. More than 400 enemy soldiers were reported killed.

February 13, 1970: At an ambush in Queson valley near Danang, 13 U.S. Marines were killed and 12 wounded. Six enemy soldiers were reported killed.

February 20, 1970: Fourteen Americans were killed and 29 were wounded when their armored unit was ambushed in the Queson valley south of Danang.

March 29, 1970: Thirteen Americans were killed and 30 wounded during an attack on a base near the Cambodian border. NVA casualties were reported at 75.

April 1, 1970: Vietcong forces launched ground and artillery assaults against 115 targets throughout South Vietnam.

April 4–5, 1970: Six U.S. soldiers were killed and 40 wounded in fighting southwest of Conthien near the DMZ.

May 3–9, 1970: The number of SVNAF troops killed in action totaled 863. That was the second highest weekly death toll of the war for South Vietnamese forces.

May 19, 1970: On the 80th anniversary of Ho Chi Minh's birth, enemy forces shelled more than 60 allied positions in South Vietnam.

July 8, 1970: U.S. rocket-firing helicopters killed 139 NVA 304th Division troops caught in the open near Khesanh after they had crossed the border from Laos.

August 26, 1970: Two U.S. helicopters were brought down by ground fire, bringing the total number of helicopters lost since January 1961 to 3,998, of which 1,777 were reported lost to groundfire.

September 5, 1970–October 8, 1971: In the last major military operations in which U.S. ground forces participated, Operation Jefferson Glen and related allied combat operations in Thauthien Province, 2,026 enemy casualties were reported. The United States reported some 200 dead and 700 wounded.

September 19, 1970: Eleven Americans were killed and 11 were wounded 1 mile south of the DMZ when NVA gunners brought down a helicopter and shelled the relief force attempting to reach the scene.

October 14, 1970: Nine American soldiers and 15 ARVN soldiers were killed, and five Americans wounded by a booby trap 66 miles southeast of Danang.

October 31, 1970: In a speech before a joint session of the National Assembly, South Vietnam's president Thieu declared that a military victory was close at hand and that "we are seeing the light at the end of the tunnel" (see Notable Phrases, p. 653-654).

November 5, 1970: U.S. troops reported killing seven NVA troops in a battle 17 miles southwest of Hué; three Americans were killed and three wounded. U.S. Marines reported killing twenty North Vietnamese in an engagement 17 miles southeast of Danang. One American was killed.

November 15, 1970: Nine Americans were killed and ten were wounded by booby traps and land mines.

November 21, 1970: Fifty American troops in ten helicopters landed at Sontay prison camp 23 miles west of Hanoi, intending to free the 70–100 Americans reportedly being held there. No U.S. prisoners were discovered; 25 North Vietnamese guards were killed and all Americans returned safely.

December 1, 1970: An ARVN force of 7,000 launched a major drive against a suspected enemy force of 3,000 in the U Minh Forest in the southern Mekong Delta.

December 2, 1970: Communist forces hit 22 targets in South Vietnam with rockets, bringing reported enemy attacks in the previous four days to nearly 100.

December 14, 1970: Six Americans in an infantry patrol were killed when they entered a U.S. minefield south of the DMZ.

December 24, 1970: Nine U.S. soldiers were killed and nine were wounded 11 miles south of Hué when a U.S. artillery shell was mistakenly fired into a group of soldiers from the 1st Brigade, 101st Airborne Division.

December 31, 1970: At year's end, there were about 334,600 U.S. troops in Vietnam. The number of Americans killed in Vietnam in 1970 was 4,204, the lowest annual total since 1965. The total number of U.S. military personnel killed in action in Vietnam to date was 44,245. Other allied military personnel in Vietnam declined to 67,700. SVNAF strength increased to 968,000; 20,914 SVNAF personnel were killed in action in 1970. More than 31,000 civilians were killed in South Vietnam in 1970.

Air War

January 28, 1970: A U.S. fighter-bomber attacked a SAM missile base 90 miles inside North Vietnam in retaliation for missiles fired at an unarmed reconnaissance plane. U.S. command denied that the attack signaled any change in U.S. policy. The North Vietnamese delegation in Paris charged that U.S. planes bombed and strafed populated areas.

February 2, 1970: A U.S. fighter-bomber attacked North Vietnamese antiaircraft positions in retaliation for antiaircraft fire at an unarmed U.S. reconnaissance plane.

February 17–18, 1970: U.S. B-52s attacked Communist forces threatening the Plain of Jars in northern Laos. The attacks provoked a wave of congressional criticism when they were made public on February 19.

May 1–2, 1970: Hundreds of U.S. planes carried out heavy bombing raids against supply depots and other targets in North Vietnam.

June 26, 1970: The U.S. government confirmed that it planned to continue bombing raids inside Cambodia after June 30, by which time all ground troops would have been withdrawn.

November 4, 1970: The U.S. turned over 31 helicopters and a Mekong Delta air base to the South Vietnamese air force as part of Vietnamization.

November 21, 1970: Some 200 U.S. fighter-bombers and 50 support planes carried out the heaviest bombing of North Vietnam since November 1, 1968.

Naval War

May 9, 1970: Thirty U.S. gunboats joined 110 South Vietnamese craft in an attempt to neutralize enemy sanctuaries along a 45-mile stretch of the Mekong River from the Vietnamese border to Phnom Penh.

May 12, 1970: Allied vessels set up a blockade along a 100-mile stretch of the Cambodian coastline to prevent enemy forces from resupplying by sea.

September 19, 1970: Two hundred South Vietnamese vessels supported by 1,500 Vietnamese marines began operations 35 miles southeast of Phnom Penh to disrupt enemy base areas and infiltration routes between the Bassac and Mekong Rivers.

December 30, 1970: The South Vietnamese navy received 125 U.S. vessels in a ceremony marking the end of the U.S. Navy's four-year role in inland waterway combat, bringing the total number of vessels turned over to the South Vietnamese navy to 650.

Cambodia/Laos

March 16, 1970: Following a week of rioting and attacks by Cambodians on Vietnamese nationals, businesses, and the embassies, North Vietnamese, NLF, and Cambodian officials met in Phnom Penh to discuss the Communist military presence in Cambodia.

March 18, 1970: In a bloodless coup, chief-of-state Prince Norodom Sihanouk of Cambodia was overthrown by Lt. Gen. Lon Nol, premier and defense minister.

March 19, 1970: Premier Lon Nol declared a state of emergency and suspended Cambodian constitutional protections for public assembly and from arbitrary arrest.

March 20, 1970: In the first Cambodian-allied operation of the war, U.S. air power and ARVN artillery requested by a Cambodian army commander helped repel 150 Vietcong attacking an outpost about 10 miles north of the Anphu district capital in Vietnam.

March 23, 1970: From Beijing, Prince Norodom Sihanouk issued a call for arms against the Lon Nol government and for the establishment of a United Front of Kampuchea (FUNK). Norodom received the immediate and enthusiastic support of the NLF, North Vietnam, and the Pathet Lao.

April 9–16, 1970: Cambodian government troops and police participated in massacres of Vietnamese civilian residents in Cambodia.

April 29–30, 1970: On April 29, some 6,000 ARVN troops launched an attack into the "Parrot's Beak" area of Cambodia along the border with South Vietnam; the ARVN forces were fully supported by U.S. warplanes, artillery, advisers, and medical evacuation teams. Then on April 30, President Richard Nixon announced that he had authorized the sending of some 8,000 U.S. combat troops into the adjacent "Fishhook" area of Cambodia. That Cambodian "incursion" was aimed at wiping out both the alleged "control center" and sanctuaries of the Communist forces.

May 6, 1970: Three new fronts opened, bringing the number of allied troops in Cambodia to 50,000, including 30,000 Americans.

May 26, 1970: Prince Sihanouk, conferring in Hanoi with North Vietnamese prime minister Pham Van Dong, Gen. Vo Nguyen Giap, and Foreign Minister Nguyen Duy Trinh, urged the people of Indochina to unite in their fight against foreign intervention.

June 29, 1970: U.S. combat troops ended two months of operations in Cambodia and returned to South Vietnam; 354 Americans had been killed and 1,689 wounded. ARVN lost 866 men; 3,724 were wounded. There were 10,000 reported enemy casualties. About 34,000 ARVN troops remained in Cambodia.

HOME FRONT

February 14, 1970: A Gallup poll showed that 55 percent of those polled continued to oppose the immediate withdrawal of U.S. troops from Vietnam; those that favored withdrawal, however, had risen to 35 percent from 22 percent in November 1969.

February 19, 1970: All defendants in the Chicago conspiracy trial were acquitted of plotting to incite riots at the 1968 Democratic National Convention.

May 2–4, 1970: Spurred by the U.S. incursion into Cambodia, large antiwar protests spread across the United States, especially on college campuses. On May 4, four students at Kent State University in Ohio were shot and killed and 11 were wounded by Ohio National Guardsmen during an antiwar demonstration.

May 9, 1970: Antiwar demonstrations continued at some 400 college campuses. In Washington, D.C., 75,000 to 100,000 protesters demonstrated at the White House.

June 24, 1970: On an amendment by Sen. Robert Dole (R–Kans.) to the Military Sales Act, the Senate voted 81-10 to repeal the Tonkin Gulf Resolution (see Home Front, August 7, 1964, p. 616). The Nixon administration announced that its conduct of the Vietnam War did not rely on that resolution but on the constitutional authority of the president to protect the lives of U.S. military forces. The repeal was approved by both houses and signed by President Richard Nixon on December 31.

June 30, 1970: The Senate passed the Cooper-Church Amendment, sponsored by Senator John Sherman Cooper (R–Ky.) and Senator Frank Church (D–Idaho). The amendment barred U.S. military personnel from combat or advisory roles in Cambodia after July 1. Although the House rejected the amendment on July 9, the Senate's action marked the first limitation ever voted by Congress on the president's powers as commander in chief during a war situation. The amendment eventually passed in a modified form on December 29; by that time, the amendment barred sending U.S. forces into Thailand and Laos rather than into Cambodia.

October 15, 1970: President Richard Nixon announced that an additional 40,000 U.S. troops would be withdrawn from Vietnam by the end of 1970.

December 31, 1970: President Nixon signed the bill repealing the Tonkin Gulf Resolution, long used as the justification for U.S. military intervention in Vietnam.

INTERNATIONAL DEVELOPMENTS

February 1, 1970: At a celebration marking

the 40th anniversary of the Indochinese Communist Party, Secretary Le Duan said that the people of Vietnam "must be prepared to fight for many more years" to force the Americans from their soil.

BATTLES AND CAMPAIGNS: 1971

SOUTH VIETNAM

January 6, 1971: The U.S. command in Saigon announced a program designed to combat widespread drug abuse among U.S. soldiers.

May 16–18, 1971: Heavy rocket and mortar fire on U.S. positions along the DMZ resulted in 30 American fatalities.

June 22–28, 1971: In a major DMZ area engagement, thousands of North Vietnamese and South Vietnamese troops clashed in a struggle centered around Fire Base Fuller. NVA casualties were reported at 500 killed with 135 wounded.

July 9, 1971: U.S. troops relinquished total responsibility for defense of the area just below the DMZ to ARVN troops.

August 18, 1971: Australia and New Zealand announced they would withdraw their troops from South Vietnam by the end of 1971.

August 31, 1971: The Royal Thai army, except for one unit, withdrew from Vietnam.

September 9, 1971: South Korea announced that it would withdraw most of its 48,000 troops from Vietnam by June 1972.

October 3, 1971: South Vietnamese president Nguyen Van Thieu, running unopposed in a highly controversial election, was elected to another four-year term.

November 12, 1971: President Richard Nixon announced that U.S. ground forces in Vietnam had a purely defensive role, and that all offensive activities were being undertaken solely by the South Vietnamese.

December 31, 1971: U.S. military strength in Vietnam declined to 156,800 by the end of 1971. The number of Americans killed in action dropped to 1,386 for 1971, bringing the cumulative total of U.S. military personnel killed during ten years of involvement in Vietnam to 45,631. SVNAF deaths in 1971 totaled 21,500, a cumulative total of 156,260 killed in action to date. SVNAF strength increased to 1,046,250, but other allied military forces declined to 53,900. Communist deaths were estimated at 97,000 for 1971.

AIR WAR

January 3, 1971: U.S. B-52s and more than 300 fighter-bombers hit sites in South Vietnam, Laos, and Cambodia with intensive bombing.

February 20–23, 1971: U.S. planes bombed North Vietnamese antiaircraft and SAM sites near the Laotian border.

April 18–23, 1971: In the heaviest protracted raids since November 1968, U.S. planes carried out their 30th raid since January inside North Vietnam.

October 7, 1971: U.S. B-52s dropped nearly 1,000 tons of bombs on targets near Krek in Cambodia and around Tayninh in South Vietnam in support of the 25,000 ARVN troops operating in Cambodia.

December 26, 1971: In the sharpest escalation of the Vietnam War since the bombing halt of November 1968, the U.S. Air Force resumed bombing of North Vietnam with as many as 250 aircraft in some missions.

CAMBODIA/LAOS

February 8–March 24, 1971: With U.S. air and logistical support, some 12,000 ARVN troops launched Operation Lam Son 719 to disrupt enemy supply lines in southern Laos. In what was described as the "bloodiest fighting" of the Vietnam War, during the last week of February, enemy troops overran two ARVN battalions 16 miles from the Laos-South Vietnam border.

March 20, 1971: Fifty-three men of the U.S. First Cavalry, in support of Operation Lam Son 719, refused orders to retrieve a disabled helicopter and an armored vehicle from a battle zone near the Laos-South Vietnam border. The soldiers were reassigned, and their commanding officer relieved of his position.

March 24, 1971: Operation Lam Son 719, scheduled to end on April 6, ended as the last ARVN units pulled out under heavy enemy assault. ARVN casualties approached 50 percent, but the ARVN claimed to have cost the enemy 13,000 casualties; U.S. casualties were 102 dead (mostly air crews) and 215 wounded. Both sides claimed "complete victory." Traffic on the Ho Chi Minh Trail soon returned to previous level.

May 11–15, 1971: More than 6,000 ARVN troops, supported by U.S. airpower, continued operations in Cambodia to destroy enemy sanctuaries used for attacks inside Vietnam west of Saigon.

October 16, 1971: Premier Lon Nol suspended the Cambodian National Assembly and announced rule by decree to facilitate fighting the Communists. On October 22, he declared a state of emergency and abolished constitutional rule. The United States declared its continuing support for his government.

December 1971: In Laos, U.S.-supported Meo troops were near defeat by the NVA.

December 17, 1971: Cambodia appeared near collapse as Communist troops continued an encircling operation around Phnom Penh. The Lon Nol government banned all anti-government and political meetings and authorized searches of private homes.

HOME FRONT

March 1, 1971: A bomb exploded in the Capitol in Washington, D.C., causing $300,000 worth of damage. A group called the Weather Underground claimed responsibility for the bombing, which the group said was intended to protest the U.S.-supported Laos invasion.

March 29, 1971: Lt. William L. Calley, Jr. was convicted of the premeditated murder of South Vietnamese civilians at My Lai (see March 16, 1968, p. 627). The defense argument that he simply was following orders was rejected, both on the grounds that no such orders had been given, and had the order to kill unarmed civilians been given, he should have known to reject it. Sentenced to life imprisonment, this was reduced to 20 years and in 1974 Nixon commuted his sentence to time served.

April 24, 1971: Some 500,000 antiwar protesters, including at least 1,000 Vietnam Veterans Against the War, converged on Washington, D.C. At least 150,000 antiwar protesters demonstrated in San Francisco.

May 3–5, 1971: Police in Washington, D.C., arrested 12,614 militant antiwar protesters, the highest number of people ever arrested for civil disturbance in the nation's history.

June 13, 1971: The *New York Times* began publishing a series of articles based on the so-called Pentagon Papers, a candid, confidential, and fully documented report of U.S. involvement in Vietnam from World War II through May 1968. The report was originally prepared for Secretary

of Defense Robert McNamara; it was secretly photocopied by Daniel Ellsberg, a disaffected former government employee and also a former supporter of the Vietnam War, who turned the report over to *New York Times* reporter Neil Sheehan. In response to government objections, on June 30, the Supreme Court ruled that newspapers may publish articles based on classified Pentagon material.

July 17, 1971: John Ehrlichman, President Nixon's chief of staff, organized the "plumbers" to investigate Daniel Ellsberg, who leaked the Pentagon Papers, and others whose loyalty to the Nixon administration was questionable.

August 2, 1971: The Nixon administration officially acknowledged that the CIA was maintaining a 30,000-man force of "irregulars" fighting throughout Laos, recruited and paid directly by the CIA. The United States had spent $284.2 million in Laos to date.

December 26, 1971: Fifteen antiwar Vietnam veterans barricaded themselves inside the Statue of Liberty and flew the American flag upside down. On December 28, they obeyed a court order to leave.

INTERNATIONAL DEVELOPMENTS

November 17, 1971: In a bloodless coup, Thai prime minister Thanom Kittikachorn ended constitutional rule and seized power. He declared martial law and pledged to continue his country's anti-Communist, pro-United States policy.

December 22, 1971: The Soviets accused China of backing U.S. policies in Vietnam.

BATTLES AND CAMPAIGNS: 1972

SOUTH VIETNAM

January 7, 1972: Eighteen Americans were wounded by a mortar attack on fire support base Fiddler's Green, 20 miles northeast of Saigon in the heaviest shelling of U.S. forces in six months.

March 30, 1972: North Vietnamese troops, crossing the DMZ and quickly overrunning northern Quangtri Province, launched the Eastertide Offensive, the largest major coordinated operation since 1968. Expanding to four fronts, the offensive eventually involved 500 tanks, 150,000 NVA troops, thousands of Vietcong, and heavy rocket and artillery fire, including the first use of heavy long-range artillery along the DMZ.

April 13, 1972: With 107 separate enemy attacks in South Vietnam in 24 hours, sustained enemy activity reached its highest level since the Tet Offensive of 1968.

April 28, 1972: Dongha was overrun by enemy troops.

May 1, 1972: NVA troops captured Quangtri city after a month of intense fighting.

May 10, 1972: Martial law was declared in South Vietnam.

June 18, 1972: The siege of An Loc, begun April 13 with 40 tanks and 3,000 NVA troops, ended as the NVA forces withdrew in defeat.

June 28, 1972: Gen. Fred Weyland relieved Gen. Creighton Abrams as commander of U.S. forces in South Vietnam (MACV).

August 23, 1972: The U.S. 3rd Battalion, 21st Infantry, the last U.S. ground battalion, withdrew from Vietnam.

September 15, 1972: ARVN troops recaptured the provincial capital of Quangtri.

October 17, 1972: Continuing enemy activity against highways around the capital began to affect the Saigon food supply and made driving outside the city dangerous.

November 11, 1972: The U.S. logistical base at Longbinh was turned over to the South Vietnamese, marking the end of direct U.S. Army combat operations in the Vietnam War.

December 31, 1972: By the end of 1972, U.S. military personnel in Vietnam numbered 24,200. U.S. combat deaths in 1972 were about 4,300, bringing the total number of U.S. personnel killed in action in Vietnam to date to 45,926. Other allied military personnel declined to 35,500. SVNAF strength increased to 1,048,000; 195,847 SVNAF were killed in action to date.

AIR WAR

January 1, 1972: U.S. planes made more than 200 strikes in Cambodia and Laos to disrupt NVA supply lines.

April 5, 1972: U.S. Air Force fighter-bombers began reinforcing units in Thailand.

April 15, 1972: Following a four-year lull interrupted by numerous "protective-reaction" strikes, the U.S. resumed heavy routine bombing of Hanoi and Haiphong.

May–October 1972: Operation Linebacker I,

tactical support of ARVN forces countering the Eastertide Offensive, was conducted by the U.S. Air Force.

May 8–October 24, 1972: On May 8, President Richard Nixon announced intensification of the U.S. bombing of North Vietnam and the mining of Haiphong harbor and all major North Vietnamese ports as well as many rivers and canals. Six U.S. carriers were stationed in the Gulf of Tonkin. The massive bombing raids continued until October 24, when Nixon ordered them stopped in response to North Vietnam's positions at the Paris peace talks (see Negotiations and Peace Treaty, p. 648).

October 11, 1972: U.S. Navy planes accidentally bombed the French embassy in Hanoi, killing Delegate General Pierre Susini. The Algerian and Indian embassies were also hit.

December 18–31, 1972: Operation Linebacker II, the "Christmas Bombing" of Hanoi and Haiphong, the most concentrated air offensive of the Vietnam War, was conducted by the U.S. Air Force on President Nixon's orders. (Nixon also authorized the Navy to resume shelling of targets in North Vietnam.) During these raids, bombs equal to half the total tonnage dropped on England during World War II hit heavily populated areas. The North Vietnamese launched their entire arsenal of some 1,200 missiles against the planes; the U.S. lost 15 B-52s; 93 flyers were downed and killed or captured.

NAVAL WAR

February 9, 1972: The *Constellation* joined two other aircraft carriers, the *Hancock* and the *Coral Sea*, off the coast of Vietnam.

April 3, 1972: The *Kitty Hawk*, the first of four additional aircraft carriers scheduled to join the three carriers already stationed off Vietnam, arrived in Vietnamese waters.

April 10, 1972: The aircraft carriers *Saratoga* and *Midway* were ordered from Florida and California to join the four other carriers and other warships engaged in the bombardment of North Vietnam.

May 8, 1972: North Vietnamese ports were mined by the U.S. Navy.

October 12–13, 1972: Racial brawls involving more than 100 sailors resulted in injuries to 46 crewmen aboard the aircraft carrier *Kitty Hawk*. Twenty-one black seamen were eventually charged with assault and rioting. Other racial incidents occurred at several Navy installations in the next few weeks.

December 18, 1972: Two sailors were killed and three were wounded when the USS *Goldsborough*, shelling North Vietnam, was hit by return fire.

CAMBODIA/LAOS

February 12, 1972: About 6,000 Cambodian troops launched an operation to expel 4,000 NVA troops that had been entrenched at Angkor Wat since June 1970. The addition of 4,000 more Cambodian troops proved futile, and the Cambodians eventually abandoned their efforts.

March 17–18, 1972: More than 8,000 ARVN troops continued their drive into eastern Cambodia. ARVN troop strength reached 10,000 over the next few days.

April 25, 1972: Communist troops were in control of all Cambodian territory bordering South Vietnam east of the Mekong River, with the exception of Svayrieng and a handful of government strongholds.

October 22, 1972: In anticipation of an Indochinese cease-fire, Communist and government troops in Laos increased hostilities in order to gain as much ground as possible.

December 21, 1972: ARVN and Cambodian troops joined in an operation to clear enemy troops concentrated in an area 35 miles south of Phnom Penh in southeast Cambodia.

HOME FRONT

January 16, 1972: Religious leaders from 46 Protestant, Catholic, and Jewish denominations met in Kansas City and asked the government to withdraw all U.S. troops and refuse aid to Indochinese governments.

June 17, 1972: In the precipitating incident that eventually forced Nixon to resign the presidency, five men—the so-called "plumbers"— were arrested for breaking into the Democratic National Committee offices at the Watergate complex in Washington, D.C.

October 26, 1972: At a press conference in Washington, D.C., National Security Adviser Henry Kissinger publicly declared, "We believe peace is at hand. We believe that an agreement is within sight." In fact, negotiations were soon again at a stalemate. Later, Kissinger was accused of making that claim to enhance Nixon's reelection chance, but he insisted that it seemed true at the time he said it (see Negotiations and Peace Treaty, October 26, 1972, pp. 647-648).

November 7, 1972: President Nixon, promising an "honorable peace," was reelected.

December 14, 1972: President Richard Nixon issued a demand that North Vietnam begin talking "seriously" or suffer the consequences, and at the same time, ordered the Joint Chiefs of Staff to prepare the most intense bombing of the Vietnam War in and around Hanoi and Haiphong, an operation the Joint Chiefs had long lobbied for.

INTERNATIONAL DEVELOPMENTS

October 17, 1972: Peace talks began in Laos between Communist and government delegates.

December 21, 1972: Referring to the heavy casualties and 1 million new refugees resulting from the renewed bombing of North Vietnam, Thich Nhat Hanh, head of the Vietnamese Buddhist delegation to the Paris peace talks, remarked that Buddhists were astonished to read that most Americans thought the Vietnam War was over, because, he said, suffering in Vietnam was at its worst in ten years.

December 31, 1972: The Hanoi delegation to the formal Paris peace talks asserted that the U.S. bombing failed "to subjugate" the Vietnamese people and called attention to the heavy loss of U.S. planes and airmen and the unfavorable world reaction to the raids.

BATTLES AND CAMPAIGNS: 1973

SOUTH VIETNAM

January 5, 1973: A letter from President Richard Nixon assured South Vietnamese President Nguyen Thieu of "continued assistance in the postsettlement period."

January 15, 1973: Anticipating the armistice negotiated in Paris, President Nixon suspended all U.S. offensive action against North Vietnam; the cessation of hostilities did not extend to South Vietnam.

January 16, 1973: President Nixon threatened President Thieu with a complete cutoff of U.S. aid if Saigon refused to "close ranks" with Washington on the peace agreement.

January 18–26, 1973: Heavy combat raged in South Vietnam as both sides attempted to gain as much territory as possible before the cease-fire went into effect.

January 27, 1973: Lt. Col. William B. Nolde, killed by an artillery shell at An Loc 11 hours before the cease-fire, became the last U.S. combat death in Vietnam. Four Americans were killed in the last week of combat.

March 29, 1973: MACV headquarters was disestablished. The withdrawal of all U.S. combat troops and the release of 590 U.S. POWs held by Hanoi was completed.

June 24, 1973: Graham Martin became the U.S. ambassador to South Vietnam.

August 15, 1973: The official end of U.S. bombing in Cambodia marked the end of all direct U.S. military action in Indochina.

October 24, 1973: According to U.S. intelligence, since the January cease-fire, North Vietnamese presence in South Vietnam increased by 70,000 troops, 400 tanks, 200 artillery pieces, 15 anti-aircraft artillery, and 12 airfields. An all-weather road from North Vietnam to Tayninh Province was nearly completed.

November 1973: In the most intense fighting since the cease-fire, NVA tanks and troops seized two ARVN camps near the Cambodian border.

December 31, 1973: By the end of 1973, the size of the U.S. military contingent in Vietnam was limited to 50. The total number of U.S. military personnel killed in action to date was 46,163. No other allied military personnel remained in Vietnam. SVNAF strength was estimated at 1,110,000; 223,748 SVNAF were killed in action to date.

AIR WAR

January 15, 1973: President Richard Nixon suspended the bombing of North Vietnam.

NAVAL WAR

March 1973: U.S. Navy Operations Market Time, Game Warden, and Clearwater were discontinued.

July 1973: The clearing of mines laid down by the United States from North Vietnamese ports, as called for in the cease-fire agreements, was completed.

CAMBODIA/LAOS

February 21, 1973: The Laotian government of Souvanna Phouma and the Pathet Lao reached a peace agreement, ending 20 years of fighting. The agreement mandated the cessation of all fighting in Laos, including all bombing and fighting by the United States and North Vietnam.

March 27, 1973: White House sources announced that U.S. bombing of Cambodia, as requested by President Lon Nol, would continue until the Communist forces there agreed to a cease-fire.

April 9, 1973: Prince Norodom Sihanouk, acting as spokesman for the Cambodian rebels, rejected Lon Nol's peace proposal.

August 15, 1973: U.S. Air Force operations Arc Light and Freedom ended as the U.S officially ceased bombing in Cambodia. That marked the end of all direct U.S. military action in Cambodia, Laos, and Vietnam.

HOME FRONT

January 27, 1973: With the signing of the peace agreement in Paris (see p. 648), Secretary of Defense Melvin Laird announced the end of the U.S. military draft; young American males would have to register in case of future emergencies and those who had refused to report for induction during the Vietnam War were still liable for prosecution. At the time, the U.S. armed forces numbered 2.5 million and there began an immediate cutback in these numbers, but many who had been inducted in the final months of the war still had to serve out their time.

June 29–30, 1973: Compromise legislation passed in Congress fixed an August 15 deadline for the cessation of U.S. bombing in Cambodia; the same bill also stated that spending for military activity in Indochina after that date must be approved by Congress. President Richard Nixon denounced Congress for undermining the "prospects for world peace."

September 22, 1973: Henry Kissinger succeeded William Rogers as secretary of state.

October 24, 1973: President Richard Nixon vetoed the War Powers Resolution, which limited the president's ability to commit U.S. armed forces abroad without congressional approval.

November 7, 1973: Congress overrode President Nixon's veto of the War Powers Act.

INTERNATIONAL DEVELOPMENTS

October 1973: In North Vietnam, the 21st Plenum of the Central Committee of the Communist Party concluded that President Nguyen Thieu could not be made to implement the Paris agreement and resolved to achieve reunification by military struggle.

BATTLES AND CAMPAIGNS: 1974

SOUTH VIETNAM

January 4, 1974: President Nguyen Thieu claimed that the war had restarted. In two clashes with enemy troops, ARVN reported 55 enemy killed.

January 27, 1974: Saigon reported that since the truce of January 1973, 13,778 ARVN soldiers, 2,159 South Vietnamese civilians, and 45,057 enemy troops had died in the fighting.

February 1974: As an ARVN offensive encroached upon areas long under Communist control, Communist forces retaliated.

March 1974: The heaviest fighting since the January 1973 cease-fire occurred. Fighting in the Central Highlands was extremely bloody.

September 20, 1974: Antigovernment demonstrations in Saigon provoked violent clashes with police.

December 3, 1974: Saigon intelligence reported it had seen documents proving that the Communists were planning an increase in hostilities for the coming season.

Also on this day, NVA troops attacked ARVN positions in Phuoc Long Province.

December 31, 1974: U.S. military strength in Vietnam remained limited to 50 advisers. Reliable estimates of SVNAF strength were no longer available. The South Vietnamese command reported that altogether 80,000 people, the highest total for any year of the Vietnam War, died in the fighting in 1974.

CAMBODIA/LAOS

January 15–28, 1974: Cambodian rebels shelled Phnom Penh.

April 5, 1974: In Laos, a new coalition government was formed with Souvanna Phouma as premier and Prince Souphanouvong, leader of the Pathet Lao, as deputy premier.

July 9, 1974: Prince Norodom Sihanouk rejected a request from Lon Nol for truce talks.

November 30, 1974: Lon Nol proposed a cease-fire in Cambodia.

HOME FRONT

February 22, 1974: In a study ordered by Congress, the National Academy of Sciences reported that U.S. use of chemical herbicides, such as Agent Orange, did damage to the South Vietnamese ecology that could last as long as a century.

April 4, 1974: Congress unexpectedly rejected a White House request for an increase in military aid to South Vietnam. On August 5, Congress voted to put a ceiling on military aid to South Vietnam.

July 30, 1974: The House Judiciary Committee voted to impeach Richard Nixon on three counts: obstruction of justice, abuse of power, and defiance of congressional subpoenas.

August 5, 1974: Congress placed a $1 billion ceiling on military aid to South Vietnam for fiscal year 1974.

August 9, 1974: Richard Nixon resigned the presidency. Vice President Gerald R. Ford became president.

August 11, 1974: Congress trimmed the military-aid ceiling to South Vietnam to $700 million. President Ford sent a letter to President Thieu reaffirming U.S. commitment and promising "adequate support" to Saigon.

September 16, 1974: President Ford signed a proclamation offering clemency to Vietnam War–era draft evaders and military deserters.

INTERNATIONAL DEVELOPMENTS

December 18, 1974: The Hanoi Political Bureau (in session until January 8, 1975), having received assurances of aid from the Soviet Union, assessed the situation as highly favorable and adopted a plan for a military campaign to overthrow the Thieu regime in two years.

BATTLES AND CAMPAIGNS: 1975

SOUTH VIETNAM

January 6, 1975: Phuoc Long Province fell to invading NVA troops. The total lack of response from U.S. forces indicated to North Vietnam that the United States would not return to Vietnam.

March 10–13, 1975: Ban Me Thuot, capital of Dar Lac province, fell to the NVA. Many ARVN soldiers deserted to rescue their families; such desertions contributed heavily to the speedy collapse of South Vietnam.

March 14, 1975: President Nguyen Thieu ordered the withdrawal of ARVN troops from the Central Highlands.

March 19, 1975: Quangtri Province fell to NVA attack.

March 26, 1975: Hué fell to the NVA.

March 30, 1975: Danang fell to the NVA.

April 1, 1975: The cities of Quinohn, Tuyhoa, and Nhatrang were abandoned, leaving North Vietnamese in possession of the entire northern half of South Vietnam.

April 21, 1975: Xuan Loc, Saigon's last line of defense, fell to NVA troops. President Thieu resigned.

April 25, 1975: Thieu fled to Taiwan.

April 29, 1975: NVA troops attacked Saigon. U.S. Marine corporal Charles McMahon, Jr. and L. Cpl. Darwin Judge, struck by shrapnel from an NVA rocket, became the last U.S. military personnel killed in Vietnam.

April 29–30, 1975: Option IV, the largest helicopter evacuation on record, evacuated all remaining Americans and select South Vietnamese from Saigon to aircraft carriers offshore.

April 30, 1975: Saigon fell. NVA colonel Bui Tin, accepting surrender from Gen. Duong Van Minh, remarked, "You have nothing to fear. Between Vietnamese there are no victors and no vanquished. Only the Americans have been beaten. If you are patriots, consider this a moment of joy. The war for our country is over."

December 31, 1975: A separate South Vietnamese government no longer existed. U.S. military aid to South Vietnam had been $300 million in 1975, down from $2.8 billion in 1973.

CAMBODIA/LAOS

January 1, 1975: Cambodian Khmer Rouge insurgents launched a final offensive and formed a siege ring around Phnom Penh.

April 1, 1975: President Lon Nol abdicated and fled Cambodia to exile in Hawaii.

April 12, 1975: The U.S. ambassador and his staff left Phnom Penh.

April 17, 1975: Phnom Penh fell to the Khmer Rouge. Over the course of the next four years, the Khmer Rouge murdered between 2 million and 3 million people (see Results of the War, pp. 648-651).

May 15, 1975: Supported by U.S. aircraft, U.S. Marines landed on Koh Tang Island to liberate the U.S. freighter *Mayaguez*, which had been seized by Cambodian Communists in the Gulf of Siam on May 12. Thirty-eight marines died rescuing 39 seamen.

December 1975: The Congress of the National United Front of Cambodia approved a new republican constitution. Cambodia was renamed Democratic Kampuchea.

December 2, 1975: Following local seizures of power by "people's committees" and November elections, Laotian communists declared the Lao People's Democratic Republic.

HOME FRONT

April 10, 1975: President Gerald Ford requested an additional $722 million emergency assistance for Saigon. The reaction from Congress was overwhelmingly negative.

April 23, 1975: President Ford declared the Vietnam War finished "as far as America is concerned. Today, Americans can regain the sense of pride that existed before Vietnam. But it cannot be achieved by refighting a war."

INTERNATIONAL DEVELOPMENTS

January 8, 1975: The Politburo in North Vietnam ordered a major offensive to liberate South Vietnam.

February 5, 1975: NVA general Van Tien Dung went south to take command of Communist forces.

April 7, 1975: Le Duc Tho arrived at NVA headquarters, Locninh, to oversee the final push into Saigon of the Ho Chi Minh Campaign.

NEGOTIATIONS AND PEACE TREATY

For the United States, getting out of the Vietnam War proved more difficult than getting in. The U.S. insistence on establishing "peace with honor" had created an embarrassing dilemma. Either of the two options—imposing a solution through absolutely overwhelming military might or simply pulling its forces out of South Vietnam—might lead to peace, but neither offered much honor. In the end, the war's conclusion had to be negotiated. Starting as early as June 1964, Hanoi and Washington made a series of surreptitious contacts through representatives of the Canadian, French, British, Italian, Polish, Romanian, Norwegian, Soviet, and Chinese governments. At times, it seemed that most of the world's leaders were trying to bring the warring parties together.

Although representatives from the United States were making little-known and unproductive contacts with representatives of North Vietnam by 1966, it was not until after the Tet Offensive in January–February 1968 that President Lyndon B. Johnson announced he was authorizing Averell Harriman to begin serious negotiations for peace. Harriman contacted the North Vietnamese at once, and after 34 days of wrangling over where to hold the conference, they finally agreed on Paris. The long road to a negotiated settlement lay ahead.

May 3, 1968: President Johnson announced that the United States and North Vietnam had agreed to begin formal peace talks in Paris.

May 10–13, 1968: After finally agreeing to meet at the Center for International Conferences in Paris, representatives of the United States and North Vietnam spent two days negotiating "procedural matters": the shape of the table (a hollow rectangle), the number of people allowed to sit at it (six for each delegation), which doors should be used to enter the room, etc. On May 13, substantive talks began. Ambassador-at-Large Averell Harriman headed the U.S. delegation; minister of state Xuan Thuy headed the North Vietnamese delegation.

May 22, 1968: The chief North Vietnamese delegate Xuan Thuy declared that negotiations would remain deadlocked until the United States halted all bombing raids on North Vietnam.

June 3, 1968: Politburo member Le Duc Tho joined the North Vietnamese negotiation team as special counselor.

July 9, 1968: The chief South Vietnamese observer at the Paris peace talks, Bui Diem, reiterated Saigon's demand for direct negotiations between North Vietnam and South Vietnam.

November 26, 1968: South Vietnam's foreign minister, Tran Chanh Thanh, declared that his government had decided to participate in the Paris peace talks.

December 23, 1968: The NLF representative in Paris, Tran Buu Kiem, rejected direct negotiations between the NLF and Saigon on the grounds that any real settlement must originate with the direct adversaries, the United States and the Vietcong.

December 27, 1968: Saigon dismissed 30 members of its 80-member peace delegation for a "violation of national discipline."

January 25, 1969: The Paris peace talks, expanded to include the Saigon government and Vietcong representatives, formally opened at the first plenary meeting.

February 10, 1969: Le Duc Tho remarked that the Nixon administration was "pursuing the same policy as the administration of President Johnson."

April 17, 1969: At the 13th plenary session in Paris, the peace talks continued to show no progress. Communist negotiators rejected proposals for mutual troop withdrawal and again demanded that the United States withdraw its forces unconditionally and immediately.

May 8, 1969: The NLF unveiled a ten-point peace plan that demanded unconditional U.S. withdrawal and a coalition government that excluded President Nguyen Thieu.

August 4, 1969: Henry Kissinger and Xuan Thuy met secretly for the first time at a private apartment in Paris.

December 11, 1969: Xuan Thuy boycotted the Paris talks to protest what his delegation called the "sabotage" and "downgrading" of the talks by the U.S. failure to name a replacement for chief U.S. negotiator Henry Cabot Lodge, who with his deputy, Lawrence E. Walsh, had resigned his post, effective December 8, on November 20.

February 20, 1970: Henry Kissinger and Le Duc Tho began secret peace talks in Paris. The third and final of these was held on April 4, 1970.

September 3, 1970: Xuan Thuy returned to the Paris talks after a nine-month boycott and observed that the positions of the United States and North Vietnam remained unchanged.

October 7, 1970: President Richard Nixon proposed a "standstill cease-fire" throughout Indochina to be followed by a peace negotiated at an Indochina peace conference. Communist delegations to the Paris talks denounced his proposals as "a maneuver to deceive world opinion." The following day, Nixon repeated the mutual withdrawal formula.

May 13, 1971: The Paris peace talks, still deadlocked, entered their fourth year.

July 29, 1971: At the Paris talks, the head of the Vietcong delegation proposed to identify all U.S. POWs as soon as the United States designated a deadline for the complete withdrawal of all its troops.

December 9, 1971: The Paris peace talks came to a standstill again when, for the first time since the talks began, both sides failed to set another meeting date after the 138th session.

January 6, 1972: Official peace talks resumed in Paris after a one-month lapse.

March 23, 1972: U.S. negotiators in Paris, as directed by President Nixon, announced an indefinite suspension of the peace talks until the Communists agreed to "serious discussions" according to a predetermined agenda.

May 2, 1972: Meeting secretly with Le Duc Tho, Henry Kissinger indicated that the United States was prepared to drop its demand for withdrawal of NVA troops from South Vietnam.

May 4, 1972: Citing a "complete lack of progress," the United States and South Vietnamese delegations called an indefinite halt to the talks in Paris.

May 8, 1972: In support of the halt in the negotiations in Paris, President Nixon announced that he had ordered the mining of major North Vietnamese ports and the intensification of the bombing of North Vietnam.

July 13, 1972: The Paris peace talks resumed following a ten-week suspension.

August 1, 1972: Kissinger and Le Duc Tho met privately in Paris to discuss peace.

October 8, 1972: Kissinger and Le Duc Tho reached agreement in principle on a "breakthrough" draft peace plan: The United States agreed to let North Vietnamese troops remain in South Vietnam while the United States completed the withdrawal of U.S. troops that had begun in June 1969.

October 22, 1972: Kissinger met with President Thieu in Saigon to try to persuade him to accept the cease-fire draft. Thieu was implacably opposed.

October 26, 1972: Radio Hanoi broadcast details of the nine-point cease-fire draft treaty and accused the United States of trying to back out of it by claiming difficulties with Saigon.

Hoping to reassure Hanoi, Kissinger announced at a White House news conference, "We believe that an agreement is within sight."

November 20, 1972: Kissinger presented Le Duc Tho with 69 amendments to their agreement demanded by President Thieu. Kissinger had previously described Thieu's terms to President Nixon as "verging on insanity" and "preposterous," and indicated that he felt they might wreck the chances for an agreement. Nixon insisted that Kissinger submit them. Secret talks continued later in November and through early December but failed to secure the agreement that had seemed so certain.

December 18, 1972: With the resumption of the bombing and mining of North Vietnam, the Paris peace talks were suspended.

January 8–19, 1973: On January 8, the peace negotiations resumed in Paris. By January 9, Kissinger and Le Duc Tho reached a basic agreement; on January 18, they announced that they would complete their agreement on January 23.

January 23, 1973: Kissinger and Tho initialed an agreement, as described by Nixon, "to end the war and bring peace with honor in Vietnam and Southeast Asia."

January 27, 1973: The peace agreement initialed on January 23, was signed in Paris by the United States, South Vietnam, the Vietcong, and North Vietnam. It became effective at 8 A.M. Saigon time, January 28. Its terms included a cease-fire throughout Vietnam, the withdrawal of all U.S. troops and advisers (by this time, numbering about 27,000), the dismantling of all U.S. bases in Vietnam within 60 days, and the release of all POWs within 60 days. It left Thieu in power, permitted North Vietnamese troops to remain in the South, and urged reunification of Vietnam by "peaceful means." As far as the United States armed forces were concerned, the Vietnam War was over.

June 6–13, 1973: Kissinger and Le Duc Tho, meeting in Paris, concluded an agreement to improve the observance of the cease-fire. The new agreement was necessitated by charges of cease-fire violations made throughout April and May by Hanoi, Saigon, and Washington.

RESULTS OF THE WAR (Casualties, Costs, Consequences)

About 59,000 American military personnel

died in Vietnam; some 47,500 of those died in combat; accidents and disease accounted for most of the other 10,500 deaths. (Some 500 U.S. servicemen died in the fighting in Laos and Cambodia.) Of the 314,000 wounded, 153,300 were classified as seriously wounded. Based on official estimates for the Vietnam War, some 15 to 20 percent of the total casualties were caused by "friendly fire," or what the U.S. military calls "incontinent ordnance delivery" (usually due to accidental "drops" of artillery or bombs.)

Some 1,269 Americans were listed as missing in action at the war's end; eventually, this figure increased to about 2,100 (including those reported dead but whose bodies had never been found); gradually, 460 were identified and their remains repatriated, but some 1,600 were still unaccounted for in 1997 (see Historical Perspectives and Controversies, pp. 657-658).

The use of helicopters and advanced medical facilities allowed 82 percent of seriously wounded Americans to be saved, the highest survival rate of any modern war; only 2.6 percent of those who reached hospitals died. The use of mines, booby traps and other such devices by the enemy's guerrilla forces, however, led to more than 10,000 servicemen losing at least one limb (more than in World War II and the Korean War combined).

The sum given for the cost of the Vietnam War to the United States varies considerably, depending on what is being included, but one estimate is about $150 billion in direct military expenses. Indirect expenses (e.g., special governmental operations in Washington, D.C., and abroad, legal expenses for antiwar movements) totaled $6 million more, and other expenses (e.g., payments on debts, payments to veterans) are ongoing. An average day of fighting cost the United States $1 million in artillery shells; a sortie by one B-52 cost $30,000 in bombs. Approximately 4,865 helicopters, at a cost of $250,000 each, were destroyed; and 3,720 other aircraft were destroyed. Eight million tons of U.S. bombs were dropped on Vietnam, Cambodia, and Laos, an amount equal to about four times the total tonnage dropped in World War II; about $6 billion was spent on those raids, which inflicted only an estimated $600 million worth of damage on North Vietnam.

The North Vietnamese and the Vietcong are reported to have lost about 1 million troops killed

in the fighting. At least as many are estimated to have been wounded. Civilian deaths in North Vietnam are estimated at about 100,000 killed, and many more wounded.

No official sources have attempted to assign a figure to the financial cost of the Vietnam War to the North Vietnamese. However, North Vietnam received an estimated total of $3 billion in military aid from the Soviet Union and China. In addition to the direct costs of the military, the North Vietnamese paid a tremendous price in the destruction of their factories, harbor facilities, irrigation systems, and infrastructure (roads, bridges, electrical power plants). And the North Vietnamese had all the usual costs of the postwar period—medical costs for veterans and civilians, survivors' benefits, and such.

The South Vietnamese military reported about 225,000 killed during the Vietnam War, and at least 500,000 wounded. Civilian deaths are estimated at some 300,000, and far more wounded.

The cost of the war to South Vietnam is incalculable, since the direct outlays for the war were largely financed by the United States and South Vietnam's postwar costs were absorbed by the unified Vietnam. However the cost is calculated, the South Vietnamese lost billions of dollars during the war. At the war's end, many thousands were homeless. The countryside was scarred by bombs and defoliation; the cities were heavily damaged; and agriculture, industry, and commerce were at a standstill.

Several other nations suffered significant casualties in the Vietnam War. South Korea suffered 4,407 service personnel killed; Thailand suffered 350 killed; and Australia and New Zealand combined suffered 475 killed and 2,348 wounded.

The most immediate consequence of the Vietnam War was the unification of Vietnam under the Communists. (On July 2, 1976, the country was reunited as the Socialist Republic of Vietnam, with its capital in Hanoi. Saigon became Ho Chi Minh City.) Laos and Cambodia fell to Communists as part of the total collapse of the Western-backed powers in Indochina.

In Laos, the Pathet Lao and the government reached a cease-fire in 1973 and formed a coalition government, but by August 1975, the Communists effectively took control. In December 1975, the Pathet Lao abolished the coalition and took full control. For some years, the Communist

Vietnamese exercised considerable control over Laos, but gradually the Laotian Communists took over; they allowed some diversity in the economic sphere but as of 1997 had not democratized the political system.

In Cambodia, during the closing years of the war in Vietnam, a Communist with the adopted name Pol Pot led his group, the Khmer Rouge, in an insurgency. Taking advantage of the disarray caused by the spillover from the Vietnam War, the Khmer Rouge gradually took control of the Cambodian countryside, and by April 17, 1975, two weeks before Saigon fell to the North Vietnamese, the Khmer Rouge captured the capital, Phnom Penh. Pol Pot renamed the country Kampuchea, forced the people out of the cities and into the countryside, and proceeded on a systematic slaughter of some 2 million to 3 million of his people. Thereafter, traditional rivalries between the Vietnamese and the Cambodians reemerged, and after several border incidents, the Vietnamese invaded Kampuchea in December 1978. By January 7, the Vietnamese overthrew the Pol Pot government and installed a government supported by as many as 180,000 Vietnamese soldiers. The Vietnamese finally withdrew in 1989, and for several years, a coalition government brought peace and order to Cambodia. However, by the mid-1990s, Cambodia's political stability was once again in question as Communists and others continued to struggle for power.

The end of the Vietnam War sent still other shock waves throughout Southeast Asia. The Chinese had supported Pol Pot and his Khmer Rouge; China also complained to the Vietnamese of "provocative" incidents on the China-Vietnam border. On February 17, 1979, the Chinese invaded Vietnam, and, before withdrawing on March 5, many thousands of Chinese and Vietnamese had died in the fighting. Meanwhile, in the wake of the Communist takeover of Vietnam, Laos, and Cambodia, hundreds of thousands of people fled from Vietnam, Laos, and Cambodia, many of them by boat. The "boat people" (as they were referred to in the U.S. media at the time) who survived made their way to lands around Southeast Asia; many of them were eventually accepted into the United States and other countries, but some still remained in refugee camps as late as 1997. Many who had made their way to Hong Kong and Thailand were eventually forced to return to Vietnam.

After 1975, Vietnam struggled to reconstruct itself: its infrastructure, industries, and agriculture were devastated; its economy was virtually bankrupt; many of its people were wounded or desolate from the years of fighting. Gradually, Vietnam began to restore its agriculture, rebuild its physical plant, and attract foreign investments. By 1997, even the United States had granted diplomatic recognition to Vietnam, and indications were that Vietnam's standard of living was slowly improving.

The consequences of the Vietnam War in the United States were also far-reaching. Among the most visible were the many thousands of Vietnam veterans who found it difficult to readjust to civilian life; in particular, there were veterans who were diagnosed as suffering from posttraumatic stress disorder—a variation of shell shock, identified in World War I (see World War I, Military Innovations, Tactics, Equipment, p. 412); some of those veterans were never able to carry on a normal life. Meanwhile, the U.S. military establishment found itself demoralized by the Vietnam War; not until the Persian Gulf War some 20 years later was the military able to regain its old sense of purpose and pride.

Among the war's casualties, too, was President Lyndon B. Johnson's "Great Society," an economic and social agenda that aimed to raise the quality of life of lower-income Americans. Johnson refused to make the choice between "guns and butter." The unpopular war in Vietnam led Johnson to decide against running for reelection in 1968. Johnson's was not the only political career damaged by the war. Vice President Hubert Humphrey, along with the convictions of old-fashioned liberalism that he championed, was pushed aside by the politics of the Vietnam War. And President Richard Nixon was at least indirectly a victim of the Vietnam War, because it was his obsession with rooting out opponents of his Vietnam policies that led to the Watergate break-in.

The Vietnam War disrupted many of the nation's institutions and attitudes. Possibly overcompensating for their failure to take responsibility for undertaking the war in Vietnam, Congress rushed through the War Powers Act in October–November 1973, greatly limiting the president's ability to commit U.S. forces. The War Powers Act has remained on the books, but presidents since have tried to avoid its conditions, and many constitutional authorities regard it as best left untested. On another level, many Americans, in response to the numerous falsehoods they learned they had been told about the extent and nature of their country's involvement in Southeast Asia, became disillusioned, even cynical. The Watergate legacy and the military's morass in Vietnam left many Americans unable to extend to their leaders—military and civilian— the trust they had shown before the Vietnam War.

One area of public life that did get a boost from the Vietnam War was journalism, both through the disclosures of the print media and the revelations of the TV coverage. Yet, even here, there was no uniformity in the reception of the message. For instance, the *New York Times*'s publication of a series of articles based on the Pentagon Papers—a clandestine, government-commissioned history of U.S. involvement in Vietnam—was hailed by some as a demonstration of Americans' fundamental right to know what their government is doing. Others saw it as a dangerous precedent that might lead to wariness on the part of government officials to commit operational details to paper for fear of leaks. Likewise, the presence of reporters and TV cameras in so many frontline situations only convinced some military authorities that this should not be repeated in subsequent conflicts: In Grenada, Panama, and the Persian Gulf War, in fact, considerable restrictions were imposed on the media.

It is too early to conclude what the long-range consequences of the Vietnam War on history will be. The world stood by as the United States got deeper and deeper into the "quagmire." The United States learned that no nation can sustain a long war without popular support. Certainly for some who lived through the period, there remains a wariness about becoming involved in foreign enterprises. To counterbalance World War II's "lesson of Munich"—that nations can wait too long to challenge aggression—the world now has the "lesson of Vietnam"—that nations can go too far in challenging aggression, especially when that aggression takes place in the context of a civil war.

MILITARY INNOVATIONS, TACTICS, EQUIPMENT

Like all major wars, the Vietnam War was a laboratory in which combatants tested their latest technology and tactics. Perhaps the most publicized combination of that was the U.S. forces' use of helicopters. Of unique utility in mobile military operations, helicopters were in their infancy in World War II but developed rapidly after the Korean War. Their ability to take troops, weapons, equipment, and supplies of all kinds to and from battles with a speed, mobility, and precision never before possible made Vietnam the "helicopter war." The UH-1 Iroquois— the "Huey"—became the primary support helicopter in Vietnam, used for everything from battlefield airborne command posts to armed assault support; the evolution of armed Hueys into the specialized gunship helicopter has been singled out by some military experts as the most important new weapon of the Vietnam War. In addition, the CH-47 Chinook, a cargo helicopter, was capable of lifting divisional artillery, and the OH-6A Cayuse, or "Loach," performed reconnaissance/scouting chores just as light horse cavalry had done a century earlier. Specialized helicopter-cavalry units played a crucial role in the Vietnam War, and every major unit in every U.S. service arm in Vietnam and in the ARVN had its own helicopter company. In addition to helicopters' performance in combat, they served in two quite special capacities: to rescue downed pilots and to evacuate the wounded (see Results of the War, p. 649).

The United States entered the Vietnam War with the first generation of post-World War II aircraft, sweptwing turbojet fighters and bombers, some capable of Mach 1 in level flight, and gradually upgraded to aircraft capable of Mach 2 equipped with advanced electronics. Late in the war laser-guided "smart" bombs were introduced, affording unprecedented accuracy. U.S. forces deployed HAWK (Homing All the Way Killer) surface-to-air missiles (SAMs) in Vietnam, but because the U.S. Air Force soon gained control of the airspace over the entire country, the HAWKs saw little action. The Soviet Union supplied the NVA with SA-2 SAMs, responsible for downing at least 200 U.S. aircraft before U.S. electronic countermeasures became effective; beginning in 1972, the Soviets supplied the North Vietnamese with lethal handheld SA-7 Strella SAMs.

Napalm, a jellied gasoline, had been used in World War II and in the Korean War, but its use in Vietnam, brought home to the United States on TV, made it emblematic of the Vietnam War, and frequent antiwar demonstrations were held against chemical companies that manufactured napalm. The cumulative effect of napalm, together with other chemical agents, such as Agent Orange, used as defoliants to remove natural tree cover from the enemy, rendered significant areas of Vietnam unusable until the late 1980s. (Twice during the war, the U.S. military sought approval to use tactical nuclear weapons but was denied.)

For the first time since the Indian Wars, U.S. forces were involved in extensive guerrilla-style fighting. The strategy and tactics of counterinsurgency (see Preparations for War, pp. 610-611; and Geographic and Strategic Considerations, pp. 613-614) were intended to confront that kind of warfare; never before had U.S. military and political missions become so intertwined; never before had the U.S. government waged a war with so many irregular and covert units and operations and with such a dizzying tangle of acronyms. The U.S. Military Advisory Assistance Group (MAAG), set up in Vietnam after the Geneva treaty of 1954 was a limited and overt operation to train South Vietnamese military forces. In 1961, it was replaced by the Military Assistance Command, Vietnam (MACV), and from that point on, it began to authorize U.S. military advisers to engage in increasingly more covert and direct actions alongside the Vietnamese military.

The Central Intelligence Agency (CIA) became involved in Vietnam in 1954 and remained heavily involved right to the end of the war. (The CIA also conducted extensive covert operations in Laos.) The CIA even ran a covert airline: Originally called Civil Air Transport, it became better known as Air America. Operated by crews of international mercenaries, its missions extended from dropping spies and supplies for covert operations to transporting both the opium that locals needed to sell and the U.S. Drug Enforcement Agency agents to cut off the drug sales. President John Kennedy committed the United States to a major increase in irregular operations in Vietnam by authorizing overt units, such as the Special Forces, and clandestine units, such as the Civilian Irregular Defense Group (CIDG) sponsored by the CIA. The CIDG was a program that organized the Montagnards (or aboriginal tribesmen in the Central Highlands) who had never identified with the ethnic Vietnamese; the goal was to turn the Montagnards' dislike of the Vietnamese against the Vietcong and North Vietnamese. Another of the most ambitious of the CIA-sponsored units was the Special Observation Group (SOG), which conducted highly classified operations throughout South Vietnam and into North Vietnam and Laos and even occasionally into Cambodia.

Television, although not usually considered a martial technology, brought home the Vietnam War to civilians in unprecedented detail and, by its daily reminders of the length of the war, which Americans had been told would end quickly, had a profound effect on American resolve. Even the stoutest defenders of the war had a hard time accepting images of the constant intrigue and infighting among the South Vietnamese leaders the United States was supporting, not to mention the destruction of defenseless villages, the napalming, defoliation and devastation of the land, and the killing of women and children. There is some basis for the view that when TV icon Walter Cronkite expressed doubts about the Vietnam War on February 27, 1968, it had more impact on President Johnson's decision to go to the negotiating table than any weapons used by the North Vietnamese.

LEGENDS AND TRIVIA

The term *fragging*, as it was used in the Vietnam War, referred to the tossing of fragmentation grenades by someone in the U.S. military in order to murder another member of the U.S. military, usually an officer or a noncommissioned leader perceived to be either incompetent or overzealous in battle. (Presumably, too, some were thrown simply out of dislike for others.) Fragging first became a concern in the late 1960s, when rapid turnover of personnel weakened unit cohesion and the sense of purpose evaporated. Official figures are hard to come by, but at least 50 officers and NCOs lost their lives in some 500 fragging incidents from 1969–1971. Although military men had probably been doing something like that since time immemorial, that particular term first appeared in print in 1970.

Meanwhile, **draft evasion** became something of an art and a science during the Vietnam War. Between 1964–1973, 2.2 million men were inducted by the Selective Service; almost 16 million youths eligible for the draft received student and occupational deferments. But 1 million committed various draft law offenses, from not registering to publicly burning their draft cards; about 25,000 were indicted, and 3,250 served time in prison. Many of those who wished to avoid induction found ways to do so. An estimated 50,000–100,000 simply went into hiding or moved to Canada or overseas. Other methods of avoiding the draft were legal or at least "winked at": getting married and/or having children, going on to graduate school in some field never intended as a personal career. If those alternatives were not available, there were methods of failing draft exams: consuming large amounts of alcohol or drugs; feigning psychiatric disorders; feigning medical problems; failing the Army I.Q. test, and a host of other ruses. (Some legendary ones such as wounding oneself or showing up in women's underwear may be more apocryphal than actual, but they convey the spirit of the times.) Some private physicians helped provide medical exemptions for their patients, and even some physicians at induction centers exempted everyone they could.

In the Vietnam War, which at least after the Tet Offensive of 1968 was opposed by a majority of Americans, returning **veterans** often became targets of antiwar sentiment. Far from receiving a hero's welcome, veterans were frequently greeted with jeers, called "baby killers," and on occasion even spat upon when returning home after demobilization. Even some of the supporters of the war felt that all they wanted to do was to get on with their lives. Communities were so polarized by the war that few found a way to honor their returning veterans. That changed to some extent after the Vietnam Veterans Memorial was dedicated in Washington, D.C., on November 13, 1982. Although the memorial's design, a simple black granite wall listing nearly 58,000 soldiers' names in order of their death or disappearance, was criticized by some for appearing to emphasize tragedy rather than heroism, it became a place of reconciliation for many who had fought in, supported, or opposed the Vietnam War. And in the years since, many Vietnam veterans proudly march in Veterans' Day parades, reclaiming the respect for their personal service if not for the war itself.

It has long been recognized that, because the Vietnam War was an "unpopular" war, while it was in progress it did not inspire what is regarded as the sure barometer of popularity in America—**movies**. One notable exception was *The Green Berets* (1968), which John Wayne co-directed (with Ray Kellogg) as well as starred in to show his personal support for the war. After a "cooling off" period, however, a number of quite ambitious films were based on the Vietnam War.

In 1978 came the breakthrough with two movies that achieved both critical and popular acclaim, *The Deer Hunter* (directed by Michael Cimino) and *Coming Home* (directed by Hal Ashby). In 1979 came *Friendly Fire* (directed by David Greene). The year 1983 saw *Uncommon Valor* (directed by Ted Kotcheff) while 1985 had one of Sylvester Stallone's "Rambo" movies, *First Blood, Part II* (directed by George Cosmatos); although the former was set in Laos and the latter in Cambodia, both dealt with MIAs in the aftermath of the Vietnam War. In 1986 there was *Platoon* (directed by Oliver Stone). In 1987 came *Full Metal Jacket* (directed by Stanley Kubrick) and *Good Morning, Vietnam* (directed by Barry Levinson). In 1989 there was *Born on the Fourth of July* (also directed by Oliver Stone) and *Casualties of War* (directed by Brian de Palma). But arguably the archetypal Vietnam War movie was *Apocalypse Now* (1979), directed by Francis Ford Coppola of *Godfather* fame. Drawing loosely on Joseph Conrad's *Heart of Darkness*, it depicts a quest (through Vietnam and into Cambodia) by a group of American special agents and soldiers for a U.S. Army officer who has become the demented ruler of his own jungle realm. Seen as a sort of allegory of America's situation in Vietnam, it has considerable power, but on another level it is also an example of a film director's (Coppola) own obsessive drive to make the ultimate movie, whatever the cost and effort. Like most of the movies inspired by the Vietnam War, *Apocalypse Now* took a critical if not downright condemnatory view of America's role in the war. Despite John Wayne's sincere efforts, the Vietnam War has not lent itself to old-fashioned Hollywood heroics.

NOTABLE PHRASES

Now we can see [success in Vietnam] clearly, like light at the end of a tunnel.

Clearly a traditional saying, in the context of the war in Vietnam, those words were first spoken by Gen. Henri Navarre when he assumed command of the French Union Forces in Vietnam on May 20, 1953. In fact, France's attempt to restore its colonial empire in Indochina was rapidly deteriorating and collapsed at Dien Bien Phu on May 7, 1954. Variations on that image were used by many prominent people in reference to events in Vietnam in the years that followed. President John F. Kennedy used the phrase in a press conference in 1962; in November 1967, on a public relations visit to the United States, Gen. William Westmoreland claimed "the end begins to come into view"; President Nguyen Van Thieu referred to the "light at the end of the tunnel" in a speech in October 1970. By the time President Lyndon B. Johnson used the phrase in a speech on September 21, 1966, however, "light at the end of the tunnel" was already becoming an ironic catchphrase for the false promises and futility associated with the Vietnam War, often expressed in the rejoinder "Yes, it's the light of an oncoming train."

the falling domino principle

Although many people had undoubtedly used that metaphor before, in the context of the Vietnam War, it was first used by President Dwight D. Eisenhower at a press conference on April 7, 1954. Dien Bien Phu was about to be overrun by the Vietnamese and President Eisenhower seemed to be suggesting that the United States might have to intervene to prevent the eventual fall of all of Asia to the Communists. He said: "You have the broader considerations that might follow what you would call the falling domino principle. You have a row of dominos set up, you knock over the first one, and what will happen to the last one is the certainty that it will go over very quickly." Although Eisenhower did not go to the aid of France, his words were used by many defenders of the United States' later involvement in Vietnam. Up to a point, they were right: Laos and Cambodia did fall to the Communists in the wake of the war in Vietnam. But no other Asian nation did.

You two did visit the same country, didn't you?

President John Kennedy sent marine general Victor Krulak and Joseph Mendenhall of the State Department to Saigon on a fact-finding mission. When they returned and reported to Kennedy on September 10, 1963, Krulak gave an optimistic account about the progress of the war and Mendenhall gave a pessimistic account of a government near collapse. Kennedy listened to both, then responded with the above words.

Declare the United States the winner and begin de-escalation.

Sen. George Aiken (R–Vt.), said that in a speech before the Senate on October 19, 1966. Aiken was no radical idealogue and spoke more as an no-nonsense elder who knew when enough was enough, but his words were gleefully taken up by those opposed to the Vietnam War. Some six years later, the treaty the United States signed in Paris in 1973 was effectively just such a face-saving gesture.

It became necessary to destroy the town to save it.

This quote appeared in an Associated Press dispatch of February 8, 1968. It was attributed to an anonymous U.S. Army major after the bombing of the town of Ben Tre. Consciously or not, it echoed the ancient Roman historian Tacitus's *Agricola*, in which he has a native Briton complain of the Roman imperial army, "Where they make a desert, they call it peace."

The Chinese are prepared to fight to the last Vietnamese.

North Vietnamese premier Pham Van Dong was quoted as saying that when commenting wryly on the likelihood of direct Chinese intervention. Had the United States understood that at the outset, it might have taken a different tack in Vietnam. Instead, the United States, overlooking the 2,000 years of intense Chinese-Vietnamese enmity, greatly feared a Korea-style Chinese invasion from the north. What the United States failed to understand was that even the Communist Vietnamese maintained a wary relationship with the Chinese.

SONGS

Like so much connected with the Vietnam War,

the story of popular music and that war is tangled and intriguing. U.S. involvement in Vietnam coincided with the great 1960s flowering of the music and culture of both folk and rock. At the same time, the perfection of economical battery-operated audio cassettes and radio technology enabled the latest music to go everywhere: The Vietnam War was literally fought to the apocalyptic strains and psychedelic lyrics of Jimi Hendrix, Santana, The Doors, and the Beatles, among others.

At home, many of the leaders of the 1960s folk music revival were prominent in the antiwar movement. The judge at the 1970 trial of the Chicago Seven (charged with conspiracy to at the Democratic convention in 1968) refused to let a number of well-known folksingers sing at the trial itself. Thus, Phil Ochs could not sing "I Ain't Marchin' Any More," Arlo Guthrie could not sing "Alice's Restaurant," Country Joe McDonald could not sing "Vietnam Rag," and Judy Collins could not sing Pete Seeger's "Where Have All the Flowers Gone?" Guthrie's "Alice's Restaurant" (1966) was both an oblique and a direct spin on the war, but more direct attacks were made by Phil Ochs's "Talking Vietnam" (1964), Malvina Reynolds's "Napalm" (1965), Pete Seeger's "Waist Deep in the Big Muddy" (1967), Joan Baez's "Saigon Bride" (1967), and Matthew Jones and Elaine Laron's "Hell No! I Ain't Gonna Go" (1967). Tom Paxton even managed to invest some mordant humor in his "Lyndon Johnson Told the Nation" (1965).

Many of the popular protest and antiwar songs seemed to transcend the war itself—such as Bob Dylan's "Blowin' In the Wind" (1964) and John Lennon's "Give Peace a Chance" (1969). Musical pleas for peace, psychedelic drugs and drug-related lyrics, were everywhere during the 1960s, although at least one authority on the subject has observed that in general the "peace" songs and lyrics of the era referred both to Vietnam and to the search for generational and spiritual peace.

Many of the grunts in the U.S. military didn't listen to folksingers and weren't much attuned to the Woodstock Festival or the hippie musical *Hair*; theirs was a different reality. Jimi Hendrix was probably the most popular among the troops, followed by Santana. The Rolling Stones and Led Zeppelin were also among the more popular bands listened to by soldiers in Vietnam.

In Vietnam, the G.I.'s had their own "hit songs" that were not even known in the States. "The Ballad of the Co Van My," for one, was written by U.S. Army advisers and sung to the tune of "The Wabash Cannonball." Airmen sang a parody of "Puff the Magic Dragon," addressed to a deadly plane with that nickname. Men of the 1st Cavalry Division sang a parody "Sorry 'Bout That, Charlie" to the tune of "Rock of Ages." "The Battle Hymn of Lieutenant Calley," sung to the tune of the "Battle Hymn of the Republic" and glorifying the officer found guilty for the massacre at My Lai, (see South Vietnam, March 16, 1968, pp. 626-627) was banned from the Armed Forces Network in 1971. And in the late 1960s and early 1970s, the South Vietnamese government tried to ban the antiwar songs by a young Vietnamese composer and guitarist, Trinh Cong Son, (reportedly heavily influenced by Dylan and Baez).

As it happened, though, the song that at least temporarily reached the most people was one of the few pro-war songs of the era: "The Ballad of the Green Berets," written by a professional soldier and self-taught songwriter, Sgt. Barry Sadler, while on duty in Vietnam (where he was wounded in combat). It was America's best-selling record in 1967.

Other wars in America's history had given rise to many popular songs. The Vietnam War was unique in inspiring so many antiwar songs, including some written years afterward. The Dead Kennedys' 1980 song "Holiday in Cambodia" about the Khmer Rouge and Bruce Springsteen's often misinterpreted 1984 hit "Born in the U.S.A." are just two examples.

HISTORICAL PERSPECTIVES AND CONTROVERSIES

Was the Vietnam War essentially a civil war, an internal struggle between two different factions of Vietnamese, in which the United States had no reason or right to become involved, or was it a proxy war for the major Communist and anti-Communist powers?

Everyone in the United States had a different opinion on that during the war; historians, political scientists, and those with a special interest in contemporary events continue to debate the question. In retrospect, it may seem obvious to say it was an internal problem, and most historians now agree that the United States, for questionable if inevitable reasons, entangled itself in a civil war in Vietnam that it did not understand. Typical would be political scientist William S. Turley's claim that "U.S. intervention transformed the conclusion of a civil and revolutionary conflict into a lethal international war of long duration." Yet at the time, the major Communist power, the Soviet Union, *was* actively intervening in other nations' internal disputes: To mention but two instances, the Soviet Union had intervened in Hungary in 1956 and intervened in Czechoslovakia in 1968. And staunchly anti-Communist Americans were not the only people in the world concerned about the "loss" of various peoples to Communist rule.

In the end, though, many informed students of the war have argued that the United States presence in Vietnam was predicated to a considerable degree on ignorance of Southeast Asia and the realities and aspirations of the postcolonial world. When the United States first became concerned with Vietnamese affairs in the closing days of World War II, its maps did not even show the existence of Vietnam. Vietnam was hidden under the colonial label French Indochina, almost suggesting that the area was an appendage of China, a misperception that existed at the very highest levels. But perhaps the most tragic of U.S. miscalculations grew from its lack of awareness of the Vietnamese identity, which, in addition to its language, tradition, and united territory, featured an ongoing myth of national indomitability and an image of heroic resistance to foreign rule. Leaders, such as Ho Chi Minh, who fulfilled that image could expect great loyalty and sacrifice from a broad spectrum of Vietnamese; leaders who succumbed to foreign pressure, collaborated with foreign rulers or foreigners, especially for personal gain, suffered from weak support as well as from self-doubt, as exemplified by Ngo Dinh Diem. Seen in the context of Vietnamese history, the Vietnam War was not so much a new war as it was the resumption of an old, unfinished war; and U.S. intervention was in effect an attempt to reverse historical trends that were firmly established long before U.S. troops arrived. Much of what ensued, in the opinion of journalist and historian Fox Butterfield, "might have been avoided if Americans had realized that Vietnam had a 2,000-year history of battling for its independence from

China, France, and Japan, and that for many Vietnamese, Ho Chi Minh was the legitimate inheritor of this tradition. The Saigon government never had this appeal to nationalism."

But if it is easy to see and say such things years removed, how real at the time was the possibility of outside intervention from the Communist Bloc? At the time, China was absorbed in its own reconstruction and was not inclined, after Korea, to let itself be drawn into another conflict (see Geographic and Strategic Considerations, pp. 613-614). The Soviet Union, for all its rhetoric, was opposed to revolutionary offensives that might require substantial commitment of its resources or draw it into confrontation with the United States. In fact, in 1957, the Soviet Union proposed admission of North Vietnam and South Vietnam to the United Nations as separate nations. Even overlooking the growing rift between the Soviet Union and China, for a long time external support for Hanoi's advocacy of reunification was quite precarious. In terms of materiel, while the United States poured hundreds of billions of dollars into the Vietnam War and sent millions of its citizens to fight there, China and the Soviet Union contributed a handful of advisers and a total of about $3 billion. The war was over for the United States in the mid-1970s, but before the end of the decade, China, which the United States had so feared as the ally of the Communist Vietnamese, invaded Vietnam with 200,000–300,000 troops along most of its 480-mile northern frontier. The Soviet Union warned China to "stop before it is too late," and Vietnam petitioned the UN "to force the Chinese aggressive troops to withdraw from Vietnam."

Why did so many young men declare themselves conscientious objectors during the Vietnam War?

Opposition to the Vietnam War took many forms, from people literally incinerating themselves to refusing to pay the special war tax on their telephone bills. Those most directly affected were the young men of draft age, and although hundreds of thousands of young Americans dutifully answered the call, there was widespread resistance to the draft. One way to resist was to claim to be a conscientious objector (CO): someone who rejects military service on the basis of a religious affiliation or strongly defined moral principle. As far back as 1661, the colony of Massachusetts exempted members of religious groups, such as the society of Friends (or Quakers) from service in the militia, and that tradition prevailed throughout all of America's wars, including World War II and the Korean War. Some COs simply refused to take up arms but were willing to serve in the medical corps or perform some other form of noncombat service; others refused to join the military and were assigned to civilian jobs, such as working in mental hospitals; a few totally committed pacifists refused to participate in any way and were sent to prison. But throughout all those wars, to be recognized as a CO, a man had to establish that he had some strong affiliation with a recognized religious group and its concept of a Supreme Being. That was the only way one could be granted CO status in the early years of the Vietnam War. Until in 1965, when the Supreme Court ruled that it was not necessary to establish a specific church-based belief in a Supreme Being to be granted CO status; individuals need only claim that their "religious training and belief" told them that war was wrong. Then in 1970, the Supreme Court further broadened the concept of Conscientious Objector to include "all those whose consciences, spurred by deeply held moral, ethical, or religious beliefs, would give them no rest or peace if they allowed themselves to become part of an instrument of war." The 1970 ruling led to a dramatic increase in the number of youths, including draftees already in service, who sought to be exempt from duty as COs. Among draftees, for example, 6 percent received CO status in 1966; by 1970, that rose to 25 percent; by 1972, for every 1,000 draftees, 130 were granted CO status. Exact and official figures have never been published because most of the decisions were made by local draft boards, but the best estimate is that about 100,000 men (both draftees and those already in-service) were granted CO status between 1964 and 1973. To put that in some perspective, during that same period, however, desertions from the military numbered some 500,000, of whom 93,250 stayed away for more than 30 days.

Why have the MIAs of the Vietnam War (those Americans missing in action) remained such a troublesome issue?

Every war has had its MIAs. Some reliable estimates state that the United States still has some 78,000 MIAs from World War II, while the Korean War left some 8,100 U.S. MIAs. Yet, few Americans have heard much about these MIAs. It has always been accepted that in the "fog" of war there are inevitably those who are killed and whose bodies are never found. (There are also always a few men who choose simply to walk away and start a new life elsewhere.) The question of the MIAs of the Vietnam War, however, continues to remain a matter of controversy. For one thing, there is no agreement on the actual figures. When the United States signed the peace treaty with North Vietnam in 1973 and agreed to a complete exchange of POWs, the U.S. authorities who negotiated the treaty chose to minimize the numbers of those missing and unaccounted for. They reported a figure of only some 1,269 true MIAs. Not long afterwards, many Americans began to claim that figure did not reflect the true numbers; eventually, as many as 2,400 MIAs were claimed. The U.S. government has never admitted to more than 2,200 and includes in that figure not only those truly lost but also those known to have died (as reported by comrades in the field) but whose bodies remain unaccounted for. As of 1997, the bodies of some 460 former American MIAs have been returned and identified; the U.S. government acknowledged 1,584 MIA's; the process of searching for remains in Indochina goes on although the U.S. government focuses on about 48 who had been reliably reported as alive when left by other prisoners. Several official U.S. delegations have gone to Vietnam and returned to report that the Vietnamese are making genuine efforts to locate American MIAs. Although that does not satisfy the families of those still listed as missing, the U.S. government continues to insist that it is doing everything possible to account for the MIAs but warns that there will inevitably be some never found.

Meanwhile, the issue of the actual number of MIAs became entwined with a related and even more controversial issue: the claim that many of those MIAs had, in fact, been alive at the time of the signing of the treaty and were simply abandoned by the United States in its haste to get out of Vietnam. The government's position has always been that, with the possibility of a few extraordinary cases it could not have known about, no living Americans were left behind. Sightings of such Americans have continued to be reported over the years, but most of those have been exposed as either complete frauds or at least lacking any hard evidence. The few instances of serious reports remain unsolved mysteries. Not all those who insist that the MIA issue has been mishandled agree that there were (and may still be) living Americans held in Vietnam. But because of the frustrating and inconclusive nature of the Vietnam War, and because the government did not always tell the true story at the time, many Americans continue to remain distrustful of the official version of the MIAs status.

Did the United States lose the war at home or on the battlefield after the Tet Offensive in 1968?

That is part of the more pervasive and still persistent controversy over whether the U.S. military would have been capable of winning the Vietnam War had it not been for the media, the dissenters, and the waverers on the home front. But setting aside that debate for the moment, it is generally agreed that the U.S. and South Vietnamese armed forces were winning the war in the narrow sense of casualty counts; even in the Tet Offensive of January–February 1968, for all the shocking events, the Communists lost far more of their forces. After the war ended, Gen. Vo Nguyen Giap admitted that his forces came close to being wiped out during that and subsequent actions. So in that sense, the United States was not losing the war on the battlefield. It is also generally agreed that the images of the Tet Offensive (North Vietnamese in the U.S. embassy compound, hundreds of civilians executed in Hué) pretty much collapsed the American people's remaining support for a military solution in Vietnam. On one level, the polls confirmed that, although not in a simplistic manner: in the immediate aftermath of the Tet Offensive, the Gallup poll reported 74 percent of Americans expressing confidence in the conduct of the Vietnam War, but that was apparently a case of rallying around a crisis. Within a month, that figure dropped to 54 percent. Outright support for the war slipped to 41 percent, and those who believed that intervention in Vietnam was a mistake rose to 49 percent. And there is no denying the impact of the Tet Offensive on the American home front, culminating in President Lyndon Johnson's

decision not to seek reelection but to work for a negotiated peace.

The debate over what the true response to the Tet Offensive should have been has never been resolved. Peter Braestrup, in a book whose title explains his subject, *Big Story: How the American Press and Television Reported and Interpreted the Crisis of Tet in 1968 in Vietnam and Washington* (New Haven, Conn.: Yale University Press, 1978), charged that the media misrepresented the actual significance of the Tet Offensive by failing to report it as a military disaster for the Communist forces. But if the effect on the U.S. home front and the Communist forces was devastating, the Tet Offensive also took a tremendous toll on the U.S. and South Vietnamese military, both in terms of personnel and equipment. The United States reported 3,895 dead between January 30 and March 31, 1968. Army historian William M. Hammond, in *The Military and the Media* (Washington, D.C.: Center of Military History, 1996), is among those who dispute Braestrup's claim. Hammond admits that there was much negative media coverage, but in the end, it was the casualty figures that undermined the American public's support for the war.

Shortly after the Tet Offensive, the official State Department assessment of March 3, 1968, put it bluntly:

"We know that despite a massive influx of 500,000 U.S. troops, 1.2 million tons of bombs a year, 400,000 attack sorties per year, 200,000 enemy KIA (killed in action) in three years, 20,000 U.S. KIA, etc., our control of the countryside and the defense of the urban levels is now essentially at pre-August 1965 levels. We have achieved a stalemate at a high commitment."

The war continued for almost five more years, and although the figures mounted, the situation on the battlefield remained essentially the same. The American home front may not have fully supported the Vietnam War, but they probably should not be blamed for losing it.

Would U.S. policy in Vietnam have been markedly different had President John F. Kennedy not been assassinated?

That question has been argued for decades, and those on both sides tend to be able to select evidence for their cause; inevitably, too, positions are often based on personal and political loyalties. In general, President Kennedy's close associates, such as Arthur Schlesinger and Theodore Sorensen, present a JFK who would have learned from history and from his mistakes and would never have led the United States into the quagmire. They argue that even though the number of U.S. military advisers in Vietnam increased during President Kennedy's "thousand days" from about 900 to 16,500, Kennedy was already preparing to withdraw 1,000 when he was killed. There are several men—Sen. Wayne Morse; Michael Forrestal, an official in the national security office; and Kenneth O'Donnell, JFK's close friend and aid—who insisted that in personal conversations just before his death, JFK let it be known he was prepared to pull back from Vietnam. Robert McNamara, JFK's defense secretary, is another who claims that "John Kennedy would have eventually gotten out of Vietnam rather than move more deeply in." McNamara also claims that he was among the first to recommend such a withdrawal. Professor John M. Newman, in his *JFK and Vietnam: Deception, Intrigue and the Struggle for Power* (New York: Warner Books, 1992), argues that it was the Joint Chiefs of Staff and senior military officers who wanted to intervene in Vietnam and were upset at JFK's plan to withdraw.

On the other side are many who point to JFK's actions and words that support the image of the "cold warrior" who expected Americans to do whatever was necessary to prevent the spread of Communism. Thomas Paterson, a history professor, in *Kennedy's Quest for Victory* (New York: Oxford University Press, 1989), is one who makes that charge. Certainly, JFK promoted the counterinsurgency programs in Laos and Vietnam, he greatly increased U.S. military aid to South Vietnam (not just thousands of advisers but helicopters and airplanes), he surrounded himself with men who proved to be hawkish on Vietnam (including Robert McNamara, Maxwell Taylor, McGeorge Bundy, Walt Rostow). And in most public speeches, Kennedy seemed to endorse the domino theory and the hard-line approach to Vietnam. In a TV interview with Walter Cronkite in September 1963, JFK referred to withdrawal from Vietnam as a "great mistake...this is a very important struggle even though it is very far away." Only a week later, in another TV interview, he referred to the "domino theory": "I believe it...China is so large [that Vietnam's fall]

would also give the impression that the wave of the future in Southeast Asia was China and the Communists." Even the speech he was scheduled to give in Dallas on the day he was assassinated had hints that he was prepared to take an active role in Vietnam: "Our assistance to these nations can be painful, risky, and costly, as is true in Southeast Asia. But we dare not weary of the task."

Again, JFK defenders argue that that was only his public posture, that he said such things to avoid a direct confrontation with the hawks, and that as soon as he was reelected in the fall of 1964 he would have revealed himself to be a dove. The opponents retort that that is an attempt to whitewash President Kennedy and to shift the blame to Presidents Johnson and Nixon. In the end, the more objective historians weigh the pros and cons of the question and conclude with two points: (1) Whatever he did or said, Kennedy did not live to fight the war in Vietnam, and (2) we never can truly know what JFK would have done had he lived.

Once committed to intervening in Vietnam, was there some other strategy that the United States might have followed? Was the war "winnable"?

While the debate continues over whether the United States should ever have become involved in Vietnam, the fact is that it did. The question then shifts to whether the United States might have conducted the war differently, more successfully. Many members of the U.S. military and, in fact, many civilian Americans, argue that the U.S. armed forces could have won the war had they been allowed to fight it without so many civilian/political constraints. The proponents of that view fall along a spectrum. At the farthest reaches are the few who advocated using nuclear weapons; taking that step was never seriously considered by responsible leaders. Close to that position was that voiced by Gen. Curtis Lemay, U.S. Air Force Chief of Staff (1961–1965): "Bomb them back to the Stone Age." That is, don't use atomic bombs but throw in everything else in the U.S. arsenal. Had that succeeded, it would have cost the United States its reputation as a civilized society. As it was, many people felt that the United States went too far in its use of weapons of destruction; in any case, massive quantities of armaments and troops were used, and they did not accomplish the task.

That shifts the argument regarding success away from an increase in quantities to a different approach in deploying them. One such strategy, promoted by many for some time, rests on the argument that the United States made a mistake in slowly escalating its commitment. The contention is that had a president dared to do what President George Bush did in the Persian Gulf—that is, raise a massive force and then commit it all at once—the Vietnam War would have ended more quickly and successfully (see Persian Gulf War, pp. 700-720). It seems a plausible scenario, but it isolates the Vietnam War from the actualities of history. Exactly when should the United States have done that? Why would the Soviets or the Chinese have stood by and watched that happen? Unlike the war in Kuwait, there was no clearly defined invasion by foreigners: The U.S. could hardly have been expected or allowed to announce in 1964 or 1965 that it was going to bring a 500,000-man army with a navy and air force and "throw out" the Vietcong and the North Vietnamese. Turmoil, conflict, and violence were rife among the South Vietnamese themselves; no U.S. task force could have stopped that. Meanwhile, the Vietcong had been gradually insinuating themselves throughout South Vietnam; the U.S. counterinsurgency forces had their chance for more than a decade and couldn't stop them.

Finally, at the other end of the spectrum of strategic changes is the argument, still made by some military men, that all that was needed was for the commanders in the field to have been allowed to pursue the Vietnam War on their own terms, that too many of the military operations were micromanaged by politicians in Washington, D.C. (President Johnson boasted that U.S. planes could not bomb a Vietnamese outhouse without his approval.) That argument seems reasonable. But if the Americans had prevailed more decisively on the battlefield in a fairly fought, less destructive war, it is still impossible to imagine that North Vietnamese Communists would ever have allowed a unified Vietnam on terms the United States would have agreed to. (Invading North Vietnam to make it totally capitulate has been ruled out by all students of the Vietnam War, for it most certainly would have brought China into the war.) Instead, the United States and North Vietnam would have sat down at a negotiating table, and the only major difference from what they did negotiate might have been that all the Vietcong and North Vietnamese forces would have withdrawn back to north of the 17th parallel. In other words, the war would most likely have ended with a situation much like that in Korea—namely, a return to a divided nation. One has only to look at Korea 45 years after the Korean War ended to question whether Americans would regard that as a more desirable outcome in Vietnam than the one that eventually prevailed.

CIVILIAN AND MILITARY BIOGRAPHIES

AMERICAN

Johnson, Lyndon Baines (1908–1973)—president: Lyndon Johnson was born in Texas. After serving in the House of Representatives and the Senate, he was selected by John F. Kennedy to be his running mate in 1960 and became president when Kennedy was assassinated in 1963. Johnson was elected president by a landslide in 1964 and used his popularity to pass such progressive social legislation as the Civil Rights Act (1964) and the Voting Rights Act (1965). Johnson's continuation of Kennedy's Vietnam policies, however, led him to a self-defeating step-by-step escalation of the Vietnam War and to misleading the public as to the war's nature and extent. Frustrated by the unsuccessful and unpopular war and his concomitant inability to pursue his "Great Society" program, Johnson announced his decision not to seek reelection in 1968 and retired from politics.

Kennedy, John Fitzgerald (1917–1963)—president: John F. Kennedy was born in Brookline, Massachusetts. After graduating from Harvard University in 1940, he served in the Navy during World War II. Kennedy, a Democrat, was elected to the House of Representatives in 1946 and to the Senate in 1952. He defeated Richard Nixon in 1960 to become the 35th president. Kennedy subscribed to the containment doctrine and the domino theory, but promoted a flexible Cold War strategy over reliance on nuclear deterrence. He and his advisers, by selecting Vietnam as a proving ground for their new emphasis on counterinsurgency, cast the die for a strategy in Vietnam that ultimately proved disastrous. Although the number of U.S. advisers in Vietnam increased from about 900 to 16,500 during his term, at the time of his assassination, President Kennedy had not yet chosen to openly commit U.S. ground forces.

Kissinger, Henry (1923–)—political scientist, public official: Henry Kissinger was born in Fuerth, Germany. He fled Nazi Germany with his family and arrived in New York in 1938. He served in the U.S. Army at the end of World War II, helping to administer Germany's temporary government. He earned his Ph.D. from Harvard University in 1954. His writings on foreign policy attracted national attention, and he served as consultant to Presidents Eisenhower, Kennedy, and Johnson. As national security adviser from 1969–1973 and secretary of state from 1973–1977, he was the chief architect of U.S. foreign policy under Presidents Nixon and Ford. The secret peace negotiations Kissinger began in Paris in 1969 led to the Vietnam cease-fire agreement of 1973 and a Nobel Peace Prize, which he shared with Le Duc Tho, in the same year. But his role in secret and illegal bombings in Cambodia and questionable associations with CIA operations tarnished his public image. In 1977, he retired to a career as a writer, lecturer, and consultant.

Lodge, Henry Cabot Jr. (1902–1985)—ambassador, peace negotiator: Henry Cabot Lodge, Jr. was the grandson of Massachusetts senator Henry Cabot Lodge (1850–1924), who led the fight against the United States joining the League of Nations. Henry Cabot Lodge Jr. was elected to the Senate in 1936, then resigned to serve in World War II. He was reelected in 1946 to the senate but lost his seat to John F. Kennedy in 1952. President Dwight Eisenhower appointed Lodge U.S. ambassador to the UN (1953–1960). Kennedy appointed him ambassador to South Vietnam in 1963. Although he was the top American on the scene when the Ngo brothers were assassinated in November 1963, he was basically a bystander. After less than a year in Vietnam, he was replaced by Maxwell Taylor; Lodge then replaced Taylor in that post in 1965. Throughout his time in Vietnam, he advocated U.S. participation in the Vietnam War but he was never really a decision maker. Lodge served as U.S. chief negotiator at the Paris peace talks in 1969 until he retired in December.

Nixon, Richard Milhous (1913–1994)—president: Richard Nixon was born in Yorba Linda, California. He gained a national reputation as an anti-Communist while serving as a California representative on the House Committee on Un-American Activities during the Alger Hiss spy case. Nixon served as Dwight D. Eisenhower's vice president (1953–1961). After losing to John F. Kennedy in the 1960 presidential election, Nixon returned to defeat Hubert Humphrey for the presidency in 1968 with a promise to "end the war and win the peace." Nixon implemented a five-part strategy, featuring Vietnamization, the reduction of U.S. troop commitments, the strengthening of South Vietnam's military, and negotiations as well as increased bombing. Reelected in 1972, Nixon enlarged and increased the U.S. role in Indochina until negotiating a withdrawal in 1973. His obsession with the antiwar elements in the government eventually led to the Watergate break-in of 1972, which in turn led him in 1974 to become the first U.S. president to resign.

Taylor, Maxwell (1901–1987)—general, adviser: Maxwell Taylor was born in Missouri. He was a 1922 West Point graduate. Taylor was a World War II hero and fought in Korea before becoming commander of the U.S. and UN forces in Korea. He had retired after serving as chief of staff (1955–1959) but came out of retirement when President John Kennedy named him chairman of the Joint Chiefs of Staff (1962–1964). In that position, and then as ambassador to South Vietnam (1964–1965), Taylor advocated a measured but finally activist role for the United States in Vietnam, and precisely because of his reputation as "the thinking man's general," his advice weighed heavily in the decisions made by Kennedy and Johnson. Almost to the end, Taylor advocated that the United States remain in the Vietnam War, but when it was over, he admitted that he had misjudged the situation in Vietnam.

Westmoreland, William C. (1914–)—general: William C. Westmoreland was born in Spartanburg County, South Carolina. He graduated from the U.S. Military Academy at West Point in 1936; he was a decorated combat hero in World War II and the Korean War. He was superintendent of the U.S Military Academy from 1960 to 1963. In June 1964, Westmoreland replaced Gen. Paul Harkins as commander of U.S. operations in Vietnam. Westmoreland's requests for more troops and greater firepower led to a troop buildup of 500,000 by 1968, but his helicopter-delivered search-and-destroy war of attrition was unsuccessful. Following the Tet Offensive of 1968 he was recalled to Washington, D.C., and reassigned as chairman of the Joint Chiefs of Staff. He retired from the Army in 1972. In 1974, he failed in his bid for the Republican gubernatorial nomination in South Carolina. Westmoreland was critical of the Johnson administration's handling of the Vietnam War after his retirement. In 1982, Westmoreland sued CBS-TV for asserting that he had manipulated intelligence data in Vietnam, but he withdrew the suit in 1985.

SOUTH VIETNAMESE

Ngo Dinh Diem(1901–1963)—president: Ngo Dinh Diem was born to a Catholic family. He served under the French as chief of Quangtri Province in 1930–1931, and later as minister of justice. He refused an offer to become minister of the interior under the Vietminh when it took control from the Japanese in 1945 and went into exile in 1950. Diem returned to Vietnam as prime minister under Emperor Bao Dai's southern government in 1954; he displaced Bao Dai in 1955. As president, Diem was unpopular and out of touch, unwilling to share power or compromise, and used most of the U.S. funds channeled to him for fighting Communists to protect himself against rivals in Saigon and to maintain his family members in dictatorial control over various provinces and offices in South Vietnam. A Catholic in a country in which 90 percent of the population was non-Christian, his heavy-handed reaction to Buddhist protests and inefficiency as an anti-Communist led to a U.S.-condoned coup that resulted in his death as well as that of his brother, Nhu.

Nguyen Cao Ky (1930–   )—premier, vice president: Nguyen Cao Ky was among the more outrageous characters to emerge from the Vietnam War. He was a young hotshot pilot when he became commander of the Vietnam air force. In 1964, he threatened to bomb the headquarters of the squabbling generals; later, he personally lead bombing raids over North Vietnam. In 1965, he became prime minister under President Nguyen Van Thieu, and in 1967, he became Thieu's vice president. Ky was outmaneuvered by Thieu, who defeated him in a bid for the presidency in 1971. When the Communists moved against Saigon in 1975, Ky fled. He ended up in California, where he opened a liquor store.

Madame Ngo Dinh Nhu (1924–   )—influential figure: Madame Ngo Dinh Nhu was born Tran Le Xuan in Hanoi to a wealthy family active in French colonial government. She spoke French fluently but was barely fluent in Vietnamese. From 1955 to 1963, she served as first lady of South Vietnam to her unmarried brother-in-law, President Ngo Dinh Diem. His brother and her husband, Ngo Dinh Nhu, headed the secret police and generally enforced control in South Vietnam, and from her vantage point she exerted considerable power. (Some Americans called her the "Dragon Lady.") Her comments on the protest self-immolation of Buddhist monks in 1963, which she applauded as "monk barbecues" ("Let them burn, and we shall clap our hands!"), received wide press coverage and helped turn American public opinion against Diem. After the deaths of Diem and Nhu in 1963, she went into exile in Rome.

Nguyen Van Thieu (1923–   )—general, president: During the Japanese occupation of Vietnam, Nguyen Van Thieu served with the Vietminh, but then joined the Vietnamese army created by the French. Thieu trained in France and later in the United States. He married a Catholic and converted to Catholicism. Thieu distinguished himself in actions against the Vietminh and became a divisional commander in the South Vietnamese army in 1959. He led a regiment against Diem in the 1963 coup and maneuvered, with U.S. backing, to become military head of state in 1965, president in 1967, and president again in 1971. Never very consistent as a leader or popular with his people, he was often regarded as intractable by the Americans on which he depended. But the United States backed him until the fall of Saigon in late April 1975, when he resigned his office and fled, eventually settling in Great Britain.

NORTH VIETNAMESE

Vo Nguyen Giap (1912–   )—commander in chief of army, minister of defense: Vo Nguyen Giap was a founding member of the Indochinese Communist Party in 1930. He graduated from the University of Hanoi Law School in the 1930s. He was a high school history teacher, and was active in the Communist underground. His wife died in a French prison. Giap helped found the Vietminh (1941), and after World War II, led it against the French. In 1954, he masterminded the siege at Dien Bien Phu that won Vietnam independence from France. He continued as chief strategist and commander in the war against the United States and South Vietnam. Although widely hailed as a military strategist, Giap's penchant for frontal assault, costing many North Vietnamese lives, opened him to criticism late in his career. He retired from public life in 1975.

Ho Chi Minh (1890–1969)—political and military leader: Ho Chi Minh was born Nguyen That Thanh. He attended a French school in Hué before setting off in 1911 on a combination exploration and exile that took him to India, France, the United States, and Great Britain. After World War I and the rejection of his plans for an independent Vietnam at the Versailles Peace Conference, Ho joined the French Communist Party (1920) and, embracing revolutionary Communism, went to Moscow to study. After writing and organizing in the Soviet Union and in China and founding the Indochinese Communist Party in 1930, he returned to Vietnam in 1941. It was then that he adopted the name Ho Chi Minh, which means "most enlightened one." In Vietnam, he helped organize the Vietminh, a successful resistance movement against the Japanese, and proclaimed Vietnamese independence in 1945. In 1954, the Vietminh expelled the French, and Ho became president and premier of the Democratic Republic of North Vietnam. He pursued his dream of a unified, independent Vietnam politically while organizing a guerrilla movement in South Vietnam. By 1960, he was engaged in armed struggle against the southern regime that soon involved the United States.

Le Duc Tho (1911–)—Communist leader: Le Duc Tho was born Phan Dinh Khai. Tho was of middle-class origins. He was an early member of Ho Chi Minh's inner circle. He was a founding member of the Indochinese Communist Party (1930) and a founder of the Vietminh (1941). More than ten years in French jails failed to dampen his commitment to independence. In the mid-1960s, Tho supervised military and political activities. He left the front to become the chief negotiator for the North Vietnamese at the Paris peace talks in 1969. A tough bargainer, he waited years for a favorable settlement, gaining Henry Kissinger's begrudging admiration, the terms he'd long sought, and a Nobel Peace Prize (shared with Kissinger in 1973), which he refused.

FURTHER READING

Bonds, Ray, ed. *The Vietnam War: The Illustrated History of the Conflict in Southeast Asia*. London: Salamander Books, 1979.

Buttinger, Joseph. *The Smaller Dragon: A Political History of Vietnam*. New York: Praeger, 1958.

————*Vietnam: The Unforgettable Tragedy*. New York: Horizon, 1977.

Caputo, Philip. *A Rumor of War*. New York: Holt, 1977.

Carhart, Tom. *Battles and Campaigns of the Vietnam War*. New York: Hamlyn, 1984.

Duiker, William. *The Communist Road to Power*. Boulder, Colo.: Westview Press, 1981.

Fall, Bernard. *The Two Vietnams: A Political and Military Analysis*. New York: Praeger, 1967.

Fitzgerald, Frances. *Fire in the Lake*. Boston: Atlantic-Little Brown, 1972.

Halberstam, David. *The Best and the Brightest*. New York: Random House, 1972.

Herr, Michael. *Dispatches*. New York: Alfed A. Knopf, 1978.

Herring, George C. *America's Longest War: The United States and Vietnam, 1950–1975*. New York: John Wiley, 1979.

Ho Chi Minh. "The Path Which Led Me to Leninism," *Ho Chi Minh on Revolution*. Bernard B. Fall, ed. New York: Praeger, 1967.

Isserman, Maurice. *The Vietnam War*. Facts On File: New York, 1992.

(Continued on p. 664)

Karnow, Stanley. *Vietnam: A History*. New York: The Viking Press, 1983.

Kattenburg, Paul M. *The Vietnam Trauma in American Foreign Policy, 1945-1975*. New Brunswick, N. J.: Transaction Books, 1980.

Lewy, Guenter. *America in Vietnam*. New York: Oxford University Press, 1978.

O'Ballance, Edgar. *The Wars in Vietnam 1954–1980*. New York: Hippocrene Books, Inc., 1981.

Sheehan, Neil, et al., ed. *The Pentagon Papers*. New York: Bantam Books, 1971.

Summers, Harry G. Jr. *Vietnam War Almanac*. New York: Facts On File, 1985.

Turley, William S. *The Second Indochina War: A Short Political and Military History, 1954–1975*. Boulder, Colo.: Westview Press, 1986.

DOMINICAN REPUBLIC INTERVENTION

DATES OF WAR

April 28, 1965–August 31, 1965

The beginning date used here was that of the landing of the first U.S. troops in the Dominican Republic. The United States never formally declared an end to its participation; the ending date used here was that of the signing of a peace agreement.

ALTERNATE NAMES

Dominican Constitutional Revolt. The Dominican Crisis.

SIGNIFICANCE

The Dominican Republic Intervention was among the largest in the long series of "interventions" during the 20th century by the United States in Caribbean and Central American states. The United States claimed that it was responsible for maintaining law and order in the Western Hemisphere. Although President Lyndon B. Johnson at first justified the sending of troops to the Dominican Republic by saying they were sent to protect Americans endangered by the rebels, he privately admitted that he was intervening to prevent a Communist takeover. Johnson was influenced by the fact that the United States was simultaneously engaged in a war against Communism in Vietnam. Johnson's decisive action in committing so many U.S. troops to the Dominican crisis was intended to send a strong message to Communists elsewhere around the world. In fact, the course of events flowing from the intervention proved all too reminescent of the origins of the war in Vietnam, as Johnson and his supporters found themselves engaged in the same kind of controversy with many of the same critics and for many of the same reasons. The result of that action was a "mini quagmire," as the United States became more and more deeply embroiled in a messy domestic dispute and eventually pulled out, as frustrated with both

sides as both sides were with the United States.

BACKGROUND

From the time the people of the eastern two-thirds of the Caribbean island of Hispaniola gained their independence from Haiti in 1844, the Dominican Republic had been an unstable, violence-torn nation. Since the early 20th century, the United States has not hesitated to step in when it decided that the Dominican Republic was on the verge of disaster. When in 1904 the Dominican Republic fell behind with its international debts, the United States stepped in to supervise payments. Then in 1916, with the Dominican Republic in the midst of bloody revolts, the United States sent in the U.S. Marines and effectively imposed a military occupation that lasted until 1924. An elected Dominican administration took over in 1924, but the U.S. government continued to control certain aspects of the country's finances. Then in 1930, Rafael Trujillo seized power. For the following 31 years, he ruled as a dictator. Trujillo brought some order and economic benefits to the Dominican Republic, but he also ordered the murders of thousands of people who resisted his rule and he clamped down on all civil rights. In May 1961, he was killed by insurgents and the country was thrown into turmoil, as various groups sought to gain power. (The U.S. Navy sent ships and planes to signal that the United States would not allow the Trujillo family to return to power.) In December 1962, the people elected as their president Juan Bosch, a leftist writer and an outspoken foe of Trujillo. Because of Bosch's progressive policies, the military and upper-class leaders cooperated in overthrowing him in September 1963 (Bosch went into exile in Puerto Rico), then set up a government with Donald Reid Cabral, an auto dealer, as the president.

CAUSES OF THE WAR

The government set up by the military coup of September 1963 was relatively benign compared to most of its predecessors in the history of the Dominican Republic. Donald Reid Cabral tried to introduce some reforms, but corruption was rampant and the military continued to plot behind the scenes. Juan Bosch had been elected legitimately, and his supporters were not willing to accept an illegal government. Not all of Bosch's supporters were Communists or even leftists, but some did belong to the 14th of June Movement, a pro-Castro group, and some were Dominicans who had trained in Cuba and had slipped back into their country. Among the dissidents were military and police officers who for a variety of reasons disliked the Reid government; at least some of them were equally opposed to Reid and to Bosch and simply wanted to gain power for themselves.

On April 24, 1965, a small group of Bosch supporters seized the government's main radio station in the capital city, Santo Domingo, and called for a "triumphant revolution to restore Juan Bosch to the presidency." Whipped up by the radio announcements, mobs took to the streets of Santo Domingo; the Dominican Republic was thrown into turmoil with no clear sense of who was on whose side. The chaos persisted throughout the following day, April 25. Some Dominican army officers installed a Bosch supporter as interim president until Bosch could return; other officers forced Reid to resign and turned power over to a three-man military junta. Some Dominican air force planes strafed the palace, and others strafed the rebels' positions. Late in the day, in Santo Domingo at least, two sides were forming: Those who supported the return of Bosch called themselves constitutionalists; those who supported the military leading the fight against the pro-Bosch officers called themselves loyalists. A Dominican army colonel, Francisco Caamaño Deñó, soon emerged as the leader of the constitutionalists/rebels, and Brig. Gen. Elias Wessin y Wessin, who had taken the lead in deposing Bosch in 1963, remained behind the scenes as the leader of the loyalists and military junta.

During the following two days (April 26–27), Santo Domingo remained in a state of chaos. Many defectors from the army began to distribute truckloads of weapons to Bosch supporters, and soon about 3,000 Bosch supporters were attacking selected points and sniping at anyone they perceived as threatening. General Wessin y Wessin called on the loyal forces in the army, navy, and air force to mount a major attack on the rebels, who by that time appeared to be in control of much of the center of Santo Domingo. Air force pilots supporting General Wessin y Wessin bombed and strafed rebel-held sections of Santo Domingo, which navy ships also bombarded. Inevitably, many innocent civilians were killed and wounded. Loyalist troops then launched an assault with tanks to make their way across the Duarte Bridge over the Ozama River, the crucial link between the center of Santo Domingo and the San Isidro Air Field. Although the rebels put up stiff resistance with Molotov cocktails and infantry weapons, the army got across and moved several blocks into the city; casualties on each side numbered in the hundreds. Many of the rebellious army officers, realizing they had no chance against the loyalist forces, began to surrender. When Juan Bosch failed to fly in from Puerto Rico and the military junta promised to hold elections in a few months, it appeared that the rebellion would collapse.

Meanwhile, U.S. embassy officials had gathered hundreds of American and other foreign civilians in a hotel in preparation for evacuation by ship. On the morning of April 27, a group of gun-toting teenage rebels burst into the hotel lobby, lined up the men against a wall, and threatened to execute them; instead, they fired into the air. At that point, a rebel army officer arrived and arranged for the civilians to be taken by helicopters and boats to U.S. Navy ships offshore, then to Puerto Rico. The evacuation was under way on April 27, but by that time, President Johnson had already decided to move in U.S. armed forces.

PREPARATIONS FOR WAR

The U.S. military had long had contingency plans for all possible kinds of crises, such as the evacuation of U.S. citizens from danger zones. Of greater relevance, because of its perception of its special role in the Western Hemisphere, the United States had long had contingency plans to intervene in Caribbean and Central American nations. The U.S. Navy and Marines, for instance, conducted frequent amphibious "demonstrations" around the Caribbean to show that they were ready to move in if the United States thought it necessary to maintain order. The crisis in the Dominican Republic in April 1965, however, burst on the scene unexpectedly, and U.S. authorities were caught off guard by the rebels' actions on April 24. (The U.S. ambassador to the Dominican Republic, W. Tapley Bennett, Jr., had just gone home to visit his mother in Georgia.) By April 26, the U.S. embassy in Santo Domingo was informing Washington, D.C., that the Dominican authorities could no longer guarantee the safety of the hundreds of U.S. citizens there. President Johnson immediately consulted with his top aides, including Secretary of State Dean Rusk and Secretary of Defense Robert McNamara. The U.S. military was placed on alert; a naval task force known as the Caribbean Ready Group was dispatched from Puerto Rico to the Dominican Republic, and the 82nd Airborne Division at Fort Bragg, North Carolina, was told to ready its men for possible action. There was little time for other preparations, but the U.S. military units assigned to go into action were more than ready to take on the minuscule, poorly trained, and poorly equipped forces they were to go up against.

DECLARATION OF WAR

There was no formal declaration of war by any of the parties involved, although the Dominican rebels did call for an uprising to restore Juan Bosch to the presidency. President Lyndon B. Johnson, once the first U.S. Marines were moving into the Dominican Republic, went before the American people on TV on April 28 and stressed one motive: "The United States government has been informed by military authorities in the Dominican Republic that American lives are in danger." He did not publicly state what he was later reported as telling his top aides when coming to his decision: "I will not have another Cuba in the Caribbean."

COMBATANTS

At peak strength, some 31,600 U.S. military served during the Dominican Republic hostilities; that included some 9,000 U.S. Navy personnel with the task force offshore. The first to go ashore were some 450 marines from the 6th Division, part of the 1,800-man force of combat-ready marines with the U.S. Navy's Task Force 124 that had been assigned to the crisis; eventually they were joined by some 6,000 marines from the 2nd Division. The United States also assigned some 12,000 men of the 82nd Airborne Division, sta-

tioned at Fort Bragg, North Carolina; the 82nd Airborne Division was one of the primary combat-ready units of the U.S. Army. No U.S. Air Force or U.S. Marine air units engaged in any combat or bombing missions, but both provided transport, reconnaissance, and other support missions.

As for the Dominicans, the active loyalists, mainly the military units fighting on behalf of Gen. Elias Wessin y Wessin, never numbered more than about 3,000, but they included most of the air force and navy and controlled all the heavy weapons, such as airplanes, tanks, and artillery. Some units, however, sat out the war.

The exact number of rebels was never known; they often exaggerated their strength, claiming as many as 47,000 active supporters. More reasonable estimates were at most 5,000 armed fighters, of whom only a few hundred had military training, although about 50 military and civilian police officers did join in at the outset. Most of the rebels were young men. They had automatic weapons, machine guns, bazookas, and mortars but little else in the way of armaments except a few captured tanks.

GEOGRAPHIC AND STRATEGIC CONSIDERATIONS

The Dominican Republic had little strategic value to the United States, either for its geographic location or its resources. Although there are some economic resources on the Dominican Republic—sugar, bananas, and bauxite (for aluminum)—the primary U.S. interest was to prevent the Dominican Republic from being controlled by hostile forces. And although the United States did not maintain any military installations there, the United States never would have tolerated Dominican Communists taking control and possibly allowing the Cubans or Soviets to establish a military presence in the Cariibbean. Moreover, the establishment of another Communist regime in the Caribbean would have been a domestic political disaster for President Johnson.

BATTLES AND CAMPAIGNS

April 28, 1965: During the night of April 27–28, the rebel forces pushed many of the loyalist troops back across the Duarte Bridge. During the morning of April 28, rebels also seized several important points in downtown Santo Domingo. The loyalists' leadership remained in disarray, and loyalist troops appeared to be weakening their grip. By late afternoon, one of the members of the antirebel junta, Col. Pedro Benoit, formally requested that the United States send in troops to prevent "another Cuba." By 5 P.M., the first of some 500 U.S. Marines were brought by helicopter from the offshore U.S. Navy Task Force 124; they landed in the western section of Santo Domingo, which encompassed the U.S embassy, other nations' embassies, a university, and the hotel where the civilians were waiting to be evacuated. The marines were under orders not to take sides and not to fire unless fired upon but simply to secure a "safe zone." By that time, the rebels had secured the southeastern section of downtown Santo Domingo bordered by the sea; the loyalists secured the section to the north. Fighting between the two factions continued, and the U.S. Marines found themselves coming under fire from the rebels, who had machine guns and bazookas.

April 29, 1965: The U.S. Marines held off an attack by the rebels on the U.S. Embassy and proceeded to secure a 3.5-square-mile zone of safety for the international community and any others who wanted to stay out of the fighting. In the rest of the city, street fighting between the two factions continued to take a heavy toll, with at least 1,000 casualties reported. In general, the rebel forces were more successful in taking control of points around downtown Santo Domingo than were the loyalists. Another 1,200 marines were flown in from the offshore task force. By the evening, some 2,500 men from the 82nd Airborne Division were flown from Pope Air Base in North Carolina to the Dominican Republic.

April 30, 1965: By 2 A.M., the first troops from the 82nd Airborne Division landed at the San Isidro Air Force Base to the northeast of Santo Domingo; during the following week, another 15,000 men from the 82nd were flown into that base. During the day, the first U.S. troops moved to clear the approaches to the Duarte Bridge; when the junta troops were unable to advance on their own, the U.S. troops moved across the bridge and secured a six-block radius around the bridgehead. Heavy fighting continued in the city, and U.S. Marines and Army troops took casualties.

The papal nuncio in Santo Domingo, Monsi-

gnor Emanuelle Clarizio, conferred with the U.S. Ambassador W. Tapley Bennett Jr., rebel leaders, and junta leaders at the San Isidro Air Field. They agreed on a cease-fire, and all signed an agreement, but it did not have much effect on individuals in the field.

May 1, 1965: Fighting in Santo Domingo was sporadic, as representatives of all sides, including various U.S. diplomats, met or spoke by telephone in an effort to maintain the cease-fire. The commander of U.S. forces, Lt. Gen. Bruce Palmer Jr., however, insisted that the U.S. Marines in the international zone and 82nd Division troops at the Duarte Bridge be allowed to link up to establish a neutral cordon between the rebels and the loyalists.

May 2, 1965: U.S. forces remained largely in place while awaiting orders from Washington, D.C., about linking up their forces. Permission was not granted until late afternoon. The two opposing factions continued their sniping and small arms fire.

The U.S. Navy announced it had evacuated about 3,000 Americans and other foreigners to Puerto Rico; from there, they went on to their home countries.

There were some 10,000 American troops in the Santo Domingo area. Official U.S. casualty figures for five days were 4 dead and some 41 wounded.

May 3, 1965: In a quick offensive shortly after midnight, U.S. Marines moved eastward and 82nd Division troops moved westward and succeeded in opening a corridor between the rebel-held section of Santo Domingo and the section held by loyalist forces. The corridor provided the U.S. forces with a clear passage between the international zone they controlled and the approach to the San Isidro Air Field. Most important, it effectively isolated the rebels in one corner of Santo Domingo.

May 4, 1965: Col. Francisco Caamaño Deñó, who had emerged as the rebel leader, took the oath as the "constitutional president." Juan Bosch, still in Puerto Rico, asked that Caamaño be given international recognition; Bosch continued to deny that the Communists were running the rebellion. Caamaño said he would not become a dictator, nor would he allow anti-Americanism to take hold.

There were 16,000 U.S. troops in the Dominican Republic. The marines went on the offensive and expanded the international zone slightly, claiming they did so to protect both sides from snipers.

May 5, 1965: Both sides signed a formal cease-fire calling for demarcation of zones and guarantees of safety, but U.S. Marines were wounded and captured by the rebels after the cease-fire was signed. The cease-fire was effectively ignored in the months that followed, but neither side gained much new territory.

May 6, 1965: In a clash in central Santo Domingo, the rebels killed three U.S. Marines, wounded two, and captured two (who, after being displayed for propaganda purposes, were released). Sniper fire continued throughout Santo Domingo.

May 7, 1965: In a surprise attempt to gain more popular support, the three-man military junta imposed on April 25, resigned and a five-man Government of National Reconstruction was formed. It was led by Brig. Gen. Antonio Imbert Barreras, a Dominican hero (and honorary general) for having been one of the assassins of the hated dictator Rafael Trujillo in 1961. Barreras, however, was no longer popular with the mass of Dominicans and was seen as a puppet of the United States and the military junta.

May 8–13, 1965: As the leaders of the two factions continued to make charges and countercharges, demands and counterdemands, snipers continued shooting at opposing forces in Santo Domingo. On May 13, the junta sent two F-51 fighters to strafe the rebels' radio station; in the course of that, some U.S. Marines were accidentally strafed. The marines shot down one of the F-51s. (The next day, the U.S. sent troops to prevent the junta from flying any more such missions.) The rebels continued to charge that the U.S. forces were making incursions into their part of Santo Domingo. By that time, there were 23,000 U.S. Marine and Army troops in and around Santo Domingo.

May 15–21, 1965: With tanks and heavy artillery, the junta forces launched a major attack to secure the northern section of Santo Domingo. Some 2,000 loyalist troops gradually drove out the rebels and seized the rebels' radio station, which had resumed broadcasting. The rebels charged that U.S. troops had participated in that attack, but the U.S. denied that its forces had taken a combat role. Hundreds of casualties were reported on both sides.

May 5, 1965—two U.S. soldiers shelter a local youth under their Jeep as they engage in a firefight in Santo Domingo, capital city of the Dominican Republic.

May 21–22, 1965: A 24-hour truce went into effect so that the Red Cross, World Health Organization, and other humanitarian agencies could make arrangements for medical and other services for civilians and military on both sides. U.S. forces set up hospitals to care for the wounded and distributed food to hungry Dominicans. When the truce ended on May 22, it was informally extended, but the fighting continued, as neither side could control individual snipers.

May 28, 1965: Gen. Hugo Panasco Alvim of Brazil took command of the OAS (Organization of American States) force in the Dominican Republic. The OAS is an association of 27 Latin American states and the United States, formed in 1948. The OAS works to ensure cooperation, peaceful settlements, and collective self-defense among its members. The crisis in the Dominican Republic was the first time the OAS deployed a military force. The U.S. military forces placed themselves under General Panasco's command. The first of a contingent of 1,600 U.S. Marines began to leave the Dominican Republic. In the ensuing weeks, troops from Brazil, Costa Rica, Honduras, and Nicaragua replaced U.S. troops.

June 6, 1965: The last of some 6,000 U.S. Marines left the Dominican Republic, but some 14,000 U.S. Army and Air Force personnel remained, along with some 1,600 soldiers from other OAS nations. Rebel snipers continued to fire at U.S. and OAS troops.

June 15–16, 1965: After rebels clashed with OAS forces along the edge of the security zone, U.S. troops advanced into the rebel zone. During 48 hours of fighting, a combined total of some 300 casualties were reported on both sides, including three U.S. soldiers killed. Each side blamed the other for initiating the clash.

June 25, 1965: In one of the few violent incidents outside the capital city of Santo Domingo, rebel sympathizers clashed with police at San Francisco de Macorís. Some 16 civilians were reported killed, 25 were wounded.

July 3, 1965: President Johnson announced that another 1,400 U.S. soldiers would be withdrawn immediately, leaving about 11,000 U.S. personnel in the Dominican Republic.

July 5–20, 1965: Incidents involving exchange of fire or minor attacks by the rebels and junta forces occurred. The U.S. and OAS troops found themselves playing the role of peacekeepers as negotiations dragged on.

August 31, 1965: With the signing of the formal accord between the rebels and junta delegates, the U.S. forces in Santo Domingo withdrew from the front lines and assumed a purely defensive posture.

HOME FRONT

April 27, 1965: At a news conference, President Lyndon B. Johnson urged an end to the violence in Santo Domingo but gave no firm answer on the question of whether the United States planned to intervene in the conflict.

April 28, 1965: President Johnson announced that the United States was sending marines to the Dominican Republic to secure the safety of Americans and other civilians trapped by the war. He said that U.S. troops would not take sides, and he urged a cease-fire. The United States offered to send the Dominican Republic food and medical supplies and promised aid as soon as a government was in place.

April 29, 1965: Supporters of Juan Bosch marched on UN headquarters in New York City to protest the U.S. intervention.

April 30, 1965: Secretary of State Dean Rusk said that although there were Communist aspects to the uprising in the Dominican Republic, it was not a Communist "second front."

May 1, 1965: The Johnson administration released a list of 58 Communists allegedly running the rebellion; later it was shown that many of those on the list had nothing to do with the rebellion (some were, in fact, dead).

May 2, 1965: President Johnson announced that the United States was sending 14,000 troops to protect the lives of civilians and to prevent a Communist takeover of the Dominican Republic. He said that Communists had usurped what began as a "popular democratic revolution."

May 3–5, 1965: Increasingly, U.S. congressmen and journalists questioned President Johnson's motives for sending troops to the Dominican Republic. In particular, he was being attacked for allowing the U.S. troops to become identified with the loyalists' military junta forces and cause while claiming that the United States was completely neutral. Another common criticism was that Johnson had not sought the support of the OAS before acting.

May 28, 1965: President Johnson, under constant attack from many quarters for his actions in the Dominican Republic, said that the "old distinction" between civil war and international war was obsolete; he specifically singled out Communist subversion as an example of that and to justify his actions.

INTERNATIONAL DEVELOPMENTS

April 26, 1965: As fighting raged in Santo Domingo, Cuba's Fidel Castro announced his support for the Juan Bosch as the rightful constitutional leader of the Dominican Republic.

April 27, 1965: Cuba charged that the United States was planning to send troops to the Dominican Republic.

April 29, 1965: The OAS called a meeting of its members. The United States agreed to shift its responsibility in the Dominican Republic to the OAS as soon as the safety of all foreign civilians was secured. The OAS asked that the papal nuncio in Santo Domingo, Monsignor Emanuelle Clarizio, report on the situation.

At the United Nations Security Council, the United States insisted that it had sent in troops only to protect American civilians. The Soviet Union, East Germany, China, Algeria, Italy, and Cuba all attacked the United States for intervening in the conflict.

April 30, 1965: Cuba called on UN Secretary-General U Thant to act against the U.S. "invasion" of the Dominican Republic.

May 1, 1965: The OAS set up a "peace commission," with representatives from Argentina, Brazil, Colombia, Guatemala, and Panama, to work out a cease-fire. Some Latin American countries, such as Chile and Peru, however, continued to criticize the United States for intervening.

May 2, 1965: W. Averell Harriman, President Johnson's ambassador at large, began a tour of several South American capitals to gain support for the U.S action.

May 3, 1965: The United States proposed that the OAS organize an inter-American military force to take over from the U.S. military in the Dominican Republic.

The UN Security Council debated the U.S. role in the Dominican Republic; the Soviet delegate attacked U.S. "militarism," but the U.S. delegate blamed Cuban and Soviet Communism for much of the unrest in the Caribbean.

The Canadian government refused to give its official support to the U.S. intervention in the Dominican Republic.

May 5, 1965: The OAS voted (14-5) to create an inter-American military peace force to replace the U.S. force in the Dominican Republic. Brazil, Costa Rica, Honduras, and Nicaragua agreed to send troops.

May 26, 1965: President Charles de Gaulle of France joined the growing international chorus of those criticizing U.S. intervention in the Dominican Republic.

June 1, 1965: The OAS voted (15-2) to send a three-man mediation team to Santo Domingo to work out a permanent peace agreement with the conflicting forces.

NEGOTIATIONS AND PEACE TREATY

From the very first hours of the uprising on April 24, there were continual negotiations involving the principals of the two conflicting sides and all the various secondary players. In fact, a fully detailed account of the days between April

24 and August 31 would devote far more space to the negotiations than to the actual hostilities. Several cease-fires were negotiated early on (see April 30, 1965, and May 5, 1965, above) but were ignored by both sides. President Lyndon Johnson and the OAS sent several special emissaries to the Dominican Republic to try to effect a truce. Not until the arrival of the three-man OAS mediation committee did serious peace negotiations begin.

June 3, 1965: The OAS mediation committee arrived in Santo Domingo. It was made up of U.S. diplomat Ellsworth Bunker, El Salvador's ambassador to the OAS, Ramon de Clairmont Dueñas, and Brazil's ambassador to the OAS, Ilmar Penna Marinho.

June 4, 1965: The OAS mediation committee held the first of many conferences with the leaders and representatives of all parties in the conflict. At the outset, rebel leader Colonel Caamaño insisted on the restoration of the 1963 constitution under which Juan Bosch had been elected, but he soon indicated that he was ready to compromise. General Imbert, leader of the loyalist junta, was less conciliatory.

June 18–23, 1965: The OAS mediation committee issued its first plan for a provisional government until elections could be held. In the following few days, both sides studied the proposal and called for clarification of some details. On June 23, the OAS put forth a new plan, calling for an OAS trusteeship over the Dominican Republic, a government with a cabinet made up of individuals not associated with political parties, and a purge of rebel officers and those in the armed forces associated with the junta. Once again, Caamaño was willing to compromise, but General Imbert insisted that his junta government had to be recognized.

July 2, 1965: Suddenly both sides agreed on most of the terms of the OAS agreement. In particular, both sides agreed to set up a provisional government to be headed by Dr. Hector Garcia Godoy, former foreign minister under Juan Bosch. New elections were to be held six to nine months after the signing of the agreement. The rebels agreed to turn over their arms to the new government. But no sooner was an agreement imminent than General Imbert and the junta indicated they were not ready to give up their role.

July 3–August 17 1965: The negotiations bogged down as each side expressed disagreement with one detail or another and distrust of the other side. At the same time, there were splits within each side between those who were ready to compromise and those who wanted to continue fighting. The United States continued to play a major role by offering to provide millions of dollars for immediate obligations and even more millions for long-term aid.

August 18–30, 1965: On August 18, General Imbert suddenly announced he was rejecting the OAS plan; the rebels responded by announcing they, too, were rejecting the plan. In the following days, even as the two sides took public stands indicating they were rejecting the OAS plan, the OAS committee applied pressure on both sides and gradually answered their objections. Then suddenly on August 29, General Imbert and his five-man junta government resigned to make way for the provisional government called for by the OAS plan.

August 31, 1965: Representatives of the rebels and junta signed the OAS-brokered Act of Reconciliation based on a provisional government. Although it did not immediately end all hostilities between the two sides, it did lead to peace and elections, and it marked the end of the U.S. forces' active involvement (although the last U.S. troops did not leave the Dominican Republic until September 19, 1966).

RESULTS OF THE WAR (Casualties, Costs, Consequences)

The United States did not calculate an official cost for its intervention in the Dominican Republic. The operation was relatively cheap because it did not involve the loss of expensive equipment such as aircraft or tanks. But in addition to the customary secondary expenses of such an operation (medical costs, insurance payments), the United States poured hundreds of millions of dollars into the Dominican Republic to keep it from collapsing into total bankruptcy. For several weeks during the war itself, the United States paid the salaries of many government employees. After the hostilities ended, the U.S. pumped many millions into aid and reconstruction projects. Some of that money was part of the usual U.S. foreign aid program; but whereas in 1964 the United States gave $12 million to the Dominican Republic, between May 1965 and June 1966, it gave $130 million.

The best estimate for what it cost the Dominican Republic was some $100 million—not that much by U.S. standards, but it was 10 percent of the Dominican Republic's gross national product for that period.

The U.S. military reported 24 dead and 149 wounded during combat; the Dominican loyalist forces never officially reported a casualty list, but they suffered at least 200 dead and 1,200 wounded. There were never any official figures for the rebels' casualties, but estimates are that the rebels suffered at least 300 killed and 1,500 wounded. In addition, there were several hundred civilian bystanders killed and wounded, as most of the fighting went on within the close quarters of the city.

The consequences of the Dominican Republic Intervention could be seen in several areas. In the weeks that followed the signing of the truce on August 31, the Dominican Republic continued to be torn by dissension and violence. U.S. personnel along with other OAS troops occasionally intervened in "incidents," but they avoided becoming involved in the major clashes between the rebels and the pro-government forces (although two more U.S. soldiers were killed and another ten wounded).

Most observers have agreed that the Dominican governments that followed the intervention did bring stability to their country, although much of that stability was due to heavy infusions of U.S. aid and to the general robustness of the international economy. Hector Garcia Godoy headed the provisional government that oversaw elections on June 1, 1966. (Juan Bosch lost to Joaquin Balaguer, who had served as president under Rafael Trujillo.) But little changed for the mass of poor Dominicans, and corruption and oppression flourished. In that sense, the major consequence of the U.S. intervention in the Dominican Republic was the restoration of the status quo in that Republic.

Many Dominicans, and Latin Americans in general, had their own special reading of the intervention. The United States had sent the message that it was prepared to intervene in Western Hemisphere countries to prevent Communists or those perceived as Communists from taking power. The converse of this was that the United States would tolerate governments of all kinds so long as they were not excessively leftist. Many Dominicans felt that at the very least the United

States had short-circuited a return to a legitimate government.

In the world at large, the unilateral military operation by the United States was most disconcerting; it made the world's other powers and international bodies wary of President Johnson's methods and leadership. That had a direct influence on the world's response to the U.S. intervention in Vietnam, which was assuming far more massive proportions than it had just a few years earlier (see Vietnam War, pp. 608-664).

MILITARY INNOVATIONS, TACTICS, EQUIPMENT

There were no new weapons or tactics used in the Dominican Republic Intervention. The war was particularly difficult for the United States military forces because they found themselves fighting in what was essentially an urban guerrilla war; there was little advantage gained by using conventional military tactics or sophisticated equipment. Most U.S. casualties were caused by snipers.

LEGENDS AND TRIVIA

There was not much about the Dominican Republic Intervention to inspire either legends or trivia, at least in the United States. After the first few days of U.S. intervention, most Americans lost interest in the long-drawn-out and obscure internal bickering, especially since they had little clear sense of the country's politics. For the most part, the Dominican Republic Intervention quickly was pushed off the front page to the inner pages of newspapers. But there was one incident that did make the front pages, and that was a microcosm of what was unsettling the United States at that time. President Lyndon Johnson was determined to show the world that he could provide both "guns and butter"—that is, he could fight a war in Vietnam and improve Americans' domestic situation. As an instance of the latter, he sponsored an arts festival at the White House on June 14, 1966, to which many of the nation's major artists in all fields were invited. On June 3, a major news story broke when Robert Lowell, a Pulitzer Prize winning poet, released a letter to the president declining to participate. Although he did not mention either the Dominican Republic or Vietnam by name, Lowell

clearly suggested them when he wrote: "What we will do and what we ought to do as a sovereign nation facing other sovereign nations seems to hang in the balance between the better and the worse possibilities." At once, an otherwise celebratory salute to the arts (and by extension, to the Johnson administration) became a political minefield, as various artists felt the need to take sides. Among others, novelist Saul Bellow issued a statement to explain why he would attend: "I consider the American intervention [in the Dominican Republic] to be indeed wicked and harmful, but the administration is more than these policies of which I disapprove." At the festival itself, writer Dwight Macdonald circulated a petition among the guests stating that their presence should not be seen as a support of all the President's policies. (Macdonald could get only three others to sign the petition.) That incident showed that many of Johnson's severest critics of his Vietnam policies—artists, intellectuals, academics, students, journalists—had been further alienated by the Dominican Republic Intervention.

NOTABLE PHRASES

What is important is that we know and they know and everybody knows that we don't propose to sit here in our rocking chair with our hands folded and let the Communists set up any government in the Western Hemisphere.

President Lyndon B. Johnson spoke those words on May 3, 1965, in a speech to the AFL-CIO construction-trade union leaders at the Hilton Hotel in Washington, D.C. The "they" and "everybody" referred to Communist nations and indeed all nations. Soon after those words were quoted, some observers suggested that Johnson was also snidely criticizing his predecessor, John F. Kennedy, for not having been bold enough during the Bay of Pigs invasion of Cuba. Kennedy had been frequently photographed sitting in a favorite rocking chair.

I realize I'm running the risk of being called a gunboat diplomat, but that is nothing compared to what I'd be called if the Dominican Republic went down the drain.

President Lyndon B. Johnson was quoted as

saying those words in *Time* (May 14, 1965). They expressed his frustration at the dilemma he felt he faced and took on a special edge because he was facing the same issues in Vietnam.

HISTORICAL PERSPECTIVES AND CONTROVERSIES

Was the intervention in the Dominican Republic justifiable under international law?

President Lyndon B. Johnson came in for a great deal of criticism for his intervention in the Dominican Republic. The harshest criticism, quite expectedly, came from those who supported the rebels and Juan Bosch, and the strongest support came from those who saw a Communist threat around the world. But even many who did not identify with either extreme were critical of Johnson's action. Although the heat of partisanship quickly died down, the issue of Johnson's "right" to intervene in the Dominican Republic has remained debatable.

On the broadest level, the justification for all such U.S. interventions in the Western Hemisphere has traditionally rested on the Monroe Doctrine (of 1823), which simply warned European nations not to interfere in the Western Hemisphere. That was followed by various extensions, such as Theodore Roosevelt's "corollary" of 1904: When it came to "flagrant cases of... wrongdoing or impotence" in the Western Hemisphere, the United States might be forced "to the exercise of international police power." But those were nothing but unilateral proclamations by the United States; they had no real standing under international law, only under power politics.

President Franklin Delano Roosevelt, in his promotion of a "good neighbor policy" during the 1930s, had said that the United States would not intervene in the affairs of its neighbors to the south. In fact, at the seventh Pan-American Conference in 1933, the United States had signed a pact agreeing to just that. Then in 1948, the United States took the lead in forming the Organization of American States (OAS). One of its most important provisions was Article 15: "No State or group of States has the right to intervene, directly or indirectly, for any reason whatever, in the internal or external affairs of any other state." In fact, that ideal was soon qualified by U.S. officials to allow for the new Communist threat. In

1961, after the failure of the Bay of Pigs invasion, President John F. Kennedy warned the world: "Should it ever appear that the inter-American doctrine of noninterference merely conceals or excuses a policy of nonaction—if the nations of this hemisphere should fail to meet their commitments against outside Communist penetration—then I want it clearly understood that this Government will not hesitate in meeting its primary obligations, which are to the security of our nation." Clearly implicit was the notion that the United States reserved the right to decide when a Communist threat in any Western Hemisphere country was a threat to U.S. security. It was that "doctrine" that President Johnson was simply reiterating when he announced in April 1965 that he was acting "to help prevent another Communist state in this hemisphere." He had a long history of precedence on his side but no known principle of international law.

The Johnson administration never really dealt with the charge that the Dominican Republic Intervention was in violation of U.S. agreements with the OAS and with the U.N. The closest it came was on June 10, 1965, when the State Department's legal adviser, Leonard C. Meeker, gave a speech in which he simply asserted that the Communists in the Dominican Republic were a threat: "International law which cannot deal with facts such as these... is not the kind of law I believe in." He said that the U.S. intervention was necessary to give the OAS time "to determine means of preserving the rights" of Dominicans. "Thus it is," Meeker concluded, "that law grows out of life and international law out of the life of nations."

CIVILIAN AND MILITARY BIOGRAPHIES

AMERICAN

Johnson, Lyndon B. (1908–1973)—president: Lyndon B. Johnson was elected to the U.S. House of Representatives in 1937, to the U.S. Senate in 1948, and in 1960, became John F. Kennedy's vice president. When Lyndon Johnson inherited the presidency in November 1963, he was probably aware that only a few weeks before a military coup had deposed Juan Bosch from the Dominican presidency. By December 14, 1963, however, Johnson approved extending diplomatic recognition to the illegal government, an action that bedeviled his presidency during much of 1965. By that time, Johnson was also coming under increasing attack for his policies in Vietnam, and he believed and acted on reports from various U.S. diplomats, military men, intelligence experts, and other official sources that events in the Dominican Republic were propelled by Communists. Johnson actually went to great lengths to minimize U.S. military action in the Dominican Republic and maximize international cooperation, but the perception of a Communist plot led to Johnson's becoming bogged down in the Dominican crisis (see Civilian and Military Biographies, Vietnam War, p. 660).

DOMINICAN

Bosch, Juan (1909–)—politician: Juan Bosch was a political theorist and novelist with a Marxist tilt. Between 1938 and 1961, he lived in exile in Cuba, where he founded the Dominican Revolutionary Party in 1939. After Rafael Trujillo's assassination in 1961, he returned to the Dominican Republic and became the country's first freely elected president in February 1963. Regarded as too sympathetic to Communists, if not one himself, he was overthrown by a military coup that September and went into exile again, that time in Puerto Rico. When the uprising of 1965 broke out, he immediately indicated he was ready to return to retake his rightful office, but as week followed week, he did not return: Some accused him of indecisiveness, but he claimed that U.S. authorities prevented him from leaving Puerto Rico. He did return from exile in September 1965 and ran unsuccessfully for president in 1966. He went to Europe in yet another exile, returning in 1970; although he ran again for president, he never again held that office.

Imbert Barreras, Antonio (1920–)—general: Antonio Imbert Barreras was an obscure small businessman when he joined three others in assassinating Rafael Trujillo in 1961. He was given the title of "national hero" and made an honorary brigadier general. He was then named to the seven-man Council of State that took over rule of the Dominican Republic in January 1962. He took charge of police affairs and cemented contacts with officers in the national police and in the armed forces and was always lurking in the background of the various plots that dominated Dominican politics during the next three years. When the rebellion broke out on April 24, 1965, he at first tried to work out a truce with the rebels, but soon cast his lot with the loyalists. On May 7 he surfaced as head of the five-man junta that took over the government, supported by the United States. But as the weeks went by, his increasingly arbitrary and intransigent ways cost him the respect and support of Americans on the scene. He became an obstacle to working out a compromise and he was pushed aside by the agreement of August 31. He was named armed forces minister in 1986 but was dismissed in 1988 and never again played an important role in Dominican affairs.

Wessin y Wessin, Elias (1924–)—general: Elias Wessin y Wessin was the son of poor Lebanese immigrants to the Dominican Republic and a devout Catholic. He rose in the Dominican military and gained a reputation for being totally uninterested in personal profit or military pomp. In 1962, he intervened to stop an attempt to overthrow the civilian council that ruled after Rafael Trujillo's assassination. But in 1963, convinced that Juan Bosch favored the Communists, he led the coup that drove Bosch out of office and into exile. Through his command of the Dominican Armed Forces Training Center, Wessin y Wessin built up what was effectively his own loyal military force. When the rebellion broke out on April 24, 1965, Wessin y Wessin remained in the background for the first 24 hours, holding his forces at the San Isidro Air Field. By midday on April 25, however, he decided that the pro-Bosch forces represented a Communist threat and committed his forces to the loyalists. For the following four months, Wessin y Wessin remained the real power behind the loyalists, but with the signing of the accord for a provisional government on August 31, he went into exile in Florida. He returned in late 1968, but when he was exposed as planning a coup in 1971, he was exiled to Spain. He returned again in 1978 and ran unsuccessfully for president in 1982. In 1988–1990, he served as armed forces minister.

FURTHER READING

Black, Jan Knippers. *The Dominican Republic: Politics and Development in an Unsovereign State*. Boston: Allen & Unwin, 1986.

Bracey, Audrey. *Resolution of the Dominican Crisis, 1965: A Study in Mediation*. Washington, D.C.: Institute for Study of Diplomacy, Georgetown University Press, 1980.

Lowenthal, Abraham F. *The Dominican Intervention*. Baltimore, Md.: Johns Hopkins University Press, 1995.

Mansbach, Richard W., and John Vasquez. *Dominican Crisis, 1965*. New York: Columbia University Press, 1983.

Martin, John Bartlow. *Overtaken By Events: The Dominican Crisis from the Fall of Trujillo to the Civil War*. New York: Doubleday, 1966.

Moya Pons, Frank. *The Dominican Republic: A National History*. New Rochelle, N.Y.: Hispaniola Books, 1995.

Palmer, Bruce A. *Intervention in the Caribbean: The Dominican Crisis of 1965*. Lexington, Ky.: University of Kentucky Press, 1990.

Schoonmaker, Herbert G. *Military Crisis Management: U.S. Intervention in the Dominican Republic, 1965*. New York: Greenwood Publishing, 1990.

GRENADA INTERVENTION

DATES OF WAR

October 25, 1983–October 27, 1983

ALTERNATE NAMES

Operation Urgent Fury. Grenada Invasion. Grenada Rescue Mission (President Ronald Reagan's preferred name).

SIGNIFICANCE

The invasion of Grenada by the United States is best understood in the context of the Cold War competition between the United States and the Soviet Union (and in this instance, the Soviets' ally, Cuba). Grenada was a Caribbean nation emerging from British colonial rule, just beginning to develop its government and its economy. The Soviet Union under Leonid Brezhnev had a policy of pursuing influence in developing countries where the balance of power was usually lopsided, with the distribution of wealth and power concentrated among a tiny elite and poverty and ignorance spread among the many. Those countries had been fertile ground for Communist ideology, and the small island nation of Grenada had come under the control of Communists.

The United States felt it held the special authority originally set forth in the Monroe Doctrine: namely, the right to make sure that no European power interfered in the independent nations of the Western Hemisphere. Beyond that, the United States saw its mission as that of keeping Soviet influence at bay and supporting the development of democracy in all developing countries. The apparently growing influence of the Soviet Union and Cuba in Grenada was incompatible with U.S. interests and goals. In addition, the Reagan administration was troubled by what it saw as instability and the threat of Soviet influence in other nations of Central and South America. So it was that President Ronald Reagan chose to launch a military operation to oust the leftist government of the tiny Caribbean island nation in what was one of the last of the proxy confrontations between the United States and the Soviet Union.

BACKGROUND

A British West Indian colony since 1763, Grenada was granted independence on February 7, 1974, but remained within the British Commonwealth. Great Britain maintained some defense and financial oversight of Grenada, as with other of its former Caribbean colonies, and continued to keep a titular representative there, a governor general. Sir Eric Gairy, the leader of the independence movement in the 1970s, became Grenada's first prime minister. His intolerance of any opposition led to the claim that he was a dictator; aside from that, his poor handling of the country's treasury (the balance of payments went from a surplus of $500,000 in 1975 to a deficit of $5.3 million in 1978) was eroding his support. Some charged that only the fear of his secret police, called the "Mongoose Gang," kept him in power.

In the 1976 elections, the New Jewel Movement (NJM), a Marxist-Leninist movement, won three seats. The NJM's leader, Maurice Bishop, took his seat in Grenada's House of Representatives, and the NJM moved to establish itself as an alternative to the Gairy government. In March 1979, the New Jewel Movement, led by Maurice Bishop and Bernard Coard, carried out an almost bloodless coup (only one person was reported killed) while Gairy was in New York; one report claimed he was intending to address the UN on unidentified flying objects, but others speculated that he had seen the coup coming. Bishop, who had popular ties with Grenadians and was more charismatic than Coard, assumed the role of prime minister of the People's Revolutionary Government (PRG). Coard was the intellectual backbone of the NJM, the Marxist-Leninist ideologist. The NJM's military arm was the People's Revolutionary Army (PRA), commanded by Gen. Hudson Austin.

The NJM under Bishop's leadership was a

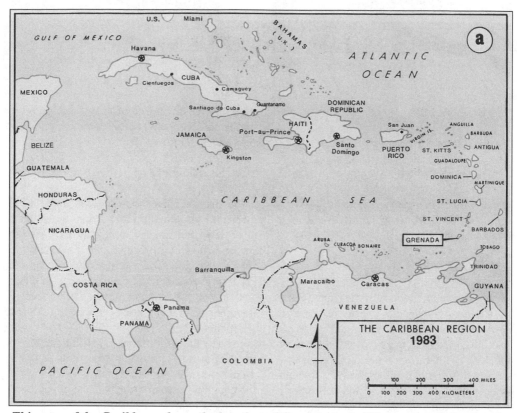

This map of the Caribbean shows the location of Grenada (only 133 square miles), one of the Lesser Antilles, off the coast of Venezuela.

blend of the democratic-socialism of the London-based Socialist International (SI) and the Marxist-Leninist ideology represented by the Communist Party of the Soviet Union. In July 1982, an agreement between Grenada and the Soviet Union established the basis for future collaboration and provided for shipments of Soviet supplies, including 5 million rubles worth of military equipment and training in their use, to the island nation. Meanwhile, tensions were developing between Coard, who favored the hard-line Marxist-Leninist stance, and Bishop, who encouraged relations with the SI, which included moderate social democrats such as Barbados prime minister Tom Adams and former West German chancellor Willy Brandt, as well as representatives from most European countries.

The main agenda of the NJM was to increase the living standards of Grenadians: Roads and schools were built and milk was supplied to young children. What caught the eye of U.S. observers of the new government in Grenada, however, was a multimillion dollar construction

project—a new airport. An airport at Point Salines at the southwestern tip of the island had been discussed for decades. The island's only airport, Pearl Airport on the northeast coast, could not accommodate international jets, night flights, or modern Grenadian air transportation needs. That shortcoming delayed Grenada's development as a tourist destination and as an exporter of agricultural produce. The Bishop government had begun the project as early as August 1979; with Cuba's Fidel Castro supplying 40 Cuban engineers to supervise and to teach the Grenadians construction skills, work began on a 10,000-foot runway. Involved in the construction, too, were technicians from the firm of Layne Dredging of Miami, Florida, and Plessey Airports, a British construction firm. Money came from various governments, including those of Venezuela, the European Community, Libya, Syria, and Algeria. As work on the airport proceeded, the U.S. government became increasingly concerned that it was being built not to accommodate Grenada's air transportation needs but to accommodate large Soviet warplanes; under a treaty of May 1980, in fact, the USSR had obtained rights to land their Tu-95 bomber/reconnaissance and airlift transports at the new airport. Concern over that development, aggravated by the presence of Cuban workers on the project, made the Reagan administration turn an even more wary eye on events unfolding on Grenada.

CAUSES OF THE WAR

Maurice Bishop, who as early as June 1980 had called on Grenadians to fight a "people's war" against imperialism, was regarded as a protégé of Fidel Castro. In addition to the construction workers, Castro had also sent military advisers to help upgrade Grenada's army. Even so, the more radical Communists were impatient with Bishop's leadership, and on October 13, 1983, Bernard Coard and Gen. Hudson Austin led a coup that placed Bishop under house arrest. That aroused the people of Grenada, for whom Bishop was a popular leader, and on October 19, Bishop was released from his house. He went to Fort Rupert, a government building (named after his father, who had been killed by Sir Eric Gairy's forces), in the capital city, St. George's, where thousands of Grenadians converged, shouting their support. While he attempted to reimpose control through loyal members of his government, members of the People's Revolutionary Army (PRA), supporting the Coard-dominated New Jewel Movement, fired into the crowd; as many as 70 citizens were reported killed (although this figure may have been exaggerated). When the PRA fired on the people, Bishop and a group of loyal officials gave up and began to file out of Fort Rupert. Bishop and reportedly nine of his closest supporters (including one woman, Jacqueline Creft, the education minister and mother of one of his children) were turned back into the courtyard and immediately executed. The new government then imposed a 24-hour curfew with orders to its forces to shoot on sight; the island was on the verge of chaos.

At that point, another element in the Grenada scene came into focus: St. George's University Medical School in and around the capital city, with its mainly American student body (see Legends and Trivia, p. 685-686). Although few Americans, probably including those in the U.S.

government, had been aware of those students until the crisis, President Ronald Reagan made their safety one of the two primary rationales for his subsequent actions. The other reason was the restoration of democracy in Grenada. On occasion, President Reagan and his spokesmen refered to 1,000 Americans on Grenada; on other occasions, they refered to 800 American medical students, implying that there were some 200 other Americans on the island. In fact, the university claimed that only 650 American medical students were in Grenada at that time (the rest were doing their internships in hospitals off the island). Reagan had some grounds for nervousness, with the image of the hostages in Tehran (1979–1981) still quite vivid. He felt the American people would never forgive him if those students came to harm during the turmoil sweeping Grenada (see Historical Perspectives and Controversies, pp. 686-687).

This outbreak of violence alarmed not just the Reagan administration but many in other Caribbean nations, in particular the prime ministers of Jamaica and Barbados and members of the Organization of Eastern Caribbean States (OECS). The OECS was made up of six small independent Caribbean nations and one British colony: Antigua and Barbuda, Dominica, Grenada, Montserrat (the British colony), St. Kitts-Nevis, St. Lucia, and St. Vincent and the Grenadines. Up to that point, the OECS nations had not shared the United States's apprehensions about Maurice Bishop's left wing government. With the outbreak of violence, however, they were galvanized into action.

October 21, 1983: Meeting in an emergency session at Bridgetown, Barbados, the prime ministers of the members of the OECS voted unanimously to send a peacekeeping force to Grenada.

October 23, 1983: Frank McNeil, a U.S. special emissary, flew to Barbados with U.S. Marine major general George Crist to meet with other U.S. officials, Barbados prime minister Adams, and OECS officials. The OECS presented the U.S. representatives with a formal written request for military intervention. The United States was reported to have had a major hand in drafting the request.

PREPARATIONS FOR WAR

As opposed to major wars the United States

had been involved in, which required a fair amount of strategic planning and military preparations, most of the elements of the Grenada invasion were in place and simply required authorization from the commander in chief to implement. In addition, because the United States had always viewed the growing influence of Communism in the Central American/Caribbean region as a threat to the United States, there were contingency plans in place. Moreover, the U.S. ambassador to France, Evan Galbraith, admitted on French television on October 26, 1983, that the United States had been planning an invasion for two weeks prior to Prime Minister Maurice Bishop's arrest.

Despite all that general "preparedness," observers agreed afterward that the operation in Grenada had been carried out too hastily. Committing modern, sophisticated military forces and equipment involves immense amounts of planning and coordination. President Ronald Reagan did not make the final decision to invade Grenada until the assassination of Maurice Bishop on October 19. By October 21, the U.S. Navy was sending two naval task forces toward Grenada; by October 24, the United States was ferrying troops and supplies into the airport at Bridgetown, Barbados. Yet the U.S. Marine Corps, which conducted the initial assault, did not even have a map of Grenada until a few hours before it went in.

As for the forces on Grenada, the People's Revolutionary Government (PRA) had some level of military preparedness in accordance with their Marxist-Leninist tenets, but the troops had minimal training and the command had no clear strategy. At least some of the Cubans, however, were disciplined fighters, and the PRA and the Cubans had heavier armaments than were expected and put up stiffer resistance than was anticipated. The Grenadians could hardly claim to have been taken by surprise because as early as October 22, Gen. Hudson Austin's government was publicly predicting that the island was going to be invaded.

DECLARATION OF WAR

There was no declaration of war. President Ronald Reagan relied on the request from the OECS nations for aid and acted under his authority to protect American lives; on the evening of October 25, he simply informed Congress that U.S. forces had landed in Grenada.

COMBATANTS

Americans: The initial invasion units involved some 500 U.S. Ranger paratroops and 600 marines; within hours, several hundred more rangers and marines went ashore on Grenada, followed in a steady stream by members of the U.S. 82nd Airborne Division (based at Fort Bragg, North Carolina). By November 4, the marines and rangers had been removed and some 5,000 82nd Airborne troops took over.

The U.S. Navy played a major role in the operation. To begin with, a unit of the U.S. Navy's elite special warfare unit, the SEALS, went ashore as part of the initial surprise attack. (SEALS is an acronym formed from sea-air-land.) The marines who went ashore were carried there by the Navy's ships. The ships were part of two U.S. Navy groups that had set out for the Mediterranean around October 18. One group was a carrier battle group of six ships led by the USS *Independence*, which carried 70 aircraft and a complement of 4,940 officers and crew; it had originally been headed for the coast of Spain, where it was to take part in a naval exercise. The other group was an amphibious assault squadron of five ships; officially labeled the 1-84 Amphibious Ready Group, it was led by the USS *Guam*, which carried 20 helicopters and had a deck large enough to launch seven helicopters at once. That squadron carried some 2,000 marines of the 22nd Marine Amphibious Unit, and when it had sailed from Virginia on October 18, it was headed for Lebanon, where it was to relieve the marines stationed in Beirut (see International Developments, October 23, 1983, p. 684). The marines carried a six-gun battery of field artillery, five M-60 tanks, a large squadron of helicopters, 13 amphibious armored vehicles, and jeeps with mounted antiaircraft missiles.

The U.S. Air Force also played a major role. The Military Airlift Command (MAC), operating out of Grantley Adams International airport in Barbados (one hour away from Grenada), dropped the U.S. Army Ranger paratroops in the initial invasion. The Air Force also provided support consisting of C-130 Hercules and C-141 transport planes. And when the Cubans turned out to have antiaircraft guns that were firing (and hitting) Army helicopters, the Air Force sent in

AC-130 Spectre gunships with their powerful weapons to take out these guns.

OECS Nations: Coming ashore shortly after the U.S. combat forces but not participating in the hostilities were some 300 policemen and soldiers (later increased by about another 75) from four countries of the Organization of Eastern Caribbean States (Antigua and Barbuda, Dominica, St. Lucia, St. Vincent) as well as soldiers from the Jamaican and Barbados Defense Forces. The OECS group were mostly untrained in warfare. Those from Jamaica and Barbados were professional soldiers who had trained at the Royal Military Academy in Great Britain; their role, however, was to guard prisoners and maintain security and order.

Grenadians: Grenada had a militia and a force called the People's Revolutionary Army (PRA). The PRA consisted of 1,000 troops whose officers had taken over the country as the Revolutionary Military Council (RMC) headed by Gen. Hudson Austin. PRA military equipment was limited but included AK-47s, 80mm light antiaircraft weapons, rocket launchers, armored personnel carriers from the Soviet Union, steel helmets, and some guns left over from the British and World War II.

Cubans: There were about 700 Cuban construction workers on Grenada; they proved to have a considerable arsenal of arms and at least some had military training. There were also some 40 Cuban military advisers on Grenada. Although all the Cubans were reported to be under orders from Havana never to surrender and many did put up considerable resistance, gradually most of the Cubans had little choice but to give up.

GEOGRAPHIC AND STRATEGIC CONSIDERATIONS

The nation of Grenada is actually composed of the main island, Grenada, and several still smaller islands; altogether, they have an area of 133 square miles and a population of 110,000. Located some 90 miles north of Trinidad and the coast of Venezuela, Grenada did not have any major economic or strategic importance. Its only products were sugar, cocoa, bananas, nutmeg, and mace; although the last two spices were valuable cash-crops, they hardly had strategic importance. But in the eyes of the Reagan administration, a move toward Communism of even one

of the smallest nations in the Western Hemisphere represented an unacceptable development. In particular, if a Communist government in Grenada allowed the Soviet Union to gain a foothold in the region of the Caribbean and Central America, it would be perceived as a direct threat to the interests of the United States.

BATTLES AND CAMPAIGNS

October 21, 1983: Just after midnight, two U.S. Navy task forces, the carrier battle group led by the USS *Independence* and the amphibious assault group led by the USS *Guam*, were ordered to turn back from their course to the Mediterranean and head for Grenada.

October 24, 1983: The two U.S. Navy forces were near the Caribbean island of Barbados. Vice Adm. Joseph Metcalf III of the U.S. Atlantic Fleet, who along with 37 of his staff had been flown in to the *Guam*, was placed in command of the forthcoming invasion.

October 25, 1983: Just before dawn, 26 members of the U.S. Navy SEALS, carried by Black Hawk helicopters, were dropped into the sea near St. George's, Grenada, the capital, and made their way to Government House. (Four SEALS drowned as they attempted the early-morning landing.) Their mission was to protect and evacuate Governor-General Sir Paul Scoon. Although they got into the building, they were soon trapped by Soviet armored personnel carriers driven by Cubans. At the same time, a second group of SEALS secured Radio Grenada.

Simultaneous with the SEALS' operation, about 600 marines from the assault ship *Guam* came in on helicopters at Pearl Airport on the northeastern coast. Meeting little resistance from the Grenadian soldiers, who surrendered quickly, the marines secured the airport within two hours.

About a half hour after those two operations (that is, about 6 A.M.), 500 U.S. Rangers, flown directly from Savannah, Georgia, by C-130 Hercules transport planes, parachuted onto the new airport at Port Salines. They were forced to jump from the relatively low altitude of 500 feet because of the unexpectedly heavy machine-gun and antiaircraft fire from the Grenadians and Cubans defending the airport. By 7:15 A.M., the Rangers had secured the airport and soon they were being reinforced by more Rangers brought

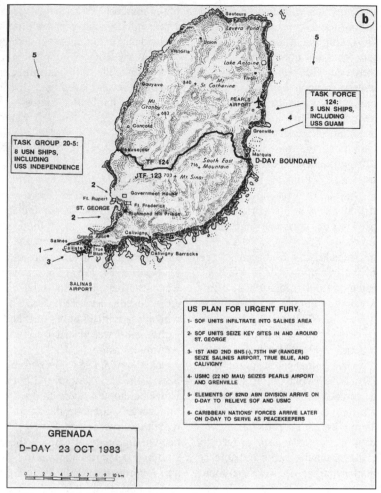

This map of the island of Grenada shows the sites designated by the U.S. military for seizing during the Grenada Intervention.

in by helicopters. In taking the airport, several Rangers were wounded, and some 20 Cubans were killed; about 200 Cubans surrendered, but more than 400 Cubans retreated into the surrounding area.

During those early hours, U.S. Navy planes bombed a military complex at Fort Frederick on the edge of St. George's and hit a mental hospital that was part of the fort. The exact number of patients killed was disputed, but the official U.S. figure was 18 killed. U.S. forces claimed the PRA had been inside the building and had fired on the Americans; not knowing it was a hospital, the Americans had called in an air strike.

By about 9 A.M., the runway at Port Salines airport was clear and the Rangers had secured the True Blue medical campus located just east of the Port Salines airport runway; medical students, meanwhile, had set up a field hospital to treat the wounded American, Cuban, and Grenadian soldiers.

By 11 A.M., some 300 members of the several cooperating Caribbean islands' police and defense forces were flown in, to be ready to perform security details when needed.

At 2:50 P.M., 750 soldiers from the 82nd Airborne Division, flown from Fort Bragg, North Carolina, landed at the Port Salines airport. As the troops got off the plane, Cuban resistance reemerged, and two U.S. soldiers were killed. Air support from the carrier *Independence* was used to drive the Cubans back.

When word reached the commander of the operation that the Rangers and the 82nd Airborne Division troops were unable to take over St. George's as expected, more Marines were sent in. At 7 P.M., about 250 marines with tanks and armored personnel carriers went ashore north of St. George's. Their goal was to relieve the SEALS trapped in Government House with Sir Paul Scoon and to take the PRA's headquarters at Fort Frederick and a prison at Richmond Hill. The U.S. troops met surprisingly heavy resistance from the Grenadian army and Cuban forces; with nightfall, the fighting halted and the U.S. command admitted that its forces had yet to take all of Grenada.

October 26, 1983: Heavy gunfire from the PRA had kept the SEALS and Governor General Scoon pinned down at Government House all night. At about 7:15 A.M, U.S. Marines stormed the area and drove off the Grenadians. Scoon was helicoptered to the USS *Guam.*

Early in the afternoon, U.S. troops from Port Salines airport moved toward St. George's about 5 miles to the north. Somewhat unexpectedly, they met resistance from the PRA and the Cubans. When the U.S. troops arrived at the Grand Anse Campus of St. George's Medical School, about half way to St. George's, they found that the Grenadian military and the Cubans had surrounded the campus and that several hundred American medical students were trapped there. The defenders had set up gun emplacements on the tops of adjacent hotels to fire on American helicopters that might try to land. The assault came at 4:30, with helicopters carrying Rangers accompanied by attack planes from the carrier *Independence;* the barrage laid down by the attack planes destroyed the hotels and gun emplacements in 15 minutes. The helicopters landed, and by early evening, the students were airlifted to the Point Salines airport, where C-141s airlifted them to safety.

Meanwhile, fighting in and around St. George's had resumed, in particular at Fort Frederick and Richmond Hill east of the capital. By evening, the U.S. forces had taken Fort Frederick but scattered resistance continued in the area around St. George's.

At midday, troops from the US Army's 82nd Airborne Division set out from the Point Salines airport to take the military barracks at Calivigny on the eastern coast of the island about 6 miles east of the airport. On their way there, they overran a military supply depot at Frequente, where they found small arms and evidence of Cuba's plans for more ambitious military activities on Grenada. Troops participating in the assault at Frequente came under fire from one of their own U.S. Navy attack planes; 16 paratroopers were wounded (one of whom died shortly thereafter). Meanwhile, in the assault at the Calivigny Barracks, three U.S. helicopters crashed, killing four Rangers.

October 27, 1983: Fighting continued at several key points throughout most of the day. The U.S. Marines captured Fort Rupert, on the edge of St. George's, site of Maurice Bishop's execution.

By the end of the day, the commander of the Atlantic Fleet reported that "all major military objectives on the island were secured." That officially marked the end of the Grenada Intervention. In fact, sporadic fighting continued for several days.

The Pentagon released videotapes purporting to show several warehouses full of Soviet-made arms and ammunition that had been seized earlier that day.

November 1, 1983: A small force of U.S. Marines went ashore on Carriacou, an islet dependency just north of Grenada. They met no resistance but reported finding a stock of small arms stored there.

November 2, 1983: The two U.S. Navy groups, with all surviving and non-wounded personnel, set sail for Spain and Lebanon.

HOME FRONT

October 17, 1983: Following news of a coup on Grenada and the arrest of Prime Minister Maurice Bishop, the U.S. Assistant Secretary of State for Inter-American Affairs formed a task force to plan the evacuation of the 1,000 U.S. citizens from Grenada.

October 19, 1983: With the announcement of the murder of Bishop and his entourage, the task force turned its attention to planning for a "nonpermissive evacuation." The State Department grew more concerned when inquiries to the Grenada coup leaders about the condition and evacuation of the Americans on Grenada were responded to "curtly."

October 20, 1983: Barbados prime minister Tom Adams, interviewed by ABC reporter Ted Koppel, said that there was great concern about

U.S. civilians who had been studying at a medical school on Grenada line up at Port Salines to be airlifted, even as the fighting was under way in October 1983. They are guarded by U.S. troops.

the events in Grenada and that West Indians hoped for military help from the United States.

October 25, 1983: At a 9 A.M press conference, President Reagan announced the invasion of Grenada by U.S. troops that morning.

October 28–November 1, 1983: The War Powers Resolution passed both houses of Congress; it authorized the president to commit U.S. troops for 60 days but required the withdrawal of U.S. troops after that time unless there was further authorization from Congress.

INTERNATIONAL DEVELOPMENTS

October 23, 1983: At a compound on the edge of the airport at Beirut, Lebanon, where U.S. Marines had been assigned since 1982, an Islamic terrorist drove a truck through the various barriers and into the building where some 300 marines and other U.S. service personnel were asleep. The truck was carrying explosives that demolished the building, killing 239 marines, 18 sailors, and 3 soldiers (and wounding 71 other U.S. personnel). Almost simultaneously, another truck crashed into a French paratroopers' bar-

racks 2 miles away; that explosion killed 58 and left 15 wounded. News of those disasters dominated the U.S. media for the next couple days so that the invasion of Grenada came as a double shock to Americans.

October 25–27, 1983: The 15-member United Nations Security Council met originally at 11:11 P.M. on the night of October 25 to debate the invasion. The vote to condemn the United States was 11 to 1, with 3 abstentions—Great Britain, Togo, and Zaire. The United States vetoed the resolution.

November 2, 1983: The United Nations General Assembly passed a resolution (108 to 9, with 27 abstentions) that called for an immediate end to the fighting in Grenada and withdrawal of all foreign troops. Voting in favor of U.S. military intervention were the Caribbean nations and Israel. Jeane Kirkpatrick, the U.S. ambassador to the UN, was prevented from giving a speech to the body by a parliamentary maneuver.

NEGOTIATIONS AND PEACE TREATY

There were no negotiations and no peace

treaty, but by the end of November, the United States committed immediate financial aid and long-term economic assistance to Grenada.

RESULTS OF THE WAR (Casualties, Costs, Consequences)

The casualties were highest among Grenadians, 45 of whom were killed and 337 of whom were wounded during the invasion; the death toll included an estimated 18 mental patients who died when American forces bombed a mental hospital in St. George's. In the fighting itself, 19 Americans were killed and about 150 were injured. Forty-five Cubans were killed and 67 were wounded.

The most reliable estimated cost of the Grenada Intervention to the United States was $75.5 million. That amount includes the loss of nine helicopters.

In the immediate aftermath of the Grenada Intervention, there could be no denying that most of the Grenadians enthusiastically welcomed the U.S. forces as their liberators. (Almost all the students of St. George's Medical School quoted in the media also expressed gratitude.) The last of the U.S. Marines and U.S. Rangers left on November 4; by mid-December, only some 300 U.S. Army Military Police and support troops were on Grenada; the last U.S. military personnel did not leave Grenada until June 1985. Some 400 members of the OECS police and defense forces performed various policing duties for several months until the Grenadians were able to take over.

Sir Paul Scoon assumed control as head of the interim government and oversaw new elections in December 1984. Bernard Coard, Gen. Hudson Austin, and 12 others most directly implicated in the deaths of Maurice Bishop and his supporters were tried; in December 1986, they were found guilty and sentenced to death, but their sentences were later commuted to life imprisonment. The new government tried to rebuild the economy, but it was not easy, as their chief sources of income—agricultural products such as cocoa and nutmeg—earned little in the international marketplace. Financial aid and loans from the United States, Great Britain, and the International Monetary Fund were necessary to help the island restore its economy and infrastructure. Gradually, the island did catch on as a tourist destination, both for cruise ships and hotel visitors; ironically, the airport, built by Cubans and with financing from various Communist nations, became what its builders claimed it would be—a tourist airport. (Its new terminal building was built with U.S. aid.) By the mid-1990s, Grenada was obtaining almost half its national income from tourism. St. George's University Medical School also continued to operate.

MILITARY INNOVATIONS, TACTICS, EQUIPMENT

The Grenada Intervention was the first combat use of the UH-60 Black Hawk armored helicopters, the most advanced, powerful, and versatile of the U.S. helicopters that had been developed in the aftermath of the Vietnam War.

Another new element in the operation was the Psychological Operations Battalion, whose job was to reassure Grenadian citizens of the humanitarian intentions of the United States and to help restore order. Their chief means for accomplishing that were carefully scripted audio tapes aired over Radio Free Grenada.

The major lesson in military strategy from the Grenada Intervention was that there was poor, indeed, almost nonexistent coordination and communication among the U.S. services involved. Although Vice Adm. Joseph Metcalf III was the nominal commander of the operation, neither he nor the other three service commanders had overall tactical authority. And lack of integrated radio communications precluded the ground forces from being able to call in naval gunfire. (One U.S. soldier used a local telephone to call his unit headquarters in the United States and call in air support.) That came about because of traditional "territorial" rivalries among the service branches and also because of an underestimation of the resistance that U.S. forces met on Grenada. The military went into the Grenada Intervention assuming the enemy would be such a pushover that there would be little or no need for such sophisticated measures as integrated radio communications.

LEGENDS AND TRIVIA

One of the surprises of the Grenada Intervention for most people was that Americans were attending medical school on the tiny island. **St.**

George's University School of Medicine on Grenada was founded in 1976 by Charles R. Modica, an entrepreneur from Long Island. Modica, rejected as a young man from medical schools in the United States, opened the school for students who could not get into U.S. medical schools. There were 1,500 enrolled students, mainly from the New York area, although at the time of the invasion, only 650 students were reported to be on Grenada. The remainder of the students were in their fifth semester on nearby St. Vincent's Island or in clinical training at hospitals in the United States or Great Britain.

Those medical professionals who knew of the existence of the school and several others in the Caribbean and in Mexico had long expressed concern about the quality of training doctors received there. The school had only a handful of resident professors, inadequate facilities and equipment, and was totally isolated from an academic and medical community. But its students were required to spend two years in a hospital gaining experience, and in 1984, nearly 80 percent of St. George's graduating students passed their qualifying exams when they returned to the United States.

NOTABLE PHRASES

This could be Ronald Reagan's "Falkland Islands' victory," signaling a welcome change in foreign policy. It is the first time in 20 years that we have tried to enforce the long-neglected Monroe Doctrine.

Sen. Steve Symms (R–Idaho) said that on October 25, 1983, after hearing that the Grenada Intervention was under way. The Monroe Doctrine was pronounced in a speech to Congress on December 2, 1823, by President James Monroe, in which he stated that countries of the "American continents" may not be colonized or subjugated by European powers. The "Falkland Islands victory" referred to the fact that British prime minister Margaret Thatcher enhanced her reputation as a decisive leader when in 1982 she sent a British force to take back the Falkland Islands from Argentina.

A brutal group of leftist thugs.

At the impromptu news conference President

Ronald Reagan held just after 9 A.M. on October 25, 1983, at which he announced that the Grenada invasion was under way, that is how he characterized the revolutionaries who had seized power on Grenada and assassinated Maurice Bishop.

To be perfectly truthful, his policy scares me. We can't go the way of gunboat diplomacy. His policy is wrong. His policy is frightening.

On October 28, 1983, Speaker of the House Thomas P. "Tip" O'Neill (D–Mass.) made that assessment of President Ronald Reagan's decision to invade Grenada. *Gunboat diplomacy*—the display of military force for political advantage over weaker powers—was a term associated by many Americans with Britain's method of controlling its large colonial empire. In fact, its first use in print (1927) was in the United States, and neither at that time nor in subsequent allusions referred specifically to the British.

It should not be difficult for any peoples to discern the difference between the force that liberates captive people from terror and the force that imposes terror on captive people.

U.S. Ambassador Jeane Kirkpatrick said that on October 27, 1983, when she addressed the United Nations Security Council. Exasperated with some members of the council who were protesting the U.S. action and comparing it to other recent military actions, she drew a contrast between the U.S. invasion of Grenada and the Soviet Union invasion of Afghanistan . The Security Council voted to censure the United States, but Kirkpatrick vetoed the resolution.

HISTORICAL PERSPECTIVES AND CONTROVERSIES

What made the U.S. invasion of Grenada so controversial?

There were several elements about the Grenada Intervention that were controversial at the time and have never been fully resolved to everyone's satisfaction. First, the United States invaded a Commonwealth nation, one that still had a direct tie with Great Britain. According to reports in the *New York Times*, Prime Minister Margaret Thatcher had urged President Reagan to reconsider his plans to invade Grenada. Her foreign secretary, who the day before the invasion assured the House of Commons that the United States had no plans to invade Grenada, was grilled for 45 minutes by Parliament following the news that there had been an invasion; Queen Elizabeth, on learning of the invasion, indicated her displeasure with events by canceling her regular Thursday meeting with Mrs. Thatcher. Heads of state in France, West Germany, and Canada, as well as in the Soviet Union and in other Communist countries, all indicated their dismay with President Reagan's action.

Second, the legality of the attack was questioned not only by individual foreign governments but also by the United Nations and by the Organization of American States (OAS). Although the Organization of Eastern Caribbean States (OECS) had petitioned the United States for help pursuant to Article 8 of the OECS treaty, the United States was not a signatory to that treaty. The United States was, however, a signatory to the Treaty of the Organization of American States (1948), in which Article 15 reads: "No state or group of states has the right to intervene, directly or indirectly, for any reason whatever, in the internal or external affairs of any other state." At the time, most of the members of the OAS condemned the U.S. action, but no formal vote was taken.

Third, President Ronald Reagan said the invasion was necessary to rescue and evacuate the American medical students and tourists on the island. However, at least two chartered planes evacuated some U.S. tourists on Monday, October 24 (the day before the invasion), and there was reason to believe that the medical students could have been evacuated without incident. The chancellor of the St. George's University medical school was quoted in the *New York Times* as claiming that the students' safety had been assured by Grenada's new military rulers (although later he said he had been persuaded by the United States government that there had been more risk than he had realized). In any case, President Ronald Reagan and his spokespeople have been accused of exaggerating the number of medical students on Grenada and the potential risk to those students.

Was the U.S. government's restriction on news coverage justified?

For many, the most troubling issue left over from the Grenada Intervention, was the total clampdown by the U.S. government and military on the media's coverage of the episode. Reporters were barred from the island until October 27, when a select pool of 15 reporters were taken to the island under the supervision of military public relations officials. (One boat containing six reporters had set out from Barbados for Grenada on the day before the invasion; the reporters arrived on Grenada the next day, but because telephones and electricity were not operating, the reporters had no way to send their stories; they were taken aboard the USS *Guam* under the ruse of gaining access to phones and were held incommunicado for 18 hours.) Naval patrol boats were ordered to shoot at unauthorized boats attempting to land members of the press. And the Federal Communications Commission (FCC) warned ham radio operators that use of their radio equipment to broadcast news was in violation of their licenses because it constituted a commercial use; later, however, the FCC explained that it had simply wanted to keep certain frequencies open for a student at the St. George's Medical School who was sending out valuable information during the operation. Whatever the motives, the United States government exercised total control on the flow of information regarding Grenada.

CIVILIAN AND MILITARY BIOGRAPHIES

GRENADIANS

Austin, Hudson (1938–)—military leader: As a young man, Hudson Austin worked as a constable and prison guard while earning an engineering degree from a correspondence course from a school on Jamaica. He ended up in the People's Revolutionary Army, a part of the New Jewel Movement, and led it in the coup against Prime Minister Eric Gairy's government in 1979. Austin shifted his support to Bernard Coard, then led the bloody coup against Maurice Bishop's government in 1983. For a few days he headed the 16-member Revolutionary Military Council that replaced Bishop's government. He was not especially committed to any ideology but simply went along with those he realized would be in charge and would reward his services. He was arrested after the invasion and tried for his role in murdering Bishop; his death sentence was commuted to life imprisonment.

Bishop, Maurice (1944–1983)—prime minister: As a young man training as a lawyer in London, Maurice Bishop was said to have been influenced by the civil rights movement in the United States. Once he had taken power in 1979, he quickly clamped down on any dissenting voices. Although he led Grenada to associate with Cuba and the Soviet Union, there were signs that he was not a rigid Communist but was seeking a more moderate course for Grenada. In any case, he was assassinated by a faction within the New Jewel Movement that wanted to enforce closer ties to the Soviet Union.

Coard, Bernard (1944–)—revolutionary leader: Bernard Coard was a university-trained Marxist economist who taught at universities in Jamaica and Trinidad. In 1976 he helped found the New Jewel Movement (NJM) and entered Grenada's legislature. He became the deputy prime minister when the NJM seized power in 1979. He pushed the NJM to pursue policies that he felt Bishop wasn't taking seriously. After Bishop reneged on a plan to share power with him, Coard plotted with some of his allies and General Austin and in October 1983 led the coup that resulted in Bishop's murder. Coard tried to govern from behind the scenes during the next week before the U.S. invasion. Arrested by U.S. Marines on October 29, 1983, he was tried in Grenada and imprisoned for his role in the coup against Bishop; his death sentence was commuted to life imprisonment.

Gairy, Sir Eric (1922–) prime minister: Eric Gairy started out as a union organizer. He led Grenada to independence in 1974 and was its first prime minister. He was a spiritualist and believer in UFOs. He became increasingly despotic (claiming he had been divinely chosen to lead Grenada) and promised the masses economic gains that never materialized. In 1979, with the country in financial ruin and living conditions deteriorating, he was deposed by the New Jewel Movement led by Maurice Bishop. After the restoration of the democratic government, he returned in January 1984 and revived his party but never again held office.

Scoon, Sir Paul (1935–)—governor general: Sir Paul Scoon was a native Grenadian. He studied in England and Canada before returning

to Grenada in 1967 to become a teacher. He was appointed (1978) governor general, the figurehead link in the formal relationship between Grenada and the Queen of England. Associated with the administration of Sir Eric Gairy, he was placed under house arrest in the aftermath of the assassination of Maurice Bishop. After he was rescued and freed by U.S. forces, he was reinstalled as head of state and remained in charge of the interim government until formal elections were held in December 1984.

AMERICAN

Kirkpatrick, Jeane (1926–)—U.S. ambassador to the United Nations: Jeane Kirkpatrick was a professor of political science at Georgetown University. She was known for her outspoken, decisive, and often acid comments on world affairs. She was appointed by President Ronald Reagan as the first female U.S. ambassador to the United Nations. Among her best known statements was her distinction between Communist "totalitarian" dictatorships and right-wing "authoritarian" governments, the latter of which, she insisted, were deserving of U.S. support. She was a staunch defender of the U.S. action in Grenada on the floor of the United Nations.

FURTHER READING

Beck, Robert J. *The Grenada Invasion: Poltics, Law, and Foreign Policy Decisionmaking*. Boulder, Colo.: Westview Press, 1993.

Kirkpatrick, Jeane J. "The U.S. Action in Grenada: Its Context and Its Meaning." *Central America and the Reagan Doctrine*. Edited by Walter F. Hahn. 137–151. Washington, D.C.: United States Strategic Institute, 1987.

O'Shaughnessy, Hugh. *Grenada: An Eyewitness Account of the U.S. Invasion and the Caribbean History that Provoked It*. New York: Dodd, Mead & Company, 1984.

Payne, Anthony, Paul Sutton, and Tony Thorndike. *Grenada: Revolution and Invasion*. New York: St. Martin's Press, 1984.

PANAMA INVASION

DATES OF WAR

December 20, 1989–January 3, 1990

ALTERNATE NAMES

Operation Just Cause

SIGNIFICANCE

The Panama Invasion was part of a long-standing tradition of sending U.S. military forces into Caribbean and Central American countries to preserve conditions or change them in the best interests of the Western Hemisphere—as perceived by the United States. That particular episode, however, had an extraordinary twist, namely, the goal of arresting a petty dictator who was under indictment in U.S. federal court for drug trafficking. Behind that stated reason for the military operation, however, lay a history of tangled dealings by the United States with that same dictator, which led many to question U.S. motives and conduct in that action.

BACKGROUND

The United States and Panama had always had a special relationship. In fact, it was the United States' determination to build a canal across the Isthmus of Panama that brought about the birth of Panama as a nation. At the outset of the 20th century, the United States began negotiating with Colombia to build a canal through the Isthmus of Panama, at that time a province of Colombia. When Colombia refused to cede sovereignty over the canal to the United States, President Theodore Roosevelt let it be known to certain people in Panama that the United States would support a move for Panamanian independence. Roosevelt sent three U.S. Navy ships to Panama. The threat of U.S. military intervention prevented Colombia from sending in its army, and Panamanians carried out a revolution on November 3–4, 1903. By November 18, U.S Secretary of State John Hay and Philippe Buneau-Varilla, the Pana-

manian ambassador to the United States who was also a lobbyist for the French company that wanted to sell its rights to the canal, signed a treaty that set up the Canal Zone. That was a strip of land 5 miles wide on either side of the planned 40-mile canal; the treaty also granted the United States exclusive control over the Canal Zone in perpetuity. The United States agreed to pay a lump sum of $10 million to Panama as well as an annual rent, which increased from $250,000 in 1913 to $2.3 million in 1979.

In 1950, negotiations began between Panama and the United States to modify the Hay–Bunau-Varilla Treaty and give Panama more responsibility for administering the Panama Canal as well as authority over the Canal Zone. In 1977, voters in Panama approved two new treaties negotiated with representatives of the United States: the Panama Canal Treaty, which reorganized operation of the canal so that by the year 2000 Panama would assume complete legal control; and the Panama Canal Neutrality Treaty, which guaranteed the canal's neutrality after the year 2000. The treaties, signed by President Jimmy Carter and Panama's president, Gen. Omar Torrijos Herrera, were ratified by the U.S. Senate in 1978. In 1979, the process under which the United States was to gradually withdraw from Panama began; the first step was the return of about 65 percent of the former Canal Zone to Panamanian jurisdiction, including the railway, 11 of 14 U.S. military bases, and the ports.

In 1981, Gen. Omar Torrijos Herrera, who was an authoritarian but popular leader of Panama, died in an airplane crash. Gen. Manuel Antonio Noriega, who had directed G-2, the intelligence arm of Panama's military, took over as head of the army and changed its name from the National Guard to the Panama Defense Force (PDF). He was also the leader of the Revolutionary Democratic Party, which through the military controlled the government. Although the 1984 Panamanian presidential elections were undoubtedly fixed by Noriega's people to guarantee the election of Nicolas Ardito Barletta, a former economist at the World Bank, President Ronald Reagan

Reagan quickly signaled his approval with a congratulatory phone call. The United States was hopeful that the economist would help Panama reverse its economic downturn.

Over the following four years, however, not only did Panama's economy fail to improve, but relations between the United States and Panama deteriorated. In part, the latter problem was due to the nature of the relationship between the United States and General Noriega, who had been recruited as a U.S. intelligence agent while still a young military student in the 1960s. He had received advanced training at U.S. military schools in Panama and in the United States, and by 1970, he had been put on the payroll of the U.S. Central Intelligence Agency (CIA); he was removed from the CIA payroll in 1977 but restored in 1981. During the years Noriega worked for the CIA, he provided information to the U.S. intelligence community on several areas of great concern, including Fidel Castro's Cuba, the Colombian drug cartel, and Central American revolutionary struggles. But it soon became clear that Noriega was serving as a double agent—that is, he was also helping Castro when he could, and he was personally profiting from the drug trade. By the mid-1980s, Noriega was clearly the person running Panama, and President Reagan's administration had become disenchanted with him; it cut aid to Panama by 85 percent and sent a top-level representative to Panama to warn Noriega to stay out of the drug trade; meanwhile, the U.S. Senate voted to investigate alleged links between the Panamanian Defense Force and drug trafficking.

In 1987, Panamanians opposed to Noriega's increasingly corrupt regime organized the *Cruzada Civilista* ("Civil Crusade"), which called for civil disobedience and a general strike, refusing to negotiate so long as Noriega was in power. In the crackdown on the *Civilistas*, a U.S. embassy official was arrested and held for several hours, and the only U.S.-civilian journalist in Panama was expelled. The U.S. Senate threatened sanctions if constitutional guarantees were not reinstated and suspended annual joint military maneuvers scheduled for 1988. Noriega declared a state of emergency, and Panamanians organized by his party stoned the U.S. Embassy and attacked U.S. banks with paint and rocks while PDF soldiers stood by and watched.

Then, on February 4, 1988, two federal grand juries, one in Miami, the other in Tampa, indicted General Noriega on drug trafficking charges. Noriega denied the charges and called for the expulsion of the Southern Command (SOUTHCOM), the U.S. military's organization in Panama. An attempt by the Panamanian president to oust Noriega was rebuffed by the PDF, which closed down opposition outlets, such as the newspaper *La Prensa*. In response to the increasing tensions, on March 3, 1988, the United States froze all Panamanian assets held in U.S. banks.

On March 16, 1988, a handful of anti-Noriega PDF officers staged a coup that was put down by loyal PDF soldiers. Anti-U.S. incidents proliferated and included a PDF takeover of a U.S.-owned striking flour mill. By March 1989, SOUTHCOM had documented more than 55 cases of harassment of U.S. military and civilians by the PDF, ranging in seriousness from stopping school buses carrying American children to armed attacks on U.S. Marines. The United States increased its economic sanctions by banning all payments to the Panamanian government and canceling purchases of sugar from Panama.

On May 7, 1989, Panama held national elections, and when it was clear that General Noriega's candidate, Carlos Duque, had lost to Guillermo Endara, Noriega's PDF raided the vote-counting centers, changed the voting returns, and announced that Duque had won. For several days after the election, demonstrators protesting the fraud were attacked by PDF squads and the Noriega-subsidized Dignity Battalions, bands of young civilians organized to show "popular" support for General Noriega. On May 9, General Noriega announced that the elections were annulled because of "obstruction by foreigners" (namely, Americans). In the demonstration on May 10, the Dignity Battalions savagely attacked Endara and one of his two vice presidential candidates, Amador Ford, and killed one of Ford's bodyguards.

In response, President George Bush sent an additional 2,000 troops to the SOUTHCOM bases, recalled the U.S. ambassador, and urged all U.S. civilians to return to the United States until the situation was stabilized. President Bush also called on the PDF to oust Noriega, but stopped short of allowing U.S. troops to assist in any coup attempt. Some U.S. civilian dependents returned to the United States, and those living off-base were ordered to move onto U.S.

military installations. Between May and August, representatives of the Organization of American States tried to negotiate with Noriega to end the crisis but without success.

On October 3, 1989, 240 PDF soldiers attempted another coup and actually had Noriega under arrest for several hours. The United States did nothing, and Noriega was able to call for rescue by his most loyal troops, the elite Battalion 2000. (Later, the United States admitted that the U.S. Army commander in Panama had been authorized to take custody of Noriega if he could do so without an overt use of U.S. forces.) On December 15, Noriega's National Assembly of Representatives voted him "maximum leader of the struggle for national liberation" and approved a resolution declaring the Republic of Panama to be in a "state of war with the United States" as a result of U.S. aggressions, specifically the economic sanctions.

CAUSES OF THE WAR

By December 15, the United States and Panama were moving swiftly on a collision course. On December 16, four unarmed and off-duty U.S. officers in a private car were stopped at a roadblock by PDF guards. When the guards began to force the Americans out of the car, they tried to drive off; the guards opened fire and killed one of the Americans, Marine Lt. Robert Paz, and wounded another. Shortly afterward, the PDF took into custody two Americans who had witnessed the incident, U.S. Navy lieutenant Adam J. Curtis and his wife, Bonnie Curtis. They were held for about four hours, during which time the lieutenant was beaten and threatened with death, and his wife was molested. They were eventually released early on the morning of December 17. On December 18, in yet another incident, a U.S. Army officer shot and wounded a Panamanian military policeman; the officer said that he thought the policeman was pulling a weapon on him.

Immediately after the incident at the roadblock on December 16, U.S. troops in Panama were put on maximum alert. On December 17, President George Bush met with his security advisers and decided to mobilize the U.S. troops in Panama and send reinforcements. On December 18, President Bush at a news conference called the killing of Lieutenant Paz "an enormous outrage" but

refused to say whether he was considering a military response, saying only that "presidents have options."

PREPARATIONS FOR WAR

The United States began expressly preparing for a military action against Panama in September 1989. The U.S. military had operational plans for various contingencies around the globe; the U.S. military had developed three possible operations to intervene in Panama, but it finally decided to go with the one called "Blue Spoon," which called for taking Noriega and eliminating the PDF. It involved five task forces from Fort Lewis in Washington State, Fort Ord in California, Fort Polk in Louisiana, Forts Benning and Stewart in Georgia, and Fort Bragg in North Carolina. Serious and focused planning by high-ranking U.S. officers continued through the autumn of 1989 and included such actions as transporting helicopters and tanks in C-5A Galaxy cargo planes and landing them at night at U.S. bases in Panama. By late November, the U.S. Army and Air Force units that would carry out the actual operation were rehearsing on several bases in the United States. At a secret midday meeting, Sunday, December 17, 1989, Gen. Colin Powell and the Joint Chiefs of Staff committed to the final plan of attack in Panama. That afternoon, General Powell presented the plan to President George Bush and his top civilian advisers; after Bush questioned Powell on various details, he simply said, "OK, let's do it." It was also at that time that the name Blue Spoon was changed to Operation Just Cause.

Because the responsibility for maintaining the neutrality of the Panama Canal was being transferred from the United States to the Republic of Panama, between 1982 and 1987, the United States gave more than $105 million in aid and credit to the Panamanian military; much of its training was conducted by the U.S. military. Gen. Manuel Noriega had militarized segments of the population by forming the Dignity Battalions, and he could count on two elite PDF units, the Battalion 2000 and *Machos del Monte*, but there is no indication that he had prepared any of his forces specifically for an invasion. And although there were rumors throughout Panama City hours before the invasion that it was imminent, Noriega took no steps to be on the alert.

DECLARATION OF WAR

President George Bush did not ask Congress to make a formal declaration of war but simply gave reasons why he ordered the action: (1) to capture Manuel Noriega and bring him to the United States to stand trial in a federal court, (2) to protect U.S. citizens who were in danger, (3) to maintain the integrity and neutrality of the Panama Canal, and (4) to restore democracy to Panama. President Bush also suggested that he was responding to a declaration of war by Noriega; by that, Bush meant the December 15 resolution by the Panamanian National Assembly, which most regarded as nothing more than bluster.

COMBATANTS

Americans: The United States had 14 military bases in the Panama Canal Zone, 11 of which had been turned over to Panama in 1979 as a result of the 1977 treaties. On the remaining three U.S. bases were stationed 12,000 personnel, most of them in the U.S. Army, but there were also some Air Force, Marine, and Navy units. Another 15,000 military personnel participated in the Panama Invasion: in addition to regular infantry troops, those included three battalions of the U.S. Army's special Rangers, various units of the Air Force, a Marine battalion, SEALs and other special forces of the Navy, and a parachute brigade of the 82nd Airborne Division.

Panamanians: The Panamanian Defense Force (PDF) numbered about 15,000 men, many of them (especially the officers) trained by the U.S. military. Its land forces included two combat battalions and eight light infantry companies. The navy had 400 personnel, with about 17 ships: 2 coast guard cutters, 2 patrol boats, and 13 launches. The air force had a staff of 500 and 20 planes: 4 armed transport craft, 8 transport planes, and 8 light planes. The Panamanian navy and air force played no role.

The Dignity Battalions were organized by Noriega in the early 1980s; ostensibly a home guard, they were armed by Noriega and allowed to do dirty work that he didn't want done by uniformed troops. In 1988, Noriega drafted civil servants to serve in the Dignity Battalions, but the ones who took to the streets were often criminals and misfits who at times behaved like little more than thugs. Their exact number was not known, but those who resisted U.S. troops were estimated at about 3,000.

GEOGRAPHIC AND STRATEGIC CONSIDERATIONS

Since 1914, when the Panama Canal opened, the isthmus of Panama had provided an irreplaceable link in international commerce, specifically between the Atlantic and Pacific, the West and East. It also had given the United States and its allies a tremendous advantage in two world wars. (In recent years, there have been increasing numbers of large ships that cannot get through the canal; there are plans to renovate the canal so that it can accommodate large ships.) Meanwhile, although the United States was in the process of transferring control of the canal to Panama, still had responsibility for ensuring the canal's neutrality and security. In any major war or action by terrorists, shutting down the Panama Canal would have a disastrous impact; there was also the possibility, although it was never actually threatened, that Gen. Manuel Noriega might have tried to take over and shut down the canal (see Historical Perspectives and Controversies, p. 698). Beyond that understandable interest in the canal, the United States had a legitimate concern over Noriega's and Panama's role in the traffic of illegal drugs into the United States. Even allowing for some exaggeration in the charges made by the Bush administration, it appears that Noriega did at least allow the drug trade and certainly profited from it.

BATTLES AND CAMPAIGNS

December 19, 1989: Guillermo Endara and the two men who had allegedly been elected as his vice presidents in the disputed May 1989 election, Amador Ford and Ricardo Arias Calderon, were invited to dinner at the Howard Air Force Base on the edge of Panama City. About 8:30 P.M., they were informed that the United States was about to invade Panama and seize Noriega and that they would be given the full support of the United States if they agreed to take over the government. They accepted and, after being sworn in, remained on the base for the next 24 hours.

December 20–21, 1989: The operations in Panama were divided among several task forces,

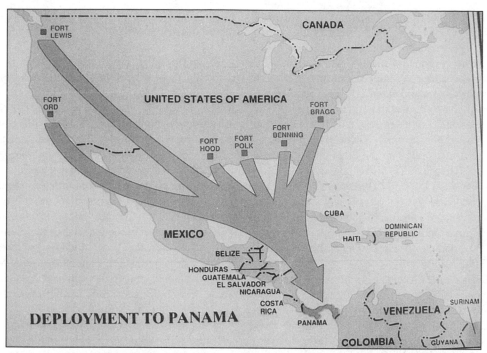

This map shows the home bases of the various U.S. troops that were deployed to join troops already in Panama in capturing Gen. Manuel Noriega. The first 9,000 soldiers either parachuted in or were flown in during the first hours of December 20, 1989, and thousands more were brought in during the next few weeks.

all scheduled to go into action at 12:45 A.M on December 20th. The main task forces and their missions were as follows:

Task Force White. That was a force of SEALs (sea-air-land), the U.S. Navy's elite commando unit. Its main mission was to deny the Panamanian military the use of its ships in the harbor of Balboa and to deny Noriega the use of his personal jet at Paitilla Airport. The SEALs succeeded in both missions. They mined various ships and by 2 A.M. succeeded in disabling them by explosions. But the SEALs who attacked the airport met unexpectedly heavy resistance by PDF forces at the airport who went on the alert when they heard the sounds of the fighting that broke out elsewhere in Panama City; although the SEALs accomplished their mission, four of them were killed.

Task Force Black. Its mission was to secure the Pacora River bridge northeast of Panama City to prevent Noriega's elite and most loyal troops, Battalion 2000, from coming to his aid. When the U.S. forces arrived at the bridge in Black Hawk helicopters about 12:45 A.M., a PDF convoy was also approaching the bridge. The U.S. forces called in AC-130 Spectre gunships, which destroyed the first trucks of the convoy. By 3 A.M., Task Force Black had secured the bridge and stopped the PDF forces from crossing; but after interrogating prisoners, the Americans learned that most of the Battalion 2000 soldiers had been assigned to Panama City the night before.

Task Force Red. That force's mission was to secure the Tocumen Military Airport, part of the Torrijos International Airport outside Panama City. The job was assigned to the 75th Rangers, which made an airborne assault and quickly secured the airport. That allowed troops of the 82nd Airborne Division to drop onto the airport 45 minutes later. Unbeknownst to the Rangers, Noriega had been at an officers' club on the edge of the airport; at the first sound of airplanes and gunfire, he jumped into a car and sped back toward Panama City. Meanwhile, some PDF soldiers had seized two young American women at the Torrijos Airport; they held them hostage until surrendering about 4 A.M. After some scattered resistance around the airports, they were declared secure about 6 A.M.

Task Force Pacific. Its mission was to seize

the PDF installations at Panama Viejo, Tinajitas, and Fort Cimmaron. The mission was assigned to three regiments from the 82nd Airborne, based at Fort Bragg, North Carolina. After a three-hour delay caused by a winter storm, the task force flew to Panama and about 2:15 A.M. began dropping on the Tocumen and Torrijos airfields. (Its vehicles and heavy equipment had been dropped ahead of the task force.) There, the U.S. forces boarded helicopters for the direct attacks on the several barracks. They met considerable resistance; it was 12 noon on December 21 before the Panama Viejo installation was secured; Tinajitas was not secured until 2:30 A.M. on December 21. Fort Cimarron was attacked at noon on December 20, and at 7:30 A.M. on December 21, it was declared secure.

Task Force Atlantic. As its name suggests, the goals of Task Force Atlantic were on the Atlantic and Caribbean sides of the canal. The task force had numerous missions, among the most important were to isolate Colon, the canal's port city; secure the vital Gatun Locks of the canal; neutralize the Panamanian marine troops at the port of Coco Solo; and capture the prison at Gamboa, midway across the isthmus, and release the anti-Noriega prisoners. The missions were assigned to units of the 82nd Airborne Division and the 7th Infantry Division. Capturing the installation at Coco Solo proved especially difficult; it was four hours before the installation was declared secure. The assault on the prison was carried out by combined amphibious and helicopter units; after considerable resistance, the prison was finally secured at 6 A.M.

Task Force Semper Fidelis. Its first mission was to block the western approaches to Panama City via the Bridge of the Americas and to protect Howard Air Force Base; other tasks included rounding up members of the PDF and Dignity Battalions. Units of the Marines, Army Engineers, and military police were assigned to that Task Force, which carried out its various tasks starting at 1 A.M. on December 20 and lasting over the course of several days.

Task Force Bayonet. That was the major task force of the Panama Invasion. Its first mission was to defend the area of Panama City, where the U.S. Southern Command and many U.S. civilians were located; that was essentially a defensive operation, and although U.S. troops came under fire from some PDF soldiers, they easily accomplished their goal. The second mission was to attack and neutralize La Comandancia, Noriega's headquarters, a compound of 15 buildings in the El Chorrillo district of Panama City. It turned out to be the most hard-fought (and controversial) action of Operation Just Cause. It involved units of the 5th and 6th Infantry Divisions, the 82nd Airborne Division, and the Marines. Most units moved into action in M-113 armored personnel carriers, light armored vehicles, and Sheridan tanks. As the armored units converged from several starting points and moved into the streets of El Chorrillo, a crowded, mostly poor residential section of Panama City, they met heavy fire from PDF troops and members of the Dignity Battalions, who had fanned out into the homes and buildings of the district. The U.S. forces were backed up by Apache assault helicopters and AC-130 Spectre gunships. In the fierce battle that ensued, the old wooden houses of the district caught fire and before La Comandancia was secured, some 50 acres and nearly 3,000 buildings were burned or bombed into rubble. Some blamed the U.S. forces entirely; others claimed that the PDF and Dignity Battalions set the fires. In any case, it was about 6 A.M. before La Comandancia was surrounded, but it had still not been taken by nightfall. The final assault began about 2 P.M. on December 21, and it was 5 P.M. before La Comandancia was finally declared secure.

December 20–21, 1989: About 6 P.M. on December 20, the U.S. forces were informed that PDF soldiers had seized about 29 Americans at the Marriott Hotel in downtown Panama City and were holding them hostage. A relief force set out about 10 P.M. and met considerable PDF resistance along the way. By about 11:30 P.M., U.S. forces had freed all the hostages—who numbered 106, of many nationalities. The PDF soldiers fled the hotel.

December 20–22, 1989: Some PDF soldiers sent a boat to the island of Tupu in the San Blas group off the Atlantic coast of the Panama Canal, where the Smithsonian Institution maintained a research institute. The PDF seized 11 research scientists and took them to the mainland, where they marched them overland some 13 miles to a remote schoolhouse. But the PDF soldiers lost interest and abandoned the scientists there; they were rescued by helicopter on December 22.

December 21, 1989: The main resistance had

been wiped out by the end of December 20, but scattered resistance continued in many places, and sections of Panama City remained in the hands of the PDF. Many PDF soldiers had long since shed their uniforms and were operating in civilian clothes alongside members of the Dignity Battalion. In parts of Panama, pro- and anti-Noriega Panamanian soldiers were shooting at each other. With Noriega still at large, a $1 million reward for information leading to his capture was offered by the U.S. government. (By that time, Noriega was hiding in the apartment on the edge of Panama City owned by the sister-in-law of his private secretary.) In Panama City, looters ransacked shops while U.S. troops stood by, under orders not to interfere.

December 29, 1989: Acknowledging that its forces had met more resistance than anticipated, the United States sent an additional 2,000 soldiers to support the ground effort. Snipers continued hit-and-run attacks that threatened to turn the invasion into a guerrilla war. Pro-Noriega PDF soldiers still had control in sections of northwest Panama.

The new Endara government dissolved the PDF and established a police force to take its place. Panamanian citizens set up vigilante groups to protect their neighborhoods from looters. The U.S. military claimed it had made significant gains in controlling the random violence in Panama.

February 13, 1990: The last of the invasion troops were withdrawn from Panama, leaving the U.S. military presence in Panama at its pre-invasion levels.

HOME FRONT

December 19, 1989: Starting about 6 P.M., President George Bush called a few Congressional leaders to inform them that the military operation in Panama was imminent.

December 20, 1989: Staying up until 4 A.M. to remain informed of events in Panama, President Bush continued to phone several Congressmen to alert them of the invasion. He also called British prime minister Margaret Thatcher to inform her of the invasion, to which Mrs. Thatcher gave her full endorsement. Meanwhile, members of the Bush administration phoned and cabled leaders of several countries around the world to inform them of the invasion, so that they would

not first hear about it from secondary sources.

At 7 A.M., President Bush addressed the American people on television to inform them of the invasion.

INTERNATIONAL DEVELOPMENTS

December 20, 1989: The Panama Canal was closed for the first time in its history because of the fighting under way in Panama and concern for the safety of ships using the canal.

December 22, 1989: The Organization of American States, by a vote of 20-1 (the United States being the sole dissenter), adopted a resolution "to deeply regret the military intervention in Panama" and "to urge the immediate cessation of hostilities and bloodshed."

January 18, 1990: The European Parliament, meeting in Strasbourg, France, condemned the Panama Invasion as a "flagrant violation of the sovereignty and integrity of an independent state."

NEGOTIATIONS AND PEACE TREATY

December 24, 1989: After arrangements had been made by Gen. Manuel Noriega's associates with the Vatican's papal nuncio in Panama, Monsignor Sebastian Laboa, Noriega drove to a Dairy Queen on the edge of Panama City and then was taken to the Vatican embassy, where he was given asylum. The U.S. authorities were soon informed and immediately surrounded the Vatican embassy with troops.

December 25, 1989–January 3, 1990: While U.S. authorities negotiated with the papal nuncio (who made it clear that he expected Noriega to surrender eventually without any need for force), U.S. troops outside began to broadcast loud rock music in an effort to wear him down psychologically (see Songs, pp. 697-698).

January 3–4, 1990: Noriega left the Vatican embassy and was escorted by U.S. Delta Force soldiers to the Howard Air Force Base in Panama City. There, he was arrested by U.S. Drug Enforcement Agency officials on charges of drug trafficking and on January 4, was flown to Miami (see Results of the War, p. 696).

There were no further negotiations and no peace treaty that came out of the Panama Invasion. Although all the basic treaties involving the turnover of the canal to Panama remained in effect, there were discussions to allow the United States to maintain a military presence in Panama after the year 2000 to ensure the security of the Panama Canal.

RESULTS OF THE WAR (Casualties, Costs, Consequences)

As a result of the Panama Invasion, 23 U.S. soldiers died, 324 were wounded, and 3 U.S. civilians were killed. According to the Pentagon, 127 PDF soldiers were killed, and 66 were wounded; some students of the invasion regard those figures as low. SOUTHCOM initially reported only 84 Panamanian civilians killed, then increased that to 202 (with many hundreds more wounded). However, even that figure was widely disputed. The Catholic Church in Panama said 655 Panamanians were killed and some 2,000 injured. Former United States Attorney General Ramsey Clark, who headed the independent (but openly critical) Commission of Inquiry on the United States Invasion of Panama, claimed there were at least 3,000 civilian deaths, but America Watch, a more detached, professional organization, counted 300. The most reasonable estimates now converge at about 500 Panamanian civilian deaths.

On June 18, 1990, a U.S. Government Accounting Office (GAO) report tallied the U.S. costs of the invasion at $163.6 million, a figure that does not include the inevitable secondary costs that follow such an action (such as veterans' medical expenses), although it did cover the period from December 20, 1989 through January 31, 1990. President George Bush promised Panama $1 billion in aid to rebuild its shattered economy and infrastructure, but less than half that amount was ever actually paid.

The full cost to Panama has never been calculated, but among other costs were the loss of some 3,000 homes and buildings and the displacement of some 15,000 residents; this has been estimated to have cost some $100 million. Estimates of the cost to the shops and business community of Panama City due to the looters range from $325 million to $1 billion. The economic sanctions in effect against Panama since 1987 were extremely costly, and unemployment levels continued to rise, as many businesses did not reopen. The best estimate of the total cost of the invasion to Panama runs to $2 billion.

The consequences of that brief military operation were relatively well defined. After Gen. Manuel Noriega was arrested and brought to Florida, he was held in prison until his trial in a federal court in Florida that began in December 1991. Although the prosecution proved its case that Noriega had participated in drug trafficking, the trial revealed some of the less savory ways that the U.S. government had behaved over the years in its dealings with Noriega. In March 1992, Noriega was found guilty of drug trafficking and money laundering, and in July 1992, was sentenced to 40 years in U.S. prison. To that extent, one of the invasion's main missions was accomplished, but the broader goal of stopping drug traffic from Central America was not even approached.

Another of the announced goals was the "restoration of democracy" in Panama. Many observers raise the question of whether Panama had ever experienced genuine democracy. However, the United States did install a civilian administration and remove the Panamanian military from the government. In the years that followed, however, the civilian administrations were not able to do much for Panama's economy or at least for the mass of poor Panamanians, and the old charges of corruption and cronyism continued. In general, there was resentment among many of Panama's people for the way the United States brought so much military force to bear on their country; some based their objections on the actuality of the destruction and disruption; others, more on the principle of interference in a foreign nation.

MILITARY INNOVATIONS, TACTICS, EQUIPMENT

The nature of the tightly focused and briefly executed Panama Invasion was such that there was no need to employ any new equipment or tactics. However, the Air Force made the first operational use of its new F-117A Stealth fighter planes, two of which were assigned to drop 2,000-pound bombs on PDF barracks; in fact, they missed their targets, due either to pilot error or to a misunderstanding in orders. Many observers believed that calling in such an advanced weapon was not required by the conditions of the engagement but was done simply to demonstrate the potential of that expensive plane.

U.S. military authorities, rather than seeing the invasion as a chance to innovate, regarded it as a successful attempt to integrate the lessons learned from mistakes made in Vietnam and the errors of the Grenada Intervention (see p. 677-688). The operation did establish two records, however, including the first time in the history of the U.S. military that a woman officially led troops in combat (see Legends and Trivia, below). The 3,000-man parachute jump into Panama City was the largest combat parachute jump since World War II, and the entire airlift was the largest since the Vietnam War.

The operation also saw the use of some unorthodox "weapons." Specially trained soldiers used tape recordings of Sherman tanks and machine-gun fire to get PDF troops to surrender. In other instances, phone calls were placed advising that if surrender were not immediate, the PDF positions would be destroyed by Spectre Gunships; those telephone calls resulted in more than 1,000 PDF troops surrendering. (The media dubbed that the "Ma Bell" tactic.) U.S. soldiers also offered money for weapons; the exchange of $150 cash for each gun netted the United States 75,000 guns, and one armored personnel carrier was turned over for $5,000.

LEGENDS AND TRIVIA

In what was a sign of the times in the traditionally masculine field of warfare, two individuals who emerged from the Panama Invasion were female.

U.S. Army captain **Linda Bray** became the first woman in U. S. military history to command troops in battle. Captain Bray was the commander of the 123-member 988th Military Police Company from Fort Benning, Georgia, which had been sent to Panama several days before the invasion. On December 20, she was dispatched with 30 other soldiers (women and men) from her military police unit to secure a kennel containing guard dogs. Intelligence reports stated the kennel was not defended, but the intelligence was wrong. The captain's efforts to secure the kennel led to a "fierce firefight," according to White House spokesperson Marlin Fitzwater, and ended with three dead PDF soldiers. No Americans were killed or wounded. Although women in the Army were not allowed to train for combat, they were allowed to serve in Military Police Units, and the

Army admitted that in the Panama Invasion there was often no clear distinction between MP duties and combat duties.

The other female who made headlines was 12-year-old **Sarah York**, a pen pal of Gen. Manuel Noriega, who lived with her parents Pauline and Mitchell York in Neganunee, Michigan. Sarah had chosen to write to Noriega after his indictment in February 1988 and accepted his invitation to visit him that October. Then in October 1989, she visited him again, accompanied by her father. Sarah's second visit with General Noriega coincided with the end of a coup attempt against the Panamanian dictator. At that time, Sarah called Noriega "a very nice man," and he named her "a meritorious daughter" of Panama City. Following Noriega's arrest and deportation to Florida, Sarah said: "I don't think he will get a fair trial. In the first place, everyone believes everything that was said against him, and then on the news today, I heard that they weren't even going to listen to what he had to say about secrets, about George Bush and the CIA."

NOTABLE PHRASES

General Noriega's reckless threats and attacks upon Americans in Panama created an imminent danger to the 35,000 American citizens in Panama. As president, I have no higher obligation than to safeguard the lives of American citizens.

President George Bush spoke those words to the American people on December 20, 1989, explaining his decision to invade Panama earlier that day.

We have decapitated him from the dictatorship of this country, and he is now a fugitive and will be treated as such.

Gen. Colin Powell, chairman of the Joint Chiefs of Staff, spoke thus in responding to a reporter's question on December 20, 1989, about the location of Gen. Manuel Noriega.

SONGS

There were no popular songs to come from the Panama Invasion. It was reported, however, that among the music blared at Noriega while he was hiding in the papal nuncio's residence were Jimi Hendrix's "Voodoo Child" and Linda Ronstadt's "You're No Good." The rock music was said to have been especially offensive to Noriega because he was an opera lover.

HISTORICAL PERSPECTIVES AND CONTROVERSIES

Did the United States have a right under international law to invade the Republic of Panama?

President George Bush listed four reasons for launching the invasion of Panama: "to safeguard the lives of Americans, to defend democracy in Panama, to combat drug trafficking, and to protect the integrity of the Panama Canal Treaty." (On occasion, he also claimed the invasion was justified by the fact that Gen. Manuel Noriega had declared war on the United States, a reference to the resolution passed by Panama's parliament on December 15, 1989.) Each of those reasons was a worthy goal, and in the realm of practical politics most people would probably approve of any action that would achieve them. But the fact is that the operation was extremely controversial, with reactions ranging from outright condemnation to qualified or full support. The Organization of American States and the European Parliament both passed resolutions condemning the invasion (see International Developments, p. 695). Several governments of countries in Latin America and the Caribbean voiced their disapproval; the president of Peru, for example, himself a strong critic of Noriega, withdrew Peru's ambassador to the United States until the invading soldiers were withdrawn from Panama. At the UN, however, a Security Council resolution to condemn the invasion was vetoed, with Great Britain and France calling the resolution unbalanced because the Noriega government was illegitimate. In the U.S. Congress, most representatives and senators supported the invasion (although they had never voted on it), but certain individuals, such as Rep. Charles Rangel (D–N.Y.), questioned its legitimacy.

Such differing opinions still leave the more fundamental question of whether the United States had a legal basis for invading a sovereign nation and abducting its leader, however serious his crimes. That is an issue that has been de-bated by academic and professional students of international affairs. In any such debate, it seems reasonable to concede that Panama is not an ordinary country: Aside from the way it was established (see Background, p. 687), the fact is the Panama Canal holds a special position in international commerce and the rest of the world expects the United States to maintain its security.

The Bush administration claimed that its actions were "fully in accordance with international law," but few authorities came forward to support that. For instance, David Cole, a lawyer with the Center for Constitutional Right, flatly stated: "It is patently unlawful under international law to invade another country in order to capture an indicted criminal." Extradition treaties exist for such situations, and when the United States does not have the right to extradite a criminal under such a treaty, it ordinarily respects that.

President Bush appealed to the need to protect the neutrality of the Panama Canal, but the 1979 treaty governing the turnover of the canal to Panama clearly prohibited "the right of intervention of the United States in the internal affairs of Panama." Furthermore, General Noriega never threatened the canal, although his presence at the helm of the nation was considered by some to be a potential threat to the security of the canal. In any case, the United States had more than enough military personnel already in Panama to protect the canal. Alfred P. Rubin, professor of international law at Tufts University in Medford, Massachusetts, further pointed out that the treaty forbade the United States "as well from any intervention in the internal affairs of [Panama]." Beyond that, the United States may well have violated provisions in the Geneva Conventions that prohibit "indiscriminate attacks" on civilians and the use of "weapons, projectiles, materials, or methods of war not justified by military necessity."

In the end, the defenders of the U.S. action in Panama were left to assert that it was a necessary response to an intolerable situation.

CIVILIAN AND MILITARY BIOGRAPHIES

AMERICAN

Bush, George (1925–)—president: George Bush was born in Milton, Massachusetts. He served as a fighter pilot in World War II and was awarded the Distinguished Flying Cross. He served two terms in the U.S. House of Representatives (1966–1970). As head of the CIA from 1975 to 1976, Bush met Gen. Manuel Noriega for the first time. Then as vice president (1981–1989), Bush met with Noriega again in 1983, allegedly to persuade Noriega to serve as an intermediary with Cuba during the invasion of Grenada, although by that time, Bush was generally overseeing the U.S. government's dealings with Noriega and Panama. When Bush became president in 1989, relations between the United States and Noriega had completely deteriorated, but those close to Bush said that what finally persuaded him to authorize a military operation was the mistreatment of the Navy officer's wife (see Causes of War, p. 691). His decision to invade Panama represented his first effort as commander in chief and substantially enhanced his standing as a man of action (see Gulf War, Civilian and Military Biographies, p. 718).

Powell, Colin (1937–   )—chairman of the Joint Chiefs of Staff: Colin Powell was born in New York City. He was a decorated veteran of the Vietnam War and served as a presidential assistant for national security affairs (1987–1989) under President Ronald Reagan before being appointed to chair the Joint Chiefs of Staff, the first African American to hold that post. Taking office on October 1, 1989, he was quickly brought up to date on the military's various contingency plans for Panama; by December 17, he found himself in charge of his first major military operation, the Panama invasion. By August 1990 he was in charge of the Persian Gulf War (see Gulf War, Civilian and Military Biographies, p. 719).

PANAMANIAN

Endara Galimany, Guillermo (1937–   )— president. Guillermo Endara was a lawyer who had studied at New York University; he served as secretary to the popular president of Panama, Arnulfo Arias. Although he specialized in labor law, Endara was regarded as the candidate of the conservative, middle-class, largely white business community when he ran for president in May 1989. International observers agreed that he was deprived of his victory by Noriega's arbitrary annulment of the election; in the ensuing protests, he was beaten so badly by Noriega's

Dignity Battalions that he was hospitalized for several days. Just prior to the invasion of Panama, Endara was sworn into office as president on a U.S. military base (see p. 693). In the aftermath of the invasion, he tried to effect some economic reforms but his administration was generally regarded as ineffectual at best, corrupt at worst, and by May 1994 he and his party were voted out of office.

Noriega Morena, Manuel Antonio (1939–   ) —general, dictator: As a young officer, Manuel Noriega was put on the payroll of the U.S. Defense Intelligence Agency and the CIA. During the rule of Gen. Omar Torrijos, Noriega headed Panama's G-2, the intelligence agency that served as a brutal secret police. After Torrijos's death in 1981, Noriega took over as head of Panama's military, then made himself the true power behind the civilian government. By 1981, Noriega was being paid $185,000 per year as a CIA informant, but by that time, he had become so enmeshed in double-dealing that it would never be clear just whose side he was on, as he provided information and aid not only to the United States but also to Fidel Castro, the Colombian Medellin drug cartel, the Nicaraguan Contras, and the Sandinistas, the Contras' opposition. In any case, Noriega personally made many millions of dollars from the drug dealers alone, and it was that that finally led the United States to overthrow him. Found guilty in federal court in Florida on drug-related charges, he was sentenced in 1992 to 40 years in prison.

FURTHER READING

Buckley, Kevin. *Panama: The Whole Story.* New York: Simon & Schuster, 1991.

Flanagan, Edward M. Jr. *Battle for Panama: Inside Operation Just Cause.* Washington, D.C.: Brassey's, 1993.

Harris, Godfrey. *Invasion: The American Destruction of the Noriega Regime in Panama.* Los Angeles: The Americas Group, 1990.

Johns, Christina Jacqueline, and P. Ward Johnson. *State Crime, The Media, and The Invasion of Panama.* Westport, Conn.: Praeger, 1994.

PERSIAN GULF WAR

DATES OF WAR

January 17, 1991–April 11, 1991

ALTERNATE NAMES

Gulf War. Desert Storm. The Second Gulf War.

SIGNIFICANCE

Although the military operations against Iraqi forces in the Persian Gulf War were extremely brief and limited, they sent a significant message—that many of the world's major nations were willing to band together and use overwhelming force to compel a military power to pull out of a smaller nation it had openly and defiantly invaded.

Whatever the motives, those allied nations demonstrated they were willing to commit personnel, material, and money to meet a clear-cut case of aggression. And although it was clearly the United States that took the lead—supported most immediately by Great Britain—the nations that joined in that action did so by utilizing the mechanisms of the United Nations (UN). That was exactly the type of test that the League of Nations had failed in the 1930s. Moreover, that was the first test of the new relationship that the Soviet Union would have with several of its former adversaries in the non-Communist world. Although that relationship was strained at some points before the actual hostilities in the Persian Gulf, in the end, the Soviet government went along with the other allied nations.

Those opposed to war against Iraq charged that the allied war effort was initiated simply to protect the oil supplies for the industrial world. But by preventing Iraq from dominating the Persian Gulf oil fields, the allied victory in the Persian Gulf War certainly avoided a worldwide energy crisis of potentially immense proportions.

BACKGROUND

The Middle East had been beset by border disputes for hundreds of years, initially because the nomadic peoples of the region recognized no fixed national boundaries. By the early 18th century, tribes from the central Arabian peninsula had settled in the region now known as Kuwait, and sheiks of the Sabah family had emerged as the most influential of those Kuwaiti Arabs. The Ottoman Turks, who claimed control over that entire area, regarded the Kuwaiti sheiks as nothing more than provincial officials within the vast Ottoman Empire. However, by the mid-1700s, the British had established an East India Company trading station on the site of modern-day Kuwait City, and they chose to treat the Sabah sheiks as independent rulers. The ensuing rivalry among foreign powers throughout that entire region ended only when Great Britain gained control over much of the Middle East after World War I. Iraq gained its independence from Great Britain in 1932, but the British attempted to resolve regional disputes by imposing essentially arbitrary borders. Although Iraq and Kuwait had agreed on a common border in 1923, artificial land borders remained an alien concept in their nomadic cultures. And Iraq was essentially left landlocked by the British officials who drew the borders: Iraq was assigned only 36 miles of marshy coastline. When Kuwait gained independence from Great Britain in 1961, Iraq immediately claimed sovereignty over the new country. A common border was once again agreed upon in 1963, after British and Arab League troops intervened, but Iraq's dreams of annexing Kuwait as its "19th province" lingered.

Iraq and Iran fought a war (sometimes called the First Gulf War) that lasted from 1980 to 1988. It ended with Iraq heavily in debt to other Arab nations and desperate for cash to rebuild its war-torn economy. Annexation of Kuwait would give Iraq control of 20 percent of the world's oil reserves, and Kuwait's coastal geography was tempting to Saddam Hussein, the Iraqi leader.

CAUSES OF THE WAR

The immediate cause of the Persian Gulf War was Iraq's invasion of Kuwait in August 1990, in clear violation of international law. Iraq's formidable military capability and Saddam Hussein's avowed ambition to dominate Middle Eastern oil production suggested that neighboring Saudi Arabia might be the next target. At first, President George Bush spoke as though the only goal was to protect Saudi Arabia by containing Iraq within Kuwait's borders. He soon broadened that goal to include removing Hussein's forces from Kuwait. As other major powers backed the United States under the auspices of the United Nations, the buildup of allied forces in Saudi Arabia, named Operation Desert Shield, confronted Iraq with the clear threat of war.

War became inevitable when Hussein ignored UN Security Council Resolution 678, issued on November 29, 1990, authorizing the use of force against Iraq if it failed to withdraw from Kuwait by January 15, 1991. The stated goal of the allies' was to reverse the invasion and destroy Iraq's ability to wage war of mass destruction. President Bush also made it clear that force would be used to protect much of the industrial world's access to the oil supplies of the region. Another implied reason for the UN-sponsored war continues to be debated: Was one aim to depose Saddam Hussein?

PREPARATIONS FOR WAR

Before Hussein turned to a military solution to solve his economic problems, he tried to intimidate Kuwait and other oil-producing nations.

February 19, 1990: Hussein told a summit of the Arab Cooperation Council (ACC) that he expected a total of $60 billion of debt forgiveness as the Persian Gulf states' contribution to the cost of the Iran-Iraq war. He called for all U.S. naval and ground forces to leave the Persian Gulf.

April 2, 1990: Hussein denied building nuclear weapons but boasted of Iraq's chemical weapons and missile capability.

May 28–30, 1990: Hussein accused oil producers that exceed OPEC (Organization of Petroleum Exporting Countries) quotas of waging "a kind of war against Iraq."

June 19, 1990: The United States announced a $4 billion arms sale to Saudi Arabia.

June 26, 1990: Iraq cautioned Kuwait and the United Arab Emirates (UAE) about their overproduction of oil and called for the price of oil to rise from $14 a barrel to $25 a barrel.

July 10, 1990: OPEC agreed on stricter enforcement of oil production quotas and a target price of $18 per barrel.

July 17, 1990: Hussein threatened military action against Arab oil producers exceeding OPEC production quotas.

July 18, 1990: Iraq accused Kuwait of stealing oil from the Iraqi side of the Rumaila oil field, a disputed area straddling the border between the two countries.

July 19, 1990: Kuwait charged Iraq with drilling wells in the Kuwaiti sector of the Rumaila oil field and asked the Arab League to settle the border dispute.

July 19–24, 1990: Iraq massed 30,000 armored troops along the Iraq-Kuwait border.

July 23, 1990: Saudi Arabia's military and the U.S. Joint Task Force Middle East were placed on alert.

July 24, 1990: U.S. warships in the Persian Gulf were placed on alert. The United States and the United Arab Emirates held joint military exercises in the Persian Gulf. Kuwait's military was placed on full alert. President Hosni Mubarak of Egypt tried to mediate the intensifying crisis.

July 25, 1990: Hussein told U.S. ambassador to Iraq April Glaspie that Iraq sought closer cooperation with the United States and wished to avoid armed confrontation in Kuwait. Ambassador Glaspie reiterated standard U.S. policy, that the United States had "no opinion on the Arab-Arab conflicts like your border disagreement with Kuwait." Iraq repeated its demand for an oil price rise to $25 per barrel.

July 27, 1990: OPEC increased its target price to $21 per barrel.

July 28, 1990: President George Bush warned Saddam Hussein against taking military action in the Gulf.

July 30, 1990: The Iraqi military buildup along the Iraq-Kuwait border reached 100,000 troops with tanks and heavy artillery.

July 31, 1990: Iraq broke off negotiations with Kuwait at Jeddah, Saudi Arabia, after only two hours.

August 2, 1990: Iraqi troops invaded Kuwait at about 2 A.M. local time. Kuwait's small defense forces were quickly overwhelmed, but thousands of troops, along with some aircraft and naval vessels, got away to Saudi Arabia. The emir of Kuwait, Sheik Jabar al-Ahmad al Jabar al-Sabah, also fled to Saudi Arabia with his family and government leaders. Within a few hours, the Iraqis seized the oil fields, occupied the capital, Kuwait City, and announced the formation of a provisional government.

Upon hearing of Iraq's invasion of Kuwait, the UN Security Council unanimously passed Resolution 660, condemning the invasion and demanding Iraq's immediate withdrawal from Kuwait. President George Bush, condemning the action as "naked aggression," ordered additional U.S. warships to the Persian Gulf, announced an economic embargo against Iraq, and froze Iraqi and Kuwaiti assets in the United States. Israel threatened a military response if Iraq deployed troops to Jordan.

August 3, 1990: The United States and the Soviet Union jointly demanded Iraq's withdrawal from Kuwait. The European Economic Community, the Arab League, and the Gulf Cooperation Council added their voices to widespread international condemnation of the invasion. Iraq said it would withdraw from Kuwait in two days "unless something happens which would threaten the security of Kuwait and Iraq." Iraq mobilized 60,000 troops in southern Kuwait near the Saudi border. Bush declared Saudi Arabia's territorial integrity to be of "vital interest" to the United States.

August 4, 1990: U.S. Central Command (CENTCOM), headquartered in Tampa, Florida, was alerted that it might be needed for Persian Gulf operations. U.S. Navy warships were ordered to the Persian Gulf, and Saudi Arabia mobilized defensive air and ground forces. Palestine Liberation Organization (PLO) chairman Yasir Arafat promoted a joint PLO-Libya peace plan favorable to Iraq.

August 5, 1990: President Bush insisted that the invasion of Kuwait "will not stand" (see Notable Phrases, p. 717).

August 6, 1990: UN Security Council Resolution 661 imposed sanctions and a trade embargo on Iraq and on occupied Kuwait. King Fahd of Saudi Arabia formally requested defensive military assistance from the United States and other countries.

August 7, 1990: Bush ordered U.S. fighter planes and troops to Saudi Arabia. Turkey cut off the flow of Iraqi oil through its pipeline. Two U.S. Navy carrier battle groups arrived in the Persian Gulf to support naval forces already stationed there.

August 8, 1990: Hussein announced the annexation of Kuwait into Iraq. In a televised address, Bush asserted that the U.S. military mission is "wholly defensive" but promised "severe" military retaliation if Iraq used chemical weapons. Great Britain committed troops to the Persian Gulf.

August 9, 1990: Operation Desert Shield, "the defense of Saudi Arabia," began. The UN Security Council unanimously passed Resolution 662, nullifying Iraq's annexation of Kuwait. The first U.S. troops arrived in Saudi Arabia. France committed troops. Jordan closed the port of Aqaba to Iraqi trade. Israel conducted the first tests of its new air defense missiles. Iraqi and Kuwaiti borders were closed to all foreigners except diplomatic personnel. Iraq ordered foreign embassies in Kuwait closed by August 24 but barred all U.S. and British citizens from leaving.

August 10, 1990: In compliance with the War Powers Act, President Bush notified the U.S. Congress of the deployment of U.S. troops to the Persian Gulf. The Arab League committed Arab troops to the coalition force. Hussein exhorted Arabs and Muslims to join in a jihad (or holy war) against the United States and the Persian Gulf emirates.

August 12, 1990: The UN naval blockade of Iraq began. Hussein declared he sought a comprehensive Middle East territorial settlement as a precondition of withdrawal from Kuwait.

August 14, 1990: The U.S. Fleet Ready Reserve was mobilized.

August 15, 1990: Bush told Pentagon employees that preventing Iraq from controlling Middle East oil reserves was vital to protect "our jobs, our way of life, our own freedom and the freedom of friendly countries around the world." Iran accepted an Iraqi proposal concluding their 1980–1988 war on Iran's terms.

August 16, 1990: U.S. naval forces began enforcing a complete blockade of Iraq.

August 17, 1990: Various units of U.S. Army, Navy, and Air Force reserves were called to active duty. The U.S. Civil Air Reserve Fleet was activated for the first time.

August 18, 1990: Iraq's parliamentary leader declared that the more than 11,000 foreign nationals in Kuwait and Iraq would be used as human shields at Iraqi military sites as long as coalition forces threatened Iraq. UN Security Council Resolution 664 demanded Iraq's immediate release of the detainees. (Two days later, President George Bush first used the term *hostages* in reference to the individuals held by Hussein.) In the first direct confrontation of the crisis, the U.S. Navy fired across the bows of Iraqi tankers.

August 19, 1990: Bush rejected Hussein's proposal to release hostages in return for U.S. withdrawal from Saudi Arabia and the lifting of the UN embargo against Iraq.

August 21, 1990: Syria and nine European Economic Community member nations committed troops to the coalition force.

August 22, 1990: Bush authorized the mobilization of 200,000 military reserves. The price of oil passed $30 per barrel.

August 23, 1990: Hussein presented himself as the "host" of foreign "guests" in a television appearance with Western hostages, including young children.

August 24, 1990: Iraqi troops surrounded several foreign embassies in Kuwait and detained U.S. diplomatic personnel in Baghdad. Iraqi troops began construction of defensive positions in Kuwait.

August 25, 1990: UN Security Council Resolution 665 authorized the use of force to enforce an embargo against Iraq. Gen. H. Norman Schwarzkopf briefed Gen. Colin Powell, chairman of the Joint Chiefs of Staff, on the plan for the Persian Gulf War before relocating his CENTCOM headquarters from Tampa, Florida, to Riyadh, Saudi Arabia.

August 28, 1990: A presidential decree by Hussein formally claimed Kuwait to be the 19th province of Iraq. Hussein declared that foreign women and children would be allowed to leave Iraq; they began leaving Baghdad on September 2. A Jordanian peace plan conciliatory to Iraq was rejected by Kuwait and Saudi Arabia.

August 29, 1990: OPEC agreed to increase oil production to compensate for the loss of Iraqi and Kuwaiti oil. Bush announced a major arms sale to Saudi Arabia.

August 30, 1990: Iraq threatened to target Israel and Saudi Arabia if war broke out.

September 1, 1990: Libya proposed a peace plan conciliatory to Iraq; Kuwait and Saudi Arabia rejected it.

September 13, 1990: UN Security Resolution 666 tightened the limits on humanitarian food supplies that could be sent to Iraq and occupied Kuwait.

September 14, 1990: Iraqi troops raided foreign diplomatic compounds in Kuwait City. Iraq rationed food.

September 15, 1990: The U.S. military presence in the Persian Gulf reached 150,000 troops and 670 combat and support aircraft.

September 16, 1990: UN Security Council Resolution 667 condemned Iraqi acts of violence against foreign embassies in Kuwait. Thousands of Kuwaitis fled to Saudi Arabia when Iraq opened the border. Coalition naval forces intercepted their 1,000th merchant ship during the blockade.

September 17, 1990: Gen. Michael Dugan, U.S. Air Force chief of staff, was fired for revealing in a newspaper interview that the centerpiece of proposed U.S. military strategy against Iraq involved the heavy bombing of Baghdad and the targeting of Saddam Hussein and his family.

September 19, 1990: The United States and Saudi Arabia rejected a Moroccan peace plan tying a resolution in Kuwait to a broad Middle East peace conference.

September 23, 1990: Hussein threatened to destroy Saudi oil fields and attack Israel.

September 24, 1990: French president François Mitterrand proposed a comprehensive Middle East peace settlement in exchange for Iraq's withdrawal from Kuwait.

September 25, 1990: UN Security Council Resolution 670 extended the land and sea embargo on Iraq to air transport.

September 27, 1990: Oil briefly reached $40 per barrel in trading in international markets.

October 1, 1990: The U.S. House of Representatives voted 380 to 29 to support President Bush's actions in the Persian Gulf. U.S. Marines practiced amphibious assault landings in Saudi Arabia.

October 2, 1990: The U.S. Senate supported President Bush's actions by a vote of 96 to 3. Amnesty International reported killings and widespread human rights abuses during the Iraqi occupation of Kuwait.

October 15, 1990: Bush accused Hussein of committing "ghastly atrocities" in Kuwait and threatened him with prosecution for war crimes.

October 16, 1990: U.S. Secretary of State James Baker told a congressional hearing that the blockade and sanctions might achieve allied goals in Kuwait.

October 23, 1990: The Bush administration

said that it might augment the 240,000 U.S. troops already in or en route to the Persian Gulf.

October 25, 1990: The U.S. Congress authorized arms sales of $7.3 billion to Saudi Arabia and $37 million to Bahrain and canceled $6.7 billion in Egyptian military debt. The United States awarded an additional $1 billion in military aid to Israel.

October 29, 1990: UN Security Council Resolution 674 condemned Iraq's "mistreatment and oppression" of Kuwaitis and held Iraq liable for damage and personal injury in Kuwait. Soviet president Mikhail Gorbachev called a military solution to the crisis "unacceptable" and asked for an Arab peace initiative; Egypt and Syria soon rejected his call. Secretary of State Baker refused to rule out military action in the Persian Gulf.

November 3, 1990: Iraq named conditions for a settlement: the withdrawal of non-Arab forces from the Persian Gulf, a pledge of nonaggression, and an agreement on Israel's occupied territories.

November 5, 1990: At the start of an eight-nation mission to discuss the possible use of military force, Baker agreed with King Fahd on a command-and-control structure for U.S. and Saudi troops in Saudi Arabia in the event of war.

November 8, 1990: Bush ordered 200,000 additional U.S. troops and more aircraft and naval vessels to the Persian Gulf to provide offensive military capability. The U.S. 7th Armored Corps was ordered to the Persian Gulf from Germany.

November 15–21, 1990: U.S. and Saudi forces conducted their first joint amphibious exercise, code-named "Imminent Thunder."

November 19, 1990: Iraq called up 100,000 reserves and deployed 250,000 additional troops to Kuwait and southern Iraq, bringing its total force there to 700,000.

November 21, 1990: Bush met in Saudi Arabia with King Fahd and Kuwaiti emir Sheik Jabar al-Ahmad al-Jabar-al-Sabah to review war plans. U.S. National Guard combat brigades were placed on active duty.

November 27, 1990: The Senate Armed Services Committee and the House Banking Committee opened hearings on the Persian Gulf.

November 29, 1990: The United Nations Security Council Resolution 678 authorized member nations to use "all necessary means" unless Iraq withdrew from Kuwait by January 15, 1991. Iraq rejected the resolution.

December 2, 1990: Iraq made its first test since April of its Soviet-supplied Scud missiles. Two days later, Iraq implemented nationwide civil defense training.

December 5, 1990: CIA Director William Webster testified before a congressional committee that 97 percent of Iraq's exports and 90 percent of its imports had been stopped. He also stated that there was no guarantee that the embargo would force Iraq to leave Kuwait.

December 6, 1990: Hussein announced the imminent release of all foreign "guests" (hostages). The last U.S. hostages and U.S. embassy staff in Kuwait were released a week later.

December 8, 1990: Bush declared that the release of the hostages would not end the crisis. The following day, administration officials went further, stating that even a withdrawal from Kuwait would not necessarily avert war, since Iraq would retain its chemical (and possible nuclear) weapons capability.

December 20, 1990: Hussein said that he would not meet the UN deadline of January 15. Bush announced that he was prepared to order military action; in the following days, U.S. government officials increasingly referred to war as inevitable.

December 24, 1990: Hussein identified Tel Aviv, Israel, as Iraq's first missile target if war broke out.

January 9, 1991: Meeting in Geneva, U.S. Secretary of State Baker and Iraqi foreign minister Tariq Aziz failed to find common ground. Hussein said Iraq was ready for war.

January 10, 1991: Many Western nations closed their Baghdad embassies. Foreigners employed by the UN left Baghdad.

January 12, 1991: After a three-day debate, House Joint Resolution 77 authorizing the use of military force in the Persian Gulf was passed in the Senate by a vote of 52 to 47 and in the House by 250 to 183. The United States closed its embassy in Baghdad.

January 13, 1991: UN Secretary General Javier Pérez de Cuéllar met with Saddam Hussein in Baghdad but made no progress in getting him to accede to the UN resolutions.

January 15, 1991: U.S. troop strength in the Persian Gulf reached offensive capability. UN Secretary General, King Fahd of Saudi Arabia, and President Mubarak of Egypt made final personal appeals to Saddam Hussein to withdraw from Kuwait. An 11th-hour French peace proposal was brought to the UN but was not regarded as viable and was never put to a vote.

January 16–17, 1991: The midnight deadline imposed by Resolution 678 passed without an Iraqi response. President Bush ordered an attack by air and missile and notified Congress of his decision.

DECLARATION OF WAR

On November 29, 1990, UN Security Council Resolution 678 authorized an international force to "use all necessary means" to evict Iraq from Kuwait. That marked the first time since the Korean War that the UN had approved the use of force to resist armed aggression (see p. 574). President George Bush had already committed the U.S. military on August 10, 1990, under authority granted him by the War Powers Act of 1973 (see Vietnam War, October 24, 1973, pp. 643-644). He never asked for a formal declaration of war. Instead, the president and Congress avoided a direct confrontation over the need to declare war by having Congress simply vote to approve compliance with UN Resolution 678. Congressional authorization for U.S. participation came after a three-day debate, when on January 12, 1991, the House approved the use of U.S. troops by a vote of 250 to 183, the Senate by a closer count of 52 to 47. No formal declaration of war was ever made by the other allied nations; they also simply went along with the UN resolution.

COMBATANTS

Iraqis: Saddam Hussein had built the largest army in the Persian Gulf: The Iraqi army numbered 1.5 million men (including reserves), supported by thousands of tanks and artillery pieces and extensive missile stocks, some with chemical and biological warheads. (UN monitors discovered after the cease-fire that in January 1991 Iraq was within a few months of acquiring nuclear capability.)

However, the long war with Iran (1980–1988) and heavy conscription had sapped Iraqi morale, few experienced generals were still in uniform, and the UN embargo (instituted in August 1990) was leaving Iraqi civilians and soldiers alike short of food, fuel, and medicine. Furthermore, most of the large army was poorly trained

for modern dynamic warfare; only the six divisions (three infantry, three armored) of the elite Republican Guard represented any real challenge to the allied powers.

The Iraqi air force comprised 40,000 personnel and 750 combat planes; despite advanced aircraft and air defenses, Iraqi pilots had performed poorly in the war with Iran. Iraq's small navy consisted mostly of vessels designed to deliver missiles and lay mines.

Americans: The United States deployed more than half a million troops to the Persian Gulf. One-third of the U.S. Army—more than 300,000 troops—was sent, along with the entire 90,000-member Marine Corps combat force, 50,000 Air Force personnel, and 80,000 naval personnel.

One hundred twenty ships from the 6th and 7th Fleets participated, including seven carrier battle groups. Those personnel were supported by a huge array of advanced military hardware and weaponry, much of it untested in battle.

Other Coalition Forces: Thirty-four countries assigned more than 200,000 air, sea, and ground forces to the Persian Gulf in addition to warships, tanks, and aircraft; several of those nations sent simply one or two token ships. The strongest contingents came from Saudi Arabia, Egypt, France, Great Britain, and Pakistan. Twelve other members of the UN coalition contributed financial support or sent tents, transport, fuel, field hospitals, and other logistical support. Ground troops and most air force personnel were based in Saudi Arabia.

GEOGRAPHIC AND STRATEGIC CONSIDERATIONS

The Middle East's vast oil reserves have long made the region a major strategic interest to the United States and other industrialized countries. The U.S. economy depends on a steady supply of Middle Eastern oil at a stable and moderate price. Elements of the U.S. 7th Fleet are routinely positioned in the Persian Gulf to ensure the security of shipping lanes. The security of the oil fields of Kuwait and of the sea route in the Persian Gulf was undeniably a major consideration in the Persian Gulf War.

Another geopolitical issue highlighted by the Persian Gulf War was the long-standing enmity between Arabs and Israelis. For 45 years of the Cold War, Arab states had manipulated superpower rivalry; the impending end of the Cold War left them anxious about the supremacy of the United States the major supporter of Israel. Saddam Hussein decided he could gain stature by leading the Arab world in a struggle against Zionism and its Western supporters. He repeatedly tried to link withdrawal from Kuwait with larger regional territorial issues, including Israel's occupied territories.

Hussein thought he could appeal to another motive to win broad Arab support of his invasion of Kuwait. He had turned Iraq into an essentially secular state and had been able to exploit that in his international relations—among other ways, by gaining some covert military support from the United States in his eight-year-long war with Iran. He had presented that war as a struggle to defend all Arabs against the expansionist ambitions of the fundamentalist Islamic republicans in Iran. He thought he could count on the other Arab states at least to sit on the sidelines as he took over Kuwait.

Instead, the multinational coalition assembled against Iraq revealed a deep and public split in the Arab world. The Arab and Islamic countries who joined the coalition did so partly out of a fear they shared with the United States: that Iraq's military prowess combined with Hussein's ambitions might escalate that minor conflict into a larger Middle East war.

BATTLES AND CAMPAIGNS

Operation Desert Storm, as the allied military campaign was called, was fought in two phases—an air war and a ground war. (In some accounts, the ground war phase is named Operation Desert Saber.) The air war began with a massive aircraft and missile bombardment of Iraq on the night of January 17, 1991. Bombs dropped by allied warplanes along with missiles launched by the allies pounded Iraq for 43 days, destroying Iraq's air force and navy and so weakening its army that the ground offensive, which began on February 24, 1991, lasted only 100 hours.

AIR WAR

The air war was planned and executed by Air Force Central Command (CENTAF), under the command of Lt. Gen. Charles Horner. General Horner's strategy was called "Instant Thunder"—

a quick, massive, overpowering strike. It called for four phases, the first three to be carried out almost simultaneously. In Phase One, the strategic air campaign, the allies were to gain air superiority, interrupt Iraqi command-and-control systems, and destroy Iraq's strategic capability. Phase Two called for the suppression of air defenses in the Kuwaiti theater of operations and the establishment of air superiority. Phase Three called for *battlefield preparation*, the military term for destruction of as much of Iraq's ground force as possible before engagement, and Phase Four called for support of the ground offensive.

The power, precision, and sheer tonnage of allied air attacks were to guarantee allied victory in the Persian Gulf. The number of sorties flown by the United States alone during the six weeks of the air war totaled approximately 110,000, an average of 2,800 a day. The United States dropped 88,500 tons of bombs on Iraq during the Persian Gulf War (including 6,520 tons of "smart" bombs), more than U.S. planes dropped in the whole of World War II.

The weather during the war was the worst in the region in 14 years. The high-tech coalition air force was repeatedly grounded, and its space-based photographic reconnaissance capability compromised by low cloud cover.

January 17, 1991: Iraqis were awakened just before 3 A.M. local time as a massive allied bombing raid and missile attack began the UN coalition's war on Iraq. The allies targeted Iraqi air defense sites, military headquarters, communications systems, electric power plants, and chemical and nuclear weapons facilities. The cruise missiles were launched from warships in the Persian Gulf. U.S. F-117A Stealth fighters carrying 2,000-pound precision-guided bombs dominated the air over Baghdad. In the first 24 hours of the air war, the allies flew 1,300 sorties against Iraq; during the first night alone, the U.S. Air Force estimated that it hit 31 percent of its Iraqi targets.

Iraq immediately responded with attacks on Tel Aviv, Israel, and Dhahran, Saudi Arabia, by Soviet-made Scud missiles—crude, inaccurate weapons whose very unpredictability made them effective weapons of terror. Saddam Hussein hoped to draw Israel into the war, thereby eroding Arab support for the coalition, but with the strong urging from the United States, Israel did not retaliate. Instead, the United States sent U.S.-

operated Patriot antimissile batteries to Israel. Iraq launched approximately 90 Scuds against Israel, Saudi Arabia, and other Persian Gulf states in the following six weeks.

January 23, 1991: The United States declared air superiority. The use of aircraft carriers in the Persian Gulf and airfields in Saudi Arabia and other Arab states, on the island of Diego Garcia in the Indian Ocean, in Great Britain, and in Turkey gave allied air forces the flexibility and rapid response capability to strive for total air supremacy throughout the theater of operations.

January 24–31, 1991: By the end of January, allied bombers had destroyed Iraq's air defense system, including its missile production and fixed launch sites. The Iraqi air force was knocked out. (During the second week of the Persian Gulf War, Iraqi pilots began defecting to Iran, where their planes were impounded.) Nearly every airfield; railroad and highway bridge; and nuclear, chemical, and biological military target in Iraq had been bombed. Iraq could barely operate its electricity plants, industry, and communications and transportation systems. Saddam Hussein was directing the war from mobile command vehicles.

February 1–10, 1991: Allied air forces turned their attention to Phase Three, battlefield preparation, with the particular goal of destroying the capabilities of Iraq's elite Republican Guard. U.S. F-111 bombers, capable of locating and destroying tanks buried in sand, destroyed up to 150 Iraqi tanks a day in an operation known as "tank plinking." Before the ground war began, thousands of Iraqi tanks, artillery pieces, armored vehicles, and ground units were destroyed.

February 12–13, 1991: The heavy bombardment of Baghdad that commenced on February 12 was the climax of the air war. On February 13, two laser-guided missiles destroyed a fortified bunker in the middle of the city, killing several hundred civilians and igniting controversy about whether the structure was a military facility, as the United States claimed, or a civilian bomb shelter, as Iraq maintained. (Eventually, the United States admitted that on the night of the destruction the facility was used as a civilian shelter but claimed that the bunker also served as an intelligence center.)

February 15, 1991: In a Baghdad Radio broadcast, Hussein indicated that he was ready to make a deal on UN Security Council Resolution 660, which called for Iraq's immediate withdrawal from Kuwait. The Bush administration dismissed the offer.

February 24–26, 1991: The beginning of the ground war triggered Phase Four of the air war, the support of the ground offensive. On February 25, Iraqi forces began to leave Kuwait in miles-long, bumper-to-bumper convoys. Thousands of military and civilian vehicles crept along several major routes, including the six-lane Highway 80 from Kuwait City to Basra, Iraqi headquarters for the Kuwait theater of operations. But coalition forces blocked every exit from Kuwait, and Gen. Norman Schwarzkopf ordered his troops "not to let anybody or anything out of Kuwait City."

As the retreating Iraqis reached Jahra 20 miles west of Kuwait City, the combined U.S. forces unleashed a ferocious attack that began on February 26 and lasted for 40 hours, turning Highway 80 into a "highway of death." Navy and air force bombers dropped thousands of pounds of bombs until the weather grounded them early in the afternoon; Army and Marine artillery continued to pound the Iraqis until the cease-fire was called. Two thousand vehicles and thousands of Iraqi troops fleeing to Baghdad were reported to have been destroyed in the bombardment. However, it was later discovered that many Iraqi troops had been withdrawn from Kuwait before the ground war started; most of the incinerated tanks were found to be empty. Only about 200 Iraqi soldiers had been killed in those destroyed columns.

February 25, 1991: The highest U.S. casualties of any single incident of the Persian Gulf War occurred when 28 Americans died and more than 90 were injured in a Scud attack on U.S. barracks at the air base in Dhahran, Saudi Arabia. The allies diverted air attacks to Iraq's mobile launchers and deployed U.S. Patriot missiles against the Iraqi Scuds.

February 27, 1991: The Air Force and Navy continued their aerial bombardment of Iraqi targets and retreating troops; Baghdad endured the heaviest bombing of the war.

U.S. Army major Rhonda Cornum went down behind Iraqi lines when the helicopter she was piloting was shot down. Cornum became the second U.S. female prisoner taken by the Iraqis (see Ground War, January 29–February 1, 1991, p. 708).

NAVAL WAR

The U.S. Navy Joint Task Force Middle East, stationed in the Persian Gulf and Red Sea, was the mainstay of the UN blockade of Iraq. During the blockade, 7,500 challenges to ships were made and 1,000 merchant vessels were boarded. Seven carrier action groups also participated in the war.

The USS *Wisconsin* and the USS *Missouri* fired more than 100 Tomahawk missiles into Iraq during the first 24 hours of the air war and continued to fire missiles for the following six weeks. The use of naval missiles and large shipboard guns was limited only by their relatively short range and lack of precision compared with the weaponry of the other services. Meanwhile, airplanes from the offshore carriers were full participants in all phases of the air war. Carrier-based aircraft flew some 18,000 sorties, nearly one-fifth of all allied missions.

Two weeks into the war, the United States claimed control of the seas, declaring the Iraqi navy to be "combat ineffective." Iraq's missile-carrying vessels and minelayers and all its ports and naval bases had been bombed. Henceforth, the three seaward sides of the Kuwait theater of operations were secured. As the ground war approached, the Navy was instrumental in deceiving Iraq into the belief that the coalition intended to liberate Kuwait with an amphibious assault; when Kuwait City was captured, the allies found that the Iraqis had assigned large amounts of armaments and personnel to defend the seacoast.

GROUND WAR

January 22, 1991: As the smoke of the first air raids began to clear, U.S. and coalition pilots reported that the Iraqis had begun setting fire to the oil fields and oil refineries in Kuwait, just as Saddam Hussein had threatened to do. The Iraqis continued to do that right up to the final days of the war.

January 25, 1991: Iraqis began to release oil from Kuwaiti storage tanks into the northern Persian Gulf. Within a few days, an 11-million-barrel oil slick threatened the regional environment and Saudi Arabia's freshwater supply, which was largely produced from seawater at coastal distilleries.

January 29–February 1, 1991: The first ground skirmish of the Persian Gulf War occurred on January 29 when Iraqi troops entered al-Khafji after a cross-border incursion into Saudi Arabia. Some U.S. forces were caught in the action and exchanged fire with the Iraqis. A U.S. Army vehicle and its two occupants were captured by the Iraqis; one of the two was Specialist Melissa Rathbun-Nealy, who became the first U.S. military female (other than medical staff) ever taken as a prisoner of war. Saudi and allied ground and air forces retook the town on February 1.

February 5–8, 1991: To prepare the U.S. public for the ground campaign, President George Bush declared on February 5 that an air war could not achieve allied objectives in Iraq. Three days later, Secretary of Defense Dick Cheney and chairman of the Joint Chiefs of Staff Colin Powell met with Gen. Norman Schwarzkopf in Riyadh to finalize plans for the ground war. Their planning was made easier by the success of the air campaign, which by February 14, had destroyed nearly a third of Iraq's armor and artillery in the Kuwait theater of operations.

Schwarzkopf's plan called for allied forces to push deep into Iraq to the west of Kuwait, encircling and trapping the Iraqi army in southern Iraq and Kuwait. From bases in Saudi Arabia, U.S. 28th Airborne Corps (along with French forces) were moved 250 miles inland from the coast along the Saudi-Iraq border, ready to move into Iraq and cut off the main roads of supply to and retreat from Kuwait. U.S. 7th Corps (along with British forces) was positioned 100 miles to the east of the 28th Corps, poised to advance deep into Iraq and engage the Iraqi army. The U.S. 1st Marine Expeditionary Force and two corps-sized units of Arab and Islamic troops under Saudi command were stationed along the southern sector of the Saudi-Kuwait border and assigned to liberate Kuwait.

February 22, 1991: President Bush issued an ultimatum setting a 24-hour deadline (local time, February 23, 8 P.M.; noon, Eastern Standard Time) for an allied ground assault unless Iraq withdrew from Kuwait. His urgency arose from the increasing threat from Iraq's use of environmental warfare: 400 Kuwaiti oil wells were on fire. Iraq's response to the president's ultimatum was to blow up more Kuwaiti wells.

February 24, 1991 (G–day): When the ground war officially began at 4 A.M. local time (eight hours were allowed to pass after the ulti-

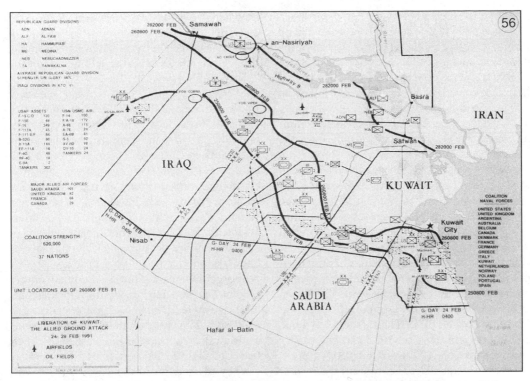

This plan shows the disposition and movement of the main coalition ground forces on February 24–28, 1991. The dark black lines show the fronts during the days indicated; the narrow vertical lines show the movement of coalition units. The broken-line rectangles indicate Iraqi units once in those positions.

matum expired), nearly a million troops were in place in the Persian Gulf. Seventeen allied divisions (eight of them American) faced 43 Iraqi divisions in the Kuwait theater of operations. The six elite Republican Guard divisions were dug in just north and northwest of the Kuwaiti border.

Later analysis showed that Saddam Hussein had withdrawn a large number of troops before the ground war began in an attempt to protect the Republican Guard, tanks, and armor. Iraqi forces in the Kuwait theater of operations numbered 336,000, with 3,400 tanks and 2,500 pieces of artillery. Many were massed along the 138-mile Saudi-Kuwait border, dug in behind berms (raised earthworks), minefields, and oil-filled trenches. Other units were concentrated in central Kuwait and southern Iraq.

Five weeks of nonstop aerial bombardment had cut supply lines and demoralized the conscripted Iraqi forces, many of whom were surviving on rice and water. The Iraqi air force was grounded, and, lacking satellite reconnaissance,

Iraqis were unaware of the massive coalition troop movements of the preceding few weeks; they were relying on information from the feints the allies were staging along the Saudi border. Four Iraqi divisions had been diverted to the defense of the coast of Kuwait by an offshore charade in which U.S. Marines pretended to prepare for an amphibious landing; to maintain that deception, G–day opened with a heavy naval barrage from the USS *Wisconsin* and the USS *Missouri*.

But the day belonged to the ground-based forces. The massive allied offensive in southern Iraq and Kuwait precisely followed General Schwarzkopf's blueprint. At 7 A.M., the allied right flank moved, with the Joint Forces Command-East (Saudi, Kuwaiti, Omani, and United Arab Emirates troops and the U.S. Marines) crossing the border into Kuwait. Half an hour later, the 28th Airborne on the left flank moved into Iraq. The Joint Forces Command-North (Saudi, Egyptian, Kuwaiti, Syrian, and Pakistani troops) advanced into Kuwait, and the 7th Corps began the main thrust into Iraq. Carried on helicopters, troops of the U.S. 101st Airborne Division established a forward operating base, code-named Cobra, 93 miles within Iraq. By the end of the day, the Iraqi army had effectively folded. Some 10,000 Iraqi troops were taken prisoner. The allies retook much of Kuwait and established an air base deep in Iraqi territory.

February 25, 1991: Coalition troops continued their rapid advance. Forward units made the first contacts with the northernmost Republican Guard divisions, and 7th Corps continued its push into southern Iraq. Iraq's main supply route was cut. The United States claimed to have taken 14,000 Iraqi prisoners of war. Massive quantities of supplies were being trucked into the forward operating base, Cobra; meanwhile, Chinook helicopters deposited huge plastic containers of gasoline at refueling stations at the forward lines of the swiftly advancing tank units. By 9 P.M., Iraqi troops were beginning to pull out of Kuwait (see Air War, p. 707). The day exacted some allied costs and casualties, too, and Iraq had by now set a total of 590 Kuwaiti oil wells on fire.

February 26, 1991: The Iraqi army was completely routed and all but encircled. At 1:30 A.M. local time, on a Baghdad Radio broadcast, Saddam Hussein claimed victory but announced Iraq's withdrawal from Kuwait due to "special conditions." The Bush administration replied, "The war continues." Convoys of Iraqis fleeing Kuwait City in military and stolen civilian vehicles were totally destroyed by air attacks (see Air War, p. 706). The 28th Corps pushed as far into Iraq as the Euphrates valley. The southern Iraqi town of Basra was heavily shelled. The Joint Command Force-East and the U.S. Marines closed in on Kuwait City as Iraqi forces continued their chaotic retreat; members of the Kuwaiti resistance movement claimed control of Kuwait City.

Some units did begin to meet serious resistance. In the afternoon, a unit of the U.S. First Cavalry Division ran into the Tawakalna Armored Division of Iraq's Republican Guard; in an engagement that lasted only a few minutes, the Americans destroyed 2 Iraqi tanks and 18 Iraqi armored personnel carriers, at the cost of 2 dead and 9 wounded. In another engagement at a locale in the desert known as 73 Easting (from its map reference), elements of the 2nd Armored Cavalry Regiment ran into other elements of the Tawakalna Division and destroyed numerous

Iraqi tanks. Rushing eastward, other units of the 2nd Armored Cavalry were joined by elements of the 3rd Armored Division, and by early evening, they were also engaging elements of the Tawakalna Division.

February 27, 1991: U.S., Kuwaiti, and Saudi troops announced their full control of Kuwait City at 4:30 A.M. local time. Throughout the day, in the Iraq desert to the northeast, the major battle of the Persian Gulf War was fought along a 100-mile-wide front, as five U.S. armored divisions confronted three armored divisions of the Republican Guard—the Tawakalna, Medina, and Hammurabi. The Iraqi forces proved powerless against the U.S. units, which destroyed practically everything in their path. In what became known as the Battle of Medina Ridge, the 1st Armored Division's tanks encountered the Medina Division dug in along a 6-mile ridgeline; the 1st Armored Division's tanks destroyed 186 tanks and 127 armored fighting vehicles.

In an afternoon meeting in Washington, D.C., Gen. Colin Powell and Secretary of Defense Dick Cheney advised President George Bush that the United States had achieved its military objectives. At 9 P.M. Eastern Standard Time (February 28, 5 A.M. local time), the president announced the liberation of Kuwait and ordered an informal cease-fire.

February 28, 1991: U.S. 1st Armored Division forces launched a final attack against the Medina Division of the Republican Guard and stopped because the cease-fire went into effect. All military operations in the Persian Gulf were suspended at 8 A.M. local time (midnight EST). Two hours later, Iraq delivered a letter to the UN agreeing to comply with all UN resolutions.

March 1, 1991: A bus full of Iraqi soldiers, stopped at a checkpoint manned by U.S. soldiers, began shooting; the Americans returned fire, killing four Iraqis.

March 2, 1991: In violation of the cease-fire, a large armored column of Iraqi troops tried to escape from Basra, a major city in southern Iraq; U.S. forces moved to stop them by destroying 187 armored vehicles, 400 other vehicles, and 43 pieces of artillery.

HOME FRONT

As the first major military operation since the Vietnam War, the Persian Gulf War offered some

A U.S. landing vehicle brings supplies to the beach at Kuwait, where a forklift will take them to troops who have liberated Kuwait City from the Iraqis.

extremely sensitive challenges to U.S. government leaders. The U.S. Congress asserted its constitutional war-making prerogatives in that war, and in accordance with Congress's January 12, 1991, authorization of force (see p. 704), President George Bush notified lawmakers an hour before the start of the Persian Gulf War. On January 17, a Senate resolution was passed commending the president and U.S. troops; the House followed the next day with a resolution supporting the war. The State of the Union address on January 29 allowed President Bush to report formally to the Congress and the nation on the progress of the war.

From the beginning, a large majority of Americans supported the president's handling of the crisis, but as early as October 20, 1990, antiwar activists conducted marches in 15 U.S. cities. In mid-November, the National Conference of Catholic Bishops and the National Council of Churches (the major Protestant association), appealed to President Bush to exercise great restraint before adopting a military solution. Immediately before the hostilities started, fewer than half of Americans favored offensive action, but once air war began in January, public support for the allied war settled at about 75 percent. Antiwar demon-

strations were held in cities throughout the country as the war began on January 17, 1991; they continued throughout the fighting, but never attained the same scale of those that took place during the Vietnam War.

The Persian Gulf War was the first U.S. war to be covered in real time on television (see Legends and Trivia, pp. 714-715). Viewers watched the bombing of Baghdad live, as Cable Network News (CNN) correspondents aimed their cameras from the al-Rashid Hotel in Baghdad on January 17. U.S. commanders released cockpit video recordings of smart bomb strikes on Iraqi targets only a few hours after the actual raids. Press briefings by U.S. and other allied military leaders in Riyadh were covered live so that Americans came to feel they had front-row seats at a war in progress. Only later did the media point out that they were actually denied unrestricted access to the units in the field and that the press briefings presented only the official military view of the war.

INTERNATIONAL DEVELOPMENTS

In early 1990, Kuwait and the United Arab Emirates deliberately increased production until oil was selling at a low $11 per barrel to $14 per barrel. After Iraq's invasion of Kuwait, market anxiety drove the price as high as $40 per barrel; some observers predicted that in the event of war, the price might reach $100 per barrel. Oil prices did surge briefly after the Persian Gulf War began, but fell back to the more ordinary level of $20 once it became apparent that Saudi oil fields would not be damaged and future supplies were assured.

Contrary to Saddam Hussein's expectation of solidarity, the Persian Gulf War divided the Arab world and set Islamic nations at odds. The Arab League passed a resolution by a 20-12 vote condemning Iraq's invasion and approving the deployment of U.S. troops to the Persian Gulf. The Gulf Cooperation Council (including Saudi Arabia, Kuwait, and the United Arab Emirates), Syria, Pakistan, and Turkey were central to the allied coalition. Jordan and Iran declared neutrality (although Jordan's leader expressed some sympathy for Iraq, and Jordanians essentially ignored the embargo). Only Libya, the Palestine Liberation Organization, and Yemen supported Iraq.

The hectic pace and variety of peace initiatives that punctuated the crisis abated only slightly during the war. In February, Iran and the Soviet Union both made serious efforts to mediate the conflict before the ground war commenced. The Soviet Union, formerly a staunch ally of and major arms supplier to Iraq, was especially intent on averting a ground offensive. Soviet president Mikhail Gorbachev, working through his personal emissary Yevgeni Primakov and with Iraqi foreign minister Tariq Aziz, negotiated a peace plan with Saddam Hussein, but it was rejected as inadequate by President George Bush on February 22; Gorbachev and Aziz came up with another peace plan but it came too late for acceptance by the United States.

NEGOTIATIONS AND PEACE TREATY

March 3, 1991: Three days after the suspension of hostilities, Gen. Norman Schwarzkopf and Saudi general Prince Khalid bin Sultan negotiated temporary cease-fire terms with Iraqi officers at the Safwan airfield in occupied territory of southern Iraq. On the same day, the Security Council passed and Iraq accepted the UN's cease-fire terms in Resolution 686.

April 3, 1991: The UN Security Council adopted Resolution 687, specifying conditions for a formal end to the Persian Gulf War. Some sanctions were to be lifted, but the ban on Iraqi oil sales was to remain in force until Iraq destroyed its weapons of mass destruction under UN supervision.

April 6, 1991: Iraq reluctantly accepted the terms of UN resolution 687. After taking effect on April 11, 1991, the official cease-fire was frequently violated by Iraq.

RESULTS OF THE WAR (Casualties, Costs, Consequences)

Of almost 800,000 U.S. and coalition troops in the Persian Gulf, only 240 were killed and 776 wounded in action; of those, 148 dead (including 6 women) and 458 wounded were American; 44 of the fatalities and 85 of the wounded were due to friendly fire; another 122 U.S. personnel died of various noncombat causes (such as accidents) during their time in the Persian Gulf.

The Kuwaiti armed forces lost an estimated 800 in the first day of the invasion. During the six months of occupation, an estimated 2,000 more Kuwaiti were killed by Iraqi forces. There were also numerous deaths from cholera due to impure water and from respiratory ailments due to the burning oil wells. (The last oil well fire was not put out until November 6, 1991.)

The precise number of Iraqi casualties is unknown. Accepted Iraqi estimates indicate that 20,000 were killed as a result of the air war, including about 1,000 civilians; another 60,000 were reported wounded. During the ground war, Iraqi military casualties were estimated at fewer than 9,500 dead and 26,000 wounded. Iraqi ground war casualties were lower than expected, mostly because the overwhelming success of the allied air war shortened the ground war. In addition, Saddam Hussein withdrew a large number of troops from the Kuwaiti theater of operations before the ground fighting began. Many more escaped before the route back to Baghdad was blocked, and thousands of Iraqi soldiers deserted or surrendered—the allies held 80,000 prisoners of war at the cease-fire.

Precise figures for Iraqi civilian casualties have never been agreed on. Iraq charged that many thousands of civilians were killed in the bombing and missile raids, but the United States estimates are considerably lower—closer to

1,000. However, reliable estimates at the end of 1991 indicated that another 70,000 Iraqi civilians had died from wounds or from deprivation of adequate water, food, and medical supplies directly attributable to the Persian Gulf War. In the years that followed, because the UN embargo cut off Iraq from virtually all imports including medical supplies, an estimated 100,000 Iraqi, mostly the very young and elderly, also lost their lives due to a lack of food and medical treatment.

The direct cost to the United States of the Persian Gulf War was relatively low, since allies paid most costs of military operations. The Department of Defense reported that the United States spent $61.1 billion; however, coalition countries offset that by contributing $48 billion in cash and $5.6 billion in materials and services, leaving the U.S. actual cost at $7.5 billion. The largest allied donors were Saudi Arabia ($16.8 billion), Kuwait ($16 billion), Japan ($10 billion), and Germany ($6 billion).

Estimates of total Arab losses from the Persian Gulf War approached half a trillion dollars. Kuwait lost an estimated $180 billion worth of oil reserves in the oil field fires, which burned for ten months. Lost oil production, infrastructure damages and continuing environmental cleanup added to an estimated total cost to Kuwait of $240 billion. Total Saudi Arabian expenses of $50 billion to $70 billion included environmental cleanup and the repair of infrastructure damaged by coalition forces stationed in Saudi Arabia.

Accurate data are difficult to come by for Iraq, but the Persian Gulf War is estimated to have cost the country at least $120 billion. Bomb damage to infrastructure and industrial plants was estimated at $50 billion; the destruction of Iraq's military arsenal, at $40 billion. Nearly 90 percent of Iraqi artillery, half of its armored personnel carriers, more than 80 percent of its tanks, and about 350 of its 750 combat planes were destroyed, captured, or relocated outside Iraq. Ongoing UN sanctions imposed annual losses of $33 billion in revenues from oil and other economic activity.

The Iraqi air force suffered such heavy losses in the first days of the war that it thereafter effectively stayed out of the air: 182 aircraft were destroyed (33 in air-to-air combat), 31 were captured on the ground, and 137 fled to Iran. The United States lost 14 fixed-wing planes in combat and another 4 in accidents; the other coali-

tion forces lost 11 planes in combat and 1 plane in an accident; most losses in combat were due to ground fire.

The real price of the war can never be assessed, for in addition to hard costs, the fighting exacted incalculable regional costs in the form of long-term environmental damage, disruption of trade, and population displacement. Kuwaiti oil wells burned for nearly a year, polluting rainfall up to 1,500 miles away. Iraq's infrastructure was devastated by allied bombing. The UN embargo continued for years, and Iraqi civilians were punished by severe shortages of basic necessities for years; limited Iraqi oil exports to pay for food and civilian aid were finally allowed beginning in December 1996. Despite U.S. hopes that Saddam Hussein would be deposed, he remained in power after the war, and his military was far from destroyed. Rebellions by Iraqi Kurds and Shiites that erupted shortly after the war ended were brutally suppressed; a million Iraqi Kurds became refugees.

The Persian Gulf War bestowed a short-lived political boost to the Bush presidency but left the U.S. economy with longer-term benefits: Oil prices remained low, thanks to the rapprochement between the Gulf Cooperation Council and the U.S. government, contributing greatly to a U.S. economic recovery.

The effects on the Middle East were similarly mixed. The advance of the Iraqi military juggernaut was temporarily halted, but the long-term implications for Iraq's political future were uncertain: Any hopes that elements within Iraq might rise up and overthrow Saddam Hussein soon faded. The United States continued to maintain a prominent and costly military presence in Saudi Arabia, Kuwait, and the Persian Gulf—at least 20 warships, hundreds of airplanes, some 40 tanks, thousands of troops. In the years after the war, those forces were put on alert on several occasions (and even supplemented by troops airlifted in from the United States) in response to what were regarded as potentially threatening moves by Hussein's military.

Although insecurity persists in that turbulent part of the world, broader Middle East relations were decisively realigned by the war. The signing of the historic Israeli-Palestinian peace accords in Washington, D.C., on September 13, 1993, was generally regarded as a direct result of the Persian Gulf War. U.S.-Arab relations assumed a new importance and trust, balancing the historically close ties between the United States and Israel.

One other consequence of the Persian Gulf War was that women in the U.S. military had new roles and opportunities. Although officially barred from serving in combat posts, they served in combat support units and ended up involved in combat: They were killed, wounded, and taken prisoner. (At least one group of women engaged in a firefight when attacked by Iraqi forces.) As a result, the "risk rule" that had kept women from serving in a combat area was rescinded by the U.S. military as of October 1, 1994, and American women can now serve as pilots of combat aircraft and helicopters and also as crew on naval warships.

MILITARY INNOVATIONS, TACTICS, EQUIPMENT

The Persian Gulf War experience made high-tech war a reality and confirmed that the nature of warfare had decisively changed. Among U.S. high-tech weapons that dominated the Persian Gulf War were precision-guided Tomahawk cruise missiles and advanced sensor and targeting systems. F-117A Stealth fighters proved the value of stealth technology—the special materials, design features, and flight methods that allowed planes to elude radar detection. Not a single F-117A was lost in action. Several of the most decisive innovations involved electronic systems, such as those that allowed the jamming of Iraq's radar and surface-to-air missiles. A tremendous advantage for the coalition forces came from the various high-tech devices that gave night vision capability to U.S. airplanes, tanks, and even infantry units.

The Patriot antitactical ballistic missile was perhaps the most publicized weapon used in the war. Twenty-one Patriot batteries were deployed in Saudi Arabia, four in Turkey, seven in Israel; none of those in Turkey fired, but those in Saudi Arabia and Israel fired some 600 Patriot missiles against Iraq's Soviet-built Scuds. During the Persian Gulf War, the Patriot missile was widely hailed for its high success rate, but it was revealed after the war that the Patriot missile had not been as effective as claimed.

Smart, or homing, bombs were first used in the Vietnam War, but those used in the Persian

Gulf War were more technologically advanced. They differed from missiles in having no propulsion system; they were essentially gravity-fall bombs, each equipped with small wings (for gliding capability and maneuverability control) and a laser system and a TV-guidance or radio-navigation system in the nose to direct the bomb onto a target. They not only provided greater accuracy but also allowed the bombers to stay at higher altitudes above artillery fire; the laser and radio-navigation systems could also be used at night.

The Persian Gulf War has been called the "first comprehensive space war." U.S. satellites provided real-time information and command-and-control capability; their functions included navigation, weather, communications, and missile defense.

An innovation then in the development stage, the battle management system, got an early field test in the Persian Gulf War, with JSTARS (joint surveillance target attack radar system), which allowed aircraft to track enemy forces, then to direct ground movements. That system was in turn part of the U.S. military's new strategy, AirLand Battle, based on lessons learned from the Vietnam War and on preparing for the possibility of a Soviet invasion in Europe. The AirLand Battle doctrine called for fighting an enemy not by the conventional way of confronting it at a front line but by mounting a more sophisticated and coordinated series of attacks by airmobile units and armored and mechanized units that strike deep into the enemy rear. JSTARS was put to its first test in the Persian Gulf War and appeared to pass with flying colors.

LEGENDS AND TRIVIA

As the United States' first live television war, the Persian Gulf War was rich in media-related stories. **Cable News Network (CNN)** war coverage was equally indispensable to average Americans and Iraqi military officials. CNN was so important to Saddam Hussein's public relations and diplomatic efforts that the Iraqi information ministry often checked the network's schedule before issuing statements. The instantaneous broadcast of war news resulted in a number of war reports filed with greater speed than accuracy. Contrary to initial reports, for example, invading Iraqis did not murder Kuwaiti babies in their incubators. In one case of Iraqi manipulation, CNN correspondent Peter Arnett (who was controversial because of his decision to stay in Baghdad throughout the war) was misled by Iraqi officials to broadcast pictures of a "baby milk factory" heartlessly bombed by the allies: In reality, the structure was a biological weapons facility. Corrections of such errors sometimes came too late to affect popular misperceptions.

Soon after U.S. forces began to be dispatched in Operation Desert Shield in the Persian Gulf, an unusual phenomenon began to be observed throughout the United States: **yellow ribbons** tied around trees and various objects in public places such as potted plants in offices. Everyone displaying those ribbons—and most Americans who were aware of them—had a ready explanation: It was an old American tradition, they said, to signify that servicemen off on a mission were not forgotten and their homecoming was awaited. But if asked just how that tradition came about, how old it was, and what the origin of the yellow ribbon was, few could answer. Nor could most experts in American folklore, because it was not, in fact, an old tradition. Its most immediate ancestor was the same practice that had appeared during the Iranian hostage crisis of 1979–1981. Various individuals took credit for being the first to do so at the time, but again, the ready explanation was that it seemed traditional to tie a yellow ribbon around a tree or some such object as a symbol of remembrance. In fact, the people doing so were inspired by a popular hit song of 1973, "Tie a Yellow Ribbon Round the Old Oak Tree," initially recorded by Tony Orlando and Dawn and later recorded by various other popular singers. The words of the song described a convict coming home after several years in prison; he tells the bus driver and fellow bus passengers that he has written to his sweetheart asking her to tie a yellow ribbon around an oak tree by the road if she will have him back; as the bus approaches the tree, a cheer goes up in the bus—there is the yellow ribbon! The creators of the song, Irwin Levine and L. Russell Brown, claimed they had been told that story by someone in the Army who had experienced such an event.

It is highly possible that the songwriters were, consciously or not, influenced by another song with deeper roots—"Round Her Neck She Wore a Yellow Ribbon." That was the theme song of a popular movie, *She Wore a Yellow Ribbon*, starring John Wayne and Joanne Dru. The movie was released in 1949, but the song had its greatest burst of popularity in 1950—coincidentally, it appears, when the Korean War broke out. The song from the movie was credited to contemporary professional songwriters M. Ottner and Leroy Parker and its words seemed to refer specifically to a young lady's wearing the yellow ribbon in remembrance of her soldier lover. In fact, the song had been around for more than a century, and it had numerous versions, not all referring to a soldier. Somehow, the notion gained currency that the song dated from the Civil War and/or referred specifically to U.S. cavalry soldiers. In fact, except for oral reminiscences, no evidence for either has ever surfaced. Instead, the song has been traced directly to a song popular in the 1830s that was sung in U.S. stage productions. In that version, however, a vegetable peddler wore a green willow around his hat, and when asked why, said, "Tell them that my true love is far, far away." In turn, scholars of old music have traced that 1830s song to English popular songs of the 1500s!

The yellow-ribbon phenomenon was related to a merchandising bonanza and a fashion trend. In the spring of 1991, chain stores in malls throughout the United States began selling clothing and jewelry not only with a yellow-ribbon motif but also with a U.S. flag motif.

NOTABLE PHRASES

This will not stand.

At an improvised news conference on the lawn of the White House on August 5, 1990 (see p. 702), President George Bush uttered this threat to Iraq: "This will not stand. This will not stand, this aggression against Kuwait." In its slightly old-fashioned tone, it expressed the public's indignation.

A line in the sand

In a televised address to the nation on August 8, 1990, President George Bush added to his prepared speech by stating, "A line has been drawn in the sand." In the context of his speech on that occasion, he seemed to be referring only to the border of Saudi Arabia as the "line" that the United States was drawing and prepared to defend. At the same time, he probably meant it in a broader, less literal sense—almost the reverse of the former meaning: It was a line that Iraq had drawn, a challenge that the United States was going to accept. In that he was employing a traditional metaphor, one that has always been a favorite of journalists, editorial writers, and politicians. On September 8, 1986, President Ronald Reagan said he had "drawn a line in concrete" when it came to Congress spending sums he disapproved of. In his autobiography, *My American Journey*, Colin Powell suggested that he was actually the first to use that phrase in a meeting with President Bush before Iraq invaded Kuwait.

A new world order

A central theme of the Bush presidency was the hope that the international community, freed from Cold War alliances and rivalries, could fulfill the UN's promise as a force for collective security and the rule of law. In an address to a joint session of Congress on September 11, 1990, President Bush laid out the first four objectives of the buildup of forces in the Persian Gulf, then concluded with a broader goal: "Out of these troubled times, our fifth objective—a new world order—can emerge: a new era, freer from the threat of terror, stronger in the pursuit of justice, and more secure in the pursuit of peace. An era in which the nations of the world, east and west, north and south, can prosper and live in harmony." President Bush returned to that theme and motto on several other occasions—particularly in his State of the Union message on January 29, 1991.

The mother of all battles

Saddam Hussein often referred to the coming showdown with the UN coalition forces in extravagant rhetoric borrowed from traditional Arabic poetry, and that was one such phrase. He actually used it on several occasions during the Persian Gulf War, but probably the most publicized occasion was his radio address to the Iraqi people on January 16, 1991, barely two hours after the beginning of the air attack on Iraq: "O great Iraqi people, sons of great people, valiant men of our courageous armed forces....The great duel, the mother of all battles, between victorious right and the evil that will certainly be de-

feated has begun, God willing." That apocalyptic phrase soon invited innumerable satirical variations by Americans, from late-night comics to Secretary of Defense Dick Cheney, who on February 27, called the Iraqi withdrawal from Kuwait "the mother of all retreats." That same day, Gen. Norman Schwarzkopf gave a presentation of the progress of the Persian Gulf War that the media dubbed "the mother of all briefings."

SONGS

Because the Persian Gulf War was compressed into such a short time frame, there was not much response—pro or con—on the part of popular musicians. On the pro side, singing the "Star-Spangled Banner" was turned into virtually a statement of support for the war; that culminated when Whitney Houston sang the "Star-Spangled Banner" at the Super Bowl in January 1991, then donated profits from the video clip and single to the American Red Cross Gulf Crisis Fund. Likewise, a popular song of 1984, Lee Greenwood's "God Bless the U.S.A" was revived and given lots of airtime. A group of well-known performers and sports stars got together in Los Angeles and recorded a single and video called "Voices That Care"; proceeds went to the Red Cross fund and to the USO. Among those participating were Billy Crystal, Little Richard, Tiffany, Michael Bolton, Meryl Streep, Kevin Costner, Whoopi Goldberg, Mike Tyson, and Wayne Gretzky. In part, that was in response to a recording produced by Lenny Kravitz, when Sean Lennon, the 15-year-old son of John Lennon and Yoko Ono updated the words of his father's antiwar song "Give Peace a Chance" and released it sung by a group that included M. C. Hammer, Peter Gabriel, L. L. Cool J., Randy Newman, and Bonnie Raitt. But neither that nor another antiwar song, "Highwire," by the Rolling Stones, received much attention. Nor did "Die for Oil, Sucker," by Jello Biafra, formerly of the Dead Kennedys. One song more pacifist than anti–Persian Gulf War that did get a fair amount of time on pop radio stations was "Song for Desert Storm," by Jim Walktendonk, a Vietnam veteran.

HISTORICAL PERSPECTIVES AND CONTROVERSIES

Might the United States and the UN have

achieved the same results with the embargo on Iraq?

That question continued to be debated long after the end of the Persian Gulf War. An embargo does not risk lives, it is relatively cheap, and has been a successful coercive tool. Iraq's near-total dependence on oil exports and imported food made it particularly vulnerable to economic sanctions, and the UN embargo imposed in August 1990 virtually cut off Iraqi trade and international finance. Scholars estimated that in time the embargo would halve Iraq's gross national product, an unsustainable drop. Most experts who testified at congressional hearings in November 1990 urged the Bush administration to rely on the embargo rather than initiate military action in the Persian Gulf.

In December, however, the Bush administration declared that sanctions alone would not force Saddam Hussein to abandon Kuwait. Although estimates varied, those endorsing that view argued that the embargo might take as long as two years to work. The coalition might have easily dissolved in the meantime, and Hussein showed every intention of waiting it out even at the expense of his people's well-being. One United Nations official said, "We...cannot be seen to use famine to bring the country down." Further, the embargo would have been unable to achieve the UN goal of destroying Iraq's weapons of mass destruction.

Those who argued against the embargo later pointed to what happened after the Persian Gulf War when the embargo, in fact, did continue: Supplies of all kinds made it through the blockade via an international blackmarket; those Iraqis with power and influence seemed relatively unaffected and even prospered; and Hussein was totally uninfluenced by its impact on the mass of his people (many thousands of whom died of malnutrition and poor medical treatment). Lawrence Freedman and Efraim Karsh have argued that the embargo and other sanctions could only have worked if they had damaged Saddam Hussein politically—and there has been little or no evidence of that occurring.

Did President George Bush stop the war too soon? After such an overwhelming military victory, why didn't he march into Iraq and remove Saddam Hussein from power?

Saddam Hussein's 12-year-rule had unquestionably been one of tyranny and international aggression, and there were times during the months leading up to the Persian Gulf War that President George Bush seemed to be saying that the goal was to get rid of "Saddam," as he referred to the Iraqi leader. However, UN Resolution 678 articulated clear and limited goals: to eject Iraq from Kuwait and "restore peace and security," which was generally interpreted to mean destroying Iraq's weapons of mass destruction. The UN and coalition members approved a war against Iraq's international aggression, not against Saddam Hussein's domestic political repression. In any case, U.S. intelligence reports were predicting (wrongly, as it happened) that the regime would not long survive the war. However ambivalent many people were about President Bush's decision to end the war when he did, most authorities have agreed that he had no legal grounds for continuing it.

Were U.S. troops in the Persian Gulf exposed to some sort of chemical or bacteriological agents that caused the symptoms known collectively as Gulf War syndrome?

Because Saddam Hussein had used deadly chemicals in his wars against Iran and the Kurds, the possibility that he might resort to chemical and/or biological warfare was considered from the outset of the planning for the Persian Gulf War. UN troops were issued gas masks and protective clothing, and there was some training in their use; some troops wore at least parts of this protective clothing throughout the entire ground war. In 1996, the United States revealed that some U.S. troops had been issued experimental drugs to protect them against deadly gasses but which instead may have caused health problems. As the war ended, however, the military reported that Iraq had not used any chemicals or biological agents.

Shortly after the war, significant numbers of military personnel who had served in the Persian Gulf began reporting a puzzling array of debilitating physical ailments, including joint pain, nausea, and fatigue. Many veterans suspected that they had been exposed to Iraqi chemical or biological weapons in the Persian Gulf War. The number of complaints, not only from U.S. veterans but from Canadians, Britons, and Australians as well, continued to rise. The Pentagon repeatedly denied that U.S. troops had been exposed, however, and numerous government studies dismissed the veterans' complaints until new studies in November 1996 finally confirmed the prevalence and seriousness of their symptoms—so-called Gulf War syndrome.

During the hostilities, chemical-weapons detectors in the Persian Gulf repeatedly read positive but were dismissed by senior U.S. officers, who disbelieved the data. (The Czech chemical weapons monitors, in contrast, routinely donned protective gear on those occasions.) Then on June 21, 1996, Pentagon officials admitted that in March 1991 some U.S. troops had been assigned to blow up an Iraqi ammunition dump at Kamishiyah that contained nerve gas weapons; the Pentagon insisted, though, that only 300–400 troops might have been exposed to any of the chemicals and that the military was still not accepting responsibility for Gulf War syndrome. On August 21, 1996, the Defense Department acknowledged that chemical weapons were detected as many as seven times during the first week of the war in staging areas in northern Saudi Arabia, where tens of thousands of U.S. troops were stationed. On September 18, 1996, the Pentagon revised its earlier figures, admitting that perhaps as many as 5,000 troops might have been exposed to the chemical agents from the ammunition dump. On September 19, 1996, newly declassified documents revealed that a battalion of U.S. troops was exposed to an Iraqi chemical attack on Jubail, Saudi Arabia, during the fighting, and that many of those troops had since reported illnesses. Although the Pentagon could not locate the detailed operations logs for the dates when the ammunition dump was destroyed, it no longer engaged in total denial of a possible link between that event and at least some of the medical problems being reported by veterans.

On the other hand, many scientists remained dubious about any connection between illnesses and chemical or biological weapons. Those scientist pointed out that the illnesses reported were more typical of those caused by stress than those that might be caused by chemical or biological weapons and that those reporting the illnesses had often been far away from any possible source of contamination.

Whatever the scientific verdict turned out to be, the fact remained that many who had served in the Persian Gulf War reported a complex of similar symptoms and disabilities. Therefore, on March 7, 1997, President Bill Clinton announced that he had authorized revising the regulations of the Department of Veterans Affairs to extend medical benefits and pensions to all Persian Gulf War veterans who reported chronic and undiagnosed maladies that appeared before December 31, 2001.

CIVILIAN AND MILITARY BIOGRAPHIES

AMERICAN

Bush, George Herbert Walker (1924–   )— president: George Bush was the youngest U.S. Navy pilot in World War II. He went on to graduate from Yale, then made his fortune in Texas oil. He served in the U.S. House of Representatives, as ambassador to the UN and to China, and as director of the CIA before serving two terms as Ronald Reagan's vice president (1981–1988). As the 41st president of the United States (1989–1993) he skillfully engaged the UN and forged an unprecedented multinational coalition to reverse the Iraqi occupation of Kuwait. His handling of the Persian Gulf War earned him the highest domestic approval rating of any president (91 percent), but a sagging economy doomed his reelection. During his last week in the White House he ordered air strikes against Iraq for UN cease-fire violations.

Cheney, Richard B. (1941–   ) U.S. Secretary of Defense: Richard Cheney was born in Nebraska. He earned his B.S. and M.S. in political science at the University of Wyoming. Cheney held several administrative positions under Presidents Richard Nixon and Gerald Ford, then served Wyoming in the House of Representatives from 1979 until 1988, when he resigned to become President George Bush's Secretary of Defense. Cheney had a reputation as a loyal team player and a hardworking, nonideological public official; as such, he worked closely with the Soviets in the first crucial years of the collapse of the Soviet Union and its military might. With the invasion of Kuwait, Cheney was thrust into the spotlight as one of the principal architects of U.S. policy and strategy in the crisis, and his calm, efficient manner helped to defuse controversy and inspire confidence. With Bush's loss in 1992, Cheney left the government and went to work in the private industrial sector.

Powell, Colin Luther (1937–   )—general: Colin Powell was born in New York City. He was commissioned in 1958 and was decorated during two tours in Vietnam. He became known for his political acumen as national security adviser to President Ronald Reagan (1987–1989). As chairman of the Joint Chiefs of Staff (1989–1993) he wielded enormous power over the United States's conduct of the Gulf War. Early in the crisis, he opposed the use of military force and urged a strategy of economic sanctions; once the military was committed, however, he argued for a quick, overpowering strike. His tact and intelligence made him a national hero, and his resignation from active duty in 1993 prompted frenzied speculation about a future political career.

Schwarzkopf, H. Norman (1934–   )—general: Norman Schwarzkopf was a New Jersey native. He graduated from West Point into an Army career that included two tours in Vietnam and the deputy command of the 1983 Grenada Intervention. As commander in chief of U.S. Central Command, he was appointed commander of Operation Desert Shield in August 1990. From his Riyadh headquarters, "Stormin' Norman" commanded the coalition forces against Iraq and personally planned and led the ground campaign. His frequent television interviews and press briefings during the Persian Gulf War showed Americans a tough, forthright, and likable character, and on his retirement from active duty in August 1991, he embarked on a second career as a public speaker and writer.

SAUDI

Ibn Abdul Aziz Fahd (?1922–   )—king: King Fahd was one of 40-some sons of Ibn Saud, the founder (1932) and first king of modern-day Saudi Arabia. He studied in universities in Europe and the United States. After his first appointment as Saudi minister of education in 1953, King Fahd assumed increasingly more prominent roles as three of his brothers and half-brothers preceded him as king; he became king in 1982. King Fahd was long a proponent of modernization in matters of developing education and the economy, but he was always careful not to challenge the more conservative religious and social elements of his society. When Kuwait was invaded, he at first was opposed to getting involved, especially to allowing U.S. and other armed forces to operate out of his country; once he was convinced that Saudi Arabia could not remain unengaged, he committed his nation's resources, money, and armed forces to the Persian Gulf War.

Bin Sultan bin Abdulaziz al Saud, Prince Khalid (1950–   )—general: Prince Khalid was a member of the Saudi royal family. He graduated from the Royal Military Academy, Sandhurst, England, and trained at the U.S. Army Air Defense Artillery School and the U.S. Air Force Air War College. As the senior Saudi royal in uniform, he was appointed commander of the Air Defense Forces in 1986. During the Persian Gulf War, he led all Arab and Muslim troops as commander of the Joint Forces Command, an appointment that made him cocommander with Gen. Norman Schwarzkopf of the allied war effort. He was dismissed in September 1991, reportedly because of the celebrity and ambition engendered by his success in the war.

KUWAITI

al-Sabah, Sheik Iber al-Ahmad al-Jabar (1926–   )—emir: A descendant of the Sabah family that had essentially been installed in power by the British, he succeeded his cousin as emir, or ruler, in 1977. He did not have much formal education, but he was regarded as a clever politician. He is said to have fathered at least 70 children and acquired a personal fortune of several billion dollars. Ruling Kuwait with an iron hand, he dissolved the token parliament whenever he chose to; when the Persian Gulf War broke out, it had not met since 1986. When the Iraqis invaded Kuwait, he barely escaped with his life to Saudi Arabia; he returned two weeks after Kuwait was liberated. The coalition suggested that he and his Sabah family would have to adopt more democratic ways to accommodate the new spirit of freedom that the war had unleashed among many Kuwaiti, but there was little sign that he or his family was prepared to share power.

IRAQI

Hussein, Saddam (1937–   )—president: Saddam Hussein was born near Tikrit, Iraq. A Ba'ath Socialist Party activist, he participated in an assassination attempt against the Iraqi premier in 1959 and a successful coup in 1963; in 1968, he helped plan the Ba'ath coup. He became president in 1979 and chairman of the Revolutionary Command Council. A ruthless dictator protected by a secret police network, he transformed his agricultural country into a military powerhouse in the hope of dominating the Arab oil-producing states. In Iraq's war with Iran (1980–1988) and in the Persian Gulf War, he miscalculated the consequences of military aggression but he remained firmly in command of Iraq.

Aziz, Tariq (?1936–)—foreign minister: Tariq Aziz's early years are somewhat clouded, but apparently he was born into a Christian family and was originally named Mikhail Yohanna; at some point, he changed his name to Tariq Aziz (Arabic for "glorious past"). He became a radical in the 1950s and joined the Ba'ath Party, the Arab Socialist Party. While working as an editor for the party's publications, he became close to a young Ba'athist revolutionary, Saddam Hussein. After the Ba'athists gained power in 1968, Aziz rose through various government posts to become the foreign minister in 1983. As Hussein's right-hand man, Aziz became the voice of Iraq after the invasion of Kuwait, traveling to Teheran, Geneva, and Moscow to try to bolster Iraq's position. In contrast to Hussein, Aziz was a man of reason, even admitting after the Persian Gulf War ended that his government had made some mistakes. But he continued to defend Hussein's positions and to fight for restoring Iraq to the community of nations.

FURTHER READING

BBC World Service, compiler. *Gulf Crisis Chronology.* Harlow, Essex: Longman Group, 1991.

Carhart, Tom. *Iron Soldiers.* New York: Pocket Books, 1994.

Dunnigan, James F., and Austin Bay. *From Shield to Storm: High-Tech Weapons, Military Strategy, and Coalition Warfare in the Persian Gulf.* New York: William Morrow &Co., 1992.

Freedman, Lawrence, and Efraim Karsh. *The Gulf Conflict, 1990-1991: Diplomacy and War in the New World Order.* Princeton, N. J.: Princeton University Press, 1993.

Gordon, Michael R., and Bernard E. Trainor. *The Generals' War: The Inside Story of the Conflict in the Gulf.* Boston: Little, Brown & Co., 1995.

Grossman, Mark. *Encyclopedia of the Persian Gulf War.* Santa Barbara, Calif.: ABC-CLIO, 1995.

Hiro, Dilip. *Desert Shield to Desert Storm: The Second Gulf War.* New York: Routledge, 1992.

Ibrahim, Ibrahim, ed. *The Gulf Crisis: Background and Consequences.* Washington, D.C.: Center for Contemporary Arab Studies, 1992.

Mazarr, Michael J., Don M. Snider, and James A. Blackwell, Jr. *Desert Storm: The Gulf War and What We Learned.* Boulder, Colo.: Westview Press, 1993.

Powell, Colin. *My American Journey.* New York: Random House, 1995.

Record, Jeffrey. *Hollow Victory: A Contrary View of the Gulf War.* Washington, D.C.: Brassey's, 1993.

Schwarzkopf, H. Norman. *It Doesn't Take a Hero.* New York: Bantam Books, 1992.

Sifry, Micah L., and Christopher Cerf, eds. *The Gulf War Reader: History, Documents, Opinions.* New York: Times Books, 1991.

Summers, Harry G. Jr. *Persian Gulf War Almanac.* New York: Facts on File, 1995.

Woodward, Robert. *The Commanders.* New York: Simon & Schuster, 1991.

GLOSSARY

Advance guard: A part of a ground combat force sent ahead of the main body for one or several purposes: to protect the main body against surprise, to gain information about the enemy's forces, to distract the enemy so as to cover the deployment or to conceal the movements of the main body, to remove obstacles and repair roads and bridges for the main body's movement. See also: **van**, **vanguard**, **scout**, and **reconnaissance**.

Air cavalry: These units make use of air mobility (usually involving helicopters) to perform such missions as reconnaissance, screening, and surprise attacks.

Aircraft carrier: A large ship with its own flat landing deck and a contingent of aircraft that serves as a mobile air base.

Amphibious operation: An operation that involves the transfer of troops between ships and land. This may involve hostile fire or not; it may also involve the withdrawal of troops.

Antiballistic missile: See **missile, antiballistic**

Armistice: An agreement by warring parties to suspend hostilities. Armistices may vary from complete cessation of all action to temporary halt of battlefield action for a limited period. See also: **truce**.

Armored unit: A ground force, usually of division size, with a combination of armed capabilities; the principal combat components are usually tank units.

Arquebus (also *harquebus*): An early type of firearm, invented in the mid-1400s; first used by the Spanish, it became common in all European armies in the 16th century. At first it had a matchlock operated by a trigger; eventually some operated with a wheel lock or a flint. Originally it was short and heavy and fired by resting it on a vertical support; later, its bent stock and longer butt allowed it to be fired from the shoulder; it was the first handgun to have a stock shaped to fit the shoulder.

Artillery: A general term that refers collectively to gunpowder weapons too large to be hand-carried and usually operated by a crew. All large, pre-gunpowder devices (such as catapults) for firing missiles are also known as artillery.

Atomic weapon: Strictly speaking, it refers only to those weapons whose explosive power derives from atomic fission—the splitting of the nuclei of atoms of elements such as uranium. In general usage it refers to the range of weapons that are based on the release of nuclear energy. See also: **hydrogen bomb** and **nuclear weapons**.

Battalion: A tactical unit of a ground army's combat force; it may vary in size, but for 20th-century U.S. forces it is generally 500 to 1,000 troops. It consists of three to five of the basic combat units of its branch—**company** for infantry, **battery** for artillery, company or troop for armor. Three or four battalions are usually combined to form a **regiment** or **brigade**.

Battery: (1) A set of guns, torpedo tubes, or missile launchers, usually of the same size or caliber. (2) The basic firing unit of artillery, usually comprising four to eight guns and their operating personnel.

Battleship: A major warship, heavily armed with the most powerful naval weaponry and, since about 1860, heavy metal-armored. See also: **capital ship**, **ship of the line**.

Bazooka: A portable rocket launcher carried by one man; electrically fired, it launched a rocket-propelled armor-piercing projectile. First used in World War II, it took its name from the musical instrument devised by an American comedian, Bob Burns.

Billet: *n.* Housing for troops in both military and nonmilitary buildings. *v.* To assign troops to housing, particularly nonmilitary lodgings.

Blockhouse: A defensive structure of substantial material, now usually concrete but earlier of heavy timbers; it has small openings or loopholes for observation and for firing weapons. In North America during the colonial and frontier periods, blockhouses were often two-story log structures, with the second overhanging the first; this allowed the defenders to fire at different angles.

Breech-loader: Any firearm, whether a cannon or a musket, which is loaded at the breech, or rear of the bore (barrel). Such firearms only came into use in the 19th century, when they replaced muzzle-loaded arms.

Brevet: A semi-temporary rank, usually assigned either because of the need for such a rank in a unit's command or to signify an honorary position. Originally used by the British, it was adopted by the U.S. Army in the 19th century; the last brevet rank awarded was in 1918. (In the U.S. military since then, the term "temporary grade" or "rank" is used.) During the Civil War, many officers held brevet rank. After a war, most officers lose their brevet (or temporary) ranks.

Brig: (1) The jail or detention room on a naval ship or naval station. (2) In earlier times, a two-masted sailing vessel with special sails, used both as naval and commercial ships.

Brigade: A military unit, the size of which has varied over time and in different armies, but which has almost always been smaller than a **division** and larger than a **regiment**. In the post–World War II U.S. Army, a brigade comprises three battalions, and three brigades make up a division.

Bushwhacker: Originally it referred to Confederate soldiers who engaged in guerrilla warfare and was based on the image of men whacking their way through the bushes and forest. The word then passed in to general usage for a guerrilla fighter but was also used for deserters and even outlaws.

Caliber: The diameter of both the bore of a gun barrel and a projectile, usually a bullet or shell. Caliber is usually expressed in millimeters, but some small arms in the United States use thousands of an inch. (Thus a .357 Magnum in the United States is slightly over one-third of an inch.)

Canister: A cylindrical metal container packed with small projectiles (called *canister shot* or *case shot*); when fired from a gun, the container bursts and the shot is scattered.

Cannon: A large gunpowder weapon, too heavy to be transported by hand, and usually having a caliber of at least 20mm. The word has traditionally been used to distinguish all larger and heavier weapons, usually artillery pieces, from small arms; in modern terminology, there are three types of cannon: **gun**, **howitzer**, and **mortar**.

Capital ship: The largest class of ship in a country's navy.

In each period of history, the biggest ships with the most guns are known as capital ships: mid-17th to mid-19th centuries, ships of the line; mid-19th to mid-20th centuries, battleships and heavy cruisers; since World War II, aircraft carriers are also designated as capital ships.

Carbine: Smaller than a rifle, larger than a pistol, this is a light, short-barreled shoulder weapon, primarily used by cavalrymen until the end of the 19th century. Carbines were among the first automatic shoulder small-arms in the mid-19th century.

Casus belli: The Latin for "occasion of war," it refers to the event, action, or circumstances that are used to justify making war. See also: **proximate cause**.

Commando: Originally associated with the British armed forces, it has come to refer to any soldier belonging to a specially selected group of combatants, trained for hand-to-hand fighting, surprise raids, and other irregular tactics. Its American equivalent is **ranger**. See also: **special forces** and **Green Berets**.

Company: A military unit, particularly in the infantry, consisting of a headquarters and two or more platoons; its size has varied, but a typical company is about 100. The next higher unit is usually a **battalion**.

Conscription: The involuntary enlisting of people into a nation's armed forces; also known as the *draft*. In the United States since World War I, it has been also known as selective service.

Corps: In the U.S. Army, a tactical unit larger than a division and smaller than a field army; usually it consists of at least two divisions together with auxiliary units.

Cruiser: A warship smaller, lighter, and with less firepower than a battleship but larger, heavier, and more heavily armed than a destroyer. Modern cruisers are classified, depending on their size and firepower, as "light" or "heavy."

Depth charge: A device designed for explosion under water; usually it has been dropped or catapulted from a ship's deck.

Destroyer: A fast warship, smaller than a cruiser; in the modern U.S. Navy it is usually armed with three-inch or five-inch guns, surface-to-surface missiles, torpedoes, and antisubmarine weapons.

Division: A basic administrative and tactical ground formation of an army, containing units of the various combat branches and large enough to operate independently. In the modern U.S. Army, a division consists of three **brigades** or **regiments**.

Dragoon: An early name for a cavalryman, or mounted infantryman; strictly used, dragoons are distinguished from cavalry by the fact that they ride into battle but then dismount to fight.

Earthworks: Any field fortification constructed primarily of earth, including trenches, walls, barriers, or dugouts; they are sometimes known as *entrenchments*.

Emplacement: A prepared position (usually in a field fortification) for housing and operating one or more weapons or pieces of equipment; they are designed to offer protection against gunfire or bombardment.

Escarpment: A steep slope, whether created by humans or part of the natural terrain, that makes for difficult access to a fortified position.

Feint: A limited movement or attack designed to distract, divert, or deceive the enemy army.

Filibuster: An adventurer who engages in a private military action in a foreign country. (The word is derived from a Spanish word for "freebooter," in turn derived from a Dutch word for "pirate.") See **mercenary**.

Fire support: The assistance or protection given ground forces in direct contact with the enemy by the firepower of ground and/or naval guns and/or by aircraft engaging in close air support.

Flank: *n.* One of the sides of a military formation or position. A flank attack is thus one directed at an enemy's side. *v.* To place one's force in position to threaten or attack the opponent's side. See also: **outflank**.

Flintlock: A small-arms ignition system, consisting of a small piece of flint held in a vise at the end of a cock; when the trigger was released, the flint struck against a piece of steel, creating sparks that ignited the priming powder; this in turn ignited the powder that fired the weapon. It is said to have been invented about 1615 by a French gunsmith, Marin le Bourgeoys. The flintlock was used on **muskets** and soon replaced the **matchlock.**

Frigate: Although used for a variety of fast, light warships, by the 18th century it usually meant a ship with 36 to 42 guns and designed to move faster than **capital ships**. In the modern U.S. Navy, a frigate refers to a class of fast, small ships with sufficient arms to operate independently or with others to counter submarine, air, and small-scale surface threats.

Front: In general, it refers to a large combat area (as the western front in World War I); it may also refer to the line of contact between two opposing forces.

Garrison: (1) A military post, usually relatively small. (2) The troops assigned to a military post.

General staff: A group of high-ranking military men whose function is to assist a nation's military leadership—or a general commanding a field force—in planning, controlling, and coordinating the activities of all subordinate military elements to achieve an assigned objective. The leaders make decisions and give commands; the general staff, after making sure that these decisions are the most effective, must see that the orders are carried out.

Grape(shot): A type of ammunition composed of a number of iron balls (usually about twice the size of a musket ball or of **canister** shot), placed inside a shell and fired from cannon. It was used in both land and naval warfare in the 18th and 19th centuries.

Green Berets: The name assigned to a branch of the U.S. Army Special Forces that was organized in 1962 to train Vietnamese forces to deal with guerrilla and unconventional forces during the war in Vietnam. President John F. Kennedy personally authorized this unit to wear a green beret. Originally the Green Berets were not expected to participate in combat except in self-defense; as the war went on, they inevitably were drawn into combat, but they retained their role as an elite and limited action unit. See also: **special forces** and **ranger**.

Guerrilla: From the Spanish for "little war," it refers to a participant in fighting not directly connected with a formal military organization or operation. More specifically, guerrilla warfare has come to refer to operations carried out by these irregulars in enemy-held or hostile territory. See also: **partisan**.

Gun: A word used in several senses. In its broadest sense, it refers to all kinds of weapons consisting of a barrel, receiver, breech mechanism, and carriage (stock or handle) using controlled explosives to shoot projectiles (or signal flares). In the precise technical sense, it applies to a cannon with a relatively long barrel, high velocity, and a consequent flat trajectory (as distinguished from a **howitzer** or a **mortar**).

Harquebus: See **arquebus**.

Howitzer: A cannon that is lighter than a gun of comparable caliber but heavier than a mortar; it delivers projectiles of medium velocities.

Hydrogen bomb: A weapon whose explosive force derives from the fusion of the nuclei of various hydrogen isotopes in the formation of helium nuclei. See also: **atomic bomb** and **nuclear weapons**.

Impressment: The forcing of service in an army or navy through kidnapping or the involuntary seizure of citizens. This was a common practice around the world well into the 19th century and was one of the major causes of the War of 1812. When carried out to kidnap crews for private or merchant ships, it is usually called "to shanghai" (from the practice of obtaining crew for ships going to China).

Insurgency: A revolt or insurrection conducted by individuals within a nation against a constituted government, but one that does not develop into a full-scale civil war.

Interdict: To stop or hinder the enemy's use of an area or route by the use of gunfire, aerial bombing, or some other means of destruction. There is usually the implication of having cut off the enemy's main force or at least prevented the enemy from assembling the full force or supplies necessary for a major action.

Irregulars: Armed individuals or groups not members of regular military forces and who often conduct warfare within enemy-held territory; also called **guerrillas** and **partisans**.

Kentucky rifle: A muzzle-loading rifle originally developed in 17th-century Germany, it was modified in the 18th century by German craftsmen in Pennsylvania, who made it lighter, longer barreled, and more accurate. Originally used for hunting, it proved highly effective in the French and Indian Wars and the American Revolution when fired by frontiersmen; since they were often associated with Kentucky, the rifle gained its popular name (although it was also known as the Pennsylvania rifle).

Lancer: A cavalryman armed with a lance—a long, metal-tipped spear. Lances were generally replaced by gunpowder weapons by the 17th century.

Letter of marque (and reprisal): A written commission from a government to the owner of a private vessel, authorizing its captain to operate against enemy ships as a **privateer**. The captain and crew of the privateer usually shared the profits from the sale of the contents of any seized ships. See also: **prize ship**.

Logistics: The activities that provide for the buildup and support of a military force so that it will be efficient and effective in both combat and noncombat operations. Included in logistics are supplies, equipment, and transportation; maintenance, construction, and operation of facilities; provision, movement, and evacuation of personnel; and other related services.

Magazine: (1) A structure or compartment for storing supplies, particularly ammunition or explosives. (2) A sometimes detachable part of a firearm that holds ammunition ready for insertion into the chamber.

Marine: One of a body of troops trained for service at sea and on land and often stationed on ships to be ready for emergency actions. In the 20th century, marines are assigned primarily to amphibious operations and are usually relieved by army units if an operation continues for any extended time.

Matchlock: A device using a match to ignite the priming powder in a weapon; the matchlock was a pivoted lever to which the soldier clipped the end of a glowing match, which the trigger released to touch the priming powder. Invented in the 14th century, it was a great advance over earlier devices; it was replaced in the 17th century by the flintlock.

Matériel: This is a French word also used by English-speaking military to refer to all those things required for the equipment, maintenance, operation, and support of military activities. In a more restricted sense, it refers only to things used in combat or logistic support operations, such as armaments, vehicles, or special clothing.

Mercenary: A soldier who hires himself out for pay to fight, usually in the army of another nation.

Militia: Part-time military or paramilitary units trained to serve in the defense of a nation in time of emergency. In the early decades of the United States they were volunteers who organized and financed their units; the Minutemen of the Revolution were such. In later times they were more like reserve units, with government support.

Missile, antiballistic (ABM): A missile designed to intercept and destroy incoming missiles, particularly those with nuclear warheads.

Missile, ballistic: In modern usage, a ballistic missile is an explosive projectile that is not fired from a gun tube but gets its thrust from a brief episode of rocket fire. (A true rocket provides its own thrust during all or most of its flight.) A missile does not rely upon aerodynamic surfaces to produce lift and so follows a ballistic trajectory when thrust is terminated. The different types of missiles are defined by their ranges: medium, intermediate, intercontinental.

Missile, cruise: A low-altitude, pilotless jet aircraft that uses terrain-following radar, which makes it highly accurate over long ranges. Its small size and low altitude make it hard to shoot down. The basic types refer to the point of origin: ground-launched, air-launched, and sea-launched. It can carry a nuclear warhead, but none so far has been used in combat.

Monitor: Originally it was a type of warship developed by the Union during the Civil War to fight in shallow harbors, coastal waters, and rivers. Its distinguishing features were that it was steam-powered, was ironclad, had a low, flat deck, and had one or more gun turrets that revolved. The term later came to be used for modern small, swift warships that also have shallow draft and are armed with guns that allow for coastal bombardment.

Mortar: A relatively small muzzle-loading cannon that fires shells at relatively short range with a high trajectory. It is usually light and easy to carry from one area to another; it is effective in firing shells over a hill or other obstruction. The name comes from its resemblance to the pharmacist's mortar.

Musket: Any of the smoothbore shoulder guns that evolved from the **arquebus** in the late 16th century. Its advantage over the arquebus was its increased range and accuracy and the greater penetrating power of its bullet. Although originally the musket was extremely large and heavy and had to be supported on a forked rest, by the late 17th century it was becoming lighter. By the late 18th century it was being replaced by the still more accurate **rifle**.

Mustard gas: A highly volatile oily liquid, its fumes cause irritation, blistering and even death. This was the poison gas that was widely used in World War I. Its chemical name is dichloroethyl sulfide.

Napalm: A jelly-like substance (which chemists know as

the aluminum soap formed by mixing naphthenic and palmitic acids); mixed with gasoline, napalm thickens it and slows the rate at which it burns, allowing it to be used in different ways. Originally developed in World War II for flamethrowers, napalm came to be used in bombs and other weapons. Napalm was especially notorious in the Vietnam War because U.S. forces used it on civilian targets.

Nuclear weapons: The generic term for all weapons whose explosive power derives from the release of nuclear energy. This would include both the **atomic bomb** and the **hydrogen bomb** as well as various kinds of shells and warheads that contain nuclear devices.

Ordnance: (1) The collective term for all military weapons, ammunition, combat vehicles, and battle **matériel**, along with the necessary maintenance tools and equipment. (2) The branch of an armed force that procures, issues, and maintains such matériel.

Outflank: To maneuver an attacking force, usually on the ground, around and behind the flank, or side, of the opposing force. This is intended to gain a tactical advantage because the opponent will be forced to divert strength from the front line to defend the flank and rear.

Palisade: A fence made of stakes placed close together to form a defensive barrier. This type of structure has not been used by military units since the early 19th century except in emergencies or in remote battlefields.

Parole: Both its meanings derive from its being the French word for "word." (1) The situation of an enemy, usually a member of the military, released from confinement or arrest on his acceptance of certain terms; the basic condition was not to return to combat until the two sides had agreed on some exchange of prisoners. (2) A password.

Partisan: A member of an irregular group operating within occupied territory to harass and inflict damage on the occupying forces. See also: **guerrilla**.

Percussion cap: A device containing a material that explodes on being struck and ignites powder or other explosive material. The first caps were developed about 1814 after the Scottish reverend Alexander Forsyth discovered (in 1807) a property of mercuric fulminate. The caps were small metal cylinders filled with the fulminate and attached to the rear end of the gun barrel; when struck with a hammer, the fulminate exploded, producing a spark that fired the powder inside the gun. Percussion caps greatly increased the effectiveness of handguns and were used until early in the 20th century.

Picket: Individuals or small groups detached from a main party and serving as outposts to guard the others from a surprise attack. The word is also applied to ships, aircraft, and even radar that serves a similar purpose of providing early warning.

Pike: A long pointed spear; it was used by infantrymen for both offensive and defensive purposes, from ancient times until the late-17th century.

Pistol: A small firearm that is held and fired with one hand. See also: **revolver**.

Pocket battleship: First used with regard to German ships during World War II, it refers to a smaller-than-usual battleship that had been built to avoid limits placed on the German navy by treaty after World War I.

Pontoon: A floating structure like a flat-bottomed boat, or even an actual boat, that supports a bridge or dock; usually these latter have had to be erected quickly for military units on the move.

Privateer: A privately owned ship commissioned by a nation at war to attack and seize enemy ships as a means of destroying enemy commerce. Privateers were abolished internationally by the 1856 Declaration of Paris, but the practice continued throughout the Civil War. See also: **letter of marque** and **prize ship**.

Prize ship (and **prize court**): A captured vessel, whether taken by an opposing naval force or privateer. Usually a "prize crew" was put aboard to take it into port. Under so-called "naval prize law," determined by "prize courts," issues of ownership of the ship and goods were determined, with the profits usually divided among the officers and crews who had seized the ships. Through the U.S. Civil War, Union and Confederate naval officers and crews continued to divide up the profits from captured opponents' ships. See also: **letter of marque** and **privateer**.

Proximate cause: The cause that directly or with no intermediate agency produces an effect; in the context of the history of wars, the event or action that is regarded as the most immediate cause of a war.

Ranger: A soldier belonging to a specially selected group in the U.S. Army, trained especially in swift raiding tactics. (The British equivalent is the **commando**.) The first such American unit was Roger's Rangers, organized by Robert Rogers in the French and Indian War. (See Civilian and Military Biographies, p. 55.) The U.S. Army revived the name during the Korean War.

Reconnaissance: A mission to obtain, by visual or other detection methods, information about the activities and resources of an enemy or potential enemy. Sometimes it is merely to obtain specific data concerning meteorological, hydrographic, or geographic characteristics of a particular area.

Redoubt: A small fortification, often temporary and often an earthwork; it is usually located outside a main fortification and guards the approaches to the areas most likely to be attacked.

Regiment: A military unit, usually of infantry, cavalry, or artillery, that can be either administrative or operational. It has varied in size over the last 200 years, but in the U.S. Army from the late 18th century to the mid-1960s it consisted of two or more **battalions**; a **division** comprised three infantry regiments (along with artillery battalions), each about 1,500 to 3,000 men. Since the 1960s, the U.S. Army has adopted the British system of treating a regiment as an administrative unit, responsible for battalions that combined into **brigades**; these latter, in size and function, are comparable to the old operational regiments.

Revolver: A handgun with rotating cylinders in which several rounds of ammunition can be placed in separate chambers; as each round is fired, the cylinder turns automatically and moves the next round into line with the barrel. Although Samuel Colt was not the first or only person to develop a revolver in the early 1800s, it was his that became among the more effective and popular.

Rifle: A gunpowder weapon with spiral grooves cut ("rifled") into the inner surface of the barrel; this causes the projectile to leave the weapon with a spinning motion that provides greater stability and accuracy. Rifled barrels were introduced in the 17th century but did not gain wide acceptance until the late 18th century. Although modern cannon and handguns have rifled barrels, the word is now usually restricted to firearms fired from the shoulder.

Riverine operations: Military operations conducted by

forces organized to exploit the special conditions of an area dominated by rivers and waterways.

Salvo: Whether by naval, air, or land forces, the firing of a number of weapons simultaneously or in quick sequence.

Scout: *n.* A person, unit, ship, or aircraft sent out from an armed force to ascertain what lies ahead in the way of terrain or enemy forces. *v.* To search for information about the enemy or the land ahead.

Ship of the line: Originally so called in the British navy, in the days of sail it was a warship that was large enough and had enough guns to form part of the principal battle line. The typical ship of the line carried over 70 guns.

Selective service: See **conscription**.

Skirmish: An encounter in which relatively few soldiers are involved and which usually lasts only a short time; it may be isolated or occur as part of a larger engagement.

Sloop-of-war: A small warship of the 17th, 18th, and early 19th centuries. Smaller than a frigate, it was usually a brig, or square-rigged, but it could also be schooner, or fore-and-aft rigged.

Smoothbore: Describing guns, from small arms to large cannon, when the bore or interior surface of the barrel is smooth—that is, not rifled. Most guns were smoothbore until the mid-19th century.

Sortie: This has different meanings for each service branch. In the army it refers to a relatively small and sudden attack made from a defensive position. (As such it can be used as a verb.) In the air force, it refers to a single mission performed by an aircraft against the enemy. In the navy, it refers to the departure of one or more ships from a harbor or anchorage, presumably for some operation. (Also used as a verb for this action.)

Special forces: The various special and small military units, mostly in the U.S. Army (such as the **Green Berets**) but also in the other branches, trained to fight the enemy using unconventional methods and often engaging in secret or behind-enemy-lines operations. (The Navy's SEALS and the Air Force's Air Commandos are two such units.) The first official Special Forces unit was formed in World War II; this was disbanded and replaced by Rangers in the Korean War; the U.S. Army then reactivated its Special Forces program in 1952, but such units did not play much of a role until the Vietnam War. See also: **rangers**.

Spike: Originally it referred to driving a spike or similar object into the vent (the hole in the breech) of a muzzle-loading cannon to render it useless. The term has come to be used for any action to disarm artillery pieces.

Squadron: (1) A naval organization consisting of two or more divisions of ships, generally of the same type. (2) The basic aviation unit of the U.S. Army, Navy, and Marine Corps as well as of the Air Force.

Status quo ante bellum: Latin for "the state of affairs before the war," it is used in the context of an end of hostilities that, whether by formal treaty or otherwise, leaves the various parties with the same territory and other conditions as before a war. See also: **uti possidetis**.

Strategic air warfare: Bombing and other air operations designed to bring about the progressive destruction of the enemy's war-making capacity. Often it involves civilian targets, including but not limited to war-production, fuel, and transportation facilities.

Strategy: In the context of the military during wartime, the planning, development, and employment of military resources and forces so as to maximize the likelihood of victory. See also: **tactics**.

Supporting artillery: Artillery that executes firing missions in support of a specific unit, usually infantry or armor, but that remains under the command of the next higher artillery commander.

Tactics: The techniques of deploying and directing military forces—troops, ships, aircraft, or combinations of these—in coordinated combat activities against an enemy in order to obtain the objectives designated by **strategy**. "Tactical" is often applied to many military terms—air control, air operations, maneuvers, even nuclear weapons—to indicate their use for these immediate goals.

Task force: (1) A temporary grouping of units under one commander, formed for the purpose of carrying out a specific operation or mission. (2) In the navy, a component of a fleet organized for the accomplishment of a specific task or goals.

Truce: The cessation of active hostilities for a period agreed upon by the belligerents. It is not a partial or temporary peace, only the suspension of military operations to the extent agreed upon by the parties. See also: **armistice**.

Turn: In combat, to lead units around the enemy's main concentration in order to strike at some point in the rear, or at least some vital and less defended point. A "turning movement" is sometimes known as a "strategic envelopment" and usually involves the attackers leaving part of their force to engage the enemy's main front while the other goes around to the side or rear.

Uti possidetis: Latin for "as you [now] possess," it is a term traditionally used in international treaties to indicate that the warring parties shall retain the territory they control at that point and the material possessions on it (unless otherwise stated by the treaty). See also: **status quo ante bellum**.

Van: The first element or portion of an advancing military formation, such as an army or fleet. Unlike the **vanguard**, it has not been sent out ahead for any special purpose.

Vanguard: See **advance guard**.

Vector: Based on the word for the course or compass direction of an airplane, "to vector" means to guide a plane or missile in flight by radioed system of directions.

SOURCES FOR FURTHER STUDY

RESEARCH WORKS

Dictionary of American Military Biography. Roger J. Spiller, ed. Westport, Conn.: Greenwood Press. 3 vols., 1984.

Dictionary of Military Terms: A Guide to the Language of Warfare and Military Institutions. Trevor Dupuy, Curt Johnson, and Grace P. Hayes, eds. New York: H.W. Wilson, 1986.

Encyclopedia of American War Films. Larry Langman and Ed Borg, eds. New York: Garland, 1989.

Guide to American Foreign Relations Since 1700. Richard Dean Burns, ed. Santa Barbara, Calif.: ABC-CLIO, 1983.

Guide to the Sources of United States Military History. Robin Higham, ed. Hamden, Conn.: Archon Books, 1992.

Guide to the Study and Use of Military History. John E. Jessup, Jr. and Robert W. Coakley, eds. Washington, D.C.: Center of Military History, 1979.

Peace and War: A Guide to Bibliographies. Berenice A. Carroll et al., eds. Santa Barbara, Calif.: ABC-CLIO, 1983.

The West Point Atlas of American Wars. Vincent J. Esposito, ed. New York: Praeger, 1959.

GENERAL READING

Bailey, Sidney. *How Wars End: The United Nations and the Termination of Armed Conflict, 1946–1964.* Oxford, England: Clarendon Press, 1983.

Barnet, Richard J. *The Rockets' Red Glare: When America Goes to War: The Presidents and the People.* New York: Simon & Schuster, 1990.

Blainey, Geoffrey. *The Causes of War.* New York: Free Press, 1988.

Brock, Peter. *Pacifism in the United States: From the Colonial Era to the First World War.* Princeton, N.J.: Princeton University Press, 1968.

Brown, Seyom. *The Causes and Prevention of War.* New York: St. Martin's Press, 1994.

Clausewitz, Carl von. *On War.* Michael Howard and Peter Paret, eds. Princeton, N.J.: Princeton University Press, 1989.

Clarkson, Jessie D. and Thomas C. Cochran, eds. *War as a Social Institution: The Historian's Perspective.* New York: AMS Press, 1996.

Cowley, Robert and Geoffrey Parker, eds. *The Reader's Companion to Military History.* Boston: Houghton Mifflin, 1996.

Dupuy, Richard E. *The Little Wars of the United States.* New York: Hawthorn Books, 1968.

Dupuy, Richard E. and Trevor Dupuy. *Military History of America.* Dubuque, Iowa: Kendall/Hunt Publishing. 2 vols., 1990–1992.

Dupuy, Trevor. *The Evolution of Weapons and Warfare.* New York: DaCapo Press, 1990.

——————— *Numbers, Prediction, and War: Using History to Evaluate Combat Factors and Predict the Outcome of Battles.* Indianapolis, Ind.: Bobbs-Merrill, 1979.

Elshtain, Jean Bethke. *Women and War: With a New Epilogue*. Chicago: University of Chicago Press, 1995.

Falk, Peter A. *Law, Morality and War in the Contemporary World*. Westport, Conn.: Greenwood Press, 1984.

Fox, William T. and Richard D. Lambert, eds. *How Wars End. Annals of the American Academy of Political and Social Sciences* (AAPSS), Series No. 39. Philadelphia: AAPSS, 1970.

Keegan, John. *A History of Warfare*. New York: Alfred A. Knopf, 1993.

Kennedy, Paul M. *The Rise and Fall of the Great Powers: Economic Change and Military Conflict from 1500 to 2000*. New York: Vintage Books, 1989.

Koistinen, Paul A. C. *Beating Plowshares into Swords: The Political Economy of American Warfare (1606–1865)*. Lawrence, Kans.: University Press of Kansas, 1996.

Levy, Jack S. *War in the Modern Great Power System, 1495–1975*. Lexington, Ky.: University Press of Kentucky, 1983.

Matloff, Maurice, ed. *American Military History*. Conshohack, Pa.: Combined Books, 1996.

O'Brien, William V. *The Conduct of a Just and Limited War*. Westport, Conn.: Greenwood Press, 1981.

Porter, Bruce D. *War and the Rise of the State: The Military Foundations of Modern Politics*. New York: Free Press, 1994.

Rinaldo, Peter M. *Unnecessary Wars? Causes and Effects of U.S. Wars from the American Revolution to Vietnam*. Briarcliff Manor, N.Y.: Dorpete Press, 1993.

Revely, W. Taylor III. *The War Powers of the President and Congress*. Charlottesville, Va.: University Press of Virginia, 1981.

Sofaer, Abraham D. *War, Foreign Affairs, and Constitutional Power: The Origins*. Cambridge, Mass.: Ballinger Publishing Co., 1976.

Sun Tzu. *The Art of War*. New York: Oxford University Press, 1984.

Waltz, Kenneth N. *Man, the State, and War: A Theoretical Analysis*. New York: Columbia University Press, 1959, 1983.

INDEX